HOW TO
INCREASE
READING
ABILITY

ninth edition

HOW TO INCREASE READING ABILITY

A Guide to Developmental & Remedial Methods

Albert J. Harris
Edward R. Sipay

Longman
New York & London

How to Increase Reading Ability, ninth edition

Longman, 95 Church Street, White Plains, N.Y. 10601

Associated companies:
Longman Group Ltd., London
Longman Cheshire Pty., Melbourne
Longman Paul Pty., Auckland
Copp Clark Pitman, Toronto

Executive editor: Raymond T. O'Connell
Development editor: Virginia Blanford
Production coordinator: Halley Gatenby
Text design adaptation: Renée Kilbride Edelman
Cover design: Joseph DePinho
Production supervisor: Joanne Jay

Library of Congress Cataloging in Publication Data

Harris, Albert Josiah.
    How to increase reading ability : a guide to developmental and
remedial methods / Albert J. Harris, Edward R. Sipay.—9th ed.
      p.   cm.
    Includes bibliographical references.
    ISBN 0-8013-0246-3
    1. Developmental reading. 2. Reading—Remedial teaching.
I. Sipay, Edward R. II. Title.
LB1050.53.H37   1990
428.4′3—dc20   89-38901
                                          CIP

ABCDEFGHIJ-MU-99 98 97 96 95 94 93 92 91 90

To Edith

Contents

List of Figures

List of Tables

Preface

The large volume of reading research published since 1985 has made necessary another thorough revision of this book. Every chapter has been comprehensively updated, so that after 50 years in print, this edition is as current as were the previous eight.

Despite many changes, the basic character of *How to Increase Reading Ability* remains the same. The book's wide use has encouraged us to maintain the guiding principles of the earlier editions: scope, balance, practicality, and clarity.

Our first principle, *scope,* requires that the book be useful to a wide range of individuals concerned with improving the reading ability of students—reading and learning disability specialists, classroom teachers, psychologists, supervisors, administrators, and researchers. This book has been used primarily as a textbook in graduate courses and as a desk reference by those who desire a comprehensive, current treatment of reading ability and disability. It has also been employed successfully in undergraduate reading and learning disabilities courses.

Our second guiding principle, *balance,* requires a commitment to present all sides of an issue. We summarize opposing theories and opinions, cite relevant research, and at times critique research findings and state our own position on an issue. Given the extensiveness of the literature, it would be impossible to summarize the ideas and findings presented in all of our references, so we provide an extensive bibliography, making it possible for serious students to locate and use original sources. All of the references appear in one alphabetized reference list, which contains some 3,000 entries. Approximately 40% of these items have been published since 1985.

The third objective was to make the book *practical* and helpful. Thus we have included succinct descriptions of diagnostic procedures and instructional and learning strategies, as well as the background knowledge needed to utilize these techniques thoughtfully.

Clarity, our fourth guideline, dictates that the book be clearly written. Technical vocabulary has been kept to a minimum; terms are defined; and explanations, illustrations, or examples are provided. We have moved coverage of some topics closer to related ones, reduced redundancies, and pointed out the relationships among concepts in order to make the flow of information easier to follow.

There are significant changes in this edition, the most important of which is the greatly expanded coverage of reading comprehension. Eighth edition Chapters 12, 13, and 14 have been divided, so that the ninth edition comprises 18 rather than 15 chapters. Chapters 1 through 5 provide background information and an overview of reading instruction from kindergarten through high school and beyond, with an emphasis on providing for individual differences in learning to read, reading to learn, and reading for enjoyment. Chapters 6 through

10 cover evaluation and diagnosis. The final chapters, 11 through 18, describe specific instructional and learning strategies.

One appendix (Appendix C, "A List of Publishers and Their Addresses" in the eighth edition) has been eliminated because of rapid changes in the publishing field that would make it too soon obsolete. To find publishers' addresses, readers are advised to consult *Literary Market Place* (Bowker, revised annually), available at any library. A list of publisher abbreviations precedes the bibliography.

We wish to express our appreciation to Mrs. Edith Harris. As for all of the previous editions, she has been helpful in many ways. We are also indebted to Mrs. Charlotte Harris Wiener for her comments about speed reading instruction in Chapter 17. Our thanks go to Donna Parent for her expert typing and to Ali Habayeb for his library research.

Albert J. Harris
Edward R. Sipay

1

Reading Ability: Its Status and Nature

Reading is a complex process. In some manner yet to be fully understood, the reader combines information provided by an author via printed or handwritten text with previously possessed knowledge to construct an interpretation of that text. Numerous factors within individuals—the skills and knowledge they possess and use while reading, their attitudes, and variables in their school, home, and sociocultural environments—probably interact in various ways to influence reading acquisition, reading development, and reading disability. This book considers most of these factors and variables and suggests how to help individuals become more proficient and efficient readers.

The purposes of this chapter are to inform readers as to why efforts should be made to increase reading ability, and to provide information that should be helpful in understanding the following chapters. The first two sections deal with the status of reading ability and its importance in today's world. These are followed by a section in which a definition of reading and models of the reading process are presented. Among the topics covered in the final section are the interrelatedness of various aspects of language, language development, differences between spoken and written language, and the nature of English orthography.

READING ABILITY AND HABITS IN THE UNITED STATES

The Status of Reading Ability

Charges that American education in general and student reading achievement in particular have declined are made from time to time.[1] These reported declines are attributed to various causes, such as attempts "to remedy the political follies and

---

[1]Declining SAT scores are frequently cited as evidence. However, the SAT is not highly influenced by reading ability per se (Farr 1984).

social irregularities of our time by obliterating academic standards" (Cahn 1981), a permissive society that produces teachers who fail to teach reading effectively (Copperman 1978), and failure to emphasize phonics in the initial stages of reading instruction (Flesch 1981). Most often, the critics cite comments of employers and college and high school teachers, compare test results with those of previous years in the United States or with those from other industrial nations, or compare private and public schools.

Although there is evidence that reading achievement was not as good in the old days as some would have us believe, it is impossible to prove whether reading performance has declined, risen, or remained stable over the years. Many more students attend school at all levels today, and the school population is much more diverse than it was only 30 years ago. Schooling was not compulsory in the early part of this century. In the 1960s, the national effort that cut the dropout rate to about one-quarter its former level had two indirect results: (1) average intelligence test scores began to decline because the former school dropouts generally had lower IQ scores than those who remained in school; and (2) average reading scores declined because of substantial correlation between IQ and reading ability. Because most dropouts are high school rather than elementary students, we should not be surprised to find that reading achievement declined more at the higher academic level (Bormuth 1982).

Although direct comparisons are questionable, comparative data can indicate trends. Based on their review of the literature, Tuinman, Rowls, and Farr (1976) conclude that a gradual improvement in reading competency took place between 1925 and 1965, and that from 1966 on there was a leveling off and perhaps a slight decline in average reading achievement in the United States. But, according to Stedman and Kaestle (1987), students' reading performance at a given age level remained stable over the years until the 1970s.

The apparent decline in American reading achievement in the 1970s is substantiated by Flanagan (1976) and seems to have been part of a nationwide trend above the primary grades in various academic areas (Harneschfeger & Wiley 1976). Although there is insufficient evidence to determine the exact causes, the decline may have reflected fewer dropouts among low-scoring students, changes in school curriculum (e.g., fewer academic courses), a decrease in average daily attendance resulting in fewer days of schooling, teenage addiction to alcohol and drugs, and changing social attitudes and trends (National Commission on Excellence in Education 1983).

A more recent study (Congressional Budget Office 1987) concludes that a wide range of social and educational factors played a role in the test score downturn during the 1960s and early 1970s and in a subsequent rebound that began in the mid-1970s. Stedman and Kaestle (1985) attribute the upswing to: (1) the increased dropout rate since the mid-1970s, which resulted in a more selective test-taking population; (2) the taking of the tests by more first- and second-born children, who tend to score higher than later-born siblings; and (3) increased attention to teaching the specific reading skills sampled by the tests. The latter practice may have negative consequences, such as uniform curricula and less attention paid to teaching higher-level thinking skills that are not sampled by the tests.

Other comparative data suggest some improvement, some stability, and some need for concern. A comparison of the National Assessment of Educational Progress test results indicates that students at age 9, 13, and 17 were better readers in 1984 than they were in 1971. The 9- and 13-year-olds improved through the 1970s, but leveled off in the early 1980s. The percentage of 17-year-olds who were proficient at the three lowest levels (Rudimentary, Basic, and Intermediate) on the *Reading Proficiency Scale* remained fairly stable over the years, but those at the upper two levels (Adept and Advanced) declined. Improvement by the 17-year-olds between 1980 and 1984 may be due in part to their earlier improvements at ages 9 and 13 (NAEP 1985b).

NAEP trend data for 1988 were not reported because there was an inexplicable precipitous decline in the average reading proficiency at ages 9 and 17 (Applebee, Langer & Mullis 1988). Care should be exercised in interpreting any change data, but one chief limitation in using NAEP data to measure change in reading ability is that it is derived from a series of cross-sectional studies, and not from a single longitudinal study (H. Braun 1988).

Even though the NAEP results are encouraging, there is need for concern. In 1984 approximately 6% of the 9-year-olds were unable to demonstrate Rudimentary reading skills and thus were in danger of future school failure. Approximately 40% of 13-year-olds and 16% of 17-year-old high schoolers had not reached the Intermediate level of reading proficiency, thereby opening to question their ability to comprehend a variety of school-related academic materials. Only 5% of the 17-year-olds had Advanced reading skills. Such findings appear to suggest the need for increased emphasis on higher-level reading skills at all age levels. Although the NAEP did not define "higher-level reading skills," Carroll (1987) suggests that they involve word meaning, understanding complex sentences and ideas, and world knowledge. But as Carroll points out, many of the tasks used at the higher levels in the NAEP assessment were similar to those on verbal IQ tests. The degree to which reading ability can be improved beyond the level of functional literacy is partly influenced by the degree to which verbal intelligence can be increased. Research findings do not suggest that significant increases in verbal intelligence can be fostered.

The NAEP data (1985b) seem to show sizable gains in the reading ability of minority-group children from 1971 to 1984. For example, the percentage of black 9-year-olds who were not functioning at the Rudimentary level dropped from 30 to 16%, and the percentage of black 17-year-olds at the Adept level rose from 7 to 16%. But his analyses of the data led Carroll (1987) to conclude that the gains were generally small and tended to occur mainly among students in the lower end of the distribution. The major improvements came in such basic skills as decoding words and in comprehending simple written language. Although the gap between minority-group students and their age peers has narrowed, on the average, minority students still read below national levels.

We should note, however, that factors other than race and ethnic background contribute to reading performance. For example, blacks in advantaged urban areas performed much closer to national levels than black students in rural and disadvantaged urban areas (NAEP 1983a). A similar situation pertained to Hispanics (Ward 1982).

Some NAEP data are disturbing in that part of the gains made by low achievers may have come at the expense of the more able students. For example, from 1977 to 1980, the lowest quartile of the 9- and 13-year-olds improved their reading skills; the 17-year-olds did not. However, the scores of the highest quartiles in each of the two oldest age groups declined (NAEP 1983b).

Other NAEP data (Kirsch & Jungeblut 1986) indicate that 95% of Americans age 21 to 25 reached or exceeded the reading ability of fourth graders, 80% reached or exceeded that of eighth graders, and 62% reached or surpassed the average reading ability of high school juniors. Only about 2% of these young adults were incapable of taking the literacy tests, and about half of these could not speak English. The English-speaking 1% of those incapable of taking the tests also responded to a set of oral language tasks. Their comparatively low performance on these tasks suggests that many had language comprehension problems that extended beyond processing printed information. An overwhelming majority of the young adults performed adequately on the Prose Literacy section that sampled skills and strategies needed to understand and use printed text often found in the home or community. However, sizable numbers of young adults did not perform adequately on moderately complex tasks in Document Literacy (understanding and using tables, charts, graphs, indexes, forms, and schedules) and Quantitative Literacy (using arithmetic operations in conjunction with printed materials).

Kirsch and Jungeblut (1986) conclude that *illiteracy* in our young adults is not a major problem, but *literacy* is. This age group was deemed to be neither totally illiterate nor fully literate for our technically advanced society. Krisch and Jungeblut further suggest that no simple step or action can allow young adults to become fully literate because becoming literate in our society is a lifelong pursuit influenced by such factors as home environment, economic situation, personal aspirations, and educational opportunities. They also warn that changing demographics and the relatively weak performance of minority groups suggests that, unless more appropriate intervention strategies are developed and implemented, there will be a less literate pool from which to fill our human resource needs in the future. A goal of improved literacy will not be accomplished easily. As Carroll (1987) points out, given the level of performance on the NAEP *Reading Proficiency Scale,* we cannot realistically expect that, in the near future, nearly all young adults will attain the Adept level of reading proficiency, even with the best possible instruction and increased instructional time. Furthermore, increasingly higher levels of literacy than those deemed adequate today may well be needed in the future.

Overall, the status of reading achievement in the United States is not as bad as some would have us believe, and some conclude that it is much better (e.g., Fay 1980). Reading achievement in the United States compares somewhat favorably to that in other countries. For example, in 1973 American 14-year-olds ranked third in reading comprehension among the 15 countries studied (Thorndike 1973), and third in the interpretation of literature and fifth in the comprehension of literature among 10 countries studied (Purves 1973). Our 18-year-olds ranked twelfth in reading comprehension, fifth in interpreting literature, and seventh in comprehending literature. More recently, Purves et al. (1981) conclude that not only do our best students read as well as, or better than, those in other developed nations, but that the United States brings a higher percentage (75%) of its age group further along in reading than any of the other 14 countries studied.

LITERACY AND ILLITERACY. There are numerous conceptual and methodological problems in studying literacy, not the least of which is its definition. No one definition of literacy or illiteracy is generally accepted. Definitions differ between and even within cultures (Tabor 1987). Illiteracy does not necessarily mean a complete lack of reading ability; there are many levels of literacy, for example, ranging from being able to read one's own name to understanding a highly technical journal article.

When literacy is defined in absolute terms, as it typically is, the criteria employed include school attendance for a particular number of years, a level of performance on a norm-referenced test, or successful demonstration of a defined set of competencies. Often those who use such definitions are referring to a minimal level of competency (see the following). But staying in school for a given number of years does not ensure that a person can read at the level of the highest grade attended. Nor does a score on a standardized test reveal what a person can comprehend.

Literacy can also be defined in relative terms. Relative definitions state that because materials vary in difficulty and are read for various purposes, a person can be literate in one situation but illiterate in another. Writers such as Bormuth (1982) suggest that persons who can read what they want to read or have to read are literate.

Within the field, different terms are used. Those who use such terms as *survival literacy* or *basic literacy* usually are referring to the application of reading skills to everyday needs like reading food labels, forms, and warning labels. They attempt to measure reading behaviors needed to maintain one's health and welfare. *Functional literacy* seems to have a broader meaning. For example, Stedman and Kaestle (1987) state that functional literacy involves the reading and writing skills needed to understand and use the printed materials normally encountered in work, leisure, and citizenship. They also distinguish between *reading achievement*—the literacy skills taught and measured in school—and *functional literacy*—the literacy skills practiced outside school. Their comment that the relationship between school and functional literacy is unclear seems to be borne out by Rush, Moe, and Storlie (1986) who found that the reading materials and processes utilized in work settings differ distinctly from those found in school settings. Occupational materials are comprehended by workers who seem to lack the necessary reading abilities, perhaps due at least in part to the frequent use of graphic aids and the application of that information to an ongoing process (their jobs). *Occupational literacy* is a subset of functional literacy. Required reading competencies vary among occupations and from job to job within an occupation (Rush, Moe & Storlie 1986).

There has been a growing concern about literacy at national and international levels. Illiteracy in the world is massive and complex. Between 1945 and 1974, world adult illiteracy dropped from 44.3% to 34.2%, but as a result of the population explosion during the same period, the number of illiterates rose from

700 million to 800 million (Corbett 1982). Internationally, illiteracy is concentrated geographically and socially. Although it appears much more frequently in emerging countries, it still occurs in highly developed industrial nations. Nationally, illiteracy is concentrated among the poor, minorities, and the elderly. Illiteracy is complexly related to cultural, social, political, and economic issues (Levine 1982, Scribner 1986).

Estimates of the number of American illiterates and semi-illiterates vary from less than 1 million to over 60 million (Ferraro 1986). For example, Stedman and Kaestle (1987) estimate that 35 million American adults have serious difficulty with common reading tasks, and another $17\frac{1}{2}$ million or so are probably marginally functionally literate. But outright, utter illiteracy is very low. Differences in definitions of literacy, the measurements used, and the inclusion of varying age groups have contributed to the widely varying estimates. Depending on which statistic you read, you could be led to believe that illiteracy is minimal or rampant.

In addition to the NAEP data reported on pages 3–4, there are other recent data on illiteracy in the United States. Using the 26-item, multiple-choice *English Language Proficiency Survey,* the Census Bureau estimates about a 13% illiteracy rate among 20- to 40-year-olds. Native speakers of English had a 9% illiteracy rate. Of these, 70% had not finished high school and 42% had not been employed in the past year. Almost half of those from non-English-speaking homes were judged illiterate, many of whom admitted to being illiterate in their native languages also (Ferraro 1986).

MINIMAL COMPETENCY.   The minimal competency movement is closely related to the concern over literacy and is part of a broad national reemphasis of basic skills. Minimal competency has had a long history in the United States, but unlike earlier responses, which involved curriculum reform, the current movement has focused on testing as the remedy. Test performance usually determines whether or not students get promoted or whether they receive a high school diploma or a certificate of attendance. By 1988, students were required to pass a minimal competency test to obtain a high school diploma (rather than a certificate of attendance) in 21 states and to be promoted from eighth grade in eight states (Goertz 1988). Although the demands that such tests place on students differ, current minimal competency tests generally attempt to determine whether specific reading, writing, and computational skills have been mastered or whether a specified level of general achievement has been attained. The arguments for and against competency testing are enumerated by Perkins (1982).

Reading Habits and Practices of American Adults

The United States is one of the highest consumers of print in the world, as judged by the number of books, magazines, and newspapers in circulation (Purves 1986a). Of Americans over age 16, 96% have reported reading books, magazines, or newspapers (Diehl 1984). But books may not be as widely read as such data suggest. Book readership declined from 75% in 1978 to 63% in 1983 for 16- to 21-year-olds; only 39% of those over the age of 60 read books (Diehl 1984).

Compared to people in other industrialized nations, Americans read less. For example, whereas Americans spend an average of 5 minutes daily reading books that are not part of their work or schooling, Russians read 29 minutes a day and Bulgarians, 20 minutes (Guthrie 1982). Reading volume, which is based on the number of books, magazines, and newspapers read monthly and is highly correlated with reading achievement, was 20% higher in New Zealand than in the United States (Guthrie 1981c). What one chooses to read during leisure time and for how long, if at all, is influenced by such factors as interest, level of reading ability, availability of materials, economic status, and sociocultural values (see pages 657–663).

The time Americans spend reading at work varies considerably. In the 10 occupations studied by Rush, Moe, and Storlie (1986), average on-the-job reading time ranged from 24 to 168 minutes daily, with an average of slightly over one hour being spent on work-related reading.

The reading habits and practices of adults (i.e., the content and type of material read, the purposes for which it is read, and the length of time for which it is read), are affected by level of education and occupation as well as by whether the reading is done at work or during leisure time. There are also interactions among these variables (Guthrie, Seifert, & Kirsch 1986). Reading interests, habits, and tastes are discussed more fully in Chapter 18.

THE IMPORTANCE OF READING ABILITY

Reading ability has academic, economic, societal, political, and personal value. Heavy emphasis is placed on teaching children to read as soon as they enter school. As students progress through school, increasing levels of reading competence are typically required for academic success in other subject areas. Students who are unable to read adequately are increasingly handicapped as they move through the elementary school. Compared to students who are making at least normal progress in reading achievement, those who cannot read adequately are more apt to meet academic failures and to repeat grades. If they get into high school, they are more likely to drop out before graduation.

Although a few illiterates have become millionaires, more frequently their fate in a modern, high-technology society is poverty. Approximately 75% of the unemployed lack basic reading and writing skills (Nickerson 1985). As technology advances, more occupations require high levels of education or specialized training for which reading ability is vital. Automation and foreign competition have eliminated many unskilled and semiskilled jobs. Many displaced workers become chronically unemployable because they do not possess the minimum reading skills required for success in new positions or job-training programs.

Unemployment cannot be solved by raising the reading abilities of the unemployed. Poor economic conditions cause lack of jobs. But, for individuals, literacy can make the difference between being able to compete effectively for available jobs or being completely out of the running (Nickerson 1985). Research suggests that individuals with limited reading skills can hold jobs, but severe reading deficiencies interfere with the ability to acquire and hold many types of jobs (Stedman & Kaestle 1987). When the economy improves, most of the newly available jobs are likely to require at least basic literacy, and many require reading skills far above that level.

Currently, more jobs are available than in past years, but there are fewer young adults to fill them. In 1981, there were more than 30 million 18- to 20-year olds available for work; by 1995, there will be only 24 million. Business and the military will increasingly compete for the 44% of that age group who do not go on to postsecondary education (Shanker 1988–1989). The difficulty of finding employees with even basic skills has caused some businesses to conduct their own basic-skills programs (Suchecki 1988).

The level of reading skills needed for satisfactory job performance is difficult to determine. The correlation between performance on reading tests and job performance is too low—about 0.25—to make an assigned reading level a credible predictor of performance. In addition, estimates of the reading level needed to perform particular jobs are especially sensitive to the criteria used to judge successful job performance (Stedman & Kaestle 1987). However, readability measures suggest that the world of work often requires a level of reading ability far above what most individuals believe necessary. The readability of over half of the training materials for seven military jobs exceeded the eleventh-grade level of difficulty (Sticht 1975). Similarly, the average difficulty of the occupational materials studied by Harste and Mikulecky (1984) was eleventh-grade level. Rush, Moe, and Storlie (1986) found that the materials actually read in 10 different occupations ranged in difficulty from the ninth-grade to the college level.

The effect of prior knowledge on comprehension must be considered in evaluating these data. For example, when given material at the eleventh-grade level, sailors who knew nothing about the topic needed to be reading above that level in order to understand the material satisfactorily. Those with the highest level of topical knowledge could read it even though they may have been measured as reading at only the sixth-grade level (Shanker 1988–1989).

Reading ability is also important for everyday functioning. Those who cannot read street or traffic signs or notices of sales, for example, are at a disadvantage. Evaluations of the readability of newspapers range from the eighth-grade (Johns & Wheat 1984) to the college level (Fusaro & Conover 1983), with the readability levels of particular articles varying considerably. Directions for preparing a TV dinner are written at the eighth-grade level; instructions for taking aspirin are at the tenth-grade level (Kilty 1976). The readability of health and safety pamphlets ranges from sixth-grade level to level seventeen (with a mean of twelfth grade); insurance policies range from the eleventh- to the sixteenth-grade level; and the old federal income tax form 1040A was at the ninth-, tenth-, or thirteenth-grade level, depending on which formula was applied (Negin & Krugler 1980).

Literacy is especially valuable in a society that has a free press. Being able to read adequately and critically allows individuals to reflect on varying political points of view, which are presented in print in much more detail than in other forms of media. Such knowledge results in political participation and efficacy.

In literate societies, a social stigma is attached to a lack of reading ability. Most individuals attempt to become literate in order to gain or preserve their

esteem among family and peers (Levine 1982). Individuals may attempt to substitute for reading ability by deceiving others into thinking they can read and
by circumventing situations that require reading. But illiterates are in constant
fear of having their inability to read discovered. Reading inability or disability
is often all too painful in school settings, and reading proficiency is essential for
self-esteem in most American subcultures.

To a large extent, those who cannot read, or who choose not to read, are
cut off, not only from possible intellectual enrichment, but also from cultural
activities, and they find it difficult to mingle with educated people. Through
reading we create the environment that shapes our minds and ourselves (Guthrie & Seifert 1983). Literacy enables individuals to conceptualize, to generalize,
to draw inferences, and to work out logical relationships among ideas in ways
that would otherwise be impossible: It alters the way people think (F. D'Angelo
1982). Reading also fulfills emotional and spiritual needs.

Technological advances have given rise to predictions that reading ability
will be unnecessary, or at least much less important, in the future. It is conceiv-
able that nonprint media may completely or largely replace printed text as a
form of communication. Material, including much of what has appeared in written format in the past, may become available in recorded voice form at a price
affordable by the masses; or computers may be able to read text aloud in other
than a dull monotone. But for the forseeable future, the ability to read such
things as labels, signs, manuals, information on a terminal screen, FAX print-
outs, forms, newspapers, textbooks, and literary works will remain important.
Currently, reading has unique advantages. Instead of having to select from limited choices, as one must when using non-print media, the reader can select
from the whole range of past and present writings. Readers can read in a place
and at a time chosen for convenience and can set their own pace—slow down,
speed up, take a break, reread, pause to think and reflect. Readers can read what,
when, where, and how they please and need not rely on others to interpret the
material. This flexibility and independence ensure the continuing value of reading ability for both education and pleasure for some time to come.

THE NATURE OF READING
AND THE READING PROCESS

A Definition of Reading

No one fully understands the extremely complex ability called reading. This is
not surprising, because reading is a cognitive activity that occurs rapidly and
privately in the mind, and is thus difficult to study. Not only is the process unob-
servable to others, but even skilled readers are hardly aware of what they do
during the reading process. Given the complexity of the human mind and our
modest, although growing, ability to understand its workings, our incomplete
understanding of the reading process is understandable (R. C. Anderson et al.
1985). Nevertheless, gains have been made in understanding the reading process, so it is possible to offer a definition of reading and the reading process that
reflects the best available information.

Reading is the meaningful interpretation of written language. In short, reading is comprehending. Others have defined reading as the process of constructing meaning from written text[2] (R. C. Anderson et al. 1985) or as thinking guided by print (Perfetti 1986a).

It cannot be overemphasized that meaningful response is at the heart of the reading process. "It [reading] can and should embrace all types of thinking, evaluating, judging, imagining, reasoning, and problem solving" (Gates 1949, p. 3). More than intellectual meaning may be involved: Feelings of considerable intensity may be aroused[3] and emotional attitudes may be profoundly altered through reading.

In constructing texts, authors present the ideas they want to express through the use of words, sentences, and paragraphs that are structured in the way they feel best allows for a flow of communication. Rarely, if ever, is a text completely explicit or self-explanatory. Authors anticipate that readers will fill in the missing information using prior knowledge and reasoning abilities.

To recreate the meaning intended by the author, the reader must, during the reading process, coordinate and integrate information that is available from various sources—the written text, the reader's mind, and perhaps an accompanying illustration. Reading comprehension is the result of the interaction between and among the reader's (1) recognition and perception of the graphic symbols used to represent language, (2) linguistic information, (3) cognitive skills, and (4) knowledge about specific topics and the world in general. Weaknesses in any of these areas, or breakdowns in processing and integrating information from any of them, can disrupt reading comprehension. The level and completeness of comprehension depends not only on the degree to which the reader's competence in the aforementioned areas meets the task demands, but also on how well the reader employs these skills and knowledge. Reading comprehension may also be influenced by the reader's motivation, interest, biases, purpose for reading, and the context in which the reading act takes place.

To obtain the intended meaning, the reader must recognize most of the printed words. The ability to recognize printed words allows readers to access their *lexicons* (mental dictionaries) in order to determine word meaning. As the reader brings prior knowledge to bear, the response to the first words sets up an anticipation for meaning that, if appropriate, aids in recognizing the words that follow. If word recognition is very inaccurate, or so slow and halting that the words are not perceived as coming in meaningful sequences, or if the sentences are run together and frequently misphrased, the resulting approximation to language is not close enough to convey the intended meaning. Accurate, automatic word recognition facilitates reading comprehension; conversely, reading comprehension facilitates word recognition and identification.

As words are identified, they are placed in short-term memory, probably in their phonological forms, and held there while the reader attempts to comprehend the idea(s) embodied in a sentence. At this point, syntactical knowledge

[2]The term *text* is used here and throughout this book to mean any series of coherently arranged sentences (Perfetti 1985). The terms *text* and *textbook* are *not* used interchangeably in this book. The latter refers to the books used as instructional tools in schools.
[3]Measurable physiological changes can occur as a reader reacts to what is being read (Nell 1988).

probably comes into play. As sentences are understood, their meanings are integrated with those of already-read sentences, as well as with the reader's prior knowledge, and a continually more complete understanding of the text emerges.

For many novice readers, speech serves as a mediator between what is visually perceived and meaning; that is, they must pronounce words orally in order to retrieve their meanings. As children become more skilled in word identification, the need for using speech as a mediator lessens; silent reading becomes inaudible, noticeable lip movements cease, and, for many an expert reader, the meaning seems to leap from the printed page with scarcely any awareness of inner speech.

Word-recognition skills continue to develop as the child's reading ability matures. Words that appear frequently in print are recognized accurately and automatically, and new words are continually added to the child's store of words recognized at sight. Skill in decoding printed words is acquired concurrently so that the child can become independent in word recognition.

As the child gets beyond the initial stages of reading acquisition, reading materials become increasingly more complex. Ideas that are outside the youngster's first-hand experience are introduced, and the text may even employ words that the child has never heard spoken, let alone seen in print. Sentences become longer and more complex and less like those heard in spoken conversation, and they represent more complex concepts. To keep up with the increasing linguistic and cognitive demands of the reading materials, children must enlarge and refine their concepts and ideas, increase their vocabularies, and master complex forms of language.

Children meet a variety of reading materials and read to satisfy many needs and purposes. Story reading becomes differentiated from reading to learn. In pleasure reading, exclusive concern with the plot is gradually enriched by the development of appreciation for humor, characterization, accuracy and vividness of description, and the sheer beauty of artistic expression. In acquiring and retaining information from expository texts, study skills and habits that differ from academic subject to academic subject must be formed. Different methods of study must be learned to cope with different phases of each subject. The efficient student learns how to locate needed information, distinguish major from minor points, follow directions, interpret, summarize, outline, and utilize information.

Finally reading becomes reflective and evaluative. To grasp the meaning and organization of a writer's ideas is important, but not sufficient. Mature readers compare the facts and arguments presented by one author with those of another, and are on the alert for errors in logic. Mature readers can distinguish factual reporting from biased propaganda and objective reasoning from wishful thinking.

The nature of the reading task changes as students progress to more mature levels of reading ability. For the novice reader, reading is concerned mainly with learning to recognize printed words and to utilize word-recognition skills in understanding printed text that employs concepts with which the reader is probably already familiar. The reasoning side of reading becomes increasingly more important as word recognition is mastered. As reading proficiency increases, individuals learn to adapt their reading strategies to their purposes for reading and to the restrictions imposed by the material.

Reading Models

Over the years, a number of models of the reading process have been formulated. Some of these have been summarized and critiqued by Samuels and Kamil (1984) and some models may be found in their original form in Singer and Ruddell (1976, 1985). Gibson and Levin (1975) are of the opinion that a single model of reading is not viable because there is no single reading process. Rather than offer a number of models, Gibson and Levin state general principles about the skilled reading processes that apply to many reading situations at various levels of proficiency.

Many of the early models were too ambitious. As Samuels and Eisenberg (1981) state, it is dangerous to attempt a description of the reading process as a whole. Comprehensive descriptions try to explain so much that they are untestable. Therefore, most models are partial in that they are concerned with specific aspects (e.g., perceptual or cognitive), stages (beginning or skilled reading), or modes (oral or silent reading) and do not attempt to account for all phases of the reading process.

Most models may be placed in one of three classes: *bottom-up, top-down,* or *interactive.*

BOTTOM-UP MODELS.   According to *bottom-up models,* reading is essentially a process of translating graphic symbols into speech during oral reading or into inner speech during silent reading. The reader then applies previously acquired listening comprehension skills. Most bottom-up theorists believe that written language is subservient to oral language; the only activity unique to reading is breaking the written code.

Sensory and perceptual processes (commonly referred to as lower-level processes) are believed to occur prior to, and perhaps independently of, cognitive processes (commonly referred to as high-level processes). The reader first picks up graphic information from the printed material (e.g., letters, groups of letters, words); after that, syntactic and semantic processing occur. As a result of this information flow, the printed material is understood. Reading comprehension is believed to be heavily dependent on rapid, accurate word recognition. Reading is controlled by textual input; the reader plays a relatively passive role in the process (Weaver & Resnick 1979). The printed material is believed to provide more information than the reader does (Strange 1980).

Some theorists and writers attribute bottom-up models to all levels of reading competence. Others suggest that bottom-up processing best describes learning to read (the acquisition stage), but that a top-down or interactive model more accurately describes skilled reading.

Two reading models often cited as bottom-up models are those of Gough (1985a) and LaBerge and Samuels (1985). Gough (1985b) concedes that there are flaws in his model, but maintains that most of it is correct. For example, while admitting that words are not always read letter by letter and that skilled readers could have direct lexical access for high-frequency words (i.e., readers could access word meanings directly from print without first having to change them into their spoken forms), Gough remained committed to the beliefs that letters mediate word recognition and that most words are recognized through phonological recoding.[4] Samuels (1985a), on the other hand, has modified the LaBerge and Samuels model so that it is now more in line with the interactive viewpoint (see the following).

TOP-DOWN MODELS.   In *top-down models* the reader's prior knowledge and cognitive and linguistic competence play key roles in the construction of meaning. Before or shortly after any graphic input, the reader generates hypotheses regarding the meaning of the printed material. These predictions are based on the reader's prior knowledge, the specific content of the material, and *syntactic parsing* (interpreting the words in their particular grammatical functions). Graphic cues are sampled only as needed. As the information is processed, the reader's predictions about meaning are rejected, confirmed, or refined. The reader, who plays an active role in the process, is believed to supply more information than the printed material. In contrast to bottom-up theorists, many top-down theorists believe that skilled readers go directly from print to meaning without first recoding print to speech.

Most top-down theorists suggest that their models are more descriptive of skilled than of unskilled readers. Some, like the Goodmans (Goodman & Goodman 1979, 1982), believe that novice readers differ from skilled readers only in their lesser command of the strategies needed to extract meaning from print.

The two models most frequently cited as representative of the top-down position are those of K. Goodman (1967) and F. Smith (1982), both of which are based on psycholinguistic theories that consider the interaction between thought and language. K. Goodman (1981, 1982), however, claims that his model is and always has been an interactive model. More recently he refers to reading as a "transactive process" (K. Goodman 1985). Some writers (e.g., Nicholson 1986) question the basic assumptions of top-down models, particularly as they apply to novice readers.

Few purely bottom-up or top-down models of reading have been proposed. It seems logical to conclude that there must be some bottom-up processing and some top-down processing in reading. The models differ in the importance ascribed to each kind of processing. Whatever model you hold, you need to remember the danger in overemphasizing either kind of processing. A proper balance must be struck between the information the text provides and that which the reader brings.

INTERACTIVE MODELS.   *Interactive models* are not merely a compromise between bottom-up and top-down theories. A hypothesis generated by top-down processing is guided by the results of bottom-up processing, and the bottom-up processing is guided in part by the expectations imposed by top-down processing. Information derived from each kind of processing is combined to determine the most likely interpretation of the printed message.

[4]Refer to pp. 436–437 for a discussion of lexical access, and to pp. 293–295 for a discussion of the need for phonological recoding.

The influence of each kind of processing is not equal in all interactive models, nor is there complete agreement among interactive theorists as to which kind of processing initiates the reading process, or if the processes occur almost simultaneously. But there is basic agreement that reading involves the skillful combination of linguistic and semantic knowledge with visual information in order to reconstruct the meaning intended by the author.

Interactive models assume that the reader takes either an active or passive role, depending on the strength and accuracy of the hypotheses generated by top-down processing (Pearson & Kamil 1978). The most widely cited interactive model is that of Rumelhart (1985).[5] His early model postulates that, at least for skilled readers, top-down and bottom-up processing occur simultaneously. When the accumulated evidence strongly supports a particular hypothesis, comprehension takes place. Because comprehension depends on both graphic information and the information in the reader's mind, it may be obstructed when a critical skill or a piece of information is missing. When comprehension is hampered, the skilled reader compensates by decoding key words, relying on context, or both. Rumelhart and McClelland (1981, 1982) proposed a more limited interactive model than the one originally formulated by Rumelhart in 1977.

Other interactive models have been developed by J. Fredericksen (1982a,b), Ruddell and Speaker (1985), and Perfetti (1985). Perfetti stresses the importance of automatic, accurate word recognition much more than do other interactive theorists. Danks and Hill (1981) present an interactive analysis of oral reading.

Although Athey (1985a) is correct in stating that none of the current models adequately explains the reading process, interactive models are by far the most favored in the literature. Despite a lack of empirical evidence, interactive models appear to be the most logical and intuitively appealing.

OTHER MODELS.   Many other models have been developed, only a few of which are mentioned here. One of the earliest models of reading was the substrata-factor theory of Holmes (1970) and Singer (1985c). Calfee (Calfee & Spector 1981, Calfee 1982) proposes a two-stage independent process model that assumes that cognitive processes can be divided into relatively independent subprocesses. E. Brown (1981) presents a model that stresses aspects of comprehending language that are unique to reading. Other models are based on eye-movement research (Carpenter & Just 1981; Just & Carpenter 1987) or artificial intelligence (Schank 1982).

Most current conceptualizations of the reading process are based heavily on the theories and findings of cognitive psychologists and information-processing theorists. *Cognitive psychology* is concerned with various mental activities related to human information processing and problem solving (e.g., perception, thinking, and how knowledge is represented, manipulated, and stored). It also is concerned with how basic component skills are organized and managed by higher-level processes, and with the reciprocal influences (operating at different levels of complexity) that these processes have on one another (Torgesen 1986a).

[5]Refer to Perfetti (1986b, pp. 47–48) for an easily understood explanation of Rumelhart's model.

Cognitive psychology currently represents the mainstream of thinking in both psychology and education (Shuell 1986).

Information processing theories deal with how sensory input is transformed, reduced, elaborated, stored, retrieved, and used. Three general components underlie information processing theory: (1) a structural component (similar to computer hardware) that sets the limits within which information can be processed at a particular stage (e.g., sensory store, short-term memory); (2) a control component (similar to computer software) that prescribes the operations at various stages; and (3) an executive process by which the reader's activities (e.g., application of strategies) are overseen and monitored. The information flow occurs in sequential stages, but there is a simultaneous flow of information among the subprocesses. At each stage, the available information is transformed and becomes the input for the succeeding stage (Swanson 1987a). Information processing models hold that the human mind has a limited capacity for processing information: Only a limited amount of information can be processed at one time. This belief implies that using the brain's limited processing capacity to execute lower-level processes (e.g., word recognition) lessens the amount available for executing higher-level processes (e.g., reading comprehension).

Instructional Implications of Reading Models

Opinions differ regarding how reading models should or actually do influence instructional practices. At one end of the argument are authors like Pearson and Kamil (1978), who believe that most teachers are guided by at least an implicit model of reading, and Singer (1985b), who states that reading models have direct instructional implications, if instruction is not defined too narrowly. At the other end of the argument are writers such as Venezky (1979a), who warn against premature leaps from theory to practice, and Duffy (1985), who claims that any theoretical knowledge possessed by teachers must, in instructional applications, be modified to fit the constraints and realities imposed by the classroom.

Beck and McKeown (1986) write that the relationship between theory and practice is not necessarily straightforward because: (1) theorists are primarily concerned with explaining how the reading process works rather than with providing explanations that can be applied directly to classroom practice; and (2) even when there is concern about relating theory to practice, exactly how such a relationship should be drawn is not clear. Suggestions for applying theory more often take the form of general recommendations than of specific concrete suggestions.

Some argue that models of reading have little, if any, impact on classroom instruction because teachers just follow whatever the basal program suggests and teachers have little input in selecting a basal series. The counterarguments are that the basal series' authors were influenced by some model and, more importantly, that the basal reader series should not be the entire reading program, nor should teachers follow the manuals slavishly.

It appears that one's point of view regarding the impact of reading models on instructional practice depends on how instruction is defined, the level at which the impact is believed to take place, and one's faith in the instructional competence of teachers. Nevertheless, adoption of one of the types of models would seem to have at least some broad implications for what is emphasized when reading is taught, especially in the case of novice readers.[6]

Adherents to a bottom-up model would place early and heavy instructional emphasis on decoding and word-recognition skills. Comprehension would not be ignored, but fast, accurate word recognition would be stressed because such reading behavior is believed necessary for reading comprehension to take place. Accordingly, teacher-centered direct instruction would be emphasized.

Top-down advocates would stress comprehension, and would keep decoding and word-recognition instruction to a minimum. Deviations from the printed words (i.e., miscues) would not necessarily be seen as disruptive to reading comprehension. The role of the teacher would be to guide and facilitate learning; instruction would be child centered. For example, rather than telling children words that they did not recognize accurately, the teacher would intervene only if the miscues were disruptive to comprehension, with "instruction" taking the form of providing cues to the reader as to how semantic and syntactic information, and perhaps even graphic information, could have been used to monitor and correct disruptive miscues. Thus, a child's mispronouncing a noun as a verb (e.g., printed word = *dog;* child's response = "dig") would likely bring a teacher response of "Does that sound right?" after the child had finished reading the sentence in which the miscue occurred.

It is difficult to state what instructional emphasis would result from following an interactive model because of the interactive effects word recognition and comprehension are believed to have on each other. It seems safe to say that neither would be overemphasized. However, followers of models such as Perfetti's (1985) would require automatic, accurate, context-free word recognition, especially during the initial stages of reading acquisition.

Despite these general instructional suggestions, it would be premature to base instruction on any particular model of the reading process. None of the models is complete, and the research evidence in support of any of them is limited. At present, no model specifies exactly *how* decoding, word recognition, reading vocabulary, or reading comprehension can best be taught and learned.

Diagnostic and Remedial Implications of Reading Models

It is not surprising to find articles that relate the diagnosis and treatment of reading disability to reading models (e.g., Rispens 1982). The approach of the diagnostician—the tests and procedures used, the interpretation of the findings, and the recommended remedial treatments—is probably influenced, at least initially, by what the individual believes the reading process involves.

Advocates of bottom-up models tend to emphasize diagnosing and treating decoding and word-recognition problems, in the belief that such weaknesses are the primary contributors to inadequate reading comprehension. Separate skills and strategies would likely be tested, and remediation would attempt to over-

---

[6]See Strange (1980) for a discussion of the instructional implications of the three types of models.

come specific weaknesses. If the initial tests did not indicate that bottom-up processes were weak, or if comprehension was still inadequate after the remediation of decoding or word-recognition weaknesses, the diagnostician would seek other causal or contributing factors.

Because word-recognition accuracy is not a primary concern, people who favor a top-down model tend to view miscues as indications of the reader's processing strategies. Thus, word recognition ability would rarely be tested by presenting words in isolation as would occur when following most bottom-up and some interactive models. Diagnoses would focus on determining the extent to which the reader was using and coordinating cues from the available sources of information, especially those "in the reader's head," in an effort to understand why top-down processing was breaking down. Remediation would play to the child's strengths and involve teaching how to generate and monitor hypotheses about the meaning of the material, as well as teaching the appropriate use of strategies for testing these hypotheses.

Followers of interactive models and some top-down advocates believe that the reading process is made up of highly interrelated subprocesses. Inability to coordinate the subprocesses or weakness in any subprocess may have a negative impact on reading comprehension. Therefore, those who abide by an interactive model would probably attempt to determine possible deficiencies in any of the information sources and discover how they might be impinging on each other. Doing so, however, may not be easy. For example, some processes appear to mediate both word recognition and text comprehension (Stanovich 1982a,b).

THE RELATIONSHIP OF READING TO LANGUAGE

As T. L. Harris and Hodges (1981) state, ". . . defining language is both a difficult and controversial effort, and a definition . . . is conditioned by the theoretical and subjective views of the definer." We prefer the *American Heritage Dictionary* (1985, p. 713) definition of language, "The use by human beings of voice sounds, and often written symbols that represent these sounds, in organized combinations and patterns to express and communicate thoughts and feelings." In short, *language* is a communication system that employs spoken and written symbols to convey a meaning to those who understand the signal system. Knowing a language involves having abstract and complex knowledge of its phonological (sound) system, word meanings (lexical and semantic knowledge), how the words may be combined into permissible, comprehensible sentences (syntactic and semantic knowledge), as well as how these various components relate to one another (Lindfors 1985). Ruddell and Speaker (1985) include knowing how spoken and written texts are structured as an aspect of language knowledge.

Typically much of this knowledge is not at a conscious level. *Linguistic awareness* is that part of one's knowledge of linguistic structures that is at least partially accessible. What a child knows about language structures is implicit knowledge, but learning to read requires that some kind of linguistic structure be brought up to a partially explicit level of knowledge. Linguistic awareness probably produces readiness for learning to read; and learning to read produces linguistic awareness (Perfetti 1985).

Spoken and Written Language

There are two forms of language—spoken and written—and each has an expressive and a receptive aspect. Spoken language includes communicating through speaking and listening. Written or printed language encompasses writing (authorship, not penmanship) and reading. When language appears in written form, the reader must also understand the relationship of written to spoken language.

In the usual sequence of language development, understanding and producing spoken language precedes understanding and producing written language. When children enter school, they have a language foundation upon which reading and writing skills can be developed. Young children typically have sufficient control of spoken language to allow them to function at least adequately in most communication situations. But such a level of language competence will not be adequate if the child is to progress much beyond the initial stages of reading acquisition. Reading development requires increasingly greater language competence.

Ruddell and Haggard (1985) hypothesized that oral and written language acquisition are parallel and interactive in their development and that oral and written language development are directly related to, and interactive with, reading acquisition and development. Language knowledge acquired through listening and speaking can, and should, help in the acquisition and development of reading ability by providing a linguistic knowledge base, which can be used to understand written language. Oral language abilities continue to grow as students encounter more sophisticated linguistic structures in written text. As exposure to more complex oral and written language forms increases, students are more likely to use such structures in their oral and written language production and comprehension (Ruddell & Speaker 1985).

As discussed more thoroughly in Chapter 8, various aspects of spoken language have been found to be related to reading ability, with the relationships often increasing or decreasing in magnitude as students get older. Such findings would seem to suggest that certain aspects of spoken language competence are more important than others during various stages of reading development. But correlational data do not necessarily indicate a direct cause-effect relationship. Furthermore, it is very difficult, if not impossible, to separate the effects of language knowledge from those of cognitive abilities, both of which seem to have a significant influence on reading acquisition and growth.

SPOKEN LANGUAGE DEVELOPMENT.   The following brief discussion is meant to provide a basic understanding of the various aspects of spoken language, their development, and how they relate to reading development. There is considerable individual variation in the rate of language acquisition (Willows & Ryan 1986).

Phonological Knowledge.   Almost all novice readers have a high degree of control over the phonological (sound) system of English (Ruddell & Haggard

1985). They can produce and understand spoken words that differ in only one *phoneme* (the minimal sound unit for distinguishing meaning). This knowledge provides the basis for the later acquisition of symbol-sound associations needed for decoding printed words.

Morphological Knowledge.[7,8]   *Morphology* is the pattern of word formation in a language, including derivation, inflection, and compounding (T. L. Harris & Hodges 1981). *Derivation* involves the use of affixes to form new words from a root or base word (e.g., *kind + ness*). *Inflection* involves adding suffixes that change a word's form or function but not its basic meaning. Inflectional suffixes include plural markers (*s, es*), verb endings (*s, ed, ing, en*), possessives (*'s, s'*), and comparative and superlative markers (*er, est*). *Compounding* is forming a new word from two or more words (e.g., *dog house*).

Although age differences affect the acquisition and control of various morphemes, most 6-year-olds have mastered the most common morphological rules of English. Acquisition of morphological knowledge continues well into the primary grades and follows a highly consistent pattern: (1) little or no use, (2) sporadic use, (3) overgeneralization, and (4) adult-like usage (Ruddell & Haggard 1985).

Morphological knowledge is used early in reading instruction when children are shown how "new" printed words can be formed by adding inflected endings to words they already know.

Syntactic Knowledge.   *Syntax* is the system of rules governing word order in clauses, phrases, and sentences. Only certain word sequences are allowable in English. Most children in kindergarten and first grade can comprehend and produce expanded and elaborated sentences. Development and control of syntax extends well into and perhaps through the elementary school (Ruddell & Haggard 1985). Children continue to make substantial gains in their ability to understand syntactic structures until at least age 13.

Syntactic knowledge allows the reader to organize information into chunks larger than single words. With increasing syntactic competence comes the ability to chunk words into larger meaningful units (Ruddell & Speaker 1985). Only a limited number of bits of information can be held in short-term memory at once. Therefore, having to deal with meaningful units larger than those conveyed by single words facilitates information processing.

Syntactic competence and comprehension are also related in other ways. For example, the sequence in which words, clauses and phrases are arranged determines the meaning of a sentence. Syntactic knowledge allows readers to predict what type of words are likely to follow in a sentence they have begun to read and when this information is combined with lexical and prior knowledge, the choices become further constrained.

---

[7]The written rather than the spoken forms are presented here to make them more easily understood.

[8]A *morpheme* is a unit of language that conveys meaning. A *free morpheme* is a whole word that cannot be further divided into meaning-bearing units (e.g., *girl*). A *bound morpheme* (inflectional endings and affixes) must be combined with a free morpheme whose meaning it changes (e.g., *girls*).

Many 4- and 5-year-olds produce spoken sentences that contain all the basic syntactic transformations that underlie adult sentence structures. This finding has led some to conclude that novice readers are linguistically mature. Such a claim is an overstatement (M. Adams 1980). Oral language syntactic competence is only moderately correlated with first-grade reading achievement (Fletcher 1981). More importantly, reading demands more syntactic sophistication than does oral language production or reception. A big difference exists between producing sentences that contain the same syntactic structures used by adults and being able to understand syntactically complex printed sentences as well as adults do.

Young children need relatively little syntactic sophistication to understand most language spoken to them because additional clues to meaning are provided by the speaker and the physical context in which the communication occurs (see page 21). Unless readers can construct syntactic structure from printed text, it does not matter if they have the syntactic competence to understand the spoken message (M. Adams 1980). The grammatical sensitivity required for reading connected discourse involves analytical knowledge of sentence structure and deliberate effort to access that knowledge appropriately, as well as to coordinate that knowledge with whatever other information is needed to interpret the text's meaning (Willows & Ryan 1986).

Novice readers are much more familiar with the less formal syntax used in spoken conversation than with the formal syntax found in written language; the latter may cause problems for some children (Rubin 1980b). Reading to preschoolers and novice readers may help to lessen such potential difficulties.

Semantic Knowledge.   *Semantic knowledge*, as it relates most directly to language development, is fairly well developed when children enter school. First graders can understand the meanings of, and use in their spoken language, many hundreds of words. Eventually they come to understand the arbitrary nature of language as they learn that words are labels for concepts and that a given label may represent several concepts, its meaning in a particular situation being dependent on the context in which it is set. With the exception of relative terms, concepts develop along a continuum from concrete through functional to abstract levels (Ruddell & Haggard 1985).

Hodges (1970), Holdzkom et al. (1984), and Lindfors (1985) discuss language development during the elementary school years. Athey (1985a) summarizes a number of language acquisition models.

Differences between Spoken and Written Language and Their Influence on Comprehension

Novice readers must learn not only that the odd-looking marks on the printed page represent the written form of language, but also that written language is meaningful and differs from oral language in certain ways. As J. Mason and Allen (1986) put it, literacy is not a simple extension of oral language; written language contains new and difficult-to-learn concepts.

When discussing differences between spoken and written language and their effects on comprehension, one must consider the purpose of the communication and the setting in which it takes place. Different discourse structures are used in formal and informal situations. For example, informal spoken conversational language tends to be repetitious, and incomplete syntax is often used. Formal written language tends to be concise and grammatically correct, and may contain syntactic structures that differ from those used to deliver the same message in spoken language. The language used in an informal letter to a friend may be similar to that found in informal spoken conversation; the language employed in a formal speech may closely approximate that found in textbooks.

Oral language, especially informal oral language, takes place in a "real-world context." Potentially ambiguous words, such as *this, here,* and *now* are readily understandable because they are usually accompanied by gestures indicating their referents, or because their meaning is clearly understood as referring to the place and time of the ongoing communication. Readers often have to infer the meanings of such words.

Oral language communication usually requires less syntactic competence than does written language because less complex sentences are used in oral language. In order to make written language as cohesive as oral language, authors, who are physically separated from their readers, must use more complex structures such as passives, a variety of tense forms, propositional noun modifiers, a variety of adjectival phrases, a variety of subordinate phrases, phrases in apposition, and logical and subordinate connectives. Furthermore, because intonational cues are not available to the reader, authors often place important information at the ends of sentences (J. Mason & Allen 1986).

In normal conversation, little question exists as to who is speaking, and the way in which the voice is used (see the following section on prosody) makes it fairly easy to understand the spoken, and perhaps implicit, message. The face-to-face interchange also provides extralinguistic cues to meaning and intent. Gestures and facial expression are especially helpful when the words do not really convey the intended meaning (e.g., a raised eyebrow can mean that the speaker questions what the words seem to say). The reader, in contrast to the listener, has to rely less on situational cues and more on linguistic cues and prior knowledge to obtain meaning. Readers must use punctuation marks as cues to who is speaking. They also must interpret the speaker's feelings primarily from applying an understanding of how a person would be likely to react and speak in a situation of that sort—although punctuation and the words used may also provide clues.

Speakers communicate with a given audience who is present and interacting directly with them. Viewing the reactions of the listeners allows speakers to adjust their manner of communicating. In addition, the listener may have opportunities to request clarification or additional information. Authors, on the other hand, write for an intended audience, and have no further opportunity to clarify their fixed written messages. Readers cannot ask the author for clarification or further information.

Lastly, the speaker greatly eases the comprehension task of the listener by pausing between thought units. Readers must chunk the information on their own.

PROSODY.   Speakers can provide three kinds of prosodic cues—pitch, stress, and juncture—that help to indicate the intended meaning of their utterances. *Pitch*—raising or lowering the voice—may provide cues as to the kind of sentence (e.g., most interrogative sentences end with a rising pitch). *Stress* involves accenting a syllable or word. Stressing a syllable can indicate the word's part of speech and sometimes its meaning (e.g., con´vict versus con-vict´). Accenting a word can modify meaning (e.g., *He* broke the glass. He *broke* the glass. He broke the *glass*.). Stressing a pronoun helps to indicate its referent (e.g., in "Rob hit Mike and then *Susie* hit him," *him* refers to Mike. But in "Rob hit Mike and then Susie hit *him*," *him* refers to Rob). *Juncture* involves slight pauses between words, longer pauses between phrases and clauses, and even longer pauses between sentences. Pauses and changes in speed often provide clues for chunking words into clauses and phrases. Generally, pauses occur at syntactic boundaries.

The ability to comprehend written language requires the acquisition of alternative strategies to compensate for the lack of prosodic features. In written language, the only available clues to pitch are punctuation marks. Occasionally, stress is cued by italics, boldface type, or the use of all capital letters. Spaces between printed words substitute for the brief pauses in speech and wider spaces, as well as periods, questions marks, and exclamation points, mark the ends of sentences. Although commas or semicolons may set off some phrases or clauses, readers often have to segment sentences into syntactic units on their own.

Punctuation marks also help identify units such as possessives, which are marked by apostrophes. Quotation marks help to separate and identify direct speech. In conversation, who is doing the speaking is clearly indicated. In the conversational dialogues that appear frequently in preprimers and primers, the characters' utterances are set off by quotation marks and phrases such as "Marcia said." The ability to interpret such cues is important for comprehension. Consider the difference in meaning between the following: Susie said, "Rob, I am here," and "Susie," said Rob, "I am here." In some reading materials, the words spoken by each character are not indicated by quotation marks, and phrases such as "asked Jim" are dropped after the first few times. As a result, it is easy for the novice reader to lose track of who said what.

Although typographical cues and punctuation marks do not reflect all the prosody of spoken language, they can be helpful to readers who understand their use. But children more than adults tend to rely on prosodic cues and are less able to employ lexical, syntactic, and semantic cues. Therefore, they may have difficulty compensating for the lack of prosody in written text.

Differences in Processing Spoken and Written Language

Opinions differ as to whether similar processing is involved in listening and reading, and if not, how important such processing differences are (see Danks & End 1987). Those who hold that listening and reading comprehension involve the same or similar processing propose that written language is parasitic on spoken language. To them, reading is decoding, a position compatible with bottom-up models of reading. They believe that once written language is recorded into its spoken form, readers apply the same processing skills as they would if they were listening to that message. Others argue that, while the use of listening skills may facilitate reading comprehension, the need for more sophisticated language skills, as well as additional processing skills, makes reading comprehension more difficult than listening comprehension.

Similarly, opinions differ as to whether oral reading and silent reading involve the same processes. Some writers (e.g., Juel & Holmes 1981) believe they do; others (e.g., Mosenthal 1976–1977) argue that important differences exist between processing oral and silent reading. Yet others (e.g., Danks & Hill 1981) feel that we understand very little of oral reading processing requirements or how they relate to silent reading. Each group offers some evidence to support its viewpoint, but definitive evidence is yet to be presented. Such debates are not merely intellectual, however; they have relevance for understanding the reading process, as well as practical significance. For instance, oral reading measures are often employed in making diagnoses. The presence or absence of certain types of processing are inferred from the overt behaviors, and the assumption is made that a similar pattern accounts for the student's silent reading processing.

English Orthography[9]

English uses an *alphabetic writing system*. Our 26 letters can be used, singularly and in combination, to represent approximately 44 sounds that can be combined to construct all the words in our language. Alphabetic orthographies may be characterized by the extent to which they represent speech sounds. A shallow orthography has spelling-to-sound correspondences that are simple and consistent. A deep orthography, such as English, has spelling-to-sound relationships that are complex. English spellings reflect not only grapheme-phoneme and phoneme-grapheme relationships, but also semantic relationships at the morphophonemic level.[10] Morphophonemes follow rules that are more complex than grapheme-phoneme correspondences, and many so-called exceptions in English orthography are actually rule governed (Venezky 1970b). The underlying regularity of spellings at the morphophonemic level aids the skilled reader in understanding similarities in meaning among words, despite changes in vowel sounds and accent shifts (e.g., *courage, courageous*).

Other spelling conventions also provide grammatical and semantic cues to the reader. For example, although the final *s* represents /s/ in *cats* and /z/ in *dogs*, the reader is cued that *s* signals pluralization of both nouns. Differences

[9]Refer to L. Henderson (1982) for a comprehensive treatment of English orthography and a brief history of writing systems. See I. Taylor (1981) for a discussion of various writing systems; Weigl (1980) for a brief history of written language leading to our use of an alphabetic writing system, and Calfee and Drum (1985) or Tompkins and Yaden (1986) for a brief history of spoken and written English.

[10]A *morphophoneme* is a unit of language that is intermediate between a *morpheme* and a *phoneme*. A *morpheme* is a unit of language that conveys meaning. A *phoneme* is the minimal sound unit that distinguishes one meaningful word from another (e.g., /b/at or /s/at). A *grapheme* is a written or printed letter or letters that represents a phoneme.

in the spellings of *homophones* (words that have the same pronunciation but different spellings due to differences in their origins) such as *hare* and *hair* provide visual cues to word meaning. Furthermore, our writing system functions well for a variety of dialect speakers because although dialect speakers may pronounce the words differently (see p. 83), printed words signal their meaning. Thus a speaker of black English whose pronunciation of *pin* and *pen* was the same would understand the meaning of *pen* in the printed sentence, "There is no ink in my pen." It should be realized, however, that although English orthography may be "near optimal" for a formal system of rules, the speaker's or reader's internalized rules are not as well defined or consistently applied as some authors suggest.

The opinion is frequently voiced that the irregularities of English grapheme-phoneme correspondences are roadblocks in learning to read. The classic example is G. B. Shaw's contention that *fish* can be spelled *ghoti* (*gh* as in tough, *o* as in women and *ti* as in nation). But such a spelling is impossible given the constraints of English orthography. At the beginning of words, *gh* never represents /f/, nor does *ti* represent /sh/ in the final position. Those who consider English orthography to be irregular often cite the finding of Hanna & Hanna (1966) that only half the approximately 17,000 words they studied could be spelled correctly by applying a series of phoneme-grapheme correspondence rules. But, as Hodges (1982) points out, about 37% of the misspelled words had only one incorrect phoneme-grapheme match. If Hanna and Hanna had accounted for morphological relationships, approximately 87% of the words would have been spelled correctly.

English spellings are constrained as to where in a word a grapheme can occur (e.g., a word never begins with *ck*) and the sequence in which graphemes can occur (e.g., *q* is always followed by *u*). The combination of letters that can occur in the spelling of a word is also restricted. For example, only 30 of a possible 441 combinations of two consonants actually occur in English spellings (L. Haber & Haber 1981).

But if English spellings are more consistent than commonly thought, why do so many English words have unusual spellings?[11]

The answer lies in the history of English spellings. In the early days of English orthography there were no commonly agreed-on spellings for large numbers of words. Nevertheless, the relationship between the ways words were spelled in Anglo-Saxon, Old English, and Middle English and the ways they were pronounced was much closer than it is for many words in Modern English. Various factors throughout the years have contributed to the straying of English spelling from its alphabetic base (Barnitz 1980, Baron et al. 1980, L. Henderson 1982, Balmuth 1982, Tompkins & Yaden 1986):

1. *Sound changes.* Although over time the pronunciations of many words changed, their spellings did not. Thus, the spellings no longer reflect pronunciation.

[11]This is especially noticeable with *function words* (articles, prepositions, conjunctions, and some auxiliary or linking verbs) that occur frequently in print because they indicate grammatical and meaning relationships (Calfee & Drum 1985).

2. *Borrowed words.* Words borrowed from other languages are usually pronounced as in the original language and retain their original spelling (e.g., *cello* from Italian, *bouquet* from French). English contains many borrowed words.
3. *Adoptions of new spellings* by scribes before spelling became standardized. For example, in 1066 Anglo-Saxon scribes began using the French distinction of hard and soft *c*.
4. *Analogy or inverse spelling.* To standardize spellings, many words that were thought to be related were respelled to match existing strong spelling patterns. Thus, the French *delite* became *delight*. However, the assumptions about relationships were not always correct. For example, the Old English word *caude* was spelled *could* when the spelling of *wolde* became *would*. During these changes, words like *come* and *love* came to be spelled with an *o* rather than with a *u* as in the original *cumen* and *luve*.
5. *Etymology.* To standardize spellings, the origins of words were employed, particularly classical Latin. At times, these efforts were misdirected. For example, the Middle English word *sisoures* acquired a silent *c* (scissors) in the belief that it was derived from the Latin *scindere* (to cut) rather than from its actual etymological source *cisorium* (a cutting tool).
6. *Homophones.* Spellings were changed to distinguish between *homophones* (words with the same pronunciation but which represent unrelated meanings). For example, we have *sum-some* and *whole-hole*. Interestingly, however, we have retained the spelling *holistic* rather than *wholistic*, which would more clearly designate its meaning.

Effect of Orthography on Reading Acquisition and Processes

Feitelson (1976) concludes that it is easier to learn to read an alphabetic language that has consistent spelling-to-sound associations than one with many irregularities because there is much less to learn and what has to be learned is less complex. Barnitz (1978) draws a similar conclusion based on cross-linguistic and bilingual studies. But although the orthography might make it easier to learn to "crack the code," it may not influence reading comprehension. For instance, written Finnish has a very consistent grapheme-phoneme relationship, yet Finnish children have as much difficulty with comprehension as those learning to read other languages (Kyöstiö 1980). L. Henderson (1982) feels that linguists' intuition that a shallow orthography might be easier for children and that a morphophonemic orthography might be more suitable for skilled readers remains untested.

The most frequently cited example of the effect of a writing system on reading achievement is Japanese. Makita (1976) attributed the low incidence of reading disability in Japan to the nature of the Japanese writing system,[12] which is

---

[12]Tzeng and Hung (1981) cautioned against accepting this cause-effect relationship for a number of stated reasons.

basically a combination of two types of symbols—Kana[13] and Kanji. In Kana, each symbol represents a consonant-vowel syllable. Rarely is a Kana syllable pronounced in more than one way. The Kanji symbols are ideographs borrowed from Chinese.[14] Kana seems fairly easy to learn (I. Taylor 1981), and because many Japanese preschoolers have informally learned the Kana system at home (Sheridan 1982), beginning reading materials, which employ only Kana, present little difficulty (Sakamoto 1976). As Kanji is introduced, reading difficulties become more frequent (Barnitz 1978).

The influence of parents on the success of learning to read in Japan cannot be overlooked. Japanese parents are strongly encouraged to prepare their children for learning to read and apparently do so by giving them books (almost half of the children's publications in Japan are written for preschoolers), answering questions about reading, and reading to their children by the time they are a year old (Sakamoto 1981).

Stevenson (1984) administered comparable reading tests individually to fifth graders in Taiwan ($N=956$), Japan ($N=755$), and the United States ($N=453$). The tests were in the students' native languages. The percentages of students reading three or more years below grade level were 9% in Chinese, 2% in Japanese and 3% in English. Stevenson concludes: "Although the form of writing used in any language may be an impediment to the efforts of certain children in learning to read, it seems very unlikely that any particular form of writing is especially conducive to the production of severe reading problems."

Aspects of Language and Their Interrelationships

Listening, speaking, reading, and writing are interrelated aspects of language. Listening begins to develop before speaking, and development in one area is thought to enhance development in the other. Both listening and speaking abilities develop naturally, in the sense that they are acquired without formal instruction. Receptive and expressive spoken language skills begin to develop early in life and continue to develop long after children enter school. Linguistic knowledge thus acquired provides the foundation upon which written language abilities develop. Receptive (reading) and expressive (writing) written language development usually is not much beyond the emerging-literacy or novice-reader stage when children enter school.

EXPRESSIVE ORAL LANGUAGE ABILITY AND READING ABILITY. Although the relationships reported between expressive oral language ability and reading ability are primarily correlational, there is more direct evidence of a causal relationship. For example, children can better comprehend printed sentences that follow the patterns used in their oral language production (Ruddell 1974). The direction of this relationship seems apparent because expressive oral language ability precedes written receptive language ability in the novice stage

---

[13]There are two types of Kana: *Hiragana*, which is used with words of Japanese origin; and *Katagana*, which is used with foreign loan words.

[14]An *ideograph* is a graphic symbol that represents an idea or an object rather than a speech sound or word.

of reading and for a period thereafter, after which the cause-effect relationship probably becomes more reciprocal. Students must often use their oral expressive language skills to demonstrate their comprehension of printed text.

Pellegrini, DeStefano, and Thompson (1983) suggest that children's ability to convey information through oral language is a necessary component for success in learning to read and write, and therefore should be incorporated into the language arts program. Yet little of such instructional practice is found in the literature, and probably a great deal less in the actual classroom. This is unfortunate: Even if oral skill demonstrated no positive impact on reading ability, developing children's oral expressive language skills would be a defensible educational goal.

RECEPTIVE ORAL LANGUAGE ABILITY AND READING ABILITY. Listening comprehension precedes reading comprehension in development and, at school entry and well into the elementary school, listening comprehension ability exceeds reading comprehension ability. The correlations between listening and reading comprehension are weak but significant in the early elementary grades, moderately strong in the middle grades, and especially strong in adults (Stanovich 1985).

Some processing skills are common to both listening and reading. Because listening comprehension is usually more highly developed than reading comprehension, attempts are made to help students transfer oral language processing skills to reading comprehension. Such attempts are discussed on pages 577–578.

SPELLING AND READING ABILITIES. Spelling is not a low-order psychomotor skill but a consequence of complex cognitive operations that only now are coming to be understood (Frith 1980). Wong (1986a) states that spelling is a cognitive act in which the speller coordinates several sources of word knowledge, including knowledge of individual sounds (phonemes) in spoken words, the relationship between phonemes in words and their orthographic or spelling patterns, and syntactic and semantic knowledge of words. Phonological-segmentation ability is highly related, perhaps causally, to the acquisition of spelling ability (Liberman et al. 1985; Mann, Tobin & Wilson 1988).

The correlations between reading and spelling range from 0.68 to 0.86 in the first grade and are around 0.66 in second grade and 0.60 in third grade (Ehri & Wilce 1987). Children are usually good readers and good spellers or poor readers and poor spellers. Some good readers are poor spellers (Frith & Frith 1980) but good spellers usually are not poor readers (Miles & Halsum 1986). Poor spellers are not always poor readers (Ehri 1987).

Childrens' early attempts at spelling reveal information regarding the nature and development of spelling ability. Some young children invent their own spellings even before they learn to read (Read 1971, 1975; C. Chomsky 1979). Their *invented spellings* reveal that these children apparently detect and use the phonetic relationships represented in English orthography. Intuitively, they devise a logical system for relating English phonology and orthography, using the letters of the alphabet to do so. Invented spellings seem to have five stages, each representing a different conceptualization of English orthography (Gentry 1982, M. Wood 1982):

1. *Deviant spelling stage.* Children use letters of the alphabet to represent words, but their spelling attempts are not readable because they do not understand the relationships of letters, letter names, and the sounds letters represent.
2. *Prephonetic stage.* The spellings begin to represent grapheme-phoneme relationships. One or more letters are used to represent a word, and a letter-name strategy is employed (e.g., R = are; LEFT = elephant).
3. *Phonetic stage.* Phonetic spellings are quite regular and all the sound features of the word are represented in the spelling.
4. *Transitional stage.* There is a marked movement toward standard spellings; a situation fostered by reading and spelling instruction. Children's spellings begin to adhere more to the basic conventions of English orthography. Vowels and consonants replace the letter-name strategy (e.g., *elephant* is spelled ELEFANT rather than LEFT, as in the second stage), common English sequences are employed (e.g., YOUNITED = united), and there is a move from phonological to morphological and visual spelling (e.g., *eighty* is spelled EIGHTEE rather than ATE, as in the second stage).
5. *Standard spelling stage.* Knowledge of the English orthographic system and its basic rules is firmly established. Children exhibit correct spellings for words that are appropriate for their grade levels.

Some writers maintain that children who invent spelling learn to read and spell more easily than through direct instruction (Clay 1975). L. Clarke (1988) reports that first graders who used invented spellings scored significantly higher than those who used traditional spellings on measures of spelling and word analysis, but not on word recognition or comprehension. However, longitudinal data regarding the possible influence of invented spelling on learning to read are not extensive enough for a conclusive answer (M. Wood 1982).

Evidence from studies of the development of spelling ability led Hodges (1982) to conclude:

1. Children make few, if any, random spelling errors. Therefore, observing and analyzing their spelling errors can reveal information about their development of spelling ability and about a particular child's own logical scheme for spelling words at a given point in development.
2. Efficient spellers seem to have visual, morphophonemic, phonetic, and semantic information about words and to use this knowledge in attempting to spell unfamiliar words. Learning to spell is, to a large degree, learning about both the phonological and the graphic structures of words.
3. Learning to spell is part of general language development, and it both draws on and is constrained by cognitive and linguistic factors inherent in the acquisition of language. Knowledge of English orthography and other writing conventions is learned continuously by an interaction with written language.

4. In learning to spell, children do not move from one aspect of the orthography to the next—from sounds and letters to syllables to words. Rather, learning to spell involves developing an understanding of the total framework of English orthography and of the interrelatedness among phonological, morphological, and other language factors.
5. A number of issues regarding spelling instruction are unresolved.

EXPRESSIVE WRITTEN LANGUAGE AND READING ABILITY. Written language production proceeds from the preliterate writing stage through the formal writing stage. Children's early written products resemble spoken language, but the complexity of the written productions increases steadily through the elementary school years (Ruddell & Haggard 1985). Initially, expressive written language ability is heavily dependent on oral language knowledge. Many young children verbalize or subvocalize what they write, thus suggesting that they are dictating to themselves. Later, written expression becomes independent in developmental stages that reflect changes in the level of acquisition of spoken and written language knowledge (Flood & Lapp 1987).

In the early 1980s, theories of reading and writing began to interface in that both stressed the active role of the reader and author and the interactive nature of both processes. Kucer (1987) indicates that: (1) readers and writers construct meanings through utilizing prior knowledge; (2) written language systems operate by feeding into a common data pool from which language users draw when constructing meaning, language users know how written language operates as a communication system, the function that written language serves, and the organizational patterns to which texts must conform, and are aware of the semantic, syntactic, and orthographic features of the written language system; and (3) readers and writers display common processing patterns when constructing meaning.

The apparent relationship between reading and writing abilities has led a number of authors to suggest that writing activities should precede or occur simultaneously with initial reading instruction, and that improvement in one area will carry over to the other even at later stages of written language development. Explanation as to why increased writing ability should have an impact on reading development range from the belief that both involve the structuring of meaning to "writing influences sight word recognition" to "writing enhances memory" (Alvermann 1987b).

F. Smith (1983) states that children can learn to write (compose written material) like a writer from what they read by "reading like a writer." Goodman and Goodman (1983), who agree with Smith, also point out that readers need not write during reading, but writers must read and reread during writing. So writing experiences are likely to have a positive impact on reading comprehension because "all of the schemata for predicting texts in reading are essentially the same as those used in constructing texts during writing."

According to Tierney and Pearson (1983), reading and writing must be viewed as essentially similar processes of meaning construction in order for the connection between them to be understood. Both are acts of composing. A similar viewpoint was presented by Wittrock (1983), who believes that good reading and effective writing involve similar processes that create meaning by building relationships between the text and what is known, believed, and experienced.

Despite these theoretical viewpoints, little is known about the exact nature of the reading and writing relationship. Her review of the literature led Stotsky (1983) to conclude the following:

1. Correlational studies almost consistently show that better writers tend to be better readers and to read more than poor writers, and better readers tend to produce more syntactically mature writing than poorer readers.
2. Experimental studies that used writing exercises primarily to improve writing did not tend to produce significant effects on reading. But almost all studies that used such procedures specifically to improve reading comprehension found small but significant gains in reading.
3. Studies that attempted to improve writing by providing reading experiences in place of grammar study or additional writing practice found reading to be as beneficial as, or more beneficial than, the experiences they replaced. But almost all studies that sought to improve writing through reading instruction were ineffective.

Flood and Lapp (1987) draw three generalizations from research findings: (1) both reading and writing are related to oral language abilities; the relations between oral and written language abilities are fundamental and reciprocal; (2) both reading and writing are cognitive/metacognitive activities requiring analysis and synthesis as well as appropriate motivation and attitudes; and (3) both reading and writing are developmental abilities whose relationships change over time.

Langer (1986), on the other hand, concludes that reading and writing skills are not as closely related as is commonly assumed. She believes that though reading and writing rely on the same knowledge and language bases, these bases are used differently because they are performed for different purposes.

Before preparing to write, students should consider the purpose of their written message and their intended audience. The steps in producing a written message include generating ideas, drafting, revising, and editing; but these steps are not strictly sequential. Writing a draft may produce new ideas and editing may indicate the need for revision. In addition to understanding the purposes for writing and the strategies that can be employed in producing a written message, students must be able to manage the conventions of written English (spelling, grammar, punctuation, and sentence construction) that allow them to communicate (NAEP 1983c). Refer to Hillocks (1986) for a review and critique of the research on written composition.

INSTRUCTIONAL INTEGRATION OF THE LANGUAGE ARTS. A number of writers suggest that because reading is a language-based ability, it should either be part of a well-balanced language arts program in which no one aspect of language is over- or underemphasized, or be integrated within the language arts curriculum (e.g., Shuy 1981b; Seaver & Botel 1983). This viewpoint is held by those who believe in the holistic nature of language. The basic premise is that the various language arts are highly interrelated and that children should be made explicitly aware of the relationships. A concomitant belief is that

contributing to successful reading acquisition could be determined, and programs formulated for developing them. How well a factor correlated with reading achievement was largely the basis for determining what should be taught in a reading readiness program. Readiness tests and programs were developed and reading instruction was delayed for the unready.

Unfortunately, as with other good ideas, the concept lost something in later translation. Some educators felt that if reading readiness activities were good for some children, they should be good for all children. This led to a requirement that particular readiness activities be completed (often one or more readiness workbooks) before starting reading instruction, even if the child was ready to read or already reading! This malpractice prevailed in many school systems for over 30 years.

The other viewpoint relied heavily on maturation theory. Thus, Hymes (1958, p. 9–11) writes, "The inescapable nature of human growth controls what can be learned, and when . . . But 'building' and 'readiness' are uncongenial terms. They clash. They contradict each other." Followers of this maturational point of view suggested withholding reading instruction until the child showed a spontaneous desire to learn to read. This "wait until ready" theory unduly delayed the start of reading for a great many children.

The 1960s saw new points of view. One trend was the development of new readiness programs, which were used sometimes in kindergarten, sometimes in first grade. A second trend was to move both readiness activities and beginning reading instruction back into kindergarten.

The 1970s and 1980s continued the trends of the 1960s. Some educators began to view readiness not as something distinct from reading that prepares the way for it, but as the teaching of specific prereading skills that merge gradually into reading. Others, who developed the concept of emergent literacy, contend that literacy acquisition begins long before the child enters school, and that traditional readiness programs focus largely on developing inappropriate skills. Advocates of emergent literacy hold that understanding the purposes and processes of using written language is much more important than acquiring such skills as visual discrimination and letter naming (Hiebert 1986).

OPPOSING OR CONVERGENT POINTS OF VIEW?

For about 60 years, the concept of reading readiness has been a part of reading instruction. The theory of emergent literacy has arisen fairly recently. Some theorists would argue that the two viewpoints are dramatically opposed. We suggest that although differences exist, they are not as great as some suppose, and that recent reading readiness theorists would not disagree with much of what emergent literacy advocates propose.

Reading Readiness

Learning to read requires adequate levels of both cognitive and linguistic development, as well as a host of specific learnings. The intimate interplay of inner growth and environmental stimulation is present in all aspects of child development, and reading development, of which reading readiness is an integral part, is no exception.

Reading readiness is a state of general maturity, based on aptitudes and learned knowledge and skills, which allows a child to profit from reading instruction under given instructional conditions. *Reading instruction* is defined here as that phase of the instructional program in which word recognition, decoding, and reading comprehension skills are introduced either informally or deliberately. According to our definition of reading readiness, a state of readiness is reached when important enabling knowledge and skills have been acquired. We do not indicate when or how such acquisition took place, nor do we specify the variables involved in reaching this developmental level. Although we can indicate the variables found to be associated with reading readiness, we cannot specify their exact relationships to reading acquisition. Many interacting factors appear to be involved in achieving a state of reading readiness, and no single factor guarantees success or failure. Some variables are no doubt more important than others, and factors can probably combine in various ways to produce a general state of readiness. Our definition also suggests that reading readiness is not an all-or-none characteristic. There are varying degrees of readiness, and all children deemed ready are not equally ready to learn everything that will be introduced in the upcoming instructional program. So the definition further implies that the degree of success in response to instruction depends on the fit of the child's knowledge and skills with what is taught and how it is taught.

A distinction should be made between reading readiness as a state of maturity and a reading readiness program. A *reading readiness program* usually consists of deliberate efforts to develop a state of readiness. Such instruction typically involves, among other things, auditory-discrimination, visual-discrimination, visual-motor-skill, and concept-development lessons, usually delivered in conjunction with a reading readiness workbook or mimeographed sheets. Recent published readiness programs also include teaching *sound-symbol associations* (the initial stimulus is a phoneme), some *symbol-sound associations* (the initial stimulus is a letter or letters),[1] and perhaps even the recognition of printed words (usually the names of story characters) which appear in the first preprimer. Manuals also suggest readiness activities similar to those recommended by advocates of the whole-language and emergent literacy points of view. It would seem, therefore, that the lines between "prereading" and "reading" instruction are blurring, and that more traditional readiness programs are borrowing from some of the newer conceptualizations of readiness and how it develops.

Emergent Literacy

Emergent literacy may be defined as literacy learning that occurs before the introduction of formal reading and writing instruction (J. Mason & Allen 1986). It occurs during the period between birth and the time when children read and

[1]See pages 457–458 for a further discussion of the distinction between sound-symbol and symbol-sound associations.

write in ways that adults would identify as reading and writing (Teale 1987). Literacy is thought of as an advanced form of language acquisition. Advocates of the emergent literacy viewpoint object to the terms "reading readiness" and "early reading and writing" because "listening to stories, learning to participate in their reproduction, and learning to retrieve them through reading-like behaviors are legitimate, appropriate, and vitally important learning-to-read strategies" (Doake 1985). To emergent literacy theorists, engaging in these strategies indicates that young children are actually engaged in the process of learning to read rather than going through a period of readiness to learn.

Emergent literacy advocates conceive of reading acquisition as a developmental continuum that has its inception long before a child enters school. What might be thought of as "prereading skills" in a traditional reading readiness program are believed to be parts of the learning-to-read process. Thus, emergent literacy advocates argue that the term "beginning reader" should be applied to children whom Chall (1983b) would classify as being at the prereading stage (Stage 0), as well as to those who are at the initial reading stage (Stage 1).[2] Although followers of the emergent literacy viewpoint might accept decoding and word-recognition skills as important parts of learning to read, they would not agree that such skills are the measure of whether a child can read. They would point out, for example, that children often are able to use some letter-sound correspondences to recognize, remember, and spell words before they are able to decode printed words (J. Mason & Allen 1986).

Comparison and Contrast of Viewpoints

Followers of either viewpoint would probably not object seriously to the definition of reading readiness presented on page 34, although emergent literacy advocates would find fault with the term itself. Individuals might disagree as to which variables make important contributions to emerging literacy/reading readiness, but such disagreements are not always the case.

Emergent literacy advocates stress the early-emerging, continual nature of the learning-to-read process, in contrast to the stage-development theory they believe reading readiness advocates hold. But development can be conceived of as continual and as proceeding through certain defined, although merging, stages. Few, if any, reading readiness theorists believe that at some point readiness miraculously ends and reading ability begins. Children continue to develop reading readiness knowledge and skills after formal reading instruction begins. Certainly the general concept of readiness to learn is applicable at all levels of reading acquisition. Reading readiness advocates would not deny that the "learning-to-read" behaviors exhibited by preschoolers contribute to reading acquisition, nor would they find fault with claims that such behaviors occur without deliberate instruction.

The most obvious differences between the two points of view are likely to emerge in instructional programming, especially if the reading readiness program consists of slavish adherence to a published separate-skills-oriented program. Rather than use workbooks or worksheets to develop skills such as auditory and visual discrimination, an emergent literacy program would attempt to

[2]Refer to pages 91–95 for a summary of Chall's stages of reading development.

structure the learning situation so that the child can learn to read naturally; reading and writing activities would be closely related. Thus, Doake (1985) writes of children "being immersed in rich and memorable written language." He suggests providing a plentiful supply of children's books of proven quality, especially predictable books whose rhyming, repetitive, and cumulative patterns allow children to gain control rapidly over their language and story structures. Doake also recommends reading Big Books (greatly enlarged copies of children's books) with enthusiasm and expression to children, and encouraging them to participate in reading the stories.[3] Heald-Taylor (1987a,b) believes that predictable stories provide emergent readers with support in gaining meaning from written text. She lists pattern books, offers ideas for their use, and presents an inventory form for keeping track of the variables associated with emergent literacy and reading readiness. Bridge (1989) also lists predictable books and discusses ways to foster literacy development.

J. Mason (1985) and Weir (1989) favor providing a "literacy-rich" classroom environment and a program of interesting activities that give young children the opportunity to talk about, listen to, read, write, and remember printed information. Such an environment and program would feature familiar printed information (e.g., labels on objects, alphabet posters, notes to and from the teacher and children); books and time to read them for uninterrupted periods in a comfortable, quiet place; reading to children and having them retell and discuss the story; and discussions of how words are written, pronounced, and used meaningfully in sentences and stories.

Individuals who are familiar with the literature realize that almost all the aforementioned suggestions are cited as aspects of a good reading readiness program.

FACTORS RELATED TO READING READINESS AND EMERGENT LITERACY

A number of variables have been shown to be related to success in learning to read and thus are often included in reading readiness programs and tests.[4] Their exact relationship to reading acquisition is not clear, however, because the data are primarily correlational. Ehri (1979) suggests four possible relationships:

- *Prerequisite* factors are those without which learning to read would be impossible. These skills must be acquired before a child can learn to read.
- *Facilitator* factors are those that allow the student to learn more quickly or easily. Although the absence of these skills will not necessarily prevent children from learning to read, teachers would be justified in teaching facilitator skills to those who have not yet acquired them.
- *Consequence* factors are those that are acquired without instruction in the course of learning to read.

[3]Refer to Strickland (1988) for suggestions on how to use Big Books.
[4]For the sake of brevity, we use the term *reading readiness* throughout the remainder of this chapter.

- *Correlate* factors are those that, along with reading ability, result from a common underlying variable.

In general, attempting to teach skills that are consequences of reading ability would serve little purpose. However, some skills or understandings may be both facilitator and consequence. Having a minimal level of skill may make it easier to learn to read, and the skill would improve later as a result of learning to read. Whether a skill is a prerequisite, a facilitator, a consequence, or a correlate of learning to read depends to some extent on the interaction between what the child already knows and the demands of the instructional tasks.

A comparison of two studies indicates some similarity, but also significant differences, regarding the relationship of various factors to reading achievement. A combination of six predictor variables plus gender and parents' language was used in a 7-year longitudinal study (Butler et al. 1985), which reveals multiple correlations with reading achievement of 0.58 in Grade 1, 0.65 in Grade 2, 0.70 in Grade 3, and 0.66 in Grade 6. The most important of the predictor variables were the child's language abilities (which was the best single predictor), psycholinguistic abilities, spatial/form perception, and figure drawing (which is sometimes used as a measure of intelligence). Perceptual-motor skills contributed little to the predictions. Prior-year reading achievement was highly related to reading achievement the following year.

Horn and Packard (1985), who used 58 studies in their meta-analysis, found that the best predictors of reading achievement in kindergarten and first grade are (1) ratings of attention/distractability (0.63); internalized problems (anxiety, personality problems, depression) (0.59); oral expressive language (0.53); receptive language (0.48); and general cognitive functioning (0.47). The correlations involving measures of sensory integration, gross motor skills, and lateral dominance range from 0.22 to 0.32. Horn and Packard conclude that, because the best predictor accounted for only about 39% of the variance,[5] these variables are only moderately useful in group prediction and of very limited value with individuals. We should also note that the extent to which distractability and emotional status interfere with reading acquisition may be a function of the instructional setting and program demands.

Neurological, Physiological, and Physical Factors

CHRONOLOGICAL AGE.   In most American school systems, children are accepted into the first grade once a year. The minimum age limit is usually 5 years 9 months when school opens, but entrance-age requirements may vary by as many as 5 calendar months (Langer, Kalk & Searls 1984). The entering class is likely to vary up to almost a full year in age, from the child who is barely old enough to the child who was almost old enough the year before. For a child whose rate of development is below average, being one of the older children is an advantage. For the rapidly developing child, age makes little difference. At age 9, children who were older at age of admission perform significantly better than those who were younger, and children who were younger at admission are

---

[5]The amount of variance is determined by squaring the correlation.

retained more often (Langer, Kalk & Searls 1984). Data indicating that the youngest children in a class are far more likely than their older classmates to repeat a grade led Ames (1986) to recommend that if chronological age (CA) is used as the criterion for entry into school, the cutoff should be set as a September birthday, or preferably at an earlier month.

When characteristics measurable before reading instruction are correlated with the degree of success in beginning reading, chronological age is one of the poorest predictors of reading achievement. Wide differences in reading achievement are found whether reading instruction is begun at age 5 as in Great Britain, age 6 as in the United States, or age 7 as in Sweden.

GENDER.   Young boys and girls do about equally well on reading readiness tests (Bond & Dykstra 1967), but American girls tend to get off to a better start in reading and have fewer failures. In Germany, on the other hand, elementary school boys read as well as girls (Preston 1979), suggesting that gender differences in early reading are more the result of school-related and cultural factors than biological factors. Gender, CA, and height and weight were found to be poor predictors in identifying at-risk kindergartners (Davies 1980).

SENSORY AND HEALTH PROBLEMS.   The sensory defects that interfere most frequently with beginning reading are poor vision and poor hearing. Such problems often go undetected.

Any marked departure from normal vision may give children hazy or incorrect images when they look at words. Comparatively few first graders are nearsighted, but many are farsighted and tend to outgrow the condition as they get older. Astigmatism and poor eye coordination are also fairly common in 6-year-olds.

A comprehensive examination by a physician for every entering first grader is a desirable practice that should be more widely adhered to. When a medical examination is not possible, an alert teacher can notice many signs that suggest physical problems. A child whose eyes water and turn pink in the classroom may need glasses. The child who repeatedly asks to have information repeated may have a hearing defect. Marked clumsiness suggests the desirability of a neurological examination. Listlessness and lack of effort may be related to anemia, malnutrition, or a focal infection.

LATERAL DOMINANCE.   The importance of lateral dominance in relation to progress in reading is a controversial issue (see pages 313–315). Part of the issue is an ambiguous terminology. *Mixed dominance* has been used to include three different conditions: *directional confusion,* evidenced by an inability to identify left and right correctly; *mixed or incomplete handedness,* ranging from ambidexterity, in which both hands seem equally proficient and are equally preferred, to a partial preference for one hand; and *crossed dominance,* in which the dominant hand and dominant eye are on opposite sides. Directional confusion and delay in establishing a consistent preference for one hand seem to be significantly related to difficulty in learning to read (Cohen & Glass 1968, A. J. Harris 1957), but crossed dominance does not.

Cognitive Factors

GENERAL INTELLIGENCE. General intelligence is an average measure of many interrelated phases of mental growth. Test results are usually expressed in terms of level of maturity (mental age, or MA) and relative brightness (intelligence quotient, or IQ). The MA increases fairly steadily until mid-adolescence but the IQ remains fairly stable in most children. About 25% of children have IQs in the bright to superior range (110 and up), about 50% are average (90 to 110), and about 25% are slow learners (below 90). Children in the bottom 3% of IQ scores are generally regarded as mentally retarded.

Correlations between intelligence scores and reading achievement in first grade tend to be substantial but not high, with a median r of about 0.50 for the combined results of 15 large-scale coordinated research studies (Bond & Dykstra 1967). Although predictions of reading achievement can be made for groups, the success or failure of individual children cannot be predicted with much accuracy from their intelligence scores.

A minimum mental age of 6 years is not necessary for learning to read, and use of such a criterion led to the unnecessary postponement of reading instruction for untold numbers of children. We have known for a long time that, with individual instruction and much patience, even children with MAs of 4 years can be taught to recognize some words (Davidson 1931). A given degree of intelligence does not guarantee success or failure, but it does influence the rate at which a child can learn. Progress in learning to read is only partly dependent on intellectual ability; the difficulty of the material, the pace of instruction, the specific instructional methods used, and the amount of individual help given all influence progress (Gates 1937).

The relation of MA to both chronological age (CA) and IQ is shown in Table 2.1. The table shows that the lower an IQ, the older a child must be to reach a particular MA. If we assume that an MA of 5 years 0 months is minimally adequate, beginning kindergartners with IQs of at least 110 have already

Table 2.1   Relation of Mental Age to Chronological Age and Intelligence Quotient

	INTELLIGENCE QUOTIENT						
	70	80	90	100	110	120	130
Chronological age	Corresponding mental age						
4 yrs. 9 mos.	3–4	3–10	4–4	4–9	5–3	5–9	6–2
5 yrs. 3 mos.	3–8	4–2	4–9	5–3	5–9	6–4	6–10
5 yrs. 9 mos.	4–0	4–7	5–3	5–9	6–4	6–11	7–6
6 yrs. 3 mos.	4–5	5–0	5–8	6–3	6–9	7–6	8–2
6 yrs. 9 mos.	4–9	5–5	6–1	6–9	7–5	8–1	8–9
7 yrs. 3 mos.	5–1	5–10	6–6	7–3	8–0	8–8	9–5
7 yrs. 9 mos.	5–5	6–2	7–0	7–9	8–6	9–4	10–1

Note: Mental ages for other chronological ages and IQs may be computed with the formula Mental Age = Chronological Age × IQ. One must remember that the IQ is really a decimal fraction. For example: To find the MA of a child who is 6 years 6 months old (6–6) and has an IQ of 85, 78 mos. × .85 equals 66.3 mos., which equals 5 years 6 months (5–6).

reached it, whereas those with IQs below 80 are at least 6 years 3 months when they reach it. Assuming that an MA of 6 years is desirable (but not essential), bright children reach it before or during kindergarten, average children during first grade, and slow learners late in first grade or during second grade.

LOGICAL THINKING.   According to Piaget (1963), children in kindergarten and first grade are in the process of transition from the preoperational stage (ages 2 to 6) to the stage of concrete operations (ages 6 to 11). Preoperational children show four kinds of immaturity in reasoning: (1) *egocentricity* (the child does not understand that his or her viewpoint may be different from that of other people and is possibly incorrect); (2) limited understanding of cause-effect relationships; (3) *centration* (focusing attention on only a limited part of a complex stimulus and ignoring the rest of it); and (4) inability to solve *conservation problems* (in which the quantity of something remains constant when its size or shape is changed). Another preoperational characteristic is a lack of *seriation* (arranging items in order of ascending or descending amounts or determining where an item belongs in a series). Young children also have difficulty understanding how items can be arranged in classes and that an item can belong to two or more classes at the same time (e.g., American, Democratic, Catholic) (Cleland 1981).

These abilities develop gradually during the period of concrete operations—termed *concrete* because the child can reason successfully about a present situation but cannot imagine a hypothetical situation and reason logically about it. According to Waller (1977), relationships between the attainment of concrete operational thought and reading achievement are low to moderate and are reduced when intelligence is held constant. Robeck (1981) suggests that the attainment of concrete operations is apparently not a prerequisite for learning to read, but there is some contrary evidence. In conducting their longitudinal study, Speece, McKinney, and Applebaum (1986) found that primary-grade, learning disabled children took about 2 years longer than their peers to attain the stage of concrete operations. Once the learning disabled children reached this stage, they acquired specific concepts at the same rate as normally developing children.

SPECIFIC COGNITIVE DISABILITIES.   Children who fail to learn to read despite apparently adequate general intelligence may have some specific cognitive deficit, dysfunction, or delay that makes learning to read difficult for them. The best available evidence indicates that in most young children traits such as memory and problem-solving ability are closely interrelated, but that does not rule out the possibility of occasionally finding a child who, in marked contrast to otherwise satisfactory abilities, shows poor memory, perceptual difficulty, inability to concentrate and pay attention, difficulty in following directions, or language disability.

VISUAL DISCRIMINATION.   Even a child with normal visual acuity may have immature visual discrimination. Some young children pay attention only to the main characteristics of visual stimuli—size, shape, and color—and ignore details. They may notice the height of a letter and ignore its other distinguishing features. When asked to match letters or words, they make many errors because they do not notice differences that are obvious to older children. The term *graphic awareness* is used by some writers (Lomax & McGee 1987) to indicate awareness of the importance of distinctive features in letters and words and awareness of their left-to-right orientation.

The tendency to make *reversal errors* is common among immature children who ignore differences in letter orientation, so that *b, d, p* and *q* are confused. Pairs of words such as *on* and *no*, and *saw* and *was*, also tend to be confused, especially when they appear in isolation. Such reversal errors result from difficulties in storing and retrieving the names of the printed words, rather than from a visual-spatial processing dysfunction (Vellutino 1987). Reversal errors tend to decrease with age, but first graders with marked reversal tendencies make less-than-normal progress (Jansky & de Hirsch 1972).

The ability to perceive visual similarities and differences is consistently related to progress in reading and practically all reading readiness tests include items to measure this ability. Visual discrimination of letters and words is a better predictor of first-grade reading ability than is discrimination of pictures and geometric designs (Barrett 1965).

VISUAL-MOTOR ABILITY.   Both visual discrimination and fine motor coordination are involved in copying designs, which may be geometric forms, irregular patterns of lines, dots or circles, or letters of the alphabet. Correlations between visual-motor scores and success in beginning reading are only moderate, around 0.40, and are not highly correlated with visual-discrimination scores. The ability to perform visual-motor tasks may simply reflect the child's general level of development.

AUDITORY DISCRIMINATION.   Many aspects of auditory discrimination are more closely related to music than to reading (e.g., pitch, loudness, rhythmic patterns). The aspects of auditory discrimination directly related to reading involve comparisons of speech sounds. Two kinds of auditory-discrimination tests for speech sounds have been developed. The first test involves listening to two words or pseudowords that either are identical or differ in only one phoneme and then deciding if they are the same or different. The second test (used in group tests) involves the use of pictures to represent words: The examiner says a word, which is pictured, then names three or four other pictures; each child marks the picture of the word that resembles the first word in a particular way (first sound or rhyming ending). Obviously this type of test makes demands on attention, verbal comprehension, and memory, as well as auditory discrimination.

Hammill and Larsen (1974b) found that correlations among different auditory-discrimination tests tend to be low and that correlations with beginning reading tend to be low to moderate. However, the Auditory Discrimination subtest of the *Macmillan Reading Readiness Test* correlated 0.65 with the reading scores of first graders (Harris & Sipay 1970). Auditory discrimination would logically seem to be more relevant when reading instruction stresses phonics, and less relevant when whole-word recognition is stressed.

Several linguists have pointed out that a child who pronounces most words correctly must have adequate auditory discrimination. This is true, but other understandings are involved in the auditory-discrimination tasks required in reading readiness tests and programs. The ability to abstract a beginning sound from a spoken word and compare it with the beginning sound of another word is a cognitive ability that many 5- and 6-year-olds have not yet developed; in Piaget's terms, it requires "decentration."

Children who speak a divergent dialect or have a foreign-language background tend to score poorly on auditory-discrimination tests because they tend to hear words as they pronounce them. Speakers of black English, for example, may not hear a difference between the spoken words *bit* and *bet* because short /i/ and short /e/ sounds are not differentiated in that dialect. The language background of the child must be taken into account when interpreting auditory-discrimination test scores.

AUDITORY BLENDING.   Auditory blending involves synthesizing speech sounds: The stimuli are auditory, but the skill is cognitive. The examiner pronounces the parts of a word with a pause between each two sounds and the child must indicate the spoken word. Auditory blending requires the child to understand that a spoken word has discernible sounds within it (phonemic segmentation awareness), that it can be spoken part by part, and that the parts can be put together mentally to form a recognizable approximation of the spoken word. Auditory blending ability is very important in decoding (see pages 467–470).

ASSOCIATIVE LEARNING.   The ability to learn associations is essential in learning to read. Such ability is demonstrated by learning to associate printed letters with their names or the sounds represented by the letters, or to associate printed words with their spoken equivalents.

Letter-name knowledge has ranked among the best single predictors of reading achievement (Bond & Dykstra 1967). For this reason almost every reading readiness test has a letter-name subtest. But although letter-name knowledge continues to be a good predictor for kindergarten children, its predictive validity has lessened for first graders because most children now enter first grade already knowing most letter names.

Predictive validity, however, does not necessarily indicate a cause-effect relationship. In fact, a number of studies indicate that teaching the names of the letters does not have a positive impact on learning to read (Groff 1984). Ehri (1983) argues that those studies are flawed and that learning the names of the letters can facilitate learning to read by providing namable referents with which to associate phonemes. On the other hand, children who can learn letter names may simply be demonstrating that they have adequate auditory and visual discrimination and memory and adequate associative learning ability, can profit from instruction, and are motivated to learn. The same factors important for learning letter names are also important for learning to read. This is not to say that children should not be taught letter names, but simply that doing so may not result in easier acquisition of reading ability. Letter-name knowledge has value (e.g., having verbal labels for letters makes it easier to refer to them), but it is not a prerequisite for learning to read.

Walsh, Price, and Gillingham (1988) found that letter-naming *speed* was strongly associated with subsequent reading achievement for kindergartners (r = 0.80 and 0.89), but not for second graders. They note that earlier studies considered only letter-name *accuracy*. According to these authors, an average letter-naming speed faster than 1.1 seconds is not an advantage; but above that threshold, that is, at speeds slower than 1.1 seconds, slowness becomes an increasingly larger disadvantage. They contend that plodding, slow letter naming hinders progress in reading achievement, even if it is highly accurate.

ATTENTION.   At any given moment, a child receives a tremendous amount of sensory stimulation—visual, auditory, touch, internal sensations—but can attend to only a small part of it. Typically, a child focuses on one main whole or pattern, within which four to seven subunits can be distinguished. The rest is background, vaguely perceived and marginally noticed or totally ignored. Difficulty in attending and maintaining concentration has been identified as significantly related to failure in first-grade reading (Malmquist 1958, Kinsbourne & Caplan 1979). This correlation is not specific to reading; a child who cannot maintain attention to the task at hand may do poorly on any test or in any learning situation.

Linguistic Factors

ORAL LANGUAGE DEVELOPMENT.   Adequate language development is one of the most important factors in reading readiness. Two major aspects of oral language development are (1) the child's vocabulary, which is very important in both listening comprehension and expressing thoughts; and (2) mastery of sentence structure or syntax, shown most clearly in children's spontaneous conversation. First-grade reading materials contain few words whose meanings are not understood by most 6-year-olds, but the materials may use unfamiliar sentence structures. Therefore, novice readers are more likely to have difficulty understanding the meanings of printed sentences than the meanings of the words used in them.

Of the many factors that influence language development, the most important are intelligence, auditory acuity (hearing ability), and home environment. Intellectual and language development are closely intertwined. For example, children have real or vicarious experiences from which they gain concepts that are given verbal labels (words). In turn, these verbal labels are essential for carrying out verbal reasoning. Children with limited intellectual ability are slow at learning to talk and to understand spoken language because language is a highly intellectual acquisition. But delayed or impaired language development or speech production may also be the result of hearing impairment or the environment in which the child was raised. Intellectual and language development often reflect the home environment.

LINGUISTIC AND METALINGUISTIC AWARENESS.   Little consensus exists about the terms *linguistic* or *language awareness* and *metalinguistic awareness*. To Mattingly (1979), linguistic awareness means understanding the concepts about language that are important in learning to read; others define metalinguistic awareness in the same way. To Liberman et al. (1980), linguistic awareness consists primarily of understanding phonemic segmentation, which others describe as but one aspect of a larger whole. Some writers attempt to distinguish between "awareness of" and "ability to use" the concepts, while others distinguish between levels of awareness, with metalinguistic awareness being a more comprehensive or higher state of development than linguistic awareness. Yaden and Templeton (1986) describe the confusion as a definitional labyrinth.

Despite the lack of agreement, some commonality occurs in the definitions and discussions of them. Certain concepts about spoken and written language are believed to be related to success in learning to read.

According to Blachman and James (1985), four categories of metalinguistic awareness are related to progressing from the stage of novice to skilled reader: (1) *word awareness*—the ability to treat words as objects of thought and to separate words from their referents (e.g., understanding that *spaghetti* is a long word because of the number of its letters or phonemes rather than because length is a physical property of spaghetti); (2) *phonological awareness*—understanding that words can be segmented into phonemes (phonemic segmentation); (3) *form awareness*—understanding the semantic and syntactic properties of sentences (e.g., knowing when a sentence makes sense and/or if it is acceptable English); and, (4) *pragmatic awareness*—understanding the higher-order structures in text and using prior knowledge to make inferences about text-based information. The first three of these seem most relevant to reading readiness.

Farnam-Diggory (1986) describes three shifts in literacy acquisition that differ somewhat from those of Blachman and James (1985): (1) the onset of *phonemic awareness*—beginning to understand that spoken words can be divided into discrete sounds; (2) the onset of *alphabetic awareness*—beginning to understand that sounds have letter counterparts; and (3) the onset of *orthographic awareness*—beginning to understand that combinations of letters represent sounds that are different from the sounds represented by individual letters, and beginning to display insight into the fact that words can be decoded. She believes these shifts are precipitated largely by instruction.

J. Mason (1981) suggests that three aspects of concept and language development are particularly significant in the early stages of reading acquisition: (1) understanding that spoken language consists of words and sentences that correspond to similar units of print; (2) becoming able to segment speech into abstract phonemic units (phonemic segmentation) that correspond to letters and letter groups; and (3) acquiring a variety of labels, rules, and procedures needed to describe and carry out reading tasks.

Thus, novice readers need to understand at least: (1) that spoken and written language are comprised of sentences, that sentences are comprised of words that can be arranged in various ways and still have meaning, and that words are comprised of sounds or letters; (2) that larger units of language can be divided into subunits; (3) that there is a relationship between spoken and written language and the units and subunits that comprise each; (4) how print is used in written language and how it is used in reading; (5) the meanings of metacognitive concepts that are needed to understand the larger concepts; and, (6) the meanings of the words and sentences employed in reading instruction.

Metacognitive Concepts.   In order to understand larger concepts about language, children must understand such basic concepts as *sentence, word, sound,* and *letter.* Novice readers may not have a firm understanding of these concepts (Yaden 1986).

The most researched of the metacognitive concepts is that of *word.* Having a concept of *word* means knowing what constitutes a word and how words are separated in sentences, for example, understanding that printed words are represented as visual configurations bound by white spaces. According to Johns (1980a,b) and Hare (1983), the concept of *word,* as it occurs in both spoken and written language, is poorly understood by many young children, especially preschoolers. But those who do not have the concept when they enter school soon gain it (Calfee & Drum 1985), and it is stabilized in most children by age 8 (M. Wood 1982).

Knowledge of the concept of *word* is highly related to reading ability (Morris 1980; Horne, Powers & Makabub 1983), but the cause-effect relationship is still open to question. Having this concept may facilitate the acquisition of metalinguistic concepts. For instance, E. Henderson (1986) suggests that having the concept of *word* precipitates awareness of phonemic segmentation. But whatever the relationship, experience with printed language and learning to read help children to develop the concept of *word.* Sulzby (1980) presents activities for assisting children who are having difficulty developing the concept.

Instructional Terminology/Language. In addition to those terms discussed in the foregoing, reading instruction often uses other terms that some children may not understand, such as *page, line; first, last, third; top, middle, bottom; right, left;* and *before, after* (A. J. Harris 1979a).

In addition to understanding the terms used in reading instruction, children must also contend with the language forms used for instruction. Styles of language usage, called *registers,* may range from highly formal to highly informal and colloquial (De Stefano 1973). A *register* is a set of linguistic forms (pronunciation, vocabulary, sentence structure) used in a given circumstance. An informal register is used in conversing with friends and relatives, but most school instruction is given in a formal style called the *language instruction register.* Children's familiarity with the language instruction register varies, but most first graders have some knowledge of it. As pupils progress through the grades, their understanding of the language instruction register generally increases. The extent to which lack of familiarity with this formal style of language interferes with the acquisition of reading ability is unknown, but it seems plausible that it may be an important factor in some cases.[6]

Auditory Segmentation. *Auditory segmentation* ability involves understanding that spoken sentences are made up of words, that words are comprised of one or more syllables, and that syllables are made up of one or more sounds.[7] When a differentiation is made between *auditory segmentation awareness* and *auditory segmentation ability,* the former refers to an implicit understanding that speech structures are comprised of discernible parts, and the latter to an explicit understanding of this concept as demonstrated by the ability to indicate the number

[6]Refer to Cazden (1988) for a comprehensive treatment of the language used in classroom instruction.

[7]The relationship of understanding certain concepts to auditory segmentation is apparent. For example, a child must know what a word is in order to segment sentences into words.

of words in a sentence, the number of syllables in a word, the number of sounds in a word, or some combination of these three. Similar distinctions are made with other aspects of cognitive or linguistic knowledge. Of the three aspects of auditory segmentation, the one receiving by far the most attention in the literature is *phonemic segmentation*—understanding that a spoken word is comprised of phonemes arranged in a given sequence.

Among the strongest advocates of the importance of phonemic segmentation is Liberman (1983). Basically, her position is that although auditory segmentation is intuitive and automatic in speech perception, it must be explicit and fully conscious in learning to read. Such knowledge is felt to be important in understanding the nature of our alphabetic writing system (see page 23).

Perfetti (1986a) also stresses that phonemic segmentation ability is fundamental to discovering and using the alphabetic principle which he feels is important to understand in learning to read. The *alphabetic principle* involves understanding that the elemental units of print (letters) represent units of speech (phonemes) rather than units of meaning.

Vernon (1971, p. 79) states: "It would seem that in learning to read, it is essential for the child to realize and understand the fundamental generalization that in alphabetic writing all words are represented by combinations of a limited number of visual symbols. . . . But a thorough grasp of this principle necessitates a fairly advanced stage of conceptual reasoning." This again suggests the interrelationship of cognitive and linguistic development.

Liberman et al. (1977) found that kindergarten children who had the greatest difficulty segmenting words into phonemes also had the greatest difficulty in learning to read. By age 4, nearly half the children studied by Liberman and Shankweiler (1979) could segment spoken words into syllables, but none could segment by phonemes. At age 5, almost half could segment by syllables and less than 20% by phonemes. By age 6, the percentages increased to 90% and 70%, respectively. Part of the difficulty with phonemic segmentation is attributable to the fact that vowel and consonant sounds in words do not have invariant sound-wave patterns (Liberman et al. 1977). The /b/ in *bed* represents a somewhat different pattern from the /b/ in *boat* or in *rob*. The sound-wave pattern depends on the sequence of sounds, not just on a single phoneme. Therefore, the concept of /b/ is an abstraction that is derived from the somewhat variable patterns that the sound has in different words. Young children also have difficulty hearing that the spoken word *bed* contains three phonemes because a spoken word is not produced one phoneme at a time, each in sequence; rather the phonemes are coarticulated so that they are thoroughly overlapped and merged, and only one pulse of sound is produced. We perceive the phonological structure of conveyed speech automatically below the level of conscious awareness (Liberman & Shankweiler 1985). Furthermore, children and adults are not used to listening for the sounds in words, but rather concentrate on the meanings conveyed by the words.

Phonemic segmentation is a good predictor of reading achievement (Calfee & Drum 1985), but the cause-effect relationship is still open to question (Yaden 1986). Elkonin (1973) developed a procedure for teaching young Russian children that spoken words are made up of phonemes in a particular sequence. Use of his procedure adapted for English did not result in improved reading ability

(Ollila, Johnson & Downing 1974), but Juel (1986) reports that learning to decode words is highly dependent on phonemic awareness, and Vellutino and Scanlon (1988) report that phonemic segmentation is causally related to learning through both a decoding approach and a whole-word approach.

Maclean, Bryant, and Bradley (1988), who found a strong relationship between knowledge of nursery rhymes and subsequent phonological development, also argue that phonemic segmentation is causally related to reading acquisition. Most of the evidence is correlation, however (Wagner 1986). There is also evidence that phonemic segmentation is a consequence of reading instruction and the acquisition of reading ability (Ehri & Wilce 1986).

Perhaps, as Perfetti et al. (1988) believe, phonemic segmentation and reading ability are reciprocally related. Learning to read may require only minimal explicit knowledge of speech segments, and a rudimentary level of ability to manipulate isolated sounds may be necessary to make significant progress in learning to read. However, reading ability may better enable children to analyze words and to manipulate their phonemes.

One of the problems encountered in interpreting the research in this area is the diversity of tasks used to assess phonemic awareness/segmentation. For example, Backman (1983) found that the ability to count the number of phonemes in a word did not predict reading or spelling achievement, but a sound-deletion task did. The two tasks were only minimally correlated, thus indicating that they placed somewhat different demands on the children. Yopp (1988) studied 10 of these tasks and concludes that the best predictor of early decoding ability is a combination of a phoneme-isolation test (e.g., "What sound do you hear at the beginning of *cat?*") and a phoneme-deletion test (e.g., "What word would be left if I took /k/ away from *cat?*").

Print Awareness.   Three factors are commonly considered under the term *print awareness:* understanding the communication purposes of written language, having concepts about print, and understanding the convention of reading.

When first confronted by reading, many children perceive it as a vague, mysterious activity (Johns 1986). This perception is understandable because the relationship between hearing a person read aloud and seeing printed words may not be clear. Children are even more likely to be mystified if they observe only silent reading. If a child wonders how the reader goes about the task of reading, the behavior must be modeled by saying the words aloud while pointing in a left-to-right direction under the line of print. If a child asks what a particular term (e.g., *word*) means, the reader should explain and demonstrate it (E. Henderson 1986).

Studies have reported that young children, even after a few years of reading instruction, do not view reading as a meaning-getting activity. Many are unsure about what behavior comprises the act of reading and the steps necessary in becoming a reader (Yaden 1986). But, under reasonably good conditions, children come to understand that written language has communication purposes and represents features of spoken language (Downing 1980). Most preschoolers have acquired information about the purposes and uses of print, and such understandings increase with age (Hiebert 1981) and with learning to read (J. Mason 1982a). They also are aware of the social contexts in which reading occurs (Templeton

1986), and why people read (Lomax & McGee 1987). Janiuk and Shanahan (1988) describe a series of activities that could be used to help children who need to become aware of the purposes of reading and writing.

Concepts about print comprise those "rules" about how print is used in written language to communicate meaning (Clay 1985). They include the knowledge that printed words are comprised of a single letter or a group of letters sequenced in a way that parallels the sounds in the spoken counterpart, and that certain graphic information, or *conventions of print* are used to represent some aspects of spoken language. These include the use of spaces between words and sentences, the role of punctuation marks, and the interpretation of underlined and italicized words.

Children do not immediately understand the convention of spacing between words as separating lexical units in print. Awareness of these spacing conventions seems to evolve from the ability to use the spaces, toward recognition of their function in segmenting written text, toward their use as indicators of word units, and finally toward recognition of words as units of meaning (Spencer & Afflerbach 1988). From age 3 through 6, the development of word consciousness occurs through a gradual process of extension and refinement of perceptual awareness, print features, and concepts about print. There is a strong relationship between word consciousness and reading acquisition (Ganapole 1987).

Children's performance on the *Metropolitan Readiness Test* correlated 0.69 with *Sands* and 0.66 with *Stone*, the two *Concepts about Print Tests* (Dirks & Moore 1985). These moderate correlations indicate that although the *Metropolitan* and *Concepts* tests were measuring some traits in common, they were each sampling different characteristics as well.

Lomax and McGee (1987) proposed and tested a model of word learning that includes a concepts-about-print component, a graphic awareness component, a phonemic awareness component, and a grapheme-phoneme association component. Some of these abilities developed early, while others emerged only at age 5 or 6.

The *conventions of reading* involve understanding that English is read from left to right and from top to bottom, and also such mechanical skills as turning a page.

J. Mason (1982a) postulates a stage theory of prereading that suggests that learning about reading is best explained in terms of changes in young children's conceptualizations about the functions of print.

Cognitive Clarity Theory.   Closely related to metalinguistic and print awareness is the *cognitive clarity theory* (Downing 1986), which holds that young children normally approach reading instruction in a state of cognitive confusion about the purposes and features of language, and gradually achieve a cognitive clarity that allows them to profit from reading instruction and reading experiences. Downing suggests that cognitive clarity develops as the child comes to understand the purposes of reading and acquires the concepts needed for reasoning about spoken and written language and their relationship. Such concepts include clear understandings of the concepts of *word* and *sentence,* awareness of their constituent parts (letters, sounds, syllables, and phrases), and the ability to associate the written word with its spoken counterpart.

A reciprocal cause-effect relationship may well exist between having concepts about spoken and written language and success or failure in learning to read and write. Children gain some insight into a concept and its name, and this insight leads to improved understanding of the tasks important to learning how to perform a reading skill. In turn, skill improvement produces greater insight into the concept and sheds new light on other concepts (Downing 1986).

Sociocultural, Social, and Emotional Factors

HOME ENVIRONMENT.   Parents lay the foundation for learning to read. Preschoolers are introduced to the use and value of written language when parents read to them; discuss stories and events with them; encourage them to learn letter names, the sounds letters "make," and words; and teach them about the world around them (R. C. Anderson et al. 1985). Some homes provide many opportunities for cognitive and linguistic development and for developing a favorable attitude toward reading; others provide very few. Children who frequently interact verbally with adults who have a rich vocabulary and who use a range of syntactic structures tend to develop the same kind of language, especially when parents explain the meanings of words and sentences in terms the child can understand. Trips provide broadening experiences and concepts upon which the child can later draw. Seeing parents and older siblings read and being read to develop a favorable attitude toward reading, and help children to value literacy. The relationship between children's exposure to written stories and their rate of literacy development is a strong one (J. Mason & Allen 1986). If appropriate verbal communication takes place between adult and child during and after the reading, children can learn how to identify story information and how to relate it to their own experiences.[8] Reading to children: (1) helps them to develop an awareness of written language, (2) helps them to learn how written language usually differs from their own oral language, (3) helps them to begin to develop a sense of story grammar (the parts found in stories), (4) provides a model of fluent reading and how the voice can be used to convey meaning, and (5) contributes to children's print awareness.

Storytelling and reading occur more frequently in middle-class than in working-class homes. Some writers have suggested that the lack of preschool, parent-supported story activities contributes to the later reading comprehension problems of working-class children. There is little direct evidence for this theory, which would be a difficult one to test because middle-class parents also engage their children in more language communication activities, own more books, model literacy activities more often, and take their children to more places (J. Mason & Allen 1986). Parents may also differ in their emphasis on the importance of learning, reading ability, and academic accomplishments. Grinnell (1984) offers general suggestions that can be shared with parents about how to help prepare their children to learn to read.

Children's expectations about reading are strongly influenced by what they hear at home. In a pioneer study (Brumbaugh 1940), 700 kindergarten children were interviewed. More children expected reading to be hard than expected it

---

[8]J. Mason and Allen (1986) offer suggestions as to how parents might foster the development of such strategies in children.

to be easy. Many expectations were based on what they had been told by older brothers or sisters: "You make mistakes and the teacher hollers at you." Some were discouraged before they even started.

The attitudes that the child brings to first grade are quickly modified by experiences in school. A good first-grade program satisfies those who expect to like reading and want to read, and changes the attitudes of those whose attitudes are negative or indifferent.

Starting in the early 1960s, many people became interested in the educational handicaps related to being economically disadvantaged. Special emphasis has been placed on compensatory education for disadvantaged preschool children. Head Start has provided federal support for preschool education for a great many of these youngsters, and TV programs such as "Sesame Street" provide stimulation for hundreds of thousands of children of all economic classes.

Early evaluations tend to show that effective preschool programs result in significant gains in IQ-test scores, language proficiency, and reading readiness and that the most effective programs present specific and structured cognitive activities (Stanley 1972). More recent findings also suggest that high-quality preschool programs, when combined with other programs such as prenatal care, dramatically reduce the need for later remediation, as well as the dropout rate (O. Butler 1989). But Entwisle et al. (1987) concludes that Head Start and other such programs have led to short-term gains in IQ scores, which soon fade, and that the major positive outcome has been the reduction of the retention rate in the primary grades. Perhaps initial gains are not sustained because appropriate follow-through does not occur in the ensuing school programs.

Chapter I funds for compensatory education were $3.9 billion in 1987, and reached one of every nine American school children. These funds are allocated and utilized in a wide variety of ways, with varying effectiveness. Children who participate in Chapter I programs show larger increases in achievement than do nonparticipants. However, these gains have not moved them substantially toward the level of achievement attained by mainstream children, and the gains do not last after the children leave the programs (Birman 1988, Goertz et al. 1988).

Emotional and Social Maturity

Five- and six-year-olds vary as much in their emotional and social maturity as they do in their intellectual and linguistic development. Some are stable, self-reliant, cooperative children who function within the classroom environment without difficulty. Others display their immaturity in a variety of ways: They need help putting on their coats; they cannot play, let alone work, independently; they cannot get along with other children; they cannot or will not follow directions; they try to monopolize the teacher's attention. These and many other forms of immature behavior may be found in many combinations and in varying degrees of severity. Some bright children lack emotional maturity and consequently make less academic progress than their level of intellect would suggest.

Three aspects of emotional and social maturity are especially significant during reading readiness instruction. The first is *emotional stability*. Rapid changes of mood, crying at little provocation, and throwing tantrums are likely to interfere with the acquisition of knowledge and skills. Not only are children not attending to the task at hand during such behaviors, but emotionally volatile children are not likely to assume much responsibility for learning. The latter is also true of children who do not assume much responsibility for their daily functioning.

Self-reliance is another aspect of maturity that is significant for school adjustment. Some parents wisely encourage their children's efforts to fend for themselves and to solve their own problems. Some neglected children become self-reliant through necessity. Other children are still very dependent when they enter school, in many cases because they were still being treated as babies at home.

The *ability to participate actively and cooperatively* in group activities is a third important aspect of social development. So much of the primary-grade instruction is done in groups that a child who is too shy, too restless, or too egocentric to take a normal part in group activities is bound to miss a great deal.

Emotionally or socially immature children can learn to read if the teacher understands their problems and makes special adjustments for them.

METHODS FOR ASSESSING READING READINESS

Reading readiness is a combination of many different characteristics. Some can be measured by standardized tests and some can be noted only by observing the child's daily behaviors and through the use of informal measures.

Intelligence Tests

Because general intelligence is one of the most important factors in learning to read, intelligence tests are obviously useful for appraising certain phases of readiness to profit from reading instruction.[9]

Most schools rely on group-administered intelligence tests because they are comparatively economical and can be given and scored by a classroom teacher. Group intelligence tests for kindergarten and first-grade children are all somewhat alike. Directions are given orally, and no reading ability is involved. Commonly included items are intended to measure such abilities as range of information, understanding of single words and sentences, memory, ability to follow directions, recognition of similarities and differences, and logical reasoning.

An individually-administered intelligence test provides a more reliable measure of mental ability than does a group-administered test. The examiner can observe and judge such things as the child's attentiveness and effort and has a better chance to keep the child doing his or her best throughout the test. The individual intelligence tests most widely used for children in kindergarten or first grade are the *Revised Stanford-Binet Intelligence Scale* and the *Wechsler Intelligence Scale for Children Revised*(WISC-R) or the *Wechsler Preschool and Primary Scale of Intelligence* (WPPSI). The WISC-R and WPPSI provide separate verbal and performance IQs as well as a total IQ. The *Kaufman Assessment*

[9]A descriptive list of tests can be found in Appendix A.

Battery for Children is becoming widely used. These tests should be administered by a person with special training.

The revised *Slosson Intelligence Test* and *Peabody Picture Vocabulary Test* are individually administered tests that are comparatively quick and do not require a trained examiner. Like the *Stanford-Binet,* both tests sample only verbal intelligence. Although not as accurate as the tests mentioned above, they can be used to rule out mental retardation; if the score is close to borderline a WPPSI or *Stanford-Binet* should be given.

Reading Readiness Tests

A number of tests designed to measure readiness for learning to read are available. In some respects, readiness tests are similar to intelligence tests at this age level, but there are important differences. Whereas intelligence tests attempt to measure general mental ability, reading readiness tests attempt to sample the particular phases of mental functioning that are most closely related to success in learning to read.

Reading readiness tests sample skills and knowledge that have been shown to correlate significantly with later success in reading. These factors include auditory discrimination, visual discrimination, general concept development (word meaning), understanding spoken language, visual-motor skills, and letter-name knowledge.

The total scores of most readiness tests correlate between 0.50 and 0.70 with reading achievement at the end of first grade. Correlations of this size allow fairly good predictions for a group but do not provide accurate predictions for individual children. There are four reasons why care should be exercised in using subtest performance as a basis for remediation, especially for individuals: (1) Subtest reliability is often not sufficiently high (at least 0.90 is needed for use with individuals); (2) the skills needed to perform the task required by the subtest may not be the same as those needed in learning to read; (3) little conclusive evidence is available regarding the level of a particular skill that is necessary for learning to read (this also may vary with the instructional approach); and (4) there is little evidence that improving a particular skills or knowledge base will, in and of itself, have a positive impact on learning to read. The possibility also exists that unrecognized variables (e.g., ability to follow oral directions, attending behavior) can influence test performance.

A few readiness tests sample the ability to learn through a whole-word approach (e.g., *Murphy-Durrell Reading Readiness Analysis, Canadian Readiness Test*) and some sample the ability to recognize words (match spoken words with their printed counterparts). Durrell and Murphy (1978) developed a *Prereading Phonics Inventory,* and a few tests measure sound-symbol association ability, auditory blending, or both. Some contain subtests that sample the child's understanding of concepts such as *letter* and *word* (e.g., *Canadian Readiness Test*) or primarily measure such concepts and/or the understanding of the functions and conventions of written language (e.g., *Linguistic Awareness in Reading Readiness, Concepts About Print Tests*). Day and Day (1986) describe and critique four published tests of linguistic awareness, including the aforementioned two.

Although standardized readiness tests have been criticized as being biased against minority-group and disadvantaged children, C. Reynolds (1980) concludes that various tests used to predict success in first grade are not racially biased. The case against readiness tests has been exaggerated.

Teacher Judgment

Teachers tend to form judgments about how ready a particular child is to profit from reading instruction. In a sense then, they are predicting how well a child is likely to succeed in learning to read. According to Cooksey, Freebody, and Davidson (1986), teachers' predictions of success in early reading are based on such cues as the child's past achievement, SES, ethnicity, behavioral patterns, and physical appearance. Teachers differ greatly in the importance they place on the various cues.

Some teachers are hesitant to trust their opinions about pupils because they feel that reading readiness or intelligence tests are more accurate and reliable predictors. But the professional judgment of competent teachers who have had time to observe pupils daily should by no means be disregarded. Teacher estimates predict future success in reading about as well as reading readiness and IQ tests do (Heilman, Blair & Rupley 1981).

This does not mean that all teachers are perfect judges or that tests are useless. Standardized tests provide a convenient basis for comparing children's status on their ability to perform whatever tasks are required by that test. However, some aspects of reading readiness are not sampled by the tests, for example, motivation to learn to read, sensory defects, and understanding the conventions of reading. These require teacher judgment based on observation, interviews, and informal measures.

Teachers can use a number of rating scales to help with their predictions. Such scales are much less useful for instructional planning. Most of the items on these scales are predictor variables, not prerequisites or even enabling skills for learning to read. It would be naive to believe that teaching children their ages or how to tie their shoes or button their coats would have any impact on learning to read. Many of the behaviors listed on these scales are simply general indicators of maturity.

Banks developed a *Kindergarten Behavioural Index* (KBI) based on a follow-up study of 2,304 Australian children. Out of 63 item tried, 37 differentiated poor readers from good readers. These 37 items, which are reproduced in Figure 2.1, "represent a diffuse syndrome of developmental functions involving sensorimotor abilities, language, perception, cognitive abilities, social attributes, and behavioral patternings" (Banks 1970). In two samples, a cutoff score of more than three checks correctly identified 78% and 82% of those who became poor readers in the first grade and misidentified 15.5% and 10% of the successful readers. The Banks KBI seems promising as a screening instrument. It can be filled out by a kindergarten teacher near the end of the year, or by a first-grade teacher 3 or 4 weeks after the beginning of the school year. A follow-up study of the children tested by Banks has shown that the KBI has a substantial correlation with failure in Grades 1–4 (J. Miles, Foreman & Anderson 1973).

A readiness rating scale that can be used in kindergarten or early first grade is shown in Figure 2.2. Although the total score of −5 indicates that Henry is

Kindergarten Behavioural Index
Enid M. Banks

INDIVIDUAL RECORD

Name...

Date of Birth.. Age............ Date of Recording..........................

- ☐ 1 Does not know own age
- ☐ 2 Is ambidextrous—uses left hand for some activities, right hand for others
- ☐ 3 Puts shoes on wrong feet
- ☐ 4 Has difficulty in hopping, changing from one foot to another
- ☐ 5 Reverses letters and numbers when copying or writing
- ☐ 6 Slow and fumbling putting on shoes, coat, etc.
- ☐ 7 Has difficulty doing up buttons
- ☐ 8 Clumsy—trips over, bumps into, knocks over, objects
- ☐ 9 Holds pencil awkwardly
- ☐ 10 Has difficulty controlling pencil—presses hard—messy work
- ☐ 11 Cannot keep within lines when colouring in
- ☐ 12 Has difficulty using scissors
- ☐ 13 Lacks sense of rhythm—keeping in time with music in running, clapping, etc.
- ☐ 14 Has difficulty pronouncing all sounds, e.g. 'wed'–'red', 'fink'–'think', 'muver'–'mother', etc.
- ☐ 15 Uses 'baby talk', e.g. 'me'–'I', 'runned'–'ran', 'dood'–'did'
- ☐ 16 Lacks verbal fluency—speaks mainly in words or phrases
- ☐ 17 Mixes up words, e.g. 'applepine' for 'pineapple'
- ☐ 18 Mixes up order of words in a sentence
- ☐ 19 Stutters
- ☐ 20 Has difficulty ordering thoughts when describing or discussing a topic
- ☐ 21 Loses main thread and goes into irrelevant details when telling a story or talking
- ☐ 22 Forgets an instruction or message and has to ask again
- ☐ 23 Cannot write own name correctly from memory
- ☐ 24 Has difficulty remembering poems, rhymes, etc.
- ☐ 25 Cannot count up to 20
- ☐ 26 Confuses names of colours
- ☐ 27 Avoids talking in front of class
- ☐ 28 Cries easily
- ☐ 29 Appears to be shy
- ☐ 30 Daydreams
- ☐ 31 Slow in carrying out commands
- ☐ 32 Overactive—always on the move
- ☐ 33 Has difficulty sitting still for very long
- ☐ 34 Fidgets with things
- ☐ 35 Lacks concentration—does not pay attention
- ☐ 36 Loses interest quickly—moves from one activity to another
- ☐ 37 Frequently loses belongings
- ☐ TOTAL

Comments...

....

Published by Australian Council for Educational Research, Frederick Street, Hawthorn, Victoria 3122.
Copyright © Enid M. Banks 1972.

Figure 2.1 The Banks Kindergarten Behavioural Index. Reproduced by permission of *The Slow Learning Child* and Enid M. Banks. Published by Australian Council for Educational Research, Frederick Street, Hawthorn, Victoria 3122. Copyright © Enid M. Banks 1972.

slightly below average in general readiness, the most helpful feature of the rating scale is calling attention to the specific items on which he was rated −1 or −2. The rating scale also points up Henry's advantages: good IQ and language development and a favorable home environment. Teachers are welcome to reproduce this rating scale without special permission.

The *Infant Rating Scale* contains 25 items on which teachers rate children on a five-point scale. It has a test-retest reliability of 0.96, and a predictive validity with reading scores 2 years later of 0.45. This British rating scale samples four factors: language, behavior, aspects of learning, and social integration (Lindsay 1980).

Whether teachers record their opinions on forms or keep them in their heads, it is advisable to reconsider them periodically and to revise ratings in light of more recent information. By amending ratings as children overcome or outgrow their difficulties, teachers can keep track of pupil progress and can get a bird's-eye view of those with readiness problems.

When teachers have had several weeks to observe their students, both kindergarten and first-grade teachers' ratings show substantial correlation with first-grade reading performance (Feshbach, Adelman & Fuller 1974). Glazzard (1979) found that teacher ratings on a five-point scale were better predictors of school achievements after 1 year but that reading readiness tests were better predictors after 2 to 3 years. Both measures were equally predictive after 4 years.

Teachers should make use of observational techniques that help them identify which children already know how to read (or at least can recognize some printed words or utilize some symbol-sound associations) and which are likely to profit from reading instruction. For example, as the teacher reads to the children, she or he can ask them to help by saying the next word after a pause or stop. Or the teacher can ask a child to perform a task that requires reacting to a printed word (e.g., "Please get me the box that has the word *pencils* printed on it."). More use should be made of experience stories (see pages 73–74) and Big Books, not only to assess who is reading or ready to learn to read, but also to determine children's concepts about print. Similarly, children's eagerness to spell and write, as well as their written products should be considered in assessing readiness.

Tests of Specific Abilities

During the 1960s and 1970s and even into the 1980s, many learning disability specialists were committed to the policy that: (1) learning disabilities result from specific deficiencies in basic cognitive skills; (2) the underlying skills should be tested and specific training should be given in those that are weak; and (3) once the underlying skills have been acquired, academic learning will improve.

The two tests most widely used by those wishing to diagnose and train underlying cognitive skills were the *Illinois Test of Psycholinguistic Abilities, Revised Edition* (ITPA) and the *Frostig Developmental Test of Visual Perception* (DTVP). Critical reviews of the ITPA (e.g., Carroll 1972) pointed out that the test is heavily loaded with vocabulary and general information, has a middle-class bias, probably taps only three or four interpretable factors rather than 12

| Name: *Henry* Age: *5–10* Rated by _____ On: *9/20* Total Score: *−5* |

Factor	Rating				
	Low −2	−1	Average 0	+1	High +2
Cognitive					
MA	___	___	X	___	___
IQ	___	___	___	X	___
Attention	___	___	X	___	___
Specific concepts	___	___	___	X	___
General conceptual background	___	___	___	X	___
Letter-name knowledge	___	X	___	___	___
Auditory discrimination	___	X	___	___	___
Visual discrimination	X	___	___	___	___
Visual perception	___	X	___	___	___
Language					
Vocabulary	___	___	___	X	___
Sentence structure	___	___	___	X	___
Listening comprehension	___	___	X	___	___
Speech production	___	X	___	___	___
Physical–Physiological					
Ability to identify left and right	___	X	___	___	___
Consistent hand preference	X	___	___	___	___
	None	left	right		
Muscular coordination	___	X	___	___	___
Visual acuity	___	___	?	___	___
Auditory acuity	___	___	?	___	___
General health	___	X	___	___	___
Social–Emotional–Cultural					
Self-reliance	___	X	___	___	___
Self-control	___	X	___	___	___
Group participation	___	___	X	___	___
Interest in being read to	___	___	___	X	___
Interest in learning to read	___	___	X	___	___
General cultural level of the home	___	___	___	X	___
Intellectual stimulation of the home	___	___	___	X	___
Column totals	−4	−9	___	8	0

Figure 2.2 A reading readiness rating scale. From A. J. Harris and E. R. Sipay, *How to teach reading* (New York: Longman, 1979), p. 61. Used with permission.

as suggested by the subtests and has some subtests with low reliability. Factor-analysis studies of the *Frostig* show that it measures one main factor and possibly a second factor, not five as suggested by the number of subtests (Hammill, Colarusso & Wiederholt (1970), and that the diagnostic value of differences among subtest scores is questionable (Mann 1972).

The main reason why use of these tests has been declining, however, is an accumulation of evidence that the training of basic cognitive skills is not an effective way to improve academic performance of young children. This issue is discussed in greater detail on pages 498–499.

Early Identification of High-Risk Children

Efforts have been made to screen young children, often preschoolers, in order to identify those who are likely to fail to learn to read by the end of first grade or who probably will learn to read adequately only with some sort of special attention. Youngsters so identified are referred to as *high-risk* or *at-risk children*. Such screening programs are based on the belief that early identification and subsequent appropriate intervention will prevent or alleviate learning problems. Many of the tasks required by the tests used in these screening batteries are similar to those found in reading readiness tests.

In a pioneering study (de Hirsch, Jansky & Langford 1966), 39 tests were given individually to kindergarten children. The *Screening Index*, which consisted of 10 tests, accurately predicted failure by the end of the second grade in a middle class population. In a second study, in which disadvantaged children also were used, the *Screening Index* was cut to five tests (Jansky & de Hirsch 1972). This revised index predicted failure for 77% of those children who did fail and for 19% of those who made successful progress in reading achievement, as measured by scores on a standardized reading test.

The original *Predictive Index* was compared with the *Metropolitan Readiness Test* in two studies. In one study, in which reading tests were given late in the first grade, the two procedures did not differ significantly in predictive power; the *Metropolitan* correctly classified 89% of the children, while the *Predictive Index* correctly classified 87% (Zaeske 1970). Using end-of-second-grade test results, the *Predictive Index* did slightly better than the *Metropolitan* in identifying future failures, but the authors doubted that the slight increase in accuracy justified the expense of individual testing (Askov, Otto & Smith 1972). Jansky and de Hirsch (1972) recommend that the *Predictive Index* be used with a flexible pass-fail cutoff that depends on local school standards and in conjunction with teachers' ratings. Satz and Fletcher (1979) point out that even with a high overall hit rate the *Predictive Index* has "little usefulness in detecting those high-risk children who would most benefit from an early intervention program."

The *Florida Kindergarten Screening Battery* was developed by Satz and his associates on the basis of a large-scale longitudinal study in which all of the kindergarten boys in a Florida school district were tested and reexamined at intervals through fifth grade (Satz et al. 1978). The five subtests were selected on the basis of good correlations with later success in reading and a minimum number of false negatives (failure predicted for those who succeed) and false positives (success predicted for those who fail). This battery also is administered individually.

Two other test batteries intended to identify probable failures in reading are the *Slingerland Prereading Screening Procedure* and the *Meeting Street School Screening Test*. According to one comparative study (Kapelis 1975), the *Slingerland* correlated 0.66 to 0.68 with first-grade reading and the *Meeting Street* correlated 0.58 to 0.62. This makes them about as good predictors as group readiness tests.

Hoffman (1971) developed a *Learning Problem Indication Index* by comparing parental information on the early development of 100 severely learning disabled children and 200 controls. Large differences were found on the following items: difficult delivery, prolonged labor, cyanosis, prematurity, blood incompatibility, adoption, late or abnormal creeping, late walking, tiptoe walking for more than 1 month, late or abnormal speech and ambidexterity after age 7. Two or more signs were present in 72% of the disability group and only 6.5% of the controls. It seems evident that this index selects mainly children whose learning problems have neurological correlates.

It is difficult to predict the future reading achievement of individuals, especially over an extended period of time. For example, Badian (1988) reports that over half the children who appeared to be at risk at age 4 were average readers by eighth grade. The accuracy of predictions for success or failure in learning to read and in later reading achievement is likely to be influenced by what is done or not done to help the child, by the instructional methodology employed, and by growth changes within the child. Changes in performance over time are much greater for children with reading problems than for those making normal progress in reading, thus making predictions for individuals even more tenuous.

Phlegar (1988) describes 16 early identification and intervention programs. Lindsay and Wedell (1982) examine the basic assumptions underlying the early identification of at-risk children and the effectiveness of screening measures for doing so. They conclude that there is a general lack of evidence for the usefulness of such screening instruments.

A Plan for Assessing Reading Readiness

Many schools routinely test all children for readiness. Although it might be advantageous to give the tests near the end of kindergarten in some schools, it is better to wait until the children are in first grade if a substantial number of children enter school without having attended kindergarten (or if there is a high degree of pupil turnover). The best time for a first-grade readiness test is 2 or 3 weeks after the beginning of the school year. This allows time for the children to get accustomed to classroom activities and teacher directions, and is early enough to make the results useful in decisions about such matters as how to group the children and when to start reading instruction.

For this form of readiness assessment, either a group intelligence test or a group readiness test can be used, preferably the latter. Not more than 10 or 12 children should be tested as a group, so arrangements need to be made to take care of part of the class while the rest are being tested. The test should be administered by the teacher or a person known to the children. After the tests have been scored, at least a sampling of them should be rescored by another person; scoring errors are made with deplorable frequency.

Some standardized tests now sample concepts about written language, or have supplementary tests that do so. If the test does not adequately consider language development and concepts about written language, the teacher should obtain such information through observation and informal measures, or from tests that sample such factors. Teale, Hiebert and Chittenden (1987) suggest ways to assess children's concepts about the functions and conventions of written language.

In most cases, an accurate estimate of each child's readiness can be made using test results in combination with teacher observation. If test and teacher judgment disagree, further study of the child is needed and further testing may be arranged. Individual testing by a school psychologist is desirable for children whose scores are low on two or more group tests.

We should note that the more effectively a teacher helps a child to improve in readiness for reading, the more inaccurate a low readiness score will be. The presence of children who succeed in learning to read despite predicted failure may be the result of good teaching rather than a shortcoming in the test. Similarly, when children do well on a readiness test but subsequently fail to learn to read, poor instruction rather than inaccurate measurement may be responsible. This principle applies to any measure of reading readiness.

FOSTERING READINESS

Misinformed Pratices

A reading readiness program should not consist of using a workbook with every child in the class for a set number of weeks. Such programs are convenient, but narrowly conceived, inefficient, and often ineffective. Fostering readiness involves more than having children complete workbook pages or worksheets. Even when a workbook is used, not every child would need the same length of time to complete it successfully. Nor should every child have to do every page. Some may not profit from any of the workbook activities because they have already mastered the skills. Paradis (1974) found that about 97% of 440 kindergartners and 69% of 128 preschoolers were successful on 80% or more of the workbook items given to them. Time spent in needless seatwork could be spent more profitably on worthwhile readiness-fostering activities.

Workbooks are not useless, but they should be used properly. They provide colorful pictures that can serve as a basis for developing concepts and oral language skills through discussions and storytelling, or for developing written language by suggesting that the pupils write words, sentences, or stories to accompany the pictures. Workbooks also contain series of exercises for developing such skills as auditory and visual discrimination and observing in a left-to-right sequence. These exercises should be used only with children who need to acquire or improve such skills. Today's children are typically more ready to learn to read than their predecessors were 40 years ago.

Suggested Practices/A Gradual Start

Soon after children enter school, they can be exposed to meaningful uses of written language and activities that foster language development. Teacher can

- place children's names on seats, desks, coat hooks, and so on
- display colorful pictures with brief titles below them
- post simple weather reports, notices of special events, alphabet posters, and messages to individual children on the bulletin board
- label items in the "store"—although simply labeling objects is insufficient. Children must have their attention called to the printed words and must interact actively with them (N. Taylor 1986)
- place book jackets and labeled pictures of storybook characters near the library corner, which contains picture and predictable books that are read to children and which they are encouraged to read themselves
- read to children and tell them stories
- encourage children to label objects and write notes and stories.[10]
- use a language-experience approach (see pages 73–74) to provide an interesting and easy introduction to reading.

Reading instruction should begin gradually. As MacGinitie (1976) suggests, "[M]eaningful reading readiness instruction means a slow and gentle introduction to reading itself—often gamelike, often hidden in other activities." A gradual approach to reading instruction with readiness skills embedded in the context of reading is preferable to a readiness-first, reading-afterwards program. When a teacher identifies a number of children who are ready to read, a group can be formed and experience stories or the first preprimer can be introduced. This may occur even before a reading readiness test is given to the other children. Language-fostering activities should continue for all children—those already grouped as well as those still deemed in need of readiness.

Rather than ask, "Is this child ready to learn to read?" the teacher should be asking, "What is important for these children to know or be able to do in order to learn to read easily?" "What does this child already know?" "What is this child ready to learn?" and, "How can this learning best be facilitated?" Based on the best available information, the teacher can then plan and conduct a readiness program that benefits each child.

Special Readiness Procedures

Kephart (1960), whose principles developed out of his work with brain-injured children, emphasizes the desirability of helping children to achieve mastery over basic perceptual-motor skills as a prerequisite for academic learning. His program involves practice in coordinated acts such as hopping, skipping, and balancing while walking on a narrow plank; training to improve laterality and directionality; and training in ocular control and visual perception. Other perceptual-motor programs that attempt to develop similar skills have emerged since 1960.

Kavale and Mattson (1983) applied the statistical technique known as meta-analysis to 180 studies of the effects of perceptual-motor training, involving 637 comparisons between trained and control groups. They found that most comparisons resulted in small differences that were not significantly different from zero.

---

[10]Most of these ideas are not new (see Harrison 1936).

There was little evidence of benefit in the perceptual-motor activities that were directly trained, and the effects on reading and other academic skills were predominantly negative. This pattern appeared at all levels of schooling from preschool through high school, and in normal as well as in several types of exceptional children. When the studies were graded for quality, the largest effects were in the poorest studies. There were no treatment effects in the medium-rated studies and negative treatment effects in the high-rated studies. The results failed to justify the use of any perceptual-motor training program, including those of Kephart, Frostig, Getman, and Delacato.

Training in visual and auditory discrimination was emphasized years ago by Durrell and Murphy (1953) as important for reading success, and is now part of the readiness procedures of most basal reader programs. When these types of training employ letters and words from the vocabulary used in the preprimers, primers, and first readers their transfer value to reading is probably enhanced. It is doubtful that intensive auditory-discrimination training beyond what is provided in conventional programs benefits early reading attainment for most children, although it can improve auditory-discrimination scores (Rosner 1973). McNeil (1967) found that Mexican-American and black children trained to hear phonemes within words did show some gain in reading, however. More evidence is needed concerning the value of training in auditory segmentation as a readiness activity.

In general, the research reviewed in the foregoing paragraphs is in harmony with long-established findings about transfer of training, which show that the more closely a learning activity resembles the activity to which transfer of learning is desired, the more likely it is that useful transfer will take place. Thus, visual-discrimination practice using letters and words is more transferable to reading than is discrimination of geometric forms. Auditory discrimination of words and phonemes is more transferable to reading than is discrimination of nonverbal sounds. The transfer to reading of gaining skill in large-muscle and small-muscle activities is doubtful. Developing listening comprehension seems more relevant to reading than does becoming a competent speaker of standard English. Viewed in the light of transfer, the research on what pays off in readiness training makes sense.

TRANSITION CLASSES.   At times a school system may have a large number of "unready" children or, in some instances, instructional adjustments for those who are not yet ready to profit from reading instruction are unlikely to be made. A potential solution in such cases may be to provide the children with another year with a carefully planned and executed readiness program leading gradually into reading instruction. Such *transition classes* have specially trained teachers and a limited number of students. Transition classes usually occur at the end of kindergarten but some follow first grade. Developmental kindergartens may also be made available for those judged to be unready for the regular kindergarten program (Durkin 1987a). The great majority of children in transition classes are promoted to the next grade, and some do so well that they "skip" a grade (e.g., a 7-year-old may not need to enter first grade but rather be promoted into second grade). The transition class was strongly recommended by Ilg and Ames (1964), who found a large percentage of middle-class children to be lacking in some aspects of readiness, despite having at least average intelligence.

Dolan (1982) reports a 6-year follow-up of children placed in a transition class after first grade. Results show a gradual blending of transition-class students with their regular peers. Rejection of transition-class placement by parents led to an increased need for special services.

Early Readers

Some children are able to read, or at least are able to recognize a number of printed words, before they enter school. Although some believe that these children learn to read "naturally" (i.e., with formal instruction), informal instruction often is involved (Durkin 1966).

Three parent behaviors have been shown to be highly related to early reading acquisition: (1) engaging their children in informal, game-like activities that promote mastery of basic phonic skills; (2) directing their children's attention to the relationships between spoken and written words; and, (3) having a feeling of responsibility for teaching their children literacy skills (Hiebert 1986). Thomas (1985) studied 15 children under the age of 6 who had begun to read at ages 2-1/2 to 4 and who were now reading fluently at the primer level. She concludes that the social interactions, the clarification of concepts, and the systematic approach to print engaged in by the parents with their children were examples of exemplary teaching. Parents, older siblings, and grandparents devoted extensive time and effort to these endeavors. Family members of early readers may provide more instruction than is commonly believed (Durkin 1987a, Teale 1987).

Tobin and Pikulski (1988) report that early readers are superior in reading achievement to non–early readers through the sixth grade.

Reading Instruction in Kindergarten

Over the past twenty years, increasingly more direct reading instruction has been occurring in kindergarten.[11] Durkin (1974–1975) summarizes her 6-year study of children taught to read at age 4 and also the research of others on the effects of teaching reading before first grade. In general, the experimental groups have had significantly higher reading scores than have control groups in first and second grades, with the differences becoming nonsignificant in third and fourth grades. Durkin suggests that the failure of teachers to provide appropriate instruction for superior readers is at least partially responsible for the fading out of the initial advantage. She concludes that "since there is no guarantee that a kindergarten start in reading will lead to greater success in later years, no school should introduce reading instruction into its kindergartens unless that instruction can be of a kind that will add enjoyment and greater self-esteem to the fifth year of a child's life" (p. 60).

More recently, Durkin (1987a) observed the teaching of reading in 42 kindergartens in one state. She found that almost 22% of the school day was devoted to reading and reading-related activities, with almost 71% of that time being devoted to whole-class instruction in phonics (including letter names). Almost

---

[11]There is some indication of "reading readiness" and even reading instruction occurring in nursery school and day-care centers.

all of what was taught came directly from workbooks, most often those that accompanied the basal series being used in the school, and worksheets. This reliance on whole-class, workbook-oriented phonics instruction appeared to be in direct contradiction to the schools' frequent use of Gesell-like developmental tests to determine school readiness.

Among the concerns expressed by the IRA Early Childhood and Literacy Development Committee (1986b) were: (1) subjecting pre–first graders to rigid formal programs that were inappropriate for their levels of development; (2) overemphasizing development of isolated skills; and (3) the pressure of accelerated programs that do not allow children to become risk-takers. This IRA committee made 15 recommendations for conducting pre–first grade reading programs. Such programs should be informal, individualized, devoid of pressure, and more like play than work. Any kindergarten reading program should be adapted to the children's intellectual and emotional stages of development and should not replace other aspects of their total development. R. C. Anderson et al. (1985) state that kindergarten reading programs should emphasize oral language development and writing as well as the beginning steps in reading. Children enter kindergarten with very different levels of knowledge about written language; instruction should be adapted to these differences.

Use of a program developed by Taylor, Blum, and Logsdon (1986) resulted in the acquisition of important preliteracy skills by kindergartners who were not exposed to a literate home environment. Their program featured a language- and print-rich environment in which the youngsters had many opportunities to observe, try out, and practice literacy skills. Active student participation was stressed. J. Mason, McCormick, and Bhavnagri (1986) describe a program through which 4-year-olds learned to assume responsibility for acquiring concepts thought to be important in emerging literacy.

Advanced language and cognitive skills and an enriched home environment can stimulate an early awareness of print, but the effects of accelerating that awareness through formal preschool instruction have not been fully explored (Collins 1986). Collins also lists the pros and cons of preschool reading instruction and briefly annotates 11 major types of such programs used in the United States.

When to begin reading instruction is still an open question, but there is strong support for an easy, relaxed introduction for kindergartners who are ready. Some research suggests that an early, slow start may be advantageous for the unready and economically disadvantaged as well. Beginning a readiness/ reading program in kindergarten and pacing instruction as slowly as necessary can provide children with more time to learn. More research is needed on this important issue.

3

Beginning
Reading
Instruction

This chapter is the second of three devoted to a description of the total reading program. Chapter 2 discussed readiness for learning to read; Chapter 4 covers reading instruction beyond the initial stages. In this chapter, a brief historical review of past methods is followed by a discussion of recent and current beginning reading approaches; teaching reading to dialect-speaking, limited-English-speaking, and non-English-speaking children; and an evaluative comparison of beginning reading approaches.

A BRIEF LOOK AT THE PAST

Over the centuries, many methods for teaching children to read have been introduced. Some gained wide acceptance, only to be replaced by other methods. Many of the changes stemmed from dissatisfaction with a prevailing method, and at times excesses in one direction were replaced by equally objectionable swings to an opposite extreme. Historical accounts of reading methodology may be found in Huey (1908), Mathews (1966), N. B. Smith (1986), and Venezky (1986). Cranney and Miller (1987) annotate a number of sources on the history of reading instruction.

Synthetic Methods

Methods that start with letters and move to larger units (syllables, words, phrases, sentences) are called *synthetic methods*.

The *alphabet-spelling method* was used from ancient times until well into the nineteenth century. Students memorized the alphabet and then drilled on two-letter combinations. In studying a word, children named the letters in sequence and then pronounced the word itself over and over. Eventually the child got to read sentences. In some languages, this procedure may be effective because the letter names are essentially the same as their sounds. In English, however, naming the letters of *cat* and putting them together gives us something like *seeaytee*. The alphabet-spelling method was mechanical, uninteresting, and difficult. "The value of the practice in learning to spell doubtless had much to do with blinding centuries of teachers to its uselessness for the reading of words and sentences" (Huey 1908, p. 266).

A number of phonic methods were developed during the nineteenth century. Their common characteristic was that they started with the sounds (rather than the names) represented by the letters and then proceeded to the sounding of consonant-vowel and vowel-consonant combinations—*ba,ca,da. . . ab,ac,ad*—then proceeded to syllables and on to words. A child who came to a new word was expected to sound it letter by letter (or by letter groups) and to blend the sounds mentally to form the whole word.

Two points are often made by critics of synthetic methods: (1) Because there are so many irregularities and complexities of English symbol-sound correspondences, an adequate phonics[1] system would have to be complicated and difficult to learn; and (2) synthetic methods encourage attention to the mechanics of word recognition and do not give enough attention to reading comprehension. To these criticisms, advocates of synthetic methods would answer: (1) English is not as irregular as commonly believed—there is sufficient regularity to allow learners to approximate closely words whose pronunciations they know; and (2) there is no evidence that early stressing of decoding adversely influences comprehension.

One effort to standardize the symbol-sound relationship was to employ diacritical markings similar to those in the pronunciation keys of dictionaries. Long vowels and silent letters were marked as long ago as 1644 (Mathews 1966). Around the beginning of the twentieth century, diacritical markings were used in the popular Ward Readers and Pollard Readers.

Another effort to reduce phonic difficulties was to modify the alphabet by adding new letter forms in order to have a separate letter to represent each sound. A modified alphabet devised by Isaac Pitman was tried in a few American school systems during the mid-nineteenth century; although reports of its results were favorable, it failed to gain acceptance and died out. This was the ancestor of the Initial Teaching Alphabet (see p. 78). A "scientific alphabet" was used for many years in readers and dictionaries published by Funk and Wagnalls.

Analytic Methods

Methods that start from larger units than letters and proceed to the study of parts are generally called *analytic methods*. They include word, sentence, and story methods.

---

[1]*Phonology* is the scientific study of speech sounds and includes phonetics and phonemics. *Phonetics* deals with the study of the sounds of speech, including their production, combination, description, and representation by written symbols. *Phonemics* is the study of the sounds (phonemes) of a particular language. *Phonics* is the study of the relationship of phonemes to the printed or written symbols that represent them (graphemes) and their use in discovering the pronunciation of printed and written words. Phonics is, therefore, the part of phonology and phonetics most involved in reading instruction.

Horace Mann advocated the word method before the middle of the nineteenth century, and primers using this method began to be used in some schools around 1850. The usual procedure was for the teacher to print or write a word on the board, pronounce it, and then combine it with other words to form various sentences. The method employed word-picture associations and used flash cards for drill.

Mathews (1966) points out two main variations of the word method: a words-to-letters method, in which words were analyzed and studied sound by sound shortly after they were introduced; and a words-to-reading method, in which word analysis was postponed for varying periods of time, and analysis was often not begun until a substantial sight vocabulary had been learned. Most basal reader systems relied heavily on the words-to-reading method until the mid-1960s when the pendulum again began to swing toward use of the words-to-letters method.

The sentence method was first advocated in the United States around 1870. Its proponents argued that because the sentence is the smallest complete unit of meaning, the child should first be taught a whole sentence at a time. The same words were presented in many different sentence arrangements, but the need for continuity of meaning from one sentence to the next was ignored in some of these systems.

The story method attempted to correct the weakness of the sentence method by introducing a whole story at a time. The teacher would read a story, usually a cumulative folktale like "The Gingerbread Boy," over and over to the children until many of them memorized it. She would then present the first few sentences in print and have the children recite the memorized lines as they looked at the print; in this way, word recognition developed. This method assumed that the child would look at the words in proper sequence and in time with the story; failure to do this produced many cases of pseudoreading in which children were able to recite a story perfectly, page by page, without having learned to recognize individual words.

Synthetic methods stressed the need to be able to work out the pronunciations of printed words. Analytic methods emphasized the need for meaningful reading and immediate recognition of words and phrases. Most current methods try to utilize the good features of these older methods and combine them into a comprehensive, flexible program that is adaptable to individual differences.

CURRENT APPROACHES TO TEACHING BEGINNING READING

In 1971 Aukerman described more than 100 beginning reading programs; in 1984 his revised book contained 165 descriptions. Various influences have converged to make the past 30 years, and particularly the last two decades, a period of change and innovation: dissatisfaction with existing programs; the contributions of cognitive and experimental psychologists, psycholinguists, linguists, and information-processing theorists; agitation by pressure groups for a return to the "basics," or to promote a particular program that will "cure the reading problem"; legal rulings; and federal funding for research, materials, and intervention programs. To those acquainted with the history of reading instruction, some of the "new" ideas and programs seem familiar.

Although the lines of distinction among commercially published reading programs have tended to blur in that they now place more stress on areas formerly emphasized by contrasting programs, most programs can be classified into one of three categories: (1) meaning-emphasis approaches; (2) code-emphasis approaches; and (3) individualized skills-emphasis approaches.

More complete discussions of the approaches and various programs may be found in Aukerman (1981, 1984) and in textbooks devoted to teaching developmental reading in the elementary school. The philosophy and methodology of a given program are best understood through studying the teachers' manuals and accompanying materials.

Basically, the approaches differ in the following ways: (1) initial and continuing emphasis on comprehension or decoding; (2) the basis on which words are selected for inclusion in the program; (3) the number of words used at a given level and in the entire program, and the rate at which these words are introduced and repeated in the selections; (4) how a child is first taught to recognize words; (5) the materials used as vehicles for developing reading skills and strategies; (6) instructional methodology; and (7) preplanned structure. Not only are there marked differences as to basic philosophy, methodology, and materials among approaches, but wide variations also exist among programs classified within the same category.

Beck (1981) enumerates specific ways in which meaning-emphasis and code-emphasis approaches differ, and the pros and cons of highly, moderately, and lightly structured programs are presented by T. Johnson, Mayfield, and Quorm (1980).

Teachers who are involved in the selection of published reading programs are more likely to implement those programs successfully (Veatch & Cooter 1986). Criteria for selecting a reading series have been presented by Dole, Rogers, and Osborn (1987) and Osborn (1989). Farr, Tully, and Powell (1987) suggest ways in which adoption committees can improve their selection processes.

Meaning-Emphasis Approaches

In basal reader programs, language-experience programs, whole-language and natural approaches, and individualized developmental reading programs, primary emphasis is placed on reading for meaning. The language-experience approach and individualized reading may be used in combination, and either or both may be combined in various ways with the basal-reader or the whole-language approach. Those who employ a basal reader series also may employ aspects of the whole-language approach, but advocates of the latter never follow a basal reader program.

BASAL READER PROGRAMS.[2] *Basal reader series,* which account for 75 to 90% of the reading programs in the United States (R. Anderson et al. 1985),

[2]Durkin (1987b) describes the forces that provoked changes in basal readers since the 1960s. Greenlinger-Harless (1987) provides a cross-referenced index to elementary school reading series, which may be used to identify the grade/reader level of textbooks as indicated by their publishers.

are preplanned, sequentially organized, detailed materials and methods to teach developmental reading skills systematically. For the past 70 years, most basal reader series have been eclectic, trying to provide a balanced developmental reading program with a broad and varied set of objectives. Many of these programs initially teach word recognition through a whole-word approach in which children learn to associate printed words with their spoken counterparts. The rationale for this procedure is that the recognition of whole words permits a quick introduction to meaningful sentences and stories. Before the mid-1960s, decoding skills were introduced very gradually, mainly at the second- and third-reader levels. Since then, there has been a decided trend toward more and earlier emphasis on decoding skills, especially so in the past 5 years. Basal series vary considerably, although they have features in common (Meyer, Greer & Crummey 1987).

Materials.   A representative series starts with one or more readiness books, usually in workbook form. The first actual reading materials are usually two or three thin paperbacks, called preprimers. To dispel the mistaken idea that a given book should be used only in a particular grade, many series number their books by levels. For example, a first preprimer that follows two readiness books would be labeled Level 3. Preprimers (Levels 3, 4, and 5[3]) are followed by the first hardcover book (primer, or Level 6), and by a first reader (Level 7), which completes the program covered by most first graders. There are usually two second readers (2[1] and 2[2], or Levels 8 and 9), two third readers (3[1] and 3[2], or Levels 10 and 11) and one text book each for the fourth-, fifth-, and sixth-reader levels (Levels, 12, 13, and 14). A few series have seventh- and eighth-reader levels (Levels 15 and 16). Some series also have transition books between reader levels or designate the textbook for possible use at two levels. Basal readers designated for the same level may differ considerably in average difficulty and in range of difficulty within each book (Bradley & Ames 1978). Stories do not systematically increase in difficulty from the beginning to the end of a text.

Each book in the series is accompanied by a consumable workbook that may provide self-help cues at the tops of pages or have recorded directions and answers for self-correction. Other accessory materials may include exercises printed on duplicating stencils; large cards for group practice with phonic elements, words, and phrases; introductory story cards or charts; correlated filmstrips and recordings; and supplementary paperback storybooks. The trend in enrichment is to provide the kinds of materials just mentioned in convenient packages as optional supplements.

Teachers tend to use the components of a commercially published reading program as a package, and their instructional procedures and materials derive primarily from those provided by the publisher, rather than from what they may have learned about teaching reading from their college professors (J. Osborn 1984a). There is little evidence as to why teachers rely so heavily on commercial reading materials (Shannon 1982).

[3]The numbering of levels varies from series to series depending on the number of books in the program. In this text, we continue to use the older terms preprimer, primer, first reader, and so on.

L. M. Anderson (1985) reports that seatwork is often heavily dependent on commercially developed materials, with each workbook page or worksheet focusing on a single skill. Children frequently perceive the goal of such assignments in terms of task completion (for its own sake), rather than as understanding or applying the skill under consideration.

Little information is available regarding the relationship of workbook content to the objectives of reading lessons, the instructional quality of workbooks, the relevance of workbook activities to the acquisition of reading ability, or the task demands that workbook exercises make on students (J. Osborn 1984a,b).

Workbook activities may: (1) require only a perfunctory level of reading; (2) provide work on skills which children do not need to learn or practice; (3) have difficult-to-understand directions; and (4) be poorly integrated with the textbooks they are designed to accompany (J. Osborn 1986). Therefore, teachers should carefully evaluate each workbook activity before assigning it. Writing activities can replace workbook activities that are not useful. Scheu, Tanner, and Au (1986) describe how to construct worksheets that not only are better coordinated with basal reader stories, but are also designed to improve reading comprehension. They (Scheu, Tanner & Au 1989) also suggest ways to use well-designed seatwork to support the goals of reading instruction.

Well-designed workbooks can be useful (J. Osborn 1986). They can help students by: (1) providing differentiated practice; (2) providing practice in writing skills; (3) providing intermittent and cumulative reviews of what has been taught; (4) helping them to synthesize information and to apply "old" information to new situations; and (5) providing practice in following written directions and in test-taking skills. Completed workbook pages can provide teachers with feedback as to how well each student can perform a particular task, and thereby aid in identifying some of the reading problems individual students are having.

Even well-designed workbooks can be overused. J. Mason (1982b) found that far more time was spent giving directions, supervising the completion of exercises, and checking workbooks than in reading instruction or reading by the students.

Each basal reader comes with a guide or manual that details the teaching method. Most manuals present a general plan and then give a detailed lesson plan for each selection. Manuals usually provide more suggestions for skill development and enrichment than are needed for most children. The teacher must therefore select activities judiciously, based on the children's needs, as well as determine the appropriate rate of presentation for different groups. Some of the suggestions made in the manuals, such as purpose-setting questions that lead children away from the important concepts in the story, may inadvertently block comprehension.

The teachers observed by Durkin (1984a) and J. Mason (1983) generally did not follow closely the instructional plans suggested by the manual; instruction in reading comprehension was noticeably lacking (Durkin 1987b). However, Russavage, Lorton, and Millham (1985) conclude that the 25 teachers they observed had a good grasp of what basal reader programs do and do not provide and that these teachers adjusted their instruction accordingly.

The trend toward progressively smaller vocabularies in basal readers extended from the 1920s through the 1950s, but has now been reversed. Current basal readers contain a much more diverse set of words than in previous years (A. J. Harris & Jacobson 1982). The number of new words per story and the number of running words has increased and the words are repeated less often (Chall 1983a).

Basal readers vary considerably in the number of new words introduced per level, the rate at which they are introduced, the number of times the words are repeated, and the total number of words employed (Willows, Borwick & Hayvren 1981). A number of words are unique to a particular series, and the vocabulary overlap between two series at a given reader level may be limited.

The language of first-grade basal readers has often been criticized as artificial, stilted, monotonous, and unduly repetitious. This criticism, although aimed at basal readers in general, has always taken its examples from preprimers, in which vocabulary restrictions are the most severe. Similar criticism can be leveled at phonic and linguistic programs that control the vocabulary on the basis of phonic regularity or spelling patterns. Many publishers now attempt to use more natural language in their first-grade basals.

Regardless of which approach is used, a limited vocabulary is employed in the initial stages of instruction. This practice may create some comprehension problems for novice readers (Beck & McCaslin 1981, McKeown 1981). Because the restricted vocabulary cannot carry the story line alone, meaning must be constructed through a combination of print, picture clues, and information provided by the pupil or teacher. Moreover, delimiting the vocabulary necessitates the use of indirect language and expressions that are semantically ambiguous and thus places additional inference burdens on young children. This is especially true in the use of first- and second-person pronouns, locational references (e.g., *here*), and demonstrative pronouns (e.g., *this*).

Basal readers now have better balance in racial and ethnic characters (Lucy Fuchs 1987); male and female characters; urban, suburban, and rural settings; and geographic locations, compared to those in previous years. They include more handicapped characters and senior citizens who are depicted favorably, but perhaps unrealistically (Fillmer & Meadows 1986); and their literary quality has improved, as has the artwork. Violence seems to have been deleted from the stories.

Basal readers and children's books have been attacked as sexist or because of insufficient cultural or ethnic pluralism. An implicit assumption of these charges is that changes in the content of reading material will result in more positive attitudes toward sex roles and minorities. As desirable as such content changes are, we cannot rely on them alone to modify attitudes. Children enter school with attitudes that have been developed over the years, and the influence of the child's family and peers continues to have a strong impact on these attitudes.

Methodology.   The typical *directed reading activity* (DRA) in a basal series consists essentially of three steps: (1) preparation, (2) reading the selection, and (3) follow-up activities. Swaby (1982) suggests ways to vary these steps to prevent boredom and Spiegel (1981b) presents a procedure for determining which of six alternatives to the DRA is best suited for a particular instructional purpose.

Wixson and Peters (1989) describe procedures for modifying basal lessons, which they feel were more consistent with current research findings.

Preparation.   Preparation to read a new selection may involve three or four main phases, all of which are not equally important for every lesson. The first phase is interest arousal, which can be accomplished by implementing the most-likely-to-be-effective suggestion(s) from among those presented in the teacher's manual. Next is the presentation of words that have not been introduced previously in the reading program. These new words are identified in the teacher's manual. The recognition of these printed words may be taught through a whole-word method, or the children may be asked to apply previously taught decoding skills to them. In some basal series, much of the decoding instruction and practice occur at this point. The meanings of these new words may be taught or the students may be asked to discuss the meanings that they know for each word, and then to select the meaning intended by the author. This word-meaning phase can be used to assess prior knowledge, if the new words represent key concepts in the passage. The third phase is getting the children to activate their prior knowledge. They should be told that using what they already know can help their reading comprehension. Students can be asked to tell what they know about the topic, or they can be asked to preview the selection and told that noting the pictures, titles, and words can help them to think about what they already know. Asking them to predict what will happen in the story or what information the passage will relate may also help them to activate prior knowledge.[4] Students may need to be told to evaluate their predictions as they read (Schmitt & Baumann 1986). The final phase may involve developing needed concepts and/or teaching the children how to activate or apply their prior knowledge.

According to R. Anderson et al. (1985), preparation for reading is the most-often-slighted aspect of DRA, especially in regard to the activation or development of background knowledge required for understanding the story.

Guided Reading and Rereading.   Usually the teacher leads a discussion of the story title and first illustration and then asks one or two purpose-setting questions. Rather than pose questions that may elicit unrelated bits of information, the teacher should get the students thinking about the direction the story will take (Beck, McCaslin & McKeown 1981). Pearson (1982) also suggests ways to formulate questions about stories. Pupils should be told that having a purpose for reading before and during reading helps them to focus their attention and enhances active comprehension (Schmitt & Baumann 1986). Teachers also need to help children learn to formulate questions for themselves. As children become more adept at doing so, teachers should provide fewer questions for them.

After a purpose for reading has been established, the students read the material silently. The amount read before the content is discussed should be

---

[4]Other suggestions for helping students to activate prior knowledge are given on page 557. In the Directed Reading-Thinking Activity, students are guided through the process of sampling the text, making predictions based on their prior knowledge and text information, resampling the text, and confirming, adjusting, or rejecting their predictions in light of new information. Haggard (1988) describes the steps in a DR/TA and offers suggestions for implementing this instructional strategy.

geared to the readers' abilities, with capable readers being allowed to read more of the text than the manual often suggests. Students should be informed that, when reading large portions of a story or the whole story, it is helpful to stop at each of the structural elements of a story[5] and to summarize[6] the important ideas covered to that point. Doing so aids comprehension by alerting them to comprehension breakdowns.

As they read, pupils should evaluate their predictions, modify them as needed, ask themselves new questions and seek answers to them, and perhaps make new predictions. They should also practice monitoring their comprehension and disruptive miscues.

After silent reading, a discussion should focus on a summary of the total selection, an evaluation of the children's predictions, a determination as to whether the purposes set for reading were fulfilled, the children's interpretations of aspects of the story, and so on (Schmitt & Baumann 1986). Among the characteristics of an effective after-reading discussion are: (1) a focus on important information, (2) requirement that students give evidence to support their responses, and (3) verbal interaction among students as well as between the teacher and students (Jett-Simpson 1986).

Oral rereading may be done for many reasons: to show how different characters felt, to read sad or funny parts that can be shared, to take parts in dramatizing the story, as a diagnostic tool, and so forth. When every story is reread orally in its entirety every day, oral reading becomes a drudgery and valuable instructional time is wasted.

Follow-Up Activities.   Follow-up activities are mainly of two kinds: (1) skills development and practice and (2) enrichment activities. In some basal reader programs, instruction in decoding skills follows discussion of the story. In almost all programs, additional practice in specific comprehension skills and use of workbook pages follow the story's discussion.

Most manuals provide suggestions for enrichment, including recommendations for stories that can be read to the children, songs that can be sung or listened to, poems or rhymes with related themes, and related art and handiwork. As children become able to read independently, suggestions are made for specific supplementary reading.

If teachers do not have time to cover all parts of the DRA, the follow-up activities are likely to be neglected. Thus, although a basal manual recommends teaching or practicing skills, the plans may not be carried out in some classrooms. Similarly, enrichment activities may be omitted by teachers who are anxious to keep to preset schedules.

Teachers who are using the same basal reader series may vary, at times considerably, in the ways in which they use the program, as well as in the amount of time spent daily on various reading activities and on reading instruction overall. Rather than make decisions in response to the demands of each lesson, teachers seem to develop routines for what to select from the teacher's manual (Barr & Sadow 1989).

[5]Story grammars are discussed on pages 564–566.
[6]Children will have to be taught how to make such summaries (see pages 616–617).

J. Mason (1982b, 1983) found that reading lessons seldom followed the pre-sumed minimal sequence of preparation, directed reading, and discussion. More often, a hurried introduction to a story was sandwiched between workbook exer-cises and the pupils reading the story at their seats. Often, either an introduction or follow-up discussion of the story was omitted. The reading lessons of these observed teachers often lacked a coherent ordering of instructional activities. Durkin (1984a) reports similar findings.

LANGUAGE-EXPERIENCE APPROACHES.   As early as the 1890s, some ex-perimental schools used short stories dictated by the children and written down by the teacher as beginning reading materials (A. J. Harris 1964). Such "experi-ence stories" have been widely used for decades to provide an informal intro-duction to reading instruction. Many teachers have also incorporated them in supplementary reading material, with particular reference to experiences in sci-ence and social studies. The experience method, now renamed the language-experience approach (LEA), rarely has the preplanned structure associated with other approaches. Generally, a *language-experience approach* is one in which

> . . . emphasis is placed on the teaching of reading in close correlation with the related activities of listening, speaking, and writing. Children are encour-aged to express their thoughts, ideas, and feelings, often stimulated by a spe-cific experience guided and developed by the teacher. The verbal produc-tions of the children are written down by the teacher in the early stages, and are used as the earliest reading materials. Pupil expression is encouraged through the use of a variety of media such as painting, speaking, and writing. Gradually, the program moves from exclusive use of reading material that is developed out of the oral language of the children, into a program of reading in which increasing emphasis is placed upon a variety of children's books. (A. J. Harris & Serwer 1966a)

Current LEA programs attempt to integrate writing, reading, listening, and speaking skills. Their implementation requires a great deal of teacher initiative, creativity, and planning. Helpful suggestions for conducting an LEA program can be found in a number of sources (Stauffer 1980, Gans 1979, Allen & Allen 1982, Veatch et al. 1979, D. White 1980). N. J. Smith (1988) suggests how word processors may be used with LEA. Commercially available language-experience programs are not based on interests that originate with the children and tend to be highly structured. Themes for experience stories can be developed from trips, science or social studies topics, and interesting happenings at home, at school, or in the neighborhood. The topics may be selected and developed by individuals or groups of pupils.

The initial teaching method resembles that of the old story-memory method, going from the teacher's reading of the entire story to the reading of single lines to phrases and words. Word-recognition and decoding skills are de-veloped from words used in the experience stories and are usually introduced as the teacher perceives a need and an opportunity rather than in any preplanned sequence. Compared to basal reader stories, experience stories may be of higher reading difficulty and contain more syntactically complex sentences (Sampson

1982). Gradually, as word recognition grows, easy first-grade books can be introduced in an LEA program and a transition made either to a basal reader program or an individualized reading program. See Reimer (1983) and Homan (1983) for suggestions.

WHOLE-LANGUAGE AND NATURAL APPROACHES.   Some writers (e.g., Holdaway 1986; F. Smith 1982; Goodman & Goodman 1979, 1982) suggest that written language can, and should, be acquired just as naturally as spoken language when the conditions for learning both forms of language are comparable. Those who promote use of a natural or whole-language[7] approach to written language acquisition hold that: (1) children have a natural facility for learning language; (2) reading and writing are natural extensions of linguistic development; (3) speaking, listening, reading, and writing are language processes that are best acquired when learning activities stress their interrelatedness; (4) children learn to read naturally if instructional practices are in keeping with their linguistic competencies and abilities; (5) children's language development is best facilitated in a learning environment that provides them with varied opportunities to use spoken and written language for a wide range of personal, social, and academic purposes; (6) language and language learning are social activities that occur best in situations that encourage discussion and sharing of ideas; (7) students must have a choice in selecting materials and activities; (8) the main role of the teacher is to structure a learning environment that encourages and allows children to "teach themselves." Learning to read is more appropriately thought of as implicit language learning than the conscious learning of reading skills; and (9) although there may be some direct teaching of skills in isolation, for the most part such instruction takes place in the context of a particular activity and only when the child demonstrates a need or a desire to acquire such a skill (Fillion & Brause 1987).

K. Goodman (1986) summarizes the feelings of most whole-language and natural learning advocates toward skill development and the need for direct instruction. He states that as children write, they develop spelling rules, invent spellings, and move toward standard spellings. As they read stories and other texts that are comprehensible and important to them, pupils develop strategies for making sense out of print. In the process, students develop phonic rules and come to know words and what they mean in a variety of contexts. Direct teaching of phonics and vocabulary are unnecessary and even counterproductive. Goodman lists three essentials for the teaching of reading: (1) Because we learn to read by reading, children should be encouraged to do a great deal of reading of whole, meaningful, relevant texts; (2) the instructional atmosphere must encourage *risk taking* in reading (trying to make sense out of text even when you are not certain); and (3) both teachers and students must focus on making sense of written language.

Whole-language and natural approaches are more implementations of a philosophy than they are methodologies (Altwerger, Edelsky & Flores 1987). Therefore, a wide range of instructional practices exist in classes in which these

---

[7]The term *whole language* is derived from one belief that emphasis should be on performing "whole" language tasks rather than on acquiring subskills. Thus it is believed that one learns to read by reading rather than by acquiring a series of component skills.

approaches are employed. Generally, however, planning, writing, editing, and revising in peer conferences are used in the writing activities. Reading activities include daily reading of trade books, newspapers, materials written by the students, and so forth. The role of the teacher differs from that of the "traditional" teacher mainly in that the responsibility for learning is delegated to the students, the curriculum stems from the student interest, and the teacher provides direct instruction only as needed (Smith-Burke 1987). Whole-language approaches are student-centered and lightly structured.

An extreme point of view (Goelman, Oberg, & Smith 1984) contends that all that is required for learning to write and read, at least during the initial stages of acquisition, is exposure to written language. But exposure to print does not assure that children will learn to read (Calfee & Drum 1985), and there is little support for the view that children move closer to acquiring reading ability after experiencing considerable print in their environments (Ehri 1987). Richgels et al. (1988) found that nonreaders paid some attention to graphic information, but attended only to individual letters and numbers.

While, under ideal supportive conditions, writing and reading abilities may arise without direct instruction, we are not sure that most children can learn in this way (Dickinson 1987). Present research on the whole-language approach describes only what happens in the classrooms, not how or why it happens (Smith-Burke 1987). See Jaggar and Harwood (1989) for a reading list on the whole-language approach.

Based on their analyses of 51 studies in which the approaches were compared, Stahl and Miller (1989) conclude that although, in general, whole-language/language-experience approaches and basal reader programs were about equally effective, their overall conclusion needed to be qualified. The more rigorous studies and the more recent studies tend to favor basal reader programs, which also produced larger effects when used with disadvantaged children. Whole-language/language-experience approaches are more effective in kindergarten or as "reading readiness" programs. Stahl and Miller suggest initial use of the whole-language/language-experience approach followed by systematic direct instruction in word recognition/decoding. We have recommended such a practice for a number of years; this allows the children to acquire first understandings regarding the functional aspects of reading (e.g., concepts about print, understanding that reading is a form of communication). But once such concepts are acquired, the children need to acquire word recognition/decoding skills to a level that allows comprehension to proceed smoothly.

INDIVIDUALIZED DEVELOPMENTAL READING.   *Individualized developmental reading* (IDR) is characterized by the elimination of systematic instruction with a basal series and the use of individual reading in a variety of reading materials as the core rather than a supplement (Hunt 1971). Each child selects the material that he or she wishes to read, sometimes with help from the teacher. During reading periods the child reads ahead silently, getting help from the teacher or another pupil when needed. At intervals (usually once or twice a week), there is a pupil-teacher conference that may involve discussion of what has been read, some oral reading, and perhaps some skills teaching. Preparation for reading is almost eliminated. Although some children are taught to set their own purposes for reading, reading is usually not guided by any specifically stated purposes except interest in the book. Comprehension is usually checked on the general plot. Rereading is often eliminated in favor of doing a large amount of varied reading. Word-recognition and decoding instruction usually consist of help given to a child as opportunities occur during the conferences, but sometimes temporary groups are formed for those children who need help on specific reading skills.

Three words often repeated by exponents of IDR are *seeking, self-selection,* and *pacing.* These concepts imply that children explore a wide range of available reading materials, choose their own reading, and proceed at their own pace. Great stress is placed on the importance of these factors in developing a spontaneous love for reading and in allowing reading to fit harmoniously into the unique pattern of growth of each child. The gradual, steady introduction of new words that can be obtained by reading a series of readers in sequence is considered unnecessary.

Many differences of opinion arise over the details of individualized developmental reading, but a knowledgeable, well-organized teacher would seem to be an absolute necessity. Some of the important issues involved in the use of IDR were discussed by Harris and Sipay (1979, pp. 89–95).

A large number of studies involving IDR have appeared, but many of them are faulty. "Much of the reported research suffers from poor research design, inadequate sampling, careless measurement, and a biased attitude on the part of the investigator" (Duker 1968). The following quotation seems to be a fair evaluation of results of research on IDR:

> An examination of the research reports leads to these tentative conclusions about individualized reading instruction: (1) Individualized reading can be somewhat successful under certain conditions. (2) It requires highly competent teachers, and those who are not particularly capable should not be asked to adopt it. (3) Children usually enjoy the personal attention of the individual conference and, as a result, develop favorable attitudes toward reading. (4) They often, but not always, read more books. (5) The less capable pupils and those having special problems are likely to be less successful in individualized reading than in more structured programs. (6) The lack of a sequential skills program and opportunities for readiness causes teachers to feel doubtful about the adequacy of skills learning. (7) Teachers are constantly pressed for time to provide conferences that pupils should have. (Sartain 1969)

Little has been written about IDR in recent years.

Code-Emphasis Approaches

Code-emphasis programs place initial stress on teaching decoding skills. Phonics programs, teaching by syllables, linguistic programs, and special alphabet and color programs are code-emphasis approaches.

PHONICS PROGRAMS. *Phonics programs* stress learning grapheme-phoneme correspondences, tend to stress phonic generalizations and ignore exceptions, tend to provide instruction in blending phonemes, and tend to provide practice in applying decoding skills to words in context. Most phonics programs use a synthetic (parts-to-whole) approach. There are wide variations among phonics programs in content and methodology. Among the differences are the sequence in which symbol-sound associations are taught, the rate at which phonic principles are introduced, the number of generalizations taught, the opportunities for reading-connected discourse, and the length and content of the connected discourse to be read.

Phonics programs intended as preliminary or supplementary materials usually appear in consumable workbook form. Other phonics programs are designed total developmental reading programs, starting with readiness material and usually going through at least the sixth-reader level. In these programs, most of the decoding skills are introduced in the first-grade materials.

TEACHING BY SYLLABLES. Based on the belief that the syllable is more easily discernible than the phoneme within a spoken word, some authors advocate teaching reading by syllables rather than by grapheme-phoneme correspondences. Rozin and Gleitman (1977) offer a detailed discussion of their 22-element syllabary approach that has been reported to be successful (Gleitman & Rozin 1973). It is difficult to evaluate the Gleitman and Rozin study, however, because of the absence of a large number of necessary controls and the probability that their curriculum was highly motivating, independent of the scripts employed (L. Henderson 1982). A syllabary approach may be useful for children who have difficulty learning phonics.

LINGUISTIC APPROACHES. Bloomfield, a noted linguist, became interested in the teaching of reading in the late 1930s and wrote an essay on the subject in 1942. However, materials based on his ideas were not published for almost 20 years (Bloomfield & Barnhart 1961). Bloomfield was highly critical of phonic methods, particularly those using a synthetic sounding-blending procedure, and even more critical of the whole-word method, which he likened to the study of Chinese ideographs. Very briefly, his recommended procedure includes the following ideas: (1) Start with teaching identification of all alphabet letters by name (not by sound); (2) begin with words in which each letter represents only one phonemic value, avoiding words with silent letters or less common sounds, so that the beginning words consist of three-letter words with a consonant-vowel-consonant pattern containing only short vowel sounds; (3) use the principle of minimal variation, employing a list of words that are alike except for one letter, such as *ban, can, Dan;* (4) do not teach rules about letter-sound correspondences, as the children will evolve their own generalizations when sound and spelling correspond in regular fashion; and (5) employ learned words in sentences, such as "Nan can fan Dan."

A few reading series are based on the above principles. They agree that translating the printed words into their spoken equivalents is the first and most important goal of a beginning reading program. Most of them use a whole-word method and the principle of minimal variation instead of teaching decoding skills directly. Programs differ on such factors as the use and teaching of high-frequency words (e.g., *the*) that are not phonetically regular. Some use illustrations from the beginning; others consider them distracting and harmful. No two linguistic series agree very closely on details.

There is some question as to how well young children abstract letter-sound associations without direct instruction (Bishop 1962), and there are possible adverse effects of not establishing a "set for diversity" caused by the use of a tightly controlled vocabulary based on a one-to-one letter-sound correspondence in set spelling patterns (Levin & Watson 1963). Questions regarding linguistic reading programs have also been raised by linguists (Wardhaugh 1969) and psycholinguists (Smith & Goodman 1971), who state that there is no such thing as a linguistic reading program but only reading programs written by linguists. Linguistic principles have been translated into diametrically opposed ideas as to how reading should be taught.

SPECIAL-ALPHABET PROGRAMS.   Based on the belief that the irregularities in the English symbol-sound system are sufficient to cause difficulty for children learning to read, there have been efforts to promote a phonetically regular alphabet for English since the middle 1800s. The idea is that a one-to-one correspondence, in which each grapheme always represents the same phoneme (and vice versa), would make it much easier to "break the code" and thus facilitate the acquisition of reading ability. Supporters of simplified and regularized spelling do not agree on details, but most advocate supplementing our 26-letter alphabet.

The best known of the special alphabets, the Initial Teaching Alphabet (i.t.a.), has 44 characters in which (1) capitals are like lowercase letters in shape, but larger; (2) there is a separate symbol for each of 44 consonant and vowel sounds; and (3) many present letters are retained, and new characters are designed to facilitate transition to traditional orthography (T. O.). The Initial Teaching Alphabet is not an instructional method but an augmented alphabet. The most widely used i.t.a. readers in Great Britain employed an eclectic methodology similar to that of most American basal series, whereas the i.t.a. series most used in the United States followed an alphabet-phonic procedure. Although fairly popular at one time, the use of i.t.a. has markedly declined in the United States, where i.t.a. materials are no longer published.

Other special-alphabet systems employed color cues rather than additional graphemes (e.g., *Words in Color*). Each phoneme, regardless of its spelling, was printed in a particular hue; color cues were gradually phased out. Research did not reveal such programs to be any more effective than programs with which they were compared. They are rarely mentioned in the current literature.

Individualized Skills-Emphasis Programs

PROGRAMMED MATERIALS.   *Programmed materials* are designed so that the user (1) encounters a series of small tasks on which success is very likely; (2) is involved in the learning process through actively responding; and (3) receives immediate feedback as to the correctness of each response. In theory, programmed materials should greatly facilitate individualized instruction because they allow each student to work almost independently with material suitable for his or her needs, proceeding at a pace commensurate with ability and interest.

Programmed reading series usually consist of consumable workbook-like textbooks, with accompanying manuals and accessory materials. Their basic method is best described as a phonic-linguistic one.

Programmed readers were found wanting by Beck (1977) for the following reasons: (1) The "missing letter technique" (the user fills in the blank space) is insufficient for developing decoding skills because it does not incorporate an auditory model or auditory feedback; (2) comprehension is interrupted because the child must stop to fill in a response, often in the middle of a sentence; (3) much of the connected discourse that surrounds the target word can be ignored, since the missing letter can be supplied from memory or by finding a copy of the complete word; and (4) very little text must be read to answer the questions correctly.

Interest in programmed reading series appears to have waned considerably, but programming principles are employed in the development of some computer software.

SKILLS MANAGEMENT SYSTEMS. *Skills management systems* (also referred to as diagnostic-prescriptive teaching, objective-based instruction, or criterion-referenced systems) place stress on diagnosing each learner's status and needs and on individualizing skill development based on diagnostic findings. Such programs usually have these characteristics: (1) a list of sequenced behavioral objectives for one or more skill areas (e.g., word recognition, comprehension); (2) criterion-referenced tests for each objective; (3) sources of instructional materials; and (4) recordkeeping procedures. A subskills orientation is believed to make learning more meaningful and easier by reducing the information load, simplifying the learning act, and allowing mastery learning (Carnine 1982).

A placement test or a series of pretests places the child along a skills continuum (perhaps at different levels in various skill areas). If the criterion for mastery is not met, the child receives instructional materials and works independently until the teacher thinks that the skill has been mastered. A posttest is then administered. If the posttest is passed, the child takes the next pretest in the sequence; if failed, additional practice is provided. Periodic mastery tests cover broader skill areas.

The teacher's role is to select, administer, and score the diagnostic instruments; arrive at diagnostic conclusions; assign appropriate practice; give individual or group assistance as needed; secure, organize, and keep track of materials; maintain motivation; and keep adequate records.

Although there are basic similarities, skills management systems differ considerably. A number of skills management systems have been described (Rude 1974, Lawrence & Simmons 1978).

Theoretically, skills management systems promote specific individualized instruction and efficient use of time (children are not required to practice skills they have already mastered). Individualized curricula relying largely on a test-teach-retest model to guide students through a planned sequence of materials place a considerable strain on teachers' recordkeeping and decision-making skills (Calfee & Brown 1979). Unless teacher aides or computer assistance for test scoring and recordkeeping are available, there may be little time for direct instruction. Such assistance involves additional expense, which many school systems cannot afford. The most frequently cited reasons for discarding skills management systems are their cost (Eveland 1975) and the demands of recordkeeping (Wirt 1976).

As with any program, there are potential disadvantages. Assigning a child to a particular exercise without determining why the pretest was failed can lead to blind repetition of the same kind of error. Instruction may also become too rigid; children do not all learn in the same way nor are all skills equally important. Then, too, there is a strong temptation to teach easily testable skills and to slight higher-level skills that are more difficult to measure. Most important, there is the danger that teaching is left solely to the practice exercises; many children need direct instruction by competent teachers.

According to Duffy (1978), objective-based instruction is not a total approach to reading instruction nor does its use dictate a particular instructional method. Rather, it is designed to help teachers organize the reading curriculum and present reading in small, logically sequenced increments. A skills hierarchy should be used as a guide; it is not infallible. Moreover, no skill is truly mastered until the student uses is consistently in independent reading. Therefore skills management systems should provide transfer activities and time for independent reading.

A term frequently associated with skills management systems is mastery learning. *Mastery learning* advocates contend that almost all pupils could learn well *if* instruction were systematic, students were helped when and where they had learning difficulties, sufficient time was provided for achieving mastery, and a clear criterion of what constituted mastery was available. Many of the tenets of mastery learning have been attributed to Bloom (1981) and Carroll (1989). Mastery learning is discussed more fully on page 142.

Use of Computers in Reading Instruction

Computers are used mainly in two ways in the teaching of reading: computer-assisted instruction (CAI) and computer-managed instruction (CMI). CAI involves the presentation of a program (software) by a computer (hardware). In CMI, computers may be utilized to generate tests and exercises, to score tests and exercises, to keep a detailed record of each student's progress in reading, and to assist in selecting appropriate instructional materials for the students. CMI programs often accompany skills management systems, but they are becoming more available for use with more conventional published reading programs.

In the pioneering CAI work of Atkinson and Fletcher (1972), emphasis was on a decoding program that supplemented classroom instruction. Reading software has improved over the years and will continue to improve; but it still has a long way to go (Balajthy 1988).

Most available software provides drill and practice in decoding, word recognition, and word meaning. Little is available for *teaching* such basic skills or for use in developing reading comprehension; most software just *measures* it (Rude 1986). Becker (1986) believes that schools use drill and practice programs because they are available, and that they are available because publishers believe that schools are likely to buy them. Drill and practice software may also be much more available because it is easier and less costly to produce as well as less likely to be pirated than costly complex programs (Blanchard, Mason & Daniel 1987).

Use of drill and practice is defensible when mastery of specific skills and concepts is critical. Most drill and practice software includes elements of programmed instruction such as moving students through a series of steps ordered according to difficulty, providing immediate feedback regarding performance, and using the student's prior performance to guide subsequent testing and practice (Becker 1986).

Research findings regarding the effectiveness of computers in reading instruction are mixed, but they seem to suggest that CAI produces a slight advantage over more traditional practice formats. Basic reading skills are mastered more readily and in a shorter period of time, and their acquisition is enjoyed more by the students. However, most of this evidence comes from studies that employed large, integrated software programs delivered on mainframe computers. The findings may not pertain to the effectiveness of programs for use with microcomputers, so we still do not know if microcomputer programs are more effective than less expensive and already available procedures (Torgesen 1986a,b; Blanchard, Mason & Daniel 1987). Most studies have been carried out by the designers of the software being tested (Balajthy 1987), but more research regarding the effectiveness of microcomputer software is being done by "outsiders." For example, Jones, Torgesen, and Sexton (1987) report that use of a published program for 15 minutes daily over 16 weeks resulted in substantial gain in decoding fluency by 20 learning disabled students who were able to transfer their newly acquired skills to unpracticed words. If computers become important learning tools, it will be because they are managed effectively to implement sound educational practice rather than because of special features of computer technology such as animation and sound effects (Torgesen 1986b).

The interactive nature of computer programs and their visually appealing displays can make drill and practice more enjoyable and thus help students stay on task. They can also provide immediate corrective feedback, thereby reducing the number of incorrect responses and cutting learning time. Computers also are tireless and nonjudgmental. They can be programmed to make corrective responses in a number of nonthreatening ways. But the following points regarding the use of microcomputers in the classroom (Goldman & Pellegrino 1987) should be considered: (1) Most currently available microcomputer software is not instructional; it does not teach. Therefore it is best suited for drill and practice of skills and concepts that have already been taught; (2) acquisition of basic skills involves more than just responding correctly. Students must acquire the ability to access acquired skills and information efficiently. Repeated practice may produce accuracy, but automaticity does not occur until performance has reached high level of accuracy. Individuals differ as to when such levels are reached; (3) the game-like format of drill and practice exercises may not be appropriate for students who have difficulty in selectively attending to task-relevant information; and, (4) it is important to determine if gains observed in microcomputer performance carry over to classroom reading situations. There is also some concern regarding the legibility of the electronic displays and the visual fatigue caused by viewing video displays (Blanchard, Mason & Daniel 1987).

Software is becoming more sophisticated. For example, one program (Olson, Foltz & Wise 1986), allows a student who cannot recognize a word simply to touch that word on the video display, and the computer pronounces it. The voice quality of most text-to-speech synthesizers is poor, but rapid advances are being made in this area as well as in having the computer respond to voice commands. Programs such as the aforementioned could help to prevent disruptions in comprehension caused by word-recognition problems. They also could allow disabled readers to utilize whatever reading skills they possess to "read" written text that they could not process on their own. If there are too many unknown words, however, comprehension is still likely to be disrupted because the message will be fragmented into a number of small difficult-to-process pieces. There is also the danger that some students will overrely on such a "quick fix" rather than learn to recognize unknown words or to use word-recognition strategies.

Computers are also used in producing written language. Some students are reluctant to write because they fear making mistakes or because they dislike having to rewrite large portions of text. Word processors can help to alleviate such fears, but they cannot get students to overcome their reluctance to organize their thoughts into coherent and systematic text. Students need rewriting skills for organizing their initial ideas and to give them confidence that they have something to say. Providing a word processor does not automatically produce skilled writers.

The potential of computers in teaching reading, writing, and literature is yet to be realized (Frase 1987), but we are embarking on an era in which teachers and computers will increasingly become partners in a learning environment (Goldman & Pellegrino 1987). Therefore, teachers and students will have to become computer literate. Geoffrion and Geoffrion (1983) explain how a computer works and its use in teaching reading. Guidelines for evaluating software may be found in Scott and Barker (1987) and Lillie, Hannum, and Stuck (1989). A number of professional journals regularly devote space to the use of computers, especially to the description and evaluation of software (see Rude 1986, pp. 164–167). Dreyer, Futtersak, and Boehm (1985) developed a list of words that primary-grade children need to recognize and understand in order to use the computer and computer software. Refer to Blanchard, Mason, and Daniel (1987) for an annotated bibliography covering a wide range of topics in computer application to reading and writing instruction, and to Reinking (1987) for discussions of issues regarding the use of computers in reading instruction.

ADJUSTING TO THE NEEDS OF DIALECT, LIMITED-ENGLISH, AND NON–ENGLISH SPEAKERS

Low-income minority students often speak a dialect or speak little or no English. Such pupils tend not only to get off to a poor start in learning to read, but also fall farther behind their age peers as they proceed through school.

A number of large-scale studies have shown that, on the average, low-income minority children are usually at the 20th to 28th percentile in reading by the third grade, approximately a year below grade level. Educational efforts to improve this situation have not been particularly effective, especially in inner-city schools (Haller 1985).

Differences between the language of the students and standard English

(SE) have been cited as having a direct or indirect negative influence on reading achievement. Obviously, not being able to speak or to understand English presents a serious problem in learning to read English. The language of instruction is very likely to be English and even if the children learn to recognize and say the words, they probably will not understand their meaning, at least initially. While the negative effects do not appear as great, differences between SE and the language of dialect and limited-English speakers may also create linguistic barriers that interfere with learning to read and reading comprehension.

Black English (BE) is the dialect given the most attention in the literature. It is not spoken by all blacks, and there are variations of BE in different communities. Most linguists (e.g., Labov 1973) believe that BE is a well-ordered, cohesive linguistic system. It has some unique features that differ from SE and have been listed as possible sources of interference for dialect speakers. These possible sources are phonological, grammatical, and lexical.[8]

The evidence for phonological interference is not convincing. In fact, Shuy (1979) flatly states that a phonological mismatch is not a cause of reading difficulty. Even though dialect speakers may pronounce words differently than do SE speakers, they evidently obtain meaning (Torrey 1983). Counting dialect renditions as word-recognition errors, however, may depress *scores* on oral reading tests (Burke, Pflaum & Knafle 1982). Dialect speakers usually become bidialectal when they enter school, and, by the middle grades, most have learned when the use of dialect is situationally appropriate (Lucas & Borders 1987). The presence of BE features in students' oral language does not insure their presence in the students' written-language production. Just as with oral language, students learn to switch codes in appropriate situations and do not improperly impose their "first language" rules on the "second language" grammar they use in writing (D. Morrow 1985). Children whose primary or second language is not English also switch codes (Martin 1989).

At times the syntax of BE could interfere with reading comprehension (Hall & Guthrie 1982). For example, there are certain differences in the ways BE and SE speakers structure prepositions (e.g., BE = "John, sit *to* the table." SE = "John, sit *at* the table.").

Lexical differences (e.g., *tote* for *carry*) are not likely to create serious comprehension problems when reading connected discourse. A restricted store of concepts and their labels is more likely to cause comprehension problems for dialect speakers.

Dialect speakers' listening comprehension does not differ significantly when material is presented in SE or BE (Cagney 1977), nor are BE speakers more successful comprehending material written in their dialect than in SE (Hall & Turner 1974). Most dialect speakers can derive meaning from selections written in SE despite surface-structure differences between their dialect and SE. Speaking SE does not seem vital for reading comprehension, although it has possible social and economic values.

Although the linguistic-mismatch theory does not appear to offer a viable

---

[8]Refer to A. J. Harris and Sipay (1979, pp. 459–481) for specific information concerning differences between SE and the languages of BE, Spanish, and Chinese speakers.

explanation for the relatively poor reading achievement of dialect speakers, it cannot be totally rejected. Our knowledge concerning the possible effect of dialect interference on novice readers is meager.

A spoken dialect or lack of English proficiency may reflect the presence of other factors that have contributed to the speaker's reading difficulties. Many dialect, limited-English, and non-English speakers are economically disadvantaged. The effects of poverty on reading achievement are pervasive, and because all the factors associated with poverty and its environment are highly interrelated, it may be impossible to isolate any single factor as *the* cause of reading problems among the poor.

The languages of children who come from minority-group, dialect-speaking, or non-English-speaking backgrounds frequently signal cultures that vary from the mainstream culture of most teachers. Misperceptions caused by language and cultural differences are possible sources of indirect interference with reading achievement. A teacher who considers children's dialects or first languages as inferior may denigrate them and their cultures, thereby causing the children to withdraw from learning situations; or, such teacher behaviors may set up teacher-pupil conflicts. Teachers' attitudes may also influence their judgements about children's learning and reading abilities, which in turn may affect expectations held for and communicated to them, the reading group in which they are placed, and so forth (see p. 133 regarding grouping practices, and page 114 regarding teacher expectations). According to Fillion and Brause (1987), cultural differences influence classroom interactions and teachers' evaluations of pupils. But Entwisle et al. (1986) report that race, which is related to language and culture, has little impact on the marks given to students by teachers in integrated schools.

Cultural variations in the function and use of language can create communication barriers between teachers and non-standard-English speakers (Toohey 1986), as can the pupils' not knowing the implicit rules of when and how to communicate in the classroom (Brause & Mayher 1982). Pupils may use "inappropriate" language or talk out at times when teachers think it is inappropriate to do so.

There are also cultural differences regarding what constitutes acceptable or desirable behaviors, as well as differences in the rules that govern interactions with others. For instance, the cultures of some Native American and Vietnamese children dictate that they remain silent in the presence of adults and that learning takes place through observing and listening. These children's silence in class could be misinterpreted by teachers as a sign of disinterest or insolence.

Nonverbal cultural differences also exist. Body language may carry different meanings, as may certain behaviors. For example, teachers may expect children with whom they are talking to make eye contact with them, but in some cultures a lowered gaze is a sign of respect.

Unrecognized cultural differences can lead to communication problems and to undesirable attitudes. The teacher may perceive the student as inattentive, disinterested, or intellectually slow. The student may see the teacher as uncaring, prejudiced, and bossy. Such attitudes may adversely influence teaching and learning (Greenbaum 1985). Teachers must be aware of and consider cultural differences in order to understand student behaviors and, in so doing, avoid misunderstandings and conflicts. R. Henderson (1980) reviews suggestions for meeting the social and emotional needs of culturally diverse students.

McDermott (1985) theorizes that the reading failure of many minority or culturally different children is best explained by the cultural makeup of the classroom.[9] When the children's culture and that of the teacher are different enough so that they are unable to make sense of each other, a cultural communication conflict emerges in the classroom. Patterns of selective attention and inattention to reading represent the culturally different child's adaptation to the politics of everyday life in class. Students take sides by attending or not, depending whether they choose to adhere to the peer group or to the teacher.

The *social organizational hypothesis* postulates that the school achievement of many minority students is related to how closely the presentation of the material and the nature of the responses allowed approximates their cultural values and norms. In a preliminary test of this hypothesis, Au and Mason (1981) found that Hawaiian 7-year-olds displayed much higher levels of achievement-related behaviors when they were allowed to enter the discussion whenever they wished and to share turns in joint performance than when they were allowed to respond only singly when called on.

Various proposals have been made as to how best to teach dialect speakers to read. However, no conclusive evidence has been presented to show that any method is more effective than the others (Sommerville 1975).

Some low-income, minority children do make normal progress in reading achievement (McPhail 1982; Durkin 1982; Larrick 1987). As for all children, the quality of reading instruction may be the key factor in the reading achievement of minority students. When first-grade black and first-grade white children of similar aptitude received high-quality reading instruction, they attained nearly equal levels of reading achievement (Dreeben 1987). Neither race nor SES was a significant factor. Providing a great deal of instructional time, using challenging materials, grouping the children by ability within the class, and matching the pace of instruction to the students' abilities resulted in higher achievement. However, as Dreeben points out, mastery of basic reading skills does not assure later academic success. Research suggests that later academic problems stem from the lack of conceptual instruction that should foster vocabulary development and the interpretation of ideas that will prepare minority children for the intellectual demands of the upper-grade curriculum. Such instruction is especially important for pupils who come from homes in which reading and the discussion of ideas are not common occurences.

In our opinion, a viable beginning reading program for dialect speakers might incorporate the following: making teachers more knowledgeable about, accepting of, and sensitive to the students' dialects and cultures; making teachers aware of how their often unrecognized attitudes may influence the reading achievement of dialect speakers; initial use of an LEA coupled with a structured skill-development program, a program for concept development, and a recreational reading program—all under the direction of skilled, effective teachers who understand and accept the pupils and who have the support of the school

---

[9]For a review of the use of ethnography in studying reading, refer to Green and Bloome (1983).

principal and the cooperation of the home. The magnitude of the correlations between third- and ninth-grade reading achievement (0.78 and 0.81) suggests that reading success or failure in the primary grades has long-term consequences for minority students (L. Meyer 1983).

Attempts are also being made to lessen failure in learning to read on the part of children whose native or strongest language is not English. In the past, most programs simply employed English as the language of instruction and utilized materials in English that depicted a culture foreign to these children. The limitations of such an approach are obvious. Instructional reading materials conceptually attuned to some minority cultures have been developed in the hope that the content would be more understandable and interesting to the learners and reflect their cultural heritage. Research regarding the effects of such materials is still lacking.

Initial reading instruction for limited-English and non-English-speakers has usually taken either of two approaches: (1) teaching them to understand and speak English before initiating reading instruction in English; or (2) teaching them to read their native language, concurrently teaching receptive and expressive English, then teaching them to read English. Early research does not clearly support either approach (Hatch 1974), but increasing evidence indicates that literacy should be taught first in the child's primary language (Freeman 1988). However, what is desirable is not always possible. Teachers who speak the language and/or instructional materials written in the child's native language are not always available. Moustafa and Penrose (1985) offer suggestions for teaching reading under such circumstances; these include developing the students' oral language through the use of pictures and concrete referents,[10] followed by the use of a language-experience approach. Moustafa (1987) describes a combination aural/oral English and LEA program for teaching non-English-speakers to read.

According to Gonzales (1981b), primary-grade children who have limited command of English should not be taught to read English until they can comprehend the syntactic and semantic structures used in the reading text. He presents procedures for assessing a child's level of competence in English and the structural level of the reading material. Ortiz (1984) discusses the wide range of communication-language skills that may be found in minority children.

The comprehension problems of nonnative speakers who are reading material written in English may be due to difficulty in understanding: (1) lexical sources (e.g., unknown word meanings, misinterpretation of figurative language, problems with connotations); (2) syntactic sources (e.g., unknown or unfamiliar grammar); (3) nonlinguistic sources (e.g., lack of familiarity with the conventions of print such as punctuation or capitalization); (4) rhetorical sources (e.g., inability to recognize transitional phrases and rhetorical clues, especially when the clues are not explicit, different discourse expectations due to cultural differences in ways of writing); and (5) cultural sources (e.g., differences in schema or prior knowledge, differences in logical thought patterns) (Lebauer 1985). Griese (1971) discusses the reading comprehension problems that Eskimo and Native American students might encounter.

[10]Teachers might find the pattern-practice approach developed by I. A. Richards and Gibson (1960) of interest.

Suggestions for teaching reading to dialect-speaking children and to children whose first language is not English may be found in Gonzales (1981a,b), Feeley (1983), and V. G. Allen (1986). Refer to Ching (1976) for an annotated bibliography on bilingual children, Harber and Beatty (1978) for an annotated bibliography on BE speakers, and Barnitz (1982, 1986) for discussions of the problems in learning to read English as a second language.

AN EVALUATION OF BEGINNING READING APPROACHES

A comparative evaluation of beginning reading approaches is not easy. The majority of children can learn to read by a variety of methods. Approaches may vary in effectiveness depending on local conditions, making it dangerous to generalize from a limited sample: Procedures that work well in a prosperous suburb may not suit the needs of children in an impoverished neighborhood.

A review of the studies completed before the mid-1960s led Chall to conclude:

> It would seem, at our present state of knowledge, that a code emphasis—one that combines control of words on spelling regularity (although not complete control of one sound for one symbol), some direct teaching of letter-sound correspondences, as well as the use of writing, tracing, or typing—produces better results with unselected groups of beginners than a meaning emphasis, the kind incorporated in most of the conventional basal-reading series used in the schools in the late 1950's and early 1960's. (Chall 1967, pp. 178–179)

She also concludes that there is no experimental basis for preferring one code-emphasis method over another. Also, it should be noted that Chall's major conclusion is stated cautiously, to the effect that methods that pay more and earlier attention to word-recognition skills than did basal readers of the 1950s and early 1960s tend, on the whole, to come out with better results than the basal readers. It is not an endorsement of procedures that ignore meaning for weeks while drilling on letters and words.

Chall also carefully discusses the great variations in results that different teachers obtain with the same method, the favorable but transient effect of novelty, the significance of the effort put forth by teachers volunteering to use a new method, the tendency to spend extra time with a new method, and other complicating factors. Accepting her main conclusion without carefully studying the many qualifications can produce a dangerously inaccurate oversimplification of a complex problem.

Chall cautions against an overemphasis on decoding when she writes: "In their enthusiasm, many authors, publishers, and teachers may be extending the decoding practice too far, and students may be spending too much time on it. This may be so both for the highly programmed decoding materials and for teacher-made exercises. Thus, stories and books, the true vehicles for reading for meaning, may be neglected in the zeal for mastery of decoding. Moderation here, as in all of life, should be valued" (1977, p. 12). Still, Chall (1983a) favors direct instruction of synthetic phonics accompanied by the teaching of blending during the initial stages of reading acquisition, with emphasis switching to the meaning and language aspects of reading after third grade.

The U.S. Office of Education supported 27 coordinated first-grade studies in 1964–1965. Summaries of all the projects appeared in *The Reading Teacher* (May & October 1966, May & October 1967) and have been gathered together in a paperback (Stauffer 1967). Results from the projects that utilized representative children and studied methods also employed in other projects were drawn together in a composite statistical analysis, summarized in two reports. The first covers 15 first-grade studies; the second, 13 studies that continued through the second grade. In the summary of the first-grade report, 15 numbered conclusions are offered. Of these, the following seem most significant:

1. Word study skills must be emphasized and taught systematically regardless of what approach to initial reading instruction is utilized.
2. Combinations of programs, such as a basal program with supplementary phonics materials, often are superior to single approaches. . . . The addition of language experiences to any kind of reading can be expected to make a contribution.
6. Reading programs are not equally effective in all situations. Evidently factors other than method, within a particular learning situation, influence pupil success in reading. . . .
9. . . . The tremendous range among classrooms within any method points out the importance of elements in the learning situation other than the methods employed. To improve reading instruction, it is necessary to train better teachers of reading rather than to expect a panacea in the form of materials.
10. Children learn to read by a variety of materials and methods. Furthermore, pupils experienced difficulty in each of the programs utilized. No one approach is so distinctly better in all situations and respects than the others that it should be considered the one best method and the one to be used exclusively.
13. A writing component is likely to be an effective addition to a primary program.
14. It is impossible to assess the relative effectiveness of programs unless they are used in the same project. Project differences are so great even when readiness for reading is controlled that a program utilized in a favored project would demonstrate a distinct advantage over one used in a less favored project regardless of the effectiveness of the program. (Bond & Dykstra 1967, pp. 210–212)

The second-grade report from the Coordinating Center essentially supports and repeats the conclusions of the first-grade report (Dykstra 1968a). Limitations of these studies have been pointed out (Sipay 1968, Lohnes & Gray 1972).

Although at the end of the second year these studies seem to support Chall's conclusion concerning the superiority of code-emphasis programs, Dykstra (1968b) cautions about the absence of any clear evidence that the early emphasis on code per se was the only or even the primary reason for the relative effectiveness of code-emphasis approaches. Other characteristics of these programs may have been more crucial in determining pupil achievement. Dykstra later writes: "We can summarize the results of 60 years of research dealing with beginning reading instruction by stating that early systematic instruction in phonics provides the child with the skills necessary to become an independent reader at an earlier age than is likely if phonics instruction is delayed and less systematic" (1974, p. 397). Current publishers have responded to this and other needs.

The early advantage of code-emphasis programs may relate to factors other than their heavy teaching of decoding. In such programs there is a great deal of direct instruction. Instruction is more systematic and focused, and lessons are more structured, provide more systematic feedback, allocate more time to reading, and maintain higher levels of time on task. Attributing effects to a particular instructional method is unwarranted unless certain variables (e.g., the amount of learning time, unusual teacher characteristics) are held constant.

The types of words appearing in preprimers may have a more powerful influence than the instructional method employed on shaping children's word-recognition strategies. Juel and Roper-Schneider (1985) found that when there was a match between the instructional method, synthetic phonics, and the decodability of the words, first graders developed a more consistent and successful use of a symbol-sound association strategy.

Of the original 27 projects, 8 followed their pupils through the third grade. In 7 of these projects, which included a variety of methods, the reading test results at the end of the third grade showed no consistent and statistically significant superiority for any method. In the eighth project, the meaning of the results is obscured by the fact that the phonic-linguistic method that achieved the highest mean-adjusted reading scores in second and third grades also had markedly higher nonpromotion rates in first and second grades; removal of the poorest readers in that method by nonpromotion would seem to have affected the results.

Thus the largest-scale studies done in America indicate no consistent advantages for any method studied when pupils are followed through the third grade. Similar conclusions were drawn in Great Britain by the Bullock Commission (Department of Education & Science 1975). There is strong evidence that the qualities of the school system, of administrative leadership, of the particular school, of the principal, of the teacher, and of the pupils (in turn related to characteristics of home and neighborhood) far outweigh differences in methodology and materials in their influences on reading achievement.

Overall, the research suggests that when skill in word recognition is the most important objective, code-emphasis programs tend to produce better results than meaning-emphasis programs, especially for low-SES students and low achievers. When comprehension is the criterion, there is no clear advantage for either approach. What is needed is a proper balance between systematic decoding instruction and attention to developing reading comprehension.

There is also evidence that none of the methods studied was able to lessen significantly the proportion of children who make disappointing progress in learning to read, let alone eliminate failure. This does not mean that all beginning reading programs are equally suitable for all children. Not all children seem able to learn through a whole-word method; others cannot learn through a phonics method. Programs also vary considerably in the conceptual demands they place on children. For instance, some first-grade programs are relatively easy in that they introduce fewer words and phonic principles; others introduce many more words and phonic principles at a more rapid pace (Barr 1982). Factors such as these should be considered in evaluating research studies and in selecting commercially published reading series.

The time has come to end the quest for the best method of teaching reading. Gross comparisons of beginning reading approaches have yielded little useful information. Efforts should concentrate on determining which aspects of a program are most effective for particular children when used by certain teachers under given conditions and, what is more important, why.

Attempts to match learner characteristics with instructional methods (aptitude-treatment interactions) in an attempt to facilitate the acquisition of reading skills have not been particularly successful. Novice readers, who are deemed to have a strong visual preference for learning, do not learn to read better with a whole-word method than with a phonics method. Nor is the reverse true for those who have supposedly strong auditory abilities (H. M. Robinson 1972b, Larrivee 1981). See page 90 for a more complete discussion of this topic. Attempts to match sensory-integration abilities (matching stimuli presented in different modalities) with beginning reading methods have also been unsuccessful (Pressman 1973).

Until more evidence is available, it seems that for most children a balanced eclectic approach that uses varied sensory cues in combination and that gives balanced attention to word recognition and comprehension seems advisable. When a child continues to fail in a particular reading program, consideration should be given to employing a program that uses a different methodology and makes different demands on the learner.

4

An Overview of Reading Instruction

This chapter is the third of three that provide a survey of the total program of reading instruction. Readiness for reading was discussed in Chapter 2, and beginning reading was discussed in Chapter 3. The present chapter provides a brief summary of the stages of reading instruction, summarizes the objectives of the reading program, discusses types of reading programs for students who are making other than normal progress in reading, covers some special issues in the teaching of reading, and considers factors that influence the effectiveness of reading instruction.

STAGES OF READING INSTRUCTION

About 65 years ago the National Committee on Reading (W. S. Gray 1925) proposed a five-stage process of learning to read: (1) readiness for reading; (2) beginning to read; (3) rapid development of reading skills (Grades 2 and 3); (4) wide reading (Grades 4–8); and (5) refinement of reading (high school and college). More recently, a six-stage classification was developed by Chall (1983b), who described the stages somewhat differently.

Chall's *Stage 0* is the *Prereading Stage*, during which understandings about reading are unsystematically accumulated over a period of years, including preschool and kindergarten.

Stage 1, Initial Reading or Decoding: Grades 1–2, Ages 6–7.

Learning the arbitrary set of letters and associating them with the corresponding parts of spoken words is the central task of this stage. In this stage, learners acquire knowledge about reading, such as how to know that *bun* is not *bug* and how to recognize when comprehension has been disrupted. By the end of this stage, learners experience a qualitative change as they develop insight into the nature of our alphabetic writing system and become able to decode printed words that they do not recognize immediately.

Stage 2, Confirmation, Fluency, Ungluing from Print: Grades 2–3, Ages 7–8.

In Stage 2 there is a consolidation of what was learned in Stage 1. Stage-2 reading is not for gaining new information but for confirming what the reader already knows. Most children in Stage 2 learn to use their decoding skills along with the linguistic information inherent in the language heard and read, gaining competence in using context and consequently improving in fluency and rate. The proper development of Stage 2 requires the reading of many easy and familiar books.

Developmental reading lessons still form the major part of the reading program, although functional reading and recreational reading gradually increase in importance. For developmental reading, the class is usually divided into groups based on reading ability.

Basal readers for these grades generally are collections of short stories arranged in groups with similar themes. Some basal readers emphasize enjoyable fiction, while others stress the social studies value of their content.

The general structure of basal reader lesson plans remains basically the same as at the first-grade level. In preparatory work, developing the meanings of unfamiliar ideas increases in importance, although providing motivation, presenting new words, and activating prior knowledge continue to be essential. Silent reading is usually a few pages or more at a time, followed by answering questions (which may be provided in the workbook), oral discussion, and oral rereading. Systematic teaching of decoding strategies is an important activity. Enrichment activities are expanded in scope because the children can read more independently.

Increasingly important in these grades is functional reading, which takes the form of reading textbooks in various subjects, or reading varied sources to obtain information needed to carry out units or projects. Weekly newspapers provide a basis for current events and other phases of the social studies in many schools.

As children become better able to read, the range of possible recreational material increases markedly. At first-grade level, the classroom library consists mainly of picture books; books at preprimer, primer, and first-reader levels; and books for the teacher to read to the class. At second-grade level, many children can read simple story books for pleasure, and at third-grade level a wide range of books and stories is suitable for individual reading.

Stage 3, Reading for Learning the New: A First Step—Grades 4–8, Ages 9–13[1]

Stage 3 fits the traditional conception that in the primary grades children learn to read, and in the higher grades they read to learn. Around the beginning of

[1]Chall does not designate grade or age levels for this stage. Those indicated are our estimates.

Stage 3, reading begins to compete with other means of acquiring knowledge. Readers must bring their knowledge and experience to their reading if they are to learn from it. Essentially, Stage 3 is for acquiring facts, concepts, and understanding of how to do things. At this stage, nuances and varied points of view are found only in reading fiction.

Developmental reading activities are concerned primarily with the refinement and improvement of skills already well started. Time devoted to developmental reading lessons decreases as more time is spent on acquiring functional reading skills and strategies. Although the basic outline of a complete reading activity persists as a desirable general plan, considerable flexibility is in order. Preparation and oral reading usually take proportionally less time than in the primary grades. Word study is concerned more with meanings than with recognition or decoding. Previously introduced decoding skills are reviewed and the use of the dictionary for both pronunciation and meanings is systematically taught. Silent reading is done in large units, often a complete selection. Comprehension may be checked by written answers to questions as well as in oral discussion, and an attempt is made to develop skill in answering different kinds of questions and in reading for different purposes. Practice to speed up silent reading may be appropriate for those who have reached an adequate level in other reading skills.

Although remedial reading instruction may be provided beyond the sixth grade, little systematic reading instruction is provided for those who are making normal progress in reading and very few programs are provided for reading in the content areas (Irvin & Connors 1989).

Stage 4, Multiple Viewpoints: High School, Ages 14–18.

Whereas in Stage 3 the student has to deal primarily with one point of view at a time, secondary school texts require dealing with a variety of viewpoints and, thus, the texts are more difficult to comprehend. Stage 4 skills are acquired mainly through reading and studying materials that vary widely in type, content, and style. These activities provide practice in acquiring increasingly more difficult concepts and in learning how to learn new concepts and points of view through reading.

Concern about reading in the secondary school first took the form of remedial programs, and in the 1960s and early 1970s secondary corrective and remedial reading programs grew dramatically (Cowan 1977). By the mid-1970s, the need for more comprehensive reading programs in the high school was widely accepted (Early 1977), but secondary school reading programs have changed very little in the past 30 years (Moore & Murphy 1987). The remedial-corrective model is still dominant. Small remedial classes are often available for severely disabled readers and/or large corrective classes for those reading 1 to 2 years below grade level. Occasionally developmental classes are available for students who are reading at or above grade level—to refine present skills and develop more advanced reading and study skills. Reading instruction as part of the instruction in the content subject is rare (Nelson & Herber 1982), as is real discussion of what has been read (Alvermann 1987a). However, emphasis on teaching reading in the context of vocational education is increasing (Derby 1987).

A comprehensive secondary school reading program should include instruction in the reading and study skills and strategies needed for success in whatever courses the pupils are taking. Herber and Nelson-Herber (1984) propose a program in which the central focus is on reading instruction in the content areas. Reading would be taught functionally. As the students read their textbooks they would be taught how to apply reading skills to them. If general reading and study skills were taught in a separate course, instruction and guided practice in applying them to the demands of each subject should be provided. The content-subject teachers should be involved in planning and conducting this aspect of the program, under the direction of a reading specialist who would offer the necessary inservice work. Provision should also be made for good readers who want to become superior readers or wish to increase their reading rate of flexibility, and for students who have moderate or severe reading problems.

Reading in the content subjects is covered more fully in Chapter 16. Farr and Wolf (1984) present a comprehensive plan for evaluating a secondary school reading program.

Stage 5, Construction and Reconstruction— A World View: College, Ages 18 and Above.

Remedial and developmental reading programs for adults have taken a number of forms. Many junior and senior colleges provide remedial programs for students who lack the reading and study skills believed necessary for college success. For those whose general reading and study skills are adequate, some colleges offer elective developmental reading courses that may focus on increasing reading rate, reading and studying efficiently, and reading selectively and critically. Out-of-school adults whose reading ability is average or above, but is deemed inadequate for their purposes, often enroll in commercial reading programs.

The longest-existing adult programs teach basic literacy and survival skills to out-of-school adults (Reed & Ward 1982). Such programs vary, but most fall under the general rubric of Adult Basic Education (ABE). Not all segments of our population value literacy as much as educators and politicians do: For as yet undetermined reasons, only 2 to 4% of the target population participate in adult literacy programs (Nickerson 1985). Motivating adults to take advantage of opportunities to acquire literacy is a problem. As Cook (1977, p. 128) lamented, "[M]illions of Americans will remain functionally illiterate by choice and their children may grow up assimilating this same indifference." With few exceptions, published evaluations of ABE programs have presented overly optimistic views of their effectiveness. Although the average gains in reading achievement were statistically significant, the majority of participants did not accomplish functional literacy (Diekhoff 1988). This failure may result, at least in part, from the programs' short duration. Many ABE programs last only 16 to 20 weeks but according to Mikulecky (1986), it usually takes close to 100 hours of instruction and feedback for an adult to gain the equivalent of one grade level in reading ability. Other factors include irregular attendance (Mikulecky 1987), the high dropout rate after the first two or three sessions (Nickerson 1985), inadequately prepared teachers, and inadequate funding.

Adult literacy programs should stress the acquisition of skills that are useful to the participants. Instructional materials should be interesting, informative, and appropriate to the adults' prior knowledge; learners should want to read them. Emphasis should always be on helping the adults transfer newly acquired skills to situations that are meaningful to them, and programs should be structured so that adult participants make a commitment to them (Nickerson 1985). Balmuth (1988) briefly discusses ways to keep students in ABE programs, and the International Reading Association (1981) presents a checklist for evaluating ABE programs.

A relatively recent interest has developed in the reading abilities, interests, and needs of senior citizens (Aiex 1987). Senior citizens report that reading provides them with relaxation, with topics to discuss, and with suggestions for strengthening their inner resources and coping with the problems of aging (Wolf 1980). Senior citizens are likely to be overrepresented in illiteracy studies, perhaps because of fewer educational opportunities in the past, but they are the least likely to participate in literacy programs (Park 1981).

OBJECTIVES OF READING INSTRUCTION

Teachers need to be definite about educational objectives. Those who list "the development of a love for reading as a form of recreation" as a major objective can find many different ways of working toward it and can achieve substantial success. But if developing a love for reading is not one of the teacher's specific goals, pupils are unlikely to acquire such an attitude as a result of the teacher's efforts. Setting clear, appropriate goals is the necessary first step in developing a sound reading program.

Developmental reading activities are those in which the teacher's main purpose is to bring about an improvement in reading skills and strategies—activities in which the primary aim is learning to read. *Functional reading* includes all reading in which the primary aim is to obtain information—in other words, reading to learn. *Recreational reading* consists of reading activities that have enjoyment, entertainment, and appreciation as their major purposes.

A somewhat more detailed analysis of these three kinds of reading, stated as general outcomes in terms of learner behavior, is as follows:

I. Developmental reading
   A. Basic or facilitating skills. The learner
      1. Has a large sight vocabulary
      2. Flexibly uses a variety of skills to recognize and decode words
      3. Reads silently with speed and fluency
      4. Coordinates rate with comprehension
      5. Reads orally with proper phrasing, expression, pitch, volume, and enunciation
      6. Self-corrects disruptive miscues
   B. Reading comprehension
      1. Vocabulary. The learner
         a. Has an extensive and accurate reading vocabulary

           b. Uses context effectively to
             (1) determine the meaning of an unfamiliar word
             (2) choose the appropriate meaning of a word
           c. Interprets figurative and nonliteral language

2. Prior Knowledge. The learner activates and utilizes prior knowledge to aid reading comprehension.
3. Literal comprehension. The learner
    a. Grasps the meaning and interrelatedness of meaningful units: words, phrases, sentences, paragraphs, whole selections
    b. Understands and recalls stated main ideas
    c. Notes and recalls significant stated details
    d. Recognizes and recalls a stated series of events in correct sequence
    e. Notes and explains stated cause-effect relationships
    f. Finds answers to specific questions
    g. Follows printed directions accurately
    h. Skims to obtain a total expression
4. Inferential comprehension. The learner
    a. Understands and recalls inferred main ideas
    b. Notes and recalls significant inferred details
    c. Recognizes and recalls an inferred series of events in correct sequence
    d. Notes, recalls and is able to explain inferred cause-effect relationships
    e. Anticipates and predicts outcomes
    f. Grasps the author's plan and intent
    g. Identifies the techniques authors use to create desired effects
5. Critical reading. The learner critically evaluates what is read.
6. Creative reading. The learner extrapolates from what is read to reach new ideas and conclusions.
7. Comprehension monitoring. The learner monitors comprehension and takes corrective action when necessary

II. Functional reading
  A. Locates needed reading material. The learner
    1. Uses indexes
    2. Uses tables of contents
    3. Uses dictionaries
    4. Uses encyclopedias
    5. Uses other bibliographic aids
    6. Scans in search of information
  B. Comprehends informational material. The learner
    1. Understands technical and specific vocabulary
    2. Applies the general comprehension skills and strategies listed above
    3. Uses the specific skills needed by special subject matter, e.g.,
      a. Reading arithmetic problems

        b. Reading maps, charts, and graphs

        c. Conducting a science experiment from printed directions

    4. Makes use of headings, subheadings, marginal notes, and other study aids

    5. Reads independently in the content subjects

  C. Selects the material needed for a purpose

  D. Organizes and records what is read. The learner

    1. Takes useful notes

    2. Summarizes

    3. Outlines

  E. Displays appropriate study skills and habits

III. Recreational reading

  A. Displays an interest in reading. The learner

    1. Enjoys reading as a voluntary leisure-time activity

    2. Selects appropriate reading matter

    3. Satisfies interests and needs through reading

  B. Improves and refines reading interests. The learner

    1. Reads different kinds of material on a variety of topics

    2. Reads materials that reflect mature interests

    3. Achieves personal development through reading

  C. Refines literary judgment and taste. The learner

    1. Applies differential criteria for various literary forms

    2. Appreciates style and beauty of language

    3. Seeks for deeper symbolic messages

These three major kinds of reading cannot and should not be kept entirely separate. In a developmental lesson children must read either narrative or expository text. An enjoyable story may be used for the cultivation of particular reading skills and developmental lessons should be planned to help pupils in their reading of content-subject material.

A sound reading program must have balance among the major kinds of reading. If the desire to read for fun is killed by an overemphasis on drills and exercises, one of the major aims of reading instruction is defeated and the result is the graduate who never opens a book after commencement. The relative balance changes grade by grade. For the novice reader, nearly all reading activities are primarily developmental; by the upper elementary grades, functional reading is most important and developmental lessons take the least amount of time.

The general learning objectives stated in the foregoing are anticipated general outcomes of a reading program. These general objectives may be subdivided and stated in varying degrees of specificity. Such specific objectives are commonly known as "behavioral" or "performance" objectives, the writing of which has been described in detail (e.g., Gronlund 1973). Although there are variations in style, a behavioral objective usually states the condition under which a specified behavior will occur (external conditions), the behavior that is to occur as a result of planned instruction (terminal behavior), and the performance level that will be accepted (acceptable performance). Some writers do not suggest stating external conditions. A behavioral objective is the result that is to follow from instruction, not the instructional activity itself. That is, the behavioral objective should be stated in terms of learner behavior (the anticipated product or outcome) rather than in terms of teacher behavior (the process of what the teacher does with the learner).

To illustrate, the general objective "Evaluates what is read" is a complex objective that calls for the use of critical thinking in reading. A number of more specific learning outcomes can be listed under this general objective:

1. Distinguishes between facts and opinions
2. Distinguishes between facts and inferences
3. Identifies cause-effect relations
4. Identifies errors in reasoning
5. Distinguishes between relevant and irrelevant arguments
6. Distinguishes between warranted and unwarranted generalizations
7. Formulates a valid conclusion from written material
8. Specifies assumptions needed to make conclusions true (Gronlund 1973)

How a behavioral objective can be developed may be illustrated with outcome 1 above. Adding external conditions to it would result in the following: Given an editorial, the learner can underline statements of opinion. Then, adding a criterion for mastery, the objective would read: Given an editorial, the learner can underline at least 9 of the 10 statements of opinion without misidentifying any statements of fact. More specificity could be added: For example, the qualifier "written at the sixth-reader level" might be added after "editorial."

It is easier to determine when cognitive objectives have been met than it is to evaluate affective objectives. Nevertheless, the latter can be stated and assessed through observation and discussion.

The sequence in using behavioral objectives is (1) to state the objectives; (2) to select and use appropriate instructional procedures, content, and methods; (3) to test to determine if the criterion for mastery has been met; and (4) to reteach if necessary. By clearly stating what a learner should be able to do under given conditions when he or she has achieved the objective, the teacher can determine the extent to which a given specific skill or ability has been mastered.

Care must be exercised, lest reading instruction be fragmented into hundreds of discrete objectives whose mastery becomes the core of the reading program. Skills can be taught and learned in isolation, but ample opportunities must be provided for utilizing them in reading connected discourse.

ADAPTED, ENRICHED, CORRECTIVE, AND REMEDIAL PROGRAMS

Most students make normal progress in developing their reading ability, but some require programs that differ from those found under the label "developmental reading." These include slow learners, the intellectually gifted, and students who are not making as much progress in reading as can be reasonably expected. It is beyond the scope of this book to discuss teaching reading to those with severe visual or auditory defects and to those who are emotionally disturbed.

Adapted Programs

The number of children with limited intellectual ability depends on how retardation is defined and the degree of retardation under consideration. The American Association of Mental Deficiency uses an IQ of 68 as the cutoff point, but the literature indicates a wide variety of practices. In addition, it should be realized that not all children who score very low on an IQ test (particularly on a group test) are mentally retarded. Severe reading disability, emotional or medical problems, sensory defects (e.g., a severe hearing loss), or language handicaps may contribute to low IQ scores or teachers' judgments of limited learning aptitude.

Slow learners need a reading program geared to their abilities, one that accepts their limitations, sets reasonable expectations, and is designed to meet their needs and interests. Such an adapted reading program should differ from the typical developmental reading program mainly in its slower pace and its use of different materials. The materials should more closely resemble those found in remedial reading programs than typical basal readers because slow learners' interests are often more mature than their reading ability. Although no conclusive evidence shows that any one reading method is most effective for slow learners (Blanton, Sitko & Gillespie 1976), supplemental instruction that provides additional time to learn and is paced properly through a sequence of tasks tends to be beneficial (Singer 1978b). Teaching slow learners to read is covered more thoroughly by Harris and Sipay (1979, pp. 481–486). A good adapted program includes adjustments in the slow learner's entire academic program, not just in reading.

Enriched Programs

At the other end of the intellectual continuum are the gifted—the 7% of our students who have IQs between 120 and 130 and the additional 3% with IQs over 130. Gifted students tend to be 1 to 3 years ahead of their age peers in academic achievement. These students need assistance in continuing their accelerated growth in reading abilities and interests. Suggestions for helping them to do so may be found in Lehr (1983), Bates (1984), and Labuda (1985).

Corrective and Remedial Programs

Children who are reading significantly below their potential should have reading programs that are planned to teach them the reading skills and strategies not yet mastered, using the best methodology, materials, and motivation possible. Efforts to help these children are broadly described as remedial reading. Under this broad heading there is a distinction between corrective and remedial reading programs. Theoretically, the two differ in four respects: (1) where the treatment takes place; (2) who provides the treatment; (3) the number of children treated in a session; and (4) the severity of the problems treated.

Corrective reading occurs within the framework of regular class instruction and is conducted by the classroom teacher for groups or subgroups whose reading-skill weaknesses are uncovered in the daily or periodic assessment of skill development. *Remedial reading* occurs away from the regular classroom, in or outside the school, and is conducted by a teacher with special training in reading (or by tutors supervised by a reading specialist) for small groups or on a one-to-one basis.

In actuality, the distinction between corrective and remedial reading is somewhat artificial. The problems treated are more likely to differ in degree than in kind, and whether a child receives corrective or remedial reading help may depend more on the resources available than on the nature of the reading problem or the instruction best suited to the child's needs.

There can be no quarrel with the proposition that major efforts should be devoted to improving the general efficiency of classroom teaching. As this takes place, the frequency of reading disabilities should diminish somewhat. Nevertheless, even with the best of teachers, children will continue to be handicapped by physical defects, to be emotionally upset, to miss school because of illness, and, for these or other reasons, to fall behind. Detecting weak points in achievement and helping the child overcome these weaknesses are integral parts of effective classroom teaching. Corrective instruction is a sort of educational first aid. It is, of course, remedial teaching, but remedial teaching conceived of without capital letters, as a normal part of good methodology. As corrective teaching in its simpler forms becomes taken for granted because it is part of every good teacher's procedure, the need for calling it by a special name diminishes. In this sense, remedial reading is losing its distinctive character by becoming normal rather than unusual procedure.

Finally, a small percentage of children will continue to have special handicaps in reading that require the application of refined diagnostic procedures by experts as well as individual teaching by skilled remedial teachers. There is, then, no conflict among the three phases of a good reading program: (1) superior first teaching adapted to the needs and individual abilities of children; (2) frequent classroom use of corrective procedures as needed; and (3) careful diagnosis and special remedial help for the seriously disabled reader.

SOME SPECIAL PROBLEMS AND ISSUES

Although each stage of reading instruction has distinct features, certain problems and issues are present at all levels and stages. A few of them are discussed here.

Oral Reading

Many years ago, instruction in reading was predominantly oral. When research showed that children taught in this way tended to be slow, laborious readers, silent reading became the vogue. In many schools, oral reading was almost completely neglected beyond the first grade. But oral reading should not be disregarded once pupils are fairly skilled readers. Reading aloud and listening to others read are features of a literate environment, whatever the reader's level of ability (R. Anderson et al. 1985). Furthermore, oral reading has many uses in the classroom, among which are: (1) to assess progress in reading skills such as word recognition, phrasing, and the use of correction strategies, especially when the student reads a fairly long, representative selection, thereby helping to determine specific instructional needs; (2) to provide a vehicle for dramatization and effective portrayal of stories; and (3) to provide a medium in which the teacher, by wise guidance, can improve the social adjustment of children, particularly the shy and retiring.

The most frequently used oral reading activity involves students taking turns reading a few sentences or a short paragraph (R. Anderson et al. 1985). Such round-robin oral reading is often overused. Two rationales are frequently offered for the almost daily use of this practice: (1) it provides diagnostic information, and (2) children expect—and want—to read orally every day. However, it is doubtful that such brief performances offer much diagnostic information, especially when few if any records are kept. Furthermore, it is doubtful that every child needs to be diagnosed every day. As for the second reason, children expect to read orally every day because it *is* such a common practice. They experience it so frequently that they come to believe that they have not had "reading" on any day they have not read orally. This belief can be overcome by explaining to pupils that silent reading is also part of their reading instruction. Every child in the class need not read orally every day. Doing so uses instructional time that could be spent more profitably.

Each oral reading activity should have a specific goal that contributes to the pupil's growth in reading. Among the worthwhile oral reading activities are:

TAKING TURNS IN SMALL GROUPS. Oral reading, when one's peers are listening, can be a stressful and anxiety-producing situation, especially for poor readers. Self-consciousness on the part of the reader is less likely when the other group members are not markedly better readers, and the pupils are allowed to prepare their oral readings. The rest of the group should not be required to follow along in their books; rather, they should provide an audience. Contrary to what some believe, having children follow along in their books does not assure that they will be learning or practicing word-recognition skills. Having the listeners try to catch the reader making a word-recognition error can only produce greater anxiety, and can be emotionally devastating to a disabled reader.

Some teachers try to reduce the anxiety caused students by not knowing when they will be called on to read by establishing a set sequence so that each child knows when his or her turn will occur. Taking sequential turns also may provide equal opportunities to read because assertive volunteers do not get to read a disproportionate number of times. Use of this procedure, however, still does not make daily round-robin oral reading by every child an educationally sound practice.

FINDING AND READING ANSWERS TO QUESTIONS OR TO PROVE A POINT. After silent reading, some type of comprehension check has become an almost universal practice. Oral reading can be brought into the task, in a natural and significant way, by having the students locate and read aloud the answers to specific questions or the part of the text that backs up a point made during a discussion of the passage. This provides purposeful silent rereading and desirable practice in oral reading. It can also stimulate interesting discussions about the appropriateness of what is read orally.

AUDIENCE READING.   Each pupil is given a chance to choose and carefully prepare a selection to read to the class, preferably from material that is *not* familiar to the other pupils. After considerable practice and, if possible, a preliminary rehearsal with the teacher, the child reads the selection to classmates. Since the material is new to them and well presented, the interest of the class is usually sustained, and the pupil experiences satisfaction from a job well done. Many good teachers make a period of audience reading a weekly event.

CHORAL READING.   Certain definite values can be derived from occasional periods in which the class reads aloud in unison. The better readers carry along the poorer ones, who may gain a better appreciation of pronunciation, phrasing, rhythm, and interpretation. This kind of oral reading is especially suitable for poetry and other strongly rhythmical material.

READING PARTS IN RADIO OR TV SCRIPTS OR PLAYS.   No oral reading is more interesting to children or helps them more to read with natural expression than reading a part in a play. When children are allowed to read their parts from the script, plays can be prepared and presented in a fraction of the time required for memorizing. See Manna (1984) for suggestions on using plays.

READING WITH VARIED INTONATION PATTERNS.   To get across the idea of how meaning varies with intonation and how the same sequence of words can convey quite different meanings, it is occasionally desirable to have children read a sentence, placing stress on different words and changing the intonation pattern and then to explain what the specific meaning of each rendition is. For example, *What* am I doing? What *am* I doing? What am *I* doing? What am I *doing?*

Other useful oral reading activities include repeated readings (see page 481), and read-along techniques (see page 482).

Silent Reading

Silent reading lessons are often designed to improve a particular reading skill. Lessons may involve finding the central idea of a selection, finding the answers to specific questions, recognizing and remembering a sequence of events, and so on. Distinctions between functional and recreational reading are made in the planning. For example, whereas dissection of plot and characters may be required in a literature lesson, it would be avoided in reading for pleasure because to do so might detract from enjoying the story.

There has been a trend toward increasing the amount and broadening the scope of the silent reading done in schools. A wide variety of materials—magazines, pamphlets, newspapers, paperbacks—are now used as instructional materials. Functional reading of many kinds takes up a large part of the school day. In literature, the "classics" have had to make room for material intimately related to contemporary life.

In *sustained silent reading,* the teacher and each student select something to read, and then they read it without interruption for a definite time period. No reports or comprehension checks are required and no records are kept. Suggestions for using this procedure may be found in Berglund and Johns (1983). The research evidence regarding the effect of sustained silent reading on reading achievement is mixed, but it does seem to foster interest in and positive attitudes toward reading (Levine 1984).

Research suggests that having children read the material silently before they read it orally improves their oral reading fluency. However, classroom observations reveal that silent prereading is frequently omitted (R. Anderson et al. 1985).

Balance of Oral and Silent Reading

A frequently made recommendation is that more emphasis should be placed on silent reading and less on oral reading. But as valid as such a recommendation may be in general, it should not be implemented without considering its basis or the degree to which it should be implemented in a given situation.

One reason for making such a recommendation appears to be the belief that too much time is spent on oral reading and too little on silent reading or, more accurately, that too much time is spent on oral reading that has little instructional value and too little time is spent on teaching students to comprehend text when reading silently. Also, too little time is allowed to read complete works silently for pleasure or to gain desired information. For example, it is very difficult to defend the oral rereading of entire basal-reader stories every day, and the daily oral reading of content-subject texbooks in a round-robin fashion.

A second reason stems from the assumption that silent reading better facilitates comprehension than does oral reading. This assumption, in turn, is based on the belief that, whereas the silent reader need concentrate only on obtaining meaning, the oral reader must convey understanding of the text to listeners, and must concentrate more closely on accurate word recognition because such behaviors are often the criteria for acceptable performance. Some individuals, however, are, or at least appear to be, much more proficient comprehenders in one mode or the other (see pages 231–232). Even on the average, silent reading does not always produce better comprehension than does oral reading. A best-evidence synthesis of 29 studies (Wilkinson, Anderson & Pearson 1988) indicates that below the third grade, oral reading produced better comprehension. At Grade 3, the results were inconclusive; and beyond that grade level, the comprehension advantage tended to be for silent reading. The effects of reading mode were conditioned by the pupils' level of reading ability, the nature of the text, and the type of comprehension measured. The students' purpose for reading (Holmes & Allison 1985) as well as the amount of practice students have had in reading in each mode also may partly account for differences in comprehension. Salasoo's (1986) study suggests that, for adult skilled readers, comprehension differences in the two modes are due primarily to differences in cognitive functioning. The relatively slower oral reading rates led to faster responses on the comprehension check than did the relatively faster silent reading.

A third reason for recommending silent reading is the finding that time spent in silent reading, but not in oral reading, is positively related to gains in reading achievement (Leinhardt, Zigmond & Cooley 1981). However, a reanalysis of the Leinhardt et al. data indicates that when the students' entry-level reading abilities are more adequately controlled, silent reading time does not significantly affect reading achievement. This reanalysis even suggests that oral reading has a greater effect than does silent reading (Wilkinson, Wardrop & Anderson 1988).

Thus, it would seem that each teacher and school should examine current practices and consider the above information before initiating change. Novice readers probably should practice more oral than silent reading, especially in the initial stage of acquisition. Novices need to understand the similarities between spoken and written language and oral reading may help them to do so. Teachers also need to monitor pupils' word recognition, how well they are applying what they know about language to the reading situation, and so forth. But more silent reading should be practiced during reading instruction in the primary grades than is often the case. Also, time should be set aside for silent recreational reading; a desire to read should be fostered early in the school years. As children become more skilled readers, increasingly more instructional time should be devoted to silent reading. Oral reading, however, should not be abandoned as it can still serve useful purposes in the intermediate and upper grades.

In general, teachers adjust the balance of oral and silent reading according to the students' level of reading ability. More oral reading is done by novice and low-ability pupils; more silent reading by skilled readers (R. Anderson et al. 1985). Children who receive remedial reading instruction probably get a disproportionate amount of oral reading practice.

Reading in Content Areas

Some children whose reading is satisfactory in basal readers and in self-chosen library books run into difficulty in applying their reading skills in the content areas. This difficulty is sometimes caused by a misfit between book difficulty and reader competence. Many content textbooks are substantially more difficult than basal readers intended for the same grade level, and children for whom the basal reader is at their instructional level may run into frustration when trying to read a difficult text- or reference book. Sometimes children attempt to read the content textbook in the same way that they read a story in a reader, resulting in superficial comprehension and poor retention. Comprehending expository texts, and retaining the information thus acquired, requires the reading and study skills, strategies, and habits discussed in Chapter 16.

Recognition of Individual Differences

Awareness of the importance of individual differences as a factor in reading is increasing. Yet some teachers still seem to believe that if their teaching is good, it should bring all or nearly all their pupils up to a fairly uniform level of achievement. Schools are realizing more and more the falsity of this belief. When children enter school, they differ widely in their abilities and in their potentialities for future development. With efficient instruction, these differences should increase rather than decrease as children progress through school. Even when, through highly efficient instruction, children with limited learning ability are brought up to the highest level that their capacities allow, they will still be far behind their brightest classmates. Uniformity of achievement in a class is more apt to indicate neglect of the abler pupils than generally effective teaching.

Recognition of the significance of individual differences has brought about all sorts of attempts to adjust the school program to the varying abilities of the pupils. These are discussed in Chapter 5.

Legal Rulings

The courts have made a number of rulings that bear on the teaching of reading (Harper & Kilarr 1977). For instance, several cases have suggested that students have a right to instruction appropriate to their educational needs and that they cannot be excluded from free public education because of organic or linguistic deficiencies (Schork & Miller 1978).

Accountability, in which educators are held responsible for the effectiveness of reading instruction, has taken on new meaning. Educational malpractice suits have blamed schools for students' illiteracy. As of 1981, the courts had rejected all claims of educational malpractice based on alleged negligent instruction by teachers. The courts, however, did not excuse the teachers from responsibility; rather, they found that the instructional-learning process was not their sole responsibility (P. Williams 1981). Legal rulings affecting educational practice continue to be made. Recently, a federal court ordered a school district to reimburse the fee paid to a private tutor by the mother of a child whom she claimed made little progress in reading before being tutored (Spofford 1986). The courts have become increasingly assertive in assessing classification practices, requiring schools to produce evidence that they are attempting to meet the needs of variously classified students, and ordering specific instructional programs and procedural safeguards to protect student's interests, especially in the area of special education (see the January 1986 issue of *Exceptional Children*). The situation caused the International Reading Association (1982) to pass a resolution that opposed extending the role of the courts in dealing with issues involving reading achievement in those areas of decision making (curriculum, methodology, and tests) that ought to be the responsibility of professionals.

EFFECTIVENESS IN TEACHING READING

Many attempts have been made to discover why teachers who ostensibly use the same methods and materials get different results. From the mid-1950s into the early 1960s, research on teacher effectiveness focused on instructional methods and materials, as well as on teacher characteristics. But no one best method or materials were identified, and effective teachers were found to possess the same characteristics as most well-adjusted people. During the late 1960s and early 1970s, research began to focus on process-product relationships (i.e, how teacher behaviors influence student achievement). More recently, research has been concerned not only with teacher behaviors but also with student characteristics (Brophy & Evertson 1981), the interactions between teacher and student behaviors and attitudes (Natriello & Dornbush 1983), and the social system in which they occur (Duffy 1982).

In interpreting the teacher-effectiveness research, four points must be remembered (Conley & Murphy 1987). First of all, different patterns of instruction generally appear to be more effective with different students. Teachers working with high-SES, high-ability pupils are most successful if pacing is rapid, students are given challenging tasks, high expectations are continually communicated, high standards are enforced, and inferior work is not accepted. Teachers who are more successful with low-SES, low-ability students are equally determined to get the most out of their students but usually do so by being warmer and more encouraging, and less businesslike and demanding than good teachers of high-SES, high-ability pupils. Successful teachers of lower-ability students take more time to motivate their pupils and to deal with their concerns. They praise more often, minimize criticism of poor work, pace instruction more slowly, and allow more time for practice and overlearning. More time is allowed to respond to questions, hints are provided for unanswered questions, or questions are rephrased (Brophy 1979b).

Second, although variables are discussed separately, they are often highly interrelated. Classrooms take on their characteristics as teachers and pupils alternatively influence, and are influenced by, one another (Copeland 1980). Effective teachers know a variety of procedures for teaching reading and possess a wide range of skills.

Third, the findings of most of the research on teacher effectiveness are limited to basic skills instruction in Grades 1–5.

Fourth, no one critical feature of instruction assures rapid progress in learning to read. Quality instruction involves many factors, and strengthening any one factor results in only small gains. Many elements must be in place for large gains to occur (R. Anderson et al. 1985).

Formal versus Informal Programs

Formal educational programs are defined as being teacher centered; the teacher follows a planned instructional sequence, often providing direct instruction. *Informal programs* tend to be student centered; students are encouraged to make choices regarding their learning, instructional sequence is not preordained, and the teacher functions largely as a facilitator and resource person. The degree of *imposed* structure is often used to distinguish between the two types of programs. It is not surprising, then, that certain instructional approaches are associated with formal or informal reading programs. For instance, use of a basal reader series is often cited as being a formal, teacher-centered program. Implementation of the whole-language philosophy, such as in the program described by Hansen (1987) in which the children have considerable control of their learning, is usually considered to exemplify an informal, student-centered program. However, in actual practice, the degree of structure and the balance of teacher-directed and student-selected activities often varies, not only among instructional approaches, but also within an approach. One should not be misled by a general label. For example, an "integrated language arts" program may range from using a whole-language approach, to a more formal program in which the teacher plans the integration of language skills but still maintains separate subject matter lessons, to the Exemplary Center for Reading Instruction (ECRI) approach (Reid 1986) which is a highly structured, teacher-directed, mastery-learning, skills-oriented approach.

Despite a continuous flow of theory and research findings in support of "natural," student-centered programs, a large body of correlational and experimental evidence supports the use of more formal programs, especially with certain types of students (Tarver 1986, Fillion & Brause 1987). Although research generally shows that reading gains tend to be greater in highly structured classes, the degree of structure should vary with the cognitive and social maturity of the students. Low-ability students and those low in self-confidence learn better under more structured conditions. High-ability and highly confident students learn better when given some choices (Greene 1980). Variability in results within formal and informal programs is marked, so it is necessary to look for specific factors that influence the effectiveness of reading teachers in both kinds of programs.

Direct Instruction

In many of the teacher-effectiveness studies, *direct instruction* meant teaching activities in which the instructional goals were chosen by the teacher and made clear to the students, the material was selected by the teacher, sufficient time was allocated for instruction, instructional pacing resulted in extensive content coverage, student performance was monitored, questions were at a low cognitive level and produced many correct responses, and feedback to the students was immediate and academically oriented (Rosenshine 1978b). These studies showed that direct instruction benefited poor readers in the primary grades and older elementary school students from low-SES backgrounds (Guthrie, Martuza & Seifort 1979). Rosenshine (1978a) warns against the unthinking application of the findings on direct instruction when he writes: "To many of us, some of the results seem grim and overbearing, and it may be possible, with due reflection, to devise instructional alternatives which are more appealing but equally effective. Furthermore, we do not know whether these direct instruction principles are sufficient to the tasks of emotional development, creativity, and enquiry skills."

Lysakowski and Walberg (1982) identify three factors associated with direct instruction that have strong effects on learning: (1) *cues* (instruction as to what is to be learned and what the student is to do in the learning process), (2) *participation* (the extent to which students are actually engaged in the learning process), and (3) *corrective feedback* (applying corrective measures as soon as a problem becomes apparent). Evans and Carr (1985) conclude that carefully organized direct instruction is an important part of beginning reading instruction because it facilitates novice readers' acquisition of a minimum level of word recognition and decoding competence. Direct instruction enhances the learning of basic reading skills and tends to produce higher academic achievement in general, but the evidence does not show that its use is more effective than other instructional approaches in developing higher-order cognitive skills (Barr 1986), and students in less-structured classes tend to be more creative and have better attitudes toward school (Peterson 1982).

More commonly, direct instruction is defined as explicit, intensive instruction in which the teacher makes clear to the students what it is they are being asked to learn, and then explains, demonstrates, or models, often in a step-by-step manner, the reading skill or strategy under consideration (Baumann 1988).

In *modeling,* teachers attempt, through what they say and do, to make as explicit as possible the thinking processes that are involved in utilizing the skills or strategy. This type of direct instruction may be used even in informal reading programs (as defined above). Good teachers who use direct instruction, realize that not all learning can be accomplished in this way. So they build into their instructional sequence increasing opportunities for their pupils to assume the responsibility for applying skills taught initially through direct instruction.

Merlin and Rogers (1981) describe a number of direct instruction strategies, and Blanton, Moorman and Wood (1986) offer a seven-phase plan for applying a direct instruction model to basal-reader lessons. Roehler and Duffy (1982) stress the need for matching direct instruction to desired outcomes.

Allocated Instructional Time

The average amount of time allocated to reading instruction in American primary classrooms is almost 2 hours a day (Squire 1980). But the amount of allocated time varies greatly (Guthrie 1980). One study, for example, found that second-grade teachers scheduled reading for from 36 to 118 minutes daily (average = 99 minutes); fifth-grade teachers, approximately 60 to 135 minutes (average = 74 minutes). It is likely that the time allocated to specific activities within these blocks of time also varies widely. Students spend about 70% of the time allocated for reading instruction in independent practice—on the average, 1 hour daily. Most of this time is devoted to completing workbook pages or worksheets (R. Anderson et al. 1985).

Correlations between learning time and reading achievement have been demonstrated repeatedly (A. J. Harris & Serwer 1966b; Guthrie, Martuza & Seifort 1979). In fact, "time to learn" correlates higher than IQ with reading achievement (Gettinger & White 1979). Generally, the more time allocated for reading, the greater the reading achievement. Allotted time alone does not account for reading gains, however. Claims of significant gains by increasing reading instructional time by as little as 5 minutes daily are probably misleading. The quality of what occurs during that time and how much of that time is used well is important. Also, the amount of time scheduled for reading may reflect the teacher's attitude toward the importance of reading, which itself can have an effect on reading achievement. Increased time alone will do little to help children learn what far exceeds their level of ability. Moreover, instructional time must be spent on relevant tasks (Hiebert 1983).

Three conditions, all of which are under the teacher's control, influence the quality of instructional time (Barr & Dreeban 1985): (1) the extent to which the teacher supervises instruction—students use their time more productively when supervised by the teacher, (2) the amount of available time that can be translated into productive time by the students—a sufficient amount of work must be provided for the students to accomplish, and (3) the nature of the assigned tasks—if the work is too easy or too difficult, pupils are less inclined to make good use of their time.

Apparently the time available for teaching is not used efficiently by many teachers. Leinhardt, Zigmond and Cooley (1981), for instance, found that learning-disabled children spent more time daily waiting (21 minutes) and preparing for or wrapping up activities (34 minutes) than in receiving reading instruction (16 minutes). More time could be devoted to reading if teachers decreased the time that children spent waiting and making transitions from one activity to another, and in the time spent coping with disruptive behavior. Improved classroom management often helps to lessen unproductive use of time. Even though the sources of "lost time" may differ from class to class, making teachers aware of how time gets eroded may enable them to adjust their activities so that there is more time available for learning.

The amount of time students spend learning is a consequence of multiple factors—the amount of time allocated to instruction, teacher competence, student aptitude, and the percentage of the allotted time that the students attend to a lesson (Karweit & Slavin 1981).

Academic Engaged Time

Rosenshine (1978b) defines *academic engaged time* (AET) as the time students spend in academically relevant activities that are at an appropriate, moderate level of difficulty. In general, the higher the academic engaged time, the higher the achievement. When students have the same rate of AET, brighter students are likely to learn more than less capable students. Reading done outside of school by middle- and upper-SES pupils probably adds significantly to their total AET; low-SES students are less likely to benefit in this way (Rosenshine & Berliner 1977).

All the observable components of AET are positively related to student achievement (R. Wilson 1987), but two have yielded the highest and most consistent correlations with achievement: the amount of content covered and *time-on-task* (the time students are actually involved in the learning task). Content coverage depends on the amount of allotted time, instructional pacing, the materials employed, and student attention (Barr 1982). Although we can measure academic learning time or time-on-task, we cannot measure what is going on in students' minds during that time, or insure that what is taking place there is addressed to learning (Carroll 1989).

Time-on-task rates vary but are reportedly higher when the teacher is working with the whole class or with large groups than in the case of individual instruction or instruction in small groups (Brophy 1979a). This finding may reflect teachers' inability to monitor the students with whom they are not working directly or inappropriate seatwork. It does not indicate that all instruction should be whole-class or large-group instruction or that there is no need to individualize instruction. At times it may be appropriate to make initial presentations to the whole class or large groups, especially when follow-up activities are individualized. But organizing the class into reading groups can be effective primarily because it allows for the use of appropriate materials and for an appropriate pace of instruction for each group (Karweit 1983). Similarly, care should be taken not to misinterpret the finding that time-on-task and reading achievement are higher when children use material that is easy for them. Although success rate is an important factor in reading achievement, students should not spend all their reading time on materials with which they are highly successful. A balance is needed between success and the use of challenging materials (Berliner 1981).

Time-on-task may be more related to the reading achievement of poor readers than of average or good readers. A 3-year study (L. Weber 1985) reveals that greater amounts of time-on-task are associated with higher reading achievement only for elementary school children whose reading ability is in the lowest quartile.

On-task behaviors increase in well-managed classes in which the teacher interacts with students, provides appropriate material, paces instruction that promotes student success, and provides feedback as to success. Teacher enthusiasm also can influence on-task behavior (Bettencourt et al. 1983). If students are already persevering to the extent needed for learning, incentives may increase time-on-task, but not the degree or rate of learning (Millman et al. 1983).

The fact that pupils learn when they are on-task and do not learn when their attention is elsewhere does not tell us how to get them to pay attention. To some extent, chronic inattention may be constitutional or psychological. But this does not explain why some whole groups or classes attend most of the time during reading lessons and others do not. Attending behavior may be a desirable by-product of effective teaching; inattention may be a signal that teaching is ineffective.

Classroom Management

A well-managed classroom runs smoothly, efficiently, and effectively. Good classroom management underlies effective teaching. It results in more academic engaged time and is thus related to student achievement. Studies suggest that classroom management skills correlate with student gains in learning not only because skilled managers maximize student time-on-task but also because good classroom managers tend to be good instructors, and vice versa. Both aspects of teaching involve similar elements of the ability to prepare and organize (Smith-Burke 1987), and many elements of classroom management are essentially instructional tasks that require teachers to show pupils what to do.

Effective classroom managers have rules and procedures integrated into a workable system that students learn early in the school year (Emmer, Evertson & Anderson 1980). They make effective use of time; transitions between activities are smooth and short, and students' on-task behaviors are maximized. Clear directions and instructions are given. Good managers structure instruction so as to avoid problems. They are aware of individual differences and adjust instruction accordingly. Pupil behavior and work are closely and consistently monitored and students are held accountable. Effective managers sense the needs of children and react quickly and positively to them. They do not treat inappropriate behavior differently than do other teachers, but they stop it sooner. The consequences of inappropriate behavior are known by the students, and the teacher applies them consistently, but with some degree of flexibility. Students expect teachers to manage their classrooms effectively, and when teachers do, children learn more easily.

Further suggestions for effective classroom management may be found in Lapp (1980) and Doyle (1985). Ideas for developing self-management skills in pupils are provided by Wang (1979), and suggestions for preventing and managing disruptive classroom behavior can be found in DeLuke and Knoblock (1987) and Stainback, Stainback, and Froyen (1987).

Attention to Pupil Needs

Effective teachers are perceptive of individual and group needs, plan and conduct instruction that meets those needs, keep a close watch on pupil progress, and provide help promptly when difficulty arises. Such teacher behaviors exists not only in teacher-directed activities but also in independent activities. When pupils are assigned independent work, effective teachers actively supervise them, giving careful attention to those who need it. Ineffective teachers assign seatwork and leave the children pretty much on their own; anyone who needs help must seek it (Medley 1977).

Difficulty of Material

Reading materials may be used under a teacher's direction or independently by pupils. Usually the materials in teacher-directed activities can be more difficult than those students use on their own. In either case, the material should be neither so difficult as to make learning or enjoyment impossible nor so easy that there is little to learn or to hold the children's interest. Attending behavior is influenced by the difficulty of the material. More off-task behavior occurs when the material is too difficult or too easy for the learner. Suggestions for selecting materials of suitable difficulty are made on pages 226–227 and 690–696.

Pacing

Pacing refers to how much is introduced in a lesson and the speed at which children are moved through the lesson and involves the rate at which new learnings are introduced over time. Pacing influences content coverage. Studies have found significant correlations between content coverage and reading achievement: the more content covered, the higher the achievement. Such findings should not mislead teachers into thinking that speeding up the instructional pace will result in higher reading ability. These findings may simply indicate that good readers move through the instructional program more rapidly than do poor readers. Instructional pacing, and thereby content coverage, should be adjusted to the rate at which the students can assimilate the learnings. Sufficient time must be allowed to absorb and master the material. Generally, more capable individuals and groups respond better to being challenged; therefore, the pace of instruction should require them to work fairly continuously at a brisk pace. Apparently, teachers do practice this principle because Borko, Shavelson, and Stern (1981) report that high reading groups are paced 2 to 15 times faster than low groups. Less capable children respond better to a slower instructional pace, and more time is allowed for learning and review (Barr 1982). In either case, however, if the material is difficult or at a high cognitive level, pacing should be slower, wait time longer, and less content covered (Smith-Burke 1987).

The pacing of first-grade reading groups is based primarily on the ease with which they can read the material orally (Calfee & Drum 1985). In general, teachers respond to the mean ability of the reading group in pacing instruction (Barr 1985).

Motivation

Increased motivation also contributes to more academic engaged time. Children are motivated to attend and learn when they achieve success, receive feedback regarding their responses and work, and are encouraged to involve themselves in the learning process. Effective teachers use praise and encouragement more than ineffective teachers do, and they avoid harsh criticism, sarcasm, or other expressions of strong disapproval (Medley 1977). If children are experiencing difficulty in learning and therefore are likely to be discouraged, praise is meaningful and motivating. Praise needs to be used *well* rather than often. Brophy (1986) provides suggestions for the effective use of praise. Although negative teacher reactions are generally undesirable, a small amount of negative affect may be effective in certain circumstances, such as to minimize disruptive behavior. Constructive criticism may serve to motivate high-ability or high-SES students (Morsink et al. 1986).

Feedback other than praise also may motivate children or keep them on-task. The teacher's verbal or nonverbal feedback provides information to the students about the effectiveness or quality of their responses, thereby allowing them to adjust and modify future responses. To be effective, positive feedback should be contingent on effortful attempts, and should convey specific information as to what would lead to improvement (Licht & Kistner 1986).

As students process written or spoken language, knowing whether they are proceeding appropriately helps to keep them on-task. Skilled readers and listeners are able to monitor their own comprehension efforts, but many less-skilled or novice readers have not developed self-monitoring strategies and require feedback from the teacher. This may involve explaining answers, discussing clues to be used in arriving at an appropriate response, and encouraging clarification of thought. Pupils can be taught strategies for monitoring reading comprehension (see pages 629–631).

Students often need to be motivated by the teacher to learn because acquiring a new skill may be difficult and take time. How teachers interact with students influences their motivation. A teaching style that combines task orientation and a human-relations orientation works best. Motivation can also be achieved using such techniques as reinforcement (rewards and punishment), contingency management (the student must do some minimal amount of work before being allowed to do a preferred activity), and work contracts (Samuels 1986).

Teacher Planning and Decision Making

Effective teaching occurs by design. It is the result of planning, carrying out the plan, and evaluating and replanning if necessary—all of which require decision making. The most general level at which effective teachers usually plan is in developing and maintaining a classroom environment that promotes learning. Such positive classroom atmospheres can be established by teachers who are knowledgeable about the content they are expected to teach and about their students; know and use effective motivational and instructional procedures; have confidence in themselves and their students and communicate this to their students; clearly establish what is expected from the students as well as what the students can expect from them; and use effective classroom management techniques.

Planning also involves deciding what to teach and how best to teach it, and evaluating how well the desired results were obtained. Decisions regarding the overall objectives of a reading program are usually made at a school or district level. However, classroom teachers can, and do, decide the relative importance of these objectives and how they are to be achieved.[2] Having ranked the objectives, teachers must decide, throughout the school year, which objectives are appropriate for each child. Because students differ in what they know and what they can do, it is unlikely that every student needs to be taught every skill and strategy suggested in the curriculum guide or teacher's manual. Therefore, teachers must determine each student's strengths and needs, and decide how best to achieve each objective—the most appropriate materials and instructional procedures to use.

In planning daily lessons, teachers must use or modify an existing plan, or devise an original plan. In doing so, they must decide such things as how the skill under consideration fits in with past and future learning, and whether or not a brief review of past learnings would aid the students.

During a lesson, a teacher often must make on-the-spot decisions. Lessons do not always go as planned; immediate adjustments may need to be made. If a teacher is aware that a plan is not working, sorts quickly through the alternatives, and makes an appropriate adjustment, the lesson can accomplish its desired aim. Such decisions are more difficult to make than those made before or after the lesson.

After a lesson is completed, the teacher must decide how well its objectives were met. If the lesson was successful, the need for further practice and reinforcement must be evaluated, and a decision made as to what to teach next. If the lesson was unsuccessful, the teacher must determine why, replan, reteach, and reevaluate.

Some teachers make few instructional decisions. They merely *go through* every lesson as prescribed in the teacher's manual with every child. This practice may occur in response to an uninformed administrative edict or because the teacher believes it to be the best or easiest way to teach. Other teachers use a *curricular domain selection* approach—if it is in the curriculum and the child cannot do it, teach it (Zigmond & Miller 1986). Perhaps the constraints imposed by time and the quantity of the content to be covered (Conley 1987b) or the realities of the classroom structure (Duffy & Ball 1986) encourage teachers to seek relatively stress-free routines for carrying out instructional goals. In any event teachers' decision making often does not correspond to the models developed by teacher educators (Barr 1986).

Most studies of teachers' decision making have examined their procedural

[2]Problems can result if teachers choose poorly and/or if their choices are in marked conflict with the beliefs of an administrator or supervisor. Teachers must also consider the possible impact of their decisions on how well the students will be able to meet the task demands imposed by other teachers or by tests used to assess their abilities.

rather than their substantive decisions. *Procedural decisions* are concerned primarily with monitoring activity flow, time allocations, pacing, and monitoring student responses and task completion. *Substantive decisions* include those dealing with what to teach and how, taking advantage of "teachable moments," qualitative restructuring of student responses, selecting alternative instructional strategies, and deciding which affective responses to make in response to student behaviors and reactions. Perhaps this is why decision making has not been identified as an important variable in teacher effectiveness (Duffy & Ball 1986).

Teacher Attitudes and Expectations

Just as attitudes can influence expectations, expectations may influence attitudes. Since *Pygmalion in the Classroom* (Rosenthal & Jacobson 1968), the term *self-fulfilling prophecy* has been widely used. According to this theory, teacher expectations indirectly influence student achievement because a teacher's expectations for students' academic success leads to differential instruction and treatment. Thus, a teacher, who believes that a certain child is not likely to achieve in school, holds low expectations for that child's reading achievement. Because she believes that the pupil's reading progress will be limited, she instructs and treats him differently than other students from whom she expects greater achievement. Accordingly, she offers the low-expectation child fewer opportunities to learn, provides lower-quality instruction, and gives him less encouragement and more criticism. As a result of these teacher behaviors, which also lessen the child's motivation to learn, the pupil learns less than he would have otherwise, and his low achievement "confirms" the teacher's expectations. Rist (1970) offers this explanation for the reading failure of the minority pupils he studied.

Although expectations based on rigid stereotypes (e.g., obese children are lazy) or bias may distort a teacher's perceptions of children to the point of inducing a self-fulfilling prophecy, such occurences are probably not as frequent as many believe. Numerous studies have failed to suppport Rosenthal and Jacobson's findings (Wineburg 1987), although Rosenthal (1987) and Rist (1987) would argue this point. In general, teacher expectations do not have much effect on student achievement because (1) their expectations are generally accurate and are based on the best available information, and (2) teachers correct inaccurate perceptions as more accurate information becomes available (Brophy 1983). Attempts to solve the ills of American schools by changing teacher expectations divert attention from social inequities by claiming that the central, if not the entire, cause of school failure rests in the minds of teachers (Wineburg 1987).

Research findings suggest that although teachers may prefer to teach good readers, their observed behaviors do not indicate favoritism for the top reading groups (Weinstein 1976). In fact, teachers are more likely to make accomodations in assigning reading materials for less-skilled readers than for students reading above grade level (Rubin 1975), and to provide more instructional time and individualized instruction for low-performing pupils (Brophy 1983). Low reading groups receive more instruction with the teacher at their side than do middle or high groups (Ysseldyke & Algozzine 1983).

Teacher expectations can also influence their own performance and effectiveness. Teachers who believe that instructing children is basic to their role, who fully expect to conduct such instruction, and who set about doing so are more successful than teachers who do not (Brophy 1979b). Teachers must believe in their ability to help students learn, and must exhibit that confidence to their pupils (Guzzetti & Marzano 1984).

Summary of Effective Teaching

Knowledgeable teachers are likely to be effective when they:

1. Plan Well
   a. Schedule enough instructional time to accomplish mastery of the reading program's objectives
   b. Vary the degree of teacher-imposed structure with the cognitive and social maturity of the students
   c. Pay close attention to pupil and group needs
2. Manage well
   a. Provide classroom conditions that are conducive to concentration and sustained attention
   b. Take steps to ensure high academic engaged time
      (1) Reinforce students for paying attention during teacher-directed and independent activities
      (2) Decrease waiting and transition time by establishing routines
      (3) Consistently monitor learning activities
   c. Establish guidelines for student behavior, assure that students understand them, are actively involved with students so as to prevent misbehavior and intervene promptly to stop misbehavior
3. Teach well
   a. Establish a work orientation, while maintaining a supportive environment
   b. Have well-planned and well-conducted lessons
   c. Present new material clearly
   d. Model and demonstrate learning behaviors
   e. Make clear to students what they are to learn, why it is important to learn it, how it relates to previous and future learning, and how they will be expected to demonstrate that learning
   f. Provide instructional materials and utilize instructional procedures that will allow students to succeed
   g. Pace the instruction to differences in the learning rates of groups and individuals
   h. Make independent seatwork worthwhile and interesting
   i. Are alert to signs of pupil difficulty and provide help promptly when needed
   j. Consistently monitor pupil work and progress and adjust instruction accordingly
4. Motivate well
   a. Show a warm interest in students and interact with them often
   b. Use praise, criticism, and challenge judiciously
   c. Provide feedback regarding student efforts, the appropriateness of their responses, and the quality of their work

   d. Are optimistic about the learning potentials of their pupils and com-
      municate that attitude to them
   e. Do not allow their perceptions of individual differences to influence
      their behavior so as to affect the morale and efforts of some pupils
      adversely (A. J. Harris 1979b, Bickel & Bickel 1986).

Effective School Reading Programs

Some of the same factors that characterize effective teachers also are displayed
by effective schools—an orderly learning environment, high achievement expectations, and emphasis on teaching basic reading skills. Effective school-wide
or district-wide reading programs also have a person, usually an administrator
or supervisor, who provides leadership. These leaders demonstrate a commitment to assuring that the goals of the reading program are met. (It is best to
have goals determined jointly by teachers and administrators.) Effective leaders
realize that positive change is more likely to occur if teachers accept and understand the program, and that it takes time and effort to improve a reading program.
They systematically monitor pupil progress and assure that the program is being
thoughtfully implemented. Slavish adherence to prescribed instructional procedures is discouraged, and alternative ways of reaching the same goals are allowed. Effective leaders also establish and maintain clear, consistent policies.
They communicate to students, teachers, parents, and the school community
that the success or failure of the reading program depends on all involved—that
the responsibility for success is shared—and they make it clear, especially to
students, that success is expected.

   The effectiveness of a school reading program is dependent on the cooperative efforts of the pupils, school, and home. But school administrators and
teachers may have different perspectives on the goals of reading instruction and
the means for attaining them. Whereas most administrators accept high test
scores as the appropriate goal and centralized planning and standard use of commercial reading materials as the appropriate means of instruction, many teachers
seek broader goals and more autonomy in instructional practices (Shannon
1986).

5

Adapting Reading Instruction to Individual Differences

Marked individual differences in reading ability occur within every school population. Such differences are not surprising in view of the fact that reading ability in particular and learning in general are influenced by a number of interrelated factors that vary among students—learning aptitude, knowledge gained from prior experiences, motivation, persistence, sensory abilities, and so on. As yet no one has devised a fully satisfactory solution to coping with individual differences.

Most attempts to accommodate instruction to individual differences involve (1) *administrative procedures* that attempt to ease the teacher's task in dealing with individual differences, (2) *classroom procedures* that involve the unit of instruction (large group, small group, individual), and (3) *instructional procedures* that attempt to match learner characteristics with instructional treatments or to vary the pace at which learning occurs. These three approaches are not mutually exclusive.

The effects of various classroom situations and instructional procedures on reading achievement are complex and far from fully understood. Variations in teacher and student abilities and in what is to be taught necessarily dictate differing strategies for optimal learning. Individual and group needs can be accommodated only as the result of careful planning, monitoring, and revising of instruction and curriculum by school personnel as they consider the goals of the reading program, the strengths and needs of their students, and the specific contexts within which instruction occurs.

We begin this chapter by establishing that children do vary widely in reading ability. Next we present the goals of any plan for accommodating the wide range in reading ability. Following this we provide three sections on administrative, classroom, and instructional procedures that attempt to help the teacher cope with the range of needs. Finally we offer a plan for combining whole-class, group, and individual instruction.

INDIVIDUAL DIFFERENCES IN READING ABILITY

Five levels of reading proficiency are defined by the National Assessment of Educational Progress (1985b). Only brief descriptors of these levels are given here,[1] accompanied by their NAEP numerical designations and their approximate grade levels as estimated by Carroll (1987):

1. *Rudimentary, 150 (Grade 1.5)*—ability to carry out simple, discrete reading tasks such as selecting the sentence that correctly describes a simple picture
2. *Basic, 200 (Grade 3.6)*—ability to understand specific or sequentially related information
3. *Intermediate, 150 (Grade 7.2)*—ability to search for specific information, interrelate inferred ideas, and make generalizations in relatively lengthy passages
4. *Adept, 300 (Grade 12.9)*—ability to find, understand, and explain the relationships within complicated information.
5. *Advanced, 350 (College senior)*—ability to synthesize and learn from specialized reading materials.

As shown in Figure 5.1, prose-comprehension ability gradually develops from age 9 through age 17. At age 9, the median performance (50th percentile) is slightly above the Basic level; at age 13, a little beyond the Intermediate level; at age 17, almost at the Adept level; and by age 23, somewhat above the Adept level. There is, however, tremendous variability in reading ability at each age level. At age 9, 93.9% reached or exceeded the Rudimentary level, 64.2% the Basic level, 18.1% the Intermediate level, and 1% the Adept level. None reached the Advanced level. Almost all the 13-year-olds reached or exceeded the Rudimentary level, 94.5% the Basic level, 60.3% the Intermediate level, 11.3% the Adept level, and 0.3% the Advanced level. All the 17-year-olds reached or exceeded the Rudimentary level; 98.6% the Basic level; 83.6% the Intermediate level; 39.2% the Adept level; and 4.9% the Advanced level (NAEP 1985b).

A great deal of overlap in ability exists between and among age levels. For example, the top 5% of the 9-year-olds scored as well as 75% of the 13-year-olds and half the 17-year-olds. Half the 13-year-olds read as well as the lowest 25% of the 17-year-olds, but 25% of them comprehended only as well as half the 9-year-olds. The bottom 5% of the 17-year-olds only read as well as about 40% of the 9-year-olds (Carroll 1987).

[1]Detailed descriptions of these levels appear on page 25 of the NAEP report. The NAEP now uses a scale of from 0 to 100 with a mean of 50 (see Applebee, Langer, & Mullis 1988).

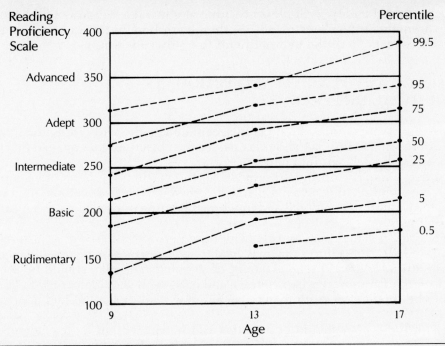

Figure 5.1. Range of reading proficiency on the 1984 NAEP *Prose Comprehension Test.* Adapted from John Carroll, The Natural Assessment in Reading: Are we misreading the findings? *Phi Delta Kappan,* February 1987, *68,* 424–430. Reproduced by permission of the author and the publisher.

The actual median and range of reading comprehension scores obtained by first through fifth graders on a standardized reading achievement test are shown in Table 5.1. Also indicated are the average level of reading textbook and range of textbooks assigned to the children. Both sets of data show a wide range of reading ability at a given grade level.

These illustrations indicate only the general level of reading achieved by

Table 5.1   Range of Reading Abilities and Assigned Reading Textbooks

Grade	N	Percentage reading below grade level	Percentage reading above midpoint of next higher grade level	Paragraph Meaning Grade-Equivalent Score Median	Range	Assigned Text Median	Range
1	1,135	3.7	16.3	1.8	1.0–4.0+	P	PP–3^2
2	894	18.1	29.4	2.8	1.0–4.0+	2^2	PP–5
3	607	24.1	28.3	3.7	1.0–7.7+	3^2	PP–6
4	342	25.1	37.1	4.8	1.8–9.5+	4	PP–JH
5	147	23.8	40.1	6.0	1.8–9.5+	5	1–JH

Source: Rosalyn Rubin, Reading ability and assigned materials: accommodations for the slow but not the accelerated, *Elementary School Journal,* March 1975.

Abbreviations: PP = preprimer, P = primer, 1 = first reader, 2^2 = high second reader, 3^2 = high third reader, 4, 5, 6 = fourth reader, etc., JH = junior high school.

the school-aged children. Students reading at a given level do not all have the same strengths or weaknesses nor do they learn best in the same ways. Such differences make it all the more difficult to optimize learning.

GOALS OF ANY PLAN TO ACCOMMODATE INDIVIDUAL DIFFERENCES

Before discussing various attempts to accommodate the wide individual differences in reading ability, we should consider the objectives for any plan that tries to do so. Such goals fall into four categories.

First, a sound plan should provide for the maximum growth of each pupil in three general reading areas. A plan concerned only with developmental reading is too limited; recreational and functional reading must also be given careful consideration.

Second, a sound plan must consider the personal and social adjustment of all the students. Procedures that may lead to social ostracism, poor self-concepts, or poor attitudes toward school should be avoided. The plan should be acceptable to administrators, teachers, pupils, and parents. It should not only help children to become better readers but also to enjoy reading, and to feel happy and secure.

Third, the plan should be one that can be carried out by teachers. Some plans need exceptionally able and creative teachers. Exhorting average teachers to adopt such a plan may discourage them from trying anything new; they may feel unable to meet the requirements. Realistic plans must be usable by most teachers and at the same time allow freedom for excellent teachers.

Finally, a good plan should fit the school and its pupils. Some good plans work well only in schools with hundreds of pupils. Others require a variety of materials beyond what the school can afford. Each school has to appraise its own situation and work out solutions to fit its needs.

ADMINISTRATIVE PROCEDURES

Various administrative procedures have been proposed to accommodate individual differences. These include promotion policies, variations in school entry ages, limitations on the number of children and/or the range of abilities with which an individual teacher has to cope, and changes in school organization and/or instructional implementation. As one reads about the various administrative plans that have been tried, the striking fact is that all of them seem to have produced favorable results in the local situations in which they were developed. Probably the enthusiasm and ability of the people who operate the plan and the appeal of novelty give any sensible innovation a temporary advantage over what was done before. In this, as in many other important questions about reading instruction, research has produced no final answers.

Acceleration and Retention

Acceleration (e.g., skipping a grade) has never been a widespread practice, but retention has, especially in first grade. Low academic achievement, especially in reading in the primary grades, was and is the most frequent basis for retention. Although retention was fairly common in the early part of this century, by 1950 many pupils were promoted regardless of achievement. This change to a "social promotion" policy was due primarily to research findings that suggested that retention did not result in improved achievement, and that nonpromoted pupils were more likely to be discipline problems, to have social difficulties, and to drop out of school (Bocks 1977). Current data are not available, but the emphasis on acquisition of "basic skills" and minimal competency has probably resulted in more retentions in the past decade. M. L. Smith and Shepard (1988) found that kindergarten teachers did not generally believe in social promotion, but rather promoted or retained their pupils on the basis of their competence or readiness.

The findings regarding the effect of retention on reading achievement are mixed. On one hand, their meta-analysis led Holmes and Matthews (1984) to conclude that nonpromotion was not beneficial and could be harmful to elementary and junior high school students; on the other hand, some evidence suggests that retention may be helpful in the elementary school (McAfee 1981), especially when low-achieving students are taught the necessary skills (Meyer 1983; Juel & Leavell 1988). A longitudinal study (Peterson, DeGracie & Ayabe 1987) indicates that retention does not have any negative effects on primary-grade children; nor does it have many long-term academic benefits. Elementary school pupils show little improvement in achievement after a second retention (Safer 1986).

Neither general plans of retention nor 100% promotion has been particularly successful (Jackson 1975) but, except for the findings of Sandoval and Hughes (1981), we know little about the factors involved in successful and unsuccessful retentions and promotions.

Each case should be decided by determining whether retention or promotion (or acceleration for high achievers) will be in the best interest of the child. Pupils should be placed where they are most likely to make the best academic progress and social and emotional adjustment. This is usually with their own age group, provided that adjustments are made in the instructional program and demands placed upon the pupils. Regardless of whether they are promoted or retained, what is done *for* the students is more important than what is done *with* them. Retention plus remediation probably leads to greater achievement than does retention alone (Peterson, DeGracie & Ayabe 1987), but social promotion plus remediation may be more effective than retention with remediation (Leinhardt 1980).

Postponing Reading for All Children

In 1898 John Dewey, one of the earliest proponents of the idea that reading is taught when children are too young, stated that "present physiological knowledge points to the age of about eight years as early enough for anything more than an incidental attention to visual and written language-forms" (quoted in Huey 1908, p. 306). Considering the difficulty of phonic methods popular at that time and the high rate of failure then prevalent, Dewey's proposal does not sound unreasonable, but methods of instruction have changed. In Sweden, beginning reading instruction at age 7 has not prevented the occurrence of reading disabilities (Malmquist 1958, 1969). Postponing reading for all children does not abolish or even lessen individual differences; it simply delays the time at which adjustment to varied learning rates will have to be made.

Homogeneous Classes

Homogeneous classes narrow the range of ability and achievement in a classroom. Among the arguments presented for homogeneous classes are that smaller individual differences result in more effective teaching and learning, the most capable students can move ahead rapidly, and the least capable are not embarrassed or stigmatized by their inability to compete. Critics of the plan argue that the less able or lower-achieving students are deprived of the stimulation provided by more able or higher-achieving pupils, homogeneous classes adversely affect pupils' perceptions of themselves and school, and teachers' perceptions and, thus, treatment of them, homogeneous grouping is elitist and amounts to *de facto* segregation, since low-SES and minority groups are overrepresented in the low classes or tracks.

There is considerable debate regarding how to interpret this overrepresentation of low-SES and minorities. To some it constitutes a form of institutional bias. Others believe it is simply the result of placing children in groups in which their needs can best be accomodated, and that the relationships between ability and racial and social factors are created by forces outside of the school (Haller & Waterman 1985).

Gross comparisons between homogeneous and heterogeneous classes generally reveal only slight mean differences in achievement, and the effects are not particularly strong or consistent (Leinhardt & Pallay 1982). Slavin (1987b) concludes that there is no research support for assigning elementary school students to self-contained classes on the basis of IQ or reading achievement test scores (the two studies that grouped children only by reading achievement showed conflicting results).

Reviewers disagree as to the varying effects of ability-based class grouping on students of different levels of ability. Some reviewers claim that ability-grouped classes benefit high-ability students and are detrimental to low-ability pupils, but Slavin (1987b) concludes that such is not the case in the elementary school. Good and Stipek (1983) report some evidence that high-ability students achieve better when grouped with others of comparable ability than when they work alone or with lower-ability students. Average-ability students tend to do better in relatively homogeneous classes than when placed with both high and low achievers. Low-ability pupils benefit more from being in classes with higher-ability students than from being in homogeneous classes. There is little evidence as to *why* such differential results are obtained.

Homogeneous classes are much more prevalent in junior and senior high schools than in elementary schools. When reading ability is one of the primary selection factors, the lowest classes usually contain considerably more behavior problems and academic failures than higher-ability classes. Often slow learners, average-aptitude students with some reading problems, and bright adolescents with serious reading problems are placed in the same classroom. Such classes are far from being homogeneous, and the teacher may be unaware of the different reasons for the students' low reading achievement.

Evertson, Stanford, and Emmer (1981) found that junior high school teachers coped with wide ranges of reading ability by (1) providing special attention and assistance in class to low-ability students; (2) limited use of in-class grouping, differentiation of material or assignments, and peer tutoring; and (3) providing frequent academic feedback and maintaining high levels of student accountability.

Homogeneous classes may have failed to solve the problem of individual differences in rate of learning because they did not improve the teachability of groups (Good & Stipek 1983). A group based on one characteristic will probably vary on other variables that influence learning, so true homogeneity is impossible. Extremely heterogeneous classes place extraordinary demands on teachers' time, attention, and skill, but good classroom managers are able to overcome most of the problems and meet individual needs (Evertson, Stanford & Emmer 1981).

Cross-Grade and Cross-Class Grouping for Reading

Plans in which children are grouped homogeneously only for reading instruction have been in operation for over 40 years. On the basis of test results and teacher judgment the pupils are divided into reading classes with a restricted range of reading ability, all of which are scheduled for reading at the same time. When the bell rings, the children go to their reading teachers; when the reading period is over, they return to their homerooms. Plans of this sort are often referred to as *Joplin Plans*.

In a small school with one class per grade, such a plan would require cross-grade grouping with, for example, the reading scores for all pupils in Grades 4, 5, and 6 placed in a single rank order. The sixth-grade teacher could have the upper range for reading, the fifth-grade teacher the middle range, and the fourth-grade teacher the lowest range (which might be a little smaller in number than the other two). In a large school with several classes at each grade, it is possible to have cross-class grouping for reading within each grade.

In a plan of this sort, the range of reading scores is reduced from about 6 years to 2 or 3 years. These groups are still far from real homogeneity: Not only is there still a 2-year-or-more span of reading levels, but individual pupils with similar scores may have different needs.

Slavin (1987b) reports that use of the Joplin plan resulted in higher reading achievement in 10 of 13 studies; the others showed no significant achievement differences. However, this finding should not be interpreted as a ringing endorsement of the Joplin plan. Almost all the studies apparently compared the Joplin plan against classes in which there was little or no grouping for reading instruction.

Hiebert (1987) argues that the effects of any grouping plan cannot be assessed or revealed simply by comparing various types of grouping practices. She contends that the role of instructional practices must be considered because grouping, in and of itself, does not produce achievement; instruction does. Any form of grouping may only provide the opportunity for better instruction. According to Slavin (1987c), no study has both compared the achievement effects of alternate grouping practices and carefully documented processes that characterized each form of grouping. Without such studies we cannot learn the conditions under which a particular grouping plan is more conducive to learning.

In recent years declining school enrollments and budget problems have led some schools to set up multigrade or multiage classes. The limited research that has compared such classes with more typical grade or age arrangements in self-contained classrooms indicates that there is no significant difference in reading achievement (Lincoln 1982).

Split-Half Classes

Some schools have half the class begin and end school an hour or so earlier than their classmates. Reading is taught to one half in the morning hour and to the other half in the afternoon, thus reducing the number of children to whom the teacher must teach reading at a given time. Favorable results have been obtained with split-half classes in Denmark (Lundahl 1976).

Theoretically, under this program teachers should individualize instruction to a greater extent than formerly because they have to deal with fewer children. But, as in any situation, what the teacher does with the time is important. If the reading instruction is the same as when many more children are in the class, the purpose for reducing class size for a given time period is defeated.

Departmentalization

Departmentalization, in which a teacher instructs only one subject or curricular area, is almost universal above the sixth grade and occurs in some middle grades. Among its claimed advantages are these: (1) Having a reading class assures that reading is taught, something that might not normally be part of the curriculum; and (2) reading teachers should be highly proficient because they are not responsible for other subjects. Lamme (1976b) found that teachers could exert more influence on children's reading habits (e.g., amount read, use of book recommendations) in a self-contained class than in a departmentalized structure.

Team Teaching

In *team teaching*, two or more teachers, working together, are responsible for all or most of the instruction provided for the same students (a greater number of students than would be assigned to one teacher). Among the advantages claimed for team teaching over the traditional classroom are more extensive diagnosis, flexible grouping, and provisions for independent study. Although few adequately controlled evaluations have been made, the findings suggest the following directional trends regarding reading achievement and student adjustment: (1) Reading achievement in traditional classrooms is usually significantly higher; and (2) the students' personal-social adjustment is similar under both team teaching and traditional teaching conditions (Townsend 1976).

The Nongraded School

The idea that children should be able to move ahead in school at their individual rates of learning and that yearly grades are too coarse a basis for pupil classification resulted in *nongraded plans* of organization, usually restricted to the primary years (Goodlad & Anderson 1959). The reading curriculum is divided into 8 to 12 instructional levels. Usually the child's assignment to a level is based mainly on informal reading tests and teacher judgment, tempered by considerations of age, social maturity, and progress in other curricular areas. Each teacher usually has no more than three adjacent levels in a self-contained classroom. A child may move to the next higher level at any time during the year, whenever he or she completes the program for the present level. There is continuous progress in that no child is ever required to repeat a level, although children move through the levels at different speeds. Thus, most children complete the primary program in 3 years; some take 4 years; a few may complete it in 2 years.

Because children who are at the same instructional level may have different patterns of reading skills and needs, a considerable amount of individualization is necessary. Careful diagnosis and planning for individuals are important in any plan for reading instruction; the need seems to be more clearly recognized and more vital for success in a nongraded plan than in a conventional school.

Early research failed to demonstrate improved reading achievement in nongraded schools compared to conventional schools (Di Lorenzo & Salter 1965). However, later studies indicate that, in general, nongraded groups achieve as well as, and often better than, graded groups (Martin & Pavan 1976).

Open Schools and Classrooms

Open or *informal schools* have the common element of replacing preplanned curriculum sequences with child-centered and, to a large extent, child-initiated learning activities.[2] The ideal classroom is seen as an active place where children choose activities and engage in them individually or in small, temporary groups. The teacher's role is one of helper and resource person rather than director of learning. Much of the American interest in open schools was generated by a desire to emulate the British informal infant and junior schools.

Usually classes are nongraded and often include children with an age range of 2 or 3 years. Team teaching and open work areas are other features commonly included. Reading instruction in open schools tends to be a combination of language experience and individualized reading approaches, with relatively little systematic attention to skills development (Moss 1972). In some schools, however, diagnosis and individually prescribed instruction are stressed (Klausmeier, Sorenson & Quilling 1971), or teachers have reading groups and use a basal series or programmed readers (Rogers 1976).

The overall findings regarding the effect of open classrooms on academic achievement and affective outcomes are mixed. Horwitz (1979) concludes that there is enough evidence to defend the concept as a viable alternative when teachers and parents are interested in its use. A meta-analysis, however, led Peterson (1982) to conclude that although open education had positive effects on affective factors, traditional teacher-directed programs had a slight advantage in reading achievement.

[2]Also see the discussion of formal versus informal programs on pp. 106–107.

CLASSROOM PROCEDURES

No one way of organizing the class serves all purposes equally well. A well-rounded reading program includes different kinds of class organization, each used in reading activities for which it is best suited. The question is not one of choosing between individualization and grouping but of how to combine whole-class, individualized, and group activities into a harmonious whole. When well implemented and suited to the learning situation, individual, small-group, and large-group instruction can have a positive effect on learning; once again, the teacher is the key. Even for whole-class instruction, there are systematic differences between relatively effective and ineffective teachers (Good & Stipek 1983).

Before discussing the various kinds of classroom activities, we must clarify a few points. Individualizing instruction means that the activity is tailored to optimize the learning of an individual; the most appropriate material and methodology are employed, instruction is paced to maximize the likelihood of learning, only what the child needs to learn is introduced, and so on. Individualization of instruction is not an either/or proposition; most often, it is a matter of degree. Theoretically, the more instruction is individualized, the more likely it is that learning will be effective and efficient. Individualization is not an exclusive concomitant of any one instructional approach or system of classroom organization.

Instruction can be individualized for a child working alone or in any size group. It is the appropriateness of the instruction and not the number of children working on an activity or the fact that each child is doing something different during the reading period that determines if instruction is individualized. The degree to which individualization occurs still rests with the skill of the teacher.

A fundamental necessity for effective individualization is a teacher or specialist who can diagnose pupil needs, abilities, and interests and can plan appropriate learning activities based on his or her findings. Unfortunately, the level of diagnostic proficiency among classroom teachers, and even reading specialists, leaves much to be desired.

Whole-Class Reading Activities

Several kinds of reading activities can profitably be carried on with the entire class. They include audience situations, choral reading, common new learnings, current events reading, and "open-book" textbook sessions. Each has a legitimate place in the total reading program. The first two activities can be used in either developmental or recreational reading, the third in any of the three strands of a total reading program, and the last two in functional reading.

AUDIENCE SITUATIONS. An oral-reading selection that has been prepared and rehearsed can be presented to the class. Materials can include poems, jokes, selections from stories and books, radio or TV scripts, or short plays. The presentation may be made by an individual or by a small group. Sessions in which children give oral book reports or present reports based on individual or committee reading can also provide whole-class audience situations. Two important requirements are (1) preparing in advance so that the performance is reasonably good, and (2) having the class act as a real audience rather than read along silently.

CHORAL READING. The occasional use of choral reading not only is helpful for the appreciation of poetry and rhythm but also assists in developing a spirit of belongingness and group cohesion in the class.

COMMON NEW LEARNINGS. On many occasions a new reading or study skill can be introduced to the whole class, even though not all will learn it with equal rapidity. Alphabetizing, the use of such aids as the table of contents, index, dictionary, and encyclopedia, and new phonic principles and word meanings are among the reading skills that can be introduced in this way. Reading strategies that are applicable regardless of the pupils' levels of reading ability (e.g., purpose setting, comprehension monitoring) also can be taught to large groups or to the whole class.

CURRENT EVENTS. School newspapers provide opportunities for current events periods in which all can participate. Weekly graded editions make it possible for all to do the same kind of reading together, although some may be reading an advanced edition and others an edition intended for lower grades. In the primary grades, experience stories can be used for the same purpose.

TEXTBOOK READING. A textbook is often the focus of instruction in a curriculum area. If the textbook is too difficult for students and if material of suitable difficulty on the same topic is not available, it may be necessary to use the textbook in a modified directed reading activity. Through listening to the explanations and discussions, the students may acquire the concepts contained in the textbook. Other ways for helping pupils for whom the content textbook is frustratingly difficult are discussed on pages 620–621.

Individualized Reading Activities

Whole-class, group, and individual activities can be employed in achieving similar general objectives of the three aspects of a total reading program. Instruction can be individualized regardless of the number of children involved. As explained on page 126, an entire class, a group, or an individual may be involved in an individualized reading activity. Individualized procedures have been developed for developmental, recreational, and functional reading, and for skills practice.

DEVELOPMENTAL READING. There are complete or partial developmental reading programs that attempt to individualize instruction to varying degrees. Many of these were discussed in Chapter 3.

INDIVIDUALIZED DEVELOPMENTAL READING (IDR) WITHIN A GROUP. A teacher who generally organizes reading instruction on a group basis might consider the use of IDR with one group rather than with the entire class. For example, it might be impossible to make group lessons profitable for a low group of six children, none of whom is reading at the same reader level. An IDR approach should be beneficial for these six. In a 35-minute period, the teacher could spend 3 to 5 minutes with each child, while the others worked on their own, asking for help as needed. The remaining time could be used for group discussions, motivation, skill development for several children, and the like. Each child could progress at his or her own rate. Whenever the range of individual reading abilities in a group is so large that it is impossible to choose a textbook that is reasonably satisfactory for all group members (and transferring the extremes to another group would not solve the problem), the possible advantages of using IDR with that group should be given serious consideration.

INDIVIDUALIZED PROGRESS IN BASAL READERS.   Individualized progress through sequential levels of a basal program is common in nongraded schools. Several programs in which individualized use of a basal reader is combined with other reading activities are briefly described by Sucher (1969). Lipson (1989) describes a number of strategies for individualizing instruction within a basal-reader program.

Bruton (1972) demonstrates how a modified systems approach can be applied to basal readers. Some publishers have incorporated similar ideas into their basal series.

RECREATIONAL READING.   Periods for recreational reading, in which children are free to read what they please (within reason), are called *free-reading*, or *independent reading, periods*. At such times the teacher can circulate among the students, spending 2 minutes with one child and 5 minutes with another. These individual contacts can be spent discussing a book already finished, considering with the child what he or she might like to read next, finding out more about the child's interests or problems, providing help on a specific difficulty, and so on. Recreational reading is covered more fully in Chapter 18.

FUNCTIONAL READING.   Modern teaching procedures create many occasions for a child to read alone to find needed information. For capable readers, this highly motivating reading provides multiple opportunities for intellectual enrichment and personal development. Less able readers who find the on-grade content-subject textbooks frustratingly difficult can be directed to material more in keeping with their reading ability.

INDIVIDUALIZED SKILLS PRACTICE.   There can be a place in the schedule for periods in which each child works on the particular reading skills in need of improvement. For this to be effective, teachers must have ways of determining individual needs, making individual assignments, and providing practice materials set up with clear, self-administering directions and scoring keys. Computer-assisted instruction offers promise in this area.

Group Reading Activities

The range of reading proficiency is wide at every age level and increases as children get older. One way to deal with these differences is to group for reading instruction. The major part of reading instruction in American elementary schools is carried out in groups (Hiebert 1983), with from three to five groups per classroom and usually with from 6 to 10 pupils in a group (Cazden 1982). Small-group instruction in the secondary school is rare (Conley 1987a).

Some teacher-effectiveness studies have reported that whole-class instruction produces more opportunities for learning than does group instruction because each child receives more instructional time. However, use of reading groups allows for greater utilization of those opportunities. Students learn more of what is taught in grouped than in ungrouped classes because the smaller unit of instruction allows the students to pay greater attention to learning or because the teacher is better able to adapt the instruction and materials to the students' needs and abilities. Small, homogeneous groups facilitate reading achievement better than do large, heterogeneous groups (Sørensen & Hallinan 1986). Methodologically-adequate studies that have compared grouping by reading ability within the class against ungrouped classes are lacking (Slavin 1987b).

Group instruction can be an efficient use of time. Usually, the group receives the same instruction initially, with all group members using the same material. However, a skill or concept may be presented in more than one way in the lesson in order to reach as many children as possible. Groups may be set up according to reading level, specific needs, or interests; the activity may be carried out with a teacher or other adult or with a pupil leader or tutor; may be self-directed or may involve supervised seatwork. Because children and teachers differ considerably, no one plan for grouping fits every situation; various group activities may be used concurrently. Whatever the grouping plans, it should be remembered that grouping for reading instruction is a means for facilitating learning; it is not an end in itself.

KINDS OF READING GROUPS.   There are basically five kinds of reading groups; the first is by far the most common.

General Level of Reading Ability.   When the range of reading ability is wide, it is usually advisable to set up reading groups on the basis of general level of reading ability. Ability-level groups are the primary instructional units, but other kinds of reading groups should be used concurrently. Use of a variety of groups also helps lessen the stigma of being in the low group. At times, students may be temporary members of more than one ability-level group. For instance, to determine whether a pupil should be placed in a higher group, the teacher may have the child participate with both groups. Or one or more children who need to acquire a skill may temporarily join the group being taught that skill. Another alternative is *open grouping* in which students are allowed to meet with any group of their choosing in addition to their own.

When there is some doubt about the best group placement for a pupil, it is advisable to place the child in the lower of the two groups being considered. This usually ensures successful participation, and it is psychologically more sound to move children from lower to higher groups than to "demote" them.

Special Needs.   Grouping mainly by levels of reading ability can profitably be supplemented by special-needs groups. Successful special-needs grouping requires a teacher who can accurately assess pupils' needs and who continuously monitors pupil progress. Children who are weak in a particular skill or strategy are grouped together. Thus, a second grade could have one group working on specific decoding skills, another group developing more fluent oral reading, and still another selecting and recalling main ideas. In sixth grade, special groups might be formed for accurate but slow readers; for rapid, inaccurate readers; for pupils who need to learn how to monitor their understanding of what is being read; and for pupils who have difficulty following printed directions. Any special-needs group might contain one or more good readers, as well as several less capable readers. As the purpose for a particular group is accomplished children can be released from it, or the group can be disbanded and a new group set up to focus on another skill area.

Temporary special-needs groups are also used regularly in some Individualized Developmental Reading programs. Competently employed, they can counteract to a considerable extent the weakness in skill development that is sometimes characteristic of that approach.

Interests. Some children may have a hobby or interest in common, such as raising tropical fish, collecting stamps, working with computers, or reading mysteries or the works of a particular author. Each group can be encouraged to meet, discover common questions, find reading material related to their special interest, read it, exchange information, and report to the class. Several interest groups may be set up in a class, with membership entirely voluntary. Such groups would not have to meet often; once a week or even once in 2 weeks might be sufficient. Interest groups can be tied in with recreational or functional reading.

Committees. Many projects, units, or activities are organized on a committee basis. Each committee usually takes responsibility for one part of the total project. Questions to be answered are decided on within the committee, and each member has responsibilities. Committees are usually set up by the teacher so that each contains a cross-section of abilities.

When reading is done to find answers to questions, a project committee consults as wide a variety of sources as it can. Better readers tackle the more difficult references; less capable readers use sources that they can understand. Those whose reading is very limited can supply information learned from illustrations. Each committee member contributes to the final report.

Cooperative Learning. *Cooperative learning* involves heterogeneous groups of four or five pupils working together on "team tasks." There are a number of variations, but most cooperative-learning plans are characterized by: (1) teacher instruction—each lesson begins with a teacher presentation; (2) team practice—the group works cooperatively to accomplish the lesson presented by the teacher; (3) individual assignments—each member of the group attempts to accomplish his or her share of the task, which is assessed individually by the teacher; and (4) team recognition—the individual grades are averaged and each member is assigned that grade for the project (Harp 1989b). The grading method motivates individuals to do their best, and group members assist one another. According to Stevens et al. (1987), cooperative-learning groups have consistently shown greater achievement than students in traditionally-structured groups. Refer to Golub (1988) for ideas on using cooperative learning.

Practical Issues

A number of practical concerns must be considered in using group activities. Most of these are discussed in this section.

CLASS SIZE.   Class size is almost always an administrative decision over which teachers have little or no control. Some research indicates that class size does not influence student performance (Bozzomo 1978), but meta-analyses have indicated that compared to larger classes, smaller classes lead to higher pupil achievement, more favorable teacher effects (e.g., morale, attitude toward students), greater attempts to individualize instruction, a better classroom climate, and more favorable student effects (e.g., self-concept, participation) (Glass et al. 1982). The findings of these meta-analyses have been questioned, however (Fillion & Brause 1987).

All else being equal (and it rarely is), the number of pupils the teacher must instruct should influence the quality of teaching and student participation, and thereby influence achievement. However, an often overlooked variable in class-size research is the quality of teaching. Small class size has little effect unless the teacher takes advantage of the situation. The same is true for grouping plans. Grouping for reading instruction is more likely to be effective when the instructional procedures, materials, and pacing are adapted to abilities.

NUMBER OF GROUPS.   There is nothing magical about having three general reading-level groups. This number is frequently employed, however, with the top group either reading more difficult material or proceeding through the material at a faster pace than the other two groups. The middle group usually works on material of intermediate difficulty, and the low group uses the easiest material.

The labels *high, average,* and *low* are relative terms. The low group in a class that has a very high overall level of reading achievement may be reading at the same level as the high group in the same grade in a school where the reading level is low. Yet the students in each school may be perceived by themselves, their peers, and teachers as low-ability readers (Hiebert 1983).

When there is an extremely wide range of reading ability, three groups may not be sufficient. In such cases, well-organized teachers may have as many as five or six groups, administrative procedures may be applied to lessen the range with which the teacher must deal, teacher aides may be employed, or individualized developmental reading may be employed for one or more groups.

At times, two groups may be appropriate, especially if the grouping is combined with some individualized reading. The upper group uses the on-grade reading textbook; the lower group, a below-grade-level reader. Children in the lower group who cannot cope with the text will need individual instruction. The best readers finish assignments quickly and use the remaining time for independent reading, or they may help one of the poorest readers. The two-group plan is appropriate for classes in which there is a limited range of reading ability or for teachers inexperienced with or unskilled at group management.

As for groups other than general-ability groups, the number depends not only on the teacher's management skills but also on the needs and interests of the pupils. It is better to have fewer efficiently functioning groups in which children are learning than to have learning stifled by a large number of groups operating in chaos.

Durrell (1940), an innovator of new patterns of class organization, advocated using five or more reading groups, with many activities led by pupil leaders and with the teacher supplying the plans and materials and exercising general supervision. Later he recommended a varied pattern of class organization involving whole-class activities, some individualized reading, heterogeneous groups for projects, small reading groups with pupil leaders, and skill practice in pairs or groups of three (Durrell 1956). Still later, Durrell (1959) reported a project that stressed team learning in groups of three to five pupils. Suggestions for using partners in reading activities may be found in Buckley (1986) and Topping (1989).

SIZE OF GROUPS.   Teachers use two strategies in determining group size. Either they establish equal-size groups because they want to be fair (unequal-size groups mean that some pupils get more attention than others), or they form a small low group based on the belief that its members need more attention (Barr 1982).

It would be undesirable to fix arbitrary rules concerning group size. Some guiding principles can be set down, however. If children require a good deal of individual attention, the group should be small; with children capable of much individual or self-regulated activity, the group can be larger. If a class has two groups, it is generally desirable for the lower group to be the smaller; similarly, the lowest of three groups should usually be smaller than the middle group. Groups set up on the basis of special needs or special interests can be of any size. Groups of two children are effective for such activities as testing each other on word cards and for some reading games. One of the pair should know the answers or be provided with them. Such "team learning" initially requires teaching direction, and demonstration of the procedures.

Some studies report differences in group size, with the suggestion that children receive more teacher-directed time if there are fewer members in the group. But evidence regarding the relationship of group size to ability level is mixed (Hiebert 1983).

BASES ON WHICH GROUPS ARE FORMED.   Borko, Shavelson, and Stern (1981) report that teachers first combine information about student characteristics into estimates of their reading ability. Groups are then formed on the basis of these ability estimates and selected school environmental factors such as the availability of resources and class size and composition. Shake (1989) offers suggestions for forming reading groups; and Wesson, Vierthaler, and Haubrich (1989) illustrate the use of competency-based measurement to form reading groups.

Studies generally report that teachers rely heavily on reading achievement indices when forming groups, but these findings are based primarily on data derived from having teachers make decisions about hypothetical cases. Shake

(1986a) reports that in a natural setting, the two most frequently used criteria for grouping are the recommendations of previous teachers (perhaps this is one reason why group membership rarely changes) and standardized test scores. Classroom teachers rely more heavily on the former; Chapter I and resource-room teachers, on the latter.

Based on interviews with 60 intermediate-grade teachers, Haller and Waterman (1985) conclude that it is misleading to think of reading groups merely as "ability groups." It would be more accurate to say that students are grouped according to their perceived capacity to profit from a preferred instructional strategy; with "capacity to profit" being a function of factors other than just aptitude, such as work habits, class-room behavior, personality variables, and home background. For instance, if a group is expected to work frequently without teacher supervision, the student's ability to work independently might become crucial in making a grouping decision. Or, if the group members would be working on a joint project, personality variables might determine placement.

Low SES and minority-group children often are assigned to low reading groups. But because reading achievement, SES, race, and cultural background are so intercorrelated, it is not clear which of these factors, or combination of factors, teachers are responding to when they form reading groups. Haller (1985) concludes that the association of race with reading-group assignment reflects pedagogical, and not racial, bias. Teachers assign students to groups in the belief that they will benefit most from the instruction provided in those groups. Dreeben (1987) reaches a similar conclusion. Haller, however, cautions that his conclusion pertains only to grouping decisions. It is possible to be unbiased in forming reading groups, and then to treat those groups in a biased manner.

FLEXIBILITY IN GROUPING.   Membership in a reading group seems to be relatively permanent (Hiebert 1983). And although various opinions have been offered as to why this situation exists, there is little clear evidence. Nevertheless, grouping should have some flexibility which can be of two main kinds.

Changing Group Placements.   Group membership should be reviewed periodically, and children should be moved to a new group whenever such a change would better meet their needs. Children differ in their rates of progress; some outgrow a low group, while others are unable to keep up with the top group. Sometimes a child who has been floundering as the poorest reader in a group gets a new lease on life as one of the best readers in a lower group. Similarly, a child who glides through group assignments with a minimum of effort may respond with redoubled energy to the challenge of working at a higher level of difficulty. In making such decisions it is often desirable to consult the children and respect their desires concerning group placement.

Using Different Groupings Simultaneously.   At least two different kinds of groupings should be in operation. In classes with a wide range of ability, grouping for developmental reading should be done according to reading level, with some use of special-needs grouping. Grouping for functional reading can often be in heterogeneous groups, especially if a project or activity unit plan is followed. Both recreational and functional reading provide opportunities for setting up interest groupings. When children belong to various groups, the possibility of developing a rigid caste system in which the poorest readers become "untouchables" is held to a minimum.

One must avoid assuming that flexibility is an end in itself, because that leads to changing groupings just for the sake of change. Under such a system, it is hard to see how either the teacher or the children will be able to settle down and get much work done. Flexibility has value when it improves learning conditions and social interrelations, but too much change can be as undesirable as too little.

EFFECTS OF GROUP PLACEMENT.   Grouping is thought by some to produce adverse affective outcomes, especially for children in low groups, but the causal relationship between reading-group placement and children's self-concepts and attitudes is unresolved (Hiebert 1983). Research does not indicate whether pupils' negative attitudes toward reading create a lack of interest in reading that contributes to lower group placement or whether lower group placement fosters negative attitudes toward self and reading. Membership in the same reading group increases the likelihood that pupils will become good friends. This unintentional consequence of grouping has possible advantages and disadvantages (Hallinan & Sørensen 1985).

There is evidence that teachers exhibit different behaviors and provide different instruction to high and low reading groups. Flexibility in procedures and assignments and more individualized follow-up tend to mark the lesson for high groups. Low groups tend to get highly structured lessons and assignments (Borko, Shavelson & Stern 1981). High groups receive more meaning-related (comprehension) activities, have their attention called to semantic cues when they make word-recognition errors, and do more silent than oral reading. Low groups tend to get more word-recognition and decoding instruction and practice, to have their attention called to grapho-phonemic cues when they err, and to do more oral than silent reading. Some writers suggest that the low achievers would become better readers if they were instructed in the same manner as good readers. However, no research evidence backs this claim, and perhaps differentiated instruction may be appropriate to meet differing needs. It is also possible, that the quality of instruction is more important than or just as important as the instructional content.

Other writers argue that differences in group treatment create the increasing discrepancy between good and poor readers as they progress through school. Apart from the fact that alternative explanations are possible, there is little information as to how this widening gap relates to differences in the experiences the reading groups have.

Teachers vary the rate at which they pace groups, but the appropriateness of that pacing is open to question. Some studies have found that teachers spend more time with high groups; other studies have not. Other studies have found that (1) teachers allow fewer interruptions when working with high groups; (2) low groups are given less time to respond to questions; (3) low groups are less frequently engaged in assigned tasks; and (4) teachers spend more time dealing with behavior and attention problems in low groups (Hiebert 1983). The latter two findings are often interpreted to indicate that children in low groups have shorter attention spans and more behavior problems. But other explanations are possible. Some pupils are in low groups because they have behavior or attention problems rather than low reading ability. Also, off-task behavior is influenced by the difficulty of the material for the child, and there is some evidence that poor readers are often given material that is comparatively more difficult for them to read than is the case for good readers.

GROUP DYNAMICS.   The manner in which group members interact with one another and the teacher can influence learning (Webb 1982). It is therefore important that the teacher understands the nature of these interactions and attempts to assure that each member plays an active, fulfilling role. The ways in which the teacher treats the group overall and its members individually, as well as the teacher's attitude toward them, can affect group participation and how children feel about themselves and others.

EQUIPMENT AND MATERIALS.   A classroom should be large enough so that the groups can be separated physically, and classroom furniture should be movable so that it can be arranged in different patterns. For any group activity involving intercommunication, the group should be seated so that everyone can see everyone else; a rectangular arrangement with desks pushed together as if to make a large table and a circle or semicircle of chairs are often used. A large area of chalkboard and bulletin board is desirable. There should be convenient shelving for books and supplies. A library corner should have in it not only space for books but also a table and chairs to encourage browsing and a colorful display of books or book jackets. These are desirable features, but none is absolutely essential.

Materials for a rich, well-rounded reading program should include the following:

1. Sets of basal readers or other materials, in numbers appropriate for the groups using them, ranging in difficulty appropriate for the lowest to the highest group.
2. A classroom library of at least 50 books, covering a wide range in difficulty and interest appeal and changed at least several times during the year. Children's magazines should also be part of the classroom library.
3. Reference works, including picture dictionaries and various dictionaries. Above the primary grades, there also should be an encyclopedia set, atlases, an almanac, and the like.
4. Workbooks that accompany the reading series and others not correlated with the series. Without these, the teacher has the additional burden of creating or duplicating seatwork.
5. Special teacher-devised materials, to fill gaps in the available commercial materials.
6. Materials that are self-administering and/or self-correcting. These may include programmed materials, computer software, boxes of exercises with answer keys, and commercial or teacher-prepared lessons on tape.
7. Individual and group reading games that can be used when an assignment is finished early.

8. Related pictures, filmstrips, slides, tapes, recordings, and movies to help provide ideational background.

In a school where supplies are meager, the teacher can provide some differentiated instruction in reading, but it is unquestionably easiest to do so with sufficient materials.

Choosing Reading Materials.   In most plans for grouping by reading levels, at least two different reading textbooks are required: one of below-grade difficulty and one of normal difficulty for the grade. The below-grade book should be at an instructional level appropriate for the low group. If there are middle and high groups, it is probably better for them to use different books, with the high group using either a comparatively difficult basal reader intended for that grade or a reader intended for the next higher grade. It is also possible to teach effectively with the middle and high groups using the same basal. In that case, the high group is given less preparation, works more independently, moves more rapidly, and has more time for supplementary and independent reading.

Some school systems use one reading series for low groups, another for middle groups, and a third series for high groups, through the grades. This has the advantage that no group has heard a story read and discussed by another group before getting to it. In such a plan, the teacher has to keep track of the skills covered in each group so that children who change groups will not miss any important reading skills. In the lower grades the frequent lack of overlapping vocabulary among reading series must be considered when a child changes groups.

Some teachers lose practically all the potential benefits of grouping by levels by having all groups use the same basal reader. This is probably even less efficient than whole-class instruction, for not only are most of the children using material too easy or too hard for best results but the amount of direct instruction each child receives is less than in whole-class instruction. For ability grouping to be reasonably effective, the reader must be suitable in difficulty for at least a majority of the group.

One of the major sources of difficulty in group management arises from giving a group a basal reader that is too difficult. This encourages restlessness, inattention, excessive requests for help, and misbehavior; what is more important, children are much less likely to progress in reading achievement.

ASSIGNMENTS.   While the teacher is working directly with one group, the other groups must have definite assignments that they can carry on without help from the teacher.

In the earliest grades, one or more groups often are unable to carry on any kind of reading activity without the active participation of the teacher. When this is the case, reading can be alternated with other activities that the children are able to carry on independently (e.g., coloring or cutting out pictures). These activities can be combined with reading in a rotating plan so that the group reads only when the teacher is with them and engages in quiet self-directed activities when the teacher is with another group. This procedure is essential in first grade and is sometimes needed in higher grades for one or more groups.

Before starting the group activities of the day, teachers should take a few minutes to clarify the specific assignments for each group. Members of a group should always have supplementary activities to which they can turn if they finish an assignment before the end of a period. For each group, have a chart that the group members can consult if they forget what to do next. With such a plan, it should be easy for the group to keep busy for a 30- or 40-minute period.

Interference between groups should be kept at a minimum. When working with a group, teachers should keep their voices low; the children soon learn to speak and work quietly also. Routines for distributing and collecting books, workbooks, paper, and other supplies quietly and efficiently need to be developed and practiced.

TIME SCHEDULE.   It is necessary to consider with care the total amount of time to be devoted to the reading program each day and each week, the duration of reading periods, and appropriate spacing of reading periods in the school day. In the primary grades the developmental reading program should take about 90 to 120 minutes a day. From fourth grade on, the amount of time specifically scheduled for developmental and recreational reading decreases grade by grade, but the amount of time spent in functional reading in a variety of curricular fields more than makes up the difference.

Each teacher has to experiment to determine the length of time that seems to work best with a particular group. When periods are too short, so much time is spent in getting materials out, warming up to the task, and putting things away again that inefficiency results. When periods are too long, children get fatigued or bored, and their increasing restlessness and noise signal an alert teacher that effective learning has stopped. Young children need shorter periods than older children. In consequence, the teacher may find it desirable to have two or three short periods a day with a group, rather than one long one. Periods devoted to easy, pleasurable activities can be relatively prolonged; periods requiring intense concentration on difficult tasks should be comparatively brief. Reading can be scheduled for both morning and afternoon.

The psychology of learning indicates that it is efficient to separate periods of similar activity by periods in which different activities are carried on. In planning a reading program it would seem desirable to interpolate nonreading activities between reading periods or to follow one reading activity by a quite different kind of reading activity.

Many teachers plan their reading as a solid block of an hour or more, during which they work with each group in turn. Reading instruction can be provided for a group while the rest of the class is working independently on other curricular activities.

There is disagreement as to whether differential amounts of time should be allotted to groups of varying abilities. Some argue that all should get approximately equal time, others that low-ability groups should receive the most instructional time because without it they will not reach their potential. Yet others contend that the best readers should have the most instructional time, because they are our future leaders. The debate is based on opinion, and any decisions about differential time allotments reflect value judgments and not research evidence.

GROUP NAMES.   Some teachers are concerned about what to call their groups. They think of them as "the high group" or "the low group," but they realize it would be bad for morale to use such terms with the children. Numbering groups is not desirable for the same reason. The assignment of names that imply relative size, speed, or competence is to be avoided. Teachers should be sensitive to the feelings of children about the traits implied by group names. Children are aware of the comparative proficiencies of groups. "The teacher calls us the red, white, and blue groups, but she might as well call us the fruits, vegetables, and nuts." Choosing names wisely does not eliminate this awareness; it merely avoids rubbing it in.

One way to select group names is to allow each group to choose its own name. During a unit on American Indians, for example, the groups may wish to choose the names of Indian tribes. This procedure avoids the dangers cited above.

Perhaps the best way of treating this problem is to make it as casual as possible. Thus, groups with chairpersons can be referred to as Billy's group or Annette's group, or the group can be named according to the title or the color of the cover of the book it is currently using. The less fuss made about group names, the better.

INDIVIDUALIZING INSTRUCTION WITHIN A GROUP.   Even though the children in a group may be reading at the same general level and using the same material, it is possible to individualize instruction, albeit to a lesser extent than under other procedures. Apart from the use of various other kinds of groups, the teacher can tailor instruction before, during, and after the lesson. Before the lesson, the teacher can develop the necessary background experience for reading a story only for those who need it or excuse those who have met the objective(s) of the lesson. During the lesson, she can match question difficulty to individual children's reading and reasoning abilities. The time given to respond also can be adjusted. In the follow-up stage, the teacher can make differing assignments in skill development and enrichment activities and allow varying amounts of time to complete the assignments.

USE OF STUDENT AND ADULT ASSISTANTS.   Students within the class, older students, and teacher aides may be used to assist teachers in individualizing instruction.

Chairpersons, Helpers, and Tutors.   In many group activities, pupils can act as group leaders, making it unnecessary for the teacher to be with the group for that activity. Often a few of the best readers are assigned to be leaders of less capable groups. Sometimes this privilege is rotated among several children so that no child gets conceited or misses too much of his or her own group's reading activities. An alternative is to let each group select its own chairperson, or to have the privilege rotate among members of the group, with each child having a turn. A chairperson who is a member of a group is often accepted with better grace than a leader who comes from another group. When a group is not yet able to function without help, it may be possible to have a chairperson from within the group, who assigns turns to read and keeps order, and a helper from a higher group who can supply assistance.

Helpers can be used during silent reading or workbook practice, as well as during oral reading. One child can be the helper for a group, or each child who needs help may be allowed to select another child as a personal helper; the helper and the child helped may be assigned adjacent seats.

Children do not naturally know how to be effective chairpersons or helpers. Sometimes they give too much help or too little, or they become officious or sarcastic. It is desirable to train helpers or chairpersons for their jobs, and it is certainly necessary to keep an eye on how they carry out their functions.

A study of peer-directed groups (Wilkinson & Calculator 1982) reveals that, in general, first graders are effective in making requests and receiving appropriate responses. Typically their requests were direct, sincere, on-task, and to a designated listener. However, the system worked less well for low-ability children.

Capable students may also be used to tutor other pupils. Peer tutoring has been shown to be effective (see page 414).

Teacher Aides. Sometimes it is possible to have two or more adults present during reading instruction. The extra people may be student teachers, volunteers, or paid teaching aides. Team teaching also makes possible situations in which more than one group at a time has adult leadership. Careful planning and supervision are necessary to ensure that what teacher aides and paraprofessionals do is beneficial to the learning of the children (see page 415).

Suggestions for Effective Teaching of Groups

Among the research-supported techniques for working with groups are the following (Brophy 1979a, 1986):

1. Use a standard and predictable signal to obtain the group's attention.
2. Teach the students to move immediately into their reading group, to bring the appropriate materials, and to make quick, orderly transitions between activities.
3. Seat the pupils in the group with their backs to the rest of the class; the teacher should face all of the class members.
4. Introduce the lesson with an overview of what is to come; this prepares the students for the presentation.
5. Demonstrate or explain any new activity before asking the children to do it.
6. Work with one child at a time when students have been asked to practice a new skill or to apply a new concept. Make sure everyone is checked and receives feedback and any needed follow-up.
7. Give the students frequent opportunities to read and to respond to questions. Give them clear feedback as to the appropriateness of their responses.
8. After asking a question, wait for the student to respond. If the child does not respond within a reasonable time (see p. 574), indicate that

some response is expected. In such instances, and when the answer is unacceptable, use a simplification procedure; do not ask another child to respond. The simplification procedure depends on the task. If the answer to the question is explictedly stated in the text (no reasoning is required), attempt to cue the child. If this does not work quickly, give the child the answer. If reasoning is involved, explain the steps to go through in arriving at the answer in addition to giving the answer itself.

9. Make sure other pupils do not call out the answer. When call-outs occur, remind the offender that everyone gets a turn and that everyone must wait for a turn.

10. Acknowledge correct responses (e.g., with a positive nod), unless their correctness is obvious. At times, emphasize the methods used to arrive at an appropriate response; this may help students who did not understand how it was done. Occasionally ask follow-up questions of the same pupil in order to help him or her to integrate information or to extend a line of questions to their logical conclusions.

11. Make sure the pupils know what to do and how to accomplish their assignments. Before releasing a group to work independently, have them demonstrate how they will accomplish their activities.

12. For students who are working independently, provide appropriate assignments, rules, and routines to follow when they need help (this minimizes interference when the teacher is working with a group), and activities which they can choose to do after completing an assignment.

McKenzie (1975) suggests ways to personalize group teaching, such as making eye contact and commenting favorably on a child's response or participation. He also provides ways to involve all group members in responding nonverbally to a question. For example, after a child responds, the teacher can say, "If you agree, raise your hand," or the children can hold up "Agree" or "Disagree" cards. In either case, it is important for the teacher to look at each child to see if a response has been made.

Reading Stations

Reading or learning stations also may be employed in differentiating reading instruction. Each station that provides for a different activity usually accommodates a maximum of five or six pupils at once, all of whom need not be working on exactly the same activity. Activities are geared to the needs and interests of individual students and need not all be directly related to reading. Whenever possible, materials used at a station should be self-administering and self-scoring. Assignments may be made according to a rotational schedule, as shown in Figure 5.2

Teacher assignments (e.g., guided reading in a textbook or workbook, teacher-pupil conference), free choice by students (e.g., recreational reading, reading games), and random assignments (e.g., using the school library) may be combined. Practical suggestions for conducting reading stations are provided by Thompson and Merritt (1975), and by Meints (1977) who describes adapting the learning-station concept for use in high school.

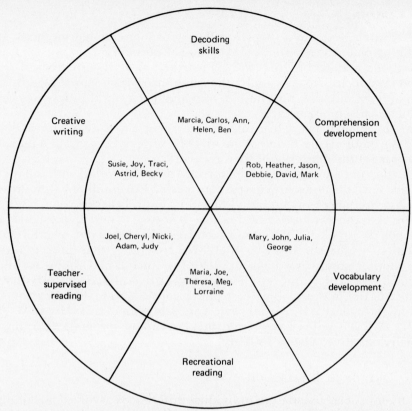

Figure 5.2.   Rotational scheduling. The rotating outer circle indicates the assignment; the inner circle shows the students selected for that activity. Adapted from E. Duval, R. Johnson, and J. Litcher, Learning stations and the reading class, in R. A. Earle (Ed.), *Classroom practice in reading* (Newark, DE: International Reading Association, 1977). The authors also provided sample forms for student recordkeeping and self-evaluations. Reproduced by permission of the authors and the International Reading Association.

INSTRUCTIONAL PROCEDURES

A number of instructional procedures attempt to accomodate individual differences to varying degrees. Many of these were discussed in Chapter 3. For example, Individualized Developmental Reading attempts to individualize every aspect of the reading program. Linearly programmed materials vary the pace at which pupils may proceed through the program, but not the program itself. Through branching, computer-assisted instruction may allow for greater individualization than programmed materials; when an incorrect response is made, the computer explains why the answer is wrong, what the correct reply is and why, and presents new material designed to help the child learn that skill or strategy. Skills management systems try to individualize instruction by having pupils work only on skills they have not mastered; pacing is also an individual matter. Two other instructional procedures are discussed here—mastery learning and aptitude-treatment interactions.

Mastery Learning

Mastery learning refers to a diverse category of instructional methods, but its chief defining characteristics are: (1) setting a criterion for mastery; (2) frequent assessment of students' progress toward mastery; and (3) corrective instruction as needed (Slavin 1987d). Generally the same instruction is received by all the students, at least initially, but the rate at which each pupil progresses through the instructional sequence varies.

In group-based mastery learning, the class or group is instructed at the same pace, and the students are tested at the end of a series of lessons or a unit. Those who do not meet the mastery criterion receive corrective help, and are retested. Those who do either are allowed to go forward or are provided with independent assignments until the nonachievers display mastery. In continuous-progress mastery learning, students work on individual units entirely at their own rate.

There is some evidence that mastery learning is effective for low-ability pupils (Good & Stipek 1983), but research findings are mixed, as are reviewers interpretations of the studies. Slavin (1987d) concludes that there is little evidence to support group-based mastery learning since it had almost no effect on standardized test scores and only moderate positive effects on tests that were closely tied to the mastery objectives under consideration. Slavin's conclusion differs from those drawn by earlier reviewers, and is challenged by L. W. Anderson (1987). A few studies have found that continuous-progress learning is instructionally effective (Slavin 1987b).

Aptitude-Treatment Interaction

Another attempt at accomodating individual differences involves matching a pupil's specific learning characteristics (aptitude) with a particular instructional method or setting (treatment); thus the term *aptitude-treatment interaction* (ATI). Instruction is adapted to capitalize on the individual's strengths or preferences and to minimize reliance on weaknesses. In theory, effectively matching learner aptitude with appropriate instructional treatment should result in improved learning.

Few reliable aptitude-treatment interactions have been found (Reynolds 1988). Among the possible reasons for a lack of positive findings are the following. ATI studies are methodologically complex and fraught with interpretation problems (Cronbach & Snow 1977), although some progress is being made in these areas. Most ATI studies suffer from methodological problems (C. Smith 1986). ATI theories assume that individuals differ in the degree to which they possess abilities thought to underlie learning, or that individuals differ in their approaches to learning, or that students are differentially influenced by instructional methods or settings. But we are a long way from being able to identify which pupil traits contribute to the need for differentiated instruction, and even a longer way from being able to measure these traits adequately. ATI is also predicated on the assumption that various instructional methods place significantly different demands on the learner. Such an assumption may not be valid. Furthermore, we are only beginning to understand the nature of effective instruction, and alternative treatments probably are not equally effective regardless of student traits (Zigmond & Miller 1986).

Refer to the indicated pages for opinions and research findings regarding ATI: beginning reading instruction (page 90), cognitive and learning styles (pages 287–289), and word recognition (pages 497–498).

ATI theory is logical, and there is sufficient evidence that not all pupils learn in the same way or respond equally to various instructional methods. ATI may be a valid but difficult-to-prove theory. Most ATI studies have compared the interactions of one or two aptitude variables (usually based on gross measures, using tests of questionable validity and reliability) and one or two treatments (almost always described only in general terms and in which such variables as instructional quality were not controlled). Comparisons of group data may have masked the effects on individuals (C. Smith 1986).

Although research findings do not support the application of ATI theory to groups of students, they do not rule out attempts to determine how a particular student learns best. When a pupil's reading progress is inadequate after a reasonable period of instruction, use of an alternate instructional method or strategy should be seriously considered.

Trial teaching may aid in this endeavor, but whatever the instruction, it is advisable to carefully monitor what does and does not work, to analyze the task demands when instruction is ineffective and to adjust future instruction accordingly.

COMBINING WHOLE-CLASS, GROUP, AND INDIVIDUALIZED READING

The plans described in this section suggest ways in which a sequential program of reading instruction, in groups based on reading level, can be combined with whole-class activities, groups based on special needs, groups based on common interests, and periods of individualized reading. Teachers who want to try more individualization than is provided in these plans can do it in more than one way. For example:

1. The reading activities of one group can be individualized. This is easiest to do with the best readers. They can often finish the on-grade reading textbook(s) early in the spring; for the rest of the year they can be given individualized reading. Sometimes the poorest readers are just too different from one another to be taught as a group, requiring that their reading instruction also be individualized.
2. Additional periods of individualized reading can be provided for the entire class, devoting more total time to the reading program.
3. It is possible to alternate days of group instruction with days of individualized reading. This plan, maintaining the program of systematic instruction but incorporating much more individualized reading than is common at present, deserves serious consideration.

Illustrative One-Week Plans

Classes at the same grade level vary tremendously, and so it is impossible to present a plan for a given grade that will suit all classes. The plans described in

Low Group (pre-primer)		Middle Group (primer)		High Group (first reader)

Whole Class: Directions and assignments to each group daily.

MONDAY

Low Group		Middle Group		High Group
	Nonreading activities	*T*	Preparation for new story	Independent reading
T	Preparation for new story		Teacher-prepared seatwork or workbook	Workbook
	Teacher-prepared seatwork or nonreading activities		Cut pictures from old magazines for picture dictionary	*T* Check workbook; preparations for new story

Whole Class: Teach symbol–sound association *m* = /m/. Teacher reads story.

TUESDAY

Low Group		Middle Group		High Group
	Visual-discrimination seatwork	*T*	Guided reading and discussion	Silent reading of story-workbook
T	Guided reading and discussion		Workbook	Supplementary reading or nonreading activities
	Workbook or nonreading activities		Paste pictures in picture dictionary	*T* Check workbook; discussion of story and selective oral reading

Whole Class: Teacher reads a poem. Children volunteer poems and rhymes. Children listen for rhyming words that teacher lists.

WEDNESDAY

Low Group		Middle Group		High Group
	Nonreading activities	*T*	Oral rereading; check workbook	Independent reading; word games
T	Oral rereading; check workbook		Duplicated seatwork	Nonreading activities
	Word games or nonreading activities		Draw a picture about the story	*T* Preparation for new story

Whole Class: Review symbol–sound association of *m*. Introduce symbol–sound association *p* = /p/. Choral reading of duplicated poem read by teacher on Tuesday.

Figure 5.3. A three-group plan for the middle of the first grade. *T* indicates the group with which the teacher is working. Each of the three daily periods is scheduled for 20–30 minutes; the whole-class period lasts about 30 minutes.

Low Group (pre-primer)		Middle Group (primer)	High Group (first reader)

THURSDAY

Low Group (pre-primer)		Middle Group (primer)	High Group (first reader)
	Cut pictures from magazines	*T* Check seatwork; related skills: decoding, comprehension	Independent reading workbook
T	Related skills: decoding, comprehension	Labeling pictures for picture dictionary	Word games or nonreading activities
	Draw a picture about the story	Duplicated seatwork	*T* Check workbook; discussion of story and selective oral reading

Whole Class: Develop experience story; practice reading it. Review the two new symbol–sound associations.

FRIDAY

Low Group (pre-primer)		Middle Group (primer)	High Group (first reader)
	High-utility word games with high group	*T* Check seatwork; preparation for new story	Team with low group for high-utility word games
T	Preparation for new story	Nonreading activities	Word games or nonreading activities
	Visual-discrimination seatwork	Silent rereading in preparation for dramatization	*T* Check seatwork; preparation for new story

Whole Class: Review the two symbol–sound associations introduced during the week. One group dramatizes a story; teacher reads a story.

Figure 5.3.   *(continued)*

Figure 5.3 are intended to be used as sources for ideas, not as specifications to be followed exactly.

In these specimen plans an attempt has been made to adhere to five basic principles: (1) Each plan combines reading by groups with some whole-class and some individualized or independent reading; (2) the teacher is with the group for those activities for which she or he is most needed; (3) expectations concerning what a group may be able to do without the teacher (but with a chairman or helper) is realistic; (4) length of periods has some relationship to the maturity of the children; and (5) all groups get a reasonable share of the teacher's attention.

Figure 5.3 shows a sample plan for the middle of the first grade. In the figure are three periods for group work or team learning and one whole-class period every day. Both developmental reading activities and some other kinds of reading and nonreading activities are included. The plan assumes that the

Very Low Group	Low Group	Middle Group	High Group

Whole Class: Directions and assignments given to each group daily as needed.

MONDAY

Very Low Group	Low Group	Middle Group	High Group
Individualized developmental reading	Silent reading of story introduced Friday	*T* Discussion and purposeful rereading of story read silently on Friday	Related workbook *GC* Check workbook
	T Discussion and purposeful rereading	Related workbook	Independent reading

Whole Class: Read and discuss different editions (levels) of weekly newspaper.

TUESDAY

Very Low Group	Low Group	Middle Group	High Group
T Teacher–pupil conferences	Related workbook *TA* Check workbook, reread and verify answers	*GC* Check workbook; related decoding and comprehension skills	Silent reading of new story (no preparation)

TA Special-needs groups; rest of class reads independently.

Whole Class: Independent reading; teacher and aide circulate, providing help as needed.

WEDNESDAY

Very Low Group	Low Group	Middle Group	High Group
TA Individualized skill practice	*GC* Plan story dramatization	*T* Check seatwork; preparation for new story	Comprehension exercises from independent workbook; self-correction
	T Check plan for dramatization; preparation for new story	Silent reading of new story	Independent reading

Whole Class: Using dictionary guide words.

Figure 5.4. A four-group plan for a heterogeneous middle grade. Periods are 20–30 minutes each. *T* = teacher works with group; *TA* = teacher aide works with group; *GC* = activity led by group chairperson.

Very Low Group	Low Group	Middle Group	High Group
		THURSDAY	
Individualized developmental reading	Silent reading of new story	*T* Discussion and purposeful reading	Independent reading
↓	*TA* Discussion and purposeful rereading	Related workbook	*T* Discussion of two stories

Whole Class: Special-interest and research groups.

		FRIDAY	
T Teacher–pupil conferences	*TA* Rehearse dramatization	*GC* Check workbook; reread to verify answers	Critical reading exercises
			T Discussion of critical reading exercises

Word-recognition and vocabulary games (team learning)

Whole Class (afternoon): Book Club meeting, audience reading, choral reading of poetry, dramatization, group reports.

Figure 5.4. *(continued)*

high group can do some independent reading in easy books that are below their instructional level but that the low and middle groups require teacher guidance for nearly all reading activities. Some workbook and seatwork periods are scheduled without the teacher, on the assumption that a teacher aide or pupil helper can be with the group; if this is not possible, there would need to be additional periods of nonreading activities for these groups, and it would take a day or two longer to complete each story.

Directions should be given to all groups at the beginning of the school day. At the start of each group period, the teacher should spend a short time with each group making sure that they have the right materials and know what to do.

The low group is guided by the teacher through the essential steps of a typical basal-reader developmental teaching plan: preparation, guided reading and discussion, oral rereading, and related skills. The group has several periods of nonreading activities but may be able to do workbook and seatwork pages with an aide or helper.

The middle group also has teacher direction through the cycle of preparation, guided reading and discussion, oral rereading, and related skills. Without the teacher, this group does workbook pages and cuts, pastes, and labels entries for a picture dictionary. The group probably needs a helper for these activities. Nonreading activities fill in the gaps.

The high group has teacher guidance for preparation, discussion of story and oral reading, and checking workbook and seatwork pages. On its own, this group does silent reading in the reader, workbook exercises, and seatwork, as well as some individualized independent reading.

Whole-class activities include work on decoding skills, the teacher reading to the class, choral reading, experience stories, and dramatization of stories. Decoding skills introduced and reviewed with the whole class have additional review during "related skills" periods for the low and middle groups.

A plan appropriate for an intermediate-grade class with a wide range of reading ability is shown in Figure 5.4. There are two daily periods for group or individualized activities and one whole-class period. The plan covers developmental reading; much additional time should be scheduled for reading in other curricular areas. Independent (recreational) reading is scheduled for all four groups. This plan makes use of a teacher aide who is available 3 days a week and group chairpersons. If a teacher aide is not available, the plan will need to be adjusted. The teacher or teacher aide works with the lowest group three times a week, with the low group four times, the middle group three times, and the high group twice a week.

Because the reading levels of the lowest group are so diverse, an individualized developmental reading approach is used. Emphasis is placed on developing needed basic skills in both individual teacher-pupil conferences and skill-practice activities.

The low group uses a below-grade-level reading textbook, and most of the group's work is closely supervised. Group members do not require the teacher's direct supervision for silent reading or for workbook and seatwork pages. The privilege of presenting a story dramatization should rotate among the groups.

The middle group, which uses the on-grade textbook, is scheduled for more self-directed reading than is the low group. The teacher is with the group for preparation, discussion, and purposeful rereading. Group members in the top three groups are expected to carry on certain activities with a group chairperson and to fill in with independent reading or other quiet activities when they complete an assignment early.

The high group uses an above-grade-level reader. Group members are expected to be able to read a selection silently without teacher-directed preparation or with a very abbreviated preparation during the giving of assignments. Workbooks are corrected by group members, either independently or under the direction of the group chairperson.

The whole-class periods accommodate a wide range of activities, not all of which can be shown in one plan and not all of which would be scheduled every week. This plan shows current-events reading. Special-needs groups and special-interest groups can be fitted into periods when most of the class is doing independent reading or other self-directed activities, or are at reading stations.

A wide range of suggestions has been presented in this chapter for accommodating individual differences in reading ability. Each school and teacher must decide what combination of procedures best produces the desired results. Whatever plan is adopted, its success will depend on the effectiveness of the teachers and their understanding of students as individuals; the support and cooperation of the school administration, parents, and community; and the desire of the students to learn.

6

What Is Reading Disability?

This chapter is the first of five concerned with the nature and diagnosis of reading disabilities. It begins with a brief history of reading disability and a discussion of its incidence. We provide a brief glossary which explains commonly used terms and pay particular attention to *dyslexia* and *learning disabilities*. The final section describes and explains various objective ways to define reading disability.

READING DISABILITY

A Brief Historical Overview

Reading failure and attempts to remediate it date back to the early seventeenth century (Pelosi 1977).[1] But the first case of reading disability was published in 1896 by Morgan, a British ophthalmologist. It describes a 14-year-old boy who had not learned to read, although he had normal intelligence. In keeping with his professional background, Morgan used the term *congenital word blindness* to describe the boy's condition. Another prominent early investigator was Hinshelwood (1900, 1917), a Glasgow eye surgeon, whose monographs attracted international attention. This early interest on the part of the medical profession in reading disability attracted little notice from psychologists and educators.

Uhl (1916) published the first report in the United States of an attempt to diagnose individual reading problems and prescribe treatment. The following year, Bronner (1917) made some interesting observations about reading problems. Schmitt (1918) described a practical phonic method for teaching nonreaders and Fernald and Keller (1921) outlined the kinesthetic method. C. T. Gray

[1]Historical developments in reading diagnosis and remediation may be found in A. J. Harris (1968), Critchley (1970), and Pelosi (1981). Refer to Hallihan and Cruickshank (1973) for a detailed history, or to Kavale and Forness (1985b) for a brief history, of learning disabilities. Monaghan (1980) provides a history of dyslexia and its treatment. A history of remedial reading in the secondary school is presented by Cowan (1977), and Cook (1977) traces the history of adult literacy in America.

(1922) and W. S. Gray (1922) published the first two books on reading disability in America, and Gates (1927) developed the first battery of diagnostic reading tests. All of these authors were psychologists or educators.

Although reading disability received a little notice from American physicians as early as 1906, it was the work of S. T. Orton (1937), a neurologist, that first attracted wide attention. Orton recognized that there were multiple causes for delays in learning to read, but believed that "*the* reading disability" was due to a failure of one cerebral hemisphere to establish clear dominance over the other.[2]

At the University of Chicago and Boston University, clinics specializing in reading difficulties became the first centers for training reading specialists and remedial teachers. New York City began the first large-scale remedial reading program in a public school system in the mid-1930s, as a federal work project of the depression era. Some secondary schools initiated remedial reading programs after World War II when they became aware of the large number of illiterates in the military forces; remedial reading programs dominated at the secondary school level during the late 1940s and early 1950s (Cowan 1977).

From about 1935 to 1955, psychoanalysts, psychiatrists, and clinical psychologists sought to explain reading disability as a symptom of emotional disturbance, and so tended to recommend psychotherapy as the preferred treatment. But the direction of a cause-effect relationship could not be established and, psychotherapy alone seemed to help only a small minority of disabled readers.

Since 1955, interest in determining the causes of and the best ways to remediate reading disabilities has grown. During the 1960s and early 1970s, neurologists and special educators proposed that the cause of reading disability was an underlying neurological or physiological defect. These theorists placed less emphasis than others on emotional and educational causes. During this time, terms such as *dyslexia* and *learning disability* came into prominence. The late 1970s and the 1980s have seen efforts by psycholinguists, linguists, neuropsychologists, and particularly cognitive psychologists to understand the reading process and thereby to gain insight into the factors that contribute to reading disability. New and more sophisticated equipment and procedures have sparked renewed interest from the medical profession.

The Incidence of Reading Disability

For several reasons, definitive information on the prevalence of reading disability is not available. First, the definitions used to indicate the populations (e.g., reading retardation, dyslexia, specific reading disability) vary considerably. Second, even when similar terms are employed, the criteria used to set a cutoff point has varied from one investigator to another. Finally, populations differ, and factors such as age of school entrance, socio-economic background, method of teaching, and degree of regularity in the symbol-sound relationships of the language produce variations. Moreover, the reported percentages are rarely based on adequate samples. The reported incidence of disability has increased

[2]Orton's theory is discussed on page 319.

as the defining criteria were broadened and as the level of severity assumed to be disabling decreased.

Estimates of reading disability reported for various countries range from virtually none in Taiwan (Kuo 1978) and Korea (Taylor 1980) to 1% in Japan (Makita 1968), 2% in Czechoslovakia (Matějček 1976), 2–3% in Russia (Chabe 1983), approximately 5% in Denmark (Jansen et al. 1976) and Norway (Vik 1976), 8% in Sweden (Malmquist 1958) and West Germany (Weinschenk et al. 1970), 10% in England (Newton 1970) and Finland (Syvälahti 1976), 13% in Israel (Gross 1978), 14% in Argentina (de Quiros & Della Cella 1959), 15% in Scotland (Clark 1970, 1979), 16% in Ireland (Swan 1978), and as high as 22% (4% having "severe dyslexia") in Austria (Schenk-Danziger 1960). That such estimates are open to question can be illustrated by the varying percentages reported for the same countries by other authors. For example, instead of 8% in West Germany, Klasen (1976) reports estimates of from 2% to 20%; Gorriti and Muñiz (1976) report 10% to 25% for Argentina rather than 14%; and Hulme (1981b) concludes that less than 4% of English children experience severe reading problems as compared with the 10% reported by Newton (1970).

A comprehensive survey of available evidence of the incidence of reading disabilities in the United States concludes that about 10% to 15% of American schoolchildren have reading disabilities. "Eight million children in America's elementary and secondary schools today will not learn to read adequately. One child in seven is handicapped in his ability to acquire essential reading skills. This phenomenon pervades all segments of our society—black and white, boys and girls, the poor and the affluent" (National Advisory Committee on Dyslexia and Related Disorders 1969, p. 7).

TERMINOLOGY

A Glossary of Terms[3]

The following glossary illustrates the confusion that exists in the literature. It also may serve as a useful reference. The terms used in this book are defined on pages 161–162.

- *Alexia:* (1) complete inability to read; (2) partial or total loss of ability to read, usually as a result of brain injury or disease; a form of aphasia.
- *Aphasia:* any receptive or expressive language disorder of neurological origin.
- *Backward reader:* an individual whose reading age (based on test scores) falls below the average performance of pupils of the same chronological age; intelligence or learning potential is *not* considered.
- *Brain damage, brain injury,* or *organic brain damage, brain lesion:* any injury to the brain structure (Strang 1968).
- *Congenital alexia:* synonym for developmental dyslexia.

[3]Refer to T. L. Harris and Hodges (1981) for a comprehensive listing and definitions of terms found in the reading and reading-related literature.

- *Congenital word blindness, word blindness:* synonym for dyslexia once favored by some medical writers (e.g., Hinshelwood 1917, Hermann 1964).
- *Dyslexia:* severe reading disability that may represent loss of reading competency following brain injury or degeneration, or it may represent a developmental failure to profit from reading instruction. Also employed broadly as a synonym for reading disability.
- *Hyperlexia:* a rare disorder, often associated with autism, in which word-recognition and decoding abilities occur before age 5 and remain very superior to reading comprehension. This disorder is usually characterized by markedly poor language, behavioral, and interpersonal skills. Hyperlexia may be a genetically-linked disorder (Healy 1982, Healy & Aram 1986).
- *Learning disability:* significant difficulty in the acquisition of listening, speaking, reading, spelling, writing, or arithmetic skills. Causation usually attributed to central nervous system deficits or dysfunctions. The disability is not the result of sensory impairment, mental retardation, emotional disturbance, or environmental influences.
- *Maturational lag:* slowness in certain specialized aspects of neurological development; concept introduced by Bender (1957).
- *Minimal brain damage* or *cerebral damage* or *dysfunction:* implies that causation is brain damage or disordered brain functioning, although clear evidence of damage or dysfunction is not present. Diagnosis is often based on "soft neurological signs" that are of doubtful validity.
- *Perceptually handicapped:* indicates a learning problem resulting from a perceptual disorder, most often noted as visual or auditory, or to a combination of disorders such as visual-motor.
- *Psycholinguistic learning disability:* weakness in processes believed necessary for learning to occur, as assessed by the *Illinois Test of Psycholinguistic Ability.*
- *Psychoneurological learning disability:* learning disability caused by a combination of psychological and neurological factors. This disability includes speech, writing, and nonverbal disabilities, as well as reading disabilities, and represents conditions in which the central nervous system is not functioning efficiently in sensorimotor, perceptual-motor, or language functions, whether because of genetic, maturational, or traumatic conditions; sociocultural deprivation; emotional problems; or a combination of some of these (D. J. Johnson & Myklebust 1967).
- *Reading difficulty* or *disorder:* synonym for reading disability; it may signify a mild to moderate degree of disability. Also used to refer to deficiency in a specific reading skill or strategy.
- *Reading disability:* reading achievement that is significantly below expectancy for both age and learning potential and is disparate with the learner's cultural, linguistic, and educational experience.
- *Reading retardation:* in the United States, reading achievement that is significantly below average and grade norms regardless of such factors as

learning potential. In England and for some medical writers, a synonym for reading disability as defined above.

- *Specific language disability:* concept similar to dyslexia but broadened to include spelling, writing, and speech problems referable to the same constitutional origin. Term often found in the Orton Dyslexia Society literature.

Cautions in Using Labels

Gallagher (1986) suggests that there are legitimate purposes for labeling pupils. He believes that studying groups with similar characteristics can lead to the discovery of the causes of the condition. Once causation is known, it may be possible to prevent or treat the condition.

Labels are commonly used in educational, psychological, and medical communities and a child must sometimes be labeled in order to be eligible for special treatment. However, there is increasing concern in educational and psychological circles regarding the possible negative impact of labeling. Labeling a child *may* result in lowered self-concept, rejection by peers, lowered levels of academic aspirations, biased responding by teachers and parents, or poor school adjustment (Palmer 1983). A movement based on the belief that labels are harmful suggests doing away with labeling and providing support for each child on an "as-needed" basis. A child who has a reading difficulty would thus be provided with the necessary educational and, if necessary, psychological services without being labeled as reading or learning disabled or dyslexic. Such a proposal calls for the blending of regular and special education and would necessitate the restructuring of existing teacher-training and school-delivery programs (see pp. 426–427). But it is unlikely that simply doing away with labels will result in quick, if any, significant changes in how pupils who vary from the norm are perceived, or in changed attitudes toward them. Even 10 years after traditional terms had been replaced by the generic term "students with special needs,"[4] their peers formed negative expectations concerning the academic abilities of students so identified. Special class placement can act as a *de facto* label (Bak et al. 1987).

Although teacher expectations are lower for labeled than nonlabeled pupils, the initial biasing effects of a label can be overcome if the teacher becomes aware that the student's actual performance is inconsistent with the label (Rolison & Medway 1985; Delclos, Burns & Kulewicz 1987). Such an awareness, however, is not likely to occur if the child is presented with low-level tasks that are in keeping with a misperceived level of ability.

Labeling a child *does not* constitute a diagnosis. As Samuels (1973b, p. 203) admonishes, labels are often pseudoexplanations:

> By identifying the problem, giving it a name, and putting the students into a diagnostic category, many educators and psychologists delude themselves into believing that they have gained insight into the causes of the problem. If we ask, "Why is the student failing in reading?" we often get the answer, "He is unable to learn because he has a learning disorder." This answer tells

---

[4] It could be argued that such a term is just as harmful a label as the ones it replaced.

us nothing about the actual sources of difficulty the students are experiencing. In fact, the answer implies circular reasoning since it is largely because of the presence of academic retardation that the label is ascribed.

      Actually, labels such as learning disorder, dyslexia, etc., provide no useful information as to why students are failing. . . . The labels do not in any way indicate where the student is having trouble, nor do they provide a clue as to how the difficulty may be overcome.

How children with reading problems are labeled and what type of instructional intervention they receive, if any, are influenced by various state and federal laws and policies. "Children experiencing reading failure may be defined quite differently depending on which school district they attend, in which state, and what financial constraints these are operating under" (McGill-Franzen 1987, p. 487).

Dyslexia

There is no unanimity concerning the meaning of *dyslexia* (T. L. Harris & Hodges 1981). The medical community and neuropsychologists tend to regard it as a severe reading-language disability for which there is a constitutional, often inherited, basis. Educational psychologists usually define it as a severe reading disability of unspecified origin. Educators tend to waver between these two positions.

      Some writers employ the term *dyslexia* broadly as a synonym for reading disability. Others offer a variety of definitions that include one or more of the following: behavioral manifestations of central nervous system deficits or dysfunctions, genetic or inherited causation, inclusion of other language disabilities along with poor reading, presence of a syndrome of maturational lag, and inability to learn to read through regular classroom methods.

      One of the more widely cited definitions is that of Critchley, a neurologist, who defines developmental dyslexia as follows:

    . . . a learning-disability which initially shows itself by difficulty in learning to read, and later by erratic spelling and by lack of facility in manipulating written as opposed to spoken words. The condition is cognitive in essence, and usually genetically determined. It is not due to intellectual inadequacy or to lack of socio-cultural opportunity, or to faults in the technique of teaching, or to any known structural brain defect. It probably represents a specific maturational defect which tends to lessen as the child gets older, and is capable of considerable improvement, especially when appropriate remedial help is offered at the earliest opportunity (Critchley 1981, pp. 1–2).

Among the symptoms of dyslexia cited by Critchley (1981) are (1) overall slowness of performance, punctuated by hesitation when unfamiliar or polysyllabic words are met; (2) confusion of mirror-opposite letters; (3) omissions of short words (articles, conjunctions, prepositions); (4) pluralization or omission or singular nouns; (5) abbreviation of lengthy words (e.g., *adolescent* is read as "adolent"); (6) overreliance on initial letter cues; and (7) substitution of synonyms.

      Dyslexia has been qualified as *specific* to distinguish reading failure from general learning failure, and *developmental dyslexia* (reading ability has been poor from the start) is contrasted with *acquired dyslexia* (loss of previously acquired reading skills).

Distinctions are also made between deep and surface dyslexia (e.g., Patterson 1981), although all theorists do not agree with them (e.g., Kremin 1982). *Deep* or *phonetic dyslexia* involves a severe impairment in the ability to decode printed words. The ability to recognize whole words and to obtain meaning from them remains largely intact. Other symptoms of deep dyslexia are reported to be semantic substitutions (e.g., seeing *dinner* and saying "food") when reading words in isolation (Siegel 1985, Farnam-Diggory 1986) and having more difficulty reading function words than content words (Schwartz 1984). In *surface* or *semantic dyslexia*, whole words are not recognized immediately, but regularly spelled words can be decoded. Irregularly spelled words are misread in a way that suggests overapplication of phonic principles (e.g., *one* is pronounced as *own*) or the use of an analogy strategy (e.g., *put* is pronounced as rhyming with *but*). The concepts of deep and surface dyslexia have been related to neurological damage and to direct and mediated lexical access (see pp. 298–299).

Taylor, Satz, and Friel (1979–1980) compared 40 boys who met all the criteria for dyslexia, as defined by the World Federation of Neurology, with 40 who failed to meet at least one of the criteria and were therefore classified as nondyslexic. Although these 80 poor readers as a group were deficient in many neurodevelopmental skills, comparisons between dyslexics and nondyslexics revealed no differences of any consequence. The authors thus conclude that there is need for a substantial revision of the concept of dyslexia.

Some writers (e.g., Morris 1966) doubt the existence of a condition such as dyslexia. Others (Yule & Rutter 1976) contend that, regardless of the label attached, there is a group of disabled readers who lie outside of normal range of variation. However, the findings on which Yule and Rutter base their claim have been questioned (Miles & Haslum 1986). Other large-scale replication studies have failed to identify a similar group (Pennington 1986).

Although committees in the United States (National Advisory Committee on Dyslexia and Related Reading Disorders 1969) and England (Tizard et al. 1972) concluded years ago that *dyslexia* was not a useful term, and despite the disagreements and ambiguities involved in its definitions, use of the term has grown in recent years. Readers must be careful to determine which of the many definitions of dyslexia a particular author is using. In this book, the term *severe reading disability* is preferred because of its relative clarity of meaning.

Our knowledge of dyslexia has not improved enough to invalidate Vernon's summary of the situation some 20 years ago:

> As to the precise nature of the disability we know little, and much further experimental investigation is required to define this and to demonstrate exactly how it operates in creating reading difficulties. And as to the ultimate cause of the disability, the evidence is too weak and conflicting to do more than suggest certain highly speculative hypotheses. . . .
>
> It is difficult in the present state of our knowledge to differentiate dyslexic from nondyslexic backward readers. Indeed it may be impossible to do so with any precision (Vernon 1971, pp. 176–178).

Learning Disabilities

The field of learning disabilities had its inception about 60 years ago (Hallahan & Cruickshank 1973), but it was not until the 1960s and early 1970s that special interest groups were instrumental in obtaining legal recognition of pupils who were having academic difficulties, but who were not covered by any existing category of exceptionality. By 1974, many states required, and provided financial support for, special education for such pupils. These state laws used a wide variety of terms (e.g., perceptually handicapped, minimally brain-damaged, neurologically impaired) to identify these pupils, and there was no uniformity in definitions or specified criteria (Gillespie, Miller & Fielder 1975).

Although the term had been used by some for years, it was not until 1975, with the passing of Public Law 94-142, that the term "learning disability" gained widespread acceptance. PL 94-142 contained a legally binding definition of a *learning disability* (LD).[5]

> "Specific learning disability" means a disorder in one or more of the basic psychological processes involved in understanding or in using language, spoken or written, which may manifest itself in an imperfect ability to listen, speak, read, write, spell, or to do mathematical calculations. The term includes such conditions as perceptual handicaps, brain injury, minimal brain dysfunction, dyslexia, and developmental aphasia. The term does not include children who have learning problems which are primarily the result of visual, hearing, or motor handicaps, of mental retardation, of emotional disturbance, or of environmental, cultural, or economic disadvantage (Federal Register, p. 65083).
>
> . . . For the purpose of these regulations, when a severe discrepancy between ability and achievement exists which cannot be explained by the presence of other known factors that lead to such a discrepancy, the cause is believed to be a specific learning disability (Ibid., p. 65085).

Specific criteria for defining "learning disability" were not indicated. And although LD is defined in terms of processing disorders, the federal regulations do not require the assessment of psychological processes in determining who is learning disabled. Such a requirement was not included simply because there was [and still is] no well-established, widely accepted method for doing so (Torgesen 1986c). The federal guidelines are general, simply indicating that children are learning disabled if there is a severe discrepancy between their learning potential and their performance in one or more of the following areas: written expression (handwriting, spelling, composition), oral expression, listening comprehension, basic reading skills, reading comprehension, mathematical calculation, or mathematical reasoning. The excluded groups—the sensory impaired. mentally retarded, emotionally disturbed, and disadvantaged—are covered either by other parts of the Education of the Handicapped Act or by Title I of the Elementary and Secondary Education Act.

The requirements of PL 94-142 state that evaluation of a child suspected

---

[5]Except for the fact that learning disabilities usually cover other academic areas in addition to reading, some definitions of LD and dyslexia are similar.

of being learning disabled is to be made by a multidisciplinary team including the child's teacher and at least one person "qualified to conduct individual diagnostic examinations of children, such as a school psychologist, speech-language pathologist, or remedial reading teacher." The team must determine if a child is learning disabled and must file a written report stating the evidence on which its conclusions are based. This evidence must include an individually administered intelligence test.

Six professional organizations, dissatisfied with the definition in PL 94-142, formed a National Joint Committee on Learning Disabilities that formulated a new definition (NJCLD 1981, 1983):

> Learning disability is a generic term that refers to a heterogeneous group of disorders manifested by significant difficulties in the acquisition and use of listening, speaking, reading, writing, reasoning, or mathematical abilities. These disorders are intrinsic to the individual and presumed to be due to central nervous system dysfunction.
>
> Even though a learning disability may occur concomitantly with other handicapping conditions (e.g., sensory impairment, mental retardation, social and emotional disturbance) or environmental influences (e.g., cultural differences, insufficient/inappropriate instruction, psychogenic factors), it is not the direct result of those conditions or influences.

This definition is an improvement in that it emphasizes the varied nature of learning disabilities, does not exclude adults, and recognizes that a learning disability may be accompanied by other handicapping conditions.

Many other definitions of LD[6] have been proposed or used; Farnam-Diggory (1986), for instance, lists 14. None, however, has gained common acceptance, and there is dissatisfaction with the prevailing definitions (Adelman & Taylor 1986). Those who label students as LD use both formal and informal measures, and attach multiple, and at times conflicting, meanings to the concept of LD (R. A. Smith et al. 1986). Defining learning disabilities will not be an easy task. The results of a meta-analysis which used 1,077 studies and which considered 38 variables across 4 domains (linguistic, achievement, neuropsychological, and social/behavioral) led Kavale and Nye (1986) to conclude that "conceptualizations of LD that include all of the necessary components will be complex and will probably require revolutionary changes to produce LD paradigms capable of explaining fully the LD phenomenon."

Writers such as Sabatino and Miller (1980) have suggested that learning disability almost defies definition. Others like Myklebust (1983) and Košc (1987) insist that it can be usefully defined. The main roadblock to formulating an acceptable definition appears to be in the conceptual frameworks upon which the various LD theories are based (Kavale & Forness 1985a,b). If people cannot agree on what a learning disability is, a commonly acceptable definition is not likely to occur. More importantly, if the conceptual underpinnings are faulty, any resulting definition cannot be valid.

The single most accepted criterion for defining a learning disability is the existence of a significant discrepancy between the pupil's measured learning poten-

---

[6]Kirk and Kirk (1983) discuss the definition of LD from a historical perspective.

tial and the pupil's current level of academic achievement (Keogh 1986). But even this criterion is not without its problems. In addition to the general difficulty with discrepancy scores (see p. 163), the potential-achievement discrepancies displayed by LD pupils may not differ significantly from those demonstrated by other groups of handicapped pupils. O'Donnell (1980) found that many children classified as having sensory impairments or behavior disorders had discrepancy scores comparable to those shown by the LD students in the study.

Two other criteria often appear in definitions of LD: (1) that the low achievement is caused by deficits or dysfunction in basic psychological processes[7] that are necessary to perform academic tasks successfully; and, (2) that these cognitive limitations are constitutional and are the result of heredity or damage, by accident or disease, to the neurological substrate that supports all intellectual activity (Torgesen 1986c). The latter criterion at least partially accounts for a fourth criterion, one of exclusion, also commonly found in LD definitions. Since the problem lies within the child, it cannot be the result of any environmental or educational factors. As will be pointed out below, the fundamental assumptions upon which these criteria are based are open to serious questions.

Despite protests to the contrary (e.g., Kauffman, Gerber & Semmel 1988), the number of students labeled as learning disabled has increased tremendously over the past 20 years, and has increased annually at a constant rate of about 3% since the mid-1970s. Recent estimates indicate that from about 2% (Messick 1984) to slightly below 4% (Keogh 1986) of the total American school population are labeled as having a learning disability. Almost 40% of the special education population are in the LD category (Keogh 1986), and in almost every state more students are classified as LD than any other category[8] of special education (Algozzine & Ysseldyke 1986). These increases are not due to more students receiving special services. The numbers in other special education categories either have remained constant (the emotionally disturbed, those with sensory or physical impairments) or have decreased (the speech impaired, the mentally retarded[9]) (Reynolds, Wang & Walberg 1987).

Between 1966 and 1985, the number of disadvantaged children receiving compensatory education under Chapter I funding declined by 42% (McGill-Franzen 1987). Because poverty has increased in our country, it is likely that some formerly "disadvantaged" students have become "learning disabled."

Among the reasons offered for these dramatic increases in LD population are : (1) the LD label appeals to parents because their children can get special help without being stigmatized by such labels as "mentally retarded"; (2) outside funding available for educating each LD child has increased; (3) there is an increased awareness that we are not successfully teaching children with mild academic problems regardless of what they are labelled or where they are

---

[7]Depending on the writer's opinion of causation, the deficits may be specified as being perceptual, perceptual-motor, attentional, neurological, conceptual, or linguistic.

[8]The percentages vary greatly from state to state. For instance, in one state, 63% of the special education students were classified as LD, but only 20% were so categorized in another (Keogh 1986). Such findings raise issues about the definitions and assessment procedures in use.

[9]Studies indicate that a number of school-identified LD students could be classified as borderline mentally retarded or as EMR (Stanovich 1986a), or at least have low IQ scores (Holcomb et al. 1987)

placed (Bicklen & Zollers 1986). The large increases in the LD category and the caps placed on funding have caused some states to tighten their criteria (Bursuck & Epstein 1987), usually by requiring a greater discrepancy between potential and achievement.

The identification of LD students is often inaccurate (Rivers & Smith 1988). Perhaps as few as half the students identified as LD meet the common eligibility requirements (Gelzheiser 1987). Interestingly, many low achievers who have not been placed in the LD category do meet the eligibility requirements (Algozzine & Ysseldyke 1986).

Many pupils who would once have been labeled as "reading disabled" are now categorized as "learning disabled." Approximately 60–80% of LD students have reading problems (Jones, Torgesen & Sexton 1987), with about 75% of them having a reading disability as their primary deficit (Kavale & Forness 1985a).

The assumptions that have guided LD theory, practice, and research since its inception have been, and continue to be, seriously questioned (Arter & Jenkins 1979, Coles 1987). Four assumptions are basic to the LD movement: (1) the psychological processes thought to cause the learning disability are valid constructs and can be measured reliably; (2) the processing deficits exhibited by LD pupils differ significantly from those found in students with other handicaps; (3) the underlying processes are amenable to training; and (4) improvement in formerly weak processing abilities will result in improved academic performance. Evidence that any of these assumptions is unwarranted is reason to question the concept of learning disabilities.

Psychological processes are not observable. Therefore, processing deficits must be inferred from performance on tests believed to measure these hypothetical constructs. There is little empirical support for the construct validity of process tests (Kavale & Forness 1985b). Tests commonly used to identify a learning disability have questionable validity and/or lack sufficient reliability (Tindal & Marston 1986). Furthermore, LD pupils are not readily distinguishable from other groups of low achievers with respect to a number of attributes (Algozzine & Ysseldyke 1986, Bicklen & Zollers 1986). Finally, although process training has been shown to result in higher scores on posttests measuring these factors, the evidence that such improvements have a positive impact on academic abilities is not convincing (Torgesen 1986c). The lack of commonly agreed-on definition, the variety of assessment procedures employed, misidentification, and the inclusion by definition of students who may have one or more of a number of different academic difficulties has resulted in the identification of a heterogenous population. Despite contentions that heterogeneity is to be expected (e.g., Shprintzen & Goldberg 1986), the diverse nature of the LD population has greatly hampered research efforts (S. D. Smith 1986). In general, the LD research has been of poor quality, and often of an atheoretical nature (Wong 1986b). A great deal of data have been reported, but little of it constitutes scientific evidence (Kavale & Forness 1985b).

Although some leaders in the LD field (e.g., Gallagher 1986) still maintain the prevailing belief that learning disabilities are neurologically based, and LD teachers frequently indicate that their pupils have processing problems, there is some movement away from these fundamental assumptions (Adelman & Taylor 1986). Consideration is now being given to environmental and educational factors (e.g., Gelzheiser 1987), information-processing theory (e.g., Swanson 1987a), and linguistic theory (e.g., C. Smith 1986) in the causation and treatment of learning disabilities. Nevertheless despite a trend away from process remediation toward the direct teaching of academic skills there is still strong belief in the process model (Bursuck & Epstein 1987).

The field of learning disabilities is in a state of considerable turmoil. Until the field puts its own house in order, the term "learning disability" can have little real meaning.

IMPLICATIONS FOR READING SPECIALISTS.   Many reading specialists have been worried about the effects of PL 94-142 on their activities and job opportunities (A. J. Harris 1980). The availability of federal funds to subsidize programs for the learning disabled, and the absence of similar support for remedial reading programs, has caused some schools to reduce or eliminate remedial reading or to shift personnel to those programs for the disadvantaged that have federal support. In some school districts, teachers for the learning disabled are being hired instead of reading specialists, especially where compliance with funding requirements mandates employment of certified special-education teachers. With reduced school budgets, fewer specialists of any kind are being hired. In some places, this situation has led to conflicts between LD and reading specialists.

Territorial conflicts are unnecessary if the decision is to make the best possible use of staff members by enabling them to do what they do best on behalf of the students. This approach involves spelling out the kinds of services needed and the professional capabilities best suited to meet those needs.

Reading specialists are likely to be involved in the diagnosis and treatment of LD pupils who have reading problems or in advising classroom, resource-room, or LD teachers as to suitable methods and materials. Because most children labeled "learning disabled" have reading problems and because reading specialists are best prepared to deal with reading difficulties, reading teachers need to demonstrate to decision makers that their expertise is valuable and effective in helping disabled readers regardless of what labels are applied. The need is there: Parents, school boards, and administrators have to be convinced. Suggestions for running effective "public relations" campaigns were made by Gaus (1983) and Goodfriend and Gogel (1987). It may also be prudent for reading specialists to become certified in learning disabilities or special education.

Terms Used in This Book

The following terms are used in this book:

- *Disabled reader* or *reading disability:* designates individuals whose general level of reading ability is significantly below expectancy for their age and intelligence and is disparate with their cultural, linguistic, and educational experience. The latter part of the definition suggests that factors other than chronological age and intelligence must be considered.
- *Severely disabled reader* or *severe reading disability:* refers to disabled readers whose general level of reading ability is extremely below expec-

tancy. Some writers apply labels such as *dyslexia* or *learning disability* to these cases.
- *Slow learner in reading*: indicates children who, although reading below age level, are generally functioning in reading close to their somewhat limited learning potential.
- *Underachiever in reading:* applies to children who, although reading at or above age or grade level, are reading significantly below their potential or expectancy level, which is often well above average.
- *Reading skill/strategy deficiency* or *difficulty:* indicates that, regardless of a child's general level of reading ability, he or she is weak in one or more reading skills or strategies. In some cases, the deficiency may be specific and may not lower the general level of reading ability. Naturally, if there are a number of skill deficiencies, if they are in basic skills, or if the skills are severely deficient, the child's general level of reading ability will be adversely influenced.

Both the disabled reader and the underachiever in reading are working below capacity. The basic difference between the two is that the disabled reader is functioning below age level, whereas the underachiever is not. Children of below-average intelligence can also be disabled readers if their general level of reading ability is significantly below potential.

Some children do not achieve in school despite adequate reading ability and study skills. Their inability to function academically in school cannot, therefore, be attributed to a reading disability. Such children may lack positive motivation or may experience interference from emotional problems. These cases should be recommended to the psychologist or counselor rather than the reading specialist.

The terms *disabled reader, underachiever in reading,* and *slow learner in reading* can be useful in that they draw attention to three kinds of learners who generally need differing treatment. Disabled readers often need intensive specialized treatment. Underachievers in reading usually need either to be better motivated or to be allowed to use above-grade-level materials. However, such students rarely receive attention because they are functioning at grade level. Slow learners should not be expected to reach grade level in reading, nor should they be written off as unable to learn. All three types of students can be misclassified by test scores; expert judgment must also be given consideration. Whatever their classification, most children, including truly slow learners, can learn more if we can determine how to teach them. We will not find out how to teach them unless we *attempt* to teach them and analyze our attempts in order to improve our efforts.

OBJECTIVE DEFINITIONS OF READING DISABILITY

Because the specific causes of reading disability vary and are often impossible to determine accurately for a given individual, most current definitions of reading disability are based on determining whether the individual shows a significant disparity between general potential or aptitude for learning, which we may call *reading expectancy*, and actual achievement in reading. This approach involves making four decisions: (1) choosing an appropriate measure of reading expectancy, (2) choosing an appropriate measure of reading achievement, (3) choosing a way to compare expectancy with achievement, and (4) deciding how large the discrepancy must be in order to be considered significant.

Even if agreement existed regarding what tests and formulas to use and the amount of difference that indicates a disability, a number of unsolved measurement problems would have to be considered:

1. No test is a perfectly reliable measure. A test score should be considered as falling within a range of scores, estimated by using the test's standard error of measurement, rather than as a specific and exact point on a scale.
2. The validity of any test (the degree to which it actually measures what it is intended to measure) is always lower than its reliability.
3. Regardless of the reliability and validity of a test, the score of a pupil who did not understand the directions or was not motivated to exert effort on the test cannot be valid.
4. Some reading tests tend to yield higher (or lower) scores than do others. The same is true of measures of reading expectancy such as intelligence tests. Therefore, the tests employed can influence decisions as to who is determined to be reading disabled, particularly when the discrepancies between the reading expectancy and reading achievement scores result in *difference scores* that are close to the cutoff criterion used to indicate a disability.
5. *Difference* or *discrepancy scores* are the result of subtracting one derived test score (e.g., grade equivalents) or normalized score (e.g., T-scores) from another. Difference scores are less reliable than either of the tests employed in their determination, and have been criticized as lacking sufficient reliability.

A related unresolved problem, and one that is concerned with validity as well as reliability, is the question of how large a difference between potential and achievement must be in order to be considered significant. Put another way, the questions become: "How can we be sure that the difference score did not occur by chance or as the result of some measurement error?" and "How large must a discrepancy be in order truly to separate those whose reading performance falls within the range of 'making normal progress' from those who should be (given our best estimates of potential) but are not?" Although related, the questions do not necessarily demand the same answer. A difference score may be reliable, but it may not distinguish accurately between who is making normal progress and who should be, but is not. The size of the discrepancy score used as the criterion can greatly influence who is determined to be reading disabled as well as how many students are so labeled. Further complicating the issue is whether or not to include students who are functioning significantly below their limited learning potential and those who are functioning at or above grade level but below their above-average or superior capacity to learn. Slow learners and underachievers are usually eliminated from consideration by employing such additional criteria as "having a least average intelligence" and "reading below grade or age level."

Berk (1984) and Reynolds (1985, 1986) suggest procedures for determining reliable and valid discrepancy scores and Reynolds (1985) notes that there are computer programs for calculating severe discrepancy. Burns (1982) presents a procedure that may be used to determine how much confidence can be placed in a predicted score.

Because all procedures for measuring reading disability have a margin of error, such procedures should not be the sole basis for determining whether to assist individuals to improve their reading skills.

In some instances, evidence of reading disability is so clear as to be self-evident. For example, a fourth grader who is known to have at least average intelligence and is reading 3 years below grade level is unquestionably disabled in reading. No computation is needed to arrive at this decision. But more exact procedures are necessary for a variety of purposes, such as (1) to arrange a number of children in order of severity of reading disability; (2) to assist in determining eligibility for inclusion in a remedial program; (3) to make statistical studies of the frequency of occurrence of reading disability; (4) to match groups of disabled readers for experimental purposes; and (5) to determine the need for remedial personnel in a school system.

Measures of Reading Expectancy

Two commonly used measures of reading expectancy are intelligence tests and listening comprehension tests.

INTELLIGENCE TESTS.[10]   Individually administered intelligence tests, such as the *Stanford-Binet* and *Wechsler* series, generally are more valid than group tests, partly because the examiner is better able to motivate the person and to note behaviors that cast doubt on the validity of the results, and partly because individual tests are less dependent on acquired knowledge and skills than are most group tests. But such tests require trained examiners, and are relatively time consuming. Certain brief individual tests, such as the revised *Slosson Intelligence Test* and the *Peabody Picture Vocabulary Test—Revised* do not require special training to administer. However, these tests sample only verbal intelligence and are less reliable than the Binet and Wechsler tests.

Many intelligence tests yield both a mental age (MA) score and an intelligence quotient (IQ). *Mental age* indicates the level of mental maturity reached at the time of testing. Children with differing IQs reach the same MA at different chronological ages (CA). For instance, a bright child with an IQ score of 129 would have an MA of 9.0 at CA 7.0; the pupil with an IQ of 100, at CA 9.0; and the child with an IQ of 90, at CA 10.0. An *IQ score* is essentially a ratio between MA and CA, and shows the average rate of mental development. Mental age is

---

[10]Most recently published tests do not use "intelligence" in their titles. Rather, such terms as "cognitive abilities" or "school aptitude" are employed. We use the term "intelligence test" because it is a generic term and, thus, likely to be understood.

the better measure for estimating present reading expectancy and for short-term prediction; IQ is the better long-term predictor.

An IQ score is a rough index of an individual's current level of overall cognitive functioning (Stanovich 1986a). Because reading is a cognitive task, it is reasonable to expect the reading achievement of pupils to be commensurate with their levels of cognitive functioning. Another reason for using IQ scores as a measure of reading potential is that the correlation between intelligence and reading comprehension is statistically significant at all ages; therefore, intelligence test scores are fairly good predictors of reading achievement. Correlations are generally in the 0.40s and 0.50s in the first grade (Bond & Dykstra 1967), rise into the 0.70s by fourth grade (Allen 1944), and tend to remain at about 0.70 into adulthood (Thorndike 1963). These correlations do not hold for disabled readers who, by definition, are reading below expectancy.

Performance on a test or subtest that samples verbal ability tends to correlate with reading ability more highly than do nonverbal intelligence tests or subtests. For example, G. Downing et al. (1965) found that the WISC Verbal IQs of black seventh graders correlated 0.78 with their scores on the *Metropolitan Reading Test*. Their WISC Performance IQs and scores on the *Cattell's Culture Fair Intelligence Test* (a group nonverbal test) correlated 0.53 and 0.56, respectively, with the same reading test.

Some individuals with reading problems score substantially higher on nonverbal than on verbal intelligence tests or subtests; for others, the reverse is true. This has led some (e.g., Brown & Bryant 1986) to suggest that the higher of the two scores should be used as an indicator of reading potential. A concomitant belief is that using a performance (nonverbal) IQ score for this purpose is legitimate because to do otherwise would unfairly prevent some pupils with high Performance IQs but low Verbal IQs from receiving needed remedial instruction. Proponents of the use of Performance IQs claim that a significant discrepancy between a child's verbal IQ score and reading test scores is not likely to occur because both tests measure similar constructs (verbal/language ability). The same inability that prevents a child from scoring adequately on the verbal IQ test also results in a low reading test score. This viewpoint also holds that although using the higher of the two scores may result in large numbers of students being identified as reading or learning disabled,[11] this situation is less serious than one in which pupils who could profit from remedial assistance are eliminated. The counter argument is that verbal scores are better predictors of reading ability because verbal scores tend to correlate with achievement more highly (0.60 to 0.80) than do nonverbal scores (0.30 to 0.50) (Heller 1986). Advocates of this point of view argue further that, because reading is a highly verbal ability, it would be unrealistic to expect an individual to achieve at a reading level commensurate with a high nonverbal score. Nonverbal tests, they say, do not adequately measure the cognitive abilities needed for becoming a skilled reader. On the other hand, a high nonverbal IQ score indicates the presence of some useful cognitive abilities, which may compensate to some extent for verbal weaknesses. Therefore, we recommend using

[11]For example, in Reed's (1970) study, when WISC Full-Scale IQs were used, 19 children were identified as disabled readers; but 29 were so identified when only the Performance IQ was employed.

the average of verbal and nonverbal IQ scores, or a total score based on both, in determining reading expectancy. Those who prefer to use either verbal or performance IQ scores should be aware that doing so can make a significant difference in estimates of reading expectancy. Disparities of 10 or more points between verbal and performance IQs are common in children and some disabled readers show differences of 30 or more IQ points between the two.

Tests that contain both verbal and nonverbal subtests include: (1) individual tests such as Wechsler's WPPSI, WISC-R, and WAIS-R, and the revised *Stanford-Binet*; (2) group tests such as the *Cognitive Abilities Test, Kuhlman-Anderson Tests,* and the *Test of Cognitive Skills;* and (3) primary-grade group tests that do not require reading, such as the *Otis-Lennon School Ability Test.*

The *Kaufmann Assessment Battery for Children* (K-ABC) yields scores for Sequential Processing, Simultaneous Processing, and Composite Mental Processing subtests. The sequential processing tasks involve integrating stimuli (usually verbal) into serially organized arrangements. Each stimulus is related in a linear fashion to the preceding and following stimuli. The simultaneous processing tasks require the child to attend to several aspects of the task at one time, and to synthesize separate elements of information into a unitary representation. The stimuli have spatial components. This individually administered battery also yields separate scores for Reading Decoding and Comprehension subtests. These two subtests sample skills that differ from those usually measured by tests with similar titles.

As might be expected, the WISC-R Performance Scale was reported to correlate 0.82 with the K-ABC Simultaneous Processing score but only 0.09 with the Sequential score for 44 learning disabled students. Somewhat surprisingly, the correlations between the WISC-R Verbal Scale and the K-ABC Simultaneous and Sequential scores were 0.50 and 0.42, respectively (Klanderman, Perney & Kroeschell 1985).

Predominantly verbal individual tests of intelligence include the 1972 edition of the *Stanford-Binet Intelligence Scale*, the *Slosson Intelligence Test* (a short test using *Stanford-Binet* items), and vocabulary tests such as the *Peabody Picture Vocabulary Test—Revised* and the *Expressive One-Word Picture Vocabulary Test.*

Usable nonverbal tests include (1) individually administered measures, such as the performance subtests of the *Weschler* scales, the *Arthur Point Scale of Performance*, and the *Raven Progressive Matrices* (which can be used with small groups above age 8); (2) group nonverbal tests, such as the *Cattell Culture Fair Series: Scales 1, 2, 3* and the *Nonverbal Test of Cognitive Skills;* and for younger children, the *Goodenough-Harris Drawing Test.*

Pupils who cannot read the IQ test items cannot score well on such tests and are thus unable to demonstrate their potential for learning. Underestimates of potential may prevent poor readers from receiving remedial assistance, either because they obtained an IQ score below the minimum set for admission to the special program or because the depressed score results in the incorrect conclusion that they are working up to their expected level. Therefore, in testing children with reading difficulties, intelligence tests that require reading ability should be avoided. Low scores, even on individually administered intelligence tests, may be due to factors such as expressive language deficits or poor motivation. If there is any reason to believe that pupils have the potential to improve their reading ability, they should be given the opportunity to do so regardless of their intelligence test scores.

When selecting tests to determine reading expectancy and achievement, it is desirable to select an intelligence or listening test and a reading test that have been normed on the same population. This practice minimizes the chance that a difference between a student's scores in the two tests might be the result of a difference in test standardization.

LISTENING COMPREHENSION. Listening comprehension *(auding, capacity level)* is recommended by some as the most satisfactory measure of reading potential:

> This ability to understand spoken English demonstrates that the child has the intelligence and perceptual abilities to handle words and sentences, the basis for all later communication skills. . . . Listening comprehension is more directly related to reading than are most tests of intelligence. Intelligence tests measure a variety of mental functions which have varying degrees of relationship to reading. Listening comprehension measures *language* acquisition, the knowledge of the very same words and sentences which are to appear later in reading (Durrell & Hayes 1969, p. 12).

Theoretically, the ability to comprehend spoken language places a ceiling on the ability to understand written language (Carroll 1977). Thus, all else being equal, a student's level of reading comprehension may match, but not exceed, his or her level of listening comprehension. When reading and listening comprehension are commensurate, children are said to be working up to their capacity to understand the language. If listening comprehension significantly exceeds reading comprehension, the reading problem is not due to language comprehension difficulties. Rather, it is caused by difficulties with skills that are unique to reading such as the ability to recognize printed words or a child's failure to apply what she or he knows about language to understanding written text (see pages 20–22). The assumption is that, if the weak mechanical/enabling skills and strategies are improved, reading comprehension will approach the pupil's level of listening comprehension.

Empirical data support using auding as a measure of reading expectancy. Sticht et al. (1974) summarize the correlations between auding and reading obtained by many researchers. The average r starts low at Grade 1 (0.35) and increases steadily to about 0.60 at Grade 4, remaining at about that level through secondary school and college. These correlations are very similar to those reported between intelligence and reading comprehension. Ruddell (1979) found that primary-grade listening comprehension scores were better than reading comprehension scores for predicting reading comprehension in Grades 8, 9, and 10.

Some standardized listening comprehension tests, such as the *Durrell Listening-Reading Series,* are available but they are at least 20 years old. Some standardized achievement tests include listening comprehension subtests, but they often require the ability to read the comprehension-check items. Listening comprehension scores also may be obtained from informal or published reading inventories, but most of these lack reliability or validity data.

Low listening comprehension scores may be due to factors other than limited intellectual ability or auditory sensory impairments, which are likely to influence language development in general. Among these are unfamiliarity with English, inattention, fatigue, and a too-rapid or generally poor rendition of the text by the examiner. Scores that are depressed for such reasons can lead to the incorrect belief that the child is reading up to capacity. On the other hand, scores may be inflated if the examiner emphasizes words or phrases that are the answers to the comprehension-check questions. A low listening comprehension score should not be the sole basis for deciding who receives remediation.

Determining General Level of Reading Ability

Standardized reading tests, well-constructed informal or published reading inventories, or cloze tests may be used to estimate an individual's present general level of reading ability. The obtained reading score should represent, as accurately as possible, the individual's instructional level. The uses and limitations of such tests for this purpose are discussed in Chapter 7.

For children who are reading below fourth-reader level and seem to have problems in reading, equal weight should be given to silent and oral reading in arriving at a composite reading score. For those reading at or above fourth-reader level, a silent reading score only may be used, but oral reading should be given at least qualitative consideration. "It is better for two reasons to use a composite of oral reading and silent reading scores, rather than silent reading alone. The first is that difficulties in word identification are central in many reading disabilities, and low comprehension scores may be the result of inability to recognize the words. The other reason is that poor readers tend to get many of their correct answers on multiple-choice tests by guessing, making their scores on such tests less dependable than the scores of normal readers" (A. J. Harris 1971a).

READING AGE.   Most reading tests provide grade norms but not age norms. For some of the computational procedures described in this section it is necessary to have a reading-age score. Since the typical child in American public schools enters first grade at the age of 6.2 years (the usual minimum is 5 years 8 or 9 months) and is promoted regularly, there tends to be a regular difference of 5.2 years between chronological age and grade placement. When a reading test does not provide age norms, grade-equivalent scores may, for the purpose of these computations, be changed into reading-age scores by adding 5.2 years. Because tests such as the informal reading inventory do not yield grade-equivalent scores, the following arbitrary grade-equivalent scores may be assigned to the instructional reading or auding level derived from these tests in order to compute the pupil's reading age or listening age:

preprimer = 1.2	low third reader = 3.2
primer = 1.5	higher third reader = 3.7
first reader = 1.8	fourth reader = 4.5
low second reader = 2.2	fifth reader = 5.5
high second reader = 2.7	sixth reader = 6.5; and so on

ESTIMATING PRESENT MENTAL AGE OR LISTENING AGE.   Unless the measure of potential was obtained recently, it is necessary to estimate a present mental age (MA) or listening age (LA) because MA and LA change with age (until about 16 for MA). This is done by using the pupil's current chronological age (CA) and the most recent IQ score in one of the following formulas (Finnucci et al. 1982). CA must be converted from twelfths to tenths by dividing the number of months by 12 (e.g., 8 years 6 months = 8.5, because 6 ÷ 12 = .5). For those under age 16, MA can be estimated with the following formula:

$$MA = \frac{CA \times IQ}{100}$$

For those 16 and older, the preferred formula is:

$$MA = \frac{16 \times IQ}{100}$$

The score from a recently administered listening comprehension test may be converted to a listening age (LA). If the score is a grade equivalent, simply add 5.2 to it (e.g., GE = 3.4, so LA = 8.6). If the score represents the pupil's level of listening comprehension that was obtained from an informal inventory (IRI) or IRI-like test, this auding level must first be assigned a grade equivalent by using the suggestions on page 168. Then add 5.2 to that GE score. For example, an auding level at the high-third-reader level would be assigned a GE score of 3.7. Adding 5.2 to this results in an LA of 8.9. If the listening score is not recent, it must be adjusted for the length of time since the measure was obtained. This is accomplished by adding the number of years and months (in tenths) that have passed to the estimated LA. Thus a listening comprehension score of 3.4 that was obtained 1 ½ years earlier would be adjusted to yield an LA of 10.1 (3.4 + 5.2 + 1.5).

Comparing Expectancy with Reading Achievement

At least six procedures are employed in comparing reading achievement with expectancy: years below grade level, mental age minus reading age, expectancy formulas, standard-score procedures, procedures using quotients, and regression equations.

YEARS-BELOW-GRADE-LEVEL PROCEDURE.   The use of a given number of years below grade level as a sole criterion for reading disability has at least two serious flaws. First, it does not consider the child's potential for learning. Thus slow learners, although reading reasonably close to their potentials, would be classified as disabled readers. Second, the distribution of achievement scores spreads out in the higher grades, so it is likely that more upper-grade than lower-grade students will fall 1, 2, or 3 years below grade level on norm-referenced tests. The meaning of the differences also changes. For example, a second grader scoring 1 year below grade level might be at the 10th percentile; an eleventh grader scoring 3 years below grade level may be at the 25th to 30th percentile (Shepard, Smith, & Vojir 1983). This method substantially overestimates disability in the upper grades and underestimates the severity of difficulties in the early grades, mainly because it uses grade-equivalent scores (Reynolds 1981)

DIRECT COMPARISON OF MENTAL AGE WITH READING AGE.   The direct comparison of MA with RA has two major faults. First, an age scale does not have equal intervals. For example, a difference of 1 year at age 7 may be comparable to a difference of 2 years at age 12. To overcome this, sliding scales are often recommended as guidelines in determining when a discrepancy between MA and RA indicates reading disability: at least a 6-month difference in Grades 1–3, a 9-month difference in Grades 4 and 5, and a 12-month difference above Grade 5. Some authors suggest larger minimum differences, such as 1 year in Grades 2 and 3, and 2 years from Grade 4 up. The MA minus RA procedure also ignores the regression effect.

EXPECTANCY FORMULAS   Reading expectancy formulas are actually variations of a general linear regression model that have been simplified by weighting the variables used in the formulas. Thus they are based on certain assumptions, such as the size of the correlation between the measures of learning potential and reading. Such reading expectancy formulas will be in error depending on the degree to which the correlation between reading and potential and/or the standard deviation of reading achievement is misestimated (Burns 1982).

The Bond and Tinker formula (Bond, Tinker, Wasson & Wasson 1989) employs years of reading instruction (YRI), IQ, and a constant of 1. Their formula may be expressed as:

$$\text{Reading Expectancy (RE)} = \frac{\text{YRI} \times \text{IQ}}{100} + 1.$$

Thus an 8-year-old whose IQ is 75 and who had received reading instruction for 2 years by the end of second grade would have an RE of 2.5:

$$2.5 = \frac{2 \times 75}{100} + 1$$

The RE would be the same if the child had spent 2 years in first grade. But if he had not received reading instruction in his first, or only, year in first grade, his RE would be 1.8. To determine if the child is a disabled reader, his reading achievement score is subtracted from his RE score. This difference score is then compared with "grade score discrepancies" which increase slightly as the grade level increases, and which range from 0.50 for Grade 1 to 2.0 for Grade 7 and above. Thus, since the "grade score discrepancy" for Grade 2 is 0.66, our sample second grader with an RE of 2.5 would be classified as a disabled reader if his reading-achievement score was 1.8 or below.

According to Burns (1982), the Bond and Tinker formula assumes an unrealistically low correlation between IQ and reading achievement. In our opinion, the formula works well for children who are close to average intelligence but sets unduly high expectations for the mentally slow and unduly low expectations for the very bright.

A. Horn (1941) developed four reading expectancy formulas based on the correlation between particular intelligence and reading tests administered in

Los Angeles. The weighting of MA and CA suggests an increase in the correlations between potential and reading as the pupils got older (0.50, 0.60, 0.67, and 0.75 respectively). Horn's RE formulas are as follows:

1. For CAs 6–0 to 8–5: $\dfrac{MA + CA}{2} - 5$

2. For CAs 8–6 to 9–11: $\dfrac{3MA + 2CA}{5} - 5$

3. For CAs 10–0 to 11–11: $\dfrac{2MA + CA}{3} - 5$

4. For CAs 12 and up: $\dfrac{3MA + CA}{4} - 5$

A constant of 5 is subtracted from the resulting formula score to provide a RE score in grade-equivalent form. For the previously cited case, application of the Horn formula 1 would result in an RE of 2.0:

$$2.0 = \frac{6 + 8}{2} - 5$$

The reading expectancy formula employed is likely to influence who is designated as a disabled reader. As with the MA minus CA procedure, the problem with the Horn formulas is knowing how much of a difference between expectancy and achievement constitutes a disability.

STANDARD-SCORE PROCEDURES.   In order to overcome the problems created by use of the grade or age scores, some writers have suggested using standard scores that express the pupil's scores in distance from the mean in standard deviation units.

Erickson (1975) suggests using Z-scores for determining reading disability. Raw scores from the two tests are transformed to Z-scores, and each pupil's Z-score for reading is subtracted from his or her potential Z-score. Erickson defines the 10% of students with the largest negative discrepancies as having a reading disability.

Winkley (1962) recommends using stanine scores obtained from reading and intelligence tests. The score for the intelligence test must be at least two stanines higher than that for the reading test in order to indicate that a child has a reading disability.

Hanna, Dyck, and Holen (1979) recommend using standardized tests of aptitude and achievement and converting the test scores into T-scores (normalized standard scores with a mean of 100 and a standard deviation of 10). The reading T-score is subtracted from the aptitude test T-score, with a difference of 8 or more points indicating fairly reliable evidence of a disability, and 4 to 8 points a doubtful range. While the T-score has some statistical advantage over age or grade scores, the recommended procedure ignores the size of the correlation between aptitude and achievement scores, as well as the regression effect.

PROCEDURES USING QUOTIENTS.   Although the idea of an accomplishment quotient in which a measure of achievement is divided by a measure of potential dates back almost to the beginning of standardized testing, its first major application to reading disability was in Monroe's classical study (1932). The Monroe expectancy formula gives equal weight to MA, CA, and Arithmetic Age (AA). An Expected Reading Grade (ERG) is determined by applying the following formula:

$$ERG = \frac{MA + CA + AA}{3} - 5$$

Monroe developed a Reading Index (RI) quotient in which the Observed Reading Grade (ORG), the pupil's current level of achievement, is divided by the ERG and multiplied by 100 to get rid of the decimal:

$$RI = \frac{ORG}{ERG} \times 100$$

Clinically referred poor readers had an average RI of only 49, while an unselected school population had a mean RI of 102. The RIs for the two groups intersected at about 80, which Monroe recommends as a reasonable cutoff quotient for identifying reading disability. Use of an RI quotient of 80 identified 12% of the unselected group as disabled readers.

Myklebust (1968) recommends use of a Learning Quotient (LQ). In reading, the LQ is reading age divided by expectancy age. The expectancy age is the average of MA, CA, and grade age (GA = the child's grade level in years and months). The MA is based on the higher of verbal or nonverbal IQ. He explains the inclusion of CA as representing physiological maturity and GA as representing opportunity for school learning. The rationale for including both CA and GA is not convincing, since the correlation between those two variables is very high. Myklebust considers LQs below 90 to indicate disability: mild or borderline between 85 and 89; and severe below 85. Because it assumes a correlation of 0.33 between reading and MA, the Mykleburst formula probably overestimates reading expectancy for pupils with IQs under 100 and underestimates it for those over 100 (Burns 1982).

Yule and Rutter criticized the use of quotients on the basis that it does not provide for the regression effect. "Thus, any measure of achievement that fails to allow for the statistical effects of regression will end up with a group of 'underachievers' in which bright children are overrepresented and dull children are underrepresented" (1976, p. 28).[12] They overlook the fact that in using an expectancy measure that is the average of three variables, the effect is similar to that of a multiple regression procedure. A more valid criticism is that both Monroe and Myklebust chose their variables on the basis of armchair reasoning and weighted them in an essentially arbitrary fashion.

REGRESSION EQUATIONS.   Regression procedures adjust for the phenomenon of regression toward the mean. Predicted scores for high scorers on the measure from which the prediction is made will be lower than if the regression effect had not been considered; the predicted scores of low scorers will be

---

[12]Finucci et al. (1982) did not find this to be the case in their study.

higher. In other words, unless the regression effect is considered, reading expectancy scores generally will be too high for bright students and too low for children with below-average IQ. This will result in overidentifying high-IQ students and underidentifying lower-IQ students. The higher the correlation between the test of potential and the reading test, the closer the predicted score will be to the potential score; the lower the correlation, the closer it will be to the mean.

R. L. Thorndike (1963) suggests using a regression-based discrepancy procedure in which the regression line is determined empirically. Aptitude and reading tests are administered to a representative sample. Then the average reading score is determined for each IQ score, and a smoothed line is made connecting each IQ point. The individual's predicted reading score is compared with his or her obtained reading score. If the discrepancy is at least as large as its standard error, the chances are at least five to one that the difference between the predicted and obtained scores is significant, thereby indicating failure to read up to expectancy. The advantages of using a regression equation may be offset by the practical problems involved (Cone & Wilson 1981), and according to Pennington (1986), the choice of what magnitude of discrepancy to use as a cutoff is still arbitrary.

McLeod (1979) advocates using data from several sources to develop a statistical model of the regression in the population under consideration. But this approach uses a potential-achievement correlation of 0.5, which is too low for older students, and the cutoff values are too stringent. Later, McLeod (1981) suggests expressing discrepancy scores as Z-scores to overcome the problems caused by the nonnormality of score distributions. A critical value of Z (cutoff score) could be set, which would identify a desired percentage of the population as disabled. McLeod's procedures do not exclude slow learners.

Regression procedures were used in several large-scale studies (Yule & Rutter 1976). Using nonverbal group IQ tests, the reality of the regression effect was demonstrated. For those with IQs above the average, the mean reading scores were less above average than the mean IQs; for those with below-average IQs, the mean reading scores were not as low as their mean IQs. A separate regression was used for each age group. "Specific reading retardation" (reading disability) was defined as a reading score two or more standard errors of prediction below the predicted score (Yule et al. 1974). This corresponded to a disparity of at least 28 months between the predicted and obtained reading comprehension score and included only 2.3% to 5.4% of the populations. Such a criterion is considerably more severe than those ordinarily used in determining reading disability.

There are several problems with the regression procedure. A regression equation is specific for the measures of potential and reading used in obtaining it and the characteristics of the population used. Certain statistical requirements about the normality of the distributions and so on should be met (Cronbach 1971). Regression equations must be derived from a large normal sample similar in CA, education, gender, and SES to the reading disabled group, and must use the same IQ and reading tests as employed in determining reading disability (Pennington 1986). Application of a regression procedure requires having staff sufficiently well versed in statistics to understand the procedure and apply it correctly. Shepard (1980), who critiqued the regression-discrepancy method, concludes that it should not be used as the sole criterion for identifying reading-disability students.

A Recommended Procedure for Identifying Reading Disabilities

We recommend a procedure for identifying reading disabilities that uses a ratio or quotient procedure but has the effect of a regression procedure. It uses the concepts of Reading Expectancy Age, Reading Expectancy Quotient, and Reading Quotient.

General intelligence, or listening comprehension, is only one of many factors that are relevant to an individual's progress in reading. The average correlation between intelligence and reading comprehension (between 0.60 and 0.75 at most grade levels) provides a little less than half of the information needed to predict reading performance with complete accuracy. Other factors that influence reading expectancy include errors of measurement and a variety of traits or abilities that improve or grow with increasing age, such as general and specific information, linguistic competence, vocabulary, and reading skills. An estimate of reading expectancy based only on intelligence or listening comprehension is likely to be less accurate than one that also gives some weight to general maturing.

Although chronological age (CA) is not in itself closely correlated with growth in reading when other factors are held constant, CA provides a time dimension within which a variety of maturing traits have the opportunity to develop. Thus CA can function as a common denominator for a variety of factors which influence growth in reading and which develop as children get older.

READING EXPECTANCY AGE.   A *Reading Expectancy Age* is an estimate of the reading age, and thereby level of achievement that a given child can reasonably be expected to attain: It is used in determining the Reading Expectancy Quotient.

A simple formula that gives priority to the importance of intelligence but also recognizes the presence of other age-related characteristics in reading expectancy involves giving mental age twice the weight of chronological age. The formula may be written:

$$\text{Reading Expectancy Age (R Exp A)} = \frac{2\text{MA} + \text{CA}}{3}$$

In this formula MA and CA should be expressed in years and tenths, giving R Exp A also in years and tenths.

This R Exp A formula yields essentially the same results as a simple regression equation for predicting reading age from mental age alone, assuming an average correlation of 0.67 between MA and RA. It is the same as one of the Horn formulas (see p. 170) but applied to a broader age range, from 8 to 14 years.[13] The assumed correlation of 0.67 does not differ considerably from 0.61, which was the median of 486 correlations between intelligence and reading reported by Hammill and McNutt (1981).

For children under age 8, the use of any expectancy formula is somewhat dubious. But if one is to be used, the Horn formula $\frac{MA + CA}{2}$ may provide a closer approximation to what would be found with a regression procedure. It assumes a correlation of 0.50 between intelligence and reading, which is not far from the 0.45 that is the median of 60 correlations for Grades 1–3 reported by Stanovich, Cunningham, and Feeman (1984). This same formula is preferable when the correlation between the intelligence and reading tests being used is close to 0.50. Determining reading disability for pupils over age 15 is covered on pages 177–178.

READING EXPECTANCY QUOTIENT. A *Reading Expectancy Quotient* (R Exp Q) expresses how a pupil's level of reading ability compares with his expected reading level. It is obtained by dividing Reading Age by Reading Expectancy Age and multiplying by 100 to avoid use of decimals. In formula form:

$$\text{Reading Expectancy Quotient (R Exp Q)} = \frac{RA}{R \, Exp \, A} \times 100$$

Reading expectancy quotients between 90 and 110 are considered to fall within normal limits. A cutoff score of 90 takes into account that part of any obtained difference may be an artifact based on chance errors of measurement. An R Exp Q below 90 indicates failure to read up to expectancy and therefore the strong likelihood of a disability or underachievement. The lower the R Exp Q, the more likely the presence of a disability and the more severe the disability. R Exp Qs below 80 almost certainly indicate disability. Finucci et al. (1982) empirically validated a zone of achievement quotients from 0.81 to 0.90 as the borderline region below which readers are "disabled" and above which they are "normal." A child with an IQ of 100 who was totally unable to read (reading grade = 1.0, RA = 6.2) at CA 7.7, would have an R Exp Q of 81. If he remained a nonreader, it would fall to 64 at age 9.7 and 53 at age 11.7. Unless a child's reading ability improves, his disability becomes progressively more severe with age.

Quotients above 110 indicate that reading is above expectancy. This may be a sign of great effort and practice, or of every superior instruction; or it may be an artifact of the tests employed (Maginnis 1972).

---

[13]Calculations using all four Horn formulas were made for hypothetical cases of children with CAs of 7, 9, 11, and 13 and with MAs 1 year below, at, and 1 year above their CAs, placing their IQs in the 90–110 range approximately. As would be expected, there were no differences in R Exp As at any age level when MA equaled CA. As the assumed correlations between IQ and reading increased from 0.50 to 0.67, the R Exp As decreased by one-tenth year when MA was 1 year lower than CA; formulas that assumed correlations of 0.67 and 0.75 essentially yielded the same R Exp As for below-average IQ children. When MA exceeded CA by 1 year, the R Exp As increased by one-tenth year as the assumed correlations increased. It would thus seem that for most children, which formula was used would make only a slight difference.

DISTINGUISHING AMONG DISABLED READERS, UNDERACHIEVERS, AND SLOW LEARNERS. It is worthwhile to make as accurate a distinction as possible among (1) disabled readers who are unable to function academically at grade level because of their poor reading ability, (2) underachievers whose reading ability is sufficient for grade-level requirements although well below their own expectancy, and (3) slow learners whose reading ability is below age level but is in keeping with their somewhat limited learning capacity. This may be accomplished by using both the Reading Expectancy Quotient and the Reading Quotient. The *Reading Quotient* is simply RA divided by CA, multiplied by 100 to eliminate the decimal point. Thus the formula for comparing the individual's present level of reading performance with that of others of his or her chronological age is:

$$\text{Reading quotient (RQ)} = \frac{\text{RA}}{\text{CA}} \times 100$$

As shown in Table 6.1, pupils whose R Exp Qs and RQs are both above 90 are making normal progress in reading ability. When children's R Exp Qs and RQs are both below 90, they are reading significantly below both their own expectancy and the normal performance for their age group. Therefore, they are classified as cases of reading disability. Those whose R Exp Qs are below 90 but whose RQs are 90 or above are usually able to cope with their reading assignments in school, although such students are apparently not making full use of their above-average or superior potential. For them, the term "underachiever" seems preferable even though such a thing may not exist in reality (see R. L. Thorndike 1963). Pupils whose R Exp Qs are at least 90, but whose RQs are below 90, are generally reading as well as can be expected. The term "slow learner in reading" is used for these students. However, when pupils with below-average intelligence are reading significantly below their potentials, they may be more appropriately referred to as slow learners who are also disabled readers.

An Example. John is 10 years 7 months old (CA = 10.6), has an IQ of 105, and is in the fifth grade. His reading grade-equivalent scores are silent reading 4.3, oral reading 3.1; he therefore has an average reading grade of 3.7, which yields a RA of 8.9 (3.7 + 5.2).

Table 6.1 Summary of Objective Definitions of Reading Ability and Disability

Classification	R Exp Q[a]	RQ[b]
Making normal progress in reading	90 or above	90 or above
Disabled reader	below 90	below 90
Underachiever in reading	below 90	90 or above
Slow learner in reading	90 or above	below 90

[a] Expresses how a learner's present general level of reading ability compares with *his or her* expected reading level.

[b] Expresses how a learner's present level of reading ability compares with that of *others of the same chronological age.*

$$MA = \frac{10.6 \times 105}{100} = 11.1$$

$$R \, Exp \, A = \frac{2(11.1) + 10.6}{3} = 10.9$$

$$R \, Exp \, Q = \frac{8.9}{10.9} \times 100 = 82$$

$$RQ = \frac{8.9}{10.6} \times 100 = 84$$

Because John is well below the critical value of 90 on both R Exp Q and RQ, there should be no hesitancy in classifying him as having a reading disability.

USING A READING EXPECTANCY AGE TABLE.   The computations explained and illustrated in the foregoing example can be greatly shortened (see Table 6.2). If you know the IQ and CA of a child, his or her R Exp A can be read from Table 6.2. If the IQ or CA falls between two values given in the table, use the nearest value and the result will usually be correct within 0.2 of a year. For greater accuracy, you can interpolate or do the arithmetic as explained above. The use of the table may be illustrated with the foregoing example. For John, CA 10.6 and IQ 105, the nearest CA column is 10.7 and there is an IQ 105 row; these intersect to give the value of R Exp A as 11.0, only 0.1 year different from the 10.9 computed with the formula.

USING A READING EXPECTANCY QUOTIENT TABLE.   Finding Reading Expectancy Quotients can be speeded up by using Table 6.3. In the left-hand

Table 6.2   Reading Expectancy Ages for Selected Combinations of Chronological Age and Intelligence Quotient

IQ	7.2	7.7	8.2	8.7	9.2	9.7	10.2	10.7	11.2	11.7	12.2	12.7	13.2
140	9.1	9.6	10.3	10.9	11.6	12.1	12.9	13.4	14.1	14.7	15.4	15.9	16.7
135	8.8	9.4	10.1	10.6	11.3	11.8	12.5	13.1	13.8	14.3	15.0	15.5	16.2
130	8.6	9.1	9.8	10.3	11.0	11.5	12.2	12.7	13.4	13.9	14.6	15.1	15.8
125	8.4	8.8	9.5	10.0	10.7	11.2	11.9	12.3	13.0	13.5	14.2	14.7	15.4
120	8.1	8.6	9.3	9.7	10.4	10.9	11.5	12.0	12.7	13.1	13.8	14.3	14.9
115	7.9	8.3	9.0	9.4	10.1	10.5	11.2	11.7	12.3	12.7	13.4	13.8	14.5
110	7.6	8.1	8.7	9.2	9.8	10.2	10.9	11.3	11.9	12.4	13.0	13.4	14.0
105	7.4	7.9	8.4	8.9	9.5	9.9	10.5	11.0	11.5	12.0	12.6	13.0	13.6
100	7.2	7.7	8.2	8.7	9.2	9.7	10.2	10.7	11.2	11.7	12.2	12.7	13.2
95	6.9	7.4	7.9	8.3	8.9	9.3	9.7	10.4	10.8	11.3	11.8	12.2	12.7
90	6.7	7.1	7.6	8.0	8.6	8.9	9.5	9.9	10.4	10.8	11.4	11.7	12.3
85	6.4	6.8	7.4	7.7	8.2	8.6	9.1	9.5	10.0	10.4	10.9	11.3	11.8
80	6.2	6.6	7.1	7.4	7.9	8.3	8.8	9.2	9.7	10.0	10.5	10.9	11.4
75	6.0	6.3	6.8	7.2	7.6	8.0	8.5	8.8	9.3	9.7	10.1	10.5	11.0
70	5.7	6.1	6.5	6.9	7.3	7.7	8.1	8.5	8.9	9.3	9.7	10.1	10.5
65	5.5	5.9	6.3	6.6	7.0	7.3	7.8	8.1	8.6	8.9	9.3	9.6	10.1
60	5.3	5.6	6.0	6.3	6.7	7.0	7.5	7.8	8.2	8.5	8.9	9.2	9.8

Note: Any expectancy age in the table can be changed into an expectancy grade equivalent by subtracting 5.2 years.

Table 6.3 Reading Expectancy Quotients for Selected Combinations of Reading Expectancy Age and Reading Age

Reading Age	Reading Expectancy Age											
	6.7	7.2	7.7	8.2	8.7	9.2	9.7	10.2	10.7	11.2	11.7	12.2
6.2	**92**	86	80	75	71	67	63	60	57	55	52	50
6.7	**100**	**93**	87	81	77	72	69	65	62	59	57	54
7.2	107	**100**	**93**	87	82	78	74	70	67	64	61	59
7.7	114	106	**100**	**93**	88	83	79	75	71	68	65	63
8.2	122	113	106	**100**	**94**	89	84	80	76	73	70	67
8.7	129	120	112	106	**100**	**94**	**90**	85	81	78	74	71
9.2	137	128	119	112	106	**100**	**95**	**90**	86	82	79	75
9.7	145	135	126	118	111	105	**100**	**95**	**91**	87	83	80
10.2	152	142	132	124	117	111	105	**100**	**95**	**91**	87	84
10.7	160	149	139	130	123	116	110	105	**100**	**96**	**91**	88
11.2	167	156	145	137	129	122	115	110	105	**100**	**96**	**92**
11.7	175	163	152	143	134	127	121	115	109	104	**100**	**96**
12.2	182	169	158	149	140	133	128	120	114	109	104	**100**

column, find the number nearest to the child's RA. Read across on that line to where it meets the vertical column closest to the child's R Exp A; the number at that intersection shows the child's approximate R Exp Q.

For our example, John, 8.7 is the number nearest his RA of 8.9. The listed R Exp A closest to his R Exp A of 10.9 is 10.7. The scores 8.7 and 10.7 intersect at 81, which is only 1 less than the Reading Expectancy Quotient computed with the formula.

The numbers in bold type fall within the normal range of 90 to 110. Numbers below 90, in the upper-right section, indicate that reading is significantly below expectancy. Numbers in the lower-left section, from 111 up, indicate that reading is significantly above expectancy. When the R Exp Q obtained from the table is close to 90, it is advisable to go through the arithmetic operations to get a more accurate result.

Reading Quotients (RQ) can also be read directly from Table 6.3. Interpret the heading "Reading Expectancy Age" to mean "Chronological Age." Find the number in the left-hand column that is closest to the child's RA and read across horizontally to where the row intersects the CA column closest to the child's CA; at the intersection is the number closest to the child's RQ.

DETERMINING READING DISABILITY FOR ADOLESCENTS AND ADULTS. The procedures described in the foregoing do not apply well above the age of 15 because mental ability does not continue to grow in approximately linear fashion during adolescence. When the reading-grade score is below eighth grade and a satisfactory IQ is available, however, the procedures described above will not be greatly in error if the CA is used up to the age of 15 and a CA of 16 is used for all ages above that.

When secondary school and college aptitude and reading tests do not have age or grade norms, it is more appropriate to use a regression equation based on the correlation between the particular aptitude and reading tests employed (see pages 172–173) than just to compare percentile or standard scores on the two tests (R. L. Thorndike 1963). Another method that works above age 15 is taking the difference between stanines on tests of reading and potential that have been normed on the same population, with a disability indicated when potential is two or more stanines higher than reading.

Some Questions about Objective Measures of Reading Disabilities

Because different procedures for identifying disabled readers can result in considerable differences as to how many and which individuals are selected (Fletcher et al. 1989), some consideration of issues concerning the application of objective measures of reading disability is desirable.

1. What is the best measure of intelligence to use? The question of using a verbal, nonverbal, or total score, or, alternatively, a measure of listening comprehension, has been considered on pages 164–167. Most of the formulas described use MA rather than IQ. If the MA is corrected for present age and the CA is also used, the difference between using MA or IQ should be inconsequential.

2. Which is better to use, age scores or grade scores? The use of grade scores seems to assume that children are equal in readiness at the beginning of first grade and start there from zero. Age scores take into consideration that children have been maturing and learning for about 6 years before reading instruction begins. The advantage is with age scores.

3. Should children of below-average intelligence be excluded? For research purposes, it is legitimate to delimit an experimental population in whatever way needed to check the validity of the hypotheses being studied. For school practice, other considerations should apply. Children who are below average in intelligence, but are not slow enough to be classified as mentally retarded, find it difficult or impossible to achieve at grade level. Many of them try hard, and some of them achieve quite well in relation to their limited learning abilities. Slow learners who are not eligible for special education should be considered for remedial instruction on the same basis of potential above achievement that applies to brighter children.

4. What does research show about the relative value of the several formulas? Unfortunately, little research has been done on the comparative merits of the several procedures available. One study (Dore-Boyce, Misner & McGuire 1975) compared the Bond and Tinker formula, Harris 1 (MA minus RA), Harris 2 (R Exp A), and the Horn formulas. The *Otis-Lennon Mental Ability Test* was used to predict SRA Total Reading scores of 733 fourth- and fifth-grade pupils. Correlations between the formula scores and the obtained reading scores were as follows: Harris 1, 0.69; Harris 2, 0.62; Horn, 0.61; Bond and Tinker, 0.47. The Bond and Tinker formula was significantly the poorest in all comparisons. The main contributor was found to be MA, with CA adding a little to the accuracy of the prediction; grade placement and gender added nothing. This study's results are limited in generalizability for two reasons: The intelligence test used required reading, making the validity of low scores questionable; and the limited age range of 2 years restricted the possible contribution of CA.

Honel (1973) compared eight reading expectancy formulas and concludes that "the R Exp Q (Harris) appeared to have the broadest application and consequently was deemed to be the preferred formula." It is questionable, however, if breadth of application is the best criterion to use. Burns (1982) concludes that the Horn formula, which we use, provides the best simplified estimate of reading expectancy.

5. *How accurate are reading expectancy formulas?* Dore-Boyce, Misner, and McGuire (1975) report standard errors of estimate of 1.3 to 1.5 grades for the formulas they studied. Yule (1967), using different tests, found the standard error of estimate to be 1.3 years for word recognition and reading comprehension. That there is a considerable margin of error in a computed reading expectancy score should be kept in mind if a child's expectancy score is close to the cutoff point.

Reading specialists should not rely exclusively on a numerical formula but should give serious consideration to teacher recommendations and the child's academic performance. If the child's reading shows very little growth each year, that reinforces the formula score in indicating a need for special remedial help.

6. *What is the best cutoff point?* For research, any cutoff score may be selected that fits the purpose of the researcher; it may be set low so as to include only severe disabilities or so high as to include mild disabilities as well.

In school practice a cutoff is usually not needed. Children are arranged in a rank order of need, considering formula scores and teacher recommendations and school policies, which may favor selecting children from certain grades. The children are chosen from the rank order until the total number that can be accommodated in the remedial reading program are selected; the rest go on the waiting list. However, if the last child chosen has an R Exp Q well below 85, the remedial reading program is not reaching all the children who need it.

For more complete explanations and critiques of the various procedures for determining reading disability, refer to Cone and Wilson (1981), Burns (1982), and Berk (1984).

7. *Is it better to use regression procedures or simplified estimates of reading expectancy?* A regression procedure provides more accurate estimates of reading expectancy, but reading expectancy formulas are quicker and easier to utilize. Each user must decide the merits of both procedures and select the most appropriate. When pupils take an intelligence test and a reading test normed on the same population, the publisher may be able to provide anticipated reading scores based on the measure of learning potential.

7

Assessing Reading Performance

Information concerning students' levels of reading achievement, reading skills and strategies, interests, and attitudes can be useful in determining if a reading program's instructional objectives are being achieved, in lesson and program planning and evaluation, in assessing students' reading progress, and in making a reading diagnosis. There are various types of tests and assessment procedures, and the specific tests or procedures within each category vary along a variety of dimensions. Some types of tests are more useful than others for particular purposes, and no single test or assessment procedure can provide all the information needed in a comprehensive reading assessment program. Furthermore, information from a variety of sources over time provides more reliable and valid data about reading ability than does information from a single testing. Decisions as to which types of tests and procedures to employ should be based on the purpose for the assessment and the type of information desired. A few examples follow.

For comparing student achievement across reading programs whether within a school, district, state, or nationally, a norm-referenced test that is not biased for or against any of the programs would be the test of choice. A similar type of test might be used in comparing the relative effectiveness of two different types of reading programs or basal reader series. If a principal wants to know whether the students are achieving the instructional goals of the school's reading program, the first choice would probably be a criterion-referenced test geared solely to sampling those objectives.

A classroom teacher might use the informal reading inventory that accompanies the reading program being used for instruction to determine into which reading group to place a new student. Or, a teacher who is using the language-experience approach might construct and administer a test of the ability to recognize high-frequency words because she knows that children are very likely to encounter those words when they read published materials. Of all the assessment procedures, the ones most likely to result in a positive impact on pupil performance over time are the informal daily assessments made by classroom teachers as they observe and interact with students who are reading complete texts (as opposed to the short paragraphs typically found in published tests) and who make use of that information in planning future lessons (Valencia & Pearson 1987). This applies both to reading from the materials being used for reading instruction and to content-subject textbooks and materials. The classroom teachers' observations, perhaps supplemented by information from the school librarian, also provide the most useful data as to whether the goals of the recreational reading portion of the total reading program are being met.

Reading specialists might initially use some of the same tests used by others, but they would be more likely than others to probe to obtain information as to how a child arrived at a particular response, or why a student could not respond acceptably to a particular task. The reading specialist's purpose would be to obtain information about the child's reading processes, not just the product of those processes. Thus, if a student performed poorly on a silent reading test, especially if it was far below what his reported daily performance would suggest, the reading specialist might have him reread parts of the test orally to see if word-recognition problems might have been a contributing factor. If he makes and does not correct disruptive miscues, the specialist might repeat some of the sentences as rendered by the pupil; asking him if they sound right and make sense (to check his ability to monitor word recognition and comprehension; and if he is aware of his errors, to correct them). Or, if the student had difficulty answering comprehension questions that called for the ability to understand textually implicit information, the specialist might determine how much of the needed textually explicit information was understood and how much information and which steps in reasoning had to be supplied before the child could answer such questions acceptably. By probing in these ways, the reading specialist has gone beyond assessment into diagnosis.

In assessing reading achievement or progress, the instructional environment also should be evaluated. The *Instructional Environment Scale* (Ysseldyke & Christenson 1987) may be used to aid in determining which factors are contributing to children's learning problems. Nicholson (1989) describes a 4-step process that teachers can use to evaluate their instruction.

Concern is growing regarding the influence of testing on school curricula. Madaus (1988) discusses how testing can and has had an effect on curriculum, and what can be done to restore the balance among instruction, learning, and testing.

TERMINOLOGY

Test users should understand the terms commonly employed in describing tests and test results. The first two terms discussed here—reliability and validity—can be in used in reference to any type of test. The other terms are more commonly associated with norm-referenced tests, although some may be used with criterion-referenced tests or even informal tests.

A test's *reliability* indicates the degree to which it yields consistent results.

No test is a perfectly reliable measure; chance errors in measurement and fluctuations in individual performance preclude this. But little faith can be placed in test results if the scores may vary greatly for an individual or even a group average. Test reliability is determined statistically, and is usually stated as a correlation coefficient or as a standard error of measurement.

There are two types of reliability coefficients. *Split-half coefficients* are derived by correlating the results of the even-numbered test items against the odd-numbered ones, and are usually higher than *test-retest reliability coefficients*, which are derived by comparing the results from two forms of the test. The higher the coefficient, the more reliable the test.

Test reliability is affected by such factors as the number of items in a test (generally longer tests are more reliable), the range of achievement of the sample in the variable being measured (the more restricted the range, the lower the reliability coefficient), and the characteristics of the group tested. Although the total score of a standardized test usually is highly reliable, subtests may not have sufficient reliability for diagnostic use with individuals.

Average test scores of groups are more reliable than scores for individuals. Opinions vary as to how reliable a test must be in order to be useful. Schwartz (1984) suggests that, for measuring reading ability, an individual test should have a reliability coefficient of at least 0.94, with the minimum increasing to 0.98 when attempting to determine changes in reading ability. Few tests are that reliable. For individual assessment, a test or subtest should have a reliability coefficient of at least 0.90 for a single age or grade level (coefficients based on a wide range of ages or grades tend to be spuriously high), or a standard error of measurement of not more than 3 months for grade-equivalent scores.

The *standard error of measurement* indicates the variation in test scores that would probably occur if that test were given repeatedly to an individual. Adding the standard error of measurement to, and subtracting it from, the obtained score, yields the range of scores in which the individual's "true" score[1] probably lies. Thus, if a child obtained a grade-equivalent score of 4.3 on a test that had a standard error of measurement of 0.2 for GE scores, the chances are about 2 to 1 that the "true" score lies somewhere between 4.1 and 4.5 (4.3 ± 0.2) and about 19 to 1 that it is between 3.9 and 4.7 (4.3 ± twice the standard error). The smaller the standard error of measurement, the more reliable the test.

Validity is the degree to which a test measures what it is intended to measure. There are different kinds of validity, each of which answers a different question about the test.

A test with low reliability cannot be valid, but high reliability does not ensure validity. Evidence about the reliability and validity of a test should be given in the test manual.

A *standardized test* is one that has specified tasks and procedures that must be followed exactly in order to assure comparable measurements whenever the test is given.

Norms are statistics that describe the test performance of the groups on whom the test was standardized. After a test has been constructed it is given to

---

[1]A true score is a hypothetical score, free of measurement error and never really determined (T. Harris & Hodges 1981).

large numbers of pupils, chosen to be representative of those for whom the test is intended. Norms are simply statements of the results obtained in the initial testing and may be used as a basis for interpreting results on the test when given to other pupils. Norms should never be considered a desired standard of achievement. The kinds of norms used in reading tests are grade-equivalent scores, percentiles, standard scores, normal-curve equivalent scores, scaled scores, extended scale scores, and stanines.

Grade-equivalent scores are based on raw scores, usually the number of correct responses. Few tests use a correction formula for guessing, although many tests have a minimum score below which no norms are assigned. A grade equivalent indicates the grade level for which the raw score was the median score actually obtained by the norming population. By definition, half the children can be expected to score above and half below the median. Grade-equivalent scores are given in years and tenths because there are usually 10 months in the school year (September = 0.0 and June = 0.9). Thus, if the average raw score obtained by the norming sample that was in the second month of third grade was 10, any pupil getting 10 correct answers is assigned a grade-equivalent score of 3.1. It makes no difference which 10 items were answered correctly.

Among the limitations of grade-equivalent scores enumerated by Hills (1983) are the following:

1. They assume that (a) the rate of growth is constant throughout the school year (i.e., equal gains are made each month); (b) there is no growth, or one month's growth, during the summer; (c) the amount of gain is the same from one grade level to the next.
2. They are not directly comparable across tests or subtests.
3. They are not equally spaced in terms of raw scores (e.g., 10 raw-score points may separate grade scores of 1.0 and 2.0, but only 4 points may separate 4.0 from 5.0). At times a small number of correct answers can greatly influence the GE score.
4. They are prone to misinterpretation. A grade-equivalent score usually does not indicate that reading material at that level is suitable for instruction, nor that the child has mastered all the reading skills taught in the reading program up to the grade level indicated by the test score.
5. The grade-equivalent scale reflects the yearly growth of achievement for average students; it is less accurate in doing so for children who are considerably above or below average in reading ability and who therefore are more likely to make yearly growth of more or less than one grade level.

Percentiles or *percentile ranks* indicate how a pupil compares with other children in the same grade or age level. These scores range from 1 to 99, with a median of 50. A percentile score of 89 means that the student did as well as or better than 89% of the group with whom the comparison is being made. It does not represent the percentage of correct responses. The distances between percentiles do not represent equal units across the entire percentile range, and so they should not be averaged or otherwise treated mathematically. A student has to answer more questions correctly in order to obtain a higher percentile in the middle range of scores than at the extremes. For instance, it might take five additional correct answers to move from the 50th to the 55th percentile, whereas one more correct response can move a pupil from the 90th to the 95th percentile or from the 1st to the 5th percentile.

Standard scores or *T-scores* are normalized scores; that is, they have been transformed to a normal distribution, the mean (usually 50 or 100) and the standard deviation (usually 10 or 15) being preassigned. A standard score of 50 (or 100) indicates average performance. Because standard scores represent equal units, they can be averaged and used to compare performances on different tests.

Normal-curve equivalent (NCE) *scores* are based on percentile ranks that have been transformed into a normalized scale representing equal units (e.g., a difference of 10 NCE units represents the same difference in reading achievement between any 2 points along the scale). NCEs, which resemble standard scores, range from 1 to 99 with a mean of 50, and describe a pupil's performance in relation to a group of pupils at the same grade level. Maintaining the same NCE score means that the student made normal growth, not that there was no growth.

Scaled scores (SS) express the results of tests at various levels within a test battery on a single common scale. Thus, scaled scores can be compared from form to form and from level to level, and are useful in measuring change in achievement over time. Scaled scores, however, are not directly comparable from one subject to another.

Extended scale scores (ESS), also referred to as *expanded standard scores* or a *growth scale*, provide a single continuous scale by which a child's or a group's progress can be followed during the school years. Because ESSs represent equal units, growth in a student's or group's reading achievement can be compared with that of other students or groups even when the initial level of achievement is not the same.

Stanines are normalized standard-score scales divided into 9 segments, ranging from a low of 1 to a high of 9. Stanines 4, 5 and 6 indicate average performance. Each stanine represents a range of scaled scores, thus avoiding some of the implied precision of other kinds of scores. However, even stanines are not perfectly reliable.

TYPES OF READING MEASURES

Information regarding students' reading skills and abilities may be obtained from norm-referenced, criteria-referenced, or informal measures. Each type of measure can provide useful information, if the particular test or procedure within a given type of measure is well chosen, and is employed and interpreted properly.

Norm-Referenced Tests

Norm-referenced tests (NRTs) are standardized tests whose directions for administration must be followed closely. If directions are not followed, the accompanying norms will not be applicable because norms are based on performances under standard conditions.

The contents of NRTs are usually based on an analysis of the reading materials and tasks required of students who are in the grades for which the test is intended. When a test is designed for use in a wide variety of school systems, it should not parallel too closely the content, style, or vocabulary of any one published reading program.

A norm-referenced test should include a sufficiently wide range of difficulty so that poor readers in the lowest grade for which the test is intended can answer some of the items correctly, and the better readers in the highest grade for which the test is intended probably cannot get a perfect score. Most NRTs have alternate forms that are comparable as to types of test items and level of difficulty. This makes it possible to retest pupils without using the same material. Using the same form of a test could result in artificially higher scores on the second administration, especially if the time between testings is short.

Some NRT publishers provide ways of using the student's performance as a criterion-referenced measure. Usually this involves identifying a cluster of test items that reportedly measure the same skill, and which can be used to determine if an instructional objective has been met by applying a criterion for mastery to the overall performance on these items.

Criterion-Referenced Tests

Criterion-referenced tests (CRTs) primarily differ from NRTs in four ways. First, whereas NRTs are designed not to be biased for or against any particular reading program, CRTs are usually deliberately designed to assess the degree to which the objectives of a particular program are being met. Second, NRTs are usually global measures of reading abilities, yielding scores in general areas such as word recognition, vocabulary, and comprehension; most CRTs measure mastery of specific skills. Third, the items in NRTs must range in difficulty because score variability is needed for test reliability. CRT items used to measure mastery of a particular objective are usually at a comparable level of difficulty, and are constructed to reduce test score variability. Finally, NRTs relate test performance to relative standards; that is, the student's performance is compared to that of the norming population. CRTs relate test performance to absolute standards; the child's performance is compared to a predetermined criterion. Mastery is demonstrated by meeting or exceeding that criterion. The ways in which NRTs and CRTs measure skills or abilities may not differ. For example, both may use multiple-choice items to measure the ability to comprehend a series of short passages.

Theoretically, CRTs should be useful in individualizing instruction. However, problems of reliability, validity, and the setting of cutoff scores are unresolved. Berk (1980) recommends that 5 to 10 items per objective should be used for most classroom tests, and 10 to 20 items per objective for school-level tests. Few, if any, CRTs even come close to meeting this suggestion. The reliability of one- or two-item samples of a specific skill (as is most often the case) is open to serious question. The reliability of the total test should also be considered. Conventional measures of test reliability require variability in scores (a range of scores), but CRTs are designed to produce low variability. Use of conventional reliability measures has been defended, and new measures have been devel-

Correlations between teachers' estimates of children's reading ability and their actual scores on various reading tests fall into the low-moderate range, usually in the 0.30s to 0.40s (Brown & Sherbenou 1981). Pupils' evaluations of their own reading abilities have not proven to be a useful source of information (Jason & Dubnow 1973).

Curriculum-Based Measurement

The term *curriculum-based measurement* (CBM) generally refers to the use of direct observation and recording of students' performance in the materials actually being used for reading instruction as a basis for gathering information to make instructional decisions. Such measurement is a form of CRT. The major advantage of CBM over NRTs is cited as being the close connection between testing and teaching. According to Deno (1987), the most common application of CBM requires that student performance be measured by a single global task repeated over time (e.g., reading orally for one minute from a basal reader). Measurement consists of repeated "probes" of the student's performance on this task. Assessment is continuous, and growth is described by an increasing score on the standard or constant task (e.g., an increased number of words read correctly in a minute).

Advocates claim that CBM provides at least as reliable and valid a measure of reading achievement as do standardized tests (Fuchs, Fuchs & Maxwell 1988) and that information gathered through the use of CBM results in better academic achievement when it is used as the basis for planning lessons (Fuchs & Fuchs 1986). Deno, Mirkin, and Chiang (1982) found that one-minute tests of reading words orally in isolation or context correlated from 0.81 to 0.87 with cloze-test performance, and even higher with standardized reading comprehension tests. Deno (1985) reports that the number of words read aloud correctly from a basal reader passage in one minute correlated from 0.70 to 0.95 with NR reading comprehension subtest scores. A similar range of correlations (most being in the 0.80s) between reading aloud from word lists and NRT performance is reported by Tindal and Marston (1986).

L. S. Fuchs (1987) discusses the four steps in developing and using a CBM procedure: (1) identifying the long-range goal; (2) creating a pool of test items or passages; (3) measuring pupil performance; and, (4) evaluating the data base. Thus, if the long-range goal was to have the student read material at a fourth-reader level at 95 WPM with less than 5 errors, a number of 200-word passages from that basal reader would be selected randomly, and the child would read one of them orally for one minute at least twice a week. According to Zigmond and Miller (1986), direct recording of the child's performance is not required, and checking reading once a week is sufficient if the data are used to modify the instructional program.

Tindal (1987), who discusses and illustrates types of charts for graphing progress when using CBM, notes that such records would indicate variability because students rarely perform exactly on the same level each day. Variation in performance may be due to differences in the difficulty of the reading passages (e.g., all the passages from a fourth reader are not at the same level of comprehensibility), in the topical knowledge of the reader, in administration and scoring procedures, and in student characteristics.

Unless comprehension is also measured, claims that a one-minute sample of word recognition can be used to assess reading ability or to monitor overall reading growth, including comprehension, are open to question. Correlations indicate only how closely two tests rank-order students. Word recognition accuracy, and speed are needed for reading comprehension, but they do not assure comprehension. It is also difficult to understand how frequent measures of word-recognition speed and accuracy can lead to meaningful instructional changes (other than adjusting the level of difficulty of the instructional material) and to instruction in word-recognition accuracy, automaticity, or strategies. Nevertheless, frequent assessments of the pupils' performance in their daily reading seem to have desirable results. Perhaps this is due, at least partially, to unrecognized variables such as making students more aware that their progress is being monitored often, thus motivating them to stay on task more frequently. Seeing their progress graphed may motivate some students to improve, and frequent assessment should certainly alert teachers to how well their instructional programs are accomplishing their aims.

Static versus Dynamic Assessment

In *static assessment*, pupils are given certain tasks to perform under specific conditions in which the examiner is not allowed to provide any help. Pupil responses to the test tasks are either "correct" or "incorrect," and their performances are rated according to the number of correct responses. Static assessment scores are estimates of the students' current, unaided level of competence. No attempt is made to assess the processes that led to that level of performance (Brown & Campione 1985). Static assessments such as standardized reading achievement tests allow for the comparison of students' ability to perform the same or similar tasks under the same conditions. What they cannot reveal is how well the students would achieve under ideal support.

Dynamic assessment evaluates the students' current status and what they are capable of learning. Attempts are made to determine if, and under what conditions, pupils can perform a novel task or one which they were previously unable to accomplish; or the level of competence at which students can achieve when provided with the most supportive learning environment possible. Thus, the examiner determines the effects of things such as providing students with information they do not have but which is necessary to perform the task; or teaching students strategies necessary to perform the task and observing their ability to profit from such instruction. Dynamic assessment is well suited to making a reading diagnosis. Refer to Campione (1989) for further information on dynamic assessment. Suggestions for making dynamic assessments of reading comprehension are offered by Paratore and Indrisano (1987).

TEST SELECTION AND INTERPRETATION

Selecting Reading Tests

In selecting reading tests, teachers should first decide what information they want to obtain, and then decide which tests will best provide the desired infor-

test and gets them all correct may be an extremely compulsive pupil who is overly concerned with getting everything right, or may be an extremely slow reader. At the other extreme is the pupil who attempts all 50 items, with the 10 correct responses scattered throughout the test. Such a score is apt to be highly influenced by guessing. How a child arrives at an answer is often more revealing than the correctness of the answer. For this reason, careful observation during testing and daily activities is strongly recommended.

OTHER FACTORS.   Any test performance can be influenced by guessing, inattention, lack of motivation, or just having a "bad day." Factors associated with test administration can also influence test scores. Pupils who know the purpose of the test and have a positive perception of the examiner tend to obtain higher test scores.

Limitations of Reading Tests

No single measure of reading is a valid measure of reading ability. A reading test indicates how well a pupil reads only from a limited perspective, under a limited set of conditions, and within a limited set of responses (Farr & Carey 1986). Furthermore, test performance can be influenced by a number of variables.

Pupils' test responses are the products of the processes they employed in arriving at their answers. A test score is a measure of those products; we must infer from the responses what took place in the reader's mind. Three attempts to gain such insights—cloze tests, miscue analysis, and eye movements—are discussed on pages 200-203, 243-245, and 341-343, respectively. Another procedure is the *"think-aloud" technique*, in which readers orally relate their recent thought processes immediately after reading a short text (often a sentence or two). The accuracy of what is related depends on such factors as the verbal ability of the readers, their ability to understand what really occurred in their minds while reading, and the relative complexity of the task (e.g., it is easier for students to explain how they decoded a word and why they did it that way than to understand and explain how they understood a text). Also, readers usually have access to only one piece of the text at a time; this excludes the use of such strategies as reading ahead to clarify a poorly understood point (although readers may relate that they would employ such a strategy). Processing such brief pieces of text may differ from what occurs in longer, more representative text; and having to report on the thought process can disrupt text processing. If the procedure calls for readers to relate their thoughts after reading a whole text, the task becomes one of free recall, and suffers from the limitations of that measure of comprehension. Many underlying cognitive processes that enter into comprehension are not available at a conscious level, and so cannot be described (Paris, Wasik & Van der Westhuizen 1988). Therefore, the think-aloud procedure probably reveals only certain elements of the reading strategies that have occurred (Berieter & Bird 1985).

Among the complaints heard about current reading tests is that they measure the comprehension only of short passages (rather than of long, complete texts as required in school) and do so in a manner that restricts thinking and responding, and they ignore the fact that materials are read for different purposes in the real world. Such complaints overlook the fact that a test should not comprise a total assessment program, and that there are reasons for constructing such tests. Publishers would argue that the use of short passages allows for wider content coverage (thus reducing the possible effect of prior knowledge on test scores); that multiple-choice tests are easier and less expensive to score; and that lengthening the passages would greatly increase test cost and administration time, thereby reducing their appeal to schools.

There is some concern that reading tests, which have not changed significantly in over 50 years in terms of what they measure and how they measure it (Farr & Carey 1986), have not kept pace with what is now known about the reading process and what influences it (Valencia & Pearson 1987). For example, at least five states are designing reading tests that use long passages, assess the pupils' topical knowledge, and attempt to measure reading strategies and attitudes toward the passages (Leslie 1989).

DETERMINING GENERAL LEVEL OF READING ABILITY

One of the most important questions to answer about a learner's reading ability is: What level of reading material is appropriate for a given purpose? Answering this question aids not only in forming instructional groups but also in selecting material appropriate for an individual. Moreover, the answer should assist in choosing material that the learner can read independently and may help to determine whether the pupil can profit from using a particular content-subject textbook. The appropriate level of reading material varies according to the kind of reading done and the degree of proficiency in reading expected. In general, material to be read under the guidance of the teacher can be somewhat more difficult than material the child is to read independently.

More Than One Level of Reading Ability

Levels of reading competence originally described by Betts (1946) are functionally useful. The *independent reading level* is the highest level at which a child can read easily and fluently, without assistance, with few word-recognition errors, and with good comprehension and recall. The *instructional level* is the highest level at which a child can do satisfactory reading provided he or she receives preparation and supervision from a teacher: Word-recognition errors are not frequent, and comprehension and recall are satisfactory. The *frustration level* is the level at which a child's reading skills break down: Fluency disappears, word-recognition errors are numerous, comprehension is faulty, recall is sketchy, and signs of emotional tension and discomfort become evident.

This useful set of concepts has helped to clarify thinking about the meaning of "reading level." For example, Susan may be able to read fifth-reader material with considerable strain, difficulty, and inaccuracy (frustration level); fourth-reader material with acceptable accuracy and comprehension after the teacher explains new words and concepts and provides guiding questions (instructional level); and third-reader material with ease, fluency, and almost complete accuracy (independent level). If the teacher assigns this child to a group using a fifth reader and expects her to do supplementary reading in fourth-reader material, her effort and accomplishment are likely to be disappointing. If she is placed in a group using a fourth reader and encouraged to read independently material of third-reader level, the results are apt to be gratifying. If all her reading is at fourth-reader level, she will probably do reasonably well in group lessons but engage in a minimum of other reading. If all her reading material is of third-reader difficulty, she may complain about a lack of challenge in her basal reader, but enjoy storybooks at that level. Gickling and Armstrong's study (1978) indicates that when reading assignments are too difficult, on-task behavior, task completion, and comprehension are relatively low; when the assignment is easy, there is a high percentage of off-task behavior.

Assessing Reading Levels

Criterion-referenced tests such as informal reading inventories (IRI), published reading inventories, and cloze tests make it possible to differentiate among a pupil's independent, instructional, and frustration reading levels. Grade-equivalent scores on standardized silent reading tests tend to overestimate the instructional reading level, particularly for poor readers whose scores may be based largely on guessing. A well-constructed, well administered, and well-interpreted informal reading inventory based on the reading series used locally is apt to indicate a child's instructional reading level more accurately than a standardized norm-referenced test.

Two standardized tests provide scores that resemble an IRI in certain respects. The *Metropolitan Reading Test* provides an Instructional Reading Level (IRL) based on the number of correct answers to a series of paragraphs of increasing difficulty. Smith and Beck (1980) found that, on the average, IRL scores were about 1 year lower than pupils' instructional levels as determined by published IRIs. The *Degrees of Reading Power* (DRP) purports to show the level of reading text that is most suitable for pupils scoring within particular ranges. Although noting that DRP scores may be valid for other purposes, Carver (1985b,c) contends that they should not be used to select reading materials by matching DRP test scores to the DRP units assigned to materials in the *DRP Readability Report*. But Bormuth (1985) suggests that Carver's contention overlooks the influence of prior knowledge on reading comprehension. Bormuth argues that when students' prior knowledge outdistances their levels of reading ability, as happens in the primary grades, they are often able to comprehend materials that are measured, by DRP units or readability formulas, to be at levels above their reading ability. On the other hand, when more skilled readers have sparse prior knowledge about topics found in upper-grade reading and content-subject materials, they would be less able to comprehend materials than their DRP scores alone would predict.

Duffelmeyer and Adamson (1986) administered the DRP and a basal-reader IRI to third and fifth graders. DRP scores correlated 0.73 with IRI scores in Grade 3 (indicating that both tests rank-ordered the students somewhat similarly), but the correlation was only 0.36 in Grade 5. The DRP-based placements were higher than the IRI placements for 13 of the 22 third graders, but were lower in 15 of the 23 comparisons in fifth grade. Differences were as large as eight reader levels. As with other such comparisons, differences do not indicate which test provides the more valid measure of reading ability. They do indicate that estimates of reading ability can be highly influenced by the test employed.

A Quick Class Survey

Dolch (1953) suggests a quick way to locate poor readers in a class. Children take turns reading orally, as fast as they can, a sentence from a basal reader. Children who refuse to read are excused cheerfully, and those who demonstrate difficulty are aided quickly. The teacher notes each child's performance. Dolch believes that since each child reads but one sentence, there is likely to be little embarrassment. Because a one-sentence sample is unreliable, we would prefer to have each child read three or four sentences and to do so only in the presence of the teacher or a small group.

Since Dolch's procedure does not include any check on comprehension, it can disclose only limited information. For a quick comprehension check, choose a short, four- or five-page selection from the basal and ask the children to read it silently. As each child finishes, she or he closes the book and looks up. This allows the teacher to spot slow readers and children for whom the text is difficult. When all the children have finished, the teacher presents a list of questions, to which the pupils write their responses. Those who score below 60% are likely to have difficulty understanding the book; those in the 60-70% range are marginal.

Combining a quick oral reading screening test with a silent reading comprehension test not only identifies the pupils for whom the book is unsuitable, but also indicates the book's suitability for the majority of the class. If teachers take the time to "try the book on for size", not only with basal readers but also with content textbooks, many frustrating experiences can be prevented.

GROUP MEASURES

Silent reading ability is measured far more frequently than oral reading ability because silent reading tests, which can be given to groups, are less time consuming and require less expertise to administer and score. However, they yield less useful diagnostic information than do oral reading tests. Nevertheless, silent reading ability, especially comprehension, is important to assess.

Standardized Silent Reading Tests

Standardized silent reading tests may be classified according to the reading functions that they purportedly measure.[2] Some measure single functions, such as reading vocabulary or rate; others measure two or more aspects of reading. This section is concerned only with the latter. Single-purpose tests are considered under appropriate headings elsewhere.

[2]Reading and reading–related tests are described in Appendix A.

There are two major kinds of norm-referenced silent reading tests. *Survey tests* sample skills and abilities that are usually taught in the grade levels for which the tests are intended. Survey tests generally allow sufficient time so that reading rate is not an important factor in the resulting scores.

All survey tests contain a comprehension subtest that requires the child to read single sentences (primary grades) or paragraphs. A few primary-grade tests sample both sentence and paragraph meaning. In addition to a comprehension subtest, first- and second-grade tests often have a word-recognition subtest and may include a decoding subtest. Third-grade tests are more likely to measure word meaning than word recognition. From the fourth grade on, the commonly used survey tests have reading vocabulary and comprehension subtests. Some also have subtests of work-study skills, reading rate, or both. A few intermediate-grade tests contain a measure of decoding.

Diagnostic reading tests provide profiles of a student's reading skills from which relatively strong and weak areas may be discovered. These tests are not diagnostic in the true sense because they do not reveal *why* the child responded in a particular way. They often contain more subtests than do survey tests, with each subtest containing more items. The number of subtests in group-administered diagnostic tests varies from test to test. Some cover a wide variety of decoding skills; others attempt to measure different kinds of reading comprehension.

In reviewing *any* test that has subtests, the following points should be considered, but they are particularly pertinent when interpreting diagnostic tests:

1. Each subtest should sample a relatively independent skill. Intercorrelations among subtests should be below 0.65; higher correlations between two subtests, suggest a greater likelihood that they are measuring similar abilities.
2. For use with an individual, the subtest reliability should be 0.90 or above.
3. Time limits on subtests may be so brief as to place an unwarranted premium on reading rate.
4. A subtest label does not necessarily indicate what is really being measured. For example, a task analysis may reveal that items in a literal comprehension subtest actually require reasoning ability or rely heavily on prior knowledge.

Criterion-Referenced Tests

Group-administered criterion-referenced tests differ widely in the number of objectives covered, the specificity of their objectives, the number of test items per objective, and what constitutes mastery. For the most part, CR group tests use the same format as NR tests—sentences or brief passages followed by multiple-choice questions. However, most CR group tests are shorter than standardized tests.

Commercially published CR tests are available, and many mastery-learning, systems-approach, and diagnostic-prescriptive reading programs employ CR tests. To construct tailor-made CR tests, appropriate items can be chosen from banks of CR test items available from state education departments, universities, and publishers. Or test users may wish to construct their own tests by employing the suggestions of such authors as Gronlund (1978). Lyons (1984) warns, however, that matching CR test items to skills does not automatically produce a valid measure of a domain. Tests like the cloze and informal reading inventory are CR tests, and brief CR tests may be found in manuals that accompany some basal reading programs.

Guidelines for evaluating CR tests have been suggested by Hambleton and Eignor (1978), who evaluated five CR reading tests and found that most fell short of the technical quality necessary to accomplish their intended purposes.

Among the factors to consider in selecting, constructing, or interpreting CR tests are these:

1. Good tests will not overcome the problem of poor objectives.
2. There is a danger that factors in the affective domain (e.g., appreciation or attitudes) might be overlooked because they are difficult to measure.
3. Objectives involving retention and transfer of what is learned may become secondary to the one-time demonstration of mastery (Otto 1973).
4. There is some question whether all measured skills are equally important, and if having to go through a specified skill sequence helps or hinders reading development (Popp 1975).
5. The skills sampled may not be relevant to reading achievement; for example, McNeil (1974) found that three skills supposedly prerequisite for decoding ability were not mastered by 75% of the best readers.

Cloze Procedure

The *cloze procedure* requires the reader to supply words that have been deleted from the passage (see Fig. 7.1). Invented by Ebbinghaus in 1897, the technique

---

Immediately the two birds changed their tactics. In an instant they _____ in front of me, _____ before my face almost _____ flycatchers, still uttering their _____ *chink* note. I stopped _____ to watch them. It _____ have been impossible to _____ fishing with that flurry _____ wings going on almost _____ my face. Once more _____ flew to a bush _____, but the minute I _____ downstream again, they _____ back around my head.

_____ put my rod down, _____ it against a bush, _____ watched them. They quieted, _____ continued to flutter their _____. It came to me, _____ I do not know, _____ they were not trying _____ lead me *from* something. _____ wanted me to come _____ them.

Deleted words in order of deletion: were, fluttering, like, distressed, again, would, continue, of, in, they, upstream, faced, were, I, leaning, and, but, wings, how, that, to, They, with.

Figure 7.1. Part of a cloze test. Reprinted from *The Gift of Reason* by Walter D. Edmonds by permission of *Cricket* magazine and the author, copyright © 1977 by Walter D. Edmonds. Taken from *Visions and Revisions*, p. 54. Copyright © The Economy Company, 1980. Reproduced by permission of the publishers.

gained popularity with its introduction as a measure of readability by Taylor (1953), and soon was also used as a measure of reading comprehension. Only its use as a measure of reading ability is considered here. Its use as a teaching device is discussed on page 578 and as a measure of readability on page 696.

CONSTRUCTION.   A passage for a cloze test on a particular book may be randomly selected; this, however, assumes that the selected passage is representative of the text's difficulty. Representative samples may be selected in the same way as selections for an IRI (see p. 219-220). Or a number of passages can be chosen randomly, made into cloze tests, and administered to students similar to those for whom the material is intended. The passage whose score (percentage of correct responses) comes closest to the average of the passage scores is used for the cloze test.

Because a minimum of 50 deletions is needed for high reliability,[3] a cloze passage in which every fifth word is deleted (the typical procedure) should be at least 250 words in length. Correspondingly longer passages are needed if the deletions occur less frequently. Often the first and last sentences are left intact to supply necessary clues. Usually deletions are made randomly (e.g., every fifth word beginning with the second word). Random word deletions provide a better measure of reading ability than do deletions of specific kinds of words (C. Robinson 1981). Studies have shown that cloze tests that delete only content words (nouns, verbs, adjectives, adverbs) measure different processes than tests in which only function words are deleted. Content words are the most difficult words to replace (Warwick 1978). Deleted words that appear often elsewhere in the text are the more likely to be replaced correctly, because more cues are available (Drum & Konopak 1987).

The selections are duplicated with equal-length lines replacing the deleted words. Use of a dash for each letter yields significantly higher scores than use of lines of equal length (Rush & Klare 1978). The purpose for testing dictates the range of selections to be used.

ADMINISTRATION.   Pupils, particularly young children, should be given guided practice in how to perform the task before a cloze test is used. Pupils do not read the original intact text before reading the cloze test passage. Before the cloze test is administered, students should be told to read the whole cloze selection silently and, while doing so, to think of words that could best complete the blanks. Then they reread the test selection silently and write in the missing words. Further rereading is allowed. A generous amount of time should be allowed to complete the test.

SCORING AND INTERPRETATION.   Because examiners may differ as to which synonyms are acceptable (thus reducing reliability), most authors suggest that only the exact deleted word should be counted as a correct response. However, based on the belief that the ability to supply synonyms indicates comprehension, some examiners may wish to accept them or to score the cloze test in

---

[3]A 50–item cloze yields a reliability coefficient of about 0.85 (Bormuth 1975a).

both ways (exact word replacements and exact word plus acceptable synonym replacements). There are, however, no criteria for determining functional reading levels when synonyms are accepted. The cloze score is the number of correct responses divided by the number of deleted items, expressed as a percentage.

According to Bormuth (1968), the instructional level is indicated by a cloze score of between 44% and 57%; scores below 44% indicate the frustration level, scores above 57%, the independent level. Very similar results with subjects of various ages are reported by Rankin (1971) and Peterson, Paradis, and Peters (1973). In these studies, every fifth word was deleted and only exact word replacements were scored as correct. Therefore, if these criteria are used, these same procedures must be followed.

There is not a consensus as to cloze criteria. For instance, Bormuth (1975a) also presents criteria that vary with grade level and kind of reading material; and Pikulski and Tobin (1982) suggest the following: Instructional level = 30% to 50%; frustration level = below 30%; independent level = above 50%. Most criteria are suggested for use with all pupils, regardless of their level of reading ability, but Peterson and Carroll (1974) report that a cloze score of between 38% and 44% indicates the instructional level of disabled readers.

ADVANTAGES.   The main advantage claimed for the cloze procedure over other measures of reading ability is that no extraneous questions of unknown difficulty act as unassessed variables. Its other advantages include: (1) It is easier and quicker to construct, administer, score, and interpret than the IRI; (2) its use requires less expertise; (3) it can be given to groups; (4) it provides a good measurement of the ability to use semantic and syntactic cues; and (5) research findings regarding its reliability and validity for children over age 8 are impressive (Warwick 1978). Additional information concerning cloze procedures may be found in Pikulski and Tobin (1982).

POSSIBLE LIMITATIONS.   All tests have limitations, and the cloze is no exception. An as yet unidentified minimum level of reading ability is necessary to employ the linguistic skills required by the cloze. Young children, and even older children, may have difficulty spelling or writing their answers. Accepting approximate spellings, spelling words for them, or administering the test individually with the answers given orally can help to overcome these possible limitations. It is often suggested that an every-tenth-word deletion pattern be used with young children because they find an every-fifth-word deletion too difficult. But it is difficult even to find a 250-word selection below the second reader level. Therefore, when used with young children, shorter and less reliable cloze tests may have to be employed.

Cloze tests provide only limited diagnostic information. If given in the usual way, as a silent reading task, cloze tests yield little information regarding the pupil's word-recognition skills, decoding skills, or relative abilities to comprehend explicit versus implicit textual information. High cloze test scores do not guarantee that the reader understood the overall meaning of the text or comprehended its main idea (Grundin et al. 1978) (see the following paragraph). Performance on the cloze is highly influenced by: (1) the reader's ability to use language, which is a combination of language development and reading ability; and (2) the reader's level of prior knowledge about the topic under consideration in the text because high topical knowledge should make it easier to predict what words have been deleted (W. L. Smith 1978). Cloze results may also be influenced by the literary style of the author (Johnston 1983) and by which words have been deleted (e.g., it is easier to replace a noun marker such as *the* than a noun that is not mentioned elsewhere in the passage).

What cloze tests really measure is unclear (Farr & Carey 1986), and there is disagreement as to whether the cloze is a valid measure of reading comprehension. Some (e.g., Warwick 1978) hold that it is a valid measure. Those who maintain that the cloze is not a valid measure base their argument primarily on the belief that the cloze task often does not require the reader to integrate information across sentences in order to be able to replace the deleted words. Chavez-Oller et al. (1985) found that about 10% of the cloze items were sensitive to constraints that reached even beyond 50 words on either side of the blank, and that although this sort of context sensitivity is inaccessible to unskilled readers, it becomes increasingly more accessible as language proficiency develops.

Cloze scores do not closely approximate the functional reading levels estimated by other procedures (Entin & Klare 1978, Smith & Beck 1980). Cloze scores correlate only 0.63 with free recall performance (Shanahan & Kamil 1982), with reading comprehension scores across a variety of tests and populations from about 0.40 to 0.80 (Shanahan & Kamil 1984), and with IRIs from 0.67 to 0.83 (DeSanti 1989).

MODIFICATIONS OF THE CLOZE. One modification of the cloze is the *maze test* in which each deletion is accompanied by three choices. Detailed instructions for constructing and interpreting a modified maze test have been presented by Dieterich, Freeman, and Griffen (1978). The criteria suggested by Guthrie et al. (1974) indicate that scores of 60% to 70% indicate the maze instructional level for disabled readers. These criteria, however, may be too low for use with children who are making normal progress in reading (Pikulski & Tobin 1982).

In the *matching cloze test*, the deleted words are clustered and placed next to the selection. This would seem to make the task easier than the normal cloze but more difficult than the maze. However, no criteria have been established for interpreting matching cloze tests.

Informal Measures

Published reading tests make demands on children that differ from those they face in their daily school programs. In order to obtain a reliable measure of silent reading ability, silent reading skills must be monitored by the teacher during daily reading activities, not just during reading instruction.

Children's understanding of what they have read is often checked by means of oral questions and answers. Oral questioning has several advantages over written questions and responses, (1) The question can allow freedom of response, (2) misunderstood questions can be detected immediately and clarified, (3) follow-up probes to incomplete or inaccurate responses are possible, and (4) socialized discussions and exchanges of opinion can occur. The major disadvantage is that usually only one child has a chance to answer a particular question.

Written comprehension checks are also desirable at times, particularly when the teacher assigns a selection for silent reading by one group while he or she is working with another group. Usually the teacher provides the group that is working independently with a set of questions to answer.

Observations that should be made while children are reading silently are discussed on pages 207-208.

Measuring Rate of Reading

Silent reading rate can be measured on a series of short paragraphs of increasing difficulty or of equivalent difficulty; we prefer the latter. Or rate can be measured on one long passage of several hundred words. In either case, if the material is too difficult for the child to comprehend, an accurate measure of reading rate cannot be obtained. Either a predetermined time limit is imposed for reading the passage(s) or the time required to complete the task is determined. On many rate tests, comprehension is checked.

A number of standardized reading tests provide measures of silent reading rate on those levels intended for use above the intermediate-grade level; a few have rate tests at the intermediate-grade level. Most rate scores on multipurpose standardized reading tests are based on reading for only a very short time period.

Informal tests of reading rate are easy to give and should be administered from time to time as a routine procedure in reading instruction above the fifth grade. Selections should be easy for the students. To obtain a fairly accurate measure, a selection should take the child 5 to 7 minutes to read.

The simplest way to measure rate is to start all pupils together and measure the time necessary for each child to finish reading the selection. Pupils should be encouraged to read as fast as they can, but informed that they will be questioned about the selection. They should be told to look up as soon as they finish reading the selection and to copy on their papers the number displayed by the teacher. The teacher should change the number at regular intervals; every 10 seconds gives sufficient accuracy. Knowing the number of words in the selection, the teacher can prepare in advance a table that gives in words per minute the rate corresponding to each number. If the number is changed 6 times a minute (e.g., 1 = 10 seconds has elapsed, 4 = 40 seconds, and so forth), the rate in WPM for any number is obtained by multiplying the number of words read by 6 and dividing by the number copied down (e.g., 200 words read $\times$ 6 $\div$ 8 = 150 WPM).

Another technique is to say "Mark" at the end of each minute and have the pupils mark the last word they read before the signal. The number of words read in each minute can be counted and averaged. This technique may reveal which parts of the selection are difficult for the children, and whether or not they are adjusting their reading rates to the difficulty. Another variation is to give only one signal to mark and then to divide the number of words read by the number of minutes allowed. This procedure is especially suitable with selection for which the cumulative total of words is given at the end of each line. After this type of rate test is over, slower readers should be allowed to finish the selection so as to have a fair chance on the comprehension test.

When a pupil is tested individually, the time taken to complete the selection can be obtained with a stopwatch, or a watch with a second hand, and the WPM computed. Norms for rate of reading are given in Table 17.1 on page 633. Because rate of reading varies according to the reader's purpose, the material read, and the reader's knowledge of the topic, any norms for rate must be considered rough approximations.

A comparison of a pupil's reading rate and comprehension may reveal various combinations ranging from very rapid rate-very accurate comprehension to very slow rate-very weak comprehension. Assuming that the tests reflect what the pupil does typically, such a comparison may suggest what needs to be done to help the student (see pp. 638-640).

Such information can also be helpful in interpreting the pupils' WPM scores, and possibly in suggesting follow-up procedures to determine the bases for the scores. For example, Steven's very slow rate with very high comprehension may indicate that he read the material more than once, or that he needs to realize that he need not read everything at the same slow rate, or perhaps that he is overly compulsive. An exceedingly high WPM rate with very low comprehension may indicate that Joan only skimmed the material. A follow-up may further indicate either that she could comprehend the text adequately when she slowed down her rate, or that the material was much too difficult for her to understand at any rate.

Particular care should be exercised in interpreting some reading-rate scores. Some rate scores are derived from the combined time taken to read the passage(s) and to answer the comprehension questions. Such scores reflect the students' speed of working, not their speed of reading (Farr & Carey 1986). At times, "efficiency" scores are derived by multiplying the WPM rate by the percent of correct comprehension expressed as a decimal. Such scores can be deceiving. For instance, a pupil who read at 50 WPM with 100% comprehension would have an efficiency score of 50 (50 × 1.00). A student who read at 100 WPM but answered only half the questions would obtain the same score (100 × .5).

At times, it is useful to measure oral reading rates also. Beyond the initial stages of reading acquisition, reading rates are normally increasingly slower for oral than for silent reading. When a student above the third grade does not generally read faster silently than orally, the reasons should be determined. A check of the student's oral reading rate may indicate a lack of automatic word recognition that is strongly contributing to the equally low silent reading rate. A measure of oral reading rate may also reveal that, although a child met the word-recognition and comprehension criteria at a particular reading level, he or she read the material at an exceedingly slow rate, thus suggesting processing difficulties. In such cases, the examiner may judge material at that level to be too difficult for instructional purposes for that pupil.

Literature

At the elementary school level, literature programs usually are conceived of as recreational reading programs whose main objectives are to develop an appreciation for children's literature, to refine interests and tastes, and to develop an interest in reading as a leisure-time activity. No standardized tests measure the attainment of these aims. Observations of children's behaviors during planned recreational reading periods and free time, as well as discussions of what they have read, are the most appropriate measures to use. Another desired outcome—personal growth—can be assessed only over time through continued observations.

In the upper grades and in high school, some standardized tests and teacher-made tests attempt to assess such things as knowledge of story characters and plots, and the ability to critique a story. Teacher-made tests are better suited for such assessments because they can be geared to the school's instructional program. No single type of assessment or single test can cover the objectives of a recreational reading or literature program. Purves (1986b) provides a procedure for specifying the objectives of a literature curriculum and for developing measures of how well the desired outcomes are achieved.

Study Skills

Norm-referenced tests designed for use at or above the intermediate grades may include subtests of study skills. These study skills tests measure a wide variety of skills and knowledge, and there does not appear to be a consensus as to what should be included in such tests and how it should be measured (Farr & Carey 1986).

INDIVIDUAL MEASURES

T. Harris and Hodges (1981) define an *individual test* as one "designed to be administered to one person at a time by a trained examiner." The key terms in this definition are *designed* and *trained examiner*. The first term implies that an individual test differs by design from a group test. For tests that measure general level of reading ability, this usually means that the test measures oral, rather than silent, reading. By necessity, group-administered reading tests must be read silently, but it is possible to design an individual test of silent reading ability. The second difference is that an oral reading test employs other criteria in addition to comprehension. Another design difference is the way in which comprehension is measured. Most group tests measure reading comprehension by using multiple-choice items. Individual tests employ free recall or a format in which both the questions and answers are given orally after either oral or silent reading. Probing of responses may also be allowed.

The second term, *trained examiner,* implies that some special training is needed to administer and interpret the test properly. Group tests require little training to administer, score, or interpret. The reliability of a score obtained from an individual test, especially if it is an oral reading test, is dependent on the skill of the examiner in giving and scoring the test. Examiner skill is even more important in interpreting performance than in giving an individual test.

Administering a group test to an individual is possible and at times desirable. For example, a student could be asked to read a norm-referenced test aloud or silently and after answering each question, she could be asked to explain why she selected that option.

General Behavioral Observations

Observing student behaviors as they read often provides useful diagnostic information. Some behaviors may appear when the pupil is reading orally or silently; others are manifested only during one mode.

SILENT OR ORAL READING BEHAVIORS. Several behaviors may occur when the child is reading either orally or silently. The following are the more frequently noted of these behaviors.

Lateral Head Movements. Moving the head from side to side may interfere with speed of reading because the eyes can move much more rapidly than the head.

Finger Pointing. Finger pointing may be manifested in various ways that may have different meanings. Some students point to each word. If word-by-word reading is also observed, the examiner should determine whether the word-by-word reading is the cause or the effect of the word-by-word pointing or if both behaviors are caused by a factor such as weak word recognition or difficulty in keeping the place. Other kinds of finger pointing include moving the finger or an object under one phrase at a time as an aid in phrasing, moving the finger under the line of print without pausing, using the hand or finger as a marker under each line of print, or marking the beginning of each line with the finger. All of these behaviors may indicate that the learner is having difficulty keeping the place on the page. Such behaviors may be helpful in avoiding faulty return eye sweeps and omissions of phrases or lines.

Inappropriate Rate. A child may read either too slowly or too rapidly. Excessively slow reading may result from weak word recognition, poor comprehension, inattention to the task, a compulsion to obtain perfect comprehension, or simply never having been instructed in reading faster. Reading too rapidly is probably a result of either the desire to get through the material as quickly as possible or the learner's mistaken belief that all reading should be done as rapidly as possible. Excessively rapid reading often results in poor comprehension and recall. It is difficult to determine the extent to which lack of attention or concentration plays a role in either too slow or too rapid silent reading. In cases where oral reading comprehension is markedly better than silent reading comprehension, it may well be that attention or concentration is lacking when reading silently.

Concentration-Task Orientation. The reading difficulties of some children are aggravated by their inability to concentrate on the reading matter. Such behavior may be a natural result of giving children reading matter that is uninteresting or too difficult and may disappear when more appropriate materials are used.

Inability to maintain attention to the task may also be caused by physiological or emotional problems (see pp. 285-286). Children who are worried about something may find their minds wandering because their problems are more important to them than reading. Other children are not task oriented; they avoid any self-investment in learning. Still others have never learned to assume the responsibility required in learning.

Tension Signs.   Signs of tension may take many forms: facial tics; a tense, tremulous, or almost inaudible voice; wiggling and squirming; shuffling the feet; body rigidity; crying; or an outright refusal to continue. Such signs are most often indications that the pupil finds it difficult to cope with the material or with the situation in general.

Personality Variables.   Impulsive children may respond quickly without giving any thought to their answers, whereas compulsive children may perform poorly because they do not move ahead unless they are certain that all their responses are correct. Strong anxiety can interfere with performance on tests or in classroom activities. The relationship of personality problems to reading disability is discussed on pages 364-369. A meta-analysis (Hembree 1988) reveals that test anxiety can cause poor performance at the third-grade level and above. Academic performance is more likely to improve if anxiety training is accompanied by counseling and reading or study-skills instruction (Derry & Murphy 1986).

Vision.   While the student is reading, the distance from the eyes to the book should be noted. Normal reading distance is approximately 12 to 18 inches. Holding the book nearer or farther than this distance may indicate a visual problem. Note also such behaviors as moving the book forward and backward from the eyes, reading with the head markedly tilted to one side, holding the book at unusual angles, and covering one eye. Even if children's reading is adequate, their vision may need professional care. Vision is discussed in greater detail on pages 343-348.

Posture and Lighting.   It is important for general hygiene, and particularly to avoid eyestrain, that the child sit or stand in a natural, easy posture while reading, with the back reasonably straight and the book held firmly or supported a proper distance from the eyes, on a proper level, and with adequate light that is devoid of glare.

SILENT READING BEHAVIORS.   Two behaviors can be observed only during silent reading. *Lip movements* (the "silent" pronunciation of words) and *vocalizations* (which may range from audible whispering to reading orally) are most often indications that either the child is making the transition from oral to silent reading or that the material is difficult for the child.

Frequent lip movements or vocalizations beyond the transition stage usually are symptoms that the material is too difficult for the pupil. Occasional lip movements or vocalization suggests that the student is having difficulty only with that part of the text.

ORAL READING BEHAVIORS.   Having the child read orally provides an opportunity to gain insights into reading behaviors that are not observable during silent reading. Oral reading is a more difficult task than silent reading because the student must not only understand the material, but must have the additional skills that allow him or her to transmit that understanding to others.

Several behaviors are readily observable during oral reading. The following are the more frequently noted of these behaviors.

Fluency.   Definitions of *oral reading fluency* generally include reference to speed, ease of reading, expressiveness, and appropriate intonation. In other words, word recognition is rapid and accurate, the words are grouped in thought units (phrased acceptably), reading flows smoothly, and the voice is used to indicate an acceptable understanding of the text. Most of these behaviors are discussed in the following sections. Hesitations and repetitions are defects in fluency. In some scoring systems, hesitations are considered to be word-recognition errors; repetitions almost always are. A lack of ease and smoothness in reading may indicate the child's nervousness or self-consciousness or it could be the result of having to read orally at sight. A lack of fluency may indicate word-recognition or comprehension problems, but fluency does not necessarily indicate adequate comprehension.

Word-by-Word Reading.   In *word-by-word reading,* the reader plods along slowly, tending to pause noticeably after almost every word. The wrong words may be grouped together, and punctuation may be ignored or misinterpreted. Finger pointing often accompanies word-by-word reading, as do lip movements during silent reading and a monotonous voice during oral reading. Word recognition, though slow, may be fairly accurate, particularly on easy materials. Some word-by-word readers have marked deficiencies in their word-recognition techniques; others have learned these strategies fairly well, but have not overcome the habit of reading one word at a time.

Word-by-word readers usually do better on vocabulary or sentence comprehension tests than on tests of paragraph meaning. Their reading rate is understandably very slow, and reading may become a distasteful activity. Understanding and recall of connected discourse is frequently poor, and material often has to be reread in order to comprehend it. Although comprehension may be adequate on material that is conceptually familiar to the child, word-by-word reading puts a strain on short-term memory and may interfere with comprehension of more difficult material.

Word-by-word reading and inadequate phrasing (see below) may result from reading orally at sight. This possibility may be checked after testing by having the child preread appropriate material silently and then reread it orally. If the undesirable behavior lessens greatly, there is no need to be concerned about it. If it persists, the causes should be determined and appropriate action taken. Some word-by-word readers need to increase their word-recognition accuracy or automaticity, or to expand their sight vocabularies. Others need to learn to group printed words into meaningful phrases.

When word-by-word reading occurs only, or primarily, on material that is frustratingly difficult for the pupil, it need not be treated directly. Providing the child with material of more appropriate difficulty will suffice.

Inadequate Phrasing.   Although the ways in which the words in a sentence may be grouped into phrases can vary slightly, each phrase usually represents a thought unit. *Inadequate phrasing* means that the reader is not grouping words into meaningful units. Grouping words into thought units facilitates comprehension by placing less of a strain on the reader's information-processing capacity. For example, a 15-word sentence chunked into three phrases means that only three bits of information need be held in short-term memory. Lack of comprehension may contribute to inadequate phrasing, or vice versa.

As with most observed behaviors, inadequate phrasing is not necessarily an either/or proposition. It may occur only during certain portions of the text. In such instances, the behavior may indicate that something in that part of the text is causing a processing problem for the child.

Ignoring or Misinterpreting Punctuation.   Ignoring or misinterpreting punctuation marks may adversely affect comprehension, especially when phrases, clauses, or sentences are run together. Such behaviors usually reflect a lack of training in the use of punctuation marks or an anxiety manifested by rushing through the reading material.

Inadequate Use of Voice.   *Inadequate use of voice* may take many forms: reading in monotone, volume too loud or too soft, poor enunciation, lack of expression, not speeding up or slowing down to portray the tempo of the story, or tense or high-pitched voice. The latter is usually a symptom of the difficulty of the material. Most of the other behaviors can be attributed to a lack of training, tenseness when reading orally, or the fact that reading is done at sight.

Speech.   The classroom or reading teacher cannot help noticing salient facts about children's clarity of speech and use of voice while listening to them read. Major speech faults such as stuttering, stammering, and lisping are easily detected. Unclear enunciation and faulty pronunciation should also be noted. The quality, pitch, and intensity of the child's voice also deserve attention. A weak, tense, strained, or high-pitched voice may be a highly significant indication that the child is nervous in the reading situation. Excessively loud, nasal, and singsong voices may also be encountered. The former may indicate a hearing loss.

The above behaviors are not mutually exclusive; they often occur together. A child may read word by word in a voice almost too soft to be heard. These behaviors may occur only when the child is reading before a group, particularly one composed of peers. Such a situation usually suggests that something in the classroom situation is inducing anxiety.

Context Readers.   Using context clues as an aid to word recognition and meaning is a desirable reading strategy that is frequently and effectively used by skilled readers. Some pupils, however, rely excessively on the general context of the passage. These *context readers* tend to read fairly fluently orally, but their word recognition is inaccurate. They go merrily along, skipping and adding words, or substituting one word for another. When there are too many unknown words or when they are no longer able to make good use of the general context, they may invent a new story that bears little resemblance to the printed text. Context readers tend to score higher on silent than oral reading tests and on tests that involve finding the general meaning of a selection than on tests calling for painstaking attention to details.

There are two general types of context readers. First are those who have the ability to read more accurately but choose not to. Often their excessive reliance on context has become habitual. They can usually reread sentences accurately after being told that they were misread. Within this first group are two subtypes, those who can read for significant details but who are content with obtaining the gist of the material, and those who do not know how to read for details.

The other type of context reader has limited word recognition and/or decoding skills. Therefore, such students must rely mainly on context for any word that is not in their sight vocabularies. If a child has sufficient cognitive and linguistic competence or can relate a great deal of prior knowledge to the passage, his or her guesses will often be accurate or at least acceptable. When too many words are unknown or when the context is not potent enough, the guesses become inaccurate and disruptive. This second type of context reader needs to improve word-recognition and/or decoding skills and learn to use them in combination with context clues.

Interpreting Observed Behaviors

When one of these behaviors occurs with material with which a child has few if any word-recognition or comprehension problems, the behavior may be a sign of overall tension or anxiety, or it may simply be a habit that has remained long after the need for it has disappeared. If tension or anxiety appear to cause the behavior, the child's overall reading performance should be interpreted cautiously: It may not reliably indicate the level at which the child could read when relaxed. Taking time to establish rapport with the child before initiating testing often relieves tension. The source of any marked anxiety should be determined and appropriate action taken. If the behavior appears to be an "unneeded carryover," the examiner must decide if it warrants immediate or eventual attention, or if it can simply be ignored. The guideline for making such decisions is: "To what extent is this behavior contributing presently to the child's reading problem, or to someone's belief that this child is a poorer reader than he or she actually is?"

Consideration should be given to the frequency and intensity of the behavior. An occasional occurence may have little significance or it may indicate a problem in processing that part of the text. Increases in a single behavior or displays of new undesirable behaviors are also symptoms that the material is becoming increasingly difficult for the child. Marked presence of one or more of the behaviors strongly suggests that the child is having difficulty processing the text.

Word-Recognition Errors and Miscues

Deviations from the printed text are commonly referred to as *word-recognition errors*. The term *miscue* (K. Goodman 1969) is more appropriate because the deviations may reflect the reader's attempt to make sense of what is being read.

There is no consensus as to which behaviors should be classified as miscues or errors. More important, most scoring systems do not consider the serious-ness of the miscue. Typically, all miscues are given equal weight in scoring a child's oral reading performance (e.g., a response of either "cat" or "go" to the stimulus *kitten* is counted as one error).[4] Simply counting the number of mis-cues has value only in determining whether a given criterion has been met. Even then, the seriousness of the miscues should be considered in judging the suitability of the material for instructional purposes or in determining the child's general level of reading ability.

A single sample of reading behaviors may not be reliable. Therefore we recommend that, whenever possible, an analysis of a student's reading behav-iors be based on a number of samples over a period of time.

MISPRONUNCIATIONS. Mispronunciations may involve whole words ("dog" for *cat*), word parts in various positions ("cap" for *cat* or "cut" for *cat*), or a combination of word parts ("cup" for *cat*). Some writers distinguish between *mispronunciations* and *substitutions*, the latter indicating that the response made sense in the sentence. Mispronunciations may be caused by inadequate word recognition, inadequate use of context clues, weak decoding skills, over-reliance on the initial elements of words, overreliance on context, or inattention to word parts. Responses that are semantically and/or syntactically inappropriate indicate that the pupil is not using context or language clues. Substitutions and mispronunciations are often the most frequent kinds of miscues.

To determine if a mispronunciation is caused by inability to recognize or decode the word, present the mispronounced word and ask the child to pro-nounce it. If her attempt is unsuccessful, and if the word is phonetically regular, ask her to decode it. Lack of success at this point suggests either that the child has a decoding problem, or that she has the necessary decoding skills but is reluctant to use them. Encouraging her to try to decode out loud may help re-solve the issue. Focusing the child's attention on the mispronounced part will help determine if inattention to word parts may be a problem. Under- or overrel-iance on context can be determined by examining the contextual appropriate-ness of the mispronunciations.

Some readers observe the first one or two letters of a word and then guess or infer the rest of it. Intelligent context readers are often surprisingly successful in their use of this strategy because their prior knowledge and facility with lan-guage allows them to predict words. Duller or less experienced children and those with limited linguistic ability also attempt to use this technique, but their predictions are often inappropriate. Among the most common errors made by those who rely on this strategy are confusions of words that begin with *wh* (e.g., *when, where, which*) or *th* (*them, then, there*). Substitutions such as "then" for *when* often result in sentences that remain syntactically acceptable.

Errors on the middles and ends of words are more common than errors in the initial position. The middles of words are especially apt to be misread.

DIALECT VARIATIONS. We do not all pronounce words in the same way. These variations reflect our exposure to regional and cultural dialects and our

[4]A scoring procedure that considers the relative seriousness of miscues is described on page 228.

personal idiosyncracies. Most dialect differences occur on vowel sounds. For example, *I* /ī/ is commonly pronounced as /ah/ in the South. In many parts of the United States, *path* is pronounced with a short vowel sound /ă/. Many New Englanders, however, pronounce *path* with an /ä/ as in *father*, while no *r* is heard in their pronunciation of words like *yard*. Short /ĕ/ is indistinguishable from short /ă/ in some regions and from short /ĭ/ in others. Sometimes words that rhyme in standard English do not rhyme in a particular dialect.

Older published oral reading tests do not take dialect renditions into consideration in scoring. This can influence test scores. For example, not counting dialect miscues as word-recognition errors increased the average scores on the *Spache, Gilmore* and *Gray* tests by slightly over a half year (Burke, Pflaum, & Knafle 1982). Dialect speakers are sometimes inconsistent in their use of dialect while reading, using a dialect rendition in one sentence and standard English in the next. When pupils read orally in accordance with their dialects, the deviations from SE should not be considered word-recognition errors. To decide if a response is a dialect variation, one must be familiar with the characteristics of the dialect and how they deviate from SE. Such information about three dialects spoken by minority children can be found in Harris and Sipay (1979, pp. 459-465, 469-472, 479-481).

WORDS AIDED. Some oral reading tests forbid pronouncing unknown words for the pupil. The number of mispronunciations or omissions is likely to be higher on such tests than on tests that allow words to be pronounced for the child. When part of the scoring system, words are usually pronounced for the pupil after a 5-second hesitation. The possible effect of pronouncing words for the child should be considered in interpreting the comprehension score: It may be inflated because without such assistance, comprehension would have been hindered.

OMISSIONS. While reading, a child may omit whole words, word parts, groups of words, or entire lines of print. Omissions may or may not be deliberate, may be caused by inattention, or may suggest a visual anomaly.

Goodman and Gollasch (1980) contend that there are two kinds of word omissions. *Deliberate omissions* are those that the reader, after consideration, chooses to make rather than make a response or ask for the teacher's help. Words that the child cannot recognize or decode may be deliberately omitted. *Nondeliberate omissions*, of which readers are often unaware, include dialect and first-language renditions, omissions of words that the author could have left out without influencing the intended meaning (e.g., noun and clause markers such as *that* in "Rob told his father that the cat was ill"), and omissions dictated by other miscues (e.g., *the dog sits* . . . is rendered as "the dogs sit . . ."). According to Goodman and Gollasch, omissions do not occur frequently (about 10% of the miscues made); nondeliberate omissions are much more frequent than deliberate omissions; and comprehension is rarely affected by omissions.

If the child correctly responds to the omitted words most of the time, word-recognition problems are not causing the omissions. At times, the pupil may not be attending to the task or to word parts, most often word endings or the middle syllable of polysyllabic words. The occasional omission of groups of words or a whole line of print may be the result of inattention to the task. Frequent omissions of whole lines of print suggest that the child has difficulty keeping the place on the page. Allowing the child to use a marker will help the examiner to decide if such is the case.

ADDITIONS. At times while reading, students add words or word parts that are not in the printed text. Most often, *additions*, or *insertions* as they are sometimes called, are in line with a previous miscue or happen because the reader has anticipated words occurring in certain patterns. Additions do not occur frequently and seldom distort the intended meaning (D'Angelo & Maklios 1983). Despite this, it is still important to examine all reading behaviors because a particular type may be disruptive for a given child.

REVERSALS. There are four kinds of *reversals:* (1) whole word ("was" for *saw*); (2) single letter ("big" for *dig*); (3) letter order (*"clam"* for *calm*); and (4) word order ("I was" for *Was I*). Reversals almost always affect the meaning adversely and therefore are usually serious miscues. The possible causes of reversals are discussed on pages 478-479.

REPETITIONS. Word parts, single words, or groups of words may be repeated. In most scoring systems, repetitions of less than two words are not counted as errors. Repetitions may be made (1) to correct a miscue, (2) to aid comprehension, (3) to regain the train of thought, or (4) to stall for time while attempting to recognize or decode a word. Any of the four possible causes, if they occur frequently, may be an indication that the material is too difficult for the pupil. Repetitions may be habitual in that the behavior persists after the original causes are no longer present. Extreme nervousness when reading orally or being tested may cause repetitions. Repetitions also occur during silent reading but can be noted only by careful observation or through the use of eye-movement photography.

OTHER BEHAVIORS SCORED AS ERRORS. In some scoring systems, not responding to a word immediately is countered as a *hesitation* error. Ignoring or misinterpreting a punctuation mark may also be counted as one error. In a few systems, each self-correction is considered to be an error. Whether or not such behaviors are considered errors may affect test scores.

SELF-CORRECTIONS. A reader may or may not correct a deviation from the printed text. At times, self-corrections occur almost immediately following a child's miscue; at other times, only after material further in the text provides information that something was wrong with the response. Pupils are more likely to correct miscues that are semantically and syntactically inappropriate than those that make sense and are grammatically correct. Syntactically inappropriate miscues are more likely to be self-corrected than are semantically inappropriate miscues. Self-correction behavior may range from correcting every miscue to rarely, if ever, making a self-correction. Both extremes are undesirable. The former suggests that the reader may be overly concerned with accurate word recognition; the latter that the child is not monitoring his or her comprehension. Generally, an analysis of when children self-correct (and when they do not) provides information about their use of semantic and syntactic cues. However, when most of the uncorrected miscues occur at the frustration level, it may simply indicate that the material was too difficult for the child. It is difficult to self-correct when the story makes little or no sense. Also, some children choose not to self-correct even though they are aware that the miscues are disruptive. Others who do not self-correct overtly may do so covertly. This may be one reason why some children can answer a comprehension question correctly, even though they have mispronounced or omitted a key word. It is also possible that such responses have been gained from redundant information in the text or from prior knowledge.

Self-corrections require a number of control strategies including awareness that meaning or syntax has been disturbed, ability to reassess the context, ability to reexamine and vary word-recognition procedures, and ability to judge the success of the attempt. Self-correction ratios are highly related to progress in learning to read during the first three years of instruction (Chittenden 1984).

RELATIVE FREQUENCY OF ORAL READING BEHAVIORS. The frequency with which various reading behaviors occur varies with reading ability, grade level, and the teaching methodology employed. Individual pupils may differ considerably from the average number of occurrences. Relative frequency also varies with the error classification used. Weber (1968), who analyzed over 50 studies of oral reading errors, points out that lack of agreement in the categories used by different investigators makes it difficult to compare their results. Despite these difficulties, it is safe to conclude that the most frequent oral reading difficulty is inadequate word recognition.

Informal Assessment

In the typical reading lesson, preparation is usually followed by guided silent reading, and oral reading is usually a form of rereading for a definite purpose. The teacher may, for example, ask a child to read orally the sentence that contains the answer to a specific question. Under these conditions, teacher and pupil are likely to focus their attention on the appropriateness of the child's choice more than on the qualities of the oral reading. When a teacher wishes to evaluate oral reading behaviors as such, the testing situation should be planned to provide optimum conditions for a careful appraisal. While one child is reading to the teacher, the rest of the class can be engaged in other activities.

The teacher should survey the major strengths and weaknesses each child shows in oral reading. For this purpose, a checklist like the one given in Figure 7.2 can be conveniently used. Copies of the checklist can be duplicated. As the child reads, or immediately after he or she has finished, the teacher runs down the checklist, marking items that are characteristic of the child's reading.

Some teachers prefer to use a briefer checklist so that the results from the group or whole class can be summarized on one sheet. A form convenient for this purpose is shown in Figure 7.3. Particular weaknesses are marked with checks, or with double checks for severe problems, in the appropriate column. A record like this makes it easy to select children who have a similar weakness and can be placed together in a special-needs group.

I. Word recognition, general
_____ 1. Inadequate sight vocabulary
_____ 2. Errors on high-utility words
_____ 3. Omits: _____ whole words; _____ word elements: _____ initial, _____ medial, _____ final
_____ 4. Inserts: _____ whole words; _____ word elements: _____ initial, _____ medial, _____ final
_____ 5. Doesn't attempt to decode unknown words
_____ 6. Tends to guess unknown words; _____ overrelies on initial elements
_____ 7. Tends to respond rapidly, with most responses being _____ appropriate _____ inappropriate

II. Use of context–language
_____ A. Relies heavily on context
_____ 1. Substitutes words of similar meaning
_____ 2. Substitutes words that are grammatically correct
_____ 3. Reads words correctly in context that are misread in isolation
_____ B. Inadequate use of context
_____ 1. Substitutes words of similar appearance but different meaning
_____ 2. Substitutes words that spoil or change meaning
_____ 3. Makes errors that produce nonsense
_____ 4. Rarely self-corrects

III. Decoding procedures
_____ 1. No apparent decoding strategies
_____ 2. Unsuccessfully attempts to decode
_____ 3. Breaks words into useful parts, such as spelling patterns and syllables
_____ 4. Uses morphemic analysis: _____ inflected endings, _____ compound words, _____ prefixes, _____ root words, _____ suffixes
_____ 5. Looks for little words in big words
_____ 6. Spells unknown words
_____ 7. Attempts to sound out: _____ single letters, _____ phonograms, _____ syllables
_____ 8. Overrelies on configuration, size, and shape
_____ 9. Attends mainly to one part of word: _____ initial, _____ medial, _____ final
_____ 10. Lacks flexibility in decoding
_____ 11. Overrelies on decoding

Figure 7.2. An oral reading checklist. This checklist does not attempt to provide an exhaustive list of oral reading behaviors. Also note that it stresses undesirable behaviors. A single check can be used to indicate the presence of a strength or weakness; a double check, a marked presence. This form may be copied without permission.

Many teachers are skeptical of the value of systematically recording oral reading behaviors. They are confident in their ability to remember important facts about their pupils without a written record. Using the checklist system often points out to such skeptics that they have either overlooked or have forgotten a number of specific points about pupils during weeks or months of work.

For a more detailed study of oral reading behaviors and miscues, it is preferable to have a duplicate copy of the reading material on which the information can be recorded. Such a procedure is described in detail on pages 222-224. With

IV. Possible specific decoding difficulties
 —— 1. Visual analysis skills: —— monosyllabic words, —— polysyllabic words
 —— 2. Symbol–sound association skills: —— consonants: —— single,
  —— blends, —— digraphs; —— vowels: —— single, —— short,
  —— long; —— final silent *e*; —— vowel digraphs; —— diphthongs
 —— 3. Blending: —— sounds into syllables, —— syllables into words
 —— 4. Reversal tendency
 —— 5. Letter confusions (list them)
V. Comprehension
 —— 1. Main ideas: —— strength, —— weakness
 —— 2. Facts: —— strength, —— weakness
 —— 3. Inferences: —— strength, —— weakness
VI. Fluency
 —— 1. Word-by-word reading
 —— 2. Phrases poorly
 —— 3. Hesitations
 —— 4. Repetitions
 —— 5. Ignores/misinterprets punctuation: —— commas, —— periods,
  —— question marks, —— other
 —— 6. Inappropriate speed: —— too fast, —— too slow
 —— 7. Rapid and jerky
VII. Use of voice
 —— 1. Monotone: lack of meaningful inflection
 —— 2. Enunciation generally poor
 —— 3. Slurs and runs words together
 —— 4. Sound substitutions
 —— 5. Stuttering or cluttered speech
 —— 6. Nervous or strained voice
 —— 7. Volume: —— too loud, —— too soft
 —— 8. Pitch: —— too high, —— too low
 —— 9. Peculiar cadence
VIII. Other behaviors
 —— 1. Finger pointing: —— word-by-word, —— by phrases, —— by lines,
  —— line marker
 —— 2. Head movements
 —— 3. Tension signs
 —— 4. Vision: holds book —— too close, —— too far away, —— at odd angle;
  —— covers left/right eye; —— loses place often; —— skips lines
 —— 5. Poor concentration
 —— 6. Poor task orientation
 —— 7. Impulsive behavior
 —— 8. Compulsive behavior
 —— 9. Lack of motivation
 —— 10. Unwillingness to try
 —— 11. Possible emotional problems
 —— 12. Poor reading posture

Figure 7.2.   (*continued*)

218

Name	Bob	Mary	Jane	Jim	Eric	Judy	Barb	Tony	Dave
Comprehension									
Literal									
Inferential									
Word Recognition/Decoding									
Inadequate sight vocabulary									
Words aided									
Mispronunciations									
Omissions									
Additions									
Inadequate use of context									
Overdepends on context									
High-utility words									
Visual analysis									
Symbol–sound associations									
Blending sounds									
Fluency									
Hesitations									
Repetitions									
Phrasing									
Word-by-word reading									
Ignores punctuation									
Inappropriate rate									
Loses place									
Use of voice									
enunciation									
expression									
volume									
Observations									
Tensions signs									
Finger pointing									
Head movements									
Concentration									
Book held too close/far									

Comments:

Figure 7.3. A checklist for recording oral reading characteristics. This form may be copied without permission.

experience, a fairly accurate list of the child's miscues can be recorded as shown in Figure 7.5 on page 223. Methods of analyzing word recognition are taken up later in this chapter.

A careful appraisal of each student's oral reading at intervals during the year tends to make the teacher more sensitive to the oral reading characteristics that appear during daily reading activities. The informal appraisal recommended here is a supplement to, not a replacement for, the teacher's daily observations. The frequency with which fairly thorough oral reading appraisals are made should vary according to the circumstances, but a 2-month interval will prove sufficient for most pupils. Children whose progress is poor need to be checked more often and more carefully than those who are making good progress. Once a high level of oral reading fluency is reached, thorough periodic rechecks may be a waste of time.

The Informal Reading Inventory

An *informal reading inventory* (IRI), the origin and development of which has been traced by Johns and Lunn (1983), is a series of graded representative selections taken from each reader level in a published reading series and used as a criterion-referenced test. It can be employed to determine a child's general level of reading ability and to yield diagnostic information. The range of the selections may be restricted to cover a limited span (e.g., five reader levels—the on-grade level and two levels below and above it); or the concept may be adapted to test the suitability of any materials, including content-subject textbooks. Because reading series and materials vary considerably in such factors as vocabulary, story content, difficulty, and instructional approaches, the IRI should be based on the material used for reading instruction.

CONSTRUCTION.   A word-recognition test for determining the reader level at which to initiate testing (it may also yield information regarding the pupil's ability to recognize or decode words in isolation) may be formulated by randomly selecting 10 to 20 words introduced in each reader level to be tested. Such new words are usually listed by the publisher at the back of the book. The words can be typed or printed on separate cards or can be organized as word lists (see Fig. 7.8 on p. 242).

Use the following procedures to select the test passages: Scan each text and choose at least five passages that seem representative of the book in content and language.[5] To these apply a readability formula (see pp. 691-696), which will assist in selecting samples that are representative of the book's difficulty. Application of readability formulas has revealed substantial intrabook variability, frequent disagreement with the publisher's grade-level designation, and the fact that books in a series are not always scaled from easy to difficult (Bradley 1976, Bradley & Ames 1977). The readability formula may also reveal whether the spread of difficulty within the text is narrow or wide and whether the selections progress from easy to more difficult from the beginning to the end of the book (usually they do not).

[5]Based on their study, Bradley and Ames (1977) conclude that 24 samples were necessary to adequately predict the readability values of a basal reader. According to Bormuth (1975a), little can be gained by using more than 12 samples.

From the selections whose readability has been determined, choose at least two selections that approximate the average readability score. One selection is to be used for oral reading and the other or others for obtaining further information about the child's oral reading ability, silent reading, or listening comprehension.

Using the average readability score means that if that text is used for instruction, the children will encounter some selections that are easy and some that are difficult for them. For example, the average sample from a text might be at the fifth-reader level; however, the range of readability of the entire text might be from the low-third-reader to the seventh-reader level.

Selections of 50-75 words usually suffice at preprimer level. At primer and first-reader levels, 100-150-word selections are appropriate, as are 250-300-word selections above that level. The selection chosen should end with a complete sentence. If narrative material is employed, it is preferable that the passage constitute an event that has a beginning, middle, and end. Many IRI passages do not follow this suggestion (Gillis & Olson 1987).

For each IRI selection, prepare a short introduction that provides the background necessary for understanding the selection, directions regarding how much to read and how (orally or silently), and a motivating or purpose-setting question. Such an introduction might read: "In this story, a boy has ignored the warnings of the older men in the village. Read orally from here to here to find our what happened to him as a result." Below the third-reader level, the characters' names should be told; the same is true for unusual names (e.g., Amyntas, Sioux) at any reader level.

Some examiners believe that unaided recall is the best way to measure reading comprehension. Thus they prefer to use a free-response comprehension check ("Tell me the story in your own words"). The major concepts and events in the selection should be listed in advance and checked off as the child relates the story. If the pupil does not mention key ideas, the examiner may ask specific questions on them. Some criterion should be set to judge whether the student successfully understood the selection; the categories *good, fair,* and *unsatisfactory* will usually be sufficient. See page 236 for a further discussion of this procedure.

If specific comprehension questions are to be asked, 5 to 10 relevant questions should be prepared in advance. Both literal and inferential questions should be used, with fewer inferential questions occurring at lower reader levels. The wording of questions should be clearly understood by the pupils; trick questions should be avoided. Questions that can be answered with a simple yes or no should be followed with a "How do you know?" question, the two parts being counted as one test item. Care should be exercised in the formulation of test questions because they can greatly influence IRI results (Peterson, Greenlaw, & Tierney 1978). Any IRI passage or comprehension-check item that proves unsuitable should be replaced.

Classification of Comprehension Question.   A number of classification systems have been presented for specifying the type of comprehension involved in answers to questions. In addition to those cited on pages 553-555 and 573, others have been described and illustrated by Pearson and Johnson (1978) and Lucas and McConkie (1980); in both these approaches, the relationship of the question to the information source is considered. The classification system employed can influence the findings of a study or interpretation of test results (see p. 573).

Use of a Story Grammar to Formulate Questions.   A *story grammar* is a description of the typical elements, and their relationships, frequently found in narratives. To determine the reader's understanding and recall of these events, it is helpful to think of the story as providing answers to five general questions (Sadow 1982):

1. Where and when did the events in the story take place, and who was involved in them? (Setting)
2. What started the chain of events in the story? (Initiating events)
3. What was the main character's reaction to this event? (Reaction)
4. What did the main character do about it? (Action)
5. What happened as a result of what the main character did? (Consequence)

McNeil (1987) also suggests questions whose answers require the ability to follow the organization of a story, to synthesize story information, and to reconstruct the story as a unit.

To get at an understanding of the relationship among these events requires posing other questions that create a "causal chain" in which one event leads to another (Pearson 1982). This necessitates asking *why* questions, such as, "What happened because . . .?" or, "What did _____ have to do before she could _____ ?"

RECORDING PERFORMANCE.   A student's IRI performance can be recorded in one of three ways, the choice depending on the purpose for testing and the amount of information desired. A detailed record form is not necessary if one is interested only in determining which book, or which level of material, is suitable for that child's instruction. A sheet of paper indicating the child's name, the date of testing, and the reader-level designation of the text will suffice. Next to each reader-level designation, the examiner tallies word-recognition errors or miscues as they occur, as well as the number of correctly answered comprehension questions. Later the examiner determines if the criteria have been met and subjectively evaluates the quality of the miscues.

If more detailed information is desired, either of two forms that allow for an analysis of the child's performance may be used. On a Listing/Tally Form, similar to the one shown in Figure 7.4, are recorded the student's name, date of testing, the student's reading levels (which are filled in *after* testing is completed), the reader levels tested, the pages on which they are located, the total number of words in each selection, and the criteria to be applied (the number of word-recognition errors and the number of correct comprehension questions are filled in at the end of each selection). Mispronunciations or miscues (see p. 212) are recorded under the *Said* column, with the stimulus word under the *For* column. Space is also provided to record words pronounced for the child (*Told*), omissions, additions, repetitions, and comments regarding fluency. If a parallel silent reading selection is administered, the reading rate, comprehension score, and qualitative observations should be recorded.

222 HOW TO INCREASE READING ABILITY

Name _Susie_			Date _8/29_	

Reading Levels: Independent _2_ (Low)   Instructional _2_ (High)   Frustration _3_ (Low)

Low second reader, pp. 18–20 (120 words)   WRE (6) _3_   Comp. (7) _10_

Said	For	Told	Omissions	Reversals
bag	bug	pony		
brown	black			

Fluency: _Very fluent_

High second reader, pp. 56–58 (201 words)   WRE (10) _7_   Comp. (7) _7_

Said	For	Told	Omissions	Reversals
later	last	every	giant	
covered	come			
our	the			
friends	family			
garden	yard			

Fluency: _Some misphrasing and hesitations_

Low third reader, pp. 31–33 (225 words)   WRE (11) _14_   Comp. (7) _5_

Said	For	Told	Omissions	Reversals
terror	terrible	patient	loose	girl-grill
begin	begun	anxious		
faster	fasten	during		
writing	written	shiny		
wake	weak	stomach		
ton	tongue			
screen	scream			

Fluency: _Word-by-word reading at times. Voice showed tension._

Figure 7.4.   A listing/tally form for recording oral reading performance. Cooper's (1952) definition of word–recognition errors and his criteria for the most suitable material (instructional level) were employed (see p. 227). The number in parentheses after *WRE* indicates the maximum number of allowable word–recognition errors. The number after *Comp.* indicates the minimum number of comprehension questions the child must answer correctly to meet the criterion.

The other form is a duplicated copy of the selection on which the child's performance is directly recorded (see Fig. 7.5). Double-spaced copy is used to allow room for recording. Placing the answers you are willing to accept in parentheses after each comprehension question encourages more consistent scoring. Good answers that were not anticipated should be accepted. Indicating the kind of comprehension questions (e.g., inferred main idea) or what the pupil must know or understand in order to be able to answer the question will aid later interpretation. A duplicated copy saves time because, if the expected responses are given by the child, they need only be checked off rather than written out. Also, knowing where miscues occurred can aid interpretation. Later, listing miscues (as in Fig. 7.4) can help in analyzing the child's performance. Recording the pupil's answers to the comprehension check can help in determining such

Name _Rob_ Date _2/8_

Level 16 *Free Rein*, pp. 100–101.

WRE: No more than (14) _____ Comprehension: At least (6) _____

Introduction. This story is about some birds that once lived in our country. Read (orally) (silently) from here to here to find out what they looked like, how they lived, and what happened to them.

No one has seen a passenger pigeon since

1914, for at that time the last one died in a
P
Cincinnati zoo. The passenger pigeon was a

graceful, and beautiful bird, resembling our mourn-
(dōve)
ing dove, only much larger. The male(bird) was

Λ handsomely feathered in slate blue and brown

on his back; his head was blue, his legs red.

On the side and back of the neck, pink, purple,

green and gold feathers glistened in the sun-

light. A long, wedge-shaped tail gave him

slenderness.

---

1. What happened to the passenger pigeon? (died out; became extinct)

2. Describe the male passenger pigeon. (For full credit, must give at least 2 of 3: 1) graceful or beautiful, or larger than mourning dove; 2) at least 4 of 8 colors; 3) long and/or wedge-shaped tail.

Figure 7.5. Oral reading performance recorded on a mimeographed form. Only one paragraph of the 279–word selection and two of the comprehension questions are shown. The performance was recorded according to the modified procedures shown on p. 225. The content was reproduced from *Free Rein*, Level 16. Published by Allyn & Bacon, 1978. Reprinted by permission of Coward, McCann & Geoghegan, Inc. from *Wildlife in Danger* by Ivah Green. Copyright © 1960 by Ivah Green.

things as whether the comprehension score was inflated by words pronounced for the child, inability to answer a question was caused by a word-recognition error, or faulty reasoning may be contributing to the child's comprehension difficulties.

ADMINISTRATION.　Select about 30 to 45 minutes during which there will be no interruptions and a setting where other children cannot hear the testing (a student may not perform well if he believes his peers can hear him). Have the necessary materials available, and sit where you can observe the child. Take time to establish rapport and put the child at ease. Explain that the purpose of the test is to determine how he can be helped to become a better reader.

If a word-recognition test is used, begin with a list below the child's estimated level of functioning (e.g., if the child is using a low-second reader in class, begin with the primer or first reader). Present each list in increasing level of difficulty until the child fails more than 20% of the words on the list. A response is considered correct if the word is acceptably pronounced within 3 seconds of initial exposure. Self-corrections are accepted as correct responses.

Initiate oral reading testing at the reader level below the highest-level list on which the child met the criterion on the word-recognition test. Thus if the highest word list on which the criterion was met was the fourth-reader level, oral reading would begin at high-third-reader level. But regardless of the child's performance on the word-recognition test, testing should not be initiated higher than the child's grade level or reading level, and preferably below that point. If you do not employ a word-recognition test, begin oral reading at least two reader levels below the reader level the child is using for instruction. Starting with an easy selection (1) helps the child overcome initial nervousness and settle down in performance before reaching levels that challenge him or her, and (2) takes into consideration the possibility that the child's word-recognition ability exceeds his or her reading comprehension skills. Oral reading is done at sight, because preparatory silent reading might conceal some of the child's problems and the strategies employed when he or she encounters difficulty.

Before commencing the test, tell the child (1) that when he or she finishes reading you will ask some questions about what has just been read or will ask him or her to retell the story, and (2) that you will take the material away when he or she has finished reading. Give the introduction, and as the child reads orally from the book, record the reading and your observations using the symbols shown in Figure 7.6.

When the child finishes the selection, take back the material and present the comprehension check. Read the questions to the child or ask for a retelling of the story, and record the oral responses. If the word-recognition and comprehension criteria are both met, present the next higher level.

After the child fails either or both criteria for oral reading, drop back two reader levels and initiate silent reading. For example, if oral reading is terminated at the sixth-reader level, begin testing silently at the fourth-reader level. Silent reading should be timed,[6] and testing continued at each higher level until

---

[6]Timing oral reading is also advisable because it can help in deciding the suitability of material. For instance, although word recognition may be accurate, it may be extremely slow. Rate of oral reading can also be compared with silent reading rate. After about the second–reader level, silent reading should be faster.

Behavior	Symbol	Sample
Hesitation	Check mark over word	✓ social
Word pronounced by examiner after 5-second hesitation by child	*P* over pronounced word; check may be changed to ✓*P*	*P* social
Mispronunciation; substitution	Child's response over printed stimulus	*buf* bough
Dialectal rendition	Child's response over printed stimulus; add Ⓓ	*des*Ⓓ *be* Ⓓ desk He is here
Reversal	Child's response over printed stimulus; may be letter, complete letter sequence; partial letter sequence; word order	*big* *clam* dig calm *was* *he was* saw was he
Omission	Encircle omitted word(s) or word part(s)	ⓕⓐⓡⓔ pant ⓢ
Addition	Child's response over caret, which indicates where insertion occurred	a *big* cat ^
Self-correction within 5 seconds	Parentheses around correction	*(dog)* puppy
Repetition	Wavy line under repeated material, with bar at left to show where repetition began	the tiny tot ﹍﹍
Punctuation ignored or misinterpreted	× through punctuation mark	He did ✗
Inadequate phrasing	Slash at pause indicating misphrasing; when frequent, IP in margin	the room into / IP
Word-by-word reading	W/W in margin	W/W
Finger pointing	FP in margin; indicate type (e.g., word-by-word)	FP (W/W)
Head movements	HM in margin	HM
Inappropriate rate	Too fast; too slow in margin	Too fast
Concentration–task orientation	Behavior that indicates inattention noted in margin (e.g., easily distracted by noise)	Easily distracted by noise
Tension signs	Tension sign noted in margin (e.g., facial tics)	Facial tics
Vision	Possible signs of visual problem noted in margin	Held book 4" from eyes
Personality–emotional problems	Possible symptoms noted in margin	Bizarre answers to number of comp questions

Figure 7.6. Symbols for recording oral reading behaviors.

the comprehension criterion is not met. Questions are asked and answered orally, or retelling is requested, after reading of each selection.

The IRI can also be employed to estimate the child's listening comprehension level. After testing silent reading, the examiner reads selections to the child, beginning at the level at which the silent reading criterion was failed. Comprehension is checked in the same manner as if the child had read the selection, and testing continues until the comprehension criterion is not met.

SCORING AND INTERPRETATION.   Material at the child's *independent level* is generally suitable for recreational reading. At times the child should be allowed to read independently materials that are below and above this level. Material at the independent level may also be used for certain instructional purposes. For example, if the child is weak at phrasing or mechanical skills, such as the proper use of the voice in oral reading, material at the independent level would be suitable for instruction because the child could concentrate on these skills; word recognition and comprehension should not create any problems. The *instructional level* indicates that the material is suitable for use under the teacher's direction. The material presents some challenge so that new skills can be acquired. Material at the *frustration level* is too difficult.

Some examiners determine separate functional reading levels for oral and silent reading; others prefer only one score per functional level, taking into consideration the child's performance in both oral and silent reading. There is no agreement on the criteria that should be used for determining these functional levels. The main criteria proposed by Betts (1946) are

1. Independent level = (a) more than 99% correct word recognition; (b) at least 90% comprehension for oral reading and, for silent reading, "a rate of comprehension higher than that for oral reading", (c) freedom from tension; (d) fluent reading.
2. Instructional Level = (a) at least 75% comprehension for oral reading and for silent reading "a rate of comprehension substantially higher than that for oral reading"; (b) at least 95% correct word recognition; (c) ability to anticipate meaning; and (d) freedom from tension.
3. Frustration level = (a) comprehension below 50%; (b) 90% or less correct word recognition; (c) slow, halting reading; and (d) signs of tension. (1946, pp. 449 ff.)

Use of almost the same criteria is still being suggested (see Johnson, Kress & Pikulski 1987).

Some studies seem to support the 95% word-recognition criterion (E. Davis & Ekwall 1976, Hoffman et al. 1984). For the instructional level, Powell (1973) suggests the following criteria: (a) at least 70% comprehension at all grade levels, and (b) correct word recognition: 87-94% for preprimer to Grade 2, 92-96% for Grades 3-5, and 94-97% for Grades 6 and up.

To date, the best study for determining IRI criteria has been conducted by Cooper (1952). His criteria for determining the instructional level are

1. Second and third grades = (a) 99% word recognition (most suitable material) or 95%-98% word recognition (material of questionable suitability)[7] and (b) a minimum of 70% comprehension.
2. Intermediate grades = (a) 97%-99% word recognition (most suitable material) or 91%-96% word recognition (material of questionable suitability); and (b) a minimum of 60% comprehension.

Word-recognition errors included only substitutions, mispronunciations, words pronounced by the examiner after a hesitation of 5 seconds, omissions, and reversals. Additions, hesitations, repetitions, and ignoring punctuation were not counted as word-recognition errors. In addition to the quantitative criteria cited above, Cooper also considered qualitative symptoms in decision making. Any two of the following behaviors combined with a borderline performance, or the presence of more than two behaviors even when criteria were met, were considered indicative of the frustration level: word-by-word reading; inadequate phrasing; slow, halting reading; ignoring punctuation; finger pointing; visible tension; and a strained, high-pitched voice.

In applying any such criteria, one must examine (and use) what the author counted as a word-recognition error. For example, Betts (1946) did not specify specific word-recognition errors. Nor did he indicate whether words could or should be pronounced for the child; and repetitions, insertions, reversals, and omissions seem to be treated as symptoms that were to be considered in making a judgment.

There is no consensus as to which behaviors should be counted as errors in scoring an oral reading test. But Dunkeld (1970) found that a word-recognition score based on a count of mispronunciations, substitutions, words pronounced for the pupil, insertions, and reversals showed a higher correlation with reading comprehension than any other combination of miscues.

Apart from the fact that there is not complete agreement as to what constitutes a word-recognition error, there is some evidence that personality variables such as impulsivity and reflectiveness may influence the kind and number of miscues a child makes (Fisher 1977). Of two studies reported by Pikulski (1974), one supported the use of Betts's criteria, the other supported Powell's (Cooper's criteria were not considered). The approach used for teaching reading may influence IRI results, and the student's level of reading ability may influence the balance of word-recognition and comprehension scores.

In almost all scoring procedures suggested for IRIs and published oral reading tests, all word-perception errors are given equal weight. Thus, both a completely mispronounced word that disrupts meaning and an omission of *the* are each counted as one error. Because a distinction between serious and minor responses and behaviors should be made, we recommend the following scoring procedure:

1. Count as one error: (a) each response that deviates from the printed text and disrupts the intended meaning; (b) each word pronounced for the child after a 5-second hesitation.

[7]The "questionably suitable" category probably indicates the instructional level of most students, but its upper limits may suggest the frustration level for some.

2. Count as one-half error: each response that deviates from the printed text but does not disrupt the intended meaning.
3. Count as a total of one error, regardless of the number of times of behavior occurs: (a) repeated substitutions, such as "a" for *the* (except when a distinction between *a* and *the* is important to obtaining the meaning intended by the author); (b) repetitions; (c) repeated errors on the same word, regardless of the error made.
4. Do not count as an error: (a) responses that conform to cultural, regional, or social dialects; (b) self-corrections made within 5 seconds; (c) hesitations; (d) ignoring or misinterpreting punctuation marks.

Use of the above suggestions probably will result in a lower total number of word-recognition errors than would occur using Cooper's scoring procedure. The comprehension score and the presence or absence of symptoms of frustration should be considered. Specific behaviors observed and recorded during testing provide information for a qualitative analysis of the pupil's reading ability. Suggestions on how to make such an analysis are found on pages 245-247.

Some conclusions can be drawn about the child's relative rate and comprehension in oral and silent reading if comprehension has been checked with similar questions on oral and silent reading selections of comparable difficulty and content, and if the reading of selections is timed.

Estimates of a child's reading level that are based on a series of short samples should be recognized as approximations. Short selections do not yield extremely reliable results. A child's performance in a test situation can be influenced by a number of variables and therefore may not be truly representative of his or her reading ability, and there are marked variations in readability within a given text. Because a student can successfully read one selection written on a certain topic in a particular style does not necessarily mean that he or she will be as successful with material that may be of the same level of difficulty but that differs in content and writing style. The child's subsequent degree of success in reading the assigned book should be monitored, and more appropriate material substituted if necessary.

The examiner's ability can greatly influence IRI results. When 17 reading specialists were asked to rate the same performance, 6 rated it at the independent level, 6 at the frustration level, and 5 at the instructional level (Page & Carlson 1975). Even when provided with information that should have led to a fairly consistent interpretation of a pupil's test performance, the participants in a study by Schell (1982) did not agree in interpreting the data. Approximately 65% of the college professors and 25% of the graduate students judged the performance to be at the instructional level; the others, at the frustration level. Because teachers are exposed to a wide variety of training programs, they may score and interpret IRIs differently. But similarly trained clinicians can obtain very similar results if they use agreed-on procedures and criteria (Pikulski & Shanahan 1982).

Criteria for determining the instructional level may be adjusted for defensible reasons. For example, with children of limited experiential background, it may be advisable to use a comprehension criterion of 50% or 60%, rather than 70%. The rationale is that more time than usual will be spent developing the concepts and vocabulary necessary for understanding the stories. On the other hand, if the children are to be placed with highly skilled readers, a more stringent criterion may be selected.

Opinions also differ as to whether students should read the passages more than once. Some suggest that the material should be preread silently before it is read orally in order to maximize oral reading performance. Others argue that to do so would mask some of the problems children encounter on an initial reading as well as prevent the examiner from gaining any insights into the strategies the children employ when they encounter reading problems. Some believe that the texts should be read and reread orally in order to obtain a more reliable measure of pupils' word-recognition ability. Betts (1960) even suggests oral rereading following silent reading. Research in this area (Gonzales & Elijah 1978, Brecht 1977) is limited and has employed only small samples. Therefore, any resulting suggestions must be considered tentative. Until prereading and rereading procedures are used in establishing new criteria for the instructional level, currently available procedures should be employed in administering an IRI.

COMPARISON OF IRI RESULTS WITH STANDARDIZED TEST SCORES. Since Sipay (1964) reported his findings, several other studies also have found that some standardized reading achievement tests tend to give grade-equivalent scores higher than the instructional level determined by an IRI. It should be realized, however, that the results of such comparisons are influenced by (1) the standardized test used; (2) the material on which the IRI is based; (3) how well the IRI is constructed, administered, scored, and interpreted; and (4) the criteria used to determine the functional reading levels.

As for tests other than standardized silent reading tests, Bradley (1976) found that over 75% of the children obtained higher scores on the WRAT and *Gilmore Oral Reading Test* than on the basal IRIs. Even when scores on two tests are highly correlated, they do not necessarily yield similar results. For example, although the *Gilmore* Accuracy score correlated 0.91 with the *Macmillan IRI,* they agreed in placement on only slightly more than 10% of the students.

Some writers suggest subtracting a constant (e.g., 1 year) from grade-equivalent scores to estimate the learner's instructional level. Such a procedure is not accurate, however (Bradley 1976).

Published Reading Inventories

A number of published reading inventories are program independent. Most of these are described in Appendix A. They are very similar in organization, administration, and scoring to an informal reading inventory, but differ widely in such matters as passage content, what is considered to be a word-recognition error, scoring criteria, and the kinds of comprehension questions posed. Almost all lack published reliability and validity data.[8] Alternate-form reliability ranging from 0.60 to 0.78 was established by Helgren-Lempesis and Mangrum (1986) for three published IRIs. They also noted that, although there were no significant

---

[8]Questions regarding the lack of reliability and validity of teacher–constructed IRIs have also been raised (see Johnson, Kress & Pikulski 1987).

mean differences between the groups' scores for any of the three tests, some students scored quite differently on the alternate forms.

In examining the labels placed on the comprehension questions, care should be taken to determine what kind of comprehension is being sampled, and to use such information in making a diagnosis. For example, Duffelmeyer and Duffelmeyer (1989) claim that less than half the passages in three IRIs were suitable for assessing the comprehension of main ideas, and Gillis and Olson (1977) report that relatively few of the questions labeled as measuring the comprehension of main ideas actually did so. Schell and Hanna (1981) conclude that the six published inventories they analyzed should not be used to determine strengths and weaknesses in reading comprehension.

In one of the few studies comparing test scores from published inventories and NR tests, W. E. Smith and Beck (1980) found that, on the average, the *Sucher-Allred* and *Rand McNally* scores were a year higher than the grade-equivalent scores on the *Metropolitan Reading Test*. Some children scored higher on the published inventory; others, on the standardized test.

Standardized Oral Reading Tests and Test Batteries

Two commonly used standardized oral reading tests are the *Gray* and *Gilmore*. The 1963 edition of the *Gray Oral Reading Test* yields a single score based on word-recognition errors and reading time. Although comprehension is measured, it is not considered in the test score. The 1986 edition of the *Gray* yields a passage score, which is based on the same type of criteria as the single score obtained from the 1963 edition, as well as standard scores and percentiles for comprehension. The *Gilmore Oral Reading Test* provides separate scores for accuracy, comprehension, and rate. The scores on the *Gray* and the *Gilmore* are based on the student's performance across selections of increasing length and difficulty.

Measures of the ability to read connected discourse orally also are part of some diagnostic reading test batteries, each of which measures a variety of reading skills in addition to oral reading. The *Gates-McKillop-Horowitz Reading Diagnostic Tests* contain an oral reading test, the score of which is based on word recognition only; comprehension is not even checked. Oral and silent reading as well as listening comprehension are sampled by the *Durrell Analysis of Reading Difficulty* and the *Spache Diagnostic Reading Scales*. The instructional and potential (listening comprehension) levels from the *Botel Reading Inventory* are based only on word recognition and knowledge of word meaning (the words are presented in isolation).

A survey (German, Johnson & Schneider 1985) reveals that a number of the same tests were used by both reading teachers and LD teachers. However, reading teachers more frequently used comprehensive reading tests such as an IRI, the *Gilmore*, the *Durrell*, or the *Stanford Diagnostic Reading Test*; LD teachers more often employed word-recognition tests (e.g., *Wide Range*), test batteries (e.g., *Woodcock*), and perceptual tests (e.g., *Bender*) or process tests (e.g., ITPA). Another survey (Irvin & Lynch-Brown 1988) found that a wide variety of tests, including perceptual tests, were reportedly used in university reading clinics.

The *Woodcock Reading Mastery Test* and the *Peabody Individual Achieve-ment Test* (PIAT) are widely used, especially by LD teachers and school psy-chologists (Caskey 1986). Reading comprehension scores on both tests are based on reading very brief materials. The use of both tests for diagnostic purposes is limited, and suggestions for using them to make an error analysis of a child's performance as a basis for instructional planning are highly questionable (Lillie & Alberg 1986).

An oral reading test's scoring system should distinguish between miscues that disrupt meaning and those that do not (see page 231). As yet, no published oral reading test has done so. If a large number of word-recognition errors are nondisruptive, the resulting test score probably underestimates the reading level at which the child is capable of functioning. However, *standardized* tests, must be scored according to the manual if the norms are to be used.

USE OF A TAPE RECORDER.   Recording a child's performance on a response sheet as he reads orally requires speed in the use of a variety of symbols that represent different kinds of behaviors. Inexperienced testers usually cannot re-cord as fast as the child reads, and so their records are often incomplete and only partially accurate. For them, it is highly advisable that the child's oral reading be tape recorded and scored later at leisure, when parts of the recording can be replayed as necessary to obtain an accurate account. The use of a tape recorder may allow even an experienced examiner to pay more attention to the child's behaviors during reading without distracting the child, who may try to watch what the examiner is writing. A tape recording provides more accurate recording and scoring of errors. It also allows children to listen to their performances and, by comparing them with recordings made after remedial help, to note their prog-ress. Nevertheless, if a child seems upset by the presence of a tape recorder, do the best you can without it.

R. Anderson et al. (1985) suggest that each pupil's oral reading performance be taped three times a year and kept on file for diagnostic purposes and for reporting to parents.

Comparison of Oral and Silent Reading Ability

As yet, no study has been conducted to show the comparability of widely used oral and silent reading tests for individuals. One way to alleviate the problem of noncomparability of existing tests is to use an informal reading inventory that has two comparable passages at each reader level (realizing, of course, that prior knowledge is always a variable). One set of passages is read orally and the other silently until the comprehension criterion is not met. At times, this necessitates having children read passages at levels above which they failed to meet the word-recognition criterion. A difference of at least two reader levels should oc-cur before the teacher could reasonably conclude that a child's oral and silent reading levels differ significantly. This two-reader-level criterion is an estimate.

When silent reading seems significantly better than oral reading, the fol-lowing possibilities, which can occur singly or in combination, should be con-sidered: (1) The reader makes numerous minor miscues that cause failure to meet the word-recognition criterion, although they do not greatly hamper comprehension; (2) the reader can reread at will in silent reading but is penalized for repetitions in oral reading; (3) the reader has good language skills and is expert at using context, thus achieving sufficient comprehension despite word-recognition weaknesses; (4) the reader is self-conscious or extremely anxious when reading orally but is more relaxed when reading silently; (5) the reader is so concerned about word recognition and "expression" in oral reading that his or her comprehension suffers; (6) the reader has benefited from extensive guessing when taking the silent reading test (which very often uses multiple-choice questions), artificially raising the score.

Oral reading may be significantly better than silent reading in some cases. This may be the result of the child's having had much more practice reading orally than silently, or being aided by the aural feedback (hearing the words makes it easier for the reader to understand the material). For older readers, the more likely reason is that they must attend to the task when reading orally, but need not when reading silently or listening.

ASSESSING READING COMPREHENSION

How well children understand what they read is the most important aspect of reading ability to assess. But, as will be indicated in this section, assessing it is not an easy matter.

All measures of reading comprehension are indirect because we cannot directly observe the actual process in the reader's mind. Procedures for testing reading comprehension may be classified as product or process measures. *Product measures* test comprehension after the child has read. *Process measures* attempt to sample comprehension as it is taking place.

There are two main types of product measures, with one having three variations: retelling, and the use of questions and answers. The question/answer paradigm has three variations: aided recall (e.g., multiple-choice questions); unaided recall (e.g., open-ended questions); and true/false items. The four types of process measures include cloze tasks, miscue analysis, eye-movement measures, and the think-aloud procedure that was discussed on page 236. Johnston (1983) and Chang (1983) discuss most of these measures, indicating their cognitive demands, advantages, and limitations. Some writers do not classify the cloze as a process measure.

Children's reading comprehension is often described in terms such as being at the *fourth-grade* or *fourth-reader level*. Such descriptors are derived from one or more of the following sources: an NR grade-equivalent score, the highest reader level at which the criteria were met on a CR test, or the level of text being used with the child for reading instruction. All these descriptors have limitations, but for the present such general statements will have to suffice.

What tests measure and how test scores are derived differ widely, as do the demands placed on pupils by what they are required to read in school. What constitutes acceptable comprehension differs from teacher to teacher. Therefore a teacher cannot rely on a single test score to predict how well a group, let alone a child, will read in various classroom situations. How well children can comprehend the materials used daily in school must be assessed using samples from those materials, and over time. Narrative and expository texts place different demands on the reader (see pp. 600-601).

In evaluating a pupil's reading comprehension, an examiner should recognize that the meaning the reader derives from a particular part of the text may be shaped by her earlier interpretations of the text, and that the meaning the reader constructs may continue to change with her interpretation of the text that follows (Langer 1985).

What Does a Reading Comprehension Test Measure?

A student's performance on a reading comprehension test and the resulting score are a function of the interactions among these factors: the complexity of the material; the pupil's purpose for reading, reading ability, reasoning ability, linguistic competence, topical knowledge, and world knowledge; the cognitive demands placed on the reader by the way in which comprehension is assessed; and the situation in which the test is taken. Thus, an oversimplified answer to the question of what a reading comprehension test measures is that it measures a student's ability to demonstrate his or her comprehension of the material contained in that test, which was read for a particular purpose and under particular circumstances. Inferences drawn from such a relatively small sample of behavior with regard to the student's ability to comprehend other materials, as well as to read for different purposes (or even to read the same material for a different purpose) and under other conditions may or may not be accurate.

What Should a Reading Comprehension Test Measure?

The answer to this question may seem obvious, but there are differences of opinion. Some writers (e.g., Carroll 1977) suggest developing reading tests that would reduce the effects of reasoning ability and prior knowledge on reading comprehension test scores. Thus, the tests would measure only literal comprehension using only passage-dependent questions. Such "purer" measures of reading might be more sensitive to gains in reading ability, as some authors suggest, but the question remains as to how well such tests would reflect normal reading in which reasoning and prior knowledge often play important roles. Furthermore, comprehension normally involves inferences that may be based on information in the text or on prior knowledge. Both kinds of inferences are central to the comprehension process (T. Carr 1981). It is almost impossible to factor prior knowledge out of measures of reading comprehension, but its effect on reading comprehension should be controlled so that it does not account for too much, or an unknown amount, of the test results (Farr & Carey 1986).

Differences of opinion as to what reading tests measure or how reading comprehension should be measured are illustrated by comparing the work of two writers. On one hand, Spearritt (1980) concludes that cloze and multiple-choice reading comprehension tests measure much the same skills. Johnston (1983), on the other hand, indicates that the various procedures for measuring reading comprehension place different demands on the testee. Spearritt based his conclusion on factor-analysis studies; Johnston's point of view is based on cognitive psychology and information-processing theory.

Cross and Paris (1987) contend that the appropriateness of a measure of reading comprehension depends on the fit between the purposes for testing and the properties of the tests. They lay out, in tabular form, the values of test properties for different test purposes.

PRIOR KNOWLEDGE.   Prior knowledge plays a major role in reading comprehension and influences comprehension at all levels of processing (Johnston & Pearson 1982). At the decoding and word-recognition level, it operates by limiting the set of words that could possibly appear in a sentence slot. At the short-term memory level, it influences the amount that can be stored in working memory. During the inference stage, it determines which, if any, inferences should be made. And at the storage level, it determines which information will be stored, in what format it will be stored, and whether it will be retrieved.

When word recognition is automatic but comprehension is weak, lack of prior knowledge may be a contributing factor. One way to assess topical knowledge prior to the child's reading of the material is to present three key content words from the passage to the student, who is asked to free-associate whatever comes to mind when hearing each word. The child's associations are scored according to prescribed guidelines, as indicating much, some, or little prior knowledge (Langer 1980). Both Langer's qualitative measure and a quantitative measure (a count of the number of associations made with a word) successfully predicted overall recall, independently of intelligence and reading level—with the quantitative measure proving to be the better predictor (Hare 1982). A less involved, but perhaps less reliable, measure or prior knowledge was developed by Zakaluk, Samuels, and Taylor (1986). In this procedure, pupils respond to a key word or phrase in a way similar to Langer's procedure. One point is given for each "reasonable idea" and the child's total score is rated as low (0-2), average (3-6), or high (7 or above). Refer to Holmes and Roser (1987) for other ways to assess topical knowledge.

One way that test constructors have attempted to lessen the possible bias created by prior knowledge is by using a number of short passages on a variety of topics. The net effect, however, has been that readers with broader general knowledge are likely to do better on the tests. Use of a series of short passages, each on a different topic, requires the readers not only to activate a different prior-knowledge network for each passage, but to shift such activation more quickly and more often than is typically required in daily reading activities.

The 1985 edition of the *Metropolitan Reading Test* gives consideration to prior knowledge by presenting a purpose-setting question before each passage. The questions that follow the passage are directly or indirectly related to the purpose question. Rowe and Rayford (1987) found that: (1) students in Grades 1, 6, and 10 could use these purpose-setting questions to activate prior knowledge; (2) for the two older groups, but not for the first graders, the activated schema were significantly related to the type of information given in the question; (3) the questions were not equally effective in performing their cueing function; and, (4) topical knowledge, the amount of information presented, and the presence of genre clues may be the text features that most influence schema activation.

An often-overlooked point is that the influence of the reader's topical knowledge on reading comprehension is itself affected by the amount and type of prior knowledge that the author assumes of the potential reader. Authors are likely to provide more information when they assume their audiences have little, rather than abundant, knowledge on a topic.

TEXT CONTENT AND STRUCTURE.   Reading comprehension can be influenced by various factors within the text (Johnston 1983), such as the quantity of information (often indicated by passage length, the density of information, the density of *new* information, the number of modifiers in clauses, sentence complexity, the familiarity of the vocabulary to the reader, the use of anaphoric terms, and cohesive ties.

Differences between test content and classroom reading materials can influence the predictive validity of a test. For example, test passages are usually shorter and have less obvious structure than classroom reading materials.

POSSIBLE INFLUENCE OF QUESTION WORDING.   There are two broad categories of question wording: verbatim and paraphrased. *Verbatim questions* use the same, or very nearly the same, wording and sentence structure as the text from which they are derived. For instance, if the text read "The regent's diadem glistened resplendently," a verbatim question would be "Whose diadem glistened resplendently?" It is possible to answer verbatim questions simply by matching the wording of the question and text. The reader being tested can provide the correct answer without understanding the text (e.g., the testee need not know what a regent is or understand that the crown shone brilliantly). One of the limitations of verbatim questions is that the tester cannot be sure if an acceptable response indicates *recall* or *comprehension*. Therefore, except when the wording of the text is the only acceptable response, it is advisable to ask pupils to put their responses in their own words.

In *paraphrased* or *transformed questions,* the words and/or the syntactic structure differ noticeably from those of the text. Paraphrased questions can be easier or more difficult to answer, depending on the wording of the text and the question. One of the limitations of paraphrased questions is that the student may understand the text but not the question.

PRODUCTION REQUIREMENTS.   The requirements imposed by the manner in which pupils have to demonstrate their reading comprehension are often overlooked in analyzing test performance. Test performance may be influenced by factors such as whether the questions are posed orally or in written form, whether the responses must be given orally or in written form, the format of the comprehension check, and the availability of the text while comprehension is being assessed. Refer to Davey (1987) for a discussion of these and other factors.

Oral questions may be easier to understand than written ones, especially for poor readers who may not be able to read the questions; they also allow for follow-up by the examiner. Simliarly, many children find it easier to respond orally than in writing. Written responses require additional skills—written language production and spelling—so that difficulty in responding in written form may indicate problems other than reading comprehension.

Reading comprehension may be checked by free recall (retelling); open-ended, multiple-choice, true-false questions; or cloze or maze tests. Each of these test methods places differing cognitive demands on the student (Johnston 1983). Probably the most demanding is retelling, followed by cloze tests, open-ended (unaided recall) questions, multiple-choice questions, maze tests, and true/false items.

In the *retelling procedure*, the testee is asked to relate the content of what has just been read. The advantage claimed for retelling over other procedures is that it allows the student to structure her response according to her own interpretation/reconstruction of the text. Some writers suggest that pupils should not be cued during retellings. More authors, however, recommend either cueing or using probe questions if the retelling is incomplete. The quality of the retelling may be judged simply on a subjective basis (e.g., adequate versus inadequate) or according to the richness of the retelling as in the procedure developed by Irwin and Mitchell (1983). Difficulties in scoring retellings include: (1) the amount of text content recalled is often quite low, especially if the text is over 250-300 words long; and (2) there is no easy way to score inferences or to evaluate attempts to link textual information to prior knowledge (Morrow 1986). Points are usually not deducted for including incorrect information in the retelling and scores are likely to be greatly influenced by the amount of experience students have had in making retellings.

Retelling is not an easy task for pupils of any age, but is especially difficult for young children and for those with little experience with retellings. Guided practice makes the task easier and increases the quality of the retellings. Refer to Morrow (1988a) for suggestions on how to use retellings for both developing and assessing reading comprehension.

Two other points about the use of retellings should be considered. First, retellings place a heavier demand on the ability to retrieve and organize the required information than do other assessment procedures. Second, children's retellings to an examiner or teacher may not indicate their complete understanding or recall of the material. When children think the person to whom they are retelling the story has already read the story (an assumption likely to be made about an examiner or teacher), their retellings are less complete than when relating the story to children who have not read it (Johnston & Pearson 1982).

Many classroom activities and group tests allow the student to refer to the reading material during the comprehension check. This makes the task easier than if the text is not available. When the text is not available to the pupil during the comprehension check, the question of whether the inability to respond correctly reflects difficulty in comprehension or in recall can be resolved by allowing the student to refer to the text to find the answers to incorrectly answered questions. If the student is then able to answer the item, or can supply the information omitted from his retelling, comprehension is not the problem.

Davey (1988) reports that good readers made more spontaneous and effective use of "look-back" strategies than did poor readers, who generally did not know how to take advantage of text availability during comprehension assessment. In another study (Rubenstein, Kender & Mace 1988), allowing the pupils to reinspect the text resulted in higher inferential, but not literal comprehension.

WHEN IS AN ANSWER CORRECT? The responses to comprehension-check questions indicated by test publishers or teachers' manuals are not always the only acceptable answers. A careful analysis of the text may reveal that the child's response is just as plausible as the "correct" one(s). For instance, the text might read, "The trip by boat was pleasant, but Adam was thrilled to be on land again." Rather than say "pleasant" in response to the question "What kind of trip did Adam have?" the pupil might say "a boat trip" (which the examiner should follow with a probe) or "long," which is based on an inference—it must have been long because he was thrilled to be on land again (the examiner should follow this response with "How do you know?"). Because pupils draw on their existing knowledge, their answers to questions or their retellings may include elaborations on what is stated in the text. Cultural differences may also influence the interpretation of text.

"Incorrect" responses that are plausible, that indicate possible misconceptions, that indicate faulty reasoning, or that are not completely acceptable should be followed up with probes.

READING ORALLY AT SIGHT. Prereading material silently before reading it orally allows the student the opportunity to work on unknown words and obtain at least a general idea of the content of the passage. Even then it is possible that the amount of attention that must be devoted to fluent oral reading may lessen the processing capacity available for comprehension. When children are required to read at sight orally, as is usually the case in testing, even more processing capacity may have to be devoted to word recognition and reading fluently. Word-recognition weaknesses may interfere with the activation of prior knowledge by reducing the amount of attention available for comprehending.

ASSESSING COMPREHENSION OF SPOKEN LANGUAGE. If the child is very weak in reading comprehension and if word recognition is not a problem, it is advisable to determine how well she understands similar material read to her. To prevent confounding, the measures of reading and listening comprehension should make similar conceptual and linguistic demands on the pupil. Reading and listening comprehension are compared to determine if the problem is one of language comprehension in general or of reading comprehension only. If the student is attending to the tasks and if her listening comprehension is as weak as her reading comprehension, she probably has a general language comprehension problem. If listening comprehension is *significantly* higher than reading comprehension, the comprehension problem is centered in reading.

If difficulty understanding syntactic structures is suspected, the child may be asked to paraphrase sentences containing such structures or asked questions that will reveal her understanding of them. For further suggestions on formal and informal tests of spoken language and the problems in devising such measures, refer to Swisher and Aten (1981) and Vellutino and Shub (1982).

ASSESSING READING VOCABULARY

Reading vocabulary refers to the ability to determine the most appropriate meanings of printed words. Although word recognition is usually subsumed under this term, a pupil can sometimes determine the meaning of a word without being able to recognize it or decode it if the context in which the unknown word appears is sufficiently revealing. Conversely, the ability to provide the oral counterpart of a printed word does not assure that the child knows its meaning.

Group-Administered Tests

Almost all published tests intended for use above the second grade sample understanding of word meanings. They do so in a variety of ways. The vocabulary subtest may require students to select synonyms, antonyms, or word classifications for words that appear either in isolation or in varying amounts of context. Some tests include vocabulary items in their comprehension subtests. The wide array of procedures used to measure reading vocabulary casts doubt as to whether any two tests measure the same behavior (Farr & Carey 1986).

Apart from the comparative data they provide and the indication as to whether or not reading vocabulary is a problem area, NR vocabulary tests provide little useful diagnostic information. The words used in NR tests vary greatly from test to test and may not adequately sample the reading vocabulary to which the child has been exposed. The same is true for published CR tests. In almost all cases, only the most common meaning of the word is measured. But many English words have multiple meanings, and the ability to determine which meaning is appropriate in a particular context is an important reading comprehension skill.

The majority of items on standardized reading-vocabulary tests appear to assess knowledge of word meanings already familiar to most of the children to whom the tests are administered. Furthermore, only a moderate amount of information about the words' meanings is needed to answer the items correctly (Curtis 1987).

Group-administered vocabulary tests require, at a minimum, that the child recognize the stimulus word and the correct answer, and the meanings of both. An incorrect response to a test item may reflect inability to recognize or decode the printed words, not knowing the meaning of the stimulus word or the correct response, or any combination of these factors. Only individual follow-up can provide information as to the reasons for incorrect responses. Having the child read the incorrectly answered test items orally will reveal if word recognition or decoding contributed to poor test performance. Asking the child to define the stimulus words and the correct responses will indicate if lack of word meaning was a contributing factor. Asking the pupil why he selected his answers is also advisable. He may have an acceptable, though unexpected, rationale or he may reveal faulty reasoning.

If word meaning is identified as an area of weakness, the child's understanding vocabulary should be sampled more thoroughly. If the pupil's understanding vocabulary proves meager, the causes for this handicapping condition should be explored. Limited experiential background and learning potential are often associated with limited understanding vocabulary.

Individually Administered Tests

Few individually administered reading tests contain a word-meaning subtest, but some have vocabulary items in their comprehension checks. Care should be exercised in interpreting the Word Comprehension subtest of the *Woodcock Reading Mastery Tests* because this subtest requires the child to make analogies, a skill that heavily involves reasoning ability.

Informal Tests

In most directed reading activities, the teacher checks the children's knowledge of the meanings of key words in the story they are about to read. Workbooks that accompany published reading programs often contain word-meaning exercises. Unfortunately, students' knowledge of the vocabulary employed in their content-subject textbooks is much less frequently assessed.

APPRAISING WORD RECOGNITION

Word recognition is defined here as the ability to determine the oral equivalent of a printed word. It does not involve determining word meaning, although word recognition usually leads to word meaning. A word can be recognized or decoded without knowing its meaning.

Word-recognition scores correlate highly (around 0.80) with reading comprehension in the primary grades and less highly (around 0.65) with comprehension in the upper grades. But although word-recognition test scores can be used to estimate an individual's level of reading ability, they cannot substitute for measures of the ability to comprehend connected discourse. Some children are much better at word recognition than at reading comprehension, and studies show that word-recognition scores often do not place children at the same levels as do IRIs or NR tests (Marzano et al. 1978).

Assessing Word Recognition

Two aspects of word recognition should be measured: accuracy and automaticity (Samuels 1983). *Word-recognition accuracy* can be measured by having the pupil read orally words presented in isolation or in context. Ability to recognize words in isolation is a purer measure of word-recognition accuracy because the pupil must rely solely on graphic information. Word-recognition accuracy should also be checked while reading connected discourse to find out about the student's use of context clues. Most students' word recognition is better in context than in isolation.

Automaticity means recognizing words with no hesitation and with minimal attention. Samuels (1983, 1988b) suggests that automaticity can be tested by having the child orally read a previously unread passage (tell the child that her comprehension will be checked). One indicator of automaticity is the degree of expression and fluency used in reading the passage. Another is the accuracy of recall, because in order to comprehend while reading orally, little attention can be devoted to word recognition. Of course, factors such as inadequate prior knowledge or syntactic complexity may also hamper comprehension, even though word recognition is automatic.

The simplest technique for measuring automaticity is to time how long it takes the child to read a list of words. Only words recognized accurately should be counted in computing the average time per word. Because no norms are available for such tests, the average time it takes good readers to read the list can be used as a guideline. When word recognition is automatic, less attention need be devoted to word recognition, but this fact does not assure comprehension.

One way to assess word-recognition automaticity and accuracy is to present each word initially for a very brief period of time and, if the word is not recognized, to show it again for a 3- to 5-second exposure. An acceptable response to a flashed word indicates that its recognition is accurate and automatic. A correct response to the second exposure indicates accurate, but slow, recognition. The words must either be placed on individual cards or exposed in a quick-flash device. Presenting only one word at a time and keeping the remaining cards from view helps the child to focus attention on the word. A word card may be exposed briefly or covered with a blank card, which is lifted quickly to expose the stimulus card and then replaced. In either case it is somewhat difficult to keep the exposure time constant. This problem is overcome by using a manufactured tachistoscope (see p. 649) or lessened by using a simple hand tachistoscope, such as the one shown in Figure 7.7.

GROUP-ADMINISTERED TESTS. Most NR and CR reading tests designed for use in the primary grades contain word-recognition subtests. These tests vary in the degree to which they sample the words that have been taught to a particular group of children (Good & Salvia 1988). Tests that accompany basal reading programs sample only the words used in their programs.

Group-administered word-recognition tests may fail to detect children with word-recognition problems because of the manner in which the skill is measured. Word recognition is usually sampled by having the child match one of three or four printed words with a picture or with a word spoken by the examiner. Scores on such tests are influenced by the degree to which the distractors (incorrect answers) resemble the correct response (Baumann, Walker & Johnson 1981). If the distractors differ greatly (e.g., *ox, elephant, dog* when the correct response is *cat*), the child need rely only on certain cues (e.g., the initial sound-symbol association) in order to arrive at the correct response. In such cases, some children who score well on the test are unable to recognize the same words in isolation or in context when reading orally.

If this situation is suspected or if a child does poorly on a group test, a follow-up procedure can be employed. Point to each correct answer and ask the child to pronounce it. A comparison of the child's performance on both formats will reveal if the initial results were accurate. An analysis of the errors may provide clues to the child's problem.

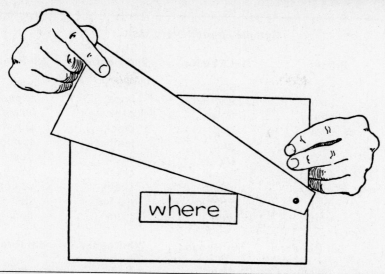

Figure 7.7.   A simple hand tachistoscope. This can be made in sizes to fit the use of 4 × 6–in. or 3 × 5–in. index cards. The shield and shutter can be cut out of stiff cardboard or the sides of a grocery carton with a sharp razor blade. To use, hold the shield upright on table top with the left hand. Pick up a card with the right hand and place it against the shield, with the bottom of the card resting on the table, so that the material to be exposed is in the opening. Place the left thumb against the card, holding it in place. With the right hand lift the shutter quickly until its lower corner is level with the top of the shield and let go; this gives a fairly rapid exposure. Very rapid exposures can be obtained by placing the left index finger across the top of the shield and bouncing the shutter against it.

INDIVIDUALLY ADMINISTERED TESTS.   Individually administered word-recognition tests make different and more revealing demands on the testee than do group tests in that they require the child to pronounce the word. The ability to recognize words in context is measured by standardized oral reading tests and informal and published reading inventories. Most oral reading tests do not yield separate scores for words recognized in context; the *Gilmore* does.

Some standardized tests measure only the ability to recognize words presented in isolation. The two most commonly used are the *Wide Range Achievement Test* (WRAT), which also tests math and spelling, and the *Slosson Oral Reading Test* (SORT). WRAT reading scores tend to overestimate the instructional levels of children (Bradley 1976, Pikulski & Shanahan 1982). Yet despite the fact that it measures only word recognition and has other limitations, the WRAT is by far the most frequently used test for measuring reading achievement in special education studies (Tindal 1985).

INFORMAL TESTS.   The ability to recognize words in context is checked frequently during classroom instruction, but there are times when the ability to recognize words in isolation should be checked. Such tests are easy to construct. A random sampling of words can be selected from the desired source. To obtain a quick estimate of the suitability of a reading textbook, a 20-word sample drawn

Sample Graded Word Lists

Pre-primer	Primer	1st Reader	2nd Reader	3rd Reader
no	box	store	zoom	peel
help	take	another	hope	depend
all	happy	flower	peek	helpless
stop	over	hop	block	apron
up	father	pan	feather	rowboat
for	saw	try	wind	trust
red	would	bone	crack	being
jump	mouse	mean	speak	ceiling
book	into	should	market	split
come	under	dark	trunk	flop

4th Reader	5th Reader	6th Reader	7th Reader	8th Reader
gulf	resign	baron	quail	yacht
tense	haze	torment	ignorant	electrified
recent	socket	originate	wrath	barnacle
occasional	admirer	soundless	bribe	spacious
coward	pianist	cruelty	solitary	obnoxious
snare	cupboard	hesitation	cultivate	trivial
broad	unaware	yield	traverse	deficiency
launch	expand	recreation	factual	legislation
exhibit	mature	locomotive	absurd	geometric
whirlwind	broth	existence	maroon	radiance

Figure 7.8. Ten–word lists at 10 reader levels. The difficulty levels are not indicated on copies presented to the pupil. The highest level at which the pupil can recognize at least seven of the words is suggestive of his instructional level. These words were taken from the Harris–Jacobson Basic Lists by Levels (1982).

from the new words introduced in that textbook will suffice (these words are usually indicated in the back of the textbook or in the teacher's manual). A child who has difficulty with more than 4 of the 20 words is likely to have difficulty reading the book from which the sample was drawn.

Multiple copies of the test can be run off so that the examiner can use a fresh copy for each pupil. What is recorded will depend on the information desired.

Word-recognition tests that are more broadly indicative of word-recognition ability may be constructed by drawing 10-word samples per level from a graded word list. Such a test is shown in Figure 7.8. A brief test of this type can also be used to estimate the ability to recognize high-frequency words or to determine which level of words should be checked out more thoroughly.

Some clinicians test disabled readers on all 220 words in the *Dolch Basic Sight Vocabulary* (see pages 441-445). Testing all 220 *Dolch* words or any list of such length is unnecessarily tedious and frustrating for most disabled readers, especially if it is done in one session. We prefer to try only a sample of any list of high-frequency words to determine if work on those words will be needed, leaving to remediation the identification of specific words that need to be learned.

Refer to Farr and Carey (1986, pp. 85-87) for other recommendations for assessing word recognition.

Miscue Analysis

Procedures for analyzing and interpreting reading miscues, called *miscue analysis,* have been developed by K. Goodman (1969) and Y. Goodman and Burke (1972). The original edition of the latter, less complex *Reading Miscue Inventory* was reviewed by Singer (1978a). Alternative procedures for using the *Reading Miscue Inventory* are also available (Y. Goodman, Watson & Burke 1987).

Miscue analysis is based on K. Goodman's model of reading as a psycholinguistic guessing game. Basically, miscue analysis is a procedure for analyzing oral reading processing. The selection must be (1) new to the pupil; (2) a complete story or passage (have a beginning, middle, and end); (3) one grade level *above* the material used by the child in class; and (4) of sufficient length and difficulty to generate a minimum of 25 miscues. Assistance in word recognition is not provided by the examiner, except for urging the reader to guess the word after a 30-second hesitation; if hesitations are continuous, the reader is told to continue reading even if it means skipping a word or phrase. Following the oral reading, the child retells the story, with some general guiding questions posed by the examiner if necessary. Comprehension is scored subjectively by the examiner, who can award up to 100 points for the retelling. The procedure does not yield a reading-level score; rather, it provides insights into the reading strategies employed by the reader.

The following is a simplified set of questions that may be asked about each miscue:

1. To what extent would the printed form of the oral response (miscue) look like the printed stimuli? [This question deals with the child's use of graphic information.]
2. To what extent does the miscue sound like the anticipated response? [This question deals with the child's use of graphophonemic (symbol-sound association) information.]
3. Does the sentence make sense up to and including the miscue?
4. Does the miscue make sense in the total sentence? [Questions 3 and 4 deal with the use of semantic information.]
5. Is the sentence grammatically acceptable up to and including the miscue?
6. Does the miscue fit grammatically in the total sentence? [Questions 5 and 6 deal with the use of syntactic information.]
7. Was the miscue self-corrected? When does the child self-correct? [These questions deal with the pupil's monitoring strategies and ability to take corrective actions.]

8. To what extent did the miscue disrupt the author's intended meaning? How important to understanding the text is that disruption?
9. Does the miscue reflect the pupil's dialect?

Miscue analysis is time consuming even when a simplified version of the procedure is used. Hood (1978) points out other limitations of miscue analysis:

1. Some miscue scores have questionable reliability because the classification of miscues varies among examiners.
2. Classification of some miscues as "good" or "bad" seems to differ with the reader's age and reading ability.
3. The relationship between passage content and the reader's background seems to influence test results.
4. Miscues made by a given reader are related to the overall accuracy level at which they were made. For example, when word-recognition accuracy was 90% or less and the passage was not closely related to the reader's experience, the proportion of nonsense-word responses or no responses was greater and fewer serious errors were self-corrected. At and above the 95% level of accuracy, proportionally more minor miscues occurred.
5. Examiners' opinions regarding the contexual appropriateness of miscues vary considerably.

According to Weber (1977), not all miscue categories are equally useful. Goldsmith, Nicolich and Haupt (1982) present an adaptation of the usual miscue taxonomy that attempts to separate the information sources employed by the reader. Refer to Sadowski and Lee (1986) for information regarding the relationships of five differing miscue scoring systems to reading comprehension.

Caution should be exercised in analyzing miscue and word-recognition patterns that occur across a series of graded paragraphs or only at the pupil's frustration level. Passage difficulty can have a significant effect on qualitative miscue or error patterns. Compared to performances on material at or below their instructional levels, at their frustration levels children tend to make more semantically and syntactically unacceptable miscues (especially the former), to correct fewer miscues that disrupt meaning, and to make more miscues that are graphically similar to the stimuli (Christie & Alonso 1980, Pikulski & Shanahan 1982). Because the frequency and types of miscues probably vary with the difficulty of the text, a miscue analysis based only on difficult material could lead to a different interpretation of the data and therefore to differing remediation than if miscues made on more suitable material were also considered. A child could demonstrate adequate use of the various cue systems on the fairly easy material but not on the difficult text. This suggests that Goodman's recommendation to use difficult material in making a miscue analysis is open to question.

Combining the miscues or word-recognition errors made across a series of passages of increasing difficulty could also lead to misinterpretation. Most of the miscues are likely to occur at the frustration level, and if they greatly outnumber those made below that level and differ in type, the data could be misleading. For these reasons, we suggest making separate analyses on miscues that occur on texts that are difficult for the child and those made on material that is of a more suitable level of difficulty.

Despite its limitations, miscue analysis has provided a useful research tool and has forced educators to reconsider beliefs about the meanings of oral reading behaviors. Miscue-analysis research has suggested the following (Wixson 1979):

1. Most readers make a greater number of semantically and syntactically acceptable miscues than miscues that are graphically similar to the stimuli.
   a. The majority of miscues are syntactically acceptable.
   b. Most readers average about 20% more syntactically acceptable miscues than semantically acceptable miscues.
   c. The proportion of semantically and syntactically acceptable miscues increases with reading proficiency.
2. Novice readers' miscues tend to include a large number of real-word substitutions (often words that have been previously taught) and "no response" omissions.
3. As readers mature, the percentage of graphically similar miscues tends to increase initially and then stabilizes at some point (. . . for good readers) [Less-skilled readers continue to rely on graphic cues (Christie 1981).]
   a. The percentage of "no response" omissions tends to decrease with age.
   b. Older readers tend to substitute nonwords or real words that may not have been previously taught.
4. Compared to proficient readers, less proficient readers
   a. tend to make a relatively higher percentage of miscues that are graphically similar to the stimuli.
   b. make fewer attempts to self-correct.
   c. tend to correct acceptable and unacceptable miscues at an almost equal rate.
5. Proficient readers
   a. omit words that are not essential to comprehension.
   b. correct unacceptable miscues at a higher rate than acceptable miscues.
6. Many of the miscue patterns that appear to reflect developmental trends actually vary as a function of the complex interaction among instructional methodology; the child's reading skills, background, and purpose for reading; and the nature and content of the written material.

Some Suggestions and Examples

If a child's word-recognition errors or miscues are going to be analyzed, the words on which the child erred should be presented after the test has been administered. Words that have been pronounced correctly most of the time should not be included in the analysis. Given a second chance, children often correct their own errors (Leibert 1982).

The student's miscues should be carefully analyzed for information about (1) use of semantic, syntactic, graphic and graphophonemic cues, as well as monitoring strategies; (2) which word-recognition and decoding skills and strategies were employed, and how well they were utilized; (3) the particular words, types of words, or word parts that may be causing problems; and (4) the impact of word-recognition errors on comprehension.

Susie's oral reading performance (see Fig. 7.4 on p. 222) indicates that at the low-second-reader level she made very few miscues and had excellent comprehension. At the high-second-reader level, both word-recognition and comprehension criteria were met. Susie made adequate use of context at the second-reader levels, at times combining graphic and context cues to keep the meaning essentially correct. At the low-third-reader level, however, almost all her miscues were serious, and five words had to be pronounced for her. When many words are unknown or mispronounced, or if the material is not understood, it is difficult to predict words and anticipate meaning. At this level Susie was unable to make much use of context cues as an aid to word recognition. Her miscues suggest little difficulty making symbol-sound associations, except possibly for vowel combinations (e.g., we*a*k, *loo*se). Most of her mispronunciations occurred on the final parts of words, but these were more likely the result of inattention to word endings and her overall difficulty with the passage than the result of an inability to decode these elements. These hypotheses can be checked out by presenting the words in isolation and focusing her attention on the ends of the words. Susie's main word-recognition difficulties seem to be with words that contain elements that cannot be decoded by applying phonic principles (e.g., g*iant*, *tongue*, pat*ient*, *st*omach) with and decoding words of more than one syllable. These weaknesses should be checked further.

Maria, a third grader, scored 3.1 on the *California Reading Test.* Her teacher, however, reported that Maria was having difficulty reading the third-grade basal reader. Her oral reading was slow and inaccurate. She responded to every word, but nearly all of her miscues were mispronunciations, and many of them were semantically and syntactically inappropriate. A representative sample of her miscues on monosyllabic words follows:

Stimulus	Response	Stimulus	Response
1. front	first	11. flow	few
2. bread	bag	12. cold	cool
3. silt	set	13. shall	shell
4. glass	guess	14. goat	game
5. spent	sped	15. shawl	shade
6. blank	back	16. gulp	gal
7. snip	snag	17. chart	champ
8. rigs	rags	18. these	that
9. there	that	19. hear	her
10. noon	neck	20. stood	stone

The above sample suggests the following: (1) Maria was overrelying on the initial letter or two and making little use of context. (2) She had difficulty making symbol-sound associations for *r* and *l* blends in the initial position (items 1, 2, 4, 6, 11) but not *s* blends (items 5, 7, 20). (3) She had difficulty making the symbol-sound associations for final blends (items, 1, 3, 5, 6, 12, 16) and vowel combinations (items 2, 10, 11, 14, 15, 20). (4) She had no difficulty making symbol-sound associations for single consonants (items 3, 8, 10, 12, 14, 16, 19), the first consonant of each initial blend, and consonant diagraphs (items 9, 13, 15, 17, 18). The errors on final single consonants were probably caused by her overreliance on the initial letters and difficulty with vowel combinations. The fact that Maria had no difficulty with single consonants in the initial position reinforces this interpretation. (5) Maria may have difficulty with symbol-sound associations for single vowels, but her over-reliance on initial consonants may be strongly contributing to such errors, and three of the single vowels (items 1, 12, 13) are nonphonetic elements. Follow-up testing with the appropriate decoding tests indicated that Maria did not have problems making symbol-sound associations for initial blends when her attention was focused on the graphemes, but did for vowel combinations and consonant blends that appear only in the final position. Follow-up testing also revealed that she had no problem with visual analysis of monosyllables or with blending.

These findings led to the recommendations that Maria's remedial program should include getting her to develop the habit of attending to the whole word rather than just the beginning; teaching her to monitor her word-recognition responses and make more effective use of meaning clues; and teaching her only those symbol-sound associations she needed to learn.

Rob, a fifth grader, obtained a score of 4.8 on the *Metropolitan Reading Test*. In oral reading, his performance was at the third-reader level in comprehension and second-reader level in word recognition. His miscues showed considerable variety, but for the most part were semantically and syntactically appropriate. Follow-up testing indicated that Rob had little trouble recognizing the words on which he miscued in context when they were presented in isolation, and that he could decode difficult polysyllabic words. When reading connected discourse, however, his tendency was to rely too much on context. Rob had to be convinced that, although at times it is not necessary to recognize all the printed words, it is very important to do so at other times. He also needed to learn when this is so, to be shown that he had the skills to do so, and to be convinced that there is a payoff for making the effort to recognize words accurately. A well-established ineffective reading strategy needed to be replaced with more effective ones.

Relationship between Miscues/Word-Recognition Errors and Reading Comprehension

Pflaum (1980) found that, for disabled readers, higher rates of errors that change meaning were associated with lower comprehension; higher rates of phonic-cue use, with higher comprehension. Also, a study by Beebe (1979-1980) reveals that, although substitution miscues generally detracted from comprehension and recall, only uncorrected unacceptable substitutions had a negative impact on comprehension and recall. Self-corrections and acceptable substitutions were associated with higher comprehension and retelling scores. It is not surprising that contextually appropriate miscues occur when comprehension is high, since comprehension can influence word recognition and the appropriateness of miscues. But miscues do not always reflect the reader's comprehension. Some children's miscue patterns suggest weak comprehension, but their retellings indicate good comprehension. Other readers produce miscue patterns that indicate adequate comprehension, but they demonstrate minimal comprehension (Wixson 1979).

When word recognition and comprehension are both inadequate on a passage, one of three situations may exist: (1) Weak word recognition is contributing to the inadequate comprehension; (2) inadequate comprehension is contributing to the weak word recognition; or (3) weaknesses in both areas are contributing to each other. Inability to recognize many of the printed words is a strong contributor to inadequate reading comprehension. To determine if poor word recognition is contributing to inadequate comprehension, the unknown words can be pronounced for the child, or the whole passage can be read to one pupil, and the impact on comprehension determined.

ASSESSING DECODING SKILLS

Various strategies may be used in attempting to recognize a word that is not immediately known. The context in which the word is set may be used to facilitate word recognition. The sounds represented by the graphemes may be determined and then blended to get the word's pronunciation. Or the resemblance of the unknown word to a known word or words may be noticed and utilized. A less desirable strategy involves spelling the word. This strategy may be used by pupils who have encountered the word in spelling lessons or by those who have been taught to read through the use of a linguistic reading program.

Good readers know a number of strategies and are resourceful in their use. They know how to utilize context clues, how to make and apply symbol-sound associations, how to determine useful word parts, how to employ graphic resemblances, and how to blend. If one strategy is not successful, they try another. Poor readers often restrict themselves to one strategy and employ even that one poorly. It is important to determine what strategy or strategies a child tries to use, as well as how successfully a strategy is employed.

Some children have laboriously acquired a small stock of sight words that is inadequate for their needs. They may or may not try to make use of context or language cues when confronted by an unknown word. They may never have learned any decoding technique thoroughly enough to use it successfully. They may not even know how to begin, or they can make few symbol-sound associations, or they have difficulty blending phonemes into syllables. They do not look for common recognizable parts in a word or for resemblances to words they know. In short, they know little about *decoding,* which we define as a mediated form of word recognition.

There are three main subskill areas of decoding: visual analysis, phonic analysis, and blending.[9] Good readers usually inspect an unknown word for parts they can utilize, make necessary symbol-sound associations, blend the parts into a whole word, and check for appropriateness. It is possible for different learners to employ different processes and information to arrive at the same final response (Sipay 1971).

A learner who cannot decode words may be deficient in any or all of the skill areas, with symbol-sound association weaknesses occurring most frequently. The examiner's task is to determine which weaknesses are creating most of the problem.

Nonwords, often referred to as nonsense words or syllables, are often employed in decoding tests to rule out the possibility that the pupil might recognize the words at sight and thus not have to utilize any decoding skills. This use of nonwords has been criticized by Cunningham (1977), who suggests that a more valid assessment of decoding skills could be obtained by first flashing real words and then allowing the child time to decode those words not recognized initially.

In assessing decoding ability, two points should be considered. First, it is easier to decode words that are in your listening vocabulary, because you have something against which to monitor a decoding effort. Second, words in context are easier to recognize and decode than words in isolation because additional

[9]These skill areas are discussed more fully on pages 462–470.

cues are available. These two points lead to the conclusion that a test employing nonwords in isolation requires a higher degree of decoding ability than is necessary for decoding real words in context. On such tests, therefore, one should be willing to accept a mastery level below that which might be desirable if real words were used.

Published Group-Administered Decoding Tests

A number of NR survey tests and CR tests contain decoding subtests (using an assortment of titles) at the primary level or at the primary and intermediate levels. Some NR diagnostic tests, such as the *Stanford Diagnostic Reading Test*, even sample decoding skills at the upper grade levels. Tests that accompany commercially published reading programs sample only those decoding skills taught at a given point in the program.

All group-administered decoding tests have a number of limitations. The tasks they require should be examined carefully, giving consideration to the following points:

1. Subtest(s) having the same label may make different demands on the learner.
2. The skills required to accomplish the test task may not be relevant to reading ability.
3. In group-administered decoding tests, it is not possible to measure the same decoding skills as in individually administered tests.
4. Subtest titles can be very misleading. One "Whole-Word Recognition" subtest requires only visual discrimination.
5. Most group tests contain too few items to provide a reliable measure of a specific skill (e.g., one item that samples the ability to make the sound-symbol association /t/ = t).
6. It is extremely difficult to measure blending skills realistically on a group test.
7. Group tests do not measure ability to combine all the skills needed for decoding. Usually a subtest measures just one aspect (e.g., syllabication).

Published Individually Administered Decoding Tests

Several published individually administered decoding tests are available. Some are part of a diagnostic test battery, such as the *Spache Diagnostic Reading Scales* (DRS), *Gates-McKillip-Horowitz, Durrell,* or *Woodcock.* Others are single-purpose tests, such as the comprehensive *Diagnostic Decoding Test,* and the much briefer *Roswell-Chall Diagnostic Reading Test.* These individual tests vary considerably as to which decoding skills are measured and how. Care must be exercised in interpreting test performance, For instance, if the task only asks the pupil to pronounce a printed polysyllabic word (this may be an item on a test labeled "syllabication"), the inability to respond acceptably may have a number of causes. The child may not know how or where to syllabicate, be unable to decode one or more of the syllables, or be unable to blend the phonemes into syllables or the syllables into words. Also, although the manual gives only one acceptable response, others may be just as permissible, especially if contrived words are used. For example, *prodisla* (a stimulus from a published test) may be "syllabicated" into *pro-dis-la*, *pro-di-sla*, *prod-is-la*, or *prod-i-sla*, with the resulting vowel sounds varying in accordance with whether they appear in open or closed syllables.

Informal Tests

Information regarding learners' decoding skills can be obtained by analyzing their word-recognition errors (see p. 246-247). Such analyses may reveal possible weaknesses or strengths in a subskill area (e.g., making vowel symbol-sound associations). The analysis can narrow down the areas requiring further investigation. For instance, it may indicate that it is necessary to check the child's ability to make symbol-sound associations for vowel digraphs and diphthongs but not for single vowels.

A pupil may be able to verbalize a phonic generalization but be unable to apply it. On the other hand, some children can apply generalizations but choose not to; some can apply phonic principles without being able to verbalize them.

Many phonic generalizations involve a two-step process. The pupil must: (1) determine which principle to apply and understand the terms used in it (e.g., in order to apply the generalization "the single vowel letter probably represents its long sound because it is an open syllable," the child must know what an open syllable is); and (2) determine what the correct sound is (e.g., long vowels say their names). A breakdown in either step can produce an error.

An informal check of visual-analysis skills can be made by presenting unknown words to the child and asking where she would divide them and why. In some cases it is preferable to ask the child what she would do first in attempting to "figure out" what the word says. Some children do not know where to begin.

Symbol-sound associations may be tested by presenting letters in isolation or in words. If words are used, they should not be in the child's sight vocabulary, since there is no need to make symbol-sound associations if the words are recognized immediately. A brief test of symbol-sound knowledge is presented in Figure 7.9.

Blending skills should be tested. Depending on which skills one wishes to sample, single letters *(g a m)*, a single letter and a phonogram *(g am)*, or syllables *(gam ble)* may be presented. Probably it is easiest to blend syllables into whole words, followed by blending a consonant with a phonogram.

Sounds are blended in the testee's mind regardless of whether the original stimuli are visual or auditory. Some children have difficulty blending auditorily even if the test is well administered.

Informal auditory-blending tests can be constructed, or a brief standardized test like the *Roswell-Chall Auditory Blending Test* or a blending test such as the one in the *Gates-McKillop-Horowitz* may be used. In an auditory-blending test, the parts of the word are spoken by the examiner with a brief pause (½ to 1 second) between each segment. The pupil's task is to blend the parts into a whole word and then say the word. The words that are used, the manner in which they are segmented (e.g., /b/-/a/-/g/ is easier to say and synthesize than /s/-/t/-/r/-/i/-/p/), the enunciation of the examiner—especially how well he can

TEST OF PHONIC KNOWLEDGE

A	h	s	v	c	z	k	w	r	f	t
	g	l	b	m	d	n	y	p	j	
B	bl	st	ch	dr	wh	fr	th	pl	sh	
	qu	str	scr	spl	spr	thr	ph	kn	wr	
C	e	o	a	u	i					
D	ee	ai	ay	oa	ou	oi	oy			
	aw	au	ea	oo	ow	ew	ey			
E	weed	dote	pan	jut	bide					
	wed	dot	pane	jute	bid					
F	de	un	re	im	pre	trans				
	tion	ful	ly	ous	ment	ance				

Figure 7.9. A brief test of phonic knowledge. *Directions:* As the child reads from one copy, the examiner records on another. The child points to each stimulus as he gives a response. For the single consonants (A) and consonant clusters (B), the child may give the sound in isolation or a word beginning with the sound represented by the grapheme. The child may be asked for the alternate sounds represented by c and g. For the single vowel letters (C), the child may be asked what sounds each letter can make, or be asked to give a word containing the corresponding sounds. The alternate sounds represented by ea, oo, and ow (D) may be requested. The two lines of words testing some spelling patterns (E) are read horizontally in pairs (e.g., *weed, wed*). This subtest is not given if the child had difficulty making the symbol–sound associations for single consonants and vowels. For children who do well, a few common affixes (F) are given.

"leave out" extraneous vowel sounds (e.g., /b/ instead of /buh/), and whether or not the word is in the child's lexicon are among the variables that can influence performance on an auditory-blending test.

Refer to Eeds (1988) for a "holistic assessment" of decoding ability and to Goodman, Goodman, and Hood (1989) for other assessment procedures that would be favored by whole-language advocates. A literacy development checklist is presented by Bailey et al. (1988).

THE USE OF CONTEXT AND LANGUAGE CLUES. The use of context and language clues can aid word recognition and decoding. Minimal visual input may be sufficient to determine an unknown word if the context and the sentence structure offer strong clues as to what the word is. In both cases experiential background plays a role. In the sentence, "The bone was eaten by the _____," the child's knowledge about animals suggests possibilities for the final word. Experience with language suggests that only certain words are likely to occur in a given pattern. Thus, the unknown word is likely to be a noun. Context and language clues are often combined with other word-recognition or decoding skills.

If the ability to use context or language clues is to be measured, the cloze test material should be at or below the child's instructional level. It is difficult to use context clues if a number of words are not recognized, and impossible to do so if most words are unknown.

FOLLOW-UP TO DECODING TESTS.   The best way to determine if a child needs to, or can, learn skills in which tests or observations have shown him to be deficient is to try to teach him these skills. If the initial lessons indicate that the tests were in error, there is no need to continue teaching a skill for which a child already demonstrates mastery. If a child cannot learn the skill after a reasonable length of time, the teacher should attempt to determine what factors are contributing to the problem. These factors may be external or within the child. Emotional stress caused by events at home or in school may be curtailing his ability or desire to learn in general. Or, something within the way the skill is presented may be a factor. Perhaps the child does not understand the directions, or there is an attempt to teach too much at once, or the pace of the lessons is too rapid, or there is a need for additional reinforcement. A child who cannot learn to make symbol-sound associations may be weak in underlying skills (see pages 456-459).

DIAGNOSTIC USE OF SAMPLE LESSONS

Years ago, tests of associative learning were used to determine why a child had trouble learning to recognize printed words. These tests involved associating nonsense or meaningful words with geometric forms, real words with squiggles that looked something like printed words, and so on (Gates 1927). These tests fell into disuse as diagnostic tools because the test results were of little help in planning remediation. Nevertheless, the idea that children's ability to learn can be tested by trying them on learning tasks has real merit.

The use of *sample lessons* for reading diagnosis was developed by A. J. Harris and Roswell (1953). The technique is sometimes known as *trial teaching* and may be used to select an approach for teaching word-recognition or decoding skills to severely disabled readers. It may also be adapted for determining which beginning reading approach is more likely to succeed for particular children. Directions for five different instructional methods follow.

Directions

The entire session should be informal, with a great deal of give and take. Because observational information is significant in interpreting the results of sample lessons, the examiner notes such factors as the speed with which the child grasps the task; task involvement or avoidance; work tempo; need for repetition of instructions; motivation; effort; sustained attention; perseverence; anxiety; reaction to success, failure, and praise; and recall of what was taught.

Several methods are tried until one is clearly successful. If time allows, a variety of materials is presented to obtain some impression of the child's reactions to books, workbooks, and game-type devices. Failure is kept to a minimum, and success is liberally praised, as is effort. In one such period it is possible to demonstrate to many children that they can learn to read. In most cases, this experience is a powerful motivator for future reading instruction.

The procedures described below should be used at the discretion of the examiner. Which methods to use and at what level to begin the trial teaching should be based on an appraisal of the child's basic reading skills.

1. WHOLE-WORD METHOD.   For the child who has few, if any, word-recognition skills, it is advisable to begin with a whole-word method, which essentially involves learning to associate printed words with their oral counterparts. Additional motivation may be supplied by teaching words that the child wants to learn.

Construct a number of picture cards, each illustrating a well-known object (e.g., a cake, a table) with the object's name printed under each picture. Also make a corresponding set of word cards that do not have any pictures. Make sure that the cards do not have any marks that could be used as cues. Use the word cards to determine which words are already known. Then select three to five unknown words for teaching. Follow-up may indicate that this is too many for the child to learn and retain in one session. On the other hand, success in learning these words does not mean that the child will learn a comparable number in every future session.

Present the first picture card, and pronounce the word while drawing your finger from left to right under it. Have the child say the word several times while looking carefully at the word. Then ask her to select the corresponding word card. When the child thinks she has learned the word, repeat the procedure with a second word. After that word has been learned, present the two word cards in random order until mastery is demonstrated. Teach a third word, followed by mixed practice with the previously taught words. Follow a similar procedure until all of the words have been taught. Then present the word cards in random fashion three times, prompting if necessary. If the child is successful, retest about 30 minutes later. If possible, check retention 1, 3, and 7 days later; long-term memory is vital in use of the whole-word method.

It may be desirable to follow up by teaching a few words from the material being considered for instructional use, followed by reading the corresponding material. If the child objects to this material, it may be necessary to avoid using any book in the early stages of remedial instruction.

Some children are distracted by the use of pictures in learning to recognize words through a whole-word approach. If use of the preceding procedure suggests this, it may be well to repeat the lesson with different words and without the use of pictures.

2. SYNTHETIC PHONIC METHOD.   The ability to synthesize or blend sounds into whole words is vital to this method. If the child shows some auditory-blending skill, it is safe to try synthetic phonics. Auditory blending may be checked with one of the available tests or informally (see pages 250-251). A reasonable criterion for adequate performance is at least 80% correct, but any correct responses indicate that a method relying on blending is not impossible.

Teach or review the symbol-sound associations of four or five consonants and one short vowel (e.g., *m, c, t, s, d,* and *a*). Each symbol-sound association is presented singly as follows: Show the lowercase letter *m* and say, "This is 'em' [use the letter name] and the sound it makes is /m/, the sound that you hear at the beginning of *man* [slightly emphasize the /m/]. Listen for the /m/ sound at the beginning of each of these words; *meat, my, milk.* Can you hear the /m/? Now you give me some words that begin with /m/."

Then say, "Now I'm going to say a word, then its parts slowly, and then the whole word again. Listen carefully; Mat; /m/-/a/-/t/; mat. This is how the word *mat* looks." Use letter cards to form the word, first saying the whole word, then each sound as the letter is put in place, and finally the whole word again. Repeat the word, sound by sound, moving your finger under each letter in the word as the sound is pronounced. Hand the child the appropriate letters and say. "Put these together to make *mat,*" Ask him to sound out the word as he does so. Help him, if necessary. Then show how to change *mat* to *cat* and *sat.*

Write a sentence containing the words, such as "The cat sat on the mat," and have him read it, providing help as necessary.

Show him how to change the final elements to form new words: *mat* to *mad, sat* to *sad.* Then provide practice in using the symbol-sound associations to form five words.

Present the five words in the same manner described above for the whole-word method. If the child recognizes and decodes four of the words successfully, he is likely to succeed with a phonic program that employs a similar method.

The number of symbol-sound associations presented in one session and the way in which they are taught are two variables that can influence the success or failure of this instructional method. If the enabling skills and understandings that are important for learning to decode are weak, it may be advisable to delay phonics instruction until they are strengthened. Auditory discrimination, which is probably an important subskill in learning symbol-sound associations, may be assessed by using a standardized test. Or, it may be checked informally by pronouncing sets of three words and having the child raise her hand when she hears a word that begins with the sound under consideration.

3. LINGUISTIC METHOD. This technique is especially useful with pupils who possess only rudimentary blending ability and are unable to cope with a synthetic-phonic method. Used solely, however, it affords only a limited degree of independence in word recognition and decoding.

Present a high-frequency word like *man.* The teach or review separately three consonant symbol-sound associations (e.g., *r, f, p*) that can be used in the initial position to form other common words. Demonstrate how initial consonants may be substituted to form new words. Provide practice in utilizing this technique, followed by mixed practice with the three words formed with the introduced consonants. Repeat this procedure for a different spelling pattern (e.g., *at* or *un*) and the same initial consonants. Learning and retention may be checked using the procedure described above for the whole-word method.

As with the other methods, variations may be tried to determine their possible effect on learning. For example, instead of using a word like *man* as a starting point, a phonogram that is a commonly known word (e.g., *an*) may be employed, and the child taught to form new words by appending initial consonants. Most linguistic reading programs do not provide direct teaching of symbol-sound associations.

4. VISUAL-MOTOR METHOD.   Choose from three to five 5- to 8-letter words which the child cannot recognize (e.g., *friend, airplane*). Print the word on a card as the child is observing. Say, "This word is 'friend.' Look carefully at this word. What is this word? Now close your eyes and try to see the printed word in your mind. Open your eyes and look at the word again. What is this word?" Remove the word card and ask the child to print or write it. Have her compare her word with the word on the card. (You will have to produce a written version if the child has chosen to write, rather than to print the word). If she is incorrect, repeat the above procedure: present the word, pronounce it, have her try to visualize it, then have her write it, and compare it against your copy. Repeat the procedure until the child can reproduce the word from memory three times in a row. Teach the other words in the same way. After a period of time, test the child's ability to recognize all of the words. A more detailed description of this procedure appears on pages 502-504.

5. KINESTHETIC METHOD.   Only the initial stages used in teaching by a kinesthetic method are presented here. A more complete description can be found on pages 500-502.

After a short orientation period, tell the child that you are going to teach him to read by an entirely new method. Assure him as to its value by telling him that others who had difficulty learning to read learned through this method. Describe the procedure to him. Ask him which words he would like to learn.

Write the word with a crayon or marker on paper in letters approximately 2 inches high. Then tell the child to trace the word with his index finger (and thumb, if he wishes), and to say the word aloud as he traces it. The word is traced until the child can reproduce the word without looking at the original copy. In case of error, or if the child hesitates and seems unable to complete the word, he has to retrace the word as a whole. Erasing to correct an error is not permitted. If the child has difficulty recalling the word, he should be encouraged to trace it a number of times and then to write it without consulting the original copy. Teach three to five words in this way, and then test their recognition as indicated above.

Because most children can learn through one of the first four methods listed in the foregoing, it usually is necessary to try the kinesthetic method only with cases of severe word-recognition disability. Regardless of which method is used initially, instruction should eventually incorporate the teaching of other potentially helpful word-recognition skills and strategies.

Mills (1956) developed a test that employs standardized sample lessons using four instructional methods: visual, phonic, kinesthetic, and combined. Ten words are taught in each 15-minute lesson. Mill's adaptation of the principle of sample lessons appears to be time consuming and fatiguing for the child, but some clinicians and remedial teachers may find it useful.

The essence of the sample lesson is a situation in which the child's behaviors as a learner can be carefully observed and evaluated. Qualitative observation and interpretation are much more important than numerical scores or ratings. A standardized procedure and scoring may not draw teachers' attention away from these qualitative factors, but the temptation to rely on scores is strong. For these reasons, using sample lessons in a flexible, unstandardized way is preferable.

8

Correlates of Reading Disability I: Cognitive Factors

This chapter is the first of three concerned with the many factors related to reading disability, some of which are also related to less serious reading problems. We open with a discussion of causation and how it is determined, and then contrast single and plural views of causation. The third section summarizes efforts to identify subtypes of reading disability; and the fourth section describes models of reading disability. The last three sections deal respectively with the relationships of intelligence, specific cognitive factors, and language to reading disability.

MEAN DIFFERENCES, CORRELATIONS, AND CAUSATION

Good readers and poor readers[1] have been compared on a myriad of cognitive, linguistic, neurological, physiological, psychological, educational, and socioeconomic variables. The performances of poor and disabled readers on measures of various reading skills have been correlated with many of the same factors. Empirical evidence concerning the factors thought to be related to reading disability is not lacking. These data have led to a plethora of explanations for reading failure, with researchers seemingly favoring their own theories of causation (Stanovich 1986a,b).

[1]The terms *good reader* and *poor reader* are defined variously in the literature. Here, *good readers* refers to students who are making at least normal progress in reading achievement; *poor readers*, to those who are not. The latter term, as used here, also includes disabled readers unless otherwise specified.

Poor readers and disabled readers, on average, display weaker performances than good readers on a wide variety of factors. An implicit assumption in much of this research is that the identification of performance differences on any component of the reading process provides evidence for causation. Despite significant mean differences between the groups, however, there are individuals in each group whose performances are comparable to those of individuals in the other group. In other words, some poor readers perform just as well as some good readers, and vice versa.

No disabled reader has all, or even most, of the characteristics reported to be related to reading disability, and some good readers often display many of the same traits. Other than their relatively poor reading ability, disabled readers have no one characteristic in common. Nor has a *syndrome* (a particular cluster of symptoms) been found.

This situation may exist for a number of reasons. The probability is strong that reading disability is not a homogeneous entity; rather, the classification could be composed of a number of subgroups, each having differing characteristics. Thus, what might be true of one type of disabled reader would not be true for all types. Research findings could be highly influenced by the relative distribution of these subtypes in the disabled-reader sample. Even statistically significant mean differences do not necessarily mean that the variable under consideration is *the* cause of differences in reading ability. Differences between good readers and poor readers may be (1) symptoms of the actual underlying component (e.g., poor eye movements usually do not cause reading disability, but they do reflect underlying cognitive processes); (2) caused by the reading problem, rather than causing it; (3) indicative that the reading problem and the other deficits cyclically reinforce one another (e.g., poor vocabulary knowledge may be contributing to the reading problem and, in turn, poor reading ability cuts the child off from opportunities to increase his or her vocabulary) (Kleiman 1982).

Perfetti (1985) suggests two possible occurrences of the latter situation, also known as *reciprocal causation.* He postulates that novice readers who do not develop rapid, accurate word recognition at the same rate as their peers find reading less enjoyable because it is encumbered by the process of "sounding out" words. Such children would not likely be motivated to read on their own, and thus would receive less practice in what they need most. Their problem would be exacerbated by the introduction of more difficult text, and their slower progress in reading acquisition would begin to have more generalized effects on processes that underlie a broad range of cognitive skills. Another reciprocal causation is the possibility that reading failure may cause motivational problems.

Another issue that complicates attempts to determine causation is the possible influence of *compensation:* the probability that strength in one trait related to reading ability can make up for a weakness in another relevant trait. It is also possible that a combination of weak abilities may have a combined causal effect that none of the weaknesses could produce by itself.

Most of the studies comparing reading or learning disabled students with those who are making normal progress in reading have been flawed (Valtin 1978–1979, Kleiman 1982). A major problem has been the selection of the disabled sample, which can vary in number and characteristics depending on the selection criteria. As Valtin (1980) points out, observed differences between good readers and poor readers can be artifacts of research methodology. If truly representative samples of good readers and poor readers are drawn, the groups will differ in variables such as IQ and SES. Consequently, they will also differ on factors that are correlated with these variables (e.g., memory, language abilities, prior knowledge). Therefore, poor readers will show a number of cognitive deficits. If only subjects whose reading ability is not commensurate with their potential are included in the study, the deficits will vary depending on whether a Verbal IQ (VIQ), Performance IQ (PIQ), or Full-Scale (FS) is used. Whereas both the average VIQs and PIQs of good readers approximate 110, the majority of disabled readers show a significantly higher PIQ (about 105) than VIQ (about 95). Therefore, if good and poor readers are matched on PIQ, poor readers will have lower VIQs and FS scores and will show deficits in factors related to verbal ability, especially language. If VIQ is used, these differences tend to disappear. If FS is used, poor readers will show better results in visual tasks. Group selection also may be influenced by the reading test employed (Silberberg & Silberberg 1977).

A second problem is the representativeness of the groups. Normally developing readers in many studies have average IQs of about 115, while disabled readers tend to have average IQs 10 to 20 points lower. Such IQ differences may account for some reported good/poor reader differences. When less skilled readers, who have mild cognitive defects, are compared with good readers whose IQs come closer to 100, it is not surprising that a large number of performance differences occur (Stanovich 1986b). In order to match good and poor readers on intelligence, one has to choose from the higher end of the disabled readers' IQ distribution and the lower end of the good readers' distribution; thus neither sample is truly representative of the population from which they were selected.

The selection of control groups is also important. Usually the control group is similar in age and IQ (and sometimes SES and gender) and much better in reading than the disabled group. Guthrie (1973) points out some advantages of using two comparison groups: a group of similar age but with much better reading ability than the disabled group, and a younger group with reading achievement equal to that of the disabled group. Mattis, French, and Rapin (1975) used three groups: disabled readers with brain damage, disabled readers without brain damage, and good readers with brain damage. The latter group served to eliminate from consideration deficient abilities that do not prevent brain-damaged children from learning to read.

Another problem is the *washing-out effect*. When two or more subgroups exist within the reading-disabled sample, the high scores of one subgroup on a particular skill or attribute may offset the low scores of another subgroup. Use of average group performance may also mask the fact that a trait was quite prominent in a few disabled readers (or good readers) but not in enough of them to have any impact on the mean of the group.

It is commonly accepted that there is an interaction between constitutional and environmental variables. So there is no way of completely ruling out the possible effects of past differences in experience on the characteristics displayed by the subjects in a study (Doehring, Backman & Waters 1983).

Many of the factors associated with reading disability have been identified from correlational data. However, *correlation*—the fact that two or more measurable characteristics tend to be found together—does not prove causation. Correlations simply indicate relationships between variables; the higher the correlation, the stronger the implied relationship. Although a cause-effect relationship may exist, causation cannot be inferred directly from a correlation coefficient; much more direct evidence needs to be established.

Even when a cause-effect relationship is strongly presumed, we cannot be sure which factor is the cause and which is the effect. Furthermore, the correlation may be the result of another factor or factors. To illustrate these points, consider the following: In a broad age range of children, a high correlation between height and reading achievement is likely, with shorter children tending to be less capable readers than taller children. But height does not cause reading ability, or vice versa. The correlation between height and reading achievement reflects the fact that taller children tend to be older than shorter children; they have not only had more opportunity to improve their reading ability but also have attained greater cognitive and linguistic maturity. For these reasons, we use the term "correlate" rather than "cause" when discussing factors associated with reading disability.

Thus, we are often faced with a child who displays characteristics demonstrably related to reading disability, but we cannot be certain that any of them caused, or are even contributing to, the child's reading problems. Yet there are logical and theoretical reasons to suspect that certain factors *might* be contributors.

This apparent dilemma is not as hopeless as it might seem. The reading ability of many disabled readers can often be improved through instruction. When remedial efforts are successful, we need not determine what originally caused the problem. Also, we have little or no control over some variables. In other instances, knowing the cause of a reading disability would be of little use because that information of itself does not tell us how best to instruct the pupil.

Something can be done about certain factors (e.g., visual problems, dietary deficiencies) that inhibit a child's progress in learning to read. If a condition cannot be corrected, possibly it can be circumvented. Even if immediate use cannot be made of the information, reading teachers should be aware of the factors that may contribute to some reading problems, if for no other reason than to understand the theoretical bases for particular remedial procedures and to appreciate the efforts being made toward differential diagnosis.

VIEWS OF CAUSATION

Two opposing views regarding causation have existed since reading disability was first studied. Although admitting that some cases of reading disability stem from other causes, physicians have tended to attribute reading disability to a basic constitutional cause, often inherited, and usually accompanied by one or more other communication difficulties in language, speech, spelling, handwriting, or composing a written text. Thus, they have looked for causes within the child. Most learning disability specialists and neuropsychologists follow this medical model. On the other hand, while granting that some cases are attributable to constitutional defects or dysfunctions, most regular-education personnel, reading specialists, and psychologists have been impressed by the wide range of factors associated with reading disability, and have tended to favor a pluralistic theory of causation and to view reading difficulties on a continuum from mild to severe.

Single-Factor Theories

The earliest literature on reading disability (Morgan 1896; Hinshelwood 1900, 1917) indicated that *the* cause of *congenital word blindness* was a deficiency in the local area of the brain where visual images are stored. Since that time, various writers have suggested that all or most cases of reading disability are attributable to a single cause. Most of these single-factor theories seem to refer to seriously disabled readers, and imply a cognitive or neurological basis for the reading disability. Thus, we have theories involving deficits, deficiencies, or dysfunctions in perceptual, visual-motor, linguistic, and psycholinguistic functioning, as well as in auditory-visual integration, memory, and attention. Similarly, different theories implicate hemispheric rivalry, incomplete hemispheric lateralization, the presence of a function in a hemisphere not best suited to subserve that function, or a problem in the coordination between the two hemispheres of the brain. Other theories involve frank or implied brain damage, vestibular disorders, or a lack of neurological organization. A few theories are related to neurological hypotheses, for example, the chemical imbalance hypothesis of Smith and Carrigan (1959).

Rather than imply damage or dysfunction, the *maturational lag* theories of Bender (1957, 1975) and Satz and his associates (1978) suggest a specialized slowness in certain aspects of neurological development. In these theories, factors such as poorly established hemispheric dominance and reading disability are thought to be the result of a developmental lag. One developmental view holds that the main cause of school failure is general immaturity (Ames 1968, 1983). Phonological coding (see pages 293–295) appears to be a recent single-factor theory. Still others argue that reading or learning disability is caused, directly or indirectly, by one or more physical or physiological factors, such as visual or auditory sensory defects, glandular disturbances, or dietary deficiencies or inclusions.

Few specific theories involving educational, socioeconomic, and emotional problems have been offered. Rather, the theories in these areas have been rather diffuse, citing such general variables as inadequate or inappropriate teaching, poverty, and emotional blocks to learning.

To us, it seems probable that each of the single-cause advocates has emphasized one part of what is really a very complex situation.

Multiple-Causation Theories

For many years, the majority of educators and psychologists have favored the view that there are many possible causes of reading disability. As Monroe (1932, p. 80) stated almost 60 years ago, "In considering the causes for a child's failure to read, we must inquire into a number of possible impeding factors, both in his constitutional organization and in his environment."

Studies of disabled readers have revealed a variety of possible causal or contributing factors. One of the most intensive studies of causal or contributing factors in reading disability to date is H. M. Robinson's study (1946) of 30 cases of severe reading disability. A social case history for each child was taken by a trained social worker, and the child was examined by a psychologist, a psychiatrist, a pediatrician, a neurologist, an ophthalmologist, an otolaryngologist, a speech pathologist, and an endocrinologist. After the examinations had been completed, a case conference was held on each child, at which the specialists came to a group decision concerning which factors were probably causal and which were merely concomitants of the reading problem. Treatment was supervised in 22 of these cases. After the results of treatment were known, another conference was held at which the conclusions previously reached about causation were reviewed and sometimes changed. A summary of causal factors was then made, based on both diagnosis and remediation.

The number of probable causal factors ranged from one to four. The most frequent were social problems and visual difficulties, followed by emotional maladjustment, neurological difficulties, speech or discrimination difficulties, school methods, auditory difficulties, endocrine disturbances, and general physical difficulty. Each handicap was present more often than it was judged to have causal significance, and each handicap was considered by the specialists to be a possible cause before remediation in more cases than it was judged to be a probable cause after remedial treatment.

A study of 34 very poor readers in Swedish first grades led Malmquist (1958) to write:

> On the basis of our results, it appears reasonable to draw the important conclusion that to attempt to find a single factor which will entirely explain the occurrence of reading errors is, in the great majority of cases, a vain endeavor. Most frequently there appear to be several factors in constellation which are related to reading failure. Many of these factors seem to be closely interrelated. There appears to be an interplay between the child's general physical, intellectual, emotional and social development, and the development of his reading ability. (1958, p. 390)

The factors that seemed most significant to Malmquist were intelligence; ability to concentrate, persistence, self-confidence, and emotional stability; spelling ability; visual perception, social status and educational level of the parents; and the teaching experience of the child's teacher.

The multiple-causation point of view contends that there is more than one cause of reading disability. As such, it is closely related to the belief that there are probably a number of types of reading disability.

SUBTYPES OF READING DISABILITY[2]

Two main approaches have been used in attempts to identify subtypes of reading disability. Representative studies of each type are summarized below.

[2]Studies in which the samples were identified as reading disabled, learning disabled in reading, and dyslexic are used in this discussion. We feel justified in including the latter two designations because most children classified as learning disabled have a reading disability, and dyslexics could not be differentiated from disabled readers on a number of variables (Taylor, Satz & Friel 1979–1980). In most cases, we have used the term employed by the researcher or author.

Clinical-Inferential Classification[3]

Clinical-inferential classification may be based on presumed causation (often believed to be an intrinsic, constitutional deficit), on different performance patterns on various neuropsychological measures (nonreading variables), or on reading achievement variables. The subtypes are derived from visual inspection of complex, multidimensional data.

Ingram and Reid (1956) studied reading-disabled children who had differences of 20 or more points between their Verbal and Performance IQs. Those with higher Verbal IQs more often showed visuospatial reading and spelling errors; this subtype was labeled *visuospatial dyslexia. Audiophonic dyslexics* had higher performance IQs and tended to have difficulty with auditory discrimination, blending, and letter-sound associations. Based on his study of speech-retarded children, Ingram (1969) concludes that the more severe the reading disability, the more likely the occurrence of both visuospatial and audiophonic symptoms in the same child. A mixed category was added later (Ingram, Mason & Blackburn 1970).

Kinsbourne and Warrington (1966), like Ingram, indentified two subgroups of disabled readers who had large differences between their Verbal and Performance IQs. The *language-retarded* group were characterized by a late onset of language, significantly lower Verbal than Performance IQs, phonetically inappropriate spelling errors, and adequate performance on math and finger localization tests.[4] The *Gerstman syndrome group* had lower Performance IQs than Verbal IQs, directional confusion, and poor performance in writing and on arithmetic and finger localization tests. These researchers concluded that a cerebral deficit may delay the acquisition of reading and writing in different ways.

Rabinovitch (1968) proposes a three-group classification that attempts to distinguish neurological dysfunctioning from brain damage. The *primary reading retardation* group has basic neurological disturbances without evidence of definite brain damage. This subtype is similar to *developmental dyslexia* as defined by Critchley (1981). *Secondary reading retardation* includes cases whose reading problems are not caused primarily by central nervous system disorders, but are the result of such varied nonneurological factors as impaired vision, emotional maladjustment, and environmental deprivation. Rabinovitch (1962), however, admits that it is often difficult to find a pure case of either type; thus, in effect, his classification also includes a "mixed" category. His third subtype is *brain damage with reading retardation.*

A viewpoint similar to that of Rabinovitch is expressed by Matějček (1977), who distinguishes between severe disabilities whose causes are constitutional in nature and mild disabilities that have variable causation influenced by teaching methods, educational pressures, and aggravating factors such as sociocultural problems, poor motivation, or poor health.

Bannatyne (1971) differs from Rabinovitch in not attempting to distinguish neurological dysfunction from brain damage and in his inclusion of an inherited cause. He lists four main categories of dyslexia: (1) *primary emotional communicative* (e.g., parental rejection or neglect); (2) *minimal neurological dysfunction,*

---

[3]This classification was suggested by Satz and Morris (1981). Other reviews of the literature regarding subtypes of reading disability may be found in Doehring et al. (1981); Rosenthal, Boder, and Callaway (1982); A. J. Harris (1982); and Lyon (1983).

[4]See page 323 for a description of finger localization tests.

involving a disorder in one or more of visual-spatial, auditory, integrative, concep-tual, or tactual and kinesthetic functioning; (3) *social, cultural,* or *educational deprivation;* and (4) *genetic dyslexia,* which is characterized by a strong tendency to run in families.

Denckla (1972) attempted to classify 190 disabled readers through an "ex-tended neurological examination." Only 30% fell clearly into one of three catego-ries: (1) those with *specific language disabilities* without perceptual deficits but with "poor visuomotor and audiovisual circuits" (15%); (2) *dyscontrol syndrome,* characterized as impulsive, "sweet, silly, and sloppy" (10%); and (3) *specific vis-uospatial difficulties* similar to the Gerstmann syndrome, with left-right confu-sion, poor finger localization, low Performance IQ, more difficulty with arithme-tic and writing than with reading and oral spelling, and emotional problems (5%).

In order to eliminate psychological deficits that do not interfere with learn-ing to read, Mattis, French, and Rapin (1975) utilized a control group of brain-injured children who could read normally. Most of their dyslexic children fell into one of three groups: (1) *language disorder,* those who had difficulty in nam-ing, along with poor auding, poor imitation, or poor speech-sound discrimination (28%); (2) *articulatory and graphomotor,* those with poor sound blending and uncoordinated writing, but normal auding (48%); and (3) a small *visuospatial* group with low Performance IQ and difficulty in visual perception and memory (14%). Mattis (1978) reports a cross-validation study that verified the three groups and added a fourth. In this sample of 165 dyslexic children, mainly from disadvantaged minority backgrounds, he found the following proportions: lan-guage-disorder syndrome, 63%; articulatory and graphomotor syndrome, 10%; visuoperceptual disorder, 5%; combination of two syndromes, 9%; and a se-quencing disorder, with poor auditory memory span and difficulty with the con-cepts of before-behind and left-right, 10%.

Boder (1973) used patterns of performance on a graded word-recognition test and written spelling of words that were and were not in the children's sight vocabularies to classify 107 children with developmental dyslexia. She was able to place 100 of them into one of three subtypes. Children in the *dysphonetic* group (N=67) had some sight vocabulary but lacked word-analysis skills and were unable to make symbol-sound associations and blend phonemes into words. Those in the *diseidetic* group (N=10) were deficient in the ability to perceive words as wholes or visual gestalts and tended to employ a phonic-anal-ysis approach to word recognition. The most severe cases were those who were both dysphonetic and diseidetic (N=23). Her research led to the development of *The Boder Test of Reading-Spelling Patterns.*

Myklebust (1978) hypothesizes five subtypes: (1) *inner-language dyslexia* in which deficits in both auditory and visual-verbal processing prevent children from understanding written language, even though they can recognize and pro-nounce printed words (a severe form of *word calling*); (2) *auditory dyslexia,* which involves the inability to "symbolize auditory information" and relate pho-nemes to graphemes; (3) *visual dyslexia (visual-verbal agnosia)* in which the child cannot attain symbolic meaning from print because of visual-perceptual deficits; (4) *intermodal dyslexia,* which is the inability to integrate visual and auditory information; and (5) a neurological deficit in storage and retrieval (a memory deficit).

Pirozzolo, Dunn & Zetusky (1983) identify two subtypes, the first being by far the more prevalent. *Auditory-linguistic dyslexics* have language disorders such as impaired expressive language, lower verbal IQs than performance IQs, agrammatism, anomia, and faulty grapheme-to-phoneme matching. *Visual-spatial dyslexics* are weak in visual-perceptual, spatial, and occulomotor skills as indicated by their directional disorientation, spatial dysgraphia, dyscalculia, and finger agnosia. Pirozzolo attributes the difficulty of auditory-linguistic dyslexics with tasks requiring rapid, complex linguistic processing to the late maturation of the nerve-fiber pathways involved in these left-hemispheric functions. He further hypothesizes that visual-spatial dyslexics are impaired on tasks requiring visual discrimination, analysis, and memory because of late maturation of the fiber pathways in the brain's visual-association areas, and possibly the corpus callosum.

Pennington and Smith (1983) report that, in a study primarily concerned with the genetic basis of reading and other language disorders, 91% of the 125 disabled readers fell into one of four subtypes: (1) a deficit in reading only (41%); (2) spatial-reasoning deficit (23%); (3) coding-speed deficit (18%); and (4) deficits in all three factors—a mixed category (9%).

Other researchers also attribute the causes of different subtypes of reading disability to brain or neural dysfunctions. For example, Smith and Carrigan (1959) attempt to explain different types of reading disability—the context reader, the word caller, and so on—in terms of an imbalance between two chemicals that influence the transmission of nerve impulses in the brain; the symptoms would vary according to patterns of excess and deficiency in the chemicals. And Rosenthal, Boder, and Callaway (1982) claim that *language-symbolic dyslexia* has its origins in the left hemisphere, and the *spatial-gestalt* subtype has a dysfunction in the right hemisphere.[5] Indeed, Gaddes (1980, p. 242) states: "The reading circuits in the brain are extremely complex, including specific centers usually in the left hemispheric cortex, with thalamic connections to other subcortical areas. There are most likely as many types of dyslexia as there are loci of cerebral lesions in this circuit and its contiguous brain tissue."

Based on observed differences in the strategies used by children with reading comprehension problems, Maria and MacGinitie (1982) suggest that poor comprehenders can be categorized into three subgroups: (1) those who interpret each sentence separately and who seem unaware of the contradictions that arise when they do not maintain a common schema for what they are reading; (2) those using a *fixed-hypothesis strategy*, who form an interpretation of one or more of the first sentences in the text and try to interpret the remainder of the text to conform with their original hypothesis; and (3) poor comprehenders who employ a *nonaccommodating strategy* and rely excessively on prior knowledge. The latter subgroup uses a few words in the text to call up related background knowledge but are little influenced by the information in the text.

Statistical Classification

Statistical classification approaches use cluster analysis and factor-analytic techniques to identify subtypes of reading disability. *Cluster analysis* is a procedure

[5]Hemispheric specialization and its relationship to reading disability is considered on pages 305–306.

that groups subjects into clusters based on each individual's pattern of performance on the tests used, in an attempt to obtain clusters that contain subjects whose tested attributes are more like one another than the subjects in the other clusters (Kavale & Forness 1987a). The *Q technique* is a kind of inverted factor analysis that analyzes correlations between individuals to classify them into groups with similar characteristics. Achievement and/or neuropsychological variables are used to make the classifications. Once subtypes are revealed, the researcher is obligated to demonstrate that they relate differentially to other variables of interest (Senf 1986).

Among the limitations of most subtyping studies were the tests employed and the apparently subjective manner in which clustered strengths and weaknesses were interpreted (Satz & Morris 1981). Reading was operationally defined by the tests in a very narrow way; rarely as being above the word-recognition level. Also, many of the nonreading tests had limited reliability and often questionable construct validity (Adelman & Taylor 1986).

Subtyping studies have offered little useful information regarding causation (Satz, Morris & Fletcher 1985), nor have they provided detailed information regarding how the identified combinations of strengths and weaknesses actually cause the disability.

A statistical and case-study analysis of severely reading-disabled boys aged 10 to 14 by Doehring (1968) reveals three subtypes: language, perceptual, and mixed. Two later studies (Doehring & Hoshko 1977; Doehring, Hoshko & Bryans 1979), which used the Q technique, identified three groups: (1) a *language deficit* type who performed poorly on the syllable- and word-reading tasks but had normal scores on all visual matching and most auditory-visual matching tests; (2) a *phonological deficit* type marked by low auditory-visual matching; and (3) an *intersensory-integration deficit* type who were almost normal in auditory-visual matching of letters but not of syllables and words.

More recently, Doehring et al. (1981), who stressed the interaction of reading, language, and neurological deficits, were able to classify 82% of 88 disabled readers into one of three subtypes. The *oral reading disability* cases tended to perform much more poorly on the oral reading of letters, syllables, and words than on "silent reading" tasks (visual and auditory-visual matching of letters, syllables, and words). Children in the *associational reading disability* group tended to perform very poorly on all auditory-visual matching and oral reading tasks. Those with a *sequencing reading disability* tended to be very weak on all tasks using syllables and words, but not when single letters were used. It should be noted, however, that 30–60% of the subjects scored within the normal range on the oral reading tasks and that the three subtypes were not distinct, since a number of the classified subjects exhibited some of the same characteristics displayed by those in another subtype.

Using the Q technique, Petrauskas and Rourke (1979) were able to place about 50% of their disabled readers aged 8–10 into one of three subgroups. Those with a *language disorder* (N = 4) were mainly characterized by impaired verbal fluency and sentence memory. The *impaired verbal coding* group (N = 13) were mildly or moderately impaired in finger localization, verbal fluency, sentence memory, and visual-spatial (sequencing) memory; and moderately to severely impaired in concept formation. The third subtype (N = 26, 92% males) showed moderate to severe impairment in sentence memory, finger localization, and visual-spatial memory. Three similar, but not as discrete, subtypes were also identified in a multivariate analysis study by Fisk and Rourke (1979) with children aged 9-14.

Two factor analytic studies by Hicks and Spurgeon (1982) reveal two subtypes of dyslexia: one with deficits in auditory processing marked by bizarre spelling, poor sound blending, and poor auditory discrimination; and the other with verbal problems characterized by poor visual memory, phonic errors, left-right confusion, and sequencing and vocabulary weaknesses.

Satz and Morris (1981) first used a cluster analysis of the achievement patterns in reading, spelling, and arithmetic (as measured by the WRAT) to classify 236 fifth-grade boys into subgroups. The data from the 86 boys in the two lowest groups were then subjected to cluster-analytic techniques based on their scores on four neuropsychological tests. Five subtypes emerged: (1) an *unexpected learning disability type* (N = 12) who did not show any neuropsychological deficits;[6] (2) a *global language impairment* type (N = 27) who scored very low on both language measures but in the average range on nonlanguage perceptual tests; (3) a *specific language (naming)* type (N = 14) who were impaired on only the verbal fluency test; (4) a *visual-perceptual-motor impaired* type (N = 23) whose performance was deficient on the perceptual, but not the language, tests; and (5) a *mixed* type (N = 10) who performed poorly on all four tests but who probably should not be classified as reading or learning disabled because they all scored poorly on the IQ test.

Lyon (1983), who also used cluster analyses, reports two studies, which reveal six subgroups. One group had minimal sight vocabularies and deficient decoding skills and were deficient in receptive-language comprehension, sound blending, visual-motor integration, visual-spatial skills, and auditory and visual memory. A second group had deficits in receptive-language comprehension, auditory memory, and visual-motor integration. A third group had problems in receptive-language comprehension and sound blending. The fourth subtype was impaired in visual perception, but without language deficits. A fifth subtype had global language problems, and the sixth group was comprised of poor readers who had normal neuropsychological profiles (unexpected learning disability).

Other Evidence of Subtypes

Possible anatomical evidence of reading-disability subtypes was obtained by Hier et al. (1978), who analyzed the computerized brain tomograms of 24 developmental dyslexics. Eight subjects exhibited normal hemispheric asymmetry (a wider left than right parieto-occipital region). Ten displayed a reversed pattern, and there was no difference between the left and right hemispheric areas in 6 cases.

There also is some electrophysical evidence. Fried et al. (1981) used event-

[6]Investigators have reported a subtype of disabled readers (on the average about 25% of the subjects) who are relatively free of cognitive and linguistic deficits, and who also show more advantageous neurological, SES, and family reading status than do the other subjects. In one study, this subtype showed increasing improvement in their information-processing abilities from kindergarten to Grade 5 (Satz, Morris & Fletcher 1985).

related potentials (ERPs) to study word and musical-chord processing in the right and left hemispheres. They conclude that dysphonetic subjects (those with auditory-verbal deficits) had failed to develop normal left-hemisphere specialization for processing auditory-linguistic material.

Lovett (1984) took a different approach to subtyping two groups of 8- to 13-year olds. The *accuracy disabled* group had inaccurate word recognition; the *rate* disabled group had accurate word recognition but slow reading rates. The two groups were comparable in reading fluency, reading comprehension, word-meaning knowledge, and word retrieval. But the accuracy disabled group was inferior in decoding and spelling, as well as understanding language structures.

Taylor, Fletcher, and Satz (1982) attempted to relate cognitive deficits as measured by neuropsychological tests to three subtypes of reading deficits: word recognition, decoding, and comprehension. They were, however, able to classify only 40% of their 45 subjects into one of the three subtypes, which did not turn out to be distinctly different in neuropsychological deficits. Other attempts to subgroup on the basis of impaired neuropsychological functions have produced contradictory findings (Obrzut & Hynd 1987).

Although most studies identify a language-impaired subtype, many also reveal small subgroups who had relatively intact language-processing ability, but who demonstrated weak visual-perceptual-motor skills (Satz, Morris & Fletcher 1985). Satz et al. hypothesize that the latter subtype includes children who were in the early stage of reading acquisition, when the development of word-recognition skills requires visual and spatial abilities.

Vellutino and Scanlon (1986a) conclude that almost all severely disabled readers can be placed into one of three subgroups: (1) deficiencies in semantic and/or syntactic development that limit the ability to use holistic, meaning-based strategies in learning to recognize printed words; (2) deficiencies in phonological development that limit the use of decoding (phonic) strategies for word recognition;, and (3) generalized language deficiencies that limit the ability to use either type of strategy for learning to recognize printed words.

Summary and Conclusions

Subtyping research is based on the belief that reading disability is not a homogeneous entity and the hope that the identification of homogeneous, independent subgroups will lead to better understanding of etiologies and to more effective treatments. But despite its promise, subtyping research has not yet provided sufficient evidence upon which to base differential diagnosis. On almost every measure, some disabled readers performed better than good readers, and some good readers scored below the average of the reading-disabled groups (Satz, Morris & Fletcher 1985; Doehring 1985). Subgrouping research has not produced any strong evidence implicating subtypes in the wide variety of deficits observed, but newer research methods in this area are just beginning to be evaluated (Stanovich 1986b).

A. J. Harris (1982, p. 459) reviewed the research on subtypes and concludes:

... the recent studies demonstrate that there are at least three subtypes and syndromes within the disabled reader populations that have been used. The first and most common shows a general deficiency in language skills (coupled with normal visual and visual-motor skills) and a lower verbal IQ than performance IQ. The language deficit is shown in poor listening comprehension, limited vocabulary, difficulty in verbal expression, limited grasp of sentence structure, poor auditory discrimination and memory, and poor blending ability.

A second pattern involves difficulty with visual perception and visual-motor tasks, coupled with relatively normal language abilities and a verbal IQ higher than performance IQ. Benton (1978) has described this group as follows: "Reversal errors, the cardinal feature of a visuo-spatial type of disability, have been found to be associated with right-left confusion in body schema performances, with left-handedness and mixed laterality, with a more generalized learning disability extending beyond reading, and with signs of neurological abnormality."

A third pattern is what Satz and Morris (1981) called an "unexpected" subtype whose cognitive abilities fail to show any significant deficits that could account for the reading failure. It may be that this group has predominantly environmental problems. . . .

A fourth type found in some but not all of the recent studies involves normal verbal comprehension and vocabulary but a deficiency in verbal fluency. These children are slow in naming tasks and have marked difficulty in segmenting spoken words and blending phonemes into words.

There are a number of less frequent findings that may indicate the reality of small but nevertheless significant subgroups. One of these is the group with difficulty in finger localization. Another such group has difficulty in identifying tactile patterns. Levinson's [1980] insistence on the importance of cerebellar and vestibular difficulties may apply to a subgroup.

The question of a genetic type of reading disability has not been resolved. Unquestionably there are some families with several disabled readers, but the degree to which this is inherited or learned within the home environment is still uncertain.

It may be that each case of reading disability involves a unique constellation of handicapping conditions—constitutional, environmental, and motivational—and that the search for a relatively small number of subtypes into which they can be pigeon-holed is futile.

One of the main reasons we have been unable to find a satisfactory explanation for reading disabilities may be the extremely complex interactive nature of cognition, language, and reading, each of which is a complex process in itself. We may well have to await a more complete understanding of each area before we can understand how deficits in any of them can interact to cause reading disabilities of various subtypes (Doehring, Backman & Waters 1983).

MODELS OF READING DISABILITY

No consensus exists as to the causes of reading disability, as the following illustrative models indicate.

Several kinds of models, starting with a single cause–single effect and increasing to multiple causes–multiple effects, are described by Wiener and Cromer (1967). They also postulate four different types of causal relationships, each having a different kind of etiology and leading to differing remedial plans:

(1) a *defect* attributable to some malfunction (e.g., sensory or physiological factors); (2) a *deficiency* attributable to the absence or low level of some function; (3) a *disruption*, which suggests that something (e.g., anxiety) is interfering with reading; and, (4) a *difference*, in which there are mismatches between the student's characteristics and his or her instructional program.

Guthrie (1973) describes two kinds of models that differ in the degree of integration or interrelatedness among relevant factors. The *assembly model* assumes that the skills involved in reading are independent and can be isolated both in diagnosis and remediation. The *systems model* views reading as involving interdependent components such that one or two severely deficient abilities could prevent the development of other needed abilities. Guthrie interprets his results as suggesting that the systems model applies to normal readers, for whom a variety of reading test scores are substantially intercorrelated; and that the assembly model fits disabled readers better, since their test scores show low intercorrelations. However, it should be noted that Guthrie did not use any measure of reading comprehension in his study.

Vernon (1977) argues that reading disability can result from a variety of dysfunctions that can induce breakdowns at critical points in learning to read. She describes four main types: (1) deficiencies in the ability to analyze complex, sequential, visual and/or auditory-linguistic structures; (2) deficiencies in linking visual with auditory-linguistic symbols: (3) inability to establish regularities in variable grapheme-phoneme correspondences; and (4) inability to group recognized words into meaningful phrases.

Doehring, Backman, and Waters (1983) list three types of models: (1) a direct, simple cause-effect model; (2) an intermediate, three-stage cause-effect model in which a specific brain deficit results in the deficient development of a nonreading ability that is essential to reading and, in turn, this specific nonreading deficit prevents normal reading acquisition; and (3) models suggesting that reading disability is not a unitary disorder.

Valtin (1980) describes five different assessment approaches (which could serve as models of reading disability) and their limitations:

1. In the *etiological approach,* attempts are made to identify the physical, environmental, or educational factors that may impede reading progress.
2. The *cognitive approach* attempts to isolate various types of reading problems by identifying cognitive deficits.
3. The *symptoms approach* attempts to analyze errors that may provide hints regarding the specific difficulty in the reading process.
4. The *process-oriented approach* attempts to identify the partial processes of reading in which the reading disabled are deficient.
5. The *task-analysis,* or *subskills, approach* suggests that one source of reading disability is a lack of integration among reading subskills (e.g., see Guthrie [1973], above).

Kinsbourne (1983) describes a number of models of learning disability that are also applicable to reading disability. Kleiman (1982) summarizes and discusses the limitations of various reading-disability models.

Models of reading ability have also been used to explain reading disability. A breakdown in any of the components theorized to be important in the reading process could cause reading problems.

Torgesen (1986b) describes three broad models that are used to explain either reading ability or disability—information-processing (see page 15), neuro-psychological, and applied behavioral analysis.

A neuropsychological model attempts to explain cognitive behavior in terms of the specific brain systems that support it. In seeking to explain these "brain-performance" relationships, references are made to the degree of intactness and to the organization of various brain systems that are purportedly involved in specific kinds of cognitive behavior. Deficient performance on intellectual tasks is usually explained in terms of damage to, or malfunctioning of, specific areas of the brain in which these systems are located. Neuropsychological theories are tested by examining the patterns of psychological test performance obtained from subjects with known types of brain damage, EEG readings during various tasks, the results of dichotic listening and visual half-field studies that attempt to assess hemispheric specialization patterns, CAT scans, positron-emission tomography, and surgical examination of the brains of deceased persons known to have had behavioral deficits.[7]

The assumption that reading problems are caused by brain deficits reasonably specific to the cognitive requirements of the reading process has been challenged by a large body of research (Stanovich 1986a), but the advent of new technologies and improved experimental methodology may allow neuropsychological theories to prove more useful than in the past.

Applied behavioral analysis attempts to explain behavior in terms of observable stimulus-response relationships. Behavior is explained in terms of the stimulus conditions that precede the behavior, or in terms of the behavior that follows the stimulus. This model is tested by carefully examining the behavioral changes that occur when the stimuli are manipulated. A functional relationship is said to exist when behavior changes reliably in response to these manipulations. Followers of this model tend to focus on the creation and validation of instructional and remedial procedures, with the treatment being closely monitored and replaced if shown to be ineffective. Although admitting that there are cognitive differences among pupils, those who believe in applied behavioral analysis tend to believe that reading failure stems from learning inappropriate responses to instructional stimuli or from a lack of properly reinforced practice. Research has consistently shown that reading disabled students' performance on reading tasks improves following modifications in either antecedents or consequences of the reading behavior. Such findings challenge the concepts of cognitive or neurological deficits because effective instruction improved reading performance without considering such variables. However, most of the successful academic interventions involved isolated, narrowly-defined skills, and their long-term effects have not been evaluated.

Spear and Sternberg (1986) postulate an information-processing model of reading disability. They believe that reading disability involves malfunctioning

[7]Most of these terms are defined and discussed in Chapter 9.

of learning processes (those employed in acquiring a new skill) and performance processes (those used in carrying out a task). Disorders in higher-level planning processes (those used in decision making and the management of mental processes) are not thought to play a central role in their model of reading disability. In this theoretical framework, there are two phases in the progression of a reading disability. The earlier phase involves disabled readers who are nonreaders or who are reading at the first- or second-reader level. Their reading disability manifests itself in a cluster of lower-level problems such as difficulty learning to decode words and deficient use of a speech-based code in short-term memory. The later phase involves disabled readers who are reading at the third-reader level or above. They are believed to have high-level kinds of difficulties, especially with reading comprehension and the use of reading and memory strategies. These higher-level difficulties are not attributed to higher-level processing deficits, but rather to at least one of three other variables: (1) an original constellation of lower-level deficits, which may affect higher-level processing and limit the ability to profit from instruction; (2) difficulty with automatic decoding of written language (the need to concentrate on word recognition leaves little processing capacity for comprehension); and, (3) disabled readers do not read as much as good readers do nor do they experience the same academic demands.

Another information-processing theory is Perfetti's (1985) *Verbal Efficiency Theory* which attempts to account for individual differences in reading comprehension.[8] His model assumes that reading comprehension depends on efficient interactions of numerous subprocesses including word identification, *syntactic parsing* (analyzing sentences by grammatical labels such as subject, predicate, and object [T. Harris & Hodges 1981]), the formation of thought units, and a group of integrative and knowledge-dependent processes used to construct a coherent interpretation of the text. The temporal courses of these subprocesses and processes overlap, so that if one of them is slow, the information it should provide will not be completely available when needed by the others. Because our capacity to process information is limited, if one subprocess is especially attention-demanding, other processes may not receive sufficient attention. Lower-level subprocesses that bring about word identification have the potential for being relatively nondemanding of processing resources. Higher-level cognitive processes that are involved in comprehension place heavy demands on processing capacity. If word identification is accurate and automatic (attention-free), the comprehension process can operate smoothly and efficiently. Comprehension processes may suffer to the extent that lower-level processes use one's limited processing resources. Thus weak or slow word identification can cause poor reading comprehension by failing to provide accurate word information fast enough (Roth & Beck 1987).

There are also developmental theories that suggest that the point at which normal reading development is disrupted has an effect on the type and severity of the reading problems that emerge.

Frith (1986) hypothesizes three overlapping phases in normal reading development. These correspond to the acquisition of *logographic skills* (instant

[8]Perfetti (1985, 1986b) also believes that individual differences in working memory capacity (but not necessarily in memory storage capacity) can produce differences in reading comprehension.

word recognition based on the use of salient graphic features), *alphabetic skills* (use of letter-sound correspondences to decode words), and *orthographic skills* (instant recognition of the morphemic parts of words. Breakdowns can occur at any of the critical points at which new skills have to be acquired. The variety of possible breakdowns results in different types of reading disorders. According to Frith, damage that occurs early in reading development is likely to have different manifestations than disorders that occur later in development. Both would be clearly distinguished from damage that happened after reading development had been completed. The later the breakdown in development, the milder the reading disorder. Arrested development in one particular area may lead to overdevelopment of an earlier-developing strategy, or it may take other forms. An adaptation or compensation whose outcome is deviant can easily be confused with the cause of the reading problem.

Similarly, Stanovich (1986b) suggests that some relationships are developmentally limited. That is, individual differences in particular cognitive processes may be causally linked to variations in the early development of reading achievement, but may have no effects thereafter. He further speculates that some differences in cognitive processes related to reading ability may be the effects of, rather than the causes of, reading deficiency. Similarly, some of the cognitive processes associated with the reading ability of adults may be remnants of their reading histories, especially if the processes responsible for reading ability variations change several times during development, leaving behind differences in cognitive processes that were causal at earlier stages. It is also possible that qualitatively different processing patterns represent alternative ways of coping with reading deficits that had a common cause.

The developmental version of the *specificity hypothesis* (Perfetti 1985) states that there is a developmental trend in the specificity of the disability. For example, a specific cognitive deficit may prevent the early acquisition of reading ability. In turn, delayed reading acquisition has adverse cognitive, behavioral, and motivational consequences that slow the development of other cognitive skills. The development of knowledge bases is also inhibited. The longer this developmental sequence is allowed to continue, the more general the deficits become. This may partly account for the failure of researchers to present strong evidence of specificity rather than for a number of cognitive deficits. Their subjects may have advanced to the point at which generalized cognitive deficiencies had begun to appear.

The *interactionist view* is that reading ability and reading disability are relative concepts (Lipson & Wixson 1986). These theorists believe that an individual's reading performance will vary across texts, tasks, and settings because of interactions among these variables. Therefore, a student's reading performance is considered to be an indication of what she or he can do under a specific set of conditions, rather than as a set of fixed abilities and disabilities. Followers of the interactionist view contend that research in reading disability must move away from seeking causative factors within the pupil, and toward specifying the conditions under which each pupil can and will learn. The need to identify the cause is eliminated, so attention can be focused on determining which set of conditions is most likely to facilitate the reading ability of each student.

An interactionist point of view is more defensible when applied to pupils who are making normal progress in reading or who have minor problems. Variation in their performance is not unusual, but they are successful in many reading situations. It is less defensible for disabled readers who show much less variation in performance, and who would fail if asked to read the same materials as their age-peers who are good readers.

An argument can be made for viewing reading disability as a social construct (see J. Downing 1977). Uniform standards for achievement, expectations for uniform performance, and uniform methods of instruction may create a group viewed as deviant.

INTELLIGENCE AND READING

Wechsler (1944) defines intelligence as "the aggregate or global capacity of the individual to act purposefully, to think rationally and to deal effectively with his environment". But intelligence is still a hypothetical construct whose definition remains elusive (T. Harris & Hodges 1981).

Most psychologists believe that intellectual functioning, however defined, is the result of the intimate interaction between an innate potential for intellectual development, which varies among individuals, and environmental conditions that strongly influence the degree to which that potential is realized.

Theoretically, intelligence places a limit on an individual's level of language ability, which in turn governs the level of reading ability (Carroll 1977). Intelligence, language ability, and reading ability are highly interrelated, so it is difficult to isolate the effects of one ability from that of the others. But it is highly likely that cognitive processes, reasoning ability, and linguistic competence influence reading ability. Children with high IQ scores tend to be the best readers; those with below average intelligence tend to be poor readers. As reading tasks require more reasoning ability, the relationships between intelligence-test and reading-comprehension-test scores are likely to increase. Although the precise nature of general intelligence is not understood, IQ tests predict reading achievement quite well (Torgesen 1985). However, the relationship between intelligence and reading is far from perfect. Other factors also enter into successful reading achievement or reading failure, but it is difficult to separate out the unique contributions of general intelligence, specific cognitive factors such as memory, and language because they are so closely interrelated. Whether intelligence is related to reading ability for pupils in a particular age group depends on variables such as the nature and difficulty of the tasks, the capabilities of the reader, the time allowed for learning, the quality of instruction, and the nature of the tests used to assess intelligence and reading ability (H. Singer 1977).

Disabled readers, by definition, are those who are reading significantly below their potential. Therefore, the high correlations between intelligence and reading ability do not hold for them. Not all poor readers are disabled readers because some are not functioning significantly below their potential levels.

Most disabled readers have average or above-average intelligence. In 13 studies summarized by Belmont and Birch (1966), the average WISC IQs for disabled readers ranged from about 92 to 110. When they studied children in the bottom of 10% in reading, those with IQs below 90 generally were reading at a level commensurate with expectancy; while those with IQs of 90 and above generally were a year or more below expectancy.

Research has begun to focus on attempts to identify cognitive abilities that vary independently of general intelligence, but that are crucial in acquiring reading skills. The standard method for this type of research is to contrast good readers and poor readers closely matched with respect to IQ and other factors shown to correlate with reading disability. But in research studies, most disabled readers score approximately half a standard deviation below the control group on IQ tests. This suggests that reading disability is characterized by a mild but generalized cognitive deficit, rather than by a specific, highly localized problem in reading. Research findings as to whether the cognitive processes that mediate inferior reading are fundamentally different from those of normally developing readers are mixed (Stanovich 1986a,b).

Many specific disabilities may actually be expressions of slight, but pervasive, general intelligence differences between samples of good readers and poor readers, rather than specific causes of reading disability that are independent of general intelligence. Heterogeneous groups of good readers and poor readers, matched on IQ scores, are likely more different from one another in true ability than their IQ scores indicate (Torgesen 1985).

There are differences of opinion as to whether to use Verbal IQ, nonverbal (Performance) IQ, or a combination of both when selecting disabled readers. We prefer the latter (see pages 164–165). The type of intelligence test score used in a research study may affect its findings. Depending on which type of intelligence is evaluated (and which intelligence test is used), the pupils identified as reading disabled will represent somewhat different samples, and the characteristics common to each group will vary accordingly. The modality deficiencies, the cognitive defects, the aptitude weaknesses, and the relation of verbal to performance abilities will vary according to the method used to identify disabled readers (Reed 1970).

Just as intelligence may influence reading achievement, reading ability can have an effect on some group-administered intelligence tests. Primary-grade group IQ tests usually present items in pictorial form and so are not directly influenced by reading ability. Such tests have statistically significant, but not high, positive correlations with reading ability. From the third or fourth grade up, most group aptitude tests contain many items that must be read by the pupil. Inability to read those tests items can result in depressed IQ scores that do not reliably indicate the student's intellectual ability. Neville (1965) found that intermediate-grade pupils who scored below 4.0 on a reading test were penalized an average of 10 IQ points on the typical group IQ test. Therefore, whenever possible, an individually administered IQ test should be used in identifying disabled readers, especially if the child has serious reading problems. Group intelligence tests that do not require reading ability are listed in Appendix A.

Patterns of Abilities on the WISC and K-ABC

Some believe that the WISC-score patterns of reading- or learning-disabled children differ from those of good readers and that such differences have diagnostic value in that they indicate specific areas of cognitive strengths and weaknesses (see Searls 1985). The patterns most frequently mentioned are significant discrepancies between Verbal IQs (VIQs) and Performance IQs (PIQs), subtest score scatter (variability), and characteristic test score profiles.

Verbal/Performance IQ differences are common in reading- or learning-disabled children, but the same is true of children without such problems (Dudley-Marling, Kaufman & Tarver 1981). In fact, 25 percent of normally developing children have differences of at least 15 points between their VIQs and PIQs. The diagnostic value of such discrepancies, as well as patterns of abilities on the WISC, is further weakened by the fact that low scores on the Information and Arithmetic subtests often distort the meaning of the VIQs of reading- or learning-disabled pupils who consistently score low on these two subtests, which are highly related to schooling (A. Kaufman 1981). Furthermore, Klasen (1972) reports that in 488 cases of reading disability, 22% had significantly higher VIQs than PIQs, 19% had significantly higher PIQs, and the scores did not differ significantly in 59%. In Scarborough's (1984) study, about 60% of the disabled readers and 25% of the good readers had significantly lower VIQs than PIQs on the WAIS. Such findings suggest that although IQ profile differences may be statistically reliable, they are of little theoretical or practical value for defining or diagnosing reading disability.

Subtest scatter (widely differing standard scores on the subtests) is supposedly typical of reading- or learning-disabled pupils. However, the average difference between the lowest and highest subtest scores was seven standard score points in the sample upon whom the WISC-R was normed (A. Kaufman 1976). So it is not unusual for children to exhibit considerable subtest scatter (Dudley-Marling, Kaufman & Tarver 1981), nor does WISC-R subtest score scatter differentiate among mentally retarded, learning-disabled, and behaviorally disordered children (Thompson 1980), or among learning-disabled, emotionally disturbed, and nonhandicapped children (Berk 1983).

Bannatyne (1971, 1974) recommends summing the WISC subtest scaled scores to form four categories: conceptual ability (Comprehension, Similarities, and Vocabulary); spatial ability (Block Design, Object Assembly, and Picture Completion); sequencing ability (Picture Arrangement, Digit Span, and Coding), and acquired knowledge (Information, Arithmetic, and Vocabulary). One of the purportedly significant diagnostic findings is the presence of significant differences between the spatial, conceptual, and sequential categories, but Dundon et al. (1986) found that only 11% of 189 LD children exhibited such differences. Bannatyne's recategorizations are of little value in distinguishing among learning-disabled, mentally retarded, and emotionally disturbed children (Webster & Lafayette 1979) or between LD and normally achieving children (Henry & Wittman 1981). Classifying pupils on the basis of Bannatyne's recategorizations is not warranted because few pupils previously classified as reading- or learning-disabled actually display the pattern. Nor is prescribing treatment based on such recategorizations warranted because a link between these scores and the most efficient reading instruction has not been demonstrated (Moore & Wilson 1987).

Regardless of the manner in which the WISC-R subtest scores are grouped or regrouped, no recategorization, profile pattern, or factor cluster has been demonstrated to be a clinically significant indicator of learning disabilities (Kavale & Forness 1985). WISC-R patterns cannot be used to classify students into diagnostic categories or to identify individuals as disabled readers (Searls 1985), nor is there is any WISC-R profile that characterizes reading or learning disabled students (Tindal & Marston 1986) or any characteristic common to all such students (Holcomb et al. 1987). Therefore, suggestions for using WISC-R profile analyses as a basis for providing treatment (e.g., Wallbrown, Blaha & Vance 1980), should be viewed with skepticism.

Some tests, such as the *Kaufman Assessment Battery for Children* (K-ABC), yield separate scores for simultaneous and sequential processing.[9] Some writers feel that such scores can be used in making a diagnosis. For example, Kirby and Robinson (1987) contend that *syntactic ability* (knowledge of the ways in which words can be sequentially arranged to form acceptable sentences) is based largely on successive processing skills, and that *semantic ability* (the ability to identify meaningful relationships among words or groups of words) is based on simultaneous processing. They further speculate that successive processing is involved in decoding words, and that simultaneous processing is involved in *direct lexical access* (going directly from the printed whole word to its meaning). But according to Hooper and Hynd (1986), performance on only one of the K-ABC simultaneous processing subtests (Matrix Analyses) distinguished between "dyslexics" and normally achieving children. And although they also stated that a sequential processing deficit was implicated in reading disability, "dyslexics" and good readers differed significantly on only two of the four K-ABC sequential processing subtests. Such hypotheses remain to be proven.

Half of the subjects on whom the K-ABC was normed had differences of 11 or more points between their simultaneous and sequential processing scores, and subtest score scatter among the norming sample was not unusual (Chatman, Reynolds & Willson 1984). Therefore, suggestions for using K-ABC patterns in the diagnosis and treatment of reading difficulties should be viewed cautiously.

SPECIFIC COGNITIVE FACTORS

Because the development of many cognitive abilities and the acquisition of reading skills usually proceed hand-in-hand, it is difficult to distinguish cognitive abilities that play causal roles in learning to read from those that are by-products of the acquisition of reading skills (Wagner 1986).

Perception

Stimulation of our sense organs, such as the eyes and ears, produces sensations. *Perception* is the interpretation of these incoming sensations by the brain, which selects, groups, organizes, and sequences them. Meaningful interpretation can then lead to appropriate responses. The perceptual aspects of reading are complex because the mind must act on a succession of stimuli in which both spatial

[9]These terms are discussed on page 166.

and temporal patterns must be perceived. "Reading is a continuing cycle of excitation and reaction in which each moment of perception produces a feedback effect which sets the person for the following perception. In this rapidly repeating cycle, the sequential perceptions are apprehended as forming linguistic sequences that convey large units of meaning" (A. J. Harris 1961).

The following terms are frequently encountered in the literature on perception and reading:

- *Figure-ground.* Normally, one major unit or group of units is perceived clearly against a background that is more vaguely perceived. In reading, the print is the dark figure that stands out from the white background of the page.
- *Closure.* There is a strong tendency to perceive wholes; the mind tends to fill in parts that are missing. Examples of closure as related to reading are the ability to understand the meaning of a sentence that contains one or more unknown words, the ability to fill in the deleted items on a cloze test, the ability to recognize or pronounce correctly a word from which some letters are missing, and the ability to recognize incompletely heard words or words from which phonemes have been deleted.
- *Sequence.* In listening, sequence is inherent in the sensory input; in reading, the sequence of the visual stimuli must be imposed by the reader. The left-to-right sequence of letters in words and words across the page, as well as the top-to-bottom arrangement of written English, are arbitrary conventions that children must learn.
- *Discrimination.* The ability to distinguish among stimuli increases with age and experience. As skills develop there is a change from vague perception of wholes, to reliance on prominent details, toward mature perception in which the whole is perceived sharply and the details within it are also clearly discerned.
- *Mind Set.* One's immediate mind set provides an anticipation of what is likely to occur next. Such anticipations can be helpful in predicting what words or concepts are likely to occur in the next portion of a text. On the other hand, it can lead to errors when the anticipation is incorrect.

VISUAL PERCEPTION.[10]   Visual perception is defined by test performance, but visual-perception tests vary widely as to what they measure (some actually sample visual-motor skills) and how reliably they do so (see Colarusso & Gill 1975–1976). In the past, the most widely used perceptual test was the *Frostig Developmental Test of Visual Perception* (DTVP) whose five subtests supposedly measured discrete skills. Remedial programs to overcome weaknesses indicated by the subtest scores were employed, particularly in the field of special education. The consensus of researchers strongly suggests that the content validity of the DTVP should be seriously questioned (Olson 1980). Coles (1978) and Beech (1985) report that visual perceptual training resulted in higher scores on tests of

---

[10]Those interested in this topic may wish to refer to the annotated bibliography by Weintraub and Cowan (1982).

visual perception, but not in significant increases in reading achievement. A meta-analysis of 59 studies led Kavale (1984) to conclude that the DTVP revealed a large common variance with intelligence and was not a useful predictor of reading ability, and that the Frostig training was not an effective intervention for improving either visual-perceptual skills as measured by the DTVP or reading achievement.

Meares (1980) reports that some disabled readers seem to have a visual-ground difficulty, which is due to perceptual instability induced by the black print on a white page. These children reported experiencing print as blurring, moving, jumping, and flickering in the absence of visual defects. Meares states that the effect was reduced and reading became easier for them with the use of light print on a darker background (reduced brightness contrast), with small rather than large print, and with a minimum of space between words and lines. Her claims need to be researched, but it is not unusual for severely disabled readers to report such symptoms.

Olson et al. (1985) do not find a significant relationship between reading disability and visual-perceptual difficulties, and Vellutino (1987) states that visual form perception did not differ in good readers and poor readers. Therefore, although it is possible that a subgroup of severely disabled readers manifest such abnormalities, visual-spatial perceptual problems cannot be considered to be a general cause of reading disability (Perfetti 1985).

THE PERCEPTUAL-DEFICIT HYPOTHESIS.   Vellutino (1977, 1979) grouped various theories dealing with the possible role of visual perception in reading disability and used the term *perceptual-deficit hypothesis* to indicate the general premise of these theories. Essentially, the perceptual-deficit hypothesis states that reading disability is caused by visual-spatial confusions stemming from a neurological dysfunction or deficiency. These constitutional disorders, which are believed to disrupt visual perception and then visual memory, are manifested in orientation and sequencing errors (e.g., reversals). But according to Vellutino and Scanlon (1982), the perceptual-deficit hypothesis can be criticized on empirical grounds. For example, findings indicate that disabled readers do perceive printed words accurately and reversal errors are manifestations of dysfunctions in verbal mediation, not of visual-spatial confusion (Vellutino & Scanlon 1987b). Other writers, such as Carr (1981), have also rejected the visual perceptual-deficit hypothesis. A more cautious stance was taken by Olson (1980), who states that perceptual deficiencies may contribute to, but not cause, reading disability.

According to Vellutino and Scanlon (1987b), reading ability can tolerate a wide range of individual differences in visual processing ability, provided that the students have acquired grapheme-phoneme correspondence rules that minimize the demands made on the visual system. Mastery of grapheme-phoneme correspondence rules depends on linguistic coding ability.

VISUAL-MOTOR PERFORMANCE.   For many years, psychologists have used tests of the ability to copy visual designs (visual-motor coordination) as diagnostic tools. The most frequently used of these is the *Bender Visual-Motor Gestalt Tests* (BVMGT). A series of designs is presented, one at a time, which the student is asked to copy. The stimuli are available to the child, so visual memory is not a factor. While the test yields an age-level score, the qualitative features of the child's productions (e.g., rotations, difficulty with diagonals, form distortions) are felt to be of more diagnostic significance (Koppitz 1964). In interpreting the *Bender*, the examiner cannot always be sure if poor performance results from perceptual difficulty, poor motor control, or the linking of motor behavior to perception.

The use of the *Bender* in the diagnosis of learning disabilities has been reviewed by Keogh (1961) and Bender (1970). There is no clear agreement as to its predictive value. On the average, the *Bender* correlates approximately 0.31 with reading achievement; but the magnitude of the relationship decreases significantly when intelligence is partialed out (Kavale 1982b). This suggests that *Bender* scores do not provide much improvement over chance in predicting the reading scores of individuals. The notion that reading problems are primarily caused by malfunctioning in visual-motor perception that can be measured by the *Bender* is incorrect. The *Bender* is sensitive to emotional problems as well as to neurological development and dysfunction (Coles 1978).

AUDITORY PERCEPTION.   Three aspects of auditory perception—segmentation (discussed on pages 291–292), discrimination, and blending—are commonly associated with reading disability.

Difficulties with *auditory discrimination*, which is the ability to perceive differences among spoken stimuli, have been cited as a strong contributor to reading disability (e.g., Johnson & Myklebust 1967). The assumption is that an auditory-discrimination disorder indicates either a neurological problem or maturational lag and creates problems with learning in general. Auditory discrimination is measured in varying ways by different tests. The *Wepman Auditory Discrimination Test* requires the pupil to listen to pairs of words, most of which differ on one minimally contrasting phoneme (e.g., thin-fin), and respond as to whether each pair sounds the same or different. The findings are mixed as to whether the *Wepman* can be used to distinguish learning or reading disabled children from those without such problems (Coles 1978). In the *Goldman-Fristoe-Woodcock Test of Auditory Discrimination*, the child selects one of four pictures (e.g., *cap, cab, cat, catch*) that represents the word spoken by the examiner. Reading readiness tests commonly ask children to indicate which of a number of pictured words begin or end with the same sound as the word spoken by the examiner. Dykstra (1966) demonstrates that different auditory-discrimination tests actually sample different skills, at least for young children.

Tallal (1984) found that good readers and poor readers did not differ on auditory discrimination and temporal-order perception tasks when verbal and nonverbal stimuli were presented at slow rates, but that the reading disabled subjects performed more poorly when the stimuli were presented rapidly. She has interpreted her findings as suggesting that some reading disabled children have a general rapid auditory-processing deficit and a limited capacity to process more than one auditory input at a time (Dickstein & Tallal 1987). Such a deficit could lead to difficulty with phonemic segmentation and could partially account for the difficulties poor readers have in segmenting and recoding phonologically, that is, they have significant difficulty keeping pace with the rapidly changing flow of sequential information entering the processing system. Tallal postulates that the left hemisphere may be specialized for rapid processing of information (and therefore language) while the right hemisphere in most individuals processes at a slower rate (and thus accommodates many of the visual-spatial demands) (Tallal, Stark & Mellits 1985). Rapid temporal analysis deficits cannot be attributed to a lack of experience with speech processing and production (Poizner & Tallal 1987).

Vellutino (1983) and others point out that children who fail auditory-discrimination tests often can verbally repeat the stimuli presented by the examiner, thereby demonstrating adequate discrimination (i.e., if they can say the word pairs exactly as given, they must be able to distinguish between the minimally contrasting phonemes). It is also suggested that children who speak clearly cannot have auditory-discrimination problems. The counter argument is that the types of auditory discrimination needed for oral language and for reading differ.

A literature review led Hammill and Larsen (1974b) to conclude that auditory-discrimination, memory, sound-blending and auditory-visual integration are not essential for successful reading. Nevertheless, failure to find average differences between good and poor readers does not negate the possibility that some disabled readers have marked deficits in one or more aspects of auditory perception that may be contributing to their reading problems.

Kavale (1981b) concludes that auditory perception is an important correlate of reading ability (correlations ranged from 0.02 to 0.81, with a mean of 0.358 and a median of 0.328) and of some use in predicting reading achievement. However, he also notes that intelligence appears to be a major component of all auditory-perceptual skills and that only auditory discrimination maintained some independence from intelligence in its relationship to reading ability.

In interpreting performance on auditory-discrimination tests, the following points should be considered: (1) Dialect speakers and nonnative speakers of English may do poorly on tests of phoneme discrimination because the sounds under consideration may differ from standard English in their dialect or first language; (2) performance on any auditory test can be greatly influenced by attending behavior; (3) the speech of the examiner can affect test scores; and (4) tests often require skills or concepts in addition to those suggested by the test title (e.g., the child must understand the concepts *same* and *different*.

Auditory blending is the ability to synthesize sounds mentally into syllables and syllables into words. Auditory blending differs from visual blending in that, in the former, the sounds are presented by an examiner; in the latter, the pupil must first recognize units of the printed word, whose sounds are then blended into a recognizable whole. At times, children are diagnosed as having blending problems when in fact their problem is their inability to make the necessary symbol-sound associations needed to decode unknown words. To rule out such possible misdiagnoses, auditory-blending tests are given. Performance on auditory-blending tests can be greatly influenced by the manner in which the words are broken up and the skills of the examiner in not distorting the separate sounds (see page 251). Apparent blending problems also may reflect poor memory for individual sounds when more than four sounds must be blended (Moore et al. 1982).

The *Roswell-Chall Auditory Blending Test* correlates significantly with reading (Chall, Roswell & Blumenthal 1963). Richardson et al. (1980) report that ITPA auditory-blending scores were significantly related to reading achievement even when IQ was partialed out. Kavale (1981b), however, does not find this to be so.

Memory

Logically, memory must be involved in acquiring, storing, and retrieving information needed for reading comprehension (e.g., language competence, word recognition, word meaning, topical knowledge).

Memory does not reside in a particular discrete area in the brain; rather, various components of memory are represented diffusely throughout the higher cortical centers (Levine 1987). Nor is memory a unitary ability: It is comprised of three processes—encoding, storage, and retrieval (Torgesen 1985). *Encoding* is the process of translating sensory input into a representational form that can be stored in memory. Almost all sensory information is stored in some coded form. *Memory storage* refers to the durability of the memory code. Coded information may last or be available for varying amounts of time in short-term memory (STM) and in long-term memory (LTM). *Retrieval* is concerned with extracting information from memory. It can occur relatively automatically, or it can involve conscious effort.

Images from the printed text enter the information-processing system as very brief visual images that are replicas of the stimuli. Each *sensory visual trace*, which is the visual information acquired during an eye fixation, lasts only about one-quarter second in *sensory memory* before being replaced or masked by the next sensory input. This sensory information must be acted on quickly, or it is lost.

Information, from the sensory memory, to which the reader has attended, enters *short-term memory* (STM).[11] Here, it is transformed (encoded) into more abstract symbolic representations. STM is a limited-capacity system. Only a small amount of information (up to seven or eight items) can be held for only a short time (usually less than 10–15 seconds) in STM before it is lost (Torgesen 1985). Only a few *propositions* (thought units) can be held in STM at one time, and this encoded information is available for only a second or two while the sentence is being processed for meaning. As new propositions are assembled, previously assembled ones are vulnerable to memory loss. The trick is to integrate quickly the assembled propositions into representations that can be held in LTM (Perfetti 1985). Connections must be built, not only among key ideas while the information is being held in STM, but also between the new information in STM and the existing information in LTM (Mayer 1987).

THEORIES REGARDING THE RELATIONSHIP OF MEMORY AND READING DISABILITY. The various hypotheses regarding the relationship between memory and reading disability fall into four categories: (1) Reading dis-

---

[11]Some writers use the term *working memory* (WM) interchangeably with STM. Others conceive of WM as a separate processing stage or memory store in which information from STM is manipulated.

ability is caused by basic or general memory deficits; (2) disabled readers have difficulty encoding, storing, or retrieving information in or from memory; (3) disabled readers' slow and/or inaccurate word recognition/identification disrupts STM processes because the encoded information decays before it can be used; and (4) the poor memory performance of disabled readers is due to not using, or inefficient use of, learning or memory strategies.

Some writers have postulated that disabled readers suffer from a general memory deficit. One extreme theory holds that an STM deficit causes severe reading disability (Jorm 1979). Jorm's theory has been challenged by Byrne (1981) and other viewpoints similar to Jorm's are undermined by the fact that disabled readers are deficient on only certain kinds of memory tasks (Sternberg & Wagner 1982). Memory problems of poor readers and disabled readers are generally specific to verbal/linguistic materials or to materials that can be represented (coded) linguistically (Crain & Shankweiler 1988).

Some hypotheses suggest that disabled readers have problems encoding information into STM, and that this difficulty is the basis for other language deficiencies. Phonological coding deficiencies are usually thought to disrupt STM processes (e.g., Brady 1986) or problems in accessing phonological word codes (see page 435) are believed to be due to phonemic segmentation difficulties (Snowling et al. 1986). Swanson (1987) hypothesizes that, whereas skilled readers have interdependent visual and verbal coding systems that facilitate lexical access, disabled readers have functionally independent coding systems—a situation that makes it difficult for them to coordinate verbal information from STM and LTM.

Other viewpoints hold that slow and inefficient encoding of new items into STM and slow clearing out of old items creates a "traffic jam" in short-term storage, which in turn interferes with comprehension (T. Carr 1981). One form of this type of hypothesis suggests that disabled readers take so long to recognize words that encoded information decays before it can be used, thereby disrupting STM processes (Davey 1987). Such views are compatible with the belief that poor readers do too much slow, attention-demanding processing (Lesgold & Perfetti 1981).

The *abstractive memory model* states that remembering is an abstractive process in which certain information is designated "to be remembered" and other information is selectively filtered out and forgotten. This model's *central-incidental hypothesis* holds that the relative importance of the material determines what is attended to, stored, and recalled, Skilled readers screen out incidental and irrelevant information, and store important information. Unskilled or disabled readers may select what is to be remembered on some basis other than its importance for comprehension or they may attempt to remember everything. The former results in the recall of less important or insignificant information; the latter in memory overload, which in turn creates weak recall (Luftig 1983).

SEQUENTIAL MEMORY.   One of the most frequently cited memory problems of disabled readers involves deficits in *sequential memory* (the ability to store and to recall items in the sequence in which they occurred). Sequential-memory-deficit theories are intuitively appealing for three reasons: (1) The order in which letters appear in a word is important to word recognition and meaning, as is the order in which a word's phonemes are blended during decoding; (2) the sequence of words and phrases in sentences bears on their syntactic acceptability and meaning; and, (3) the sequence in which information is presented and processed can influence comprehension.

Auditory sequential memory is often measured by digit span tests such as those in the WISC-R and ITPA. Interpreting performance on such tasks presents some problems (Torgesen 1978–1979). Visual sequential memory is frequently sampled by the ITPA subtest of the same name, which requires the child to reconstruct abstract designs comprised of a series of geometric designs, each shown for five seconds.

Poor readers are reported to be deficient in the ordered recall of nameable objects, letters, digits, nonwords, and sequences of words in spoken utterances (Mann 1986). These data are interpreted by some to mean that inefficient or deficient sequential memory (e.g., Bakker & Schroots 1981) or insensitivity to order information (M. Singer 1982) is a cause of reading problems. Such beliefs are based on the assumptions that general memory ability and sequential memory ability are supported by neurologically separate memory systems, or that the brain is equipped with an "ordering mechanism" that is responsible for putting information in its proper sequence. Neither case is likely. Research evidence does not confirm the view that disabled readers suffer from a fundamental and independent deficit in sequential memory (Vellutino & Scanlon 1987b). Observed good/poor reader group differences in auditory memory and auditory sequential memory are largely attributable to differences in encoding speed, when memory span or capacity limits have been exceeded (Vellutino & Scanlon 1987a). Performance differences on visual STM tasks appear to be the result of differences in the ability to label and to store items in some form of verbal code (Hicks 1980).

There is considerable belief that verbal information is normally held in STM through use of a phonological code and that use of this code is STM's best hedge against the loss of serial information. This has led some researchers to suggest that sequential-memory difficulties are probably the result of inefficient or deficient phonological recoding or verbal encoding (e.g., Torgesen & Houck 1980; Mann 1986; Vellutino & Scanlon 1987a).

RESEARCH FINDINGS. Research evidence that memory problems are a cause of reading disability is inconclusive and the evidence that poor readers have STM deficits is largely correlational (Stanovich 1986a). Furthermore when verbal IQ is controlled, the relationship between memory and reading ability is reduced considerably (Bowers, Steffy & Tate 1988).

It has been suggested that memory dysfunctions are rooted in inherent neurological limitations; however, research data rule out the idea that disabled readers have a structurally deficient memory system (Howe, Brainerd & Kingsma 1985). Visual and auditory traces in sensory memory do not dissipate any faster in disabled readers than in good readers (Vellutino 1987), nor do disabled readers necessarily forget more rapidly than do good readers. Reported memory problems could be due to unrecognized variables such as test anxiety, auditory or sensory acuity losses, inattention, or failure to understand the task requirements. Furthermore, memory depends on the effective operation of a large array of cognitive processes (Torgesen 1985).

Memory is not a unitary ability. Findings are equivocal regarding which, if any, encoding, retention, or retrieval processes are deficient in disabled readers (Aaron & Baker 1983), but encoding and retrieval processes are the most likely to be implicated.

Three factors influence encoding and retrieval processes (Torgesen 1985). The first is the status, or intactness, of the basic processing operations and capacities (e.g., the ability to recognize an item as having been previously seen).

The second factor is the use made of *control strategies*, which are sequences of mental operations that can be consciously employed to enhance memory. They include: (1) *rehearsal* (repeating the items aloud or to oneself); (2) *elaboration* (thinking of verbal or visual associations for the information under consideration); (3) clustering items by meaningful relationships; (4) chunking (e.g., rather than trying to remember six separate numbers, chunk them into two groups of three); and (5) proper apportioning of study time. Not all disabled readers are strategically deficient or inefficient. But as a group, they are less efficient than good readers in their use of, or willingness to use, a wide variety of memory strategies even when the strategies are within their capabilities (Stanovich 1986a, b) and they do not tend to use rehearsal strategies spontaneously (Lorsbach & Gray 1985). Rehearsal strategies can be taught to disabled readers. and such instruction results in their increased use (Haines & Torgeson 1979) and in improved recall (Moore et al. 1982).

Selective reminding of items not recalled on previous trials permits the separation of the storage and retrieval aspects of memory. Fletcher (1985) found that disabled readers did not differ from the control group in storage, but they did display retrieval difficulties with verbal material.

The third factor influencing encoding and retrieval processes is differences in the readers' knowledge base. Many of the developmental differences once attributed to memory capacity differences are now thought to be age-related differences in prior knowledge (Torgesen 1985).

Attention

A distinction should be drawn among *attention*, which in the broad sense refers to noticing stimuli; *selective attention*, which is the ability to select and maintain focus on particular stimuli and to disregard or suppress other stimuli; and *sustained attention*, which involves the ability to concentrate or stay on task over a period of time. Selective attention is basic to efficiency in perception, learning, memory, and information processing. Selective and sustained attention normally improve with age (Prior & Sanson 1986), and both are mentioned as possible causes of reading or learning disability (e.g., Denckla 1985).

A lack of attention is sometimes attributed to, or equated with, distractability, but a distinction should be made between a lack of selective attention and the extreme distractability associated with brain damage, which is at times listed as a symptom of hyperactivity. Neurologically impaired children may have marked difficulty suppressing distracting external stimuli as well as maintaining attention to relevant stimuli. Disabled readers are not more distractable than normally achieving students under all conditions; rather, their episodes of distractability are task- or situation-specific (Krupski 1986).

Although disabled readers or LD children may display attentional problems (e.g., Moore et al. 1982; Cherry & Kruger 1983), this does not mean that their low academic achievement is a result of an attentional deficit. Little evidence supports an attentional-deficit hypothesis. Studies have not revealed major sustained attention deficits in disabled readers (Samuels & Miller 1985, Krupski 1986), nor do disabled readers, as a group, exhibit basic or pervasive deficits in selective attention (Bauer 1982). Both good readers and disabled readers perform similarly on selective attention tasks that do not require reading (Vellutino & Scanlon 1982). The poorer performance of disabled readers on verbal selective attention tasks may result from (1) their weak reading ability, which causes them to disengage from reading; (2) looking at other words or pictures in an attempt to find clues to unknown words; or (3) attempts to escape the frustration and anxiety cause by repeated failures in reading (Morrison & Manis 1982). Differences in attention between good readers and poor readers may be due at least in part to differences in rapid, automatically functioning information-processing skills (Torgesen 1978–79). Tarver et al. (1977) attribute inattention to a lack of verbal rehearsal and Eliason and Richman (1987) conclude that the disabled readers whom they studied did not have attentional deficits, but either did not allocate their processing resources efficiently or did not apply processing strategies efficiently.

Selective attention can be improved by teaching children how to use verbal rehearsal (Tarver et al. 1977), by using a reward system (Hallahan et al. 1978), or by teaching them self-monitoring strategies (Hallahan, Marshall & Lloyd 1981). Although self-monitoring is effective at increasing on-task behavior, children must be taught not only how to attend, but also to what they should attend. Attention deficits may reflect the inability to perceive what is relevant in academic tasks (Snider 1987). The fact that such teaching approaches improve selective attention strongly indicates that the attentional problems of reading disabled students are not neurologically based.

Lack of attention can be situational or created by such external factors as poor instructional practices. As Wittrock (1983) states, attention is influenced by the questions teachers ask, the textbooks they use, and the directions teachers provide to pupils as to the relationships the pupils must construct between the text and their prior knowledge. Attentional processes are also subject to psychosocial influences, including social class, culture, home environment, and style of mother/child interactions (Prior & Sanson 1986). The degree to which the material used for reading instruction is of an appropriate level of difficulty for the pupils also influences attending behavior (Gambrell, Wilson & Ganitt 1981).

We do not yet have sufficient knowledge for defining an attentional deficit (Prior & Sanson 1986); it is difficult to determine with any certainty what constitutes a normal level of distractability (Levine 1987); and many uncertainties are involved in the measurement of attention (Krupski 1986, Eliason & Richman 1987). Nevertheless, it seems clear that getting students to focus on the task at hand is an important responsibility of any teacher and is particularly vital in remediation.

Integration between Modalities

Reading appears to require the integration of information from the auditory and visual sensory systems—the association between graphemes and phonemes, between printed and spoken words, between the written and spoken forms of language. The ability to integrate sensory information is known as *auditory-visual integration* (AVI).

Birch & Belmont (1964) believe that a major cause of reading disability is the inability to associate and to integrate representations stored in different cognitive systems. But the notion that basic deficits in sensory integration cause reading disability has received little support (Vellutino & Scanlon 1987b). Furthermore, poor readers perform as poorly on intramodal (auditory-auditory, visual-visual) tasks as they do on AVI (Van de Voort, Senf & Benton 1972).

On the other hand, Kavale (1980) somewhat cautiously concludes that AVI is sufficiently associated with reading ability to be considered in the prediction of reading achievement. AVI correlates about 0.34 with various measures of reading, except for vocabulary (0.13). The correlation is higher for good readers (0.35) than for disabled readers (0.21). Intelligence appears to be a component of AVI.

A number of factors have been suggested as influencing AVI performance. Blank and Bridger (1966) implicate attention and verbal labeling, but Drader (1975) failed to find evidence of a verbal labeling deficiency among disabled readers. Rudel and Denckla (1976) found that whether the stimulus pattern was simultaneous or successive was more important than whether the sequence of stimuli was auditory-to-visual or visual-to-auditory. Badian (1977) interprets her data as indicating that poor AVI is the result of inferior auditory sequential memory. But poor performance on a sequential-memory test may reflect a number of factors, as indicated above.

At present it appears that although AVI ability is related to reading ability, a cause-effect relationship has not been established. Evidence does not show that AVI training has any benefit for growth in reading skills (Calfee & Drum 1978).

Cognitive Style

Cognitive style has been characterized in a number of ways, but all of them deal with individual differences in the ways in which information and experiences are organized and processed (Messick 1982). Guilford (1980) believes that cognitive styles are personality traits regarding preferences for information processing. Three aspects of cognitive style that are relevant to reading are field dependence–independence, reflectiveness-impulsiveness, and modality preference.

Field dependence–independence refers to a dimension at one end of which are the field dependent, who are socially sensitive, conforming, and easily influenced. At the other end are the field independent, who tend to be impersonal, analytical, and not easily influenced. Most people fall between the extremes and are somewhat variable according to the situation (Witkin et al. 1977). Keogh and Donlon (1972) found LD boys to be highly field dependent, but no direct relation to reading disability has been established, and the implications of this dimension for teaching are not clear. Although some studies have shown that field-independent pupils scored higher on standardized reading tests than did field-dependent students, other studies have found no significant differences between the two groups; the possible effect of intelligence has been ignored in most of these studies.

Conceptual tempo (reflectiveness-impulsiveness) refers to a dimension having the reflective (slow but accurate) at one end and the impulsive (fast but inaccurate) at the other. Most people fall between the extremes, and many are slow and inaccurate or fast and accurate. Recommendations concerning use of reading approaches that are congruent with a student's cognitive style are premature (Roberge & Flexer 1984). Impulsiveness and reflectiveness may influence the kind and number of miscues a child makes; impulsive children in the early grades tend to rely on the first letter of a short word or the first or last syllable of a long word (Fisher 1977). Considerable evidence indicates that inactive or impulsive learning styles are the consequences of an inadequate understanding of the relationships among tasks, strategies, and outcomes (Ryan, Weed & Short 1986).

The following are among the problems encountered in trying to interpret conceptual-tempo studies. Conceptual tempo is often measured by the *Matching Familiar Figures Test* (MFFT), in which the subjects are classified by a double-median-split method (slow but accurate, slow and inaccurate, fast and inaccurate, and fast and accurate). Use of such a classification procedure means that conceptual tempo is a relative term, the meaning of which shifts depending on the subjects being tested. Test-retest reliability for the MFFT is questionable. In one study (Walker 1985), less than half of the 20 subjects were classified the same on both MFFT administrations. Finally, inpulsivity is typically said to be due to an inability to inhibit responding, but it may also be caused by an unwillingness. Reflectivity requires more effortful processing than impulsivity, and some children may be less willing to exert such effort (Prior & Sanson 1986).

The idea of matching a child's *modality preference*, that is, his or her strongest learning aptitude or preferred modality for learning, with a corresponding teaching method has not been supported by research (see page 90). Most children do not show a significant preference for either the visual or auditory modality. Among those few who do show preference, those with strong visual preferences do not do better learning to recognize words through a whole-word approach than through a phonics method—as the theory would suggest. Those with strong auditory abilities do not show a special advantage when a phonics method is employed (H. M. Robinson 1972). Based on their meta-analysis of 39 studies involving aptitude-treatment interaction, Kavale and Forness (1987b) conclude that neither modality assessment nor instruction based on supposed modality preferences is warranted. Perhaps the modality-preference model is invalid because reading requires both visual and auditory abilities.

Learning Styles

Learning style is the aggregate of a student's opinion about the conditions under which he or she learns best. Learning style is most often determined by a questionnaire, the *Reading Styles Inventory*. Elements sampled include: (1) the instructional environment (noise level, lighting, temperature, and furniture design); (2) emotionality (motivation, persistence, responsibility, and need for either external or internal structure); (3) the people with whom one learns most easily (alone, in pairs, with peers, or with an authoritative or permissive adult); (4) physical charactistics (perceptual strengths, energy levels during the day or night, intake needs, and mobility requirements); and (5) psychological and cognitive inclinations (global/analytical, hemispheric style, and impulsive/reflective) (Dunn (1988). Dunn (1988) and Carbo (1988) are the strongest proponents of learning styles. Despite their contention to the contrary, White (1983) cautions that there is no agreement about what constitutes learning style, and that research on its identification and use in reading instruction is still in its infancy are still valid.

Before accepting Dunn's and Carbo's viewpoint, we should examine the assessment instrument critically, consider whether it would be physically possible to accommodate the possible permutations of learning styles that might exist in a class, and consider the fact that almost all the research in this area has been done at one institution, by the chief proponents of this theory or by their graduate students. An examination of these studies led Stahl (1988) to question seriously Carbo's claims, at least for novice readers.

LANGUAGE ABILITIES

Distinctions need to be drawn among the terms *language, inner speech, language competence, language usage,* and *speech* before discussing the relationship of language to reading disability. *Language* is a communication system that employs spoken and written symbols that convey meaning to those who understand the system. *Inner speech,* which includes most thinking, is an important aspect of language. In turn, language is an important underlying aspect of intelligence that facilitates cognitive functioning (Stanovich 1986a). *Language competence* involves knowing, to varying degrees and often implicitly: the language's phonological, morphological, and orthographic systems; word meanings; how to combine words into permissible, comprehensible sentences and text; how to interpret the spoken and written forms of the language; and how these various components of language are interrelated.

There is a difference between language competence and *language usage.* Individuals may have the competence necessary to process a wide range of spoken or written language, but they do not necessarily display such competencies in their use of oral or written language. For example, children understand the meanings of many words that they do not commonly use when speaking to others.

Speech refers to the neuromuscular activities that produce oral communication. There is some evidence of a relationship between articulatory speech defects and reading problems (Young & Tyre 1983). Of the 242 learning-disabled 8- to 12-year-olds studied by Gibbs and Cooper (1989), 23.5% had articulation problems. The speech of some disabled readers is indistinct with blurred sounds and a generally "thick" quality; or it may be rapid, jerky, and stumbling (sometimes referred to as *cluttering*). Others may stutter, lisp, make speech-sound substitutions, or slur their words. But most disabled readers do not have speech defects; nor do all children with speech defects have reading problems. Therefore, it should not be assumed that speech defects cause reading disability. Speech can be significantly abnormal without any concomitant disturbance of language or thought (Benson 1983), and some defective speech patterns are learned behaviors. Also, it is possible that the speech defect and the reading problem have a common underlying cause. A hearing loss may be the cause of the speech problem, and difficulty hearing the teacher's instruction is likely to hamper reading acquisition. Or both problems may be caused by a language deficit. Any speech defect may produce embarrassment in attempting to communicate orally, and thus have an indirect, but adverse, effect on language development. A speech problem may also produce a dislike for reading, especially if the child is asked to read orally in front of his or her peers. Some decoding skills may be difficult to learn for speech-impaired children, especially if a synthetic phonics approach is employed with a child who is also hearing impaired.

Given the important role of language in reading ability, it is not surprising that their interrelationships have been studied and that language deficits or dysfunctions have been suggested as causes of reading problems. Bottom-up theories suggest that printed words are almost always phonologically recoded, with all subsequent language processing occurring through the spoken system. These code-emphasis theories predict that any specific effect of language deficiencies on reading ability would involve language abilities at or below the level of phonological recoding (see page 293–295): Lexical, syntactic, and semantic-level deficiencies would occur in both spoken and written language.

Top-down theories postulate that in reading there is direct access to meaning. Therefore, effects of language deficiencies on reading ability would involve language deficits at or above the lexical level. Top-down theorists also postulate that poor readers fail to use their linguistic knowledge to increase *unitization* (chunking information into fewer linguistic units); or fail to use context clues to make better predictions concerning the information that is likely to be coming up next (Morrison & Manis 1982).

As for interactive models, Roth and Perfetti (1980) suggest that the severity of language dysfunctions within a complex processing system (such as in reading) may be a matter of the degree to which a dysfunction has affected other subsystems and the degree of compensatory processing that has emerged.

Children who are slow in language development have been found to have later reading problems (de Hirsch, Jansky & Langford 1966; Young & Tyre 1983). However, because language development is usually measured by the ability to understand and use spoken language, the slow development of such skills and of reading ability may all be related to underlying linguistic deficiencies.

Numerous studies have found that disabled readers are less proficient than good readers on a wide variety of language skills.

First graders who were good readers performed better than poor readers on a variety of auditory/oral tasks. The groups did not differ in their ability to judge the semantic acceptability of sentences (Blachman & James 1985). In their study of 8-year-olds, Morice and Slaghuis (1985) found that: (1) children who had both language comprehension and language production problems were the poorest readers; (2) those with either problem had average reading ability; and, (3) children with neither problem were the best readers. By age 9, the combined-problems group and the low-language-comprehension group were further behind in their reading achievement than were the other groups. The performance of the low-language-comprehension group may reflect an underlying cognitive, rather than language, deficit. Stahl and Erickson (1986) report that LD third graders performed similarly to normally achieving first graders, but significantly more poorly than third-grade good readers on tasks of phonological awareness, speed of access to semantic information, knowledge and use of syntactic structures and morphological rules, and use of story grammar. Primary- and intermediate-grade poor readers were less proficient than good readers in their knowledge and use of inflectional morphemes, judgments of grammaticality, sentence imitation, use of such complex syntactic structures as embedded sentences, detection of ambiguity, and the ability to paraphrase (Vellutino & Scanlon 1986b).

Doehring et al. (1981) gave 22 language measures to 88 disabled readers. Many of them showed marked weaknesses in phonemic segmentation and blending, serial naming, morphophonemic knowledge, syntactic usage, and following spoken instructions. However, half the subjects scored within the normal range on these language tests, and there was considerable variability from test to test and from subject to subject. None of Doehring's three identified subtypes of reading disability could be clearly differentiated solely on the basis of the language skills measured.

Disabled readers do not always have language deficits (Newcomer & Magee 1977), and it is unlikely that reading disability is associated with a generalized language impairment (V. Mann 1986). Nevertheless, linguistic skills may be factors in some cases of reading disability.

Growth in oral language development during the primary grades is marked, and language development correlates fairly highly with reading achievement during these years. Some have interpreted such relationships to indicate that language development influences reading acquisition. But other interpretations are plausible: (1) Reading experiences might contribute to linguistic sensitivity and competence; (2) the relationship may be reciprocal; or, (3) both oral language and reading development may reflect growth in underlying language-processing efficiency (Willows & Ryan 1986). There may be developmental changes in the linguistic correlates of reading achievement (Fletcher, Satz & Scholes 1981).

Vellutino and Scanlon (1987b) offer a developmental hypothesis in which the nature of language deficits that lead to reading difficulties change along an age continuum. Disabled readers who are at the initial stages of reading acquisition have particular difficulty in utilizing phonological and/or syntactic components of language (the purely linguistic attributes) to code, store, and retrieve information. Such deficiencies are not as pronounced in older disabled readers.

Auditory Processing

Auditory-processing difficulties have been suggested as contributing to reading disability. One hypothesis holds that a deficient auditory sensory memory causes auditory traces to dissipate faster than they normally would. Another suggests that auditory-processing disorders limit the ability of poor readers to attend selectively to auditory stimuli. Yet a third hypothesis states that disabled readers are generally limited in their ability to store acoustic information in LTM. There is little research support for these theories (Vellutino 1987).

Auditory Segmentation

Auditory segmentation is the ability to segment spoken language into its constituent parts. There is some belief (e.g., Liberman 1983) that auditory segmentation in general and phonemic segmentation in particular are related to reading disability. This view holds that in order to become skilled readers, children must be aware that English is an alphabetic language in which spoken words are comprised of phonemes arranged in a particular sequence, and that this metalinguistic awareness is best demonstrated by the ability to segment syllables into phonemes.

Weak auditory segmentation ability is believed to be related to reading disability at the word-recognition level. Inadequate phonemic segmentation is thought to make it difficult to encode words phonemically (see the following), which in turn disrupts reading comprehension at the sentence level by hampering lexical access and retrieval (Liberman & Shankweiler 1985; Corley 1988). Teaching phonemic segmentation had a positive effect on good and poor readers in the second grade: It made them more aware of the grapheme and phoneme units contained in words, and they began using these units in word recognition (Vellutino & Scanlon 1986a).

Oral Narrative Ability

Reading- and learning-disabled pupils do not differ greatly from their normally achieving peers in their use of a story grammar in telling and in retelling stories (Ripick & Griffith 1988). But their self-generated narratives are not as long or as structurally complex as those of their peers, are told in less age-appropriate narrative styles (Roth 1986), and are less coherent (Stahl & Erickson 1986). Even when they can nonverbally demonstrate their comprehension of stories, reading-disabled children have difficulty orally retelling them (Feagans & Short 1984).

Linguistic Coding/Verbal Processing

Linguistic coding is defined broadly as the use of language to symbolize information. More specifically, it involves the functional use of the phonological, syntactic, and semantic attributes of units of language in storing and retrieving both the units themselves and the information within them (Vellutino & Scanlon 1986b).

According to some researchers, reading disability is largely attributable to inadequate use of language as a coding device. For example, Vellutino and Scanlon's (1986b) basic premise is that disabled readers have great difficulty processing spoken and written words, and that such difficulty is causally related, not only to poor performance on such reading tasks as word identification and comprehension, but also to inept performance on any task that involves the use of words and other units of language to code information.

Verbal processing plays a key role in Vellutino's (1979, 1983, 1987) *verbal-deficit hypothesis.* Basically, the theory suggests that severe reading disability is caused by a variety of linguistic impairments, which are often subtle rather than obvious; and is a consequence of limited facility in using language to code information and of deficiencies or inefficiencies in processing verbally coded information (Vellutino & Scanlon 1988). Vellutino's verbal-deficit theory has received widespread, but not unanimous, support (Zecker & Zinner 1987).

Remedial suggestions based on the verbal-deficit hypothesis tend to emphasize direct instruction and practice on component reading skills, as opposed to practice in general language skills in a context outside reading.

There are two other types of language-deficit models (Stahl & Erickson 1986). The *speed-of-processing* model states that disabled readers are slower at retrieving information from STM, and that this slowness creates a bottleneck in STM, which in turn encumbers both language processing and reading comprehension. The *rule-abstraction model* (e.g., Morrison 1984) holds that disabled readers have difficulty abstracting rules from exposure to language, probably because they either lack the ability to reflect on their language (metalinguistic awareness) or because they have a specific deficit in inductive reasoning.

Some studies (e.g., Stahl & Erickson 1986) support the contention that disabled readers have a general deficit in rule learning; others do not. For instance, Treiman and Hirsh-Pasek (1985) interpret their findings as supporting the developmental lag theory. Vellutino and Scanlon (1987b) state that there is no support for a rule-learning-deficiency hypothesis.

A variety of terms are used in the literature on linguistic coding and the distinctions among them often are not clear. As with other terminology in the field of reading, the same term can have various meanings, and different terms can have the same, or a similar, meaning. Some authors use the descriptors *phonological* and *phonetic* almost interchangeably; others consider them to be different types of coding.

T. Harris and Hodges (1981) define *coding* as changing "information into a code," *encoding* as changing "a message into symbols" or as giving "a deep structure to a message," and *recoding* as changing "information from one code to another (e.g., changing written to oral language). Some authors use these terms to define differing processes; others do not.

Information is *coded* (transformed) from one form into another. For instance, incoming sensory information is thought to be coded into a phonological code in STM. At some point in the information-processing system, the phonologically-coded information is *encoded* into a semantic code for storage in LTM. However, phonological information about words is also stored in LTM, and some theorists believe that it is such information that must be accessed for word identification to occur.

Phonological coding refers to the acquisition and application of phonologic and morphophonologic[12] rules for ordering the phonemes that comprise words. It also involves the ability to represent and to assign phonetic descriptors to spoken and written words, parts of words, and strings of words to aid in distinguishing and remembering them (Vellutino & Scanlon 1986b). Theoretically, after the sensory images of printed words enter the information-processing sys-

---

[12]*Morphophonologics* involves the relationship between morphemes (minimum units of language) and the phonemes which represent them (T. Harris & Hodges 1981).

tem during reading, they are coded in terms of their phonological features. Phonological coding is believed to insure the retention of verbal information in STM, and STM is thought to rely on phonological coding to hold a sufficient number of words and their sequences in memory long enough to process sentences. Words are stored in LTM along with their various attributes (e.g., phonological features, orthographic structure, meanings). It is believed that, except for highly familiar words, readers transform a written word into a string of phonemes, which is compared with phonemic strings in their lexicons. If a match occurs, word identification takes place (Wagner 1986). These phonologically based codes can be activated either by hearing the words spoken or through subvocal articulation (Torgesen 1985). Thus, phonological coding assists the storage and retrieval of information.

Phonological processing plays an important role in learning to read (Frith 1986, Wagner 1986). Novices who encounter problems learning to read often have difficulty using phonological information for verbal coding[13] (Corley 1988).

Phonological-processing deficiencies are thought to be related, perhaps causally, to reading disability, with the problems of disabled readers in the phonological domain not restricted to reading tasks (Brady 1986). According to Liberman and Shankweiler (1985), poor readers have three problems in the phonological domain: (1) difficulty becoming aware of the sublexical structure of words (phonological awareness); (2) unreliable access to the phonological representations in their lexicons (lexical access); and (3) deficient use of phonetic properties as a basis for STM operations that underlie the processing of connected discourse (phonological coding). Good readers and poor readers tend to differ in the rate at which they develop phonological processing skills (Mann, Cowin & Schoenheimer 1989), and although older good readers and poor readers may be comparable in their use of phonological coding, good readers code more rapidly (Corley 1988).

The phonological-core, variable-difference model suggests that problems in processing phonological features of language are the basic causes of most reading disability. This type of disability primarily limits the acquisition of fluent word recognition. If this model is valid, why do disabled readers perform lower than good readers on so many different tasks? There are two possible answers. First, phonological-processing problems, through their direct effects on higher level language-processing tasks, have a broader effect on cognition than believed. Second, reading failure itself may have broad negative consequences for cognitive and behavioral development in young children, and so, the characteristics of reading disability are consequences and not causes (Torgesen 1989).

Severely disabled readers perform poorly on tasks requiring verbatim retention of strings of verbal items. Such tasks require storage in, and retrieval from, STM (Torgesen 1985). Phonological problems could also lead to difficulty learning to make symbol-sound associations and to recognize words through a whole-word instructional approach. If a word is stored without complete phonological codes, a reader cannot call it up because not enough clues to the name of the word have been retained (Vellutino 1987).

---

[13]See page 292.

Evidence for a causal relationship between phonological coding difficulties and reading disability are of two types. First, relatively weak evidence suggests that individual differences in phonological coding, which exist before reading instruction is initiated, can be used to predict success in learning to read. Second, substantial evidence indicates that poor readers have slower rates of verbal articulation than do good readers. Because it is unlikely that reading instruction has an effect on simple articulation rate, it is possible to make a causal inference even though the data are correlational (Torgesen 1985). Olson et al. (1985) claim that although there are substantial individual differences, deficient phonological coding seems to be the most distinctive characteristic of disabled readers, and may be the cause of the most severe deficits in reading ability. Vellutino and Scanlon (1987a) agree that severely disabled readers are especially deficient in phonological processing and that there is probably a causal relationship.

Phonological-coding facility varies with intelligence and general verbal skills, and it is difficult to determine the independence of phonological skills from skills in the other two areas. Brady (1986) interprets her data as suggesting that the critical differences in phonological processing between good and poor readers were the accuracy with which phonetic representations are formulated and the rate at which they are processed. Torgesen (1985) attributes the language comprehension problems of disabled readers to insufficient general knowledge or to control-strategy deficits rather than to difficulties in the verbatim retention of language strings.

Among the unresolved issues regarding the role of phonological coding in reading disability are: (1) Little is known about the developmental course of phonological-coding difficulties; (2) the exact relationship between coding deficits and other kinds of phonological processing problems is not clear; and (3) the causes of phonological-coding deficits are unknown (Torgesen 1985). We have yet to determine the effects of training phonological processing, especially for disabled readers (Wagner 1986).

Deficiencies in phonological processing are postulated as sources of reading disability in auditory-discrimination-deficiency theories and the phonemic-segmentation-deficiency theory.

Syntactic coding involves acquiring and applying implicitly known rules for ordering words in a language and for representing and understanding structural differences in sentences.

Studies indicate that poor readers and disabled readers are not as proficient as good readers on a variety of syntactic tasks in both listening and reading (e.g., A. Glass & Perna 1986, Willows & Ryan 1986). Disabled readers demonstrate sensitivity to basic grammatical structures significantly later than do their peers who are making normal progress in reading achievement. This lag remains throughout middle childhood (Siegel & Ryan 1988). But not all poor readers have weak syntactic skills. For example, 6 of the 18 poor readers in Morice and Slaghuis' (1985) study performed above the mean attained by the good readers on a syntactic comprehension test.

Syntactic weaknesses may be a cause of reading difficulties since they appear before children are taught to read (Vellutino 1983), or they may be a consequence of lack of reading experiences because not reading cuts children off from opportunities to increase their syntactic knowledge through reading (V. Mann 1986). Syntactic-processing deficits could result from a lack of the syntactic knowledge needed to process language efficiently or from an inability to access and use syntactic information efficiently during sentence comprehension (Corley 1988).

SEMANTIC CODING AND PROCESSING.   *Semantic codes* are linguistic representations of meaningful concepts, as encoded in both individual words and groups of words. Word meaning comes to exist in a complex network of interrelated associations, stored in LTM, that become more elaborated and better defined during the course of lexical development. *Semantic coding* is the process whereby meanings are attached to and conveyed by certain language components. Semantic coding involves the use of words, phrases, and sentences to code and process meaningful information (Vellutino & Scanlon 1986b). Without *semantic processing* (abstracting meaning from verbal stimuli), it would be impossible to remember the words in a sentence or sentences in a paragraph clearly enough to extract the intended meaning.

Disabled readers have displayed semantic coding and processing difficulties, but there is no evidence that poor readers lack semantic knowledge or competence. In fact, poor readers may rely more than good readers on semantic representations, perhaps to compensate for weaknesses in other areas. For instance, Vellutino and Scanlon (1986b) report that poor readers in Grades 1–4 were more attuned to the semantic (meaning) component than to the phonological, syntactic, and orthographic (structural) components of spoken and written words; good readers were attuned to both meaning and structural components. Some disabled readers are not impaired in semantic processing; but when group differences are compared, it is the speed at which semantic information can be accessed, rather than the amount of information available to be accessed, that distinguishes disabled from skilled readers (Zecker & Zinner 1987).

GRAPHIC AND ORTHOGRAPHIC CODING AND PROCESSING.   As children learn to read and spell, the use of graphic and orthographic codes enter into language processing. *Graphic codes* are representations of the unique visual patterns formed by the particular arrangement of letters that define a given word (its configuration and length) and by the varied patterns formed by the letters themselves. *Orthographic codes* are representations of the structural attributes of written words. Orthographic rules constrain the spatial ordering of graphemes within English words (i.e., the sequence of letters that is permissible). Only certain letter sequences are allowable (e.g., *ble* is a legal sequence, *grt* is not), and certain sequences can occur in only a particular position in an English word. (e.g., *ng* can occur in the final, but not the initial, position).

In order to learn to identify words and to spell, children must store representations of the graphic and orthographic features of words. Fluent word identification also requires storage of the orthographic features that a word has in common with other words. When reading, semantic and syntactic codes must be activated, phonological codes maintained long enough for sentences to be fully processed, and graphic and orthographic codes activated for lexical access (Vellutino & Scanlon 1987b).

Lexical Knowledge

As concepts are learned, verbal labels (word names) are attached to them and stored, along with other information about the words, in out LTMs. The words in our *lexicons* (mental dictionaries) are complex mental representations that symbolize concepts, entities, attributes, and ideas taken from our experiences (Vellutino & Scanlon 1987b). These representations have been coded into units of language using *linguistic codes* (see the foregoing), which are complex representations of the physical properties that define these words and of the rules that constrain their use. All lexical items (words) have substantive and structural components. The *substantive components* of a word are a collection of memory codes that signify the meanings embedded in that word (i.e., its semantic features). During the course of lexical development, these semantic codes become increasingly more elaborated, more highly differentiated, and better integrated. They come to exist in a complex network of hierarchically ordered associations that are connected in varying degrees. Students who have highly differentiated and elaborated inventories of semantic codes, as shown by a rich fund of world knowledge and verbal labels for that knowledge, are better able to make functional use of semantic (meaning-based) strategies in storing and retrieving spoken and written words.

The quality of children's verbal concepts may be revealed by their definitions of words. Preschool children usually explain words in terms of their function or use—a ball is to throw. Primary-grade pupils are apt to add some description—a ball is a round thing you play with. Intelligent older students usually state a category to which the item belongs and then indicate one or more ways the item can be distinguished from other members of that category—a ball is a plaything and is usually round; it can be thrown, caught, or kicked. As children get older and have more experiences, concepts are refined and broadened.

Bright children usually acquire concepts rapidly and have large vocabularies. Thus, vocabulary knowledge is a good indicator of learning ability in general and of probable success in school. It also suggests the child's level of topical knowledge. Breadth and depth of word meaning are important for reading comprehension.

The *structural components* of a word are a collection of memory codes that refer to the formal properties of words that define the word as a meaning unit. The formal properties of spoken words are defined by the coded representations of their phonological and syntactic attributes; those of written words by the coded representations of their graphic and orthographic attributes.

The *syntactic features* of a word are the part(s) of speech it may serve. Some words have only one grammatical function; others more than one (e.g., *can* may be either a noun or verb). The *phonological features* of a word are defined by the unique sequence of phonemes that comprise that word. Children acquire implicit knowledge about the syntactic and phonological features of words through experiences with language.

As children are exposed to printed words, they add information about the graphic and orthographic features of words to their lexicons. A word's *graphic features* are the visual patterns formed by the word and the letters that make up the word. Its *orthographic features* are the sequences of letters that constitute that word.

In general, disabled readers are not deficient in their knowledge of word meanings (Swanson 1986). But even though their understanding vocabularies may be comparable to good readers of the same age, many of them understandably have weak knowledge of the graphic, orthographic, and phonological features of these words. The understanding vocabularies of disabled readers in the early stages of reading acquisition tend to be less deficient, compared to those of their normally achieving age peers, than those of older disabled readers (Vellutino & Scanlon 1987b). A study by Snowling et al. (1986) indicates that older, severely disabled readers' lexical knowledge approximates that of younger children. Snowling et al. attributes this to a developmental lag, but it also may be that relatively weak understanding vocabularies are due in part to the reading disability. Since disabled readers generally do not engage in wide reading, they are cut off from one source of vocabulary development.

LEXICAL ACCESS.　Information about words stored in the lexicon has to be accessed in order for reading comprehension to occur. *Lexical access* refers to the point at which information stored with the lexical items becomes available for use by other comprehension processes (Foss 1988). Two forms of lexical access have been theorized. In *direct access*, words are identified by finding a direct match between the printed word and a lexical entry, or printed words are converted to a visual code that is spatially defined and which involves word shape and length, letter features, and the features of letter sequences and groupings (Katz & Feldman 1981). In the latter case, the visual-orthographic code is matched with the lexical entry. In *phonological access*, the printed words are first converted to a phonological code, which is then used to search the lexicon for a match.

Disagreement among theorists concerning lexical access seems to center on two main points: (1) whether phonological recoding is necessary for lexical access; and (2) when the phonological identities (properties) of words are determined. There are wide differences of opinion concerning how the lexicon is accessed. At one end of the continuum are those who believe that skilled, and perhaps unskilled, readers can and do go directly from print to meaning.

At the other end of the continuum are theorists who claim that graphic information must be recoded into phonological information. If the lexical entry for a word is jointly constituted by its four defining properties (phonological, visual, grammatical, and meaning), as some think it is (see Foss 1988), then at some point the word must be "pronounced" because it is a necessary part of the word. There is disagreement whether this takes place pre- or postlexically. Some argue that it must occur after the word has been accessed in the lexicon, otherwise a reader could not differentiate between such words as *dough* and *cough*. Others conclude that phonological encoding is prelexical for all situations; or that it is prelexical for tasks involving single words in isolation, but postlexical when reading words in context. Some evidence indicates that phonological codes are activated postlexically in order to maintain verbatim information in STM long enough to allow a sentence to be processed (Vellutino & Scanlon 1987b). Some theorists suggest that even in skilled reading there is a form of phonological recoding, however abbreviated, that precedes comprehension. One subgroup believes that phonological memory serves as a link between visual memory and semantic memory. When a unit is selected from visual memory for processing, it is recoded phonologically and then phonological memory is searched for a counterpart. This phonological information is passed on to semantic memory where it is processed for meaning (Samuels & Eisenberg 1981). Another subgroup holds that phonological coding facilitates reading by providing a stable code for information that must be held in STM until the meanings of segments (e.g., clauses, sentences) can be extracted (e.g., Liberman et al. 1980).

A third point of view is that novice readers may, or may need to, use a mediated access, but that skilled readers can use direct access. Once orthographic images are established in the lexicon (this is believed to occur through extensive lexical access for a word), the need for mediated access ceases. There are, however, unanswered questions as to how this transition takes place and whether phonological recoding continues to serve some role subsequent to lexical access (e.g., as an aid to memory) even after orthographic images have been established (Lesgold & Perfetti 1981). Within this viewpoint are those who believe that skilled readers revert to phonological recoding when the material is difficult for them. Venezky (1981) points out the weaknesses in phonological-mediation hypotheses.

Yet others (e.g., Glushko 1981), propose that, in reading, all the paths that can be used are used for lexical access. In dual-process, independent-channel models of word identification, both routes are activated simultaneously, with the first to produce a match in the lexicon being acted on by the reader (Juel 1983).

There is growing evidence that either pathway may be utilized, with the choice depending on various factors (Haines & Leong 1983). Novice readers may be more reliant on direct access when reading familiar words (Katz & Feldman 1981), or when they have been instructed through a whole-word method or have had little instruction and practice in decoding (Barron 1981a). Research strongly supports the position that direct access is possible for skilled readers, but that they use a mediated access when confronted by unknown words (Kleiman & Humphrey 1982). Word familiarity has a significant effect on lexical access and language processing. A word's syntactic and semantic complexity does not affect the time it takes to access it in the mental lexicon. A word's phonological or orthographic organization as well as its relation to other words in the lexicon may influence access time (Foss 1988).

Some writers (e.g., Mitterer 1982) suggest that there are two types of poor readers—*recoding-poor readers* who rely excessively on phonological recoding, and *whole-word-poor readers* who make little use of it. Others (e.g., Shankweiler et al. 1979) state that disabled readers are unable to make adequate use of the phonological route, primarily due to phonological recoding problems. Ellis (1981), on the other hand, is of the opinion that severely disabled readers are deficient in the use of both routes for lexical access. Perhaps the severity of the reading problem accounts for the difference between these two views. Swanson (1986) suggests that disabled readers fail to activate a critical number of word features from semantic memory, and therefore resort to alternative means of processing information.

According to Vellutino and Scanlon (1985), the facility to store and to retrieve items from one's lexicon requires a functional acquaintance with multiple attributes of the items—their semantic, phonological, syntactic, graphic, and orthographic features. A reader must be able to activate and cross-reference individual words for lexical storage and retrieval. Reading disability may be caused by deficiencies in lexical access that create word-identification problems (Vellutino & Scanlon 1987a).

Rapid Automatic Naming

Rapid Automatic Naming (RAN) refers to the ability to name things (e.g., depicted objects, colors) accurately and quickly.[14] As such it is a measure of lexical access or name retrieval speed.[15] Its use as a measure of verbal ability evolved from the common finding of *anomia* (loss of the ability to recall the names of common objects) in adults with an acquired reading disability known as *alexia without agraphia* (Denckla 1983).

Reading and learning disabled pupils have been found to be impaired on a number of word-finding, naming, and speed-of-naming tasks (V. Mann 1986; Bowers, Steffy & Tate 1988). But the correlations between RAN scores and reading comprehension reported by Morrison and Hinshaw (1988) were either nonsignificant or in the low negative range (-0.29, -0.30). Finding that performance on the *Boston Naming Test* correlated only 0.36 with scores on the *Gates-MacGinitie Reading Test* and 0.34 with performance on the *Gray Oral Reading Test*, after IQ was parcelled out, led Wolf and Goodglass (1986) to conclude that access-speed disorders could not explain the retrieval problems of all severely reading disabled children, nor could it be eliminated as a possible explanation for some of them. Wolf and Goodglass also note that the relationship between name-access speed and reading ability varies with the pupil's level of maturation (it becomes less important in semantic processing by the end of the second grade), the type of stimuli and their presentation (there were only small good/poor reader differences in speed of naming when one stimuli at a time was presented but large differences when the task required serial recall) and that the relationship is complicated by the multiply determined nature of both naming and reading ability. Furthermore, the use of various tasks and scoring procedures in measuring naming ability (e.g., the number of pictures named correctly; the speed with which the stimuli in display are named; same/different reaction time to pairs of letters) makes it difficult to generalize from the findings in this area (Jacobwitz & Haupt 1984). Rudel (1980) reports that, on RAN tasks, learning-disabled children tend to *circumlocute* (give a function rather than name— e.g., "to sit" for *chair*), reverse syllables (e.g., "shoehorse" for *horseshoe*), or name another object in the same category (e.g. "sink" for *faucet*).

Speed-of-naming and naming problems have been variously attributed to: failure to seek or to find an appropriate single word or phrase for encapsulating information (Denckla, Rudel & Broman 1981); incomplete specification of the word's phonological properties; deficient storage or processing of stored phonological information (Liberman & Shankweiler 1985); deficient speed of access

---

[14]Items that should be highly familiar to subjects in the age group studied are used to control for the possibility that the word name is not in the child's lexicon.
[15]RAN tasks require the subject not only to retrieve the name of the visual stimulus, but also to produce the name, while preparing to encode the name of the next stimulus. (Perfetti 1985). Difficulty with any of these components could result in a weak performance.

to stored phonological codes; and slow activation of articulatory codes (Olson et al. 1985). According to Pennington (1986), the available longitudinal evidence suggests that *lexical retrieval* (speed and accuracy of naming) is a persistent and possibly intrinsic deficit in severe reading disability. He states that, neuroanatomically, both lexical retrieval and reading ability appear to require coordination between the visual-association areas and the posterior-speech areas. Pennington also notes that in both processes, a visual stimulus evokes a phonologic name code from the lexicon. However, unlike printed words, picture naming depends on a semantic rather than a graphic or phonological access route to the lexicon. Therefore, a comparison of reading and naming performance may help to specify the cognitive deficit in disabled readers.

Ackerman and Dykman (1982) contend that the speed-of-naming hypothesis as a explanation for reading disability is weakened by the fact that some studies did not find good/poor reader differences in naming speed. General name-retrieval speed is not a critical determinant of learning to read (Stanovich, Nathan & Vala-Rossi 1986); nor is it a major source of reading problems, although it may be a factor in severe reading disability (Perfetti 1985). Speed-of-name-retrieval-deficit hypotheses should be accepted cautiously because: (1) the relationship between reading ability and speed of lexical access is strong only when children at the extremes of reading ability are included in the sample; and (2) the magnitude of the relationship may be task dependent—continuous tasks (e.g., serial naming of a list of words) tend to yield higher correlations than discrete tasks (reaction time to a single stimulus). The latter situation probably exists because continuous tasks involve many other reading-related processing operations in addition to name access. Speed-of-name retrieval is linked in some way to reading ability; however, whether it is a cause of reading ability or disability or whether the greater amount of reading done by good readers better enables them to name stimuli more efficiently is an open question (Stanovich 1986a). Name-retrieval speed is not likely a critical determinant of initial reading acquisition (Stanovich, Nathan & Vala-Rossi 1986).

Sentence Comprehension

Skilled comprehenders segment incoming discourse into syntactically and semantically defined units (clauses and sentences) and hold two types of information about sentences in memory: (1) verbatim information (the surface structure), and (2) gist information (the deep structure). A verbal code of the discourse, usually coinciding with a clause or sentence boundary, is maintained until semantic coding can occur. Verbal coding is usually considered a STM process; semantic coding, a LTM process. Surface representations deteriorate quickly in memory; deep structures are retained over time (Corley 1988).[16]

Research suggests that poor readers are less proficient than their normally achieving age peers in comprehending both spoken and written sentences (Corley 1988). Poor readers have more difficulty than good readers in understanding syntactically complex sentences, and sentences containing relative clauses (e.g.,

---

[16]See pages 282–285 for a discussion of the relationship of memory to reading disability.

The girl *who is drinking the soda* is my sister.), and double object constructions (Liberman & Shankweiler 1985, V. Mann 1986).

Two explanations are commonly offered for good/poor reader differences in sentence comprehension. The *phonological-encoding-deficit hypothesis* states that inadequate encoding of the phonological components of words is a primary cause of poor sentence comprehension (see pages 293–295). The syntactic-processing-deficit hypothesis holds that sentence comprehension difficulties stem from insufficient processing of the syntactic components of language (see page 295). Although normally developing first and second graders rely heavily on semantic strategies for comprehending sentences, by the fifth grade they develop more sophisticated strategies that balance and integrate phonological, syntactic, and semantic information. Poor readers continue to rely on immature semantic strategies in the later grades. This sustained reliance on semantic structures is related to weak phonological and/or ineffective syntactic processing, but the direction of this relationship is not clear (Corley 1988).

Psycholinguistic Abilities

Psycholinguistics is the "interdisciplinary field of psychology and linguistics in which language behavior is examined" (T. Harris & Hodges 1981). Thus, in its broad definition, psycholinguistic ability refers to one's use of language. In practice, however, the term is most frequently defined operationally by performance on the *Illinois Test of Psycholinguistic Abilities* (ITPA). Since the advent of the ITPA, the relationship between psycholinguistic abilities and reading ability and disability has received considerable attention.

Reviews of the ITPA (e.g., Carroll 1972) indicate the following: (1) Only half of the subtests involve the use of language; (2) ITPA total scores are highly related to intelligence; (3) the 12 subtests do not measure discrete abilities; (4) the norms are based on middle-class children; (5) several subtests penalize dialect speakers; (6) the test has good internal reliability but only fair retest reliability; and (7) there is no particular pattern of high and low subtest scores that characterizes the reading disabled.

An analysis of 28 studies in which ITPA subtests were correlated with reading (Newcomer & Hammill 1975) reveals that only the Sound Blending (auditory blending) subtest correlates significantly (0.38) with reading ability, and that no subtest consistently distinguishes between disabled readers and those progressing normally in reading development. Newcomer and Hammill (1975) conclude: "There appears little doubt that, when used with school-aged children, . . . its [the ITPA's] use for individual diagnosis is neither supported nor recommended."

9

Correlates of Reading Disability II: Neurological, Physiological, and Physical Factors

This chapter is the second of three on the correlates of reading disabilities. The main topics discussed are the role of the brain in language and reading abilities, which covers subtopics such as laterality and hemispheric specialization; as well as the role in reading disabilities that is played by neurological damage and dysfunction, eye movements, sensory defects, and other physical conditions.

THE ROLE OF THE BRAIN IN LANGUAGE AND READING

The human brain is an incredibly complex organ whose role in language, and therefore reading, is not fully understood.[1] But given the cognitive factors related to reading that were discussed in Chapter 8, it is reasonable to assume that language and reading require a brain that is functioning within normal limits, and that deviations from these limits may result in reading problems. In the following discussion, a distinction is made between brain structure and brain function.

[1]For more information about the brain and its functioning, refer to Masland (1981), Downing and Leong (1982), Kirk (1983), or Benson (1983).

Brain Structure

The human brain, which contains billions of nerve cells that are interconnected in extremely complex ways, is divided into two cerebral hemispheres connected mainly by a band of nerve tissue called the *corpus callosum*. Collectively, these three parts of the brain are referred to as the *cerebrum*, which forms almost 70% of the central nervous system (CNS) (T. Harris & Hodges 1981). The *cerebral cortex* (the outer layer of the cerebrum) is important in the production and understanding of language.

STRUCTURAL DIFFERENCES.   The right and left cerebral hemispheres differ anatomically in a number of areas. For instance, the language area of the left hemisphere is usually larger than the corresponding area in the right hemisphere (Pirozzolo & Hansch 1982) and the left hemisphere has a number of components that are thought to be specialized for processing spoken and written language (Trevarthen 1983).

Although the exact locations and boundaries of the cortical areas important for language remain vague, two areas within the left hemisphere are widely acknowledged as important for language functions. Both are shown in Figure 9.1. *Broca's area* is vital for speaking (motor-speech functions); *Wernicke's area*, for understanding language. Damage to Broca's area may adversely affect oral reading ability but does not disrupt comprehension. Damage to Wernicke's area is more likely to be associated with listening and reading comprehension problems (Hanley & Sklar 1976).

Anatomical differences in the hemispheres have led to *structural differ-*

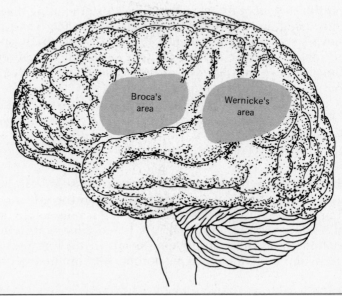

Figure 9.1.   Language areas of the cortex in the left hemisphere of the human brain. From T. Teyler, *A primer of psychobiology: brain and behavior* (San Francisco: W. H. Freeman, 1975). Used by permission of the author and publisher.

ence theories, which postulate that cognitive performance is superior when processing takes place in the hemisphere best suited anatomically to performing that function. Thus, for example, the left hemisphere is believed to be structurally better equipped than the right hemisphere for language functions.

STRUCTURAL LOCALIZATION THEORIES. *Structural localization theories* state that specific language functions are located within certain identifiable areas of the brain. Attempts to provide evidence for such a link, however, have not been successful. The exact locations of specific language areas in the cortex vary considerably among individuals (Ojemann 1983). Tools for studying the brain are available (see pages 307–311); however, all such tools are incapable of determining the precise area of the brain where a given function occurs. Even postmortem examinations of the brain are inadequate because they can demonstrate only structural changes, not functional disturbances. A structural change may not have been the cause of a functional disturbance (Benson 1983).

Hemispheric Specialization

TERMINOLOGY. Before reading the upcoming section, it is important to understand three key terms, the definitions of which are based on those of Hiscock and Kinsbourne (1982):

- *Laterality* or *lateral dominance* refers to the degree to which a receptor or effector organ on one side of the body is superior to, or is used in preference to, its counterpart on the other side. Laterality, which is often described by such terms as *handedness* or *eyedness*, is measurable. But laterality does not provide direct evidence regarding brain structure or cognitive functioning (Hiscock & Kinsbourne 1987).
- *Lateralization* is the state of cerebral organization in which there are thought to be qualitative and quantitative differences in functions between the two hemispheres of the brain. A function is said to be "lateralizing" when it is in the process of becoming a specialized function of one of the hemispheres. When a hemisphere plays a dominant role in that function, it is considered to be "lateralized." Lateralization may involve physical (e.g., use of body parts) or cognitive (e.g., language) functions. Lateralization refers to hemispheric specialization (a preferable term), rather than to one hemisphere exercising control over the other.
- *Hemispheric specialization* indicates that one hemisphere plays a major role in performing a particular cognitive or physical activity. It should be understood, however, that in a complex cognitive task such as reading, we probably use the processing specializations of both hemispheres. The term *hemispheric specialization* is preferable to *cerebral* or *hemispheric dominance*[2] because the latter two terms incorrectly imply the general mastery of one hemisphere over the other.

[2]Refer to pages 313–315 for a discussion of how these terms evolved and were used at one time.

FACT AND THEORY.   Each cerebral hemisphere controls motor and sensory functions on the opposite (contralateral) side of the body. For example, certain areas of the left hemisphere control the movements of the right arm, hand, or leg. Damage to generally identifiable areas in the left hemisphere results in paralysis of body parts on the contralateral side.

The role of each hemisphere in cognitive functioning is less clearly established. There are a variety of theories and atheoretical beliefs in this area. Some theories propose that hemispheric specialization occurs during particular stages of information processing. Others hold that each hemisphere specializes in a particular, characteristic type of processing, irrespective of the stimuli. Thus, left-hemispheric processing is supposedly sequential, temporal, or analytic; right-hemispheric processing, parallel, gestalt, or holistic (Shucard et al. 1985). However, sweeping generalizations about such cognitive differences between the hemispheres are unwarranted (Hiscock & Kinsbourne 1987).

There is also some belief that the degree to which the functions are lateralized distinguishes disabled readers from good readers (Shucard et al. 1985). But the neural substrate of certain cognitive functions is lateralized long before these cognitive functions are measurable. This fact casts doubt on the assumed relationship between the degree of hemispheric specialization and the level of cognitive performance (Hiscock & Kinsbourne 1987).

It is generally believed that the left hemisphere is highly involved in linguistic functions, with the right hemisphere participating in a limited manner during reading (Moscovitch 1981). Estimates suggest that 95–99% of right-handed persons and 60–70% of left-handers have left-hemispheric-specialization for language functions. The right hemisphere is believed to specialize in performing perceptual tasks, such as recognizing faces or geometric forms.

Complete agreement has not been reached regarding the role of each hemisphere in reading. Levy (1985) writes that the left hemisphere is believed to be more active than the right in processing verbal information; the right, in processing spatial information. During reading, the left hemisphere is thought to play a special role in such functions as understanding syntax, encoding written words into their phonemic representations, and drawing meaning from the complex relationships among word meanings and syntax. The right hemisphere is believed to be concurrently involved in decoding visual information, maintaining story structure, appreciating humor and emotional content, deriving meanings from past associations, and understanding metaphors. Benson (1983) states that silent and audible vocalization during reading may depend on left-hemisphere activity; whereas associating printed words with their visual images may be right-hemisphere function. Word recognition itself may involve reciprocal contributions from both hemispheres: feature analysis by the right hemisphere and decoding and naming from the left (Leong 1980).

LANGUAGE LATERALIZATION AND BRAIN PLASTICITY.   Some theorists hold that both hemispheres have equal potential for assuming language specialization; others, that the left hemisphere is, or begins to be, specialized for language at or before birth (Trevarthen 1983).

According to Masland (1981), the cutoff point for the right hemisphere to assume language functions is around ages 8–12, but this plasticity may cease to occur at much earlier ages. Most theorists consider language lateralization to be underway by about age 5, and many believe that hemispheric specialization for language is well developed by age 12 (Benson 1983). Recent research suggests that the two hemispheres are less rigidly specialized in their functions during the early and middle years than they are after age 15 (Obrzut & Hynd 1987).

EDUCATING EACH HEMISPHERE SEPARATELY. Proposals to educate one hemisphere at a time are based on the erroneous assumption that, because there is hemispheric specialization, each hemisphere must function as a separate brain. The opposite is true of normal brains—hemispheric functions are often integrated in performing cognitive tasks. No evidence supports the view that students are purely "left-brained" or "right-brained" (Levy 1985). Suggestions for educating each hemisphere separately can be safely ignored.

Medical Procedures for Studying Brain Structure and Function

Two basic types of procedures are used to study brain structure, brain function, laterality, and lateralization. *Invasive procedures* are those in which surgery is employed or a foreign substance is introduced to disrupt normal brain functioning. Almost all the early medical procedures were of this type. More recent procedures are noninvasive.

AUTOPSIES. Early methods involved noting the particular behavioral changes that followed brain damage from a stroke or wound and comparing them with later autopsy findings. Such medical research helped identify the brain areas in which language, sensations, or movements are generally located.

ELECTRICAL STIMULATION. Penfield and Roberts (1959) developed the technique of opening the skull and electrically stimulating tiny areas of the cerebral surface to determine the possible effects of surgical removal of these areas. Their results agree with those of Wada Tests (see the following) in showing that the left hemisphere is usually specialized for language regardless of the individual's handedness.

SPLIT BRAINS. In the 1960s, a few patients with severe intractable epilepsy were treated by severing the nerve fibers that connect the two hemispheres (commissurotomy), thus, in effect, producing "two brains." Studies of these *split-brain* patients (Sperry, Gazzaniga & Bogen 1969; Searleman 1977) reveal that usually: (1) Receptive and expressive language, analytical reasoning, and sequential processing are left-hemispheric functions; (2) simultaneous perception of visual forms, such as faces or geometric figures, are functions of the right hemisphere; and (3) the right hemisphere is not wholly nonverbal, but it cannot produce connected speech once speech has been firmly lateralized in the left hemisphere (see Fig. 9.2). While noting that information from split-brain studies has provided valuable information (the data are largely in accord with that of studies involving normal subjects), Beaumont (1982b) warns of considerable problems in interpreting the data. For example, most of the conclusions are based on data from only two of the seven split-brain patients.

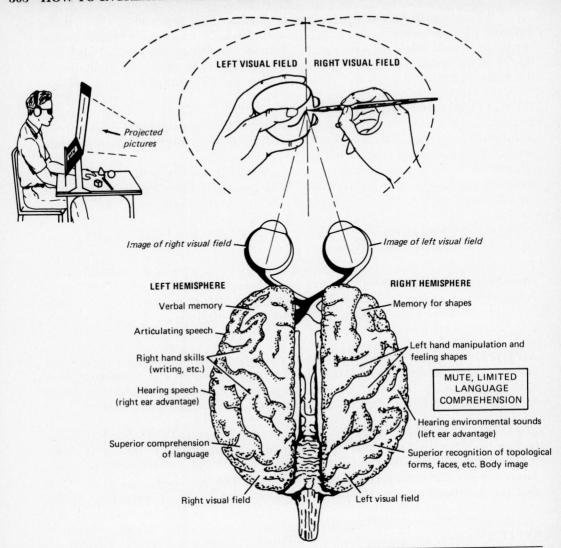

Figure 9.2. Hemispheric functions revealed by psychological tests of commissurotomy patients, carried out with orientation controlled as shown on the left. From C. Trevarthen, Development of the cerebral mechanism for language, in U. Kirk (Ed.), *Neuropsychology of language, reading, and spelling* (New York: Academic Press, 1983). Used with permission of the author and publisher.

WADA TEST. The *Wada Test* (Wada & Rasmussen 1960) involves injecting sodium amytal into the carotid artery that conveys blood from the aorta to the cerebral hemisphere on the same side of the body. If the injection produces a temporary *aphasia* (loss of speech or reading ability), the hemisphere is specialized for language functions; if not, the language functions are assumed to be centered in the other hemisphere. According to Rasmussen and Milner (1975),

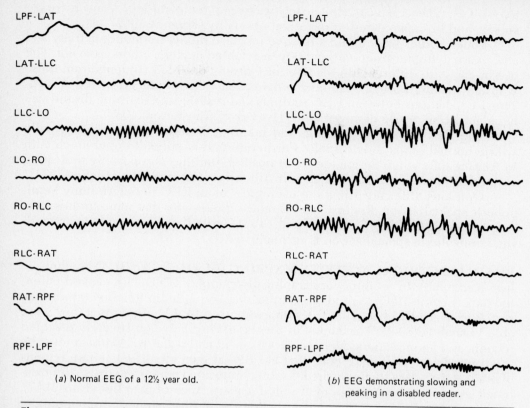

LPF-LAT

LAT-LLC

LLC-LO

LO-RO

RO-RLC

RLC-RAT

RAT-RPF

RPF-LPF

(a) Normal EEG of a 12½ year old.

(b) EEG demonstrating slowing and peaking in a disabled reader.

Figure 9.3.   Examples of normal and abnormal EEGs.   From H. Goldberg, G. Schiffman, and M. Bender, *Dyslexia: Interdisciplinary approaches to reading* (New York: Grune & Stratton, 1983). Reproduced by permission of the authors and publisher.

Wada Test results show that language is centered in the left hemisphere in over 95% of right-handers and about 70% of all others.[3] In only about 2–3% of the general population is language centered in the right hemisphere or in both hemispheres.

Hiscock and Kinsbourne (1982) warn, however, that findings based on pathology, temporary incapacitation of most of one hemisphere (Wada Test), electrical stimulation of cortical regions, and so forth are not generalizable because such invasive techniques are not used to study normal brains.

ELECTROENCEPHALOGRAPHY.   By placing electrodes on various parts of the scalp, the electrical activity of the brain nearest these points can be measured. The resulting electrical bursts and rhythmic waves are amplified and traced on moving graph paper, resulting in an *electroencephalogram* (EEG), as shown in Figure 9.3. Four types of EEG findings indicate abnormality: (1) posi-

---

[3]Benson (1983) states that over 99% of right-handers and about 60% of left-handers have left-hemispheric specializations for language.

tive spikes; (2) excessive occipital slow waves; (3) temporal-lobe sharp waves or spikes; and (4) generalized or diffuse abnormality (Hughes 1982).

Some studies have found a relative increase in low-frequency activity and a decrease in higher-frequency activity in disabled readers; others have not. The use of EEGs to differentiate reading- or learning-disabled students from those who are making normal academic progress has also produced mixed results. Thus, associations between EEG findings and reading and learning disabilities have not been clearly demonstrated (Hiscock & Kinsbourne 1987).

The EEG results of reading- and learning-disabled children are usually within normal limits (Boyle 1982). Furthermore, it is difficult to put much faith in EEG results when the incidence of positive findings (supposedly indicating abnormality) occurs in 20–30% of normally achieving students (Hughes 1971).

Opinions differ regarding the usefulness of an EEG in determining hemispheric specialization. For instance, Hughes (1982) states that some studies indicate its usefulness, but Doehring et al. (1981) write that EEG evidence regarding hemispheric specialization is inconclusive.

BRAIN ELECTRICAL ACTIVITY MAPPING (BEAM).   The BEAM technique uses a computer to combine topographically mapped EEGs with evoked-potential data (Levine 1987) to produce graphic displays of brain function rather than structure. F. Duffy et al. (1980a, 1980b), who used BEAM, report that they were able to achieve 80–90% accuracy in distinguishing between severely disabled readers and good readers. Denckla (1985), who notes that BEAM data must be interpreted with caution, reports that her BEAM data identified certain regions of brain activity that distinguished disabled from good readers, and also differentiated among three subgroups of disabled readers. According to Vellutino (1987), evidence from BEAM studies suggests that the left-hemispheric functioning of severely disabled readers is qualitatively different from that of good readers, especially in areas known to support language functions. BEAM data and data from blood-flow measures reflect brain activity in different ways; thus their combined use may provide further insights into brain function (Coppola 1985).

EVOKED RESPONSE (ER).   *Evoked-response* data are obtained by taking EEG recordings while the person is exposed to auditory or visual stimuli.[4] Evoked-response studies indicate that some disabled readers have abnormal EEG recordings in the left angular gyrus (the cerebral cortex area usually involved when adults lose the ability to read as a result of brain injury or a stroke), while others show greater electrical amplitude in the hemisphere opposite that in which such activity occurs in good readers. However, there are discrepancies in the reported findings (Pirozzolo & Hansch 1982, Harter et al. 1988); the findings have been inconsistent; and none of the ER studies attempted to examine brain activity during the ongoing processing of connected text (only single words were used) (Shucard et al. 1985).

NEUROMETRICS.   *Neurometrics* (John 1981) is a quantitative method that uses EEG recordings and evoked potentials to obtain information about brain

---

[4]See Rugg (1982) for a description of the nature and methodology of evoked responses.

functions. A microprocessor system controls the stimuli and sets up 58 different standardized conditions in John's *Neurometric Test Battery*. The scores of the child being tested are compared against norms based on 600 normally functioning children aged 6–10.

POSITRON EMISSION TOMOGRAPHY (PET).   The PET procedure uses radioisotope labeling and detection to follow ongoing brain processes. Changes in the body's chemistry are recorded (Fincher 1984) and three-dimensional graphics of metabolic activity and blood flow are obtained (Coppola 1985).

CEREBRAL ARTERIOGRAPHY.   Blood flow can be used to study the brain's functions (Lassen, Ingvar & Skinkøj 1978). A small amount of radioactive gas is inhaled, and its flow can be followed through the brain's blood vessels with the use of a radiation detector and a computer.

COMPUTER-ASSISTED TOMOGRAPHY (CAT SCAN).   CAT scans employ multiple x-ray beams and computer processing of the data to produce three-dimensional images of the body (Fincher 1984). CAT scans, as well as *nuclear magnetic resonance*, can provide information about the structure of the brain, but not about its functioning (Coppola 1985). There is no reason to expect that substantial numbers of disabled readers have gross abnormalities of brain structure.

Behavioral and Psychometric Procedures for Determining Laterality and Hemispheric Specialization.

Noninvasive techniques are used to determine laterality and hemispheric specialization. Handedness, eyedness, and footedness are behavioral measures of laterality from which lateralization or hemispheric specialization is inferred. Visual half-field and ear-advantage tests are psychometric or perceptual measures and are thought to be more direct measures of hemispheric specialization than are behavioral measures.

HANDEDNESS.   Assessments of handedness are usually made by asking the child to perform certain tasks (e.g., to use a toy hammer) or by observing which hand is more commonly used in daily activities. The more frequently used hand is said to be the preferred, or dominant, hand. It is not uncommon to find that a child does not always use the same hand. Handedness may be a matter of degree; therefore, the term should be operationally defined in studies involving handedness. Measures of handedness that employ only a single task, or even a few tasks or observations, are not reliable. More reliable estimates can be obtained by administering such tests as the *Harris Tests of Lateral Dominance*.

According to some theories, a pupil who does not show a right-hand preference or superiority is likely to be a disabled reader. The notion is that any deviation from right-handedness indicates that the left hemisphere is not lateralized for language due to damage, dysfunction, or delay; and because language is the basis upon which reading ability is developed, reading problems are likely to occur. A concurrent assumption is that "incomplete hemispheric dominance" (as indicated by mixed-handedness) or the presence of language lateralization in the right hemisphere (as indicated by left-handedness) also will cause reading difficulties. In the former case, the cause is believed to be a lack of sufficient neurological development. In the latter situation, having the language function in a hemisphere that is not well designed to subserve that function is thought to be the cause of reading difficulties.

Mixed-handedness, or *mixed-hand dominance*, usually refers to a lack of consistent preference for either hand. Mixed-handedness is believed by some to indicate a lack of cerebral lateralization, a neurological lag, or incomplete neurological organization; and thus is linked, perhaps causally, to reading disability. Studies of clinic populations have tended to find large numbers of disabled readers with mixed-handedness, often accompanied by directional confusion (A. J. Harris 1957, Zangwill 1962, Ingram 1969). But many children in the general population who do not show a consistent hand preference make normal progress in reading ability.

Language functions are centered in the left hemisphere in approximately 95% of right-handed and 70% of left-handed individuals (Rasmussen & Milner 1975). Given these data, proportionally more left-handers than right-handers should be disabled readers, if the aforementioned theory is correct. However, in the general population there is not a significantly greater proportion of left-handers who are disabled readers (Swanson 1986); nor is there any apparent association between left-handedness and reading ability in general (Obrzut & Boliek 1986; Hiscock & Kinsbourne 1987).

At times, left-handers are overrepresented in clinical populations. There are two possible reasons for such findings (Hiscock & Kinsbourne 1987). First, the samples included a disproportionately high number of children who became left-handed as a consequence of early brain damage. Brain damage that produces shifts from right- to left-handedness can also contribute to cognitive deficits, so both can be consequences of early brain damage. Second, genetic/familial sensitivity seems to predispose some children to cognitive deficits as well as to diseases of the immune system.

The observation that left-handed persons have more immune disorders led Geschwind (1983) to speculate that both the immune disorder and reading disability are the result of a *hormonal imbalance*. He suggests that an elevated quantity of testosterone in the developing fetal brain slows the growth of the left hemisphere and also accounts for the higher incidence of reading disability in males. There is, however, no empirical support for the claim that testosterone selectively inhibits maturation of the left hemisphere (Hiscock & Kinsbourne 1987).

An explanation sometimes offered as a cause of reading disability is the changing of a child's handedness from left to right by the use of coercion, punishment, or ridicule. Supposedly, the way in which the change is made and not the fact of changed handedness produces an emotional block that disrupts learning. There is little data to confirm this hypothesis.

DIRECTIONAL CONFUSION. Some evidence supports a relationship between confused knowledge of left and right and reading disability, at least in young children (A. J. Harris 1957, Benton 1959, Belmont & Birch 1965) or in specific subtypes of reading disability (Mattis 1978). Inability to differentiate right and left should not be regarded as clinically significant before age 8, however (Clark 1979). To assess knowledge of left and right, the brief tests of the *Harris Tests of Lateral Dominance* are sufficient for young children; for older pupils, the more comprehensive tests developed by Benton (1959) are more satisfactory. Directional confusion is most likely to occur in children with mixed-handedness as measured by the *Harris* tests.

When children enter school, directional confusion is typically shown by reversals in reading but may also appear in spelling, writing, or in producing Arabic numbers. Some directional confusion accompanied by reversal tendencies is so common among preschool children, especially with letters such as *b*, *d*, *p*, and *q*,, that it has to be considered a normal characteristic up to age 6 or 7. Only when such confusion persists after considerable instruction in the left-to-right direction in reading and writing does it require careful consideration.

The cause of directional confusion is unknown. At times a physiological basis for it is inferred from a history of difficult birth, delayed or irregular maturation, or a familial growth pattern characterized by a delay in establishing handedness, a strong reversal tendency, some speech difficulty, and early difficulty in learning to read.

EYEDNESS. Whereas each hand is controlled by the contralateral hemisphere, each eye is connected to both hemispheres (see Figure 9.4). This fact does not preclude the measurement of eye preference or eye superiority. But because each eye sends signals to both hemispheres, eye-preference tests (e.g., sighting a gun) and eye-superiority tests (visual acuity, retinal rivalry, controlling eye) are of no use in determining cerebral lateralization or hemispheric specialization. This fact of anatomy also brings into question the practice of patching one eye to establish "eye dominance" on the same side of the body as the dominant hand (see page 315).

Measures of preference and measures of superiority may not yield similar results and the same eye may not be the controlling eye at both near and far points.

FOOTEDNESS. At times, foot preference is used as a measure of laterality. Tasks such as kicking a ball are employed in these tests. The rationale for determining footedness is the same as for handedness but unlike handedness, foot preference is not likely to be subject to use or change by cultural pressures. The limited available findings on footedness approximate those for handedness; and the correlation between footedness and handedness is positive (Hiscock & Kinsbourne 1982).

LATERALITY AS AN INDICATOR OF "HEMISPHERIC DOMINANCE" AND HEMISPHERIC SPECIALIZATION. Each cerebral hemisphere controls motor and sensory functions on the opposite (contralateral) side of the body. This neurological connection apparently led to the once widely held belief that laterality—as demonstrated by hand, eye, ear, or foot preference or superiority—indicated that the hemisphere on the contralateral side was the "dominant hemisphere." Two terms, *hemispheric dominance* and *cerebral dominance*, were commonly used with this theory. Both terms incorrectly imply a general mastery of one hemisphere over the other, with such mastery applying to cognitive as

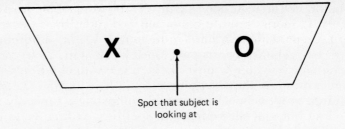

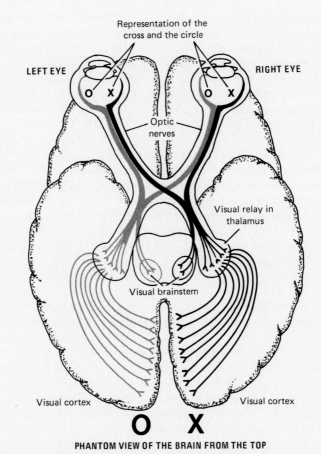

PHANTOM VIEW OF THE BRAIN FROM THE TOP

Figure 9.4. The visual pathway of humans. Images from the right half of the visual field are focused on the left side of each retina. The information from these two left sides travels to the left hemisphere of the brain via a relay in the thalamus. Similarly, images from the left half of the visual field are processed in the right cerebral cortex. The retina also sends axons into the visual area of the brainstem. Adapted from "The Neurophysiology of Binocular Vision" by J. D. Pettigrew. Copyright © 1972 by Scientific American, Inc. All rights reserved.

well as motor and sensory functions. Rather than thinking of one hemisphere as being dominant, it is more accurate to conceive of each hemisphere as being primarily involved in particular cognitive functions (i.e., hemispheric specialization).

At times, the child's handedness was used as the sole criterion for "hemispheric dominance." If one hand was clearly preferred, the hemisphere on the opposite side was judged to be "dominant." Or, two or more sensory or motor functions were used. Thus, if the preferred hand and eye were on the same side of the body, the child was said to be either *right-sided* or *left-sided*. Either finding was considered to indicate "hemispheric dominance," or a high degree of neurological organization (Gaddes 1980). Children with the preferred hand and the preferred eye on opposite sides of the body were considered to have *crossed eye-hand dominance*, and attempts may have been made to establish both preferences on the same side by employing such techniques as patching the "offending" eye. The concept of crossed eye-hand dominance is of little value. About a third of the general population is left-eyed; of those, approximately 90% are right-handed (Hiscock & Kinsbourne 1982). Therefore, many good readers would show crossed eye-hand dominance.

"Hemispheric dominance" was usually measured for two reasons. First, it was believed that language functions were centered in or controlled by the "dominant" hemisphere, and if the left hemisphere was not dominant, the child was likely to have reading problems. Second, "hemispheric dominance" was thought to indicate a high level of neurological development. In both cases, use of laterality as a indicator of "dominance" is open to question.

Apart from the cautions mentioned in the preceding discussion of laterality, using measures of laterality would not greatly increase the odds of choosing the correct hemisphere much over what could be predicted from available data. Language functions are lateralized in the left hemispheres of about 97–98% of the general population (Rasmussen & Milner 1975). Therefore, a prediction that a person's left hemisphere was "dominant" would likely be accurate without measuring laterality. Knowledge of handedness will not improve the prediction of language lateralization until we can distinguish between those left-handers who have left-hemisphere language specialization and those who do not (Hiscock & Kinsbourne 1982).

VISUAL HALF-FIELDS.   Visual information can be presented to only the right or only the left hemisphere because the left half of the visual field of each eye is connected to the visual area in the right hemisphere; the right half-fields with the left hemisphere (see Fig. 9.4). In the *visual half-field* (VHF) technique, the subject is instructed to fixate on a dot on the screen. Digits, which the subject must report, may also be placed near the fixation point.[5] Visual stimuli are then flashed very quickly to the left or right of the fixation point. Because of the way in which the visual pathways are connected to each hemisphere, it is possible to compare the processing of the stimuli by each hemisphere (Beaumont 1982a).

[5]The visual pathways are such that each hemisphere receives sensory input from the opposite visual hemifield, with the exception of the midline vertical meridian, approximately ± ½ degree, which projects bilaterally (Hermann, Sonnabend & Zeevi 1986).

Results of VHF studies are inconsistent, but they generally indicate that words are identified better in the right VHF (left hemisphere); the results are less clear for other verbal stimuli such as letters. With nonverbal stimuli, only faces yield a consistent left-VHF superiority; when geometric forms are used, the evidence is less certain (Beaumont 1982a).

Methodological problems are involved in arranging for presentation of the stimuli at a specific locus in one of the visual fields. Problems in interpretation also exist as a result of what the viewer does during the presentation and because a variety of theories explain what happens after the information is received by the visual cortex (Beaumont 1982a). VHF findings can be, and probably are, influenced by biases that direct the subject's attention to the stimuli (Hiscock & Kinsbourne 1982, Obrzut & Boliek 1986) and by differences in the processing strategies adopted by the subject (Underwood & Root 1986). The need to present the stimuli tachistoscopically limits the number of stimuli that can be shown and, therefore, inferences cannot be drawn regarding information processing beyond the word level.

The low reliabilities (typically 0.50 to 0.65) of VHF and dichotic listening tests limits their utility in determining hemispheric lateralization or specialization (Reynolds 1982). In VHF studies, only about 70% of the individuals who show left-hemisphere specialization for language (as measured by the Wada Test) exhibit a right-VHF (left-hemisphere) advantage (G. Cohen 1982). VHF differences between disabled and good readers have not been found consistently (Doehring et al. 1981). Caution should be exercised in equating anomalous performance on a VHF or dichotic listening test with anomalous hemispheric specialization (Hiscock & Kinsbourne 1987). Therefore, any reported relationship between lateralization or hemisphere specialization, as measured by the VHF procedure, and reading disability must be considered inconclusive.

EAR ADVANTAGE. As shown in Figure 9.5 not all the auditory pathways to the brain are crossed, but the most powerful auditory input goes to the opposite hemisphere (Teyler 1985). Ear advantage is measured by the *dichotic listening technique,* in which different stimuli are presented simultaneously to each ear through stereophonic earphones. The stimuli may be verbal (e.g., phonemes, words) or nonverbal (e.g., musical notes, two-note melodies). Scoring can be based on which stimuli are heard first, the completeness and accuracy of reporting the stimuli presented to each ear, and so forth. The ear with the higher score (ear advantage) is assumed to indicate that the opposite hemisphere is specialized for the class of stimuli used. In general, dichotic listening studies show a right-ear advantage (left-hemisphere lateralization) for verbal material and left-ear advantage for nonverbal stimuli.

Among the perplexing results obtained from dichotic listening studies is that only 65–85% of the subjects show a right-ear advantage (REA) for verbal stimuli (G. Cohen 1982) as compared to the 90–98% revealed by other measures. Dichotic listening studies also suffer from methodological problems (Leong 1980).

The reliability of dichotic listening tests tends to be moderately high, reaching as high as 0.70. But about 30% of the subjects reverse their ear advantage from one testing to the next. The concurrent validity of dichotic listening

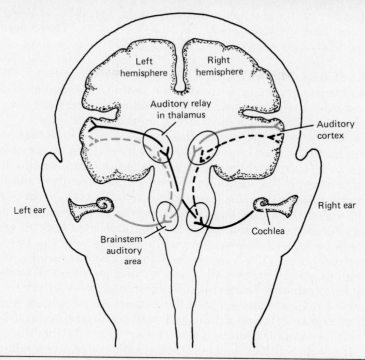

Figure 9.5.   Auditory pathways in the brain. All of these pathways are not crossed (notice dashed lines), but the most powerful auditory input goes to the opposite hemisphere, that is, right ear to left hemisphere. Adapted from "The Asymmetry of the Human Brain" by D. Kimura. Copyright © 1973 by Scientific American, Inc. All rights reserved. Taken from T. Teyler, *A primer of psychobiology: brain and behavior* (San Francisco: W. H. Freeman, 1975). Used by permission of the author and publisher.

tests is not impressive, and their scores are susceptible to a number of influences extraneous to hemispheric lateralization (Hiscock & Kinsbourne 1987).

Disabled readers are reported not to show the usual REA effect for verbal stimuli (Pirozzolo & Hansch 1982). This fact has led to the inference that they lack left-hemispheric specialization for language. There is, however, little support for the hypothesis that the superiority of each ear for verbal and nonverbal stimuli reflects the functional specialization of the contralateral hemisphere (Obrzut & Boliek 1986). In fact, most disabled readers probably have left-hemisphere language lateralization (see page 315). V. Mann (1986) believes that most of the reported ear-advantage differences between good and disabled readers may reflect the short-term memory problems of disabled readers, because such good/poor reader differences tend to occur only on dichotic listening tasks that stress STM.

Bakker (1982) and his associates (Bakker, Teunisson & Bosch 1976) speculate that the ear asymmetry/reading ability relationship changes with the level of reading ability. They hypothesize that lack of a REA is not particularly important during the initial stage of reading acquisition because the right hemisphere can handle word recognition. At the later stages of reading development, when linguistic processing becomes the more important variable, a REA/left-hemi-sphere-language-lateralization would be more necessary. There is no satisfactory empirical basis for such a claim (Hiscock & Kinsbourne 1982).

OTHER MEASURES OF LATERALIZATION.   Silver and Hagin (1982) claim that the *arm-extension text* can be used to determine if hemispheric dominance has been established. The arm-extension procedure suffers from the same limitations as does handedness as a measure of lateralization.

Hiscock and Kinsbourne (1982) briefly describe a *dual-task measure* of functional lateralization that requires the child to perform motor tasks with either the right or left hand while reading. The assumption on which dual-task methodology is based is that individuals usually cannot perform simultaneously two tasks programmed in the same hemisphere as well as they can perform each task by itself or as well as they can perform two tasks programmed in different hemispheres. For instance, concurrent reading and right-hand finger tapping should be more disruptive than reading while tapping with the left hand. Stellern, Collins, and Bayne (1987) report finding good/poor reader differences in functional lateralization but, overall, studies using measures of *verbal-manual time sharing* have produced mixed results (Obrzut & Boliek 1986).

Most recent reviewers have noted the inconclusive findings regarding the relationship of cerebral lateralization and reading disability, and have questioned the role of lateralization as an important factor in reading or learning disabilities. Hiscock and Kinsbourne (1982) believe that even when students are classified into more homogeneous subgroups, it remains unclear how the characteristics of any subgroup may be related to cerebral lateralization. The degree of reading disability may be a variable contributing to the inconclusive findings. For example, Garren (1980) found that a significant relationship between reading disability and lateralization did not occur unless the subjects were 18 months or more below their expected reading level.

DEGREE OF LATERALIZATION.   There is some belief that at least some disabled readers can be distinguished from good readers by the degree to which the groups differ in functional, usually language, lateralization. Because the degree of lateralization is almost always measured by visual half-field or dichotic listening tests, such beliefs are open to serious question. VHF and dichotic listening tests are not particularly reliable measures of hemispheric specialization, and certainly lack the sensitivity needed to differentiate among degrees of specialization (Shucard et al. 1985).

LATERALITY, HEMISPHERIC SPECIALIZATION, AND READING DISABILITY.   A thorough presentation of the various viewpoints regarding the relationship of laterality and hemispheric specialization to reading disability cannot be done in a few pages. Those interested in obtaining a better understanding of these theories should read the original sources cited here and in the reviews by Leong (1980) and Hiscock and Kinsbourne (1982, 1987). A number of these theories are summarized below in order to indicate their diversity. The summaries are followed by a classification framework into which most of the hypotheses could be categorized.

Dearborn (1933) emphasizes a motor conflict when he indicates that, when writing, humans tend to pivot at the elbow and find it easier to move outward from the middle of the body than across its midline. Dearborn believes that when a person is not definitely right- or left-sided (i.e., has not achieved lateral dominance), competing motor tendencies develop. These, in turn, produce inconsistent eye movements and confused visual perception, which results in reading difficulties.

Orton (1937) proposes that visual stimuli are received simultaneously by both hemispheres and that each receives a memory trace (*engram*), one being the mirror image of the other. If the left hemisphere is clearly dominant, the memory trace in the nondominant right hemisphere is suppressed, and normal perception results. But if hemispheric dominance is incomplete or inconsistent, the right hemisphere (the one containing the mirror image) could at times gain control of the output channel and thus cause the spatially reversed engrams to be expressed as reversals. Orton states that poorly established or mixed handedness or -eyedness reflects a lack of "lateral dominance."

Zangwill (1962) theorizes that children who lack strong and consistent "lateral dominance" may be particularly vulnerable to stress. Similarly, Leong (1980) notes that poorly established laterality patterns in combination with other factors may make such pupils more vulnerable to learning disorders.

Yeni-Komshian, Isenberg, and Goldberg (1975) conclude that reading disability is related to a right-hemisphere processing dysfunction or to impaired transmission of information from the right to the left hemisphere.

Witelson (1977) claims that disabled readers have normal left-hemisphere linguistic functions but that spatial functions (normally right-hemisphere functions) are represented in both hemispheres. She argues that this bilateral representation of spatial functions interferes with the left hemisphere's ability to carry out its language functions. She also thinks that location of spatial functions in both hemispheres causes disabled readers to read with a predominantly spatial-holistic strategy and to neglect a phonetic-sequential strategy.

Masland (1981) postulates that reading disability is caused by a left-hemisphere dysfunction in which the overdevelopment of the right hemisphere impedes the functional development of the left hemisphere. According to Kershner (1983), a learning disability appears to involve reduced left-hemisphere processing capacity, severe right-hemisphere-directed attentional disorders, and the inability to coordinate the simultaneous processing of linguistic information between the hemispheres.

Bakker (1982) proposes two hemispheric-related etiologies of reading disability. L-type disabled readers are theorized to have an overdeveloped, language-mediating left hemisphere that causes them to rely on left-hemisphere processing too early in their reading development and to rely too heavily on such strategies in their later school years. L-type disabled readers, those who show a right-ear advantage, make a relatively high proportion of word-recognition errors (e.g., omissions, additions) and have fast, but inaccurate, word recognition. P-type disabled readers are thought to be overly sensitive to the perceptual aspect of the text and to continue to rely on strategies generated by the right hemisphere, often failing to adopt left-hemisphere strategies (which should be developed at about Grade 3). P-types, those who show a left-ear advantage, tend to have slow, but accurate, word recognition and make a high proportion of time-consuming "errors" such as repetitions (Bakker & Vinke 1985).

Satz et al. (1985) suggest that lesions in the peri-Sylvan and/or peri-Rolandic regions of the left hemisphere, which occur before age 6, lead to the development of speech and language functions in the right hemisphere, or in both hemispheres.

Hiscock and Kinsburne (1982, 1987) identify four classes of hemispheric-related models of reading disability.

1. Anomalous hemisphere models presuppose that an otherwise normal processor may perform inadequately if it is located in the wrong hemisphere (e.g., if language functions are centered in the right, rather than the left, hemisphere), or if a processor must share its territory with another processor (e.g., if the same function is duplicated in both hemispheres or if hemispheric specialization is incomplete). So many different anomalies are possible that at least one such model could be contrived, post hoc, to "explain" almost any data obtained (Hiscock & Kinsbourne 1987).

2. Unilateral-deficit models suggest that reading disability is due to a deficit in one hemisphere. For instance, one theory holds that although the left hemisphere participates sufficiently in reading, the right hemisphere is somehow deficient (Keefe & Swinney 1979). Such theories have received little research support (Pirozzolo & Rayner 1979).

3. Callosal models hold that there is a deficit in the corpus callosum, resulting in too little or too much information being transferred between the hemispheres, distortion of information, or transmission of information to the wrong hemisphere. Obrzut and Boliek (1987) contend that a deficient callosal function interferes with the ability to use simultaneous processing of verbal information. Little evidence supports callosal-deficit theories (Levine 1987).

4. Output-completion models include ideas about independent processing in the left and right hemispheres, quantitative or qualitative differences between the hemispheres in information processing, or the tendency of one hemisphere to suppress the activity of the other or to deny the other hemisphere access to output mechanisms.

To the foregoing list may be added theories involving maturational lag in hemispheric development (see pages 325–326).

GENDER, READING DISABILITY, AND CEREBRAL LATERALIZATION. One theory holds that differences in hemispheric lateralization may account for the larger number of males who are reading disabled. According to Bakker, Teunissen, and Bosch (1976), girls pass through the successive laterality-reading stages faster than boys. As a consequence, boys run the risk of getting stuck in the early reading strategies generated by the right hemisphere. (See page 319.)

Hier (1979) states that gender differences in hemispheric specialization for verbal and spatial processing underlie the prevalence of reading disability in boys. Males show a strong left-hemisphere specialization for verbal processing, whereas females show greater bihemispheric participation in both verbal and spatial processing.

Masland (1981) suggests that certain male characteristics might predispose them more than females to reading disability: (1) less well developed left-hemisphere language functions; (2) greater specialization of spatial skills in the right hemisphere; and (3) an earlier start in lateralization of functions but, in general, a slower maturation of them. Hormonal imbalance theories may be added to this list (see page 312).

Little firm evidence supports any of the foregoing hypotheses.

REMEDIAL PROCEDURES BASED ON LATERAL DOMINANCE. Delacato (1966) theorizes that poor intellectual and educational development results from a failure to achieve neurological integration at a subcortical level of the brain. He advocates a treatment program that emphasizes activities such as sleeping in a particular position, creeping, and crawling. For children who have achieved subcortical integration, he attributes reading disability to a lack of "clear and consistent cerebral dominance," usually shown by crossed eye-hand dominance. For them he recommends treatment procedures to compel the child to rely on the eye on the same side as the dominant hand by occluding the other eye (see page 315), eliminating music, and so forth. Apart from the fact that his theoretical basis is open to serious question, independent research evidence does not support the Doman-Delacato treatment (Robbins 1966). In fact, "without exception, the empirical studies cited by Delacato as a 'scientific appraisal' of his theories of neurological organization are shown to be of dubious value" (Glass & Robbins 1967). Eight major medical and health organizations issued a joint report that describes the theory underlying the approach as being without merit and charges Delacato and Doman with making undocumented claims of cures (*New York Times* 1968). Reading specialists can safely ignore the Doman-Delacato approach (L. Silver 1987).

Van den Honert (1977) reports a procedure based on the assumption that the disabled reader's left hemisphere has insufficient dominance over the right hemisphere. Using stereophonic earphones, she directed reading instruction to the right ear (left hemisphere) and popular music to the left ear in order to keep the right hemisphere busy and prevent it from interfering with the left hemisphere's control of reading. A blackened lens was used to block out the vision of the left eye. She reports a great improvement in her pupils' rate of learning to read, although the instructional procedure (intensive phonics) was the same as before. In response to an inquiry from this book's senior author, Van den Honert wrote: "If I use either the glasses alone or the auditory setup alone, nothing much happens. It is only when I do both over a period of time that I begin to get dramatic results." To the best of our knowledge, nothing concerning this technique has appeared in the literature since 1977.

NEUROLOGICAL DAMAGE, DEFICITS, ANOMALIES, AND DELAYS

Various hypotheses attempt to relate brain deficits to reading disability; the following discussion illustrates some of them. Geschwind's (1965) *disconnection theory* proposes that a lesion within the corpus callosum disconnects the right visual cortex region from the left angular gyrus. Jorm (1979) states that severe reading disability is the result of genetically based dysfunction of the inferior parietal lobe, the region believed important for short-term memory and reading. Another hypothesis (Denckla 1983) suggests that a "pure dyslexic, with no deficit in spoken language," appears to have verbal learning deficits associated with a left-frontal-lobe anomaly. And Tarnopol and Tarnopol (1979) argue, rather unconvincingly, that learning to read may be adversely influenced by dysfunction in the sensorimotor areas of the brain. Other theories contend that reading disability is caused by delayed development of the angular gyrus. All these hypotheses lack conclusive empirical evidence.

Medical evidence, primarily from postmortem examinations, supports neuroanatomical bases for various forms of *alexia* (loss of already acquired reading ability). These have been well described by Benson (1981, 1983). Basically, the findings indicate that damage to particular areas of the brain results in the predictable loss of certain language, cognitive, and motor functions in particular combinations (e.g., alexia without agraphia). Such findings have led some authorities to infer that an inability to acquire reading ability must be due to similar deficits or to subtle brain damage in the language areas.

Rare cases of congenital and acquired brain deficits of a specialized kind have also been diagnosed in living persons. For example, skull x-rays revealed a large undeveloped area in one part of the brain (*porencephaly*) of a dull-normal teenage nonreader who had been referred to one of the authors.

There are structural differences in comparable areas of the left and right hemispheres of normal brains. Variations from such normal asymmetries have been found in the brains of some disabled readers. For example, 10 of the 24 disabled readers studied by Hier et al. (1978) exhibited wider right than left parieto-occipital regions (the reverse of what is normally found); and in two cases, there were no differences in the widths of these areas. However, the reversed structural pattern occurs in 10–12% of the general population, and Hier's findings have not been confirmed by other investigators (Shaywitz & Waxman 1987).

Postmortem examinations of brains of five dyslexics (all males aged 12–36, two of whom were left-handers, but all five were from families with strong histories of left-handedness) by Galaburda (1985) revealed two types of structural anomalies. First, there was a deviation from the standard asymmetrical pattern for the language areas. Instead of the usual larger language area in the left hemisphere, the size of the temporal language areas was the same in both hemispheres. Second, there were distinct abnormalities in the ways in which the cells were arranged (*disordered cellular architecture*).

Some form of cerebral damage or abnormality may be the cause of reading disability in some children, and the number of such children has probably increased over the years. Improved medical knowledge and care have greatly increased the number of children who survive brain injury at birth or later brain tissue damage from high-fever diseases such as encephalitis. There are many varieties of brain damage, and its functional consequences can range from such observable difficulties as cerebral palsy, complete or partial paralysis, or profound mental deficiency to a lack of any discernible abnormality. Pirozzolo et al. (1981) review some of the basic causes of cerebral dysfunction in children and their consequences.

In spite of the probability that more children than formerly may now have neurological impairments, there is little evidence that such impairments are a major cause of reading disability (Hiscock & Kinsbourne 1987). Actual injury in particular areas of the cortex occurs in only a few cases (Vernon 1971), and cerebral lesions and firm neurological signs are not apparent in most reading or learning disabled pupils (Fletcher 1981, Coles 1987).

The typical neurological examination does not reveal much about the neurological basis of higher mental processes. Nevertheless, at times a child should be referred to a pediatric neurologist. Symptoms that suggest the need for such a referral include a history of difficult birth as indicated by prolonged labor, instrument delivery, marked head deformity, difficulty in starting to breathe, cyanosis, difficulty sucking or swallowing, and so on; prematurity or low birth weight; poor equilibrium and general awkwardness; delayed speech development in the presence of otherwise normal mental ability; a history of convulsive seizures or lapses of consciousness; and extreme restlessness or distractability. *Petit mal*, a mild form of epilepsy, may not be detected because the overt signs are subtle (unconsciousness is momentary and there are no convulsions).

One neurological test often mentioned in the literature is *finger localization*, the ability to detect which finger has been touched when the examinee cannot see the touching taking place. In adults, failure in finger localization tests is a symptom of Gerstmann's syndrome, which is thought to be indicative of neurological dysfunctioning. In children, such failure has been found to be characteristic of disabled readers with low performance IQs (Kinsbourne & Warrington 1966). Satz et al. (1978) reports that kindergarten finger localization scores (based partly on number knowledge) were the best predictors (in their battery) of reading disability in Grades 2–5. Fletcher et al. (1982), however, report that finger localization does not have any specific relationship to reading achievement.

Minimal Brain Dysfunction and Soft Signs

Minimal brain dysfunction (MBD), also known as *minimal brain damage*, is a suspected neurological problem whose existence cannot be proven by existing medical tests. The two main concepts of MBD suggest that it is (1) a lesser variant of brain damage or (2) the result of a genetically determined disorder rather than a brain injury (Rutter 1982). Diagnoses of MBD are based on *soft signs*, which are physical characteristics and responses considered to be developmentally abnormal (that is, to be present beyond the ages at which they generally disappear). Such soft signs include fine and gross deficiencies in motor coordination, defective or delayed speech, short attention span, poor balance, gait disturbance, inadequate muscle tone, and general awkwardness. Refer to Levine (1987) for more complete discussions of assessing and interpreting soft signs. Children with *Strauss syndrome*, which is thought to indicate MBD, are described as being hyperactive, impulsive, distractable, emotionally changeable, perseverative (i.e., the child perseverates), and perceptually disordered.

According to Gaddes (1985), 2% of the school population have hard signs and another 5% have soft signs of neurological impairment. These estimates seem high to us. Spreen (1982), among others, argues that soft signs are of diagnostic significance, but research has not supported their use as indicators of neurological dysfunctioning (Kavale & Forness 1985b). Soft neurological signs are present in 10% of normallly developing children (Dulcan 1986), and their presence is not uncommon in children under age 7. Definitions of MBD are more speculative than definitive, and learning disabled students cannot be reliably distinguished from normally achieving pupils on the basis of soft signs (Kavale & Forness 1985b).

Some clinical and school psychologists and most neuropsychologists interpret certain kinds of performance on various psychological tests as indicating brain damage or dysfunction (*organicity*). Such soft signs should always be regarded as suggestive, not conclusive. Even when evidence pointing to neurological dysfunctioning is strong, psychological testing cannot as yet distinguish accurately between MBD and delayed or irregular neurological development. Some physicians suggest that the paradoxical effect of a stimulant drug on a hyperactive child demonstrates a neurological etiology; a contention not fully supported by the evidence (Dulcan 1986). Similarly, many child neurologists regard a language or learning disorder to be a soft sign of CNS impairment (Shprintzen & Goldberg 1986).

Neuropsychological Anomalies

The *neuropsychological model* contends that all behavior is mediated by the CNS and its integrated and supporting subsystems, and that the relationship between brain functioning and behavior is causal. It is believed that when the physiological system does not function properly, disruptions in perception, cognition, and motor responses can occur (Obrzut & Hynd 1987). The theoretical basis of neuropsychology appears to stem from Luria (1973). Basically, Luria believes that reading ability is dependent on a complicated "functionalization of cooperating zones of the cerebral cortex and subcortical structures. Accordingly, a deficit in any one, or several, of these zones may impede learning and/ or performance of fluent reading behavior" (Lyon 1983, p. 104).

Neuropsychologists use traditional psychometric tests, interviews, and observations. The typical neuropsychological battery contains tests of gross and fine motor coordination, auditory and visual perception and sequencing, and visual-motor coordination (Morrison & Hinshaw 1988). According to Obrzut and Hynd (1987), such tests do not attempt to determine where a particular psychological function is located in the brain, but to determine which group of brain zones working in concert are responsible for mediating behavior, as well as the unique contribution made by each zone. Obrzut and Hynd also indicate that the relationships between neurological and cognition functions are still not understood well enough to provide a definitive assessment of learning deficits or to prescribe a remedial program. However, the neuropsychological literature suggests that at least some neuropsychologists think that the field has progressed far beyond this point. Neuropsychologists also appear prone to diagnosing neurological dysfunctions on the basis of psychological test performance.

Doehring et al. (1981) found low correlations (none exceeding 0.41) between 37 neuropsychological tests and reading test scores. Even lower and less significant correlations were found between the neuropsychological tests and reading-related skills. Reynolds (1982) correctly cautions against drawing unwarranted conclusions from neuropsychological tests. Schwartz (1984) goes even further in his criticism. He considers naive the assumption that there are cortical centers for every language and reading function.

Hynd and Hynd (1984) present a *neurolinguistic model of reading* which describes the major cortical regions thought to be involved in normal reading. For example, they believe that: (1) The mechanisms for making symbol-sound associations are in the angular gyrus, (2) word identification and reading comprehension take place in Wernicke's area; and (3) oral reading results from participation by Broca's area. Hynd and Hynd clearly attribute severe reading disability to neurological causes, and imply that each specific reading problem is due to a lesion or malfunction in a particular cortical zone.

In a severe criticism of the Hynd and Hynd article, Dorman (1985) makes the following points: (1) The definition of dyslexia cited by Hynd and Hynd is mix of objective diagnostic criteria with a hypothetical etiological formulation. This definition prompted Hynd and Hynd to insist on a diagnosis of the hypothetical etiology where there are no objective criteria for such a diagnosis; (2) although there is general agreement, at least among neurologists, that there must be something wrong with the brains of extremely poor readers, there is no agreement as to what that something is; (3) the authors did not review all the evidence for or against a neurological basis for severe reading disorders; and (4) it is not at all clear that traumatically injured adults are the appropriate examples when searching for an analogue for childhood reading disorders. Most disabled readers do not have histories indicative of any postnatal trauma. Neither is there any reason to believe that the causes of aphasia also prevent a child from acquiring reading skills for the first time.

Delayed and Irregular Neurological Development

There is substantial medical opinion to the effect that severe reading disability is often the result of some delay in the maturing of the central nervous system—slight enough to allow the development of normal general intelligence, but severe enough to slow the development of certain cerebral areas that are critical for acquiring reading ability. Developmental lag theories have been expressed by Bender (1957), Rabinovitch (1962), and Bakker (1982), among others. Maturational lags would not necessarily all be alike, so the concept allows for more than one pattern of deficits.

Satz et al. (1978) interpret the results of their longitudinal studies as showing that severe reading disabilities are related to a lag in brain maturation that differentially delays those skills that normally develop during a certain period. The skills in which disabled readers were deficient changed as the children got older. Perceptual skills tended to be delayed in young reading disabled pupils. As the disabled readers got older, their perceptual skills developed, but they were likely to show lags in linguistic and conceptual skills.

The developmental lag theory predicts that, as disabled readers reach about age 10, some or all of the previously lagging neurological areas will have developed sufficiently to allow improved reading ability. Studies have supported not this prediction (Miles & Haslum 1986) but rather a permanent-deficit hypothesis. For example, Rourke and Orr (1977) found that only about one-quarter of the cases they studied showed enough improvement over 4 years to be considered as having had delayed maturation. Satz et al.'s (1978) data do not support the developmental lag position because less than 6% of their subjects attained age-appropriate reading achievement after 6 years of school (Fletcher & Satz 1980).

There are at least two possible reasons for such findings.

First, a distinction was not made between severe and mild cases of reading disability. Stanovich, Nathan, and Vala-Rossi (1986), who distinguish between "garden-variety poor readers" and severely disabled readers, state that the vast majority of school-labeled poor readers are characterized by a generalized developmental delay, whereas the rarer, severely disabled readers have cognitive skill deficits that present long-term difficulties. Results of a study by Stanovich, Nathan, and Zolman (1988) support the developmental lag theory for "garden-variety poor readers" whose rapid growth in reading ability from the third to the fifth grade was accompanied by superior growth in word recognition.

Second, if we assume that there are subtypes of reading disability, it seems probable that some disabled readers have maturational lags and others have permanent deficits. As yet, we are unable to distinguish prior to remediation, the "late bloomers" from those with more lasting handicaps.

Vestibular Disorders

The vestibular system, which is bilateral, performs three major functions: control of balance and posture, control of eye movements, and conscious perception of space. Balance and posture are dependent on sensory impressions from the vestibular canals of the inner ear and from muscles in the neck, coordinated by the cerebellum and other brain centers below the level of the cerebral cortex. When the automatic, reflex control of balance is deficient, eye movements are affected. According to de Quiros and Schrager (1978), vestibular dysfunction disrupts this automatic control and creates a need for conscious control. The requirement of conscious effort for postural control and balance puts an added burden on the cerebral cortex thereby interfering with its efficiency in processing language and thought. De Quiros (1976) suggests that evidence of a vestibular disorder in newborns is predictive of a learning disability and that the disability could be prevented through specialized therapy.

Frank and Levinson (1975–1976) mainly used a "blurring speed" test to diagnose a condition they labeled *dysmetric dyslexia with dyspraxia*, which they claim is caused by a cerebellar-vestibular dysfunction. This condition is said to exist when moving targets against a fixed background are seen as blurring at a comparatively low speed. Frank and Levinson report finding this condition in 97% of 250 consecutively referred cases of dyslexia. However, because the "blurring speed" test is a visual stimulation test, rather than a vestibular test, it cannot indicate vestibular dysfunction (L. B. Silver 1987). In a later paper, Frank and Levinson (1976) report that some cases of dysmetric dyslexia are good readers, and that the condition tends to be outgrown during preadolescence.

Frank and Levinson (1977) also state that dysmetric dyslexia can be treated with anti-motion-sickness medication, but recent studies of vestibular disorders have not supported the use of such drugs (Helveston 1987). These authors have yet to issue detailed statistical data to substantiate their claims; Levinson's (1980) book provides no new useful information. Other studies report negative or equivocal results regarding the role of vestibular disorders in dyslexics (L. B. Silver 1987).

Ayres' (1978) *sensory-integration theory* holds that reading and learning disabilities result from the failure to integrate proprioceptive, kinesthetic, visual, and auditory information at the brain-stem level. Ayres attributes such a failure to vestibular dysfunctioning. She devised a battery of tests to identify such problems and a treatment program to remedy them through stimulation of the vestibular and positional awareness systems. *Nystagmus* (an involuntary oscillation of the eyes, which is characterized by alternating slow and rapid ocular movements) is considered to be the most objective sign of a vestibular dysfunction.[6] However, Ayres' *Southern California Postrotary Nystagmus Test* is not a valid measure of vestibular function (L. B. Silver 1987). No firm evidence supports Ayres' theory (Vellutino 1983) and independent confirmation that her treatment results in improved reading ability is lacking (L. B. Silver 1987). Helveston (1987) reports that pupils with nystagmus or gross extraocular-movement disorders display normal reading achievement. B. Brown et al. (1985) did not find any significant differences between reading disabled and normally achieving 10- to 12-year-olds in their performance on the *Romberg Test*, a crude, but widely used, clinical measure of vestibular and cerebellar function and postural compensation. After reviewing the 12 studies conducted prior to her own, Polatajko (1985) concludes that there is inadequate information to reach any conclusions about either the presence of abnormal vestibular function in learning disabled children or the role of vestibular disorders in academic learning. Her own study reveals that: (1) there were no significant differences between normal and LD children either in the intensity of vestibular responsivity or the incidence of vestibular dysfunction; (2) children categorized as having low, average, or high vestibular responsivity did not differ in word recognition or reading comprehension; and (3) there were no significant correlations between measures of academic performance and vestibular function. In short, there was no support for either the idea that vestibular function is related to academic performance or for vestibular-dysfunction theories.

The presence of primitive reflexes is also considered by some to be a sign of neurological impairment. *Primitive reflexes,* such as an asymmetrical tonic neck response, are predominantly subcortical. Their presence after about age 1 is often interpreted as an indication that higher-level cortical development has not progressed normally. As primitive reflexes become less salient during the course of normal development, equilibrium reactions emerge and provide the body with an adaptive response to changes in the center of gravity. Compared to the control group, disabled readers demonstrated more frequent primitive reflexes and fewer instances of adaptive equilibrium reactions (Morrison, Hinshaw & Carte 1985).

Reading clinicians should rely on neurologists to interpret the meaning of deviations in posture, balance, oculomotor reflexes, and primitive reflexes.

Heredity

Hinshelwood (1917) and Critchley (1981) believe strongly that severe reading disability is inherited—a belief that is widely held within the medical commu-

---

[6]Refer to Polatajko (1985) for a more complete discussion of this topic.

nity. Other authors suggest that there is a genetic basis for only one type of reading disability (Bannatyne 1971) or for a right-hemisphere asymmetry that causes reading disability (H. Gordon 1983).

In looking at the issue, one must distinguish between inheritability and familial incidence. There is evidence that reading disability tends to run in certain families (Walker & Cole 1965, DeFries 1985) and that it does not (de Hirsch, Jansky & Langford 1966; Clark 1970). These conflicting results may be due to various reasons, including the possibility that the incidence of affected families varied in the populations studied and that, in some samples, the incidence was too small to be statistically significant. Reading disabled fathers are more likely than reading disabled mothers to have a reading disabled child (DeFries 1985). However, reading disabled parents have more normally achieving than reading disabled children (Loehlin, Willerman & Horn 1988).

Although familial incidence argues for a genetic determination, it does not provide sufficient evidence (DeFries 1985). Familial cultural transmission remains a possibility (Benton 1978) as do other environmental factors.

Because familial similarity may also be attributed to a shared environment, twin studies can provide better evidence for assessing genetic contributions to reading disability (Decker & Bender 1988). Five studies found higher concordance rates for reading disability (that is, both twins either were or were not reading disabled) in identical twins, who share a common set of genes, than in fraternal twins, who, on average, share only 50% of the same genes. A sixth study (Stevenson et al. 1987) reveals that at age 13, genetic factors play only a moderate role in reading backwardness (IQ was not considered) and reading retardation (IQ was considered), but do exert a strong influence on spelling ability. Overall, these findings suggest a possible heredity component in reading disability. However, in some sets of identical twins, only one was reading disabled. This reveals the existence of important nonfamilial, environmental factors in addition to genetic factors in the causation of reading disability (E. L. Harris 1986). Perhaps as Young and Tyre (1983) comment, some children inherit a predisposition toward reading difficulties, and their environment does the rest.

There is little evidence of sex-linked inheritance (Pennington & Smith 1983), although there is some evidence for autosomal[7] recessive inheritance in the families of reading disabled girls (DeFries 1985). Despite the fact that over three times as many boys as girls were identified as being reading disabled in the Colorado Reading Project (DeFries 1985), on average, reading disabled boys were impaired no more nor less than reading disabled girls.

Most children with sex-chromosome abnormalities have learning disorders (B. Bender et al. 1986). Eleven of 14 boys with an extra X chromosome, who were studied by Decker and Bender (1988), were reading disabled, but there was considerable variability in the severity of their reading disabilities. Hier, Atkins and Perlo's (1980) failure to detect any sex-chromosome abnormalities in 20 reading disabled, male adults may simply reflect the rarity of such genetic disorders in the reading disabled population.

One study (S. D. Smith et al. 1983) suggests that a gene on chromosome 15 plays a major causal role in one form of reading disability. However, other at-

---

[7]An *autosome* is a chromosome that is not sex-linked.

tempts to fit single-gene models of inheritance to the data have yielded contradictory results (Decker & Vandenberg 1985). Even if the presence of a "reading disability gene" on chromosome 15 is confirmed, it would likely account for only a small percentage of disabled readers.

The evidence suggests that reading disability may be the additive result of many genes acting together. It is likely that there is more than one type of genetically based reading disability, and that multiple genetic and environmental factors interact to produce a continuum of overlapping subtypes that are behaviorally indistinguishable (Decker & Bender 1988).

Even if there were a substantial inherited component in reading disability, it is not clear that genetic influences are related to a specific type of reading disability (Decker & Vandenberg 1985).

Perinatal Complications and Stress

Since Kawi and Pasamanick (1958) first reported that adverse prenatal conditions and prematurity had been relatively more common among disabled readers than among good readers, many other studies have examined the relationship between reading disability and the conditions before, during, and soon after birth. Reading difficulties are associated with problems during pregnancy such as pre-eclampsia, hypertension, bleeding, and maternal ingestion of alcohol, drugs, or toxins; forced labor and traumatic delivery; prematurity; smallness for gestational age; and low birth weight (Levine 1987). Such factors are likely to influence reading ability years later only to the extent that they cause neurological damage (Balow, Rubin & Rosen 1975–1976). For example, because the brain is very sensitive to *anoxia* (the lack or reduction of oxygen), any condition that causes anoxia in the fetus or newborn could cause brain damage. The ultimate effects of perinatal stress can be mediated by the child's environment, with low-SES children most likely to have subsequent developmental and educational problems as a result of perinatal complications (Levine 1987). Some children who have histories of perinatal stress do not become disabled readers and some disabled readers had no known perinatal complications. All that can be said with some degree of certainty is that perinatal complications probably result in some children having reading difficulties (Young & Tyre 1983).

Hyperactivity

Estimates of hyperactivity in school-aged children range from 3–15%, with four to eight times as many boys as girls being labeled hyperactive (Cotugno 1987). This wide discrepancy in estimated incidence is largely due to problems in defining and identifying hyperactivity. A study by Holborow, Berry, and Elkins (1984) illustrates the identification problem. The identification rates obtained from three different rating scales ranged from 6–12%, but only about 3% of 1,908 elementary-school children were rated as hyperactive by all three scales.

A variety of definitions exist, but even the American Psychiatric Association's definition for *attention-deficit disorder (ADD) with hyperactivity* (there is also one "without hyperactivity") has not been completely accepted within that profession (Prior & Sanson 1986). The primary symptoms used to identify *hyper-*

activity (hyperkinesis, ADD with hyperactivity) are overactivity, inability to focus or sustain attention, impulsivity, and distractability. Use of these general categories of behavior to discriminate hyperactive from nonhyperactive children is open to question (Schworm & Birnbaum 1989). Other symptoms may be acquired (e.g., irritability) as a result of the social or familial milieu in which the child is raised. Any of these symptomatic behaviors could interfere with the acquisition of reading ability. Other characteristics, such as perseveration, could make the child's behavior unacceptable to the teacher (Simms 1985). In either case, the cause would be indirect.

One problem with identification is that such symptoms are also manifestations of other childhood conditions (e.g., depression or anxiety). Some professionals differentiate between *impulsivity,* which is a kind of "driven" behavior that is internally determined and does not seem to be triggered by particular stimuli, and the kind of hyperactivity and distractability that involves excessive responses to stimuli most children can ignore. The former corresponds to Keogh's Type I (see the following) and is the more serious.

Most of the scales used to determine hyperactivity have moderate reliability and validity, but are subject to rater bias; often contain vague, leading questions; and primarily cover negative symptoms (Prout & Ingram 1982). Questionnaire rating scales measure adults' perceptions of a child's behavior, not some absolute truth (Dulcan 1986).

Hyperactivity appears to be a relative condition—what is considered excessive activity by some is thought to be within normal limits by others. Furthermore, hyperactivity is often situational, and the few studies that have used direct measures of overt behaviors have not found significant differences between children who have and have not been labeled hyperactive (Simms 1985). The term is best reserved for that small percentage of children whose activity levels are excessive across all settings and situations (Cotugno 1987).

Among the etiologies postulated for hyperactivity are minimal brain damage, birth complications, biochemical abnormalities, and genetic factors. However, there is no solid evidence that any of these factors accounts for more than a small percentage of the cases (Prior & Sanson 1986), nor does any substantial evidence support the view that hyperactivity is caused by food allergies or fluorescent lighting. Lead toxicity is not a likely cause, but the possibility should be considered, especially if there is a history of *pica* (a craving for unnatural food such as paint) or evidence of a significant environmental exposure to lead (L. B. Silver 1987).

Keogh (1971) proposes three main types of hyperactivity: (1) an accompaniment of cerebral dysfunction; (2) excessive activity that disrupts attention and interferes with learning, without any evidence of cerebral dysfunction; and (3) impulsiveness in decision making, similar to Kagan's (1965) impulsivity dimension in cognitive style. Keogh proposes that the first type be treated by medication; the other two, by behavior management. A study by Keogh and Glover (1980) found differential effects of medication, behavior modification, and cognitive control training on the behavior of hyperactive children.

The extensive body of literature on hyperactivity cannot be adequately summarized here. For a summary of the research findings and a discussion of the causes, diagnosis, and treatment of hyperactivity, refer to Schworm (1982), who notes that efforts to determine the cause of, diagnose, and prescribe treatment for hyperactivity have been fraught with inconsistencies and confusion.

Some children outgrow their hyperactive behaviors by adolescence, but 30–60% of the children diagnosed as hyperactive reportedly continue to show similar symptoms as adults (Dulcan 1986). Hartlage and Telzrow (1982) caution that many adolescents can inhibit excessive activity, but continue to experience attentional difficulties. This may be one reason why many parents and physicians believe that adolescents have outgrown their hyperactivity but that teachers continue to report its presence and that the students still have academic difficulties. On the other hand, these differences in perception may simply reflect a situational bias. Different demands are placed on the child at home and in school, and it is quite possible that the child lacks the reading skills and concepts needed to perform the tasks required in school.

PSYCHOSTIMULANT MEDICATION.   Stimulant medication has a paradoxical effect on many hyperactive children, although scientists cannot fully explain its effects biologically or physiologically (Dulcan 1986). Among the stimulant drugs most commonly prescribed for hyperactivity or attention disorders are methyphenidate (Ritalin), dextroamphetamine (Dexedrine), and pemoline (Cylert) (Levine 1987). All the major stimulant drugs provide equally effective treatment; caffeine is less effective (Kavale & Forness 1985b). Positive responses are reported to occur in from 60–70% (Prior & Sanson 1986) to as high as 80% of cases (Haney 1988); but about 40% of hyperactive children also show improvement on placebos (Dulcan 1986).

Possible side effects of stimulant medication include appetite loss, irritability, depression, headaches, and insomnia (Simms 1985). These side effects are usually dose-related and diminish or disappear within 2–3 weeks after the dosage is reduced (Dulcan 1986). Serious side effects are uncommon, but high-normal doses over time may moderately suppress growth (Roche, Lipman & Oaerall 1980), with very high doses of Ritalin over a prolonged period most likely to produce the greatest decrements in height (Levine 1987). The overall effects of treatment during pubescence and early adolescence are unknown (O'Donnell 1982), but it does not lead to drug abuse or dependency in adolescence (Levine 1987).

Improved academic performance is usually attributed to increased attention and reduced impulsivity, which are the results of the medication. Although logically such behavioral changes should better enable a child to profit from instruction, other factors also may be operative. When the effects of attention were held constant, the positive effect for achievement was reduced by only 20%. This suggests that variables in addition to attention enhanced academic performance (Forness & Kavale 1988). Little evidence is available regarding the effects of medication on long-term academic gains and behavioral adjustments. Lack of academic improvement may be due in part to not receiving appropriate remediation (Dulcan 1986). Opinions differ as to whether combining stimulant medication with psychological intervention produces better results than either form of treatment alone (For example, compare Whalen, Henker and Hinshaw 1985 with Dulcan 1986).

Most states do not have laws or regulations dealing with the use of medication in schools. In these states, school personnel involved in stimulant-medication therapy are open to a number of legal risks (Courtnage 1982). Standardized evaluation instruments for assessing the effects of pharmacotherapy are rarely used, and communication between the school and physicians is almost nonexistent (Dulcan 1986). We believe that the use of stimulant medication should be carefully considered before it is initiated and if it is employed, its effectiveness should be objectively measured. Medical supervision is necessary to monitor undesirable side effects and to adjust dosage as necessary. Levine (1987) discusses how to select and monitor such medication. The Council for Exceptional Children (1986) publishes a booklet that describes the characteristics of various classes of drugs, examines their effects on behavior and cognition, and indexes the most frequently used stimulant medications by trade and generic names.

Biochemical Bases

Inadequate brain functioning may result from a biochemical imbalance, without any structural defect in the brain. D. E. P. Smith and Carrigan (1959) attempt to explain various kinds of disabled readers—the context reader, the word-caller, and others—in terms of an imbalance between two neurochemical transmitters (acetylcholine and cholinesterase) that are probably involved in the conduction of nerve impulses in the brain. Using a special battery of tests, they differentiated five subtypes and provided a physiological explanation of each. They also tried, unsuccessfully, to demonstrate a relationship of these patterns to endocrine functioning. Although their research is open to criticism and their explanations fall into the realm of unproved hypotheses, Smith and Carrigan opened up a new area for research that may yet prove fruitful (A. J. Harris 1960).

Buckley (1981) proposes that the integration of two neurotransmitters (dopamine and norepinephrine) is disrupted in children labeled as having minimal brain dysfunction. Serotonin levels are typically lower than normal in MBD children (Brase & Loh 1975). *Neurotransmitters* are chemical messengers located in the axon terminals which provide neurons, (nerve cells) the means by which they communicate among themselves. Neurotransmitters are directly responsible for emotion, mood, behavior, and cognition. There is some evidence of possible neurotransmitter difficulties in severely disabled readers, but a cause-effect relationship has not been established (Levine 1987). Firm conclusions regarding the biochemical bases of reading or learning disabilities cannot be drawn, but the area merits further research.

EYE MOVEMENTS

In 1878 Javal published the first account of systematic observations of eye movements during reading. His work stimulated other studies, so considerable information on eye movements had been gathered by the time Huey (1908) published his classic book on the psychology of reading. Early investigations were handicapped by clumsy, sometimes painful, apparatus. After Dodge invented an eye-movement camera, many important studies were made, notably by Buswell (1922).[8]

[8]A brief history of eye-movement research has been given by Weintraub (1977).

Although readers feel that their eyes are moving most of the time during reading, eye movements actually take up less than 10% of the reading time. During reading, the eyes periodically make a quick, jerky movement known as a *saccade*. Skilled readers make about four saccades per second, each requiring an average of about 35 milliseconds[9] between fixations (see the following). A saccade covers an average of about 8 to 10 letter-character spaces (McConkie 1982), but may range from 1 to 20 character spaces (Rayner 1985). Each saccadic movement serves to bring a new region of text into foveal vision. *Foveal vision* is the area of central vision, where vision is the clearest. *Parafoveal vision* extends farther out, and stimuli seen in this area are seen less clearly than in foveal vision. In *peripheral vision*, which extends out even farther than parafoveal vision, vision is the least clear.

The bases on which the mind decides when to make a saccade and where to make the next eye fixation are not well understood. There is some disagreement regarding both the nature of the information used in deciding where to send the eyes next and how soon that information is utilized in making the final decision (e.g., compare Rayner 1983b, McConkie et al. 1985, Foss 1988).

There seems to be more agreement as to where the next fixation is placed. According to Rayner (1983a,b), information obtained from parafoveal vision regarding word length seems to be the primary determinant as to where to make the next fixation. If the upcoming word is long, the eyes will probably be sent near the center of the word (McConkie & Zola 1984). There is also a tendency to avoid blank spaces and not to fixate *the* as often as other three-letter words. Words that are "skipped" tend to be high-frequency words (Hogaboam 1983).

Sometimes the eyes move backward to get another look at something that was not understood clearly. Such a backward eye movement is known as a *regression*. As shown in Table 9.1, the average number of regressions is high in

Table 9.1 Eye-Movement Norms

	GRADE												
	1	2	3	4	5	6	7	8	9	10	11	12	Col
Fixations per 100 words (including regressions)	224	174	155	139	129	120	114	109	105	101	96	94	90
Regressions per 100 words	52	40	35	31	28	25	23	21	20	19	18	17	15
Average span of recognition (in words)	.45	.57	.65	.72	.78	.83	.88	.92	.95	.99	1.04	1.06	1.11
Average duration of fixations (in seconds)	.33	.30	.28	.27	.27	.27	.27	.27	.27	.26	.26	.25	.24
Rate with comprehension (words per minute)	80	115	138	158	173	185	195	204	214	224	237	250	280

Source: Sanford E. Taylor, Helen Frackenpohl, and James L. Pettee, *Grade Level Norms for the Components of the Fundamental Reading Skill*, Research Information Bulletin, No. 3 (Huntington, N.Y.: Educational Developmental Laboratories, Inc., a Division of McGraw-Hill Company, 1960), p. 12. Reproduced with permission. These norms are based on students who scored 70% or better in comprehension when reading material of average difficulty for the grade.

[9]A *millisecond* is a thousandth of a second. Thus, 250 msec = ¼ of a second, 500 msec = ½ of a second.

first grade and declines to a fairly constant percentage at about the eighth grade. Regressions is skilled college readers occur, on average, about 15% of the time but may vary from 0–40% (Rayner 1983a,b). Fewer regressions are made on very easy text; considerably more on text that is difficult for the reader (Rayner 1985).

When the reader comes to the end of a line of print, there is a smooth, continuous left-to-right diagonal movement to the beginning of the next line. This movement is called a *return sweep* (see Figure 9.6, on page 335).

The pauses between saccades are called *fixations*. During a fixation, the eyes are relatively still. They do show small drifts and tremors, which are critical to proper vision and without which the visual stimuli would appear to fragment and disappear (McConkie 1982). Although the eyes are relatively still during a fixation, the mind is actively processing the incoming information and deciding where to send the eyes next. During a fixation, the reader has available to him or her all of the information obtained from reading up to that point and information obtained from the current fixation (R. Haber & Haber 1981a,b), plus whatever prior knowledge is brought to bear.

The *duration of a fixation* is the amount of time from the beginning of a fixation to the decision to move the eyes (McConkie & Zola 1986). A fixation lasts about a quarter-second for skilled readers, but may range from a tenth to over half a second (Rayner 1985). McConkie and Zola (1986) report that not only were there wide variations in the average fixation durations among third graders, but also for each child. Fixations during regressions are shorter than those following forward saccades (Underwood & Zola 1986).

The duration of a fixation is probably influenced by information acquired in previous fixations (Underwood & Zola 1986), and is related to the characteristics of the words being fixated.[10] Unusual words receive longer fixations: common words, shorter fixations. Words important to understanding the text tend to be fixated longer than unimportant words. In short, how long a fixation lasts is probably related to both perceptual and psycholinguistic factors (Kliegl, Olson & Davidson 1983). What is less clear is the extent to which the processing of information is completed before the eyes make another saccade. Probably the relationship between the duration of a fixation and the amount of time required to process the information acquired during the fixation is not a simple one. Termination of a fixation is the result of a decision that it is time to move the eyes to a new location (McConkie & Zola 1986). On average, the duration of fixation changes very little from first grade through college (see Table 9.1).

Each fixation provides the mind with a slightly different image of the stimuli.[11] Yet, although each fixation is discrete and provides some overlapping as well as new visual information to the mind, the reader is unaware of any discontinuity from one fixation to the next. It is not known whether the brain actually integrates the visual images obtained in successive fixations into a single image; McConkie and Zola (1986) could not find any evidence of this. If the brain does integrate these input differences to give the appearance of a single flowing experience, the mechanisms by which the integration occurs is largely unknown (see McConkie 1982, L. Haber & Haber 1981).

[10]Information available during a fixation can also influence the length of the immediately following saccade (McConkie et al. 1985).

[11]See L. Haber and Haber (1981) for a schematic representation of this phenomenon.

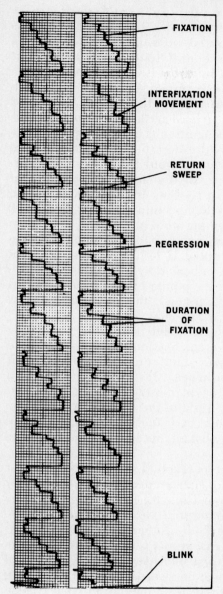

Figure 9.6. Diagram showing how eye-movement characteristics are represented in a Reading Eye II recording. From *Eye-Movement Analysis with the Reading Eye II*, by Helen Frackenpohl Morris. New York: McGraw-Hill Inc., 1973. Reproduced with the permission of EDL/McGraw-Hill, a division of McGraw-Hill Book Company.

A distinction should be drawn between span of recognition and span of perception. The *span of recognition* is what the reader sees, or reports seeing, during one fixation. As shown in Table 9.1, the average span of recognition is about a half-word in first grade (the novice reader averages two fixations per word) but increases only to about one word at the college level. A recognition span is influenced by such factors as word length, the type of reading material, and the reader's purpose for reading.

The *span of perception* is the region from which the reader acquires *and uses* visual information during a fixation (McConkie 1982). Disagreements regarding the size of the span of perception for skilled readers of English may be more apparent than real. According to Rayner (1983b), the perceptual span extends from the beginning of the currently fixated word, or no more than 3–4 letter spaces to the left of the fixation point, to about 15 letter spaces to the right of the center of the fixation. But according to Underwood and McConkie (1985), the region in which letter distinctions are made by skilled readers, who are reading carefully, is from 4 letter spaces to the left and 8 to the right of the fixated letter. These apparent differences may be due, at least partially, to how the information is used. Information useful in word recognition is obtained from the foveal region and the beginning of the parafoveal vision (6–8 letters around the center of fixation; one to two words depending on word length). Some letter-feature information is obtained from the region slightly farther to the right, but it is not useful in word recognition during that fixation. In many fixations, the fixated word, along with the first few letters of the upcoming word, is processed. This preliminary letter processing of the upcoming word presumably speeds up the reading process. Word-length information, which is useful in guiding the eyes to their next fixation, is acquired out to about 15 letter spaces to the right of the fixation (Rayner 1983a,b). If the region indicated by Rayner as being important to word recognition (14 letters around the point of fixation) is compared with that of Underwood and McConkie (12 letters), the difference is less marked.

Underwood and Zola (1986) report that even though poor readers read only about 70% as fast as good readers and had average fixation durations that were 22% longer than those of good readers, the span of letter recognition was about the same for good and poor readers while reading easy text. Both groups of fifth graders acquired letter information from the region of text extending from 2 letter spaces to the left and 6 or 7 spaces to the right of the fixation point. These data are comparable to those reported for adults by Underwood and McConkie (1985). The span of perception is not a fixed constant, but varies from fixation to fixation (Hogaboam 1983).

Rayner (1985) indicates that the average perceptual span is 0.46 word for second graders, 0.78 for fourth graders, 0.84 for sixth graders, and 1.08 words for adults. These data are similar to those shown in Table 9.1 for recognition spans.

Different methods have been used to determine recognition and perceptual spans, and their use has led to differing findings (Samuels 1985b, Underwood & Zola 1986). When the total number of words read is divided by the number of fixations made, the recognition span increases from an average of about one-half word in first grade to a little over one word in college (see Table 9.1). This method incorrectly assumes that there is no overlap in what is seen with each fixation.

When the stimuli are presented tachistoscopically for a quarter-second (the average duration of a fixation), good readers report seeing more information than do poor readers. This good/poor reader difference may reflect the limitations poor readers have in encoding and reporting information, rather than true differences in span of recognition. A general problem with this technique is that the amount of visual information on the retina fades very rapidly following each rapid exposure. Therefore, much of the information is lost by the time children process the information and report what they saw.

Another way to measure recognition span is to determine how far from the fixation point (center of vision) individually presented letters or words can be identified. The stimuli are flashed to the left and/or right of the point on which the pupil is fixating. Studies in which this technique has been used, report mixed findings regarding good/poor reader differences in span of recognition. Good readers and poor readers may differ in the amount of meaning they can obtain from the stimuli during an exposure, rather than in the size of their recognition spans.

A fourth procedure involves the disruption of text by techniques such as omitting or filling in the spaces between words, or by presenting text in alternating upper- and lower-case letters. Use of visually disrupted text is based on the belief that good readers have a wider span of recognition and thus make greater use of their peripheral vision (or vice versa), and that therefore they should be more negatively affected than poor readers by such disruptions. The problem is that the procedure may also disrupt visual information in foveal vision. Therefore, the obtained effects may not be due to differential use of peripheral vision.

A recently developed procedure uses complex computer-aided equipment to restrict the reader's visual field and to make display changes contingent on the position of the reader's eyes. See Underwood and Zola (1986) for a more complete description of this procedure, which is used to measure perceptual spans, as well as other eye movements.

Another measure used to assess perceptual span is the eye-voice span. The *eye-voice span* (EVS) is the distance that the reader's eyes are ahead of his or her voice while reading orally. A rough measure of a person's EVS is obtained by suddenly covering the portion of the text after the word last spoken by the person who is reading orally; the EVS is then the number of words following the last word spoken that the reader can report. The EVS, which is normally the amount a person can read in one second (Geyer 1968), shows that material already perceived is stored in short-term memory until the vocal response is made.

The eye-voice span is longer for meaningful text than for unrelated words, and with meaningful material the span tends to stop at a phrase boundary rather than within a phrase, showing that it is controlled to some extent by the grasp of meaning (Levin & Kaplan 1970). A large eye-voice span tends to accompany skilled reading; a small span often goes with slow, choppy, word-by-word reading. This finding is in harmony with evidence that good readers tend to respond to cues at the intersentence, sentence, phrase, and word levels; poor readers tend to respond mainly to part-word and word cues (Clay & Imlach 1971). The fact that good readers have longer eye-voice spans (EVS) than do poor readers is sometimes used to argue that good readers actually see more in a fixation. However, an EVS is probably the result of at least two fixations, because a single fixation lasts only about 250 milliseconds, and an EVS lasts 640–700 milliseconds (Underwood 1982).

The length of the eye-voice span is usually reported in terms of number of words. The average EVS across all ages is 2.19 words for meaningless strings of words, and 3.91 words for meaningful strings. The average EVS increases from 3.19 words for second graders to 5.02 words for adults (Samuels 1985b). The eye-voice span tends to increase with age (Buswell 1922, Levin & Cohn 1968) and is influenced by the meaningfulness of the material (Morton 1964) and by linguistic constraints (Fusaro 1974). Reviews of the research on eye-voice span have been given by Gibson and Levin (1975) and Levin and Addis (1979).

The EVS may not be synonymous with the span of recognition, because eye-movement data suggest that the span of recognition (the amount seen in one eye fixation) is not more than a word even in skilled readers (see page 336). Eye-movement data do not support interpretations of EVS findings that words are sometimes identified beyond the location of the eyes (McConkie & Hogaboam 1985).

The main limitation of the EVS procedure is that successive eye fixations have considerable overlap, and the eyes are more than one fixation ahead of the voice. Also, since the EVS is measured in continuous oral reading, it may reflect output restrictions rather than perceptual processing (Underwood & Zola 1986).

It is difficult to generalize about readers' perceptual spans from data derived from all but the computer-assisted procedure. The other five procedures may provide information about the region within which letters or words can be identified if the reader desires to use the full region available. They do not provide data that indicate whether this full region is actually used.

As reading ability increases, there are fewer fixations per line, fewer regressions, and shorter duration of fixations (see Table 9.1 and Figure 9.7). Eye-movement patterns also become more regular with increasing reading ability.

Eye-movement patterns differ among not only individuals, but also for a given individual at various places in a text. McConkie and Zola (1986) suggest that what readers do with their eyes as they read reflects the ways in which they are attending to the text. Their oculomotor behaviors are, in turn, assumed to reflect both the nature of the processing of visual information and the pupils' abilities to coordinate the controlling processes necessary to provide information as it is needed.

One school of thought holds that skilled readers rely minimally on visual information from the text, sampling graphic information only as needed to confirm or reject their hypotheses about meaning (e.g., K. Goodman 1967, F. Smith 1982). Eye-movement data, however, do not support models of reading that suggest that skilled readers form hypotheses about meaning and anticipate upcoming text, and that such behaviors facilitate word recognition. Nor do these data support models that stress the extensive use of peripheral vision for acquiring cues from upcoming words.

Instead, eye-movement studies indicate that printed words are attended to and identified in a small visual area, and that the reader has little or no visual information about other words, even when they lie within the fovea itself (McConkie & Hogaboam 1985). Eye-movement data indicate that, at least when reading carefully, skilled readers perceive no more than one or two words at a time (McConkie 1982). They sample text frequently, usually fixating adjacent words or skipping no more than one word (Carpenter & Just 1983). Contrary to the foregoing data, Shebilske & Fisher (1983) report that readers fixate only one-half to two-thirds of the words in many situations.

Olson et al. (1985) interpret their eye-movement data as revealing two types of reading styles. "Plodders' make relatively few regressions or word-skipping, forward eye movements. They tended to move steadily forward, with more frequent saccades within words and to the immediately-following words.

MATURATION OF READING PERFORMANCE

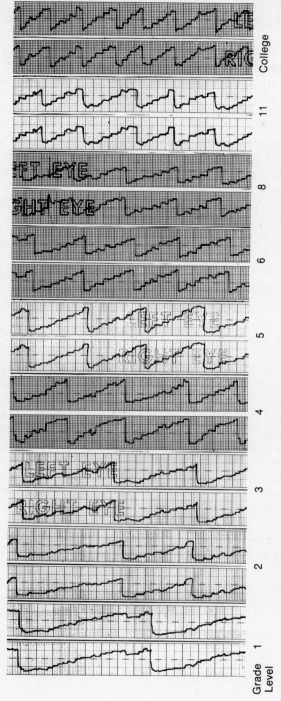

Grade Level   1   2   3   4   5   6   8   11   College

These graphs reveal the progressive development of reading performance. As the student advances academically, his pattern reflects fewer fixations per line, fewer regressions, a shorter duration of fixation, and a more rapid rate of reading. In general, the pattern becomes more regular and uniform, reflecting an improvement in perceptual accuracy, directional attack, and reading fluency.

Figure 9.7. Samples of eye-movement photographs, showing development through the school years and in college. From a photograph supplied by Educational Developmental Laboratories and used with their permission.

"Explorers" make relatively more regressions and forward word-skipping eye movements. They have relatively fewer intraword and word-to-word forward movements.

There is also some belief that fixation duration can be used as a measure of processing time. Thus, attempts are made to relate fixation duration and processing time to the difficulty of particular syntactic structures or to the conceptual difficulty of the text. McConkie et al. (1985) contend that such studies assume that the processing of visual information perceived during a fixation is completed by the time a decision is made to move the eyes to the next location. They believe that such an assumption is untenable for two reasons. First, the time between the arrival of retinal information at the brain and the point of no return is 90 milliseconds less than the duration of a fixation. Second, the assumption requires that the period from a point of no return until the time when the brain is stimulated by the visual pattern present on the next fixation must be dead time, during which no processing occurs. To assume that there is such dead time is to suggest that, during reading, the mind spends only half its time in processing activities.

Measurement of Eye Movements

Portable eye-movement cameras are available, such as the *Reading Eye II* (EDL) and *Eye-Trac* (Applied Science). An optical system positions images of the reader's eyes on a ground-glass screen, and two pairs of photocells monitor eye movements. The photocell signals are amplified and recorded on heat-sensitive paper. The movements of both eyes are monitored simultaneously and, in smooth reading, their parallel movements give a sort of descending staircase effect (see Figure. 9.6). The duration of each fixation is shown by the length of the vertical line. The amount of print taken in during a fixation is indicated by the length of the horizontal line representing the movement between fixations. A regression is shown by a short horizontal movement to the left, and a return sweep, by a long horizontal movement to the left.

Young and Sheena (1975) reviewed the eye-movement measurement techniques available at that time; but in the last decade, more sophisticated equipment has become available for research purposes (refer to McConkie 1982; McConkie, Wolverton & Zola 1984). New equipment and techniques make use of scleral or corneal reflection techniques and a computer that continually checks the position of the eyes and can measure eye movements precisely. The reading material is usually presented on computer-controlled displays, and the text can be altered for various reasons without the reader being aware of it, even to the point of changing aspects of the text display contingent on the reader's eye movements.

Three informal procedures are used for observing eye movements. Although none is as revealing or reliable as the computer-aided procedures described in the foregoing, they may provide some useful information and should certainly be informative for anyone who has never observed a pupil's eye movements while reading.

In the *mirror method,* the child is seated at a table on which the book is held in a reading position. The observer sits slightly behind and to one side of the child, also facing the table. A rectangular mirror is placed on the table fairly close to the book and held or propped at an angle so as to allow the child's eyes to be observed.

To use the *Miles Peep-Hole Method* (Miles & Segel 1929), an appropriate reading selection is mounted in a sheet of pasteboard. A quarter-inch square opening is made near the middle of the page between two lines. The observer is positioned so that he or she can look through the opening as the child reads the selection. The peephole method gives a clearer vision of the eye movements than does the mirror method, but it requires special preparation.

In the procedure that we prefer, the child sits and holds a book on a level with his eyes as he reads. The observer sits across from the child and watches the reader's eyes across the top of the book. Because the reader's eyes begin to be obscured by his eyelashes when he nears the middle of the page, this procedure can be used only for the top half of each page.

The Significance of Eye Movements

When selections of sufficient length are used, eye-movement photography gives reliable and valid measures of reading performance (Tinker 1946). However, the expense of the apparatus alone may make eye-movement photography impractical for most school and clinical situations.

Photography or informal observation of eye movements discloses *what* the eyes do while the person reads; it does not provide an explanation of *why* they move as they do. The eyes are the servants of the brain. Discovering that there are many regressions in a person's reading, for example, does not in itself explain the difficulty or indicate the specific nature of the remedial work needed.

In all but a few cases, poor eye movements are not the cause of poor reading; they are symptoms of the fact that the reader is reading poorly. Tinker studied the question of training eye movements for over 35 years and summarizes his conclusions as follows:

> Actually, there is no evidence to support the view that the eye movements determine reading proficiency. . . . All experimental evidence derived from well-designed studies shows that oculomotor reactions are exceedingly flexible and quickly reflect any change in reading skill and any change in perception and comprehension. . . . Real progress in programs of teaching reading would be achieved if the term and concept of rhythmical eye movements were abandoned, if eye-movement photography were confined to the research laboratory, and if the use of gadgets and other techniques to train eye movements were discarded. (Tinker 1965, pp. 111–112)

Good readers are not aware of what their eyes do when they read. If they try deliberately to control their eyes while reading, comprehension suffers and reading efficiency deteriorates. If comprehension and rate are satisfactory, eye movements can be safely ignored. If eye movements are poor, the remedial work should usually stress the basic elements of good comprehension: accurate word recognition, knowledge of word meanings, phrasing, good concentration, and so on. Very few students need training to overcome specified poor eye-movement habits.

Eye Movements, Poor Reading, and Reading Disability

Compared to good readers, poor and disabled readers show longer durations of fixations, shorter saccades, many more regressions, and generally more erratic-looking eye movement patterns (McConkie 1982, Underwood & Zola 1986).[12]

Data such as the foregoing have been interpreted in ways that are diametrically opposed. Eye movements are believed to be either the cause of reading disability or simply an effect. The former viewpoint is discussed first.

Lefton et al. (1979) found that, in addition to the differences mentioned above, disabled readers made significantly more fixations than did good readers and showed relatively unsystematic eye movements, which varied considerably from line to line. They conclude that disabled readers are severely hampered by "chaotic oculomotor control." Similar, but not as dramatic, conclusions have been reached by Elterman et al. (1980).

Pavlidis (1983; 1985) claims that eye-movement performance can be used to differentiate between dyslexics, other disabled readers, and good readers by requiring them to track light sources that are illuminated sequentially.[13] Pavlidis also reports that the duration of the dyslexics' fixations was highly variable, that they made significantly more right-to-left saccades (and these regressions often occurred in clusters of two or more), that their eye movements were erratic and idiosyncratic, and that the narrow perceptual span of dyslexia is a consequence of their erratic eye movements and excessive regressions. He further claims that the dyslexics displayed the same eye-movement patterns when reading easy material and when performing nonreading tasks. Although Pavlidis (1983) suggested that it was as yet impossible to tell which of five possible factors caused these erratic eye movements, he appears to favor strongly a malfunctioning oculomotor control system, a general sequencing problem, or an interaction between the two. Black et al. (1984), however, conclude that underlying oculomotor-control abnormality cannot be the explanation for the reported abnormal erratic eye movements exhibited by disabled readers while reading. Pavlidis (1985) later attributed the erratic eye movements to "an as yet undetermined brain malfunction."

Pavlidis' claims are controversial. A number of studies have failed to replicate his findings (Rayner 1985), and his conclusions have been questioned by other findings (e.g., Olson, Kliegl & Davidson 1983). McConkie (1982) writes that the aberrant eye-movement patterns of disabled readers indicate that processing is not flowing smoothly but that, at present, the eye movements themselves do not indicate the nature of the problems. Most studies have found that when given material of appropriate difficulty, the eye movements of poor readers do not differ significantly from those of good readers of the same age (Rayner 1983a).

Perhaps, as Rayner (1983a) suggests, Pavlidis' subjects were a different subtype of disabled readers than those found in other studies. Only further studies will clarify the issue. There is, however, some evidence of differences in eye movements between two subtypes of disabled readers (Rayner 1983a, Pirozzolo 1983). Whereas audiolinguistic dyslexics do not show evidence of eye-movement disorders, visual-spatial dyslexics do (their eye movements are similar to

---

[12]Various patterns of eye movements in disabled readers have been reported by Olson, Kliegl, and Davidson (1983).

[13]The "nonreading lights test" he used is described in Pavlidis (1985) on page 47.

those reported by Pavlidis). But neither Rayner nor Pirozzolo agrees with Pavlidis that such eye movements are causal. Eye-movement patterns reflect the moment-to-moment cognitive changes induced by an interaction of the visual stimuli and the task of comprehending (McConkie & Zola 1984).

In almost all eye-movement research, a single eye has been monitored. For this reason, it is impossible to utilize most existing eye-movement data to test the hypothesis that some cases of reading disability are caused by a failure to coordinate the simultaneous activities of both eyes (McConkie & Zola 1986).

At present, even with the most sophisticated equipment available, little diagnostic or remedial information can be gained from eye-movement photography. A number of issues remain to be resolved, but with the emergence of more testable models of the reading process and with the availability of highly sophisticated technology, the future looks promising.

Geiger and Lettvin (1987) studied five university students who were good readers, five adult "residual dyslexics" (they had had dyslexia, but recovered), and one dyslexic adult who was reading at the third-reader level. Geiger and Lettvin compared their subjects' ability to identify individual letters and short strings of letters presented briefly in their peripheral fields at the same time a single letter was presented to a fixation point. They reported that the dyslexic and recovered dyslexics had markedly wider peripheral areas in which they could correctly identify the stimuli (i.e., they had wider recognition spans than the good readers), but had a "masking" of the letters in foveal and near-peripheral vision. Geiger and Lettvin conclude that dyslexics see more clearly in their peripheral vision than in foveal vision (the opposite of what occurs in normal vision) and that this caused them to learn to read outside of foveal vision and to use different perceptual strategies for task-directed vision. The dyslexics reportedly benefited from a treatment that involved placing a sheet of white paper over the text and then reading. On the sheet was a fixation point (a dot) and 35 millimeters to the right of the dot was a rectangular hole, eight to nine letter-spaces long and only slightly higher than the line of print. The subjects looked at the dot but used their peripheral vision to view the text that appeared in the hole in the paper while reading at a comfortable speed. In their critique of Geiger and Lettvin's study, Shaywitz and Waxman (1987) seriously question their interpretation of the data, and offer alternative explanations.

SENSORY DEFECTS

Kinds of Visual Defects

Of the many different kinds of visual defects, some seem to be more important than others in the causation of reading difficulties.

The three defects best known to the layperson are *nearsightedness (myopia), farsightedness (hypermetropia),* and *astigmatism.* All are usually caused by structural deviations from the normal shape of the eye. The myopic eye is too long from front to back, and so light focuses in front of the retina and tends to produce a blurred impression. The farsighted eye is too short from front to back; light coming from a source near the eye focuses behind the retina. It is possible for the moderately farsighted person to get near objects into clear focus, but long-continued attention to near objects, as in reading, tends to produce eyestrain with accompanying fatigue and headaches. *Astigmatism* is usually the result of uneven curvature of the front part of the eye so that light rays coming into the eye are not evenly distributed over the retina; the results are blurred or distorted images and eyestrain. All three conditions can be corrected with prescription lenses.

The eyes have to make four major adjustments for clear vision. The first of these is an automatic reflex adjustment of the size of the pupillary opening to the amount of illumination *(pupillary reflex);* this permits a larger amount of light to enter in dim light and protects the eye against the dazzling effect of bright illumination. Second, an automatic reflex adjusts the shape of the lens to the distance of the object being looked at; this *accommodation reflex* acts like the adjustment for distance in a camera. Third, an automatic reflex controls the degree to which the eyes turn in so that both focus on the same spot (the *convergence reflex);* the eyes are almost parallel when viewing an object more than 10 feet away but turn in noticeably when aimed at a target a foot away. Fourth, the eyes must be aimed so that the objects the viewer wishes to see most clearly are in the center of the visual field, where acuity is greatest. This requires smooth, continuous movement when following a moving object and quick, jerky movements *(saccadic movements)* with intervening pauses *(fixations)* when observing stationary objects. These movements are not easily seen in casual observation but are easily noted in eye-movement photography or when making special observations of eye movement.

Some defects cannot be detected when each eye is tested separately, but do appear when the eyes are used together. For normal binocular vision, both eyes must be focused accurately on the same target. This allows the brain to fuse the slightly different images from the two eyes. Fusion difficulty is often the result of paralysis of an eye muscle. When fusion does not occur, the person sometimes sees double (as when under the influence of alcohol) but, more commonly, the image from one eye is ignored or suppressed. Continued suppression of the vision of one eye for a period of years may eventually produce loss of vision in that eye. It is therefore important to detect cases of visual suppression early.

Partial or imperfect fusion is more apt to interfere with clear vision than a complete absence of fusion. When fusion is incomplete, a blurred image is likely, even though the person may see clearly with either eye separately. Some people can fuse the images, but do so slowly. This problem may not be a handicap in the ordinary use of the eyes but may interfere with clear vision when rapid, precise focusing is needed, as in reading (Brod & Hamilton 1973). There has been no research follow-up on the finding by Witty and Kopel (1936) that slow visual fusion was present in 29% of 100 poor readers and in only 1% of the control group of normal readers.

Poor fusion is often associated with a lack of proper balance among the six pairs of muscles that turn the eyeballs. When the lack of balance is extreme, the condition is called *strabismus (cross-eyed* or *walleyed).* The person with strabismus usually ignores one eye completely to avoid interference with the vision of the other eye. Milder cases of poor muscle balance *(heterophoria)* also occur, such as *esophoria,* in which one eye turns in too much; *exophoria* in which one eye turns out; and *hyperphoria,* in which one eye focuses a little higher than the other. Most people with these defects are able to obtain proper fusion when the eyes are not tired, but get blurred vision after extended reading or other close and exacting visual work. When the eyes are tired, they may get blurred images or may see a combination of the things each eye is looking at. Complete suppression of one eye may occur.

Color blindness of the usual type, which involves difficulty or inability to distinguish reds from greens, is found in 4–8% of boys and is rare in girls. No evidence indicates that color blindness has any effect on reading ability. Weakness in the ability to perceive depth *(astereopsis)* has been mentioned as possibly being involved in reading disability cases; it is related to poor fusion. *Aniseikonia,* a condition in which one eye forms a larger image of the object than the other eye, has been found to cause visual disturbance in some individuals; it would seem to be a reasonable cause for poor fusion in some cases.

As yet, little is known about the possible importance for reading of the speed and precision with which the pupillary, accommodation, and convergence reflexes adapt the eyes to new targets or to a changing target. Vision tests currently in use do not attempt to measure these factors.

The Significance of Visual Defects for Reading[14]

Although many studies have investigated the relationship of visual defects to reading ability, an exact statement on the degree to which poor reading is caused by poor vision cannot yet be made. Studies can be found to support or to deny (1) the contention that a particular visual defect is more prevalent in disabled readers than in a random group, and (2) the hypothesis that remediation of a particular visual dysfunction has a positive effect on reading achievement (Suchoff 1981).

There are at least three possible reasons for the lack of any conclusive evidence. First, the subjects and tests employed in the studies varied widely. Second, and more fundamentally, people vary in their ability to adapt to handicaps. For instance, two people can have the same moderate degree of exophoria, but the condition may not cause a problem for the person who is able to compensate. Third, poor vision is only one of the handicaps that may interfere with reading. If poor vision is the only handicap, the child may be able to become a good reader in spite of it; with several additional handicaps, the combined effects may be too much.

There is general agreement that myopia and astigmatism are no more prevalent among disabled readers than among good readers; myopia actually occurs more frequently in good readers. Hyperopia is more frequent in poor readers. The relationship between astigmatism and reading difficulties is unknown; too few studies have been made (Grisham & Simons 1986). However, low to moderate astigmatism does not cause sufficiently blurred vision to interfere with reading; high amounts of astigmatism may. Total lack of binocular vision, as evidenced by strabismus, does not appear to be characteristic of reading disability. In general, research has demonstrated few one-to-one relationships between particular visual conditions and reading (Suchoff 1981). Refractive errors (near-

[14]Research on this topic is too extensive to review here. Those interested may wish to refer to the annotated bibliography by Weintraub and Cowan (1982 pp. 13–26), and to the summaries by Hartlage (1976) and Suchoff (1981).

and farsightedness, astigmatism) are correctable with lenses; rarely are they responsible for impaired reading (W. Smith 1984). Wharry and Kirkpatrick (1986) report that the severity of refractive errors had little relationship to the performance of learning-disabled pupils on standardized word-recognition and oral reading tests.

Ophthalmologists tend to minimize the significance of visual problems in the causation of reading disability (e.g., Metzger & Werner 1984; Beauchamp 1987). Optometrists, on the other hand, tend to stress the importance of binocular vision, accommodation, convergence, and ocular motility (e.g., Allen 1977, W. Smith 1984). Optometrists schooled in developmental vision emphasize the value of *orthoptic training* (e.g., Solan 1981, Getman 1985)—the idea being that specialized visual exercises will improve visual and perceptual abilities, thereby making it easier to learn to read. At least part of this professional difference of opinion reflects differences in the education of each type of vision specialist. Nevertheless, their disagreement makes it difficult to know to whom a child with suspected visual problems should be referred.

Keogh and Pelland (1985), who made an extensive review of the literature, state that it is impossible to draw any firm conclusions regarding the efficacy of visual training. A clear-cut decision is impossible due to the ambiguous and equivocal findings reported, the widely varying content of the visual training programs, the differing natures of the subjects, and the use of inadequate or inappropriate research methods.

The truth regarding the relationship of visual defects and reading probably lies somewhere between two extreme points of view—absolutely no relationship versus a major cause. The answer awaits future research that is better conceived and conducted than in the past. For the present, it seems reasonable to conclude that visual defects may contribute to the reading problems of some children. But even if definitive evidence indicated no relationship between vision and reading, it would still be prudent to suggest that teachers be alert to possible signs of visual problems and that children be screened and referred to vision specialists when necessary.

With the advent of mainstreaming, regular classroom teachers have had more visually impaired children in their classrooms. Dequin and Johns (1985) describe various equipment that can be used to assist visually-impaired students when reading. Among these are the *Kierweil Reading Machine* which actually produces an oral interpretation of the written text, the *Optacan Print Reading System* which converts images of printed letters into a vibrating form that can be felt with one finger, and *Visuscan* which magnifies print up to 64 times. They also list other sources of information for helping the visually impaired to read better or more easily.

The Detection of Visual Defects

Schools commonly give simple visual screening tests in order to select children whose vision requires careful professional examination. Usually, this is done with the *Snellen Chart* or some similar test. The child stands 20 feet from the chart and tries to name letters of different sizes, with one eye covered. Thus, the Snellen measures monocular acuity at far point. In addition to the fact that reading is normally done at 12 to 18 inches using both eyes, the Snellen has other drawbacks: (1) A child can memorize the chart and thus simulate adequate distance vision; (2) the chart fails to detect moderate degrees of farsightedness or astigmatism; and (3) it fails completely to detect even severe cases of poor fusion and eye-muscle imbalance. Eames (1942) reports that Snellen tests had suggested the presence of defective vision in only 48 of 100 children who had visual defects as determined by an ophthalmological examination.

Visual screening tests that include measures of acuity for both near and distance vision, eye-muscle balance, and binocular coordination are available. These tests, which use stereoscopic instruments, include the *Massachusetts Vision Test* (Welch-Allyn, American Optical, Keystone), *Keystone Visual Survey Tests* (Keystone), *School Vision Tester* (Baush & Lomb), *Sight Screener* (American Optical) and *Titmus School Vision Tester* (Titmus). The *Modified Telebinocular Technique*, which does not call for specialized training, supposedly provides superior results (Schubert & Walton 1980), but independent verification of this claim has not been made.

Jobe (1976) explains why the results of screening tests may not agree with the findings of vision specialists. Ophthalmologists, whose backgrounds are medical, tend to emphasize far-point measurements and structural eye defects. Optometrists tend to put greater emphasis on near-point measurements and disorders of fusion and coordination. Some tests depend on the subjective judgment of the examiner. The lack of agreement in findings may also result from errors in administering and scoring the screening tests or from inherent differences between stereoscopic and clinical testing procedures. Jobe recommends that if a school vision screening program is to be set up, a committee including optometrists, ophthalmologists, and parents should settle in advance the questions of what procedures to use, how to train the examiners, and how to interpret the results in order to make appropriate referrals.

Teachers should always be alert to signs of visual discomfort in children's appearance or behavior. Among the things to note are bloodshot, swollen, teary, or discharging eyes; excessive rubbing of the eyes; recurring sties; inflamed eyelids; complaints of sleepiness, fatigue, headache, nausea, dizziness, or vision that is blurred, double, or distorted; pain or a feeling of dryness, itching, burning, or grittiness in the eyes; strained or tense facial expressions; rapid blinking or facial twitchings; and such habits as holding the book very close to or far from the eyes, or off to one side; moving the reading material alternately toward and away from the eyes; holding the head to one side of the book; and covering one eye while reading.

No matter how complete school visions tests may be, no teacher, nurse, or psychologist should attempt to diagnose visual defects or prescribe treatment for them. Their responsibility is to identify those children who probably need expert attention and to refer them to a vision specialist.

Kinds of Auditory Impairments and Their Significance for Reading Ability and Instruction

A relatively slight hearing impairment can have marked negative effects on the acquisition of communication skills and verbal knowledge, particularly when hearing is defective in both ears (Owrid 1970). The degree to which poor hearing impacts reading ability may depend on the type of instruction provided for novice readers. Bond (1935) found significant differences in hearing between good and poor readers in the second and third grades and reports that partly deaf children were seriously handicapped in classes where oral-phonetic methods were stressed, but made normal progress in classes that stressed visual teaching materials and silent reading.

Otitis media (an inflammation of the middle ear) or *middle-ear effusion* (fluid in the middle-ear space) during the formative years from birth to age 6 may have adverse effects on the development of cognitive and language skills (Denk-Glass, Laber & Brewer 1981) and, later, in reading ability (Silva, Chalmers & Stewart 1986). Almost 16% of the 242 LD children studied by Gibbs and Cooper (1989) had middle-ear function defects, but such problems often go undetected. Recurrent ear infections during the school years produce varied results, which may depend on factors such as the severity and length of the hearing loss, the importance of the information that the pupil missed, and whether or not such losses were recognized and remediated. Intermittent hearing losses may cause the child to become confused.

Although the majority of children with impaired hearing show lessened acuity across the full range of pitch represented by the piano keyboard, there are others whose deficiency is concentrated in the higher frequencies. An example of high frequency hearing loss is shown in Figure 9.8. High frequency losses may prevent students from hearing or distinguishing among consonant sounds;

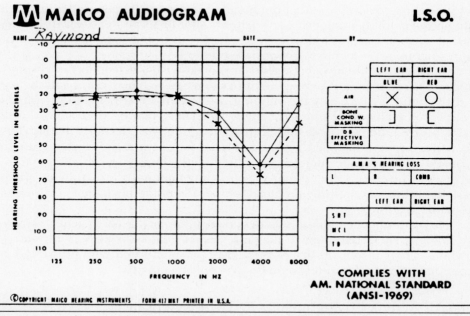

Figure 9.8. Audiogram of a 10-year-old with a severe reading disability. The chart shows an impairment of acuity in the higher frequencies in both ears, with the left ear slightly poorer than the right. Reproduced by permission of Maico Hearing Instruments.

low-frequency losses may impair their ability to hear or distinguish vowel sounds (Young & Tyre 1983).

The handicapping effect of a partial hearing loss is much greater for some people than for others. Some make up for their sensory weaknesses by concentrating intently and getting the greatest possible meaning from what they do hear; others, combining inattention or disregard for small differences with their sensory loss, are more greatly handicapped.

Increasingly more hearing-impaired children are being placed in regular classrooms for at least part of the school day. Accommodation must be made in their instructional programs. Not all hearing-impaired children are alike. Their hearing losses may range from moderate to severe, some may have and use residual hearing, a few may even be oblivious to sound, and most will have some type of hearing aid. Some have limited speech; some sign using American Sign Language (ASL) or Signed English; and some have little ability to communicate.

Among the problems in learning to read encountered by the hearing impaired are limited understanding vocabularies and differences between the syntax of the sentences used in their reading textbooks and that of the language system they have learned. They may transliterate the written text into the syntax of their language system. For example, a child schooled in ASL may change *I haven't eaten* to "I eat not yet." There is no consensus as to how best to teach hearing-impaired pupils to read (Carlsen 1985).

Testing Hearing

Some conditions that lead to progressively increasing deafness can be cured if treated early enough, and careful periodic tests of hearing should be part of the routine health procedure in every school. Teachers should watch for signs of poor hearing in a child's general behavior. Children with inflamed or running ears should be referred for medical treatment. Poor hearing should be suspected if a child has delayed language development, asks to have statements repeated, cups a hand behind an ear, scowls, or otherwise shows intense effort in listening, confuses words of similar sounds, or has indistinct speech. Teachers sometimes mistakenly decide that a child lacks intellectual ability because his face has a "blank expression" or he does not respond to their questions or instruction, when in fact, such behavior is due to the student's impaired ability to hear.

By far the most satisfactory way to measure hearing is to use an audiometer. For the purpose of singling out pupils who need careful medical examination to their hearing, audiometers are available that can be used to test as many as 40 children at one time. In such a test, each child listens through an earphone and writes down the numbers he or she hears. The numbers, spoken with different degrees of loudness, are played on a special phonograph, and from the child's written answers the degree of hearing loss can be readily calculated. For individual testing, an audiometer that measures amount of hearing loss for pure tones of low, medium and high pitches should be used. In one study of LD children (Gibbs & Cooper 1989), about 7% of the 8- to 12-year-olds failed a pure-tone hearing test.

Frequency (Hz), or pitch, is the number of vibrations per second produced by the sound source. The range of human hearing is 20–20,000 Hz; audiologists typically test the 125–8,000 Hz range. *Intensity* or loudness is measured in decibels (db). A loss of 21–40 decibels constitutes a mild hearing loss. A moderate hearing loss (41–55 db) makes it difficult to hear normal conversation, and may be accompanied by speech articulation problems. Children with hearing losses in the 56–70 dbs range are candidates for hearing aids, and those with a severe loss (71–90 db) have difficulty understanding speech and their speech may be unintelligble (Hinds 1986–87). Because ear infections and other temporary conditions can cause a transitory hearing loss, it is advisable to retest, two months later, a child who has failed an audiometric test.

OTHER PHYSICAL CONDITIONS

Illness

There is no evidence that any common infectious diseases of childhood are directly related to reading disability. Diseases might, however, predispose children to learning problems, especially those of the central nervous system such as meningitis and encephalitis. The ultimate developmental effects of such diseases depend on their severity, the child's initial response to treatment, and the age of onset (Levine 1987).

Prolonged illness of any kind may influence reading ability if the child is out of school for a long period of time and misses important work. A history of a series of long absences in the first and second grades is found fairly often among children with severe reading handicaps. Many children show no lasting scholastic effects of such absences, either because they were ahead of the class or because their mothers and teachers gave them special help to make up the lost ground. When neither of these conditions is present, the child may not catch up.

Certain chronic conditions lower a child's general vitality so that he or she tires quickly and cannot put forth a normal amount of effort. Rheumatic fever, asthma, heart trouble, sinus trouble, other chronic infections, and malnutrition are conditions that cause intermittent absence and lower the child's energy output. Lack of energy can also be the result of insufficient sleep.

Coordination

A number of poor readers are generally clumsy. They are below average in athletic skill, are awkward in walking and running, and make poorly formed letters and numbers in writing. Although there seems to be no direct causal connection between awkwardness and poor reading, in some cases both may result from the same condition. Mild injuries to the brain or delayed neurological maturation may be responsible both for poor muscular coordination and for speech and reading disabilities.

Glandular Disturbances

The endocrine glands are small organs that have tremendous influence on human growth and efficiency. Marked thyroid deficiency is usually accomplished by obesity and mental sluggishness; an overactive thyroid gland may cause loss of weight, fatigue, and nervous irritability. Abnormalities of the pituitary gland may cause dwarfism and gigantism, obesity, or sexual immaturity. Each of the endocrine glands has important regulative functions, but medical authorities are still far from a complete understanding of them. The frequency of endocrine deviations is reported to be greater in poor readers than in the normal child population. Most of these children have been overweight, with signs of either thyroid deficiency or a general endocrine disturbance involving the thyroid, pituitary, and sex glands (Eames 1960). Many of these children have shown marked improvement in mental alertness, effort, and learning ability after appropriate endocrine treatment. Park and Schneider (1975) report markedly elevated thyroxine levels in 53 children with severe reading disabilities. However, controlled experimentation has generally resulted in frustration when attempting to apply biochemical therapy to learning (Green & Perlman 1971).

Diet, Nutrition, and Malnutrition

Feingold (1976) asserts that the use of synthetic food colors and flavors is responsible for many cases of hyperactivity and learning disability. The Feingold diet eliminates all foods containing additives, dyes, and natural salicylates. Other physicians criticize Feingold's claims as being based on faulty or insufficient evidence and call for a moratorium on use of the diet (Spring & Sandoval 1976, Sieben 1977). In rebuttal, Feingold (1977) points out that one questionable food at a time could be eliminated to determine its effect and that his limited diet is not harmful. The research findings on the diet's effects on hyperactivity are mixed; however, methodologically satisfactory studies indicate that 5–10% of hyperactive children may show behavioral improvement on the Feingold diet, with preschoolers being more likely than older children to respond positively (Dulcan 1986). Dietary treatments have little apparent influence on cognitive functions (Kavale & Forness 1985b).

Levine (1987) states that there is no rigorous evidence that hypoglycemia (low blood sugar) or carbohydrates (e.g., the sugar in chocolate) cause learning problems. On the other hand, Powers (1975) contends that excessive intake of sugar or other carbohydrates, especially in combination with the caffeine in coffee, tea, and soda, tends to make children overwrought and overstimulated. Powers' evidence comes mainly from his private cases, and in other studies caffeine has been shown to reduce hyperactivity (e.g., Firestone et al. 1978), not stimulate it. Perhaps the keys to this medical controversy are the amount of intake and its combination with other factors. More conclusive evidence is needed.

The physiological mechanism for the relationship between diet and behavior is unclear, but some evidence indicates that abnormal or unstable blood glucose levels may be responsible (Fishbein & Meduski 1987).

There are indirect and direct relationships between nutrition and learning (Grohens 1988). Examples of an indirect relationship are the possibility that poor nutrition leads to absenteeism and that an iron-deficient diet and its consequent anemia reduces the child's energy level, thus leading to a low level of attention in school (Levine 1987). An example of a direct relationship is the research finding that protein-poor diets produce children who have lower IQs, are less able to learn, and have poor language development.

Little is known about the adverse effects of mild degrees of malnutrition (Levine 1987) and it is difficult to establish a direct relationship between an inadequate diet and academic achievement because mild or moderate malnutrition is so closely bound up with the environmental effects of poverty. Severe malnutrition during the prenatal and perinatal periods and/or during infancy adversely affects brain development and behavior (Read 1976) and negatively affects both mental and physical growth (Perkins 1977). The nutrition of pregnant women is vitally important because the child's brain begins to develop long before birth.

ORTHOMOLECULAR OR MEGAVITAMIN THERAPY.   Another controversial medical issue involves giving massive doses of vitamins and minerals to hyperactive or learning disabled children. The aim is to produce optimum concentrations of certain substances normally present in the human body. For the pros and cons of this issue, see Cott (1985), Sieben (1977), and Adler (1979). In response to Sieben's criticism, Cott writes: "The efficacy of these various treatment modalities has not been supported overall by incontrovertible evidence. But that is not reason to dismiss the possibilities." According to L. B. Silver (1987), no biochemical studies have documented Cott's claims.

HAIR MINERAL ANALYSIS.   Another controversial issue is the analysis of trace minerals in the hair. *Hair mineral analysis* is used to detect excessive amounts of trace elements that may be harmful such as lead, arsenic, mercury, cadmium, and aluminum. It can also be used to obtain information regarding the overall balance of nutrient mineral levels in the body. Such minerals as calcium, magnesium, copper, and zinc are necessary for maintaining normal physiological functions. Dietary deficiencies in these nutrients and Vitamin C enhance the toxicity of lead and cadmium, and therefore should be considered in hair mineral analyses. Hair-sample analysis is a much better indicator of the long-term exposure of low levels of lead than is blood (Thatcher & Lester 1985), but it should never be used as the sole indicator (Baker 1985). According to L. B. Silver (1987), there is some question as to how accurately hair analysis measures the levels of trace elements in the body.

In five of nine studies, learning disabled pupils were found to have significantly higher levels of lead and/or cadmium than were present in the control groups (Moon et al. 1985). Moon et al. (1985) found that increases in arsenic and the interaction of arsenic with lead were significantly related to decreased word recognition and spelling performance on the WRAT. Thatcher and Lester (1985) report higher levels of lead and cadmium in low achievers than in achieving students. Another study (Struempler, Larsen & Rimland 1985) reveals that Navy recruits with high hair magnesium levels tended to be poor readers (an unexpected finding since magnesium is a nutrient mineral) and that those with high levels of cadmium tended to have reading and behavioral problems. But the presence of excessive trace minerals does not provide causal evidence.

It is generally accepted that high levels of lead or other metallic pollutants can cause neurological damage. However, there is considerable debate regarding the effects of low doses of such pollutions (for example, compare Fishbein & Meduski 1987 versus Ernhart, Landa & Wolf 1985). There are no data to support the contention that deficiencies in nutrients cause learning disorders and there is little evidence that modifying low levels of mineral concentrations affects learning (Sieben 1977).

ALLERGIES.   There is some medical opinion (e.g., Mayron 1979) that allergies cause learning problems. But, as Levine (1987) points out, two of the most common chronic disorders in childhood are allergies and learning problems. It is not surprising, therefore, that they coexist in some students. Although there may not be a direct causal relationship, there may be an indirect contributing one. Allergies cause wheezing and scratching, two behaviors that may make it difficult to concentrate in school (Levine 1987).

APPLIED KINESIOLOGY.   Some chiropractors claim that learning disorders are caused by the displacement of the sphenoid and temporal bones, which causes neurological problems by creating unequal pressure in areas of the brain. Proponents of this theory use "applied kinesiology" to treat reading and learning disorders. However, their basic premises run contrary to concepts held by most anatomists, and outside research has not replicated their reported cures (L. B. Silver 1987).

The aforementioned medical issues are controversial and not for the reading specialist to decide. Parents are responsible for choosing their physicians and for following or not following the medical advice received. When asked, however, the reading specialist may wish to relate to parents and other educators both sides of the issue and the research findings on the topic.

Favorable articles on a health topic are likely to appear in popular magazines and in some journals aimed at educators. Fewer research studies testing the hypothesis, and conducted by objective researchers, are likely to be published. Establishing clear causal relationships between health-related factors and reading disability is difficult. These health factors probably interact with preexisting CNS strengths and weaknesses, as well as with environmental factors. A skeptical attitude toward health-risk factors is advisable. Medical explanations are easy to sell, but apparently logical and appealing explanations for phenomena often fail to survive rigorous scientific inquiry (Levine 1987).

10

Correlates of Reading Disability III: Educational, Sociocultural, and Emotional Factors

The preceding two chapters explored the cognitive, neurological, and physical factors that may be correlates of reading disability. This chapter discusses educational, sociocultural, and emotional factors. The chapter concludes with a consideration of the interrelationships of factors as they may occur in a disabled reader, and with directions for making a reading diagnosis and a case study.

EDUCATIONAL FACTORS

Information from School Records

Cumulative school records can provide information useful for understanding a child's current reading problems, for example: What was the child's age on entering school? (Was he too young to profit from typical instruction? Was she much older than average? If so, why was school entry delayed?) When was poor academic progress first noted and what, if anything, was done? Which grades, if any, were repeated and why? And how often was there a change of school or teacher, possibly exposing the child to differing methods of reading instruction? (It is not the moves themselves that are important, but the causes or consequences of those moves.) Attendance records can indicate if learning opportunities were disrupted by frequent or prolonged absences, and this information may indicate illness or truancy. Teachers' annual ratings of conduct, effort, and personality may be significant. Achievement and intelligence test scores should be noted, although low IQ scores on group tests may show only that the child could not read the test. A clean health record, including satisfactory vision tests, should not be taken at face value; a thorough physical examination should, if possible, be part of the diagnostic study whenever physical or neurological problems are suspected.

Teachers who have previously taught the child should be consulted for information not entered on records. It may be important to find out what methods of teaching reading have been used with the child, especially in first grade. The child's former teachers can also contribute information about his behavior in class, attitude toward reading, and home conditions; and their impressions of the child's intelligence and language facility. Attempts should also be made to determine the child's academic values. Students who do not value school, who see little purpose in reading, or who enjoy other activities in preference to reading are unlikely to develop a high level of reading achievement (Athey 1982).

Instructional History

An instructional history can cast light on how a reading disability started and developed, but it is usually impossible to obtain an accurate history. Parents can recall what they thought of the first-grade teacher, but they never knew the details of what went on day by day in class. The child's recollections of early schooling are apt to be vague, and many children are unwilling to confide information about their true feelings to an inquisitive adult. The teacher's view of the child may have been biased, and teachers rarely realize their own possible contributions to the failure of children.

Teacher effectiveness has a strong influence on how well children learn to read (A. J. Harris 1979b).[1] It seems reasonable to conclude that some children who have become disabled readers might have fared better with different teachers. But if most children learn reasonably well with a particular teacher, the child who does not may have handicaps that prevent her from responding to instruction.

Teacher Practices That Contribute to Failure

According to McDermott (1977, 1985), communicative barriers between teachers and pupils can create hindrances to learning: ". . . any kind of classroom talk can do the instructional job as long as mutual trust and mutual accountability between the teacher and the child are achieved." Children "respond most often not to the activity but to the feeling that the adult displays about them in the course of asking them to do whatever it is the adult has in mind."

A similar point of view is expressed by Larsen and Ehly (1978), who discuss the damage that can be done by inaccurate and inflexible opinions about children's capabilities. The danger lies in the creation of a self-fulfilling proph-

[1]See pages 105–116

ecy, which can be especially damaging when it is based on a stereotype of an ethnic or racial group as capable of only inferior learning.

Teacher practices that aggravate learning problems include (1) failing to ensure readiness for learning a new skill or strategy; (2) using materials that are too difficult for the child; (3) instructing the child or group at a pace that is too fast for acquiring new learnings; (4) ignoring unsatisfactory reading behaviors until they become ingrained habits; (5) rarely calling on a child to perform tasks required of other group members; (6) answering questions herself or asking other pupils to answer questions to which the child did not respond soon enough or answer acceptably (rather than giving the child time to think and then assisting the child to think the task through and arrive at an acceptable response); (7) failing to give recognition and approval when the child makes an effort to perform a task or makes a correct response; (8) expressing disapproval or even sarcasm when the child makes mistakes; (9) allowing or encouraging other children to express disdain or derision for the child's efforts; (10) requesting that a child perform tasks that he or she cannot do well in the presence of peers (This practice embarasses the child, can lead to or reinforce a poor self-concept, and may encourage negative attitudes toward the child on the part of peers.); and (11) expecting a student to perform poorly because his or her older siblings did not perform well academically. When pupils sense that they habitually fail to satisfy the teacher's standards, and they receive more disapproval than approval, their efforts and attitudes are likely to deteriorate.

Spelling

The correlations between reading and spelling ability range from approximately 0.5 to 0.8 (Malmquist 1958). These correlations suggest that good readers tend to be good spellers, and poor readers to be poor spellers, but that there are many exceptions. Frith and Frith (1980) indicate three major patterns of reading-spelling relationships: (1) good reader and speller; (2) poor reader and speller; and (3) good reader but poor speller (estimated at about 2% of the population). Apparently children who are poor readers but good spellers are rare.

Good readers are less likely to misspell phonetically regular words than *phonetically-irregular words* (i.e., words in which one or more of the phonemes are represented by graphemes that do not ordinarily represent those sounds, such as the *o* and *f* in *of*.

The misspellings of good readers are usually phonetically accurate (e.g., S-E-D for *said*) (DiStefano & Hagerty 1985).

The misspellings of some disabled readers have been described as unrecognizable (Carpenter 1983) or bizzare (Fox & Routh 1983), but the misspellings of most disabled readers are usually only phonetically inaccurate (Frith 1980). However, whether disabled readers' rates of phonetically inaccurate misspellings differ significantly from those of good readers is an open question because the research findings are mixed (Bruck 1988). Not all, or even most, disabled readers produce phonetically inaccurate misspellings. For example, the misspellings made by about 60% of the disabled readers in Finucci et al.'s (1983) study were primarily phonetically accurate. The degree to which misspellings are phonetically inaccurate may vary with the seriousness of the reading disability, with the most deviant and inconsistent misspellings being made by the most seriously disabled readers. Horn, O'Donnell, and Leicht (1988) state that phonetically inaccurate spelling reflects an underlying language disorder. However, such difficulties may be due, more specifically, to problems in acquiring and utilizing sound-symbol-association knowledge. Ehri (1989) contends that teaching children to spell phonetically has a positive effect on word-recognition ability.

Poor reading ability may have some effect on the development of spelling ability because it limits the opportunities to learn. But spelling disability is unlikely to be accounted for mainly in terms of a secondary effect of reading disability (Nelson 1980).

Spelling tests are used by many European and some North American researchers to identify cases of dyslexia. But the ability to spell words that are in an individual's sight vocabulary does not reliably discriminate dyslexics from good readers because some good readers spell as poorly as dyslexics (Scarborough 1984).

Some procedures delineate subtypes of readers in terms of the types of spelling errors made (see page 264). The finding that the types of spelling errors made by disabled readers vary (Finucci et al. 1983) lends some support to such procedures. Reading specialists may want to assess a child's spelling ability, as well as his writing and computational skills, in order to assess his level of literacy or to obtain information against which to compare his progress in reading.

Handwriting

Poor penmanship occurs with some degree of frequency among disabled readers. In order to test handwriting independently of spelling ability, a teacher can present a printed or typed selection to be copied. Poor penmanship may be an expression of a dislike for reading and everything that goes with it, or it may be a sign of an underlying visual-motor deficit or of neurologically based poor coordination.

Arithmetic

Disabled readers are often below average in arithmetic ability as well, although not as far below average as in reading and spelling. For reading diagnosis, it is not necessary to use an elaborate battery of tests such as the *Key Math Diagnostic Arithmetic Test*. A selection of examples ranging from simple two-digit addition to computations taught at the child's grade level is usually sufficient to disclose any weakness. Asking the child to do each incorrectly answered item out loud often pinpoints specific difficulties, such as gaps in knowledge of basic number combinations, adding or subtracting starting at the left instead of the right, saying a correct number but writing it incorrectly (saying 71 and writing 17), or using the wrong operation (adding when the item calls for multiplying).

The child who is poor at solving written arithmetic problems should be asked to explain her procedure step by step. This makes it possible to identify specific sources of difficulty, such as incorrect word recognition, lack of word-meaning knowledge, choice of a wrong operation, skipping or not understanding an essential step, errors of computation, or failure to check if the answer is reasonable.

SOCIOCULTURAL FACTORS

Three topics are discussed in this section. First, various opinions are presented as to why girls are better readers and have fewer reading disabilities than boys. This is followed by a discussion of the role of the family in promoting reading achievement. Last is a discussion of the relationship of socioeconomic status and minority-group membership to reading disability.

Gender Differences in Reading Ability and Disability

In the United States, girls 17 years of age and younger generally score higher on the NAEP reading tests than do boys of the same ages (Holbrook 1988).[2] They receive higher grades in reading than boys do (Johnson & Greenbaum 1980); boys constitute 70–75% of reading-disability cases (Asher 1977); and the preponderance of children classified as learning disabled are males (Leinhardt, Seewald & Zigmond 1982). Such data have led to various speculations as to the cause of the apparent gender differences in reading achievement.

Research findings suggest that maturational or biological explanations are not viable because similar female superiority does not exist in other countries (Preston 1979, Downing, May & Ollila 1982). Nor can the apparent female superiority in reading be attributed to the feminization of American schools because, on the whole, male and female teachers do not differ significantly in their perception or treatment of boys and girls (Stake & Katz 1982). No bases have been found for beliefs that (1) the contents of basal readers favor the interests of girls; (2) boys achieve more when taught by males; and (3) female teachers structure classroom situations in ways that alienate boys (Johnson & Greenbaum 1980). It may be that, at least in the elementary school, girls are more motivated to succeed academically, they try harder, complete their assignments, are less disruptive, and so forth; and these behaviors account for the higher reading grades assigned by teachers. It does not, however, account for the female superiority on standardized reading tests, and the question of why girls are more motivated or conforming than boys remains unanswered.

Cultural and sex-role expectations probably contribute to gender differences in reading achievement. School-age girls in North America view reading as femininely appropriate. Young North American boys (i.e., those in the early primary grades) accept reading as an appropriate masculine activity (May & Ollila 1981), but they rapidly learn to perceive reading as feminine. In other countries, males perceive reading as an appropriate masculine activity throughout the school years. But because of methodological difficulties, the findings of

[2]According to Downing, May, and Ollila (1982), when girls reach the secondary school, they lose any significant superiority in reading achievement that they may have had in the elementary school.

cross-cultural studies have not offered definitive evidence that cultural differences are the main cause of gender differences in reading achievement (Downing, May & Ollila 1982).

Cultural influences on sex-role expectations appear to begin early. For instance, in one study, girls obtained higher scores than boys on the *Preschool Inventory*, a difference Laosa (1981) attributes to differential home instruction: Parents involved their 3-year-old girls in school-relevant activities more than they did boys of the same age. When children enter school, they are expected to act in the "appropriate" student role that typically emphasizes obedience, conformity, and learning by listening and reading rather than by active participation. These expected behaviors fit the traditional female sex role better; young boys who are highly accepting of the traditional masculine sex role are more likely to experience conflict and stress in school (Johnson & Greenbaum 1980).

Two hypotheses suggest that gender differences in reading ability are genetically linked: (1) The odds are stacked against males because sex-linked defects are transmitted only on X chromosomes; and (2) boys develop more slowly in spatial perception and language ability, and are more vulnerable to pre- and perinatally acquired deficits (Young & Tyre 1983). Various neurological and biochemical hypotheses as to why more boys than girls are disabled readers have also been offered (see pages 320–321). Additionally, Goldberg, Shiffman, and Bender (1983) suggest that one reason for the higher proportion of reading disability in males is the greater incidence of trauma of the central nervous system experienced by males. But, contrary to what would be expected from theoretical speculation regarding gender differences in hemispheric specialization, Canning, Orr, and Rourke (1980) found that male and female disabled readers did not differ significantly on a number of perceptual, visual-motor, language, and concept-formation abilities. There may also be a referral bias, as suggested by findings that the actual ratio of intermediate-grade boys to girls who were reading two or more years below grade level and potential level was only 3 to 2 (Naiden 1976), 10 to 7 (Scarborough 1984) or 3 to 1 (Maughan, Gray & Rutter 1985; DeFries 1985). This contrasts sharply with reported ratios as high as 10 to 1.

The reasons for gender differences in reading ability are of interest for a number of reasons; however, the issue may be irrelevant for classroom and reading teachers because the range of individual differences in reading ability within each gender is so wide that average differences between the sexes are almost meaningless for educational planning.

Home and Familial Influences

Children are raised in families and in home environments that vary widely with respect to a number of factors. Family values and practices as well as home conditions can influence students' attitudes toward reading and can exert a major influence on reading achievement. Variables within the home that are related to school learning fall into two categories (Fotheringham & Creal 1980): (1) status variables (e.g., SES), which, although positively correlated with school achievement, are of limited value in explaining how the effects of the family are passed on to the child; and (2) process variables (e.g., achievement press, providing rich language environments), which indicate what parents do to encourage and support academic achievement by their children.

Familial influence seems to operate through the initial level of learning ability with which the child enters school, which is partly inherited, and through opportunities for learning and attitudes toward education (Fotheringham & Creal 1980). Child-rearing attitudes and practices can influence preschool children's intellectual development (Laosa 1981) and their later academic achievement (Banner 1979), as can helping children with their reading at home, or listening to them read books sent home by the school (Tizard, Schofield & Hewison 1982).

The following process variables associated with the family are likely to have a positive influence on cognitive development and reading achievement (Sartain 1981, Greaney 1986, Samuels 1986):

1. Interact verbally with the child. The higher the quality and frequency of these parent/child interactions, the more likely the child is to develop linguistic and cognitive skills that are important for reading. Parents can also present good language models for their children.

2. Demonstrate an interest in and a favorable attitude toward reading. Children who come from homes that contain abundant reading materials score significantly higher on reading tests than children who have few books or magazines in their homes (NAEP 1985b). The presence of reading materials is not as important a factor as what their presence probably indicates. Families that value and enjoy reading are more likely to have many reading materials in their homes. Parents who are observed reading widely and who discuss what they have read are developing positive attitudes toward reading.

3. Provide opportunities for reading. The presence of books in the home does not insure that they will be read by any member of the family. Parents can encourage their offspring to read by buying children's books and magazines for them, by taking them to the library, and by discussing what the children have read with them. Parents can also provide a quiet place for children to read and do their homework.

4. Provide a home environment that is psychologically comfortable and supportive.

5. Provide cultural and learning experiences such as taking children to places that will help them to establish backgound knowledge. During such events, parents should help their children to acquire verbal labels for the concepts that they acquire on these trips.

6. Provide tutoring as needed. This should be done without inducing anxiety; it may be done by siblings and relatives.

7. Show an interest in children's academic performance. Discuss the children's school programs and progress with them, and reward their efforts and successes. The importance parents place on academic achievement can be a potent determinant of school success (Levine 1987).

8. Read to children. Reading to preschoolers is linked to their initial attempts in learning to read. Important competencies are more likely to be acquired if, in reading to the child, adults or older siblings: (a) interact

verbally with the child; (b) make references to the child's experiential background before reading and relate it to the story content; (c) provide positive reinforcement when the child becomes actively involved in the story; (d) answer the child's questions; (e) present and discuss evaluative questions after the reading. (Teale 1981, Shanahan & Hogan 1983)

Parents with a high level of education are more likely to provide the above-mentioned assistance, but parental influences may vary for different children in the same family. Home environment tends to have a stronger effect on reading achievement than on reading habits (Greaney 1986).

Parental influence can also be negative. Abusive, dominating, overly demanding, disapproving, overprotective, rejecting, or affection-lacking parents tend to have an adverse effect on their children's reading achievement. The same is true of homes that are characterized by domestic turmoil or intensive sibling comparisons or competition. Children whose lives are heavily programmed by their parents often find it very difficult to plan or organize activities independently (Young & Tyre 1983, Levine 1987).

Some life events within the family constellation may also have a negative impact on academic performance. These include such potentially disruptive events as a death or a divorce in the family. Children respond differently to such events (Levine 1987), and although stress from family problems may aggravate school problems, it is seldom the sole cause of school failure.

Rules that define allowable and expected behaviors are developed and enforced in homes and in classrooms. Hansen (1986) reports that the greater the discontinuity between the "rules of interaction" in the home and in the school, the lower the child's academic performance. Children fare best in school situations in which the interactive rules parallel those in their homes. Pupils from any type of home can be relatively disadvantaged in some classrooms, and relatively advantaged in others. Familial interactive rules are likely related to SES. For example, low-SES parents are more likely to be authoritarian; middle-class parents to be more democratic and permissive.

Most parents are interested in their children's reading ability and are concerned about their progress in reading. Parents need to know what the school is attempting to accomplish for their children, how it is trying to do so, and how they can assist the school. Practical suggestions for getting parents involved and communicating with them are presented by Vukelich (1984), Fredericks and Taylor (1985), and Rasinski and Fredericks (1988); and for conducting effective parent conferences, by B. Barron and Colvin (1983). M. Harris (1981) offers suggestions that families can use to help their children in language and reading development, and Rhodes and Hill (1985) present ideas as to where parents can locate information about children's reading and how they can help them. Refer to Boehnlein and Hager (1985) for an annotated bibliography on parental involvement.

Socioeconomic Status and Reading Achievement

Correlations between socioeconomic status (SES) and academic achievement range from about 0.35 to 0.50 (Fotheringham & Creal 1980). But SES is not a unitary factor; rather, it is comprised of a number of variables so highly interrelated that it has been impossible to separate out the effect of each on reading achievement. No one is certain as to the precise mechanisms through which SES exerts its influence on reading achievement. Nevertheless, high-SES children tend to be good readers, and a large proportion of poor readers come from low-SES families. When low-SES pupils develop learning difficulties, their prognoses for academic success are poorer than for middle- and upper-SES pupils who have the same learning problems (Schonhaut & Satz 1983).

There are a number of minority groups in America, which are primarily non-white, although caucasians in some inner-city and isolated rural areas may also be considered minority groups. The term "disadvantaged" is often applied to minority-group members who also have a low SES (as commonly defined by family income, parental occupation, residence, and other such variables).

There is ample evidence that disadvantaged children tend to have low reading achievement (see page 82). The causes of this situation are probably multiple and varied (M. Fry & Lagomarsino 1982) (refer to pages 82–85). Also, although there is little difference in the early grades among SES groups in terms of their self-concepts, the self-concepts of low-SES children tend to decline more quickly over the ensuing years (Wigfield & Asher 1984).

Disadvantaged children can become good readers, as illustrated by the CRAFT Project (A. J. Harris et al. 1968). At the beginning of first grade, the median reading readiness test score of 20,000 inner-city pupils in their study was at the twentieth percentile. However, with experimental teacher training and the use of motivational techniques, these children scored close to national norms in reading comprehension in second and third grades. More recent evidence also indicates that disadvantaged children can increase their reading achievement (see page 85). The same factors are related to reading disability across the range of SES, but low-SES pupils are more likely to be severely disabled readers because they have additional factors working against them.

FAMILY INFLUENCES.   Children from the same cultural, ethnic, and racial backgrounds, who live in the same neighborhood, and who attend the same school can vary widely in reading achievement. As indicated above, the family can have an important influence on reading achievement. Differences in parental involvement in reading activities and the value parents place on school success give rise to achievement motivation, which in turn influences children's efforts and successes or failures. Middle- and upper-SES students are more likely to enter school with the idea that reading is important, and to have been exposed to activities that foster school-relevant cognitive skills and motivational styles (Wigfield & Asher 1984).

Disadvantaged students who become good readers are most likely to come from families in which the parents value education, have a strong desire for their children to succeed in school and express that desire to them, provide emotional support, and provide guidance without strict domination.

Middle- and upper-SES families can also contribute to low reading achievement. For example, being an "average reader" is not sufficient in the eyes of some parents, so they place extreme pressure on their child to achieve far above what he or she may be capable of accomplishing. The increased anxiety created by this situation may cause the child to perform at an even lower level than before.

PEER INFLUENCES.   As children move through the grades, peer systems become important influences on students' learning (Hiebert 1983). According to Entwisle et al. (1986), peer influences were operating in the integrated and black working-class schools they studied, but not in the white middle-class schools. Peer influence can be positive, but if the pupil belongs to a gang or club whose code is antagonistic to school and derogates school success, it becomes almost obligatory for a member to neglect learning. Peer groups exert a negative influence on the school achievement of low-SES students (Wigfield & Asher 1984).

It may be, as Labov (1973) suggests, that low-achieving, inner-city children will continue to fall further behind in reading as they get older unless the aims of the peer group and school are brought into harmony, or until peer-group antagonism to schooling is neutralized. Labov's viewpoint is limited in application, however. Some gang members learn to read well, and others remain nonreaders. This would not happen if gang influence were the only important factor.

HEALTH FACTORS AND SES.   In general, health problems of many kinds tend to be more common among the poor; and health problems of poor children are more likely to be neglected or to receive poor attention and treatment. One might expect, for example, that poor maternal health during pregnancy, and the resulting possibility of neurological damage to the baby, is more common among the poor than in the general population. In a study of 2,000 black children in Chicago, prematurity and poor maternal health during pregnancy were significantly related to later school adjustment (Kellam & Schiff 1969). Intensive clinical studies were made of 29 children chosen at the end of first grade as the poorest readers in a school with mainly black and Puerto Rican children, from a low-income neighborhood. "A comparatively large proportion of the first-grade children in this study gave evidence of constitutional difficulties or developmental lag. The difficulties discovered were of several types and the etiology in most cases was not clear. Emotional and social factors compounded the difficulties in almost every case and complicated the diagnosis" (Fite & Schwartz 1965).

There is little reason to believe that the health situation has changed in the past 25 years or so. When disadvantaged children are reading well below the norm for their peers, as well as below their expectancy levels, a search for persisting handicaps and inhibiting factors beyond those common to the group is recommended.

EMOTIONAL AND SOCIAL VARIABLES

Whereas case studies may reveal concurrent reading problems and personality or emotional problems, research studies comparing good versus poor readers have not found any consistent group differences. The latter probably reflect misguided attempts to find a common personality type or emotional problem in students who have reading problems or disabilities (A. J. Harris 1971b).

Poor readers display a wide range of personalities and mental well-being. There are poor readers who are emotionally healthy; inhibited, but considered to be "good children" because they do not cause any trouble; disruptive in class; adjudicated delinquents; extroverts; introverts; braggarts; self-effacing; and psychotic. Affective factors play a role in reading ability and disability (Athey 1985b), and therefore need to be considered in diagnosing and treating reading problems and disabilities.

Personality Theories

Many personality theories have been proposed, and each expresses a point of view that may be true of some children. Athey (1985b) provides excellent short summaries of several personality theories. For each theory, she indicates some implications for reading ability and the results of research relating the theory to reading problems. The brief descriptions below are oversimplified versions of the theories. To be understood fully, each theory must be studied carefully in greater detail.

Lecky's (1951) *self-consistency theory* explains resistance to learning to read as a conflict between the child's belief structure regarding what he wants to be (and how he wants to act) and what the school expects of him. For example a first-grade boy's notions of how a boy should behave may cause him to reject stories whose content runs contrary to his beliefs, and may thus adversely affect his reading acquisition.

Developmental-task theory (Erikson 1950, Havighurst 1953) states that at each stage of development, the accomplishment of certain tasks is central to healthy personality growth. "In American society, learning to read is the *major* developmental task of the elementary school years" (Athey 1985b, p. 538). Those who succeed tend to develop feelings of autonomy, a sense of mastery of their environment, accurate perception of reality, and low anxiety; those who fail show the opposite traits.

Expectancy theory emphasizes the importance of the teacher's beliefs about children's abilities. This theory suggests that pupils' self-perceptions tend to be influenced by their perceptions of the teacher's feelings toward them. Teachers' perceptions of their students may be accurate or inaccurate, flexible or fixed. An inaccurate, fixed opinion about a child may do real damage (see pages 114–115, 356).

There are several theoretical, psychoanalytic explanations of ways in which personality dynamics can influence learning. For example, one theory suggests that inhibition of sexual curiosity as a result of real or imagined parental threats can be overgeneralized by the child to an emotionally based inhibition of intellectual curiosity in general (Strickler 1969).

Effect of Reading Failure on Personality

Children who are outdistanced academically by their peers are apt to be disturbed by their lack of progress. Although they might try harder at first, if their efforts fail to bring improvement, strong feelings of stress eventually develop. When called upon to read, such children become tense and, as a result, their performance deteriorates even further. They may become convinced that they are "dumb," and generally build up a strong dislike for reading that may lead to either "fight" reactions (e.g., refusing to carry out the reading assignment, engaging in disruptive behavior during reading activities) or "flight" reactions (refusing to attempt challenging reading tasks) (Gentile & McMillan 1987). As they fall further and further behind in their academic achievement, they lose interest in classwork and become inattentive. Their parents are likely to show strong disappointment and may nag, threaten, or punish them. These behaviors, in turn, tend to intensify the children's negative emotional reactions and to increase their dislike for school. Thus, a vicious cycle becomes established. Gentile and McMillan (1988) present ways of helping disabled readers to deal with stress during reading.

Disabled readers are very sensitive to the opinions of others and usually feel keenly the criticism of teachers, classmates, and parents. These feelings can be aroused even when the critical attitude is not directly stated, but only implied in actions or facial expressions. Unsympathetic reactions to children's problems can cause students to become bitterly resentful.

Children differ in how they interpret and respond to failure (Licht & Kistner 1986). Some children attempt to make themselves as inconspicuous as possible by developing a meek, timid attitude that seems to say "I hope nobody notices me." These pupils often daydream to excess. Others attempt to protect their ego by denying that their failure is important to them (you cannot be hurt by something about which you do not care). Still others adopt a truculent, defiant pose, as if to dare anyone—teacher included—to make fun of their failure or even to try to teach them. A few children attempt to compensate for their shortcomings by boasting, bluffing, or exaggerating (e.g., telling tall stories). Some children may exhibit physical reactions such as facial tics, nail biting, or stuttering. Some complain of headaches or dizziness or even resort to vomiting in order to avoid reading tasks. Some may become truant. Fairly satisfactory compensations can be achieved by some children through becoming highly proficient in school subjects such as arithmetic or art, or by becoming outstanding in mechanical work or athletics.

Even if children are emotionally well adjusted when they enter school, continued failure in reading tasks is very likely to have unfavorable effects on personality. The meaning of any maladaptive reaction to reading failure can be understood only if the teacher is willing to look for the reasons behind the objectionable behavior before taking disciplinary measures.

Self-Concept, Attribution, Motivation, and Learned Helplessness

The direct and specific causes of self-concept have not been determined (Quandt & Selznick 1984).[3] But according to *self-concept theory*, children who feel adequate, self-confident, and self-reliant tend to be good readers; poor read-

---

[3]Quandt and Selznick state that there are problems in assessing "self-concept" with both self-reports (e.g., respondents are not always truthful) and observations (e.g., data are highly influenced by the observer's objectivity). But Marsh, Parker, and Barnes (1985) report that the ll subscales of the *Self-Descriptive Questionnaire II* were reliable and fairly independent. At grades 7–12, the academic, but not the nonacademic, subscales were significantly correlated to academic achievement.

ers tend to have negative self-concepts, particularly in relation to school achievement. According to Hansford and Hattie (1982), the correlations between self-concept and reading achievement are low, but Marsh, Parker, and Barnes (1985) report that self-concept, as measured by a newer test, correlated 0.78 with reading in Grades 7 and 8. As with other variables, the cause-effect relationship is not clear, but is likely influenced by factors such as personal and family aspirations, peer accomplishments, and the expectations of teachers (Serafica & Harway 1979).

A number of studies have reported that reading- and learning-disabled students have low self-concepts; however, self-concept is not a single entity, but a system of concepts about one's "self" assuming different roles in various types of situations (Athey 1985b). It is more accurate to state that reading- and learning-disabled pupils have low academic and intellectual self-concepts; they may, and often do, have high self-concepts for other situations (Cooley & Ayres 1988, Chapman 1988).

Many preschoolers and first graders have high, positive self-concepts regardless of their achievement or ability level. Around the third grade, pupils with learning problems begin to lower their academic self-concepts. Preadolescents with learning problems appear to be the most susceptible to the negative impact of school failure on academic self-concept (Quandt & Selznick 1984).

Rist (1970) believes that low self-images or negative expectations dampen reading performance. Entwisle et al. (1986) found that the expectations of first graders were amorphous, even though they had positive ideas about themselves. There was little variability in these beliefs across SES levels and racial groups. Coleman (1985) reports that high-SES low achievers had significantly lower self-concepts than low-SES low achievers who had been mainstreamed.

Reading- and learning-disabled pupils tend to be rejected by their teachers and classmates (Horne 1982). They are often reported to occupy an inferior social status in school (e.g., Gottlieb et al. 1986); but, at least in some cases, their apparent low social status may have to do with how well they are known by the other children (Cohen & Zigmond 1986). There is little direct evidence regarding the relationship between their low sociometric status and the behaviors of LD children. However, their lower social status may be due, at least in part, to subtle conversational behaviors, which are yet to be identified, but which apparently elicit negative first impressions from others (Pearl, Donahue & Bryan 1986). Many low achievers have low opinions of their cognitive abilities, and are aware of the negative attitudes toward them (Siperstein et al. 1978). The former point is important because a feeling of competence is a source of satisfaction, which is independent of extrinsic rewards, punishments, and social expectations (Athey 1985b).

Although research suggests that school success increases the probability that students will develop positive self-images and that repeated failure or low performance increases the likelihood of low self-concepts (Braun, Neilson & Dykstra 1976), the evidence strongly suggests that attempts to enhance students' feelings about themselves may not lead to improved academic achievement (Scheirer & Kraut 1979). It may be that in addition to improving self-concept, the intervention must also improve the child's reading ability. In our experience, the disabled reader's self-concept often improves as a result of improvement in reading.

Attribution theory holds that an individual's motivation and behaviors are influenced by the factors to which the person attributes success or failure. *Locus of control* refers to whether a person believes that outcomes are the result of his or her control (internal control) or of factors beyond control, such as the actions of others, task difficulty, or luck (external control).

According to attribution theory, attributing success to ability and failure to lack of effort leads to willingness to try more challenging tasks. It also leads to task persistence and continuing motivation because the student believes that effort will result in success (Willig et al. 1983). Children who attribute outcome to effort are likely to work harder and longer than those who attribute outcome mainly to ability. Students who attribute failure to lack of ability are likely to be less persistent at tasks (the feeling is that effort will not make much difference); and the less persistent child tends to take less personal responsibility for both success and failure (Thomas 1979). Attributing one's academic failure to poor ability is significantly related to low expectancy and poor achievement.

Children under the age of 7 or 8 are less likely than older students to conclude that they are low in ability and to decrease their efforts as a result of failure. After the age of 10, failure is much more likely to have seriously debilitating effects on performance (Licht & Kistner 1986). Students with low self-concepts are more likely to attribute failures to lack of ability and to explain their successes as being caused by external factors. Both attributions could lead to lowered motivation (Cooley & Ayres 1988).

Compared to children who are making normal progress in reading, disabled readers tend to believe that success is caused by external factors (Hiebert 1983) and reflects more a lack of ability than a lack of effort (Hill & Hill 1982). Disabled readers are also less likely to attribute failure to a lack of effort than to task difficulty or luck (Pearl, Bryan & Donahue 1980). In general, high reading achievement scores are significantly related to high self-concept and internal locus of control; low reading scores to low self-concept and external locus of control (Rogers & Saklofske 1985).

Research findings regarding the locus-of-control beliefs of learning-disabled adolescents is mixed (Bender 1987b). Children with low self-concepts who attribute failure to a lack of ability or to an external locus of control are not apt to be highly motivated to perform reading tasks. Some observed performance deficits could be the result of failure-induced motivation problems that negatively affect performance on all school-related tasks (Stanovich 1986a).

Johnston (1985) suggests that rather than accepting neurological or processing-deficit explanations of reading disability, we should consider explanations that stress the combination of attribution, anxiety, maladaptive strategies, inaccurate or nonexistent concepts about aspects of reading, and motivational factors. Kavale and Forness (1986) describe the LD child as a *disassociated learner;* that is, one who is not actively involved in the learning process. A lack of motivation could lead to a lack of involvement. Johnston and Winograd (1985) believe that many problems exhibited by poor readers are related to their passive involvement in reading. They suggest that a key factor underlying *passive fail-*

ure appears to be the child's perception that responses and outcomes are independent and, therefore, remediation must force the passive learner to focus on the response/outcome relationship. In other words, their attribution needs to be retrained. Because disabled readers often do not understand the relationship between effortful, strategic behavior and successful performance, Borkowski, Wehing and Turner (1986) suggest a program that combines strategy instruction and attributional retraining. Bender's (1987a) findings partially support the concept of LD children as inactive learners.

Attribution plays a key role in learned-helplessness theory. *Learned helplessness* is the phenomenon in which children come to believe (learn), as a result of repeated failures over time, that their efforts have little or no effect on outcomes (Pearl, Bryan & Donahue 1980). This attribution results in increased expectations for failure, passivity, decreased efforts and persistence, anxiety or depressed affect, lower self-esteem, and self-blame (Friedman & Medway 1987). Compared to achieving students, children who have developed learned helplessness tend to place significantly less emphasis on the amount of effort required for success (Thomas 1979) and may react with impaired performance even when success is clearly within their capabilities and even in areas in which they do not have a learning disability (Pearl, Bryan & Donahue 1980). Learned helplessness may lead to an increasingly generalized inability to deal with academic tasks of all types (Perfetti 1985).

A study by Friedman and Medway (1987) reveals that fourth- and fifth-grade LD children did not consistently demonstrate learned-helplessness behaviors. Friedman and Medway interpret their findings as being more in keeping with *low achievement motivation theory*, which states that pupils are driven more by the need to avoid failure than by the need to attain success.

Although many remedial approaches suggest providing students with opportunities to experience success as a means of improving their self-concepts and developing a more positive attitude toward tasks, such experiences can be ineffective with children who underplay the role of their effort in success. Negative attribution can be reversed (Willig et al. 1983), but not all attempts are successful (e.g., Pflaum & Pascarella 1982). *Attribution retraining* primarily involves getting pupils to accept responsibility for their successes and failures, and to understand that effort and persistence may help to overcome failure (Stipek & Weisz 1981; DeSanti & Alexander 1986–87). Attribution retraining is less successful when it consists only of admonishing students to try harder than when it includes instruction in how to direct effort to strategic processing (Pressley, Johnson & Symons 1987). Unless increased effort and persistence result in improved performance after treatment has ceased, positive treatment effects are likely to be short lived. To insure long-term maintenance of new, more desirable attributions, pupils must be trained on a variety of tasks, across a variety of settings, over a long period of time (Licht & Kistner 1986). Pupils with learned helplessness need a positive remedial approach that increases their motivation through the setting of attainable goals.

RELATIONSHIP OF CONSTRUCTS   A possible oversimplification of the theoretical relationships among self-concept, attribution, motivation, and learned helplessness is as follows: Children with poor self-concepts tend to attribute their failures to lack of ability or to factors beyond their control. The belief that they cannot do anything to overcome their failures leads to decreased effort and eventually to a feeling of helplessness. Poor self-concept, external locus of control, negative attribution, poor motivation, and learned helplessness are associated with poor reading achievement. What is not known, however, is the direction of the relationships. For example, are poor self-esteem, negative attribution, and lack of effort a cause or an effect of reading disability? Or are the conditions mutually reinforcing?

Anxiety

It is not surprising that many disabled readers rate high in school-related anxiety. A high level of anxiety has a debilitating effect on school performance (Willig et al. 1983); but in general, anxiety affects individual children differently. For some, it causes distress that disrupts performance; for others, it presents a challenge that enhances performance. The optimal level of anxiety probably varies with individuals and types of tasks, as does the role of anxiety in reading success and failure (Athey 1985b). Research suggests that anxiety interferes with learning by causing some children to divide their attention between the task at hand and their preoccupation with how well they are accomplishing that task (Wigfield & Asher 1984).

Emotional Problems

Disabled readers often have some emotional maladjustment, especially if the disability has been present for a number of years, although, such emotional problems are usually not severe.

It is difficult to determine the cause-effect relationships between reading and emotional problems for a number of reasons. First, similar emotional problems occur in both good and poor readers. Second, the causes of a reading disability are usually not investigated until a few years after it has occurred. Retrospective data are not particularly reliable and, because the reading and emotional problems have probably been mutually reinforcing, it becomes almost impossible to disentangle the cause-effect relationship at that late date. Two studies have attempted to determine whether emotional/behavioral problems appeared before the reading problems (and thereby, whether the emotional problems *could have* caused the reading problems). McGee et al. (1986) found that behavior problems were present at school entry, and that reading failure exacerbated the existing behavior problems. Jorm et al. (1986) report that backward readers,[4] already had behavior problems at school entry. But the retarded readers did not evidence such problems at school entry nor did they exhibit behavior problems after a reading problem developed. Both studies, however, have a few recognized, serious limitations. Third, professional opinion regarding the role emotional problems play in reading disability frequently var-

[4]The term *backward reader* refers to a child whose test score was below the average attained by children of the same age; the child's learning potential (e.g., intelligence) is not considered. A *retarded reader* (Americans use the term *disabled reader*) is reading significantly below age level and learning potential.

ies according to particular professional backgrounds. For example, a psychiatrist is more apt to attribute a major causal role to emotional problems than would a behavioral or cognitive psychologist. Finally, both sets of problems could be due to a third factor such as an inherited predisposition toward both conditions, or an adverse social environment (McGee et al. 1986).

Whether an emotional problem causes or contributes to a reading problem (or vice versa) probably depends on such factors as how long the problem has existed, the pupil's ability to cope with problems, the severity of the problem, and the treatment and support received by the student.

The attempt to describe carefully and accurately the different emotional problems that can contribute to reading disabilities is only in its early stages. Nevertheless, several different problems can already be distinguished.

1. Conscious refusal to learn. The child feels real hostility to parents or teachers or both—hostility consciously realized and readily expressed—and rejects reading because it is identified with the adult or adults against whom these feelings are directed. This frequently occurs when there is a conflict between the cultural values of teacher and pupil; a child from a minority background may not be willing to accept the goals that teachers approve, perhaps because doing so might jeopardize the child's social standing in the gang. Or the child may be imitating an admired parent who frequently voices contempt for "book learning."

2. Overt hostility. In some children, self-control is hard to maintain because they have built up intense feelings of resentment and their angry feelings are apt to break out with relatively little provocation. Such children are generally regarded as "bad," and for them school tends to become a continuing series of skirmishes and battles, interrupted by punishments. For these children, the teacher-pupil relationship is rarely conducive for learning.

3. Negative conditioning to reading. The child has built up a negative emotional response to reading (fear, anger, dislike) through the normal working of learning by association. Reading, having become associated with someone or something already feared or disliked, becomes able, by itself, to produce negative emotional reactions. As an example, one child had a first-grade teacher who walked around the room rapping knuckles with a ruler, and who placed great stress on reading. The child's panic-like reaction to the teacher continued in response to reading lessons from other teachers in later years.

4. Displacement of hostility. The child may be jealous of a favored brother or sister who is good in reading. In this case, the child's hostility becomes transferred to the act of reading, which is the sibling's strong point. Another pattern is that of the child who is unable to express hostility toward the parent, who is an avid reader, in any open and direct fashion. The hostility may be expressed indirectly by failure in reading, which is so important to the parent. Displaced hostility is rarely recognized as such by either parent or child.

5. Resistance to pressure. Mothers who are overanxious about a child's eating and try during early childhood to cram as much food as possible into the child, often find their children becoming feeding problems. Similarly, overambitious parents, who want their child to be a genius, can develop in their children a resistance to pressure for intellectual attainment that may take the form of lack of interest in reading. Reading in such cases becomes the main battle-ground on which children fight for their "rights."

6. Clinging to dependency. Children who are consciously or unconsciously overprotected and babied may prefer to remain infantile and get attention through helplessness. Learning to read may mean growing up and becoming self-reliant, which the child is not yet ready to attempt. This pattern is common among children who were the only child for 4 or 5 years before they entered kindergarten or first grade. Such children may interpret being sent to school as an attempt to get them out of the house so mother can give her full attention to the new baby.

7. Quick discouragement. Some children start off with a desire to learn to read but meet with initial difficulty and quickly give up and stop trying. These children, as a rule, come to school with marked feelings of inferiority and insecurity already well established. Their home life fails to provide them with security and affection. Often they come from broken homes or homes in which much quarreling goes on. Many of them have the feeling (justified or unjustified) that their parents do not care for them. In various ways, their lives have failed to give them wholesome feelings of self-confidence and self-respect. For this reason they are easily convinced that they lack intellectual ability and accept inferior status in reading as natural, when other, more self-confident children would exert extra effort.

8. Success is dangerous. For some children with deep-lying emotional problems, almost any successful form of self-expression may stir up feelings of intense anxiety and distress, related to unconscious fears of destruction or damage. For such a child, success in reading may symbolize entering into an adult activity and therefore attempting to compete as a rival with a parent. Such competition, in turn, implies the possibility of dreadful forms of retaliation. On an unconscious level, the child feels that safety lies in self-restriction and passivity. This reaction, based on deep-lying unconscious conflicts, tends to be resistive to remedial help unless psychotherapy is also provided.

9. Extreme distractibility or restlessness. A high degree of tension in a child may build up an uncontrollable need for relief in the form of physical activity. The child who is unable to sit still is likely to fall behind in learning, and once aware of being behind, quick discouragement is likely to set in. Distractibility is often closely related to restlessness and complicates the picture, because the child's attention is pulled away from the reading task by almost any stimulus. In cases of neurological deviation, distractibility is one of the main problems to be overcome and often requires that the remedial work be completely individual, be conducted in a distraction-free place, and be done calmly, because high motivation may bring about disorganization.

10. Absorption in a private world. Some children are absorbed in their own thoughts to such an extent that they can give only intermittent attention to their environments and cannot devote to reading the sustained attention needed for good learning. Many of their daydreams and reveries are of a wish-fulfilling type in which they hit home runs, score touchdowns, and achieve other romantic ambitions. Sometimes their ruminations are of a morbid character. In either case, their inner preoccupation interferes with the attentive concentration that good reading requires. When retreat into fantasy is severe enough to interfere with progress in a good remedial situation, referral for study by a clinical psychologist or psychiatrist is desirable. Some children who seem merely to be inattentive insofar as the teacher is concerned are found to have severe mental disturbances (obsessive-ruminative psychoneuroses or schizoid states) for which intensive psychotherapy is urgently needed. If the condition is severe (e.g., autism, childhood schizophrenia), residential care may be required. But some schizophrenic children can respond to remedial reading help on an outpatient basis (Levison 1970).

Psychotic children often perform poorly on cognitive and information-processing tasks, so their reading failure may mistakenly be attributed to mental deficiency. Some emotionally disordered children are good readers. Others have excellent word recognition but little comprehension. Still others can understand what they read, but are so impaired in their social relationships that their idiosyncratic responses to questions make teachers doubt their reading comprehension ability.

11. Depression. Substantial evidence indicates that major depressive disorders and learning difficulties are associated, but that the nature of the relationship is not clear (Livingston 1985). Nevertheless, emotional depression, especially when severe and long-lasting, can have a marked negative influence on learning or can prevent a pupil from demonstrating what has been learned.

A diagnosis of depression requires that the child display for a period of at least two weeks, a sad or irritable mood or a loss of interest or pleasure in activities that usually elicit such responses, as well as the presence of at least eight other symptoms (e.g., changes in appetite, weight, or sleep patterns; feelings of guilt; apathy) (Livingston 1985). Childhood depression may not be recognized by parents or teachers.

The incidence of childhood depression is unknown, but estimates of its presence in LD children range from about 2% (Brumback & Staton 1983) to as high as 54% (Colbert et al. 1982). Differences in identification criteria likely account for such widely varying estimates.

In describing emotional problems that may be found in disabled readers, an attempt has been made to make the problems understandable. More technical descriptions have been given by Pearson (1952). Kaye (1982) reviews the literature on the psychoanalytic perspectives of learning diabilities. Not all cases fit into any of these categories.

Disabled readers who come to the attention of psychiatrists and clinical psychologists are likely to have marked emotional problems. Those who are not referred outside of the school system usually have less serious emotional difficulties. Many more disabled readers likely fall in the latter category.

Parental Reactions

Some children react negatively to reading in response to a home situation for which the parents are primarily responsible. Going beyond that, it is important to inquire how parents react to the discovery that their child has a reading problem.

In a follow-up study of over 200 cases, it was concluded that severe reading disabilities caused emotional problems in families more often than family emotional problems caused reading disabilities. The parents were especially hurt by three problems: (1) frustration in the attempt to find good diagnostic and treatment resources; (2) the ignorance, hostility, and defensiveness of some teachers and principals; and (3) actual cruelty to the child in the classroom (Kline & Kline 1975).

Efforts to get accurate information from parents, and to convey diagnostic conclusions and recommendations to them, sometimes fail because the parents are unable to respond.

> Parental reactions of denial, projection, helplessness, and hopelessness are equally common and equally deterrents to adjustment. Denial is a basic form of self-protection against painful realities. Some parents are unable to face the facts; they cannot "hear" the diagnostic interpretation; they "shop around" for magical cures; they acknowledge physical defects but are oblivious to mental disability. . . . The tendency of some parents to project blame elsewhere for the child's shortcomings is further symptomatic of stress. The obstetrician is blamed for inducing labor prematurely, the pediatrician is blamed for improper treatment of infection and injury, and sometimes parents blame each other. When the teacher is included as a target for blame, an effective partnership with the parent is difficult to achieve. In denial or projection, the child is the ultimate loser. (Begab 1967)

Abrams and Kaslow (1977) point out that family dynamics can play a significant role in reading disabilities and that different family constellations provide clues to the best kind of intervention for each family. They discuss seven intervention strategies, ranging from educational help only to psychotherapy involving both the child and the parents, and suggest criteria for deciding which intervention may be best in each case. Kronick (1976) lived with the families of three learning-disabled children and described the sometimes destructive interaction among the family members. Parents' perceptions of and reaction to the child's reading difficulty may be contributing to the child's problem and, therefore, may have to be attended to while the child is receiving remedial instruction (Rourke & Fisk 1981).

Juvenile Delinquency

An estimated 26–85% of delinquents have a reading or learning disability (Nickerson 1985, Larson 1988). Maughan, Gray, and Rutter (1985) found that about 67% of their sample of disabled readers had records of juvenile delinquency.

Even when backgrounds are controlled, learning disability and juvenile delinquency are significantly related (Dunivant 1982). Five hypotheses attempt to explain the reading/learning disability–juvenile delinquency link: (1) The reading disability leads to school failure, which leads to a negative self-image, which, in turn, results in school dropout and delinquency; (2) some reading- and learning-disabled pupils possess antisocial characteristics that contribute to their academic problems; (3) both the antisocial behavior and school failure are consequences of adverse family backgrounds or peer relationships; (4) reading/learning-disabled youths are at increased risk for delinquency because they: a) are low in social skillfulness, b) have certain personality characteristics (e.g., impulsivity, poor reception of social cues); or c) are more likely to be ineffective in problem solving; and (5) reading-disabled and non-reading-disabled children engage in the same rate and kind of delinquent behaviors but are treated differently by social workers, the police, and judges (Schonhaut & Satz 1983, Larson 1988). However, a causal relationship between reading disability and delinquency has neither been established (Larson 1988) nor disproved (Keilitz & Dunivant 1986).

Investigating Emotional and Social Conditions

An understanding of the child's emotional makeup is best acquired by learning his past history and from day-to-day contact with him. The first, and perhaps most important, phase of gathering data is to gain the child's friendship. A teacher who is accepted as a friend can usually get the child to talk with some freedom about him- or herself—likes and dislikes, fears and hopes, hobbies and interest, friends and enemies, family; in fact, about nearly anything. Since many of these children regard themselves as friendless, the remedial teacher is in an ideal position to become a sympathetic listener.

Personality tests of the paper-and-pencil questionnaire type often are not very helpful with reading-disability cases. Frequently it is necessary to read the questions to the child—a procedure that is time consuming and probably less revealing than the information that can be obtained using the same time for informal talks. On the other hand, some children find it difficult to talk about their feelings but have less difficulty answering the more impersonal printed questions. An incomplete-sentence test like the one in Figure 18.2 on page 672 may be very useful with them.

The psychologist, who has only a limited time in which to try to understand the child, relies on interviews and observation of the child's behavior during testing, supplemented by case-history material and possibly by projective test results. Projective techniques must be administered by a trained examiner, and the resulting data interpreted with great care. Parents can provide important information. As with children, it is important in interviewing parents to be understanding, sympathetic, and noncritical if true feelings are to be expressed. Even when a cordial relationship has been established, the interviewer must remember that self-protection and self-deception are not uncommon and that what the parent says must be interpreted with discriminating judgment.

Among the questions to which interviewers should try to obtain answers are the following:[5]

1. Who are the other people in the home? What are their ages? How much education have they had? Which ones work? What are their outstanding traits? What languages are spoken in the home?
2. What is the social and economic status of the family? What sort of house or apartment and neighborhood do they live in? Are they living

[5]The use of male pronouns in this list is arbitrary; all questions, of course, apply equally for girls.

at a poverty, marginal, adequate, comfortable, or luxurious level? Has the status of the family changed markedly since the child's birth?

3. How adequate is the physical care given the child? Is he provided with suitable food and clothing? Does he get proper attention when sick? Have physical defects been corrected?

4. What intellectual stimulation is provided in the home? What newspapers, magazines, and books are available? How much has the child read or been encouraged to read?

5. How is the child treated by his parents? Do they love him, or are there indications of rejection or of marked preference for other children? What disciplinary procedures do they use? Do they compare him unfavorably with other children or regard him as having low intellectual ability? Are they greatly disappointed in him?

6. How is the child treated by his brothers and sisters? What do they think of him? Do they boss him or tease him about his poor reading ability?

7. How does the child feel about his family? Does he feel neglected or mistreated? Has he feelings of hatred or resentment against family members? Does he resort to undesirable behavior in order to get attention?

8. What efforts have been made to help at home with his schoolwork? Who has worked with him? What methods have been used? How has the child responded to this help? What have the results been?

9. How does the child spend his spare time? What interests does he show? Does he have any hobbies? Does he show any special talent? What are his goals for the future?

10. Who are his friends, what are they like, and how does he get along with them? Does he play by himself? Does he prefer to associate with younger children? Is he a leader or a follower?

11. What signs of emotional maladjustment does he show? Has he any specific nervous habits? Is he a poor eater or poor sleeper? What variations from normal emotional behavior does he show?

12. How does he feel about himself? Has he resigned himself to being "dumb"? Does he give evidence of open feelings of inferiority and discouragement? If not, what substitute forms of behavior has he adopted? Does he engage in lying, stealing, fire-setting, or vandalism?

13. How does the child feel about school? Classmates? Teachers? Which subject does he like best? Least? How does he think the teacher(s) feels about him? What does he think his classmates feel about him? Does he try to evade going to school?

14. How does the teacher feel about the child? His learning ability? His effort? His conduct? His status among his classmates? Does the teacher try to provide help? In what way? Has the school provided remedial help? If so, how, when, by whom, and with what results?

When evidence seems to indicate marked emotional disturbance, the teacher should call the child to the attention of the person responsible for working with such problems. This may be the school guidance counselor, school psychologist, principal, or school social worker. Intensive study in a child guidance clinic or examination by a clinical psychologist or psychiatrist is probably needed. Decisions about what kind of treatment should be started first and whether or not to proceed with remedial teaching, should preferably be made by the specialist or the clinic. If, however, there would be a delay of several months before the special diagnostic study could be carried out, it is better to try remedial instruction than to wait and do nothing.

Those who are interested in delving further into the relations between reading disability and social and emotional problems will find helpful integrative summaries and discussions, accompanied by useful bibliographies, in Connolly (1971), A. J. Harris (1971b), and Athey (1985b).

INTERRELATIONSHIPS OF CAUSAL FACTORS

Diagnosis would be comparatively easy if one could expect to find only one important causal factor in each disabled reader, but such an expectation would be mistaken. A number of possibly causal or contributing factors, any one of which could be an important drawback to progress in reading, are likely to be found in most cases of reading disability, especially when it is severe.

Mitchell was 7½ years old and had just completed second grade in a private school. His teacher did not think that his reading was very poor, but his mother was worried about it. During a morning of testing and interviewing, the following significant facts were discovered:

(1) Mitchell's general intelligence was slightly above average. (2) His speech was somewhat indistinct, and a slight hearing loss was suspected. (3) He had entered the first grade in public school when he was only 5½ years old. His teacher rated him as immature and inattentive, and he missed several weeks because of scarlet fever. He was transferred to a private school and entered the high first grade with zero reading ability. Lack of reading readiness was obvious. (4) He had been taken to an eye specialist, who prescribed stereoscopic exercises to correct a marked difficulty in binocular vision, but Mitchell's mother had had difficulty getting him to do the exercises and had discontinued them. (5) Mitchell could not remember which was his right hand and which was his left and could be considered a case of directional confusion. (6) The combination of indistinct speech, immaturity, inattentiveness, poor eye coordination, and directional confusion strongly suggested delayed and irregular neurological maturation. (7) He had been exposed to teaching that was undoubtedly ineffective and unsuited to his needs. Although the class was small, there was no individualization of work. The teacher used the now-outmoded story-memory method: One day the teacher would read a selection to the class, and the next day the pupils would take turns orally reading the same selection. Mitchell had good auditory memory and, by listening carefully, he had been able to "read" well without paying attention to the printed words. Actually he was unable to read pre-primer material satisfactorily, but he had been trying to read first and second readers. No training in decoding had been given. (8) There were several sources of emotional difficulty. Mitchell had been a nervous, overactive child since babyhood. His mother had taken him to a child guidance clinic when he was 4 years old because she had trouble trying to get him to mind. He had one older sister whose good behavior and excellent schoolwork were frequently held up to him as exam-

ples. His father had been in the army for 3 years, stationed away from home. Because Mitchell was much more attached to his father than to his mother, this separation was undoubtedly a source of anxiety. (9) Mitchell had never shown evidence of a strong desire to learn to read.

In Mitchell's case, as in so many others, there was more than enough causation to create a severe reading disability, and it was impossible to determine the relative contribution of each handicap to the total outcome. Was Mitchell reacting with immaturity to the loss of his father's attention and his mother's favoritism toward his sister? Would he have developed a reading disability because of delayed and irregular neurological maturation regardless of the family picture? We will never know. The number of different, possibly contributing factors he displayed is not unusual in severe cases of reading disability.

From a practical standpoint, the aim of a thorough diagnosis is not to fix the blame for the child's difficulties but to discover each of the many conditions that may require correction or consideration. A person who develops an enthusiasm for any theory of causation can frequently find evidence of that handicap but is likely to overlook many other significant complications. An unbiased search for every possible handicap is needed for a really comprehensive and satisfactory diagnosis. This usually requires the combined efforts of several different professions.

It is satisfying to a diagnostician to come out with a definite conclusion about causation in each case but, from a practical viewpoint, this is unnecessary. The practical value of an intensive diagnostic study depends on the degree to which answers are provided to the following questions: (1) What persisting and present factors are likely to interfere with responsiveness to remedial instruction? (2) What can be done to eliminate these factors or lessen their impact? (3) Should remediation be started as soon as possible, or should it be delayed until other forms of treatment help the child to be more responsive to instruction?

Among the forms of noneducational treatment to be considered are correction or control of medical conditions, correction of visual problems, speech correction, social service assistance to the family, and counseling or psychotherapy for the child, the parents, or the family. Aside from remedial instruction, educational recommendations may involve a change of school, class, teacher, or program and may require providing information about the child to the school staff in a way that should improve their treatment of him or her.

MAKING A READING DIAGNOSIS

Reading diagnoses are conducted to determine how best to assist students to improve their reading abilities. In making a diagnosis, facts must be collected from tests, observations, and records. However, the heart of diagnosis is not testing or fact gathering, but the intelligent interpretation of information by a person who has both the theoretical knowledge and the practical experience to know what questions to ask about each child's reading problem and, therefore, what information to obtain; how to obtain valid, reliable information efficaciously; and how to interpret the data intelligently.

Reading diagnoses can be carried out to various degrees of completeness, with the amount of diagnostic information obtained being dependent on the seriousness and complexity of the individual reading problem.

If provided with appropriate reading instruction and frequent opportunity to read, most pupils become increasingly skilled readers. But all students do not progress at the same steady rate, nor is an individual's progress always even. In the daily course of events, some students do not perform assigned reading tasks acceptably. At such times, perceptive, knowledgeable classroom teachers utilize diagnostic techniques to determine what can be done to improve learning. Thus, classroom teachers ask themselves such questions as, "What does the pupil need to know or be able to do in order to perform this task?" "Which of these skills and pieces of information does the student possess?" and "How can I modify my instruction to accommodate this pupil's abilities and needs?"

At other times, the teacher may suspect that a child has a specific problem (e.g., decoding previously unencountered printed words of more than two syllables). So, the teacher selects or constructs an appropriate test to check this hypothesis. Depending on the task(s) required by the test and the knowledge of the teacher, the test results may simply confirm or deny the hypothesis or may provide information regarding the child's specific strengths and weaknesses in decoding polysyllabic words. In the latter case, the teacher must devise and deliver an instructional program individualized for that child or for others with very similar needs. If the results indicate that the child can perform the task, the next step is to determine why the pupil does not employ those skills in the classroom. It may be necessary, for example, to convince the student that he or she can perform the task, and that there is a payoff for taking the time to do so when reading.

A classroom teacher who wants to know whether a book is of a suitable level of difficulty for a particular purpose with a child, need not construct or administer an informal reading inventory (IRI); use of a more easily constructed, administered, and scored cloze test may provide sufficient information to make the decision. Nevertheless, knowing how to make and interpret the observations usually made during the administration of an IRI can be useful to the classroom teacher in daily lessons and in instructional planning.

Good classroom teachers can identify and correct many reading difficulties and problems, thereby preventing them from worsening and accumulating, and causing a reading disability. However, teachers should not be expected to make detailed comprehensive reading diagnoses; most of them have neither the expertise nor the time to do so. When a classroom teacher cannot determine why a student is not progressing in reading ability, the pupil should be referred to a reading specialist.

The first phase of the reading specialist's diagnosis should be based on the stated reasons for the referral. Thus, if the referral suggests a severe reading problem (e.g., "Jamie can't read anything," or "I think Max is learning disabled"), or if the principal requests a list of disabled readers, the reading specialist must obtain current measures of the students' general level of reading ability and of their potential for improvement. In other words, the first question to be answered is "Does the pupil read significantly below his or her potential?" If the student is a disabled reader, the diagnostician must then attempt to make three determinations: (1) the level of material that is most appropriate for reading instruction; (2) specific strengths and weaknesses in comprehension and word recognition skills and strategies; and (3) where to begin the remediation (i.e., what is most important for this child to learn first, second, etc.). For some referred students such information can be obtained quickly, but it may take longer to do so for those with serious reading problems.

If a new teacher requests help in placing a recently arrived student in the most appropriate reading group, the specialist should find out which materials each group is using. Then he or she would determine, on the basis of the child's performance on samples of these materials, which of the groups to recommend. If the first-grade teacher says, "This child can't learn to read any words," the specialist determines exactly what instructional procedure the teacher is using, tries them with the child, and observes the child's reactions to the tasks. If the procedure can be modified to accommodate the child's learning, the specialist informs the teacher of this modification and may help the teacher put it into practice in the classroom. If the instructional procedure is judged to be inappropriate for the child, the specialist would employ trial teaching to determine the best way to teach this child to recognize printed words. Or, an intermediate-grade teacher may refer a student who "can't understand anything he reads unless it is stated directly and simply in the book." Then the specialist's tasks is to determine under what conditions and why the student is having difficulty making inferences or understanding implied relationships. If an upper-grade teacher reports that "Sherri can't remember much of what she reads from her science textbook," the reading specialist first determines if the student can comprehend the text. If she is unable to understand the text adequately, the specialist then seeks to determine why. If Sherri's comprehension is adequate, the reading specialist explores such possibilities as weak or unused study skills or habits, lack of motivation, or poorly constructed teacher tests.

The reading specialist may decide that a pupil's problems can be handled by the classroom teacher, with varying degrees of support. The degree of backup needed is a function of such factors as the classroom teacher's instructional ability, the number of pupils in the class who require extra or special assistance, the severity of the pupil's problem, and the availability of appropriate instructional material.

If the reading specialist determines that the classroom teacher could not follow through on his or her suggestions even with assistance, or would not provide the appropriate instruction that is needed, the specialist may decide to work with the child directly. Such situations are more likely to occur when the pupil has a serious reading problem. Should the specialist be unable to determine how to help the pupil, he or she may refer the pupil to other professionals who may either provide useful information or take over the case.

Pupils may display markedly different levels of performance in the classroom and reading center. A child who is relaxed and in a supportive learning environment may demonstrate greater reading ability than in a tense, anxiety-provoking situation. Being in a one-to-one situation, as opposed to a group or class situation, can also influence performance. In a one-to-one setting, the variables that can influence performance are easier to control. Some students also work better when they have the undivided attention of an adult, something that they relish. Or, a child may stay on task more because she or he knows that the specialist is quickly aware of off-task behavior. It is also possible that the following other situational differences might account for differences in performance: peer pressures in and out of the classroom, a conscious or unconscious decision not to perform well in a certain subject area or for a particular teacher, or a lack of motivation to succeed academically. If the classroom learning environment is not conducive to learning, the specialist should tactfully attempt to change it. Understanding and changing the student's unwillingness or inability to perform in the classroom may require the assistance of the school psychologist or counselor.

Referrals may be based on questionable, uninformed, or faulty criteria. For instance, a child may be referred as being a nonreader, not because he or she cannot read, but for not choosing to do so as a leisure-time activity. Although such a problem needs to be addressed, the teacher should learn to provide more accurate reasons for her referrals. Occasionally, teachers believe that children have reading problems because they do not complete, or complete inaccurately, their workbook or homework assignments. Follow-ups often reveal that the children did not understand how to perform the task, did not have the skills to do so, or were bored by the tasks. A teacher may think that dialect renditions constitute word-recognition errors and, therefore, mistakenly think that a child has a serious word-recognition problem. In some cases, the problem is that the teacher is asking the student to read materials that are much too difficult, or to perform tasks for which he or she does not have the prerequisites. Occurrences such as these are matters for in-service education.

The Need to Determine Causation

Attempts to determine the causation of a child's reading difficulty are based on the belief that knowing the causes will enable the teacher or reading specialist to provide the most appropriate treatment. But the term "cause" is variously defined in the literature on reading disability; little evidence supports a direct cause-effect relationship between reading disability and almost all its hypothesized causes; and no one cause is likely to account for all or even most instances of reading disability.

The term *cause* may refer to factors, usually cognitive or neurological in nature, believed to be the basic underlying reasons why pupils have difficulty learning to read through the use of instructional methods that work with most pupils. Such underlying causes are commonly associated with severe reading disability, and usually with children who have limited word-recognition ability.

Low intellectual ability can contribute to *poor reading ability* (i.e., reading ability that is significantly below age level) because, for example, language and concept development are slower and more limited than normal, and because reasoning ability is limited. But not all poor readers are disabled readers. Poor readers whose level of reading ability is commensurate with their reading potential (which is usually assessed by means of an intelligence test) are not disabled readers because they are not functioning below what could reasonably be expected of them. Slow learners could be classified as disabled readers if they were reading significantly below their capacity *and* if the statement, "has at least average intelligence," were not included as one of the criteria. But even then, low intellectual ability would not be considered a cause of the reading disability. By definition, a disabled reader is not functioning at or near age level, even though she has the general intellectual ability to do so. Measures of general intelligence can be used to separate those who are functioning reasonably well in reading from those who are not. However, the fact that a student has the general intellectual ability to be reading at a significantly higher level does not rule out the possibility of specific cognitive deficits or dysfunctions that could be contributing factors. The problems lie in the difficulty of obtaining reliable measures of these variables and in proving a cause-effect relationship (see Chapter 9). At present, classroom and remedial teachers should not be concerned with making such determinations.

Because reading involves written language, it is natural to assume that language deficits or dysfunctions might be causing or contributing to a pupil's reading difficulty. Listening comprehension is used as a measure of general language comprehension and to estimate reading potential. The rationale for both usages is that general language ability is a good indicator of the level of reading ability a pupil can reasonably be expected to achieve. As a measure of reading potential, the results of listening comprehension tests are interpreted similarly to those of IQ tests. Comparing listening and reading comprehension allows one to determine if poor *reading* comprehension is due to weak *language* comprehension, or is specific to processing written language. If listening and reading comprehension are commensurate, and if both are below age level, poor reading comprehension is likely due to poor language comprehension. In such cases, one should decide whether other variables (e.g., familiarity with English, intelligence, linguistic experiences) are contributing to the language comprehension problem and what can be done to help the child. If reading comprehension is significantly lower than listening comprehension, the child is said to have a reading comprehension problem. The examiner should then determine which of the variables that are unique to reading are contributing factors. One other possibility should be considered. Regardless of the student's general level of listening (language) ability, certain aspects of language (e.g., anaphora, embedded clauses, words signaling "thought reversals") may be causing problems for the pupil, and could be impinging on reading comprehension. Such possibilities can be checked out by using informal measures and observations, or through the use of standardized tests that purportedly sample these skills. In the latter case, care should be exercised in test selection.

By most definitions, children who have severe sensory impairments cannot be classified as reading or learning disabled. This restriction does not mean that visual or auditory deficits or dysfunctions cannot cause or contribute to a child's reading problems. Obviously, blind children cannot learn to read printed text, and those with limited sight would find it difficult to learn to read print unless adjustments were made in the materials used for reading. Somewhat similarly, a child who has been profoundly deaf from birth is much more likely than a normally hearing child to have reading comprehension problems. Students may have less severe visual or auditory losses, many of which can be compensated for through corrective lens or hearing aids. Reading teachers and specialists need to be alert to past and present sensory problems, to consider such problems in their teaching, and to refer pupils to vision or auditory specialists as needed.

By definition, students often cannot be classified as reading or learning disabled if the "primary" cause of their reading disability is believed to be socioeconomic (sociocultural, environmental), emotional, or educational.

The question of how to determine if low SES is a "primary" or "secondary" cause is rarely even addressed, and the issue is often overlooked in practice. Low SES, in and of itself, is unlikely to cause reading disability, and it is probably impossible to separate out the interrelated factors associated with low SES and minority-group membership that "caused" or contributed to the child's low reading achievement. Therefore, because teachers cannot change a child's SES and cannot determine exactly which aspects of low SES cause or contribute to the student's reading problem, the best policy is to try to understand how any of these factors are presently contributing to the reading problem; what, if anything, can be done to overcome or bypass them; and, as with any child, to develop and deliver a reading program adjusted to the child's strengths and needs. Evidence indicates that low-SES students do respond to quality reading instruction (see page 85).

Children with recognized severe emotional problems rarely attend regular schools, but reading specialists may encounter children who were once emotionally disturbed or whose emotional problems are now under control. The emotional problem may have prevented the pupil from acquiring important reading skills, but there is no way of being certain that the emotional problem was indeed the cause. What the teacher or reading specialist needs to determine is the extent to which the emotional problem is presently impacting on the child's performance so that she can consider this in planning and delivering reading instruction. Such information is best obtained from the professional who is treating the student.

A reading teacher is more likely to encounter students who have the less serious emotional problems that accompany failure. If she is unable to cope with them or if achieving success in reading does not improve the pupil's emotional well-being, the reading teacher may wish to refer the child to a psychologist or counselor, or seek their assistance in working with the child.

Educational factors are usually not considered in defining reading disability. Nevertheless, it is possible that poor, inadequate, or inappropriate instruction contributed to the child's reading problems.

In many cases, the adequacy of past reading instruction cannot be reliably determined. But knowing what the instructional program required may assist in making a diagnosis by providing such information as the ways in which word recognition was supposed to have been taught or the words that were introduced in that basal series. If records indicate that a disproportionate number of referrals of disabled or poor readers come from a particular teacher, the reading specialist should attempt to determine the reasons for that situation. The purpose is not to assess blame, but, if the situation warrants it, to help that teacher to improve his or her reading instruction. The emphasis here is on prevention.

Little can be done by classroom teachers and reading specialists to change certain causal or contributing factors. The findings of other professionals may help them to understand why the child is not making progress in reading, and such findings should be considered in planning and conducting remediation. But there are no reliable neurological or psychological tests that can help to plan a particular child's program. A neurologist may prescribe medication that helps the child to attend to the task; a psychologist may help the child to improve his self-image or to assume more responsibility for learning; a social worker may obtain financial aid for the family or enlist the parent's cooperation in developing the child's motivation; or a vision specialist may prescribe corrective lenses that make it much easier for the child to see the print on a page. However, in the end, it is the classroom teacher or reading specialist who must design, deliver, and evaluate a child's reading program. Effective instruction, especially for severely disabled readers, may result only after extensive trial teaching.

The term "cause" also may refer to either general areas of reading ability (e.g. weak word recognition; inadequate comprehension; lack of study skills); or, to types of skills or strategies within a general area (e.g., inability to recognize high-frequency words; inability to understand textually implicit information; inability to organize and recall information from a textbook); or, to specific skills or strategies (e.g., inability to decode polysyllabic words comprised of two or more affixes and a root word; difficulty synthesizing information across paragraphs due to a weak understanding of cohesive ties; incorrectly assuming that a single reading of a textbook chapter will suffice for comprehension and delayed recall). In this sense, the term "cause" is used to mean that the noted weakness is causing or at least strongly contributing to the child's relatively poor reading performance. In some instances, once the weakness is defined (e.g., the child cannot make the symbol-sound association for any of the short vowels), the next step is to teach these skills to the child. If the child proves able to learn them, there is no need to determine why they were not learned earlier. In other instances, it may be necessary to continue looking for causes before initiating instruction. For example, if the child cannot recognize any of the words shown him, the teacher would first determine if those words were ever taught to the child. If not, then the child's recognition of words that had already been introduced should be assessed before a statement can be made that weak word recognition is causing his reading problems. Or, if a child has difficulty comprehending textually implicit information, the diagnostician should determine if the child comprehends the textually explicit information needed to make the inference, has the topical knowledge that may be necessary to make such an inference, and has the ability to reason through the steps needed to comprehend the textually implicit information. The more specifically the examiner can determine at what point and why information processing is breaking down, the more likely she will be able to treat the problem. As logical as this approach might seem, there is little empirical evidence that improving the skill(s) in one area results in increasing the child's general level of reading ability.

A RECOMMENDED PROCEDURE. Because reading is such a complex ability, comprised of many interrelated processes that must be coordinated, it is not easy to make a reading diagnosis. We have no way to know directly what is going on inside a reader's mind as she attempts to process written language; we must infer what is taking place from test performances and observations of pupil behavior. Furthermore, students' reading problems can vary considerably, ranging from mild to severe, and can be the result of numerous factors and situations.

The length and nature of a reading diagnosis depends on the complexity of the reading problem. At times, it is necessary to determine only the student's general level of reading ability or certain reading skill and strategy strengths and needs. In other cases, it may be necessary to delve deeper into exactly why the child is having difficulty processing the text, and perhaps to consider variables that may currently be interfering with the child's reading progress. Determining the original or basic cause of the reading disability or why skills were not previously learned is often impossible. Opinions about underlying causes differ, and remain largely in the realm of unproven hypotheses. Therefore, differential diagnosis is very unreliable, as are programs based upon such diagnoses. Most reading problems are not severe, and can be treated without knowing exactly what caused the reading problem initially. This does not mean that basic research in these areas is unwarranted. On the contrary, we strongly support such efforts and feel that educators and psychologists should keep up with this body of research.

Reading specialists, teachers, and psychologists would be well advised to employ the following sequence in making a diagnosis:

Step 1: Determine the student's general level of reading ability and compare it with his potential for learning, giving consideration to other factors that may also have influenced his level of reading achievement. If the reading specialist's and the classroom teacher's estimates of the pupil's reading ability differ, the reasons for the difference should be explored cooperatively. Determine if the materials being used in the classroom are at an appropriate level of difficulty for the child; if not, advise the teacher as to what level of material would be more suitable. If the child's reading ability is commensurate with his level of learning aptitude, employ Steps 2, 4, and 5 only as needed. If the pupil is functioning significantly below his potential, proceed to Step 2.

Step 2: Determine the student's specific reading strengths and needs. An analysis of the pupil's performance on an individually administered reading test may suggest whether to begin assessment in the general area either of word recognition (including decoding) or of comprehension (including knowledge of word meanings). If the student has an apparent reading comprehension problem, determine if the problem occurs only during reading or is common to both listening and reading. The latter situation suggests a language comprehension and not a reading comprehension problem. The reason for this language comprehension problem should be investigated (e.g., Is the problem due to limited intellectual ability? Does the child have difficulty understanding certain syntactic structures? Is the child having difficulty comprehending because he does not understand the meanings of key words or lacks the level of topical knowledge needed?)

Step 3: Determine which factors, if any, are probably hampering the child's progress in reading at this time. Emphasis should be placed on determining the adequacy of reading instruction and the learning environment in which it is provided. At this point, the reading specialist may either report her diagnostic findings and recommendations for remediation to the appropriate school personnel; or, she may opt to initiate remediation or to conduct a complete remedial program. Diagnostic findings and recommendations may be summarized using a form such as the one shown in Figure 10.1 (pages 386–387) or a more detailed report may be needed, especially if a case study is conducted.[6]

Step 4: Remove or lessen those factors that can be controlled or corrected, either before or during remedial treatment. In planning and conducting the remedial program, consideration should be given to those factors over which educators have no control.

Step 5: Select the most effective and efficient ways to teach the needed important skills and strategies, and then teach them until they are mastered. Provide the pupil with ample opportunities to apply these skills to new situations, and monitor his application of them. Constantly evaluate your instructional program, and make adjustments as needed. Also, allow time for the pupil to read interesting materials of his choice. Suggestions for conducting an effective remedial program are considered in the chapters that follow.

Step 6: Refer to an appropriate professional, clinic, or agency any student who does not respond to treatment after a reasonable period of time.

How to Make a Case Study

At times it is necessary to conduct an intensive study of a child's reading disability. Before seeing the disabled reader, the reading specialist should consult available records in order to obtain as much initial information as possible. The first session or two with the child should be devoted to establishing rapport, gaining information about the pupil and his or her reading disability, and leading the pupil into the proper frame of mind for the diagnostic and remedial work. Testing may be started as soon as the student is ready to cooperate. Testing and data gathering can be spread out over a number of sessions, and may continue after remediation has begun. It is advisable to initiate remediation as soon as possible, even though changes may have to be made when more complete diagnostic information is obtained. Disabled readers need to believe quickly that they can improve their reading ability.

The task of the person making the case study is to obtain an overall impression of one child and his or her needs. After sufficient diagnostic information has been collected, conclusions must be drawn regarding: the child's reading strengths and weaknesses, which reading needs should be addressed first, the most reasonable explanation of the causes of the reading disability, which factors may still be impeding reading progress, and what remedial procedures should be tried first. After remediation is underway, the remedial lessons should provide continuous diagnostic information, but more complete periodic checks should also be made to assess the program's effectiveness and to determine the need for changes in materials or methodology. Before releasing the pupil from the remedial program, progress since the beginning of remediation should be assessed and reported.

If a formal case report is to be submitted, it is desirable to follow a definite

[6]Many psychoeducational reports are not read or are ignored. Williams and Coleman (1982) discuss the reasons for these problems as well as ways of overcoming them.

SUMMARY OF READING DIAGNOSIS

Name _____ Date of Birth _____ CA ____ Grade, Class _____

Teacher _____ School _____ Examiner _____ Date ____

Reading Levels   Oral   Silent
     Independent   _____   _____
     Instructional   _____   _____
     Frustration   _____   _____
Listening Comprehension Level _____

Reading Expectancy Quotient _____Reading Quotient _____
Classification: Normal Progress _____Disabled Reader _____
Severely Disabled Reader _____Underachiever _____
Slow Learner _____

Test Results

Reading Test	Form	Date	Scores

Intelligence Test	Form	Date	MA	IQ	Subscores

Other Tests	Form	Date	Results

Comments on test results: _____
_____
_____

Reading Skill Strengths and Weaknesses
Word recognition _____
_____
Decoding _____
_____
Vocabulary _____
_____
Comprehension _____

Figure 10.1. A two-page record form for briefly summarizing the results of a reading diagnosis.

Rate _____

Oral Reading _____

Silent Reading _____

Health: Vision _____
Hearing _____
Present physical condition _____
Health History _____
Home Background: Cultural _____
Socioeconomic _____
Family _____
Siblings _____
Treatment of child _____

Personality: Personality traits (temperament, mood)
Self-esteem _____
Interests _____
Emotionality _____
Attitude toward reading _____
Relationship w/adults _____
Relationship w/peers _____
Remarks _____
School History: Grade progress _____
Attendance _____
Marks in reading _____
Methods of reading instruction _____
Marks in other subjects _____
Conduct & behavior _____
Possible Contributing–Causal Factors: _____

Recommendations
Reading _____
_____
_____

School adjustment _____

Advice to parents _____

Other exams or treatment _____

Figure 10.1. *continued.*

outline. This practice is good insurance against omitting important information, as well as an aid to the person reading the report. The outline that follows can be useful to teachers as a guide in writing up remedial reading cases. The amount of space given to a heading does not indicate its comparative importance; headings H, I, and J are much more important in a case report than the space allocated to them in the outline would suggest.

A. Objective Data
   1. Child's name
   2. Date of birth and age at beginning of study
   3. School grade at beginning of study
   4. Intelligence test data, including name of test and form, date of administration, MA, and IQ
   5. Silent reading test scores, including name of test and form, date of administration, reading age, and reading grade
         When separate norms are available for parts of the test, the scores on the parts should be listed as well as the total score.
   6. Oral reading test scores, including name of test and form, date, and reading grade
   7. Results of standardized tests in other school subjects if such tests have been given
   8. Results of informal testing and observations
   9. Examiner and date of report
B. Reasons for referral
C. Health data
   1. Results of vision tests and other evidence about vision
   2. Results of hearing tests and other evidence about hearing
   3. Summary of child's present health status
   4. Summary of child's health history
D. Home background
      The questions listed on pages 374–375 may be used as a guide in summarizing information about home background.
E. Child's personality
   1. Statement of outstanding personality traits, with illustrations
   2. Child's interests in reading, school, and play
   3. Child's attitudes toward teachers, classmates, and family
F. School history
   1. Record of progress through the grades
   2. Marks in reading and other subjects
   3. Attendance record
   4. Notations about conduct and general behavior
   5. Methods of teaching reading used by former teachers
G. Interpretation of reading-assessment results
   1. Interpretation of silent reading performance
   2. Interpretation of oral reading performance
H. Summary of diagnosis
   1. Summary of outstanding strengths and difficulties in reading
   2. Summary of factors related to the child's difficulties

I. Recommendations for remedial treatment
  1. Recommendations concerning reading instruction
  2. Other recommendations for school adjustment
  3. Recommendations to the parents
  4. Recommendations for medical examination or treatment
  5. Other recommendations
J. Description of remedial treatment
     The description of treatment should be given in detail. Preferably, a chronological order should be followed, describing procedures used at the beginning of remediation and explaining changes made in procedure as the remedial work progressed. Methods should be described in sufficient detail to allow others to reproduce them. The materials used should be indicated.
K. Evaluation of results
  1. Tabular summary of initial test scores and retest scores
  2. Evaluation of progress shown by formal and informal tests
  3. Evidence of change shown in the child's general schoolwork
  4. Evidence of change shown in the child's personality and behavior

Rigid adherence to an outline such as this is not absolutely necessary, but a systematic procedure should be followed. Some cases are more complex than others and need to be described in greater detail. Refer to Salend and Salend (1985) for other suggestions for writing and evaluating assessment reports, and to Abrams (1988) on how to take a case history.

11

Basic Principles of Remedial Reading

The suggestions for individualizing reading instruction discussed in Chapter 5 are based on the assumption that a good developmental reading program must provide for marked differences in rates of learning. Plans for individualizing instruction also include provisions for giving specific corrective help as needed. This type of instructional planning makes it possible to provide much of what was formerly considered corrective reading within the framework of the regular classroom program. *Remedial reading* means giving special help to students whose progress in learning to read is not commensurate with reasonable expectations.

In many ways, remedial reading resembles good classroom teaching. Both have the same desired outcomes, and both involve application of the same basic principles of learning and motivation. Many of the factors that contribute to teacher effectiveness (see pages 105–106) also contribute to effective remediation.

The main differences between classroom instruction and remedial teaching are in opportunity and competence. Remedial teaching allows for diagnosis of individual needs and instruction tailored to those needs to a degree that few classroom teachers can match. Skilled remedial teachers are more expert than most classroom teachers at both diagnosing reading problems and individualizing instruction.

Even in schools where well-differentiated reading programs are in operation, some pupils still need remedial help. The program of the lowest reading group in the class may be frustrating for the least capable readers, and the teacher may find it impossible to give them enough individual attention to meet their needs. Detailed diagnoses are needed when dealing with severe cases of reading disability. A classroom teacher, even one who is capable of conducting such a diagnosis, may not be able to spare the time.

GENERAL CHARACTERISTICS
OF REMEDIAL TEACHING

Basing Remedial Instruction on Needs and Strengths

Good classroom instruction commonly uses a "teach, test, reteach" pattern. This practice points up the importance of determining whether new skills or strategies have been mastered and providing review or reteaching for what was not learned. In remediation, however, the more common pattern is "test, teach, re-test, reteach." Because the pupils have been exposed to a number of reading skills and strategies, the remedial teacher starts by determining what has been mastered and what needs to be improved. Not only can such determinations enable more efficient use of the time available for remediation, but they prevent needless repetition that might bore the child. On the basis of test results, observations, discussions with the child,[1] and pertinent information from other professionals, the reading specialist formulates a plan of teaching to overcome difficulties and make use of strengths. After proceeding with this instructional plan for a time, it becomes necessary to determine whether the instruction has been effective. If the plan has been effective, new skills or strategies can be introduced; if not, additional instruction and practice is probably necessary, or a different instructional approach may be needed.

Starting from What the Pupil Knows

Laying the foundation before putting up the superstructure is as important in remedial reading as it is in building construction. A 12-year-old who is reading at the first-reader level likely needs instruction in basic reading skills. Marked weaknesses in word recognition must be overcome before satisfactory results can be expected from instruction designed to improve reading comprehension. On the other hand, it would be foolish to teach high-frequency words to a child who does not have a word-recognition problem.

Selecting Appropriate Materials and Methods

Selecting appropriate instructional materials is extremely important for the success of a remedial program. Guidelines for doing so have been provided by Roberts (1980) and Cunningham (1981). Three points should be considered in selecting material: (1) its level of difficulty, (2) its interest to the pupils, and (3) whether it lends itself to the teaching and acquisition of the desired learnings. All three criteria need not be met in making every selection.

Prior to receiving remediation, many disabled readers are asked to read text that is too difficult for them. Not only does such "overplacement" lead to feelings of failure, incompetence, and frustration; but it prevents students from acquiring the skills and strategies they need to learn in order to improve their reading ability. Disabled readers do not possess many of the skills and strategies

---

[1]Indrisano (1982) outlines an interview procedure for eliciting from children information about themselves.

necessary for meeting the objectives of the program that accompanies the reading textbooks used in the classroom, which are above their instructional levels, nor can they practice the skills and strategies they do possess if the material they are working with is too difficult for them to read.

Because it is important to convince the student that he can read successfully and to have him read as much as possible, the first connected discourse (e.g., story, short book) the child is asked to read should be well within his instructional level. It should contain few words that he cannot recognize fairly rapidly, and the content should be interesting and easily comprehended. At times, instruction with material below the child's instructional level is warranted, for instance, to ensure that the child will achieve success, or when the teacher does not want word-recognition or comprehension problems to interfere with the acquisition of particular skills (e.g., learning to phrase appropriately) or strategies (e.g., how to understand inferred ideas).

Use of interesting material helps to attract and hold children's attention and, thus, helps to get them actively involved in reading and to keep them on task. Because children usually know more about things they are interested in, the use of interesting material also increases the chance that students will have topical knowledge that can facilitate their reading comprehension. Reader interests are discussed on pages 657–658. The interest value of the content is particularly important when working with older disabled readers who often express disdain for books written for young children. For them, high-interest/low-vocabulary books may be of use (see page 687 and Appendix B).

Selecting materials for initial skill or strategy instruction is relatively easy. However, such materials, as well as those typically used for practice, are almost always brief—usually a sentence or so. The sentences are often contrived to make the skill easier to understand and apply. Use of brief text for some instructional purposes is legitimate, but instruction and practice cannot end there. Children need a number of opportunities to apply newly introduced skills and strategies to natural, complete text. But finding longer, interesting material that both represents an appropriate level of difficulty and requires the application of target skills is not always easy.

Another point to be considered in selecting introductory and practice materials is how much faith can be placed in the title of the exercise or the objective of the lesson as stated by the publisher. It is advisable to analyze materials to determine the actual demands they make on the user. Such analysis reveals whether the exercise is appropriate or whether skills other than those indicated are necessary for successful task completion.

An overall instructional approach is usually selected and this choice depends on factors such as the level of success the child has had with previously utilized approaches or programs, the child's and the reading specialist's attitudes toward the approach, and the availability of materials. If the child is willing to accept its use, the program currently employed in the school's core reading curriculum (and its accompanying approach) can be used, with modifications, in the remedial program. The advantages of utilizing the same program are the congruence between the remedial and core-curriculum programs, and the likelihood that this congruence will facilitate the child's reentry into regular classroom reading instruction. Remediation should begin with the level of reading textbook that is judged to be most appropriate. The child would be instructed only in the important skills and strategies, introduced at or below that level, for which he or she could not demonstrate mastery. One or more stories can be read in a single session, and every story need not be read. The pace of instruction should not exceed the child's ability to assimilate the target skills; but once basic skills have been mastered, it may not be necessary to pace instruction at the same rate as in a developmental reading program. Doing so could prevent the child who is making rapid progress from ever catching up (e.g., a fifth grader reading at the low-second-reader level, who is paced as a normally achieving second grader, would get through only the second-reader program that year, the third-reader program the year after, etc.).

If the child has negative feelings about a program's materials, a program that employs a similar instructional approach may be utilized for remediation or the instructional approach employed in the core curriculum can be used with materials from another reading program or with trade books. Possible problems with using such adaptations include finding material that has sufficient overlap with the vocabulary used in the core curriculum program (this becomes less of a problem at about the third-reader level) and whose content lends itself to the skill-development program of the core curriculum.

Some poor readers are immature enough to enjoy stories written for children several years younger, but many balk initially at using "baby books." This attitude can be overcome by explaining the reason for their use or by employing face-saving techniques (e.g., asking them to prepare a story that will be read to younger students). Most likely the experience of being able to read anything with ease and fluency more than makes up for immature content. The sense of success on completing a reading textbook, no matter how low its level, proves to children that they can improve their reading ability and thereby generates interest. Completing a textbook fairly quickly and being promoted to a higher-level textbook is especially likely to increase motivation.

Almost every type of reading program cited in Chapter 3 can be adapted for use in remediation. For example, individualized reading could be used in conjunction with the skill-development sequence found in the core curriculum. A special-alphabet program might be successful with pupils who have extreme difficulty learning to decode, and linguistic reading materials might provide useful practice for those who need a vocabulary that is tightly controlled for vowel symbol-sound associations. A whole-language approach would require the most modifications because disabled readers seem to profit most from direct instruction.

At times, disabled readers present a dilemma: They reject material that is easy enough for them to read and all the books they are willing to try are too difficult for them. Usually their insecurity makes it difficult for them to acknowledge and accept the low level at which they are functioning in reading. A few disabled readers build up an extreme aversion to any published book. In either case, a modified language experience approach (LEA) may be the answer (see pages 73–74). The emphasis placed by Fernald (1943) on the use of stories created by children is probably as great a contribution to remedial procedures as the kinesthetic methods she advocates.

In using an LEA, children are encouraged to talk about anything of interest to them. With inarticulate or inhibited children, it may be necessary to provide pictures that can stimulate discussion. The teacher selects one of the topics, and suggests that the child might like to make up a story about it. Depending on the child's writing abilities and inclination, the pupil may write the story independently or with the teacher's assistance, or the teacher may write the story initially. Early selections should be kept short. When children produce written stories, there is no need to emphasize correct spelling or to attempt to improve such things as the story line. No attempts should be made to control the wording or vocabulary in the students' initial oral or written attempts. The children are using language that they understand, and perhaps they are proud of any long or unusual word they are able to employ. As the children become more secure, they can select favorite stories for editing.

Initially, the children are simply encouraged to write and to read their creations. Later, the selections are used as a vehicle for teaching reading skills. An LEA can motivate children who are resistive or antagonistic to easy or published materials. Its drawbacks are the heavy demands it makes on the teacher and the possibility that the child's stories do not lend themselves well to the acquisition of targeted skills and strategies. Therefore, it may be necessary to combine use of an LEA with other instructional materials, especially after basic reading skills have been acquired.

In addition to selecting an overall instructional approach, other decisions must be made. For instance, should the remedial program play to the child's strengths or attempt mainly to overcome weaknesses? A number of remedial techniques or methods are available from which the reading specialist must select the ones she believes will probably be the most effective. Trial teaching may help to narrow some of the choices (see pages 252–256). If the technique or procedure does not promote the desired effects after a reasonable time, modifications should be employed or the method should be replaced.

Care should be exercised in developing skills and strategies: Each should be explicated when it is first introduced. A thorough explication contains: (1) the name of the skill or strategy (this helps the child to remember and to apply it); (2) a thorough explanation and demonstration of the steps required to apply the skill or strategy; (3) an explanation of why the skill or strategy is important (how it can help the reader); and (4) discussions and continuing demonstrations of the situations in which its application is or is not appropriate (Blanton, Moorman & Wood 1986).

Reading skills and strategies are often introduced in isolation in order to allow the learner to focus attention on the specific task. Although this practice is acceptable initially, it is rarely sufficient for learning. Guided practice must be provided, followed by wide reading (i.e., reading on a variety of subjects, types, and/or themes) in which the student has multiple opportunities to apply the skill or strategy independently. *Guided practice* involves giving the child ample experience in applying the recently introduced skill or strategy while reading previously unread text under the direct observation of the teacher. Through questioning, the teacher can determine how well the skill or strategy was applied; and can then provide assistance as needed. In providing guided practice: (1) work on only one skill or strategy at a time; (2) link practice to the initial instruction; (3) inform the student as to which skill or strategy is being practiced; (4) provide substantive feedback as to why the child's application is or is not correct (this should help the pupil to establish criteria for determining how appropriately he is applying skills and strategies); and (5) if possible, change to less difficult materials when the child's applications are not at least 80–90% correct (Blanton, Moorman & Wood 1986). Refer to Blair and Rupley (1988) for guidelines in planning, delivering, and evaluating practice activities.

Pacing, Practice, and Review

In remediation, particularly during the early stages, it is important to present instruction in steps small enough for the child to understand and master, and to pace instruction at a rate that will facilitate learning. Pacing involves controlling, not only how much is taught at once, but the rate at which new skills are introduced. A skill should be practiced until the child can utilize it with a comfortable degree of facility before new, related skills are introduced. One factor contributing to the child's reading problem may be that someone has tried to teach her too much too rapidly. On the other hand, pacing should not be too slow.

Once a skill has been taught, it should be practiced and integrated with previously taught skills. The teacher should, therefore, teach only one short-vowel symbol-sound association in an introductory lesson, rather than attempt to teach all five at once. After the child is fairly secure with the first, another symbol-sound association can be taught. This would be followed by practice involving both skills, and so forth. There should also be periodically spaced review of previously taught skills.

Too many remedial reading programs are concerned only with skill development. Although this aspect of remediation is important, recreational reading and functional reading should not be ignored. Children improve their reading ability by reading. Therefore, it is important to: (1) provide time during some remedial sessions for the child to read text that is of interest to him and that is not used for instructional purposes, and (2) encourage the child to read widely and often. The suggestions found in Chapter 18 are just as useful, if not more so, in teaching disabled readers. Ford and Ohlhausen (1988) offer guidelines for motivating disabled readers to read.

Students who receive remediation are usually held accountable for acquiring the concepts taught in the content subjects. Whenever possible, students should be shown how what they are learning in the remedial program can be applied to their content-subject textbooks.[2] If the difficulty of the content-subject texts prevents the students from acquiring the information they contain, adjustments should be made in their functional reading programs.

ENLISTING AND MAINTAINING THE CHILD'S ACTIVE PARTICIPATION

Most disabled readers are aware that they have failed to achieve proficiency in an ability that our society regards as a criterion of general academic competence.

[2]This suggestion should also be followed if a different reading textbook is being used in the regular classroom.

Moreover, they are aware that most of their peers have succeeded where they have failed. Knowing this often leads to self-doubt and beliefs of intellectual inadequacy. Such feelings can start a vicious cycle. The need to protect a damaged or frail ego and feelings of inadequacy may lead to the avoidance of reading tasks whenever possible and/or to being a "disengaged" or "passive" participant when required to perform reading tasks. As a result, these disabled readers practice their reading skills minimally and fail to acquire new skills. They make minimal, if any, gains in reading ability and continually fall further and further behind their peers. The realization that the reading ability gap is widening in turn leads to lower self-esteem and effort; and so the cycle continues.

Remedial intervention can break this cycle, but only if the child's will to learn is aroused and maintained. Motivating a disabled reader to take an active role in a remedial program is not an easy task. Many disabled readers have failed so often and for so long that they believe they are beyond help. Furthermore, some of the things they need to learn are neither easily acquired nor innately interesting. Disabled readers are more likely to participate actively in the remedial program if the following suggestions are implemented: (1) make every effort to demonstrate to the pupils that they are accepted and understood; (2) structure the remedial program so that success occurs far more often than failure; (3) help the students learn to attribute success to their effort and ability; (4) use both intrinsically interesting reading materials and extrinsic incentives; and (5) involve the children in determining their reading problems, planning their remedial program, and evaluating their progress. These suggestions address the need to restore the child's self-confidence and self-concept, retrain attribution, and initiate and maintain motivation.

Acceptance and Understanding[3]

The child must accept himself and the teacher, and the teacher must accept herself and the child. The child's parents also need to accept and understand the child. A child's acceptance of himself is tied to self-concept (see pages 365–369). Quandt and Selznick (1984) offer a number of suggestions for building positive self-concepts. In general, the best way to raise self-esteem is to ensure that children experience success (Scheirer & Kraut 1979). But some children are so deeply discouraged that they have given up trying and have resigned themselves to chronic failure (see the discussion of learned helplessness, page 368). For extremely discouraged pupils, it is advisable to delay reading instruction until they achieve success in at least one other activity for which they have received merited approval and recognition. It makes sense to deal with deep discouragement first by building success in an area where good results can be obtained more quickly than in reading.

Teachers can help disabled readers to overcome often-prevalent and potentially interfering feelings by conveying to them that: other children also have reading troubles; a person can be intelligent and still have difficulty learning to read; reading disability is not caused by some mysterious, life-threatening malady or deficit; and reading problems can be overcome by working together, but

[3]Refer to page 112 for a discussion of the use of praise

it will take time and effort. Axelrod (1975) provides suggestions for dispelling misconceptions disabled readers have about themselves and remediation.

The child's acceptance of the teacher comes about as a result of her ability to interact positively with him (see the following section) and to demonstrate to him that their remedial plan is working. An effective teacher believes in herself and her ability to teach; these beliefs must be conveyed to the child. She must also convince the child that he is accepted, and that negative comments about some of his behaviors do not mean that she no longer accepts or believes in him, but that such behaviors are making it more difficult for him to learn. Disabled readers desperately want to be understood. They often feel shunned, hurt, discouraged, or angry. A teacher who recognizes these feelings and their causes can help children get their emotions under control by demonstrating that her friendly interest is not shaken by awareness of their feelings. Teachers can also help other children to accept a disabled reader by involving the disabled reader in group activities in which he is skilled.

During the course of a remedial program, there are inevitable downs as well as ups; discouragement returns and effort slackens. These periods may be induced by events outside the remedial program, such as a quarrel at home, insufficient sleep, a sarcastic remark by another teacher, or being excluded from a game. At these times, the remedial teacher can provide invaluable support by slowing the pace and maintaining a steady faith in the child. Occasionally, being a sympathetic listener for a child who wants to pour out her troubles can also serve a useful purpose, provided the teacher does not trespass into psychotherapy.

Temporary setbacks can be portrayed in terms of problems to be solved. During these periods, it is important for a teacher to convey to students his trust in them and his readiness to provide support and help as needed (Deci & Chandler 1986).

The Remedial Teacher as a Person

The most important characteristic of a good remedial teacher is a real liking for children. The liking must be genuine; children are quick to detect the difference between a warm, friendly person and one who puts on a show of friendliness without really feeling that way. Appearance, dress, age, speech, theoretical knowledge, experience—all these are less important than a genuine fondness for children as they are, complete with their faults and annoying habits.

Good remedial teachers convey a note of optimism and good cheer to children. The teachers may be full of contagious enthusiasm, or they may be quiet people who create a calm, relaxed atmosphere. They try to avoid any display of vexation or irritation with the children. They create opportunities to praise and try to make criticism kindly and constructive.

Good remedial teachers are sensitive to the emotional needs of children. They do not ask embarrassing questions and accept confidences with friendly interest. Confrontations are avoided by arranging activities in which the child will participate willingly.

Teachers who are naturally endowed with warmth, tact, and sympathetic understanding usually get good results in remedial work. Individuals who are completely insensitive to children should avoid all branches of teaching. Teachers who fall between these two extremes—and they constitute the majority—can greatly improve their relationships with pupils.

Each teacher who succeeds with poor readers finds ways of dealing with the children that are compatible with her personality. A quiet teacher who creates a calm and relaxed atmosphere, a vivacious teacher who stirs children up, and a strong teacher whose self-assurance conveys a sense of security to children may all get fine results although their ways are different.

Cooperation between Teacher and Learner

One vital ingredient of a well-motivated remedial approach is the learner's feeling that the program is his program, not something imposed on him by somebody else. This can be achieved if the reading problem is approached as something on which teacher and pupil can work together. For this to succeed, there must be a teacher-learner relationship in which the learner trusts the teacher's good intentions and wants to help himself. Under these conditions the learner can take an active part in discussing his problems in reading, in trying to select the particular weaknesses that are most urgently in need of attention, in the selection of materials to be used, and in evaluating progress. This is particularly true with adolescents.

The degree of insight into their own difficulties that some children possess is amazing. Sometimes they not only can pick out the major weak points in their reading skills but have intelligent ideas about how they came to be poor readers. Such children can often be given wide latitude in selecting their own materials. They delight in devising ways of checking their work and in constructing charts to record their progress.

This does not mean that the teacher adopts a passive role. On the contrary, the teacher is responsible for the entire process. She encourages the learner to make suggestions, but is obligated to point out important issues the learner may have overlooked, to correct erroneous interpretations and proposals, and to provide helpful guidance at every stage. Encouraging the learner to help in planning does not mean abdication of responsibility, but the creation of an atmosphere of truly cooperative work.

Occasionally pupils resent the implication that anything is wrong with their reading. "Why pick on me? I can read all right," is a familiar complaint, particularly to junior high school teachers. In a way, many of these pupils are right. They can read well enough to plow through a passable portion of the assigned reading. But their reading is likely to be laborious, halting, slow, full of minor inaccuracies and misunderstood words, and only partially understood. They are aware that they are not particularly good readers, but usually do not realize how faulty their reading actually is.

Rob, an eighth grader, was resentful about having been singled out of his class for special help in reading. "Maybe you are right," said the teacher. "You can take a reading test if you want to, and we can score it together. After that you can decide whether or not you want to work on your reading." Rob took the *Iowa Silent Reading Test*, on which his subtest grade scores ranged from 3.3 in Rate to 7.6 in Use of Index. A bright boy of 13, he was shocked at his poor showing. But he had checked the scoring himself, and soon he and the teacher were discussing possible reasons why his reading was so slow and listing some of the things he could do to increase his rate.

Learning exactly where one stands is not a good stimulus for some poor readers. To a sensitive, easily discouraged child it may be disheartening. It is also inadvisable for those who are already reading nearly up to capacity. For them, emphasizing their poor reading may be a form of needless cruelty. For pupils like Rob, however, the opportunity to learn just where they stand on objective standardized tests may be exactly what is needed to break through the crust of real or assumed indifference.

Children sometimes develop the notion that the main reason for learning to read is to please the teacher. The teacher shows pleasure when the child reads well and shows or implies displeasure when reading is poor. If the child wants to retaliate against the teacher, it may seem logical to get even by not reading or by reading poorly.

Such an attitude is usually a transfer to the classroom of attitudes learned at home. Many children eat, not because they are hungry, but to please mother. Such children can often beat their mothers in a contest of wills by refusing to eat. If a child who has learned this technique has a mother who is quite concerned over his or her reading, the child is likely to experiment to find out if rejecting reading can be used in the same way as rejecting food. Often the experiment is successful. Not progressing in reading can become a way of keeping mother's attention centered on the child, and this may be more important to the child than the satisfactions of successful learning. Because teachers are to a large extent substitute parents, the child may be attempting to capture a larger share of the teacher's attention.

If the child thinks he can control his mother and teacher through not reading or by not improving in reading, the first step is to demonstrate to him that it will not work. Mother and teacher must both switch over to the attitude that they are not going to try to make Johnny read—if he does not learn, he is the one who will be hurt—and must maintain this attitude steadily for a period long enough to convince him. This plan should not be attempted unless there is good reason to believe that it will be carried through without faltering. In class, the teacher must be able to put across the idea that Johnny doesn't have to read if he doesn't want to, and that while she likes him and would like to see him succeed, Johnny himself is the only one who loses out if he doesn't improve his reading ability.

The underlying cause of this problem, the need for attention, will persist unless treated. Therefore, the child must be provided with better ways of obtaining the attention and affection he craves. Approval must be given for commendable things that the child does if he is to give up less praiseworthy means of attracting notice. When resistance to reading arises out of the child's fundamental emotional needs, more than a change in teaching technique is required.

Social Recognition

Social recognition is very important. Opportunities can be created for the poor reader to demonstrate his growing competence before classmates whose generosity in commending him for improvement can usually be counted on to bolster his shaky self-esteem and serve as a further incentive. The school principal and other teachers may provide appreciative audiences. It is especially valuable to keep parents well informed about the child's progress and to send commendatory notes home at frequent intervals. For many children, the anxiety of parents, shown in nagging, threats, punishment, and ineffectual attempts at tutoring, is a major deterrent to progress. When parents relax such pressures at home, the child is able to function better in school.

The Parents' Role in a Remedial Program

The relationship of the home environment to reading disability was discussed on pages 359–361. When a child enters a remedial program, the parents' continuing attitudes toward, and treatment of, him can significantly influence his progress.

In talking with the parents of a reading disabled child, it is advisable first to inquire about their ideas concerning the causes of his difficulty. Sometimes parents bring out many complaints about the child—he is lazy, he will not work, he must be "stupid." Sometimes they blame the school or a particular teacher. Very often their attitude is defensive, and they attempt to prove that his poor work is not their fault. After the parents have made their suggestions, the teacher can try to correct their misconceptions. In general, an attempt should be made to restore the parents' confidence in the child and to convey the impression that neither the parents nor the child should be blamed for his failure. Refer to Price and Marsh (1985) for suggestions on planning and conducting parent conferences.

It may reasonably be assumed that the parents of most disabled readers have tried to help them. Even with the best of intentions, however, parents can aggravate the problem, particularly by inappropriate efforts at motivation. Most family attempts at remediation are unsuccessful. Parents usually lack teaching skills, and their instruction is often at odds with what the school is teaching and, therefore, is confusing to the child. Many parents are anxious for success, expect too much too soon, and become easily discouraged and emotionally tense when their remedial efforts fail. Often these sessions end with the parent angry and the child crying. Many parents nag, scold, and exhort disabled readers to be like a scholastically successful sibling; some even resort to physical punishment. Siblings often make things worse by sarcastic comments and uncomplimentary remarks. The problem of how to discuss these issues with parents without antagonizing them requires more understanding than could be imparted in a sentence or two here. Refer to Lieben (1958) for ideas on how to conduct such discussions. The main idea to remember is that the parents have been trying to do the right thing.

Parents should be given encouragement to believe that there are important things they can do to help the remedial program. Particularly with younger children, the importance of continuing (or resuming) the reading and telling of stories to the child can be stressed. Many parents do not realize the value of conversation, visits to places of interest, and trips, in helping the child to enrich ideas, expand vocabulary, and provide a base for improved comprehension. Sharing these and other activities with the child may improve the parent-child relationship.

Many overanxious parents are unable to stop their attempts to teach the child to read, even after they have agreed to do so. When this seems likely, they can be given very limited jobs to do. The task should be one that can be completed in 5 to 10 minutes and should consist more of review than of new learning. The exact procedure the parent is expected to use must be explained in detail and demonstrated in a sample lesson.

As the child progresses in remedial work, it is desirable to send notes home at frequent intervals, praising the child's efforts and mentioning some new achievements. Sometimes a lessening of parental dissatisfaction with a child induces further helpful changes in the home situation. Flood and Lapp (1989) offer suggestions for reporting reading progress to parents.

Group counseling for parents can be helpful. Counseling may consist of a structured series of parent meetings, each starting with a short lecture, followed by discussion, and concluding with instruction about specific activities the parents are encouraged to engage in with their children (McWhirter 1976). Or the counseling sessions may be more like group psychotherapy, in which parents are encouraged to talk about their feelings about school, teachers, and the child. They learn that their child's problems are by no means unique, and after giving vent to feelings of frustration and anger, they can begin to explore with other parents ways in which they can become more helpful (Bricklin 1970). Unfortunately, many parents are unable to participate in such programs because of jobs or small children at home, and some just refuse to get involved.

Motivating Participation

In addition to the affective factors discussed in the preceding pages, students can be motivated to participate in the remedial program by using interesting materials, structuring the program so that the child achieves success, avoiding monotony, making learning fun, and dramatizing progress.

THE INTEREST FACTOR.   Overrelying on drill and repetition, which remedial teachers tend to do, makes learning dull and uninteresting. There are two main ways to make remediation interesting: (1) employing reading materials that are intrinsically capable of attracting and holding the pupil's interest, and (2) using material in ways that foster interest.

It is not always possible to find intrinsically interesting material for introducing and teaching reading skills and strategies. But stories and books that are interesting to poor or disabled readers and to which they can apply their skills and strategies can be found. The teacher who has obtained magical effects when just the right book is placed in a child's hands cannot ever again disregard the importance of matching the book to the child. To find the right book, the teacher must know both the child and the books. This issue is treated in detail in Chapter 18. When material to fit the child's known interests cannot be found, the resourceful teacher must sometimes be able to stimulate interest in material that is available. In attempting to sell a book in a new category, it is advisable to use stories and books known to have wide appeal.

Reading to disabled or poor readers should not be overlooked as a motivating device.

NOTHING SUCCEEDS LIKE SUCCESS. A remedial program must be initiated using reading materials and specific tasks that are easy enough so that successful performance is virtually certain. Large amounts of success are especially important for pupils with histories of low achievement (Marliave & Filby 1985). Inexperienced remedial teachers often fail to recognize fully the extent of the students' reading problems and tend to overestimate the level at which the pupils can experience success. Standardized test grade-equivalent scores are not a safe guide in selecting remedial material. More reliable choices can be made on the basis of information obtained from an informal reading inventory or application of IRI procedures or a cloze procedure to materials under consideration (see pages 219–229, 200–204). If the teacher opts to begin remediation before such information is available, the child can be asked to read a page or so from books of different levels of difficulty (see page 198). As a last resort, she might consider using material that is at least one or two years below the child's grade-equivalent score or the level of reading textbook that the child is using in the regular classroom.

The first reading skill or strategy taught should be one that the child can master fairly quickly and, if at all possible, one that will be immediately helpful. It may be prudent to begin with a skill in which the student has some ability but has not yet mastered.

Teachers who are willing to begin at a level almost guaranteed to assure success and to proceed slowly at first are often rewarded by accelerated progress later. As the remediation continues, good judgment is needed in deciding how much to cover, how fast to go, and how soon to move to a higher level of text difficulty. The student's responses to the tasks, materials, and pace of instruction provide cues to the alert teacher. After the child has achieved a high level of success at the beginning of remediation and his self-concept and belief in his ability to succeed have improved, there is less need for making sure that he will be successful on almost every task. More challenging tasks and materials can be introduced gradually. When conditions are right, the remedial teacher may start presenting occasional tasks on which the child is likely to fail; the child may need to develop a tolerance for failure. This practice may also help prepare the child for his return to regular classroom reading instruction, where he may not be successful as often as in the remedial program.

AVOIDING MONOTONY. Variety adds spice to the remedial program. Children often get tired of doing the same thing again and again, even if they are highly motivated to improve their reading. Each lesson should be subdivided into at least three different activities. Having some variation in the plan from lesson to lesson and introducing an occasional surprise are also desirable.

Another reason for variety during a remedial lesson is the desirability of keeping *retroactive inhibition* to a minimum. When the same kind of learning activity is continued for some time, the material learned last tends to blot out or inhibit memory for what was learned earlier in that lesson. Poor readers show more retroactive inhibition than do good readers (Otto 1966). As a poor reader continues uninterrupted with the same learning task, the effect of more practice is increasingly canceled by retroactive inhibition, and the net gain may be very little. Retroactive inhibition can be held to a minimum by introducing short rest periods and by shifting from one learning task to a quite different one. The duration of the task should be geared to the child's needs. Some children welcome frequent shifts of activity, and others are bothered by them.

TRANSFORMING PRACTICE INTO GAMES.   Many kinds of practice that are not intrinsically interesting can be made into games, thus becoming play rather than distasteful work. Adaptations of Bingo are easily constructed or can be purchased. Card games such as rummy and poker are adaptable as word or phrase cards. A magnet on a string can catch "fish" (word cards decorated with paper clips) from a "pond" (desk top). The rules of baseball, football, and basketball can provide scoring systems for competitive contents between two players or two teams, or between pupil and teacher. Other ideas for reading games may be found in the sources listed on page 484, and in the "Classroom Reading Teacher" section of *The Reading Teacher*. Snyder (1981) discusses the pros and cons of teacher-made and commercially published games.

DRAMATIZING PROGRESS.   The learner's competitive urge to improve his own record can be a most effective form of motivation. This urge is what gives motivating power to activities in which the learner can keep his score in comparable units, lesson after lesson. For example, graphing rate and comprehension scores is effective both in increasing the rates of excessively slow readers and in improving the accuracy of fast but careless readers.

Because most disabled readers lack self-confidence, visible evidence of their improvement is more important than it is with good readers. The principle of celebrating a child's successes is essential in remedial teaching. At first, every little improvement should be noted and praised. As the child becomes more accustomed to success, procedures for recognizing progress over weeks and months become more important.

Records and charts can be devised to track progress in any phase of reading. Different charts can be constructed for number of pages, stories, or books read; number of new words learned; number of phonic elements mastered; increased word-recognition accuracy; increased comprehension; gradual elimination of a specific fault, such as confusing *then* with *when*; rate of reading; and so on. Having a separate record for each objective emphasized is desirable. At any one time a remedial pupil should be keeping track of improvement toward three or four major objectives. After an objective has been attained, a new one should be selected.

There are many kinds of progress records. Colored stars, writing *"Good,"* or some similar word of recognition can be placed on young children's daily work or on a chart for a particular objective. Older children require more sophisticated rewards.

Charts and graphs that have been used successfully include:

1. The *thermometer chart*. As the cumulative total goes up, the red moves up the center of the thermometer. This type of chart is useful for record-

ing cumulative results, such as number of words learned or stories read. A variation attractive to many children is a *rocket chart*. A small cutout paper rocket is fastened to the chart by tape that is sticky on both sides and can be lifted up and replaced higher on the scale.

2. The *skyscraper chart*. As a unit of work is completed, the child adds a window to the outline of a skyscraper.
3. The *racetrack chart*. Progress is recorded by moving a tiny auto or horse around the track. A variant is to have a swimmer complete laps back and forth across a swimming pool.
4. A *map chart*. A trip across country, the world, or outer space is divided into units, and each completed exercise is noted by filling in another unit until the trip is completed.
5. A *bar graph*. This can be used for a group, with each child having a column, which is filled in as another unit is completed, or it can be used with an individual as suggested for a line graph.
6. The *airplane* or *ship chart*. The outline of a plane or ship is fastened to a cardboard base to make a pocket. The child records progress by placing "passengers" (slips of paper) into the pocket.
7. A *bookcase chart*. This type of chart is used mainly for independent reading; the child adds another book to the bookcase each time another book is finished. (See Figure 18.3 on page 679.)
8. The *line graph*. This type of graph, which takes note of decreases as well as increases, is most useful for recording rate and comprehension scores.

The child may be asked to choose and to make the progress chart, rather than use a more polished chart made by the teacher. Although the child's chart may be less attractive, it will mean more to the child.

Use of wide, rather than narrow, spaces between units of increment (e.g., an inch rather than a quarter-inch on a line graph) gives the child the impression of greater progress. Units of improvement to be recorded on the progress chart should be small enough so that progress can be recorded at frequent intervals. It is more desirable to have a child compete with her or his own record than to compete with other children. If a group is fairly homogeneous, however, a chart that compares the progress of all children in the group sometimes aids motivation.

Facilitating Participation

At times, teachers need to utilize techniques that will better enable students to profit from remedial instruction. These include stress-relieving procedures, behavior modification, and psychotherapeutic-like understanding on the part of the teacher.

RELIEVING STRESS. Reading problems and failure can create stress. Students must learn to deal directly with such stress by reappraising the threat and developing ways of coping with it. Stress-reducing methods, either direct or self-regulating coping skills, can be taught. These involve helping students: (1) to set explicit, reasonable, attainable short-term goals; (2) to establish incentives to work and to provide themselves with tangible rewards when the goals are met; and (3) to monitor the behavior they seek to change (i.e., their reactions to stress). Before a positive change in reading performance can occur, stressed students must recognize that a stress problem exists, acknowledge the nature of the problem, and gain control using adaptive stress-reducing behaviors. Refer to Gentile and McMillan (1987) for more specific suggestions on reducing stress.

The following techniques also have been used to assist poor or disabled readers.

HYPNOSIS. Hypnosis has been recommended as an aid to improving study habits, improving concentration, reducing test anxiety, increasing motivation, and facilitating learning (Krippner 1971). Self-hypnosis can be taught to highly susceptible subjects and reportedly can be used to improve rate and comprehension (Willis 1972). However, not all people are hypnotizable; the value of hypnosis in treating cases of severe reading disability has not been explored sufficiently, and even if it were shown to have favorable effects, properly trained hypnotists are scarce. In a small-scale study (Oldridge 1982), disabled readers who received hypnotic suggestion did not score higher in reading achievement than a control group.

SUGGESTOPEDIA. *Suggestopedia* and *suggestology* are alternative names for a system of instruction developed by Lozanov (1975). The system assumes that most individuals have great potential for improved learning and that a combination of positive suggestion and relaxation can overcome barriers to high-speed learning. The key components of suggestopedia are: (1) suggestions that emphasize the worthiness of the individual; (2) relaxation and imagery (breathing exercises, progressive muscle relaxation, tension-releasing exercises, imagining a pleasant place, etc.); (3) exciting presentations of lessons and active learning; and (4) music and environmental sounds (Brownlee 1982). Lehr (1987) discusses the American form of suggestopedia entitled *Suggestive-Accelerated Learning and Teaching* (SALT). Pritchard and Taylor (1978) describe the application of suggestopedia to 17 poor readers ranging in age from 8 to 13. After 4 months of instruction, most of the group improved a year or more in oral and silent reading, less in word recognition. Their statistical treatment was meager, and there was no control group other than the same teacher's previous results with (possibly) similar children. This is a development to be watched, but it needs to be researched by nonpartisans. The limited research to date suggests that suggestopedia has some promise for students with negative attitudes toward reading and for disabled readers.

REALITY THERAPY. *Reality therapy* is a nonpunitive approach designed to help reading and learning disabled students acquire strategies that will assist them in dealing with their social and emotional hurts and rejections. It focuses on personal interaction. Fuller and Fuller (1982) describe a 10-step approach to reality therapy.

RELAXATION TRAINING. *Relaxation therapy* attempts to help individuals relax, usually by employing self-suggestion. Biofeedback-induced relaxation training decreased impulsivity and increased attention to task in learning disabled children (Omizo & Michael 1982). Carter and Russell (1985) report that reading and learning disabled children who received relaxation therapy made small but statistically significant gains in reading achievement.

Such therapies probably do not improve reading ability directly; rather, their successful use may allow students to attend better to learning tasks and/or to demonstrate their reading ability.

BEHAVIOR MODIFICATION. *Behavior-modification* attempts to change behaviors by systematically rewarding desirable behaviors and either disregarding or punishing undesirable ones. Such techniques are based on operant conditioning, the learning model from which B. F. Skinner developed teaching machines and programmed instruction.

A general description of the steps to be taken include: (1) Specify carefully the behavior to be modified and the outcomes desired, in the form of behavioral objectives; (2) collect data on the occurrence of this behavior under present conditions (often called "establishing a baseline"); (3) change the environmental setting, using stimulus change and reinforcement, to induce behavior change in the desired direction, (4) continue to collect data to show degree and direction of change until the objective is reached; (5) if the change is insufficient, modify the program (Knowles 1970).

Positive reinforcement seems to work best with most individuals. Among the effective reinforcers are tokens (e.g., chips, beans) that are exchangeable for prizes (e.g., candy, money) or privileges (e.g., free time), feedback on progress, and praise and encouragement. The reinforcement schedule is changed as progress toward the desired behavior occurs. At first, every desired behavior may be reinforced. As the child improves, reinforcement occurs for larger numbers of the targeted behaviors. Bannatyne (1972a) provides a list of reinforcers that may be useful to remedial teachers. Reinforcers operate differently among individuals.

The importance of social reinforcers is stressed by Kuypers, Becker, and O'Leary (1968). They favor giving praise and privileges for improvement in behavior as well as for academic learnings. Deviant behaviors should be ignored unless someone is being hurt or prevented from learning, in which case the offender is simply removed temporarily. It is important to find something the child does that can be rewarded, even if in the beginning, this "something" is nothing more than staying in her seat. Not talking to her neighbor, having the right materials in front of her, paying attention, and working can all be reinforced even if the child is not yet showing much academic progress.

It is important to choose the right behaviors for reinforcement. Deaton (1975) compared the results of reinforcing poor readers for accuracy with reinforcing a comparable group for percentage of time-on-task. The accuracy group became more accurate and also remained on- task 97.5% of the time. The on-task group improved its on-task time to 99.7%, but decreased in accuracy to 88%. Programmed material was used, and the author comments that "the problem of cheating is prevalent and offers a challenge to those who teach problem readers with programmed materials." Apparently an unintended result of the reinforcement procedure was to reinforce cheating as an easy way to get 100% accuracy.

Stott (1978) describes a procedure for classifying faulty learning patterns found in learning disabled children and outlines a treatment program for each maladjustment pattern, based on behavioral-modification procedures.

It is evident that reinforcement theory provides one theoretical explanation for the strong emphasis that good remedial teachers placed on motivation long before the concepts of behavioral modification were developed. Teachers emphasized starting at levels low enough and with small enough steps to ensure success. They made the work interesting with games and carefully chosen materials. They provided frequent feedback on successful tries ("That's fine!" "OK!" "Terrific!" "Very good!") and provided encouragement and praise for effort when the going was hard. They arranged for social reinforcement through praise from classroom teachers, parents, classmates, the principal, and so on. They used progress charts and records to make progress vividly visible. To them, behavior modification is just new terminology for long-established practices.

Some cautions about behavior modification have been expressed. Although token economies are usually successful while they are in operation, the continuation of gains afterward, and the generalization of gains to other learning situations, often have not been checked (Kazdin & Bootzin 1972). The concept of "classroom engineering" or "precision teaching" may lead to a coldly mechanical application of reinforcement. Instead, the use of specific reinforcements should take place in an atmosphere that focuses on trust, positive attitudes, and empathy toward the child (Griffiths 1970–1971). According to Rose, Koorland, and Epstein (1982), most of the studies of reinforcement strategies have been methodologically flawed.

A more complete understanding of behavior modification can be gained from a book by Axelrod (1977). But knowing about a technique does not provide skill in applying it. It is helpful to be able to try behavior modification with the aid of an expert consultant. Without such help, trial-and-error learning may contain serious errors, and a teacher without guidance may not be able to recognize and correct the errors.

COGNITIVE BEHAVIOR MODIFICATION. Affect plays a role in the cognitive functioning that underlies learning (Meichenbaum 1977). Children's negative beliefs regarding their likelihood for success can deter or prevent them from activating and employing the skills they possess, thereby adversely influencing learning. Such negative ideation reflects the students' executive-control processes that determine when to change, interrupt, or continue a thought. By rehearsing positive self-talk and other behaviors that are inconsistent with self-defeating attitudes, pupils gradually achieve *cognitive restructuring* that supports attitudes more conducive for learning (Derry & Murphy 1986). Procedures that attempt to achieve cognitive restructuring are referred to as *cognitive behavior modification* or *cognitive behavioral therapy*.

Cognitive behavior modification has four common characteristics: (1) Pupils are active participants; (2) overt verbalizations are required, at least initially (they usually give way to *internal dialogue*); (3) the target strategy is identified as a series of discrete steps that are modeled by the teacher and later imitated by the students; and (4) the goal of the training is to develop in the student a positive, reflective response style (Ryan, Weed & Short 1986). Cognitive behavior modification can be used to address two common problems found in reading and learning disabled students—a lack of motivation and failure to use self-directed learning strategies.

An example of the use of this technique for motivational purposes would involve teaching the pupil to recognize negative, self-defeating statements (e.g., "It's too hard for me, why try?") and their adverse effects on performance, and to replace them with positive statements (e.g., "It's hard, but I can do it if I really try."). An illustration of the use of cognitive behavior modification to overcome the inadequate use of strategies is Carlton, Hummer, and Rainey's (1984) four-step instructional procedure in which pupils are taught: (1) to think through what must be done before attempting a task ("To get ready for this assignment I must do ———."); (2) to think statements that help them to analyze the task ("First I must ———, then, ———, etc."); (3) to think statements that guide them through the task ("I still have to ———.") and provide for taking corrective actions ("That's not right, I'd better go back and ———."); and (4) to praise themselves after completing part or all of the task ("I've done a great job!"). The aforementioned procedure teaches the child a general strategy that can be applied across a variety of situations. Another type of general strategy involves assessing a problem situation, determining its requirements, and selecting and applying a specific strategy to solve the problem. The cognitive behavior modification literature reveals a trend away from teaching general strategies toward an increasing emphasis on teaching strategies needed to solve particular problems (Tarver 1986). Meichenbaum (1977) gives detailed descriptions of many variations of cognitive behavior therapy, and outlines guidelines for maximizing the likelihood that strategies acquired in training will transfer to new situations (Meichenbaum 1980). Refer to Derry and Murphy (1986) for other suggestions.

There are conflicting interpretations of the effectiveness of cognitive behavior modifications. According to Whalen, Henker, and Hinshaw (1985), cognitive behavior modification (1) has been effective in circumscribed contexts for brief periods of time, primarily with nonclinical cases who have deficient self-control; (2) has not produced strong, consistent results that are easy to replicate; and (3) has not been effective over time or had a positive effect on academic performance. On the other hand, Ryan, Weed, and Short (1986) state that: (1) evidence that cognitive behavior modification is effective in modifying impulsivity and attentional deficits is gradually accumulating; (2) in general, longer studies that employed specific task strategies showed greater change in the targeted behaviors; and (3) there is only slight evidence of maintenance and generalization to new situations.

Remedial Reading and Psychotherapy

Good remedial teaching has some characteristics of good psychotherapy. It is based on the development of a friendly, warm, comfortable relationship between teacher and pupil—a relationship described by the term *rapport*. It employs reassurance to express the teacher's faith in the child's ability to improve. It provides the child with the security of feeling that the adult knows what she is doing and can be relied on and, at the same time, that the child has some choice of activities. It requires that the teacher be clear about what kinds and degrees of freedom the child can be allowed, and be pleasantly firm in maintaining the particular limits she or he feels it necessary to employ. It requires sufficient objectivity on the teacher's part to avoid becoming involved as a partisan in the child's struggles with parents or complaints about teachers. It is intended to strengthen the child's self-respect so that he becomes able to attack problems with courage, energy, and persistence.

There are, however, some important differences. A remedial situation must have a definite structure of planned activities, and the freedom allowed the child involves choosing among approved learning activities, whereas in psychotherapy much wider freedom of action is permitted (especially in play therapy). The major difference, though, is in regard to interpretation. A major goal of most forms of psychotherapy is the development of insight and self-understanding through the therapist's interpretations of remarks and actions. The remedial teacher should generally avoid interpreting to the child what she thinks the true significance of the child's remarks or conduct may be, or giving advice outside the field of reading and schoolwork.

The child may want to spend time talking about problems or pleasant experiences. "If the child chooses to do so, the tutor should listen respectfully and make natural comments, expressing sympathy, understanding, happiness for the child's triumphs, or whatever would be appropriate between any two people who respect one another and have something in common" (Dahlberg, Roswell & Chall 1952). When in doubt, the safest procedure is to say, "You think that . . ." or "You feel that . . ." and to complete the sentence by restating the gist of the child's statement to you. This is one way to use the technique called "reflection of feeling" by C. R. Rogers (1942), whose nondirective methods can be useful to remedial teachers.

Children react differently to remedial teachers and programs. Teachers must try to understand the real meanings of these behaviors and cope with them accordingly. Some pupils do not accept their remedial teachers at face value, but test them repeatedly to find out what they are really like. This practice can try a teacher's patience, but she must remain calm and demonstrate her acceptance of the students, while maintaining the guidelines she has established for acceptable behavior. Usually, this type of "testing the limits" abates after awhile. When it persists to the point of becoming disruptive to the teaching/ learning environment, it is advisable to have a private conference with the perpetrator and ask why she is behaving in this unacceptable manner.

Other students who are usually guarded, conforming, and polite may let a bit of hostility show or may become critical or argumentative. It is important to recognize this for what it is: a venture in the direction of self-assertion and overcoming shackling inhibitions. It is important for the child to feel that he can be liked even when he wants to do objectionable things; this helps to set the teacher's response, which should be to show liking for the child while firmly drawing the line against unacceptable behavior. Similarly, expressions of jealousy of other pupils point to a need for reassurance about the teacher's interest in the jealous one. Attempts to prolong lessons beyond their time limits should be understood partly as a play for more teacher attention and partly as a challenge of the limit set. The setting of limits in a kindly, but firm and consistent, manner is in itself a therapeutic process, which provides some children with a feeling of security and safety that they have lacked in their relationships with other adults.

Some psychologists have explored the possibilities of therapeutically oriented remedial settings in which the teacher is very permissive and the child may choose freely among reading and play activities and is encouraged to express her feelings about reading, school, and her family. A skillful and well-trained psychotherapist may be able to get good results with such a combined approach. Our limit observations of such efforts lead us to believe that results in both reading improvement and better adjustment come faster when remediation and psychotherapy are carried on concurrently by different people and are coordinated.

Relatively few studies on the value of counseling or psychotherapy with disabled readers have been undertaken, and most of their findings are limited in applicability because of the small undertaken size of the groups studied, the difficulty of matching groups, and the difficulty of controlling the quality of treatment. Pumfrey and Elliott (1970) review the evidence on the value of psychotherapy as a treatment for reading failure and conclude that unequivocal proof of its effects on adjustment and reading skills has not been shown.

Published case reports describe various ways to combine remedial instruction with individual or group counseling or psychotherapy (A. J. Harris 1970, cases 1, 5, 6, 7, 14); Edelstein 1970; Wright & McKenzie 1970). Such case reports provide persuasive evidence of the value of combined approaches in specific cases.

Although successful remedial reading can improve the adjustment of many children with emotional problems, psychiatric intervention is needed for psychotic children. Emotional problems that are secondary to reading failure may require professional treatment in addition to reading remediation. The parents of children with severe, long-standing reading problems may require counseling to deal with their own feelings of guilt and despair.

ROLES AND RESPONSIBILITIES
OF READING SPECIALISTS

The roles and responsibilities of reading professionals are affected by a number of factors such as the size and type of school, financial exigencies, and the professional's personality (Bean & Eichelberger 1985). Attempts to standardize titles and to define the roles and responsibilities of particular types of reading professionals have not been successful. Reading professionals with the same title often serve different functions, just as those with different titles perform similar duties. Nevertheless, the International Reading Association (IRA) (1986a) has specified the roles and responsibilities for elementary and secondary classroom teachers, reading specialists (diagnostic/remedial teacher, developmental reading/study-skills teacher, reading consultant/reading resource-room teacher, reading coordinator/supervisor, and reading professor), and for those in special education, administration, and support services. This IRA publication also suggests the minimal academic preparation in reading required for each position, as well as the competencies that each type of reading professional should possess.[4] The IRA Code of Ethics appears in the November, 1987 issues of *The Reading Teacher* and the *Journal of Reading.*

Structuring the Position

Before accepting a new position, the reading specialist should determine what roles and responsibilities are expected of her. These should be in the form of a written job description. It is also advisable to determine if expectations differ from those stated in writing. Classroom teachers often perceive reading specialists as important, even necessary, personnel who spend most of their time working directly with children but who are available for consultation (Pikulski & Ross 1979). Reading specialists and school administrators may differ widely in their perceptions of the specialist's role (Rupley, Mason & Logan 1985). The same is true for resource teachers and their administrators. (Friend & McNutt 1987). For instance, administrators indicated that reading consultants should spend most of their time making diagnoses and providing reading instruction and the least time as inservice leaders and resource persons. Reading consultants saw their roles as being just the opposite (Mangieri & Heimberger 1980). Conflicting expectations can lead to serious misunderstanding. It is important to determine how other school personnel (including teachers, administrators, and supervisors) envision the role and responsibilities of the reading specialist, and how open to change their ideas are.

Reading specialists also need to know what written and unwritten policies have been established and how specific they are. Policies cover such items as the objectives of the remedial program, pupil referral and selection procedures, evaluation procedures, caseload, restrictions as to how many children a teacher can work with during a remedial period, the length of time a child can stay in the program, and so forth. These policies may be district-wide or may differ from school to school within the district. It is also prudent to determine the extent to which established policies are followed. In a new situation it is advisable for the reading specialist to adhere to existing policies until she is fairly secure in the position before working for policy changes.

Closely related to the policy issue is the need for a clear understanding of the lines of authority. The reading teacher is usually supervised by the school principal but may be directly answerable to an assistant principal, the district reading consultant or supervisor, a director of pupil personnel services, or the person in charge of special services or special education. Optimally, clashes will not occur among personnel with whom the reading teacher must deal; if they do, the reading specialist needs tactfully to avoid taking sides or being caught in the middle.

Other things the reading specialist needs to know include which reading program is employed in the school; the availability and usefulness of existing records; the use made of tutors and aides; the availability of space, supplies, and

[4]Rupley, Mason, and Logan (1985) present a brief history of reading specialists' job responsibilities.

equipment; and how previous reading teachers related to other school personnel.

MAKING AN INVENTORY.   One of the first steps is to inventory available space and materials. There may be books, workbooks, games, and audiovisual equipment in the reading room or elsewhere in the school. A simple coding system can be employed to indicate the approximate difficulty level of an item, the specific purposes for which it can be used, and whether it requires teacher direction or can be used independently.

USING A PREPARATORY PERIOD.   An experienced reading teacher may need 1 week to prepare for the coming school year; new teachers may require a 2- or 3-week preparatory period. Pupil selection always takes time. Even if selection was done during the previous term or semester, vacancies may have occurred; filling them will probably involve studying pupil records, some diagnostic testing, and conferring with teachers and parents. Record folders have to be started for newly admitted pupils, and the records of continuing pupils must be updated. Groups need to be organized, sessions scheduled, and lesson plans developed.

The physical setup of the reading room or center also must be organized. Instructional materials should be arranged for easy access and convenient use. Space must be planned for individual and group activities, a listening center, a visual-aids center, and a comfortable browsing area. Volunteer helpers can be useful during this aspect of the preparatory period.

Pupil Selection

In selecting students for the remedial program, a minimum IQ is not a desirable criterion for two reasons. The chance that the IQ score from a group test is inaccurate is far greater for a disabled reader than for a pupil who is making normal progress in reading. Moreover, the correlation between IQ and ability to profit from remedial help, although positive, is low (Frost 1963). The objective measure of reading disability described on pages 173–178 can be used to rank referred students as to the severity of their reading disabilities. However, use of statistical procedures such as the R Exp Q should be tempered by giving consideration to the child's age and grade placement, teacher recommendations, and so forth.

Prereferral systems, such as those described by Graden, Casey, and Christenson (1985) and Bicklen and Zollers (1986), can reduce the need to classify students in order for them to receive special services, as well as reduce the number of cases a reading specialist has to remediate. Basically, the plans call for screening and intervention in the regular classroom setting and curriculum prior to referral.

When a remedial program is started, it is probably desirable to take the most serious cases first, regardless of grade level. Admission to the program should not be limited to the beginning of the school year or semester; rather, it should be on a need–space availability basis throughout the school year. In deciding how many and whom to admit, slots must be reserved for continuing pupils. Some places should also be left open for newly admitted students who need help in reading and for children whose problems have become more acute because they have not received remedial help.

School policies may give priority to children in specific grades. Some remedial programs concentrate on second and third graders, hoping to overcome problems before they become too serious. Above the primary-grade level, remedial efforts are often concentrated on students in the first year of a particular school: for example, seventh graders in a junior high school and freshmen in a four-year high school.

Efficient Use of the Remedial Teacher's Time

INSTRUCTIONAL BLOCKS. Many remedial teachers have found it useful to divide the school year into four blocks or terms of approximately equal duration. In a typical school year of 38 weeks, there can be four teaching blocks of 8 weeks each, with a nonteaching week for preparation, testing, conferring, record keeping, and planning before each block and 2 nonteaching weeks at the end of the year. Alternatively there can be 2 preparatory weeks at the beginning and 1 week at the end.

THE REMEDIAL TEACHER'S SCHEDULE. Remedial periods usually last from 30 to 45 minutes, depending on the school situation. In departmentalized schools or grades, the remedial period conforms to the school-wide schedule. Where there are self-contained classrooms, shorter periods can be used for younger children and somewhat longer periods for older children. This type of scheduling provides the remedial teacher with five teaching periods a day plus a lunch period and a nonteaching period (usually the last one) for correction of tests and exercises, record keeping, instructional planning, and conferences. Often the completion of the jobs for the nonteaching period will keep the remedial teacher busy until well after school.

Five teaching periods a day, or 25 periods a week, can best be utilized by having some groups twice a week and other groups three times a week. Having five groups on three days and another five groups on the two intervening days is possible whether the teacher is located in one school or divides time between two schools. The scheduling should be cleared with classroom teachers to insure that no child will miss too much of another important subject. Sometimes neatness of scheduling has to be sacrificed in order to minimize the inroads into children's other schoolwork.

Guthrie, Seifert, and Kline (1978) conclude that although groups of four to eight pupils achieved good results in remedial reading programs, tutoring from one to three children at a time produced still better results. The results of the studies they reviewed, however, may have been influenced by the fact that the smaller groups tended to have brighter children in them. Nevertheless, highly individualized remediation becomes increasingly more difficult as the size of the group increases.

From the standpoint of both financial cost and professional time, tutoring a child on a one-to-one basis is expensive. Yet, at times, individual tutoring is the only way to produce results. Some disabled readers cannot work in even a small group; they need intensive, highly individualized instruction over a period of time by a skilled teacher who can keep them on task. Unfortunately, few schools are able to provide such remediation. Parents must often turn to remedial reading teachers who are in private practice or work in privately operated clinics. The competence of these tutors varies greatly, as does the degree to which they work with the school.

Duration of remediation is also important. Guthrie, Seifert, and Kline (1978) found that a minimum of about 50 instructional hours seemed necessary for significant and lasting improvement. Although rate of improvement is not closely related to age, older pupils usually have greater disparities between their initial performance and normal performance than younger children do and, therefore, require a longer duration of remedial help to come up to grade level.

GROUP MANAGEMENT.   Members of a newly formed group may naturally compete with one another. Some have learned previously that the only way they can win is to cheat, and some try to establish their superiority by calling attention to blunders made by other group members.

The teacher should repeatedly point out that what counts is each individual's progress and not who makes mistakes. Making mistakes is a normal part of learning. Group members keep records of their own progress, and the teacher praises each child's improvement and expresses no interest in comparing one child's record with another.

Praising group members who encourage, support, or help others is advisable, as is ignoring derogatory remarks. Gradually the group will become mutually supportive. Including some games in which chance rather than ability determines the winner can help every child in the group win occasionally.

UTILIZING THE REMEDIAL PERIOD.   In an efficiently planned remedial period, every child is doing something useful nearly all the time. The following plan has worked well for a 40- to 45-minute period:

5 min.	Assignments, getting materials, and so forth.
10 min.	Teacher-led group lesson, often introducing a new skill or strategy.
15 min.	Follow-up practice, applying what was taught in the group lesson. Teacher uses time to work individually with 2–3 children.
10–15 min.	Children who have finished the follow-up exercise move to an individual activity, often self-chosen.

Such a plan allows considerable flexibility. A child who does not need the group lesson may use the time for individual activities; five minutes may be reserved for the teacher to read an exciting story; group games or recreational reading may replace all or part of the time for individual activities.

The Use of Tutors and Paraprofessionals

Classroom and remedial teachers who have assistants may provide more individual help than they could single-handedly. Peer and cross-age tutoring has positive effects on the reading achievement and attitudes of both the tutored and the tutors, particularly when the programs are structured (Cohen, Kulik & Kulik 1982). There is wide speculation (see Nevi 1983) as to why tutors improve their academic skills as much as, or more than, the tutees. Although much of the research indicates that tutoring is effective, the specific circumstances under which tutoring is most effective are still not completely known, nor is it clear if tutoring is more effective than other procedures. Many researchers are convinced of the merits of tutoring, regardless of whether or not their studies show empirical support for their opinions (Scruggs & Richter 1985).

Student tutors can help provide the individual attention needed by other pupils, but they must be trained in tutoring skills and techniques, must clearly understand what is to be done and how it is to be accomplished, and must be supervised carefully (King 1982). These requirements are the same for adult volunteers or paid paraprofessionals as well. According to Ellson (1976), the critical conditions for successful tutoring by nonprofessionals are either intensive training and supervision by professionals in unstructured tutoring programs or highly structured programs that tutors are required to follow in detail. Boomer (1980) presents ideas for interviewing, selecting, training, and using paraprofessionals. Other suggestions for tutoring programs and the use of paraprofessionals may be found in Mavrogenes and Galen (1979), Rauch and Sanacore (1985), and McKenzie and Houk (1986).

The introduction of nonteachers into the instructional-social structure can create problems. One of the potential dangers is that the tutee and tutor may come to believe that the child being tutored is incapable of being taught if some real progress is not shown. On the other hand, tutees who make progress are likely to attribute the outcomes to their ability, resulting in an improved self-concept (Medway & Lowe 1980).

Out-of-School Assignments

Children become better readers by reading. Often those who like to read do more reading outside of school than in school, and this voluntary reading is an important factor in their continued improvement. If poor readers can be convinced to read extensively between lessons, their progress will likely accelerate.

It is not advisable, however, to insist that children read at home, especially at the start of a remedial program. The teacher should wait until children demonstrate confidence in their reading ability and find that they can get pleasure from it. Then it may be suggested that the child might like to do some reading between lessons. The importance of doing as much reading as possible can be discussed, and a progress chart for outside reading can be started. At first these stories should be short, of interest to the pupil, and well within the child's independent reading level. Reports on outside reading should be kept to a minimum; when used, they should be required only from the standpoint of discussing what the child enjoyed about the story. As a check on progress, the child can be asked to read a particularly enjoyable or interesting part of the story to the teacher.

Workbook exercises are less interesting than stories and usually should not be assigned for completion outside the tutoring situation unless the child enjoys doing them. The same principle—that the pupil should want extra practice—should govern decisions about any homework assignment.

There is a relationship between reading proficiency and the amount of assigned and completed homework (NAEP 1985b), but we do not know whether the relationship is causal, let alone its direction. Jongsma (1985) makes a number of recommendations about the use of homework for pupils in general.

Record Keeping

Keeping useful records is important in any phase of a total reading program, but it is vital for a successful remedial reading program. Well-kept records help in making instructional decisions and provide feedback on program management, a concrete measure of accountability, and a record of each pupil's program and progress. A basic record keeping system should be manageable by the teacher, fairly easy to use, provide only for the collection of useful data, and give a simple means of displaying the data. Records should indicate student strengths and needs, exactly what activities have been attempted, how successful they were (along with any changes that should be made), and the need for any follow-up (Memory 1980). Many of these requirements can be met by use of a form such as that shown in Figure 11.1.

Different kinds of records can be kept. Records kept by the teacher include checklists or other summaries, such as those found in cumulative records, detailed profiles as found in a case study (see page 585), anecdotal notes, and comments written on lesson plans. If children in the remedial group are working on different activities during the allotted time, the teacher needs to have a master schedule of what each pupil is doing.

In individual tutoring, it is desirable to keep a day-by-day diary that contains notations about children's behavior and feelings as well as their reading. If such a detailed record is impractical, significant changes in performance, unusual behavior, the effectiveness of a particular technique, and so on can be noted briefly on a handy pad and dated. These notes should be placed in the child's file and reread periodically. Each child's records (including diagnostic summaries and recommendations, an outline of the teaching plan, and notations about progress) should be kept in a separate file folder or envelope. Use of abbreviations and checklists can reduce the amount of writing necessary.

Records should also be kept of the assignments given to each child. These should contain notations as to when they were begun and finished and comments about how well they were accomplished (see Figure 11.2). Each child should have a notebook in which to do written work and a large envelope in which to keep notebook, assignment sheets, progress charts, word cards, and so on.

Individual Educational Programs

Public Law 94-142 mandates that an *Individual Educational Program* (IEP) be written for each handicapped student. Although there is some evidence that reading teachers are not perceived as contributing much to, or exerting much influence on, IEP committee decisions (Gilliam & Coleman 1981), they should be involved in the development, conduct, and evaluation of IEPs for children who have reading problems. Even if a disabled reader is not classified as handi-

PROGRESS REPORT

Name _Marcia_

Objective _Will recognize, within 1 second each, 3 of the Harris-Jacobson Core pre-primer words (list attached)_

Date	Method–Material	Evaluation

9/9	1. T: a. Show ball printed on card — no time limit
	  b. "This word says _ball_."
	  c. "Look carefully at this word."
	  d. Repeat a + b.
	  e. "What does this word say?"
		c. S has difficulty maintaining attention

	2. S: Responds orally	2. ball
	3. T: Repeat 1a–e	
	4. S: Repeat 2	4. ball
	5. Repeat 1–4 with _can_.	5. Still difficulty with attention. Correctly responded to _can_ on both trials.
	6. Provide mixed practice with _ball_ and _can_.	6. Responded correctly to both words on first 3 trials.
	7. Repeat 1–4 with _play_.	7. Attention slightly better. Correctly responded to _play_ on both trials.
	8. Provide mixed practice with all 3 words.	8. Unable to respond correctly to all 3 words in 3 trials. Responses suggest S isn't using initial consonants as cues.
9/10	1. Repeat 9/9 plan, but call S's attention to use of initial consonants as aid to word recognition.	1. S responded to all 3 words correctly on first 3 trials.
	2. Combine ball, _can_, play with previously learned words _I_, _big_, _my_, _a_, _have_, _is_ in sentences.	

	Have S read
	  a. I can play ball.
	  b. I have a big ball.
	  c. My ball is big.
		a. Responded correctly to all words.
		b. Ditto
		c. Ditto

Figure 11.1. A form for a progress report. A separate set of forms is used for each objective. The form also may be modified for use as a daily lesson plan. If so, all the objectives for a lesson would be stated and the plan laid out in the sequence in which the lesson would be presented. T = Teacher, S = Student.

READING ASSIGNMENT SHEET

Name _____

Date Assigned	Assignment	Date Completed	Comments

Figure 11.2.   A form for individual reading assignments.

capped, reading specialists may want to use IEPs to help plan and evaluate their remediation.

The majority of parents ask few questions and respond little during initial placement/IEP conferences. However, they are satisfied for the most part with the conferences. Vaughn et al. (1988) discusses the possible reasons for this passive role taken by parents.

Apparently, there is some confusion over what constitutes an acceptable IEP (Kammerlohr, Henderson & Rock 1983), as well as some question as to its utility (Calfee 1982). Each IEP must include: (1) a statement of the student's present level of educational performance, (2) annual goals and short-term instructional objectives that lead to the attainment of the annual goals, (3) the specific educational services the child will receive to achieve those goals, (4) the duration of services, and (5) a method of determining whether the goals are attained (Bierly 1978). There is no standard IEP from, and a new IEP need not be written annually; however, it must be revised as needed and kept up to date.

Trumbell, Strickland, and Hammer (1978a,b) provide a concise description of the PL 94-142 regulations pertaining to IEPs and describe how to formulate IEPs that are in compliance with the legal requirements. There are also suggestions for developing databased IEPs (Deno, Mirkin & Wesson 1984), developing IEPs based on a whole-language model (Hassilriis 1982), evaluating IEPs (Freasier 1983), involving students in the formulation of their own IEPs (Salend 1983), and using microcomputers in writing IEPs (Gore & Vance 1983). The aforementioned should be read carefully and critically. For example, the contention by Salend that students can determine their own instructional levels accurately is open to question; and although computers may be useful in developing and monitoring IEPs, presenting a menu from which goals are to be selected may lead to stilted, mechanical procedures that bypass the thought that is often necessary to formulate a useful IEP.

Discharging Students from a Remedial Program

Two practices can defeat the aims of remedial reading program in the long run: (1) setting an arbitrary time limit for which the child may receive remediation, and (2) giving in to pressure to remediate more children than may be accommodated by the available personnel and resources. In both cases, pupils are usually released from the program too early, which greatly increases the probability that they will not continue to improve in their reading ability, or that they will fail to maintain their gains.

Two criteria should be applied in judging when a child is ready to leave a remedial program: (1) Does the child have the ability to read classroom assignments with adequate comprehension? (2) Has the child established the habit of reading for pleasure? The first criterion implies that the teacher must know what demands will be placed on children in the regular classroom and prepare them to meet these demands. Anderson-Inman (1986) provides strategies that promote application of skills learned in the remedial program to the classroom program. The second criterion suggests that the child is practicing newly acquired skills. Failure to meet either criterion may mean that progress in reading will come to a halt when special help is stopped.

Before pupils are discharged from the remedial program, the teacher should wean them from any dependency and convince them that they can be successful in the regular classroom program. The time needed to accomplish this depends both on the degree of the child's dependency and personality. The transition should be planned with the classroom teacher also. As pupils are released, they should be replaced by others with reading problems.

If pressure from a long waiting list makes it necessary to discontinue children before they are ready, the remedial teacher should confer with the classroom teacher and provide both teaching suggestions and appropriate materials. Allowing the child to return to the remedial room for an occasional visit also helps.

Providing Support in Other Curricular Areas

Sometimes children make good progress in a remedial program and gain confidence as they experience successful learning, only to be crushed when they fail in other subject-matter areas. The remedial teacher should try to prevent this by conferring with the classroom teachers and suggesting the possibility of shorter and more appropriate assignments, arranging to have assignments read to the children by other students or family members, providing them with taped recordings of the textbooks, and possibly arranging to have tests given orally. When the required reading tasks are well above the children's frustration levels, giving them the same opportunities to learn that would be given a children with severely defective vision seems reasonable. Further suggestions about content-subject instruction for disabled readers may be found on pages 620–621.

Consultation

When a reading specialist is employed as a reading consultant, working with and through classroom teachers is typically the specialist's main responsibility. Reading consultants may carry out diagnostic studies of individual children in order to make specific recommendations for the teacher, may demonstrate how to teach a group of poor readers, or may provide individual help for a small number of children to get them started. But the main responsibility for teaching rests with the classroom teachers.

Robinson and Pettit (1978) discuss ways in which a remedial teacher can expand her role in the school's total reading program. Skill in human relations is a prerequisite. At Level 1, acceptance by classroom teachers is improved by volunteering to share such chores as lunchroom duty, conferring regularly with teachers who have children in the remedial program, and offering to demonstrate new reading materials and techniques. At Level 2, the remedial teacher accepts an invitation from a teacher to visit her classroom during reading instruction in order to suggest ways of improving that teacher's reading program, and serves on such faculty committees as curriculum, textbook selection, and library committees. At Level 3, the remedial teacher, with administrative approval, serves at least half time as a reading consultant.

It takes from 3 to 6 years to make substantive changes in existing reading curricula. Therefore, whoever takes the lead in securing such changes must make a long-term commitment (Samuels 1988a). In attempting to evoke curricular change, the following should be considered: (1) obtaining whatever administrative permission is necessary; (2) obtaining administrative, parental, and teacher support; (3) securing needed funding; (4) establishing a steering committee whose membership includes classroom teachers, parents, and perhaps even a board of education member and a student; (5) holding committee meetings to assess needs, to determine priorities, and to plan, implement, and evaluate the targeted changes; and (6) planning, scheduling, and conducting inservice meetings to change existing beliefs, attitudes, and instructional practices.

Supervision and Staff Development

Some reading specialists are responsible for a school- or district-wide reading program and thus have to supervise classroom and reading teachers. Space does not allow these topics to be treated adequately here, but some references are indicated for those interested.

Rauch (1982) discusses the characteristics of a good directed reading lesson, Sanacore (1981) presents a checklist for observing remedial reading lessons, Bagford (1981) developed a procedure for evaluating the teaching of developmental and functional reading, and Bell (1982) puts forth a five-stage model for helping teachers to analyze and improve their teaching of reading. Staff development is the subject of publications by Shanker (1982) and J. L. Vacca (1983). Suggestions for conducting inservice problems are made by Siedow, Memory, and Bristow (1985) and Lutz (1987). Ideas as to how a reading specialist can effect changes in existing reading programs are offered by Carnine (1988); Gallagher, Goudvis, and Pearson (1988); and Meyer (1988).

Accountability and Remedial Reading

With increasing frequency, reading specialists are being asked to demonstrate the worth of their remedial programs. Retesting at appropriate intervals is one way to determine how much children have improved. What is measured and how depends on what has been taught, test content and demands, and the purpose of testing.

Norm-referenced tests are not appropriate for measuring gains over short periods of time, especially for individuals. They are not sensitive to small but meaningful changes in reading skills or behaviors. NR tests may not measure the skills taught or may sample them in a way that differs from that in which the skills were practiced. NR tests may provide reliable measures of change for groups over a fairly long period, but growth in general level of reading ability is perhaps better demonstrated through the use of individually administered tests.

Informal or criterion-referenced tests are more likely to be useful in evaluating the effectiveness of a remedial program. The development of particular skills or strategies can also be documented through keeping records. It is advisable to obtain baseline data on each child and compare progress against these starting points. For example, a child may recognize at sight only eight words from a list of high-frequency words. If he learns one additional word a day over a 6-week period (30 days), the child will have almost quadrupled his sight vocabulary (such gains may not result in significant gains on an NR test).

"Rate of progress" scores can be used to obtain a rough approximation of program effectiveness. The gains made by the child before and after remediation are changed to percentages and compared. For example, if Susie had a reading score of 1.5 in September of the third grade, she would have made a half-year (5 months) of progress in 2 years of instruction (grade-equivalent scores start at 1.0). Her rate of progress was only 25% of normal. If, after 10 months of remedial help, she scored 2.8 on the posttest, her gain would be 1.3 years. This indicates a rate of progress of 130%. Put another way, during regular classroom instruction she made an average gain of a quarter-month for each month of instruction. With remediation, she made an average gain of 1.3 months for each month of remediation.

Another usable procedure is to compute a Reading Expectancy Quotient for the pupil before and after remediation. If Susie's IQ was 100 and her MA and CA were both 8.2, her R Exp Q before remediation would have been 81.7 ($6.7 \div 8.2$). After 10 months of remediation, it would have been 87.9 ($8.0 \div 9.1$), showing progress toward normal reading but still some disability.

Other ways to evaluate growth as a result of remediation are to use single-subject, multiple-baseline data (Johnston & Afflerbach 1983), or the number of children who have been successfully returned to the regular classroom program.

Use of "rate of progress" scores and the R Exp Q have been criticized (Yule & Rutter 1976, McLeod 1979) on the grounds that such criteria do not allow for regression effects. Usually when a group is retested with an equivalent test, the average score for those who were very low at the first testing tends to be somewhat closer to the average; it regresses toward the mean. This phenomenon should occur regardless of whether remediation was provided. Yule and Rutter recommend computing a regression equation, using it to find an expected score for each child, and then comparing the obtained score with the expected score.

The trouble with this procedure is that disabled readers who do not receive remediation do not as a group regress toward the mean. Instead, they tend to fall further behind each year. The expected score from a regression equation sets an unrealistically high expectation, and in some cases actually converts a real gain in reading into a theoretical loss.

REMEDIAL READING DELIVERY SYSTEMS

Model Programs

From the remedial reading programs financed by the federal government from about 1965 to 1970, the American Institute for Research in the Behavioral Sciences selected those with superior results that might serve as models. These reports are available through the ERIC system; in the brief mentions that follow, their ERIC order numbers are given instead of the usual citations. The model programs were of many kinds and included the following: programmed tutoring of disadvantaged first graders individually by paraprofessionals a few minutes each day (ED 053 883); a reading center for each elementary school in a large district, which provided both small-group remedial instruction for children and inservice training and consultations for teachers (ED 053 885); Intensive Reading Centers providing concentrated instruction for disadvantaged first graders in groups of 10 or 11, for a full morning each day for 10 weeks (ED 053 886); a remedial reading program for Hispanic children in Grades 2–4, 30 minutes a day in small groups (ED 053 890); summer sessions providing individualized and small-group instruction, for elementary (ED 053 884) and junior high school students (ED 053 882); a county reading-learning center to which children were bused for hour-long lessons 4 days a week, and in which classroom teachers were trained as reading specialists (ED 053 887); a multilevel program including a diagnostic clinic, small-group remedial reading instruction in the schools, and inservice teacher training (ED 053 888); and a high school program including a reading clinic, a reading laboratory open to good readers as well as poor readers, and a program of individually prescribed study (ED 053 881). Other innovative programs have included the use of fully equipped reading clinics or laboratories in buses that travel from school to school; programs to train and use volunteers, high school pupils, or paraprofessional teacher aides as reading tutors; after-school study centers, some of them located in churches or empty stores; and the like. Remedial reading services in secondary schools have been described by Palmer and Brannock (1982); E. Webber (1984); and Schumaker, Deshler, and Ellis (1986).

Remediation outside the Regular Classroom

Most commonly, disabled readers leave their classrooms to receive all or part of their reading instruction. Such delivery systems are referred to as *"pull-out programs."* These programs are of three basic types, which function within a school: reading rooms, resource rooms, and reading labs. Out-of-school resources include reading clinics, reading schools, and summer reading programs.

READING ROOMS.   Many schools have remedial-reading teachers who work primarily with students in one or more schools. They work with a small group or an individual in the room set aside for such activities. The pupils come mainly from regular-education classrooms, although some may come from special-education classes. These children need not come from the same classroom or grade level during a remedial session.

RESOURCE ROOM.   As a result of PL 94-142, a number of students are receiving their reading instruction outside of their special education classes, either in a regular-education classroom, a reading room, or a resource room. *Mainstreaming,* as this practice is called, has occasioned a number of problems for pupils and regular-education teachers (Horne 1985). In addition to having to provide educational programs for the mainstreamed students, a teacher also needs to be concerned about their social and emotional well-being. Little attention has been paid to the mainstreamed child's ability to function in a regular-education classroom and to prepare regular-education teachers and pupils to accept and interact with mainstreamed children (Lipson & Alden 1983).

In some schools, special education students receive instruction in one or more subjects in a resource room from a teacher who has been trained to provide for their needs. Ideas for developing and operating resource rooms can be found in J. Cohen (1982); and Cheyney and Strichart (1981) outline a plan for using learning stations in a resource room.

In the 23 resource rooms studied by Haynes and Jenkins (1986), a daily average of about 47 minutes (range = 11–180 minutes) was scheduled for reading instruction. But only about 44% of the scheduled time was used for instruction by the teacher and reading by the children. More time was spent on such activities in the children's classrooms. In both settings, there was little relationship between the amount of time devoted to reading instruction and the severity of the reading problems but, in general, the reading instruction in the resource rooms was less geared to the students' instructional needs. Receiving insufficient instructional time and inappropriate instruction may help to explain why resource rooms often fail to help children to close the gap between their level of reading achievement and that of their peers who remain in the classroom, despite a low (6 to 1) teacher-pupil ratio.

According to Madden and Slavin (1983), research findings favor the placement of learning disabled students in regular-education classrooms in which reading instruction is individualized or supplemented by well-designed resource programs. Affleck et al. (1988) found that LD pupils who remained in regular classrooms that were staffed by selected teachers and teacher aides, performed as well in reading after three years as those who were instructed in resource rooms.

READING LABS.   Some schools have found it efficient to combine remedial reading and enrichment for good readers in one setting, which is sometimes called a *reading lab*. At times, writing instruction is also provided, and the term *language lab* is employed. In an interesting example from a middle school (Grades 6–8), each of two reading labs was staffed by a reading specialist and a corps of volunteer student aides. The lab offered three kinds of programs: a remedial program for those who needed it; minicourses in specific reading and study skills for average and above-average readers; and a recreational reading program, open to all students (Crawford & Conley 1971). This kind of program deserves emulation.

EVALUATION OF PULL-OUT PROGRAMS.   Among the most frequently cited shortcomings of pull-out programs are: scheduling problems, the time children lose in getting to and from their classrooms and where the remediation is provided, the academic instruction pupils miss when they are out of the classroom during times other than the reading period (and the difficulty of making up such losses), and the lack of congruence or coordination between the child's core instructional program and the remedial program (Bicklen & Zollers 1986). Such potential problems can be greatly lessened, if not overcome, by careful and cooperative planning. Unfortunately, such planning does not seem to occur very often (see the following).

According to Idol, West, and Lloyd (1988), pull-out programs have not produced many positive results. If Haynes and Jenkins' (1986) and Allington et al.'s (1986) findings are typical of remedial reading, a lack of positive results is not surprising. Haynes and Jenkins' results are summarized on page 423. In the remedial programs observed by Allington et al. in four schools over 6 months, remediation consisted mainly of completing workbook or worksheet skill lessons. There was little direct instruction, and only a small amount of time was devoted to having the children read anything other than very brief pieces of connected text.

Allington (1986) states that remedial instruction is typically independent of, and different from, that received in regular classrooms,[5] but Haynes and Jenkins (1986) report that the nature of reading instruction and eight reading activities were similar in the resource rooms and regular classrooms they studied. Differences in reading instruction in the two settings *may* indicate that remedial work is more in keeping with the child's needs than the classroom program, or vice versa. In either case, the child may become confused if the instructional procedures, terminology, or the ways in which reading skills are to be performed or strategies applied differ significantly in the two settings.

The reported lack of congruence has led to suggestions which closely approximate those made by advocates of the REI movement (see the following). Having the reading specialist work with children in their classrooms can facilitate the coordination of remedial and core-curriculum reading programs. But it may also present some drawbacks. A portion of the reading specialist's time is spent getting from one classroom to another; in a given class, only one or two children may have a serious problem or there may not be children with similar needs who could be grouped for instruction; the typical classroom stimulations and distractions make it difficult for some children to concentrate; and, being watched by their classmates severely inhibits the performance of some disabled readers. In one newly established "within class" remedial program, one of the main problems was whether the reading specialist or classroom teacher should exert leadership and control (Bean & Eichelberger 1985). These problems are

[5]Refer to Johnston, Allington, and Afflerbach (1985) and Allington (1986), for the possible causes of this lack of congruence.

not insurmountable, but they need to be considered. A collaborative reading program that requires all support personnel to integrate their services is described by Idol, West, and Lloyd (1988), and Proctor (1986) presents an in-class team approach that whole-language advocates would find acceptable.

READING CLINICS AND CENTERS.   Children with severe reading disabilities and those who fail to respond to remedial efforts in their schools should, when possible, be referred for more intensive and complete diagnosis to a reading clinic or center. Many of these facilities are run by universities or colleges and combine training of graduate students as reading specialists with research and service to clients. Some are outpatient clinics located in the neurological, psychiatric, or pediatric services of a hospital. Others are organized within the pupil personnel services of a school system. A few are privately operated. Many children with reading disabilities are also seen in child guidance clinics, in which a psychiatric orientation usually predominates. Several clinics and their procedures are described in the May 1982 issue of the *Journal of Learning Disabilities.*

In addition to a director and one or more reading specialists, a clinic or center should have on its staff other professionals from such fields as clinical psychology, psychiatry, neurology, pediatrics, social work, ophthalmology or optometry, and speech and audiology; or should refer children to such specialists for examinations or consultations as needed. After clinical findings have been interpreted and integrated, recommendations are made both about the treatment of handicaps that interfere with learning and about the kind of remedial instruction the child needs. Treatment is often given in the same clinic. Muia and Connors (1978) provide a useful discussion of legal requirements concerning confidentiality and obtaining client permissions.

REMEDIAL SCHOOLS.   A few full-time schools take children with severe reading disabilities. Some of them are sponsored by universities; other are under private auspices. There are also schools for children who need special education, including those with learning disabilities. Unless a remedial school is heavily endowed, tuition is necessarily high.

SUMMER PROGRAMS.   That some pupils show a decline in reading skills over the summer is fairly well established. But summer reading programs may prove helpful to these students (Cornelius & Semmel 1982), if for no other reason than that they get the children to practice their reading skills. Well-designed and operated summer-long remedial programs may help some children make significant gains in reading. However, the permanence of gains from programs lasting only a few weeks is questionable. Summer reading programs have been described by Zeller (1980) and Gambrell and Jarrell (1980).

Remediation in Regular Classrooms

Remediation may be provided within the regular-education or special education classroom. It may be provided by the teacher, with or without backup services from the reading specialist or by a tutor who receives consultation and direction from the teacher or reading specialist. Teachers either must have the ability, time, and inclination to conduct remediation on their own or to follow through on the reading specialist's recommendations. Students placed in this option are not likely to be severely reading disabled.

In the integrated classroom model, all of the children are instructed by the regular class teacher, without any assistance from outside specialists. There are fewer students than in ordinary classrooms, and teacher aides are provided. Research suggests that integrated classrooms are as effective as other in-class models at promoting student achievement (Jenkins & Heinen 1989). Such plans are not new (see A. J. Harris & Sipay 1975 [1980, 1985], p. 92).

Remediation can also be conducted in the classroom by the reading specialist. This plan may facilitate coordination of the child's remedial reading and classroom reading programs. This option is discussed in more detail in the next section.

REGULAR EDUCATION INITIATIVE.　A number of special education and other educational programs are based on the assumption that different potentially handicapping conditions create different educational needs, and that these specialized needs can best be addressed through programs specifically designed to meet those differing needs. However, opinion is growing that programs that require the categorization and labeling of these children, especially those who are mildly handicapped, should be replaced with a unified educational delivery system that is more efficient and effective than the myriad of existing programs (e.g., Reynolds, Wang & Walberg 1987). As Bickel and Bickel (1986, p. 497) state, "The natural and artificial distinctions that exist between special and regular education at the classroom level have come under growing scrutiny in the context of mainstreaming large numbers of special-needs students. The press for mainstreaming is forcing an examination of many current assumptions on both sides." This movement, which is commonly referred to as the *Regular Education Initiative* (REI), would result in many formerly categorized children being placed in regular-education classes, with their educational programs designed and delivered cooperatively by regular and special education teachers as well as support personnel. A basic belief of REI advocates is that improved learning for *all* children can be delivered in regular classrooms *if* instruction is adjusted to meet individual needs.

The REI movement seems to have arisen from a number of dissatisfactions, including: (1) a belief that labeling children is harmful; (2) suggestions that learning disabled and other special education students simply receive the same instruction that has already failed in regular classrooms, only in smaller classes or groups at a slower pace (Reynolds 1988); (3) the lack of congruence between regular-classroom and remedial instruction (Johnston, Allington & Afflerbach 1985); (4) the lack of coordination between the regular-class core curriculum and that of the school's remedial and/or special education programs (Idol, West & Lloyd 1988); (5) the lack of individualized instruction for children who are removed from the regular class (Farnam-Diggory 1986); (6) the belief that special-education and compensatory-education programs are often conflicting classification and intervention systems that have evolved to serve an overlapping population of low achievers (McGill-Franzen 1987); and (7) dissatisfaction with the results produced by pull-out programs (see the foregoing).

Opponents to REI focus on such arguments as the difficulty in retraining teachers and eliciting cooperative efforts; existing programs *are* serving special-needs children (the research findings are mixed); problems with funding if existing categorized programs were abolished; and questions regarding the validity of research studies on which REI is based (e.g., Kaufman, Gerber & Semmel 1988; McKinney & Hocutt 1988).

Whether remedial reading is conducted in or out of the regular classroom, it is important that the children's teachers communicate about their reading instruction. Each should know what methods and materials the other is using, and work cooperatively to design the best possible program for each student. The reading specialist must understand the reading program(s) used in the regular classrooms in order to develop a program that will enable the children to enter that program satisfactorily when they are released from the remedial program.

Students' preferences for a particular delivery model are not only influenced by their experiences with a model and their age, but also by a complex array of factors including their perceptions of the teacher's knowledge of their instructional needs and the quality of the learning environment. Regardless of the delivery system or the classification of the children, students (especially older ones) do not want to draw attention to their academic difficulties. Most children prefer to receive any needed extra help from their classroom teacher; but when they have to see a specialist, they prefer a pull-out over an in-class model (Jenkins & Heinen 1989). Differences in achievement cannot be traced unambiguously to the use of a particular delivery model (Birman 1988).

Effectiveness of Remediation

The evidence on the effectiveness of remediation is mixed. Kline and Kline (1975) report that private tutoring four to five times weekly resulted in improved reading for 95% of the 92 dyslexics studied. Most of them required from 1 to 3 years of treatment, with the amount of reading gain positively related to the length of treatment. In contrast to several other studies, older children improved more than younger pupils. Gittleman and Feingold (1983) also found that remediation was effective.

In order to make the results of the 15 studies in their analysis comparable, Guthrie, Seifert, and Kline (1978) changed all the results to learning gains (gains in months divided by the number of months of remedial help). Using only studies with satisfactory control groups, they found that the tutored groups showed significantly greater improvement in reading. Under favorable conditions, a learning rate double that of normally achieving children with classroom instruction was obtained in several studies. The following characteristics were found in programs that had both high learning rates during remediation and continued improvement at least at a normal rate for 2 years after remedial help was stopped: pupils of elementary school age; students of middle-class SES; students with IQs of 90 or over; those who were given more than 50 hours of remedial help; certified, experienced remedial teachers or trained, supervised tutors. Secondary students learned at about the same rate as did elementary school children, but the former had much more to learn and so needed much more time.

The general conclusion reached by most reviewers is that reading and spelling disabilities persist long after childhood; and in many cases, in spite of intensive remediation (LaBuda & DeFries 1988).

Of the 18 follow-up studies reviewed by Schonhaut and Satz (1983), 4 showed favorable gains in reading, 12 did not, and the findings of 2 were mixed. They conclude that the academic outlook for children with early reading problems is poor, unless the pupil comes from a high-SES family and/or is exposed to an intensive remedial program such as the Orton-Gillingham (see pages 504–505), in which case the outlook is good. The two variables that Schonhaut and Satz credit for successful remediation should not be accepted too readily as causes. SES is not a unitary factor, and there is no evidence regarding which of the many facets of SES were operative. Reading gains may be the direct result of using a particular program, but they also might be due to skilled instruction by understanding teachers who made other adjustments in the students' reading and academic programs.

Other researchers report more negative results. According to Spreen (1982), rather than catch up to their peers in reading ability, the reading problems of most disabled readers who are referred to a reading clinic are more likely to worsen over time. Spreen claims that the positive effects of remediation were minimal at best, except for high-SES, high-verbal-IQ students who attended private schools. Other studies also suggest that the gap between the reading achievement of good and disabled readers widens over time. However, in one study (LaBuda & DeFries 1988), the average rate of growth was similar for both groups over an eight-year period.

Reading gains may not be lasting. Ito (1980) reports that although reading instruction in a resource room had a positive effect on reading performance at the end of the study, the gains were not maintained after 1 year in the regular classroom program. H. C. M. Carroll (1972) also found that there was a slowing down or loss of reading gains after remediation was discontinued. Such results may partly reflect failure on the part of the classroom teachers to provide for students whose reading ability was marginal at best when they were released from the remedial programs. Pupils can make significant gains in reading, but still be reading at a level that would not allow them to continue making progress in programs that did not address their needs.

A longitudinal study (Balow & Blomquist 1965) also casts some light on why the positive effects of remediation sometimes do not last. Children given remedial help for long periods (2 to 3 years) tended to continue to improve; those given short-term remediation (e.g., summer school) did not. Those whose remediation tapered off gradually and who had opportunities to see the remedial teacher about once a month, were more likely to have continued improving than were those whose remediation ended abruptly.

The amount of reading improvement that can reasonably be expected probably depends on many variables and their interactions. Among these factors are: (1) the severity of the reading disability, (2) the child's intellectual ability, (3) the accuracy of the diagnosis, (4) the appropriateness of the remediation, (5) the quality of the reading teacher, (6) the intensity of the remediation (two 15-minute periods per week for a seriously disabled reader is almost a waste of time and may have negative a effect if the child does not improve), (7) the duration of remediation, (8) whether the child was taught to transfer skills to the regular school program, (9) the child's desire to improve his reading ability, and (10) the emotional support the child receives from his teacher, peers and family.

Schonhaut and Satz (1983) contend that we still do not know whether early identification and treatment improves the chances of successful remediation. There is, however, some evidence that it does (Valtin 1984, Clay 1985). All else being equal, it would seem logical to assume that early intervention would produce better results; the problem is less likely to be severe and the child has not failed continuously over a number of years. If intervention occurs early in the child's school years, care must be taken to prevent the feeling that such an "early failure" indicates that there is something radically wrong with the child.

We are of the opinion that there would be many fewer disabled readers if what was known about diagnosis and remediation were applied in order to prevent reading difficulties from becoming reading problems and reading problems from turning into reading disabilities. Prevention should begin in the first grade. Clay (1987a) reports positive results for her Reading Recovery Program, which provides for early, individual treatment. Positive outcomes also were found for the Ohio Reading Recovery Project, which involved supplementary one-to-one tutoring 30 minutes daily for the poorest readers in first grade (R. C. Anderson 1988).

Long-Term Effects of Reading Disability

Reading disability seems to persist in many children throughout the elementary school (McGee et al. 1986) and secondary school years and into adulthood (Scarborough 1984; Finucci, Gottfredson & Childs 1985; Buchanan & Wolf 1986). The more severe the reading disability, the longer it seems to persist. Maughan, Gray, and Rutter (1985) report that only 2½–9% of severely disabled readers were reading at or above the population mean at the time of follow-up. A group of third graders whose word-recognition ability was at the primer level were reading only 1 or 2 years below grade level when tested as adolescents. However, those who were at the preprimer level in third grade were still seriously disabled readers as adolescents. Both groups reportedly had received individualized remediation consistently during the intervening years (Forell & Hood 1985).

Although reading and learning disabled students may make continual progress in reading, they usually still have problems with academic subjects throughout their school years. Unless they are high-SES pupils, their academic careers are often cut short with early entry into low-paying, low-status jobs (Spreen 1982). They also tend to have considerably higher unemployment rates than the general population after leaving high school. Their persistent reading problems play a role in both their unemployment and restricted job opportunities (Maughan, Gray & Rutter 1985). Generally, severe reading disabilities limit educational attainment (Finucci 1986).

There are, however, wide differences in how disabled readers turn out in later years. Many intelligent disabled readers, who received high-quality remediation long enough for them to gain sufficient reading ability to handle school assignments, have completed high school, college, and even graduate school (Finucci, Gottfredson & Childs 1985; N. C. Goodman 1987), although it may have taken them longer than usual to attain their degrees (Finucci 1986). Those who went on to college tended to concentrate in academic areas that did not require extensive reading, and many of them had residual problems such as slow reading. Even readers who had once been severely disabled, although still not reading up to expectations, can be successful in occupations that require less intensive reading than other positions having similar pay and responsibility (Finucci 1986). What appears to account for the differences in attainment in academic and occupational success are the family's SES (and the myriad of interrelated factors associated with it); the child's learning potential; the quality, intensity, and duration of remediation; family support and encouragement; the student's motivation to succeed; and the adjustments made in the child's academic curriculum after being discharged from the remedial program. Generally, studies that show good academic and occupational outcomes have tended to base their conclusions on high-SES samples. Most studies have either improperly controlled for SES, or have not even considered it (O'Connor & Spreen 1988).

12 Developing Word-Recognition Ability

This chapter is the first of two on word recognition. We begin this chapter by placing a number of definitions into a conceptual framework that should prove helpful in understanding both chapters. We then discuss the importance of word recognition and conclude that it is important to, but not solely sufficient for, reading comprehension. Third, we deal with theoretical issues; fourth, with instructional issues. The last two sections cover the two most commonly used methods for teaching children to recognize printed words. These are followed by a detailed treatment of decoding, and a suggested scope and sequence for teaching decoding.

TERMINOLOGY IN A CONCEPTUAL FRAMEWORK

Before children learn to read, they can recognize and understand the meanings of many spoken words. A major step in reading acquisition is learning to recognize the printed representations of spoken words.

Two general types of instructional methods, each of which has variations, are commonly used initially to teach novice readers to recognize printed words. In the *whole-word method*, children are taught to associate whole printed words with their oral counterparts. In *decoding* or *code-emphasis methods*, pupils learn to associate single letters or letter combinations *(graphemes)* with the sounds they represent in spoken words *(phonemes)*, and to blend the phonemes into words. *Phonics* is the use of *symbol-sound associations (grapheme-phoneme correspondences)* in decoding printed words.

Rarely is either instructional method used exclusively. A number of the written words children need to recognize are *phonetically irregular;* that is, applying phonic principles to them would not result in the oral equivalent of the word. For example, *of* would be decoded as /of/, not /uv/. So phonetically irregular words must be learned in some way other than through a decoding method. On the other hand, children cannot be taught directly every word they will encounter in print; therefore, they must learn to decode unknown words if they are to become independent readers. Efficient, fluent reading requires both an extensive *sight vocabulary* (all of the printed words that a reader can recognize immediately) and the ability to use other word-recognition skills, including decoding, when needed.

Regardless of which instructional method is employed initially, children encounter whole words when reading. While whole-word and/or decoding instruction is continuing, and well after it ceases, pupils learn, through various word-recognition strategies, to recognize written words that have not been part of their instructional programs. Often this occurs as a result of decoding *unknown words* (words that are not recognized at sight) the first time or so they are met in print. *Decoding*[1] is a mediated form of word recognition. It involves using a variety of skills, including phonics, to approximate the spoken form of a printed word.

No matter how a student learns to recognize written words—whether initially through a whole-word or a decoding instructional method, or independently through the use of word-recognition strategies including the application of decoding skills—after a word is seen in print enough times, it becomes part of the reader's sight vocabulary. Children's sight vocabularies vary widely with age and reading ability (Adams & Huggins 1985).

Word recognition is the ability to associate a printed word with its spoken counterpart either instantly or through some mediated process. Understanding the meaning of the word is not included in this definition. However, if the appropriate word meaning is in the reader's *lexicon* (mental dictionary), word recognition is likely to lead to word identification. *Word identification* usually subsumes word recognition and definitely involves word meaning. A distinction is drawn between the two because it is possible to determine the spoken form of a printed word without understanding even its most common meaning. For instance, most readers could arrive at the oral counterpart of *kine* the first time they see it in print, but not understand that it means cows. On the other hand, the meaning of a previously unencountered word can be derived without knowing or determining its spoken equivalent if the word appears in sufficiently potent context (e.g., The *kine*, or cows as we call them, were being milked").

THE IMPORTANCE OF WORD RECOGNITION
TO READING COMPREHENSION

Opinions differ regarding the importance of word recognition in the reading process. Some theorists believe that skilled readers make minimal use of printed

---

[1]The term *decoding* is used in the literature to define different processes. In addition to the definition used here, it has been employed to mean "to identify a word's pronunciation *and* meaning," "to convert printed words into spoken language, either orally or subvocally," or "to comprehend written language."

words, sampling them only as needed to construct or confirm their hypotheses about text meaning. Other theorists contend that word-recognition ability is extremely important, and that even skilled readers attend to the vast majority of the words in a written text. Our position is that word recognition provides a necessary foundation for reading comprehension, that accurate and automatic word recognition facilitates reading comprehension, but that even perfect word recognition does not assure reading comprehension. Teaching must reflect a reasonable balance between attention to word recognition and obtaining meaning. If too much attention is focused on word recognition, obtaining meaning may be hampered. If too little attention is paid to word-recognition accuracy, meaning can be distorted.

There is increasing belief (e.g., Perfetti 1986a, Stanovich 1986a,b) that context-free word-recognition ability best distinguishes good from poor readers. Successful readers have usually gained automatic word-processing skills by second or third grade, but disabled readers find it difficult to acquire fluent word-recognition and identification skills (Torgesen 1986a). Seidenberg et al. (1985) report that disabled readers' word recognition is slower and less accurate than that of poor readers, whose word recognition is slower and more error-filled than that of good readers. They also conclude that the three groups studied did not differ significantly in their word-recognition proccesses. Szesulski and Manis (1987) and Bruck (1988) agree with this conclusion; Wolf (1986) does not.

In discussing its relationship to reading comprehension, two aspects of word recognition are considered—accuracy and speed. Common sense suggests that inability to recognize accurately most of the words in a written text is likely to disrupt reading comprehension. At times, even the inaccurate recognition of one or two key words in a text can have adverse effects on understanding.

Correlations between word-recognition accuracy and reading comprehension tend to be about 0.80 in the primary grades and approximately 0.65 in upper grades. Higher correlations in the primary grades are not surprising, since early reading materials usually employ a limited number of different words, sentence patterns that are within most young children's syntactic competence, and concepts that are likely already understood. The relationship between reading comprehension and word recognition decreases and its relation to cognitive and linguistic abilities increases when texts utilize many different words, more words with unknown or abstract meanings, more syntactically complex structures, and more difficult and unfamiliar concepts. The magnitude of the correlations indicate that factors other than word recognition enter into reading comprehension.

In general, accurate word recognition lays the foundation for fluent word identification, which is important for reading comprehension. But the importance of accurate word recognition depends on the relevance of the word(s) to understanding the text. Nouns and verbs usually are more meaning-bearing than are other categories of words, but not all nouns and verbs are equally important for comprehending a particular text. The necessity for accurate word recognition also depends on the level of comprehension desired. Accurate word recognition is more important for the precise type of comprehension required in understanding content-subject textbooks than it is for global comprehension tasks, such as getting the gist of a story.

Various theories suggest that word recognition must be not only accurate, but automatic, before the reading comprehension process can be fully developed (Torgesen 1986a). Gough (1985a) theorizes that words cannot be organized into meaningful groups unless word recognition is accurate and fast enough to avoid exceeding the limits of short-term memory (STM). Five to ten bits of information can be retained in STM for about 10 to 15 seconds. If the words in a sentence are recognized too slowly, its structure collapses and meaning is lost (Calfee & Drum 1985). According to Perfetti (1986a), speed of word identification reflects the accessibility of lexical information (see page 436); the richer the word representations, the more quickly lexical access is obtained. Both Perfetti's (1985) verbal efficiency theory and LaBerge and Samuel's (1985) limited-attentional model hold that the amount of processing or attentional capacity available for reading comprehension is limited by the amount used for word recognition/identification. Rapid, accurate word recognition frees space in working memory for the higher-order processes involved in comprehension. This theory is supported by the repeated finding that less skilled readers recognize printed words more slowly than do skilled readers at early and later stages of reading acquisition (Manis 1985).

A lack of automatic word recognition can cause reading difficulty. However, even though novice and poor readers typically allot a considerable portion of their processing capacity to word recognition, this fact may not hamper their comprehension greatly if the text does not require a great deal of attentional capacity to obtain meaning (e.g., as when the reader has high level of relevant topical knowledge). Nevertheless, having to constantly switch attention back and forth between word recognition and comprehension places heavy demands on memory (Samuels 1987b).

Correlations between word-recognition speed and reading comprehension range from about 0.50 to 0.80 in Grades 1–6 (Stanovich, Cunningham & West 1981). Studies have shown that word-recognition speed usually increases with age; is significantly faster in good than in poor readers, except for high-frequency words; and is faster in context than in isolation, especially for poor readers (Lyon 1984). Skilled readers have faster word recognition than less-skilled readers at every grade level (Stanovich 1986b).

Lovett (1987) found that pupils identified as being accuracy-disabled (having inaccurate, slow word recognition) produced more word recognition errors, read more slowly, and comprehended less than those labeled as rate-disabled (accurate but slow word recognition) and pupils with fluent word recognition. The accuracy-disabled group also had difficulty making symbol-sound associations, were inferior in phonemic segmentation, were the slowest at verbal-naming tasks, and had marked deficiencies in understanding morphological and syntactic conventions that mediate comprehension. The slow word-recognition speed of the rate-disabled group appeared to have an adverse effect on their reading comprehension.

Torgesen (1986a) believes that, although a number of questions are unanswered, substantial evidence indicates that fluent word recognition is a crucial prerequisite for reading comprehension. However, research findings regarding the influence of rapid, single-word training on reading comprehension are mixed (A. J. Harris & Sipay 1985). Perhaps, as Resnick (1979) writes, instruction in any one subskill alone is unlikely by itself to change poor readers into good readers because the observed skill difference is but one indicator of many differences between good and poor readers.

THEORETICAL ISSUES

Printed words are used by readers in attempting to understand written texts. But words are just symbols. What information do words represent? How is this knowledge acquired? How does one store, access, and utilize this information? Presently, the answers to these questions must be based primarily on theory.

Word Representations

Through experiences with spoken and written language, we acquire information about words. The exact nature of this information and how it is learned and stored are largely unknown. It has been theorized (e.g., Ehri 1980, Vellutino 1983) that we have various kinds of information, to varying extent, filed in our long-term memories. Each *lexical entry* is thought to contain information about the word's meaning(s), syntactic properties, pronunciation, and orthographic structure. These types of information are variously referred to as the word's *identities*, *features*, *properties*, or *representations*. Information about grapheme-phoneme relationships is also stored in LTM.

As we hear and speak words, we acquire information about their phonological, semantic, and syntactic properties. We learn the "names" of words (i.e., their spoken or acoustic forms). As we say the words, we gain information about their articulatory features. At some later point, we become aware that spoken language is comprised of various-sized units, and we eventually acquire information about the phonemic structures of words. We also learn the unique ordering of phonemes comprising a word, and that phonemes can be rearranged in various ways to form different words. Together, this information is referred to as the word's *phonological representation*. A word's *semantic representation* includes all of its possible meanings that we have learned, as well as knowing which of its meanings is appropriate for a given context. A word's *syntactic representation* specifies its characteristic grammatical function(s).

When we learn to read, we add new words to our lexicons, as well as further semantic and syntactic information about words that are already in our mental dictionaries. As we learn to recognize printed words, orthographic information about these words is stored in our lexicons. *Orthographic representations* are learned as sequences of letters bearing systematic relationships to acoustic or articulatory segments already stored in long-term memory. A word's orthographic form is secured to its phonological form when at least some of its letters come to represent phonemic segments. Gradually, a complicated associational network is built up in which various word representations are interrelated and synthesized. Once established, each of the available representations is activated whenever the printed word is seen, thereby providing alternative means by which the word may be recognized (Ehri 1980, 1987). Repeated exposure to whole printed words results in rapid, accurate word recognition because all the sources of information about a word are consolidated into a single, highly cohesive representation (Ehri & Wilce 1982). Thus, a printed word becomes a symbol for its phonological, semantic, syntactic, and orthographic information.

Lexical Access

Reading comprehension requires that lexical information be accessed because semantic and syntactic information is used in understanding the text. *Lexical access* is the process of retrieving information about word representations from memory. According to Perfetti (1986a), lexical access initiates the critical process of *semantic encoding* (attaching contextually relevant meanings to words during text processing) and it must occur at high rates because even skilled readers take in only a limited amount of visual information in each fixation. Inefficient lexical access disrupts the temporary representations of text in working memory, and thus competes for processing resources.

Two routes to the lexicon are thought to exist (Leong 1986). In *direct access,* words are identified by finding a match between the visual or orthographic pattern of the printed word and the spelling pattern of a lexical entry, or printed words are converted to a visual code that is matched with a lexical entry. If a match occurs, information about the word is immediately available to the reader. In direct access, printed whole words are used to retrieve semantic and syntactic information as well as *postlexical phonological representations* (retrieving the name of the word after the lexicon has been accessed). Thus, direct-access models postulate that words are first recognized visually, with the phonological code being subsequently obtained from LTM (Waters, Bruck & Seidenberg 1985). Reading teachers would say that the word was in the child's sight vocabulary.[2] Another form of direct access involves the use of word parts that are comprised of frequently encountered spelling patterns. This type of access would probably involve either use of an analogy strategy (see page 464) or morphemic analysis (see page 463). An extreme version of the dual-access theory (see the following) holds that word recognition occurs only by analogy. Among the problems with this view is that it ignores the significant individual and developmental differences in the processing units used by children (R. Olson 1985).

Mediated access (also known as *phonological or indirect access)* involves recoding graphic information, on the basis of grapheme-phoneme correspondence knowledge, into a phonological code which is used to access the lexicon. Access to lexical meaning is mediated by prelexical phonological representations. Reading specialists refer to this as decoding. Use of an indirect access route requires that the reader understand how our orthographic system maps onto spoken language, and have the skills necessary to decode the word. Initially, a match with the word's pronunciation makes semantic and syntactic information available to the reader. After the word has been encountered in print a number of times, its orthographic representation is established in the lexicon, and the direct access route can be used by the reader (Ehri 1987).

There are also *dual-process theories* of lexical access in which both the direct and mediated routes are activated simultaneously (Juel 1983, Baron 1985).

[2]Although a word may be recognized immediately and one of its meanings activated, word identification cannot be said to have taken place unless the meaning is contextually appropriate.

In some theories, they operate in parallel and are used simultaneously; in others, the first pathway to produce a match in the lexicon is acted on by the reader. Some dual-process theorists would allow that task demands, word familiarity, and developmental differences influence the reader's relative dependence on each of the routes (R. Olson 1985).

Some advocates of top-down models of reading suggest that skilled readers, and perhaps even less skilled readers, almost always go directly from print to meaning. At times, this belief is used as a rationale for not teaching decoding skills. At the other end of the continuum are those, usually followers of bottom-up models, who believe that all, or almost all, printed words must be recoded into a phonological code in order to access the lexicon (see Weaver & Resnick 1979). More commonly, it is believed that although skilled readers make frequent use of the direct-access route, they also have the skills required to use the mediated route when necessary (Kleiman & Humphrey 1982, Stanovich 1986b). There is some belief that novice readers rely on phonological access while they are learning to associate written with spoken language, but Barron (1986) contends that neither route predominates during early reading acquisition.

There is some evidence for the existence and use of both a direct and a mediated pathway to the lexicon (Glushko 1981, Barron 1981b). Some research findings suggest that either pathway may be used, with the choice depending on various factors (Haines & Leong 1983). Carr and Pollatsek (1985), however, conclude that an expanded and complex version of the dual-process model best accounts for the existing data on the recognition of words in isolation, but that none of the theories are adequate for words in context. The dual-process theory has been challenged (Humphreys & Evett 1985).

Other Word-Recognition Models

Obtaining reliable information as to how words are recognized is extremely difficult because our minds tend to make only the final product of their processing available to conscious awareness; the intermediate processing steps are usually hidden from us (J. C. Johnston 1981). Therefore, it is not surprising that the word-recognition process is not yet well understood. But there are a number of word-recognition models in addition to the lexical-access theories discussed above. Although there is some commonality, a comparison of existing models reveals a lack of agreement as to what is involved in word recognition. Foss (1988) summarizes a number of word-recognition theories.

There appears to be greater consensus regarding the strategies that may be used to recognize or identify printed words. These closely approximate theories of lexical access. Children may use a whole-word, analogy, or phonologically mediated strategy. According to Ehri (1987), novice readers initially recognize a printed word by accessing remembered associations between a few letters in the word and the sounds in its pronunciation. But although she notes that novice readers may employ other strategies, Barr (1974–1975) concludes that they usually employ the word-recognition strategies taught to them (either a whole-word or mediated strategy). Children's word-recognition strategies may change with reading experience (Patberg, Dewitz & Samuels 1981).

Opinions differ considerably regarding the unit of perception in reading.

Early studies (Cattell 1885, Huey 1908) are often cited as evidence that the word is the unit of perception in reading.[3] The data from these studies, however, do not support this contention (Kamil 1980), nor can findings indicating that individuals *can* use letter or letter-cluster information to recognize words (e.g., Mewhort & Campbell 1981) be taken as proof that such units actually *are* used during normal reading (N. F. Johnson 1981).

Vellutino (1982) summarizes and critiques feature-analysis, component-letter, letter-group, and whole-word theories of word recognition and concludes that the unit of perception used in reading is relative. He states that all the visual information contained in a word is apprehended by the reader, but that the unit of focal attention at the time when word identification is finalized is variable and depends on the nature of the stimulus, the context in which the word is perceived, and the information available to, and typically used by, the reader. For example, printed words that are easily discriminated from other words or words that are highly constrained by context may be recognized by only their salient features. Less easily discriminated words must be processed more carefully, especially when they appear in isolation or in ambiguous or uncertain contexts.

Reading proficiency may also influence the unit of perception in word recognition. Novice and poor readers use units smaller than the whole word, possibly as small as a single letter. Skilled readers may use the word or smaller units, depending on their familiarity with the word or their purpose for reading (Samuels 1987). Disabled readers tend to process words in smaller units than do good readers, and therefore are more affected by increases in word length (Manis 1985). These viewpoints run counter to that of Marmurek (1988) who contends that both good and poor readers process words holistically.

METHODOLOGICAL CONSIDERATIONS

Factors That Influence Word Recognition

Many factors influence the recognition and retention of printed words. One of these is teaching methodology. Children taught initially with a phonic method: (1) are less likely to guess unfamiliar words; (2) are more likely to recognize phonetically regular words than irregular words; (3) are likely to make mispronunciations that are graphically or phonemically similar to the stimuli, but which may be semantically inappropriate; and (4) are likely to make little use of semantic and syntactic cues (Barr 1972, 1974–1975, 1975; Dank 1977). Children taught initially with a whole-word method (1) are likely to guess unfamiliar words; (2) rely heavily at first on context clues, at times disregarding graphic cues; (3) often substitute a previously taught word for the stimulus; (4) tend to apply decoding skills as they are acquired; and (5) increasingly combine contextual and graphic cues as reading ability improves (Biemiller 1970).

Some words tend to be learned more easily by children.[4] These include

[3]These studies also were cited as justification for the introduction of the whole-word instructional method.

[4]Use of closed-caption TV programs improved the word recognition, but not the fluency, of LD students (Koskinen et al. 1986). Suggestions for using closed-caption TV for teaching word recognition may be found in Koskinen and Wilson (1987).

words that children want to learn and that are meaningful to them (Brescia & Braun 1977), have strong emotional overtones (Adams 1974),[5] or evoke imagery (Terwilliger & Kolker 1982). Van der Veur (1975) lists the imagery ratings of 1,000 high-frequency words.

Content words (nouns, verbs, adjectives, adverbs) are meaning-bearing words. *Function words* (prepositions, conjunctions, pronouns, auxiliary and linking verbs, and articles) have no clear lexical meaning, but have grammatical meaning. Content words are learned more readily than function words. Functors are often troublesome because they have abstract meanings and because of their graphic similarity (e.g., a number of functors begin with *th—that, this, there;* or *wh—what, which, who, why*). Yet function words must be mastered because they serve to organize content words into meaningful phrases and sentences as well as to provide text cohesion. Function words appear much more frequently in print than do content words (Blank 1985). Jolly (1981) offers suggestions for teaching function words.

Jorm (1977) found that high-frequency words were easier to learn; Horodezky (1979) did not. In learning to recognize words, children with high reading ability are less affected by word frequency than are less skilled readers (Blank 1985).

Repetition and Reinforcement

Practice does not necessarily make perfect. Mere repetition is not a sufficient basis for learning. Nevertheless, repetition has some relevance. Children differ greatly in how quickly they learn to recognize printed words. Some children can remember a word easily after a few exposures; others need many repetitions. To be effective, repetition should not be monotonous drill but should be presented so as to maintain the child's interest and encourage accurate perception. After a word is introduced in a reading series, it is usually repeated a number of times in differing contexts in the reading textbook. Correlated workbooks can furnish additional repetitions and an abundance of easy, pleasurable reading provides an excellent way to practice word recognition.

Word cards[6] can be used to introduce words, to build sentences, to test word-recognition accuracy, and in quick-exposure techniques to develop speed of recognition after word-recognition accuracy has been fairly well developed by the child. Care should be exercised to prevent dependence on accidental or incidental cues, such as a smudge on the card or a dog-eared corner. Opportunities must be provided to meet, in context, words which have been introduced and practiced in isolation.

Picture-word cards that can be used for independent study and self-teaching can be made by the teacher or pupils. The word is printed on one side of an opaque card, and an illustrative picture with the word below it is on the other

[5]One of the basic tenets of the language-experience approach is that the students should be taught the words they want to use in creating their stories. The belief that words that carry high emotional charges and interest for the children are easier for them to learn is the basis for the development of an "organic vocabulary," first advocated by Ashton-Warner (1959) and later systematically developed by Veatch et al. (1979).

[6]The term *word card* is more appropriate than *flash card* since the card can be displayed for any length of time and can be used for other than quick exposures.

side. Clipping one corner makes it easier to keep the cards right side up. After studying the picture-word side of a few cards, the cards are turned over and the child tests himself, checking the correctness of each response by looking again at the picture.

Nouns are easiest to depict. Fry (1987) presents a list of 100 nouns that can be depicted. Action verbs and direction words (e.g., *above, to, from*) may be represented by using stick figures, arrows, and so forth. Abstract words (e.g., *an, is*) are difficult to picture and usually must be placed in a phrase or sentence in which context is the main cue to the underlined word (e.g., The girl *is* running.).

Word cards for high-frequency words are available from various publishers, as are cards for the specific words used in the beginning reading materials in most published reading programs. Teacher-made word cards can be used to provide practice on words that need special attention. Auditory cues can also be provided by commercially available machines that employ cards on which strips of magnetic tape are mounted. The child can look at the card; attempt to read the word, phrase, or sentence; then place it in the machine and listen as a recorded voice provides the oral counterpart. The child's response can also be recorded and compared with the recorded voice. Both printed, prerecorded magnetic cards and blank magnetic cards can be purchased.

As words are encountered repeatedly in print, they become sight words. If slow word recognition persists and becomes a real handicap, a child may need special practice (see pages 480–481).

Which Words Should Be Taught?

Children should be able to recognize most of the words used in their instructional materials, but, because all words are not equally important for obtaining meaning, all are not equally important to teach. More instruction and practice should be provided for frequently occurring words and for those whose meanings are important for understanding the text.

The words that occur in a basal series or in a textbook do not occur with equal frequency. Some words appear much more often than others. For instance, in the materials examined by Goodman and Bird (1984), about 55% of the words occurred only once, and 25 words accounted for 36% to 40% of all of the words in a text.

Function words occur frequently across various texts because English syntax requires their use. Furthermore, there are a limited number of functors, and only a few words can fulfill each grammatical function. Although functors have no lexical meaning, they are important for reading comprehension because they are needed to tie ideas together.

If information about word frequency is not available from the publisher or some other source, a list of high-frequency words may be used as a guideline. Teacher judgment is needed to determine a word's importance to text comprehension.

Remedial reading teachers have a number of options. They may choose to teach first the words the child wants to learn and gradually introduce other words or they may opt to start with high-frequency words and a few content words in order to get the child quickly into reading meaningful material containing words that are likely to have high transfer value. At times, high-frequency words containing the same phonic element may be taught together and then used as a basis for teaching decoding through an analytic method. If a phonics method is more viable than a whole-word method, the teacher may first instruct the child in those skills that will allow him to decode phonetically regular, high-frequency words.

Word Lists

A relatively small number of the over 600,000 English words appear frequently in print. Johns (1981) states that 13 words (*a, and, for, he, is, in, it, of, that, the, to, was, you*) account for over 25% of the words in print. Fry, Fountoukidis, and Polk (1985) estimate that 100 words make up half of all the words in written material, and 1,000 words account for over 90%. High-frequency word lists are not in complete agreement as to the rank order of such words, nor do they all contain exactly the same words. For descriptions and comparisons of word lists, see A. J. Harris and Jacobson (1973–1974), Hillerich (1974), and Monteith (1976).

Since E. L. Thorndike (1921) compiled the first word list, numerous others have appeared.[7] The most recent comprehensive lists are based on Grade 1–8 textbooks (A. J. Harris & Jacobson 1982); the preprimer, primer, and first-reader lists of which are shown in Figure 12.1. Other comprehensive lists include one based on a wide variety of materials used in Grades 3–9 (Carroll, Davies & Richman 1971),[8] and one based on adult reading materials (Kucera & Francis 1967). A 9,000-word list that includes 6,530 words with multiple meanings was compiled by Johnson, Moe, and Baumann (1983).

Other lists have been developed for specific purposes. For instance, an oral vocabulary of 6,442 words used by first graders was compiled by Moe, Hopkins, and Rush (1982). There are also lists of survival words and phrases (e.g., Danger, Don't Walk) (Polloway & Polloway 1981), road-and-traffic-sign words (McWilliams 1979) that can be successfully taught to disabled readers (Test & Heward 1983), and the 100 words most-frequently used in each of 10 occupations (Rush, Moe & Storlie 1986). Young and Tyre (1983) list the most frequently occurring two-, three-, and four-letter words. Eeds (1985) compiled a list of 227 words that appear 20 or more times in 400 children's books. She also suggests 50 books in which these words appear frequently.

The old, but still frequently used, *Dolch Basic Sight Vocabulary* contains 220 words exclusive of nouns. The fact that after over 40 years these words still accounted for over 50% of the words found in reading materials (Johns 1976) attests to their high utility. Johns (1981) uses four word lists published between 1957 and 1971 to update the Dolch list. He eliminates 31 and adds 37 words. These 226 words account for over 55% of the vocabulary in four basal series.

Dolch (1939) suggests that the "easiest" 110 words on his list should be mastered by the middle of second grade and the "harder" 110 by third grade. These 220 high-frequency words appear much earlier in current basal reader programs (see Figures 12.1 and 12.2). About 20 years ago, the number of Dolch words at

---

[7]Refer to A. J. Harris and Jacobson (1982) for a brief history of reading vocabulary lists.
[8]The Carrol, Davies, and Richman *American Heritage Word Frequency Book* (1971) was used by Fry (1980b) to develop a 300-word list and by Walker (1979) to produce a 1,000-word-list.

PRE-PRIMER LIST

a*	come*	here*	of*	the*
all*	day	hide	old*	they*
am*	did*	home	on*	thing
and*	do*	I*	out*	this*
are*	dog	in*	pet	time
at*	don't*	is*	pig	to*
be*	down*	it*	play*	too*
bear	fish	it's	read*	up*
big*	fly*	jump*	red*	want*
blue*	for*	let*	ride*	we*
book	from*	like*	run*	what*
boy	game	little*	said*	where*
but*	get*	look*	say*	who*
by*	girl	make*	see*	will*
came*	go*	man	she*	with*
can*	good*	me*	sit*	yes*
can't	have*	my*	so*	you*
car	he*	no*	stop*	your*
cat	help*	not*	that*	

PRIMER LIST

about*	cut*	frog	how*	mother
after*	dad	fun	I'll	mouse
an*	didn't	funny*	I'm	Mr.
animal	does*	good-by	if*	Mrs.
as*	door	got*	into*	much*
ask*	duck	green*	just*	must*
away*	each	grow*	know*	name
back	eat*	had*	lake	need
bad	end	happy	last	new*
bag	every*	has*	laugh*	next
ball	fall*	hat	liked	night
bat	fast*	hello	lion	nothing
bed	father	hen	live*	now*
bee	feel	her*	lived	oh
bird	feet	hid	lost	one*
bob	find*	high	lot	open*
box	fire	hill	made*	or*
call*	fix	him*	many*	other
city	found*	his*	may*	over*
could*	fox	hot*	maybe	paper
cow	friend	house	more	park

Figure 12.1. Harris-Jacobson word lists for first grade. Words that are also in the Dolch Basic Sight Vocabulary List are marked with an asterisk. Note that many of the words in the H-J but not the Dolch list are nouns; the Dolch 220 does not contain any nouns. From *Basic reading vocabularies* by Albert J. Harris and Milton D. Jacobson. Copyright © 1982 by Macmillan Publishing Co. Reproduced by permission of the authors and publisher.

pat	saw*	sun	today*	water
people	school	surprise	took	way
pick*	seed	swim	top	well*
place	show*	take*	tree	went*
plant	sing*	talk	trick	were*
put*	sky	tell*	truck	when*
rabbit	sleep*	thank*	turtle	why*
rain	slow	that's	two*	window
ran*	small*	them*	under*	woman
road	some*	then*	us*	won't
rock	something	there*	very*	work*
sad	sometime	think*	wait	would*
same	still	thought	walk*	you're
sat	street	three*	was*	youth

FIRST READER LIST

again*	bone	draw*	great	let's
ago	breakfast	drink*	grew	letter
alone	brother	drove	ground	light*
along	brown*	even	guess	line
always*	bus	ever*	hand	long*
another	cake	everyone	he's	love
ant	care	everything	head	lunch
any*	cave	everywhere	hear	making
anything	chair	eye	heard	mayor
apple	children	face	helper	mean
aren't	class	family	herself	men
around*	clean*	far*	hi	might
ate*	close	faster	hold*	miss
bake	cloud	feed	hole	mix
bark	clown	fell	hop	mom
beautiful	coat	fill	horse	money
because*	cold*	fine	hungry	morning
been*	color	first*	hurt*	most
began	coming	floor	I've	move
begin	cook	flower	inside	moved
being	couldn't	food	isn't	myself*
best*	country	gave*	jay	named
better*	cry	give*	keep*	near
bike	dance	glad	kind*	never*
birthday	dark	glass	king	nice
bit	dinner	gold	kite	noise
bite	doctor	gone	kitten	nose
black*	doesn't	grandma	leave	note
boat	don	grass	leg	off*

Figure 12.1. (continued)

only*	sang	someone	teacher	until
our*	sea	song	than	use*
outside	seat	soon*	their*	wasn't
paint	secret	sorry	there's	watch
pan	seen	sound	these*	we'll
part	sheep	squirrel	those*	wet
party	shoe	stand	tiger	what's
picture	shop	star	tire	which*
plan	should	start*	together*	while
please*	shout	stay	told	white*
pot	side	step	tonight	wind
pound	sign	stick	town	winter
pretty*	sister	stone	toy	wish*
push	six*	store	track	without
quiet	smell	story	train	wood
ready	smile	stuck	tried	word
real	smiled	sure	trip	worker
right*	snake	table	try*	yell
room	snow	tail	turn	yellow*
rope	someday	tall	TV	zoo
sandy				

Figure 12.1.   (continued)

each reader level was: preprimer = 53 (24%); primer = 47 (21%); first reader = 78 (36%); second reader = 40 (18%); and third reader = 2 (1%) (A. J. Harris & Jacobson 1972). Ten years later, the numbers were preprimer = 76 (35%); primer = 76 (35%); first reader = 47 (21%); and second reader = 21 (9%) (A. J. Harris & Jacobson 1982). Earlier introduction of these words is probably an advantage for novice readers who can assimilate them into their sight vocabularies fairly quickly, but it can be a disadvantage for children who have difficulty mastering them because they now have less time to do so. In setting up an instructional sequence from any word list, it may be helpful to compare it against the words introduced at the various reader levels in the materials from which the child is being instructed.

Because words appear on a word list or are called "basic" or "sight" words does not mean that a particular child can recognize them. Neither should it be

before	eight	its*	shall
both	five	once	ten
bring	four	own	upon
buy	full	pull	warm
carry	goes*	round	wash
done	going*	seven	write

Figure 12.2.   Dolch Basic Sight Vocabulary words that are not in the Harris-Jacobson (1982) first-grade lists. Words marked with an asterisk are inflected forms of words on the H-J preprimer list. The remaining 21 words are on the H-J second-grade list.

assumed that children know the meanings of these high-frequency words. Such words may have multiple meanings and function as different parts of speech. Although the multiple meanings of a given word rarely occur in the same text (K. Goodman & Bird 1984), shifts in word meaning can cause comprehension problems for the reader, especially when common words represent uncommon meanings.

Simms and Falcon (1987) divide the Dolch 220 into semantic categories for easier learning. The same can be done with other word lists.

Word Recognition Clues

There are basically four sources of information that can aid word recognition—visual-graphic, graphophonic, syntactic, and semantic cues. Illustrations also may provide word-recognition cues. Although discussed separately, such cues are likely to be used in combination, particularly by skilled readers. Children should be made aware of these cue systems and instructed in using them effectively and efficiently.

VISUAL-GRAPHIC CUES.   Among the types of visual-graphic cues are conventions of print, word length, word configuration, letter information, and orthographic knowledge.

Print Conventions.   Convention dictates that printed words are separated by spaces wider than those between letters, but narrower than the spacing between sentences.[9] Once aware of this convention, visual segmentation of sentences into words should not be a problem for children with normal vision.

Word Length.   Word length does not seem to be significant factor in word recognition (Jorm 1977). But at times it may provide a visual cue to the reader by helping to delimit the possible choices, especially when the words begin with the same letter (e.g., *me, mean, morning*).

Configuration.   The outline, or general shape, of the word may be of some assistance if the visual differences are significant, such as between dog and cat, and when word length is also a factor (e.g., egg, elephant). Word-shape information, when combined with other cues, can help reduce the number of alternatives from which the reader has to choose. For example, in "The cat drank the m⬚ ", the initial letter plus the configuration rule out semantically and syntactically appropriate possibilities like *water*. And although both words begin with the same letter and have similar shapes, prior knowledge suggests the answer is more likely *milk* than *meat*. Words similar in shape, length, and component letters (*want/went, saw/was*) can cause problems for novice readers who do not notice small visual differences and who are relatively insensitive to letter sequence in words. Calling their attention to the sequences of letters in such word pairs may help them to overcome such confusions and, when used as a general practice in intro-

---

[9]Other printing conventions also provide visual information to the reader. For instance, sentence boundaries are also marked by capital letters and punctuation marks, and quotation marks aid in determining who is saying what. See R. Haber and Haber (1981b).

ducing new words, may help novice readers to rely less on initial letters and more on orthographic structure as an aid to word recognition. Terwilliger and Kolker (1982) found that the subsequent learning of words was faster for first graders who were first taught words beginning with similar initial letters than for children who first learned to recognize words beginning with different letters.

Opinions differ as to the value of configuration in word recognition. According to Katz and Feldman (1981) and Perfetti (1986b), word shape and length provide some word-recognition cues, but they are not greatly relied on. Other researchers conclude that configuration is an ineffective and seldom-used cue (Timko 1970; Williams, Blumberg & Williams 1970). Because the latter studies used only words of equal length, the findings cannot be generalized to normal reading where word length is a major factor in configuration. Groff (1975) argues that the number of words represented by unique shapes is too small to provide enough visual information for accurate word recognition. But R. Haber and Haber (1981a,b) contend that the shapes of high-frequency words differ sufficiently to provide useful visual information, especially when combined with context and other cues. A few studies (e.g., Haber, Haber & Furlin 1983) show that adult readers can make use of configuration and word-length cues, but they have not revealed how important such information is to such skilled readers. Specific letter information may provide more useful cues than does configuration (Barron 1981a).

Children should not be encouraged to rely heavily on word shape or length as word-recognition cues. The same is true for certain letters in words (e.g., "The *oo* looks like two eyes, so that should help you to remember *look*") because the cue is not generalizable (e.g., the cue would have little value in recognizing words like *tool*).

Research indicates that initial letters are used more frequently as visual cues in word recognition, than are final letters, which are more frequently relied on than medial letters. This may be due to the fact that initial letters in words are more predictable. Also, initial and final letters in words are less subject to lateral masking because they are not completely surrounded by other letters (Barron 1981a). Word endings may receive attention because they convey linguistic information (e.g., pluralization) (Gibson & Levin 1975). Novice readers, who lack more reliable graphic information, may find partial graphic information (e.g., an initial letter) salient, but insufficient for word recognition (Barron 1981a).

Theorists such as K. Goodman (1973) and F. Smith (1982) have suggested that skilled readers sample only a few visual features of words as they read. Recent findings, however, indicate that skilled readers sample graphic information rather completely, even when reading predictable words (Nicholson 1986).

Information from Letters.   Theories regarding how readers extract and use letter-shape information fall into two general categories (R. Haber & Haber 1981b). *Template* or *protype models* suggest that the description of a letter is holistic and gestalt-like. In *feature models,* the description of a letter is a list of the features that make the letter unique and different from all other letters. R. Haber and Haber (1981b) believe feature models to be more tenable, and that only one or two features of a letter are often sufficient to identify it.

The physical properties of letters, such as the ascending and descending features of some lowercase letters, assist word-recognition in a limited way. There are more visual cues in lowercase than in capital letters, so words printed in lowercase are easier to recognize. The upper halves of lowercase letters provide more visual information than the lower halves do (see A. J. Harris & Sipay 1979, p. 248). Reading with vowels omitted is easier than with consonants deleted (Carroll & Walton 1979):

Th_ f_t d_g _t_ _ b_n_. versus
__e _a_ _o_ a_e a _o_e.

Orthographic Knowledge.   The spellings of English words are constrained by the positions in which letters can occur (e.g., *ck* can occur in the final, but not the initial, position) and the allowable sequences of letters (e.g., *sm* is a legal sequence, *sx* is not) (Venezky 1981). There is also a high likelihood that certain letters will follow others (e.g., only three consonants, *h*, *r*, and *w* can follow an initial *t*, with *h* occurring 65% of the time) (L. Haber & Haber 1981). Expectations for letter sequences develop over time from repeated experiences with printed words (Venezky 1979b). Knowledge of permissible letter patterns is important. In learning specific word forms, children acquire information about letter patterns that occur in a number of words, thus aiding word recognition (Perfetti 1986b).

The degree to which letter strings conform to the rules of English spelling influences the perception and processing of the stimuli (Barron 1981a). Regularly spelled letter strings (*blost*) are perceived better than those that violate spelling rules (*stobl*), which are more readily recognized than letter strings that greatly violate spelling regularity (*tsxbl*). The degree to which the stimuli are similar to known words also influences their decodability.

Children's sensitivity to orthographic structures usually increases with age and reading ability. Disabled readers use orthographic structures to the same extent as good readers do, and under some circumstances, to a greater extent (Horn & Manis 1985). However, some disabled readers do not seem to generalize from the orthographic structures of words in their sight vocabularies to related but unfamiliar words (Zivian & Samuels 1986).

It is difficult to establish precisely which aspects of orthographic regularity are used in word recognition, and the overall impact of sensitivity to orthographic knowledge on various experimental tasks has been relatively small (Juel 1983). The apparent developmental nature of sensitivity to orthographic structure suggests that orthographic knowledge is a consequence rather than a cause of word-recognition ability (Henderson & Chard 1980, Leslie & Shannon 1981).

English orthography preserves morphophonemic information. For instance, pluralization is marked by *s* in both words, even though it represents /s/ in *cats* and /z/ in *dogs*. Our spellings also assist in distinguishing between homophones (e.g., *hare* vs. *hair, band* vs. *banned*).

GRAPHOPHONIC CUES.   In our writing system, letters are used to construct words that represent their spoken counterparts. Although the relationship between graphemes and the phonemes they represent is not entirely consistent, the letters in words can provide information useful in word recognition. Knowledge of grapheme-phoneme relationships may be acquired informally or as a result of direct instruction. These symbol-sound-association skills can be used as an aid in recognizing a word that is not firmly fixed in one's sight vocabulary, especially if used in conjunction with other cues. For instance, determining the sound of the initial letter or two and the use of context may be all that is needed to recognize a word. When a word is met for the first time in print, it may be necessary to decode it more fully.

SYNTACTIC CUES.   *Syntactic* or *grammatical cues* involve implicit knowledge of word order and the functions of words. Only certain word sequences are allowable in English, and only certain kinds of words fit into particular slots in our sentence patterns. In "The baseball player _____ the ball," the missing word must be a verb, and the alternatives are restricted to such verbs as *saw, threw, caught,* and *hit.* Additional visual cues could further restrict the possibilities, as could semantic cues within the sentence. Thus, if *yesterday* appeared at the end of the sentence, only a past tense verb could be used, and the addition of "with his bat" would exclude such words as *saw* or *threw.*

Changes in word order can influence meaning greatly (Susie saw Rob vs. Rob saw Susie) or subtly, as a change in emphasis (Rob saw Susie vs. Susie was seen by Rob).

Most children enter school with the ability to understand most English syntactic structures, and they understand more of these structures than they use in their oral language. The formal syntactic patterns that often occur in written material differ from those commonly used in spoken language and may cause problems for some novice readers. But children learn early to expect that what they find in print differs from their oral language. Children continue to make substantial gains in their ability to understand syntactic structures until about age 13 (M. Adams 1977), and many continue to refine these skills through extended experiences with spoken and written language. Syntactic sensitivity is significantly related to reading ability (Bowey 1986, Willows & Ryan 1986).

SEMANTIC CUES.   *Semantic cues* involve word-meaning knowledge and a general sense of the text's meaning. Semantic knowledge serves as the basis for determining if the text, or one's interpretation of the text, makes sense. Thus one would realize that the following sentence, although syntactically appropriate, does not make sense: Footless animals win races because they can run very rapidly.

CONTEXT EFFECTS AND CONTEXT CLUES.   Studies have generally shown that word recognition is more accurate and faster in context than in isolation (Lyon 1984), especially for high-frequency words (Schatz & Baldwin 1986). One explanation for these findings is that the information obtained from what has been read, when combined with the reader's semantic, syntactic, and topical knowledge, as well as with at least some graphic information, enables the reader to predict upcoming words, primarily by reducing the uncertainty as to which words are likely to appear (Ehri 1987).

The contexts in which printed words are set can influence word recognition. This phenomenon is known as *context effects*. Context effects arise primarily from the *local context*, the phrase or sentence containing the target word (West et al. 1983). Whereas the effect of the local context probably has an important syntactic component, the effect of *global context* (e.g., the paragraph in which the word appears) is probably semantic (Gough, Alford & Holley-Wilcox 1981). Semantic and syntactic cues usually function together and are referred to as *context clues*. Sensitivity to contextual constraints increases with age (Ehrlich 1981). However, exactly how context facilitates word recognition is largely unknown.

Miscue analysis studies[10] (e.g., Leslie 1980) frequently find that good readers' miscues are more often semantically and syntactically appropriate than those made by poor readers. Compared with good readers, poor readers are less aware of the extent to which their miscues disrupt meaning, are less effective in using multiple clues and alternative strategies for preserving meaning (Aulls 1981), and, unsuprisingly, make fewer self-corrections (Bowey 1985). These data have been interpreted as indicating the need to teach poor readers how to make better use of context. Such instruction may prove of value, but it is also possible that poor readers' weak word recognition interferes with their use of context clues, and therefore needs to be addressed. The word recognition of poor readers is facilitated by context when the content of the text is within the pupils' conceptual grasp and when the number of unknown words does not exceed their word-recognition ability (Kibby 1979b, Adams & Huggins 1985, Stanovich 1986a). When these two conditions are not met, slow and/or inaccurate word recognition may degrade the contextual information to a point where it is useless.

Pupils with high topical knowledge may be able to overcome some word-recognition problems by filling in, from prior knowledge, the information that the printed words would have supplied. But topical knowledge cannot compensate for the effects of text difficulty caused by a high number of unknown words.

There are contrasting opinions concerning the differences between good and poor readers in their relative use of context clues versus graphic or graphophonic cues. Many believe that good readers make greater use of contextual information, and that poor readers make more use of graphic or graphophonic cues. But it may be that the apparently greater use of context made by good readers is due to their decreased need to rely on graphic or graphophonic cues because their word-recognition processing is so efficient. According to Stanovich (1986b), poor readers often rely more on contextual than graphic information. Stanovich's (1980, 1982c) *interactive-compensatory theory* states that graphic and contextual information interact and contribute to word recognition. It predicts that a deficiency in either information source results in greater reliance on the other. Thus, students with weak word recognition would rely more on contextual information than on graphic information to achieve word recognition/identification. A number of researchers (e.g., Simons & Leu 1987; Bruck 1988) have interpreted their findings as being consistent with an interactive-compensatory model. There is some indication that the level of text difficulty may differentially influence the word-recognition strategies employed by good readers and poor readers (see Fleisher 1988).

[10]Stanovich (1986b) questioned the use of misuse analysis to examine individual differences in the use of context.

Novice readers may not make maximum use of context clues because: (1) their word-recognition skills are just developing, so they focus on graphic rather than contextual information; (2) they may not understand how to apply the information they use to understand spoken language to aid their comprehension of written language; or (3) the context clues available in beginning-reading materials may not be sufficiently potent to aid word recognition. The linguistic structures employed in early-reading materials may also come into conflict with the kinds of linguistic knowledge novice readers attempt to utilize during the reading process (Simons & Ammon 1988). Samuels (1980) suggests that novice readers have difficulty using context to facilitate word recognition because they attempt to process units smaller than the whole word. He believes that such attempts result in filling STM with meaningless information, so that meaningful context is not available for use. Text difficulty has a greater negative impact on the use of context by younger students than older students (Schwantes 1981).

ILLUSTRATIONS.   One rationale for using illustrations is that they initially aid in learning to recognize printed words and later may facilitate recognizing previously taught or unknown words that appear in context. But research findings regarding the contribution of illustrations to word recognition are mixed.

The *focal attention hypothesis* states that although pictures and context ease the initial learning task, in the long run it is more effective to present words in isolation initially because it forces children's attention onto graphic cues that will be helpful in recognizing the words in different contexts (i.e., it facilitates transfer of training) (H. Singer 1980b). Some studies support this hypothesis; others do not. Ceprano (1987) attributes the mixed results to: (1) differences in the instructions given to the picture-treatment group, (2) the types of words used (similar or dissimilar in visual attributes), (3) the confounding problem caused by using the trial-to-criterion paradigm, and (4) differences in the content and mode of presentation of the illustration used to cue the word. Ceprano (1981) concludes that learning to recognize printed words was best facilitated by a procedure that focused pupils' attention on graphic cues and at the same time enhanced word meaning through picture clues. Unfortunately it would be difficult, if not impossible, to employ this procedure for all new words.

If a child becomes overdependent on picture cues (e.g., looks for a picture as soon as he meets an unknown word), the teacher should determine if the child has more efficient word-recognition strategies. If he does, the teacher will have to convince him to use them, perhaps by covering the pictures. If he does not, the needed skills should be taught.

THE WHOLE-WORD METHOD

The *whole-word method* is an instructional procedure through which children are taught to associate whole, printed words with their spoken counterparts and, if necessary, with their meanings. Most published reading programs suggest employing some variation of the whole-word method when first teaching children to recognize printed words. Almost all basal reader series begin to combine whole-word methodology with the teaching of decoding and other word-recognition skills early in their programs, but they vary in the degree to which they do so.

There are three commonly-stated rationales for initially employing a whole-word instructional method. First, most children find it the easiest method through which to learn. Second, its use allows children to begin reading for meaning sooner than would other methods because fewer subskills have to be taught and learned. Pupils quickly learn to recognize a number of printed words that can be used to formulate meaningful texts. Third, because over half of high-frequency words are phonetically irregular (e.g., *said*) (Lewandowski 1979), they must be learned as wholes rather than through a decoding method. Learning phonetically irregular words is particularly troublesome for disabled readers (Manis 1985, Seidenberg et al. 1985).

New words[11] may be introduced in context or in isolation. Some authorities believe that introducing words in context makes their meanings more clear, thus facilitating learning to recognize them, and encourages later use of context as a word-recognition cue. Others advise against use of this procedure because, like the use of illustrations, it lessens the likelihood that children will focus on the graphic information contained in printed words—information that will be helpful in recognizing these words later in novel contexts. Research has not clearly supported either procedure (Wiesendanger & Bader 1987).

Introducing words in isolation or in context may make a difference in what gets learned. Whereas first graders who learned to recognize words embedded in sentences learned more about the words' semantic and syntactic identities, those to whom words were introduced in isolation remembered more about their orthographic properties (Ehri & Wilce 1980).

Exclusive use of either instructional practice is not advisable, rather, it is probably more productive to combine their use, basing decisions when to use each on the purpose of the instruction and the nature of the words.

A printed word may be presented initially in isolation, may be shown to the pupils as it is being spoken in an oral context, and soon thereafter may be presented in a printed phrase or sentence. Practice in recognizing the word in isolation may precede and follow its presentation in printed context. Words first introduced in isolation must be read in connected discourse shortly thereafter if the child is to learn that reading is a meaning-getting process.

When words are presented in isolation, the oral form is spoken by a person or audio device. ("This word says _____.") while the printed form is shown. Whether the word is shown in isolation or context, the children should be instructed to look at the word carefully while saying it, and to note the sequence of the letters and sounds within the word.

New words presented in context can be highlighted (e.g., underlined or color coded), printed in isolation above the word in the sentence or near the sentence, or the word can be shown in isolation immediately following its presentation in context. Cunningham (1980) developed a context-isolation-context procedure that may be helpful. When new words are presented in context, all or almost all the other words in the printed sentence should be in the children's

[11]The descriptor "new" means that the words are introduced for the first time in that particular reading program. Some children may already be able to recognize some "new" words.

sight vocabulary so they can concentrate on learning the new word. The context should be rich enough so that the intended meaning of the new word is clear, but not so potent as to require little attention to the word's graphic information.

Two other considerations are involved in formulating contextually potent sentences (Duffelmeyer 1982b): (1) Use language structures that are within the children's syntactic repetoire, and concepts to which the children can relate their prior knowledge; and (2) embed the new word in the middle or end of the sentence in order to provide more semantic and syntactic information before the target word is met. The sentence may be read first by the teacher and then orally by some pupils, or it may be read silently first by all the children, then orally by a few. Pupils may be asked how they "figured out" the new words, and the teacher may point out how previously taught skills can be used to aid in recognizing the new word and demonstrate how the new word is similar to or different from previously taught words, especially if such words are likely to be confused.

Practice with new words may involve selecting the word spoken by the teacher from several word cards, matching the word card with the word in a printed phrase or sentence, or arranging word cards to form different sentences. In the first two types of exercise, the child should say the word while making his choice. Workbook exercises may involve matching the word to a picture, selecting the sentence containing the new word that matches a picture, writing the word into an incomplete sentence, selecting which of two or three words best completes a sentence, reading the word in a question that can be answered briefly, or reading the word in a context that differs from that in which the word was introduced. Children may keep packs of cards on which the words they have mastered have been printed, or they may construct their own picture dictionaries and learn how to use them.

In the "every pupil" response technique (Hopkins 1979), each child in the group responds simultaneously to the task set orally by the teacher by displaying the appropriate response from a set of word cards (e.g., "Show me the word *dog*."). This technique encourages active participation and increases the number of responses a child makes in a given amount of time. By scanning the raised cards, the teacher can immediately detect which children are responding correctly or are slow to respond.

For most children, recognition of a word becomes automatic as a result of reading it in a wide variety of contexts. If a child has difficulty learning through a whole-word method, such variables as the number of words introduced in a session and the amount of reinforcement provided should be considered. Trying to accomplish too much too quickly can prevent learning.

DECODING AND THE DECODING METHOD[12]

In this book, to *decode* a printed word means to approximate its spoken form through the use of various skills (see pages 462–470), often relying heavily on symbol-sound associations.

---

[12]Johnson and Pearson (1984, p.14) summarize various instructional programs as to their use of analytic or synthetic phonics, early and intensive teaching or gradual introduction of decoding skills, whether or not generalizations are taught, and whether an inductive or deductive approach is used.

The *decoding method* is an instructional procedure that is used to teach novice readers how to recognize printed words. There are variations of the decoding method but, in general, children are taught to use units smaller than the whole word to recognize printed words. This involves teaching them analysis, phonic, and blending skills, which can be used during the initial stage of reading acquistion to recognize words that are used in their reading program and/or whenever they encounter printed words that they cannot recognize immediately.

There is some disagreement regarding points such as how much emphasis to place on teaching decoding skills, which skills should be taught, and when they should be taught. Goodman and Goodman (1982) claim that there is no need for phonics instruction because children learn their own rules for relating print to speech as they read meaningful texts. Most authorities, however, believe that some sort of decoding instruction is necessary for most pupils. For example, Chall (1987) states that early and explicit instruction in word recognition and decoding is more effective in developing reading ability than is assuming that children will acquire such skills "naturally" through experiences with print. Learning decoding principles has advantages and no known disadvantages (Perfetti 1986a), but decoding should not be overemphasized because it may encourage children to focus on visual or phonological information at the expense of contextual information (Barron 1981a).

Should a Whole-Word or a Decoding Method Be Used for Reading Instruction?

For most children, it probably matters little which method is emphasized initially. Regardless of the instructional program employed, children are likely to be taught some words through a whole-word method as well as how to decode printed words. The differences among programs that employ these two instructional methods lie in when the skills are taught and the relative emphasis placed on them.

Some disabled readers learn to recognize words more successfully through use of one method or the other; a few, with neither. At present there is no way other than trial teaching to predetermine which method is more likely to be successful.

Just as with students who are making normal progress in reading, it is desirable to incorporate both methodologies at some point in programs for disabled readers. Each method has positive and negative features. Their combined use may allow us to capitalize on the strengths of each, while compensating for their weaknesses.

Values of Decoding Ability

A unique advantage of an alphabetic writing system is that it enables us to approximate the spoken forms of many English words from their spellings. English uses 26 letters, singly and in combination, to represent the 40 or so phonemes that occur in spoken English words. The grapheme-phoneme relationships of English are sufficiently consistent to make knowledge of them useful. Such knowledge, plus a few other skills, allows one to decode many words that are not recognized at sight. Decoding ability has other benefits also.

Learning to decode provides children with insights into the alphabetic nature of English. These insights facilitate mastery of the alphabetic principle[13] (Vellutino & Scanlon 1987b), a step that is important for learning to read an alphabetic language (Perfetti 1985). An early understanding that letters represent sounds in words encourages children to look for the regularities of English, and to infer grapheme-phoneme relationships on their own (Carrol & Walton 1979).

Decoding instruction calls pupils' attention to the sequences of letters in printed words. This helps them to understand the left-to-right sequence of letters used in English, and it aids them in the acquisition of orthographic representations of words. The teaching of decoding also focuses children's attention on the phonemes in spoken words, and their sequence, which may facilitate phonemic awareness and phonemic segmentation (see pages 45–47).

Children could probably learn to read initially without having explicit knowledge of phonics. On the average, however, children taught decoding skills get off to a better start in learning to read. (R. Anderson et al. 1985). One study (Juel & Roper-Schneider 1985) reveals that, regardless of whether a code-emphasis or a meaning-emphasis basal reader program was used for instruction, first graders who developed strong decoding skills recognized significantly more words than did weak decoders.

Third graders who were good readers and spellers had better phonic ability than did those who were good readers but poor spellers, who displayed better decoding skills than did those who were both poor readers and poor spellers (Waters, Bruck & Seidenberg 1985). More direct evidence of the value of decoding ability is revealed by training studies that have indicated the advantage of decoding skills for improving reading and spelling ability (J. Mason & Allen 1986).

The Relationship of Decoding Ability to Reading Ability and Disability

Moderate to high correlations (0.43 to 0.86) have been reported between decoding ability and reading achievement in the primary grades (Fletcher 1981, Calfee & Piontkowski 1981, Durkin 1984b). The relationship diminishes after the primary grades (Rosso & Emans 1981), but mastery of letter-sound correspondences is still related positively to reading ability in the secondary school (Ryder & Graves 1980).

Children who are making normal progress in reading achievement are characterized by developmental increases in decoding ability and in the size of their sight vocabularies. Some disabled readers, however, lack the decoding skills that normally accompany a given level of reading ability. For example, disabled readers displayed much weaker decoding ability than did younger chil-

---

[13]Mastery of the *alphabetic principle* means that the child understands, at least implicitly, that a letter (the minimal unit of print) represents a phoneme (the minimal unit of speech) rather than a unit of meaning (Perfetti 1986a).

dren who had the same level of word-recognition ability as the disabled readers (R. Olson 1985).

Research findings support the contention that weak decoding ability is a major factor in reading disability (Vellutino 1987). Indeed, one of the reading tasks that best differentiates good from poor readers in the elementary school is the ability to decode *phonetically regular pseudowords* (nonwords that can be decoded by applying decoding principles taught to, or "rules" that have been inferred by, the pupils). Good/poor reader differences in decoding ability are especially striking in novice readers and, although the differences lessen, they do not disappear with age (Torgesen 1986a).

Decoding ability varies directly with knowledge of symbol-sound associations (Gough & Tunmer 1986). Severely disabled readers are less proficient than good readers in acquiring and using grapheme-phoneme correspondences to decode unknown words (Manis et al. 1986, 1987). This deficiency is believed to be rooted in more basic difficulties with phonological coding ability (Stanovich 1986a), as indicated by studies that have shown disabled readers to have weaker recall of spoken words than did good readers (Vellutino 1987). Severely disabled readers are not incapable of learning and using phonics. They do attempt to apply whatever phonic skills they possess (Waters, Bruck & Seidenberg 1985) but their weak knowledge prevents them from attaining rapid, automatic decoding ability (Manis 1985). Some disabled readers can decode a word, but do not recognize it at the next encounter, even if it occurs within seconds (Zivian & Samuels 1986). This is not surprising, because the children have not established an orthographic representation for the word in their lexicons on the basis of a single exposure.

The Decoding Ability of Children

The limited data available suggest that there is a wide range of decoding ability at various grade levels, but that, in general, decoding ability seems to increase with age, and therefore with reading ability. When given a 50-item test that primarily required the ability to decode consonant-vowel-consonant pseudowords, the 20 highest-scoring first graders acceptably decoded about 30 items, on average. Twenty of these first graders were unable to decode any of the 50 items. Scores ranged from 0 to 35 (Juel, Griffith & Gough 1985).

Durkin (1984b) gave a much more difficult 29-pseudoword decoding test to third, fourth, and sixth graders. Their performance indicated less variation in decoding ability than was displayed by first graders in the Juel et al. study. In general, Durkin's subjects: (1) seemed to lack an understanding of the significance of syllables for decoding (they often tried to use "recognizable parts" of words even when these crossed syllable boundaries), (2) had difficulty determining when *c* and *g* likely represented their "soft sounds" (their "hard sounds" were usually given); (3) had difficulty making the appropriate symbol-sound associations for: (a) the vowel sounds represented by *y*, (b) r-controlled vowels, and (c) *x* in the initial position (this occurs so infrequently that such a weakness is not a serious one); (4) often did not treat the letters that form a consonant digraph as a grapheme (e.g., *t* and *h* were treated as separate graphemes); and (5) had difficulty blending phonemes into words. In regard to the latter finding, our clinical experience does not indicate that blending is a frequent problem among disabled readers.

In another study (Seidenberg et al. 1985), good readers made significantly fewer symbol-sound-association errors than did poor readers and disabled readers. Whereas good readers made approximately equal numbers of consonant and vowel errors, poor readers (and disabled readers in particular) had much greater difficulty making vowel grapheme-phoneme associations. Most of the vowel errors made by good readers and poor readers reflected difficulty determining when a vowel letter represented its long or short sound; disabled readers frequently made totally inappropriate vowel responses.

Readiness for Decoding Skills

A study by Dolch and Bloomster (1937) had a significant effect on phonics instruction for many years. They found that first and second graders with mental ages below 7 years performed very poorly on a decoding test that required the application of phonic principles to uncommon, monosyllabic words presented in isolation. This led them to conclude that the ability to learn and apply phonic principles requires a higher level of mental maturity than that needed for learning through a whole-word approach. They recommend that the major part of phonics instruction be placed in the second and third grades because the majority of first-grade pupils were not ready to profit from such instruction. But the Dolch-Bloomster decoding test presented the children with a more difficult task than they faced in reading connected meaningful material, and thus their findings underestimated the readiness of first graders. More recent research demonstrates that code-emphasis programs can be used successfully with first graders.

AUDITORY AND VISUAL DISCRIMINATION.   Children who have difficulty discriminating among letter forms *(visual discrimination)* or phonemes *(auditory discrimination)* may have difficulty learning phonics. For example, not being able to distinguish between *m* and *n* makes it difficult to learn with which letter the sound /m/ should be associated.

Those who need visual discrimination training may receive exercises that require them to mark the letter or word that is the same or different from a target letter or word. Opinions differ as to whether visual-discrimination training should employ letters that are highly similar visually in order to help children to learn the distinctive features of each letter (Samuels 1976) or whether maximally contrastive letters should be used initially and later those that require more demanding discriminations (M. Singer 1982). Research indicates that it is desirable to point out to the child the specific feature or features that distinguish that letter from all others (Samuels 1973a).

Auditory discrimination of speech sounds can be weak even when auditory acuity is normal. It is not a matter of sensory acuity, but of hearing selectively the beginning, middle, or end of a spoken word and comparing it with the sounds of the corresponding parts of other words, thus providing the basis for comparison and the recognition of both similarities and differences.

Poor auditory discrimination is often accompanied by inaccurate or indistinct speech. The child who pronounces *with* as /wiv/[14] is not likely to notice any difference between final /v/ and /th/ in words. It is hard for many children to discriminate among short-vowel sounds because those sounds do not differ greatly. Poor test or exercise performance may be the result of not understanding the directions or concepts (e.g., *same* and *different*) or a lack of attention.

The discrimination aspects of phonic readiness, listed roughly in order of increasing difficulty, appear to be the ability to: (1) discriminate between printed words as well as letters; (2) determine whether a difference exists between two spoken words that may differ in only one phoneme (/had/–/had/, /had/–/hat/, /had/–/hid/); (3) detect whether two words begin with the same sound; (4) listen to a word and supply two or three words that begin with the same sound; (5) determine whether two words rhyme; (6) supply a word that rhymes with a spoken word (numbers 5 and 6 are important in teaching the use of vowel-consonant phonograms or word families); (7) detect similarities and differences in the ends of spoken words; and (8) detect similarities and differences in the middle of spoken words. All these skills can be improved somewhat through direct instruction and practice, but the impact of such improvement on decoding ability has not been established.

A variety of procedures can be used to develop auditory discrimination. The general technique is to provide a list of spoken words containing (usually beginning with) the element to be taught, to focus the children's attention on that particular sound in the words, to get them to compare words and determine which words contain the target sound, and to encourage them to think of additional words that contain the sound in a particular position. In teaching auditory discrimination involving /f/, for example, the technique would encompass the following:

1. Have the children listen carefully to a short list of words (/fun/, /fox/, /field/) and explain how they sound alike.
2. Play listening games in which the children signal which words begin with the same sound as words spoken by the teacher (teacher says /fat/, /fur/; children respond to /fun/, /make/, /toy/, /fig/).
3. Ask the children to suggest words that begin like /fat/ and /fur/. To make this more challenging, the words may have to fit a category, such as the name of a person or animal.
4. Give incomplete oral sentences or riddles that the children are to finish or answer with a word that begins like /fat/ and /fur/. For example, "Susie's cat is skinny, but Rob's cat is _____," or "What pets can you keep in water?" (fish)

SOUND-SYMBOL ASSOCIATIONS. Whereas *symbol-sound associations* involve seeing a grapheme and then determining the phoneme it represents,

---

[14]Although slashes usually are not used to indicate spoken words, we use them here and elsewhere to make it easier to distinguish between spoken words and written words, which are italicized. Except when used to make a point, real words are not respelled phonetically so that they can be recognized more easily.

sound-symbol associations means hearing a phoneme and then associating it with a grapheme. Sound-symbol-association instruction and practice may precede introduction of symbol-sound association and thereby be considered a readiness activity or it may be given concurrently with phonics instruction in an effort to reinforce symbol-sound associations. On average, children score higher on phoneme-grapheme tests than on grapheme-phoneme tests (Filp 1975). Learning sound-symbol associations may be more helpful in developing spelling than reading ability. However, it may help to make children more aware that the sounds in spoken words can be represented by graphemes.

To introduce a sound-symbol association:

1. Tell children that all the words you are going to say begin with the same sound (or end with, or are the same in the middle).
2. Pronounce three words, slightly emphasizing the target sound (/fig/, /fur/, /fat/). You may need to separate or isolate the target sound slightly in order for some children to understand the concept.
3. Print the letter that represents the sound on the board (e.g., *f*) and tell the children, "The sound that you hear at the beginning of *fig, fur*, and *fat* is made by[15] this letter, the name of which is /ef/." You may add, "The sound /f/ is made by this letter," while pointing to it.

Practice in making sound-symbol associations can be given by having children hold up the appropriate letter card, write the letter, or say the letter name when asked what letter makes the sound heard in a particular position in the stimulus word. Other exercises include having the children place appropriate pictures on a peg below which the letter is printed; or having them select the letter that "makes the sound" at the beginning of a pictured word.

CONCEPTS AND UNDERSTANDINGS.   It is believed by some (e.g., Liberman et al. 1980, Perfetti 1985) that in order to acquire decoding skills children must attain some minimal level of *phonological awareness* (understanding that a spoken word, which is heard as an unbroken continuous pattern, can be segmented into phonemes) and understand the *alphabetic principle* (that graphemes represent phonemes, rather than units of meaning). It is further believed that inadequate phonological awareness makes it difficult to grasp the alphabetic principle (Perfetti 1985) and to acquire auditory segmentation skills. Suggestions for facilitating phonological awareness may be found in Mann and Liberman (1984).

SEGMENTATION SKILLS.   Both visual- and auditory-segmentation skills are related to reading acquisition. Visual-segmentation studies have dealt mainly with segmenting printed sentences into words, a skill which also requires the concept of *word* (see page 45). Most novice or disabled readers have been read to and exposed to print, so they are likely to be aware that a printed word is marked on either side by spaces that are wider than the spaces between the

---

[15]Letters do not "make" sounds, but the terms *stands for* and *represents* are not understood by many children.

letters in words. Therefore, difficulty with visual segmentation of sentences into words is not likely to be a cause of word-recognition problems. Although children are more likely to have difficulty segmenting words into their component graphemes (this requires the concept of "letter" and the understanding that some graphemes are comprised of more than one letter), decoding and spelling instruction probably makes them sufficiently aware that printed words are made up of graphemes. Therefore, if the children have the motor skills required by the task, they could mark off the separate graphemes.

There is some belief that phonemic segmentation may be a prerequisite for decoding ability, but it may also be a facilitator or a consequence of decoding ability. Having some phonemic segmentation skill may make it easier to learn how to decode, and being taught decoding skills may improve segmentation ability.

The findings of studies by Vellutino and Scanlon (1982, 1986b) indicate that phonemic segmentation is amenable to training in both good and poor readers and that such training may facilitate learning to read through a whole-word method as well as through a decoding method. Segmentation training may also have helped to establish a left-to right sequence, since those who were taught to segment made fewer reversals than the control group.

The following procedure may be used to demonstrate the concept that words are comprised of phonemes. Tell the children to listen carefully as you "take a word apart and then put it back together again." First, say the word normally as a whole, then pronounce each phoneme in the word (distorting each as little as possible), with a half-second pause between each. Then reverse the process, starting with the separate sounds and speeding up gradually so that the relationship between the phonemes and the pronunciation of the word as a whole can be understood. Have the children repeat the process, because understanding the concept requires attention to articulatory as well as to auditory clues. The same procedure can be used to demonstrate auditory blending. Those who have difficulty with the concept may be aided by segmenting only the initial sound from the word or segmenting words that contain only two phonemes. Later, consonant-vowel-consonant words can be segmented.

LETTER-NAME KNOWLEDGE.   Although letter-name knowledge correlates highly with success in learning to read in first grade (see page 42), training experiments have indicated that it does not facilitate the acquisition of word-recognition or decoding skills (Beck 1981). Durrell (1980, 1984), however, defends the value of letter-name knowledge in learning to read and spell. He points out that the awareness of letter names at the beginning of spoken words is among the earliest developmental abilities on which reading acquisition is based (e.g., the young child hears "bee" in "beaver" and expects the word to begin with *b*). Durrell also cites as evidence the use of letters containing their names in children's invented spellings (e.g., *engine = njn*). Durrell and Murphy (1978) state that except for *h, q, w,* and *y,* consonant letter names are made up of the basic phoneme plus a vowel (e.g., /b/ + /ē/, /ĕ/ + /f/, /j/ + /ā/), and that the names of the vowels are their "long sounds." Venezky (1975, 1979b) disputes this statement.

There is also disagreement about whether letter names should be used in teaching phonics. Some writers contend that learning the letter names and symbol-sound associations concurrently ("This letter is 'bee' and it makes the sound /b/") places an additional burden on the child. Others suggest that the concurrent use of the letter name and sound confuses the child as to which is which. Most children already know the letter names before being taught to decode, so their use is not likely to provide an additional learning task. Because children have such knowledge, it is important to make clear to them the distinction between letter names and the sounds that letters represent. If their combined use produces a problem for the child, the name of the letter can simply be deleted ("This letter makes the sound /b/").

Regardless of the various disagreements, there is no evidence that teaching letter names is harmful. Furthermore, even if such knowledge were completely unrelated or even useless in learning to read, letter-name knowledge can serve other useful purposes.

Decoding Instruction in Meaning-Emphasis Approaches

In meaning-emphasis programs, phonics is taught along with other decoding strategies, but less initial emphasis is placed on making symbol-sound associations and blending techniques. The procedure frequently used is *analytic phonics*, in which children are helped to understand the relationship of letters and phonograms to the sounds they represent and to use that knowledge to decode unknown words by comparing and contrasting sounds in whole words. Rather than learn, for example, "*M* says /m/," pupils are taught that the letter stands for sound heard at the beginning of *mother* and *me*—words that are already in their sight vocabularies.

The teacher may emphasize the target sound in the words while pronouncing them or may slightly segment the sound from the rest of the word. Although some analytic phonics proponents oppose ever mentioning the phoneme in isolation, such a prohibition is decidedly questionable. Some children have difficulty segmenting the target sound from the rest of the word. The teacher has no control over what the children are thinking or saying to themselves, and so the children are better off if given a model to imitate.

Cue words may also be used in teaching symbol-sound associations (e.g., ' "Em," /m/, is for milk). A picture of the cue word (a carton with the word "milk" on it) accompanied by the lowercase, and perhaps the uppercase, letter can be shown and then displayed in the room so that the children can refer to it as needed. Simply thinking of the cue word may help some children to remember the sound represented by the letter. But being able to think of the sound without referring to a cue word is preferable.

The following substitution procedure may be taught in analytic phonics: (1) Think of known words that begin like and words that end like the unknown word, (2) use the known parts to determine the sounds represented by the similar elements in the unknown word, (3) mentally blend the parts, and (4) say the word aloud or to yourself. Thus, if the unfamiliar word was *mast*, the child might think: *m*ilk and *l*ast; /m/, /ast/; /mast/. Or the child may quickly perceive the parts, be aware of their sounds, and decode the word without having to think of known words that are similar in some respect. The substitution technique also can be used for final consonants and medial vowels. Substitution seems to work satisfactorily for a majority of children, but experimental comparisons of the relative effectiveness of different kinds of phonic methods are not available. It is probably much easier for children to respond correctly to a new word when the teacher changes the initial consonant (*last* is shown; the *l* is erased and replaced with *m*) than to use substitutions on their own.

Decoding Instruction in Code-Emphasis Approaches

Three major types of methods are used in code-emphasis reading programs. Each has certain advantages and limitations.

SINGLE-LETTER PHONICS.   Probably the oldest of these approaches is *single-letter phonics* in which children learn to make successive symbol-sound associations and to blend the resulting phonemes into words, as /k/ + /a/ + /t/ = /cat/. This method teaches a systematic left-to-right sequence in decoding the word and requires initially teaching a relatively small number of phonic elements. Its four main possible disadvantages are: (1) Extraneous sounds added to the phonemes (e.g., /ə/ is added to certain consonant sounds) may hamper recognition of the oral word (e.g., the result of blending /kuh/ + /ă/ + /tuh/ does not sound like /cat/); (2) blending single phonemes is comparatively difficult for young children, even when extra sounds are minimized; (3) a number of words are not amenable to single-letter phonics (e.g., *elephant*); and (4) it may be more useful for short words because in longer words the child may forget the symbol-sound associations made for graphemes at the beginning of the word. Successive blending of each phoneme with the preceding sound or group of sounds might lessen the latter problem.

INITIAL CONSONANT PLUS PHONOGRAM.[16]   The grapheme-phoneme relationship for the initial consonant is made and the rest of the word is sounded out as a phonogram unit or spelling pattern of two or more graphemes, usually a vowel and consonant (e.g., /k/ + /at/ = /cat/; /p/ + /ik/ = /pick/). Word families, such as *at, bat, cat, fat, hat, mat, pat, rat, sat*, are taught. Because many one-syllable words belong to such word families, this has been a popular procedure. Blending is easier than in single-letter phonics because only two parts need to be fused together. Use of this procedure can result in these problems: (1) adding a /ə/ (schwa) to the initial consonant, thus making it difficult to blend; (2) practice on word families in list form may have little transfer to recognition of these words in context; and (3) many commonly taught phonograms (e.g., *ap, end, ist*) occur infrequently in words of more than one syllable.

PHONOGRAM PLUS FINAL CONSONANT.   The initial consonant and following vowel are sounded as a unit, and the phoneme for the final consonant is added, as /ka/ + /t/ = /cat/. Cordts (1955) claims that this procedure avoids adding extraneous sounds, makes blending comparatively easy, and prepares the

---

[16]Lists of word families may be found in D. Johnson and Pearson (1984) and Fry, Fountoukidis, and Polk (1985).

way for syllabication of longer words. Critics have pointed out that: (1) A very large number of consonant-vowel combinations would have to be taught; (2) it is difficult to know whether to give the vowel its long or short sound because that usually depends on what follows the vowel letter; and (3) if followed exclusively, the method prevents teaching such phonograms as *ight, ind, ound,* and *old,* which are best learned as units.

Since flexibility is needed in decoding, exclusive devotion to any of these three procedures is less desirable than a varied approach.

A few important points greatly influence the success or failure of teaching decoding:

1. Give attention to the development of adequate readiness skills and concepts.
2. Try to avoid adding extraneous sounds to the phonemes.
3. Sound out words continuously, with the sound of one phoneme running into the next phoneme. If it is necessary to pronounce the phonemes separately, the time interval between the sounds should be as short as possible.
4. If the skills developed in phonics lessons are to function in connected reading, provide abundant in practice in the application of the skills to unknown words in reading easy, interesting material.

SKILL AREAS IN DECODING

In order to decode a word completely, children must be able: (1) to divide it mentally into usable parts, (2) to determine the sound(s) each part represents, and (3) to blend the sounds mentally in correct sequence into a recognizable whole word. These three areas are referred to as visual analysis, symbol-sound association, and visual blending.

Visual Analysis

Competent readers try to analyze unfamiliar printed words into some component parts that they recognize or find useful in decoding. Although the term *visual analysis* is used, it should be realized that, except when words are syllabicated at the end of a line, the stimuli are seen as whole words. The stimuli are visual; the process is mental. The term is used to distinguish it from auditory analysis, in which no printed stimuli occur.

MONOSYLLABLES.   Children instructed in single-letter phonics or the use of phonograms or spelling patterns are likely to receive instruction in how to analyze one-syllable words. Depending on the instructional methodology employed, they may separate the word into single graphemes; a consonant and vowel-consonant phonogram; a consonant-vowel phonogram and final consonant; or grapheme and spelling pattern (*m all*). Although phonograms and spelling patterns are fairly consistent in the sounds they represent in monosyllabic words, looking for that part, or looking for the "little word" in the "big word" can be misleading (e.g., *alliga*tor, *fat her, fi*nal).

MORPHEMIC ANALYSIS.   *Morphemic analysis* means analyzing words into their morphemes, or meaning units. *Free morphemes* are whole words that cannot be further divided into meaning-bearing elements. *Bound morphemes* are ones that must be combined with a free morpheme to change meaning. Children are taught early to recognize such endings (bound morphemes) as *s, es, ed, er, est,* and *ing.* Unknown words divided into their meaningful parts can often be decoded quickly because the parts are already familiar. Morphemic analysis should be tried before other analysis skills are attempted.

Dividing compound words into their component words is another form of morphemic analysis that is taught early. Initial use of this technique should be limited to words that naturally separate into known meaningful words (e.g., *cow girl, some thing*). Exercises for teaching compound words appear in D. Johnson and Pearson (1984, pp. 132–136).

A third form of morphemic analysis involves the use of familiar or decodable prefixes, root words, and suffixes (*re pay, excite ment, un truth ful*). Polysyllabic words are typically composed of monosyllabic content words to which affixes have been added.

There are two useful morphemic-analysis generalizations:

1. Divide between the words that form a compound; other divisions may occur in either or both parts.
2. Divide between the root word and an affix; other divisions may occur in the root or affix.

SYLLABICATION.   A *syllable* is an uninterrupted unit of speech that contains one vowel phoneme, forming either a whole word or part of a word; also the grapheme(s) that represent the spoken syllable. A syllable may consist only of a vowel or of a vowel preceded and/or followed by one or more consonants.

By second or third grade, children meet many printed words of more than one syllable. By at least second grade, the children's attention should be called to the fact that some words are made up of more than one syllable by giving them practice in noting the number of syllables heard in a word.

Children can learn to recognize a word that has been divided into syllables for them long before they can make independent use of syllabication generalizations. Often children who have difficulty blending single phonemes find it easier to blend syllables to make a spoken word. It is not necessary, therefore, to wait until generalizations are taught before using syllabication as an aid in word recognition.

Syllabication generalizations should be worded as clearly as possible, and their application rather than their recitation should be stressed. Only generalizations that have wide application and relatively few exceptions should be taught. These include the following:

1. Usually divide between two consonants that are not a digraph or a blend (e.g., meth-od).

2. A single consonant between two single vowels may go with either syllable.
3. Final *le* and the preceding consonant usually form the final syllable.

Note that the first generalization does not suggest whether the blend or digraph goes with the preceding or following syllable. It does assume that the child knows what blends and digraphs are.

In some programs, separate generalizations are taught for dividing between *unlike consonants* (e.g., but-ler) and *double consonants* (e.g. but-ter). Occasionally, children are taught to divide *after* a double consonant because the two letters usually represent one phoneme. This practice may cause problems when the child encounters words in which each letter of the double consonant represents a different sound, as with *cc* in *success* and *gg* in *suggest*.

Consonant digraphs must be treated as a unit because they represent a speech sound that is not represented by either of the letters individually. However, we can often "divide" between the two consonants that usually form a blend and yet closely approximate the word's pronunciation, especially if the word name is in our lexicon. A child who is having trouble with the generalization can be taught to "divide between two consonants unless they are *ch*, *ph*, *sh*, *th*, or *wh*."

McFeeley (1981) reports that the first vowel in over 2,000 VCV spellings represents its long sound 55% of the time; in 95% of the rest of the items, it represents its short sound. In applying the second generalization above, then, the child should probably be told first to try the long sound of the first single vowel and, if the result doesn't make sense, to try its short sound.

Although teaching syllabication generalizations has been criticized (e.g., Groff & Seymour 1987), the fact remains that, properly taught and used, they can provide guidelines for dividing "big words" into decodable units. Children can divide the same word in various ways and still closely approximate its oral equivalent. For example, *treaty* may be analyzed as *treat-y*, *trea-ty*, or *tr-ea-ty* (but the *ea* must be treated as a unit) and the word can be acceptably decoded. The fewer parts into which the word is analyzed, the more efficient the decoding.

The research findings regarding the value of teaching syllabication are mixed.

USE OF COMPARE-CONTRAST OR ANALOGY STRATEGIES.   Some evidence suggests that rather than use phonic and syllabication generalizations when decoding or attempting to recognize unknown words, students may search for familiar letter clusters or word parts (Hardy, Stennett & Smythe 1973) or compare the unknown word to known words or word parts (P. Cunningham 1980). According to Baron (1985), individuals decode pseudowords by: (1) analogies; (2) large-unit "rules" (e.g., knowing that *oad* can be pronounced as in *load* or *broad*); or (3) small unit "rules" (e.g., applying separate "rules" for *oa* and *d*.). It would be difficult to distinguish between use of the first two strategies. Glass (1973) developed a teaching procedure using letter clusters as a decoding strategy.

According to P. Cunningham (1979), children should be taught to segment an unknown word into the largest manageable parts derived by using the compare-contrast strategy. Her suggestions do not differ greatly from our recommendations that morphemic analysis should be applied first and that the largest possible units be employed in decoding.

Compare-contrast strategies are applicable to phonemically regular words but may result in incorrect responses with irregular words (e.g., *put* pronounced as rhyming with *but*).

Manis et al. (1986) found that severely disabled readers produced fewer analogy-based responses in a decoding task than did good readers of the same age or younger readers who were reading at the same level as the disabled readers. Perhaps, as the researchers suggest, the results were influenced by the instruction received by the pupils. But it is also possible that one needs to develop a stock of words that can be recognized at sight in order to make much use of an analogy strategy.

ACCENTING.   *Accent*, or stress, is the emphasis given to a syllable in a word (or to a word in a sentence) that makes it stand out in comparison to adjacent syllables (or words). In most two-syllable words, one of the syllables is accented. In words of three or more syllables, one syllable has primary accent (') and there is sometimes a secondary accent (') on another syllable. Shifts in accent can influence word pronunciation and meaning (*rec'-ord, re-cord'*).

Only two accenting generalizations merit being taught: (1) Usually the first syllable of a two-syllable word is accented; and (2) affixes are usually not accented. Resourceful readers try to accent one syllable to see if this results in a word they know that fits the meaning of the sentence; if it does not, they try accenting another syllable.

Symbol-Sound Associations

Our alphabetic writing system attempts to codify the relevant sounds of English into distinctive graphic symbols. Knowledge of these grapheme-phoneme correspondences can be quite useful. At times it may be necessary to determine all or most of the grapheme-phoneme relationships in an unknown word; at other times, only one or two such associations will trigger recognition.

Some children infer symbol-sound associations before they are introduced. For teaching phonics and other decoding generalizations, there are two general procedures. The children can be led to infer the generalization from specific instances which are presented by the teacher or the generalization may be introduced first, followed by examples of its applications. Because children do not all learn the same way, both the inductive and deductive approaches should be incorporated into the teaching of decoding generalizations. The exact wording of a generalization need not be required of the children, if the concept is accurate. The emphasis should be on application of the generalization, not on the ability to verbalize it. Pupils should also be informed that generalizations do not always work and should be taught strategies to employ when the generalizations do not result in an acceptable response. The aim is to have application of the generalization so automatic that its wording need not be brought to the level of conscious awareness.

Letter-sound patterns of English may be classified as invariant, variant-predictable, and variant-unpredictable (Venezky 1981).[17] Symbol-sound associations that are invariant or for which there are few exceptions are the consonants *f, j, ph, qu* (which usually represents /kw/), *sh, v, wh,* and *z*. The variant-predictable class includes most of the other consonants and a few vowels. The position of the letter, adjacent letters, and morphemic identification influence letter-sound associations.

There are two types of consonant combinations: *consonant blends* (e.g., *bl, st, cr, spl*) and *consonant digraphs* (e.g., *ch, sh, th, wh,* and *ph*). Although it is more efficient to treat a blend as a unit, it is possible to decode a word successfully by making an appropriate symbol-sound association for each letter in the blend. But because a digraph represents a single sound, it must be treated as a unit. In some programs the term *silent consonants* is used, and symbol-sound associations are taught for them (e.g., *kn, wr, mb*). In other programs such graphemes are referred to as consonant digraphs. Some "silent letters" are not always silent. For instance, the *b* in *mb* is silent in the base word (*bomb*) and before inflectional suffixes (*bombed*), but not before other letters (*bombard*).

For historical reasons, vowel symbol-sound associations are more variable than those for consonants (Calfee 1982). Single vowel letters usually represent either their long or short sounds, but they may represent other sounds when followed by *r* (e.g., *car*) or *l* (e.g., *call*). These spelling patterns are sufficiently consistent to be useful in decoding. *Vowel digraphs* are two letters that represent one phoneme (which usually could be represented by one of the letters in the digraph). In *diphthongs*, the vowel sound could not be represented by either of the letters alone. Only four vowel digraphs (*ai, ay, ee,* and *oa*) are consistent in their symbol-sound associations and occur relatively frequently. The common diphthongs (*au, aw; oi, oy;* and *ou*) are also consistent. The "two-vowel rule" (the first letter says its name and the second is silent) is of little value and could be very misleading. A few common vowel combinations (*ea, oo, ow*) most likely represent one of two sounds; others, such as *ew, ey,* and *ie*, although fairly common, are much more inconsistent in their symbol-sound associations. Some vowel combinations are fairly consistent but appear infrequently (e.g., *oe*); others are unpredictable and/or uncommon. In our opinion, only the common and at least fairly consistent associations should be taught.

Research studies have shown that many of the once commonly taught phonic generalizations are not very useful. There are, however, four phonic principles that may be useful. They concern the effect of position on vowel symbol-sound associations and are often taught in conjunction with syllabication and accenting generalizations:

1. A single vowel letter at the end of an accented syllable usually represents its long sound. Syllables that end with a vowel are called *open syllables.*
2. A single vowel letter followed by a single consonant other than *r* usually represents its short sound in an accented syllable. Syllables that end with consonants are called *closed syllables.*

[17]Refer to Venezky (1970) or Sipay (1973, 1990) for a more complete discussion of the frequency with which graphemes represent particular sounds.

3. A single vowel letter followed by a single consonant (other than *v*) and a final *e* usually represents its long sound and the *e* is silent.
4. Vowel letters in many unaccented syllables represent a schwa sound (/ə/)[18]

Few phonic generalizations deal with consonants, but children are commonly taught that *c* and *g* usually represent their "soft sounds" (/s/ and /j/ respectively) when followed by *e, i,* or *y.* When followed by any other letter or when they end a syllable, *c* and *g* usually represent their "hard sounds" (/k/ and /g/). According to Venezky (1979b), children and adults have a strong bias toward associating *c* with /k/ regardless of the spelling pattern in which it occurs.

There is no evidence that the ability to state a decoding generalization facilitates the ability to apply it (Beck 1981), but bringing it to the level of conscious awareness may help some pupils. Many children can apply decoding generalizations without being able to verbalize them (Rosso & Emans 1981). Some children abstract and apply phonic generalizations before such skills are taught, but reading disabled students are much less likely to do so. The inability to make vowel symbol-sound associations is more common among poor readers than among good readers (Smiley, Pasquale & Chandler 1976).

After a decoding generalization or principle has been taught, practice in applying it to unknown words in context should be provided. This may be done by using single sentences containing the target word. Children can be asked if the sentence makes sense (e.g., The mane ate the food"); to indicate yes or no to such sentences as "A bug can run" or "A rug can run"; or to select, then write in, the word that best makes sense ("The man used his _____ to help him walk" [*can* or *cane*]).

Heavy emphasis on phonic generalizations does not seem justified. It is more advisable (1) to teach the phoneme most commonly represented by a grapheme; and (2) to teach the second-most-likely sound for those letters that can represent more than one sound with some degree of frequency. Children who have difficulty learning or applying even a few generalizations may be taught the long and short sounds of the vowels and the alternate sounds represented by *c* and *g*, and may be instructed that if their first attempt does not result in a satisfactory response, "Try the other sound."

Blending

Two terms are used in reference to the ability to blend or synthesize phonemes into syllables and syllables into words. In *auditory blending* the examiner or teacher provides the sounds to be fused; there are no visual stimuli. In *visual blending* the pupil must first make the appropriate symbol-sound associations and then blend the results into a recognizable whole.

Auditory-blending ability is significantly related to scores on reading readiness tests (Rohrlack, Bell & McLaughlin 1982) and to reading ability (Richardson, Di Benedetto & Bradley 1977). The correlations in the 21 studies reviewed by Whaley and Kibby (1979) ranged from 0.19 to 0.67. Sound blending tends to

---

[18]The schwa can be represented by any single vowel letter and some vowel combinations (e.g., fam*ou*s).

be more highly correlated with decoding and word-recognition skills than with reading comprehension (Backman 1983).

Roberts (1979) reports that of 168 English 5-years-olds, 36% were competent in auditory blending (got at least 16 of the 20 items correct), 46% were not competent (4 or fewer correct responses), and the rest were in a state of transition. She also found that using voiced consonants (*b* = buh) did not necessarily affect performance negatively; so did Haddock (1978). Sound-blending ability increases quickly in the primary grades (Backman 1983).

Haddock's (1976) suggestion that teaching children to blend auditorily might facilitate acquisition of visual-blending ability seems logical because once the grapheme-phoneme correspondences have been made, the same cognitive tasks come into play. Suggestions for teaching auditory blending may be found in Liberman and Shankweiler (1979), Samuels (1981), and some phonics manuals.

Despite Groff's (1976) doubts about the usefulness of teaching children to blend, blending is an important decoding skill that may require direct teaching for some children. Few meaning-emphasis programs and only some decoding-emphasis programs attempt to develop blending skills in any consistent or systematic manner (Meyer, Greer & Crummey 1987). Whaley (1975) indicates how blending was taught in a number of different reading programs and offers suggestions for teaching blending.

In single-letter phonics programs children are usually taught to make all the necessary symbol-sound associations and then to blend them into a word (c = /k/, a = /ă/, t = /t/; /k/ + /a/ + /t/ = /cat/). This creates problems for some children because it puts a strain on their short-term memory, especially when more than four or five phonemes are involved. The child may forget the symbol-sound associations she made for the beginning of the word by the time she makes the association for the last letter. Use of a successive blending procedure may be more useful for many children because they need hold only two bits of information in STM at any one time. As soon as two sounds are produced they are blended together, and each additional phoneme is blended to what has already been fused. For example, *cat* would be decoded and synthesized as follows: c = /k/, a = /a/; /k/ + /a/ = /ka/; t = /t/; /ka/ + /t/ = /cat/.

In another blending technique, the vowel in a syllable is pronounced first, then the preceding consonant is added to it, and finally the final consonant is added (/ă/, /kă/, /cat/). The serious drawback of this procedure is that it disrupts a systematic left-to-right sequence.

Some children who have difficulty in grasping the concepts of segmentation and blending are helped by constructing a word with separate alphabet letters. For segmentation, place a word like *man* on the table. Explain that you are going to show how the word can be taken apart. "This word says /man/. I am going to shown you how to take it apart." Move the *an* to the right and say /m/ /an/. For blending, say "Now we can put the sounds together again; /m/ /an/." Move the *m* to the right and as you do so say, "/m/ /an/, /man/." Have the child imitate the whole procedure. For initial consonants, it is desirable to begin with those that are easy to blend with vowels, such as *f, l, m, n,* and *r,* postponing the stop consonants until the child is getting the idea. Repeat the procedure, changing the initial consonant and final phonogram, and continue until the child can sound and blend without the help of the movable letters. Hoogeveen and Smeets (1988) present a series of steps that may help children who have difficulty blending phonemes.

Some writers theorize that phonological awareness is related to blending ability. The belief is that before individuals can synthesize sounds and recognize the result as a specific word, they must grasp the concept that a spoken word can be segmented into phonemes.

Spelling as a Word-Recognition Strategy

In many linguistic reading programs (see page 77), children are encouraged to spell, letter by letter, any word that they do not recognize. Apparently it is believed that spelling the word will help the child recognize the spelling pattern, which is fairly tightly controlled in these programs (e.g., Nan can fan Dan.).

According to Durrell (1980), spelling out an unknown word is usually more effective than "sounding it out" because (1) spelling forces close examination of the word with every letter being noted; and (2) most letter names contain their phonemes. In our opinion, spelling is relatively ineffective word-recognition strategy, especially with words of more than four letters, and it interferes with the use of more effective word-recognition strategies.

SCOPE AND SEQUENCE IN TEACHING DECODING SKILLS

Many different sequences are used in teaching decoding skills, particularly phonic skills. There is no conclusive evidence indicating which is the most effective. In attempting to devise a sensible sequence for introducing decoding skills, the major guiding principles are to introduce early those skills met frequently in primary-grade words, and to teach those skills most readily learned and useful in decoding a reasonable number of words. If one adheres to these commonsense ideas, a number of different sequences can achieve satisfactory results.

Probably the ideal time to introduce a new decoding skill is when the child has a need for it and is ready to learn it. If these conditions are met, teachers should not hesitate to teach a new skill, even though it deviates from a previously planned sequence.

In our judgment, Table 12.1 (pages 470–471) suggests a reasonable sequence of skills and reader levels by which these skills should be acquired. No attempt has been made to indicate a sequence in which the skills should be taught at a particular reader level. This table is intended to provide a list from which behavioral objectives can be derived or a checklist to determine what needs to be reviewed or first taught, rather than to provide an instructional sequence. Many children will not master a particular decoding skill the first time it is introduced; therefore spaced review at that and higher reader levels is a necessity. No attempt has been made to indicate specific readiness activities at the different levels.

Table 12.1 Desirable Decoding Skills by Reader Level[a]

Preprimer

Grapheme-phoneme associations for consonants: *b, c /k/, d, f, g /g/, h, j, l, m, n, p, r, s, t, w*
Substitution: substituting initial and final consonants in known words
Context cues: using context and consonants to recognize unknown words
Morphemic analysis: inflectional endings *s* (plural marker—*dogs*) and *ed* (*called*)

Primer

Grapheme-phoneme associations:
 consonants: *k, v, y, z*
 consonant digraphs: *ch, sh, th*
 consonant blends: *pl, st, tr*
 short vowels: *a, e, i, o, u*
 spelling patterns: *er, or, ur, ar, ow, et, an, ight, at, ay, all*
Substitution: using grapheme-phoneme associations and parts of known words to
  recognize unknown words
Context cues: using semantic and syntactic cues to monitor responses to unknown printed
  words
Morphemic analysis:
 inflectional endings: *s* (3rd person singular verbs—*eats*), *d* (*liked*), *es* (*boxes*),
  's (possessive—*Ann's*), *er* (comparative—*faster*)
 suffix: *er* (as agent—*farmer*)

First Reader

Grapheme-phoneme associations
 consonant: *x*
 consonant digraphs:[b] *wh /h/, kn /n/, wr /r/, ck /k/*
 consonant blends: *br, cr, dr, fr, gr, bl, cl, fl, sl, sc, tw, ld, nd*
 short vowels: *y*
 long vowels: *a, e, i, o, u, y*
 vowel digraphs: *ay, ea /ē/ & /ĕ/, ee, oa, ow /ō/*
 vowel diphthongs: *oi, oy, ow /ou/*
 spelling patterns: *alk, eigh, ind, old, ook*
 generalization: In the initial position, *y* represents a consonant sound; in other
  positions, a vowel sound
Morphemic analysis:
 inflectional endings: *ing (walking), est (fastest)*
 compound words: compounds comprised of 2 known words
 contractions: *not = n't (doesn't), will/shall = 'll (I'll)*[c]
Structural analysis:
 separating monosyllables into parts
 counting the number of vowel sounds in a word as a clue to the number of syllables
Synthesis: blending sounds into syllables; syllables into words

Second Reader

Grapheme-phoneme associations:
 consonants: *c /s/, g /j/*
 consonant digraphs: *ph /f/, tch /ch/, gn /n/, mb /m/, dge /j/*
 consonant blends:[b] *gl, pr, qu /kw/, sk, sm, sn, sp, sw, scr, sch, str, squ, thr, lk, nk*
 vowel digraphs: *ai, oo /o͞o/ & /o͝o/, ey, ew, ei, ie, ue*
 vowel diphthongs: *ou, au, aw*
 schwa: */ə/ as represented by an initial vowel (ago)*

Table 12.1 *continued*

r- controlled vowels: *ar, er, ir, or, ur, oor (door, poor) ear (year, earn, bear, heart), our (hour, four)*

spelling pattern: *ough (through, though, thought, rough)*

generalizations:

1. When *c* and *g* are followed by *e, i,* or *y* they usually represent soft sounds
2. A single vowel letter at the end of an accented syllable usually represents its long sound
3. A single vowel letter followed by a consonant other than *r* usually represents its short sound in an accented syllable
4. A single vowel letter followed by a single consonant, other than *v,* and a final *e* usually represents its long sound and the *e* is silent

Morphemic analysis:

inflectional endings: *s' (boys'), en (beaten)*

prefix: *un*

suffixes: *ful, fully, ish, less, ly, ness, self, y*

contraction: *have = 've (I've)*[c]

generalizations:

1. Divide between the words that form a compound; other divisions may occur in either or both parts
2. Divide between the root word and an affix; other divisions may occur in either the root or affix

recognizing words with spelling changes made by adding suffixes when: the final *e* has been dropped *(hide—hiding), y* has been changed to *i (baby—babies),* and a final consonant has been doubled *(sit—sitting)*

Accenting: hearing and marking accented syllables

Third Reader

Grapheme–phoneme associations:

consonant blends: *spl, spr, ng, nt*

generalization: A single vowel letter or vowel combination (danger*ous*) represents a schwa sound in many unaccented syllables

Morphemic analysis

prefixes: *dis, ex, im, in, post, pre, re, sub, super, trans*

suffixes: *or* (as agent—*actor*), *ous, tion, sion, ment, ty, ic, al, able*

contractions: *are = 're (they're),*[c] *would/had = 'd (I'd)*[d]

Structural analysis: Syllabicating words of more than 2 syllables

Accenting generalizations:

1. Usually the first syllable in a 2-syllable word is accented
2. Usually affixes are not accented

---

[a]Refer to Ekwall (1988) for charts indicating the levels at which basal reader series teach specific decoding skills.

[b]Silent consonants are included under consonant digraphs.

[c]More words with this contraction are likely to be encountered at higher reader levels.

[d]Most contractions of *would/should* (*'d*) and *is/has* (*'s*) are likely to be encountered above the third reader level.

13

Dealing with Word-Recognition Problems

In this chapter, we consider ways of understanding and treating specific word-recognition problems, and provide a description of materials that can be used to improve word recognition. The remainder of the chapter is devoted to ways of helping students who find it extremely difficult to acquire word-recognition skills through conventional instructional methods.

SPECIFIC WORD-RECOGNITION PROBLEMS

Most children who need corrective help in reading have only a few specific word-recognition weaknesses. One pupil may have a reversal tendency; another, difficulty in making vowel symbol-sound associations. Yet other students may need help in recognizing certain high-frequency words or in making better use of context clues.

Understanding a child's word-recognition strengths and needs is usually based on an analysis of her oral reading. For this reason, the headings in this section use the terms that correspond to these behaviors.

General Comments

Rather than repeat a comment a number of times or suggest the same procedure each time it may be applied to treat a word-recognition problem, some general comments are enumerated in this section.

1. There is no need to be concerned about
   a. occasional miscues that disrupt comprehension
   b. relatively infrequent miscues that do not disrupt comprehension
   c. dialectal renditions
2. There is a need to treat frequent reading behaviors that disrupt comprehension.
3. Although, in general, remedial techniques may not differ greatly from classroom procedures, the following suggestions tend to make learning more effective:
   a. Teach only one skill at time
   b. introduce skills at a pace that allows for mastery
   c. reinforce initial learning in a variety of ways
   d. teach the skill until it is overlearned
   e. provide guided application of the skill to words in context
   f. have periodically spaced reviews

Before attempting to teach a skill, an effort should be made to determine if the student really is weak in that area or is simply not using a skill that he has in his repertoire. In the former case, the skill needs to be taught and practiced; in the latter, an attitude change is needed.

Refusal to Attempt Words

A fairly common oral reading behavior is reluctance or refusal to try to read an unknown word. The child may stop and wait for the teacher's reaction, may try to omit the word without the omission being noticed, or may simply say that he or she does not know that word. The majority of refusals are caused by inadequate word-recognition skills or strategies; they diminish in frequency as word-recognition skill improves.

Some children, however, do not try unknown words even when they have the skills to recognize or decode them. This may reflect a lack of confidence in their own abilities that is the result of a long period of frustrated effort. Other pupils are not risk takers,[1] do not want to assume the responsibility needed for learning, or have other personality traits that lead to such behaviors. Lack of confidence can be overcome by demonstrating to children that they can be successful. Some children do not attempt unknown words because they have learned that the teacher will provide the word for them.

Decoding Skills

Many pupils have inadequate knowledge of symbol-sound associations. They may know the majority of correspondences for single consonants but have difficulty with vowels and consonant clusters. Knowledge of common phonograms may be uneven, and a strategy for decoding multisyllabic words is often unknown territory. Some of these gaps represent deficiencies in previous instruction, but many of them are the result of attempting to teach skills which the child was not

---

[1]Refer to Spiegel (1985) for suggestions on how to develop risk taking.

ready to learn. It is desirable to find out by preliminary testing and observation which associations are known and which need to be taught; those that seem most urgently needed should be given priority in the teaching sequence.

PROCEDURAL PLANS.   Schell (1978) developed a PPARR cycle for teaching decoding to poor readers, which involves: (1) Presenting the skill and tying it to the child's prior knowledge; (2) providing structured Practice; (3) showing the child how to Apply the skill; (4) providing frequent Review by giving the child opportunities to apply the skill in a variety of contexts; and (5) providing cumulative Rereview in which two or more "new" skills have to be used.

Bryant (1980, 1981) outlines a nine-step plan for using a whole-word or phonic method. It is based on direct teaching of specific skills, controlling the amount to be learned in one lesson, reducing response competition (words or phonic elements are dropped out of a lesson as they are mastered so the child need concentrate on fewer items), providing immediate feedback, providing immediate and distributed review, mastery learning, and teaching for transfer.

VIVID CUES.   For children who have difficulty in remembering phonemes, it is important to provide vivid associations that can be used to recall the sound. Picture cards representing cue words are often helpful. If a child comes to the word *met* and has difficulty remembering the short *e* sound, he can look at the picture of the egg (accompanied by *egg* and *e*). Saying "egg" to himself can remind him of the sound. Cue cards can be mounted above the chalkboard for reference, or each child can have a personal set. Sometimes cue cards made by the children are more effective than commercially available ones.

At times it is effective to dramatize phonemes. Each sound can be associated with a situation in which the sound is made, as /s/, the hissing of steam or a snake; /t/, the tick of a clock; /ō/, what we say when we are surprised; and so on. Tracing and writing the letter can be used for reinforcement. Schmitt (1918) advocates teaching symbol-sound associations by employing a continued story, in which cows mooed /m/, for example. One new sound is added each day. This is followed by practice in which the teacher pronounces unblended parts of words in giving short directions (/R//un/ to me.; /F//old/ your hands.) as a readiness activity for blending instruction.

LETTER OR WORD CONFUSION.   Monroe (1932) points out that many children who confuse letters do not hear the differences between phonemes clearly. She therefore advocates preliminary training in auditory discrimination, which starts by presenting pictures of several objects, some of whose names begin with the sound. The child is taught to discriminate sounds in the following way: The child looks at the pictures and says, "/s/—soap, yes, soap sounds like /s/; /s/—man, no, man doesn't sound like /s/," and so on. A child who has difficulty producing such accoustically similar sounds as /d/, /t/, and /th/; /s/ and /sh/; /r/, /l/, and /w/; or /f/ and /v/ is taught the differences in the lip, tongue, and throat movements involved in making the sounds. After the phonemes can be distinguished and produced clearly, their associations with the printed letters are taught.

A persistent tendency to confuse two letters or letter combinations can be treated by following a sequence of five steps:

1. Point out the visual differences in the letters.
2. Present a printed list of words, all of which contain one of the graphemes under consideration. For consonants, use words beginning with the letter; for vowels, use one-syllable words with the vowel at the beginning or in the middle. Present a similar list for the other grapheme. Have the child read each list; help him when necessary.
3. Use the principle of minimal variation to present pairs of words that are alike except for one grapheme as *h*ill, *b*ill; h*a*t, h*i*t; ca*n*, ca*m*.
4. Give the child silent reading exercises of a multiple-choice or completion type: The cat ran after the (nouse, mouse); The cat ran after the —ouse.
5. Have the child read orally sentences that contain many words in which the two letters are used.

Pupils can be assisted in overcoming confusion between or among visually similar words by using the following techniques. Differences between the printed words can be pointed out (e.g., differences in letter sequence) and highlighted (e.g., by placing one word above the other— $\frac{that}{what}$ —and comparing them; coloring the target letters in different colors). Forced-choice exercises, such as those indicated above, may also prove useful. Use of the visual-auditory-kinesthetic—tactile (VAKT) technique with only the target words may help to clear up the confusion.

DIFFICULTIES WITH WORDS OF MORE THAN ONE SYLLABLE. Above the second- or third-reader level, difficulties in word recognition are apt to involve words of more than one syllable. Word-recognition skills that have been successful in learning such words as *went* and *their* do not seem to work when employed on such words as *migration, provocative, theoretical,* and *constitutionally.* In fact, difficulties in word recognition may arise during the middle grades in children who have previously had little difficulty with reading.

Many of these children have few decoding skills or do not employ those they possess. They developed satisfactory sight vocabularies as long as the new words were taught to them; and their sight vocabularies, aided by guessing from the context, kept them going fairly well. Nevertheless, their lack of decoding knowledge makes it impossible for them to work out the correct pronunciation of the separate syllables in a long, unfamiliar word. They may not know how to analyze the word into usable parts. They soon form the habit of guessing from the context, aided by the general appearance of the word, with perhaps a more careful inspection of the word's beginning. Sometimes they form the habit of skipping long words altogether, filling in during oral reading with a vague mumble. Analysis of the words on which the errors occur and follow-up testing will suggest what needs to be taught.

Positional Errors in Words

Errors on the beginnings of words are relatively infrequent. Those that do occur are likely to be letter reversals (*b-d*), confusion of similar words (*when, then*), words beginning with single vowels that represent a schwa sound *(again, other)*, or one phase of a serious general weakness in word recognition. Helping children to overcome reversal tendencies is discussed in the following. Pupils who consistently err on initial consonants need to learn those symbol-sound associations and how to combine this knowledge with other cues to recognize unknown words. Calling attention to the fact that certain high-frequency words begin with a schwa sound (which they do not expect to hear for that vowel letter) may help children overcome such errors. When the errors are caused by inattention to the beginnings of words, forced-choice exercises that draw attention to the initial word elements may help, as may teaching the child how to monitor his word recognition. Exercises in alphabetizing and the use of dictionaries also call attention to the beginning of the word.

Many unskilled readers observe only the beginning of an unfamiliar word and guess at the rest. This behavior is common in context readers and is found in children who get little or no help from the context. In either case, such errors may alter the intended meaning of a passage. Demonstrating how such miscues disrupt meaning and teaching monitoring strategies often help these children.

Medial errors usually involve an inability to make vowel symbol-sound associations; therefore, unknown correspondences should be taught. After the associations have been learned, and their application practiced, provide exercises in reading words that are alike except for their medial vowels. For example, the sun is (hat, hot, hut).

A form of medial error found in individuals of fairly advanced reading ability is the confusion of multisyllablic words that have similar beginnings and endings, such as *commission* and *communion* or *precision* and *procession*. These pupils must be taught to make better use of context and how to decode such words systematically. It is often helpful to insert vertical lines between the syllables, or to emphasize the part omitted or misread by underlining it.

Some errors on word endings are caused by a failure to note inflected endings or suffixes. Usually specific practice is sufficient to overcome such behaviors. After pointing out how the ending can change the meaning of a word, provide practice in reading sentences like these: There are many *(horse, horses)* in the barn; I can run *(fast, fastest, faster)* than you. Multiple-choice exercises that compel the child to pay careful attention to the total word can also be employed: The lady put her money in the *(benk, bank, balk)*. In other cases, the behavior indicates that the child cannot recognize the element as a unit (e.g., *tion*) or does not possess the skills necessary to decode it. In some cases, the miscue merely reflects the reader's dialect.

Mispronunciations and Substitutions

Mispronunciations and substitutions are responses that differ from the spoken word signaled by the stimuli. When a distinction is made between the two, the term *mispronunciation* means that the miscue violated the context (e.g., "dig" for *dog*); *substitution* implies that the response made sense (but did not necessarily represent the meaning intended by the author) and was syntactically acceptable (e.g., "cat" for *kitten*). An analysis of these and other miscues may reveal information that is useful in providing treatment. For example, a number of mispronunciations may have occurred on high-frequency, phonetically irregular words; or a number of the stimuli may contain vowel combinations and/or be polysyllabic. Frequent mispronunciations may indicate that the material is too difficult for the child, or that she is not using context to monitor her word recognition. In the latter case, the next question becomes, "Can she?" (see page 483)[2] If the child makes use of context when the material is of suitable difficulty, the "cure" is simply to use material of an appropriate level of difficulty and to teach the child the skills or knowledge needed to deal with more difficult text. If the child can use context, but is not doing so, she must be convinced that there is a payoff for taking the time to do so. Some poor or disabled readers can benefit from instruction and guided practice in using context cues.

Pupils who make frequent substitutions may be overrelying on context. Treatment for overreliance on context is covered on page 483.

Additions and Omissions

Additions occur less frequently than omissions, and most often do not disrupt meaning. Additions may be inserted to make the sentence flow more easily for the reader, or to make it more grammatically acceptable or more in keeping with the child's oral language pattern.

Omissions of whole words usually indicate that the child is "editing out" words that are not needed to obtain meaning or is translating the passage into his dialect. In either case, there is no need for concern. Words may also be omitted because they are not recognized or because the child lacks the necessary skills or inclination to decode them. In these cases, the treatments are obvious.

Letters and syllables are more likely to be omitted at the end or middle of a word than in the initial position. Such errors may result form inattention, reading too rapidly, the inability to recognize or decode that element, or a dialectal rendition. As the inattention, recognition, or decoding problem is overcome such omissions and additions usually disappear. Frequent omissions of whole lines of print may indicate a problem with return sweep (see page 333) or with keeping one's place on the page. The use of a marker, which is moved down one line at a time, provides "first aid" until the basic cause is overcome.

Reversals

The term *reversal* may refer to: (1) a confusion of single letters (e.g., *b-d, p-g, n-u*); (2) a complete reversal of letter sequence in a word (e.g., *on-no, saw-was*); (3) a partial reversal of letter sequences or transposition of letters (e.g., *ram-arm, ate-tea, girl-grill*); or (4) a reversal of the word order in a sentence (e.g., "The boy saw the dog" for *The dog saw the boy*). Bannatyne (1972b) distinguishes three types of letter-orientation reversals: (1) mirror images *(b-d)*; (2) inversions *(u-n)*; and (3) rotations *(b-p)*.

Reversals are fairly common among young children, who apparently tend to think that differences in the spatial orientation of letters or the order of letters in words are relatively unimportant. They take the same attitude as they do to-

---

[2]Difficulty using context may occur only when the material contains too many unknown words, or when it is conceptually or linguistically too complex for the child.

ward a picture of a person, which they can recognize about as well when it is sideways or upside down as when it is right side up. As Downing and Thackray (1971) put it, before entering school, children have learned to ignore such things as mirror images—a stick is a stick no matter in which direction it is presented. Children must learn that, in reading, direction does matter.

Preschool children, particularly those under age 5, have great difficulty discriminating among visual stimuli that differ only in orientation, whether the stimuli are horseshoes or letters like *b-d-p*. Ability to discriminate between *up* and *down* improves with age, but differentiating between *left* and *right* continues to be a problem until about age 6 (Ross 1976). Thus first graders are less likely to confuse *b* and *p* than *b* and *d*. Only when reversals persist much beyond age 7 is there need for concern.

Reversals usually do not occur in reading with much frequency beyond the initial stages of acquisition. They tend to occur more frequently with certain letters and words (Liberman et al. 1971), are influenced by context (Y. Goodman 1976), and are less likely to occur in context than in isolation.

For years, reversals have been considered symptomatic of, or associated with, reading disability. But, as a proportion of total word-recognition errors, reversals are no higher in poor than in good readers (Stanovich 1985; A. Adams 1988). Although there are a number of theories about the cause of reversals (lack of cerebral dominance, directional confusion, sequencing problems), all lack firm research evidence to support them (Stone 1976). One of the earliest theories to appear in the United States was that of S. T. Orton (1937), who postulates that reversals were the prime symptom of "the reading disability," which he termed *strephosymbolia* (twisted symbols). According to Orton's theory, reversals reflect failure to develop a clear dominance of one cerebral hemisphere. Each hemisphere receives an image, but the one in the "less dominant" hemisphere is a reversed image. The dominant hemisphere normally suppresses the reversed image, but when the less-dominant hemisphere takes over sporadically, reversals occur. Because not all reversals involve mirror images, Orton's theory cannot be considered definitive. Some evidence indicates that reversals are not caused by inadequate perception or a neurological deficit (Cohn & Strickler 1979). According to Vellutino (1987), reversals result from difficulty in storing and retrieving word names rather than from a dysfunction in visual-spatial processing. Stanovich (1986a) also attributes sequencing and reversal errors to verbal linguistic factors. When Deno and Chiang (1979) provided incentives for accurate responses, there was a rapid decrease in reversals by children who previously made such errors. Other studies (Liberman et al. 1971) found that letter-orientation reversals were not significantly correlated with letter-sequence reversals, suggesting that the two may have different causes.

Factors other than immaturity may cause reversals. Failure to develop consistent left-to-right eye movements in reading may result in reversals. Because of regressive movements, the letters or parts of the word may be interpreted in the wrong direction or order, or words may be scanned in the wrong direction or order. Other possible causes of reversals are difficulty with fusion and eye coordination and directional confusion.

The general principles described in this chapter for overcoming letter confusions usually suffice to overcome letter reversals. The need for tracing and writing letters is greater for children who reverse letters than it is for those who make other letter errors, and more intensive drill is usually necessary before reversals are eliminated.

Reversals of words, parts of words, and the order of words in sentences usually indicate that the child needs training to develop a consistent left to right sequence in reading. The need for such a consistent direction should first be explained to the child, with illustrations of how the words and meanings are changed when the correct order is not maintained. Various methods may then be employed to build up proper directional habits. Among the devices found to work well in overcoming reversal tendencies are the following:

1. Tracing, writing, and sounding out words that are frequently confused. These procedures automatically enforce using the correct sequence of letters. Cursive writing is more helpful than manuscript writing.
2. Covering a word with a card which is moved slowly to the right so that the letters are exposed in proper sequence.
3. Underlining the first letter in the word. Underlining the first letter in green and the last letter in red—"traffic lights"—may be effective. The child is told to start on green and stop on red.
4. Encouraging the child to use a finger or pencil as a guide in reading along a line. This practice is helpful as a means of teaching the proper direction for eye movements.
5. Exposing a line of print a little at a time by means of a card or an opening cut in a card, by opening a zipper, or by use of a controlled reader set at slow speed.
6. Drawing an arrow pointing to the right under words that are frequently reversed.
7. Allowing the child to use a typewriter. This practice has favorable effects on spelling and composition, as well as on word recognition.

Fernald (1943) states that reversals quickly disappeared when children were taught by the kinesthetic method, making sure that they started to write at the left edge of the paper. Monroe (1932) found that systematic letter-by-letter phonic training, combined with tracing, had a similarly beneficial effect on a reversal tendency.

Teaching the use of context to monitor responses while reading can also aid children with reversal tendencies. Children with *b-d* problems who monitor the appropriateness of their responses are not likely to accept *done* for *bone* in the sentence "The dog ate the bone." Forced-choice exercises in which the context is revealing can also be used for this purpose. When letter reversals do not seem amenable to training, children can be taught a compensation strategy that may help. Knowing, for example, that they confuse *b* and *d*, the children say to themselves, "If the word isn't *bump*, it must be *dump*."

Repetitions

The oral reading of some children is marred by frequent repetitions. These may be repetitions of part of a word, a whole word, a phrase, or the entire sentence.

For example, a child may read "The boy went for a walk with his spotted dog" as follows: "The boy—the boy want for—the boy went for a—a walk—with his stop—spotted dog."

Some repetitions are caused by slowness in word recognition: The child repeats a preceding word or two, or part of a word, to have more time for decoding. These repetitions drop out as greater skill in word recognition is attained. Another cause of repetitions is the realization that the first reading did not make sense; two instances of this type, involving *want* for *went* and *stop* for *spotted*, occur in the foregoing example. Although repetitions caused by self-corrections are desirable behaviors, their frequent occurrence indicates a need for more automatic word recognition. Sometimes a child loses the trend of thought and goes back in order to pick up the meaning. As comprehension improves, the need for repetitions of this sort lessens. Frequent repetitions may also indicate that the material is too difficult for the child. Regressive eye movements accompany repetitions, but the need to repeat usually causes the regressive movements, rather than vice versa.

Many children repeat words because of nervousness during oral reading. As their confidence is built up, their hesitations and repetitions diminish. These pupils should be given opportunities to rehearse easy selections carefully and then read the selections to children who are unfamiliar with the story. They also need large doses of encouragement and praise.

Occasionally a child tends to overcorrect; that is, the child compulsively corrects every miscue, even minor ones. Again, a balance needs to be struck. The child needs to learn that, at times, 100% correct word recognition is not necessary.

Slow Word Recognition

Some children recognize words accurately but slowly. This fact is apparent on tests using words in isolation, when a number of their correct responses are made very close to the time limit allowed (often 3 seconds), or they can recognize the words when given additional time. Lack of automatic word recognition can also be noted when reading in context; reading rate is slow and often word by word. Slow word recognition can adversely affect both fluency and comprehension (Beck 1981).

Slow word recognition is not unusual in children who are just learning to read. Word-recognition accuracy may be acquired quickly; but rapid, automatic recognition follows a slow developmental trend (Samuels 1981). With progress in reading, word recognition becomes faster and more automatic. Reading a great deal of easy, interesting material also tends to increase word-recognition speed. Repeated readings also may help (see page 481).

Samuels (1988b) suggests two informal measures of automaticity. The first involves having the student read a passage at sight. If it is read with expression and with few hesitations and pauses, word recognition is probably automatic. Alternatively, the child may read orally a passage on which he has little topical knowledge, and then retell what he has read. If comprehension is adequate, word recognition must have been automatic for the child to have understood the text while pronouncing the words aloud.

At times, children who have been given intensive phonic training develop the habit of trying to sound out most words. This behavior, referred to as an *overanalytical set,* keeps their speed far below what it would be if they responded immediately to words as wholes. Although they attempt to decode almost every word, these children often can recognize a number of these words when they are presented for a brief amount of time. Quick-flash techniques can be used to demonstrate that they need not decode every word. The advantage of recognizing words at sight should also be discussed.

Another helpful procedure for increasing word-recognition speed is the use of flash cards (see page 439) or a tachistoscope (see page 649). Start with one-syllable, high-utility words to which the child has already been exposed. At first the words should be of different shapes, such as *all, father, house,* and *they.* Longer and more visually similar words can be introduced gradually. If phrases (e.g., to the store) are shown, more time should be allowed, because even excellent readers usually do not take in much more than two short words with one fixation. The emphasis in quick-exposure practice should be on changing "two-look" words to "one-look" words.

Because high-frequency words make up more than half the running words of most reading material, speeding up children's recognition of them often improves reading fluency, rate, and perhaps comprehension. The attention previously spent on recognizing or decoding words can be shifted to attaining meaning.

Lack of Fluency[3]

Current models of reading and data from information-processing studies of skilled readers suggest that fluent reading greatly aids comprehension (Torgesen 1986a). *Reading fluency* is the ability to read smoothly, easily, and readily; and it involves freedom from word recognition/identification problems (T. L. Harris & Hodges 1981). Inadequate fluency is marked by such behaviors as hesitations, word-by-word reading, improper phrasing, repetitions, and inadequate use of voice (e.g., lack of expressiveness or intonation)—almost all of which are caused by inaccurate or slow word recognition. Once word-recognition/decoding problems are overcome, work on developing fluency can proceed if it is needed. For example, the child may need work on skills such as proper phrasing or how to use her voice to demonstrate her understanding of the text. When lack of fluency is a symptom that the material is too difficult for the student, the "cure" is obvious. Lack of fluency may also result from reading orally at sight. In such cases, fluency improves after prereading silently.

A great deal of easy reading probably increases fluency. But because disabled readers are not apt to do much recreational reading, direct instruction aimed at overcoming the underlying causes is needed. The most common methods of increasing fluency involve overlearning word-recognition skills. Modeling fluent reading may also assist pupils who lack fluency.

One procedure used to develop fluency involves *repeated readings*. The

---

[3]Fluency is almost always measured through oral reading. It is assumed that fluency carries over to silent reading.

child reads a short selection until fluency on a given passage is satisfactory, as determined by reaching a criterion of 85 WPM. Then the technique is repeated with new material. Reading speed, rather than accurate word recognition, is stressed (Samuels 1979). Before initiating the procedure, the child should be told that a number of rereadings may be necessary to reach criterion. During the repeated readings, frequent feedback regarding gains in rate should be provided (Dowhower 1987). O'Shea, Sindelar, and O'Shea (1985) obtained the best results when each passage was read about four times and the child was cued to reading for meaning. Use of the latter instructional strategy is based on the possibility that pupils may not automatically shift to concentrating on comprehension after fluency is established. Dowhower (1989) offers other suggestions for using repeated readings.

Dowhower (1987, 1989) states that strong empirical evidence supports the use of repeated reading to develop reading rate and word-recognition accuracy. But according to Otto (1985), little experimental evidence demonstrates this method's effectiveness. Torgesen (1986a) notes that the primary effect of repeated readings was to increase the rate of word recognition for specific words in the passage. Whatever skills are acquired may transfer only to the same type of material as that used in the repeated readings and the technique may not be useful for students reading above the fifth- or sixth-reader level (Carver & Hoffman 1981). Increases in word-recognition speed influence reading rate on other passages only to the extent that the practiced and new passage contain the same words (Rashotte & Torgesen 1985).

A modification of the repeated readings technique involves having the child read along silently while listening to a taped version of the text. Then the story is read silently without the recording, until it can be read orally with satisfactory fluency (Samuels & Eisenberg 1981). Kann (1983) recommends combining repeated readings with the Neurological Impress Method (see p. 508), Lauritzen (1982) describes how the technique could be used with groups, and Koskinen and Blum (1986) make suggestions for using paired repeated readings.

According to Schreiber (1980), repeated readings and similar methods are effective either because they help children to discover the appropriate prosodic pattern of the reading material or because the massive practice helps them to transfer prosodic skills to novel passages. Refer to Miccinati (1985) for suggestions on developing fluency through teaching children to make use of prosodic cues in choral reading.

Use of Context Cues

Use of context cues in word recognition/identification refers to utilizing information from the immediate setting in which the word occurs. These cues include the surrounding words, phrases, or sentence; illustrations; syntax; and typography (T. L. Harris & Hodges 1981). The meaning of the less immediate text can also aid the process. Context can assist in predicting what words are likely to occur next, in recognizing or identifying words, and in verifying predictions or responses. As with any cue system, there must be a balance in the use made of context. Neither overreliance on, nor inadequate use of, context cues is desirable, although the former is the lesser of two evils under certain conditions.

Some students overrely on context, even though they need not. They make frequent substitutions that often begin with the sound represented by the first letter(s) in the stimuli; and which, although contextually acceptable, vary in the degree to which they alter the author's intended meaning. Very often, these *context readers* can supply the miscued word when their attention is focused on it. They may be able to obtain meaning from the selection, particularly if they have sufficient topical knowledge. However, at times, the obtained meaning may be inaccurate. For example, substituting "dog" for *pup* will probably distort meaning if the animal is a baby seal. Such behaviors may not be too disruptive when one is reading to get an overview or the gist of the text, or when reading for pleasure, but they could have a negative impact on comprehension when the task calls for careful reading.

Treatment involves attempting to change what is probably a well-ingrained habit. Context readers should be made aware of what they are doing (e.g., by reading their renditions to them as they follow along in the text); the possible consequences of such behaviors (how meaning is changed); and that at times (and told when) it is important to read all, or almost all, of the words accurately, such as in reading a math problem or a science experiment. The need for exact reading can be demonstrated, for instance, by having the child read and follow a set of directions that must be read carefully in order to complete the task successfully.

Pupils cannot or do not use context cues to their advantage for a number of reasons. If many of the words are not recognized, little or no context is available to the reader. In addition to the need for adequate word recognition, the use of context requires the availability and utilization of semantic, syntactic, and topical knowledge. Apparent inability to use context may reflect a weakness in one or more of these areas. Accurate but slow word recognition may also be disruptive. The reasons for inadequate use of context should be determined and appropriate remedial action taken.

Contextual information can be used to monitor word recognition by making use of one's semantic and syntactic knowledge to tell when word recognition responses make sense or "sound right." In addition to being generally aware of the appropriateness of their word recognition, readers can make specific checks. After responding to a word that was not recognized immediately, pupils may ask themselves: "Does it sound like a word I know?" (use of lexical knowledge); "Does it make sense?" (use of semantic knowledge); and, "Does the sentence sound right with this word in it?" (use of syntactic knowledge).

In order to make a needed self-correction, readers must be aware when a miscue is disruptive, be interested in taking corrective action; and know some self-correction strategies. Children who are reading above the first-reader level can be taught to distinguish between disruptive and nondisruptive miscues as well as how to use self-correction procedures (Pflaum & Pascarella 1980).

Children can be helped to become aware of disruptive miscues by having them: listen to material containing disruptive miscues, indicate when such miscues occur, and tell why the miscue is inappropriate (at first they may need help in doing so). Later they can be given practice in deciding between disruptive and nondisruptive miscues, and in "fixing up" the disruptive ones. Instruction should begin with sentences containing very obvious disruptive words.

The value of making the effort to monitor one's word recognition and taking the time to self-correct when needed can be demonstrated to students by showing them how doing so helps them to understand the text more accurately. D'Angelo (1982) suggests ways to develop self-correction behaviors.

When encountering an unknown word in context, or on becoming aware that a disruptive miscue has occurred, the first strategy to employ is to finish reading the sentence because it may provide additional information. A *place holder*—a word that makes sense and is syntactically appropriate—can be used until new information makes it necessary to try a new response. If neither strategy works, rereading the sentence containing the word may help. But before doing so, the word causing the problem should be checked for graphic or graphophonic cues that could be used in combination with contextual cues to aid word recognition. If this does not result in an acceptable response, and if the word is important to meaning, an attempt should be made to decode it. At times it may be prudent to apply this strategy earlier in the sequence, especially if the word is important for understanding the text. If none of these strategies triggers word recognition or identification, rereading some of the text preceding the sentence containing the target word may provide useful information, or may reveal that a previously unidentified miscue contributed to the miscue on the word under consideration (i.e., one error led to another). At times, reading more of the text following the sentence containing the target word proves helpful. There are benefits and consequences attached to the use of each strategy.

Taylor and Nosbush (1983) recommend a four-step procedure for encouraging students to correct their disruptive miscues: (1) The child, on a one-to-one basis, reads a 100- to 300-word passage at his instructional level to the teacher, who provides as little feedback as possible; (2) the teacher praises the child for something done well in oral reading, especially for self-correcting disruptive miscues; (3) one or two uncorrected disruptive miscues are pointed out to the child by reading his rendition to him and having him tell what word did not make sense or sound right; and (4) the child is helped to recognize the miscued words by demonstrating how graphic and context clues could be employed.

As the occasions arise during reading lessons, the teacher can model how to use context as an aid to word identification by saying out loud the thoughts that occur in her mind as she goes through the process. Specifically constructed cloze or maze exercises or sentences containing nonsense words (e.g., "I knew the girls were happy because they were plinking") could also be provided, and the pupils asked to explain the bases on which their responses were made. If their choices are unacceptable, the teacher should explain how to arrive at a better prediction. Strategy lessons based on an analysis of pupils' miscues may be found in Goodman and Goodman (1982), Y. Goodman (1970, 1975), and Y. Goodman and Burke (1980).

Dahl and Samuels (1977) present a hypothesis-test strategy for using context to aid word recognition. The steps in the strategy are as follows: (1) Use information from the passage (and, we would add, from conceptual background and language cues); (2) make a prediction (the hypothesis) as to which word is most likely to occur; (3) compare the printed and predicted words (testing the hypothesis) for goodness of fit; and (4) accept or reject the prediction. Rejection should lead to another attempt. Samuels (1981) suggests teaching the hypothesis-test strategy after the child is fairly proficient in decoding. His rationale is that knowledge of symbol-sound associations could be combined with context to make more accurate predictions.

Combining Context Cues, Graphic Cues, and Phonic Skills

Because the goal is to recognize words as quickly and efficiently as possible, the less the child has to do, the better. Thus, instantaneous recognition of the whole word is highly desirable.

When immediate word recognition does not occur, the combination of an intelligent prediction based on context and whatever familiar part(s) of the unknown word are immediately discernible is often sufficient. The general category of the unfamiliar word may be suggested by the rest of the sentence, or the preceding sentence (e.g., Henry went into the _____ to buy some candy). Use of syntactic cues indicates that the unknown word is almost certainly a noun. The term *noun* need not be known, but the child's past experience with spoken language suggests the kind of word that grammatically fits the sentence. Past experience and semantic cues further limit the words that can make sense in this sentence and uncertainty about the specific noun in question can be reduced further by employing as many additional cues as necessary. The initial letter alone (e.g., *s*) may narrow the possibilities, but the reader may need to go to the second letter (e.g., *st*) or beyond to rule out *shop*. Word length and configuration clues may rule out some possibilities (e.g., *stadium*).

If the use of context and partial graphic information is not sufficient (context is not always potent enough to cue the reader, or the number of unfamiliar words in the sentence make it difficult to use context clues), the reader needs to be able to apply additional decoding skills, going only as far as necessary to achieve word recognition. Skilled readers use only as many cues as necessary to recognize words, but they possess highly developed decoding skills and employ them flexibly.

Morphemic analysis may be sufficient when all or most parts of the word are already known at sight. However, morphemic analysis is frequently used in combination with context and phonic cues beyond the initial stage of learning to read. The unknown word is divided into reasonable parts; the parts are sounded out and blended. The resulting response is then tested to determine its appropriateness in the sentence. If the unfamiliar printed word is one the child has heard or uses, a close approximation of the spoken equivalent, or even a partial decoding of the word, is often sufficient for recognition. If the word is completely new, the child has to infer both its pronunciation and meaning, and neither is any help in determining the other. Thus, a word like *incognito* may be correctly divided into syllables, each of which is sounded in a reasonable way, But the wrong syllable may be accented, and wrong vowel sounds may be tried, because the word is entirely unfamiliar to the reader.

As a last resort, the interested reader may turn to a dictionary or glossary to determine the pronunciation of the unfamiliar printed word. This requires the ability to understand the phonetic respelling code used in that dictionary. At times, readers are surprised to find in the dictionary that they have heard or used that word before and know its meaning but have never encountered it before in print (e.g., *island, depot*).

Reading skills are usually taught separately but used in combination. The ability to combine various word-recognition skills can be developed by the use of materials that demand careful attention to both meaning and word details. This exercise, in its many variations, requires the reader to understand the sentence as a whole, to predict what word to expect, and to choose correctly from among words that look very much alike. A modified cloze procedure in which various graphic cues are provided is another method for helping children combine cues (e.g., It is foolish to go into the pool if you can't sw__ __).

An effective word-recognition program teaches children to employ a variety of skills flexibly; no one strategy is overemphasized. The goal is to equip learners with a variety of strategies and let them select the ones that work best for them in a given situation.

Corrective Feedback

As it relates to word recognition/identification, *corrective feedback* refers to teacher behaviors in response to children's miscues while reading orally. Researchers have focused on what the teacher does or does not do, when such reactions take place, differences in teacher behaviors when responding to good readers and to poor readers, and the effect of teacher feedback on what children do and learn. Corrective feedback can be immediate or delayed, *terminal* (telling the word to the child) or *sustaining* (providing cues that can help the child to recognize or decode the word), and it may vary with the perceived seriousness of the miscue, as well as with the child's level of reading ability.

Terminal feedback may involve: (1) the teacher naming the word for the child, who repeats the word and continues reading or rereads the whole sentence; (2) the child being told the word by the teacher, who lists the unknown words and (a) reviews them with the child after a short time (e.g., at the end of a page) or (b) later provides continual practice until the words are mastered; and (3) the teacher tells the child the word and defines it. Examples of sustaining feedback include: (1) the teacher asking the child to "sound out" each letter or word part as she points to it; or (2) the teacher using a *corrective-cues hierarchy,* which starts by attempting to get the child to assume the responsibility for recognizing the unknown word. If that fails, the teacher provides increasingly more cues until the word is recognized by the child or named by the teacher. Thus, the sequence of teacher statements might be: (1) "Try some ways to recognize the word."; (2) "Finish reading the sentence to see if it will help you to recognize the word, then guess what the word is."; (3) "Break the word into parts and sound out each part."; (4) "Look at what I point to, and tell me what each part says."; (5) "What sound does _____ make?" (6) Put the sounds together."; and, finally, "This word is _____." (McCoy & Pany 1986).

Advocates of corrective feedback believe that it helps pupils to develop word-recognition monitoring and self-correction behaviors, thus increasing word-recognition accuracy, which they feel is important for comprehension. Opponents contend that corrective feedback disrupts the comprehension process, focuses the reader's attention on graphic information rather than on attending to meaning, develops dependency on external monitoring of word recognition, and curtails the development of self-corrective strategies. We feel that it is not an either/or proposition, but that the appropriateness of corrective feedback varies with the instructional situation.

One study (Hoffman, O'Neal & Baker 1981) found that teachers made overt responses to only 37% of the children's miscues. Their responses were divided almost equally between terminal and sustaining feedback. Immediate terminal feedback appears to interfere with learning to monitor one's word recognition (McNaughton 1981). It also increases the likelihood that, on the next unknown word, the child will wait for the word to be supplied by the teacher, who obliges. Thus, a vicious cycle is established (Hoffman et al. 1984). Delayed feedback is likely to result in increased self-monitoring and self-corrections (Shake 1986b).

Teachers are prone to provide feedback when the miscue disrupts meaning, when the child is struggling with the word, or after the child has made a number of miscues on the passage (Shake 1986b). However, when a child stops at an unknown word in an otherwise strong performance, the teacher is apt to direct the student's attention to graphophonic cues or root words or to remind the student of the story's gist (Chittenden 1984).

Apparently, teachers adjust their responses to the qualitative characteristics of the miscues (Hoffman et al. 1984). They tend to disregard nondisruptive miscues, and either to supply the word or to attempt to cue the child when the miscue is disruptive or when the child does not respond or has made a number of unsuccessful attempts (Lass 1984).

The child's level of reading ability appears to enter into the decision. Observational studies suggest that when miscues occur, poor readers are likely to be interrupted more often, and more quickly, than are good readers. Poor readers are usually told the word or have their attention drawn to graphophonic or visual cues. Good readers are more often told to attend to context clues (Shake 1986b). At times, such differentiated teacher practices are interpreted as reflecting poor instructional practice. But it is possible that, at least for some students, the differentiated feedback is appropriate. It is impossible to make judgments as to the appropriateness of corrective feedback practices unless the teachers' reasons for making them are also understood. This factor is rarely addressed in the research.

Corrective feedback enhances the word recognition of disabled readers more than does receiving no feedback (McCoy & Pany 1986), but simply acknowledging correct word-recognition and correcting word-recognition errors does not (Kibby 1979a). According to one study (L. Meyer 1982), it did not seem to make much difference for word-recognition accuracy whether unknown words were supplied by the teacher or children were encouraged to use previously taught decoding skills. Another study (McCoy & Pany 1986) reveals that practicing miscued words until they were mastered produced the best results.

Two studies found that corrective feedback aided the reading comprehension of disabled readers. Two other studies, which used average readers, produced mixed results (McCoy & Pany 1986). Another study (Pany & McCoy 1988) reveals that corrective feedback had significant positive effects on the word-recognition accuracy and reading comprehension of third-grade disabled readers.

The following behaviors are most likely to produce desirable results:

1. Ignore occasional nondisruptive miscues as well as rare disruptive miscues.
2. If the child makes frequent nondisruptive miscues, point out the possible negative consequences of such reading behaviors under given circumstances and provide guided practice in more exact reading.
3. Teach strategies for monitoring word recognition and for dealing with miscues.
4. When a child makes a disruptive miscue, allow about 5 seconds for him to realize it and to take corrective action.
5. Supply the word quickly if
   a. the miscue is disruptive but the word is phonetically irregular and/or the context is not sufficient to aid word recognition
   b. the child does not possess the skills needed to decode the word or make use of contextual information
   c. the pupil has previously made a number of disruptive miscues or if a number of previous words have caused him difficulty (either may indicate that the material is too difficult for the child)
   e. if the child is upset by his weak performance
6. If the word is decodable and/or if context cues can be used to aid word recognition, cue the child to the usable information using a "corrective-cues hierarchy" (see page 486).
7. If the student has made a few disruptive miscues which he has "ignored," wait until the sentence containing the next such miscue has been completed and cue the child to the use of monitoring and cognitive strategies (e.g., "You read that sentence as _____. Did that make sense? What part doesn't fit? What word that begins like _____ would make sense in this sentence?)
8. If the word is supplied by the teacher or if the child recognizes it after awhile, encourage him to reread the sentence in order to assist him to assimilate the word and to recover the meaning of the sentence
9. Try to determine why the child is having word recognition problems, and provide the necessary instruction and guided practice.

Modeling of the appropriate strategies to employ when a child encounters unknown words may also assist children with word-recognition difficulties. Shake (1986b) presents a useful plan that teachers can employ to monitor their reactions to miscues.

MATERIALS FOR IMPROVING WORD-RECOGNITION SKILLS

Manipulative Devices and Games

Many manipulative devices and games can be used to add variety and interest to word-recognition and decoding programs. They serve to break the monotony that may otherwise cause a pupil's effort to slacken. Depending on the task and

the nature of the stimuli, most of these devices can be used for teaching or reinforcing either word-recognition or decoding skills. The following descriptions
are representative of materials that may be made or purchased. Blank or reusable
game boards also are available from some publishing companies.

Use of games can improve word recognition (Kirby, Holborn & Bushby
1981). Games involving physical-activity (e.g., Word Toss) were found to be
more effective than passive games (e.g., Go Fish) in increasing the word recognition of inner-city children (Dickerson 1982).

DIRECTIONS FOR USING GAMES

1. Lucky Wheel. Two circles, one smaller than the other, are fastened together through their center so that each can be rotated freely without disturbing
the other (see Figure 13.1). Initial consonants or consonant clusters are printed
around the outer circle, and phonograms are printed around the edge of the
inner circle; in this way, different words can be formed. By rotating the outer
circle, different initial elements can be combined with the same phonogram; by
rotating the inner circle, the same initial element can be combined with different phonograms. Many variations of this general idea have been devised. Such
a wheel can be used as a basis for competitive games.

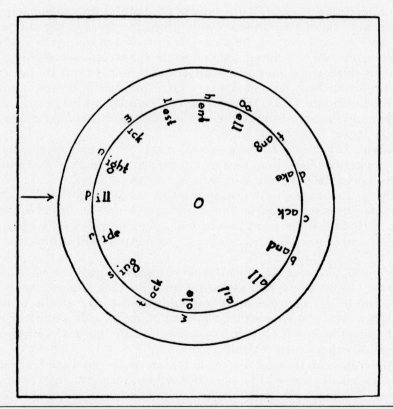

Figure 13.1.   "Lucky Wheel" for phonic practice. Both outer and inner circles can be rotated.

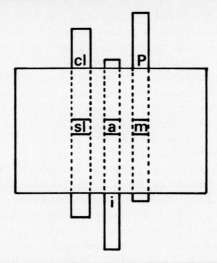

Figure 13.2. A phonic card, showing how strip inserts can be used to form a variety of words.

2. Phonic Strips. Three horizontal slits, close together and in line, are made across a 4 × 6-inch index card. Three other slits are made directly below them. A number of thin strips are prepared (by cutting up another index card); the strips should be of a width that can be threaded through the slits in such a way that only a small part of the strip is exposed. On one strip a number of initial consonants can be printed, one below the other; on a second strip, middle vowels; on a third strip, common word endings; and so on. By inserting the strips and moving them up and down, a large number of different words can be formed (see Figure 13.2). This device can be adapted for practice on word beginnings, middles, or endings and can be used with phonograms as well as with single letters.

3. Rhyme Making. Lines from several verses are printed on separate strips. The child picks out all the lines that end in the same sound and assembles them into a little poem. High poetic standards are not necessary.

4. Darts. An inexpensive dart-and-target set is used. Small cards, each with a single phonogram, are pasted to the target, and an initial consonant is pasted on each dart. If the word formed when the dart hits a phonogram is read correctly, a point is scored. A beanbag-toss game may be substituted for the dart set.

5. Word-O. Game cards, modeled after Bingo or Lotto, can be made, using words instead of numbers, and the usual rules for such games can be used or modified. The leader says the word and holds up the card, or the word is said but not shown. The players look for the word on their cards and cover it if they find it. The first player who covers five words in a row, column, or in a diagonal and can identify them correctly wins.

6. Anagrams. An inexpensive anagram set can be purchased, or letters can be printed on small pasteboard squares. Word-building games of several kinds can be played. Phonic elements can be color coded (e.g., consonants on white cards, vowels on blue).

7. *Spin the Pointer.* Words are arranged around the outside of a circle, and the child tries to read the word at which the pointer stops. Failures and successes can be scored according to the rules of games like baseball and football. In baseball, for example, correctly recognizing the word is a hit and failure to do so is an out; the score is kept in terms of runs. By making slits into which word cards may be inserted, the same circle and pointer can be used indefinitely.

8. *Fishing.* One word, phrase, or sentence is printed on each of a number of cardboard cutouts in the shape of fish, to which paper clips are attached. The child picks up a fish by means of a horseshoe magnet on a string, and keeps the fish if the word is read correctly. Similar games can be devised involving taking leaves off a tree and so on.

9. *Racing.* A large racetrack is drawn and divided into boxes, in each of which a word is placed. Each child has a car, horse, or the like, of a different color. Each player, in turn, spins a pointer, which indicates a move of one, two, three, or four boxes. If the word is read correctly, the marker is advanced that many spaces; if not, the player waits for his next turn.

10. *Word Hospital.* Words that cause persistent difficulty are called "sick" words, and the child, as doctor, puts them to bed in a word hospital until they are cured (see Figure 13.3).

11. *This to That.* Starting with one word, one of the letters in the word is changed each time, making a series of words: *his, him, ham, ram.* The game can also be played allowing changes of two-letter combinations: *shook, spook,*

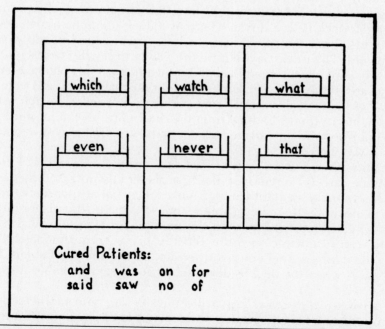

Figure 13.3. A "hospital" for "sick" words. A word with which the child has persistent difficulty is printed on a small card and is put to bed (inserted in the slit corresponding to the mattress of the bed). When a sick word is cured, its name is entered at the bottom of the chart.

speak. Reading such a sequence is a welcome change from the monotony of word families and provides an interesting form of review.

   12. Word Tic-Tac-Toe. One of nine practice words is printed into each space on a blank form, or word cards are fitted into slots cut into a form made of oak tag. The game is played like Tic-Tac-Toe, but the player must acceptably pronounce the word in the square in order to place her or his X or O in that space.

   13. Alphabet Pyramid. A word beginning with *a* is written by the first player. The next player must add a word that begins with the next letter of the alphabet. The player who is able to add the last word is the winner.

   14. Card Games. Packs of blank playing cards, with decorative backs but no printing on the face side, are available from some playing-card manufacturers, or oak tag can be cut into rectangles of appropriate size. By printing the same word on four cards, it is possible to make a "rummy" deck containing a given number of words or adapt the deck to the rules of other simple card games such as Go Fish or Old Maid.

   Self-correcting materials. Picture-word cards are cut so that only the correct word can be inserted to complete the picture-word matching. Such cards and other self-checking materials are illustrated in Figure 13.4.

   Change Over. In this teacher-made game, which is played like Crazy Eights, each card has a word that contains one or more symbol-sound associations to be practiced; the same word may appear as more than one card in the deck. Five cards have "Change Over" printed on them; these may be used to change the choice to any other consonant or vowel sound. Each player is dealt eight or fewer cards and the top card from the remaining deck is turned over; the rest of the deck is face down. The first player attempts to match a word in his hand with either the initial consonant or vowel sound in the word on the turned-up card. The rules may require the player to say the words on the target card and the word chosen from his hand or just to place his choice on top of the turned-up card. If the player makes an appropriate match, the card from his hand is placed over the turned-up card. If the player cannot make a match with a word in his hand, he continues to draw from the deck until he can, or until the cards are used up. Then the next player takes a turn. The first player to get rid of all his cards is the winner.

   Synonyms/Antonyms. Target words are printed on cards and placed in a deck. When a card is turned over, the first player attempts to provide orally an acceptable synonym or antonym and must tell if her response is the same or opposite in meaning. If an acceptable response is made, the player picks up the card. A new card is turned up, and the next player takes a turn. If the player cannot make an acceptable response, the next player tries. If none of the players can "win the card," a new one is turned up. The winner is the child who has the most cards when the deck is depleted or no more acceptable responses can be made.

   15. Crossword Puzzles. Crossword puzzles can be constructed to provide practice in either word recognition or decoding or to develop word meaning.

   16. Letter-Word Cubes. Letters, phonograms, word parts, or words may be attached to, or printed on, the side of 1-inch or larger cubes. The cubes are cast like dice; the learner's task is to form as many words or sentences as possible.

cat

_at   front

hat   back

The cat drank the m____.   front

ilk   back

Figure 13.4. Examples of self-checking materials. Adapted from C. Mercer and A. Mercer, *The development and use of self-correcting material with exceptional children, Teaching Exceptional Children,* Fall 1978.

Task difficulty can be controlled by limiting or increasing the possible number of responses. For example, if practice with only three initial consonants is desired, each consonant letter would appear twice on the cube, thus limiting the number of words that can be formed when added to the vowel-consonant phonogram(s) on the other block(s). Among the activities for which cubes can be used are (1) Single letter and/or multiple letters (e.g., blends, digraphs, diphthongs) on all the cubes can be used to form as many words as the player can think of; (2) single consonants and/or consonant clusters on some blocks, and vowel-consonant and/or consonant-vowel phonograms on the others can be used to practice substituting initial and final consonants to form words; (3) root words on some blocks, affixes on the others can be used to practice use of prefixes and suffixes (this can be made into a vocabulary exercise by having the learner define the words constructed); and (4) words on all the cubes can be used to practice word recognition, "sentence sense," or comprehension. Commercially prepared cubes under various trade names are available.

17. Flip Cards. Cards that have flip folds can be used for practice in substituting word beginnings and endings or to aid morphemic analysis. One part of the card can be folded over to form a new word.

18. Concentration. Pairs of words, one per card, are printed on 3 × 5-inch cards. The cards are shuffled and placed face down on a hard surface. Each player (two to four can play) takes a turn exposing two cards. If the words match and are pronounced acceptably, the player keeps the cards and takes another turn. If the words do not match, or the word is not pronounced acceptably, the cards are returned to their original place. When all the cards are gone, the player with the most cards is the winner.

Intensive practice in the application of phonic skills may be provided by using materials in which the vocabulary contains only certain phonic elements (e.g., consonant-short vowel-consonant trigrams; single consonants and particular vowel combinations that represent certain long vowel sounds).

Many other teacher-made games and devices for developing reading skills, particularly word-recognition and decoding skills, can be found in Russell, Karp, and Mueser (1975); The Reading Development Centre (1976a,b); Vail (1976); E. Spache (1982); Herr (1977); Burns and Roe (1979); McCormick and Collins (1981); and Kaye (1988). Canney (1978) suggests ways for turning commercial games into reading games.

Workbooks

The workbooks that accompany commercial reading programs have many pages of practice material on word-recognition and decoding skills. Independent workbook material can be helpful in remedial and corrective work and in teaching children who seem to need a more systematic phonic procedure than a meaning-emphasis approach may provide. It should be clearly understood, however, that simply having a learner complete workbook pages or exercises does not constitute teaching. The child who can complete the task successfully probably has whatever skills are required to perform that task. For the child who cannot perform the task, the teacher must seek to determine *why* he cannot, if the skill is an important one to learn. Even when the student can demonstrate skills in workbook or other exercises, the teacher cannot be assured that the child will apply the new skills in the actual act of reading. Opportunities for doing so must be provided and monitored, with guided practice provided as necessary. Periodic checks must be made to determine if the skills are being employed. The same is true in teaching vocabulary, comprehension, and study skills. The output of phonic workbooks and boxed sets of phonic practice materials has been so great in recent years that a comprehensive listing would run on for pages. In selecting workbooks and exercises, careful consideration should be given to the tasks they require and to the relevance of the tasks for improving word-recognition or decoding ability.

Even if lack of funds prohibits the purchase of consumable workbooks, the resourceful teacher is not entirely prevented from making some use of them. From single copies, which are generally inexpensive, the teacher can get ideas that can be incorporated in board work or developed in duplicated worksheets of her own construction. Note, however, that imitation is permissible, but outright copying is plagiarism and is a violation of the law.

Many successful remedial teachers have developed files of useful practice exercises. They order two copies of each of a number of workbooks and cut them up (two copies are needed because pages are printed on both sides). Each page is mounted on heavy paper or oak tag and can be covered with transparent plastic for permanence. By assembling pages from several workbooks, a comprehensive series of exercises can be built up. Exercises constructed by the teacher can be inserted into the series at any time. A carton or box can be used as a file drawer. The exercises should be classified by type and number within each type. Care in classifying and numbering exercises makes it possible for a student librarian to keep the collection in order and select for each pupil the exercises assigned by the teacher. A separate file of answer keys, corresponding to the exercises, makes it possible for the teacher to correct written work quickly, or for pupils to correct their own work.

Programs and Kits

Programs and kits primarily designed for developmental reading also contain material and procedures that may be used in corrective or remedial work. It should be realized, however, that the pace suggested by the manuals may be inappropriate, the materials may provide too little or too much skill practice, and that the materials require various levels of reading ability. Unless the student is very deficient, it is more efficient to work only on the skills in which she is weak, rather than take her through an entire program. The *Reading Teacher* staff (1978) found that middle-grade, high-ability students performed reasonably well with self-teaching kits; low-ability students did not.

Multimedia Materials

An increasing number of programs, including computer software, use two or more media. Most of these combine tapes or records with one or more forms of reading material. New multimedia learning packages will unquestionably continue to be placed on the market faster than their usefulness can be determined. Because the cost of such materials tends to run high, it is desirable to arrange for a careful local evaluation and, if possible, for a trial use on approval before investing in such programs. When trained remedial personnel are scarce, materials that allow the teacher to give remedial help to more children by providing self-directing and self-checking learning experiences may justify their cost.

A number of films, filmstrips, and recordings are based on children's books. Their main purpose is to motivate children to read. Some tapes dramatize parts of the stories; others record parts of the whole selection with which the children are to read along. Although such materials are apparently used widely, information is lacking regarding how and why taped books are being used in the classroom and how effective they are.

WORD-RECOGNITION METHODS
FOR SEVERE DISABILITIES[4]

Some children have serious, pervasive word-recognition difficulties. After a number of years of schooling, they can recognize or decode only a small number of printed words; a few nonreaders cannot even recognize their names in print. Disabled readers, especially the seriously disabled, are much more likely to have weak word-recognition than basic comprehension problems. Once they "break the code," many disabled readers show progress in reading comprehension.

Choice of Methodology

Cumulative records and interviews should reveal the method(s) used in attempts to teach the child to recognize printed words. Diagnostic testing may indicate that the method was inappropriate for the child or that the child became confused because many different or conflicting methods were used. In the latter situation, it is not uncommon to find that when one method was unsuccessful after a short time, another was initiated. In many cases, there was no coordination between classroom and remedial reading instruction.

What cumulative records and interviews are not likely to reveal is that (1) the pace of the program was too rapid to allow the child to learn and retain the skills; (2) the teacher attempted to present too much for the child to absorb in a lesson; (3) skills were not reinforced or periodically reviewed to check maintenance; (4) opportunities were not provided for the child to apply the skills in reading interesting, connected discourse; and (5) the child simply was not ready to learn the skill at the time it was introduced. For the most part, diagnosis and remediation should be concerned with the child's present abilities and needs.

Basic Instructional Strategies for Remediation

Broadly speaking, there are two basic instructional strategies that are used to teach individuals who have difficulty recognizing printed words. The chief difference between the two lies in when word-recognition instruction is initiated. Whereas in the *direct-treatment strategy* word-recognition instruction is begun almost immediately, in the *indirect-treatment strategy* it is delayed until the pupil has developed adequate "enabling abilities."

Direct-Treatment Strategy

There are two versions of the direct-treatment strategy. They differ in their underlying assumptions and the bases on which the instructional method is chosen.

One version makes no assumptions as to the cognitive abilities needed to learn through a particular instructional method. Rather, the various instructional methods are assumed to place similar cognitive demands on the learner, and

---

[4]According to Pelosi (1982), most current remedial techniques are actually only slight adaptations of those recommended years ago. For example, Huey (1908) mentioned "imitation reading" long before the Neurological Impress Method became popular.

whatever variations exist are handled by modifying instruction. Instruction begins as soon as a viable instructional method is selected. Usually, the choice is based on information gathered through trial teaching (see pages 252–256).

Trial teaching may begin with the method currently being employed to teach word recognition to the child (e.g., a whole-word method). This is done to determine if use of this method is contributing to the child's word-recognition problems. If not, its use may continue, likely with modifications revealed by trial teaching to be necessary for learning (e.g., introducing only one new word in a tutoring session, wording the decoding generalizations so the child can understand and apply them, working in a one-to-one situation). However, even though the child may be able to learn through a method, it may not be the method of choice because the child has an aversion to it (e.g., he associates his reading failure with the method or he finds its procedures tedious) or the method may be very slow and time-consuming (e.g., the VAKT). In such a case, further effort is made to determine if another method is also viable. If the first method assessed it not effective or desirable, another commonly used method (e.g. decoding) is next used in trial teaching. If that proves effective, it is used; if not, the selection process continues.

Some reading specialists prefer to start trial teaching with whichever of the two most commonly used methods (whole-word or decoding) has not been used for instruction in the immediate past. The rationale goes like this—apparently the method being used isn't working, so let's try the other less time-consuming method. If that doesn't work, we'll try one of the more time-consuming ones.

Once the instructional method is begun, what are commonly referred to as readiness activities may take place concurrently with the teaching of word recognition, but these activities usually take up a minor part of the remedial period and are tied as closely as possible to the word-recognition programs. For example, visual-discrimination would emphasize noting the similarities and differences among the letters or words being taught, and auditory discrimination practice would involve the phonemes and words being introduced that day.

After some initial success with a method, other word-recognition skills are taught. For example, if a decoding method is employed initially, a whole-word method is introduced later. If the child cannot learn through a whole-word method, either a VAK or VAKT method (see page 500–504) is used to teach recognition of phonetically irregular words.

The other version of the direct-treatment strategy assumes that matching the instructional method with the student's strong or intact perceptual, psycholinguistic, or cognitive abilities will result in faster and better learning of printed words. Like advocates of the indirect-treatment strategy, followers of this version of the direct-treatment strategy assume that different instructional methods place differing demands on the learner. So, a method is selected that will match the learner's strengths, bypassing or minimizing the need for abilities in which the child is weak. For instance, if modality preference or strength is the ability under consideration, a child with a strong visual preference (a *visual learner*) or with weak auditory abilities (e.g., an *auditory dyslexic*—see D. J. Johnson 1979), or a child with an "articulation and graphomotor dyscoordination syndrome" (see Mattis 1981) would be taught through a whole-word approach, which is assumed to require stronger visual than auditory abilities. A pupil deemed to have strong auditory abilities (an *audile learner*), or weak visual abilities (e.g., a *visual dyslexic*), or with a "language disorder syndrome" would be instructed initially through a decoding method. Students with strong kinesthetic abilities or with a visual-perceptual disorder would learn to use a VAK or VAKT method. Little or no attempt is made to develop weak abilities initially, although such efforts may occur later.

This type of direct treatment, like indirect treatment, is based on three unproven interrelated assumptions: (1) We can validly measure the underlying abilities and distinguish among various types of learners; (2) specific ability strengths are needed for success with a particular instructional method; and (3) different instructional methods make differing demands on the learner. It also appears to assume that nonreading deficiencies of neurological origin are irreversible and cannot be improved by training (Doehring et al. 1981) or that it is more efficient to play to the strengths and bypass the weak processes.

There are measurement problems in distinguishing among various types of learners, and relatively few children can be so classified (E. Miller 1974). Both auditory and visual abilities seem important in almost all methods of teaching word recognition. For example, printed words are visual stimuli, but auditory skills also are required to learn through a whole-word method because an association must be made between the visual and auditory forms of the words. Learning phonics may require a high degree of auditory abilities, but visual skills also must be used because letters must be associated with sounds.

P. G. Aaron, Grantham, and Campbell (1982) claim that a decoding method is more effective than a whole-word method with diseidetics (see page 264). Two studies reported by Satz, Morris, and Fletcher (1988) suggest that disabled readers are more likely to improve their skills when taught through a method that allows them to utilize their strengths than by those that attempt to strengthen their weaknesses. However, because most aptitude-treatment interaction (ATI) studies have not supported basing instruction on modality preference (see pages 90 and 142), the question of whether a learner's traits interact with the instructional method is still open.

Indirect-Treatment Strategy

The second basic strategy, the *indirect-treatment strategy*, involves training what are believed to be prerequisite or facilitative abilities *before* attempting to teach word recognition. The belief is that training perceptual, psycholinguistic, or cognitive abilities will either alleviate the reading problem directly or set the stage for learning to read (Wiederholt & Hale 1982). The basic problem is seen as existing within the child rather than in the reading instruction so initial treatment emphasizes the development of deficient processing abilities. There appears to be a shift away from this process-oriented treatment in the field of learning disabilities.

Weaknesses in the process-oriented viewpoint have been pointed out by Coles (1978, 1987), and Arter and Jenkins (1979), (see page 160). It is difficult to obtain valid measures of the processes thought to cause reading disability and to specify the relationship between deficit processes and reading disability, because most of the processes cannot be observed directly (Doehring et al. 1981). The empirical evidence supporting indirect-treatment programs is not convincing (Beech 1985). None of the reviewers of the research in this area found that emphasis on perceptual, perceptual-motor, or motor training had any advantage over direct teaching of needed reading skills (e.g., H. M. Robinson 1972a; Hammill, Goodman & Wiederholt 1974; Kavale & Forness 1985b). Research findings have not provided sufficient evidence that any of the indirect methods improve reading ability (Wong 1986b). If better reading is the goal of treatment, then reading should be taught directly.

It is possible that process training is a valid procedure for a limited number of individuals. However, it should be coordinated with direct reading instruction (Clements & Barnes 1978). Frostig (1972), whose name is associated with the perceptual-deficit hypothesis, also advocates the simultaneous teaching of specific reading skills according to whatever abilities the child can use, as well as activities to strengthen weak perceptual abilities.

Process-oriented remediation may not have been successful because: (1) the tests and treatments were based on theoretical constructs which have not been adequately defined or whose validity has not been well established (Doehring et al. 1981); or (2) cognitive processes operate in an interrelated and interactive way, not in isolation as suggested by the theories on which the treatments are based; or (3) there is no causal link between a particular processing deficiency and a reading problem (Wong 1986b).

Wilson, Harris, and Harris (1976) found that remediating auditory-perceptual difficulties was not effective in developing word recognition.

The effectiveness of training psycholinguistic skills is questioned by Hammill and Larsen (1974a), but the general conclusion reached by Kavale (1981a) on the basis of a meta-analysis is that psycholinguistic training was effective. Sternberg and Taylor (1982) found several serious methodological and interpretive flaws in Kavale's review and note that even though the differences reached statistical significance, the impact of psycholinguistic training lacked practical significance (the effect was small, especially in light of the amount of time devoted to such instruction). A meta-analysis using six additional studies to those employed by Kavale led Larsen, Parker, and Hammill (1982) to reaffirm their position: "To date, the cumulative results of the relevant research (no matter how they are statistically analyzed) have failed to demonstrate clearly that psycholinguistic training has value. Consequently, programs and techniques designed to improve the types of skills measured by the *Illinois Test of Psycholinguistic Ability* (ITPA) should continue to be viewed with caution and monitored with care." More recently, Kavale and Forness (1985) write that psycholinguistic training was effective for a few of the areas measured by ITPA.

Multisensory Techniques

Pupils who are unable to recognize words after painstaking teaching efforts, likely have failed to develop a mental image of the words that can be recalled at a later time. Many severely disabled readers first perceive a word in a very incomplete and hazy fashion, and additional exposures to the printed word do little to improve their first impression. In some cases the initial perception is fairly good, but the child has little or no visual image of the word when she closes her eyes and tries to "see" it mentally.

Methods that have generally succeeded with such severe cases involve the use of additional sensory and perceptual cues that lend vividness to the visual image of the word so that it can be stored and retrieved from memory.

THE KINESTHETIC METHOD.　In 1921 Grace M. Fernald and Helen B. Keller described a method that emphasizes tracing and writing as basic procedures for teaching nonreaders. The following description of the method is based on the account given in Fernald's book (1943):

Description.　At first the child is asked to tell the teacher a few words he would like to learn. These are taught one by one. As soon as a few words have been learned, the child is encouraged to compose a little story and is taught any words in the story that are not already known. At first the compositions are dictated to the teacher and later they are written by the child. After the story has been read in written form, it is typed so that the child can read it the next day in printed form. The child's own compositions are the only materials used until a fairly large sight vocabulary has been learned.

The method of teaching words changes as the child's ability to learn words improves. Four stages are distinguished.

Stage 1. Tracing.　The word is written for the child on a strip of paper about 4 inches by 10 inches, preferably in large cursive writing. The child traces the word, with his finger in contact with the paper, saying each syllable of the word as it is traced. This is repeated until the child can reproduce the motions of writing the word from memory. He writes it on scrap paper and then in his story. Later the story is typed and read in typed form. The child places each new word that is learned in an alphabetical file. The following points of techniques are stressed: (1) Finger contact is important; tracing in the air or with a pencil is less useful; (2) the child should never copy a word, but always writes from memory; (3) the word should always be written as a unit; (4) the child must say each syllable of the word either to himself or out loud as he traces it and writes it; and (5) whatever he writes must be typed and read before too long an interval; this practice provides transfer from the written to the printed form.

Stage 2. Writing without tracing.　After a while (days in some cases, weeks in others) the child does not need to trace most new words. He looks at the word in script, says it to himself several times, tries to "see" the word with his eyes shut, and writes it from memory. If he makes an error, he compares his result with the model, paying particular attention to the part or parts he missed. This is repeated until he can write the word correctly from memory. Index cards with the words in both script and print form are substituted for the large words strips and are filed alphabetically. Essentially this procedure is the same as the VAK method described on page 502–503.

Stage 3. Recognition in print.　It becomes unnecessary to write each new word on a card. The child looks at the word in print, is told what it says, pronounces it once or twice, and writes it from memory. Reading in books is usually started about the time that this stage is reached.

Stage 4. Word analysis.　The child begins to identify new words by noting their resemblance to known words, and it is no longer necessary to teach each new word. Although phonic sounding of single letters is not taught, skill in word analysis gradually develops through noticing grapheme-phoneme correspondences that are met repeatedly.

Total nonreaders are started at Stage 1; children with partial disabilities are often started at Stage 2. No special techniques are used to overcome such difficulties as reversals or omissions; these are believed to drop out without special attention, since the tracing-writing process enforces a consistent left-to-right direction and requires correct reproduction of the entire word.

Unique features in Fernald's method are the emphasis on tracing and writing, the teaching of difficult as well as easy words from the beginning, the use of the child's own compositions as the only reading material in the early stages, and the beginning of book reading at a fairly difficult level.

Although research evidence regarding its effectiveness is equivocal and inconclusive, the kinesthetic method has produced successful results with many severe disability cases who had histories of repeated failure (Myers 1978). In addition to the many cases in Fernald's book, cases using the Fernald approach have been described by Kress and Johnson (1970), Berres and Eyer (1970), and Cotterell (1972).

The approach has several desirable features: (1) It enforces careful and systematic observation and study of words; (2) it makes necessary a consistent left-to-right direction in reading; (3) it provides adequate repetition; (4) errors are immediately noted and corrected; (5) progress can be noted by the child at practically every lesson; and (6) the sensory impressions from tracing, writing, and saying the words reinforce visual impressions.

Nevertheless, there are several limitations of the use of the kinesthetic method as outlined by Fernald:

1. The teacher has to direct and check every step in the child's work and teach every new word until the child has progressed far along the road to skilled reading. During the early stages, the child is unable to do any independent reading. The method is well suited for use in a special clinic school such as the one supervised by Fernald, in which the children were with the remedial teacher for a full school day 5 days a week, but is not so well adapted to a remedial setup in which the child has only a small number of remedial periods each week.
2. The majority of nonreaders can learn to recognize words by methods that are faster than the cumbersome tracing-writing procedure. The VAK method of word study (Fernald's Stage 2) is often helpful, however.
3. We see no advantage in avoiding the use of easy books in the early stages of remedial work unless the child has a strong resistance to them. It is desirable to start reading in books as early as possible, even if pre-primers must be used, provided the child's cooperation can be obtained and the words are pretaught.

It has become customary to call tracing methods VAKT (visual-auditory-kinesthetic-tactual) methods. Actually, the child (1) sees the teacher write the word; (2) hears the teacher say the word; (3) says the word; (4) hears himself say the word; (5) feels the movements made as he traces the word; (6) feels the surface with his fingertips as he traces; (7) sees his hand move as he traces; and (8) says and hears himself say the word (or syllables) as he traces.

Witman and Riley (1978) describe a method that differs from Fernald's in a number of ways, including tracing the word written in chalk (thereby allowing easy detection of faulty tracing) and spelling the word after pronouncing it. Other authors have suggested such variations as tracing over the raised effect created by writing the word on a screen with a crayon, tracing the word in the air with the eyes opened or closed, and tracing the word in a sand tray. No data suggest which variation is likely to work best, but observational reports suggest the VAKT is more successful with children aged 8 and above (Miccinati 1979) than with younger children. Knowing a number of variations and ways to reinforce initial learnings increases the likelihood of success with the VAKT method.

Various explanations have been offered as to why a VAKT approach is effective for some learners. Hulme (1981a) concludes that tracing verbal material benefits disabled readers because they are reluctant or unable to use phonological coding and, instead, rely heavily on a visual code. Tracing is thought to improve visual-memory processes.

Peters (1981) hypothesizes that a VAKT method could work with children who do not have clearly defined functional lateralization of the hemispheres for the processes involved in reading and spelling. His reasoning is that use of kinesthetic and tactile components forces a clear lateralization of the visual and auditory processes. Whereas the auditory and visual sensory channels provide information to both hemispheres simultaneously, kinesthetic and tactile information is transmitted only to the contralateral hemisphere. Thus, when the left hand is stimulated kinesthetically and/or by touch, the information is registered in the right hemisphere.

Thorpe and Borden (1985) theorize that a VAKT method might be effective because: (1) it provides maximum sensory input to the brain; (2) kinesthetic and tactile sensory input compensates for weak visual or auditory input; (3) the auditory, kinesthetic, and tactile information provides support for visual information; and (4) following the VAKT procedure requires the child to attend to the task, and on-task behavior increases the likelihood of learning.

VISUAL-MOTOR METHOD. Many children do not need extensive practice in tracing but are helped greatly by a visual-motor, or VAK (visual-auditory-kinesthetic), method that combines visual observation while saying the word with writing the word from memory. The procedure is as follows:

1. Select a few unknown words to teach. Words may be from the story about to be read, from an experience story, or simply words that the child wants to learn.
2. Introduce each word in meaningful context; check the child's understanding of its meaning(s) (it may be used in a less common manner); and teach the meaning if necessary.
3. Present the word in a printed sentence, emphasize the word as in the whole-word method.
4. Pronounce the word while holding up a word card. As the child looks

carefully at the word, he pronounces it aloud softly and then a few times to himself. Caution the child not to spell the word letter by letter.

5. Tell the child to shut his eyes and try to "make a picture" (visual image) of the printed word (not the object it represents). Tell him to open his eyes and compare his mental image with the original model on the card.

6. Cover or remove the word card and tell the child to print (or write) the word.

7. Expose the word card and have the child compare his reproduction with the original, paying particular attention to any parts not reproduced accurately.

8. Repeat the process until the child can reproduce the word correctly from memory.

9. Teach the other words in the same way.

10. Shuffle the word cards and use them to provide practice in recognizing the new words, and later to develop speed of recognition.

11. Have the children read the words in meaningful context.

After using the VAK method for a month or so, children usually no longer need to write the word in order to remember it. At this point, the whole-word method may be introduced. Gradually, phonic skills also should be developed.

The VAK or VAKT methods may also be used selectively to teach specific words (e.g., *when, then*) that are causing problems for the child. Some workbooks provide large copies of the words for tracing as part of their regular instructional procedures.

According to Fernald, who originated it, the VAK method is a modified kinesthetic procedure in which the motor imagery of the movements involved in writing the word reinforces the auditory-visual association between the sound of the word and its printed form. The kinesthetic element is probably of minor importance. It seems likely that writing helps the child remember the word because the printed form must be perceived correctly in all its details in order to reproduce it accurately. The method seems to work as well whether the child prints the work, writes it, or types it. Whatever the true explanation may turn out to be, many children who have difficulty learning through a whole-word or phonic method can learn and remember words when a visual-motor method is employed.

Roberts and Coleman (1958) found that poor readers who had normal visual perception were not aided by kinesthetic cues. Berres (1967) found that motoric reinforcement did not help disadvantaged disabled readers in speed of learning, but did improve their long-time retention; tracing and writing helped more than writing without tracing, and both improved retention over visual study without motor reinforcement. On the other hand, Vandever and Neville (1972–1973) report that poor readers tended to learn more words when visual and auditory cues were stressed than when tracing cues were emphasized. Ofman and Schaevitz (1963) compare two tracing methods with learning nonsense syllables through a whole-word method. Tracing with the eye was as effective as tracing with the finger; both were superior to "look-and-say." They speculate that enforced attention to details in sequence rather than tactual-kinesthetic sensation is the significant aid to learning. This would seem to explain the success of VAK for many children; it does not rule out the need for VAKT by a few.

Zorotovich (1979) reports the unique case of a left-handed child who seemed unable to learn by tracing with his left hand. She tried having him trace with his right hand, which was easy for him; but he could not write legibly with that hand. He began to make real progress when she had him trace with the right hand and write with the left.

"Blind" Tracing and Writing

A little-researched procedure involves tracing three-dimensional letters while blindfolded and drawing letters on the child's back (Blau & Blau 1968). The rationale offered for this auditory, kinesthetic, tactile (AKT) "modality blocking" technique is that it allows development of clear kinesthetic perception, imagery, and memory without interference from deficient or distorted visual perception. Blau and Loveless (1982) suggest use of the tactile modality with severely disabled spellers. Based on the assumption that it makes use of right-hemisphere processing, two fingers on the left hand are used to trace the letters while blindfolded. Such a procedure *might* work in some cases because it avoids neurological overloading, which may happen in an immature or damaged brain when several sensory avenues are stimulated simultaneously (D. J. Johnson 1979). Of course, after the "feel" of the word has been learned, it will still be necessary to build a visual-kinesthetic association. Frostig (1965) also recommends a blind-writing procedure for use with children who have inferior visual perception.

A comparison of VAKT, AKT, and other methods did not indicate any superiority for any of the methods when used with children in a special education class (Koepsel 1974). On the basis of his short, small-scale study, Maginnis (1986) concludes that if the AKT method had any value at all, it was probably as a change of pace. Nevertheless, this procedure deserves further study, particularly in very severe cases in which progress with VAKT or with phonics is extremely slow.

Methods Based on Sounding Out and Blending

Some reading specialists, particularly those influenced by S. T. Orton, advocate synthetic-phonics methods through which children are taught to make symbol-sound associations and to blend the resulting phonemes into words (i.e., how to "sound out" words). The instructional method may also be supplemented by use of kinesthetic procedures. Refer to J. Orton (1966) for a clear and relatively brief summary of Orton's point of view, or to the lengthy and detailed manual (Gillingham & Stillman 1966), which has been the main training textbook for followers of Orton. Programs that adapt the approach for use in the primary grades have been developed by Slingerland (1976) and Traub (1982). J. Orton (1976) and Cox (1977) have written somewhat briefer manuals on how to use the Orton approach. Research on the Orton-Gillingham approach has been extremely limited (Ansara 1982).

The basic common features of the approaches used by followers of Orton have been briefly summarized by J. Orton (1966, p.144) as follows:

Their common conceptual background can usually be seen in their introduction of the kinesthetic element to reinforce the visual-auditory language associations and to establish left-to-right habits of progression. Their phonetic approach is generally the same: teaching the phonic units in isolation but giving special training in blending; introducing the consonants and the short sounds of the vowels first and building three-letter words with them for reading and spelling; programming the material in easy, orderly, cumulative steps.

According to Gillingham and Stillman (1966), the method requires five lessons a week for a minimum of two years. Drill on symbol-sound associations and blending is the main activity for many weeks. The first group of correspondences taught includes *a, b, f, h, i, j, k, m, p, t*. After these have been learned (usually not more than one new association a day) and used in blending and spelling short words, simple sentences using only words containing these letters may be introduced. Gillingham prefers to sound the initial consonant and vowel together, then add the final consonant (/ba/ /t/). She emphasizes the importance of simultaneous oral spelling (saying the sounds in sequence, then saying the letter names in sequence while writing them). Kinesthetic procedures are used to teach words with irregular grapheme-phoneme relationships. Other points stressed by Gillingham include the following: (1) Parents are advised to read all homework to the pupil until she becomes able to read with reasonable fluency; (2) teachers are asked to excuse the child from written tests and to test her orally; and (3) independent reading is not allowed until the major part of the phonic program has been covered.

If, on the basis of diagnostic testing and sample lesson tryouts, it seems likely that a child may make more rapid progress with a systematic phonic approach than with a whole-word or kinesthetic method, many different phonic systems can be used with success. The considerations that apply when phonics is used for remedial work are no different from those that apply in developmental instruction. At this point, therefore, it is desirable to review pages 462–470. As much practice as possible should be given in applying phonic skills in meaningful context rather than concentrating on drill with isolated words. As soon as is feasible, words that have to be sounded out should be practiced for immediate sight recognition.

For the majority of reading disability cases, phonic instruction is more effective when it is used in combination with other procedures than when it is made the almost exclusive method of learning words. With some children, however, previously disappointing progress becomes very rapid when they are changed to a systematic phonic method and when instruction is paced to their ability to master the skills.

Methods Stressing Visual Analysis and Visualizing

In addition to the kinesthetic and phonic methods just described, there is a third basic method that emphasizes visual analysis and visualizing. Such a procedure is described and advocated by Gates (1947). Words are taught as wholes, and illustrations are used freely as ways of introducing and giving clues to words. The pupil is encouraged to close his eyes and visualize words, first part by part in left-to-right order, and then as wholes. Then he is asked to pronounce the word softly, part by part, while writing it; this is essentially the VAK procedure. Phonic work and writing are used as supplementary devices when pupils seem not to be progressing satisfactorily without them. Familiarity with word elements is developed through finding similarities and differences in words already learned.

Essentially this program is similar to that used for teaching normal beginners with most basal readers. It differs mainly in that the pupil's learning is more carefully supervised and more attention is devoted to making sure that new words are really learned than is the case in most classroom teaching. The program assumes that the child has the capacity to learn as normal readers do, but has been handicapped by such factors as immaturity when first exposed to reading instruction, inefficient teaching, or something else that does not affect the child's present learning ability.

A Combination Method

The vast majority of children with reading disabilities do not have special cognitive or neurological defects; the disability results from causes such as lack of reading readiness when first exposed to reading instruction, uncorrected sensory defects, discouragement, emotional problems, and poor teaching that is sometimes aggravated by linguistic and cultural mismatches between teachers and pupils. Therefore, remedial work with these cases should not be radically different from the general methods used with primary-grade children.

The majority of severe cases of reading disability (those who are reading at the first-reader level or below) show inattention to details in visual perception and have poor phonic aptitude. Such children can be started at the beginning of the easiest preprimer in an unfamiliar set of readers, using the "begin-over" explanation to make the low-level materials acceptable. In the "begin-over" procedure, the teacher explains the reasons for using the "easy" books in the basal-reader series employed in the core curriculum. The children are told the importance of learning the words in these books, and that they will probably learn them more easily now that they are older, and smarter. Instruction should not be paced as slowly in a developmental reading program once basic skills have been mastered.

These children need to be carefully pretaught the new words that they will meet in the next few pages of connected reading. Each new word is printed on a card and studied by a whole-word or VAK method, whichever seems to suit the child better. After a few words have been taught, the cards are shuffled and reviewed. The child then reads the connected material in which the new words appear and reviews the new-word cards again. The workbook provides practice in matching the few words in the preprimer vocabulary with pictures; between the repetitions in the workbook and those in the preprimer, the child learns the words by being prompted every time she stumbles or forgets. The number of repetitions needed to learn new words gradually lessens. The cards are reviewed in the next few lessons. When the child recognizes a word without prompting, a little checkmark is made on the back of the card. Three checks, on different days, indicate that the word has been learned.

Rather than depend exclusively or primarily on a whole-word method, phonics is taught early and systematically. However, the majority of reading disabled children require a good deal of phonic readiness work before they can begin to apply phonics in word recognition. By the time the child has finished reading one or two preprimers, she has usually become sound conscious and pays attention to initial consonants. Readiness activities (see pages 456–460) may be continued throughout the phonics program. Systematic teaching of phonics accompanies the use of a primer and first and second readers, with adaptations for individual differences. Some children catch on to blending and can learn to use a "single-letter phonics" procedure, Others never become proficient at blending and are taught decoding through the use of a large number of phonograms or by initial consonant-vowel combinations.

On the other hand, some children seem, right from the start, to have excellent phonic aptitude. With such children, it seems sensible to follow a synthetic phonic procedure with emphasis on the teaching of symbol-sound associations and blending. Phonetically irregular words have to be learned by these children also, and many of them need the VAK method because they lack success with a whole-word method. A hard part of the remedial job is to persuade some children to give up the practice of spelling words letter by letter, in favor of a sounding-out procedure.

Few children that we have seen needed tracing of the sort emphasized by Fernald. The VAK method has been helpful to many, however, and supplementary practice in writing words from dictation on paper and at the board has been used considerably.

When resistance to the reading textbooks normally used in first or second grade is strong, it is advisable to give up the books entirely for the time being, using instead a combination of experience stories and teacher-devised material. In such cases, much time can be spent in the early stages playing word-recognition or decoding games. If a typewriter or computer is available, the opportunity to use it is welcomed by most children. Children are started on easy books as soon as they are receptive to their use.

Other Materials and Methods

Linguistic basal-reader programs stress regularity of spelling patterns and, in beginning reading material, use words with irregular grapheme-phoneme relationships only as necessary (see page 77). Such materials can be used with disabled readers, with emphasis on spelling patterns in whole words, and can also be employed as supplementary reading in a synthetic-phonics program. Their possible value in the initial stages of instruction lies in the consistency of the symbol-sound association in the words employed, particularly for vowels. The child does not have to decide which of the possible sounds a letter represents, and massive practice on the associations is provided. Contrary to their use in developmental reading, many remedial teachers provide direct instruction in symbol-sound association *before* the element is met in the program. The possible disadvantages to linguistic basal-reader materials are: (1) some children are confused by the repetitiveness of only short-vowel words; (2) the language structure and story content are restricted and often artificial; and (3) no set for diversity is established. As yet no research on the value of linguistic readers in remedial reading has appeared.

A "massive oral decoding technique" makes simultaneous use of several series of linguistic readers (R. J. Johnson, Johnson & Kerfoot 1972). After a spelling pattern has been introduced with one series, the pages emphasizing the same pattern in several other series are read before introducing a new pattern. The teacher guides oral reading of selection after selection, providing reinforcement of correct decoding responses. No phonic generalizations are taught, and no comprehension questions are asked. R. J. Johnson, Johnson, and Kerfoot indicate that the procedure is effective across a considerable range of disabled readers. Janicke (1981) reports that the technique was successful with 10 disabled readers in the seventh and eighth grades.

Material printed in i.t.a. has also been used in remedial reading. Gardner (1966) reports that it worked better with disabled readers with at least average intelligence than with mentally slower children. Mazurkiewicz (1966) recommends the use of i.t.a. in remedial reading, but presents little evidence in support of his claims. The problems that might arise when disabled readers learn to read in i.t.a. and then must transfer to the conventional alphabet have not been studied sufficiently.

Two systems that use color as a clue to grapheme-phoneme relationships have been described and advocated for use as remedial materials by their originators (Bannatyne 1966, Gattegno & Hinman 1966). As yet there is no well-controlled research on the value of these color systems in remedial teaching. Other authors, such as Frostig (1965, 1972), recommend color coding the letters to aid in learning symbol-sound associations. Attention can be focused on a grapheme by coloring it differently from the rest of the word.

Programmed instruction would seem to have considerable promise in remedial reading, particularly in providing self-correcting work that the pupil can do while the teacher is working with another child or group. The principle is attractive, but the remedial value of any particular set of programmed materials still needs to be verified. Programmed tutoring, shown to be effective with slow first graders when provided by paraprofessionals (Ellson, P. Harris & Barber 1968), can be helpful when volunteers or aides can be trained to employ it.

In the *Neurological Impress Method* (NIM) (Heckelman 1969), the teacher and student read aloud simultaneously for 15 minutes daily. The teacher, who is slightly behind the child, directs her voice into the student's ear. As the words are spoken, the teacher, and later the child, slides her finger along smoothly under the words. No attention is called to the pictures, no direct attempt is made to teach word recognition or decoding, and comprehension is not checked. The material is reread until fluency is attained by the pupil. The simultaneous seeing of the printed word and hearing the spoken word supposedly produces a neurological memory trace.

According to Kann (1983), research findings regarding the effectiveness of NIM are mixed; but Bos (1982) states that, for the most part, its use has resulted in significant gains in both word recognition and comprehension for disabled readers. Bos also indicates, however, that the studies often lacked control groups and used small samples, and that NIM may be more effective for severely than for moderately disabled readers. Henk (1983) suggests replacing the guided silent reading step in the directed reading activity with NIM.

Other "listening-reading" or "read along" or "imitative reading" techniques have three elements in common: (1) The reading is modeled either by a person or a tape; (2) the line of print is tracked by the child with a finger or marker; and (3) the child reads the same material to which he has listened (Janiak 1983). According to Henk, Helfeldt, and Platt (1986), imitative reading improves word-recognition accuracy and encourages proper phrasing and intonation. In *Prime-O-Tec* (Jordan 1967), which is an adaptation of NIM, individuals or groups listen to a taped story through earphones while following the written text with their finger. *Echo reading* (B. Anderson 1981) involves the teacher reading the material to the child, who then repeats (echoes) it; later the child listens to a taped story while reading it. In C. Chomsky's (1978) technique, the child listens to a tape while reading and rereads the story until it can be read fluently to the teacher. Stage 1 of *assisted reading* is like echo reading. In Stage 2 the teacher reads to the child and pauses at words that she thinks the child can recognize; the child is instructed to pronounce the word when the teacher pauses. During Stage 3, the child reads orally and the teacher supplies help as needed. Assisted reading has been promoted by Hoskisson (1979) as a supplementary procedure for initial reading instruction. Cunningham (1988) offers suggestions for working with older pupils who have severe word-recognition problems.

The Choice of Method

Although we may have knowledge of individual differences among children, possession of such knowledge is not particularly helpful in selecting the best instructional procedure in advance of actual tutoring. Currently, no reliable guidelines indicate how student characteristics will interact with a particular method. With many children, it is helpful to try brief sample lessons with each of several word-recognition procedures (see pages 252–256) in order to determine which method should be used initially. As lessons proceed, the child's rate of learning and emotional responsiveness should guide the teacher in modifying instruction.

The remedial teacher must be resourceful. If the pupil has not made adequate progress after a fair attempt to utilize one method, he must be willing to try something else. Adapting to the pupil's needs is far more important than devotion to a particular procedure. For most case, the preferable strategy is to use a method that takes advantage of the child's relatively strong abilities and minimizes use of his weak ones and at the same time provides training to develop the weak abilities without postponing reading instruction.

It seems likely that any remedial program in word recognition that provides good motivation, ensures careful observation of words and word parts, and enforces consistent left-to-right habits in reading will succeed in most cases. The specific details of the method are less important than the fact that the major objectives are attained in one way or another.

14 Reading Comprehension I: Vocabulary Development and Sentence Comprehension

Reading comprehension is typically a slowly developing ability. Achievement varies enormously, but the average student takes about 14 years to progress from just above the Basic Level to a level of competence just above Adept.[1] For most pupils who achieve above the 50th percentile, the rate of development is fairly constant. For those below the median in performance, progress in reading comprehension falls further and further behind that of their age peers as they get older (Carroll 1987).

Some of the factors associated with reading comprehension, including word recognition, have been covered in previous chapters. This chapter is the first of four concerned with understanding and improving reading comprehension. In this chapter, we devote our attention to vocabulary development because word-meaning knowledge influences reading comprehension. Sentence comprehension is discussed because understanding single sentences and their relationships enables one to comprehend longer units of discourse.

VOCABULARY DEVELOPMENT

Types of Vocabulary

The four types of vocabulary include listening, reading, speaking, and writing. The former two are referred to as *receptive vocabularies;* the latter two, as *expressive vocabularies. Listening vocabulary* includes all the spoken words a

[1]Refer to page 118 for a description of these levels.

510

person can understand. Its acquisition begins early in life and increases greatly during the school years. Listening vocabulary usually serves as a basis for the development of other types of vocabulary. *Reading vocabulary* encompasses all the printed words that a reader can recognize and whose meanings she understands. Word meanings acquired through reading are often added to one's listening vocabulary. *Speaking vocabulary* includes all the words a person can use appropriately in oral communication. Individuals usually know the meanings of more words than they commonly use in speaking. *Writing vocabulary* encompasses all the words a person can use appropriately in composing a written text.

The Word-Recognition/ Word-Identification Continuum

Novice readers can understand the meanings of thousands of spoken words, but they can recognize relatively few of their printed forms. Their listening vocabularies far surpass their reading vocabularies. Therefore, in the early stages of reading instruction, the emphasis is on helping children to recognize printed words whose meanings are already known. There is little need to teach word meanings, at least in the materials used for reading instruction, because the vast majority of the words used in the textbooks were selected because their meanings were probably known. Once the printed forms of words whose meanings are already known can be recognized, the child can access their meanings, so word recognition quickly leads to word identification. The typical child takes about 3–4 years to learn to recognize the 3,000 words and their derivatives that can be recognized by about 80% of fourth graders (Chall 1987).

By the third or fourth grade, children begin to encounter an increasing number of words whose printed forms they cannot recognize immediately and whose meanings are unknown (Nagy 1988), as well as printed words that represent meanings other than their most common ones. The teaching/learning task shifts from primarily one of word recognition to word identification. At about Grades 3–4, a shift also takes place in pupils' ability to define words.

Children's Definitional Abilities

Children's early attempts to define words are more like descriptions of things and events than they are like definitions. Their early "definitions" emphasize functional characteristics of the referent, rather than the word's meaning (e.g., *cat:* "You pet it"). At about age five or six, the structure of their definitions begins to change. Subordinate categories begin to replace functional definitions, and their definitions become more elaborate, complete, and closer to dictionary definitions (e.g., *cat:* "It's an animal"). Such paradigmatic responses predominate until age ten (Watson & Olson 1987). After that, children's definitions move from the concrete to the more abstract and general, and pupils can define more abstract words (Chall 1987).

Estimates of Vocabulary Size

Vocabulary size is estimated by sampling word-meaning knowledge and inferring, from the obtained data, the number of additional words whose meanings would probably have been known had they been tested. All four types of vocabulary have been estimated. Only listening and reading vocabulary are considered here.

Estimates by various researchers of the average number of words, the meanings of which are known at a given age or grade level, vary considerably (Nagy & Anderson 1984). For instance, such estimates range from 3,562 to 26,000 words at Grade 1; from 2,000 to 25,000 at Grade 3; and from 4,750 to 51,000 at Grade 7 (Anderson & Freebody 1985). Various factors probably account for such diverse findings, including what was counted as a "word" (e.g., only root words vs. root words plus their inflected and derived forms) and differences in the ways in which word-meaning knowledge was sampled (e.g., generating a definition vs. multiple-choice items).

What is meant by "knowing the meaning of a word"? Many English words have a number of meanings, and some serve different grammatical functions. Yet vocabulary-size studies, as well as almost all vocabulary tests, consider only *extensiveness or breadth of vocabulary;* that is, the number of words for which one appropriate meaning (usually the word's most common meaning) can be indicated. *Depth of vocabulary* (the number of meanings known per word) and *flexibility* (the ability to select the appropriate meaning of a word in a given context) are rarely considered;[2] yet both are important factors in reading comprehension.

Despite differences in estimated vocabulary size, vocabulary knowledge grows rapidly during the school years. Pupils appear to learn an average of about 3,000 words annually, so that the average high-school senior is estimated to have a vocabulary of about 40,000 words (Nagy & Herman 1987). Word meanings may be acquired through self-instruction (e.g., looking up word meanings in a dictionary); through direct instruction (e.g., children are told definitions and/or provided with labeled examples); or through indirect learning—the use of spoken or written context or morphological analysis (e.g., knowing the meaning of *refer* allows one to deduce the meanings of such derivations as *reference* and *referral*). Exactly how, and the extent to which, each method contributes to vocabulary development is largely unknown. Vocabulary development probably involves the methods' combined use, but it is likely that most word meanings are acquired through indirect learning.

Self-instruction probably accounts for only a small share of newly-acquired words meanings, and only about 200–300 of the new words acquired annually could be attributed to direct instruction (Nagy, Herman & Anderson 1985b). The time required to produce vocabulary learning and the available instructional time preclude acquisition of large numbers of words through direct instruction. Moreover, direct vocabulary instruction in schools seems to be sparse and not particularly effective (Jenkins & Dixon 1983). Therefore, pupils must learn most new word meanings by inferring them from context while listening and reading (Nagy, Herman & Anderson 1985b; Nagy, Anderson & Herman 1987).

FACTORS THAT INFLUENCE VOCABULARY SIZE.   At every level of development, children show large differences in vocabulary size. For instance, children scoring at the 25th percentile might know the meanings of about 4,500

---

[2]Breadth of vocabulary is a prerequisite for flexibility.

words; those at the 50th percentile, about 5,400 (Nagy & Herman 1984). Among the reasons for wide differences in vocabulary size are intellectual ability, experiences, and motivation.

Intelligence is highly related to vocabulary size and the rate at which new word meanings are acquired. Low verbal intelligence generally leads to delayed and limited language development and to difficulty understanding and acquiring word meanings, particularly those that represent abstract or complex concepts. Compared with children with less learning capacity, bright pupils are more likely to profit from instruction, to make more effective use of context, to learn new word meanings, and to read more widely and often. Thus, they are likely to know the meanings of many more words and more meanings of a specific word, as well as how to select the most appropriate meaning of a multiple-meaning word. When older children of the same chronological age are asked to define a word, bright students tend to give abstract or generalized definitions; slow learners, to define words in terms of use or function.

Experience also plays a role in vocabulary growth and size. Individuals who have been intellectually stimulated, exposed to a rich and varied vocabulary and to a variety of experiences, and who have had extensive practice using spoken and written language are more likely to have more extensive and deeper vocabularies than those who have not. Speech and hearing problems can also interfere with vocabulary acquisition because they cut off many opportunities to learn from oral language experiences.

Vocabulary size also varies with SES. For instance, whereas the reading vocabularies of middle-class children were estimated to be 2,711, 4,038, and 4,656 words in Grades 1, 2, and 3, respectively; those of disadvantaged pupils were 1,791, 2,800, and 2,842 words (Graves, Brunetti & Slater 1982).

Children who easily and successfully acquire new word meanings are apt to be motivated to learn even more words, especially if they are reinforced in some way. Those who see little use in increasing their vocabularies or who find it difficult to do so are much less likely to have extensive word-meaning knowledge.

Vocabulary Knowledge and Reading Comprehension

Vocabulary knowledge plays an important role in models of the reading process. It has been theorized that, as word meanings are accessed from our mental lexicons or are revealed by context, they are integrated to form in our minds representations of clauses and sentences. These integrations are guided by syntactic knowledge. The clauses and sentences are organized systematically to form an encompassing representation of the entire discourse (Danks & End 1987). At the least, word-meaning knowledge would seem to allow us to gain a more complete understanding of the text than if word meanings were vaguely known, and rapid access to accurate word meanings could greatly facilitate comprehension. On the other hand, reading comprehension would suffer if most of the word meanings or a few key word meanings were unknown. Indeed, evidence indicates that, although pupils may be able to obtain a rough understanding of text that contains a high proportion of unknown words, they are more likely to have difficulty comprehending and recalling central and supporting information (Stahl et al. 1989).

The statistical relationship between vocabulary knowledge and reading comprehension is well documented. Factor analytic studies have consistently shown that word-meaning knowledge accounts for substantial proportions of the variance in reading comprehension, with vocabulary factor loadings ranging from 0.41 to 0.93 (Mezynski 1983). Moderate to high correlations between vocabulary and reading comprehension have also been reported. For example, in his study of reading comprehension in 15 countries, Thorndike (1973) found median correlations of 0.71, 0.75, and 0.66 for 10-, 14-, and 17-year-olds, respectively.

A definite cause-effect relationship between vocabulary knowledge and reading comprehension has not been firmly established, in part because vocabulary, comprehension, and cognitive ability are so highly intercorrelated (Calfee & Drum 1985). For example, there are robust correlations (0.71–0.98) between vocabulary and general intelligence (Anderson & Freebody 1985).

There are four main theories regarding the relationship between vocabulary and reading comprehension. The *instrumentalist theory* posits that vocabulary has an enabling effect on reading comprehension. Greater knowledge of word meanings enables better comprehension of language. This theory predicts that reading comprehension can be increased either by replacing words whose meanings are likely unknown with synonyms whose meanings are known, or by teaching the meanings of difficult or unknown words before the text is read.

Research findings suggest that replacing difficult with easy words improves text comprehension (e.g., Stahl & Jacobson 1986), but the effect of this practice is seldom large and a number of words have to be replaced to improve comprehension (M. Graves 1986).

Reviewers (e.g., Mezynski 1983, Ruddell 1986) typically report that research findings regarding the effect of vocabulary instruction on reading comprehension are mixed or inconclusive. Some of the studies actually deal with word recognition, not with word meaning. A distinction may also need to be made between the effect of vocabulary instruction on comprehension of text containing all the target words and of novel text in which only some of the target words appear. A meta-analysis of 52 studies led Stahl and Fairbanks (1986) to conclude that vocabulary instruction has a significant positive effect on the comprehension of passages containing the target words but only a slight transfer effect.

According to the *knowledge theory*, prior knowledge serves as the basis for both vocabulary and comprehension ability and thus accounts for the relationship between the two (Nagy & Anderson 1984). This theory assumes that vocabulary size indicates the number of concepts understood, and because concepts are derived from experiences, a large vocabulary indicates considerable likelihood that an individual has had experiences that can be drawn upon to understand written texts. Children who understand words relevant to a specific topic are likely to have the topical knowledge needed to understand the text. Advocates of this theory would devote school time to building up children's knowledge through first-hand and vicarious experiences.

The *aptitude theory* states that word knowledge and reading comprehension are indicators of cognitive ability, which to a large extent determines one's level of ability in each. The theory suggests that highly intelligent pupils have

larger vocabularies and higher reading abilities than those with low learning aptitude.

A fourth view holds that there is a *reciprocal relationship* between word-
meaning knowledge and reading comprehension. Pupils who have large vocabularies are good readers who read extensively; in doing so, they increase their
vocabulary knowledge and become even better readers. Students with inadequate vocabularies read slowly and with difficulty. For them, reading becomes
less enjoyable because they have to expend increasingly more time and effort to
read material that gets more and more difficult for them. They avoid reading and,
as a result of having less practice, they have slower vocabulary development. This
inhibits their growth in reading comprehension ability, and the gap in achievement between good and poor readers widens (Perfetti 1985, Stanovich 1986b).

Probably no one of the aforementioned theories alone accounts completely
for the word meaning/comprehension relationship, and all may contain part of
the "truth."

**WHY VOCABULARY INSTRUCTION MAY FAIL TO IMPROVE READING
COMPREHENSION.**   The possible reasons why vocabulary instruction fails to
improve reading comprehension fall into five general overlapping categories:
the level of word meaning needed to improve comprehension, the word meanings taught, the number of word meanings that must be known, the need for
additional skill improvement, and the way in which the influence of vocabulary
instruction on comprehension is measured. A distinction also needs to be drawn
between improving the understanding of the text in which the target words appear and increasing a pupil's general level of reading ability. The latter would
call for a significant transfer effect.

Most vocabulary instruction fails to produce the level of word meaning
needed to improve reading comprehension. Reading comprehension depends
on having a wealth of encyclopedic knowledge (e.g., knowing a great deal about
whales), not an merely knowing a definition (a whale is a mammal) (Nagy 1988).

Even if word-meaning were developed adequately, the words taught may
have little, if any, measurable impact on comprehension. If many of the word
meanings were already known or if they could be derived from context, "preteaching" their meanings would have little effect on differences in comprehension. Also, all words are not of equal importance for understanding a text; some
are more central to obtaining meaning. It may be possible to understand a passage without knowing the meaning of every word in it. Freebody and Anderson
(1983) found that reading comprehension was not decreased significantly when
approximately 15% of the content words were replaced with more difficult synonyms, but Stahl et al. (1989) reports that replacing every sixth content word did
have a negative impact on comprehension. If not knowing the meanings of a
number of words does not *measurably* affect comprehension, teaching word
meaning may not measurably improve it either.

The lack of significant differences in some research studies may be due
to what was measured. If few of the instructed word meanings needed to be
understood in order to demonstrate comprehension, their acquisition would not
have influenced the results. In other words, the test may not have been sufficiently sensitive to measure the impact of vocabulary learning.

Teaching the meanings of key words might improve the comprehension of selections containing those words, but it may not have great transfer value because the words may have different meanings in other contexts. Overall improvement of reading comprehension may require not only development of a wide range of concepts, but also increasing reading skills and strategies.

The point at which unknown word meanings begin to interfere with comprehension is apt to vary with such factors as the importance of the word meaning to understanding the text; the pupil's topical knowledge, purpose for reading, and level of reading ability; and the overall difficulty of the selection.

In general, vocabulary programs that stress breadth of word-meaning knowledge, provide extended and intensive instruction and learning opportunities, and get students actively involved in processing and learning word meanings seem to have a positive impact on reading comprehension.

Developing Vocabulary Knowledge

Over the years, classroom observations generally have revealed that the little vocabulary instruction that did take place was inadequate for the development of word-meaning knowledge (Durkin 1978–1979, Calfee & Drum 1985, M. Graves 1986). Even today, vocabulary instruction largely involves some combination of the teacher mentioning the word's meaning in a single-sentence explanation or providing a brief definition or synonym, the pupils looking up word meanings, and the students writing and memorizing definitions (Nagy 1988). Such limited instruction could result in the acquisition of hazy, superficial, or inaccurate word meanings. Thus, a child who has been told that *frantic* means "wild" may talk about picking "frantic flowers."

The amount of time spent on vocabulary instruction correlates 0.65 with the effectiveness of the instruction (Stahl 1986), but how the time is spent is a more important variable. Blachowitz (1987) reports that three to five times more time was being devoted to vocabulary instruction than in the past. But the quality and type of instruction still appear to be wanting. Almost all the instruction took place as a prereading activity, little or no time was spent refining word meanings after the selections were read, and very little time was given to developing independence in gaining word meanings.

A well-planned, systematic, continuous program is required for vocabulary instruction to be effective (Dale & O'Rourke 1971, 1984). Such a program should include concept development, generating and sustaining an interest in words and a desire to increase one's vocabulary, direct teaching of word meanings, helping pupils learn how to determine word meanings on their own, and providing frequent opportunities for reading. Beck, McKeown, and Omanson (1987) describe what they considered an ideal vocabulary-development program.

CONCEPT DEVELOPMENT.   *Words* are verbal labels for concepts. As children mature, their concepts gradually become more accurate and refined. Thus, the concept represented by the word *dog* is vaguely understood and often overgeneralized by tots who are just beginning to use oral language, as indicated by their application of the term to any four-footed animal. Over time, children learn to exclude other animals from the "dog" category. Later, they learn that the word "dog" can also be a verb (e.g., He dogged it.) and that it can have other meanings (e.g., a hot dog in a bun and hot dog on a ski slope are not the same). It takes a number of experiences to develop and refine a concept.

In general, concepts that represent things (nouns), actions (verbs), or observable qualities (adjectives, adverbs) are comparatively easy to develop. Concepts representing relationships (e.g., conjunctions, prepositions) are more difficult to teach and acquire. Ease of acquisition can vary within a category. For example, nouns that represent physical objects or that can evoke visual imagery (e.g., *table*) are easier to teach and acquire than are those representing abstract concepts such as "democracy" (Schwanenflugel & Stowe 1989). The depth or precision of meaning that needs to be developed also influences how difficult a concept is to teach (Graves 1987).

Children should be provided with meaningful experiences that allow them to refine existing concepts and to acquire new ones. Vivid, first-hand sensory experiences are excellent for developing accurate concepts. Such experiences can occur during or outside of the school day, such as during intelligently planned and conducted trips and follow-ups. Teachers and parents should decide beforehand which concepts they want to introduce and the most appropriate words to use to represent those concepts; make certain that the concepts are discussed and the verbal labels applied before the trip, especially while the experiences are occurring; and encourage the children to use the words as the concepts are being discussed before, during, and after the trip.

Because first-hand experiences are not always possible, it is also necessary to provide vicarious experiences through the use of movies, videotapes, filmstrips, pictures, and so forth. Storytelling and reading to pupils also can foster concept development, especially in the primary grades. Older children can gain concepts through reading. Practice using the words is highly important. Naturally occurring opportunities in which the words can be used for speaking, listening, and writing arise in discussions, conversations, and reports.

Rentel (1971) recommends the following guidelines for teaching concepts: (1) Establish the proper word labels for the concept and its attributes; (2) emphasize the significant characteristics that differentiate that concept from related concepts; (3) provide examples and instances of the concept; (4) encourage and guide discovery of the concept's essence; and (5) provide opportunities for applying the concept. Graves and Prenn (1986) provide a six-step procedure for teaching a concept.

Concept acquisition is facilitated by having pupils generate examples of the concept, and by providing exercises that require them to discriminate examples of the concept from minimally different nonexamples (Dixon 1987). The latter should be followed by discussions as to how the nonexamples differ from the target concept. Among the ways (Nagy (1988) suggests for focusing on concepts rather than on their labels is occasionally to start developing the word meaning without mentioning the word itself. Thus, as an introduction to "déjà vu," the teacher might say "Have you ever had the feeling that something you knew you were experiencing for the first time had happened to you before?"

MOTIVATION. Interest and motivation often determine how individuals allocate their time and effort. Therefore arousing and maintaining in students both an interest in words and a desire to increase their word knowledge is important. Teachers should talk to children about the importance of knowing the meanings of many words and demonstrate to them how knowing the best word to fit an idea can improve their ability to communicate. The teacher's use of words and her enthusiasm for words also can motivate children. Pupils must also understand how newly acquired vocabulary may benefit them if long-term acquisition of word knowledge is to be achieved (Ruddell 1986).

Among the ways of stimulating a desire to learn new words are staging word contests, using word puns, and playing word games (see Lake 1967, Wise 1972) and by personalizing vocabulary development (see Bougere 1968, Haggard 1982). Some children get "turned on to words" by being introduced to euphemisms; word origins;[3] *palindromes* (words and phrases spelled the same way forward and backward, such as *radar* and "Madam I'm Adam"), coined words (e.g., *blurb*); *portmanteau words* (words formed by merging portions of other words, such as *brunch*); slide words (e.g., *jeep*); and so forth (see Pilon 1978). Achievement-oriented students may be prodded by discussing with them their less-than-desirable vocabulary-test results. Tompkins and Yaden (1986), who provide information about how words and their spellings came into our language, also suggest activities for developing an interest in words.

DIRECT TEACHING OF WORD MEANINGS. English has approximately 100,000 distinct word meanings (Nagy & Herman 1984). Students need to know considerably fewer, and many word meanings are apparently acquired indirectly from context. Nonetheless, there is a place for the direct instruction of word meanings. Research suggests that direct instruction is more effective than extensive reading for learning word meanings when the teacher wants to make certain that particular words and their meanings are learned by students, especially when those word meanings are needed to comprehend particular texts (Nelson-Herber 1986). Direct instruction may also involve word meanings that are not of immediate use but which may be of later value (e.g., root words that allow pupils on their own to gain the meanings of the words' derivatives or that are useful in demonstrating the relationships among word meanings).

Because instructional time is limited and it may take a long time to develop some word meanings, it is important to decide carefully which word meanings to teach, the depth of meaning that needs to be developed, and the most appropriate and efficient instructional strategies for doing so.

Deciding Which Word Meanings to Teach. Basal reader manuals usually indicate which words and word meanings[4] to teach, but the final decision rests with teachers. They may know, for instance, that their students already understand the meanings of certain target words, or that a less common meaning of a high-frequency word is used in the upcoming selection, even though the manual does not mention it. Except for technical vocabulary, content-subject textbooks usually do not indicate important word meanings. Even then, teachers must decide

---

[3]Refer to Pilon (1978), Gold (1981), or Johnson and Pearson (1984) for lists of children's books on etymology. Also see Limburg (1986).

[4]Word-recognition and word-meaning instruction may occur concurrently, particularly beyond the primary grades.

whether the definitions provided by the textbook are sufficient for understanding the word's meaning. Definitions, even some in dictionaries and glossaries, are not always very revealing (see Nagy 1988).

Teaching and learning *technical vocabulary* (content-subject words that have specialized meanings) are difficult for a number of reasons (Nelson-Herber 1986). In addition to the fact that many technical words are polysyllabic, their meanings not only are unknown but must be learned in relationship to concept clusters represented by other multisyllabic words whose meanings are also often unknown. For instance, a student can memorize the definition of *photosynthesis* but usually cannot understand the concept without understanding the meaning of such words as *chlorophyll, oxygen, carbon dioxide*, and *catalyst*. Furthermore, students rarely encounter or use the words outside of the class in which they are taught. Nelson-Herber (1986) presents and illustrates a model for teaching technical vocabulary.

Some teachers prefer not to preteach vocabulary but to have pupils read the selection and then indicate which words caused them problems. Two advantages are claimed for this procedure. First, it supposedly saves time and effort because students ask about fewer words than would be selected by the teacher. Second, pupils are apt to invest more effort in acquiring word meanings that they select to learn. The procedure may work with achievement-oriented, good readers. But novice readers and poor readers often fail to ask about many of the words they do not know because they are unaware or do not care that the word meanings are unknown or because they are embarrassed to admit it.

At times, word lists (see pages 441–445) are used to select the words to be taught. Almost all word lists are based on the frequency with which the words appear in print. Only *The Living Word Vocabulary* (Dale & O'Rourke 1981) indicates the percentages of students who, at various grade levels, knew the meanings of the words, including various meanings of the same word. However, word-frequency lists may be of some use in determining the likelihood that a common meaning of a word, but not necessarily the appropriate meaning in a given context, is known. The most common meanings of high-frequency words are probably known, but not their uncommon meanings (e.g., a *run* on a bank). The probability that any of a word's meanings is known decreases as the frequency with which it is used in print decreases.

In deciding which word meanings (and perhaps word recognition as well) to teach, the following questions may be used as guidelines: (1) How important is the word's meaning to an understanding of the text? (2) How likely is the word's particular meaning to be understood? (3) Does the context reveal the meaning and, if so, do the students have the skill to use that contextual information? (4) Does the text define the word and, if so, how adequate is the definition? (5) How important to future learning is the word's meaning?

A word that appears only once in a text is probably not significantly related to the comprehension of that text. On the other hand, a word with a generally low-frequency count may be relatively common to a particular text. In such cases, it is important to know the meaning of that word. A high-frequency word may appear often in a text but may cause difficulty because it represents different meanings (e.g., Mary will *run* to the bank even though she has a *run* in her stockings because she heard that there was going to be a *run* on the bank.).

Common words tend to have more meanings per word than do low-frequency words (e.g., *run* vs. *neuroanatomy*) (Calfee & Drum 1985).

Selecting Instructional Strategies.[5]   For instructional planning, words may be classified into one of four categories. Once categorized, appropriate instructional strategies can be selected. See Graves (1984) for sources that suggest how to teach words in the different categories.

Category-1 words are high-frequency words, the most common meanings of which are likely known by the children. Instruction should focus on helping pupils to recognize the printed forms of these words. The instructional techniques discussed in Chapter 12 may be used for this purpose.

The printed forms of words in Category 2 are recognized by students who know the words' common meanings, but not the less common ones need to understand the text. Instruction should involve teaching new meanings for these words and expanding the pupils' word-meaning knowledge. Category-2 words may occur frequently because there are many *polysemous words* in English. For example, about one-third of the words in *The Living Word Vocabulary* (Dale & O'Rourke 1981) and over 70% of the 9,000 words in the *Ginn Word Book for Teachers* (Johnson, Moe & Baumann 1983) have more than one meaning. Searls and Klesius (1984) list 99 words found at the first-reader level that have four or more definitions and are used as more than one part of speech, and suggest ways to teach these words. Some students may need to be shown that words have more than one possible meaning.

The two types of Category-2 words include: (1) those that have more than one common meaning and possibly a number of uncommon ones (e.g., *run*); and (2) high-frequency words that have different restricted meanings when used in various content subjects, such as *bar* in *bar graph* (math or social studies), *sand bar* (social studies or literature) and "Crossing the Bar" (literature). Students who know more than one meaning for the first type of word may be able to determine its appropriate meaning from context. It is usually necessary to teach specific word meanings for the second type.

The printed forms and the meanings of words in both Category 3 and Category 4 are unlikely to be known. Words in these two categories differ in that, whereas Category-3 words represent concepts that are developed relatively easily, it takes considerable time to understand the concepts represented by Category-4 words because they are abstract and/or complex. For both categories, instruction involves both word recognition and word meanings. Teaching sets of related concepts is best accomplished through intensive integration (Graves & Prenn 1986) (see pages 521–522).

The aforementioned categories may also be useful in diagnosis and remediation. There are at least three possible interpretations of a child's statement "I don't know that word": (1) The word's meaning would be known if the printed form were recognized (Category 1); (2) the printed form is recognized, but the word's particular meaning is unknown (Category 2); or (3) neither the word's printed form nor its meaning is known (Categories 3 and 4). Frequent word-recognition or word-identification problems may indicate either that the text is

[5]Ruddell (1986) sets forth criteria for evaluating vocabulary-development strategies.

too difficult for instructional purposes or that a great deal of teacher support will be needed for the pupil to understand the text. Numerous Category-3 or Category-4 words suggest that the content of the material surpasses the child's knowledge base. If the number of new concepts that need to be taught greatly exceeds the number that can be taught easily, the subject matter is too difficult for the students (Graves 1987).

Levels of Word Meaning. Beck, McKeown and Omanson (1987) suggest that there are five levels of word-meaning knowledge: (1) no knowledge, (2) general information, (3) a narrow understanding that is context bound, (4) the need to pause momentarily before knowing the meaning, and (5) full, rich knowledge that is accessed rapidly, even when the word is not set in context. They hypothesize that the semantic processes involved in reading comprehension require word knowledge at the highest level and that failure to develop vocabulary to that level accounts for the failure of vocabulary instruction to improve reading comprehension.

Brief explanations, definitions, or synonyms may provide sufficient word meaning if the concept is already partially known or is easily understood, or if the meaning is peripheral to understanding the text. Providing such brief information is also appropriate when it allows the child to continue reading for meaning. Struggling over a word meaning can disrupt comprehension. Learning a definition may provide a good start in learning the word's meaning if the definition is accurate and explains the meaning in terms understood by the child (Nagy 1988). However, such brief instruction should not constitute the bulk of the vocabulary-development program. At times, illustrations, pictures, or schematic drawings are more effective than words in developing word meaning.

If the instructional goal is higher-order processing that involves integrating words and context, then richer instruction involving elaborated word meanings and encountering the words in diverse contexts is required. Such intensive vocabulary instruction is appropriate for developing understanding of conceptually difficult words and for words whose meanings are central to understanding the text at hand or which will be of value in expanding word-meaning knowledge. (McKeown 1985b).

Intensive or *knowledge-based vocabulary instruction* assists pupils in developing word-meaning knowledge to a level likely to help improve reading comprehension.[6] Nagy (1988) uses three descriptors that research has indicated are important aspects of such instruction: integration, repetition, and meaningful use. The three are interrelated.

Integration refers to establishing ties between new word meanings and children's existing knowledge. Studies suggest that developing vocabulary through the association of new terminology with familiar concepts encourages

---

[6]Acquisition of such word-meaning knowledge *alone* may not improve reading comprehension because a child may be deficient in other areas important to comprehension. Such acquisition will probably have a greater effect on understanding texts containing the particular words than on students' general level of reading ability, due to such factors as topical knowledge requirements. On the other hand, extended intensive vocabulary instruction may not only serve to increase knowledge of the target words but to assist pupils in learning word meanings on their own because certain attitudes and strategies have been developed in the process.

construction of rich semantic networks[7] that enable students to understand word meanings more fully. Such increased understanding has been effective in improving vocabulary retention and, in some cases, passage comprehension (Carr & Mazur-Stewart 1988).

Among the techniques for getting children to make connections between and among words are the use of: (1) classification activities such as those found on page 537 (children should be eased into dealing with complicated classifications by explaining to them how two words are related); (2) semantic mapping (see page 538); (3) synonymic webbing (see page 539); (4) semantic feature analysis (see page 539 and Nagy 1988); (5) Venn diagrams, hierarchical arrays, and linear arrays (see page 540 and Nagy 1988); (6) concept ladders, which show how a single word that represents a main concept is related hierarchically to already-known words; and (7) predict-o-gram charts, which indicate the relationship of the vocabulary employed in the text to the text structure (see Blachowicz 1986). It is not necessary to restrict vocabulary instruction to only the words found in a text. Other words related to those word meanings or to the theme may be included. Refer to Marzano and Marzano (1988) for suggestions on presenting words in semantically related categories and for lists of words that may be presented in such clusters.

Research suggests that vocabulary instruction is effective when it provides both definitional and contextual information (Reutzel & Hollingsworth 1988). *Definitional information* is knowledge about relationships between the target words and words whose meanings are already known. It can be provided through the use of definitions, synonyms, antonyms, root words and affixes, as well as through use of the procedures on pages 537–540. *Contextual information* is knowledge about the core concepts represented by the words, and how word meanings may change in different contexts. Contextual information is derived from experiences with words in context. It is first acquired in relation to a particular context, and retrieval of the word meaning may require contextual support. A concept/word becomes "decontextualized" only after a number of exposures to the word in different contexts (Stahl 1986).

Repetition refers to frequent encounters with the words in order to develop and reinforce definitional and contextual information. Repetition also helps to develop word-meaning accuracy and speed to a level that makes it easy to access lexical information, thereby facilitating the comprehension process. To achieve a transfer effect, vocabulary instruction must provide numerous opportunities to meet the words in varying print contexts over an extended period of time (Graves 1986). In addition to reading, writing, and speaking activities that take place in school, pupils should be encouraged to use the words outside of school (Beck, McKeown & Omanson 1987).

Repetition alone is insufficient; students need to process the words meaningfully. *Meaningful use* means that pupils are actively involved in processing word meanings; that is, they are required to make inferences about words based

---

[7]Knowledge is hypothesized to be an associative network of concepts. Individuals vary in the number of concepts known, in the ways in which the concepts are organized and linked, as well as in their ability to access the concepts. When a word or group of words is encountered, corresponding concepts in memory are activated. This activation automatically spreads from that concept to related concepts in the network (Garner 1987).

on their meanings. Rich and varied word information is developed through deep processing. *Depth of processing* involves thinking deeply about word meanings and their relationships. It requires greater cognitive effort and involvement than does, say, learning only a brief definition. Stahl and Fairbanks (1986) refer to how three levels of word knowledge, each requiring succeedingly deeper processing to acquire, are demonstrated:

1. *Association*—Having learned simply to associate a word with one of its brief meanings, children can state a verbatim definition or the synonym taught.
2. *Comprehension*—Having a deeper understanding than just an association allows pupils to apply a learned association, such as in filling in a blank to complete a sentence or in finding an antonym, and
3. An even more complete grasp of the concept permits students to define a word in their own words or to create original sentences using the target words. It should be noted, however, that successful completion of the latter two tasks does not necessarily mean that the child possesses a level of word knowledge that will improve comprehension.

Deep-processing tasks require students to use, rather than just state, word meanings. In addition to most of the above-mentioned activities, deep processing can also be encouraged by having pupils describe how target words relate to other words and to their own experiences (Beck, McKeown & Omanson 1987). Relating word meanings to their own experiences makes words personally meaningful for children (Carr & Wixson 1986). Other suggestions may be found in Carr and Wixson (1986) and Nagy (1988).

Oral and written activities in which pupils use the target words to generate novel responses may not be the only ways to foster deep processing. Stahl and Clark (1987) found that participation in classroom discussions was not necessary for learning science vocabulary *if* students anticipated being called on to respond. Anticipation may cause covert rehearsal of responses, thus forcing deep processing of target word meanings.

HELPING STUDENTS LEARN WORD MEANINGS ON THEIR OWN. Because the bulk of word-meaning knowledge comes from sources other than direct instruction, students should be taught ways to increase their vocabularies on their own and should be provided with numerous opportunities to do so. Pupils need to acquire strategies for dealing with unknown word meanings while they are reading, learn how to use context clues and morphological cues, and be given school time to read materials other than their textbooks as well as opportunities to use newly acquired word meanings.

Strategies for Dealing with Unknown Word Meanings. Children who are monitoring their reading behaviors usually know when they encounter an unknown word meaning. When such situations occur, they must decide quickly whether knowing that word meaning is important for attaining the desired level of comprehension and whether they want to do anything about inferring its meaning. A negative answer to either question leads to ignoring the word. If the answers to both questions are positive, the child should quickly review the preceding context to see if it can help infer the word meaning or if a synonym or antonym has been provided. If the word meaning is deemed very important, the reader may make use of morphological cues either before or after rereading. A great deal of time should not be spent on this or any other step because it can disrupt reading comprehension. If the preceding context or morphological cues do not help, the student should continue reading, being alert to any clues that may supply useful information. When continuing to read does not help and the word meaning is still deemed important, the student may opt to return to the unknown word and attempt to determine its meaning through morphological analysis is he has not already done so. If this does not work and if comprehension is still extremely hampered by not knowing that word's meaning, an expert source should be consulted. Asking for and receiving a quick definition from the teacher is less disruptive than consulting a dictionary or glossary. If comprehension is acceptable to the student, he may wish to note the word and consult an expert source at a nondisruptive point while reading (e.g., at the end of a headed section) or after the whole passage has been read. A glossary may be quicker to use than a dictionary because it contains fewer entries, and may restrict the meaning to the one used in the text.

Use of Context Clues.   There is an important distinction between *deriving* the meaning of an unfamiliar word from context and *learning* the meaning of that word. Students may successfully infer a word meaning and utilize it to understand the text; however, that meaning may be forgotten soon thereafter (Jenkins & Dixon 1983). A single encounter with an unknown word's meaning results only in a small gain in knowledge of that word. Learning the meanings of previously unknown words from context typically occurs in small increments (Nagy, Herman & Anderson 1985b). It takes a long time for full concept knowledge, unprompted recall (i.e., the ability to identify a word meaning without reference to a context), and rapid lexical access to develop (Kameenui, Dixon & Carnine 1987). The strength of learning word meaning from context lies in its long-term cumulative effects (Nagy, Herman & Anderson 1985a). In general, studies report that students are not particularly adept at using context clues to determine word meanings (e.g., Carnine, Kameenui & Coyle 1984). However, the context itself may have contributed to such findings. Context determines word meaning but only infrequently reveals the meaning of an unknown word (Deighton 1959).

When children are taught to use context clues, the target words are usually set in a *pedagogical context* (one contrived to illustrate clearly how a particular kind of context clue can be used to deduce the meaning of an unknown word. But *natural context* (the context of most published materials) usually does not provide appropriate cues to word meanings because the primary purpose of the material is to communicate ideas, not to increase word-meaning knowledge (Beck, McKeown & McCaslin 1983).[8]

[8]The apparent inconsistency between natural context not supplying clues to word meaning and the strong possibility that most new word meanings are acquired from context is taken up on page 523.

Yet at times authors do provide clues to word meaning, primarily because they think that those word meanings are important for comprehension and are probably not known by the intended readers. Even though the following types of context clues currently do not appear frequently in natural contexts, students should be made aware of them and taught how to use them.

1. Synonym. A more commonly occurring synonym for the unfamiliar word may (1) appear in parentheses—*avarice* (greed); (2) appear in apposition—He did not *repent*, regret, his actions; (3) be embedded in a sentence—Tom was *exhausted* and Fred was tired too. At times the use of a synonym is too subtle for children to apprehend easily—Rare books cost more because they are *scarce* and in demand.

2. Antonym. The unfamiliar word is contrasted with an antonym whose meaning is more likely known—Dolores *hastened* to complete the job, but Alice took her time. A key to understanding the use of this technique is recognition of such "thought reversing" cues as *but.* An author who thinks a word meaning is important may employ a synonym + antonym technique—Mary's speech was *concise;* it was brief, but John's speech was too long.

3. Definition. The unfamiliar word is defined: (1) in parentheses—the *caboose* (the last car on the train); (2) in apposition—*polygamy*, the custom of having more than one wife at a time; (3) embedded in a sentence—The male principal of a private school is often called the *headmaster*—or in a subsequent sentence— Blood flowed from the *lesion.* This wound . . .; (4) by supplying examples (usually introduced by "such as" or a similar phrase)—*odd numbers*, such as 1, 3, 9; (5) by a restatement (often introduced by "that is")—she was *wan;* that is, very pale; and (6) in a footnote.

4. Experiential background. The cue is based on the child's past experiences, either with life in general (The horselike animal with black and white stripes is a *zebra.*) or language (Nickie was *as quite as a mouse.*). Past experience also may lead the reader to anticipate words occurring in conjunction with other words and, although their printed forms may not be recognized, their meanings may be inferred if the child has sufficient topical knowledge.

5. Summary. The preceding information is summarized by the unfamiliar word—First they saw an elephant. Then they saw lions and tigers in cages. Adam liked the *zoo.*

6. Reflection. The general situation or mood of the sentence or paragraph provides the cue—The eerie music made me shudder. And when the candle went out, a strong feeling of *trepidation* came over me.

The first three types of context clues are more likely to appear in expository texts; the latter three in narratives. Children also need to understand the amount of flexibility allowable in assigning meanings to words in context (McKeown 1985a).

Research suggests that: (1) contextual information can assist in deducing word meanings under certain conditions; (2) where more clues are available, word meaning is more likely to be derived; (3) clues closer to the target word are more likely to be helpful; (4) greater topical knowledge is more likely to enable the reader to derive word meaning; (5) a higher proportion of unknown words makes it harder to derive a word meaning; (6) meanings of more conceptually difficult words are harder to learn from context; (7) meanings of words met frequently in variable contexts are more likely to be learned; (8) gaining word meaning from context is not an automatic process, especially for poor readers; (9) good readers are more sensitive to contextual information than are poor readers and they make more effective use of it; (10) the ability to use context clues increases with age and reading ability; and (11) instruction in the use of context clues has a positive effect on their use (Graves 1986; Wysocki & Jenkins 1987; Drum & Konopak 1987).

Some of the abovementioned findings must be interpreted in light of the fact that most studies either used a cloze task in which high-frequency words were deleted (and therefore the word meaning was already known) or asked the students to derive the meaning of a specified low-frequency word. In both cases, the deletion or target word usually appeared in constrained, often contrived, contexts (Herman et al. 1987).

Many of the types of context clues that children are taught to use do not occur frequently in natural text and, in general, words that contribute a great deal of information to the understanding of a passage are less likely to have their meanings revealed in context. This situation has led some authors (e.g., Schatz & Baldwin 1986) to contend that teaching the use of context clues is unjustifiable or at least questionable.

Few studies have investigated the incidental learning of word meaning from natural written text when children read for such normal purposes as to enjoy a story or to understand and remember textual information (Herman et al. 1987). The findings have been mixed, but some evidence indicates that word meanings are learned incidently by reading materials whose contexts are not very informative (Nagy, Herman & Anderson 1985a) and that there are qualitative differences in the ways in which word meanings are learned from expository and narrative texts (Nagy, Anderson & Herman 1986).

Research studies may fail to demonstrate appreciable learning of word meanings from context if their vocabulary-knowledge tests are insensitive to small increments in learning (i.e., to partial word-meaning knowledge) (Nagy, Herman & Anderson 1985a). Furthermore, the acquisition of word knowledge generally occurs in small increments. When unfamiliar words are first encountered, pupils may grasp only part of their meanings. Acquisition of only partial word-meaning knowledge may also be due to the fact that most natural texts reveal, at best, only some aspect of the word's meaning, and then only to an alert reader (Herman et al. 1987). The number of word meanings learned from reading depends on three factors: (1) the volume of exposure to written language, (2) the quality of the text, and (3) the child's ability to infer and remember the meanings of new words met during reading. The single most important factor is probably the volume of exposure (Nagy, Anderson & Herman 1986).

An attempt at making it easier to learn word meanings during reading involves writing elaborated texts. Compared with natural texts, *elaborated texts* provide more thorough descriptions of important concepts, clearly explain their relationships, and give examples of concepts that may be difficult to understand or are unlikely to be known by students. Some studies have shown that elaborated text significantly increases the incidental acquisition of word meanings (Herman et al. 1987; Konopak 1988a, b).

Cloze exercises are often used to develop the use of contextual information.

Their use is based on the premise that the information surrounding the deleted words may allow the reader to predict the missing word. The use of cloze exercises, however, is not likely to increase a child's vocabulary knowledge because, in order to fill in the blank, the word must already be in the reader's understanding vocabulary. The potential value of these exercises lies in learning to use whatever contextual information is available. Students should be informed as to how what they learn from cloze exercises can be useful in determining the meaning of an unknown printed word.

Exercises for teaching the use of context clues may be found in D. Johnson and Pearson (1984, pp. 114–147). Many of the prediction and verification exercises suggested by Y. Goodman and Burke (1980) may also be helpful.

Use of Morphological Cues.   The use of morphological cues as an aid to gaining word meaning requires skill in morphological analysis (see page 463) and knowledge of the meanings of the separate word parts because it involves mentally separating an unfamiliar word into its meaning units (e.g., prefix–base word–suffix), which are then used to derive the meaning of the unknown word. Meaning units include the words that form a compound word, base words, Latin or Greek roots, and affixes.

It is theorized that incidental learning of word meanings from context depends on the ability to combine information from morphology and context. However, the few studies that have been undertaken in this area suggest that students did not combine information from both sources, but rather relied on one or the other (Nagy, Anderson & Herman 1986; Wysocki & Jenkins 1987).

Children are usually taught compound words fairly early in their reading programs. There are three kinds of compound words, those in which: (1) the meaning is the sum of its parts (*houseboat*); (2) the meaning is related to, but not completely represented by, the meaning of its components (*shipyard*); and (3) the meaning is not literally related to the meaning of its parts (*moonstruck*) or the compound has more than one meaning (*doghouse*) (Moretz & Davey 1974). If a child encounters *doghouse* for the first time in print, dividing it into *dog* and *house* will likely reveal its meaning quickly because its most common meaning (a place where a dog lives) is probably already known. However, its nonliteral meaning (to be in disfavor) is not readily apparent from morphological clues alone, but when combined with the use of contextual clues, its meaning may be inferred (e.g., The man was in the *doghouse* because his wife was angry at him for not mowing the lawn.).

Inflectional endings (*s, es, en, 's, s', ed, ing, er, est, ly, y*) are understood in speech by practically all children entering first grade. Children are usually taught to recognize their printed forms and interpret them in first and second grades. Because the addition of an inflectional suffix does not change the basic meaning of the base word, inflected words are not very useful in expanding one's vocabulary. But in about the third or fourth grade, children begin increasingly to encounter more *derived words*—base words or stems to which prefixes and/or suffixes have been added to form other words, which, although semantically related to the base words, are definable new words. Refer to Tyler and Nagy (1985) for a discussion of the role of derivational suffixes in sentence comprehension.

Although writers apparently do not agree as to what constitutes a prefix,

Table 14.1   A Recommended List of Prefixes

Prefix	Meaning(s)	Examples
ab[2]	away from	abnormal
ad, ap, at[2]	to, toward, nearness or addition to	admit, appear, attract adjoin, adrenal
be[2]	by	beside
com, con, col, co[2]	with, together	combine, concur, collect, cohere
de	from	detract
	reverse, undo	defrost
dis, dif	not	dishonest
	reversal	disappear
	cause to be the opposite of	disable
em, en	in, into	embrace, enclose
	cause to make to be	endanger
ex[2]	out	expel
	former	ex-boxer
	beyond	excess
in, im	in, into	infuse
	not	incorrect, impure
mono[1,2]	one	monochrome
bi[1,2]	two, happening every two or twice during	biped, biweekly, bimonthly
tri[1,2]	three	triangle
ob, of, op[1,2]	against	obnoxious, offend, oppress
	to, toward	object
post[1,2]	after	postdate, postpone
pre	before	prewar
	in front of	predict
pro[2]	in favor of	prolabor
	before, ahead of	promote, prologue
re	back	repay, refer
	again	reappear
sub	under	subsoil
	to a lesser degree	subtropical
super[1]	over, above	superscribe
	higher in rank	supervisor
	surpassing, greater than normal	superhuman
trans[1]	across	transport, transatlantic
un	not	unhappy
	do the opposite of	untie

[1] Not among the 15 prefixes cited by Stauffer (1942)
[2] Not among the 20 prefixes cited by White, Sowell, and Yanagihara (1989).

there is agreement that many English words start with prefixes, and that relatively few prefixes account for most of those found in prefixed words. Stauffer (1942) found that 24% of the first 20,00 words in the Thorndike list have prefixes. The 15 prefixes, which account for 82% of the prefixed Thorndike words, are shown in Table 14.1.

White, Sowell, and Yanagihara (1989) report that 20 prefixes account for about 97% of the prefixed words in the *Word Frequency Book* (WFB) (Carroll,

Table 14.2 The Most Common Latin Roots in the Vocabulary of Children

Root	Meanings	Examples
fac, fact (facere)	to make or do	facile, factory
fer (ferre)	to bear, carry	transfer, ferry
mis, mit (mittere)	to send	admissible, transmit
mov, mot (movere, motus)	to move	movement, motion
par (parpare)	to get ready	prepare, repair
port (portare)	to carry	export, portable
pos, pon (posito, ponere)	to place, put	position, opponent
spect, spic (specere)	to look	inspect, conspicuous
stat, sta (stare)	to stand	station, stanza
tend, tens (tendere, tensus)	to stretch	extend, tension
ven, vent (venire)	to come	convention, event
vid, vis (videre, visus)	to see	provide, vision

Source: L. C. Breen, Vocabulary development by teaching prefixes, suffixes and root derivations, *The Reading Teacher,* November 1960.

Davies & Richman 1971). The nine that were not cited by Stauffer (1942) are: *non, over, mis, inter, fore, semi, anti, mid,* and *under.* A number of the prefixes cited by Stauffer do not appear in the White et al. list (e.g., *ad, com, mono*) because they are not considered prefixes by White's definition or, more probably, because they occur in less than 1% of the prefixed WFB words. By far the most common prefix is *un,* which appears in 26% of the WFB words. Four prefixes (*un, re, in* [not], *dis*) account for 58% of the prefixed WFB words, and 48% of them begin with one of four negation prefixes (*un, in, dis, non*).

Some prefixes have more than one meaning and some meanings are represented by more than one prefix. The former is much less of a problem in determining word meaning because the meanings do not differ that greatly. But the alternative spellings of some prefixes are not likely to be recognized by students (or even most adults). Because of the phonetic structure of English, the final sound of some prefixes is absorbed or "assimilated" into the word or root to which it is attached (Hodges 1982), and this results in spelling changes. Instead of *ad* + *pear* (to + become visible), we have *appear; different* rather than *dis* + *ferent;* and *illegal,* not *in* + *legal.* Some children may overgeneralize, which can lead to errors such as thinking that *invaluable* means "not valuable."

Most pupils probably find it difficult to make use of prefixes attached to Latin or Greek roots, especially when the prefix has a less common spelling. Prefixes are more likely to be useful when they have been added to a base word that the child already knows. For instance, it is easier to perceive the meaning units in *unhappy* and *remake* than in *appear* or *collect.* It is easier to build on prior knowledge, and teachers should take advantage of this fact. Therefore, it is advisable to introduce prefixes in connection with known words, to teach those that have the most transfer value (those that occur most frequently and are consistent in meaning), and to leave the more difficult prefixes for individual study by the most capable upper-grade students. Suggestions for teaching prefixes may be found in Graves and Hammond (1980) and D. Johnson and Pearson (1984).

Knowledge of the meanings of the more common Latin roots shown in Table 14.2 can help mature, bright students determine the meanings of unknown

Table 14.3   Fairly Common Suffixes That Have a Reasonably Consistent Meaning

Suffix	Meanings	Examples
er, or	one who does	teacher, sailor
ist	one who does or practices	pianist, dentist
	one who believes in	abolitionist
ian	one who is expert in	musician, statistician
tion, sion	act of	creation, decision
ment	result of	judgment
	act of	management
ence, ance, ancy	act of	persistence
	state of	repentance, truancy
ness	state of being	sadness
ty, ity	condition of, quality of	safety, purity
al	pertaining to	musical
ic, ical	pertaining to	historic, historical
	like	angelic
ous, ious	like	laborious
	full of	joyous
ful	full of	painful
	pertaining to, tending to	forgetful
ly, y	in the manner of	truly, windy
ble, able, ible	capable of being	adaptable, permissible
less	without	homeless
ward	in the direction of	westward

Note: Some of these suffixes have other meanings in addition to those indicated.

words and thus increase their word knowledge. Only 82 Latin roots and 6 Greek roots occur 10 or more times each in children's vocabulary (Breen 1960). Roots like *port* (to carry) and *fac, fact, fic* (to make or do) are fairly easy to learn and use; for example, the meaning of *export* is easily perceived. Templeton (1983) suggests that the study of roots should begin with those for which meaning is relatively constant. These roots are *spect* (to look), *press* (to press), *port* (to carry), *form* (to shape), *pose* (to put or place), *tract* (to draw or pull), *spir* (to breathe), and *dict* (to say). O'Rourke (1974) lists 21 roots having at least five applications. The use of roots and affixes as an aid to understanding word meaning requires a fairly high level of reasoning ability; even then the meanings of many words are not easily determined (e.g., con spic uous = together + look + full of = easy to see).

English has many suffixes, but the majority of them have more than one meaning, so teaching only the most common meaning may create some confusion. Suffixes that are both fairly common and have a reasonably constant meaning are shown in Table 14.3. Inflectional endings are suffixes.

Nagy and Anderson (1984) estimate that, for every word learned, a pupil should be able to understand one to three semantically related words, depending on the child's ability to use morphological and context clues. Therefore, it is advisable to demonstrate to students how some words are related and how their commonality can be helpful in determining word meaning. This can be done by building groups of semantically related words. Start with a word whose meaning is known by the pupils (e.g., *porter*) and have them add to the list (e.g., *export, transport, portable*). The visual spelling-cue that is common to all the words on the list should be pointed out. How the word meanings and perhaps how their parts of speech are changed by the affixes should be discussed.

Teaching words together as a "family" has advantages: (1) If the most frequent words in the family are already known, bridges can be built between the old and the new; (2) such teaching calls attention to the word-formation process that relates different words within the family so that students are more likely to take advantage of such relationships on their own; and (3) such teaching familiarizes students with the kinds of meaning changes that often occur between related words (Nagy & Anderson 1984).

Skill in using morphological cues increases with age, and research findings generally suggest that the ability to use such cues may contribute to increasing vocabulary knowledge, especially if the pupils have had prior experience with related words. But, in general, elementary and secondary school students are not very sophisticated in the use of morphological cues. (Wysocki & Jenkins 1987).

Use of some word-part cues can be taught, and pupils can learn to use these units to determine the meanings of unfamiliar words and to retain their meanings. But precisely which morphological cues can be learned at the various grade levels is unknown (Graves 1986). Research regarding the effects of teaching children to use morphological cues has been minimal (Moore 1987).

Use of the Dictionary. Although readers may not use a glossary or dictionary while reading to determine the meaning of an unknown word, the fact remains that the dictionary is an excellent source of word meaning, as well as of other useful information. Picture dictionaries can be used as early as the first grade and are helpful additions to the library table through the primary grades and in remedial work beyond that level. Meyer (1980) presents criteria for selecting children's dictionaries.

A good dictionary definition usually has two elements: (1) It states a class or category to which the concept belongs, and (2) it gives one or more descriptive characteristics that distinguish this concept from other members of the category. Thus, a *fanatic* is defined as "a person with an extreme and unreasoning enthusiasm or zeal, especially in religious matters." The category is "person"; the rest tells how fanatics differ from other persons. Children can be helped to analyze definitions, to construct their own definitions for familiar words, and to compare their definitions with the definitions in the dictionary.

Synonyms are often given as definitions. This is fine when the synonym is already understood or is clearly and understandably defined. Learning synonyms is a good way to enlarge vocabulary, especially when the dictionary explains fine distinctions, as among *ancient, antique, antiquated,* and *old-fashioned.* Fortunately, circular definitions (fantasy—hallucination; hallucination—a form of fantasy) are rare in today's dictionaries.

A dictionary is a complex work, and in order to get children to use it willingly, it is advisable to prepare a planned sequence of lessons to teach dictionary skills. The following outline lists the major dictionary understandings and skills. The simplest ones can be started in first grade; the more difficult ones can be taught in fourth, fifth, and sixth grades.

1. Locating words
   a. Understanding alphabetical sequence and its purpose
   b. Ability to use alphabetical order
      (1) Determining quickly which letters come immediately before and after a given letter
      (2) Finding words with differing first, second, third, and fourth letters[9]
      (3) Using a thumb index
      (4) Opening to a page near the one containing the target word
      (5) Use of the guide word(s) at the top of the pages
   c. Finding words whose exact spellings are unknown
2. Determining word pronunciation
   a. Understanding the parts of a dictionary entry
   b. Understanding and using the abbreviations employed
   c. Locating, understanding, and using the pronunciation guide
   d. Understanding and using: (1) the syllabications provided, (2) phonetic respellings, (3) diacritical marks, and (4) accent marks
   e. Understanding alternate word pronunciations
3. Determining word meaning and usage
   a. Understanding the abbreviations employed
   b. Understanding the effect of syntactic category on meaning
   c. Interpreting typical dictionary definitions
   d. Selecting the appropriate word meaning
   e. Relating derived forms of words to their base word
   f. Distinguishing among acceptable usage, obsolete usage, slang, and unacceptable usage
   g. Determining etymology

Refer to Cooper (1986, pp. 176–178) for suggestions on teaching the use of a dictionary. Dictionary exercises can be found in many workbooks and in Crisculo (1980), and D. Johnson and Pearson (1984). The most valuable practice probably occurs when pupils use the dictionary to find information they want. E. F. Miller (1962) discusses ways to use a dictionary to stimulate reading.

Wide Reading.   Years ago, E. L. Thorndike (1936–1937) concluded that it is impossible to teach directly all the words that children will encounter in reading. His solution—to have pupils read a variety of interesting books that are sufficiently comprehensible to allow for the learning of new ideas and words— has received support from recent theory and research. A major factor in vocabulary development after third grade is the amount of independent reading done by students (Nagy & Anderson 1982, 1984). The amount of free reading was found to be the best predictor of vocabulary growth between Grades 2 and 5 (Fielding, Wilson & Anderson 1986).

[9]One way to help develop these skills is to provide practice arranging lists of words alphabetically by first letter; and then later, by second, third, and fourth letters when the preceding letters are the same in all of the listed words.

In response to the question, "If learning new word meanings from context is a relatively ineffective method, how can context be the largest source of vocabulary growth?" Nagy (1988) replies, "Sheer volume." By reading a great deal in a variety of areas, a large number of unknown word meanings are encountered. Even if only a relatively small percentage of these words are learned, children can increase their vocabularies significantly. Many new word meanings are probably derived initially from spoken context, and only later are the printed word forms recognized and identified. Thereafter, the combination of encounters with spoken and written contexts may facilitate learning the word's meaning(s). Reading to children also can increase their vocabulary knowledge (Eller, Pappas & Brown 1988) especially when unknown word meanings are explained (Elley 1989).

Vocabulary learning does occur in the absence of instruction, and this growth is impressive (Kameenui, Dixon & Carnine 1987). When compared with almost any instructional approach, incidental learning of vocabulary appears to be ineffective in the short run, but even a moderate amount of regular reading is beneficial (Nagy & Herman 1987). Research suggests that vocabulary growth through wide reading is cumulative and especially noted in terms of its long-term effects (Castle 1986).

Wide reading not only increases word-meaning knowledge but can also produce gains in topical and world knowledge that can further facilitate reading comprehension. Acquisition of new word-recognition and word-meaning skills also broadens the base of words that students can use in employing morphological cues, thus making their use even more effective. By providing extensive practice, wide reading can lead to the automatization of enabling skills (e.g., rapid word recognition and lexical access) that also may improve reading comprehension. Therefore, extensive reading should be encouraged by employing the suggestions offered in Chapter 18.

The influence of wide reading on vocabulary acquisition varies depending on the amount of reading done, the overall difficulty of the text, the number of words in the material for which meanings are unknown to the reader, how well context reveals meaning, and the child's ability to infer word meaning from available contextual or morphological information. Bright, motivated students who read well and enjoy reading are apt to read a wide variety of materials and have the ability and desire to deduce word meanings; such students will profit most. Poor or reluctant readers are much less likely to increase their vocabulary knowledge through wide reading. Those most in need of increasing their vocabularies are least likely to avail themselves of the opportunity to do so through reading, thus establishing a vicious cycle. Limited reading restricts the opportunity to learn new words, and failure to build up vocabulary knowledge hampers reading improvement.

RELATIVE EFFECTIVENESS OF INSTRUCTIONAL STRATEGIES. Over 20 years ago, Petty, Herold, and Stoll (1968) concluded that the research comparing the effectiveness of different vocabulary-development strategies was inconclusive. The situation has not changed. Recent comparisons also have produced mixed results. Results with specific methods have not always been replicated, and methods shown to be superior in one study may be shown inferior in another. No one method is superior in all circumstances and for all purposes

(Graves 1986). Few of these comparative studies used more than 100 words (Nagy & Herman 1987) and there have been very few long-term studies (Jenkins & Dixon 1983). The conflicting results are likely due to: the use of instructional treatments that vary widely in nature and length, the degree of teacher/pupil interactions generated by the instruction, and variations in research designs. The problem is compounded by the lack of theoretical bases that could account for vocabulary learning in the context of reading instruction (Ruddell 1986).

Research suggests that explicit instruction is more effective than incidental learning for the acquisition of specific vocabulary (Reutzel & Hollingsworth 1988), but the combination of incidental learning from context and direct instruction is likely to be more effective in increasing overall vocabulary knowledge than is relying on either approach alone (Nagy & Herman 1987; Jenkins, Matlock & Slocum 1989).

Consideration should be given to the costs and benefits associated with the various methods of teaching vocabulary. The tasks in learning word meanings vary considerably depending on the pupil's word-recognition and word-meaning knowledge as well as how thoroughly the word meanings need to be known. Also, the amount of time needed for teaching particular words varies. Therefore, different instructional methods are appropriate under different circumstances. Intensive long-term instruction is needed to develop the mastery of word meanings and the development of rich conceptual networks that are likely to improve reading comprehension. But "brief" instruction can get children started on the road to mastery and prevent them from stumbling over unknown words during reading (Graves & Prenn 1986).

INSTRUCTIONAL ACTIVITIES.   The following are among the many activities that can be used to develop and refine word meanings. Many of these activities can also be used to increase listening vocabulary, which can lay a foundation for the acquisition of reading vocabulary. Almost all can be group or individual activities.

General Suggestions.   Preteaching word meanings in order to develop greater understandings than would result from following the instructional suggestions found in the typical teacher's manual can improve children's comprehension of basal reader selections (see Thames & Readence 1988). When new words are introduced, children should be encouraged to ask themselves, "What do I know about these words?" and should be asked to predict how the target words relate to each other or to the theme of the text. After the passage has been read, students can be asked to confirm, revise, or reformulate their predictions (Blachowicz 1986).

If worded properly, questions can also encourage students to think about the relationships among words. Rather than ask, "What does superannuated mean?" some better questions would be, "Can a toddler be superannuated? and Why?" (Nagy 1988).

Concept-of-definition instruction (Schwartz & Raphael 1985) stresses the importance of being able to figure out the meaning of an unknown word on your own. Children are taught what type of information makes up a definition and how to use definitional information, context clues, and prior knowledge.

Synonyms and Antonyms. Studying and using synonyms and antonyms can help pupils to expand their vocabularies, assist them in understanding that no two words have exactly the same meaning, and aid them in learning fine discriminations among word meanings.

Note the differences in task requirements among the following examples of synonym and antonym exercises:

1. Underline the word that means almost the same as *quiet:*
   pretty   still   yet   surrender _____
2. What word means the opposite of *huge?*
3. A *courteous* remark is: rude   polite   deceitful   lawful
4. List all the words you can that mean about the same as *happy.* _____
5. Are these two words synonyms or antonyms?
   animated   lethargic _____

A concept and one label for that concept must be understood in order for synonym instruction to be of value. If the child does not understand a synonym, a simpler one may be used; however, such simplification is limited (Dixon 1987). Refer to Powell (1986) for suggestions on increasing vocabulary through the use of antonyms.

Analogies. Analogy exercises can present problems for pupils because their successful completion requires reasoning ability, prior knowledge, and more word-meaning knowledge than needed for other types of vocabulary activities. Therefore, the steps required to complete analogies should be demonstrated clearly, and guided practice in their application should be provided prior to assigning such exercises to children. As shown below, the relationships that must be understood are not the same in all analogy items. Analogy items may appear in different formats, such as: *good* is to *bad* as *light* is to: (a) bright (b) naughty (c) dark (d) happy; or *foot* is to *hand* as shoe is to _____. Analogies may also involve other types of analysis (Ignoffo 1980):

Part to whole	lead : pencil : : ink : _____
Object to function	refrigerator : cold : : oven : _____
Object and its composition	car : metal : : book : _____
Worker and tools	mechanic : pliers : : sculptor : _____
Size or degree	stream : river : : sea : _____

Denotations and Connotations. A *denotation* is the literal meaning of a word (yellow = color); a *connotation* refers to an implied nonliteral meaning (yellow = cowardly). Children can be helped to distinguish between literal and emotional tones of words by using exercises such as those suggested by D. Johnson and Pearson (1984) and Baldwin, Ford, and Readence (1981).

Learning Fine Shades of Meaning. Many children fall victim to the insidious use of a small number of stock words rather than attempt to state an idea as clearly or descriptively as possible. Some pupils are unaware of fine shades of word meanings; others have the necessary vocabulary to distinguish nuances but opt not to.

One of the best ways to awaken children to the desirability of stating their meanings with precision is to take advantage of a pupil's use of a word whose generalized meaning has been worked to death. If a student describes a party as being "lousy," the teacher might ask, "Was it boring, dull, disappointing? Were the refreshments insufficient, unappetizing? Were the people covered with lice?" Discussion of this sort can lead to exercises such as the construction of a *word line* (see Hofler 1981), which depicts the relationships among words in a single category on a graduated line. For example, a word line dealing with size might have *minuscule* printed at one end and *colossal* at the other. In between would be words indicating increasing changes in size. Pictures rather than printed words can be used in the lower grades. The *concept attainment strategy* (Thelen 1982) also stresses the hierarchical arrangement of words. Upper-grade students should be shown how to use and encourage to use an appropriate-level thesaurus.

Homographs, Heteronyms, Homonyms, and Homophones[10]   *Homographs* are words that are spelled the same but have different pronunciations and meanings (e.g., *bow*, *lead*). A list of 86 homographs appears in D. Johnson, Moe, and Baumann (1983). W. R. Johnston (1988) lists 547 heteronyms, which are defined as being synonymous to homographs (T. L. Harris & Hodges 1981). *Homonyms* are spelled and sound alike but have different meanings (e.g., *pool* can mean a place to swim, a game of billiards, or to combine resources). *Homophones* are words that are pronounced alike but are spelled differently and have different meanings (e.g., *you, yew, ewe*). Refer to D. Johnson and Pearson (1984) or to Fry, Fountoukidis, and Polk (1985) for lists of homophones.

Initial instruction with the aforementioned types of words should focus on preventing problems with understanding their meanings. Pupils need to understand that context determines the pronunciations and meanings of homographs (e.g., the *bow* in the girl's hair vs. the *bow* of a ship). Context also determines the meanings of homonyms; but, as with homographs, does not necessarily reveal their meanings. Students may be more confused by the unknown meaning of a word for which other meanings are known than by a word that is totally new to them. A child who knows that *strike* means "to hit" may need help understanding its use in such expressions as "strike it rich," "go on strike," or "strike a camp." Learning new meanings for "old" words is an important part of vocabulary development. Multiple-meaning words are best learned by encountering them in a variety of meaningful contexts. Unlike homographs and homonyms, the spellings of homophones help to indicate their meanings. Children can be made aware of this by discussing the different spelling and meaning of each word as the pupils are looking at its printed form and then by comparing the spellings and meanings of the homophones.

Figurative Language.   Authors frequently use words and phrases the intended meanings of which differ from their literal meanings. These figurative expres-

[10]Dictionaries and authors are not in complete agreement as to how these four terms should be defined, nor are the distinctions that should be made among them clear.

sions include idioms, similes, metaphors, *personification* (attributing human characteristics to a nonhuman), and *hyperbole* (great exaggeration: The suitcase weighed a ton.).

In *Amelia Bedelia* (Parish 1963), the central character is very literal-minded. She "trims" a steak with ribbons and "dresses" a chicken in clothing. This book provides an excellent steppingstone to the study of uncommon secondary meanings, idioms, and other figurative language. For suggestions on ways to interest children in, and help them to understand, figurative language, see Turner (1976) and Howell (1987) on figurative language; Forester (1974), Edwards (1975) and May (1979) on idioms; Sherer (1977), Thompson (1986), and Readence, Baldwin, and Head (1987) on metaphors; Readence, Baldwin, and Rickelman (1983a) on similes; and McKenna (1978) on portmanteau words. Refer to Ortony (1984) for a discussion of children's understanding of figurative language.

The ability to interpret ideas presented through analogies, similies, metaphors, euphemisms, and circumlocutions grows from meeting such forms of expression repeatedly in contexts that make their meanings clear. Few adults are deceived by the "great regret" with which a public official's resignation is received by his or her superior.

Sensitivity to implied meanings requires a fairly high level of verbal intelligence. Individuals who easily recognize analogies and readily note similarities and differences between concepts are likely to understand implied meanings. Those who lack facility in understanding verbal relationships are likely to grasp only obvious, stated meanings.

One way to develop an understanding of figurative language is through practice in paraphrasing. Being able to restate another's thoughts in one's own language clearly and unambiguously is a crucial test of whether the thoughts were understood. Erroneous interpretations can be discovered and correct ones provided and explained.

Metaphors have received a great deal of research attention. *Metaphors* are nonliteral comparisons in which two things that are not alike can be compared because they share some attribute (Readence, Baldwin & Head 1987). Pupils may fail to understand a specific metaphor because they: (1) interpret it literally, (2) fail to identify the appropriate shared attribute, or (3) lack sufficient word-meaning knowledge to identify the critical matching attribute. The latter is the most likely cause in older students (Ortony 1980; Pearson et al. 1981; Readence et al. 1986). Poor readers are less skilled than good readers in interpreting metaphors (Seidenberg & Bernstein 1988). Refer to O'Brien and Martin (1988) for summaries of theories as to how metaphors are understood. The ability of young blacks to engage in ritual insults that require a high degree of skill with figurative language, especially metaphors, suggests that comprehending figurative language may depend largely on having appropriate experiences (Ortony, Turner & Larson-Shapiro 1985; DeLain, Pearson & Anderson 1985).

Categorization.   Categorization exercises require the systematic arrangement of objects, pictures, or words into groups or categories in accordance with some predetermined criterion (e.g., things that fly). A modification of this technique involves placing the items into as many different categories as possible (e.g., a *fork* may be classified under "things used in eating," "metal objects," "sharp objects," etc.)

Categorization of classification exercises include the following:

1. Name the parts of an automobile.
2. A wing is a part of:
   (a) an animal   (b) a bird   (c) a fish   (d) a plant
3. Place the following words under either <u>vegetables</u> or <u>fruits</u>:
   orange   potato   pineapple   lettuce.
4. List all the words you can under the following headings:
   <u>Animals</u>   <u>Food</u>   <u>Clothing</u>

Many other types of vocabulary practice also require classification skills, such as the three-component categorization technique described by Readence and Searfoss (1980).

Keyword Method.   The *keyword method* involves selecting a familiar word that is visually and/or acoustically similar to the unknown word and then linking the two words by creating an interactive image (thematic relationship) between the two terms. The mental image is used to learn and to remember the new word meaning. It was originally used for teaching foreign-language vocabulary; for example, to learn the Spanish word *carta* ("letter"), one would think of a *cart* and then imagine a *letter* being transported in a shopping cart.

According to Guthrie (1984), the keyword method is an effective technique for learning word meanings, and has been reported effective for LD students (Condus, Marshall & Miller 1986). The technique is also reportedly useful for learning content material (Levin et al. 1986, Konopak & Williams 1988) and in acquiring associations between pieces of information that may not have an obvious relationship (Pressley, Johnson & Symons 1987).

Use of the keyword method with children under age 11 may require the teacher to provide illustrations of the keyword and definition referents. Maximum facilitation may occur only if the child is provided with illustrations in which the interactions between the keyword and its referent are explicit (Pressley, Levin & Miller 1981). Refer to Mastropieri (1988) and Konopak and Williams (1988) for information regarding how to use the keyword method.

The keyword method has not received universal endorsement. Sternberg (1987) points out that it requires one to know in advance a meaning of the target word and is therefore of little use in learning new word meanings independently. The effects on reading comprehension of vocabulary knowledge acquired through the keyword method have not been studied adequately (Stahl & Fairbanks 1986). According to Moore (1987), who refers to it as cumbersome and artificial, the value of the keyword method on learning subject-matter vocabulary is yet to be shown. Pressley, Levin, and McDaniel (1987) defend its use.

Semantic Mapping.   Vocabulary instruction that focuses on building rich semantic networks of related concepts facilitates transferable growth in both vocabulary and comprehension (Pearson 1985). *Semantic mapping*, the categorical structuring of information in a graphic form, can be used before or after reading. The procedure can be used to develop vocabulary or comprehension, to activate or assess prior knowledge, to organize ideas in preparation for writing, or as a

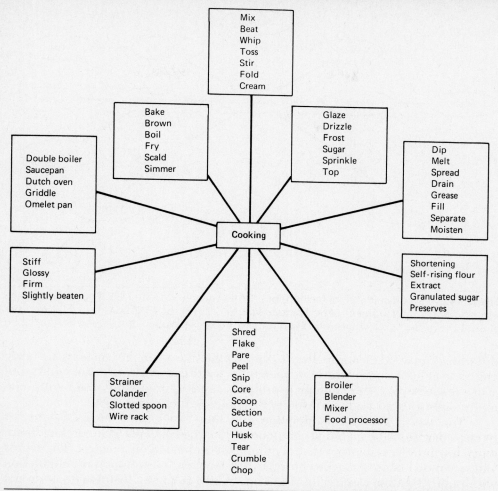

Figure 14.1. Semantic map for cooking. Figure from *Teaching Reading Vocabulary*, Second Edition, by Dale Johnson and P. David Pearson, copyright © 1984 by Holt, Rinehart and Winston, Inc., reprinted by permission of the publisher.

study aid to organize and integrate information. The resulting semantic map (see Figure 14.1) depicts relationships among words and concepts. As a vocabulary-building strategy, semantic mapping provides anchor points to which students can attach new concepts (see McNeil 1987). A completed semantic map reveals to the teacher anchor points on which new concepts can be built (D. Johnson, Pittleman & Heimlich 1986).

Another form of semantic mapping is the synonomic web (see Figure 14.2). For suggestions on the construction and use of semantic mapping, refer to Heimlich and Pittleman (1986), McNeil (1987), and Nagy (1988).

Semantic Feature Analysis. Semantic feature analysis goes beyond semantic mapping in that it focuses on specific relationships and distinguishes similarities and

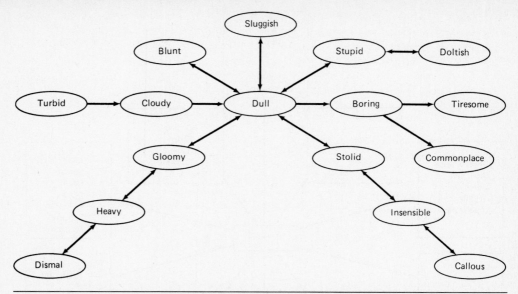

Figure 14.2. Synonymic web of relationship. From Joseph P. O'Rourke, *Toward a science of vocabulary development* (The Hague: Mouton, 1974), p. 75. Reproduced by permission of the author and Mouton de Gruyter, a division of Walter de Gruyter & Co.

differences in word meaning. Its use is most effective when the concepts are fairly close and at least some of the word meanings are already known by the pupils. Because it is complex, this strategy is probably more appropriately used with relatively sophisticated students (Moore, Readance & Rickelman 1989).

The words under consideration and their *semantic features* (words or phrases that describe meaning components that the concepts share or that distinguish a word meaning from that of others) are indicated on a matrix. The words and semantic features may be chosen by the teacher or developed in conjunction with pupils through discussion. Deciding which semantic features do or do not apply to a word is done by the students. Anders and Bos (1986), McNeil (1987), and Nagy (1988) offer suggestions for using semantic feature analysis, as do Moore, Readence, and Rickelman (1989), who also suggest other instructional strategies for teaching word meaning.

The *Venn diagram* is another semantic-feature-analysis technique. Semantic features that the words and concepts have in common appear in the portions of the two or more circles that overlap. The feature unique to a concept appears in the unconnected part of each circle (see Nagy 1988).

Vocabulary Materials and Games.   Vocabulary-building activities are provided in workbooks correlated with basal readers and in independent workbooks designed to develop only vocabulary or reading comprehension in general. Multimedia materials and computer software are also available Each set of materials should be evaluated before it is used with students. Many commercially published vocabulary programs introduce obscure word meanings (Graves 1984).

Many word-recognition games (see pages 488–494) can be adapted for vocabulary development. Vocabulary games also are available from various publishers. A variety of vocabulary games and exercises can be found in Platts (1970); Dale and O'Rourke (1971); O'Rourke (1974); Wagner, Hosier, and Cesinger (1972); Criscuolo (1981, 1984); and D. Johnson and Pearson (1984).

SENTENCE COMPREHENSION

Sentence comprehension involves the use of both linguistic information (e.g., knowledge of word meanings and syntactic structures) and nonlinguistic information (e.g., world knowledge) (Richgels 1986). The importance of accurate, automatic word recognition and knowledge of word meanings for reading comprehension has already been discussed. This section deals with the factors that influence sentence difficulty and how to improve sentence comprehension.

Factors That May Influence Sentence Difficulty

Some sentences are more difficult than others to understand. The following are some of the factors that influence the comprehensibility of sentences.

SURFACE VERSUS DEEP STRUCTURE. Transformational-generative linguists stress that every sentence has a surface structure and a deep structure. A *surface structure* refers to what is actually written, a *deep structure* to what the sentence means. A sentence is said to be understood when the meaning of its deep structure is grasped.

Two sentences may have very similar surface structures but different meanings (as in sentences a and b below). Two or three sentences may have different surface structures and have the same meaning (as in sentences b, c, and d below)

    a. He painted the house red.
    b. He painted the red house.
    c. He painted the house that was red.
    d. The house that he painted was red.

The deep structure of a sentence may not be apparent from its surface structure. The closer the match between the surface and deep structures of a sentence, the fewer transformations the reader has to make and, therefore, the easier the sentence is to understand (McNeil 1987). "Judy fed the dog" is easy to understand because children have had numerous experiences with such simple active sentences of the subject-verb-object type, and so it is clear as to who did what for or to whom. Other kinds of sentences require the reader to carry out special mental operations to make the transformation. For example, passive sentences (e.g., The dog was fed by Judy) can cause problems because the sequence of words in the sentence is an inversion of the basic subject-verb-object word order, and a form of *be* is introduced. Children below seventh grade usually have more difficulty understanding passive than active sentences, especially when the syntax is complex (Richgels 1986). Passive sentences focus attention on the recipient of the action; active sentences focus attention on the subject of the sentence. Many readers, even those who are fairly skilled, fail to understand this subtle difference in meaning. Refer to Harris and Coltheart (1986, pp. 223–227) for information about when and why passive sentences are used.

There may also be a discrepancy between the surface and deep semantic structure of a sentence (McNeil 1987). An author may intend an entirely different meaning for a sentence than its surface structure suggests. Thus, "That's nice" can be a positive comment by a story character, or it can be a sarcastic remark. The alert reader infers the appropriate meaning from the context. Conflicts in semantic structure (e.g., I'm not unhappy) require the reader to transform the sentence into its opposite meaning (McNeil 1987).

SENTENCE LENGTH.   Long sentences are often more difficult to understand than short sentences because they contain one or more dependent clauses, embedded phrases or clauses, or plural subjects or predicates. Such constructions increase the syntactic complexity of the sentence. It is the syntactic and semantic complexity of the sentence and not its length *per se* that makes it difficult to understand.

Short sentences are not necessarily easy to understand. For example, in early-reading materials that contain a great deal of dialogue, the speaker of a sentence is often not clearly marked (e.g., "Jane said" is not continuously repeated). Other short sentences require the reader to infer missing words (e.g., in " 'Shut the door,' said Mother," the reader must infer to whom Mother was speaking). Sentences may have a number of possible meanings. For example, "It is hot in here" may be a simple statement of fact or a subtle request to open a window.

A series of short sentences is not necessarily easier to understand than a longer sentence expressing the same idea. For instance, "The tired fisherman caught a huge sailfish" is probably easier to understand than "The fisherman was tired. The fisherman caught a sailfish. The sailfish was huge." The longer sentence is easier to process because the information is chunked into two phrases and the relationships among the ideas are more explicit. Similarly, it is easier to grasp the meaning of "The machine stopped due to an electrical power failure" (even though the effect precedes the cause) than "The electrical power failed. The machine stopped." The cause-effect relationship is explicitly marked by "due to" in the longer sentence; the reader must infer the cause-effect relationship between the concepts revealed by two short sentences.

CONCEPT DENSITY.   Sentences of relatively equal length may vary considerably in the number of concepts they contain. Densely packed idea units are difficult to understand because they place more of a burden on our limited cognitive processing systems (Samuels & Eisenberg 1981). Children who lack adequate reading fluency may find it difficult to retain enough incoming information to establish a relationship among the concepts. Concept density is more likely to be a problem in expository than in narrative text.

SYNTACTIC COMPLEXITY.   *Syntax* is the primary means by which the intended relations among words are specified. Therefore, understanding the syntactic structure of a sentence is important to reading comprehension.

In most cases, the reader's level of syntactic competence exceeds the level of syntactic complexity used in the material being read. But it should be remembered that, for the most part, syntactic competence is based on experience with oral language. The syntactic structures found in written material tend to be more complex than those used in the informal oral language experiences of children. Also, some written syntactic structures occur only rarely in spoken language: For example, spoken sentences rarely contain a number of embedded clauses. The large amount of processing capacity necessarily devoted to word recognition also detracts from the novice reader's use of her knowledge of phrase and sentence structures (Ryan 1981).

Children in Grades 2–6 are not adept at interpreting complex syntax, so they rely heavily on their world knowledge to comprehend such sentences. But when sentences cannot be interpreted properly without having the necessary syntactic knowledge, their reading comprehension suffers. Elementary school children usually understand complex active sentences better when they are spoken than written, but even spoken complex passive sentences cause problems (Richgels 1986). Disabled readers generally have difficulty understanding complex syntax even in spoken language (Stanovich 1986a).

In general, the more syntactically complex the sentence, the more difficult it is to understand. However, a potentially difficult structure may not cause a problem if the reader's topical knowledge matches the sentence content (Barnitz 1979). Syntax can also be a problem when complex structures are used to express semantic relationships that are, in themselves, too advanced for the reader (Huggins & Adams 1980). Sentence comprehension can be limited by the reader's lack of familiarity with the concepts the sentence is attempting to reveal.

Direct measures of sentence complexity or depth have been devised (Yngve 1962, R. L. Allen 1966, Botel & Granowsky 1972), but they are not commonly used. A less complex measure of sentence difficulty is the *kernel distance theory* (Fry, Weber & DePierro 1978). It suggests that the greater the number of words between the subject and predicate of the sentence and between the verb and the object, the more difficult is the sentence to understand.

Some students have difficulty understanding negative or complex verbs (Hildyard & Olson 1982). Mathewson (1984) provides examples of typical negative sentence structures (e.g., We never want to go; None of us wants to go), discusses why children find them difficult to comprehend, and offers suggestions for helping pupils grasp their meaning.

Other pupils have difficulty understanding dependent or subordinate clauses in general.[11] Many of these problems are caused by not understanding the *signal words* that introduce, connect, order, and relate ideas to larger concepts. Signals words can occur within a sentence or act as cohesive ties between sentences. Poor comprehenders often fail to attend to signal words (Maria & MacGintie 1987). Among the signal words children are likely to encounter are the following:

- *More information to follow:* also, and, another, as well as, besides, finally, furthermore, in addition to, in conclusion, moreover
- *Opposite idea to follow:* although, as a matter of fact, but, either . . . or (im-

[11]Kachuk (1981) discusses how to help children overcome problems understanding relative clauses.

plies alternative), even if, however, in spite of, instead of, nevertheless, on the other hand, rather, still, yet
- *Cause indicated:* as a result of, because, due to, in order to, on account of, since
- *Effect indicated:* as a consequence, as a result, consequently, so, so as to, so that, therefore
- *Exceptions to follow:* all but, except
- *Conditions to be met:* after, as soon as, before, following, if (also may indicate a supposition), provided that, should, while, without, unless, until
- *Comparison to be made:* as, before . . . after, like, once . . . now, some . . . others, than
- *Examples to follow* (these words are often followed by *is* or *are*): examples, for example, kinds, ordinal numbers (e.g., (1) . . .; (2) . . .), others, several, some, such as, the following, types, ways.

Stoodt (1972) reports that the best-understood signal words through fourth grade were *and, for,* and *as;* those that were comparatively difficult were *when, so, but, or, where, how, that,* and *if.* Robertson (1968) found that sentences containing clauses introduced by *however, thus, which, although,* and *yet* were difficult for intermediate-grade children; understanding of these connectives was closely related to intelligence and listening comprehension, and correlated 0.83 with reading comprehension. Implicit connectives are more difficult to understand than explicitly stated connectives.

Readers who fail to note or who do not recognize a conjunction may interpret the ideas it connects as either unrelated or related in ways that the author did not intend. Thus, they may comprehend each clause or sentence but fail to understand the passage as a whole (McClure & Steffensen 1985).

Primary-grade children understand time relationships better when the sequence of events in the sentence matches the sequence in which the events usually occur in the real world (e.g., I ate lunch before going out to play) than when the time sequence is reversed in the sentence (e.g., Before going out to play, I ate lunch) (Distad & Paradis 1983).

Other syntactic structures that can cause comprehension problems are appositives (Rob, my son, is an electrical engineer) and clauses that are the subjects of sentences (Skiing all day tired Susie). Research on teaching children to understand syntactic structures is sparse (Jenkins & Pany 1981).

ANAPHORA. This term refers to the substitution of one word for another word or group of words.[12] Its use allows authors to avoid repeated use of the same word. But anaphora can create comprehension problems for readers who do not infer the relationships between or among anaphoric terms and their referents.

In general, inferring the relationship between an anaphoric word and its referent is more difficult when: 1) more than one anaphoric term occurs in the text, especially when they have the same gender and/or number; 2) the term

---

[12]Linguists distinguish between *anaphora* and *cataphora.* In anaphora, the referent comes before the substitution; in cataphora, the reverse is true. We use *anaphora* to refer to both terms because it is more commonly used in that way.

precedes its referent; or 3) many words come between the two, or the anaphoric word and its referent are in different sentences. Such generalizations must be tempered by the fact that other variables also influence the ease with which the relationship can be understood. In the sentence, "John saw Mary and he said hello to her," the parallel construction of the two clauses and the pronoun gender differences make it comparatively easy to relate the pronouns to their referents, even though the closest antecedent to *he* is *Mary*. Because the referents are not clear in "John saw Tom and he said hello to him," the sentence is ambiguous.

Regardless of age, the *canonical order strategy* is preferred for assigning pronoun referents. The noun that provides an interpretation that is most consistent to what is most likely to happen in the real word is selected as the pronoun antecedent. Thus, in the following example, *Mother* rather than *Winnie* is selected as the referent for *she:*" Mother sat next to her two year-old daughter Winnie. She began to read the book." When the text is not semantically biased toward a "Most-likely-event" interpretation, two other strategies may be employed. In using the *minimum distance principle* (MDP), the nearest syntactically appropriate noun preceding the pronoun is chosen as its antecedent. The literature suggests that children below age 10 prefer to use the MDP; after age 12, they are able to use strategies that violate the MDP. Use of the *parallel function strategy* (PFS) requires that the person be capable of violating the MDP. In using the PFS, the antecedent of a pronoun is assumed to be the subject of the recent discourse. The age at which pupils begin to prefer the PFS has not been determined, but adults prefer to use it about 70% of the time. A. Adams (1986) did not find a developmental sequence in preferred strategies. The MDP strategy was not preferred by children younger than 10, nor was the PFS preferred by those over age 12.

Personal pronouns are the most common form of anaphora. Baumann (1987) found, for example, that about 42% of the anaphora used in basal reader selections were accounted for by five personal pronouns (*he, I, it, she,* and *you*). About 13% of the basal reader words were anaphoric terms. Other types of pronouns are *demonstrative pronouns* (e.g., *this, that,*[13] *these, those*) and *relative pronouns* (e.g., *who, whom, whose, which*). Locatives (e.g., *here, there*) often refer to phrases (Julia eats *in the kitchen*. It is warm *there*.). At times a pronoun may refer to a whole sentence (*Helen eats noisily. This* annoys Ben).

By the sixth grade most pupils are able to comprehend all but a few types of pronouns (Barnitz 1981). Novice readers (Baumann 1987) and some disabled readers (Fayne 1981) may not have mastered even commonly occurring forms of anaphora. Children can be taught strategies that help them to resolve anaphoric relations (Baumann 1986c).

Some structures can cause comprehension problems because they require making difficult inferences. A verb may have a verb-phrase referent (Marshall *eats too much*. Marge knows that he *does*.), or the reader may need to infer one or more words that have been omitted. For example, "he" must be inferred as occurring between *and* and *said* in "John saw Mary and said hello to her," and

---

[13]*This* and *that* may also be used as locatives that suggest distance (e.g., "I want *that* book" indicates the book is farther away from the speaker than in "I want *this* book."

"wash the floor" must be inferred as what Barbara did in "No one else would wash the floor, so Barbara did." (Bormuth 1975b).

Referring terms that may cause comprehension difficulty, especially for novice readers, include: (1) temporal references (e.g., the *next* day); (2) locational references (e.g., *under* the table); and (3) discourse references, in which third-person pronouns represent nouns (e.g., Give *this* to *them*) (Samuels & Eisenberg 1981). Even some older pupils get confused when more than one term is used to represent a story character (e.g., Dr. Smith, Jim, Nancy's husband, the only psychiatrist in town, etc.).

Pearson and Johnson (1978) suggest ways to use questions to determine if anaphoric relationships are understood, and offer suggestions for teaching anaphora, as do McNeil (1987) and Baumann (1987).

Improving Sentence Comprehension

Psycholinguistic research points to the sentence as the fundamental unit in discourse comprehension. It also suggests that sentence comprehension skills usually continue to develop until at least age 10 (Corley 1988). However, some children can profit from instruction and practice aimed at improving their ability to understand various types of written sentences. Some suggestions were given in the foregoing; others follow.

Many novice readers do not make adequate use of their spoken language skills when first learning to read. They need to be encouraged to read using the same intonations they would use in telling the story. Doing so should help them to understand the relationships between the spoken and written forms of language, and to use their language competence to understand written sentences. Teachers can provide models of good oral reading. And, because many of the stories they are asked to read contain dialogue, children can be encouraged to take cues from the events in the story or from accompanying illustrations to "read it, just like _____ would say it."[14]

Too often, sentence comprehension practice relies heavily on workbook or worksheet exercises. Such materials can be useful if used judiciously, and if remediation based on determined causes is provided. Children who consistently make few errors on such exercises should be excused from them. Rather than do boring busywork, their time can be spent in reading for pleasure.

Misunderstood sentences can be followed up with appropriate questions. Understanding of essential factual content of most sentences can be checked by asking *who, what, where, when,* or *how.* Comprehension of causal relationships can be assessed by asking *why.* Questions such as "Who did _____?" "What did _____?" do and "To whom (or what) did _____ do it?" can be used to check the child's understanding of the relationships among subject, verb, and object of the sentence. Following up an unacceptable response with "How do you know?" or "Why do you think so?" may reveal the source of the comprehension difficulty or that the child's interpretation is perfectly logical, although unexpected.

Exposing children to oral language that is richer and more complex than

---

[14]When a first grader was asked to read the sentence just as the story character, a duck, would say it, his response was "Quack, quack!"

what they presently understand may lay the groundwork for comprehending reading material of similar complexity. For example, some children have difficulty understanding sentences containing embedded clauses because they are not accustomed to hearing or using such structures. However, some written language patterns do not occur frequently in spoken language. This is another reason for reading to children. Learning to write increasingly more complex sentences also may aid sentence comprehension. Weaver (1979) found that having third graders construct sentences using word cards while applying a word-grouping strategy (which is clearly outlined in the article) improved their reading comprehension. "Sentence sense" or sentence-organization skills can also be developed by having students manipulate phrase cards to make meaningful sentences (Greenewald & Pederson 1983).

Manipulating sentence structures may provide insight into the internal workings of sentences. Combining simple sentences into a more complex sentence, or the reverse, may help some children to better understand complex or compound sentences. Sentence-combining ability seems to improve with age; nevertheless, only 20% of the 13-year-olds and 44% of the 17-year-olds responded correctly to the more difficult sentence-combining items on a national assessment test (NAEP 1982a).

Most studies have shown that the use of sentence-combining exercises has improved various aspects of student's writing ability (Hillocks 1986), such as increased use of syntactically complex sentences (W. L. Smith & Combs 1980). Findings regarding the effect of such exercises on reading comprehension are inconclusive (Stotsky 1982). That such programs have not been particularly effective may in part reflect the use of measures that were not sufficiently sensitive to gains in sentence-combining or sentence-reduction ability or to the fact that such training can help only those who could profit from it (Tierney & Cunningham 1984). Neville and Searls (1985) report that training in sentence combining and kernel identification enabled sixth graders to comprehend syntactically more complex text than could the control group.

Suggestions for sentence-combining exercises have been provided by Chomsky (1981), and Strong (1986); and for improving sentence comprehension in general, by Barnitz (1979), and McNeil (1987).

USE OF PUNCTUATION.   *Punctuation marks* are used to clarify the meanings of sentences and to give speech characteristics to written language (T. L. Harris & Hodges 1981). Most children learn early how to use their voices in response to punctuation. For example, they pause briefly at commas and longer at dashes; stop at periods; and, in response to the punctuation marks at the end of sentences, they use their voices to differentiate among declarative, interrogative, and exclamatory sentences. Simple explanations, modeling, and supervised practice usually help children who have difficulties in these areas. At times, it is necessary to use such techniques as color coding (e.g., commas are yellow, periods are red).

Children's oral reading can provide information about their use of some punctuation marks, but not others (e.g., possessives). And appropriate use of the voice does not necessarily mean that the pupil understands the purpose of the punctuation (e.g., commas may indicate apposition rather than a listing of items). Some pupils may not understand, for instance, that colons may be used to separate the main part of a sentence from an explanation or example or to indicate that a list is to follow, or that a semicolon can indicate separate independent clauses in structurally complex sentences. Pupil understanding of such punctuation marks can be determined through appropriate questioning.

Ability to Read in Phrases

Grammarians often define a phrase as a group of two or more words not containing a subject or a predicate. Here, we use the term *phrase* to indicate a thought unit. *Reading in phrases* means dividing a sentence into thought units. Phrasing is indicated during speaking or oral reading by pauses (The gracious hostess moved quietly   among her guests.). There is no "rule" that governs how a sentence should be phrased; at times the same sentence can be phrased differently yet appropriately. The key is that the words in the phrase are related in some meaningful way so as to form a thought unit.

Grouping words into phrases can facilitate language processing. One reason why spoken language is often easier to understand than written language is that the speaker pauses between phrases, thus separating the message into thought units for the listener. Given the limited amount of information that can be stored in STM, a smaller number of units to process, allows for more efficient processing: In the example above, it is more efficient to process three phrases than eight words. Encouraging pupils to read in phrases forces them to look for relationships among words and larger units of meaning. Reading phrases facilitates fluency.

Most children begin to acquire the concept of phrasing by being read to well. Phrasing ability is developed by being encouraged to read orally with natural expression (since speakers often pause at the ends of phrasal units, reading "just as you would talk" results in phrasing) and through other instructional activities.

New words are often introduced in phrases or sentences. Phrase cards can be used in various ways, such as in constructing sentences or in answering questions. Children's attention can be directed to phrases by posing oral questions that require the reading of phrases as meaningful units. For example, if the written sentence was "Nora bought the door at the lumberyard," the teacher may ask, "Where did Nora buy the door?" Written exercises, such as the following, that require the pupil to write in or select the correct phrase also may be employed:

Nora bought the door _____.

Nora bought the door

____ in the woods   ____ in the grocery store

____ at the lumberyard   ____ from her father

Adequate phrasing usually indicates reading comprehension, but inadequate phrasing has a number of possible causes. It is not unusual for children who are just learning to read to demonstrate inadequate phrasing while reading. They are just learning to recognize printed words, and, with appropriate guidance and practice, their phrasing becomes increasingly more appropriate. Children who are making normal progress in reading achievement usually do not need much work on phrasing; poor or disabled readers often do.

Special work on phrasing should not be given before considering the possible causes of the behavior. Nervousness may cause inadequate phrasing. When the child is more relaxed and confident, phrasing becomes adequate. Nervousness is often the reason when a pupil's phrasing is inappropriate on the first passage or so read during testing, but improves considerably thereafter. Reading orally at sight can also contribute to inadequate phrasing because appropriate phrasing is often dependent on understanding the material, and at times it is difficult to do so before the whole text or a majority of it has been read. This possibility can be checked out by having the child preread silently material at his instructional level, telling him beforehand that he will be asked to reread it orally and that his comprehension will be checked. Work on phrasing would be provided only if the inadequate phrasing persisted on the oral rereading.

When phrasing is generally inadequate only on passages that exceed the child's word-recognition or comprehension abilities, it is a symptom. Providing material of a more appropriate level of difficulty will solve the "problem." At times, phrasing is inadequate only on a section of the text.

If it is determined that the child needs special work in phrasing, the treatment should be based on the most probable cause(s). A child whose word recognition is good may simply need to understand the concept of phrasing and how it can help her, and be given guided practice. Inadequate phrasing is frequently due to weak, inaccurate, or slow word recognition. A pupil who cannot recognize many words needs to have her sight vocabulary increased before work on phrasing is provided. When word recognition is accurate but slow, efforts can be made to improve both word-recognition speed and phrasing ability.[15] Unless instruction and practice in phrasing is provided, inadequate phrasing may persist even after the word-recognition problem is overcome.

Word-by-word reading, which is the most extreme form of inadequate phrasing, is likely to have an adverse influence on reading comprehension unless the material is conceptually easy for the child. Reading with marked pauses between each two words places a strain on one's information-processing system. Treating each word individually makes it difficult to make use of syntactic and semantic information.

Cromer (1970) distinguishes between two kinds of poor comprehenders. His "deficit" group was poor in both reading vocabulary and paragraph comprehension; the "difference" group was poor in comprehension but had normal reading vocabularies. When they read material that was marked off in phrases, the reading comprehension of only the "difference" group improved. Segmenting written text into phrases (and thus organizing the material into thought units for the reader) has been shown to improve the reading comprehension of 9-year-old disabled readers (McBride 1976), children with slow, but accurate, word recognition (O'Shea & Sindelar 1983), high school sophomores (Stevens 1981), and hearing-impaired second graders (Negin 1987). But N. Taylor, Wade, and

---

[15]Care should be exercised in attempting to use phrase cards to develop word-recognition speed and phrasing ability concurrently. Even skilled readers can see only a word or so in one fixation (see page 336). Therefore, it would be impossible to see all of the words in most phrases that were shown very briefly. Phrase cards should be exposed for longer periods of time than one-word cards.

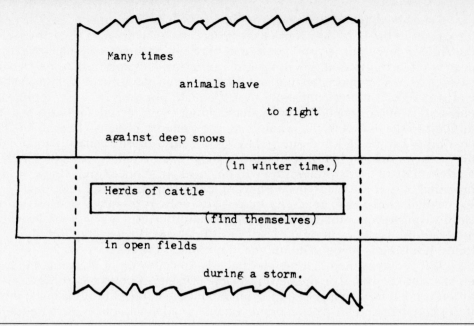

Figure 14.3. One type of practice material for reading in phrases. A strip of paper with one phrase typed per line is placed flat on the reading surface and a strip of stiff paper with a rectangular opening is moved steadily down the page, exposing one phrase at a time. Phrases in parentheses are concealed by the strip.

Yekovich (1985) found that the use of phrased material did not improve the comprehension of fifth-grade poor readers.

Among the more helpful suggestions for improving phrasing ability are:

1. Explain and demonstrate to the child what a phrase is, why it is important, and how to phrase.
2. Model good phrasing. Read sentences orally with somewhat exaggerated phrasing; then have the children imitate your renditions. Having the child read in unison with the teacher, and the alternate reading of sentences aloud by teacher and pupil are also helpful.
3. Use reading material that is well within the word-recognition and comprehension abilities of the child.
4. Provide practice in reading material in which the phrases have been marked off by vertical lines (The boy/ is going/ to the store.), by underlining each phrase (The boy is going to the store, or by spaces (The boy   is going   to the store.) Phrasing practice can also be given using the device shown in Figure 14.3.
5. After the pupil has developed some skill in the use of material that has been phrased for him, he can be asked to mark off the phrases on unmarked selections. His ability to group words into phrases can be checked, and assistance provided as needed.
6. It is important for children to use their newly acquired phrasing skills in their everyday reading. Without frequent practice, they may lose whatever gains were made.

15 Reading Comprehension II: Comprehension beyond the Sentence Level

This chapter deals with beliefs about the nature of reading comprehension; the relationship of prior knowledge to reading comprehension and how knowledge is represented in the mind (schema theory); text coherence; text structure; whether reading comprehension is taught in the schools; and suggestions for developing reading comprehension. Components of reading comprehension are considered separately because it make it easier to discuss them; they actually function in highly interactive ways during reading.

THE NATURE OF READING COMPREHENSION

Durkin (1986) draws an important distinction between testing comprehension and teaching comprehension—the difference between process (the how) and product (the result). Whereas instruction is concerned with the process of reading comprehension, testing is concerned with measuring the product of reading comprehension. Whereas the aim of reading instruction is to have a positive effect on students' cognitive activities as they read, the purpose of testing is to obtain data on which to base informed judgments regarding the outcomes of instruction. Chapter 7 was concerned with measuring reading comprehension; here we discuss the comprehension process and the factors that may influence that process.

Research on reading comprehension and ways of improving it has been going on for over a hundred years (see Singer 1981), and reading comprehension has been variously defined and taught over the years (see Pearson 1985). Between 1978 and 1982 there was more research on reading comprehension processes and instructional practices than during any previous time period of any length. Numerous new theories attempted to explain the comprehension process (Pearson & Gallagher 1983).

Attempts to understand the reading process are important from an educational standpoint because knowing what goes into and happens during reading comprehension should lead to improved instructional practices. Various theories and their instructional implications were covered in Chapter 1. Here, we concentrate on differences of opinion as to whether reading comprehension is a unitary process or one that consists of distinguishable underlying skills or subprocesses.

The Unitary Point of View

Those who believe that reading comprehension cannot be "broken up into small parts" point primarily to researchers' lack of success in identifying truly distinct components of reading comprehension and to the lack of evidence that even improvement in a factor that has been identified (e.g., word-meaning knowledge) results in improved comprehension. They also state that: (1) there is little or no evidence that teaching the numerous reading skills outlined in reading programs improves reading ability; (2) attempts to demonstrate a hierarchical arrangement of reading skills have not been successful; and (3) teaching so many skills misleads children into believing that reading is the mastery of fragmented skills rather than a thought-getting process. Adherents to the unitary viewpoint are prone to say that children learn to read by reading meaningful material. Many of them recommend use of the whole-language approach.

The Subskill/Subprocess View

Belief that the reading process is comprised of subskills or subprocesses is based on statistical analyses, logical analyses, or on theoretical models. There is some belief that skills and/or knowledge are needed for the subprocesses to function optimally (Cooper 1986).

STATISTICAL ANALYSES OF READING COMPREHENSION.   Factor analysis, a statistical technique for analyzing the intercorrelations of test results, has been used to determine whether there are distinct comprehension subskills. F. B. Davis (1968, 1972) analyzed a large battery of test results obtained from high school students. He concludes that the following subskills are identifiable: recalling word meanings and drawing inferences about a word from context; getting the literal sense of details and weaving together ideas in the content; drawing inferences from the content; and recognizing an author's purpose, attitude, tone, mood, and technique.

Spearritt (1972) employed factor-analytic procedures that differed from those used by Davis, to reanalyze Davis's data. He identifies four distinguishable skills: recalling word meanings; drawing inferences from the content; following the structure of a passage; and recognizing a writer's purpose, attitude, tone, and mood. However, Spearritt concludes that, aside from word-meaning knowledge, the other skills are so highly intercorrelated that they could best be described as "reasoning in reading." A reanalysis of Davis's data led R. L. Thorndike (1973–1974) to a similar conclusion. In a later study Spearritt (1977) gave a large battery of tests to sixth graders and found three subskills: knowledge of word meanings, sentence comprehension, and grasp of semantic content. He found no difference between literal and implied meanings. These findings suggest that word-meaning knowledge is an important determiner of comprehension and raises the question of whether the often-listed comprehension subskills are genuinely distinct from one another.

A number of problems are associated with the use of factor analysis to attempt to solve the holistic–subskill debate (P. Johnston 1981). The findings revealed by factor analysis are highly influenced by the items chosen to measure the traits and by the intercorrelations among those traits. The search has attempted to find *independent* comprehension skills, but there is no reason to suppose that different comprehension skills should not be correlated. Furthermore, there is some reason to doubt that the test items that supposedly measure literal or inferential comprehension are "pure" measures of these traits.

LOGICAL ANALYSES OF READING COMPREHENSION.   Unlike statistical-analysis studies that are primarily concerned with identifying separate skills or subprocess, logical analyses of reading comprehension are concerned with *levels* of comprehension. The *Taxonomy of Educational Objectives: Cognitive Domain* (Bloom 1956) is a classification of objectives designed to systematize the desired intellectual outcomes of education in a comprehensive and logically sound hierarchical arrangement. Barrett adapted the Bloom taxonomy to produce a classification of reading objectives (R. J. Smith & Barrett 1974). He uses four main headings (literal recognition and recall, inferential comprehension, evaluation, and appreciation), each of which has subheadings and finer subdivisions. Ruddell (1978) revised Barrett's classification. As shown in Figure 15.1, most of the seven comprehension subskills can be addressed at a factual, an interpretative, or an applicative level.

Another widely used classification employs four main headings: (1) literal comprehension (understanding important, explicitly stated textual information; (2) interpretation (probing for greater depths of meaning); (3) critical reading (evaluating and passing personal judgment); and (4) creative reading, which starts with an inquiry and goes beyond implications derived from the text (N. B. Smith 1972). Still another classification identifies three levels of comprehension: literal, interpretative, and applied—students read to find out what the author said, what the author meant, and how to use the ideas (Herber 1978). These level-of-comprehension classifications do not differ greatly. Literal and factual comprehension are synonymous, as are evaluative and critical reading. Inferential comprehension may mean the same thing as interpretation, but it may include or primarily refer to understanding implicit textual information. Creative reading and application are somewhat alike, but not identical.

Hillocks and Ludlow (1984) established seven hierarchically ordered lev-

| | COMPREHENSION LEVELS | | |
Skill Competencies	*Factual*	*Interpretive*	*Applicative*
1. Details			
a. Identifying	✓	✓	
b. Comparing	✓	✓	✓
c. Classifying		✓	✓
2. Sequence	✓	✓	✓
3. Cause and Effect	✓	✓	✓
4. Main Idea	✓	✓	✓
5. Predicting Outcome		✓	✓
6. Valuing			
a. Personal judgment	✓	✓	✓
b. Character trait identification	✓	✓	✓
c. Author's motive identification		✓	✓
7. Problem solving			✓

Figure 15.1. Classfication of reading comprehension subskills. From R. B. Ruddell, Developing comprehension abilities: implications from research for an instructional framework, in S. J. Samuels (Ed.), *What research has to say about reading instruction* (Newark, DE: International Reading Association, 1978), p. 112. Used by permission of the author and the International Reading Association.

els of fiction comprehension: (1) basic, stated information, (2) key details, (3) stated relationships, (4) simple implied relationships, (5) complex implied relationships, (6) author's generalizations, and (7) structural generalizations. This sequence of comprehension skills appears to begin with low-level literal comprehension and move to understanding more important directly stated information at Level 2. At Level 3 (stated relationships), reasoning ability begins to enter into comprehension and becomes increasingly involved in text processing with each higher level. High school students who could answer questions higher in the sequence could answer all the questions dealing with lower-level comprehension, but the reverse did not occur. Perhaps this is one reason why studies have failed to find separate literal and inferential comprehension. Those who are good comprehenders are usually adept at both types of comprehension; poor comprehenders are inept at both. Furthermore, the ability to make inferences often depends on understanding explicit textual information.

What are typically called comprehension *skills* are really comprehension *tasks* (see pages 586–598) that require (1) application of differing reading strategies, (2) various levels of enabling skills and abilities, and (3) focusing attention on and coordinating, as needed, information that is available from the text, prior knowledge, and illustrations. Learning any one task alone is unlikely to improve a student's overall level of reading ability. Furthermore, teaching reading comprehension involves more than teaching discrete skills or tasks; it also involves teaching the processes of comprehension and how to use them (Cooper 1986). Teaching and practicing a "separate" reading task is educationally defensible because it allows students to focus on learning that skill. But because reading skills usually are utilized in concert during the reading process, children need to be shown how and when to use that skill when reading texts other than the short, single-purpose ones often used in initial instruction, especially those contrived to clearly illustrate use of that skill.

Thinking of comprehension skills as tasks and differentiating among different levels of comprehension can be useful in employing questioning as an instructional strategy, as well as in attempting to understand where and why a child is experiencing comprehension difficulties. Both uses require analysis of task demands, which involves determining what the reader must already know, be able to do, and be able to reason out in order to comprehend the text or to be able to answer comprehension questions acceptably. Knowing, for example, that the reader must infer a cohesive tie in order to understand the relationship between two ideas in contiguous sentences should make the teacher aware of why a pupil probably did not understand that relationship. A question can be formulated that requires the student to focus on an important explicit detail in the text or that requires the pupil to integrate textual information and prior knowledge. Posing such questions for pupils provides them with models of questions to ask themselves while reading.

THEORETICAL FRAMEWORKS.   Carroll (1977) discusses three bases for reading comprehension: cognition, language comprehension, and reading skill. The three are interrelated but are distinguished from one another for the purpose of discussion. *Cognition* (knowing, reasoning, inferencing, and the like; that is, intelligence) cannot be taught directly but sets limits to the individual's ability to develop language comprehension. In turn, language comprehension, which is teachable, limits the level of reading comprehension possible. Carroll recommends the use of parallel auding and reading comprehension tests to distinguish between comprehension difficulties that reflect a lack of sufficient language competence and those that are caused by a lack of reading skills.

A number of writers believe that reading comprehension is a complex process in which a number of functionally defined, information-processing components (subprocesses) interact with one another. As Perfetti and Lesgold (1979) put it, these components are not functionally independent but mutually facilitative. The subprocesses can be isolated in principle, but they are interrelated in practice. In order to specify the effect of any of the myriad of factors involved in the reading process, one would have to know how that factor interacts with all the other factors. At present, it is impossible to describe all these interactions. Therefore, the complexity of the reading process and the interactive nature of the subprocesses seem to preclude the identification of separate comprehension skills. They may exist, but we simply cannot separate them out.

Subprocess theories, such as the interactive theories mentioned in Chapter 1 and the componential theory of reading (Fredericksen, Warren & Roseberg 1985) and the separable-processes model of Calfee, Henry, and Funderberg (1988) suggest that gains in one subprocess allow for gains in others and that insufficiently developed or dysfunctioning subprocesses may limit development of other subskills. Following this line of reasoning, attempts to improve reading comprehension would involve improving the various subcomponents, as well as the abilities and knowledge needed to perform them.

KEY FACTORS IN READING COMPREHENSION

A wide range of variables can influence reading comprehension. These cognitive, linguistic, neurophysiological, and sociocultural factors have been discussed in detail in other chapters. Reading is often described as an interactive process involving what is in the reader's head and what is on the printed page. This section is concerned with key factors involved in this interaction—the reader's prior knowledge and how that knowledge is organized, text coherence, and text structure.

Prior Knowledge

All the information stored in an individual's long-term memory can be described as *prior knowledge.* It includes information about such diverse things as events one has experienced; what words mean; what constitutes an acceptable English sentence; that gold is a precious metal; where Sri Lanka is located; what is likely to be said, done, and felt by characters in a particular situation, as well as how they are probably attired; how to decode unknown words; and when to apply a particular study strategy. In short, prior knowledge includes information about what, how, and why.

Three other terms are sometimes used in this and other contexts: *declarative knowledge* (knowing what, that, or where); *procedural knowledge* (knowing how); and *conditional knowledge* (knowing when and why). Sometimes the term *world knowledge* is employed as a synonym for prior knowledge; at other times it appears to have a more restricted meaning, for example, only declarative knowledge. *Topical knowledge* refers to the information one has concerning a specific topic. Topical knowledge not only increases comprehension and recall of textually explicit information, but enables the reader to fill in information that the author did not supply directly. Topical knowledge is not an either-or proposition, but a matter of degree. Some children have only bits and pieces of fragmented information (Gordon & Rennie 1987).

The importance to reading comprehension of what is already known before reading is not a recent discovery (see W. S. Gray 1948). For years *background knowledge,* as it was frequently called, was considered important and, therefore, influenced instructional practices. It was generally accepted in 1948, as it is now, that the extent and quality of prior knowledge influences the facility with which individuals can understand a text and how well the reader understands the author's message. What is relatively new are the theoretical bases for, and research evidence to support, what was once an intuitively based concept.

Research findings suggest that: (1) Children are not adept at spontaneously drawing on their prior knowledge while reading (R. Anderson et al. 1985); (2) prior knowledge is a better predictor of comprehension than either IQ- or reading-test scores (Pearson 1985); (3) high topical knowledge enhances sensitivity to the relative importance of textual information (Winograd & Newell 1985); (4) differences in levels of prior knowledge account for differences in reading comprehension (Marr & Gormley 1982), independently of IQ (Langer & Nicholich 1981); (5) prior knowledge has a large effect on the level of reading ability needed to comprehend difficult text (Sticht et al. 1986); (6) children with significant prior knowledge make fewer miscues that disrupt meaning (Taft & Leslie 1985); (7) teaching topical and world knowledge prior to reading improves reading comprehension (Ruddell & Speaker 1985, Stahl & Jacobson 1986), perhaps more so for poor readers than for good readers (Calfee & Drum 1985); and (8) making connections between prior knowledge and explicit textual information improves reading comprehension (Beck, Omanson & McKeown 1982). Differences in prior knowledge created by cultural (Barnitz 1986, Ohlausen & Roller 1988) and religious (Lipson 1983) differences, as well as differences in expectations for text content or in frames of reference (R. Anderson & Pearson 1984), can influence text interpretation.

The role of prior knowledge should be considered in planning and conducting reading lessons as well as in assessing reading comprehension. When planning a lesson, it is advisable for the teacher to read the text to determine: (1) which concepts and which relationships between concepts are important to comprehending the material; (2) which concepts and relationships the author provides; (3) how clearly they are provided; (4) which concepts and relationships the author expects the readers to provide; and (5) which concepts and relationships are likely to cause problems for the pupils.

At times teachers may wish to assess children's prior knowledge and to develop the understandings important for text comprehension before the children read the text. The procedures summarized by Holmes and Roser (1987) may be used to make such assessments and to activate prior knowledge (unless readers activate their prior knowledge, it is of little use to them). Three other activities for activating prior knowledge involve (1) having the pupils rate their knowledge of the meanings of important words contained in the text; (2) brainstorming (see Blachowicz 1986), which also helps build rich semantic networks for increasing word-meaning knowledge (Carr & Wixson 1986); and (3) using the *Anticipation Guide* (Duffelmeyer, Baum, & Merkley 1987), which consists of a series of teacher-generated statements to which students respond individually. These assessment/activation procedures usually reveal more about children's grasp of concepts than about how well they will understand the relations between those concepts. Determining the latter often requires additional questioning. To provide practice in independently using prior knowledge, teachers should suggest that the children activate their prior knowledge, have them read, and then discuss how prior knowledge could have been used when it apparently was not.

There are no specific guidelines for developing background knowledge (Tierney & Cunningham 1984). Preteaching vocabulary and related concepts may help (see pages 520–523). Guidelines for preparing and conducting discussions aimed at building background knowledge are offered by Cooper (1986). Students have also been helped to understand new and possibly difficult information by comparing and/or contrasting it with something the pupils already know or can understand more easily (Vosniadou & Ortony 1983). Brief discussions at certain "break points" during reading may be used to reinforce important understandings (see Beck & McKeown 1986).

Activating prior knowledge and building background knowledge prior to reading facilitates comprehension and helps students realize the importance of relating what they already know to textual information. Occasionally a pupil's topical knowledge is so deficient that it precludes adequate comprehension. In some cases, the child can simply be asked to read something else or excused from reading that text at present. If reading a particular piece of literature is required, the teacher can attempt to find a more comprehensible edition. For an expository text, the teacher may need to supply the information that an elaborated text would offer (see page 604) or to develop the concepts through a means other than having the child read the text.

PRIOR KNOWLEDGE AND READING COMPREHENSION PROBLEMS. Reading comprehension may be hampered because readers lack sufficient topical knowledge or fail to activate the relevant knowledge they possess. Poor readers use their prior knowledge less well than good readers do, especially when reading expository texts (B. Holmes 1983b). Poor readers may have an impoverished understanding of the relationships among the facts they do know about a topic. In addition, authors may fail to provide enough clues to activate pupils' prior knowledge (L. Baker & Brown 1984b) or may not explain important concepts and their relationships sufficiently to overcome the pupils' lack of familiarity with the topic (Herman et al. 1987).

Comprehension problems can also occur when readers fail to maintain a proper balance between the information in their heads and that in the written text. Some pupils rely too much on text-based information and fail to use their world knowledge to guide their text processing. Other readers rely too heavily on their prior knowledge and fail to consider textual information.

Maria & MacGinitie (1982, 1987) identified two types of poor comprehenders who overrely on top-down processing. Type 1 readers employ a *fixed-hypothesis strategy*. They form an initial interpretation based on an early portion of the next and then try to interpret the rest of the text to conform to their initial hypothesis. Often, Type 1 readers give far-fetched interpretations of later portions of the text or may "change" the details in the text to make them conform with their initial interpretation. They lack flexibility. Kimmel & MacGinitie (1985) suggest ways to help Type 1 readers.

Type 2 readers use a *nonaccommodating strategy*. They read the text as though it simply repeated what they already know and fail to take account of the textual information or fail to use it to modify their existing schema. When the text does not conform to their prior knowledge, they may ignore or misinterpret that textual information. Thus, Type 2 readers may find it difficult to learn effectively from text that contains new information. This type of comprehension problem is compounded by the fact that the reader often does not know that she doesn't know.

To help children who rely too heavily on prior knowledge, the teacher can (1) demonstrate the need to read more carefully; (2) teach strategies for monitoring comprehension; (3) have the pupils read material that must be read carefully in order to perform some activity successfully; (4) provide activities that require careful reading, such as outlining and notetaking; and (5) use teacher questioning to force students to construct the author's intended meaning (Tierney & Spiro 1979). Showing the pupils what they are doing and how it can cause comprehension problems may also be helpful.

Kimmel and MacGinitie (1984) identified a group of children who used a *perseverative text-processing strategy*. These pupils employ either an inductive or deductive comprehension strategy, regardless of how the text is organized. The variability within Gold and Fleisher's (1986) data suggests that factors in addition to employing a perseverative stategy may have been operative.

Other pupils have comprehension difficulties when the text is not compatible with or contradicts their prior knowledge or beliefs (Alvermann, Smith & Readence 1985; Maria & MacGinitie 1987). Some studies show that such students are likely to let their prior knowledge or beliefs override textual information; other studies do not (Gordon & Rennie 1986). There is evidence that some readers intentionally reconstruct a text when they disagree with its message (Spivey & King 1989).

Schema Theory

Schema theory attempts to explain how knowledge is represented in the mind and how those representations facilitate comprehension and learning. According to schema theory, all knowledge is packed into units referred to as *schemata*. (Schemata is the plural form; schema, the singular.) Some writers use the term *frame* or *script* rather than *schema*. The notion of schema is not new; Bartlett (1932) used the term in its present meaning almost 60 years ago. A schema is more than just a definition of a word: Each schema represents a "packet of knowledge" that summarizes what one knows about the concept and how these pieces of information are related. In addition to the generic concept itself, a schema includes other information related to the concept and information about how this knowledge is to be used (Rumelhart 1984). For example, a schema for *giraffe* may include knowledge of what it eats, where it lives, how it is able to drink, and so forth. A schema may represent all we know about an event (e.g., a parade); a situation (e.g., what it feels like to experience physical or emotional pain); an action (e.g., dancing), a sequence of actions (e.g., eating in a restaurant involves being seated, receiving a menu, reading the menu, making a decision, etc.); a role (e.g., mother); or an abstract idea, Schemata are thought to be hierarchically arranged networks of concepts (Durkin 1981).

A schema is believed to develop by abstracting the common characteristics of events and experiences, which leads to a representation of generalized knowledge. Schemata can remain stable (Ruddell & Speaker 1985); new schemata can develop; and existing ones can be modified, restructured, or fine tuned (Gordon & Rennie 1987).

Schemata are of two types (Mavrogenes 1983). *Contextual schemata*, with which we are primarily concerned in this section, refers to the person's knowledge of real or imaginary worlds. Contextual schemata are used by the reader during and after reading to help recall what has been read. *Textual schemata* involve knowledge of discourse conventions (see pages 564–570).

According to schema theory, comprehension depends on a person's schemata and textual information and how the individual relates the information from these two sources. Thus, reading comprehension involves simultaneous top-down and bottom-up processing. As a person begins to read (or listen), a search begins for a schema to account for textual information. Words referring to any component of the schema will probably activate the schema as a whole; once the schema is activated, the reader can retrieve the desired information (R. C. Anderson & Pearson 1984). On the basis of the schema first activated, the reader constructs a partial model of meaning, which in turn provides a framework for continuing the search for other appropriate schemata (Gordon & Rennie 1987). As information is gathered and processed, the reader constructs hypotheses about the interactions between his schemata and the textual information. These hypotheses are progressively modified, refined, or discarded (J. Mason et al. 1984) until a plausible, coherent interpretation is achieved (Rummelhart 1984). Because no one schema is likely to contain all the information that would be useful in constructing meaning, more than one schema can be evoked concurrently (Samuels & Eisenberg 1981) or in some sequence. The reader's task is to determine and select which schemata are needed.

Readers may fail to understand a text for three reasons: (1) The reader lacks appropriate schemata to understand the ideas being communicated; (2) the clues provided by the author are not sufficient to suggest selection of appropriate schemata that the reader does possess; and (3) the reader may discover a consistent interpretation of the text, but not the one intended by the author (the reader "understands" the text, but misunderstands the author) (Rumelhart 1980).

Because schemata contain information generalized from experience and because few people have had exactly the same experiences, schemata are usually idiosyncratic. This is one reason why two individuals may have differing interpretations of the same text.

Schemata have "slots" that readers expect to be filled by textual information. Information that fills these slots is easily understood and remembered. Schemata also facilitate the selective allocation of attention (i.e., they guide the search for the important ideas that should be attended to and remembered). Focusing on important information, in turn, facilitates such skills as summarizing (Pearson 1985).

Research findings suggest that both the ability to make inferences and the nature of those inferences are influenced by prior knowledge. Schemata allow the reader to understand far more that what is stated in the text. They allow readers to fill in the information not provided by the author, as well as to infer what the author means by the use of certain words or phrases (e.g., figurative language). Readers are not consciously aware of the *inferential elaborations* (integrating information from prior knowledge with textual information) they make while reading. That such elaborations are made can be demonstrated by reading the following sentences:

1. The punter kicked the ball.
2. The golfer kicked the ball.

Assuming that the reader has the necessary topical knowledge, the differences in the size, color, and shape of the ball in each sentence are known to the reader and can be used in understanding the sentence and later parts of the text. Moreover, the reader can infer that (1) the game being played in the first sentence is football; (2) the punter's team has failed to make a first down or is using the punt as a defensive strategy; (3) the play is probably not a field-goal attempt because place kickers, not punters, are used in such situations; and (4) this is a routine occurrence in a football game.

In the second sentence the reader will probably infer that the golfer had some reason for kicking the ball, because such an action is not the way the game is played. For instance, the reader might infer that the golfer missed an easy putt, got angry, and kicked the ball in anger or that the ball was lying in an disadvantageous spot so the golfer kicked it to give himself an advantage. His cheating allows one to infer something about the golfer's character.

Another form of inferencing based on prior knowledge is referred to as *instantiation*, which involves activating a relevant schema that functions to guide comprehension (Whitney 1987). For example instantiation occurs when we encounter a general noun in context (the *bird* spoke three languages) and use context plus prior knowledge to generate a particular instance of that noun (parrot). Evidence indicates that spontaneous instantiation occurs (Dreher 1985).

While schema theory can account for individual differences in the text comprehension that depend on specific knowledge, its application to reading ability in general is limited (Perfetti 1985). Differences in comprehension cannot be attributed solely to the availability of schemata. Use of schemata may be hampered by weaknesses in skills such as word recognition. Because printed words are the triggers that activate appropriate schemata, weak word-recognition can interfere with the process (Perfetti 1986a). Critics of schema theory also point out that our knowledge is often used to understand information for which we have no obvious schema (Foss 1988). Beers (1987) raises other questions about schema theory.

Connecting, Selecting, and Organizing Reading Processes

A widely held notion is that reading involves constructing a mental representation through an interaction between the reader and the written text. The reader "makes meaning" by integrating textual information and prior knowledge through the processes of connecting, selecting, and organizing information. Readers (1) connect related ideas by discovering and generating links—both internal connections among ideas in the text and external connections between ideas in the text and their prior knowledge (Muth 1987b); (2) select which content to process on the basis of some criterion; and (3) organize that content by applying their knowledge of text structure. Both the author and reader are involved with the use of text coherence and text structure.

When creating text, authors organize it by providing a variety of information. Readers cannot, or may not want to, retain all the information available to them while reading. Therefore, they tacitly or consciously select certain information, on the basis of some criteria as to its importance. A criterion may be textual—that is, it may be based on how high in the text structure the information occurs (see pages 566–567), contextual—that is, based on how salient the information is for accomplishing the reading task; or based on the reader's specific interest. World knowledge also is used in selecting which textual information is important (Ohlausen & Roller 1988).

Readers organize the selected content through their knowledge and use of the conventional patterns employed by authors to structure their messages. These schemata for text structure are used to guide comprehension. Barring any overriding purpose or perspective, skilled readers usually employ the same structure as that of the text when reading well-organized narrative or expository texts. Skilled readers also impose a conventional organization on disorganized or even scrambled text. (Spivey & King 1989).

TEXT COHERENCE.   Reading comprehension can be influenced by the ways in which the textual information is presented by the author, as well as by factors that lie within the reader. To be comprehensible, a text must be coherent and describe a plausible set of ideas or sequence of events (Bock & Brewer 1985). A coherent text is cohesive. *Cohesion* refers to the relationships of ideas within a text—which describe it as a text. Cohesion is significant when the interpretation of some element in the text depends on understanding another concept. For instance, parts of clauses and sentences "cohere" with each other by virtue of the fact that all such grammatical units are structured (Halliday & Hasan 1976). *Text coherence* refers to how well the author has woven together ideas to allow the reader to make logical connections between and among the ideas presented. All else being equal, more coherent text makes it easier to maintain the flow of meaning from one idea to another, thereby making it easier to process the information (Armbruster & Anderson 1984).

Coherence operates at both local and global levels. At the local level, various semantic and grammatical devices are used to help readers comprehend the text. Cohesive ties (see the following) are used to establish relationships between ideas; and cohesive chains are built by employing pronouns, key content words, and varied sets of terms that are semantically related (Foss 1988).[1] At the global level, text is coherent to the extent that it facilitates the integration of key ideas across the discourse. Global coherence is a function of the overall structure or organization of the text (Armbruster & Anderson 1984). Text structure is discussed on pages 564–570.

Cohesive Ties.   Intrasentence cohesion is determined primarily by syntactic structures, but relationships within the sentence may be "marked" by cohesive ties that are either explicit (e.g., a conjunction) or must be inferred (e.g., an ellipsis). In either case, the relationships that they link must be inferred. Such *bridging inferences* enable the reader to form connections between text elements.

Intersentence cohesion is achieved by cohesive ties that integrate semantic relationships between sentences. Except for the first sentence in a paragraph, every sentence contains at least one cohesive tie that connects it, usually with what has gone before, and less often with the information to follow.

Halliday and Hasan (1976) described five categories of cohesive ties, which

[1]Refer to the discussion of anaphora on pages 544–546.

signal that information also has to be retrieved from elsewhere in the text. *Referential ties* embody semantic relations that allow some words in the text to co-refer to others. Readers must infer that the different terms refer to the same referent. The three kinds of referential ties (personal, demonstrative, and comparative) usually are expressed as pronouns, adjectives, and adverbs.

The use of *substitution* and *ellipsis* involves replacing one linguistic unit with another structurally equivalent lexical term, or implying a relationship with a previous one.[2] An example of a substitution is: My *hat* blew away. I must get a new *one*. In an ellipsis, part of the message is omitted but can be inferred from the text as in: "Did you find your dog?" "Yes, I did [find my dog]." A *conjunctive tie* specifies the way in which what is to follow in the text connects to what was said before the conjunction. There are *additive* (e.g., *and*), *adversative* (e.g., *but*), *causal* (e.g., *because, as a result of*), and *temporal* (e.g., *then, next, first, finally*) conjunctions.[3] In *lexical cohesion*, the effect is achieved by the selection of words that in some way are related to information which has already been presented. *Reiteration* is a form of lexical cohesion which involves use of such devices as repetition of the same word, synonyms, or *superordinate terms* (a general term used in place of a specific term). In *collocation*, cohesion is achieved through the association of lexical items that regularly co-occur (e.g. *dollars, cents; basement, roof*).

Research findings support the contention that text coherence affects its comprehensibility. Among the aspects of coherence that make material less comprehensible are: (1) use of terms whose referents are ambiguous, distant, or indirect; (2) inclusion of concepts unfamiliar to the reader; (3) lack of a clear relationship between story events; and (4) inclusion of irrelevant ideas or events (Beck et al. 1984). For a further discussion of coherence, refer to L. Chapman (1983, 1984).

Bridge and Winograd (1982) found that, in general, both good and poor readers in the sixth grade understood the cohesive ties used in their study. However, some students do not understand how cohesive ties indicate relationships until they are in the secondary school (L. Chapman 1984) and poor readers may have particular difficulty with them (J. Smith & Elkins 1985).

Conjunctions appear to cause problems for children, especially for poor readers. McClure and Steffensen (1985) report that the ability to use conjunctions correctly improved between Grades 3 and 9 and that correct usage was correlated with reading achievement. When reading expository text, average readers and, to a greater degree, poor readers in Grades 5 and 7 demonstrate difficulty understanding logical relationships across clauses explicitly marked by the conjunctions *because, although, since, but,* and *so.* Highlighting the conjunctions called the students' attention to them, and improved their comprehension (Geva & Ryan 1985).

Some studies indicate that the presence of explicit connectives facilitates comprehension; other studies do not. However, poor readers find it more difficult to infer implied relationships than to understand those marked by explicit

[2]It may be difficult to distinguish among these categories from the information presented here. Halliday and Hasan (1976) make the distinctions much clearer.
[3]See the discussion of signal words on pages 543–544.

connectives (McKenzie, Neilsen & Braun 1981). The density of cohesive ties and the distance between them does not seem to affect reading comprehension or recall (Neilsen 1981).

TEXT STRUCTURE.[4] Good writing is well organized. Authors start out knowing what they want to say; think through the relative importance of the specific ideas they want to communicate, the sequence in which they are to be presented, and how to interrelate these ideas; and develop their texts accordingly. In fiction there are characters to be introduced, settings to be described, and well-planned lines of events that lead up to a climax. Expository text usually contains an introduction, a body, and a conclusion or summary. Headings, subheadings, material in bold type, marginal notes, and so forth may be added to assist the readers.

Text structure refers to how the ideas in a text are organized by the author. Over time and through exposure, readers gradually become familiar with the general structures of written texts and develop mental representations of them in the form of *text-structure schemata.* By activating these schemata, students become aware of the probable structure of the text they are about to read or are reading and use that knowledge as a framework for forming expectations as to how the content is organized (Ruddell & Speaker 1985). Text structure provides an organizational framework that can be used to help judge the relative importance of information, to organize incoming information, and to order recall (B. Meyer 1984).

Although narratives differ in structure, they are often described in terms of a story grammar. Expository texts are generally described in terms of a hierarchical structure or in levels of information. There are major structural differences between narratives and expository texts, and expository texts are conventionally organized in more ways than are narratives. Also, the particular text structures employed by a writer can vary considerably. Nevertheless, in well-written text the pattern or plan of the text is discernible.

Awareness of expository-text structures begins later than for narratives: at about third-grade level rather than before school entry as is the case with story schema (Gillis & Olson 1987). The ability to capitalize fully on expository-text structures is probably a late-developing skill (L. Baker & Brown 1984b). Many pupils need help in learning how to use their implicit knowledge of text structure to facilitate their comprehension and recall.

The primary purposes of texts are: (1) to tell a story *(narration);* (2) to provide rich sensory images *(description);* (3) to set forth or to explain information *(exposition);* and (4) to argue a particular point of view, and in doing so, to persuade or sway the reader *(argumentation).* Realizing the author's purpose for writing the text can help the reader understand and evaluate the message.

Story Grammar and Story Schema. A *story* is a series of events related to one another in specified ways (Sadow 1982). Theorists have described the common

---

[4]The oft-cited prose-analysis procedures of Fredericksen, Kintsch, and Meyer are described, compared, and critiqued by Meyer and Rice (1984). These and other systems are summarized by Downing and Leong (1982) and Matsuhaski and Quinn (1984). Other types of text analyses are discussed by Tiernay, Mosenthal, and Kantor (1984).

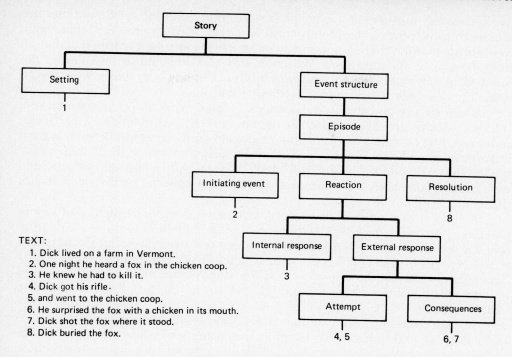

TEXT:
1. Dick lived on a farm in Vermont.
2. One night he heard a fox in the chicken coop.
3. He knew he had to kill it.
4. Dick got his rifle.
5. and went to the chicken coop.
6. He surprised the fox with a chicken in its mouth.
7. Dick shot the fox where it stood.
8. Dick buried the fox.

Figure 15.2.   An example of a basic story structure. From R. Tierney, J. Mosenthal, and R. Kantor, Classroom applications of text analyses: toward improving text selection and use, in J. Flood (Ed.), *Promoting reading comprehension* (Newark, DE: International Reading Association, 1984). Reproduced with permission of the authors and the International Reading Association.

components of a story and how these relate to one another. The resulting *story grammars* indicate that well-formed stories from Western cultures have all or most of the following key elements: (1) a setting (time, place, major characters); (2) a plot that generally involves an initiating event (the problem is identified); (3) the protagonist's reaction to the problem and her or his goal; (4) the protagonist's attempt(s) to achieve the goal (to solve the problem); and (5) the resolution, or lack of resolution, of the problem. Figure 15.2 illustrates a basic story structure. In reading a story, it is important to understand the actions of the main characters because the relations among them are central to understanding the plot and theme of the story. Knowledge of human motivations and actions also serve as a guide to comprehension because it enables the reader to link together various story components in a causal manner (Wixson & Peters 1987).

Hearing and reading stories enables children to develop a *story schema*,[5] which consists of an implicit understanding of *story* that includes a hierarchical ordering of story elements, with the basic components of a story being causally or temporarily related (Rand 1984). By the time they enter school, most children

[5]Gates (1947) stressed the value of "story sense" to comprehension almost 45 years ago, but not until fairly recently have story grammars been described and their influence on comprehension tested empirically.

have adequate implicit knowledge of story structure (Perfetti 1985), but they are unable to recall stories completely until about age 8 (Pellegrini & Galda 1982). As children mature, their concept of story becomes more sophisticated and more fully developed (Whaley 1981, Williams, 1986a). Older pupils have better defined story schemata than do younger children, but how and under what conditions this develops is still not clear (Rand 1984).

Children use their story schemata as a framework for comprehending a story by setting up expectations for certain contents occurring in a particular sequence. Story schemata also enable readers to know what information is most important for understanding a story, thereby helping them to focus their attention on those elements (McConaughy 1982). Young children should be provided with reading selections that conform to their expectations for well-formed stories (Brennan, Bridge & Winograd 1986).

A child's story schema may or may not match the ideal structure of a story grammar (McConaughy 1985). If the story does not conform to the reader's story schema, comprehension is likely to be decreased or even seriously impaired (Calfee & Spector 1981). The ease with which a young child understands a story depends, not only on how well formed the story is, but on how well the child understands the social situations and interactions in the story (Stein & Trabasso 1981).

Research findings indicate that story-grammar instruction does not necessarily improve children's ability to comprehend stories. Pupils who already have a keen sense of story structure are not likely to benefit from such instruction, but it may help poor comprehenders of narratives (Tierney & Cunningham 1984). Story-grammar instruction should be a short-term intervention aimed mainly at helping pupils learn to *apply* their knowledge of story structure. There is no basis for making story-grammar instruction the central focus of a remedial program (Perfetti 1985). In fact, the story-schema organization of poor readers equalled that of good readers when they were required to summarize what they thought important rather than to recall as much of the story as possible (McConaughy 1985).

Ibn *story mapping*, children are taught a strategy for using the structural framework of a story for drawing together textual information and prior knowledge (Idol 1987). For information on using story mapping, refer to Reutzel (1985), and Bergenske (1987).

Other suggestions for helping students to develop, refine, or use their story schema to aid their comprehension are offered by Rubin (1980a), Spiegel and Fitzgerald (1986), and Gordon (1989). Children understand stories better if asked questions that focus their attention on integrating story parts. Beck and McKeown (1981), and Pearson (1982, [1984]) suggest ways to formulate such questions.

Because story grammars are based on folk and fairy tales, they do not fit narratives with more complex structures (Schmitt & O'Brien 1986). Refer to Foss (1988) and Fitzgerald (1989) for other possible limitations of story grammar.

Expository-Text Structures.   One way of describing expository-text structures is in terms of levels of information, or *top-level structure* as it is called. At the top of the content structure are main ideas. Ideas at the middle level correspond to supporting details, and the concepts at the low end of the structure correspond to very specific details. Top-level concepts dominate the subordinate ideas, with each lower structural level providing further information regarding the ideas presented in the level(s) above it (Wixson & Peters 1987).

Research findings suggest that: (1) there are structural features of text that operate independently of the text's content to facilitate text processing; (2) information appearing in high levels of text-structure hierarchy is consistently rated as "most important" by readers; (3) top-level ideas are recalled and retained better than are lower-level ideas;[6] (4) students who use top-level structure or other structural schemata demonstrate better comprehension and recall than those who cannot or do not; (5) failure to use top-level structure has a more negative impact when the topic of the material is unfamiliar to the reader than when the reader possesses appropriate topical knowledge; (6) competency in the use of text structures generally improves with age and ability; (7) students can be taught to identify top-level structure; and (8) training in the use of top-level structure improves reading comprehension (B. Meyer 1984, Ohlausen & Roller 1988, Henk 1988).

In general, many students lack sufficient awareness of how ideas are organized in expository texts (Armbruster, Anderson & Ostertag 1987; Garner & Gillingham 1987), with their levels of awareness varying among the different types of expository text structures (Richgels et al. 1987). At various age levels, good readers have better knowledge of, and make more use of, expository text structures than do poor readers (Gillis & Olson 1987).

Text structure is also viewed in terms of its microstructure and its macrostructure. A text's *microstructure* describes the interrelationships of ideas within a paragraph. The aspects of a text's microstructure that influence comprehension are the logical and temporal relations between *propositions* (thought units), which are expressed through cohesive ties (Herman et al. 1987). A text's *macrostructure* describes interrelationships among larger and more general text units such as paragraphs and the gist (McCown & Miller 1986). Macrostructure is expressed in text through the use of titles and topic sentences and by the overall organization and flow of information. Skilled readers may use these cues to gain an initial understanding of the textual information. Awareness of a text's macrostructure leads students to expect information relevant to that framework (Herman et al. 1987). From sixth grade through college there is a developmental trend in the ability to use expository text structure to facilitate comprehension and recall (L. McGee 1982).

Students should understand that different rhetorical structures are used in texts and learn how they may be used to facilitate comprehension and recall. Among the ways to help students understand text structures are the use of graphic representations (pages 609–612) and having pupils write paragraphs employing a specific structure (see Piccolo 1987; Muth 1987a). T. Bean (1988) illustrates a procedure for introducing children to text structures, and Richgels, McKee, and Slaton (1989) suggest a seven-step procedure for helping students

[6]Although levels of structure are used more frequently in discussing expository text, the concept also applies to narratives. Information that is more important for understanding stories (e.g., setting, main characters) is more likely to be recalled than less important information such as a character's emotional responses. (Fitzgerald 1989).

identify and use expository text structures. Flood, Lapp, and Farnan (1986) describe a reading and writing procedure that may help pupils understand text structures.

Although authorities do not agree on the categories of rhetorical style, there is sufficient commonality to warrant discussion of the following types. *Temporal-order* patterns are used in narratives (Horowitz 1985a). Signal words (e.g., *then, finally*) may explicitly mark the sequence of events, or the reader may have to infer the temporal order. Temporal-order structures may be used in some expository texts (e.g., historical accounts).

The following rhetorical styles are often used to hold together segments of an expository text (Meyer & Rice 1984, Calfee, & Curley 1984, Cooper 1986, Richgels et al. 1987). In a *description*, information about the topic is provided by presenting attributes, explanations, settings, or specifics. Such information has only one organizational component, grouping by association, in which one element is subordinate to another. Descriptions may identify features, uses, or relationships with other objects, events, or ideas. Unlike other rhetorical structures, descriptions do not include signal words that may facilitate comprehension. Readers must note the details and select the important information.

A *collection* structure includes more than one description. Ideas, events, or groups of objects are grouped together on the basis of some commonality. Collection structures may involve the ordering of events, such as sequencing by time. Signal words may be used to denote related points, but the reader must infer the relationships between the listed points and the overall topic (e.g., Alligators and crocodiles differ in a number of ways. First, . . .").

A *cause-effect (antecedent-consequence)* structure shows that a causal relationship exists between topics. The cause may be given before the effect, or vice versa. At times, the causal relations are marked by signal words such as "therefore" or "as a result of"; in other instances, the relationships must be inferred. Although used in a wide variety of texts, cause-effect structures are troublesome for many readers from the early elementary grades through college (Horowitz 1985b).

The *response* structure makes use of question-answer or problem-solution formats. Signal words (e.g., the problem is) are often provided.

In *comparison/contrast* patterns, similarities and/or differences between two or more topics are pointed out. Use of this rhetorical style requires the reader to note the likenesses and/or differences between the ideas or things being compared or contrasted, perhaps aided by such clue words as "resembles" or "differs from."

Sample passages of the last five types of structures are shown in Figure 15.3. Others may be found in Richgels et al. (1987).

Authors may also organize their texts so as to present an argument or to attempt to persuade (Calfee & Curley 1984). An argument in which generalities lead to a particular (the conclusion necessarily follows from the premises), requires the reader to use *deductive reasoning. Inductive reasoning* is required when the argument leads from a particular to generalities (e.g., a concept is developed and followed by examples of it). In *persuasion*, the author sets out a line of argument that presents the ideas in the most convincing manner. The presented argument may or may not be correct.

Structure	Sample Passage
Description	The Summer Olympic Games are the biggest entertainment spectacles of modern times. Every four years they offer two weeks of nonstop pageantry and competition.
Collection	The Summer Olympics have so many different things to offer. First, there are many kinds of events: big shows like the opening and closing ceremonies, pure competitions like the races and games, and events that are partly artistic and partly competitive like the subjectively scored diving and gymnastics contests. There are old things and new things, like the classic track and field events staged in 1984 in the same stadium where they were held in 1932, and the almost bizarre sport of synchronized swimming first presented in 1984.
Causation	There are several reasons why so many people attend the Olympic Games or watch them on television. The first Olympics were held in Greece more than 2,000 years ago. As a result of hearing the name "Olympics," seeing the torch and flame, and being reminded in other ways of the ancient Games, people feel that they are escaping the ordinariness of daily life. People like to identify with someone else's individual sacrifice and accomplishment; thus an athlete's or a team's hard-earned, well-deserved victory becomes a nation's victory. There are national medal counts and people watch so that they can see how their country is doing. Because the Olympics are staged only every four years and maybe only once in a lifetime in a particular country, people flock to even obscure events.
Problem/Solution	One problem with the modern Olympics is that they have gotten so big and so expensive to operate. A city or country often loses a lot of money by staging the Games. A stadium, pools, and playing fields are built for the many events and housing is built for the athletes but it is all used for only two weeks. In 1984, Los Angeles solved these problems by charging companies for permission to be official sponsors and by using many buildings that were already there. Companies like McDonald's paid a lot of money to be part of the Olympics. The Collseum, where the 1932 Games were held, was used again and many colleges and universities in the area became playing and living sites.
Comparison	The modern Summer Olympics are really very unlike the ancient Olympic Games. Individual events are different. For example, there were no swimming races in the ancient Games, but there were charlot races. There were no women contestants and everyone competed in the nude. Of course the ancient and modern Olympics are also alike in many ways. Some events are the same, like the javelin and discus throws. Some people say that cheating, professionalism, and nationalism in the modern Games are a disgrace to the ancient Olympic tradition. But according to ancient Greek writers, there were many cases of cheating, nationalism, and professionalism in their Olympics too.

Figure 15.3. Sample passages illustrating types of expository text structures. From L. M. McGee and D. J. Richgels. Teaching expository text structure to elementary students. *The Reading Teacher*, April 1985, 38, 39–48. Used by permission of the authors and the International Reading Association.

Text must also be structured in functional ways (Calfee & Curley 1984). An author may use an opening statement, an *introduction*, that indicates a point of view and perhaps how the subject will be developed. *Transition* establishes a framework for integrating information already given with forthcoming information. Relationships among ideas are emphasized or changes in theme are explained. A *conclusion* generally includes a review of the ideas, in which any uncompleted lines of thought are tied together.

GENERAL PROCEDURES FOR DEVELOPING READING COMPREHENSION

This section begins by considering two questions: "Can reading comprehension be taught?" and "Is it being taught?" We then discuss various general instructional procedures that may be used to help students develop their reading comprehension.

Can Reading Comprehension Be Taught?

Some authorities (e.g., Carver 1987a) would argue that the research evidence supporting the contention that reading comprehension strategies can be taught is "frail at best." Others contend that little or nothing can be done to teach reading comprehension because reading is reasoning, and you cannot teach reasoning. Our position is that although you cannot teach children something they are incapable of learning, a number of things can and should be done to improve most children's abilities to understand and recall written text. It is important—and possible—to help pupils develop a conceptual and linguistic knowledge base on which they can draw while reading. The same is true of word-recognition and identification skills and of knowledge of text structure. Such knowledge and skills are enabling factors that facilitate comprehension. As such, they may be developed before or concurrently with attempts to improve comprehension. What children often need to learn is how to employ what they already know when attempting to understand what they are reading. Reading comprehension instruction should focus on teaching children how to: use textual features, relate textual information to their topical and world knowledge, use strategies for linking ideas from various sources of information, monitor their comprehension, and employ corrective strategies when there is a comprehension breakdown. Pupils often profit from guided practice in reading different kinds of texts for different purposes. Skills and strategies may be taught in isolation, but they should be practiced in context.

Is Reading Comprehension Taught in the Schools?

Observations of third- through sixth-grade classes indicated that reading comprehension instruction was rare (Durkin 1978–1979). Rather than teach relevant skills and strategies and help children understand how their application can facilitate reading comprehension, comprehension activities were found to consist mainly of assessing how well the reading material was understood and providing massive doses of often unguided practice in the form of completing workbook pages and duplicated exercises. Social studies lessons concentrated on acquiring the facts to be learned, with much oral reading by the good readers of materials deemed too difficult for the poor readers. Hardly any effort was made to teach comprehension or study skills during these social studies periods. Similar findings are reported by Neilsen, Rennie, and Connell (1982) and Armbruster and Gudbrandsen (1986). Thus it would seem that in both reading and social studies periods, the emphasis was on the *product*, rather than the *process*, of reading comprehension.

Durkin's study has been criticized on methodological grounds by Heap (1982) and for using too narrow a definition of reading instruction. Using Durkin's data, but a broader definition of reading instruction, C. Hodges (1981) found that approximately 23% of the reading period (as opposed to the less than 1% reported by Durkin) was devoted to teaching reading comprehension.

That little has been done to teach reading comprehension is not surprising. Until fairly recently, very little was known about the reading comprehension process that could be translated into instructional practices.

Questioning

Comprehension questions can serve two purposes. First, they can be used to assess comprehension; this is by far their more common use (Beck & McKeown 1981). Second, questions can be employed as an instructional device to help students clarify meaning or to organize and integrate textual information. We are concerned here with the latter. Questions may be posed by the teacher, text, or reader. Well-formulated teacher and text questions can serve as models for self-questioning by students.

PLACEMENT OF QUESTIONS.   Questions may be posed before students begin to read the text; while the text is being read, either before or after the needed information is provided by the text; or after the entire selection has been read. The choice of placement often depends on the purpose of the questions.

Questions may be asked before children begin to read the passage in order to activate, review, or develop background knowledge; to preview key concepts; or to set one or more purposes for reading. Use of the latter form of prereading questioning is based on the belief that having a purpose for reading helps pupils to maintain and focus their attention while reading and thus facilitates their comprehension. Purpose questions may also help pupils activate and use the appropriate schema needed for comprehension.

Questioning during reading is a fairly common practice, especially on the part of primary-grade teachers. At various points in the text, the teacher may pose a question that can provide guidance in comprehending what is about to be read or in relating what has been read to upcoming information and/or to prior knowledge. If worded properly, these questions can also help pupils to understand the processes needed to comprehend the upcoming text, or to understand the upcoming text structure and how to use it in selecting and organizing important ideas. Formulation of such during-reading prequestions requires skill and knowledge, if the questions are to be effective. Muth (1987b) illustrates how to use questions that prompt students to identify relationships among ideas in expository texts. Asking students to predict upcoming information or content is another form of prequestioning that can occur either before or after reading is begun. (See Nessel 1987). Postquestions may be posed during reading to determine if the material has been understood, so that comprehension problems can be cleared up before they interfere with understanding the rest of the passage. Postquestions may also help pupils to monitor and learn to monitor their comprehension and prompt them to take any needed corrective action on their own.

Questions that are posed after the passage has been read can serve as a measure of comprehension or as a means for organizing and interpreting what has been read. They also can provide students with opportunities to rehearse text information, to increase associations between text information and prior knowledge, to summarize what has been read, and to apply that information in an extended fashion.

Hamaker (1986) defines *factual questions* as those that require students to repeat or to recognize information exactly as presented in the text; *higher-order questions* as those that require the mental manipulation of information to create an acceptable response or to support an answer with logically reasoned evidence before the needed information appears in the text, whether such questions are posed before or during reading; and *postquestions* as those that are presented both during and after reading. Based on his review of the literature, Hamaker concludes that: (1) factual prequestions (a) facilitate the acquisition of information that is directly related to or cued by the questions but (b) have a negative effect on recalling information unrelated to the questions; (2) factual postquestions (a) facilitate the learning of material covered either directly or indirectly by them but (b) have a negative effect on unrelated test questions when study time is controlled (when study time is not controlled, there is a positive effect); (3) questions have a stronger facilitating effect in a short-answer test format than in a multiple-choice format; (4) effect sizes are related to text length, density of questions, question format, the test format, and the level of the control group's performance; (5) effect sizes are not related to students' ages, the interval between reading and testing, whether "look backs" are allowed during testing, the average distance between the questions and the relevant textual information; and (6) high-level questions may have a more facilitating effect overall than factual questions on comprehension, recall, and learning. Questions that force the reader to process more than small pieces of the text can be formulated (see Cooper 1986 and McNeil 1987).

Massed prereading questions rarely enhance learning of the desired information (Memory 1982); and the few studies that considered how making predictions affects reading comprehension produced mixed results (Shanahan 1986). According to J. L. Vaughn (1982), research findings consistently favor the use of during-reading questions over pre- and postreading questions. However, Tierney and Cunningham (1984) state that while research has generally indicated that inserted questions facilitate the recall of factual information, students apply textual information better when they have to respond to both inserted and post-reading questions.

Different types of postreading questions require different kinds of processing. In general, higher-order questions result in a general review of the material; lower-order questions require a review of only the questioned information (Wixson 1984). When using postquestions, teachers typically provide feedback that informs students about how well they have responded. Research generally supports this practice.

TEACHERS' QUESTIONS.   Weber and Shake (1988) found that second-grade teachers asked an average of almost 27 questions per reading lesson. The children responded, on average, to 19 questions; the teacher accepted 18 of their responses. Most often the teacher did not respond verbally to a response (but perhaps did so nonverbally), repeated the question, or rephrased the student's response.

The kinds of questions posed by teachers may influence what children learn to consider when they read. Repeatedly asking the same kinds of questions focuses students' attention on the information needed to answer them, and students allocate their attention accordingly. So, for example, if the teacher asks only literal comprehension questions, children attend to details as they read. Research suggests that asking well-crafted questions can promote reading ability (R. C. Anderson et al. 1985).

The questions found in basal reader manuals vary from series to series in terms of the degree to which they emphasize literal or inferential comprehension. The same is true of workbooks and worksheets.

Some teachers prefer to formulate their own comprehension questions. But whatever the source of the questions, studies report that teachers' questions largely call for understanding textually explicit information or literal comprehension (Raphael & Gavelek 1984). According to O'Flahaven, Hartman, and Pearson (1988), however, the proportion of teacher questions that call for literal comprehension has decreased dramatically over the past twenty years, and has been replaced by inferential questions and questions that call for paraphrasing different portions of the text.

The results of such studies appear to be highly influenced by the classification system employed. When they used Guszak's (1967) classification, Hare and Pulliam (1980) classified about 75% of the teacher's questions as literal, 10% as inferential, and 15% as reflective. But when they used Pearson and Johnson's (1978) system, the results were about 27% literal (textually explicit) and 73% inferential (textually and scriptually implicit). When Shake (1988) applied Pearson and Johnson's taxonomy, the greatest percentage of question/answer relationships involved the use of scriptually implicit information (relying heavily or completely on prior knowledge), but use of Barrett's classification system (R. J. Smith and Barrett 1974) resulted in the majority of the questions being labeled as literal comprehension. As Shake notes, however, although many literal questions were posed, the children's responses indicated that they had integrated textual information and prior knowledge. Any analysis of questions also needs to consider the pupils' responses to them.

High reading groups are more likely to be asked questions calling for evaluation, explanation, or conjecture. Low reading groups are asked mainly recognition and recall questions. According to Medley (1977), this adjustment to pupil abilities is helpful to both the high and low reading groups. Others would contend that unless you also ask some high-level questions of poor readers, they will never raise their level of reading comprehension.

Literal comprehension is the simplest level of comprehension because it makes the least cognitive demands on the reader. But, as Pearson (1982) points out, understanding details is crucial to building a coherent representation of text (i.e., to achieving reading comprehension). Questions whose answers require literal comprehension are needed because the main focus of some texts is factual information (e.g., a science textbook). At times it is necessary to establish whether the child's inability to make an inference is base on a lack of literal comprehension. For the most part, literal questions should be links in a chain of questions that lead to an inference or to understanding relationships or the text as a whole.

Among others, Pressley, Johnson, and Symons (1987) believe that asking questions that require inferencing or reasoning rather than literal comprehension produces greater gains in reading comprehension. Indeed, Pearson (1985) states that instructional emphasis on making inferences results in growth in inferential thinking, without a loss and perhaps even with a gain, in literal comprehension. Nevertheless, the balance between literal and inferential questions must be equitable. In the *Reflective Reading-Thinking Activities* that are part of the Junior Great Books program, the teacher starts with factual questions, proceeds to interpretation questions, and concludes with evaluative questions (Biskin, Hoskisson & Modin 1976).

Teachers typically do not allow much time for children to think before they respond to comprehension questions and they tend to provide feedback immediately after a child responds. Neither practice is desirable. Research evidence suggests that allowing five seconds of "wait time" after asking a question as well as after the pupil's initial response results in: (1) a decrease in failure to respond; (2) an increase in appropriate and longer responses; (3) higher-level thinking and the making of more inferences that could be supported by evidence and logic; and (4) teachers becoming more adept at using pupil responses to ask for clarifications, invite elaborations, and so forth (M. Rowe 1987). Repeating part or all of the students' responses tends to inhibit the number and quality of future responses.

Ruddell (1978) considers four kinds of questions to be most useful for developing comprehension.

> *Focusing* enables the teacher to immediately establish a mental set, a purpose for reading. *Extending* allows the teacher to elicit additional information at the same comprehension level. *Clarifying* enables the teacher to encourage returning to a previous response for further clarification, explanation, or redefinition. *Raising* allows the teacher to obtain additional information on the same subject but at a higher comprehension level.

Other suggestions for formulating and using comprehension questions may be found in Christenburg and Kelly (1983), Ruddell (1984), McNeil (1987), and Wixson and Peters (1987).

In order to answer a question, children must: (1) understand the question; (2) remember the question if it is posed orally; (3) determine where the information needed to answer the question may be found; (4) retrieve the information; and (5) have some criteria for determining when the obtained information is sufficient for answering the question adequately (Raphael & Gavelek 1984). Davey (1989) reports that good readers could effectively integrate textual information with prior knowledge, and could differentiate between the task demands of questions requiring the comprehension of explicit versus implicit textual information.

In the *Question-Answer Relationships (QAR) strategy* developed by Raphael (1986), pupils are taught to identify the kinds of information required to answer questions, as well as the sources of that information and how to retrieve it. The QAR procedure begins by teaching children that there are two general sources of information "In the book" and "In my head." When the pupils have a clear understanding of the difference between textual information and prior knowledge as the sources of information needed to answer questions, each category is further divided. Two "In the book" sources—explicit ("Right There") and implicit ("Think and Search") textual information—are then introduced. Later children are taught that in order to answer a question, they may have to combine textual information and prior knowledge ("Author and you") or that the answer may be passage independent, requiring only prior knowledge ("On my own"). Refer to Raphael (1986) for illustrative QAR lessons. Research indicates that: (1) teachers can be trained fairly quickly and easily in how to teach QAR; (2) learning the QAR strategy results in improved ability to answer questions, especially for average and low-average students; and (3) the strategy can be learned by (a) fourth and fifth graders with about a week of instruction plus six to eight weeks of practice, (b) sixth graders in four days, and (c) older students with only a ten-minute orientation (Raphael & Pearson 1985).

If students do not possess a particular reading skill, asking them questions that require application of that skill is nonproductive. Herber and Nelson (1975) propose the following instructional sequential steps in such cases: (1) give the students statements that are the answers to the questions and tell them where the supporting evidence can be found in the text and have them locate it; (2) provide statements without indicating the locations of the answers; (3) provide questions, and locations where the answers are given; (4) provide questions only; and (5) have the students formulate their own questions.

STUDENT-GENERATED QUESTIONS. Students can generate their own questions before (e.g., What do I know about _____?), during (e.g., What is the main idea? Did I really understand this?), or after (e.g., Can I summarize the important parts?) reading (Wong 1985). Student-generated questions serve the same purposes as those asked by teachers. The value of getting students to generate their own questions is that it places the responsibility for learning on them, thus enabling them to learn how to comprehend text independently. There are two kinds of student-generated questions (Raphael & Gavelek 1984). *Reflective* *questions* involve asking how well previously read material was understood. Such questions could be asked of any material (e.g., Who are the main characters?). *Prospective questions* are more content specific and are generally of a predictive nature (e.g., What is _____ trying to accomplish?). Student-generated questions are an integral part of the Directed Reading-Thinking Activity (Stauffer 1969) and the Request procedure (Manzo 1985).[7] The latter involves reciprocal questioning in which the teacher models questioning behavior; as sections of the text are read silently, the teacher and pupils take turns asking and answering questions. The *active comprehension strategy* (Nolte & Singer 1985) involves setting a purpose for reading, determining what content is important, generating questions throughout reading, and searching for the answers to them. At first, the teacher models questions at pertinent points in the passage in order to shape and guide thinking while reading. Teacher-questions are phased out as pupil-questions are phased in, until the students take over the questioning entirely.

Reviewers differ in their conclusions about the value of student-generated questions. H. Singer (1985a) concludes that their value had been documented. But, according to T. Anderson and Armbruster (1984b), the research findings are mixed. The success of student-generated questions probably depends heavily on the quality of instruction. Research suggests that, in general, self-questioning improved students' text processing when the pupils were provided with clear instructions in formulating self-questions, were trained to criteria, and were given sufficient time to actively process the text and to generate questions (Wong 1985).

Reciprocal teaching of comprehension strategies is an instructional procedure in which the teacher and pupils take turns assuming the role of teacher. It occurs in a cooperative learning situation[8] that features guided practice in applying strategies to the tasks of reading comprehension. Reciprocal teaching is based on five principles. First, the teacher actively models the desired comprehension activities, making her thought processes overt, explicit, and concrete. Second, the strategies are modeled in appropriate contexts, never in isolation. The four key structures of predicting, questioning, clarifying, and summarizing are embedded in the dialogue that takes place during the lesson. *Predicting* means that the pupils hypothesize what the author will discuss next. Successful prediction requires pupils to activate relevant prior knowledge. Predicting gives them a purpose for reading—to confirm, refute, or adjust their hypotheses. It also presents opportunities to link new textual information with prior knowledge, and facilitates the use of text structure because students learn that headings, embedded questions, and so forth are useful in anticipating upcoming information. *Generating questions* provides students with opportunities to identify the kinds of information about which questions should be asked, to frame these questions, and to engage in self-testing. Self-questioning involves pupils more actively in the reading process. As the students proceed through the passage, the teacher guides them at first in integrating information across paragraphs and other sections of the text. *Summarizing* involves identifying and paraphrasing main ideas and is an excellent vehicle for integrating textual information. *Clarifying*, which is especially important to

[7]Tierney, Readence, and Dishner (1985) describe how to use these and other instructional strategies.

[8]Refer to Uttero (1988) and K. Wood (1988) for suggestions on using cooperative learning as a means of improving reading comprehension.

use with children who have a history of comprehension difficulty, helps pupils discern when their comprehension is breaking down and alerts them to take corrective action. When children are asked to clarify their responses, they become aware that there may be a number of reasons why text is difficult to understand (Palincsar & Brown 1986).

Third, the discussions focus on both the text content and the students' understanding of the strategies they are using to comprehend the text. Fourth, the teacher provides feedback tailored to the students' levels of competence. Fifth, the responsibility for comprehension activities is transferred from the teacher to the students as soon as possible. The last principle deals with the instructional strategy known as *scaffolding* or the *gradual release of responsibility model*. The teacher provides whatever assistance students need to perform a task they could not accomplish on their own. The teacher uses a balance of explanation, instruction, modeling, and guided practice, and steadily withdraws more of the "support system" until the child is successful on his own (Brown & Palincsar 1986). Refer to Slater and Graves (1989) for a more complete description of the gradual release model.

Reciprocal teaching would seem suitable for children who have adequate word recognition but inadequate comprehension. Refer to Palincsar (1984) and Brown and Palincsar (1985) for further information on how to use their eight-step teaching strategy. Material is suitable for use in reciprocal teaching if the pupils can read it at a rate of at least 80 WPM, with no more than two word-recognition errors per minute (Palincsar 1986).

Research findings suggest that reciprocal teaching results in significant improvements in comprehension monitoring and comprehension (Paris, Wixson & Palincsar 1986). Daily use of reciprocal teaching for 3 to 6 weeks was effective in improving the listening comprehension of first graders and the reading comprehension of narrative and expository texts by elementary school pupils and poor readers in the junior high school, when used with small groups, large groups, or in peer instruction (Brown & Campione 1985; Palincsar & Brown 1986; Palincsar Brown & Martin 1987). Paris, Wasik, and Van der Westhuizen (1988) question the generalizability of the research findings in this area.

Listening Comprehension

The correlation between reading and listening comprehension increases from 0.35 in first grade to about 0.60 in fourth grade, and remains fairly constant thereafter (Sticht & James 1984). This change in relationship has led some to believe that once word recognition has been mastered, both reading and listening are controlled by very similar cognitive processes. Others hold that different cognitive processes are required because of the significant differences in grammar, vocabulary, and style between written and spoken language. The present data are insufficient to resolve the issue. Nevertheless, a prevailing belief is that comprehension skills acquired in one mode should transfer to the other mode. Most frequently, the training occurs in the auditory mode because of the belief that aural comprehension skills are more advanced than reading comprehension skills.

Boodt (1984) found that a critical-listening program improved the ability of disabled readers to read critically, and Sticht and James (1984) state that 10 of 12 studies report a successful transfer of skills from auding to reading. Pearson and Fielding (1982) indicate that it is fairly safe to conclude that: (1) Direct instruction resulted in the improvement of specific listening comprehension skills at almost any age level but there was not much transfer from one listening skill to another; and (2) after students became mature readers, whatever training benefited listening comprehension also benefitted reading comprehension and vice versa, but prior to that stage, transfer from one mode to the other was possible but less likely. Cunningham (1975) provides suggestions for helping children transfer comprehension skills from listening to reading. The differences between comprehending spoken and written language are enumerated on pages 20–22 and should be considered in any attempt to transfer any comprehension skill from listening to reading.

We are in firm agreement with those who suggest that schools should place more emphasis on developing listening comprehension. Even if its development does not improve reading comprehension, listening comprehension ability is important. Suggestions for improving listening comprehension may be found in Devine (1987) and Hyslop and Tone (1988).

Cloze as an Instructional Tool

The use of cloze exercises to help children improve their reading comprehension is based on the belief that filling in the blanks forces the reader to process the information surrounding the deletion and that doing so requires similar cognitive processes to those used in reading unmutilated text. Use of cloze exercises further assumes that the skills learned in completing cloze tasks will transfer to normal reading.

On the basis of a literature review, Jongsma (1980) concludes the following: (1) Cloze can be an effective teaching technique but is no more nor less effective than many other widely used instructional methods; (2) cloze is most effective in developing certain comprehension skills and least effective in developing word-meaning knowledge; (3) there is no evidence that the cloze is more effective with narrative or expository text; (4) cloze is not more effective for any one age or grade level or for any level of reading ability; (5) although findings are mixed, cloze instruction is likely to be more effective when discussion is focused on clues that signal appropriate responses; (6) cloze materials that are carefully sequenced as to difficulty are more effective than undifferentiated exercises; (7) the quality of cloze instruction is more important than the length of the program; (8) there is no firm evidence regarding the minimum amount of instruction needed before cloze instruction is effective; (9) selective deletion systems aimed at particular contextual relationships are more effective than random deletion systems; and (10) semantically acceptable responses should be encouraged (there is no need to demand exact word replacements for instructional purposes).

For further suggestions on using the cloze for instructional purposes, refer to McKenna and Robinson (1980); McNeil (1987); and Carr, Dewitz and Patberg (1989).

Improving Reading Comprehension through Writing Activities

The author-reader relationship has been well described by Tierney and Pearson (1983). Basically, they stress that reading (comprehending text) and writing (authoring text) involve essentially similar cognitive processes in the construction and reconstruction of meaning.

The basic premise underlying most attempts to improve reading comprehension through writing is that expressing one's thoughts clearly in writing requires the ability to organize and relate information in an understandable manner. It is hoped that having to use such skills in writing will improve pupils' abilities to "read like a writer" or make them more aware of how authors organize their ideas, and thus help them to become more sensitive to text structure. There is only limited evidence that skills transfer between writing and reading. Shanahan (1988) contends that reading and writing are not as similar as is widely assumed. He argues that, although reading and writing have some similar components, there is no set of variables that completely defines the reading-writing relationship. Furthermore, the correlations between the two are only low to moderate (in the 0.25 to 0.40 range) and rarely reach as high as 0.60.

Suggestions for using writing activities to develop reading comprehension can be found in Cooper (1986), Shanahan (1988) and Moore, Readence, and Rickelman (1989). Refer to Tway (1985) for suggestions on using children's literature to combine reading and writing activities.

Illustrations

Theoretically, illustrations could facilitate reading comprehension by repeating information occurring in the text, by providing information that clarifies or expands on textual information, or by attracting and holding the reader's interest. Although the number and types of illustrations vary among publishers, pictures are quite common in beginning-reading instructional materials. Because only a limited number of words are used in the stories, illustrations may provide or maintain the story line. Illustrations may substitute for or repeat the meanings of words or groups of words, make clear who is speaking and their emotional state, provide the setting for the episode, and suggest the genre of the story (e.g., fiction) (Elster & Simons 1985). Thus, illustrations can provide novice readers with information that facilitates comprehension and, also, how the material should be read orally so as to reflect what is happening in the story. For instance, "Look at this!" should be rendered with a different intonation when accompanied by a picture of a mother scolding the pet dog as opposed to one depicting a child who has just opened a birthday present. Pictures may also provide word-recognition and word-identification cues (see page 450). Children should learn to make optimal, efficient use of illustrations, but should not overdepend on them.

Reviewers have decided that the evidence regarding the influence of illustrations on reading comprehension is generally inconclusive. (Grinnell 1982, O'Donnell 1983). Some studies show that illustrations enhance reading comprehension, at least for some students under certain conditions. For example, Habayeb (1988) found that illustrations facilitated the comprehension of textually explicit and textually implicit information by both high- and low-topical-knowledge fifth graders. For both topical-knowledge groups, illustrations that clarified textually implicit information were of more assistance than those that repeated the same information as the text. Illustrations helped the low-topical-knowledge pupils more than the high-topical-knowledge students in answering the questions on textually explicit information, but they aided both groups equally well in responding to questions based on textually implicit information. Other studies report little, if any, positive effect or suggest that illustrations actually hinder comprehension. Many of the studies failed to consider important variables or were methodologically flawed (Habayeb 1988). In the studies, narratives were used more frequently than expository texts.

The ability to learn from illustrations may increase with age (O'Donnell 1983) but opinions differ as to whether graphic aids (pictures, diagrams, maps) facilitate the comprehension of expository text. Writers such as Levin (1981) suggest that illustrations do help under certain conditions; others (e.g., Pressley, Johnson, & Symons 1987) believe that, at least for representational pictures, the effect on learning is unclear. Researchers have found that graphic aids have not been of similar value to all readers. Due to differences in background and personal predilections, some pupils (especially poor readers) make little or no use of graphic aids. Explicit oral cueing can increase good and poor readers' attention to graphic aids and their recall of information shown in both media (Reinking, Hayes & McEneaney 1988).

Reading comprehension may be hindered when children misinterpret pictures (O'Donnell 1983) and when illustrations contain information that contradicts textual information (Grinnell 1982). Novice readers are often required to integrate depicted and textual information in order to understand a story. Teachers should be alert to such situations, and provide assistance as needed.

In general, illustrations have little motivational effect (Levin 1981; Willows, Borwick & Hayvren 1981). As long as the material itself is sufficiently interesting, there is no reason to believe that illustrations will increase interest. However, there is little doubt that children like pictures in books (O'Donnell 1983).

Mental Imagery

Mental or *visual imagery* involves forming, in the mind's eye, images of story characters, events, and so forth when reading or listening to narratives, or of information to be learned from expository text. Some studies suggest that attempting to read and image at the same time presents difficulties for both children and adults. J. Levin (1981) states that self-generated mental imagery usually does not improve reading comprehension or recall; and that when it does, the effects are small or limited in the extent to which they can be generalized. Tierney and Cunningham (1984) concur with Levin. It should be noted, however, that few of these studies established that imagery actually occurred. In almost all of them, the passages were read to the students, who followed along in their written texts. Having to shadow the oral rendition may have suppressed mental imagery.

It is frequently reported that readers, especially poor readers, do not spontaneously evoke mental images while reading, but there is some evidence that imagery does occur while children are reading in a natural situation and that imagery can be an effective comprehension and recall strategy (Sadowski 1985). Pupils report inducing mental imagery when specifically directed to do so. Induced mental imagery results in significantly higher comprehension monitoring by poor readers (Gambrell & Bales 1986) and enhanced reading comprehension (Gambrell, Kapinus & Wilson 1987). Children under age 8 have difficulty creating images that mirror text content (Pressley, Johnson & Symons 1987). Teaching a modification of the keyword method (see page 538) as a comprehension strategy resulted in improved prose comprehension (Peters & Levin 1986). Refer to Gambrell, Kapinus, and Wilson (1987) for an instructional strategy that may be useful in teaching children to evoke mental imagery.

Elaboration

The term *elaboration* has two meanings. It is used to refer to information that does not appear in the text but that students provide from their prior knowledge when they retell what they have read. *Elaboration*, as a comprehension strategy, refers to deliberately forming logical relationships between new information and prior knowledge by evoking mental images, using verbal elaborations such as inferences and analogies, or paraphrasing text. The purpose of elaborative techniques is to make information more understandable or memorable by embellishing what is presented in the text. Elaborations may be provided to pupils in the form of illustrations as well as by adjunct questions or statements in the text or by teachers, or children can generate their own. For example, pupils may attempt to picture in their minds what is occurring in the story, or they may try to put the author's ideas in their own words or try to relate them to their own experiences. Students may make elaborative inferences: For example, "The woman bought the food" could be elaborated by thinking, in line with the story content, that the woman must have been very kind because she was buying the food for a hungry family.

The limited research dealing with elaboration as a study technique has produced mixed results (T. Anderson & Armbruster 1984b) and has been concerned with understanding sentences or short paragraphs (Pressley, Johnson & Symons 1987). Teaching children how to use and choose from a variety of elaboration strategies may prove useful. See Reder (1980) for a critical review of the research on the role of elaboration in the comprehension and retention of information. For further information on elaboration, refer to Bransford, Vye, and Stein (1984), and McNeil (1987).

Appropriate Reading Rate

Comprehension may suffer when the rate of reading is either too fast or too slow. Some inaccurate readers need to be temporarily slowed down until they reach a satisfactory standard of accuracy; when that result has been attained, they can gradually speed up again while maintaining the newly achieved precision. Some very slow readers do poorly in comprehension because their many repetitions and hesitations, which often are symptoms of weak word recognition or conceptual or linguistic difficulties, break up the continuity of thought. The relation between rate and comprehension, and procedures that are effective in coordinating them, are treated in detail in Chapter 17. For practice materials, timed reading exercises with comprehension checks are usually desirable.

Concentration

The inability to concentrate on obtaining meaning during reading is a frequent cause of poor comprehension. But inability to concentrate is not an explanation for poor reading comprehension; it is itself a result of causes. The individual is unable to adjust to the requirements of the reading situation. Before initiating treatment, the teacher should find out what makes it difficult for the child to concentrate. The causes can usually be found in the answers to one or more of the following questions:

1. Does the pupil have visual problems? Visual difficulties are a frequent and often unsuspected cause of concentration difficulties. Examination by a vision specialist is desirable.
2. Is the pupil physically below par? Many physical conditions lower vitality and impair the ability to exert effort.
3. Is the student generally overworked? Accumulated fatigue, which results from an effort to carry too heavy a load, may bring on a decline in ability to concentrate.
4. Is the material much too difficult or much too easy for the child? Providing material of more suitable difficulty may improve concentration.
5. Is the pupil interested in the content of the text? A marked improvement in concentration sometimes occurs when more interesting material is provided.
6. Does the pupil's reading take place under suitable physical conditions? For most efficient reading, the reader should sit upright or bending slightly forward in a straight-backed chair, with good, glareless lighting, in surroundings free from distracting sights and sounds. Although some people can read well in unfavorable surroundings, poor readers should give themselves the benefit of good working conditions.
7. Do other thoughts keep running through the reader's mind? Attention can be focused well on only one thing at a time. To read well, the student must be able to exclude other thoughts for the time being. When questioning discloses that the reader's mind runs off on other things when she is supposed to be reading, the teacher must try to determine whether this problem is a superficial habit that can be broken or a symptom of an emotional difficulty that needs expert treatment.

In helping a child to develop better concentration, it is sometimes desirable to start with very small units. For example, 2 or 3 minutes of intensive silent reading are followed by discussion of the meaning of the material and then a brief period of relaxation before another practice exercise is tried. For work of this type, exercises such as those found in *Standard Test Lessons in Reading* (Teachers College Press) can be used to good advantage. When proficiency is attained in handling brief assignments, longer selections can be introduced gradually.

DEVELOPING LEVELS OF COMPREHENSION

Four levels of comprehension are commonly discussed—literal comprehension, inferential comprehension, critical reading, and creative reading. The first two levels deal with reading comprehension *per se*. Critical reading is based on reading comprehension, but the key ability at this level is critical thinking. In creative reading, the key ability is thinking creatively.

Literal and Inferential Comprehension

There is some debate as to whether reading comprehension can even be separated into two levels of comprehension—literal and inferential, and, among those who believe that there is a difference, there appears to be no consensus as to what constitutes each. We believe that a distinction can and should be made.

Literal comprehension means understanding explicit textual information; that is, the meaning is directly stated (e.g., "Jim is the Smiths' only son.") or a relationship is marked by graphic cues such as signal words. The information always appears in one sentence.

Inferential comprehension involves applying reasoning ability in order to understand the idea and events or their relationships. There are at least three types of inferential comprehension. *Bridging inferences* refers to inferring (reasoning out) relationships, between two or more pieces of information that are not explicitly stated or marked. Thus, we consider understanding "The woman opened her umbrella because it started to rain" as involving literal comprehension because the effect-cause relationship is supplied by the author through the use of *because*.[9] Inferential comprehension is involved in understanding "It began to rain. The woman opened her umbrella," because readers have to infer the implied cause-effect relationship and supply *"so"* on their own. Other examples of bridging inferences are understanding cohesive ties (see pages 562–564). *Contextual or elaborated inferences* refer to relating background knowledge to textual information or to filling in, from one's schemata, information that the author did not provide: for example, knowing how a story character would feel or act in a given situation or how a log cabin would be furnished.[10] *Structural inferencing* involves applying what one knows about text structures to guide comprehension (see pages 564–570).

In addition to having to understand at least some related textually explicit information (literal comprehension), inferential comprehension may require: (1) reasoning ability, (2) topical knowledge, (3) vocabulary knowledge, (4) knowledge of social interactions and the motives behind human actions, (5) knowledge

[9]It could be argued that the reader must still infer what is being related by the cohesive ties.
[10]Refer to (J. Allen 1985) for a taxonomy of inferences that may be drawn while reading a story.

of causal relationships, and (6) knowledge of how authors organize text. How the process of inferencing is accomplished is largely unknown (Trabasso 1981).

Two possibilities may account for at least some of the disagreement regarding the existence of separate literal and inferential levels of comprehension. First, the ability to make an inference often depends on first understanding textually explicit information. Individuals who are skilled at inferential comprehension are almost certainly skilled at literal comprehension. Individuals who cannot understand textually explicit information are unlikely to demonstrate adequate inferential comprehension. Therefore, it may be difficult to show statistically that differences between literal and inferential comprehension abilities exist. Second, although the textual information may be explicit, the wording of the comprehension question may in fact call for the child to make an inference in order to answer acceptably, or the child's response may indicate that an elaboration was made during reading.

Text is difficult to comprehend when pupils are required to make a number of causal inferences (Kemper 1988). Studies have shown that when logical and temporal relations between and within sentences are made explicit, sentence comprehension improves, especially for poor readers. When texts are longer, the effects of explicit and implicit relationships on comprehension are not as clear-cut. Most of the studies that report little difference between the comprehension of explicit and implicit relations used only skilled readers. Studies using less skilled readers report mixed results (Herman et al. 1987).

Research suggests that some children do not draw inferences spontaneously while reading, even though they have the mental ability and memory capacity to do so (Dewitz, Carr & Patberg 1987). Older pupils make more spontaneous inferences than do younger children, but the reason for this difference is not well understood (Pearson & Gallagher 1983). J. Allen (1985) found that primary-grade children's ability to draw inferences was influenced by their word-recognition ability and that they were better able to make inferences when reading material that they had dictated than when reading text authored by others. Failure to make inferences may also be due to limited topical knowledge, not having or not utilizing apropriate inferencing strategies, or failure to attend to relevant textual information (Reutzel & Hollingsworth 1988).

Research also suggests that inferential comprehension of narratives can be improved, even in fairly young children (Hansen 1981; Dewitz, Carr & Patberg 1987; Reutzel & Hollingsworth 1988). Among the instructional techniques that have been employed successfully are: teaching children to identify key vocabulary for specific inferential operations (see Johnson & Johnson 1986); explicit instruction of inferential strategies; having students generate inferential text; a mutual exchange between teacher and pupils in solving and explaining the solutions of inferential text; building topical knowledge; discussing background knowledge and using it to make predictions; teaching children to use self-monitoring checklists; and the use of the cloze procedure and structured overviews (Reutzel & Hollingsworth 1988). Often these procedures are used in combination. Refer to Beck (1989) for suggestions on developing reasoning skills through reading.

Suggestions for teaching inferencing in the primary grades are offered by K. Carr (1983), and Hansen and Hubbard (1984) describe how to help poor readers learn to make inferences while reading. Holmes (1983a) relates a procedure for helping poor readers improve their ability to answer inference questions.

Critical Reading

Critical reading involves analytical thinking for the purpose of evaluating what is read (Ericson et al. 1987). An important kind of critical reading involves comparison of two or more sources of information. Children are usually amazed when they first find two texts that contradict each other. Such an experience can serve as a preliminary to discussion of such questions as the reputation and prestige of authors, their impartiality or bias, the comparative recency of the two sources, and so on. Reading experiences of this sort develop naturally when children do wide reading to find data on a problem. The teacher should be alert and should make use of such occasions as steppingstones toward a more mature attitude toward the credibility of reading matter. In the study of current events, comparison of the treatment of an event by two newspapers or magazines of opposing points of view can form an effective point of departure.

A second kind of critical reading involves considering new ideas or information in the light of one's previous knowledge and beliefs. Thoughtful readers ask themselves: Is it reasonable? Is it possible? They do not, of course, automatically reject the unfamiliar idea or challenging conclusion, but they become doubly alert when they find disagreements with what they have previously accepted as true.

One of the most important aspects of critical reading is the ability to detect and resist the influences of undesirable propaganda. In recent years, the molding of public opinion has become tremendously important in political and social affairs. While the term *propaganda* has sometimes been defined to include all activities intended to influence people in a given direction, concern has been centered mainly on attempts to persuade people to believe or act in a biased fashion.

There is reason to believe that teachers, by the kinds of discussions they lead, influence the degree to which children read critically (Davidson 1967). It is not easy, however, for teachers to change their established personal habits of questioning, especially when it comes to critical reading (Wolf, King & Huck 1968).

Refer to the following for teaching suggestions regarding the indicated topics: propaganda analysis (A. J. Harris & Sipay 1979); use of advertisements and commercials to teach critical reading (Tutolo 1981; Allen, Wright & Laminack 1988); checking the reliability of a source of information (E. Ross 1981); distinguishing fact from opinion and identifying bias and slant (Hillerich 1980a,b); judging the authenticity and accuracy of fictionalized biographies (Storey 1982); how to use conflicting accounts of the same topic to develop critical reading (Frager & Thompson 1985); using humor to teach critical reading (Whitimer 1986); constructing and using anticipation-reaction guides, text previews, and study guides to increase critical reading (Ericson et al. 1987); how to develop critical thinking with the DRTA (Haggard 1988); and activities to promote critical thinking (Golub 1986). Valeri-Gold (1988) presents a "critical reading skills ladder" that consists of specific critical-reading skills and corresponding questions students can ask themselves while reading.

Creative Reading

Creative reading may be described as going beyond an understanding of reading matter to arrive at new ideas or conclusions. The encouragement of creativity has been a major goal in recent years. Psychologists and educators contrast *convergent thinking* (arriving at a specific correct answer) with *divergent thinking* (developing alternative answers, none of which is incorrect); divergent thinking is a synonym for creative thinking.

Creative reading can be encouraged through procedures, such as the following:

1. Stop the students at a given point in the story and ask them to think of an ending for the story. Compare their endings with one another and with the one provided by the author. Discuss the basis for the students' endings.
2. After finishing a story, ask children to devise endings for it that are different from the author's ending. Let them devise as many different endings as they can.
3. Ask pupils to use the plot of a given story, but to change the setting to a different time and place. Discuss what changes may need to be made.
4. Change a specific event (e.g., a character finds money instead of losing it). Discuss how this could have changed the rest of the story.

Procedures such as these can enliven the reading period and provide needed practice in applying creative thinking to reading. Other ideas are discussed by Martin, Cramond, and Safter (1982).

DEVELOPING SPECIFIC COMPREHENSION SKILLS

Few comprehension skills have been shown to be statistically independent, and there is some doubt as to the value of teaching separate comprehension skills (e.g., Winograd & Johnston 1987). Nevertheless, the teaching of separate comprehension skills is justifiable *if* their relationship to each other is properly conceived and *if* a reasonable number of them are taught properly.

During the reading process, reading comprehension skills probably do not operate in isolation but in concert, and the same or very similar cognitive and language abilities may underlie all or most of them. However, teaching separate skills allows children to focus their attention on a specific task, and when taught as a strategy, skills teaching points out important aspects of text processing. Focusing on one skill at a time emphasizes the different types of processing that may be required while reading connected discourse. All students need not be taught every comprehension skill to the same extent. Although a technique may be taught in isolation as a separate skill, pupils will need varying degrees of guided practice in applying it and integrating it with other comprehension skills while reading natural text.

Furthermore, the teaching of separate comprehension skills and the reading of connected discourse need not be an either/or proposition. Both can be done, with the proportional share of time devoted to each varying with individual needs. Finally, instruction should be purposeful. Having children complete innumerable worksheets that require few of the skills needed to comprehend natural text should be avoided.

Selecting and Generating Main Ideas

Given our limited cognitive capacity to process text, it is reasonable to assume that focusing selectively on important textual information facilitates reading comprehension. Selectively attending to text requires the reader to discern among various levels of textual importance. There is evidence of both developmental and ability differences in sensitivity to the importance of textual information (Roller 1985). Such sensitivity is very poor in novice readers and increases only gradually with reading experience (M. Adams 1980). Skilled readers are more adept than less skilled readers in determining textual importance (Spivey & King 1989), but whether the ability to select and attend to the most important information is a cause or an effect of reading ability is an open question. It is possible that sensitivity to gradations in the importance of ideas may be a cause, a facilitator, or a consequence of reading ability, depending on the child's level of sensitvity and reading ability. Nevertheless, being able to select and to generate main ideas while reading are important comprehension skills. Once identified, main ideas provide the reader with "mental hooks" to which and around which relatively less-important information can be related and organized. Identifying main ideas also allows readers to focus their attention on those concepts. When readers are able to organize the textual information and main ideas receive extra attention, important text elements are better understood and remembered. Furthermore, the ability to identify main ideas is a prerequisite for such skills as outlining and note taking as well as for the use of self-questioning strategies (Derry & Murphy 1986).

Exactly how main ideas are identified is largely unknown, but the following is a simplified version of a generally accepted theory. While reading, individuals mentally parse the text into idea units (e.g., clauses and sentences). These idea units are coded into mental representation known as *propositions*. Each of these idea units is processed to some minimal level, and tacitly graded for importance. Criteria for judging its importance are provided by: (1) the conceptual and structural schemata to which the text is being assimilated and compared; (2) already-processed information; (3) a prereading analysis of task demands; and perhaps (4) the reader's interests. Idea units that meet or surpass the criteria for importance that the reader has set receive extra attention. As readers proceed through the text, propositions are deleted and integrated. At some point, the reader selects a single proposition that either represents the most important textual information or that brings cohesion to the remaining, less important information (R. Anderson & Pearson 1984; J. Williams 1986b; Reutzel, Hollingsworth & Daines 1988).

As shown in Figure 15.4 the term *main idea* has been variously defined. The

Term	Definition	Example
Topic Sentence	The sentence that tells most completely what the paragraph, as a whole, states or is about.	When birds land, they have to slow down so they won't get hurt when they hit the ground.
Gist	A summary of the explicit contents achieved by creating generalized statements that subsume specific information and by then deleting redundant information.	Birds land in a way such as not to get hurt.
Instantiated Rhetorical Predicate	A statement produced by selecting and combining the most superordinate and important words and phrases from a passage.	This passage is about how careful birds have to be when they land and how they slow dow to land.
Topic	A single word, term, or phrase labeling the subject of a passage without revealing specific content from the passage.	How birds land.
Topic Issue	A single word, term, or phrase labeling a conceptual context for the passage.	Birds
Interpretation	A summary of the possible or probable contents of a passage.	Birds land carefully and slowly and open their wings until they land.
Theme	A generalization about life, the world, or the universe that the passage as a whole develops, implies, or illustrates but which is not topic or topic-issue specific.	Nature prepares animals to cope with their environment.

Figure 15.4. Definitions and examples of seven types of main ideas in paragraphs. Adapted from D. W. Moore, J. W. Cunningham, and N. J. Rudisell. Readers' conceptions of the main idea. In J. A. Niles & L. A. Harris (Eds.), *Searches for meaning in reading, language processing, and instruction* (pp. 202–206). Thirty-second yearbook of the National Reading Conference. Rochester, NY, 1983. Reproduced by permission of the authors and the National Reading Conference.

confusion about and multiplicity of definitions makes it difficult not only to interpret the literature on main ideas (Reutzel, Hollingsworth & Daines 1988), but also to translate research findings into practice. Communication problems can result when teachers and pupils are using different definitions. A *main idea* may be defined generally as the concept that summarizes all the other textual information in that unit of discourse. In terms of text structure, main ideas are at the top level, they are the superordinate concepts and other related ideas are subordinate to them. As Hare, Rabinowitz, and Schieble (1989) put it, the main idea is the proposition that subsumes all the other propositions in that discourse unit.

There are main ideas of paragraphs and of longer units of text. Main ideas may involve literal comprehension (i.e., they are textually explicit) or inferential comprehension (i.e., they are textually implicit or require readers to combine textual information and prior knowledge). Rarely is a main idea completely explicit (e.g. "The main idea of this paragraph is _____.") The closest example of an explicit main idea is the topic sentence.[11] But even then, the ability to select the topic sentence requires some degree of reasoning because the reader must determine which sentence encompasses the subordinate details. Topic sentences are discussed more fully in the following.

Some authorities (e.g., Baumann 1986a), indicate that children are not particularly adept at identifying main ideas. But, according to Reutzel, Hollingsworth, and Daines (1988), research findings regarding the ability of young children to identify main ideas in narratives are mixed, and intermediate-grade students can be taught to select and to generate main ideas in expository texts. Junior-high pupils of at least average reading ability selected explicit main ideas twice as well as they were able to generate statements for implicit main ideas. Well-organized text facilitated both abilities (Hare & Chelsa 1986). Because the ability to identify main ideas usually requires a form of reasoning involving comparison and selection, it is not surprising that children of below-average intelligence often have more difficulty with this comprehension skill than with understanding details, especially if the main idea is textually implicit.

Children must initially grasp four concepts: (1) Some information they hear or read is more important to understand and remember than other information; (2) very important pieces of information are known as main ideas; (3) a *main idea* is a single word or a statement that summarizes or tells all about the other information in that unit of text; and (4) main ideas may be stated in the text or have to be inferred by the listener or reader.

Development of the first concept can begin in the early grades by discussing and demonstrating the relative importance of information in stories the children hear, read, tell, and write. The term *main idea* can be introduced and the concept demonstrated by showing children how the ideas in a paragraph or short story can be summarized. Then the pupils can be provided with guided practice in making summaries. For example, after discussing the unstated emotion felt by the main character during or after a significant event in a story, the teacher can have the children summarize the emotion in one word or so. Categorization exercises, in which the reasons for placing items under a given heading are discussed, can also be helpful, as can later exercises in which the pupils have to supply the heading (superordinate word) for a related group of words (e.g., *cat, horse, chicken* = animals).

Discussions can center on why authors chose the titles for their stories, but it should be realized that title/story content relationships are not always obvious. Similar discussions can involve the use of newspaper headlines. Such exercises can be followed up with activities in which students select the "best" title or headline from two or more choices and explain their decisions. At first, short passages should be employed.

Because generating a story title, a one-sentence summary of a story event, or a headline is a more difficult task than selecting a response from the choices

---

[11]Titles and center and side headings also may come close to being explicit main ideas, depending on their wording.

offered, such exercises should be delayed until a fair level of competency with the easier task has been demonstrated. Actual newspaper articles, without their headlines, can be read to the children; or the pupils can read the article if it is of a suitable level of difficulty. Students can generate headlines, compare theirs with the originals, and discuss any possible differences.

There are various types of cues that can signal textual importance, which children should be taught to use: (1) graphic (e.g., type size, italics);[12] (2) syntactic (e.g., word order can signal the relative importance of ideas in a sentence); (3) lexical (e.g., use of such words as *important, relevant to*); (4) semantic (e.g., use of thematic words); and (5) schematic (e.g., story grammar and expository-text structures) (J. Williams 1986c).

The use of titles and headings has not proven to be particularly effective in improving the comprehension of natural text, perhaps because unambiguous text is sufficiently redundant (i.e., the important information is repeated often enough) to eliminate the need for explicit titles and headings (Herman et al. 1987). *Signaling* involves adding a word or statement (e.g., a heading or logical connective) that announces upcoming content or a relationship before it actually occurs in the text. In theory, signals should aid students in selecting an appropriate schema, in deciding which information is important, in forming a hierarchical framework in which to store information, and in checking the correctness of information in memory. However, the effects of signals have not been conclusively demonstrated (Spyridakis & Standal 1987). This does not mean that teaching children to note such clues and how to use them should be abandoned; rather it suggests that doing so does not necessarily improve reading comprehension.

One of the most frequently taught main-idea skills is locating and using the topic sentence. Topic sentences occur most frequently in the beginning or end of a paragraph, but they may occur in the middle or be split into two sentences. In *deductively organized paragraphs* (a generalization followed by specifics), the topic sentence is usually the first sentence, which is followed by supporting details. In *inductively structured paragraphs* (specifics lead to a generalization), the topic sentence is usually the last sentence. Some paragraphs do not contain a topic sentence; instead they require the reader to infer the main ideas from the details provided by the text.[13] Yet other paragraphs have neither an explicit nor an implicit main idea. They serve functions such as providing further or more specific details or clarifying previously presented information.

Of the 169 students in one study (Gold & Fleisher 1986), 95% performed significantly better on deductively than on inductively structured paragraphs. In another study (Hare, Rabinowitz & Schieble 1989), the developmental trend in the ability to identify main ideas was highly influenced by text structure, but only when the main ideas were classified as explicit. At all three grade levels (four, six, and eleven), the students had so much more difficulty with implicit than with explicit main ideas that it overrode differences in performance due to text structures.

The ability to select the topic sentence is a slowly developing skill that

[12]There has been little research on the use of italics and boldface as typographic cues to word importance. Nevertheless, italics have been used successfully to stress certain words in order to enhance a particular perspective on a passage (Hartley 1987).

[13]Some authors include such paragraphs in the inductively structured category.

may not be in the repertoires of young pupils. Creation of topic sentences from explicit textual information is a problem even at the college level (Hidi & Anderson 1986).

The children in Gold and Fleisher's (1986) study inappropriately relied on a "first-sentence" strategy 17–47% of the time. Some children, perhaps due to inaccurate instruction, believe that the first sentence of a paragraph is always the topic sentence. They are likely to have difficulty comprehending inductively organized paragraphs or ones without a topic sentence. Other students fail to employ any strategy, or initially select an inappropriate schema and interpret the passage in line with it, even in the face of disconfirming textual information. According to Derry and Murphy (1986), research strongly suggests that the ability to identify main ideas can be enhanced by training in which text processing is primed by heeding topic sentences and headings. However, Herman et al. (1987) state that the degree to which topic sentences aid reading comprehension is not clear.

Although the texts used in workbooks and other such exercises may be helpful in getting across the idea of "topic sentence," care should be exercised in their use. Workbook passages are usually contrived so as to highlight the skill under consideration and to make it fairly easy for children to understand the task. However, they usually do not represent the task requirements of comprehending naturally occurring texts. A few years ago, clear topic sentences were rare in general prose (Moore & Readence 1980) and appeared in less than half the paragraphs in social studies textbooks (Baumann & Serra 1984). There is little evidence that this situation has changed. Furthermore, textbooks are likely to use a variety of text structures, thus increasing the processing demands over those of single-purpose exercises.

Care also should be taken in interpreting children's performance on workbook pages. B. Taylor et al. (1985) found that fifth and sixth graders who successfully completed typical main-idea worksheets had difficulty answering main-idea questions and generating main-idea statements. Such differences in performance were likely due to differences in task demands. Workbook exercises should be followed up by providing guided practice in identifying main ideas in the actual textbooks being used by the students.

Outlining is not likely to help students identify main ideas because a student must be able to discriminate important from less important information in order to construct an outline. However, outlining can provide practice in identifying main ideas (at first the related details can be provided by the teachers in a partially completed outline), and it can be used as an informal measure of pupils' sensitivity to the relative importance of ideas.

Cooper (1986) suggests that pupils be taught the following strategy for identifying a main idea: (1) Determine the general topic by noting which ideas are related to one another and decide which are the most relevant details; (2) find the sentence that summarizes the relevant, related details; and (3) if there is no topic sentence, use the relevant, related details to formulate a main idea statement in your own words. Application of such a strategy may help a pupil to identify the main idea *after* the text has been read. Hopefully, guided practice in the use of such strategies will help lead to spontaneous identification of main ideas while reading.

Berkowitz (1986) presents a procedure for helping students to discriminate main ideas from details, and Jenkins et al. (1987) reports that teaching pupils to write brief restatements of the important ideas in paragraphs as they read narratives resulted in improved comprehension, which transferred to new tasks. Baumann (1988) devised a scope and sequence chart that can be used to help guide the nature of main-idea instruction at various grade levels. Other suggestions for teaching main-idea skills are offered by Duffelmeyer (1985), Erickson and Stephenson (1985), and Baumann (1986b).

Noting, Relating, and Recalling Significant Details

In many reading situations, it is important to note details sufficiently, to understand how they are related, and to be able to recall them. This is especially true when studying, in which the purpose is to assimilate, as thoroughly as possible, the ideas presented by authors.

Details in narratives enable readers to imagine more fully how characters look, feel, or act; the appearance of a setting; or exactly what occurred during an event in the story. In expository materials, details serve various functions. They provide examples that make a generalization more comprehensible, provide evidence to support a conclusion, or show ways a concept can be applied.

Details should not be treated as isolated bits of information. Rather, instructional emphasis should be on relating significant details to each other and to the main ideas they support. Far too many questions ask who, what, when, and where; too few ask how and why details are related.

Two extremes should be avoided—paying too little attention to significant details and paying too much attention to insignificant ones. Some pupils are skilled at obtaining the gist or general meaning of a text but pay little if any attention to details. They need to accept the fact that details can provide important information, and be provided with guided practice in selecting and recalling details that are significantly related to understanding the text more thoroughly. Other pupils try to remember everything or are overly concerned with noting minutiae. This tendency is encouraged by teachers who consistently ask questions on details that have little to do with comprehending the material. Two things need to happen in such situations: Teachers must be shown how to improve their questioning, and children have to be broken of the habit of focusing on minor details.

To enhance student's skills in noting details, practice of the following types is suggested:

1. After the pupils have finished reading, have an informal discussion. First discuss the main ideas; then call attention to significant details by posing questions such as:
   a. What did _____ do when _____? Why did she do that?
   b. How did _____ feel when he heard that news? Why?
   c. What did _____ have to do before she could _____?
   d. What examples for that generalization did the author provide? Name a few examples that wouldn't fit.
   e. What evidence did the author provide to substantiate her conclusion? Do you accept the conclusion? Why?

    f. What applications of that concept were provided by the author? What other examples could have been given?

2. Straightforward questions about significant details can be used at times, but they primarily serve to assess, rather than to develop, comprehension. Multiple-choice questions are quicker to score, but completion and short-answer questions can be more revealing.

3. Provide students with an incomplete outline of a text. Only the main ideas are provided and there are an appropriate number of blank spaces under each, on which the students are to record the related details after they have read the text.

4. At times announce beforehand that the pupils will not be allowed to look at their texts when answering comprehension questions.

5. Ask children to retell what they have read, and probe for important details when they are not supplied by the child.

    Details are not always directly stated in the text (e.g., Mike was a very disagreeable person.). At times, the reader must infer details (e.g., Mike argued with everyone. He never had a smile or kind word for anything or anyone.). Unlike some other types of comprehension skills, literal details (explicit information) are not marked by signal words.

Scanning and Skimming

At times, individuals read for one of these two purposes: to find a specific piece of information or an answer to a specific question, or to get an overall impression of the content. Achieving either purpose involves rapid reading, but the ways in which the purposes are achieved differ.

    To find a specific bit of information (e.g., a name, date, phone number) or the answer to a specific question (e.g., Why is oxygen essential for combustion?), the reader uses a process known as scanning. *Scanning* involves knowing exactly what you are looking for, noting the key words in your question, and selectively finding those words as rapidly as possible. In scanning, there is no intent to absorb the meaning of the text. So, for example, in looking for the date of the Battle of Waterloo, the reader knows that the answer has to be a number. Therefore, all the words in the text except *Waterloo* are ignored as the eyes move rapidly over the text, and stop only when an Arabic number appears near the word *Waterloo*. When a key word is spotted, it seems to stand out almost as if it were in bold type, and the scanner reads the content around it to determine if it contains the answer to the question. Scanning speeds can be extremely fast, but they need to be adjusted to the reader's purpose. Finding a particular name usually can be done with more speed than finding an answer to a question.

    Children often need to learn the purposes for scanning, and exactly how to go about it. Initial practice can entail presenting a single item and having the children respond orally when they find the answer. To curtail answers coming from only the best scanners, children should not be allowed to respond before, say, 45 seconds have passed. Later practice in scanning can be provided by presenting a list of questions of the following types and encouraging the pupils to find the answers as quickly as possible:

1. Which state produces the most wheat?
2. What is the atomic number of gold?
3. Why did the pilgrims leave England?
4. At what theatre is the movie "_____" now playing?

After completing the exercise, the students can be asked to respond orally and their responses can be discussed, or they can write the answers, and thus provide an assessment. In either case, the teacher should observe the children's behaviors while they are supposed to be scanning. Later, in order to encourage speed, time limits may be placed on completing the exercises. The items may be drawn from various sources such as the pupils' textbooks, reference materials, newspapers, and phone books.

Skimming involves superficial, rapid reading to get a general overall impression of the material. More attention is paid to obtaining meaning than in scanning, but less so than in normal reading. Skimming is most often done to determine if a more thorough reading is desirable. Some of the purposes for which skimming is done are:

1. Previewing a textbook chapter in order to obtain an overview of its contents and to activate prior knowledge. This may involve skimming only the title, headings, introductory statements, and the first sentence of each paragraph, and reading the summary or conclusion more carefully.
2. Sampling a few pages at random to decide whether one would enjoy reading the book.
3. Looking rapidly through material to judge if it is likely to contain the information sought, or if it contains information that differs from that in another source.
4. Going quickly through a controversial article to determine the author's point of view, without noting any specific arguments.
5. Examining material to decide if it is of a suitable level of reading difficulty.

As with other reading skills, improved efficiency in skimming comes gradually with motivated practice. Motivation is best achieved by encouraging the pupils to skim when doing so will be of practical importance to them.

In one study (Kobasigawa, Ransom & Holland 1980) virtually all the eighth graders but only two-thirds of the sixth graders and half the fourth graders were able to describe how to skim. The pupils at all three grade levels could skim when explicitly instructed to do so, but skimming as a spontaneous strategy based on an implicit task assignment did not occur until eighth grade. Memory and Moore (1981) offer suggestions for developing skimming skills.

Understanding Cause-Effect Relationships

Cause-effect statements may appear in single sentences or separate sentences. The relationship may be explicitly marked or have to be inferred. Either the cause or effect can come first, but usually the cause comes first in inferred statements. Cause-effect relations expressed through subject and predicate may be difficult for children to understand, especially if the passive form is used (e.g., Irene's inability to concentrate caused her to fail the test.). Even when the relationship is marked, certain constructions seem to cause difficulty for children. For example, a construction with an "effect" marker (*so, then*, etc.) in the middle of a sentence is more difficult to comprehend because the reader must wait to be informed that the second clause is an effect (e.g., Bill left, so Zeb put down his rifle). Part of the problem may be that *so* is not interpreted as *therefore*.

Other statements, similar to those of cause-effect, also create comprehension problems for pupils. These include *conditionals* (e.g., If I run fast [then] I will win; Unless I run fast, I will not win.) and *concession,* which often indicates a lack of cause-effect (e.g., She wept, but she was not sad). Refer to Cronnell (1981) for further information on cause-effect statements.

Providing open-ended *why* questions that require pupils to identify cause-effects in short paragraphs improved the ability of low-average readers, but not of good readers, to understand such relationships (Memory 1983a,b).

Following the Sequence of Events

The comprehension of texts such as narrative and historical accounts relies on the ability to note the sequence of events and to grasp any relationships between or among that sequence. Sequence may be marked by words such as *first, finally, next, following that, before,* and *later,* or by numbers; or it may be marked in ways that also require reasoning ability to follow the order of events—dates, the changes in seasons, or the passage of time on a clock. At times readers must completely infer the sequence from the relative position of sentences of paragraphs containing the events (e.g., Winnie dashed into the house. She quickly opened all the windows.) or by understanding from prior knowledge the sequence that is most likely to occur in real-life situations.

In the normal course of reading such texts, these various sources of information regarding sequence can be brought to students' attention and discussed. As with other types of comprehension skills, whenever a child has difficulty understanding or recalling the sequence of events, the reason for that problem should be determined and appropriate practice and instruction provided. Flashbacks in narratives give even older students difficulty, especially when they first encounter the technique.

In reading narratives, readers can be helped by anticipating upcoming events. Teachers can help children learn to make predictions by asking them at critical points in the story, "What do you think is going to happen next?" and "Why do you think so?" Refer to D. Baker (1982) for other suggestions for developing sequential concepts and skills.

Following Printed Directions

Printed directions are used daily by a wide variety of people in numerous situations—the auto mechanic attempting to repair a type of ignition system that he has never worked on, the physician learning a new surgical procedure, the parent assembling a child's new bike, and the child learning to play a new board game. The goals of reading to follow directions are to do or produce something once, or to learn how to do something that will be used again in the future. If the task will rarely be attempted or if the consequences of failure are not serious, there is no need to be able to recall each step; the procedure can be completed and forgotten. If learning is the goal, there an intent to remember each step, and each step must be read more carefully (and perhaps the relationship between steps understood). In either case, each step must be understood so that it can be carried out accurately and in sequence.

Slightly different procedures for reading directions have been offered. Rush, Moe, and Storlie (1986) suggest the following: (1) Read the instructions completely once in order to develop a mental set for what is to be done; (2) read the first step carefully and do what it directs; (3) reread the first step and check your work; (4) read, do, reread, and check each of the remaining steps in sequence; and (5) reread and check the entire set of directions. Henk and Helfeldt (1987) recommend this procedure: (1) Survey any available illustrations to get a quick overview of the scope and complexity of the task; (2) read the set of instructions "once over lightly"; (3) read each step carefully and relate each to any corresponding illustration; (4) skim the whole set of directions again to help synthesize and fix the overall procedure; (5) actively do the task.

The best practice in reading to follow directions is provided through the use of activities that students want or need to do. Content-subject textbooks, especially those in math and science, contain directions; and children may like to work on directions in the *Scout Handbook*, magazines like *Popular Mechanics*, or numerous "how to" articles and books on activities such as making toys, cooking, and conducting experiments. If the task is easily repeated or if errors are easily corrected, children can attempt to carry out the task on their own. If the task is long, involves expensive materials, or contains some danger, it is desirable to discuss the directions with the pupils and to clear up any problems through rereading and discussion before they attempt the task. Closer monitoring of each step by the teacher may also be prudent. When additional practice seems needed, workbook exercises may be employed.

Written directions can cause problems for adults, let alone children. Directions are not always well written. The reader must be sensitive to sequence cues (e.g., *then, next*), but there may be no explicit links between the steps. Directions may call for understanding locational propositions, complex spatial relationships, and a technical vocabulary. They often contain telegraphic sentences, implied procedures, and abbreviations.

Marshall (1984) provides suggestions for helping students to learn how to read directions by asking questions that both focus on the unique characteristics of written directions and provide information that facilitates their comprehension. Other useful suggestions may be found in Henk and Helfeldt (1987).

Filling out applications and forms can be a unique form of reading to follow directions. M. Smith and Schloss (1986) developed a form that can be used to help individuals complete approximately 80% of the items on any job application, provided that the vocabulary used in them is understood.

Remembering What Has Been Read

Children and adults complain that they understand what they read when they read it, but cannot remember it later. This complaint is serious and deserves careful consideration.

There are large individual differences in both speed of assimilation and permanence of retention. Some people's memories are naturally better than others. However, the correct application of known and generally accepted principles of learning would enable most complainers to remember what they read far better than they do at present.

The principles listed below can be found in almost every educational psychology textbook:

1. Ease of recall is directly proportional to how well the information was understood originally. It is difficult to recall ideas that have been only partially understood or not understood at all.
2. Material that is well organized in the reader's mind is easier to remember than material that is unorganized. The efficient reader tries to grasp the author's plan and understand the relationships between ideas and the relations between the major ideas and the facts or details that give them definite meaning.
3. Remembering what has been read may be aided by outlining, summarizing, or taking notes during or after reading. Similar benefits may be derived from underlining significant points or writing comments in the margin.
4. An active intention to remember aids recall. A reader who is determined to remember, better concentrates his or her attention and tends to read more effectively.
5. Recall should be selective. A person cannot hope to remember everything read. The points that are most important to remember should be singled out for special attention.
6. A single reading is rarely enough. Most people have to do some reviewing and rereading if they want to remember for any length of time.
7. After reading, the reader should try to recall the points worth remembering and recite them to him- or herself. If there is time, it is desirable to check recall by rereading and then reciting again. At least half the time spent (after the first reading) in trying to fix the material in memory should be spent in active recitation. Omission of this procedure is one of the most frequent errors of those who complain about their poor memories.
8. What we learn, but never review or use, is gradually forgotten. What we really want to remember must be refreshed by review from time to time. Derry and Murphy (1986) discuss strategies that may be used for short-term and long-term retention.

Poor memory for what has been read results from an unselective, passive, single reading followed by failure to review the points the reader wishes to remember. Both of these major faults are correctable. Other procedures for improving retention of information include mnemonic strategies, visual imagery, associating new information with what is already known, and overlearning (see Devine 1987).

Some teachers encourage reading without the intent to recall by the kinds of reading practice they give and the kinds of questions they ask. In most exercises, children are free to look back into the material if they cannot remember the answer. Unless some practice is given in answering questions with the book closed or the page covered, pupils may become excessively dependent on rereading. They may also learn to read the questions first and then read for the answers, a desirable procedure in many situations, but not suitable when one is trying to stimulate the ability to recall. Excessive reliance on multiple-choice or true-false questions may also be harmful to recall, because such questions require only recognition of the correct answer, and pupils may become quite skillful at recognizing what they cannot remember. It is therefore important to ask recall questions and to provide at least some practice in reading with the intent to reproduce the gist of the material. Study skills and habits that can influence recall are discussed on pages 604–618.

16

Reading Comprehension III: Learning through Reading

This third chapter on reading comprehension considers studying—a special form of reading that is used to learn from text. Studying involves not only comprehension but storage and recall of information. Following an introductory section, we discuss content-subject textbooks and the demands they place on students. The rest of the chapter is devoted to ways of helping pupils to learn from their textbooks and to become independent learners. Topics included in these sections are instructional and learning activities, using graphic aids, locating information, study habits, content-subject instruction for disabled readers, and metacognitive and cognitive strategies.

HELPING STUDENTS LEARN FROM WRITTEN TEXT

In the primary grades, the instructional emphasis is on helping children learn how to read; that is, how to comprehend written text. Narrative texts are primarily used in this endeavor, and the teacher has the major responsibility for the children's learning. Beginning at about the fourth grade, the instructional and learning emphasis begins to shift, until much of what is commonly referred to as reading is actually studying and critical thinking (A. Brown 1985). Reading becomes a vehicle for learning new information. Narrative texts become more complex, students more frequently encounter various types of expository-text structures, the ideas presented in the texts become more complex and abstract, and the responsibility for learning shifts from the teacher to the students.

Learning from written text necessitates studying. Studying involves reading, but it requires more thorough comprehension than what is needed to read a basal reader in a directed-reading activity or a story for pleasure. A detailed memory representation must be developed, so that the information can be retrieved easily at some future point. Studying also requires the ability to concentrate simultaneously on understanding the text and on one's self as a learner, as well as more detailed use of strategic behaviors (A. Brown 1985).

The outcome of studying—learning—is a function of the interactions among student-status, text-status, and processing variables. *Student-status variables* include the student's (1) knowledge of the purpose for reading and of what is required to complete the task successfully; (2) general level of reading ability; (3) ability to use cognitive strategies; (4) prior knowledge and use of that information; and (5) motivation. Among the more important *text-status variables* are the text's content and structure. One of the most important processing variables is the processing-load demand. Processing demands in studying can be quite heavy. For instance, a subject-matter textbook page may contain 50 idea units that are related in a number of ways (T. H. Anderson & Armbruster 1984b).

Teachers can help children learn from written texts by improving their general reading comprehension skills and by teaching them: (1) to recognize and use expository-text structures, (2) how to read their content-subject textbooks (see Gee and Raskow 1987), (3) how to study, and (4) how to become independent learners.

CONTENT-SUBJECT TEXTBOOKS

Narrative and expository texts place different demands on students. Narratives often require the reader to supply or infer main ideas and to fill in a number of details from their background knowledge, as well as to understand connotative and literary usages of words and phrases. The text structure used in narratives is usually a sequence of events leading to a climax or conclusion. A major exception in this regard is the use of flashbacks, which often cause comprehension problems for students. Narrative texts read in literature classes are typically longer and more complex than those used in developmental reading lessons. These pieces of literature do not necessarily follow the story grammar children have come to expect, and understanding them is made even more difficult by the fact that writing styles differ not only among the various kinds of narrations (e.g., short stories vs. autobiographies) but among authors within a genre.

Typically, the ideas presented in expository texts are readily identifiable because the author has made them explicit. Expository text is characterized by content that is often unfamiliar to the readers; heavy concept density and loads; technical vocabulary; high-frequency words with meanings other than their common ones; long sentences with complex syntactic structures; abstract content; and varied and changing text structures, often in combination within a given text (Muth 1987a).

Given these differences in task demands, it is not surprising that both good and poor readers, in general, have more difficulty understanding exposition than

narration (M. Olson 1985, Muth 1987a). Pupils have more problems comprehending both explicit and implicit relationships in expository texts than in narrative texts. Such differences may be due, at least partially, to the availability of
background knowledge. It may be relatively easier to integrate information
when reading narratives because they deal with more familiar topics or events
than do expository texts (Geva & Ryan 1985).

Two points need to be made regarding differences between narratives and
expository texts. First, the purpose for reading determines the reader's desired
level of comprehension as well as what is understood and remembered. For example, levels of comprehension and recall are likely to differ when a narrative is read
in a reading lesson, for enjoyment as a free-time activity, or in a literature class.

Second, there is more latitude for differences in interpretation of narratives
than of expository text because of differences between the two in text content
and in what the reader has to "fill in" from prior knowledge. Students are likely
to interpret text in a manner consistent with their schemata. So, because individuals' schemata are varied and unique, it is possible for pupils to interpret parts
of or even the whole story differently from one another, the teacher, and even
the author. Differences in background knowledge may also explain why some
pupils focus on and remember certain text information and overlook seemingly
more significant information (K. Wood 1985).

Different strategies are needed for reading various narrative and expository
materials. These are discussed by Beach and Appleman (1984). Forgan and Mangrum (1981) list the reading skills needed for the content areas. Useful suggestions for developing reading-to-learn skills may be found in: Graham and Robinson (1984); Wong and Au (1985); Singer and Bean (1988); Singer and Donlan
(1988); Ogle (1989); and Schuder, Clewell, and Jackson (1989).

Vocabulary Burden in Textbooks.

Beginning-reading materials usually contain only words whose meanings are
already familiar to children or that can be explained easily. Therefore, word
meaning is rarely a problem for novice readers. As the levels of the basal reader
materials get higher, progressively more new words and ideas are introduced,
and more meanings of a particular word are employed.

The vocabulary burden is more acute in content-subject textbooks than in
general reading materials. Each content area has an extensive specialized vocabulary that must be learned if the student is to understand the content. Successful
teachers take pains to introduce new concepts and the verbal labels that represent
them with meaningful illustrations and examples, guide the formulation of a statement as to what the term means, and then check carefully to see if the concept has
been understood and the printed word recognized. Technical vocabulary is of two
main kinds: (1) words that are specific to that content field, such as *divisor* and *lon-
gitude;* and (2) words whose meanings change from subject to subject, such as
group in biology (a large number of plants or animals related to each other because of a common similarity) or in social studies (a number of persons gathered
together and forming a unit) or in chemistry (a radical—a group of two or more
atoms that acts as a single atom and goes through a reaction unchanged or is replaced by a single atom). Many pupils experience semantic confusion when a

high-frequency word has an uncommon, technical meaning such as *left* meaning *remainder* instead of a direction, *coast* meaning a *shore* and not something done with a sled, or *subject* used as a verb.

Lists of content-subject words are available. Subject-area vocabularies are listed by broad grade ranges (e.g., primary, intermediate, secondary) by Fry, Fountoukidis, and Polk (1985). A. J. Harris and Jacobson (1972) provide lists of the technical vocabularies in four subject areas, and the *EDL Core Vocabularies* (S. Taylor et al. 1979) have mathematical word lists for Grades 1–3 and 4–6, and social studies and science lists for Grades 3–6. Swett (1978) presents a brief list of essential math terms, and O'Mara (1981) lists mathematical words and terms. Reutzel (1983) indicates the words that signal the types of computations required to solve a word problem. Lists of high-frequency technical vocabulary for each of 10 occupations have been provided by Rush, Moe, and Storlie (1986). These lists may be helpful in identifying the important technical terms in each subject area. Dupuis and Snyder (1983) describe and illustrate an approach to teaching technical vocabulary as a part of concept development, and Lloyd and Mitchell (1989) suggest a three-step procedure for deciding which concepts to teach when a textbook contains too many ideas for the pupils to absorb. A test of the important vocabulary and concepts used in primary-grade mathematics was developed by J. Cox and Wiebe (1984).

Organizational Patterns in Textbooks

The various types of text structures were covered on pages 564–578. Here, the concern is primarily with the relative frequency of these structures in textbooks and the content areas in which they occur.

An analysis of 142 content-subject textbooks (Cheek & Cheek 1983) reveals three main organizational patterns: (1) *enumeration*—a topic immediately followed by information that expands on it (e.g., a main idea followed by descriptive details); (2) *relationships*—including cause-effect (often used in social studies textbooks), compare-contrast (often found in science textbooks), and classification; and (3) *problem-solving*—the problem presented has to be solved in order to demonstrate understanding of a concept (used in mathematics, science, business education, and vocational textbooks). One study of science and social studies textbooks indicates that cause-effect, compare-contrast, and simple listings were the most frequent types of text structure (Colwell & Helfeldt 1983). Another study of commonly used social studies textbooks found the enumerative structure to be the most common. In most of the passages examined, the theme was implied rather than stated, and explicit connections were not used to mark the relationships between superordinate and subordinate concepts (Risko & Alvarez 1986).

MacGinitie, Kimmel, and Maria (1980) report that many of the textbooks used in Grades 3–6, were written in an inductive style—supporting or descriptive information leading up to the main point in the paragraph.

Demands Made by Various Content-Area Textbooks

Textbooks in some content areas seem more difficult to comprehend than those in others. They also seem to place different demands on the reader.

Material used in mathematics is more difficult to read than in any other content area (V. Schell 1982). Dunlap and McNight (1978) demonstrate with many examples the difficulties that children experience in trying to translate mathematical language into their everyday language in order to comprehend it. They also show how drawings and diagrams can be used to clear up many of the problems.

One of the biggest problems children have in mathematics is solving word problems. Usually the difficulty lies in comprehending the written problem and not in performing the calculations. Earp (1970) suggests the following five-step procedure for reading math problems: (1) Read to visualize or grasp the situation presented; (2) reread to note the specific facts given; (3) note any difficult concepts or terminology and get help if needed; (4) reread to select the operations to be used and to plan the solution; (5) after finding an answer, reread again to check the process chosen and the reasonableness of the solution. Another plan is offered by Kreese (1984). Word problems can be made more understandable by simplifying the syntax and resequencing the information in the problem to match the order in which it will be needed to solve the problem (O'Mara 1981). Refer to Stein (1987) and Muth (1988) for other suggestions on how to teach children to read word problems.

Science is another area in which exactingly slow, careful reading is necessary. Suggestions for how to read science material may be found in Thelen (1984). Teachers should be aware that students' comprehension of science material is often adversely affected by their prior beliefs and preconceptions that are at odds with accepted scientific thinking (C. Anderson & Smith 1984).

Many social studies textbooks are difficult to read because they are not well written (Armbruster & Gudbrandsen 1986b). Armbruster et al. (1984), who found that many of the questions posed in history texts were hard to understand, present a taxonomy of American History questions and give examples of what students must know or be able to do in order to answer each type of question. Suggestions for teaching reading in the social studies may be found in Lunstrum and Taylor (1978).

Research has indicated that providing reading- and study-skill instruction in the social studies can raise achievement scores in both reading and social studies to levels higher than those attained by students who did not receive such instruction. The successful instructional programs were the ones in which (1) the teachers played an important role in designing the program; (2) there were more than just a few activities and materials employed; and (3) the teachers played an active role in instruction and did not simply rely on written overviews and exercises (Wade 1983).

Questions on narratives should tap information central to the development of the story. Questions should guide the students in understanding the important story concepts and highlight the interrelationships of these concepts and events, rather than seek discrete bits of information. Ringler and Weber (1982) suggest how to help students make the inferences that are often necessary to comprehend narratives.

Inconsiderate, Considerate, and Elaborated Texts

Textbooks have come under close scrutiny in the past few years and have been found wanting by some (e.g., T. H. Anderson & Armbruster 1984a) but not others (e.g., Dreher, Singer & Letteer 1987). Among the criticisms hurled at history textbooks are the following: their prose style is bland, the excessive coverage makes them boring, coverage of most topics is superficial, and their format and graphics diminish the style and coherence of the text content (Sewall 1988). As a result of their thoughtful analysis of the coverage of the American Revolution in fifth-grade textbooks, Beck and MeKeown (1988) conclude that the textbooks: merely give information rather than engineer it to bring about understanding; assume unrealistic levels of prior knowledge on the part of the intended readers (". . . a text that may seem to an adult to contain reasonable content with which to build a coherent representation may seem incomprehensible to a 10-year-old"); often did not explain major concepts and events; and fail to explicate how ideas and events are connected.

The degree to which *inconsiderate text*, that is, text not well written, hinders comprehension is not well understood, but it appears to suppress performance (Herman et al. 1987). There has been some effort to make textbooks more "considerate," that is, more comprehensible, by such modifications as making the text structure more obvious and making the concepts and their relationships more explicit. The latter approach often requires longer texts and is therefore referred to as an *elaborated text.* Elaborated text could be especially helpful to students who have limited topical knowledge and therefore might have difficulty understanding how the network of concepts fits together, particularly if doing so requires a great deal of inferencing.

Guidelines for examining the comprehensibility of textbooks are provided by Clewell and Cliffton (1983), and a Textbook Evaluation Checklist and accompanying discussion may be found in T. H. Anderson and Armbruster (1984a). Refer to Armbruster and Anderson (1984) for an example of a textbook chapter that was written to maximize its comprehensibility.

Sundbye (1987) reports that reducing the inferential load in basal reader stories by adding large amounts of information (i.e., creating an elaborated text) increased the overall comprehension of third graders, but had no effect on the amount of important information included in their retellings or on their reading rates. Asking inferential questions at the end each episode, which guided the children in making the same connections as did the elaborated text, produced comprehension gains similar to those that resulted from the use of the elaborated text.

INSTRUCTIONAL AND LEARNING ACTIVITIES

That pupils are not very adept at learning from their textbooks (Schumaker 1987) is not surprising because they receive little if any instruction in adapting their general reading skills to task requirements or instruction that could help them to acquire or employ the specialized reading/study skills and strategies often needed to comprehend and to learn from content-subject texts (Pearson & Gallagher 1983).

Many teachers have not learned how to provide the necessary instruction; and some, especially content-area specialists, believe that it is not their responsibility or that the textbooks are much too difficult for the students to understand so they have to "spoon feed" the information to them. But reading specialists can demonstrate to teachers the value of skill and strategy instruction, how to use comprehension/study aids appropriately, and how to plan lessons to accomplish their goals. They can work *cooperatively* with classroom teachers to deliver an effective reading/study program, which many of them can eventually conduct on their own. Dennis, McKenna, and Miller (1989) discuss how content-subject teachers might be encouraged to instruct their students in how to comprehend their textbooks.

Some instructional procedures are aimed at helping children to understand a particular text; others, such as teaching metacognitive and cognitive strategies, are taught so that pupils can apply them independently in any learning situation.

In planning a lesson, teachers should decide what they want their pupils to learn and how they will structure the lesson to achieve that learning. Teachers can manipulate five variables to promote students' learning from text (Moore, Readence & Rickelman 1989): content knowledge, motivation, attention, instructional/learning strategies, and expected learning outcomes. Only the latter is discussed here; the other variables are covered elsewhere in this book.

Expected learning outcomes may be concepts, principles, attitudes, or strategic behaviors. Having an instructional goal helps to structure the lesson. For example, teachers should determine what assistance, if any, pupils will need to comprehend the text at a level that will allow them to attain the desired goal. An examination of the text will reveal the amount of *content knowledge* needed to comprehend the text. Knowing what information the text provides and how it is presented, what the author expects the readers to provide, and the background knowledge of the students allows teachers to determine the kind and amount of prereading or during-reading assistance that will have to be provided. Such knowledge can also help in selecting a procedure that may facilitate the students' comprehension or in deciding whether the text lends itself to the use of a study aid or the learning of a cognitive strategy. Strahan and Herlihy (1985) present a model for analyzing textbook content.

If the teacher wants his pupils to acquire understandings other than those emphasized by the author, he has to decide how best to direct their attention to the text information he thinks is important. The anticipated outcome of the lesson also enters into planning postreading activities—what should be reviewed and how, how to assess the degree to which the goal has been attained, and so forth.

The following activities are divided into prereading, during-reading, and postreading procedures; but some of them can be used in more than one of these periods.

Prereading Activities

Three instructional/learning strategies can be incorporated into prereading activities (Moore, Readence & Rickelman 1989). *Predicting*, which is anticipating upcoming text content, calls for thinking ahead before and during reading. Having a set of expectations helps students to focus their attention because they need to determine which expectations are correct and what unexpected text information should cause them to modify or abandon and replace their predictions.

Among the activities that include predicting are the SQ3R, PReP, and webbing. Predicting can also be used as a during-reading activity. *Organizing* means arranging information in a meaningful fashion. Webbing and graphing activities capitalize on using prior knowledge to organize information. Organizing also involves following the pattern of the author's ideas. Surveying and outlining can help students to identify and use text structures. Concept mapping and thematic organizers can also help pupils to detect and use text structures, but they are difficult to use without a teacher (Muth 1987b). *Connecting* involves relating new text information to what is already known. Strategies that promote predictions also promote connections; other connection activities are considered in the following section. These three activities tie in nicely with the three cognitive processes important to reading comprehension: (1) attending to incoming information; (2) organizing incoming information into a coherent structure; and (3) integrating incoming information with existing knowledge structures (Mayer 1987).

Behavioral objectives are sometimes used as a prereading procedure. Their use is based on the assumption that knowing what one is expected to learn and how that learning will be assessed allows pupils to study more systematically. Just as with prereading questions, objectives seem to focus the students' attention on the targeted information but have a negative effect on the acquisition of other text information (Tierney & Cunningham 1984). The influence of stated objectives on the acquisition of targeted information decreases as the reading material increases in length. Objectives are less effective than prereading questions (Klauer 1984).

The major purpose for prereading activities is to increase the probability that the reading material will be understood by the pupils. Prereading activities may be grouped into general study strategies, procedures for relating prior knowledge to upcoming textual information, and graphic representations; these activities are not mutually exclusive.

GENERAL STUDY PROCEDURES.   The five-step SQ3R procedure (F. P. Robinson 1970) is widely used. *Survey* involves quickly reading the table of contents, the introductory and summary paragraphs, the headings and side headings,[1] marginal notes, and pictorial aids. The purpose is to obtain an overview of the author's purpose and the structure used to transmit that message. It should also serve to activate topical knowledge. *Question* means to turn each heading and side heading into a question before that section is read; where such typographical aids are not present, the topic sentence may be used. Generating questions provides a purpose for reading, helps readers focus their attention, and supplies a means for self-monitoring comprehension. *Reading* must be an active process in which readers relate what they already know to textual information. Care must be taken, however, not to overlook any important information not covered by the self-generated questions. *Recite* means stating the obtained information to oneself subvocally or in some more permanent form such as under-

[1]Students of all ages do not take full advantage of headings in expository textbooks (Hare & Lomax 1985).

lining, note taking, or informal outlining. Recitation allows one to check how well the material was understood and recalled, and may suggest the need to reread. Understanding can be checked by expressing the author's ideas in one's own words. This immediate review helps to store the information in memory. Written forms of recitation require the pupil to determine the relative importance of information and to organize it in some fashion that can be used later as a review. *Review* involves spending appropriate amounts of time to go over the material immediately after reading and at appropriate intervals thereafter. Review not only helps to retain information over time but provides a continual check as to how well the material is still understood.

The SQ3R procedure seems well grounded in the psychology of learning; and as indicated above, it can accommodate many of the more recent ideas on cognition and metacognition. Based on their review of 27 studies, Gustafson and Pederson (1986) conclude that the SQ3R method is as effective as, but no more effective than, other study procedures.

A number of minor modifications of the SQ3R have been developed. Pauk (1984) suggests an SQ4R technique: Survey to get started, Question to focus attention, Read with concentration, Record by taking succinct notes, Recite by covering the whole page except for your marginal notes and then reciting aloud using the notes as a cue, and Reflect by thinking about the information. G. Powell and Zalud (1982) describe an adaptation for use with older poor readers. It uses a worksheet that the students complete. A PQ5R study method was proposed by Graham and Robinson (1984), and a PSRT strategy by S. Simons (1989).

PReP is a three-step study procedure developed by Langer (1982). First, the students free-associate with key words, phrases, or pictures from the text. This serves to activate relevant prior knowledge and allows the teacher to assess the extent of that prior knowledge and thereby to judge the need for establishing additional background knowledge before having the pupils read the material. This first step is similar to the *brainstorming* technique discussed by Tierney, Mosenthal, and Kantor (1984). Next, the teacher encourages the students to reflect on their initial associations by asking questions such as "What made you think of ____?" This allows the students to become aware of their network of associations and to evaluate and monitor the adequacy of their topical knowledge. Finally, the students are encouraged to reformulate their ideas by questions such as "Based on our discussion, what new ideas do you have?" PReP has been shown to help increase text comprehension (Langer 1984).

K. Wood (1985) illustrates the use of an instructional procedure in which students are presented with a list of key concepts in the order in which they occur in their textbook chapter. The students are told that these concepts and significant supporting details will form the basis for a chapter test. During reading, the students take notes by organizing the details around the major concepts. No more than 24 hours later (to curtail forgetting), the pupils try to associate all the text information they can with each key word.

Presenting key words that appear in the text can serve to activate prior knowledge. The *Directed Reading/Thinking Activity* (Stauffer 1969) attempts to get children to relate prior knowledge and new information. Summaries of the DRTA strategy and many other strategies may be found in Tierney, Readence, and Dishner (1985) and Moore, Readence, and Rickelman (1989). A modification of the DRTA is the *Direct Inquiry Activity* (DIA), which Thomas (1986) suggests has particular utility when the text contains a great deal of factual information, much of which the students are expected to retain. In the DIA, pupils are encouraged to predict responses to six key questions: Who? What? When? Where? How? and Why?

Advance organizers are short introductory passages intended to facilitate learning. They are based on Ausubel's (1960) theory, which holds that "cognitive structure is highly organized in terms of highly inclusive concepts under which are assumed less inclusive subconcepts and informational data." In other words, knowledge is organized hierarchically. Ausubel's theory is generally consistent with schema theory (Ausubel 1980) in that it assumes that new information is learned and retained to the extent that it can be related to one's existing cognitive structure. The function of advance organizers is to encourage the development of the ideational or organizational framework needed to facilitate comprehension and learning (C. Clark & Bean 1982).

Most studies regarding the effectiveness of advance organizers have used college students. High school students have been used occasionally; elementary school children, rarely. Since 1975 there have been at least seven literature reviews, but their conclusions have differed widely. About all that one can safely say about advance organizers is that they tend to help some readers, but their effects vary (Pearson & Gallagher 1983). An even less positive conclusion was rendered by Tierney and Cunningham (1984). The most comprehensive of the reviews, a meta-analysis of 135 studies (Luiten, Ames & Acherson 1980), indicates that the average advance organizer study shows a small but facilitative effect on learning and retention of content-subject material with pupils of all grade and ability levels (although they are generally more beneficial to lower-ability students). The short duration of many of the studies (one or two class periods) may have contributed to the small treatment effects. Other possible explanations are that the advance organizers used in the studies did not assist the pupils to relate new information to existing knowledge or that the pupils already had the knowledge developed by the advance organizer (Jenkins & Pany 1981). It would seem that a single advance organizer may not be appropriate for use with a group simply because of wide individual differences in prior knowledge, reading ability, and reasoning ability. The major problems seem to be the lack of a clearly specified definition of an advance organizer and the global nature of the questions researchers have tended to ask (Lenz, Alley & Schumaker 1987). Mayer (1979) provides a checklist that may be used to produce effective advance organizers.

An *anticipation guide* combines pre- and postreading activities by encouraging students to elaborate on concepts in the text that are already in their knowledge base; having them predict, from various cues provided by the teacher, the contents of the material; and, finally, having pupils evaluate their predictions. Unlike typical study guides, this instructional strategy asks students to react to statements, not all of which are supported by the text (Nichols 1983). Suggestions for constructing and using anticipation guides may be found in K. Wood and Mateja (1983), Bean et al. (1986), and Moore, Readence, and Rickelman 1989).

Thelen (1982) presents a procedure that combines the format of a structured overview (see the following) and a model of concept attainment. It is designed to help guide students to organize their prior knowledge into a conceptual framework, to fill in informational gaps in the students' background knowledge, and to blend past experiences with the new content.

Bean and Ericson (1989) illustrate the use of an activity that combines the use of a text preview, which is an introductory paragraph designed to provide a detailed framework for comprehending the selection, with a three-level study guide, which asks students to react to text concepts at various levels of comprehension. Armstrong, Patberg, and Dewitz (1988) describe how to construct and use a reading guide, which is in effect a "walk through" of the reading processes needed to comprehend the text.

GRAPHIC REPRESENTATIONS.   *Graphic representations* attempt to depict key concepts and their relationships visually. As a prereading activity, their purpose is to help students comprehend the material by clarifying new ideas and by indicating the structure of the text. As a postreading activity, they help students learn to organize textual information, and the finished product can be used as a review aid. When used before reading, graphic representation is a teacher-directed activity, although pupils may participate. When employed after reading, the students may play a major or independent role in their construction. In either case, the hope is that the graphic representations and the accompanying discussions will help students acquire comprehension skills that will transfer to new situations. There is some belief that diagrammatic representations transform the information into a symbolic representation that more closely represents the way in which knowledge is stored in memory and thus make it easier to activate prior knowledge and incorporate new information into existing knowledge (T. Anderson & Armbruster 1984b). The following examples of graphic organizers are currently in use.

A *structured overview* attempts to provide cognitive readiness for reading by presenting major concepts and key terms in a schematic diagram that conveys their relationships through the use of connecting lines (see Figure 16.1). As an instructional strategy, this approach involves teaching the vocabulary and discussing the relationships among the concepts. (see Readence & Moore 1979, R. Vacca 1981). It provides a hierarchical structure that readers can use to organize ideas and to assimilate information more easily. Structured overviews also help to establish relationships between new information and prior knowledge (Dewitz, Carr & Patberg 1987).

Although used primarily with secondary-school students, structured overviews have been employed successfully as low as in the fourth grade (Moore, Readence & Rickelman 1989). Research findings suggest that their use is effective under certain conditions with certain pupils. In general, students with high verbal IQs seem to benefit most (Tierney & Cunningham 1984), and the overviews appear to be more effective when pupils participate in their construction (J. L. Vaughn 1982). Studies have not adequately addressed the possible influence that the quality of the structured overview has on performance.

Cognitive or *semantic mapping* involves visually displaying superordinate text concepts and some important subordinate ideas so that the relationships among them are made explicit (see Figure 16.2). Differing symbols and shapes can be used to demonstrate how the ideas are linked and also to show the organi-

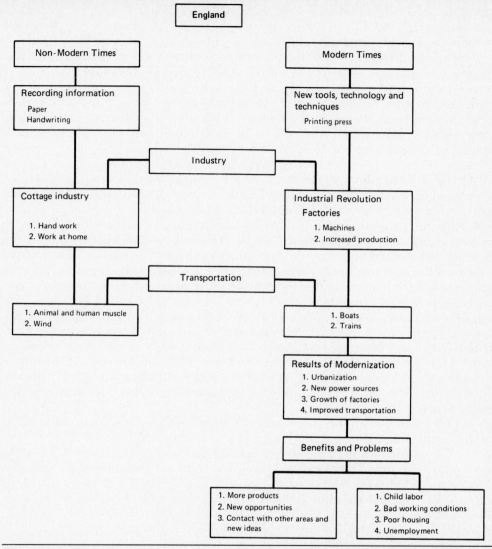

Figure 16.1. A structured overview. From E. Carr, P. Dewitz, and J. Patberg, The effect of inference training on children's comprehension of expository text, *Journal of Reading Behavior* 1983, *15*, 3. Reprinted by permission of the authors and the National Reading Conference.

zational pattern of the text (Armbruster & Anderson 1982). The maps can take a variety of shapes and designs, but usually the information is arranged hierarchically and words are kept to a minimum. Research has shown mapping to be an effective instructional strategy for improving the text comprehension of readers from the middle grades through adulthood (Miccinati 1988), but studies have shown mapping to have only modest transfer effects. Mapping has been shown to be more effective than rereading or notetaking (Pearson & Gallagher 1983, Tierney & Cun-

Reading selection

The snake plant is very easy to grow. It has erect long leaves that grow 12"–18" tall. It is usually dark green with bands of light green. One variety has a gold band.

The snake plant is easy to take care of. It will grow in any part of the home that has a window. Don't water it a lot. It should be kept dry. It grows in soil of loam, sand, and peat moss. To propagate the snake plant, divide clumps of older plants or take leaf cuttings.

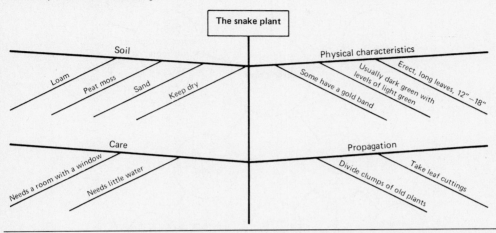

Figure 16.2.   An example of semantic mapping. From P. Gold, Cognitive mapping, *Academic Therapy*, January 1984, *19*. Reprinted by permission of the author and *Academic Therapy*.

ningham 1984). As a postreading activity, semantic mapping can be used by students to recall, organize, and graphically represent pertinent information (D. Johnson, Pittleman & Heimlich 1986). Mapping procedures are described and illustrated by McNeil (1987), Muth (1987a), Miccinati (1988), and Flood and Lapp (1988a).

   Webbing is a graphic way of showing the important relationships that define the text structure (see Figure 16.3). At the center of the web is the topic or main idea (selected by the teacher) and the spokes contain the related ideas (generated by the pupils). The procedure can be used to demonstrate or identify specific text structures (Clewell & Haidemenos 1983). The web also may contain "strand ties," which depict the relationships between and among strands. Webbing procedures can also be found in Widomski (1983). Friedman and Reynolds (1980) illustrated the use of webbing with basal reader stories.

   In *pyramiding*, the levels of information (main ideas, middle-level ideas, specific details) are shown graphically. Pyramiding can be used to illustrate superordinate and subordinate information, to help students become more sensitive to the relative importance of information, as a review of content, and to prepare students for learning to outline or to take notes (Clewell & Haidemenos 1983).

   The effects are greater when students produce a graphic organizer after the text is read than when they only interact with a graphic organizer before the text is read. Graphic organizers benefit college students substantially more than elementary and secondary school pupils (Moore 1987). Bergerud, Lovitt, and Horton (1988) report that graphic aids were more helpful than either study

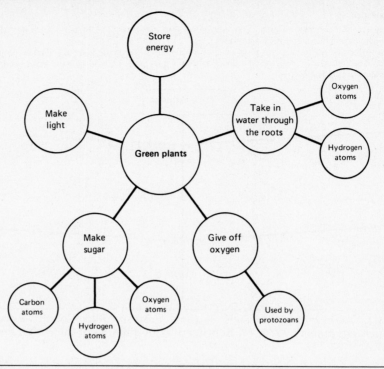

Figure 16.3.   An example of webbing. From S. Clewell and J. Haidemos, Organizational strategies to increase comprehension, *Reading World*, May 1983. Reproduced by permission of the authors and the College Reading Association.

guides or self-study in the comprehension of life-science textbooks by learning-disabled, high school students.

Muth (1987) describe two other text-structure strategies. A *hierarchical summary* is an outline created from the headings in an expository textbook. *Thematic organizers*, written by the teacher at the students' ability levels, have two parts. A set of analogous situations, which are related to the students' prior knowledge, is used to explain the text's central theme, to show relationships among text ideas, and to connect textual information to prior knowledge. There also is a set of instructional statements (elaborations of the text's main ideas) that the pupils read to verify during or after reading. Risko and Alvarez (1986) described their successful use of thematic organizers, which are used to explicate the cohesion among the ideas presented in the texts.

Other prereading activities may be found in Neuman (1988b) and in Moore, Readence and Rickelman (1989), who also offer guidelines for selecting the most appropriate activity for a particular purpose.

During-Reading Activities

A *study guide* is a teaching aid prepared by the teacher and used by students. Its purpose is twofold: to facilitate the student's comprehension of the text and to develop comprehension skills. A study guide is usually a typewritten copy, keyed to the textbook, that can be placed beside the textbook and referred to while studying. The study guide, which is used to help meet individual differences, identifies a reading task and presents a plan or strategy for the student to follow. The assumption is that comprehension will be enhanced when the directions that stipulate goals are in clear proximity to the textual material containing the relevant information (Tutolo 1977). Use of study guides enhances teaching, but does not replace it (Cooper 1986). Suggestions for developing and using study guides can be found in McClain (1981) and M. Olson and Longion (1982). Few studies have evaluated the effectiveness of study guides, but the available evidence generally suggests they facilitate comprehension (J. L. Vaughn 1982, Tierney & Cunningham 1984).

Because students do not often apply skills learned in isolation, Otto, White, and Camperell (1980) developed the *gloss* procedure. It uses marginal and other notations that tell the students how to apply specific skills and strategies. The gloss procedure directs the students's attention to places in the text where certain kinds of thinking would facilitate comprehension. The dual focus on content and process acts as a guide for integrating new with known information. A detailed description of the technique and examples of gloss appear in Otto et al. (1981), and guidelines for preparing gloss may be found in Richgels and Hansen (1984) and Richgels and Mateja (1984). An example of gloss is shown in Figure 16.4.

A *guide-o-rama* can be used to help students process major points in a text by highlighting significant ideas (see K. Wood & Mateja 1983). A guide-o-rama presents a general purpose for reading the text and indicates the pages on which the information needed to answer a series of stated questions appears. It also may suggest the rate at which a section of text should be read.

UNDERLINING.   This technique is one of the most popular studying techniques. As with other strategies, underlining requires that the student be able to distinguish important from less important and unimportant information. Students tend to underline too much. Among other things, they should be told not to underline until they have finished reading a headed section because waiting may reveal a summary statement that would be the only part of the section to need underlining. Pupils should also be taught to develop at least a two-tiered system of differentiating between important information; some information can be marked with a star or double underscoring; less important information, with only a single underscore. Refer to McAndrew (1983), Podstay (1984) and Blanchard (1985) for ideas on teaching underlining. Many young pupils do not grasp the importance of underlining without instruction in its function (Hartley 1987).

Overall, underlining as a study strategy has some research support and some theoretical support. Its successful use probably depends on the quality of what the students choose to underline and how much they underline (L. Johnson 1988).

NOTE TAKING.   This strategy is a form of summarizing and has to be used in place of underlining when the student does not own the reading material. Notes can be taken as the student reads or may be delayed until a section of the text has been read. Note taking is an important skill when the reader has to consult a number of sources from which information has to be obtained and retained.

Gloss	Text
1. Notice that the topic of this passage is given in the heading and by the bold print word *oxidation*. You need to find out what oxidation is.	21:1 Oxidation (a) The term *oxidation* was first applied (b) to the combining of oxygen with other elements. There were many known
2. This sentence gives you a defintion of oxidation. Oxidation is _____ . But notice the word *first*—there must be a second or later definition of oxidation.	instances of this. Iron rusts and (c) carbon burns. In rusting, oxygen combines slowly with iron to form Fe_2O_3. In burning, oxygen unites rapidly with carbon to form CO_2. Observations of these reactions gave
3. The final, better definition is going to be similar to the first, but that means that it will not be exactly the same, but also what is changed in the later definition of oxidation.	rise to the terms "slow" and "rapid" oxidation. Chemists recognize, however, that (d) other nonmetallic elements unite with substances in a manner similar to that
4. This sentence tells what observations led to the later definition of oxidation. What is the same is that something is _____ . What is different is that there is no _____	of oxygen. Hydrogen, antimony, and sodium all burn in chlorine, and iron (e) will burn in fluorine. Since these reactions were similar, chemists formed a more general definition of oxidation. Electrons were removed from each free element by reactants O_2 or Cl_2.
5. Since oxygen is not always involved, you will end up with a "more general" definition of oxidation. The more general definition is given in this sentence. It is that oxidation is _____	Thus, oxidation was defined as the (f) process by which electrons are apparently removed from an atom or ion.

Figure 16.4. Text and accompanying gloss sheet with example of developmental gloss. Text from R. C. Smoot, J. Price, and R. G. Smith, *Chemistry: A modern course*, 5th Ed. (Columbus, OH: Charles E. Merrill Publishing Co., 1979), p. 488. Reprinted by permission. Figure taken from D. Richgels and J. Mateja, Gloss II: Integrating content and process for independence, *Journal of Reading*, February 1984. Reproduced by permission of the authors and the International Reading Association.

In addition to its value for review or in preparing a report, note taking performs a useful function in enforcing selective, thoughtful reading. To take good notes, one must select what is worth recording by separating major from minor points, must consider the relation of one idea to another, and must condense the author's ideas into accurate restatements in one's own words. Taking good notes while reading passively is impossible. The further students move from verbatim to elaborative notes, the greater the benefits. *Elaboration* involves paraphrasing, indicating relationships among ideas, and adding one's own comments and examples. As such, it requires deep text processing, which increases the likelihood of comprehension and retention (P. L. Smith & Tompkins 1988).

Learning to take efficient notes is not easy and perhaps is better introduced as a strategy after the pupils have some skill in summarizing and outlining. Student-generated notes vary tremendously in volume, quality, and character (P. L. Smith & Tompkins 1988). Many students leave out so much important information that the notes could not be substituted for a rereading of the material. Other pupils take such voluminous notes that they are difficult to use. In both cases, the cause is usually the inability to determine what information is important. In the latter situation, the child also may need to learn that "more is not better."

The overall research literature, which deals primarily with taking notes from lectures, suggests that note taking can be a useful learning strategy, especially when notes are reviewed before taking a test (Rickards 1979, Hale 1982). The few studies dealing with reading and note taking have produced mixed findings, with most showing note taking to be neither more nor less effective than other studying strategies. Refer to P. L. Smith and Tompkins (1988) for a discussion of a structured note-taking strategy that can be used for reading in the content-subject areas. Research has begun to concentrate on the cognitive processes involved in note taking (Beecher 1987).

Postreading Activities

A number of instructional strategies and learning activities that serve their purposes best when they are applied after the pupils have read the material. The following are among these procedures.

RETELLINGS.   Research suggests that having children retell stories they have heard or read can facilitate their future comprehension (Morrow 1989b). Accurate retellings require pupils to organize textual information, and thus to have focused their attention on comprehending the text in a holistic fashion (Kapinus, Gambrell & Koskinen 1987). Koskinen et al. (1988) describe a verbal rehearsal procedure that reportedly improved retellings.

DISCUSSIONS.   Research findings indicate that young readers and poor readers of every age do not consistently understand the relationships among items of text information and between text information and their background knowledge. Appropriate questioning during discussions can help them see such relations. Such questions should lead students to understand how the text's central points are related as well as how to integrate their prior knowledge with textual information. They should probe for the major elements of a story's plot and for the interrelationships of events and actions. If the story has a moral, the discussion should lead to understanding this deeper meaning (R. C. Anderson et al. 1985).

To be classified as a a discussion, an activity must meet three criteria: (1) Multiple points of view should be put forth by the discussants who keep an open mind regarding the topic under consideration; (2) the students should interact with one another and with the teacher; and (3) contributions should exceed the two- to three-word phrases common to recitations. Suggestions for using postreading discussions to promote reading comprehension are presented by Alvermann, Dillon, and O'Brien (1987).

SUMMARIZATION.   A *summary* is a brief statement that represents a condensation of information and that reflects the gist of the text. The ability to summarize requires comprehension, evaluation, and condensation skills, as well as frequent transformations of presented ideas. Inadequate summaries are most likely to stem from inappropriate choices as to what is important in the original text and from the inability to integrate information from different parts of the text (Hidi & Anderson 1986). Intermediate-grade pupils' summarization problems may also be due to their inability to find and express main ideas (K. Taylor 1986) or to make use of the text structure (B. Taylor 1985).

Research findings suggest that: (1) short passages are easier to summarize than long ones; (2) narratives are easier to summarize than exposition, especially for children; (3) complex text is more difficult to summarize than easy text; (4) it is easier to summarize when the text is available, especially if it is lengthy (Hidi & Anderson 1986). The instructional implications of these findings are obvious.

Brown, Campione, and Day (1981) identify six rules essential to summarization: (1) Delete unnecessary or trival information; (2) delete material that is important but redundant; (3) substitute a superordinate term for a list of items (e.g., *pets* for *cats, dogs, goldfish,* etc.); (4) substitute a superordinate term for the components of an action (e.g., "Carol went to New York." for "Carol left the house. She got on the bus, etc"); (5) select a topic sentence; and (6) invent a topic sentence if one is not given.

Summarization skills develop slowly. Although proficiency generally increases with age, even college students are not truly proficient at summarization (Garner 1985). Children were able to use the two deletion rules given in the foregoing paragraph (numbers 1 and 2) at a relatively early age, but fifth and seventh graders had problems with the generalization and integration rules (numbers 3 and 4) and with the topic-sentences rule (number 5). The invention rule (number 6) was the last to develop and was the most difficult to apply, even for junior college students (A. Brown & Day 1983).

Overall, research regarding the effectiveness of summarization as a study technique has been sparse, and its findings are mixed (A. Brown, Campione & Day 1981). There is a modest transfer of summarization ability within a content area but not across content subjects (Tierney & Cunningham 1984). Armbruster, Anderson, and Ostertag (1987), who offer suggestions for summarizing different types of text structures, found that summarization instruction improved learning from expository text. Rinehart, Stahl, and Erickson (1986), who present a summarization checklist to be used by pupils, found summarization training to be effective in improving reading and study skills.

K. Taylor (1984) suggests that pupils be taught the following strategy in writing summaries: (1) Read carefully to identify the structure and content of the material; (2) check your comprehension of the material; (3) write a first draft; (4) check the first draft against the original article; (5) write a second draft; and (6) check the second draft against the original article. Hare and Borchardt (1984) present general steps to help in applying specific rules for writing a summary.

Ideas for helping students with précis writing are offered by Bromley and McKeveny (1986).

Self-directed summarization can be an excellent comprehension-monitoring activity. As students go along, they attempt to summarize what they have read. Writing a one-sentence summary following each paragraph read has been shown to increase retention (Hidi & Anderson 1986). Inability to produce an adequate synopsis should be a clear sign to the reader that comprehension is not proceeding smoothly, and that corrective action is called for. Poor readers do not readily engage in self-directed summarization (Palincsar & Brown 1983).

Summaries provided by authors can aid recall of salient information, although there is some debate as to whether they are more effective when placed at the beginning or end of the text. *Overview summaries* describe, in general terms, what is to follow; *interim summaries* sum up the arguments made by the author so far; and *review summaries* sum up what has gone before, often using more technical terms than those introduced in the body of the text (Hartley 1987).

OUTLINING. An *outline* is a hierarchical organization of major concepts and important supporting details. When first introducing outlining, the teacher should discuss the importance of being able to outline what one reads. She can point out that an outline shows the relative importance of each idea, its relation to other ideas in the material, and can show that the outline is, in effect, the framework of ideas that the writer has "dressed up" by expressing them in well-written sentences and paragraphs. The teacher can then demonstrate the procedure by outlining some well-organized expository text that the children have read. She should model how and why she selects certain ideas to place in the outline and how the outline format signals the importance of ideas and relationships between them. This demonstration outline should not be complex.

Once motivation has been established, a series of graded exercises in outlining, in which pupils are initially given a great deal of help, can be presented. For the first two or three sessions, the teacher should display a complete outline of the material. After the students read the text, the outline is discussed, and the teacher answers any questions that are raised. In this meaningful setting, it is easy to explain the system of progressive indentation, the sequence of roman numerals, capital letters, and so on. When the plan of a formal outline has been learned, the second stage is to assign outlines on which the complete skeleton is shown, but only part of the outline itself is provided. Some of these incomplete outlines contain only the main headings; the details are to be filled in. In others, the details are provided and the headings have to be inserted. After reading the accompanying material, the children complete the outline, and discussion follows. In the third stage, the structure of the outline is given, but no slots are filled in by the teacher. In the fourth stage, only the number of main headings is given, and in the final stages the pupils produce a complete outline without assistance.

Learning how to condense a sentence into a few words can be achieved through discussion of the most satisfactory way to state a given part of the outline. Different statements can be compared as to clarity and conciseness and the best ones selected. The writing of acceptable incomplete sentences in a telegraphic style can be taught in a meaningful situation.

It is desirable to teach the use of the formal outline before teaching children to use informal outlines. The basic difference between the two forms is the absence of the number-and-letter scheme in the informal outline. Once a student has learned to think in outline terms, the trappings can be discarded without losing the ability to reduce what has been read to its essential structure.

A teacher-prepared outline can serve as a prereading activity, to activate students' prior knowledge, to develop expectations, and to provide a structure that can be used to guide the pupils' reading. As a postreading activity it can help students learn to separate important from less important information and to organize information. The outline can also be used as a study aid.

Insensitivity to the importance of textual information is probably more detrimental to outlining than to summarizing ability. Whereas summarizing requires the ability to identify and represent main ideas succinctly, outlining requires the student to identify and represent the entire hierarchy of passage ideas. Summarization stipulates that unimportant information be identified and eliminated, without having to explain why. Outlining asks pupils to lay out explicitly not only the most important ideas, but also subordinate and sub-subordinate ideas (Hare & Borchardt 1984).

In two studies in which students were trained to outline, outlining was more effective than the strategies to which it was compared. The pupils were not trained to outline in any of the four studies that showed no significant difference between treatments (T. Anderson & Armbruster 1984b).

REREADING.   Several studies have found that students' comprehension of expository text improves when they reread it (Flood 1986). Good comprehenders make spontaneous use of *lookbacks* (rereading parts of the text) both during and after reading. See Alvermann (1987c) for guidelines in using a lookback strategy.

READING MAPS, GRAPHS, CHARTS, AND TABLES

A large amount of information can be presented concisely in visual form through the use of maps, graphs, charts, and tables. Charts are used to express complex information in visually simple forms: They summarize detailed information. Graphs are used to summarize written or tabular information. Bar graphs show differences in amount, line graphs display increases or decreases, and circle and pie graphs indicate proportional distribution of variables. Tables are employed to summarize numerical or statistical information (Rush, Moe & Storlie 1986). Pupils frequently fail to make use of these aids.

There are wide variations as to types and purposes within each of these four kinds of graphical representations: Learning to make use of any one of them requires the acquisition of a number of skills. Teaching children how to interpret these graphic aids and encouraging their use should be the responsibility of each content-subject teacher. Fry (1981) offers excellent suggestions for developing graphic literacy. The *Visual Reading Guide* (Moore, Readence & Rickelman 1989) may be used to show students how to formulate predictions regarding text content based on information obtained from examining the accompanying visual aids. Reinking (1986) presents a *Graphic Information Lesson* that may be used to teach students to connect information from graphic aids, the text, and their prior knowledge.

LOCATING INFORMATION

Locating information is a form of strategic reading that differs from the comprehension and recall of prose in general in that it is more goal directed, more selective in the use of text, and less dependent on declarative knowledge (i.e., on knowing *about*, opposed to knowing *how* or *why*). Locating information requires that the students: (1) formulate a goal (e.g., have a question that they need or want to answer); (2) select a category of text for inspection (e.g., almanac vs. encyclopedia); and (3) extract the desired information from the text. Locational skills are important to success in the content subjects but are rarely taught (Guthrie & Mosenthal 1987).

Two locational skills can be great timesavers—using a table of contents and an index. The use of a table of contents is usually introduced early in the primary grades. Once children understand its use they have little difficulty employing it to locate a particular story or section in a book. Those who have not acquired skill in using a table of contents should be provided with instruction and guided practice in its use.

The first index encountered by children is usually one in which the topics are arranged alphabetically by topic and subtopic. This fact should be explained to children, as well as the meanings of the numbers and other notations (e.g., *see also*) that may accompany an entry. By the time indexes appear in their books, most children are fairly advanced in their knowledge of alphabetization. Therefore, the instructional emphasis should be on locating information. In an introductory lesson, children can be asked to suggest headings under which information appears in their textbooks. For example, information on the number of cattle raised in Colorado may be found under several possible headings: Cattle, production of; Colorado, cattle raising in; and so on. After discussing why some of the suggestions are better than others, the possibilities can be listed on the board. Then each pupil checks his textbook to see if it contains those entries. When the page references have been found, the information under the various headings can be located and reported to the group. After the general procedure has been learned, periodic practice in using an index can be provided, but its use will probably be learned best as children employ it to find needed information on their own.

After they have mastered the use of a book index fairly well, pupils should learn the value of and how to use reference resources such as encyclopedias, almanacs, atlases, a library card index, and the *Readers Guide to Periodical Literature*. Encouraging them to use their index skills to find information in these references often serves as a good introduction. A suitable teaching sequence should include: (1) teaching students what kinds of information are contained in the different reference works; (2) practice in thinking of relevant headings or entries under which the information might be found; (3) teaching students how to choose the correct volume when the reference has more than one; and (4) interpreting commonly used abbreviations. M. J. Miller (1979) lists the library skills and understandings that should be developed in the primary grades.

STUDY HABITS

Students vary in their study habits—the amount of time they spend studying, the promptness with which they get to and complete work, the conditions under which they study, their degree of concentration, and the study strategies they employ. Many students who fail or marginally pass in various content areas have adequate reading skills and perhaps knowledge of appropriate study skills. What they lack are good habits.

Pupils generally do not perceive their reading assignments to be either a meaningful or a necessary activity (F. R. Smith & Feathers 1983). Students report that their textbooks are boring and difficult to understand and that at best they read a textbook assignment only once (Tierney & Schallert 1982, Chall & Conrad 1984). It is, therefore, little wonder that they also report that they have difficulty remembering what they read. Making students aware of the need to continue to study until they are ready to be tested on their understanding and recall of that information improves study performance (L. Baker & Brown 1984b). To remember, good students review before reading, take notes on their reading, review for and know how to take tests, and study systematically (Estes & Richards 1985).

Allocation of study time is something few students do well, but skilled readers are more likely than less skilled readers to allocate more time for studying when they encounter a difficult task (Palincsar & Brown 1987). Time allocation is a metacognitive skill based on knowing what needs to be learned and how long it will take to learn it. Refer to Rogers (1984) and Thelen (1984) for informal ways to assess study skills, and to A. J. Harris and Sipay (1979, pp. 390–394) for suggestions on assessing and developing study habits.

CONTENT-SUBJECT INSTRUCTION FOR DISABLED READERS

Some teachers, particularly subject-matter specialists, feel that little can be done to assist students to learn if they cannot read the on-grade textbooks. Thus, disabled readers and at times even average readers, are left to flounder and fail because they cannot cope with reading assignments. Contrary to such a belief, things can be done to assist disabled readers to develop the concepts and attitudes called for by the curriculum. When less competent readers are faced with reading a mandated text, teachers can facilitate comprehension by highlighting important text information through aids such as study guides, thematic organizers, and gloss. Suggestions for helping disabled readers learn content-subject material by also are presented Darch and Carnine (1986), Lovitt et al. (1986), and Bristow (1988).

At times, material more appropriate for the pupil's level of reading ability can be obtained. Although the content may not treat exactly the same topics as the on-grade textbook, an increased amount of content-area material is available from various publishers for use with students who are reading below grade level. For example, a series of 12 physical science textbooks, *Pathways in Sci-*

ence (Globe), is available for junior and senior high school students who are reading at the fifth- or sixth-reader levels. There are three books each for earth science, chemistry, physics, and life science. Other materials include the Reader's Digest *Science Readers* (Random House), the reading levels of which go from the third- to the sixth-reader levels, and *Wonders of Science* (Steck-Vaughn), which is a six-book series intended for middle and secondary school students who are reading at the second- to third-reader levels. Some of the materials found in the series listed in Appendix B also may be appropriate.

In the social sciences, similar programs are available, such as *World History* (Scholastic). *America's Story* and *World Geography and You* (Steck-Vaughn) are both written at the second- to third-reader levels. Other high interest/low readability books are in series such as *How They Lived* and *Living in Today's World* (Garrard). Both written at the fourth-reader level, the former deals with documentaries of America's growth and heritage; the latter, with people of other cultures.

Similarly, programs are available for the English curriculum, such as *Scope English Anthologies* (Scholastic), and *Activity-Concept English* (Scott, Foresman). In the area of literature, either adapted classics may be read or other titles can be substituted for those called for by the curriculum.

It is highly advantageous for disabled readers to receive content-subject information through nonprint media. Textbooks may be read to, and their content discussed with, these students at home or by volunteers during school time, or recorded textbooks may be utilized. When such assistance is provided, listening comprehension lessons also should be built into the child's program. "Learning through listening" programs, accompanied by appropriate instruction and discussion, would help disabled readers to acquire the same understandings required of other students. Acquiring such understanding would serve a dual purpose: First, it would allow the pupils to experience academic success (especially if adjustments were made in the ways in which their knowledge was measured); second, it would provide background knowledge that may be needed to comprehend more difficult texts in future years. Some disabled readers will acquire the necessary enabling reading skills (e.g., word recognition) that would allow them to read the texts on their own, but they will have difficulty understanding the texts unless they have the necessary topical knowledge.

Whatever adjustments are made, it is equally important to allow disabled readers opportunities to demonstrate their newly acquired knowledge. This can take place during classroom discussions; but because course grades are often based on test performance, it may be necessary to administer teacher-made tests (and perhaps other tests) orally. If students cannot read the test, they cannot demonstrate their knowledge—a situation that can be frustrating and that can kill the motivation to learn.

METACOGNITION AND COGNITIVE STRATEGIES

Successful reading comprehension requires active participation by the reader; to become an independent learner, one must be able to "self-initiate and self-regulate" reading and learning behaviors (Tierney 1982). Active reading comprehension and control over one's reading and learning outcomes requires meta-cognition and use of cognitive strategies.

No definition of metacognition is commonly accepted (Paris, Wasik & Van der Westhuizen 1988). The term *metacognition* has been defined as generally as "thinking about thinking" (Jacobs & Paris 1987), but it usually refers to the awareness, monitoring, and regulating of one's cognitive processes (Haller, Child & Walberg 1988). A clear distinction between metacognition and cognition is rarely drawn in the literature. When such a distinction is made, it appears that *cognition* refers to "ongoing mental operations" or "actual mental processes and strategies"; metacognition, to controlling cognition. Thus it seems that met-acognition underlies the effective use of reading comprehension and learning strategies. *Cognitive strategies* are systematic plans geared toward improving performance (Schunk & Rice 1987).

Two broad but closely related categories of metacognition can be distin-guished (A. Brown & Palincsar 1982). *Knowledge about cognition* involves an awareness of, and reflection on, one's thinking processes. *Regulation of cogni-tion* involves control of cognitive processes. It is with the latter category that cognitive strategies are associated. Whereas knowledge about cognition may be tacit, metacognitive control refers to the *conscious* direction of thinking pro-cesses (Duffy, Roehler & Hermann 1988).

As it pertains to comprehending and learning from written text, metacogni-tion appears to involve *awareness* of one's thinking processes, one's self as an active processor of information, what is to be learned and why, how well one is equipped cognitively to accomplish the task; and specific cognitive strategies that could be employed and when to apply them. Such awareness and knowl-edge serve as a basis for planning a cognitive course of action (e.g., setting a goal, selecting strategies). As the plan is being implemented, comprehension/study is *monitored,* as is the plan. When reading is completed, the adequacy of the comprehension or learning is evaluated by the student. *Regulation* involves taking corrective action when comprehension difficulties are noted or modifying all or part of the comprehension/learning plan. Planning, implementing, and monitoring are sometimes referred to as *executive control* processes (see Wagner & Sternberg 1987). Some writers include coordination of the various functions and/or evaluation of the plan as executive control processes. There is some question as to whether all of the perceptual and cognition operations performed during fluent reading could be under direct executive control throughout the entire course of their functioning (see Masson 1987). Ellis, Deshler, and Schumaker (1989) describe how to teach an executive-control strategy.

Classroom observations reveal that teachers usually neither facilitate nor monitor students' use of cognitive strategies in accomplishing learning tasks (Fillion & Brause 1987).

Types of Cognitive Strategies

There are various types of strategies that readers can employ and that can be taught. The following are among these types (Jones, Amiran & Katims 1985; Weinstein 1987; Duffy & Roehler 1987b):

1. *Prereading strategies* involve activating topical and text-structure knowledge, setting a purpose for reading, and predicting text content and structure.
2. *Rehearsal strategies* emphasize the use of repetition and in general are designed to facilitate verbatim recall. Examples of rehearsal strategies are verbal repetition, rereading parts of the text, taking notes, and underlining. Rehearsal strategies allow the reader to hold onto new information so that elaboration, organization, or comprehension-monitoring strategies can be employed.
3. *Elaboration strategies* require the reader to expand on text information so as to make it more meaningful by associating new with existing information in some organized fashion. Imagery, paraphrasing, summarizing, and use of analogies are examples of elaboration.
4. *Organizational strategies* involve transforming incoming information into more easily understood formats, for example, categorizing items by features they have in common and using a time line to organize events sequentially. The benefits of using organizational strategies accrue from the processing involved in transforming and organizing the information.
5. *Monitoring strategies* include self-questioning, paraphrasing, and summarizing. Other types of monitoring include relating details to main ideas and confirming predictions.
6. *Constructive strategies* involve the use of reasoning and synthesis to construct meaning from multiple sources or from inadequate or ambiguous text.
7. *Affective strategies* are those that help the reader to create and maintain a climate conducive to reading comprehension and learning. They include positive self-talk to reduce anxiety, finding a quiet place to study, and establishing and maintaining a study schedule.

All the aforementioned strategies may be referred to collectively as *learning strategies*. More specifics regarding these strategies were presented earlier in this chapter. Refer to Garner (1987a) for a comprehensive coverage of metacognition and reading comprehension and to Alvermann (1987c) for a discussion of the role of metacognition in the secondary school.

An Illustration of the Use of Metacognition and Cognitive Strategies

The following description of purposeful reading illustrates how metacognition and cognitive strategies are believed to function during reading/studying.

First, the purpose for reading is determined and clarified by identifying the explicit and implicit task demands (i.e., knowing exactly what must be known or done in order to perform the criterion task successfully). Knowing why the material is to be read and how comprehension of the text will be assessed allows the student to set a goal. Setting a goal, in turn, suggests which reading strategy to employ initially, provides a criterion against which ongoing comprehension can be monitored, and helps to determine which text information is most important so that attention can be allotted accordingly. Previewing the text before reading provides an idea of text content and how it is organized. Once the text has been previewed, the plan for learning continues by activating relevant prior knowledge. This helps further to predict text content and structure. Awareness of the task demands and the text content helps readers assess their own competence to perform the tasks necessary for accomplishing the goal. When combined with other information, this assessment of self-competence helps to select reading strategies (e.g., I'm inclined to overlook the reasoning used by an author in reaching a conclusion; but because I'll need to know that for the test, I'd better read that part carefully—perhaps even a few times—to make sure I understand it well enough to critique it).

While reading, relevant background and text-structure knowledge are used spontaneously to guide and construct meaning and, along with the purpose for reading, to determine the relative importance of text information and thereby to allot processing attention accordingly. Incoming text information is related to prior knowledge, and is evaluated critically for internal consistency, compatibility with prior knowledge, and common sense. As reading progresses, attempts may be made to enhance comprehension by employing imagery or elaboration or to organize the information so that the interrelationships among ideas are clearly understood. Outgoing cognitive activities are monitored to assess how well comprehension is progressing, by engaging in such activities as periodic self-reviews. Inferences are made and tested, and newly acquired information is refined and extended by thinking about uses of the information, or is critiqued by considering counterexamples of the text information. If comprehension falters, corrective action is taken.

When the first reading is completed, a determination is made regarding the degree to which the purpose for reading has been met. This might be accomplished by strategies such as determining how well the reader can elaborate on her notes, or by outlining the text information and seeing how often she has to look back at the text to complete the outline; or by constructing a semantic web. If comprehension and recall are determined to have been inadequate, corrective action (e.g., rereading the text) is taken. If the goal for reading has been met, the means of having made that assessment may have provided sufficient immediate review. If not, another postreading strategy such as verbal rehearsal might be employed. The choice of postreading strategy may depend on its cost effectiveness (Is it worth the time it takes?) (Tierney & Cunningham 1984, Derry & Murphy 1986, Weinstein 1987).

Metacognitive- and Cognitive-Strategy Deficiencies

Compared to older and more skilled readers, young pupils and less skilled readers often demonstrate deficiencies in one or more of the following: (1) predicting task difficulty and realizing when task difficulty has changed, (2) systematically attending to text structure, (3) selectively attending to the most important textual information, (4) adequately monitoring their comprehension, (5) choosing strategies to maximize learning, (6) distinguishing between useful and harmful strategies, (7) determining the success of a chosen strategy, (8) knowing or applying corrective strategies, (9) allocating sufficient study time, and (10) knowing when a task has been completed successfully (Ryan, Weed & Short 1986; Wagner &

Sternberg 1987; Davey 1987). In short, they may lack the metacognitive skills needed to plan, monitor, and evaluate their cognitive performances.

At times, lack of strategic behavior on the part of poor and disabled readers is attributed to the passive role pupils assume in the reading/learning process (de Bettencourt 1987). However, the findings of one study (Shepherd, Gelzheizer & Solar 1985) question such a broad characterization of reading and learning disabled pupils. Furthermore, the majority of the evidence cited to support this claim has focused on documenting developmental and ability-level differences, without determining whether the student's poor performances could be improved. Evidence suggests that teaching poor or disabled readers to use efficient cognitive strategies improves their school-related performances (Duffy 1986).

All poor or disabled readers have not been found to suffer from comprehension-strategy deficits, and the studies that report such deficiencies did not consider the students' word-identification fluency (Perfetti 1985). Researchers frequently have assumed that comprehension strategies and cognitive monitoring during reading are cognitive abilities that are separate from those linked with word-recognition skill. Therefore, it is possible that some of the observed differences in the use of comprehension strategies may be due to differences in word-recognition and/or word-identification abilities. Skilled readers could be recognizing and identifying words more efficiently than poor readers, thereby having more cognitive-processing resources available for comprehension. But, more likely, comprehension-strategy differences are the result of a combination of cognitive-monitoring differences and differential resource availability due to word-recognition/identification differences (Stanovich 1986b).

Some students' comprehension/learning problems may be due, at least in part, to the mistaken assumption that their "everyday" thinking skills are sufficient for academic success. In general, the thinking skills employed in day-to-day functioning are executed relatively automatically, so cognition is effortless. Academic success, on the other hand, requires deliberate, effortful thinking, which places a far greater emphasis than does "everyday" thinking on precision, accurate comprehension, and monitoring of performance. Opting to read passively, in the hope that learning will occur as easily as it does in daily functioning, is likely to lead to difficulties. Learning effectively from written text requires readers to focus on the material to be learned, while simultaneously monitoring their comprehension and retention of the information. It also requires readers to determine if they are employing the mental operations that will produce learning (Reeve, Palincsar & Brown 1985).

Assessing Strategy Awareness and Knowledge

Information regarding student's metacognitive and cognitive-strategy awareness and knowledge may be obtained by asking questions such as, "How do you know when you don't understand something you have just read?" or "How can you make sure you will remember what you read in your science book?" Alternatively, a pupil may be asked to tutor a younger child with a comprehension problem; the directions, hints, and cautions provided by the tutor can suggest the comprehension strategies he believes important (Palincsar & Ransom 1988).

The *Reading Comprehension Interview* (Wixson et al. 1984), which is shown in Figure 16.5, can be used to assess how well pupils understand reading tasks, the demands such tasks place on them, and which strategies may be used to accomplish the tasks. The *Index of Reading Awareness* (Jacobs & Paris 1987) is a 20-item, multiple-choice questionnaire designed to measure four aspects of metacognition. As with any such instrument, the items should be carefully evaluated. Duffy et al. (1987a) discuss and evaluate four measures of strategy awareness and use.

Use of a structured interview to evaluate students' self-regulated learning strategies allowed Zimmerman and Pons (1986) to predict, with 93% accuracy, whether high school sophomores were in a high- or low-achievement track. High achievers reported significantly greater use of strategies in 13 of 14 categories.

Instructional Programs and Procedures

Cognitive-strategy instructional programs are designed to develop thoughtful and conscious reasoning while reading (Duffy & Roehler 1987b). This goal is achieved by teaching pupils, through direct instruction, to plan, implement, and evaluate strategic approaches to comprehending written text, learning from text, and problem solving (Palincsar 1986).

Strategy-instruction programs may be of three types. First, strategies that have wide applicability may be taught in a separate program, apart from any specific content-subject matter. Alternatively, teaching of strategies may be incorporated into various existing subject-matter courses, with the strategies geared to the specific subject matter. A third plan consists of a short general instruction phase, followed by "unobtrusive prompting in actual instructional environments." Refer to Derry and Murphy (1986) for the advantages and disadvantages of each plan.

Palincsar and Ransom (1988) illustrate how to apply the following criteria in deciding which strategies to teach. The strategy should: (1) have the potential to be used flexibly across a range of reading situations; (2) promote student interaction with the text; (3) encourage students to monitor their comprehension; and (4) have a favorable cost/benefit ratio (the "payoff" for using the strategy should be worth the time and effort it takes to apply it).

DIRECT INSTRUCTION.[2]   This term, as used in conjunction with the teaching of cognitive strategies, refers to three overlapping stages: (1) demonstration, during which the strategy is defined and modeled, and its use is discussed (basically procedures 1–5 below); (2) guided practice, which involves the strategy being applied by the students under the teacher's supervision, teacher feedback, and possibly reteaching (procedures 6–10 below); and (3) independent application, during which students come to apply the strategy automatically on their own (procedures 10–14 below) (Moore, Readence & Rickelman 1989).

Successful cognitive-strategy instruction includes the following proce-

[2]For a model of how to use direct instruction in developing reading comprehension strategies refer to Mason, Roehler, and Duffy (1984); or Duffy and Roehler (1987b). Cooper (1986) also provides a model of direct instruction.

Name:

Classroom teacher:

Date:

Reading level:

Grade:

Directions: Introduce the procedure by explaining that you are interested in finding out what children think about various reading activities. Tell the student that he or she will be asked questions about his/her reading; that there are no right or wrong answers, and that you are only interested in knowing what s/he thinks. Tell the student that if s/he does not know how to answer a question s/he should say so and you will go on to the next one.

General probes such as "Can you tell me more about that?" or "Anything else?" may be used. Keep in mind that the interview is an informal diagnostic measure and you should feel free to probe to elicit useful information.

1. What hobbies or interests do you have that you like to read about?
2. a. How often do you read in school?
   b. How often do you read at home?
3. What school subjects do you like to read about?

Introduce reading and social studies books.

Directions: For this section use the child's classroom basal reader and a content area textbook (social studies, science, etc.). Place these texts in front of the student. Ask each question twice, once with reference to the basal reader and once with reference to the content area textbook. Randomly vary the order of presentation (basal, content). As each question is asked, open the appropriate text in front of the student to help provide a point of reference for the question.

4. What is the most important reason for reading this kind of material?
   Why does your teacher want you to read this book?
5. a. Who's the best reader you know in _____?
   b. What does he/she do that makes him/her such a good reader?
6. a. How good are *you* at reading this kind of material?
   b. How do you know?
7. What do you have to do to get a good grade in _____in your class?
8. a. If the teacher told you to remember the information in this story/chapter, what would be the best way to do this?
   b. Have you ever tried _____?
9. a. If your teacher told you to find the answers to the questions in this book, what would be the best way to do this? Why?
   b. Have you ever tried _____?
10. a. What is the hardest part about answering questions like the ones in this book?
    b. Does that mean you do anything differently?

Introduce at least two comprehension worksheets.

Directions: Present the worksheets to the child and ask questions 11 and 12. Ask the child to complete portions of each worksheet. Then ask questions 13 and 14. Next, show the child a worksheet designed to simulate the work of another child. Then ask question 15.

11. Why would your teacher want you to do worksheets like these (for what purpose)?
12. What would your teacher say you must do to get a good mark on worksheets like these? (What does your teacher look for?)

Ask the child to complete portions of at least two worksheets.

13. Did you do this one differently from the way you did that one? How or in what way?
14. Did you have to work harder on one of these worksheets than the other? (Does one make you think more?)

Present the simulated worksheet.

15. a. Look over this worksheet. If you were the teacher, what kind of mark would you give the worksheet? Why?
    b. If you were the teacher, what would you ask this person to do differently next time?

Figure 16.5. Reading comprehension interview. From K. Wixson et al., An interview for assessing students' perceptions of classroom reading tasks, *The Reading Teacher*, January 1984, 37. Reprinted by permission of the authors and the International Reading Association.

dures and activities[3]: (1) clear identification of the strategy (e.g., naming it); (2) explicit description of the component steps in the strategy; (3) modeling the strategy (see the next section); (4) clear explanation and demonstration of how and why its use can be beneficial; (5) clear explanation and demonstration of when the strategy is best used and when its use is not advisable; (6) guided practice in applying the strategy in school-related situations; (7) appropriate teacher feedback when children apply the strategy; (8) encouragement of pupils to master the strategy; (9) clear explanation and demonstration of alternate ways to solve a problem (e.g., overcoming a comprehension problem, see page 630); (10) scaffolding (see page 577); (11) instruction and guided practice in self-regulation—overseeing, orchestrating, and monitoring the strategy (see page 629); (12) multiple opportunities for independent practice using a variety of texts (in order to promote generalization of strategy-use across the curriculum); (13) maintenance of procedures (see page 631); and (14) assessment of student progress toward mastery, in which students participate (Baumann & Schmitt 1986; Gersten, Woodward & Darch 1986; Duffy & Roehler 1987b; Palincsar & Brown 1987; Palincsar & Ransom 1988; Baumann 1988). Because the development of metacognitive skills may be facilitated by social interactions, programs aimed at fostering these skills should focus on interactive instructional procedures (see pages 576–577). Such programs should be sensitive to the children's current levels of metacognitive functioning (Reeve & Brown 1985). Motivation can play an important role in metacognitive and cognitive strategy training (see Ellis (1986).

Instructional strategies and procedures for improving comprehension and learning may also be found in Eeds (1981); Baumann (1983); Paris, Wixson, and Palincsar (1986); Pressley, Johnson, and Symons (1987); Montague and Tanner (1987); and Palincsar and Ransom (1988).

MODELING.   Modeling, which some consider a component part of direct instruction, is more than just telling or showing pupils how to do something or verbalizing the procedural steps in completing a task. *Modeling* involves making explicit, through "thinking aloud," the cognitive processes used in a particular reading act. Modeling reading behaviors can take various forms. The teacher may model appropriate use of the voice during oral reading. This does not mean simply saying "Listen to me. This is the way you should read it." Rather, the teacher first demonstrates how the voice can be used to depict various emotions or meanings and explains why it is important to do so. Next, she tells them that she is going to say out loud what she is thinking as she decides how to read something aloud. For example, "Dot must have been mad when Ray broke her favorite doll. So, I'll use an *angry* voice when Dot says to him, 'Ray, why did you do that!'"

Modeling may involve making explicit the thought processes used while attempting to decode a word, figure out a word meaning from context, and so on. Comprehension processes also can be modeled. For instance, the teacher

[3]These could also apply to the teaching of a skill. Duffy and Roehler (1987b), who differentiate between skills and strategies, define a *skill* as an overlearned procedure in which the same response is given repeatedly, accurately, and automatically; and a *strategy* as a systematic plan for achieving a goal, which can be used flexibly in different situations.

verbalizes the bases on which he generates a hypothesis about the meaning of the text. As he reads, he points out supporting and disconforming information, expresses occasional confusion and doubt about the meaning (as if he were experiencing the problem), and makes critical comments (Derry & Murphy 1986).

Nist and Kirby (1986), who provide examples of "thinking aloud," suggest that, for modeling to be successful, the teacher must go through these interrelated steps with the pupils: (1) Use an activity or statement to focus the students' attention on what the teacher is about to do; (2) provide a general overview, telling the students what they are going to do; (3) introduce and develop any new terms in the context of how they will be used in the lesson; (4) demonstrate how to perform the task, by going through the procedures, step-by-step, by saying out loud what is being thought while each step is being performed; (5) have the students repeat what the teacher demonstrated, but in new situations; and if necessary, (6) demonstrate the procedure again. Pupils are most likely to learn and apply demonstrated procedures or strategies if the teacher models them using materials which the children are asked to read and provides numerous opportunities for application by the students in a nonthreatening atmosphere. Herrmann (1988) illustrates an eight-step decision-making process that can be used for modeling "thinking while reading." Refer to Heller (1986) for a transcription of a teacher's verbalization of her metacognitive processing.

COMPREHENSION MONITORING. This strategy may take various forms, but some sort of self-questioning is involved. For example, in the SQ3R procedure, headings are turned into questions to be answered while reading. Alternately, children may monitor their ongoing comprehension by carrying on an internal dialogue such as the one taught successfully by Meichenbaum and Asarnow (1979). Pupils might employ clarifying questions ("Is that clear to me?") or formulate and answer questions that their teacher is likely to ask. Other forms of comprehension monitoring involve pausing at various points in the text either to summarize important text information or to predict upcoming content (Cooper 1986).

Descriptive research has demonstrated a developmental trend in comprehension monitoring and that it usually is a late-developing ability—one that generally does not emerge fully until late adolescence. Differences in comprehension monitoring also differentiate skilled from less skilled readers. Young pupils and less skilled readers are less likely than older and skilled readers to monitor and regulate their comprehension spontaneously or to detect and correct breakdowns in their comprehension (Chan, Cole, & Barfett 1987). Research findings suggest that the comprehension difficulties of many poor readers are related to their limited use of self-regulatory strategies, such as failure to detect when their comprehension has been impeded (Miller, Giovenco & Rentiers 1987).

Instructional interventions do not always improve the comprehension monitoring of young or less skilled readers (G. Miller 1987), but instructional studies generally show that comprehension-monitoring strategies can be developed and refined in pupils at various age levels (Devine 1987, Schmitt 1988), and that the effects are large, durable, and transferable (Palincsar & Brown 1986) and result in improved reading comprehension (Mier 1984). Self-monitoring instruction may be most relevant for poor readers who tend not to be aware of their comprehension breakdowns (Wong 1985).

STRATEGIES FOR DEALING WITH COMPREHENSION DIFFICULTIES. Research suggests that when the structural or conceptual load of a text becomes sufficiently complex to block comprehension, skilled readers use strategies to restore meaning. Poor readers often do not know of these strategies or are unable or unwilling to apply those of which they are aware. Often they possess only partial knowledge of the strategies (Duffy et al. 1987b).

There are basically six strategies that can be employed when comprehension breaks down (Baker & Brown 1984b): (1) Ignore the breakdown and just continue reading; (2) suspend judgment as to meaning and continue reading to determine whether the upcoming text helps to clear up the problem; (3) form a tentative hypothesis regarding meaning and continue reading to determine if it can be confirmed or if it needs to be modified or replaced; (4) reread the current sentence to determine if helpful information was missed or if meaning was misapprehended perhaps due to inaccurate word recognition; (5) reread part or all of the preceding text; or (6) seek clarification or guidance from an expert source (e.g., the teacher). Another strategy that readers might employ when they begin to sense that comprehension is faltering is to slow down their reading rate. The degree to which each of these strategies disrupts the flow of reading increases from the first to the last strategy, but the sequence in which they appear does not indicate the order of desirability or likely effectiveness. Discussing and demonstrating the use, advantages, and limitations of these strategies may help students to use them effectively.

FACTORS THAT MAY INFLUENCE USE OF COGNITIVE STRATEGIES. Failure to employ cognitive strategies is not always due to a lack of awareness or knowledge of strategic behaviors; their use can be influenced by personality and affective factors. Some pupils opt not to utilize strategies that they have in their repertoires.

For instance, some students may have difficulty monitoring their comprehension because they are unwilling to admit, even to themselves, that they do not understand something. These children are reluctant to ask questions for fear that they will be ridiculed or because they perceive asking for help as a sign of weakness. Other personality variables such as cognitive style may influence use of strategies and learning, as may factors such as dogmatism and closed-mindedness (Athey 1982, Baker & Brown 1984b).

Acquisition and use of cognitive strategies can be influenced by affective factors such as self-image, attribution, and *perceived self-efficacy,* which is the result of the beliefs students have regarding their capabilities to organize the actions necessary to attain designated levels of performance (Borkowski, Wehing & Turner 1986; Schunk & Rice 1987). Any affective factor that diminishes or rules out students' active involvement in their learning is likely to result in weaker use of metacognitive and cognitive strategies as well as poorer academic performance (Athey 1982, Johnston & Winograd 1985).

IS COGNITIVE-STRATEGY INSTRUCTION EFFECTIVE?   There appears to be agreement that it takes an extended period of time to develop cognitive strategies that can impact on comprehension and learning. But views as to the effectiveness of cognitive-strategy training vary widely. Some contend that only a few studies have resulted in significantly greater reading comprehension ability (e.g., Jacobs & Paris 1987) or that the research findings are mixed (e.g., Alvermann & Swafford 1989). On a more positive note, Pearson (1985) and A. Brown (1985) believe that strategy instruction resulted in long-lasting, significant improvements in reading comprehension and learning. On the basis of their meta-analysis of 20 studies, Haller, Child, and Walberg (1988) conclude that metacognitive instruction had a substantial positive effect on reading comprehension.

Strategy-training does not assure that students will continue to employ the strategies after their application is no longer required by the teacher. Greater strategy use and maintenance can result from continually informing students that employing the strategies can improve their performance and by providing feedback linking improved performance to their use of the strategies (Schunk & Rice 1987).

17 Reading Comprehension IV: Reading Rate and Reading Flexibility

Today's literate adults probably encounter more reading materials in a week than their great-grandparents did in a year, so the ability to read rapidly has become an important asset. But going through material with little or no comprehension is just as wasteful as unnecessarily slow reading. Skilled readers adjust their reading rates to maintain the desired level of comprehension.

In this chapter we consider ways to improve students' abilities to read rapidly and flexibly. The first section is devoted to the relationship between reading rate and comprehension and includes discussions of how fast individuals can read and of factors to consider in deciding who should receive instruction in reading rate and flexibility. The other two sections consider, respectively, reading behaviors thought to contribute to slow reading rates and various ways to increase reading rate.

RELATIONSHIP OF READING RATE TO COMPREHENSION

One of the questions studied by early reading researchers was the relationship between reading rate and comprehension. Their findings suggested that the relationships varied with the age and intellectual ability of the subjects, as well as with the type of reading materials.

The obtained correlations were generally higher in the primary than in the other elementary school grades. This is understandable because word-recognition ability plays such a key role in both reading rate and comprehension at the early age level. Furthermore, the text content is usually well within the conceptual grasp of novice readers. At the secondary school and college levels, most correlations tended to be positive but quite low, about 0.30 (Tinker 1939). Among bright students, faster readers tended to have higher comprehension than did slow readers. At lower intelligence levels, slower readers tended to comprehend better than fast readers did (Shores & Husbands 1950). Although such were the findings when general measures of comprehension were employed, different results were obtained when specific types of material were read. When mathematical and science texts were used, the correlations tended to be low and negative. Although there were many exceptions, faster reading generally meant lower comprehension (Blommers & Lindquist 1944).

The data obtained from these early studies were largely correlational, and factors such as prior knowledge and purpose for reading were rarely considered. Nonetheless, three general conclusions, which are still valid, may be drawn from these data: (1) It is impossible to state, without qualification, that fast readers are better (or poorer) comprehenders than are slow readers; (2) skilled readers do not always read rapidly; and (3) slow reading rates do not necessarily lead to poor comprehension. The rate at which we can process the ideas in a text places an upper limit on our reading rates, but reading rate should also be influenced by factors such as the purpose for reading.

Because certain distinctions must be made when discussing reading rate and its relation to comprehension, the following subsections deal with how fast pupils *do, can,* and *should* read, whether they *should* and *can* be trained to read faster, and whether students *should* and *can* be taught to read more flexibly.

How Fast Do Pupils Read?

This question is the easiest to answer, but the answers must be qualified. Data from a number of different standardized tests are shown in Table 17.1. Because these data are from norm-referenced tests, each figure represents the median number of words read per minute (WPM). The figures do not indicate the rates attained by the fastest, average, and slowest reader at each grade level. Not only did some individuals read much slower or faster than the indicated WPM, but the task demands differed from test to test. Norms for reading rate can be misleading because they vary considerably with the nature of the material. The fact that task demands vary widely is one of the reasons why the typical reading rates reported by different investigators differ markedly. As yet, no one has established rate norms for reading the same kinds of material for different purposes, nor has the influence of topical knowledge on rate been considered. Furthermore, the rate at which pupils read under test conditions may not be the same as the rate that they employ in their daily reading in school.

Nevertheless, the data from Table 17.1 provide some useful information. There is a difference of roughly 50–80 WPM between the highest and lowest median WPMs at each grade level. This variation may reflect factors such as differences in task demands and the subjects on whom the tests were normed, but considering that there were faster and slower readers than the medians indicate, the data suggest a fairly wide range of reading rates at each grade level.

The data in Tables 17.1 and 9.1 (page 334) generally indicate a steady up-

Table 17.1 Median Rates of Reading for Different Grades as Determined by Several Standardized Reading Tests

	\multicolumn{9}{c}{Grade}								
	2	3	4	5	6	7	8	9	12
Highest test	118	138	170	195	230	246	267	260	295
Median test	86	116	155	177	206	215	237	252	251
Lowest test	35	75	120	145	171	176	188	199	216

Note: The number of tests included in the table is 7 for Grades 2, 3; 8 for Grades 4, 5, 6, 7; 6 for Grades 8, 9; and 3 for Grade 12.

ward trend in WPM from the primary grades through Grade 9. They differ, however, in that the data in Table 17.1 indicate a leveling off at 250 WPM in Grades 9 and 12, whereas Table 9.1 shows a continuing increase from Grade 9 (214 WPM) to Grade 12 (250 WPM). The NAEP (1972) results show the average 17-year-old reading at 195 WPM (material at the tenth-grade level was used), with only 25% of the students reading at 250 WPM or higher (only 10% read at 300 WPM or above). It would appear that the average American high school student reads at about 200–250 words per minute.

How Fast Can a Person Read?

The answer to this question depends primarily on how reading rate (and reading) is defined and how it is measured. Opinions vary widely as to how fast an individual can read. Some authorities contend that reading rates of 2,000–3,000 WPM or even higher can be achieved with the proper instruction and practice. Others state that such claims are unfounded because the individuals tested were actually skimming and not really reading (e.g., Carver 1985a) or because questionable comprehension measures were employed. It has been argued that it is physiologically impossible to take in every printed word on the page at such high speeds and counterargued that a reader need not perceive every word in order to comprehend the material.

Eye-movement data indicate that speed readers do not use exotic scanning strategies, nor do they sample only the more important words in a wider-than-normal perceptual span (Just & Carpenter 1987). Both average and rapid readers are twice as likely to sample content words as function words. But whereas those with average reading rates sample text fairly densely, fixating on about 80% of the content words; rapid readers fixate on about only 30–40% of the content words and for about only two-thirds of the average fixation duration per word. The fact that speed readers are comparatively better at comprehending information high in text structure (i.e., main ideas) from texts on familiar topics suggests that speed readers have sufficiently detailed schemata that allow them to support rapid inferencing. In effect, speed readers do more top-level processing (using prior knowledge to infer textual information) and less bottom-up processing (e.g., perceiving word sequences) than do those with average reading rates.

Sticht (1984) writes that, although high rates of skimming can be accomplished, there is little or no evidence that people can or typically do read at rates far above those at which they can *aud* (listen with comprehension) or speak.

According to Sticht (1984), the maximal auding and reading rates are probably the same because they use the same language base (lexicon and syntax) and conceptual base (semantic memory). Sticht (1984) concludes that once word recognition has been mastered, speed of reading is limited by the individual's ability to process language and that the maximal rates for auding and reading are both about 250–300 WPM, with comprehension falling off after 300 WPM.

Similar conclusions were reached by Carver (1982, 1984). In one study, Carver (1982) found that for college students there was a consistent optimal rate at which comprehension efficiency was maximal regardless of the difficulty of the material. Carver also reports that when college students had to read and later estimate the percentage of the total number of complete thought units in the material they understood (reading for general meaning), their comprehension was about 80–90% when reading between 62 and 250 WPM, dropped off to 40% at 500 WPM, fell further to 15–20% at 1,000 WPM, and was practically nil above 1,000 WPM. When reading to find the missing verb (reading for details), the comprehension scores were even lower at the various rates. Both Sticht and Carver, therefore, would contend that reading faster than 300 WPM is likely to result in considerable loss in comprehension.

Carver (1988) argues that there is no sound evidence that individuals can operate their normal reading processes at rates higher than 600 WPM and still consistently comprehend more than 75% on even relatively easy material. He states that rates above 600 WPM actually represent skimming and scanning.

Fullmer (1980) found that the maximum rate, defined as the rate at which comprehension is no better than chance, is around 700 WPM for reading and approximately 500 WPM for auding. Her findings are in contrast with Sticht's hypothesis that one's levels of auding and reading comprehension are basically the same.

Tinker (1958) concludes that 800 WPM is about the fastest rate possible for genuine reading and that rates faster than that are based on skimming. Spache (1962) insists that while rates of several thousand WPM can be attained by rapid skimming or scanning, genuine reading (in which most of the words are perceived) cannot proceed faster than 800 to 900 WPM. These calculations are based on the assumption that 10-word lines are read with an average of three fixations per line, with each fixation averaging about a quarter of a second. Also considered in the calculations were the very brief times needed for moving the eyes from one fixation to the next and from the end of one line to the beginning of the next line.

It seems that the question of how fast individuals can read is still far from being answered. Whether speeds of over 600 WPM should be called reading or skimming is still an open question. The fact is that, for some reading purposes and for some material, such speeds are both possible and desirable. But the goal should be flexible adaptation to one's purpose for reading and the nature of the material, not a uniformly very high rate of reading.

Almost all reading-rate research has involved silent reading. But Carver (1988) reports that adults and college students had an average *Maximum Oral Reading Rate* (reading aloud as fast as possible) of about 200–250 WPM. It is interesting that this rate does not differ greatly from the 250–300 WPM rates for auding and silent reading arrived at by Sticht (1984).

How Fast Should a Person Read?

Reading rate is often defined as the number of words per minute, but it would more appropriately be defined as the speed with which a person can gain the desired information from the written text. This definition implies that no one rate of reading is appropriate in all situations. Rather, reading rate is relative and depends on the reader's cognitive and reading abilities, their purposes for reading, and the difficulty of the material.

Yoakam (1955) distinguishes four major rates of reading and indicates some of the kinds of reading situations in which they are appropriate.

1. Skimming rate
   a. Work-type reading: to find a reference; to locate new material; to answer a specific question; to get the general idea of a selection
   b. Recreational reading: to go through a book or magazine to get a general idea of the contents; to review a familiar story
2. Rapid Reading
   a. Work-type: to review familiar material; to get the main idea or central thought; to get information for temporary use
   b. Recreational: to read narrative material primarily for the plot; to read informational material for pleasure; to reread familiar material
3. Normal rate
   a. Work-type: to find answers to specific questions; to note details; to solve a problem; to grasp relation of details to main ideas; to read material of average difficulty
   b. Recreational: to appreciate beauty of literary style; to keep up with current events; to read with the intention of later retelling the story
4. Careful rate
   a. Work-type: to master content including details; to evaluate material; to get details in sequence, as in following directions; to outline, summarize, or paraphrase; to analyze author's presentation; to solve a problem.
   b. Recreational: to read material with unusual vocabulary or style; to read poetry; to read with the intent of memorizing; to judge literary values

Carver (1988) defines five basic reading processes. Each process is used for a different purpose (e.g., to recall the facts; to understand the complete thought the author intended to communicate); is comprised of from one to five components; and operates at a different typical rate, ranging from 138 to 600 WPM. He believes that skilled readers do not adjust their reading rates to changes in reading difficulty but alter their reading processes, which operate at different rates. Thus, he speaks of "processing" not "rate" flexibility.

Efficient readers vary their reading processes or rates widely in accord with their purposes and with the difficulty of the text. In reading light fiction or easy nonfiction, a rapid rate is highly advantageous. A skilled adult reader should be able to go through material of this sort at a rate of at least 400 WPM. A person's normal reading rate, for somewhat more careful reading, may be only two-thirds as fast as the most rapid rate. For very careful reading or when the text is very difficult, it may be prudent to slow down to less than one-third one's rapid rate.

Choice of a reading rate that is inappropriate for successful task completion can be an important factor in comprehension problems. Selection of an inappropriate rate may be due to the pupil's past reading experiences. Children whose reading diets consist almost entirely of light, easy fiction, often become rapid, fluent readers whose comprehension is adequate for that task. When faced with texts that require careful reading, they attempt to read at the same rate and with the same purposes in mind that allowed them to be successful in the past. The results are predictable. At the other end of the continuum are those children who have been asked nothing but numerous detail questions. In order to be "successful," they read slowly so as to note even the trivia. As a result, they come to believe that everything should be read slowly and meticulously, and they often find it difficult to understand the central thought of a passage.

Should and Can Students Be Taught to Read Faster?

There appears to be common belief that most individuals can learn to read faster (Farr & Carey 1986) and that most individuals are probably capable of reading material of easy and average difficulty far faster than they do. But whether attempts should be made to increase a pupil's rate of reading depends on a number of factors. Students may show one of four patterns in regard to their reading rate and comprehension: (1) adequate rate and at least adequate comprehension; (2) satisfactory comprehension but slow rate; (3) rapid rate and poor comprehension; or (4) slow rate and poor comprehension. These categories assume that the reading behavior is typical and does not occur only occasionally.

Students falling in the first category are likely to benefit from improving their reading rates. Their comprehension is at least adequate, and almost all of them could increase their rates without decreases in comprehension (unless of course, the material is too difficult for them to understand). They are also likely candidates for learning to read more flexibly.

When reading comprehension is generally satisfactory but rate is well below normal, treatment can *usually* concentrate on increasing reading speed. Often these pupils have to be convinced that they can read faster without a loss of comprehension. Before working on reading rate, it is a good idea to tell them that it is not unusual for comprehension to drop off at first when they attempt to read faster but that comprehension will pick up again in a short time. Charting their rate and comprehension can be used to demonstrate this. Some children read slowly because they have the misconception that every word must be read regardless of the purpose for reading. These pupils must first be convinced that at times it is not necessary to read every word; they need to become more flexible readers. Exercises in which many of the less important words have been deleted can be used to get across the idea that one can read for meaning without reading every word (see Figure 17.1). Teaching these children to skim also helps. Once their misconception is cleared up, work on reading rate can begin.

Rapid readers with poor comprehension may mistakenly believe either that "fast reading is best" or that their rapid rate has little, if anything, to do with

EXERCISE 7

This exercise will show you how much meaning you can get by concentrating on important words. In the selection below, only the important words are given. Skim quickly over the selection. Work for speed.

Directions: Number your paper 1–8. Write the word or words that complete each of the sentences on page 168. Do not write in this book.

_____ coyote _____ always _____ considered _____ villain _____ western plains. _____ recent years, _____ moved east _____ become _____ problem _____ Adirondacks _____ New York State. No one _____ sure _____ coyote _____ travel _____ _____ far _____, but hunters, cattlemen _____ poultry keepers _____ hate _____ animal as _____ westerners _____.

_____ coyote _____ larger _____ fox _____ more crafty. _____ eat _____ anything _____ sheep, calves, chickens _____ mice. _____ everything _____ available. _____ will eat berries, grasshoppers _____ June bugs. _____ hard _____ trap _____ will not rush _____ bait. _____ Conservation Department _____ worried _____ coyotes _____ increasing _____ number.

_____ no one _____ reported _____ coyote _____ harmed _____ human _____. Perhaps _____ coward, or perhaps _____ too smart _____ close _____ man. _____ places, _____ bounty _____ $25 _____ paid _____ killing _____ coyote.

1. The coyote is described as a   ?   .
2.   ?   is now troubled by coyotes.
3. Men who deal with   ?   hate the coyotes.
4. A reward of   ?   is often paid for killing a coyote.
5. A coyote will eat   ?   .
6. In this article he is compared to the   ?   .
7. The   ?   Department is worried about the increasing number of coyotes.
8. Coyotes are not known to attack   ?   .

Figure 17.1. An exercise giving practice in gaining meaning using only the more important words in a selection. From *Advanced Skills in Reading*, Book 1, 2d Ed., by Joseph C. Gainsburg. Copyright © 1962, 1967 by The Macmillan Co., Inc. Reprinted by permission of the publishers.

their weak comprehension. It is also possible that their comprehension would not improve if they read more carefully at a slower rate. This latter possibility should be checked out first. These children can be asked to read more slowly, and told that the material will be taken away from them and their comprehension will be checked when they finish reading. A measure of listening comprehension may provide information useful in making this decision. If focusing these students' attention on comprehension rather than on speed does not result in improved comprehension and their reading comprehension is commensurate with their listening comprehension, reading too rapidly is probably not the cause of the poor comprehension. If, on the other hand, slowing down the rate results in significantly improved comprehension, the first step in treatment has already been initiated—convincing the pupils that speed without comprehension is self-defeating and that they can comprehend better simply by reading more slowly and carefully. These children need to learn to be flexible readers and often need to learn strategies for monitoring their reading comprehension. Such pupils require guided practice in the application of their newly acquired skills and need to have their comprehension checked frequently to make sure the skills are being applied.

If assessment reveals that trying to read too fast is not causing the comprehension problem and if a child does not have a language comprehension problem, other reasons for the inadequate reading comprehension must be sought. Some students read rapidly (or even within normal limits) and accurately but have poor comprehension because they have learned that reading is "saying the words right." These children need to learn that reading is comprehending. The recommended treatment is the same as that indicated in the preceding paragraph. In any case, care must be exercised not to shift reading speed to the other extreme—slow reading is just as undesirable. The stress should be on "read as fast as you can, but make sure you understand what you are reading." It often helps to inform these pupils that as soon as their comprehension improves, they can go back to reading faster. Almost all these pupils need to learn to become flexible readers. As students learn the degree of comprehension necessary for different kinds of reading, their ability to adjust rate to the task requirements should improve.

Word callers are individuals with adequate enabling skills, who may even "read" with appropriate intonation, but who have extremely poor comprehension across a variety of topics. Evidence does not support a view that many children are word callers. In one study (R. K. Olson et al. 1985), only one of 140 disabled readers was identified as a word caller. Perfetti (1986a) tested nine students who reportedly were word callers. One of these students did not have a comprehension problem. The other eight had very slow word-recognition (one standard deviation below that of the comparison group) and tended to have below-average listening comprehension. The latter may indicate a language comprehension problem. Word recognition may be accurate but so slow as to disrupt comprehension. Excessively slow reading caused by excessively slow word recognition can interfere with reading comprehension by making it difficult to use semantic and syntactic information. Because the needed information enters STM so slowly, it is lost from working memory before it can be fully processed.

When reading speed is slow and comprehension is poor, the reasons for the latter should be sought first. If the poor comprehension is the result of limited learning aptitude, the pupil should be given an adjusted reading and academic program. If the child's intellectual and language abilities are at least within the normal range, providing material that causes fewer mechanical problems may solve the problem temporarily. Once the probable interfering factors are identified, correctable underlying weaknesses should be improved to the point where they no longer hamper comprehension. More accurate, automatic word recognition can be developed, and pupils can learn to read in thought units rather than word-by-word. Treatment can then concentrate on developing fluency and its by-product, reading rate. One of the best ways to develop fluency is to provide children with abundant opportunities to read interesting materials that are easy for them. Overcoming basic skill deficiencies often results in increased reading speed; it does not, however, assure reading comprehension. The suggestions put forth in Chapter 15 for improving comprehension may have to be employed.

There are numerous accounts of successful reading-speed programs (e.g., Pauk 1964, J. Brown 1976), but the degree to which the increased rates carry over to other reading situations varies considerably. Not only do individuals differ widely in reading rate, but they differ in their abilities to increase their rates. Reading rate is related to rate of thinking. Of two pupils who both read at 150 WPM, one may be able to improve her or his rate tremendously, while the other may already be close to the maximum rate at which he or she can process the information. All slow readers cannot be brought "up to average." Students who were faster readers originally usually gain more than slow readers from reading-rate practice.

Should and Can Students Be Taught to Read More Flexibly?

Over a decade ago, T. L. Harris (1976) bemoaned the fact that reading flexibility was a neglected aspect of reading instruction. To a large extent, it still is. *Reading flexibility* is often defined as adjusting one's rate of reading to the purpose for reading, to one's prior knowledge, and to the nature of the reading material. But how do readers know when to adjust their reading rates? The answer is that reading flexibility is a metacognitive skill (see pages 621–625), which is one aspect of monitoring one's reading comprehension. When the reader knows the purpose(s) for which the material is to be read (including how comprehension and recall are to be assessed), and how comprehensible the material probably is in light of her level of reading ability and prior knowledge, then she can decide at which overall speed the material probably should be read. Flexible readers adopt a comprehension strategy that best accommodates all the variables of which they are aware and which they can control. At one extreme of the continuum is the situation in which the excellent reader's purpose is simply to obtain the gist of some very familiar material that is to be reported orally to the teacher immediately after the material is read. All the reader probably needs to do is to skim the material very rapidly. At the other extreme is the poor reader who knows that he will be asked to produce a detailed account long after he has first read the material, whose content is unfamiliar to him and poorly written. Such a situation calls for slow, careful reading, and rereading.

Reading flexibility does not involve only reading different kinds of materials at various speeds or reading the same kind of material at different rates for differing purposes. Flexibility also means that, despite the overall rate at which the student chooses to read, at times within the material reading should speed up or slow down. This, in effect, means adopting a different, usually temporary, reading comprehension strategy. The flexible reader reads as fast or as slowly as needed to comprehend what needs to be understood. Reading rate varies substantially even when reading for pleasure (Nell 1988).

Are Students Flexible Readers?

The answer depends on which research one reads. Some studies indicate that students do not adjust their reading rates. McDonald (1965) found that over 90% of the 3,000 readers at various age levels whom he studied tended to maintain a characteristic approach and invariant rate with all types of material, despite being told to read for different purposes and in spite of variations in the difficulty, style, and content of the materials. Carver (1983) interprets his data on 333 fourth- through twelfth-grade pupils and 102 college students as indicating that they read at a constant rate instead of adjusting their rate for the difficulty of the reading material. Carver (1984) also reports that the comprehension of 102 college students was not substantially affected by the purpose for which they were directed to read. On the other hand, some studies indicate that readers showed some flexibility in modifying rate to purpose. Intermediate-grade children tended to read faster for details than for main ideas, and faster for main ideas than for sequence (Otto, Barrett & Harris 1968), and both fourth graders and college students read faster when reading for general ideas than for details (Samuels & Dahl 1975). Seventh and eighth graders read passages faster and with better comprehension to get an overview than passages they read to find details (P. DeStefano, Noe & Valencia 1981). Both disabled and normally achieving readers showed flexibility when reading to answer general, as opposed to specific, questions at Grades 4 and 7; but at Grade 10, only the good readers varied their rates (Dowdy, Crump & Welch 1982). Rankin (1970–1971) found that college students varied their rates within a selection, slowing down for difficult portions and reading faster when the material was easier.

These differences in findings may be the result of methodological differences among the studies or students may have reacted differently from study to study. In fact, they may behave very differently under research conditions than in normal classroom situations. Then again, inflexibility of rate may simply reflect a lack of appropriate instruction; not much effective teaching of reading flexibility takes place in schools. This fact may explain why many adults complain that they read everything with the same slow, careful rate that they use to read materials in their professions.

To some extent, this individually characteristic and relatively invariant rate of reading may be constitutional. Buswell (1951) found a substantial correlation between reading rate and rate of thinking on nonreading tasks. H. Brown (1970) reports that the reaction times and movement times of seventh-grade boys correlated significantly with both oral and silent reading rates. Quickness or slowness may be a characteristic common to reading and to many other categories of human responses. There may be an optimal reading rate for comprehension beyond which skilled readers do not tend to pass; if true, this may have a ceiling effect in studies of reading flexibility with skilled readers. Both Carver (1982) and Sticht (1984) postulate that reading comprehension tends to deteriorate above 250–300 WPM. Carver (1988) further hypothesizes that it would not be appropriate for good readers to adjust their rates as the material decreases in difficulty because it would be inefficient for them to do so, since the optimal rate for reading efficiency is constant.

There is evidence that children can be taught to be flexible readers. P. Miller (1978) discusses the complications that have made research on reading flexibility difficult to conduct, and provides sensible suggestions for developing flexibility in the classroom. Other suggestions are offered by Schachter (1978), and J. Hoffman (1979). The suggestions for developing metacognitive skills also pertain to the development of reading-rate flexibility.

ELIMINATING READING BEHAVIORS THAT MAY CONTRIBUTE TO SLOW READING

Experienced teachers in any area know how important it is to perform correctly and smoothly before trying for speed. Music teachers know how ruinous it is to allow a child to increase tempo too quickly. Golf pros caution their pupils against trying to hit the ball hard. What they want is a smooth, easy swing that sends the ball a satisfactory distance without disrupting coordination. In all complex abilities, the basis of a highly expert performance is not the expenditure of a great deal of effort but the attainment of a smooth, graceful, easy, relaxed, well-coordinated performance.

Reading is no exception to the principle that an emphasis on rate should be postponed until good form has been achieved. Before trying to increase a student's reading rate, the teacher should be assured that the pupil can read fluently. A number of reading behaviors can interfere with fluency in reading, and these should be eliminated or a least greatly reduced before any pressure is exerted for greater speed in reading. It is assumed that word-recognition accuracy and comprehension are adequate.

Excessive Decoding

Occasionally a child reads at an extremely slow rate because she attempts to decode every, or almost every, word encountered. She may inspect each word by syllable or even letter by letter. This is the kind of child referred to as having an *overanalytical set*. Such pupils must first be convinced that they can recognize words as wholes (and many of them can when forced to). This ability can be demonstrated to them using quick-flash techniques. Once the child is convinced, work on phrasing can begin.

Slow Word Recognition

Speed of word recognition can be increased gradually by direct practice in recognizing known words that are exposed for only a brief duration. The use of word cards for this purpose is discussed on page 439, and an easily made hand tachistoscope is illustrated in Figure 7.7 on page 241. A great deal of easy, interesting reading is an excellent way to make word recognition more automatic.

Word-by-Word Reading

The harmful effect on comprehension of reading each word as a separate unit was discussed on page 282. Word-by-word reading obviously results in a slow reading rate. If weak word recognition is not the cause of the word-by-word reading, the usual initial treatment is to develop the child's ability to group the words into thought units and to read in phrases, as described on pages 548–550.

Increasing Perceptual Span

There is some belief that increasing the amount that a reader can see in a fixation will result in the need to make fewer fixations and thereby increase reading rate. Such attempts are almost always a waste of time. There is little difference between the perceptual spans of good and poor readers, and even very skilled readers take in only one or two words in a fixation (see page 336). Work with rapid recognition of single words is just as productive as attempts to increase the span of perception by showing increasingly longer words or a line of numbers in tachistoscopic devices.

Audible Whispering, Lip Movements, and Subvocalization

Teachers and diagnosticians often note audible whispering, lip movements, and perhaps subvocalization as children read silently. Such reading behaviors are believed by some to cause or contribute to slow silent reading rates. But more often than not, these behaviors are either natural occurrences or symptoms that do not require remediation.

Novice readers are encouraged to use their knowledge of spoken language when learning to read, and hearing the words while reading orally probably facilitates their reading comprehension because they are more familiar with processing spoken language. Furthermore, they are given a great deal of oral reading practice. So it is not unusual for novice readers to read softly orally (i.e., to display *audible whispering*) when first introduced to silent reading. With increased silent reading experience, audible whispering is gradually reduced to mouthing the words, to lip movements, and finally to subvocalization while reading silently. *Subvocalization* is defined here as "silent speech" in which the mechanisms normally used in producing speech are activated but the words are not spoken or whispered. As the silent-reading rate rises significantly above a comfortable rate of speaking, signs of subvocalization (e.g., movements of the tongue or larynx) becomes unnoticeable to the human eye.

Visible signs of subvocalization may diminish, but it rarely, if ever, disappears entirely. When reading silently, even adults who are highly skilled readers show tiny changes in the electrical activity of the muscles normally used in the production of speech (Edfeldt 1960). The electrical activity that indicates activation of the speech muscles is usually so slight that it takes sensitive electrodes to detect them. "Going through the motions" of speaking the words that are being read silently is a natural occurrence. Subvocalization is often accompanied by *"inner speech."* Many readers report hearing the words as if they were spoken by an inner voice. This phenomenon is similar to the inner speech that occurs in the mind during thinking and may be a similar process.

Increases in subvocalization, after the initial stage of learning to read, are symptoms that the material is becoming, or has become, difficult for the child to process. Research suggests that a decrease in subvocalization occurs naturally when children are provided with ample experiences silently reading materials that are at their independent and instructional levels (Pomerantz 1971).

Subvocalization can be suppressed by using auditory feedback. Tiny electrical currents are picked up by electrodes attached to the throat, and are fed to an amplifier. The amplified sound makes the reader aware of the subvocal activity. However, suppression is only temporary. Opinions regarding the effects of subvocalization vary widely (Cloer 1977). Subvocalizations are variously believed: (1) to harm comprehension in general (McGuignan 1973); (2) to interfere with comprehension when the material is difficult for the reader, but not when it is easy (Samuels 1985b); (3) not to interfere with either rate or comprehension (Bergering 1976); and (4) to aid comprehension (Carver 1988). Not only is the relationship between subvocalization and rate unclear, but its relation to reading comprehension is poorly understood (Riley & Lowe 1981). Nonetheless, research provides no support for trying to suppress subvocalization in elementary school pupils (Bruinsma 1980), and the value of suppression at any age is debatable.

When children who usually do not display such behaviors makes lip movements or whisper audibly during silent reading, it is a symptom of text difficulty. When these behaviors are frequent, a temporary "cure" is to provide more suitable reading material. The causes of the comprehension difficulty should be determined, and appropriate instruction provided. When lip movements and audible whispering occur consistently on material that the child understands easily and well, it probably indicates habituated behaviors that are no longer needed. These children can be informed of what they are doing and that they no longer need these "crutches," and children may wish to remind themselves by putting a finger to their lips when these behaviors occur. But there appears to be little need to be concerned about them. Persistent use of a crutch often means that the child still needs it, and premature efforts to stop its use could be harmful.

Finger Pointing

Finger pointing is a generic term used to refer to a number of behaviors—pointing to each word; moving a finger smoothly under separate phrases or under a line of print without stopping at the end of each phrase; placing part of the hand under each line of print; or placing a finger or thumb at the beginning and/or end of each line of print. Finger pointing may be a consistent, an occasional, or a situational behavior; and the speed with which it is done can vary markedly from child to child. It could be a symptom, unneeded habit, contributor, or a cause of reading problems. These variables should be considered in deciding what, if anything, to do about finger pointing.

Finger pointing is often considered to be an undesirable behavior because it is believed to cause, or strongly contribute to, slow reading rates or poor comprehension. The basis for the belief that it causes slow reading is that the eyes could move across the lines of print much more rapidly if they did not follow the movements of the finger or hand. If in fact the eyes do follow the finger, word-by-word finger pointing is likely to result in a slow reading rate. As for the other forms of finger pointing, the reading rate would be influenced by the speed with which the finger or hand movements occurred, and whether they occurred before, during, or after the words were processed. In any case, it is more likely that whatever is causing the finger pointing (e.g., slow or inaccurate word recognition, difficulty in processing the information) is also causing the slow reading. Only when such is not the case, can finger pointing be considered a direct cause of slow reading or poor comprehension.

As for a causal relationship to poor reading comprehension, it is believed that finger pointing causes one to read so slowly that it is difficult to understand the relationship among words, which makes it difficult to construct and retain idea units, thereby making it difficult to obtain meaning.

More often than not, finger pointing is a symptom. Consistent word-by-word finger pointing usually suggests current or past word-recognition problems. The other forms of finger pointing most likely indicate present or past difficulties in maintaining left-to-right eye movements or in being able to keep the place on the page. Finger pointing is not unusual in novice readers who typically outgrow the behavior as their word-recognition ability and skill in reading from left to right improve. If testing reveals that word recognition is not a problem, attempts can be made to eliminate the finger pointing. Children can be told why eliminating this behavior may help them. Teaching them to group words into phrases may also help. They can be slowly weaned from finger pointing by allowing them to use a marker (usually a card placed under the line of print and moved quickly to the next) as an intermediate step. Later, the marker can be discarded. Some children are reluctant to give up finger pointing, especially while their word recognition is still weak. Therefore teachers should not be quick to forbid its use. If faulty left-to-right eye movements are suspected, exercises such as those indicated on page 479 may be used. Use of a marker may allow children who are worried about losing their place to devote more attention to comprehension and thus increase their reading rate.

There is no need to be concerned about occasional finger pointing. An examination of the point in the text at which the behavior occurred may reveal a syntactic or semantic complexity that caused the finger pointing. When finger pointing occurs only when the material is difficult for the child, it is simply a symptom of that difficulty; the treatment in such cases is obvious.

Head Movements

Moving the head from side to side while reading may help children with mild binocular-coordination problems, but very few others. Head movements may slow down reading rate because the eyes can move across the page much more rapidly than the head can move from left to right. Head movements over a long period of reading can cause neck muscles to tire, so the person may avoid reading because it actually causes a "pain in the neck." Pointing out the possible negative effects of head movements and providing readers with ways to remind

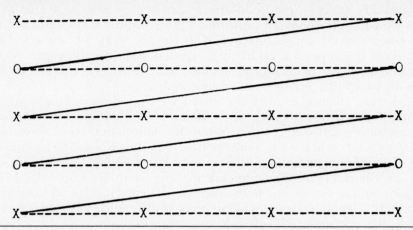

Figure 17.2.   Several lines of a cross-line exercise prepared on a typewriter, triple-spaced.

themselves to stop head movements (e.g., placing a hand on one's chin) often serve to eradicate the behavior.

Regressions

Regressions are backward eye movements that occur during the silent reading of connected discourse; that is, just as in repetitions during oral reading, some of the text is covered again. As shown in Table 9.1 on page 334, regressions decrease in frequency with age and reading ability, but they are still not uncommon even in skilled readers. Although an unusually high number of regressions curtails reading rate, the regressions are symptoms of the real cause of the slow rate—difficulty processing the text. Regressions are usually caused by word-recognition or word-meaning problems, unfamiliar or complex syntactic or semantic structures, or by attempts to clarify or regain meaning. Removing the causes of the regressions lessens their occurrence, and reading rate increases accordingly.

If a tendency to excessive regressions persists[1] as a lingering undesirable habit in a reader whose word recognition and comprehension are at a high level, specific exercises aimed at overcoming the regression may be advisable. Sometimes the use of *cross-line exercises* is helpful in reducing unnecessary regressions. Practice begins with the use of a typed page, as shown in Figure 17.2. The pupil is instructed to follow across the top line with his eyes, taking one look at each letter, then to follow the diagonal to the second line, and so on down the page. During each practice session, the student goes over the page three to five times, gradually speeding up each time. When this page format no longer presents a challenge, a second page is introduced on which single words replace the letters. A third stage uses widely spaced phrases, three or four to a line. Cross-line exercises mainly serve to convince individuals that they can go

---

[1]Only eye-movement photography can yield reliable evidence of regressions during silent reading. Regressions also may occur during oral reading, as indicated by some repetitions of words in the text.

smoothly across lines of print without looking back. A direct transfer of the steady left-to-right eye movements built up in this exercise to connected, meaningful reading is not usually achieved. Follow-up using a controlled reader (see page 648) may facilitate transfer. Pacing exercises in which the pacer is set at a comfortable rate and which do not allow one to look back at previously exposed text may also help to reduce regressions or repetitions.

A second exercise that may be helpful in reducing regressions involves use of a blank 4 × 6-inch card that has a slightly lower left than right bottom corner. This slant allows the reader to cover the beginning of each line before reaching the end of the line. As the pupil reads, the card is gradually moved down the page so as to cover what has already been read, thereby preventing regressions. This exercise, which can be used with any printed text, should result in greater transfer than the cross-line exercise because it utilizes a normal reading situation to which only a slight addition has been made. This type of exercise can be used as a rate-building exercise as well.

Difficulty Making a Return Sweep

Some children have difficulty making a return sweep with their eyes from the end of one line to the beginning of the next. At times they may jerk their heads in a right-to-left diagonal rather than making the movement just with their eyes. Some of these children skip a line or two, become confused, and begin to read again from some earlier point. Others just ignore any disruption in comprehension and continue reading. A few pupils, after reading a line, look back along the same line of print to its beginning and drop vertically to the beginning of the next line. This habit increases reading time. The possibility should be investigated that difficulty in making return sweeps are due to eye-muscle problems or slow fusion.

To develop greater skill in making the return sweep, which should be a single quick diagonal movement, one can use a page containing widely spaced lines, with diagonal lines connecting the end of each line with the beginning of the next line. The child is instructed to try to look along the diagonal when going from line to line. There is very little prepared material of this sort available; usually it is necessary to make up special material on the typewriter, starting with triple spacing and reducing to double spacing as the child improves (see Fig. 17.2). Often only a few days of practice are needed. The addition of finger pointing may make it easier for the child to master the return sweep. Pointing can continue after the diagonal lines are discontinued, and will eventually be discontinued without pressure from the teacher. The use of a marker may help.

INCREASING READING RATE BY DIRECT PRACTICE

Once slow readers have reached satisfactory levels in word recognition and comprehension and have begun to eliminate specific interfering reading behaviors, they are ready for practice aimed directly at speeding up their reading. Four main ways are used to increase rate of reading: pacing by mechanical devices, tachistoscopic training, motivated reading, and the so-called dynamic method and other speed-reading courses.

Mechanical Pacing Devices

Three mechanical pacing devices are employed to increase reading rate—motion pictures, specialized projectors, and pacers. All three attempt to increase rate by forcing students to read as fast as the print is exposed; all employ continuous discourse. The rate at which the material is exposed can be adjusted but remains uniform for the entire selection to be read. The typical procedure is to start at a fairly comfortable speed and decrease the viewing time (increase the number of words shown per minute) as the students become proficient at a given speed.

Motion pictures present one phrase at a time, brilliantly lit against a fainter background of the rest of the page. Two such sets of films have been produced. One is the *Harvard University Reading Films* (Harvard); the other, the *Iowa High School Training Films* (Iowa State University). The levels for which they are intended are indicated by their titles.

A line or part of a line, which is on a filmstrip or slide, may be displayed at varying speeds through the use of specialized projectors (e.g., a controlled reader). Devices for group or individual use may be purchased from various companies. Each machine has its own accompanying reading materials, which adds to its expense.

A method for controlling reading rate without imposing a set pattern of phrasing was worked out by Buswell (1939). It involves a shutter that gradually covers a page from top to bottom at a speed that can be regulated. Such reading pacers are sold today by a few companies. They provide individualized practice in which learners can set their own rate at each practice session and can use their own reading materials, including their textbooks (which could be a big advantage). A desirable aspect of the *Shadowscope* (Psychotechnics) is its use of a beam of light to pace the reader. The illumination of the beam can be reduced until it is barely perceptible, thereby producing an almost natural situation. When the practice is followed by adequate comprehension checks, it provides what seems to be a well-motivated procedure for guiding the learner toward gradually increased rate without sacrificing comprehension. The same could be true of other specialized devices if used individually.

One of the main problems with using mechanical pacing devices with groups is that it is impossible for a reading selection to be of suitable difficulty and, for the pacer, be set at a speed suitable for every member of the group. Another possible problem with all these devices is that of presenting an entire selection at the same rate, making it impossible for readers to slow down when they meet with difficulty or to reread as they might under normal reading conditions. This problem is somewhat lessened when the equipment is used by an individual who can stop the machine or reset the rate. The value of pacing devices may lie in forcing students to attend to the task, because they know that they will not get a second chance to read something.

Still another problem is that there is often little carry-over to natural reading situations. More carry-over is likely if the pupil's own materials are used with the pacing devices. It may be helpful to have students attempt to read material of their choice at the speed just imposed by the pacing device immediately after the paced exercise ends. How much of any favorable effect is the result of controlling the rate and how much is due to motivation that could be secured by nonmechanical procedures is impossible to estimate. Some students are intrigued with the machinery and are motivated by its use. Other students increase their reading rates only if a reading speed is imposed on them. The machine does this for them. It is still too soon to comment on the use of the computer to increase reading rate, although the possibilities seem exciting.

Tachistoscopic Training

A *tachistoscope* is a device that allows the presentation of visual material for brief intervals of time ranging usually from one second to $\frac{1}{100}$ of a second. Some tachistoscopes have a fixed exposure time, but most have variable exposure times. They can range from a simple handmade device (see Fig. 7.7 on page 241) to complex instruments for controlling the exposure time. Inexpensive small tachistoscopes for individuals are available from various companies. Projection tachistoscopes have two parts: a slide or filmstrip projector and a shutter-like device that can be set for different exposure speeds. These devices range widely in cost.

Research findings have failed to indicate any positive impact of tachistoscopic training on reading speed or comprehension (e.g., Kleinberg 1970). Learning to recognize words in less than $\frac{1}{25}$ of a second is irrelevant to continuous reading because most of the fixation time in reading is required for the brain to process the incoming visual information. Attempts to increase the span of perception or to develop the ability to recognize complete phrases at high speeds are questionable, because even skilled readers usually take in only one or two words in a fixation. The value of tachistoscopic training lies mainly in its effects on motivation and attention.

Increasing Rate through Motivated Reading

Another technique for overcoming slow reading rates is to motivate students to do large amounts of easy reading, which will provide the abundant practice needed to develop fluency. The absence of vocabulary and comprehension difficulties allows these materials to be read easily, with little need to hesitate in order to recognize words or determine word meaning, or to pause or reread to obtain meaning as must occur in reading difficult material. If the content is sufficiently interesting, the children will be attracted to the materials and their interest will be maintained while reading. They will read quickly to find out what comes next, and the absence of pressure to read at a rate set by someone or something else eliminates strain and tension. Methods for developing greater interest in voluntary reading are discussed in Chapter 18.

Rereading a favorite story or book a number of times should be encouraged. The repeated-reading procedure may be employed but should be used judiciously (see pages 481–482). With each rereading, fluency is likely to improve. As children find that they can read easily and fluently, their self-confidence and motivation are favorably affected.

A second phase of this technique involves a series of timed silent reading exercises with comprehension checks. Either workbook exercises or general

4

Who would ever have thought that the old trolley car, with its bell clanging for joy, might return to our city streets? Your grandparents could tell you that most trolleys were long ago replaced by buses and cars.

What's wrong with buses and cars? If everyone used private cars, our city streets would become choked with traffic. Both buses and cars produce unhealthy air pollution. The government wants to find a new way to move lots of people quickly, cheaply, and quietly.

Since the trolley car runs on electricity, it is quiet and does not produce clouds of exhaust fumes. Shiny new trolley cars, which are called *light rail vehicles*, are now being built for many cities. Do not be surprised if older folks smile when they see this new "vehicle of the future" clanging down the street.

---

1. **Trolley cars**   Ⓐ are a new invention   Ⓑ were used many years ago   Ⓒ will never be used again   Ⓓ are found only in museums
2. **Most trolleys run on**   Ⓐ steam   Ⓑ coal   Ⓒ electricity   Ⓓ gasoline
3. **What is the best reason for using trolleys?**   Ⓐ they can reduce air pollution   Ⓑ they are old   Ⓒ they are fun to ride   Ⓓ they run on tracks
4. **One problem with using buses is that they**   Ⓐ are too small   Ⓑ cause traffic jams   Ⓒ help cause air pollution   Ⓓ do not have a bell
5. **Trolleys are now called**   Ⓐ light buses   Ⓑ heavy rail vehicles   Ⓒ rail buses   Ⓓ light rail vehicles
6. **This story says that most old trolleys**   Ⓐ remained in use   Ⓑ were replaced by buses and cars   Ⓒ were painted red   Ⓓ were too expensive
7. **Choose the best title:**   Ⓐ The End of the Line   Ⓑ The Happy Return of the Trolley   Ⓒ The History of Railroads   Ⓓ Private Cars Are the Answer
8. **According to this story**   Ⓐ cities are too large   Ⓑ cities should build more parks   Ⓒ old ideas sometimes give new solutions   Ⓓ older people should own cars

---

No. right	1	2	3	4	5	6	7	8
G score	2.7	3.3	3.7	4.2	4.7	5.4	6.0	6.7

Figure 17.3.   A page from the McCall–Crabbs *Standard Test Lessons in Reading*. Reprinted by permission of the publisher from *McCall–Crabbs Standard Test Lessons in Reading*, Book C (New York: Teachers College Press, Copyright © 1979, 1978, 1961, 1950, 1926 by Teachers College Press, Columbia University. All rights reserved.) Reduced in size.

reading matter of a comparatively easy nature may be used. These timed exercises and the charting of progress strengthens motivation to increase reading rate and emphasizes the need to remember comprehension.

An example of workbooks that may be used for timed reading in the upper grades and secondary school are the McCall-Crabbs *Standard Test Lessons in Reading* (see Figure 17.3). Each page contains a brief selection followed by multiple-choice questions. A total of three minutes is allowed for reading the selection and answering the questions. If the passage is read too slowly, there is little or no time to answer the questions; if reading is careless or too rapid, many answers will be incorrect. Knowing what needs to be done to improve performance allows students to improve their scores on subsequent exercises. The approximate grade scores that accompany each exercise can provide an incentive to raise scores. Use of the McCall-Crabbs and similar materials greatly improved the balance between rate and comprehension, as well as the total reading scores of ninth graders (Green 1971). The more important but unanswered question is to what extent such improvements transfer to daily reading.

Provided that a teacher is willing to count or estimate the number of words, almost any material of suitable difficulty for which a good comprehension check can be divised can be used in timed reading exercises. Suggestions for computing WPMs appear on page 204. Time limits can be imposed or children can impose their own or strive to read each passage faster than the last. Fluctuations in performance are not unusual; they are likely to occur for a number of reasons (e.g., difference in text difficulty, interest, comprehension-check difficulty). Efforts should be made to use materials of similar difficulty.

The "Dynamics" Method and Other Speed-Reading Programs

The "dynamics" method attempts to replace the usual reading pattern of reading across each line in a series of fixations by a variety of patterns in which the reader's eyes follow her finger down the page. The Evelyn Wood organization's advertising asserts that the typical graduate reads at 1,200 WPM with 70% comprehension. The materials used for testing are easy, or of moderate difficulty, usually taken from general adult nonfiction. It is not clear whether time spent in previewing before reading the selection is counted in the computation of rate.

Because no detailed description of the "dynamics" approach has ever been made public, we asked Charlotte Harris Wiener, who taught the Evelyn Wood method for 3 years, to write a brief description of her procedures. Her account follows:

> My work with about a thousand students over the last decade has convinced me that speed reading is an invaluable technique, although it must be used with discretion. Whether my students have been well-educated adults, sixth graders with diverse socioeconomic and racial backgrounds, or "educationally disadvantaged" inmates in prison, the results are strikingly similar. Almost all have learned to speed-read on materials that for them are easily comprehended. Almost all have found that practicing speed techniques has increased their normal reading rate while allowing them a satisfactory level of comprehension.

The following is an outline of one of the basic drills I use for improving rates and for teaching skimming and scanning:

1. Choose an easy novel for beginning practice (in a class it is desirable for all to use the same book).
2. Read about 10 pages, underlining each line with a finger and keeping pace with the eyes.
3. "Practice read" the same 10 pages, using a finger pattern to guide the eyes. The first three times are done at 12 seconds per page, the fourth time at 6 seconds per page, and the fifth at 4 seconds per page. After the first "practice read," write down any words or ideas that you recall. After each subsequent "practice read," add to the notes. Have someone count the seconds until the reader gets the rhythm.
4. Repeat Steps 2 and 3 with consecutive sections of the book for about a half hour daily. Marked improvement in rate of reading and in recall will be noticed within 1 or 2 weeks. Practice should be continued until the reader is satisfied with his performance.

In applying speed reading to nonfiction, previewing the section very briefly before starting to read it and writing a very brief summary after reading are desirable accompaniments of the procedure.

While speed reading is possible without using one's hand, it is easier to learn and maintain if one uses a finger as a pacer and guide for the eyes. A variety of patterns for moving the hand down the page may be used, although the zigzag, curving, and looping patterns seems to be the most popular. The reader is encouraged to keep the eyes relaxed so that he can see an area of the page, not just a portion of a line. It takes hours of practice before one can see all of the words.

Training in speed reading should be combined with training designed to improve flexibility, comprehension, and study skills. A speed reader should adjust his rate according to his purpose; the style and difficulty of the reading material; and the reader's experience with the vocabulary, concepts, and general informational background relevant to the subject matter. He might read a difficult selection in an unfamiliar field at one fifth his rate for easy narrative fiction.

Speed reading feels subjectively different from skimming, although the rates attained may be similar, the scores may be similar on short-answer tests, and skilled readers often use a combination of speed reading and skimming.

Four studies of the "dynamics" method cited by Cranney et al. (1982) question the claims of extremely high rates made by advocates of the method. Their study, however, found that the five university students trained in the "Reading Dynamics" program read five to six times as fast but with the same comprehension as the control group when allowed to read at their own space. When paced at 2,600 and 3,000 WPM, the "dynamics" group had significantly higher comprehension than the control group. The training program involved (1) using the hand as a pacer, initially line by line and later in a vertical fashion; (2) mapping—the student notes the main idea and fills in other ideas in a diagram fashion (two-tiered notes are taken); and (3) using an add-a-page drill in which the students are extolled to reread very rapidly (double or triple the speed) material that they had just finished reading. Six hours a week were devoted to practice.

OTHER SPEED-READING PROCEDURES. Schale (1965) describes a procedure called the "2R-OR-ALERT method." The symbols stand for Reinforced Reading; Overview, Read rapidly; Answer questions, Locate mistakes, Examine mistakes, Reread at the same rate (if comprehension is unsatisfactory), and Transfer adjustment of comprehension to rate to another article. Emphasis is placed on using "inclusive skimming" (reading only the first sentence of each paragraph horizontally, and skimming the rest vertically for key words). Schale reports a gain for one group of 24 students from a pretest mean of 506 WPM to a posttest mean of 2,313 WPM. This group obviously had a superior rate on the pretest. In a later paper, Schale (1972) reports that two girls reached speeds of over 20,000 WPM after training in her program. One reportedly was able to read vertically, taking in two columns at a time! Schale's procedure has not been evaluated by other investigators.

Berger (1968) reports a comparison of four methods for increasing rate of reading, used in a one-semester reading–study skills course for college freshmen who were below average on their entrance-test scores. The four methods were tachistoscopic training, use of the Controlled Reader, controlled pacing, and paperback scanning. In the latter method, the reader was required to scan each page vertically under time pressure: first at 2 minutes, 8 seconds per page; next at 2 minutes, 7 seconds per page; and down to 2 seconds per page; then up to 10 seconds per page. Significant gains in rate were made by all four groups as compared to the control group; the tachistoscopic group made the smallest gains and the paperback scanning group made the largest gains, not only in rate but also in reading flexibility.

J. Brown (1976) in discussing techniques for increasing reading rate, emphasizes the importance of student and teacher expectancies and attitudes. The instructor's beliefs about how much the students could improve seemed to set limits on how much they did improve. Such student attitudes as "fear of missing something," "lack of confidence," and "the faster you read, the less you comprehend" inhibit progress unless the student is helped to overcome them. Brown emphasizes the importance of active self-discoveries and the use of "visual expediters." He reports results from three kinds of courses, each of which carried college credit. In each course, rate increased while comprehension remained constant. In a college course with direct student-teacher interaction, rates increased from an initial 252 WPM to 1,548 WPM; in an independent study–cassette version of the course, from 314 WPM to 889 WPM; and in a TV course of 12 sessions, each lasting 30 minutes, from 293 WPM to 903 WPM.

Implications for School Practice

Despite occasional reports of increasing reading rate through direct instruction as low as in the second grade (R. Rowell 1976), it is extremely doubtful that such efforts should be made in the primary grades. Berquist (1984) interprets the findings of 12 studies, including his own as indicating that intermediate-grade children can be taught to increase their reading rates without loss of comprehension. But a reanalysis of the data led Carver (1987b) to seriously question Berquist's conclusion. So there is some doubt about the advisability of aiming at greater speed through specific practice in Grades 4 and 5. Indeed, Farr and Carey (1986) state that there is no evidence that reading rate should be a part of reading instruction below the sixth grade. For the majority of students below that level, satisfactory reading rates should emerge as a by-product of a well-conceived developmental reading program that creates fluent readers through balanced attention to word recognition and comprehension, oral and silent reading, and careful directed-reading instruction and extensive independent reading.

Use of motivated, timed reading with comprehension checks seems to improve reading rate as much as does the use of expensive equipment, but use of individual pacers may benefit some students. In terms of transfer of training, procedures that most closely resemble normal reading situations seem to have an advantage over those that utilize artificial conditions. Flexibility of reading rate should be emphasized.

After an initial flurry of interest during the 1960s, researchers have largely ignored reading rate. Considering the practical importance of being able to read at rates several times faster than current average rates, the scarcity of research in this area is difficult to understand.

18

Fostering the Desire to Read Voluntarily

Reading can foster personal, academic, and intellectual growth. It can be a source of entertainment, inspiration, information, and insight into ourselves and others. Frequent reading can facilitate growth in reading ability by providing the practice needed to solidify reading skills; and reading extensively allows the reader to refine existing, and to acquire new, word and world knowledge.

Such benefits accrue maximally only if pupils choose to read during their free or leisure time. Unfortunately we have apparently produced what Huck (1971) refers to as a nation of "illiterate literates"; that is, individuals who can, but choose not to, read. For instance, a recent study (R. C. Anderson, Wilson & Fielding 1988) reveals that the daily amount of out-of-school time fifth graders spent reading books ranged from 0 to 65 minutes. However, 70% read an average of less than 10 minutes a day; half, less than 5 minutes; and 10% hardly ever read voluntarily. Voluntary reading among school-age children and their enjoyment of reading decline with age (NAEP 1982b, Telfer & Kann 1984). When asked to choose among going to a movie, watching TV, reading a book, and reading a magazine, half of the 9-year olds and almost two-thirds of the teenagers opted for the movie (NAEP 1981). Various theories have been offered to account for this situation (see Beentjes & Van der Voort 1988). On the positive side, the sale of children's books represented 7% of all books sold in 1988, up 2% from 1986 (Micklos 1988a).

It would be unrealistic to think that we could turn every child, or even a vast majority of pupils, into avid readers. Nonetheless, we probably could improve the present state of affairs considerably. A successful reading program not only turns out children who can read, but also builds a favorable attitude toward reading, develops a lasting interest in reading, and improves reading tastes. It takes superior materials, clever teachers who love to read themselves, time, and effort to develop the reading habit in children. But if we fail to develop this habit, much of our reading instruction will have been wasted. So, this chapter stresses finding "the right book for the right child" as a way of increasing children's desire to read voluntarily.

The following statement deserves wide attention:

> At all times and with every means at her command, the teacher must learn how best to counteract the attitude that reading is for school only; that reading is a second-hand, and, therefore, an inferior form of experience. Reading must be understood and interpreted as a tool of invention, relevance, and creativity, as a sort of depth-perception device that gives dimension to firsthand experience; and as a principal means by which the intellectual inheritance is tested and developed. (Dietrich & Mathews 1968).

PLANNED RECREATIONAL READING PROGRAMS

The two basic approaches to teaching literature are best viewed as complementary. The *structural approach* (literary analysis) provides the terms and concepts that help students interpret and discuss literature. In the *reader-response approach*, students' personal responses to the text are emphasized. It is preferable to initiate instruction with a reader-response approach and, as the pupils mature and develop analytic skills, to incorporate the structural approach into the literature program. Users of a structural approach often include in their programs the development of a *cultural heritage*—the acquaintance with works that adults often assume have been read by children; knowledge of the various genres; and the formal features of literature (Pugh 1988).

Few programs at the elementary school level emulate the formal study of literature found in secondary schools. Most books are read on a voluntary, unplanned basis, and a distinction is usually not drawn between recreational reading and a literature program (Hardt 1983). Therefore, we use the term *planned recreational reading program*, which has as its purposes to develop favorable attitudes toward reading, an interest in reading as a voluntary activity, and an awareness of what is considered to be good children's or adolescent literature. In short, its basic purpose is to motivate children to read and to help them expand their reading interests and tastes. This is accomplished by promoting the concept that reading can be a pleasurable, rewarding activity; by exposing pupils to various kinds of works, writing styles, topics, and authors; and by providing them with abundant, appropriate materials to read and with the time to choose, read, and discuss them. One of the important aspects of a planned recreational reading program is the allocation of time *during* school to conduct the program. If we do not demonstrate that reading is a worthwhile activity by providing school time, how can we expect children to value reading? Allowing children to read material of their choice only after school assignments are completed does not help to develop a desirable attitude toward reading as a leisure-time activity.

A planned recreational reading program incorporates the following activities in a flexible overall plan: (1) *free reading periods* in which children are allowed to read materials of their own choice, as in sustained silent reading (see page 102); (2) the teacher *reading to the students* (see page 675); (3) *guided supplementary reading* in which the pupils are helped to select materials but during which the teacher does not deaden interest by dominating the choices; (4) *topic units,* which utilize a subject, type of literature, style of writing, and so forth as a coordinating theme;[1] and (5) *creative sharing,* which is accomplished through discussion, oral reading, storytelling, and creative activities (Huus 1975).

According to Odland (1979), four major concentrations should form the framework for a program that allows for flexibility in both methods and materials and provides for the direct teaching of literature:

1. *Children's interests* provide excellent motivation for reading and the serious study of literature.
2. *Study of literary types* should include myths and legends, folk tales, contemporary and historical fiction, fantasy, science fiction, poetry, biographical fiction, and nonfiction.
3. *Literary elements* should focus on exposure, through listening and reading, to the elements that are part of the composition of a work. Children learn to examine their responses to the material and perceive what it is in the literature that causes these responses.
4. *Creators of books* involves learning about the contributions of authors, illustrators, and others involved in the production of literary works.

Practical ideas for incorporating literature into the total reading program are offered by Cullinan (1987), Huck and Hickman (1987), and Stewig and Sebesta (1989). Galda (1987a,b,c) suggests ways to teach higher-order reading comprehension skills with literature.

Planned recreational reading programs are effective in increasing the quality and quantity of voluntary reading. Children become more skilled readers by reading, and learn to love to read when pleasure is the purpose for reading (Pillar 1983). But, in order to accomplish the aims of a planned recreational reading program, teachers need to know about the reading interests of children, how to determine reading interests and attitudes toward reading, the affective aspects of reading, how and where to locate materials, and how to estimate the difficulty of reading materials.

READING INTERESTS

Definitive statements about the reading interests of children and young adults should be viewed with caution. It is difficult to compare the findings of studies because they vary widely as to the characteristics of the samples employed and

[1]Moss (1984) presents 13 focus units designed to motivate children to read more widely and to develop critical-thinking and creative-writing skills. Each unit contains a bibliography on that topic and classroom activities (e.g., drama, music).

the methods used to determine interests. A few writers (e.g., Summers & Luka-sevich 1983) make an important distinction between reading interests and reading preferences. Basically, the two differ in the ways in which they are determined and thereby in the reliability of the obtained results. *Reading interests* can be demonstrated by the materials individuals actually, or probably, have already read. Thus, a child who has borrowed or purchased books and/or magazines about animals, or who could demonstrate having read such materials, would be said to have "animals" as a reading interest. *Reading preferences* are usually determined by having individuals select from or rank a number of options (e.g., types of stories, titles of books). Their responses may indicate what they might like to read; but they do not necessarily mean that the respondents have read or will read such materials. If we accept this distinction, then most of what are referred to as "reading interests" in the literature are actually "possible reading preferences." We use the term "interests" in this chapter because it is by far the more commonly employed.

Frequently, there are marked differences between what children would prefer to read and what teachers and librarians recommend (Nilsen, Peterson & Searfoss 1980). Many of the books selected as the best of the year by adults have been ignored by children (Terman & Lima 1937, Vandament & Thalman 1956). Children's choices of the best books published annually do not agree closely with the interests revealed by various studies (Greenlaw 1983).

Probably the most important finding about reading interests is the tremendous range of individual differences both in amount of voluntary reading done and specific interests expressed. Even in groups of children who are similar in intelligence, age, and cultural background, the range of individual preferences is tremendous. Although a knowledge of general trends may help teachers to anticipate the interests of pupils, it does not relieve them of the responsibility of trying to discover the particular interests of each pupil.

A number of factors have been found to be associated with reading interests, none of which can easily be separated from the others. Nevertheless, they are discussed here in isolation for reasons of clarity.

Age

There are some similarities in reading interests across age levels, but there are differences in age-level interest categories. For instance, children and young adults demonstrate an interest in stories that have characters of their own age. But, whereas young children also readily identify with fantasy figures (usually animals) who participate in childlike experiences, older pupils prefer more realistic stories that portray children of their ages who are involved in suspenseful adventures.

As children age, their interests generally expand; but narrow again by the last two years of high school. At about the eighth- or ninth-grade level, motivation for reading begins to shift from reading for pleasure to reading for self-understanding, and reading interests begin to approximate those of adults. Reading interests usually do not change considerably after age 16, but they can be greatly affected by education or employment.

The limited research on the listening/reading interests of preschoolers is inconclusive. Perhaps their interests are fleeting or do not stabilize until children have acquired sufficient ability to read independently. Illustrations have as much as or more appeal than story content, but very young children like repetition and repeatedly ask to hear familiar stories. An analysis of children's favorite picture books reveals that the story structures children liked best (in descending order of preference) were: confrontation and solution of a problem; episodic, usually a series of adventures; contrasts, in which characters have opposing points of view; plotless, a catchall category for alphabet books and the like; and travel, in which the character embarks on an adventure. Young children like fantasy, humor, and realistic fiction (Abrahamson 1980).

Primary-grade children are strongly interested in make-believe, animals, and children's activities. These preferences were expressed by children in 10 different countries (Kirsch, Pehrsson & Robinson 1976). Middle-class first graders prefer the pranks theme over the pollyanna theme, and peer interaction over parent-child interactions (Rose, Zimet & Blom 1972). Interest in the fanciful usually increases until the age of 8 or 9 and then gradually declines.

Most preschool and primary-grade children seem to prefer humorous poems, followed by poems about animals and poems related to their own experiences. Although studies show a considerable range of opinion expressed when poetry was read to them, primary-grade children's order of preference for poetic form was: narrative poems, limericks, rhymed verse, free verse, lyric poetry, and haiku. There was a strong preference for poems that rhymed and that used sound (alliteration, onomatopoeia). Poems relying on metaphor, similes, or personification were generally disliked. Traditional poems were preferred over modern ones (Fisher & Natarella 1982).

Intermediate-grade pupils have a greater variety of interests than do younger children. By age 9 or 10, gender differences in interests become more marked (see p. 660), but both genders tend to like exciting and humorous stories (Lauritzen & Cheves 1974) and stories in which the characters have to struggle with problems similar to the ones they face in their own lives (Worley 1967). Jose and Brewer (1983) report that fourth- and sixth-graders' identification with the story character increased their liking for the story, but there was a difference in their preference for story endings. Fourth graders preferred positive outcomes regardless of whether the character was good or bad (in the sense of being socially or culturally acceptable); sixth graders preferred positive endings for good characters but negative endings for bad characters. Most middle-grade children enjoy comic strips and comic books. They also read magazines and newspapers (A. Miller 1967).

For intermediate-grade children, the most popular poems tend to be those related to children's experiences, those with humor, and those having strong rhythm and rhyme (Bridges 1967). Limericks and narrative poems are popular in the middle grades; haiku, serious or sentimental poems, and poems that are difficult to understand are not (Terry 1974).

The fact that poetry is not popular with children has been well documented (W. S. Gray 1960). Unimaginative, burdensome, and joyless teaching of poetry may contribute to its relative lack of popularity. An observational study by Baskin, Harris, and Salley (1976) reveals three major teaching faults: (1) using poetry to achieve unrelated academic purposes (e.g., a handwriting exercise);

(2) overloading children with a certain type of poetry; and (3) assigning poetry memorization as punishment. Children may find poetry difficult because it often requires a high level of thinking but uses devices that make it look easy, thus misleading them (Marston 1975). An analysis of sixth-grade basal reader manuals (Shapiro 1985) reveals that they generally do not suggest using the instructional procedures recommended by poetry authorities.

At the junior and senior high school levels, studies have shown a continuing trend toward individual differentiation in interests. But humor is an important element in what teenagers choose to read (Nilsen & Nilsen 1982). They also like books with teenage protagonists and realistic fiction. Adolescents express a strong preference for themes in which the central problem is resolved successfully (B. Samuels 1989). Young adults dislike many of the titles considered classics by their English teachers (Norvell 1972), and high school students are generally negative toward poetry (Elliott & Steinkellner 1979), perhaps because understanding poetry is one of their main sources of frustration (Seminoff 1986b).

The amount of voluntary reading usually increases until the age of 12 or 13. In some schools, there is a marked decline in voluntary reading, which coincides in time with both increasing homework and the teaching of literature. In other schools, teachers successfully maintain the amount of voluntary reading done by adolescents, and help them mature in their tastes.

Norvell (1966) explored the popularity of magazines with about 6,000 pupils. Intermediate-grade students read a variety of magazines but showed a strong preference for nonfiction and humor magazines. There were marked gender differences in choices, but *National Geographic* was popular with both boys and girls. Seven of the ten magazines that were most popular with children in Grades 4–6 were adult magazines. The extent to which this early preference for adult magazines was influenced by the availability of adult magazines and the absence of children's magazines in their homes and schools is unknown. Below Grade 7, boys read more magazines than girls did; after that, girls read more of them. On the whole, interest in magazine reading was lower in the 1960s than it had been in the 1930s. Comparable data for the 1970s and 1980s were not available. It would appear, however, that magazine reading is still popular, since 13 magazines for young people rank among the top 200 magazines in circulation in the United States (Monteith 1981a).

Newspaper reading increases with age until about age 17, but the sections of the newspaper reportedly read most often change substantially with age. There also are some gender differences as pupils age. The trend for boys is from the comics to sports, and finally to the news. For girls, it is from the comics to a diversity of personal- and social-development information, which is finally combined with reading the news. Readership is influenced by availability and whether reading a newspaper is required by teachers (Guthrie 1981a). Approximately 69% of seventh graders and 78% of eleventh graders reported reading a newspaper at least weekly (Applebee, Langer & Mullis 1988).

Gender

Primary-grade children prefer to read stories in which the characters are of the same gender as the reader (Rose, Zimet & Blom 1972). There is some belief that differences in story preference occur when the main character is the same gender as the reader because the reader identifies with the protagonist. Bleakley, Westerberg, and Hopkins (1988) found that fifth-grade boys strongly preferred stories with male protagonists over those whose main character was female. Girls also displayed a same-gender preference, but it was not as pronounced. Boys' preference for a male protagonist becomes significantly stronger between Grades 7 and 11, while girls' preference for female protagonists decreases as grade level increases (Beyard-Tyler & Sullivan 1980).

Gender differences in interest categories are not very strong in the primary grades (Kirsch 1975). More marked gender differences in reading preferences begin to appear by about age 9 or 10, and increase during the intermediate grades (Summers & Lukasevich 1983). They become even more pronounced in the junior high school, and usually lessen in the senior-high years, although Elliott and Steinkellner (1979) report clear gender-preference differences in Grades 11 and 12.

Intermediate-grade boys generally become absorbed in adventure, sports, and mystery stories. They also read fictionalized history and biography, and perhaps read extensively on mechanics, science, invention, and their hobbies. Girls seem to prefer sentimental stories of home and school life as well as animal stories. They usually develop an interest in romantic fiction between the ages of 11 and 14. A phenomenon of the early 1980s was the proliferation of contemporary teen-romance novels aimed at adolescent female readers. These books received a great deal of adult criticism, but teenage girls read them (Parrish 1983). At this age level, girls share the boys' liking for mystery and adventure, humor and fantasy, but usually do not care to read about science and invention. Boys, on the other hand, generally tend to ignore human-interest stories, and to avoid anything that seems "feminine" to them.

At the junior and senior high school levels category preferences are less marked. For boys, they roughly include adventure, sports and games, science fiction, historical novels, humor, mystery, and war. The rough categorical preferences for girls include books about people and social relationships, romance, humor, and mystery without violence.

There have been quantitative and qualitative improvements in the portrayal of females in children's and adolescent literature (Frasher 1982). Gender differences in reading preferences seem to be lessening (Feeley 1982), but reading interests still seem to be selected in accord with sex-role expectations (K. P. Scott 1986). As cultural attitudes change, children may be given more opportunities to read about males and females in nontraditional gender roles and be encouraged to read in areas previously considered more appropriate for the opposite gender. As such changes occur, expressed reading interests may change as well. But as desirable as these changes may be, reading alone is not likely to significantly alter sex-role attitudes, which are fairly well developed before children enter school and are reinforced through the years by family and peer beliefs.

Based on their review of the literature, C. Johnson and Greenbaum (1982) conclude that: (1) Girls will read about boys and their activities; (2) boys will read about girls and their activities, *if* the story content appeals to them; (3) girls have a wider range of interests than boys do; and, (4) the genders share many areas of interest. Their most important conclusion is that reading interests are so unique that the only to be sure of a given pupil's interests is to determine them for each individual.

Intelligence

A relationship between intelligence and reading interests has not been clearly established. It appears, however, that bright children read more voluntarily than do other pupils, have a wider range of reading interests, and are usually one to two years ahead of average students in interest maturity. Mentally slow children often do not choose to read, and usually have preferences that, although slightly immature for their chronological ages, are more mature than those of younger children with the same mental ages (R. L. Thorndike 1941). At the secondary school level, Norvell (1973) found little relationship between IQ level and reading preferences.

Reading Ability

Some evidence suggests that the reading interests of pupils whose reading ability is two or more years below grade level are more influenced by reading age than by chronological age (Geeslin & Wilson 1972). But our clinical experience suggests that disabled readers most often have interests more in keeping with their chronological ages. Good, average, and poor readers who were in Grades 4 and 6 expressed similar reading interests (G. Anderson, Higgens & Wurster 1985).

Poor readers and high school students of below-average intelligence tend to give high ratings to materials that have main characters with whom they can easily identify (Emans & Patyk 1967). The same principle probably applies to young poor readers. McKenna (1986) found that gender differences in reading interests appeared to peak for poor readers during the junior high school years and that the number of their reading interests declined with age. Gender preferences did not differ greatly from those of good readers at these age levels.

Although good readers tend to read more than others, they are not necessarily avid readers (Lamme 1976a, L. Morrow 1985).

Psychological Needs

One of the major determinants of reading interests is theorized to be the satisfaction of psychological needs, including the need to develop self-concept, intellectual needs, emotional needs, social needs, and aesthetic needs. Whether or not elementary school children read to satisfy their psychological needs remains an unanswered question. Their reading interests do not seem to correspond very closely to their expressed needs. They frequently turn to sources of information other than reading when they need information. Children tend to regard reading primarily as a recreational activity (Rudman 1955). However, individual differences vary so considerably that it is impossible to generalize about the relationship of needs and interests. Students may turn to other media to satisfy their needs if the expectations of reward from reading are not high.

Socioeconomic Status

Most studies have found that socioeconomic factors do not significantly affect reading interests. When intelligence and reading ability are factored out, low-, middle-, and upper-SES students express similar reading preferences. Similarly, when other variables are considered, there seems to be little difference among the reading interests of rural, suburban, and metropolitan pupils (Huus 1979). The high relationship between SES and cultural/ethnic background makes it difficult to separate out the influence of each of these two sets of variables.

Cultural/Ethnic Background

The research findings in this area are mixed. Some studies have shown significant differences in reading interests among cultural/ethnic groups at all age levels, with the widest differences occurring in the intermediate grades. For instance, Lewis (1970) found that black kindergartners strongly favored books about children in ghetto areas, whereas white children disliked such books. It is impossible, however, to state what other factors may influence these choices. Lickteig (1972) found that although there were some similarities between inner-city and suburban children, such as preference for science fiction at both fourth and sixth grades, inner-city children tended to prefer black fiction more than suburban children did, while white suburban children preferred horse stories more than inner-city children did.

Other studies have not found such differences. Considerable similarity of interests across races and cultures has been reported by Kirsch, Pehrsson, and Robinson (1976); and Asher (1978). Contrary to prevailing beliefs, intermediate-grade, inner-city children (most of whom were black) preferred stories containing middle-class settings, characters with positive self-images, and characters in positive group interactions (Johns 1973).

When reading content provide opportunity for minority-group identification, however, children's expressed interests were more different than alike. Minority-group children expressed a high degree of interest in topics related to their own ethnic group and immediate environment, but generally low interest in topics related to other minority groups. Certain titles were of high interest to all groups, particularly fiction stories combining minority culture with suspense and adventure, folk tales, and certain biographies, sports books, and cookbooks. Although the genders shared many common interests (mystery or adventure, humor, animal stories, and child's immediate environment), sports and science topics were of more interest to boys. A wide range of individual interests was found within each ethnic and gender group, with much overlapping of interests among all groups (Barchas 1971).

Influence of Other Individuals

Peers, friends, parents, and teachers influence reading interests directly through recommended or assigned reading and indirectly by serving as models. Friends and peers played an important role in influencing fifth graders' reasons for selecting certain books to read, whereas television and movies did not (Lawson 1972).

Nonprint Media

The effects of nonprint media on reading interests, on the choice of reading as a free-time activity, and on reading achievement are not well understood, primarily because of the interrelated nature of the variables involved. Almost all of the current literature has centered on the impact of TV viewing.

In the mid-1960s, elementary school children viewed television an average of 20 hours weekly; slightly less in the primary grades, slightly more in the intermediate grades (Witty 1966). In the 1970s and early 1980s, children ages 6–11 watched television an average of 24 hours per week; teenagers viewed almost 20 hours (Lamb 1976, Larrick 1983). More recently, fifth graders were found to spend about 15 hours weekly watching TV (R. C. Anderson, Wilson & Fielding 1988). Viewing time generally diminishes with age (Neuman & Prowda 1982). For the majority of students, media choices change with age, and time spent watching TV is tempered by the increasing demands of school and the onset of social activities. TV viewing is tied to a different set of needs and satisfactions than are leisure-time reading, sports, and time with friends (Neuman 1988a). Nevertheless, on average, children spend more time watching TV than they do on homework and recreational reading combined (Gough 1979); and by age 18, they will have spent 50% more time watching television than they will have spent in school (Carnegie Corporation 1977).[2]

In general, correlations between reading achievement and the amount of time spent watching TV have indicated either that the two are not significantly related (Wagner 1980; Searls, Mead & Ward 1985) or that higher viewing time tends to be associated with lower reading achievement (P. Williams, et al. 1982). Although most of the findings have fallen in the latter category, the relationship is not straightforward and its magnitude and direction are influenced by variables such as the amount of daily TV viewing, the viewer's IQ and SES, and the types of programs watched. In any case, a cause-effect relationship has not been established (NIMH 1982). TV viewing, in and of itself, seems unlikely to lower reading achievement. Poor readers may simply choose to watch more TV than good readers do. But heavy watchers (6 hours or more daily) cannot have much time for reading, homework, or with their families and friends (NAEP 1985b). Children appear to internalize the media-related behaviors and attitudes of their parents (Neuman 1986).

When students are grouped according to their hours of TV-viewing time, opinions differ slightly as to when TV viewing becomes "harmful." According to P. Williams et al. (1982), moderate viewers (usually defined as those who watch 1 to 2 hours daily) tend to have higher achievement than do light or heavy viewers. For 9-year-olds the relationship is positive up to 5 hours daily (NAEP 1985b). Beyond 10 hours per week (an average of 2 hours per school day), achievement tends to decrease as viewing time increases. Neuman (1988a) reports that children who watched TV from 2 to 4 hours daily did not differ greatly in their reading scores; but that beyond 4 hours, the relationship became increasingly negative. Beentjes and Van der Voort (1988) conclude that the relationship became strongly negative after 3 hours of daily viewing.

[2]There is little reason to believe that these estimates have changed greatly in the past decade or so.

For high-IQ students, heavy TV watching is usually related to low reading achievement; but the relationship is not significant for those in the average and low-average IQ ranges (Beentjes and Van der Voort 1988). Low-IQ children who watch more television seem to have wider reading preferences (NIMH 1982). For high-SES children, reading achievement tends to decrease as TV-viewing time increases; for low-SES pupils, reading achievement increases as TV viewing increases. There is little evidence of age or gender effects (Beentjes & Van der Voort 1988).

The effects of TV viewing may vary with the types of programs watched and the skill level of the viewers. There is, for example, some evidence that shows like "Sesame Street" and "The Electric Company" have had a positive effect on the acquisition of basic reading skills. Listening to spoken English may help non- or limited-English speakers to acquire the language (Zuckerman, Singer & Singer 1980). There is a negative relationship between watching entertainment programs and reading achievement, but a positive relation for watching the news (Beentjes & Van der Voort 1988). Television can expose viewers to experiences they might not otherwise have, and thus contribute to concept development and attitudes.

After the telecast of some shows, the borrowing and sales of books related to the programs increases (Shoup 1984, Dougan 1988); but interests whetted by television simply redirect reading choices because there is not an accompanying significant increase in recreational reading (Hornick 1981). And although TV viewing may alter some reading choices, there is no clear evidence that it has either stimulated or hindered an interest in reading as a leisure-time activity (Wagner 1980). Whether or not watching television influences reading tastes is an open question (Feeley 1974).

The effects of TV on reading performance may be more subtle than the simple displacement of one activity for another. Television habituates the mind to "short takes" rather than to the continuity of thought required by reading. (Purves 1984).

The attraction of television is beautifully expressed by one youngster: "It gives you stories like a book, pictures like movies, voices like radio, and adventure like a comic. Television has action while you stay in one spot" (Shayon 1951, p. 29). As Witty (1966) and Shayon (1951) both point out, television is filling otherwise unmet needs. Regulating the amount of time spent watching TV is highly desirable but does not solve the problem completely. A comprehensive approach would require working with parents to develop more active and creative forms of recreation in the home, helping children develop and apply criteria for evaluating and selecting TV programs, and using television for motivating and enriching reading. Suggestions for using TV viewing to stimulate reading interests may be found in Becker (1973) and Solomon (1976), and a curriculum guide for developing TV viewing skills appears in Ploghoft and Sheldon (1983). Instructional television programs, which dramatize exciting excerpts from stories and introduce authors to children, are available for motivating children to read (Gough 1979).

Before the advent of television, the failure of many children to read at home was blamed on radio, the movies, and comic books. But these activities have often been replaced by TV watching (Hornick 1981, NIMH 1982), which is now blamed. The fact is that children who do not like to read will find other things to do with their spare time. Children who find reading easy, interesting, and pleasurable and to whom appropriate reading materials are made available, will find time for reading no matter what the competing attractions.

Witty (1966) inquired about movies, radio, and voluntary reading. The majority of children went to the movies biweekly; about one-third went every week. Radio listening (mainly popular music) averaged about 7 hours a week in elementary school and 12 to 14 hours a week in high school. Children in the 1960s were doing a little more voluntary reading than in the 1930s, even though the hours per day for reading were only one-third the time spent watching television. Comparable data are not available for the 1970s or 1980s, except from parts of two studies. In one study (Telfer & Kann 1984), eleventh graders reported spending more time watching television than listening to the radio. In another (R. C. Anderson, Wilson & Fielding 1988), fifth graders spent about a half hour daily listening to music—less than 25% of the time they watched TV. Perhaps with the advent of MTV (Music Television) teens are turning more to television than to radio to fill their "popular music need."

For the most part, average and superior readers who use one or more other media widely, tend to spend more time reading. Inadequate readers have less interest in reading than in nonprint media (H. M. Robinson & Weintraub 1973).

Magazines and the Comics

As TV viewing has increased, time spent reading the comics and pulp magazines seems to have decreased permanently. Over the long run, the reading of better magazines and newspapers seems to have held their own as leisure-time activities (Hornick 1981).

Many teachers are concerned over the great interest shown by children in comic books and comic strips. Comic book popularity increases through the elementary school years and peaks at about age 12–14. Although many high school and college students read comics, the major consumers are in the 9- to 13-year-old bracket (Dechant & Smith 1977). About 39% of third graders reported reading comic books (Applebee, Langer & Mullis 1988), but the fifth graders in another study (R. C. Anderson, Wilson & Fielding 1988) reported spending only an average of two minutes daily reading comics. Comics are read as frequently by good readers as by poor readers (Swain 1978), and there is no evidence that reading comic books, in and of itself, has a negative impact on reading achievement (Hornick 1981). Irish children who read the comics had relatively good reading achievement, while those with low reading ability devoted little time to reading the comics or books (Greaney 1980).

Preventing children from reading comics may well be impossible. Instead, we should attempt to help them discriminate between the better and poorer types, and to use their comic-book reading as a springboard toward reading stories and books that will satisfy the same interests and needs. Freedom to criticize and compare comic books during a book club meeting provides a basis for developing a group opinion that almost inevitably will frown on the worst specimens. In the upper grades, a skillful teacher can lead the more voracious readers of comics into reading books of the *Tom Swift* and *Tarzan* varieties and later to

Jules Verne, H. Rider Haggard, and H. G. Wells. Comics can be used to initiate an interest in reading.

Comics can be used to teach reading skills such as left-to-right progression, use of picture clues, and distinguishing reality from fantasy. Kossack and Hoffman (1987) offer suggestions for using comics to develop comprehension skills. The readability of comic books ranges between 1.8 to 6.4, according to the Fry formula (G. Wright 1979).

Availability of Reading Materials

Availability of reading matter probably has a strong influence on children's attitudes toward reading and on their reading choices. Numerous studies have shown a significant relationship between children's reading habits and the amount and kinds of reading materials available in their homes. Children's use of a public library is directly related to its distance from their homes and schools, and interest in reading is highest when there are both school and classroom libraries (Schulte 1969). Books are usually available to schools that lack their own library facilities. Mobile libraries provide library services to rural schools, and urban teachers can borrow, and periodically change, large assortments of books from the local public libraries.

Another aspect of availability may have influenced the findings of reading-interest studies. In most studies, the choices from which children had to make their preferences were limited. If more or other options had been available, different results may have been obtained. If book titles were used as choices, pupils might have picked those with which they were familiar as a result of having heard or seen them. Also, titles are not always revealing of the text content.

Effect of Interest on Reading Comprehension

The basis for expecting interest to have an effect on reading comprehension is that interest influences attention to the task and effort, which, in turn, influences comprehension. It also is likely that interest in a topic is accompanied by topical knowledge, which could facilitate comprehension. But findings regarding the influence of interest on reading comprehension are inconclusive.

Three studies (Brooks 1972; Schultz 1975; Bleakley, Westerberg & Hopkins 1988) did not find a significant relationship between topic interest and text comprehension. Scott's (1986) study produced mixed results. Although use of interest-evoking strategies made expository text more interesting to fourth and sixth graders and facilitated their recall of some textual information, it did not improve their recall of important content (Hidi & Baird 1988).

Three studies reported by Asher (1980) and the NAEP (1982b) study found that topic interest was related to reading comprehension. Both good and poor readers performed significantly better on high-interest than on low-interest materials. Schnayer (1967) and Belloni and Jongsma (1978) report that students who are interested in the material could satisfactorily comprehend material which ordinarily would be considered to be above their instructional levels. There are a number of reasons for such findings, not the least of which is that interest and topical knowledge are not clearly separable. Dull material is difficult to attend to no matter how great the topic interest; and, if it also is poorly written, it is even more difficult to understand. On the other hand, it is unlikely that material that a reader has difficulty comprehending would be judged to be interesting. Interest *may* affect comprehension, or vice versa. Interest alone, however, may not be sufficient to overcome word-recognition problems or the conceptual or syntactic complexities of a selection.

Findings regarding the relative influence of interest on good versus poor readers are inconclusive. Schnayer (1967) and Vaughn (1975) found that interest had a more positive effect on the reading comprehension of poor than of good readers. Another study (Stevens 1979) reveals just the opposite, and Asher (1980) concludes that interest did not help one group more than the other. Girls perform better then boys on low-interest material, but there are no gender differences on high-interest material. Both black pupils and white pupils comprehend more of high-interest than low-interest material, but interest does not differentially affect the reading comprehension of these racial groups (Asher 1980).

ATTITUDES TOWARD READING

Pupils' attitudes toward reading can be an important factor in their voluntary reading and reading achievement. Studies have shown that preschoolers have positive attitudes toward reading, but that negative attitudes toward reading develop in the primary grades (Shapiro 1979). A number of opinions have been offered to account for such changes, but there is little hard evidence. The change in attitude may be partly due to the fact that primary-grade teachers spend little class time attempting to develop positive attitudes toward reading (Heathington & Alexander 1984).

Attitudes toward reading are influenced by children's self-concepts, levels of reading ability, and interests, as well as by the attitudes and behaviors of their parents, peers, and teachers. Students' gender, intelligence, and socioeconomic status are less likely to impact on these attitudes (Alexander & Filler 1976, Athey 1985b).

It is difficult to separate self-concept from reading ability. Good readers are likely to have high self-concepts; poor readers, poor self-concepts (see pages 365–369).

Studies generally show that good readers have a more positive attitude than poor readers toward reading, but the correlations are modest, ranging from 0.20 to 0.40 (Wigfield & Asher 1984). Not all good readers have a positive attitude toward reading, nor do all poor readers have a negative attitude toward reading.

As for interest, pupils are likely to have a favorable attitude toward tasks they find interesting and to avoid those that are dull, uninteresting, or difficult. It is also difficult to separate reading ability from interest. Good readers are apt to be more interested in reading because they find it an easy, enjoyable task. Poor readers are not prone to choose reading as a leisure-time activity. For example, 40% of the poor readers studied by Juel (1988) said they would rather clean their rooms than read. Poor readers report spending less time than good readers reading independently in and out of school (Applebee, Langer & Mullis 1988).

But if provided with material they find interesting, unmotivated readers may develop an interest in, and a favorable attitude toward, reading.

Attitudes in general are influenced by those around us. Parents who enjoy reading or who place a premium on reading ability pass these attitudes on to their children. If the peer group rejects reading, children must display a negative attitude toward reading if they desire to remain in group favor. Gender-role attitudes are a result of culture. If, for example, reading is looked on as a feminine activity, males in certain cultures are likely to reject reading as an appropriate activity for them.

Teachers who provide appropriate instruction and who display their love of reading usually develop in children favorable attitudes toward reading. Teachers who consistently require pupils to do tasks that are too difficult for them, or who give them difficult or dull books, or who do not provide opportunities for recreational reading may even foster negative attitudes toward reading. Children or adults are not likely to choose reading as a free-time activity if they associate reading with failure and perceive it as an unrewarding activity.

Attempts to improve attitudes toward reading can be, but are not always, successful; nor do improved attitudes necessarily result in increased reading achievement (Alexander & Filler 1976). In what appears to be the only study of its kind, (Manning and Manning 1984) compared four models of recreational reading in terms of their impact on attitudes toward reading. They found that the peer-interaction and teacher-pupil conference groups scored significantly higher on their reading attitude scale than did the sustained-silent-reading and control groups. Perhaps verbal interaction helps develop a more favorable attitude toward reading. The peer-interaction group also scored significantly higher than the other three groups on a measure of reading achievement.

Attitudes are personal and unpredictable, but if reading fulfills a need, positive attitudes toward reading usually develop.

METHODS OF DETERMINING READING INTERESTS AND ATTITUDES TOWARD READING

Interests

Many techniques have been used to determine reading interests: compiling circulation data for newspapers and magazines; assessing the popularity of particular books by counting withdrawals from libraries; and analyzing extensive questionnaires. But most of these methods are too complicated and time consuming for the classroom teacher.

The simplest and most effective way to determine children's reading interests is simply to watch their daily behavior and listen to their conversations. Children who are encouraged to be spontaneous display their preferences in many ways: through conversation, art, play, and other activities that encourage self-expression. Lillian's absorption in aviation shows in her drawings and in the many airplane models she builds; Donald's devoted care of the class rabbits suggests a potential interest in animal stories. Alert teachers may find many leads about reading interests by observing their pupils.

Establishing a hobby club or a period during which children talk about their spare-time activities not only informs the teacher about the leisure activities the students enjoy but can help popularize certain interests. An enthusiastic report about stamp collecting or a home aquarium may start several other children on the same activity. Groups with similar hobbies can be established and reading material supplied for each group.

Teachers can arrange quiet interviews with each child, in which students are encouraged to talk about their likes and dislikes, what they want to be when they grow up, their concerns and problems, and so on. Children will confide in a teacher they like and trust. A mimeographed record form provides a convenient written record and helps the teacher keep interviews more or less uniform in terms of the questions asked.

Pupils can also be asked to complete a checklist like the one developed by Eberwein (1973) for junior high school students (see Figure 18.1). Students are asked to read a list of book titles and check those that sound interesting, or that they think they would like to read. A simple interest questionnaire appears in A. J. Harris and Sipay (1979, p. 406), and Heathington (1979) developed an interest checklist for the middle school. The *Dulin-Chester Reading Interests Questionnaire* (Dulin 1979) is designed for elementary schools; and Heathington and Koskinen (1982) developed an inventory for adult literacy programs, which assesses topics about which students would like to read, preferred format (e.g., comics, newspapers, etc.), and the functional materials needed to read in their everyday lives. Such information can be helpful in planning a reading program and increasing its chances for success.

If a questionnaire study by Mangieri and Corboy (1981) is indicative of what exists nationally, teachers know very little about children's literature (only 9% of 571 respondents could name three children's books written in the past 5 years) or how to promote recreational reading (only 11% could name three or more such activities). There is also evidence that teachers lack knowledge of their pupils' interests (Byers & Evans 1980). Given these two probabilities, it is unlikely that teachers often match children's interests with reading material.

Attitudes

An *attitude* is a disposition to respond in a favorable or unfavorable manner. It is a mental construct that cannot be measured directly but must be inferred. There are three general methods for determining attitudes. *Observations* are the most useful because they can be used easily over time, but their reliability and validity are highly dependent on the skill of the observer. *Self-reports* can be useful if the scale or questionnaire is reliable and valid. However, pupils tend to respond in ways they believe will place them in a favorable light rather than express how they really feel. *Projective techniques* (e.g., sentence-completion items) are less likely to evoke socially desirable, but unreliable, responses. However, care must be exercised in interpreting the meanings of the responses. Use of all three procedures constitutes the best overall procedure (Teale 1980).

The *Incomplete Sentence Projective Test*, reproduced in Figure 18.2, can be used over a wide range of ages. If used as a group test, the children write the answers. The teacher can read the items to them and help them with spelling if

Reading Interest Inventory

Directions: Below are the titles of some books that you might like to read or use during the next year. If you think you would like to read or use the book, make a $\sqrt{}$ mark on the line in front of the title. If you are fairly sure that you would not like to read or use the book, or if you do not know if you would like to read or use the book, leave the line blank. Please be sure to read all the titles and decide if you would, would not, or do not know if you would like to read or use each book during the next year.

_____ 1. Bionics, The Science of Living Machines 001.5

_____ 2. Reference Books, a Brief Guide for Students 016

_____ 3. Books for the Teen-Age 028.52

_____ 4. How to Use the Library 028.7

_____ 5. The World Book Encyclopedia 031

_____ 6. Readers' Guide to Periodical Literature 051

_____ 7. Museum, The Story of America's Treasure Houses 069

_____ 8. Behind the Headlines, The Story of Newspapers 070

_____ 9. Witches 133.4

_____ 10. How to be a Successful Teen-Ager 155.5

_____ 11. The Tree of Life, Selections from the Literature of the World's Religions 208

_____ 12. The Story of the Dead Sea Scrolls 221.4

_____ 13. Jesus of Israel 232.9

_____ 14. Prayers for Young People 242

_____ 15. Religions in America 280

_____ 16. Heroes, Gods and Monsters of Greek Myths 292

_____ 17. Questions Teen-Agers Ask 301.43

_____ 18. Black Pride, A People's Struggle 301.451

_____ 19. Information Please Almanac 317.3

_____ 20. Petticoat Politics, How American Women Won the Right to Vote 324.73

_____ 27. How to Study Better & Get Higher Marks 371.3

_____ 28. For Good Measure, The Story of Modern Measurement 389

_____ 29. Fashion as a Career 391.069

_____ 30. Manners Made Easy 395

_____ 31. King Arthur and His Knights of the Round Table 398.2

_____ 32. All About Language 400

_____ 33. Egyptian Hieroglyphs for Everyone 411

_____ 34. Webster's Third New International Dictionary of the English Language 423

_____ 35. The New Cassell's German Dictionary 433

_____ 36. Mansion's Shorter French and English Dictionary 443

_____ 37. Cassell's Spanish Dictionary 463

_____ 38. Cassell's New Latin Dictionary 473

_____ 39. The Russian Alphabet Book 491.7

_____ 40. 700 Science Experiments for Everyone 507.2

_____ 41. The Wonderful World of Mathematics 510.9

_____ 42. Exploring Mars 523.4

_____ 43. The Riddle of Time 529

_____ 44. Push and Pull, The Story of Energy 531

_____ 45. Inside the Atom 539.7

_____ 46. The A B C's of Chemistry 540.3

_____ 47. World Beneath the Oceans 551.4

_____ 48. Instant Weather Forecasting 551.59

_____ 54. The Wildlife of South America 591.98

_____ 55. Field Book of Insects of the United States and Canada 595.7

_____ 56. The Birds of America 598

_____ 57. The World of the Opossum 599

_____ 58. The Young Inventors' Guide 608

_____ 59. The Wonderful Story of You, Your Body—Your Mind—Your Feelings 612

_____ 60. Human Growth, The Story of How Life Begins and Goes on 612.6

_____ 61. Drugs, Facts on Their Use and Abuse 613.8

_____ 62. Here is Your Hobby, Amateur Radio 621.3841

_____ 63. Motors and Engines and How They Work 621.4

_____ 64. Your Future as a Pilot 629.13

_____ 65. How to Build Hot Rods and Race Them 629.22

_____ 66. Walk in Space, The Story of Project Gemini 629.45

_____ 67. The Book of Horses 636.1

_____ 68. Young America's Cook Book 641.5

_____ 69. Strictly for Secretaries 651

_____ 70. The Story of Glass 666

_____ 71. Cloth from Fiber to Fabric 677

_____ 72. Model Making 688

_____ 73. Careers in the Building Trades 690.69

_____ 74. The World of Art 709

_____ 75. Old Cities and New Towns, The Changing Face of the Nation 711

Figure 18.1. Part of a *Reading Interest Inventory* for use in junior high school. From Lowell Eberwein, What do book choices indicate? *Journal of Reading*, December 1973, *17*, 186–191. Reproduced by permission of the author and the International Reading Association. Approximately two thirds of the items are shown.

1. Today I feel _____
2. When I have to read, I _____
3. I get angry when _____
4. To be grown up _____
5. My idea of a good time is _____
6. I wish my parents knew _____
7. School is _____
8. I can't understand why _____
9. I feel bad when _____
10. I wish teachers _____
11. I wish my mother _____
12. Going to college _____
13. To me, books _____
14. People think I _____
15. I like to read about _____
16. On weekends I _____
17. I'd rather read than _____
18. To me, homework _____
19. I hope I'll never _____
20. I wish people wouldn't _____
21. When I finish high school _____
22. I'm afraid _____
23. Comic books _____
24. When I take my report card home _____
25. I am at my best when _____
26. Most brothers and sisters _____
27. I don't know how _____
28. When I read math _____
29. I feel proud when _____
30. The future looks _____
31. I wish my father _____
32. I like to read when _____
33. I would like to be _____
34. For me, studying _____
35. I often worry about _____
36. I wish I could _____
37. Reading science _____
38. I look forward to _____
39. I wish _____
40. I'd read more if _____
41. When I read out loud _____
42. My only regret _____

Figure 18.2. Incomplete sentence projective technique. From Thomas Boning and Richard Boning, I'd rather read than . . . , *The Reading Teacher*, 1957, *10*, 197. Reproduced by permission. The items are adapted from an earlier version by Ruth Strang.

necessary. Used individually, it can be read to poor or disabled readers, and the responses recorded by the teacher. Children's responses can reveal their true feelings about reading. The question "I'd read more if _____" has brought such answers as, "I liked to read," "books weren't so hard," "I could read better," "I had time." In answer to "I'd rather read than _____," a child wrote, "I wrath get bet by a snake." Positive ideas and feelings are expressed just as freely. A device like this can help a trusted, knowledgeable teacher greatly in the effort to understand students' attitudes toward reading.

Among the available self-reports is the *Wisconsin Reading Attitude Inventory* (Dulin 1979), which was designed for use in the elementary school. The *Estes Attitude Scales* (Estes 1981), which was part of the *Wisconsin Inventory*, has separate forms for use in the elementary and secondary schools. Lewis and Teale (1980) contend that secondary school students' attitudes toward reading are multidimensional and suggest that the reason for much of the conflicting research data is that the studies treated "attitude" as unidimensional. Thus, the *Teale-Lewis Attitude Scale* measures three dimensions: the value placed on gaining insight into oneself or others; the value placed on the role of reading for attaining educational success; and reading for pleasure. In a series of studies, Wallbrown and his associates (e.g., Wallbrown & Wisneski 1982) gathered normative and reliability data for the eight-dimensional *Survey of Reading Attitudes*. It is meant for use with intermediate-grade pupils. Another attitude scale was developed by Summers and Lukasevich (1983).

Many measures of attitude toward reading are available and have been described by Alexander and Filler (1976).

CREATING AN INTEREST IN READING AND ENRICHING READING INTERESTS

One of the most important goals of a reading program is to develop and maintain an interest in reading as a leisure-time activity. Progress in reading ability is likely to remain slow if the only reading a child does is in his textbooks. The most carefully planned reading lessons may bring disappointing results unless the teacher ignites a spark of interest in reading and then nurtures it carefully into a clear flame of enthusiasm for reading. Spectacular gains in reading ability can result when children voluntarily read a book or two a week.

Children's willingness to read during their spare time is primarily based on factors such as their age, attitude toward reading, level of reading ability, the satisfaction gained from earlier leisure reading, the attractiveness of alternate pursuits, interests, and friendships (Greaney 1986). Teachers have an important influence on how much reading children do out of school. Their attempts to increase the number of books read on a voluntary basis often have the desired effects, but studies to date have not been completely convincing about such efforts (R. C. Anderson, Wilson & Fielding 1988). A literature program resulted in significantly greater use of a classroom library center by second graders, but had no effect on attitudes toward reading or reading habits at home (Morrow & Weinstein 1986).

Teachers can help to develop a positive attitude toward reading, and thus an interest in it, by creating lessons and situations that consider the student's personal needs, aspirations, and attitudes. Motivation to read occurs when the teacher focuses on students' areas of greatest interest, matches the material to their levels of reading ability, displays a high regard for reading, and makes the students aware of their success (Betts 1976).

A classroom environment that nurtures an interest in reading is one in which (1) the teacher is enthusiastic about books; (2) the classroom is full of well-selected books to which the children have easy access; (3) the children have time to browse, choose, and read; (4) children get personal introductions to special selections; (5) books are the subject of much comment and discussion; and (6) appreciation for reading is developed through cumulative experiences (Hickman 1983).

Creating an Interest in Reading

The basic principles that underlie the successful development of an interest in reading have been admirably summarized as consisting of a "lure and a ladder." The *lure* may be any of a variety of ways of enticing children to begin pleasurable reading. The *ladder* involves providing suitable reading matter that will intensify the children's interest in reading and in which they can progress gradually to reading material of superior quality.

Classroom libraries have a positive influence on children's reading habits (Wilson, Anderson & Fielding 1986). The first essential is to provide physical surroundings in the classroom that will create an atmosphere favorable to reading. There should be a "reading corner" in every classroom. Its furnishings do not have to be elaborate. A table or two, a few chairs, a rug on which to sit or lie, and bookshelves are the essentials. Interest can be stimulated if, at the beginning of the term, the children build or paint the bookcases, make and hang curtains, place colorful jackets on the books, and so on.

A class library should contain at least 50 books. They should range in difficulty from easy and interesting enough for the poorest readers in the class to others that will appeal to the most advanced readers. There should be special collections of books of varied difficulty relating to the activity units that are currently engaging the attention of the class. In addition, there should be fairy tales and legends, animal stories, adventures, stories with foreign settings, humor and nonsense, nature study and science, and some poetry. Current and back issues of good children's magazines should find a place also. Larrick (1978) critiques the 45 best-selling children's magazines. Refer to *Children's Magazine List* (Educational Press Association of America 1987) for a comprehensive list of publications that appeal to children and young adults ages 2–18, to Katz (1987) for evaluations of about 1,200 periodicals listed alphabetically under 73 subject categories, to Seminoff (1986a) for children's periodicals published throughout the world, and to Olson, Gee, and Forester (1989) for magazines that can be used in content-subject areas. Guides to magazines for children and young adults have been developed by S. Richardson (1983, 1985).

A simple classification scheme makes it easier for children to select books. The books can be arranged under a few simple headings: *Make Believe, Real Life Stories, Animals, People and Places,* and so on. Some teachers use colored tabs, a different color for each reading group in the class, to help the children find books of appropriate difficulty, but they should be allowed to choose any book. The daily class schedule must provide free time for browsing and independent silent reading if the reading corner is to serve its purpose.

A teacher who regularly reads fascinating stories to her class usually has no trouble arousing interest in reading. Pupils of any age love to listen to a lively tale. A good book or story that the teacher has read to the class will find many readers when it is placed in the library collection. Teachers who take the trouble to study the art of telling and reading stories to children reap dividends in improved attention, listening comprehension, and interest in reading (McCormick 1977). Reading to pupils can expose them to *literary-style language* (written language must employ techniques to convey meaning that could be otherwise conveyed in an oral-language situation see Purcell-Gates 1989); allows them to gain control over more vocabulary; and broadens their world knowledge (Dickinson 1987). It also can provide a model of good oral reading.

Frequent exposure to story reading has a positive effect on some aspects of literacy acquistion (e.g., see Chapman 1986), but being read to, in and of itself, does not necessarily enhance literacy development. Certain methods, environmental influences, attitudes, and interactions between adult and child may (Morrow 1988b). Refer to Green and Harker (1982) and Roser and Wilson (1986) for suggestions on what to read to children. Trelease (1985) not only provides excellent ideas for reading to children but a detailed guide to over 300 read-aloud books. Hough, Nurss, and Enright (1986) suggest ways to read to children who have limited-English-speaking ability so as to help them acquire English proficiency. Teachers who wish to become good storytellers will profit from referring to Nessel (1985), Baker and Greene (1987), and Aiex (1988). Recorded and taped stories can also be used, with the child or group either listening or following in the book while listening. Many commercially prepared taped books are paced too quickly for poor readers. Carbo (1981) relates how story books can be recorded for use with such children.

Book-talks also can interest children in reading voluntarily. The teacher or librarian attempts to make reading seem desirable and worthwhile by communicating enthusiasm and providing some honest, low-keyed guidance to well-written books. Following a 20-to 30-minute book-talk in which four to eight books are presented, the children are invited to take a book that interests them. Witucke (1979) and Bodart-Talbot (1988) offer sample book-talks and techniques for conducting them. Refer to Spirt (1988) for suggestions on introducing book plots.

Audience reading can be used to good effect to foster independent reading. The nature of audience reading has been described on page 102. The desire to find and prepare a suitable selection to read to the class is a powerful incentive for many children and creates a natural motive for reading with an evaluative attitude. Through the short selections presented in an audience-reading period, the listeners are exposed to samples from many different sources and may have their interests awakened in books and stories that they might otherwise have overlooked.

Many teachers have made excellent use of a book club. Membership is open to the entire class with the usual requirements being possession of a library card and being ready to report on one book. The club elects officers, ordinarily a president and a secretary, and sometimes a treasurer. At each weekly meeting, a few members are given the privilege of reporting on books they have read, telling whether or not they recommend the book, and if they wish to, reading to the club some especially delightful portion. Greatly increased liking for book reading and marked improvement in critical ability and taste are the normal results of a well-run club.

Some book clubs decide to have dues, which are used by a purchasing committee to buy materials for the class library collection. The judgment shown by a pupil committee in selecting materials is often amazingly good, and the experience the children gain in visiting bookstores and inspecting books for possible purchase is invaluable. The handling of the funds also provides a real situation for the use of functional arithmetic. At the end of the year, the purchases can be distributed to the members of the club or left behind for the next class.

A *reading conference,* which is often student-directed, involves a pupil presenting a book she has read, followed by peer responses and discussion. It not only offers children a way to share what they have read, but fosters language development, and critical thinking skills as well (Strickland et al. 1989).

The use of paperbacks in the schools has been increasing steadily. These relatively inexpensive books have been employed successfully to stimulate interest in a variety of classrooms (J. Davis 1970) and even in a reform school (Fader 1977). *Reading is Fundamental* (RIF), a voluntary national program, has distributed millions of free paperbacks. Matching funds for purchasing books for a school reading-motivation program are available through a program administered by RIF. Federal funds for paperback libraries are available under the National Reading Improvement Program and Title IV-B (School Libraries and Instructional Resources) of the Elementary and Secondary Education Act.

The key elements of a good reading-motivation program in which free books are given to children are these: (1) Children are allowed to make their own selections; (2) there are related motivational activities before and after the books are distributed; (3) parents are involved in the program; (4) there is a special book-selection committee; (5) there is a wide variety of books; and (6) more than one book is provided for each child (Zuckerman 1977).

Most trade-book publishers produce paperbacks, some of which are aimed at the reluctant or disabled reader. Helpful references include *The Elementary School Paperback Collection* (Gillespie 1985a), which lists nearly 4,000 paperbacks, arranged by subject area, for use with preschoolers through sixth graders, and Ammons and Larrick (1987), who list 70 favorite paperbacks of children under age 13. Kies (1987) lists 500 supernatural-fiction paperback titles, which are suitable for teenagers; and Gillespie (1985b; 1986) developed paperback collections for use in junior high and high schools. There are numerous creative ways to use paperbacks in the primary grades (see Dutt 1980) and middles grades (see Hellriegel 1980).

Intermediate-grade pupils indicated that allowing them flexibility and independence, in determining what they could read, best motivated them to read more. They were also motivated by having the teacher tell them something about books or reading from the book to them when it was introduced. Postreading motivators included reading more about the topic or theme and hearing about or from the authors. These children disliked being tested on a book's content and having to write book reports (Wiesendanger & Bader 1989).

Among the other ways for stimulating interest in books and voluntary reading suggested by Roeder and Lee (1973) are: (1) Have the students "advertise and sell" books, each trying to prove that the book they read is the best; (2) display colorful posters to advertise a specific monthly topic; (3) have a read-in in which children select partners and time is set aside for them to read to each other; and (4) read to the students, stopping at an exciting point, then provide several copies of the book for them to read. Numerous other suggestions have been made by Criscuolo (1982), Mason and Mize (1978), Ciani (1981), Spiegel (1981a) Morrow (1987), and Aaron (1987). Even book reports need not be deadly dull. Many imaginative ideas for using them to stimulate student involvement in reading have been offered (Nichols 1978, Fisher 1979, L. Robbins 1981). Many of these suggestions have been summarized by A. J. Harris and Sipay (1979, pp. 420–430). Yet another way of interesting some students in reading books is to allow use of kits such as the *Pilot Library Series* (SRA) that contain short excerpts from books and then provide the books in which students express an interest.

With a little planning and effort, the summer can be an ideal time for recreational reading. Aasen (1959) planned a real sales campaign. She promoted the idea of summer reading by having the librarian speak to the children about books and use of the library, providing a recommended list of books, arranging for Bookmobile service, a setting up a system for students to record their reading.

Ideas for promoting voluntary reading in the junior and senior high school appear in Alvermann (1987a), Matthews (1987), and Meyers (1989). Bishop (1981) describes a motivational technique that uses paperbacks related to the topics under consideration in the content areas, and Lunstrum (1981) describes how to use controversy to encourage secondary school students to read. Stahl, Henk, and King (1984) list three readability scores for drivers' manuals throughout the United States.

Reluctant Readers

There are at least three types of students who do little voluntary reading. First are the *reluctant readers* who have the necessary reading ability, but who simply opt not to read very often during their spare time. They do not dislike reading, but simply find other activities more appealing. The above-described procedures usually work in getting many of them to read more on their own volition.

There also are *reluctant readers* who have a confirmed dislike of reading. The majority of this type of reluctant reader are children who are or were poor or disabled readers and who found reading a difficult unenjoyable task to be avoided whenever possible. Their dislike for reading often was reinforced by being asked to read material that was far above their level of reading ability. In addition to helping them to develop their reading skills, they also need assistance in improving their self-concepts as well as a warm, accepting atmosphere in which they can learn that reading can be a pleasurable activity.

The other subtype of reluctant readers includes those who for one reason or another dislike reading even though they have at least average reading ability. Their negative attitude toward reading may have been caused by such events as having been derided by a teacher who was trying to force them to read required literature, or by overanxious parents who continually harped on them to "read more." Their families or peers may have a disdain for reading, which they acquired. The sources of their negative attitudes should be determined if possible, so that efforts can be made at least to lessen them. Individual discussion with the child may reveal the source of the problem and help to overcome the negative attitude. These reluctant readers also need understanding and an accepting teacher.

The first step in introducing a reluctant reader to pleasurable, voluntary reading is to locate an easy and brief book that will attract and hold his interest. Content should be chosen in relation to what is known about the child's interests, but humorous books usually make an excellent start. Few children can resist *The Cat in the Hat,* Bennett Cerf's *Book of Riddles,* the Curious George books, or *Mr. Popper's Penguins.* After a first taste, children are likely to want several more books of the same type before venturing into different content. Gentile and McMillan (1978) list the types of humor that appeal to children at various age levels; Moe and Hopkins (1978) compiled an annotated list of 150 short, light, humorous materials (joke books, riddles, puns); and Wendelin (1980) lists 50 humorous books and concludes that taste in humor is highly individual. Bennett and Bennett (1982) found that humorous books appeal to intermediate-grade pupils, but that most of the humorous books recommended for this age group are too complex and subtle for fourth graders.

In introducing a new book, show the cover and a few illustrations, and read enough aloud to arouse the desire for more. Then ask the child or children if she or they would like to read five or ten more pages before the next meeting. If a child reads more than the suggested amount in the agreed-on time, the procedure has been successful. From this point on, the problem is primarily one of keeping the child supplied with suitable books.

Older children are sometimes reluctant to take "baby" books home for fear that other children will make fun of them. Supplying a large manila carrying envelope minimizes this difficulty.

After the pupils have made a good start in voluntary reading, introduce them to the school or public library. If possible, the teacher or an aide should accompany them on their first visit, help them through the formalities of getting a library card, and show them where to look for books and how to borrow them. They may need the assistance of a specific list of four or five books at first; otherwise, the long rows of books may be bewildering. If the first few attempts at selecting their books on their own turn out poorly, they may become discouraged.

Until the habit of voluntary reading is well established, teachers should make recommendations for reading based on the child's interests or preferences. Even though their interests may be narrow, they should be respected insofar as possible.

A librarian can be of invaluable help to both teacher and child in suggesting suitable books. A teacher of reading, however, should regard a continually enlarging knowledge of children's books as an essential part of her own profes-

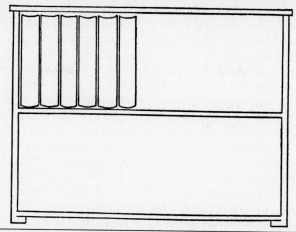

Figure 18.3.   A bookcase chart for recording independent reading. As the child finishes a book he draws another book in his bookcase. If the bookcase is made about 6 × 9 inches, the books will be large enough to allow printing the author and title on each, and the date completed. Coloring the books in crayon adds to the attractiveness of the chart.

sional development. Aids for locating reading matter of various kinds are discussed in the last part of this chapter.

Although primary motivation to read voluntarily comes from enjoyment of the reading itself, individual progress charts may help. An individual progress chart that appeals to all ages consists of a bookcase, with books filled in as they are completed. (See Figure 18.3.) Titles may be placed on the spines and coloring the books adds to the chart's attractiveness. Wiesendanger and Bader (1989) cautions against using competition and public displays of the amount of reading done. These practices do little to motivate good readers and have a negative impact on poor readers.

Expanding and Improving Reading Interests

Although it is vitally important to help children find reading matter closely related to their present interests, and although pupils' interests may change over time, teachers should also try to broaden children's reading horizons.

Ingenious teachers can find many ways of awakening curiosity about new areas of interest. Putnam (1941) found that her pupils were reading nothing but fiction. To stimulate interest in nonfiction, she asked them to write on slips of paper the topics or questions about which they would like to find information. A card index of topics was set up, with book references listed for each topic. A marked increase in the reading of informational material was the result.

Near the beginning of the term, another teacher gave her class a little talk on "Your Reading Diet." She started by reviewing the need of a proper diet of food for proper physical nutrition and growth. Then she drew an analogy to reading. "What would happen if you ate nothing but desserts and candy?" After some discussion, the class, who found the idea novel and stimulating, drew up a plan for a balanced eight-course reading meal: fruit cup—poetry; soup—current events; fish course ("brain food")—science and nature study; meat—biography and history; vegetable—special practice exercises in reading; dessert—fiction; milk—sports and hobbies; after-dinner mints—comics. Each child drew up a menu and filled in the titles of his or her reading as the term progressed. The children could take as many helpings as they wished of the courses they liked best, provided that they "ate at least one dish of every kind."

An intelligent interest in current events should be one of the outcomes of education. Interest in news events can be encouraged through the regular reading and discussion of one of the newspapers published for use in the school, such as *Scholastic News* (Scholastic). These newspapers make it possible to introduce reading about current events as early as the first grade and continue it with reading matter of appropriate difficulty through the elementary school because different editions are published for each grade level. Refer to the following for ideas on using newspapers: for teaching reading skills (Cheyney 1984); in social studies classes (Wells et al. 1987); and as effective teaching tools (Aiex 1988).

At the upper-grade levels, some of the social studies period can be devoted to current events. Each child could be expected to present a brief oral report about some recent, interesting development in the news. This combines motivated independent reading in newspapers and news magazines, practice in organizing a summary, and effective oral language development. Such assignments may also require students to compare and evaluate critically the coverage of a topic as presented in various sources.

Poetry has been somewhat neglected in reading programs in recent years. There are many ways in which teachers can awaken and develop an appreciation of poetry. One of the most important is the reading of well-chosen poems to the class by the teacher. A teacher who loves poetry and can read it well can make poems come alive for children (Jacobs 1959). A second useful procedure is choral reading and speaking. Poems that the children enjoy can be prepared for group presentation. Choral reading is ideally suited to the development of an appreciation of poetry. At a simple level, the whole class can read the poem in unison. As the children become more expert, delightful effects can be achieved through a balancing of solo parts and choral effects. A third way in which interest in poetry can be developed is through encouraging children to prepare poems for presentation in audience reading periods. Refer to Blackburn and Blackburn (1989) for an annotated index to poetry for children and young adults, and to Hopkins (1987) and Larrick (1987) for ideas on teaching poetry. Shapiro (1985) sets forth criteria for judging good poetry teaching.

Use of Literature in the Content Subjects

Not only can reading accurate historical fiction make history "come alive" for students, but it can develop concepts that help them to understand their textbooks better (see Cianciolo 1981). Brozo and Tomlinson (1986) offer procedures for selecting and using trade books in content areas. The American Library Association publishes a series of annotated bibliographies that focuses on the history and character of different geographic areas in the United States, and the Children's Book Council has published *Notable Children's Trade Books in the Field of Social Studies*. Among other useful resources for history classes are Van Meter (1989) and Howard (1988). Guidelines for the selection and use of fictionalized biographies are provided by Storey (1982). When students are asked to read narratives from which they are to obtain factual information, teachers should make explicit the purpose for which the text is being read, lest it be considered "just a story" by the pupils (Gordon & Rennie 1987).

Dole and Johnson (1981) offer a number of suggestions whereby science literature would be read more widely through the cooperative efforts of science teachers, librarians, and the reading teacher. Guerra and Payne (1981) suggest ways in which popular science books and magazines could be used to develop pupil's interest in general science. Smardo (1982) annotates books, with reading levels of third reader and below, that could be used to clarify science concepts for young children. Wilms (1985) annotates science books for children, and Butzow and Butzow (1989) discuss the use of children's literature in science classes.

Radenbaugh (1981) recommends specific books that might be used to develop various math concepts for young children.

Home Environment and Children's Reading

The impact of the home on readiness for reading and the relationship between home conditions and reading disabilities have been discussed earlier in this book. Obviously, the attitudes of parents and older siblings toward books and reading have an impact on young children. Several studies have shown that, in general, the parents of good readers have read to their children and have provided models for them by reading themselves at home (Goldfield & Snow 1984).

Few solid cause-effect relationships have been established between home-environment variables and reading achievement and attitudes. Most of this research has been correlational (Teale 1981), and such links may simply reflect underlying causes such as attitudes toward education and expectations for children (Weber 1985). Longitudinal ethnographic studies may yield more valid information regarding specific causal relationships (Morrow 1985).

Most parents need guidance concerning their role in the development of their children's reading achievement and voluntary reading. Helpful ideas for parents are available in Larrick (1975), Boehnlein and Hager (1985), Reed (1988), and Roser (1989). Ways of involving parents in their children's voluntary reading are offered by Sittig (1982). Burgess (1985) suggests a plan for modifying leisure-time reading habits at home.

AFFECTIVE GROWTH THROUGH READING

As H. M. Robinson and Weintraub (1973) point out, few would disagree that reading may change attitudes and behaviors, since reading offers an opportunity to identify with a character or to solve a problem. Yet, most of this "conventional wisdom" is based on opinion. The few studies conducted in this area neither support nor refute these possible values of reading. Perhaps, attitudes are changed more often through reading followed by discussion that by reading alone. At present, it is difficult to assess attitudinal or behavioral changes because of the complexity of the behaviors themselves and the inadequacies of available instruments to measure such changes.

Bibliotherapy

One of the possible values of reading is therapeutic. *Bibliotherapy* is the attempt to promote mental and emotional health by using reading materials to fulfill needs, relieve pressure, or help an individual in her development as a person. Basically, the process involves three steps: identification, catharsis, and insight. Theoretically, the reader identifies with the story character, thus lessening her sense of isolation; catharsis occurs as the reader vicariously experiences the motivation, conflicts, and emotions of the character. Identification and catharsis lead to insight, through which the reader's tensions are relieved.

Evidence on the value of bibliotherapy is mixed (Tulman 1984), and interpretations of research findings differ. According to Purves and Beach (1972), bibliotherapy can be useful in group psychotherapy, but the results of classroom studies are mixed. On the other hand, Narang (1977) concludes that when properly conducted with any age level, bibliotherapy is likely to produce a positive change in attitudes and self-concept and can lead to improved social and emotional adjustment. Schrank, Engels, and Silke (1983) conclude that the research evidence suggests that: (1) bibliotherapy may, but does not always, change attitudes; (2) bibliotherapy may, but does not always, help to reduce fears; (3) it is impossible to determine its impact on mental health because the findings are so contradictory; and, (4) bibliotherapy has no effect on school achievement. Lenkowsky's (1987) literature review led him to state that there was insufficient evidence regarding the value of bibliotherapy.

There is some evidence that bibliotherapy may have undesired effects. Not only did bibliotherapy *not* reduce fears of second-grade children, but it actually induced them in many of the children who had never thought about such fears before (Newhouse & Loker 1984). The casual use of bibliotherapy can make a bad situation worse.

Those who wish to learn more about bibliotherapy may refer to Clarke & Bostle (1988). Bibliotherapy will not take the place of psychotherapy for those with serious emotional problems. It is probably most effective when combined with discussion and counseling by a knowledgeable, sensitive person.

The techniques used in bibliotherapy may be useful in helping less seriously troubled pupils gain some insights into their problems and perhaps gain some relief. Annotated guides and bibliographies, as well as suggestions for using the material, are available on a variety of themes: children's needs and problems (Dreyer 1977); troubled or broken homes (Haley 1975); life crises such as death and hospitalization (Hormann 1977); health, illness, and disability (Azarnoff 1983); separation and loss (Berstein 1983); divorce (Monteith 1981b); teenage problems (Halpern 1978); everyday problems (Cuddigan & Hanson 1988); the single-parent family (Horner 1978); school adjustment (Jalongo & Renck 1987), and desirable character traits (Stephens 1989).

Improving Attitudes Toward Others

Pupils can benefit from reading about and discussing story characters who differ from them in some way. A better attitude toward others, such as the handicapped (Salend & Moe 1983), can be developed. Techniques for using books to promote sensitivity and empathy have been recommended by Tway (1981). Lass and Bromfield (1981) suggest guidelines for evaluating children's books about the handicapped and provide annotated lists of such books. Other annotated bibliographies on the disabled and suggestions for using the material may be found in Baskin and Harris (1984). Dobo (1982) lists sources of literature on the handicapped. Refer to Horne (1985) for a comprehensive treatment of attitudes toward, and of, the handicapped.

Annotated bibliographies of materials dealing with the aging and the elderly, and suggestions for their use have been provided by Trusty and Link (1980), and Watson (1981). Materials for helping students to understand minorities are indicated on pages 688–690.

Responding to Literature

Because individuals have had different experiences and because they may focus on different aspects of a story, their responses to literature may differ widely *if* the teacher allows open discussion rather than imposes one particular interpretation on the pupils. The ways in which students respond to literature, both verbally and otherwise, have begun to be investigated (e. g., Golden & Guthrie 1986). Studies have revealed that (1) children can respond to what they read but often cannot document the reasons for their responses; (2) pupils focus on the content when they respond to literature; (3) the better one understands the story, the better one is able to comment on it; and (4) different pieces of literature promote different kinds of responses (Galda 1982). Reading stories individually to low-SES 4-year-olds had a positive effect on expanding their responses to the stories (Morrow 1988b).

Reader response theory holds that (1) meaning is derived from interaction between the content and structure of the story and the prior knowledge of the reader; (2) individuals comprehend differently because each is culturally and individually unique; and (3) examining readers' responses to literature is more valid educationally than establishing one correct interpretation of the text (Chase & Hynd 1987). Beach and Wendler (1987) determined that there were developmental differences in reader responses.

In underscoring the contention that only after we understand, analyze, and appreciate students' responses to literature will we be able to expand and extend their ability to respond, Galda (1982) makes three major points:

1. Readers should not be penalized when their responses differ from those expected.
2. Teachers should seek the reasons behind their pupils' responses, and should teach students to do so as well. Knowing what in the text or in the reader (or oneself) evoked a particular response should result in more flexible and knowledgeable readers.
3. Before assessing any response, the teacher must consider his degree of involvement with his pupils and his understanding of them.

Teachers should encourage children to respond to literature and help them evaluate their responses. Alvermann (1987a) presents ways to get children to respond to what they have read; other such suggestions may be found in Nelms (1988). Galda (1982) discusses ways to encourage children to make flexible responses and to document them, as well as how to assess these responses. Those interested in the topic may wish to refer to Hickman (1980, 1981), Cianciolo (1982), Benton (1984), Chase and Hynd (1987), and Flood and Lapp (1988b).

Censorship

Attempts to censor reading materials and textbooks used in schools have increased markedly. E. Jenkinson (1980) describes two of the main censorship efforts in the United States and lists 20 organizations that protested the use of certain books in the schools and the 40 topics they opposed most often.

The National Council of Teachers of English issued a pamphlet, *The Student's Right to Know* (Burres & Jenkinson 1982), which provides a constitutionally based rationale for freedom to read without censorship and suggests a plan of action for dealing with the problem. It stresses the link between freedom to read widely and the breadth of learning needed by students if they are to become informed, thinking citizens. Although recognizing the right and responsibility of parents to monitor their children's education, the International Reading Association (1989) also opposes policies that deny pupils access to certain reading materials.

The Supreme Court ruled, in *Island Trees vs. Pico,* that although a school board has discretion over curricular matters, including the books assigned for classroom reading, it could not remove books from the school library where "voluntary inquiry holds sway." The Court, however, was split evenly on the issue of whether students had the constitutional right to have specific books available for their use in school libraries. The Court further ruled that the constitutionality of the school board's action rested on their motivation for removing the books from the school library and returned the case to a federal court for a thorough examination of the facts. But, before the matter came to trial, the Island Trees school board dropped its ban on the books and instead required parental notification when those books were checked out by students. The Supreme Court ruling did not set a precedent for future cases, but it seems to have offered some protection against the capricious removal of books from a school library. It also suggested the need for written school policies for evaluating and acting on challenges to school materials (Micklos 1983).

Suggestions for dealing with attempts at censorship are offered by Palmer (1982) and Reichman (1988). Basically, they deal with developing written policies that specify guidelines for book and material selection, establish a rationale for their use, specify procedures for dealing with legitimate complaints, and indicate a policy for handling censorship efforts. They also suggest the need to promote community support for freedom to read.

The contention of the would-be censor is that certain themes or content are inconsistent with the values of parents or the community at large and that students will acquire wrong values through reading books containing such unacceptable ideas. Behavioral science data, however, suggest that reading about an idea that runs contrary to one's beliefs is not likely to change those beliefs (Guthrie 1983).

LOCATING READING MATERIALS

There is such a wealth of reading matter for children and young adults that the task of selection is by no means easy. This section acquaints the reader with sources that can be used to locate recommended books and materials to meet all sorts of reading needs. The references are grouped in four categories: for elementary school children, for secondary school, for disabled or reluctant readers, and for special purposes. Hughes (1987) and Pillar (1987) list sources that may be used to locate literature for children and young adults.

Book Lists for Elementary School Children

The following references are useful primarily for selecting books for children who are average or above-average readers, and for locating books to read to children. The age or grade designations they give are usually quite broad, covering 3 or 4 years, and are more likely to underestimate than overestimate the level of reading ability required to read the books independently.

Good literature for 8- to 11-year-olds is not abundant, but Cianciolo (1989) lists over 60 titles and discusses the use of literature with this age group.

- *Adventuring with Books* (Monson 1985). An annotated list of nearly 1,700 books for preschool–Grade 6 with suggested difficulty and interest levels by category. Titles organized by genre, with subcategories, and by particular subject or theme.
- *A Multimedia Approach to Children's Literature* (ALA). Guide to book-related nonprint materials for use in preschool through Grade 6. 1983.
- *Best Books for Children: Preschool through the Middle Grades* (Gillespie & Gilbert 1985). An annotated bibliography of nearly 9,000 books arranged by subject areas and grades levels. Annual supplements.
- *The Best in Children's Books* (Sutherland 1986). Contains about 1,400 titles of outstanding children's books published from 1979–1984.
- *Bibliography of Books for Children* (Suderlin 1983). About 2,000 books arranged by subject; particularly good for preschool and primary levels.
- *Booklist* (ALA). Bimonthly reviews of children's books and nonprint media recommended for purchase. Once a month it includes reviews of easy-reading books keyed to both reading and interest levels.
- *Children's Book Review Index* (Gale). Series of annual volumes that cite the sources of all reviews of children's books (K–5) published that year.
- *Children's Catalog* (H. W. Wilson). A comprehensive listing containing reviews of about 5,700 titles for preschool to sixth-grade children. Revised every 5 years. Published 1986.
- *Children's Literature Review* (Gale). Series of annual volumes that excerpt significant book reviews and commentaries.
- *Classroom Choices* (Children's Book Council). An annual annotated list of books chosen by children. Also appears in *The Reading Teacher,* usually in the October issue. A composite list covering 7 years appears in Roser and Frith (1983).

- *Literature and Young Children* (NCTE) Includes an annotated bibliography of 100 books and suggestions for their use. Published 1977.

Reviews of the most recent books for children can be found in such publications as *Horn Book, Junior Libraries, Language Arts, The Reading Teacher,* the *Bulletin* of the Center for Children's Books (Chicago), and the children's book section of the *New York Times.* Teachers' choices of the best children's books published in 1986 and 1987 may be found in Kloefkorn (1988). The International Reading Association annually publishes "Children's Choices" and "Young Adults' Choices" in their journals. Parents will find E. Lipson (1988) useful in selecting books for their children.

Booklists for Secondary School

The following are representative of book lists for use with or by junior and senior high students.

- *Book Bait* (Walker 1988). A detailed annotation of almost 100 books that have immediate and strong appeal to 13- to 16-year-olds who are average readers in Grades 10–12.
- *Books for Secondary School Libraries* (Bowker). A computerized list of over 4,000 titles, no fiction included. Published 1981.
- *Books for the Teen Ager* (New York Public Library). Approximately 1,250 titles with brief annotations. Published 1988.
- *Books for You: A Booklist for Senior High Students* (Abrahamson & Carter 1988). Nearly 1,200 books published between 1985 and 1987 are described. Titles are divided into 48 wide-ranging categories. Designed primarily for student use.
- *Junior High School Library Catalog* (H. W. Wilson). Contains reviews of 3,200 books for Grades 7–9. Published 1988; annual supplements.
- *Senior High School Library Catalog* (H. W. Wilson). Contains reviews of approximately 5,000 titles. Published 1987; annual supplements.
- *Your Reading: A Booklist for Junior High and Middle School Students* (Davis & Davis 1988). An annotated list of over 2,000 books, most of them published between 1983 and 1987. Titles are classified into 61 wide-ranging categories. Designed for student use.

Refer to Greenlaw and McIntosh (1987) for how to teach science fiction to teenagers.

Book Lists for Disabled and Reluctant Readers

The following references are helpful in selecting materials for disabled and reluctant readers:

- *Good Reading for Poor Readers* (G. Spache 1974, 1978). Discusses principles of choosing books. Contains listings of trade books useful with poor readers; adapted and simplified materials; games; magazines and newspapers; series books; book clubs; and reading lists.

- *High-Interest Books for Teens: A Guide to Book Reviews and Biographical Sources* (Gale). Over 2,000 books identified as high-interest/low-reading-level books. Information provided for each title. Published 1987.
- *High Interest-Easy Reading for Junior and Senior High School Students* Matthews 1988). An annotated list of 300 easy-to-read books for use by reluctant, not disabled, readers, listed by 23 subject categories; broad range of reading levels indicated.
- *High/Low Handbook: Books, Materials and Services for the Teenage Problem Reader* (Bowker). An annotated bibliography of 175 high-interest/low-reading-level titles arranged alphabetically. Each entry includes a plot synopsis, interest level, and reading level. Also annotates 100 other titles for slightly better but reluctant readers. Published 1985.
- *Read-Ability Books for Junior and Senior High Students* (Walch). Briefly annotated list of approximately 2,000 books grouped by reading levels (Grades 1–9); interest levels also indicated (Grades 1–12). Published 1978.

An increasing number of books, including paperbacks, are both easy enough for, and interesting to, disabled readers. A list of "high interest, low-vocabulary-load series" is given in Appendix B. Other such materials have been annotated by Ryder, Graves, and Graves (1989); LiBretto (1985); Pilla (1989); and Carter and Abrahamson (1986), who also critique "high/lo" books for the young adults.

Many simplified and shortened versions of famous books frequently used at the secondary school level are also available. Appendix B lists some of them. Some of these adaptations are well done; others are poor. They range in difficulty from the second- to the eighth-reader level, and so the fact that a book is a simplified version gives no indication of its actual difficulty. *Treasure Island*, for example, is available in four different versions that range from the fourth- to the eighth-reader level in difficulty.

Not all high-interest/low-vocabulary books are well written, so they should be examined carefully before purchase. G. Mason (1981) provides a history of high-interest/low-reading-level books and discusses their future.

Materials Written by Teachers and Pupils

It is often necessary to use stories written especially to appeal to a particular child. The first step is to find out what the child would like to talk about. It is easy to get the child's cooperation in such an undertaking, and he is usually very proud to dictate a story to the teacher and later read his own words. In addition to their interest value, such stories have an important advantage in that all the words, syntactic structures, and concepts are likely to be understood by the child. Stories written by one child are often enjoyed by other children. Scrapbooks of stories written by the children themselves have great appeal as supplementary reading in remedial classes. The stories should be typewritten or printed. See pages 73–74 and 393–394 for more information on the Language-Experience Approach.

Because of a scarcity of suitable books, a remedial teacher may also find it advisable to rely largely on material that he has prepared. Unless a teacher has considerable originality, he ordinarily will be more successful in adapting the writings of others than in attempting to write completely original material. It is possible to rewrite difficult stories and material from textbooks to levels understandable to most disabled readers. Because writing special materials is time consuming, however, efforts should be made to utilize available published materials, if they are well done.

Materials for remedial pupils should be written in a simple and straightforward style and at a level of complexity within the grasp of the pupil. Compound and complex sentences may be used in moderation, provided that they do not contain many inversions of normal word order or very involved syntactic constructions. High-frequency words should be used in place of a more difficult synonym whenever possible. After the material has been written, its vocabulary may be checked against one of the word lists (see pages 441–445) to make sure that it does not contain an unreasonable number of unusual or difficult words. Word meaning should also be considered. The best test of the text's suitability is the ease with which the pupils can read it.

In planning story-type or informational material for disabled readers, it is a good idea to make each unit short enough so that it can be finished in one remedial period. Appropriate prereading, during-reading, and postreading instructional procedures, selected from those suggested elsewhere in this book, should be employed in using the materials.

Material on Minority Groups and Other Cultures

Although research does not clearly indicate that minority-group students prefer to read material pertaining to their own cultural or ethnic backgrounds, a large amount of such material has been published. Probably many children do like to read about characters similar to themselves and perhaps about those who are different as well; so ethnic materials may be of interest to both minority- and majority-group children. These materials may also be useful in developing sensitivity toward others (see pages 682–683).

Beauchamp (1970) studied the reading interests of minority-group ninth graders who were disabled readers. Among his findings were: (1) Their reading interests did not vary substantially from those of their age-level peers; (2) these students could and did read books that "ought to be too difficult" for them *if* the books had extremely high interest (but see page 668); (3) they preferred books with fewer characters but did not have a clear preference for characters similar to themselves; (4) they tended to reject love and romance themes, preferring those of perseverance, physical strength, triumph over adversity and obstacles, and detective stories; and (5) adapted classics could be used successfully, provided that description was minimized and action and suspense maximized.

Among the materials published for and about minority groups are:

- *Open Door Books* (Children's Press). Thirty-six books that contain realistic autobiographies of minority-group men and women who have been successful in modern society. Written at about the fifth-reader level; interest level, Grades 5–12.

- *Target Today Series* (Benefic). Series of four books, each containing 100 short story-lessons that use urban life as the main theme Reading levels 2–5; interest levels 4–12.
- *Americans All* (Garrard). Biographies of great Americans of all races, creeds, and national origins; emphasis on character and personal determination. Reading level about 4; interest level 3–6.
- *We Are Black* (SRA). Selections of 300–900 words taken from books and periodicals. A reading-skill program accompanies the materials. Reading levels 2–6; interest levels 4–8.
- *Ethnic Reading Series* (Book Laboratory). Twenty short booklets focus on the lives of black, Jewish, Italian, and Puerto Rican Americans of both genders. Reading levels 3–5; interest levels 7–12.
- *Contributors to American Life Series* (Benefic). Three books (*Afro-Americans, American Indians, Hispano-Americans*), each containing at least 20 biographies and each with three parts at second-, third-, and fifth-reader levels. Interest levels 4–9.
- *Indians* (Garrard). Factually accurate, unstereotyped; American history from the Indian's viewpoint. Reading level about 3; interest levels 2–5.
- *Indian Culture Series* (Montana). Authentic, interesting books depicting the life of the Indians before the coming of white people and present-day life. Reading levels 2–5; interest levels 4–12.
- *Folk Tales and Legends* (Montana). Eleven authentic tales and legends from different Indian tribes. Written at reader levels 1–4, the books should interest elementary and junior high school children.
- *Indian Children's Books* (Montana). Annotated list of books judged to be accurate in their interpretation of Indian cultures. Books are listed by tribe, region, and subject. Interest and reading levels are indicated. One chapter discusses how to use the books.
- *Indian Reading Series* (NWRL). A supplementary reading program containing 142 stories written by Indians of 16 reservations. Organized into six levels for the elementary school.

Books of interest to and about minority-group children have been listed by Archer (1972), Strickland (1973), and G. Spache (1975). Lass (1980) lists books that use black English (primarily in dialogue) and indicates the interest and reading levels of each. Children's literature dealing with interracial families is discussed and annotated by Long (1978). Refer to Brooks (1985) for a variety of ideas offered by black educators for preventing black students from losing interest in the language arts.

Annotated bibliographies of literature by and about American Indians were prepared by Stensland (1979), Westcott (1982), and Gilliland (1982). Vugrenes (1981) lists sources of North American Indian myths and legends, and Blair (1982) examines the readability and content of adolescent literature about the Indians in northern and western Canada. May (1983) describes a literature and film approach to promote a better understanding of and appreciation for Native Americans. An annotated listing of over 750 books, each dealing with some aspect of the life of American Indians and Eskimos, was edited by Lass-Woodfin (1978). Stott (1983) discusses the folk tales of one Eskimo tribe that have been adapted for children.

Schon (1981) provides critical reviews of the children's literature dealing with the customs, life styles, folklore, and history of Mexicans and Mexican Americans. Wagoner (1982) presents an annotated bibliography of children's books containing Mexican-American characters and discusses the common themes found in them. Schon (1987) lists informational books that may be used by children who can read Spanish but not English.

Suggestions for using Asian-American children's literature may be found in Aoki (1981). Algarin (1982) presents an annotated bibliography of Japanese myths, legends, and fairy tales.

Also available are an annotated bibliography of the biographies of 1,100 women (Siegel 1984), an annotated bibliography dealing with Cajun themes Cox & Wallis 1982), and a series of annotated guides to children's fiction (in English) from Czechoslovakia, Hungry, Poland, the Soviet Union, the Ukraine, and Yugoslavia (Povsic 1980a,b,c; 1981a,b; 1982a,b). Auten (1984) annotates ERIC articles on developing an understanding of other cultures through literature, and Bishop (1987) suggests ways to accomplish this.

Schlichter (1989) lists trade books that would be interesting and challenging to gifted children in the elementary school. Almost 500 children's books suitable for the visually impaired may be found in *Large Type Books in Print* (Bowker).

ESTIMATING THE DIFFICULTY OF READING MATERIAL[3]

The difficulty of reading materials can be estimated in three ways: (1) considered judgment; (2) use of a readability formula; or (3) use of a cloze or informal reading test. Judgment and readability formulas are used to predict how readable the material will be in general. These two methods have the advantage of being less time consuming, but they are less accurate in determining the difficulty of a given selection or book for a particular individual. Because the child must actually read the material in a cloze or an informal reading test such as an IRI, its use is more likely to reflect how well the student can read that material and material similar to it. Direct testing, however, has the disadvantages of being time consuming. All the procedures have uses and limitations, and none is perfectly reliable or accurate.

Considered Judgment

Jorgenson (1975) reports that teachers' judgements regarding the difficulty of reading materials may vary considerably from other estimates (by as much as

[3]For comprehensive treatments of readability, see Klare to (1974–1975, 1984). Refer to Selden (1981) or to A. J. Harris and Jacobson (1979) for historical accounts of readability formulas.

six grade levels). But, generally, the correlations between readability ratings by teachers, cloze tests, and readability formulas are moderate to fairly high. For example, teachers' rating correlated between 0.60 and 0.77 with readability-formula scores and between 0.51 and 0.69 with cloze-test scores (Harrison 1979).

The above data do not necessarily indicate that teachers' judgements regarding text difficulty are less accurate than readability-formula or cloze-test scores in predicting how difficult material will be to comprehend. The opposite may be true. There is no evidence as to which procedure actually leads to the most frequent selection of material that is of generally appropriate difficulty for a given group of children.

Readability Formulas

Readability formula developers have examined over 250 variables as possible predictors, but, in general, two factors have stood out—semantic difficulty and syntactic difficulty—with semantic difficulty typically being the better predictor of the two (Klare 1984). The most widely used readability formulas employ vocabulary difficulty and sentence length as indirect measures of semantic and syntactic difficulty. Passages with low-frequency words and difficult syntax require more cognitive effort than equivalent passages with common words and simple syntax (Britton et al. 1982). These two factors are valid measures of readability (A. J. Harris 1976, Klare 1976), account for most of the variance in readability measurement (Klare 1984), and suffice for most purposes except for doing exacting research (Klare 1974–1975). They are also better indicators of learnability (the extent to which new learning results from reading a passage) than are linguistic measures (Guthrie 1972).

Well over 50 readability formulas have been developed (Schuyler 1982). Some are meant for special purposes, such as FORECAST (Sticht 1975) for determining the readability index for job-related reading materials and the Automated Reading Index (ARI) (E. Smith & Kincaid 1970) for technical materials. Most formulas, however, are designed to be used across various kinds of materials, although many are applicable only to certain ranges of difficulty.

Among the most widely used formulas are those by Spache (1978) for the primary grades[4] and by Dale and Chall (1948) for Grades 4 through college.[5] The Harris-Jacobson Wide-Range Readability Formula yields readability scores from 1.0 to 11.3, and is easier to apply than the aforementioned formulas (see Appendix C). The Spache tends to rate material at each reader level as somewhat less difficult than does the Harris-Jacobson formula (A. J. Harris & Jacobson 1980).

Fry's Readability Graph is also easy to apply and has been extended to cover Grades 1–17 (Fry 1977). The Fry Graph overestimates the difficulty of second- and third-grade materials (A. J. Harris & Jacobson 1980) and has very low validity at high school levels (A. J. Harris & Jacobson 1976). Fry (1980a) claims that other data indicate that his formula compares quite well with the Harris-Jacobson and Spache formulas. Longo (1982) reports that the Fry yielded scores that compared closely with those of three formulas when applied to college texts, and Fusaro

[4]Burmeister (1976) formulated a table that makes the Spache formula easier to apply.
[5]Tables for rapid determination of Dale-Chall scores were developed by R. T. Williams (1972) and Layton (1980).

(1988) found that it provided an accurate measure of readability within one grade level. But G. Fitzgerald (1980) questions the reliability of Fry scores based on only three samples, as the manual suggests, and indicates that even taking a much larger sample may not increase its reliability sufficiently.

The SEER technique (Singer 1975) and the Rauding Scale (Carver) 1975–1976) do not involve any computations. Rather, the passage of unknown difficulty is compared to passages of known difficulty, and one subjectively decides which passage of known difficulty the passage in question most closely represents. Froese (1981) and Duffelmeyer (1982a) disagree as to how well the SEER technique and Rauding Scale compare in determining readability. Other easy-to-apply formulas are the Rix and Lix (J. Anderson 1983), which Kretschmer (1984) reports as comparing favorably with three other easy-to-apply formulas, and Raygor's (1977) formula, which Baldwin and Kaufman (1979) report yields scores within one year of the Spache in over 90% of the comparisons. Two other relatively easy-to-apply formulas are the Fog Index (Gunning 1979), the use of which is supported by Nell's (1988) data, and the SMOG (McLaughlin 1969), for which Maginnis (1982) developed a table for even quicker use. It should be noted, however, that the easiest formulas to apply also yield the most erratic results (Schuyler 1982).

CRITICISMS OF READABILITY FORMULAS. Readability formulas have come under recent attack. For example, Bruce and Rubin (1988) write that readability formulas account only indirectly for factors that make a particular text easy or difficult to comprehend. R. C. Anderson and Davison (1988) go even further and question the two variables used in most readability formulas. They state that word difficulty predicts comprehension as well as it does only because it is an indirect measure of background knowledge that exerts a powerful influence on comprehension. Sentence length, they argue, accounts for only a small proportion of the variance in reading comprehension; and, although longer sentences may be more syntactically complex than short sentences, they are not more difficult to understand because the relationships between clauses, for example, are explicitly marked. Fry (1989) counterargues that, *on average,* word difficulty and sentence length do accurately predict how easily a given passage will be understood *by the average reader.*

Basically, the criticisms have centered on two points: (1) Readability formulas do not indicate very well how comprehensible a text is going to be for an individual; and (2) the formulas are poor guides for writing comprehensible material. Many of the points regarding comprehensibility are well taken, but their attacks would often be better directed at misapplication of readability formulas. In regard to the first point, Klare (1984) states that a readability formula is a *predictive* device intended to provide a quantitative, objective estimate of reading difficulty. Much of the controversy reflects a failure to recognize the implication of the term *predictive.* Modern readability formulas have achieved extremely high correlations with their criteria. In other words, they do what they were designed to do—predict how difficult material is likely to be as compared with the criterion measure. Klare (1984) contrasts *prediction* with *production.* In the latter, the goal is to produce more comprehensible reading materials. Prediction research only need show relationship to the criterion. Production research must demonstrate a causal relationship in that a manipulation of variables produces a significant increase in pupils' comprehension. Klare (1988) reports that in only 19 of 36 studies did reducing the readability scores of the texts significantly improve text comprehension.

There are variables within the child (e.g., prior knowledge, motivation) and within the text (e.g., vocabulary, text structure and cohesion, concept load and density, grammatical complexity) that must be considered in attempting to select material of suitable difficulty because they interact to determine how comprehensible that material is for a particular pupil. Readability is not an inherent property of written text, but the result of interactions between text characteristics and the information-processing characterization of the reader (Zakaluk & Samuels 1988). Contrary to current criticism, readability researchers have been aware of this fact for at least 50 years (Chall 1988). It would be foolhardy simply to match a readability grade score with a child's grade-equivalent score from a standardized test, as some critics (e.g., Dreyer 1984) suggest is done.

Attempts to increase the predictive power of readability formulas by adding linguistic measures have not been particularly successful (Binkley 1988). For instance, adding a measure of syntax increased the predictive power of a readability formula for older readers using more difficult texts but had little effect for younger readers (Selden 1981). Bormuth (1966) found that the number of words per sentence correlated 0.86 with a formal measure of word depth. And Bamberger and Rabin (1984) report that in about 70% of the cases, use of their *Readability Profile* (subjective judgment of text content, organization, print, style and motivation) did not add to or detract from the estimate of difficulty indicated by the readability formula score.

The criteria against which readability formulas have been validated have also come under fire. It has been argued that to use the publisher's grade-level designation is tantamount to circular reasoning because publishers use readability formulas to determine the levels of their basal readers. A number of formulas have used the *McCall-Crabbs Standardized Test Lessons* as their criterion. Stevens (1980) claims that the McCall-Crabbs is not based on extensive testing, that the grade-equivalent scores lack reliability and comparability, and that complete technical data are not available from the publisher. On the other hand, Selden (1981) writes that the McCall-Crabs has the advantage of having been normed on a large population and that there seems to be some empirical basis for the grade placement of the passages. Furthermore, Selden indicates that, although the McCall-Crabbs was originally normed in 1925, a fairly recent study indicates that its norms are still indicative of performance, except at the twelfth-grade level.

Two formulas may be highly correlated, but that fact indicates only that the rank order in which they place the passages shows high agreement. When applied to the same materials, readability formulas consistently disagree as to the levels of difficulty they assign (Klare 1984). The degree to which formula scores disagree (and they have been shown to disagree from one to six or more grade levels) varies with the formulas used and the materials to which they are applied. Some formulas yield consistently higher scores than do other formulas. For example, when eight formulas were applied to the same 16 passages, the ARI yielded the lowest ratings in 15 comparisons and the Fry indicated the highest scores in 9 (Schuyler 1982).

As for the second main criticism, most readability formulas were never meant to provide a guide for readable writing (Fry 1989). Over the years, readability researchers and scholars have cautioned editors, publishers, and educators that readability formulas should not be used mechanically to simplify texts (Chall 1988). Readability formulas were intended to be indices of the difficulty of the passage but were never meant to provide specifications of text characteristics that contribute to text difficulty (Selden 1981). As demonstrated by Davison and Kantor (1982), attempts to simplify text may well result in less comprehensible material. Replacing a compound or complex sentence with a number of short, simple sentences often makes the relationships that link ideas together more vague, and may require the readers to make additional inferences; for instance, having to infer a deleted connective that originally signaled a cause-effect relationship. Deleting details may not clarify meaning, and replacing low-frequency but precise word with "easy" words may blur the intended meaning. Furthermore, condensing ideas may increase their density to a point that causes conceptual overload for the student (T. Anderson, Armbruster & Kantor 1980).

Nonetheless, writers (e.g., Ostertag & Rambeau 1982) still recommend that all one need do to make material "easier to read" is make the sentences shorter and replace the hard words. Such changes will probably reduce the readability formula score, but they may make the material less comprehensible. As Shuy (1981a) points out, simplicity is not necessarily equivalent to clarity of writing.

Suggestions for rewriting materials that go beyond the usual ones mentioned above have been provided by Charry (1975) and Fry (1988). It is of interest to note that in two studies (Funkhouser & Maccoby 1971, Shaffer 1977) comprehension improved most when both word difficulty and sentence length were manipulated, rather than either factor alone.

PROPER USE AND INTERPRETATION OF READABILITY FORMULAS. Readability formulas have value, especially when their intended purpose and limitations are understood (Fry 1989). It would be impossible to test directly every potential reader with each piece of reading material, so estimates of difficulty are useful in initially selecting materials.

Klare (1988) makes the following comments that may help to prevent readability formulas from being misused: (1) Readability formulas can be useful as screening devices in the prediction of readability; (2) a larger number of samples than the formula manual suggests should be taken (see page 219); (3) readability formulas are poor predictors of text difficulty at the higher grade levels, especially college, because of the text content; (4) other variables that contribute to text comprehensibility should be considered when selecting reading materials; (5) after a text has been used with pupils, it may be necessary to shift its readability estimate up or down: and (6) readability formulas should not be used in the production to text, except to gain feedback *after* the text is written.

Formulas do not necessarily yield similar levels of difficulty when applied to the same material, so the predicted difficulty of any passage or book may well depend on which formula is used. Educators would be well advised to use the formula that best predicts the difficulty of the material being used by their pupils who are reading that material.

It may be advisable to supplement the data provided by a readability formula with information about the text's comprehensibility. A checklist may be used for this purpose. The checklist presented by Clewell and Cliffton (1983) is based on the premise that text comprehensibility is influenced by the reader's prior knowledge, text coherence, the degree to which the author sticks to the topic, and text structure. Irwin and Davis's 5-point rating scale (1980) considers the relationship between text information and the reader's conceptual development and prior knowledge, as well as syntax; how clearly main ideas are stated; the inclusion of irrelevant details; and the exclusion of explicit connectives. Among the problems with such checklists are that they require a knowledgeable user and that subjective judgment is used to rate information that is not readily apparent or available (e.g., the reader's prior knowledge). Reliability of such assessments could vary widely.

Among the findings of readability studies summarized by Klare (1976) are the following:

1. At times, motivation can override the effects of readability on comprehension.
2. Easier readability may increase the likelihood that pupils will continue to read, even when it does not result in better comprehension.
3. It is more important to improve the readability of low-preferred than high-preferred material.
4. The grade-equivalent scores provided by readability formulas are not precise values.
5. Readability formulas may (a) underestimate the difficulty of material in which a pupil has limited background information; and (b) overestimate the difficulty for highly intelligent and well-informed readers.

COMPUTER APPLICATIONS.   With the increased availability of microcomputers, it is inevitable that computer programs would be developed to save time in applying readability formulas (see Blanchard, Mason & Daniel 1983). Microcomputer programs are available for the RIX readability index (Kretschmer 1984) and the Fog Index (Gross & Sadowski 1985). Schuyler (1982) covers eight readability formulas. Other sources of computer programs for readability are listed by Kennedy (1985). One of the apparently unanswered questions about using the microcomputer to apply certain formulas is how the application of certain rules is taken into consideration. Manual procedures produce more accurate scores than do computerized versions of readability formulas (Blanchard, Mason & Daniel 1987).

CURRENT STATUS OF READABILITY.   Interest in readability is alive and thriving (Klare 1984). This interest has spread to the development of readability formulas for languages other than English. The Fry has been modified for use with Spanish (Gilliam, Peña & Mountain 1980). Readability formulas for estimating the difficulty of texts written in 12 languages other than English may be found in Rabin (1988), who also provides a brief history of these readability formulas.

Interest in readability/comprehensibility is also indicated by publications such as *Simply Stated* (American Institute for Research), a monthly newsletter that tells of efforts to make documents more readable. As of 1983, 27 states had laws requiring the use of "plain language" in insurance policies.

In response to the question "Have we gone too far with readability?" Klare (1984) replies in the negative with regard to research. He also indicates that research has clearly begun to move in the direction of attempting to understand how changes in readability can work for individual readers. As for whether the application of readability has gone too far, Klare offers a cautious "sometimes yes, sometimes no." We can go too far in attempts at predicting and producing readable writing, but we need not. If readability formulas are selected and used properly, they can be helpful screening devices. But they cannot serve as guides for readable writing because humans and language are too complex to expect simple cause-effect relationships.

Other Measures of Comprehensibility/Readability

An estimate of how comprehensible a given text is for a particular child can be obtained by employing an informal reading inventory (see pages 219–229) or a cloze test (see pages 200–205).

Cloze scores and readability formulas do not yield similar results (Schlief & Wood 1974, Froese 1975). Correlations between readability formula scores and cloze ratings range from 0.35 to 0.62 (Harrison 1979). The cloze also has limitations. Cloze tests lack *face validity;* that is, they do not look like measures of readability. Cloze scores are greatly influenced by the kind and number of deletions. For example, deleted content words (nouns, main verbs, adverbs and adjectives) are probably more difficult to supply than function words are; and, an every-fifth-word deletion may not be suitable for everyone. Also, the ability to complete many items successfully depends more on the reader's experiential background and general language ability than on the content of the material itself (Hittleman 1978). It also may depend heavily on the reader's verbal problem-solving ability (Selden 1981).

This chapter has stressed the importance of finding "the right book for the right child" as a way of increasing children's interest in reading for pleasure and providing a basis for the gradual maturing and refining of taste and critical standards. The child who reads extensively will make his or her own comparisons and will, in the long run, prefer sound writing to trash. Even if she or he does not, an omnivorous reading diet is far superior to none at all. In the face of the competition from mass media such as television, it takes both superior materials and clever salesmanship by teachers to develop the reading habit; without this habit, much of reading instruction is wasted. For the disabled reader, fluency and ease in reading can develop only through much reading of interesting, easy material.

APPENDIX

A Descriptive Listing of Tests by Types

The lists that follow give pertinent information about the tests mentioned in this book and in the literature or that may be found in diagnostic reports. A few tests are listed because of their historical interest. The exclusion of a test does not mean that we consider it to be an inadequate test, and test inclusion does not indicate our endorsement.

Within each category, the tests are listed alphabetically. When a test is part of an achievement battery, only the reading and reading-related tests are described. Test authors and acronyms are mentioned when such information may be helpful in identifying the test. Information about the test that appears in its title is not repeated in the description. Oral reading tests must be administered individually; therefore the word "individual" is omitted from their descriptions. Unless otherwise indicated, you may assume that in all but obvious cases a test is group-administered, norm-referenced, and read silently. Projective tests must be interpreted by a trained examiner.

Each description is brief and not evaluative. In order to determine what a test really measures and its adequacy, you must analyze the tasks required by that test or rely on the judgments of others. More detailed descriptions and critical evaluations may be found in journals (many of these are listed in *News on Tests*), and in Buros (1968, 1972, 1975, 1978) and Mitchell (1983, 1985), Conoley et al. (1988), and Conoley and Kramer (1989). British reading tests and assessment procedures are reviewed by Vincent et al. (1983).

Before deciding which test to use, make a tentative selection of a few tests that might be suitable and order a specimen set of each for careful study. For large-scale testing, also consider such factors as how well the test measures the objectives of the school's reading program, the practicality and cost of hand-scoring versus machine-scoring (all tests cannot be machine scored), and the test–result reports that publishers can provide (and the cost of such).

The names of the test publishers are abbreviated. The full names of those whose abbreviated names may make them difficult to identify are given on pages 751–752.

READINESS AND EARLY IDENTIFICATION
OF HIGH-RISK CHILDREN

Analysis of Readiness Skills: Reading and Mathematics (1972). Five scores: visual perception of letters, letter identification, mathematics (identification, counting), total. Directions and norms for both English- and Spanish-speaking children. Grades K–1. Riverside.

Anton Brenner Developmental Gestalt Test of School Readiness (1964). Visual-motor copying test. Rating scale yields 2 scores: achievement-ability, social-emotional. Ages 5–6. WPS.

Aston Index (1972). Battery of tests designed to identify "at-risk" children who have a predisposition to dyslexia-type language difficulties. Verbal and perceptual tasks; family history included. Aston.

Beginning Assessment Test for Reading (1975). Criterion-referenced. Measures understanding of spoken words, visual and auditory discrimination, classification, rhyming, sequencing, riddles, letter names, sound-symbol associations, picture-word and picture-sentence matching, spelling, sentence completion, oral production and comprehension, and color naming. Placement test measures 12 objectives with 2–6 items for each. Comprehensive test measures 19 objectives with 2–6 items each. Grades K–1. Lippincott.

Boehm Tests of Basic Concepts (1986). Assesses mastery of concepts fundamental to understanding verbal instructions and necessary for early school achievement. Grades K–2. Psy Corp.

Braun-Neilsen Pre-Reading Inventory (1979). Subtests: conventions of language (basic literacy concepts, speech-print association, spoken word boundaries), semantic-associational relationships (classroom concepts, classification), and graphophonemic (letter recognition, visual discrimination, beginning sounds). Supplementary tests: listening for sequence, listening for meaning, auditory discrimination, and rhyming elements. Two forms. Grades K–1. Ginn (Canada).

Brigance Screen for Kindergarten and First Grade (1983). Primarily individual. Brief criterion-referenced battery of 18 tests (only 12 or 13 given to each child). Seven tests given to both kindergarten and first-grade children: personal data (child gives name orally, etc.), color recognition (names 10 colors), picture vocabulary, visual-motor skills (copying 5 geometric shapes), rote counting, numerical comprehension (associating quantities with numerals), and printing personal data. Curriculum Associates.

Circus (1979). Measure of reading and school readiness. Levels A (Grades pre-K to K) and B (K–1) contain 12 or 14 tests covering a variety of areas (e.g., receptive vocabulary, quantitative concepts, perceptual-motor coordination, expressive language, visual memory, and problem solving) and 2 or 3 teacher-completed inventories. Levels C (1–2) and D (2–3) contain measures of phonetic analysis, oral reading, vocabulary, and sentence and reading comprehension. Two forms. Grades K–3. CTB.

Concepts about Print Test (1982). Individual. *Sand* and *Stones* are 20-page paperbacks that are used to observe and evaluate child's concepts about: book orientation (e.g., when pictures and print are right side up); whether print or pictures carry the message; directionality of lines of print, words, and page sequence; relationships between written and spoken language; words, letters, capitals, space, and punctuation. Ages 5–7. Heinemann.

Contemporary School Readiness Test (1970). Subtests other than reading test can be group administered. Subtests: name writing; colors; science, health, and social studies;

numbers; handwriting readiness; reading; visual and auditory discrimination; listening comprehension. Grades K–1. Montana Council on Indian Education.

CTBS Readiness Test (1977). Six subtests: letter names, letter forms, listening for information, letter sounds, visual discrimination, and sound matching. Grades K–1. CTB.

Dyslexia Schedule (1969). School-entrance questionnaire (89 items) completed by parents. Score based on 23 discriminating items, 21 of which are on *School Entrance Check List*. Also used to elicit information about children referred because of reading disability. K–1. EPS.

Dyslexia Screening Survey (Valett 1980). Checklist of neuropsychological skills thought to be involved in the reading process. Covers phonetic-auditory, visual, and multisensory processing skills. Grades 1–6. Fearon.

Florida Kindergarten Screening Battery (1982). Designed to detect young children "at risk" for subsequent reading disability. Includes *PPVT-R*, recognition-discrimination (visual perception of rotated figures), *Beery Visual–Motor Integration Test*, alphabet recitation, and finger localization. Used in studies by Satz (see pp. 325–326). ATP; PAR.

Gesell Preschool Tests (1980). Series of individual test situations that reveal child's relative maturing in 4 basic areas of behavior: motor, adaptive, language, and personal-social. Ages $2\frac{1}{2}$–6. Programs for Education.

Harrison-Stroud Reading Readiness Profiles (1957). Five subtests: using symbols, visual discrimination, using context, auditory discrimination, and using context and auditory clues. Also includes test of letter names. Grades K–1. Riverside.

Kindergarten Behavioural Index: A Screening Technique for Reading Readiness (1972). Behavior rating scale designed to aid in identifying children with potential learning problems. Grades K–1. Australian Council. A copy of the KBI is shown on page 54.

Lee-Clark Reading Readiness Test (1962). Four subtests measure visual discrimination of letter forms (2 subtests), concepts, and visual discrimination of word forms. Grades K–1. CTB.

Let's Look at Children (1981). Procedures for assessing and developing school readiness of children, especially minority children. Based on works of Piaget. Grades K–3. Addison-Wesley.

Linguistic Awareness in Reading Readiness Test (1984). Subtests: recognizing literacy behavior (extent to which child can recognize kinds of activities involved in reading and writing); understanding literacy functions (understanding of varied purposes of reading and writing); and technical language of literacy (knowledge of technical terms such as *letter, word,* and *top line*). Two forms. Ages 4–8. NFER–Nelson; Psy Corp.

McCarthy Screening Test (1978). Criterion-referenced adaptation of *McCarthy Scales of Children's Abilities*. Six tests: right-left orientation, verbal memory, draw-a-design, numerical memory, conceptual grouping, and coordination. Percentile cutoff scores used to identify "at-risk" children. Ages 4–$6\frac{1}{2}$. Psy Corp.

Meeting Street School Screening Test (1969). Individual. Designed to identify children with potential learning problems. Three subtests: motor patterning (bilateral sequential movement patterns and spatial awareness), visual perceptual-motor (visual discrimination, visual memory, eye-hand coordination, spatial and directional concepts), and language (listening comprehension, auditory memory, and language formulation). Also includes behavior rating scale. Ages 5–$7\frac{1}{2}$. Meeting Street.

Metropolitan Readiness Test (1986). Level I (K.0–K.5) subtests: auditory memory, beginning consonants, letter recognition, visual matching, school language and listening, and quantitative language. Level II (K.5–1.5) subtests: beginning consonants, sound-letter correspondences, visual matching, finding patterns, school language, listening, and quantitative concepts and operations. Both levels have optional copying test. Grades K–1. Psy Corp.

Monroe Reading Aptitude Tests (1936). Group and individual subtests. Measures 5 factors: visual perception and memory, auditory perception and memory, motor control, oral speed and articulation, and language. Grades K–1 and nonreaders to age 9. Riverside.

Murphy-Durrell Prereading Phonics Inventory (1978). Five subtests: identifying letters named, letter names in spoken words, phonemes in spoken words, writing letters from dictation, and syntax matching (examiner reads sentence, child points to target word in printed sentence as directed by examiner). Grades K–1. Borg-Warner. Also part of *Durrell Analysis of Reading Difficulty.*

Murphy-Durrell Reading Readiness Analysis (1965). Yields 6 scores: sound recognition, letter names (capitals, lower case, total), and learning rate (ability to learn to recognize printed words). Early first grade. Psy Corp.

Prescriptive Reading Inventory (1977). Criterion-referenced tests covering 10 objectives each for Levels 1 and 2. Level 1 (K.0–Grade 1.0): sound discrimination, sound matching, form matching, visual reasoning, sound-symbol correspondence, letter names, oral language, literal comprehension, interpretative comprehension, and attention skills. Level 2 (K.5–2.0): 8 areas, same as in Level 1; sight vocabulary and initial reading replace form matching and letter names. Grades K–1. CTB.

Pupil Rating Scale: Screening for Learning Disabilities (Myklebust 1981). Child's behavioral characteristics rated (5-point scale) on 24 items in 5 areas: auditory comprehension and memory, spoken language, orientation, motor coordination, and personal-social behavior. Ages 5–14. WPS.

Quickscreen (1981). Brief screening test to identify children with potential learning problems. Kindergarten level: name writing, figure copying, story, and sentence repetition. First-grade level: name writing, figures, words, story, and sentences. Second-grade level: name writing, figures, story, and sentences. Four forms at kindergarten level; 2 forms at others. Cutoff scores used. Grades K–2. WPS.

Rhode Island Profile of Early Learning Behavior (1982). Forty items divided into 9 areas of behavior: body perception, sensory-motor coordination, attention, memory for events, self-concept, visual memory, spatial and sequential arrangements of letters and symbols, and memory for symbols. Five-point scale used to rate behaviors over 4 observations. Grades K–2. Jamestown.

School Readiness Survey (1975). Administered and scored by parents with school supervision. Yields 8 scores: number concepts, form discrimination, color naming, symbol matching, speaking vocabulary, listening vocabulary, general information, and total. Also includes general readiness checklist. Ages 4–6. Consulting Psychologists.

School Readiness Test (1974). Classifies children into 6 levels of readiness based on the total score of 7 subtests: word recognition, identifying letters, visual discrimination, auditory discrimination, comprehension and interpretation, handwriting readiness, and number readiness. Grades K–1. Spanish Language Edition (1977). STS.

SEARCH (2nd ed.) Individual. Designed to identify "high-risk" children. Ten subtests: visual perception (discrimination, recall, visual-motor), auditory perception (discrimination, sequencing), intermodal (articulation, auditory, and initial consonants), and body image (directionality, finger schema, pencil grip). Ages 5–6. Walker.

Slingerland Pre-Reading Screening Procedures (1977). Measures auditory, visual, and kinesthetic skills. Twelve subtests: visual perception 1 & 2 (visual discrimination), visual perception and memory (visual memory), near- and far-point copying, auditory-visual association (understanding spoken sentences), letter recognition (letter names), visual-kinesthetic memory (visual-motor integration), auditory perception with comprehension (understanding a short oral story), auditory discrimination, auditory-visual-kinesthetic integration (matching spoken letter name with its printed form and then copying it), and auditory-visual association (sound-symbol association). Grades K–1. EPS.

Slingerland Screening Tests for Identifying Children with Specific Language Disability (1974). Attempts to identify children who have or are likely to have disabilities in reading, spelling, speaking, or handwriting. All levels contain 8 subtests: copying from near- and far-point, visual memory, visual discrimination, visual-kinesthetic memory, auditory kinesthetic memory, auditory analysis (with written response), and auditory-visual integration (matching spoken and printed words). Form D also has subtests to identify possible confusion in orientation in time and space and to determine written expression. Three subtests given individually: echolalia (echoing words and phrases), word finding (auditory cloze), and storytelling (retelling of story read by examiner). Form A (Grades 1–2), B (2–3), C (3–4), D (5–6). EPS.

Spanish Reading Criterion Referenced Test: Kindergarten (1971). Measure of readiness to learn to read in Spanish. National Hispanic Center.

SRA Achievement Series: Reading (1978). Level A measures visual and auditory discrimination, letters and sounds, listening comprehension, and mathematical concepts. Two forms. Grades K–1. SRA.

Stanford Early School Achievement Test (1987). Levels 1 (K.0–K.9) and 2 (K.5–1.9) have subtests: sounds and letters (auditory perception, letter names, sound-symbol associations), word reading (word recognition), and listening to words and stories (understanding vocabulary and listening comprehension). Level 2 also includes sentence-comprehension subtest. Grades K–1. Psy Corp.

Test of Early Reading Ability–2 (1989). Measures ability of preschool, kindergarten, and primary-grade children. Yields information about child's letter-name knowledge, conventions of reading (e.g., book orientation and format), and reading comprehension. Two forms. Ages 3–9. Pro-Ed.

Walker Readiness Test for Disadvantaged Preschool Children (1972). Individual. Subtests: likenesses or similarities (visual discrimination), differences (distinguishing size, shapes), numerical analogies, and missing parts (visual closure). Directions available in English, Spanish, and French. Two forms. Ages 4–6. (ERIC number ED 037 253.)

READING

American School Achievement Tests: Reading (1975). Primary II (Grades 2–3), Intermediate (4–6), Advanced (7–9) levels each yield 4 scores: vocabulary, sentence meaning, paragraph comprehension, and total score. Two forms. Grades 2–9. Bobbs.

Analysis of Skills (ASK): Reading (1974). Criterion-referenced. Each of 4 levels (Grades 1–2, 3–4, 5–6, 7–8) measures 43–48 objectives of the total of 60 covered by the series. Each skill sampled by 3 items; mastery equals all 3 correct, or 2 of 3 including most difficult item. Three main areas tested; word analysis, comprehension, study skills. Grades 1–8. STS.

Analytical Reading Inventory (Woods & Moe 1989). Individual. Commercially published IRI. Each of 3 forms consists of 17 graded 20-word lists (primer–Grade 6) and 10 graded passages (primer–9). Six comprehension questions at primer and first-reader levels; 8 at others. Question types: idea, factual, terminology, cause-effect, inference, and conclusions. Two expository subtests consist of graded social studies and science passages (9 each, Grades 1–9). Oral reading and listening comprehension measured; silent reading optional. Grades 1–9. Merrill.

Bader Reading and Language Inventory (1983). A series of graded 10-word lists (primer–Grade 8) and 4 supplementary word lists (words used in instructional materials, tests, and words encountered in daily living), 3 sets of graded reading passages (preprimer–Grade 12), 14 phonic and word-analysis subtests, 7 spelling tests, 4 cloze tests (to assess semantic, syntactic, and grammatical processing), visual- and auditory-discrimination tests, an interest test, an estimate of language abilities (receptive and expressive language, handwriting), and a brief arithmetic test. Grades 1–12, adult. Macmillan.

Basic Achievement Skills Individual Screener (BASIS): Reading (1983). Individual. Yields both norm- and criterion-referenced information. Test items grouped in grade-referenced clusters ranging from readiness to Grade 8. Readiness measured by letter identification and visual discrimination. At lower levels, decoding, word recognition, and sentence comprehension assessed. Reading test assesses comprehension of graded passages (primer–Grade 8), using a cloze procedure (child reads orally and supplies missing words). Grades 1–12. Psy Corp.

Basic Reading Inventory (Johns 1988). Individual. Commercially published IRI. Each of 3 forms consists of 10 graded 20-word lists (preprimer–Grade 8) and 10 graded passages (preprimer–Grade 8). Words on lists first shown quickly; unknown words presented again untimed. Four comprehension questions at preprimer level; 10 at others (1 main idea, 5 factual, 2 inference, 1 vocabulary, 1 experience (evaluation). Instructional level: 91–98% word recognition, 55–85% comprehension; preferably 95% word recognition and 75% comprehension. Grades 1–8. Kendall/Hunt.

Basic Reading Rate Scale (Tinker & Carver 1970). Measure of rate when reading very easy material. Yields 3 scores: number correct, number attempted, and percent accuracy. Grades 3–16, adults. Revrac.

Basic Word Vocabulary Test (1975). Measure of word-meaning knowledge. Printed words presented in isolation. Testee selects 1 word (4 choices) whose meaning most similar to target word. Number of words range from 55 at Grade 3 to all 123 for adults. Yields Vocabulary Age score and Vocabulary Development Quotient. Estimated Vocabulary Size score is obtained by multiplying raw score by 100. Grade 3–adult. Jamestown.

Boder Test of Reading-Spelling Patterns (1982). Individual. Used to identify 4 subtypes of disabled readers: dysphonetic, diseidetic, dysphonetic and diseidetic, and nonspecific (see p. 264). Reading subtest has 13 graded lists (preprimer–adult), each containing 10 phonically regular and 10 irregular words. Words are flashed and each unknown word presented again for 10 seconds. Reading level = highest word list with at least 50% words correct when flashed. Reading Quotient = 5 years + reading age + CA × 100. Spelling subtest individualized; 10 correctly recognized words (5 regular, 5 irregular) and 10 words incorrectly recognized on reading subtest. Subtypes determined on basis of RQ, percent of known and unknown words spelled correctly or as good phonic equivalents. Disabled readers of all ages. Psy Corp.

Brigance Diagnostic Comprehensive Inventory of Basic Skills (1983). Informal, individual battery of criterion-referenced tests covering a wide range of skills. Reading subtests include word recognition, word analysis, vocabulary, and oral reading. Spelling and study skills measured by other tests. Grades K–6. Curriculum Associates.

Burt Word Reading Test—New Zealand Revision (1981). Individual. Measures ability to recognize words presented in isolation. Consists of 110 words printed in different-size type and graded in difficulty. Ages 6–13. New Zealand.

California Achievement Tests: Reading (1987). Norm-referenced, but yield criterion-referenced information. Levels 11 (Grade K.6–2.2), 12 (1.6–3.2), and 13 (2.6–4.2); subtests: phonic analysis, vocabulary, and comprehension. Level 13 also has structural analysis subtest. Levels 14–16 (Grades 3.6–7.2) and 17–20 (6.6–12.9) have vocabulary and comprehension subtests. Two forms. Grades K–12. CTB.

Canadian Test of Basic Skills (1981). Levels 5 and 6 (Grades K–1) are readiness tests. Levels 5–8 (K–3) assess listening, word analysis, vocabulary, reading, oral and written language, work-study skills, and math. Levels 9–14 (Grades 4–8) measure vocabulary, reading, writing mechanics, study skills, and math. Levels 15–18 (Grades 9–12) have 4 tests: reading, math, written expression, and using sources of information. Normed on same population as *Canadian Cognitive Abilities Test.* Two forms. Grades K–12. Nelson Canada.

Carver-Darby Chunked Reading Test (1972). Criterion-referenced. Measures rate and retention. After reading each of 5 passages, student is presented "chunks" (groups of meaningful related words within a sentence). From each set of chunks, the reader marks the one whose meaning has been changed from that of the original text. Yields 3 scores: rate (number of answers given), accuracy (number of correct answers), and efficiency (accuracy ÷ rate × 100). Two forms. Accuracy 7–16, adults. Revrac.

Classroom Reading Inventory (Silvaroli 1986). Individual. Commercially published IRI. Each form has 8 graded 20-word lists and 8 to 10 graded passages (preprimer–Grade 8 or Grades 1–8). Each passage followed by 5 comprehension questions (factual, inference, vocabulary). Instructional level: 95% word recognition, 75% comprehension. Oral reading measured; silent reading, listening comprehension, and spelling optional. Forms A and B for Grades 1–6; C for junior high; and D for senior high and adults. Grade 1–adult. William C. Brown.

Comprehensive Tests of Basic Skills: Reading (1985). Levels A and B (K.6–1.6) have 3 subtests: word attack, oral vocabulary and comprehension. Levels C (Grades 1.0–1.9), D (1.6–2.9), E (2.6–3.9) measure word attack, vocabulary, and reading comprehension. Levels F–K (3.6–4.9, 4.6–6.9, 6.6–8.9, 8.6–12.9, 11.0–12.9) have vocabulary, reading comprehension, and reference skills subtests. Two forms. CTB.

Computer-Based Reading Assessment (1986). Individual. Commercially published IRI. Each of two forms consists of graded word lists and 8 graded passages. Each passage followed by 8 multiple-choice questions and 10 probed recall questions. Not completely computer administered. Spanish edition available. Grades 1–8. Kendall/Hunt.

Contemporary Classroom Reading Inventory (Rinsky & de Fossard 1980). Individual. Commercially published IRI. Each of 3 series consists of graded 20-word lists (primer–Grade 7) and graded passages (primer–9). One series each for fiction, social studies, and science. Primer and first-reader passages have 5 comprehension questions; second reader has 6; third reader, 7; fourth reader, 7 or 8; all others have 8. Types of questions: main idea, detail, inference, sequence, vocabulary, reasoning/conclusion, and evaluation. Instructional level: 92–96% word recognition, 60–79% comprehension. Oral reading measured; silent reading not indicated; listening comprehension optional. Also contains cloze tests in the same 3 content areas. Grades 1–9. Gorsuch Scarisbrick.

Content Inventories, English, Social Studies, and Science (McWilliams & Rake 1979). Group. Criterion-referenced. Cloze placement inventories and group reading inventories in English (Grades 7–12), social studies, and science (Grades 4–12). Instructional level on cloze tests: 37–57% exact replacement. Passage in Group Reading Inventory is read silently, then taken away. Student answers 14 questions in writing (2 main idea, 3 use of context, 5 details, and 4 inference). Unlike other inventories, only 1 passage given. Instructional level: 64–79% comprehension (9–11 answers correct). Also contains study skills assessment (use of book parts, locational skills, note taking, interpreting graphic aids, reading for different purposes, attitudes, habits, and interests). Grades 4–12. Kendall/Hunt.

Cooper-McGuire Diagnostic Word Analysis Tests (1972). Primarily group-administered. Criterion-referenced. Readiness test samples letter names, auditory and visual discrimination, and sound blending. Seventeen phonic analysis tests (e.g., sound-symbol associations, initial consonant with context, auditory perception of vowels, decoding nonsense words) and 10 structural-analysis tests (e.g., inflected endings, root words, number of syllables heard in words). All subtests need not be given. Two forms. Grades 1–6; disabled readers. Croft.

Criterion Reading (1971). Criterion-referenced. Five levels (K, 1, 2–3, 4–6, 7–adult) covering 451 overlapping specific-objective subtests. Level 1 has 90 subtests: motor skills, visual matching, and auditory matching. Levels 2–5 have 361 subtests in 5 areas: phonics, structural analysis, verbal information, syntax, and comprehension. Grade K–adult. Random House.

Criterion Test of Basic Skills: Reading (1976). Individual. Criterion-referenced. Measures 18 objectives dealing with letter recognition, letter sounds, writing letters, phonics, and word recognition. Average of 13 items per objective. Grades K–8. ATP.

CTBS Espanol. Spanish-language adaptation of 1978 CTBS test battery. Levels 1 (Grades 3–4), 2 (5–6), and 3 (7–8). Grades 3–8. CTB.

Davis Reading Test (1958). Provides scores on level of comprehension and rate of comprehension. Series 2 (Grades 8–11); Series 1 (11–13). Two forms. Grades 8–13. Psy Corp. Out of print.

Decoding Inventory (1979). Group screening test used to determine level of test to be administered individually. Criterion-referenced. Level R (Readiness) measures auditory and visual discrimination. Level 1 (Basic) (Grades 1–3) has 10 subtests; Level 2 (Advanced) (Grades 4 and up) has 17 parts. Grades 1 and up. Kendall/Hunt.

Decoding Skills Test (Richardson & DiBenedetto 1985). Individual. Criterion-referenced. Three subtests: (1) Basal vocabulary—11 10-word lists; (2) phonic patterns (range from CVC to CCVVCC)—6 10-word lists each for monosyllabic and polysyllabic words; and (3) contextual decoding—target words set in context; preprimer–high fifth reader. Yields reader-level scores, profiles of decoding deficiencies, and assessment of effect of context. See Richardson (1985) for more detailed description. Grades 1–5. York.

Degrees of Reading Power (1989). Measure of reading comprehension that uses maze format. Each form contains series of graded passages, with total of 42–77 deletions. Six forms: Grades 1–3, 3, 4–6, 6–9, 9–12, 12–14. Yields 3 scores in DRP units that translate to independent, instructional, and frustration levels. Readability data (in DRP units) on reading materials available. Grades 1–14. TASA.

Diagnosis: An Instructional Aid—Reading (1974). Criterion-referenced. Covers 306 objectives at Level A (Grades 1–4) and 224 at Level B (Grades 3–6). Skill areas measured: phonic and structural analysis; comprehension, vocabulary, study skills, and use of sources. Almost three-quarters of the objectives are sampled by only 1 or 2 items. Grades 1–6. SRA.

Diagnostic Achievement Battery (1984). Primarily individual. Reading subtest measures: letter names, phonics, word knowledge, and reading comprehension (text read silently, oral questions and answers). Listening comprehension subtest samples story comprehension. Other subtests: speaking, writing, and math. Ages 6–14. Pro Ed.

Diagnostic Achievement Test for Adolescents (1986). Primarily individual. Word identification subtest samples word-recognition and decoding abilities. Reading comprehension subtest contains 7 passages for silent reading, each followed by 6 literal and 6 inference questions. Uses IRI format. Also has spelling and reference skills subtests. Grades 7–12. Pro Ed.

Diagnostic Analysis of Reading Errors (DARE) (1979). The 46 words in the WRAT spelling test (Level 11) are read to students, who select the word spoken by the examiner from 4 printed choices. Four scores: number of correct responses, sound substitutions, omissions, and reversals. Ages 12–adult. Jastak.

Diagnostic Analysis of Reading Tasks (1976). Criterion-referenced. Uses nonsense words. DART 1 (Grades 2.5 and below) yields 3 scores: encoding (spelling), decoding, and auditory screening (number of syllables heard in a word). DART 2 (Grade 2.5 and above) yields 6 scores: encoding (sections A, B), decoding (sections A, B), medial diphthongs and digraphs, and irregular letter clusters. Grades 1 and up. Slosson.

Diagnostic Decoding Tests (Sipay 1990). Individual. Criterion-referenced battery of tests from which examiner selects one(s) needed to provide desired information. Measures decoding ability in 1 or more of 3 areas: visual analysis, symbol-sound associations, and blending; also ability to combine skills. Each specific skill (e.g. symbol-sound association for *t*) measured by at least 3 items on any test. Answer sheets designed to facilitate detailed analysis of child's performance that provides information on specific strengths and weaknesses. Report Forms specify whether a skill has been mastered, needs guided practice, or needs to be taught. Grades 1–3, disabled readers. EPS.

Diagnostic Reading Inventory (Jacobs & Searfoss 1979). Individual. Commercially published IRI. Eight graded, 20-word lists (Grades 1–8) and 8 graded passages (1–8), one each for oral reading, silent reading, and listening comprehension. Twelve questions for Grades 1–3; 20 questions for Grades 4–8 (literal, inferential, critical/evaluative, vocabulary). Instructional level: 92–97% word recognition, 60–89% comprehension. Two levels of a decoding inventory also included. Optional phrase list. Grades 1–8. Kendall/Hunt.

Diagnostic Reading Scales (Spache 1981). Individual. Criterion- and norm-referenced battery. Three word lists (40–50 words each), two sets of 11 graded passages (preprimer–seventh reader) with 7–8 comprehension questions each (primarily literal details) and 12 supplementary decoding tests. Word-recognition criterion for oral reading is norm-referenced (mean plus 1 standard deviation). Comprehension criterion for oral and silent reading, and listening comprehension is criterion-referenced (60%). Instructional level is based on oral reading, independent level on silent reading. Decoding tests yield grade-equivalent scores. Grades 1–7; disabled readers. CTB.

Doren Diagnostic Reading Test of Word Recognition Skills (1973). Criterion-referenced. Twelve subtests measure beginning and ending sounds, sight words, rhyming, whole-word recognition, words within words, speech consonants, blending, vowels, discriminate guessing, letter recognition, and spelling. Scoring based on number of incorrect items; 7 or more errors on a subtest indicates need to teach those skills. Grades 1–6. AGS.

Durrell Analysis of Reading Difficulty (1980). Battery of individually administered diagnostic tests. Five primary and 3 intermediate-level paragraphs, each followed by 5–9 primarily factual detail questions. Instructional level (oral reading) based primarily on reading time, with comprehension given consideration. Five different primary- and 3 intermediate-level passages for silent reading. Independent level (silent reading) based on reading time and recall (comprehension measured by retellings). Six passages (Grades 1–6) available for listening comprehension, each followed by 7–8 questions. Criterion for listening comprehension: no more than 2 incorrect answers (72%, 75%). Word-recognition/word-analysis test consists of 4 50-word lists. Words are first flashed, and unknown words are shown untimed. Listening-vocabulary test consists of 5 15-word lists (same words as in word-recognition test); student indicates in which of 3 categories word belongs. Listening vocabulary also used as measure of reading potential. Sounds-in-isolation test measures symbol-sound associations. Spelling test consists of 2 20-word lists; and 15 words are dictated on the phonic-spelling-of-words test. Also included are visual memory for words and identifying sounds in words, as well as prereading phonic abilities inventories. Grades 1–6; disabled readers. Psy Corp.

Durrell Listening-Reading Series (1970). Vocabulary and sentence comprehension subtests in both reading and listening. Provides for comparison of pupil's reading and listening abilities. Primary level (Grades 1–2); Intermediate (3–6); Advanced (7–9). Two forms. Grades 1–6. Psy Corp.

ECRI Informal Reading Inventory. (1981). Individual. Criterion-referenced oral reading test. Separate tests for Grades 1–6 and Grade 7–adult, each with 17 graded passages (preprimer–Grade 12). Six comprehension questions per passage. Instructional level: 91–95% word recognition, 50–75% comprehension. Grade 1–adult. Cove.

Edwards Reading Test (1980). Individual. Commercially published IRI. Eight graded word lists and 8 graded passages (Ages 6–13). Four to 10 questions per passage. Instructional level: 90–95% word recognition, 70% comprehension. Oral reading, silent reading, and listening comprehension measured. Two forms. Heinemann.

Ekwall Reading Inventory (1979). Individual. Commercially published IRI. Each of 4 forms consists of 11 graded word lists (primer–Grade 9) and 11 graded passages (preprimer–9); there is no primer level. Five comprehension questions at preprimer level; 10 at others (factual, inference, vocabulary). Instructional level: 95–98% word recognition, 60–89% comprehension. Oral and silent reading measured; listening comprehension optional. Also contains Quick Survey Word List and the El Paso Phonics Survey. Grades 1–9. Allyn & Bacon.

Formal Reading Inventory (Wiederholt 1985). Each of 4 forms has 13 graded passages, with 5 multiple-choice questions following each. Forms A and C are for silent reading and yield a Silent Reading Quotient. Forms B and D are read orally and the results are used for a modified miscue analysis. Grades 1–12. Pro Ed.

Fountain Valley Reading Skills Tests. Criterion-referenced. For Grades 1–6: series of 77 one-page tests covering 367 objectives (number of objectives per test level range from 33 to 125, with 2 to 12 items per objective). Skill areas sampled: phonic and structural analysis, vocabulary, comprehension, and study skills. For Grades 7–12: 61 specific-objective subtests, usually with 4 to 6 items each. Measures vocabulary, comprehension, and study skills. Grades 1–12. Zweig.

GAP Reading Comprehension Test (1970). Cloze technique with approximately every tenth word deleted in each of 7 brief paragraphs. Yields a reading age. Australian and British editions. Two forms. Grades 2–7. GAPADOL for ages 10–16. Heinemann.

Gates-MacGinitie Reading Tests (1989). Separate levels for Grades 5 and 6, 7–9, and 10–12. Vocabulary subtests contain 45 multiple-choice items. Comprehension subtests consist of a series of narrative and expository passages; 46 items sample understanding of explicit and implicit information. Grades 5–12. Riverside.

Gates-McKillop-Horowitz Reading Diagnostic Tests (1981). Test battery contains 15 individually administered tests. Oral reading test has 7 paragraphs; score based on number of word-recognition errors (reading comprehension questions are not even asked). Reading sentences test has 4 sentences that are read orally; score based on word recognition. Words: Flash consists of 4 10-word lists; Words: Untimed uses same words. Knowledge of word parts: Word attack measures syllabication, recognition, and blending of common word parts, decoding nonsense words, making symbol-sound associations for single consonants, and naming upper- and lowercase letters. Recognition of visual form of sounds measures sound-symbol association of single vowels. Auditory tests measure blending and discrimination. Spelling and writing skills are sampled by written expression test. Grades 1–6; disabled readers. Teachers College Press.

Gillingham-Childs Phonics Proficiency Scales (1967). Individual. Criterion-referenced tests of letter-sound correspondences, syllabication, and decoding of real and nonsense words. Series 1 contains 17 subtests each in reading and spelling. Series 2 has 20 subtests in reading. Grades 1–6. EPS.

Gilmore Oral Reading Test (1968). Individual. Ten graded passages (preprimer–high school; 5 literal questions on each. Scores (based on performance across passages) for accuracy (word recognition), comprehension (literal), and rate of reading. Performance ratings (e.g., above average) also provided. Two forms. Grades 1–8. Psy Corp.

Gray Oral Reading Test (1967). Thirteen graded passages in each of 4 forms. Child continues reading until 7 or more word-recognition errors on 2 consecutive passages. Four factual comprehension questions per passage, but score does not consider comprehension. Score based on time taken to read each passage and number of word-recognition errors per passage; based on performance across passages. Separate norms for girls and boys. Grades 1–12. Bobbs; WPS.

Gray Oral Reading Tests—Revised (1986). Thirteen revised, graded passages in each of 2 forms. Five questions per passage. Passage Score, which is derived in same way as original *Gray,* reported now in standard scores and percentiles. Unlike original, GORT-R yields scores for comprehension, as well as an Oral Reading Quotient. Provides for modified miscue analysis. Ages 7–17. Pro Ed.

Gray Standardized Oral Reading Check Tests (1923–1955). Set 1 (Grade 1); Set 2 (2–3); Set 3 (4–5); Set 4 (6–8). Each set contains 5 passages of approximately equal difficulty (used to measure progress). Yields 2 standard scores; reading rate and accuracy (word recognition). Grades 1–8. Bobbs.

Gray Standardized Oral Reading Paragraphs (1915). Twelve graded paragraphs (Grades 1–12). Yields 3 scores: paragraph, total raw, and B-scores (grade equivalents). Comprehension is not measured. Grades 1–12. Bobbs.

Group Assessment in Reading (1984). Battery of criterion-referenced tests. Series of graded passages (preprimer–Grade 12) for silent reading (instructional level = 75–96% comprehension). Cloze tests (primer–Grade 12) require exact word replacement (instructional level = 40–60%). Also measures specific comprehension skills (word meaning, literal and inferential comprehension, critical reading), work-study skills (locating information, reference sources, pictorial and graphic materials, organizing information), attitudes, and interests. Grades 1–12. Prentice-Hall.

Group Diagnostic Reading Aptitude and Achievement Tests (Marion Monroe & E. Sherman 1939). Yields 15 scores: reading (paragraph comprehension, rate), word discrimination (vowels, consonants, reversals, additions, and omissions), arithmetic, spelling, visual ability (letter and form memory), auditory ability (letter memory, discrimination, and orientation), motor ability (copying, crossing out letters), and vocabulary. Grades 3–9. Nevins.

Individual Evaluation Procedures in Reading (1983). Criterion-referenced. Battery consists of 9 graded 20-word lists, 11 graded passages (primer–Grade 10) in each of 3 content areas (literature, science, history), 6 visual-discrimination tests, 1 auditory-discrimination test, 2 auditory memory tests, 1 phonic and structural-analysis test, 2 lists of survival words, and an interest inventory (used to determine in which content area to test reading). Separate instructional levels for word recognition in isolation (at least 75% of 20 words correct) and in context (88–90% correct; dialectal renditions *are* deliberately counted as errors), and for oral reading, silent reading, and listening (60% criterion). Of the comprehension items, 20–40% for each passage measure word meaning. PAL score is Projected Achievement Level. Two forms. Grades 1–12. Prentice-Hall.

Individual Phonics Criterion Test (1971). Criterion-referenced. Covers 99 phonic skills in 14 areas such as single consonants, long and short vowels, consonant digraphs and blends, and schwa sounds. Grades 1–6. Jamestown.

Individual Pupil Monitoring System: Reading (1974). Criterion-referenced, but a mastery level is not suggested in the manual. Separate test booklets for word attack, vocabulary and comprehension, and discrimination/study skills for each grade level (1–6). Each of 343 overlapping objectives measured by a 5-item test. Two forms. Grades 1–6. Riverside.

Informal Reading Inventory (Burns & Roe 1989). Individual. Commercially published IRI. Two graded word lists (preprimer–Grade 12) and 4 sets of graded passages (preprimer–12). Eight questions at preprimer–second reader; 10 at others (6 types on each passage—main idea, detail, sequence, cause-effect, inference, and vocabulary). Instructional level: 85–95% word recognition (Grades 1–2) or 95–98% word recognition (Grades 3–12) and 75–89% comprehension. Oral reading measured; silent reading and listening comprehension optional. Grades 1–12. Houghton; Nelson-Canada.

Instant Words Criterion Test (1980). Individual. Criterion-referenced. Consists of 300 high-frequency words presented in isolation. Quick survey and suffix tests included. Grades K–3. Jamestown.

Iowa Silent Reading Tests (1973). Measures ability to apply reading skills to different kinds of reading tasks. Reading Efficiency Index indicates relative effectiveness of reading rate and comprehension. Level 1 (Grades 6–9) and Level 2 (Grades 9–14) include subtests of vocabulary, comprehension (including items on which the student is not allowed to look back at the selection), directed reading [work-study skills including locational skills, skimming, and scanning, and reading efficiency (6 short easy passages)]. Level 3 (academically accelerated high school students and college students) does not include a directed reading subtest. Two forms. Grades 6–14. Psy Corp.

Iowa Tests of Basic Skills (1986). Levels 5 (K–1.5), 6 (K.8–1.9), 7 (1.7–2.6), and 8 (2.5–3.5) measure listening, word analysis, and vocabulary. Levels 6–8 also sample reading comprehension. Levels 9–14 (Grades 3, 4, 5, 6, 7, 8–9) have vocabulary, comprehension, and reference materials subtests. Lists behavioral objectives to which test items written. Grades K–9. Riverside.

IOX Basic Skills Competencies in Reading (1984). Criterion-referenced test with 2 forms. Competencies assessed include: decoding, word meaning, comprehension of main ideas and details, drawing conclusions, and using references. Grades 1–8. IOX.

IOX Objectives-Based Tests: Reading (1973). Criterion-referenced; mastery level not specified. Consists of 38 word-attack skills tests (objectives) and 40 comprehension tests. Manual does not suggest which tests should be given at a given grade level. Most word-attack tests have 10 items; most comprehension tests, 5. Two forms. Grades 1–6. IOX.

Johnson Basic Sight Vocabulary Test (1976). Measures recognition of 300 high-frequency words; 10 30-item subtests. Two forms. Grades 1–3. Personnel.

Kaufman Test of Educational Development (1985). Individual. Decoding subtest (66 items) assesses letter-name knowledge, word recognition, and decoding skills. Reading comprehension subtest (50 items) uses sentences and short paragraphs, each followed by 1 or 2 questions. Also has spelling and math subtests. Grades 1–12. AGS.

Kennedy Institute Phonics Test (KIPT). Individual (production) and group (recognition) tests. Measures variety of decoding skills, (symbol-sound associations, blending) and sound-symbol associations. Ages 5 and up. Test Collection.

Library Skills Test (1980). Forty-five-item test designed to locate strengths and weaknesses in working with library materials, including terminology, card catalog classification system, filing, parts of a book, indexes, reference tools, and bibliographic forms. Grades 7–13. STS.

Macmillan Diagnostic Reading Pack (1980). Stage 1 (Reading ages 5–6); item scores in 3 areas: visual skills (e.g., 32 key words, letter matching, visual-memory reproduction), auditory skills (e.g., sound values of letters, auditory discrimination), and phonic blending (auditory blending, blending two- and three-letter words). Stage 2 (Reading ages 6–7); item scores in 5 areas: key words (68 and 32), phonic recognition (e.g., blends and digraphs), phonic blending, phonic spelling (two- and three-letter words), and oral reading (accuracy, comprehension). Stage 3 (Reading ages 7–8); 5 areas: key words, phonic recognition, phonic blending, phonic spelling, oral reading. Stage 4 (Reading ages 8–9); 4 areas: phonic recognition, phonic blending, phonic spelling, oral reading. Ages 5–9. Macmillan England.

McGuire-Bumpus Diagnostic Comprehension Tests (1979). Criterion-referenced. Measures 12 skills in 4 types of comprehension: literal (selecting details, translating details, identifying signal words, selecting main ideas), interpretive (determining implied ideas, identifying organizational patterns, inferring main ideas), analytic (identifying the problem, developing hypotheses, determining relevant details), and critical reading (selecting criteria for judgment, making a judgment). Each type is measured at 3 levels; the level used is dependent on the child's level of reading ability: Early primary (1^2–2^2), primary (2^2–3^2), and intermediate (4th–6th reader levels). Each objective is sampled by 12 multiple-choice questions. Two forms. Grades 1–6. Croft.

McLeod Phonic Worksheets (1987). Criterion-referenced. Measures 6 areas: initial and final single consonants, single vowels, consonant blends and digraphs, vowel blends, and auditory discrimination. Computer-assisted error analysis available. Grades 1–3. EPS.

Metropolitan Achievement Tests: Reading Diagnostic Tests (1986). Primer (Grades K.5–1.9) and Primary 1 (1.5–2.9) subtests: auditory discrimination, word recognition, consonant phoneme-grapheme correspondences, vocabulary in context, and comprehension.

Primer also samples visual discrimination and letter recognition. Primary 1 also has word part clues and vowel sound-symbol association subtests. Primary 2 (Grades 2.5–3.9) has same subtests as Primary 1, except auditory discrimination. Elementary Grades (3.5–4.9), Intermediate Grades (5.0–6.9), and Advanced 1 (Grades 7.0–9.9) subtests: vocabulary in context, rate of comprehension, comprehension, and skimming and scanning. Elementary and Intermediate Grades also have consonant and vowel sound-symbol association and word part clues subtests. Test yields instructional reading level (IRL) score based on child's raw score on reading comprehension subtest. Normed on same sample as *Otis-Lennon*. Grades K–9. Psy Corp.

Mills Learning Methods Test, Revised Edition (1970). Trial teaching procedures. Used to determine comparative effectiveness of 4 methods of teaching word recognition: visual, phonic, kinesthetic, or a combination. Grades K–3; disabled readers. Mills Center.

Monroe Diagnostic Reading Test (Marion Monroe 1928). Preliminary tests include Stanford-Binet, Gray's Oral Reading Paragraphs, Haggerty Reading Examination, Monroe Silent Reading Test, Ayres' Spelling Scale, and Stanford Achievement Test in Arithmetic. Analytic tests include alphabet repeating (alphabetic sequence) and reading (letter-name knowledge), iota word test (recognition of words in isolation), reversible-letters test, mirror reading, mirror writing, number reversals, word discrimination (reversible words), sound blending, and handedness. A profile of word-recognition errors is suggested. Grades 1–4; disabled readers. Stoelting.

Monroe's Standardized Silent Reading Test (Walter Monroe 1919). Very brief tests of rate of comprehension. Test I (Grades 3–5): 17 paragraphs each followed by 1 multiple-choice item; Test II (6–8): 16 paragraphs; Test III (9–12): 12 paragraphs each followed by 1 completion item. Tests I and II are self-scoring. Two forms. Grades 3–12. Bobbs.

MULTI SCORE (1984). Criterion-referenced tests customized to match local school programs. Covers reading readiness, sound-symbol associations, word meaning, comprehension, study skills, and classifying and analyzing forms of literature. Grades K–12. Riverside.

Neal Analysis of Reading Ability (1966). Yields 3 scores: accuracy, comprehension, rate of reading. Three optional tests: names and sounds of letters, auditory discrimination through simple spelling, blending and recognition of syllables. Ages 6–13. Macmillan England.

Nelson Reading Skills Tests (1977). All levels measure word meaning and reading comprehension. For Level A (Grades 3.0–4.5) sound-symbol correspondences, root words, and syllabication are optional. For Levels B (4.6–6.9) and C (7.0–9.9), reading rate is optional. Two forms. Grades 3–9. Riverside.

Nelson-Denny Reading Test (1981). Measures vocabulary (50 prefixed and 50 nonprefixed words), reading comprehension (8 passages with a total of 36 questions—18 each literal and interpretation), and reading rate based on the first minute of the reading comprehension test. Two forms. Two levels: Grades 9–12, 13–16. Riverside.

New Sucher-Allred Reading Placement Inventory (1981). Individual. Commercially published IRI. Each of 2 forms has 12 word lists and 12 oral reading selections (preprimer–9). Five comprehension questions per passage (literal, inferential, cause-effect, main idea). Instructional level: 92–96% word recognition, 60–79% comprehension. Grades 1–9. McGraw-Hill.

Objectives—Referenced Bank of Items and Tests: Reading and Communication Skills (ORBIT) (1982). Customized, criterion-referenced tests (4-item, single-objective subtests) covering up to 50 objectives chosen by the school district to match those of their reading program. Grades K–12. CTB.

Oral Reading Criterion Test (1971). Individual. Criterion-referenced. Consists of 10 brief passages (Grades 1–7). Independent, instructional, and frustration levels based only on word recognition. Grades 1–7. Jamestown.

Peabody Individual Achievement Test Revised (PIAT-R) (1989). Individual. Wide-range screening test: reading, arithmetic, spelling, and general information. Reading recognition includes readiness skills (e.g., visual discrimination, letter names) and words in isolation that the student attempts to read aloud. Reading comprehension contains sentences that are read silently; after each, the student selects the picture (4 choices) that best illustrates the meaning of the sentence. Grades K–12. AGS.

Prescriptive Reading Inventory (PRI) (1977). Criterion-referenced. Covers 30 objectives for Levels 1 (Grades K.0–1.0) and 2 (K.5–2.0) and 90 objectives for Levels A (1.5–2.5), B (2.0–3.5), C (3.0–4.5), and D (4.0–6.5). Reading readiness skills at Levels 1 and 2. Other 4 levels measure phonic and structural analysis; translation (vocabulary); and literal, interpretive, and critical comprehension. Over 80% of pretest objectives are measured by 3–4 items; mastery defined as not more than 1 error. Grades K–6. CTB.

Prescriptive Reading Performance Test (1978). Individual. Uses child's performance on graded word lists (Grades 1–12) and spelling of words that are and are not in the child's sight vocabulary to classify students as normal or into 3 subtypes of reading disability. WPS.

Primary Reading Profiles (1968). Each level has 5 subtests: aptitude for reading, auditory association, word recognition, word attack, and reading comprehension. Level 1 (Grades 1.5–2.5); Level 2 (2.5–3.5). Grades 1–3. Riverside.

PRI/RS (1984). Criterion-referenced. Measures 4 skill areas: oral language at Levels A (Grades K–1) and B (1–2); word attack and usage—word analysis, vocabulary, word usage at Levels A, B, C (Grades 2–3), and D (4–6); comprehension—literal, interpretive, and critical reading at Levels B, C, D, and E (Grades 7–9); and application—study skills, content-area reading at Levels C–E. Measures 171 objectives across the 5 levels. Grades K–9. CTB.

Prueba de Lectura (1978). Assesses reading comprehension in Spanish. Grades 3 and 6. Test Collection.

Primary Reading Test (1981). Assesses ability to apply reading skills to comprehend words and simple sentences. Ages 6–12. NFER-Nelson.

PRISM: Reading 1 (1982). Microcomputer-based software. Criterion-referenced test based on diagnostic-prescriptive approach. Item bank contains over 2000 items in 3 skill areas: word identification, comprehension, and study skills. Levels C, D, E: Grades 3, 4, 5. Psy Corp.

Rauding Efficiency Level Test (Carver). Individual. Eighteen graded passages (Grades 1–18), each with comprehension questions. Efficiency level based on performance on 3–7 passages. Grades 2–18. Revrac.

Reading Diagnosis: Informal Reading Inventories (Fry 1981). Primarily individual. Criterion-referenced. Battery measures oral reading, silent reading comprehension (2 10-item multiple-choice tests: literal and inferential comprehension), phonics (symbol-sound associations of various elements in isolation; decoding nonsense words), recognition of words in isolation, word meaning, letter and number recognition, spelling, handwriting, vision, hearing, and interests. *Oral Reading Criterion Test* has 2 passages for Grades 1–3 and 1 passage for Grades 4–7. Instructional level based only on word recognition (criterion varies from approximately 71% to 97%). *Brief Reading Comprehension Test* read silently; Primary (Grades 1–2) and one test each for 9- and 13-year-olds. Criterion for primary grades is 75% comprehension, 70% for others. Grades 1–6. Jamestown.

Reading Skills Inventory: A Portfolio of Tested Diagnostic and Remedial Techniques (1980). Series of group or individual informal reading inventories in social studies, literature, science, and mathematics. Identifies instructional level and suggests remedial activities. Grades 4–12. Prentice-Hall.

Reading Yardsticks (1981). Criterion-referenced but supplemented by NR information. Level 6 (kindergarten) assesses visual and auditory discrimination, letter and word matching (and identification), vocabulary (understanding spoken words or sentences), and literal and interpretative comprehension of phrases, clauses, and sentences. Levels 7 and 8 (Grades 1 and 2) test auditory and visual discrimination, phonic analysis, vocabulary (meanings of printed words), and comprehension. Level 8 also measures structural analysis. Levels 9–14 (Grades 3–8) measure structural analysis, vocabulary, comprehension, and study skills. Reading rate is assessed at Grades 5–8 (average WPM over 2 passages). Number of subtests in a skill area for a given level range from 4 to 8; number of objectives range from 17 to 46. Specific objectives measured by 3–5 items each. Grades K–8. Riverside.

Roswell-Chall Auditory Blending Test (1963). Brief individual test of ability to hear the sounds of a word pronounced separately by the examiner and then blend them into a whole word, which the testee pronounces. Grades K–2; disabled readers. Essay.

Roswell-Chall Diagnostic Reading Test of Word Analysis Skills (1978). Individual. Brief measures of fundamental skills. Yields 15 scores: high-frequency words, decoding (10 subtests), letter names (upper- and lowercase), and spelling (single consonants, phonically regular CVC words). Two forms. Grades 1–6; disabled readers. Essay.

Sequential Tests of Educational Progress (STEP): Reading, Series III (1979). Measures vocabulary in context and literal and inferential comprehension. Vocabulary test samples knowledge of synonyms. Study skills and listening test measures listening comprehension, following directions, dictionary usage, library skills, and reference skills. Levels E (Grades 3–5), F (4–6), G (8–12). Two forms. Grades 3–12. CTB.

Silent Reading Diagnostic Tests (1976). Eight subtests of word recognition and phonic skills. Measure ability to recognize words in isolation and in context; identify root words; syllabicate and apply syllabication rules; blend word parts; distinguish beginning and ending sound, vowels, and consonant sounds. Grades 3–6. Rand McNally.

Sipay Word Analysis Tests (SWAT) (1974). Out of print. See *Diagnostic Decoding Tests*.

Slosson Oral Reading Test (SORT) (1981). Individual. Brief test of ability to recognize (respond orally to) words presented in isolation. Grades 1–12. Slosson; AGS.

SOBAR (System for Objective-Based Assessment: Reading) (1976). Criterion-referenced test for each grade (K–9). Each contains 23–35 3-item, single-objective subtests (criterion for mastery usually 100%). Skills areas measured: letter recognition (kindergarten), phonic analysis (K–4), structural analysis (1–9), vocabulary (1–9), comprehension (K–9), and study skills (1–9). Also 9 selected short SOBAR reading tests for Grades 3–9. Tests in either English or Spanish can be customized to fit school objectives. SRA.

Spandafore Diagnostic Reading Tests (1983). Individual. Criterion-referenced. Assesses decoding, word recognition, and oral reading, silent reading, and listening comprehension. Grades 1–12. ATP.

Spanish Criterion Referenced Test (1974). Designed to determine mastery of Spanish in reading program for bilinguals. Covers phonics, structural analysis, and comprehension. Grades K–5. Test Collection.

Spanish Oral Reading Test (1982). Individual. Designed for use with native Spanish speakers. Consists of 2 word lists, 2 paragraphs at each of 6 grade levels, and 6 phonics tests (includes English sounds frequently distorted by Spanish speakers). Grades 1–6. Paradox.

Spanish Reading Comprehension Tests and English Reading Comprehension Tests (1978). Spanish tests standardized and normed in Mexico. English tests translated from Spanish tests. Elementary level (Grades 1–6) consists of 73 items; Secondary level (Grades 7–12, adult) consists of 81 items. Designed to determine degree of bilingualism or to evaluate bilingual programs. Grades 1–12. Moreno Educational.

SRA Achievement Tests: Reading (1978). Levels B (Grades 1–2) and C (2–3) subtests: letters and sounds, listening comprehension, vocabulary, and reading comprehension. Level B also measures auditory discrimination. Levels D (Grades 3–4), E (4–6), F (6–8), G (8–10), and H (9–12) sample only vocabulary (word meaning) and comprehension. Separate reference materials tests in Levels E–H. Two forms. Grades 1–12. SRA.

Standard Reading Inventory (McCracken 1966). Individual. Commercially published IRI. Each of 2 forms has 11 graded word lists (preprimer–Grade 7), 11 oral reading passages, and 8 silent reading passages. Five comprehension questions at preprimer level; 13–15 at others (literal, inferential, vocabulary). Yields independent, minimum instructional, maximum instructional, and frustration levels. Instruction level can have "no subtest rated as frustration." Also yields 6–9 subtest scores: word recognition in isolation and context, total oral reading errors, recall after oral and silent reading, total comprehension, word meaning, oral and silent speed, as well as various ratings and check lists. Grades 1–7. Klamath.

Standardized Reading Inventory (Newcomer 1986). Individual. Commercially published IRI. Word lists and 10 graded passages (preprimer–Grade 8). After a passage has been read orally and silently, 5 to 10 open-ended comprehension questions are posed. Instructional level defined as highest level at which child's score is within ± 1SD of mean obtained by standardization sample. Two forms. Grades 1–8. Pro Ed.

Stanford Achievement Test: Reading (1987). Norm-referenced but provides criterion-referenced information. Levels: Primary 1 (Grades 1.5–2.9), Primary 2 (2.5–3.9), Primary 3 (3.5–4.9), Intermediate 1 (4.5–5.9), Intermediate 2 (5.5–7.9), and Advanced (7.0–9.9). Skill areas and grades at which measured: Word-study skills (sound-symbol association, structural analysis)—Grades 1.5–7.9; word reading (matching spoken and printed words or printed words with pictures)—Grades 1.5–3.9; reading comprehension (literal and inferential)—Grades 1.5–9.9; vocabulary (understanding *spoken* words)—Grades 1.5–9.9; and listening comprehension—Grades 1.5–9.9. Normed on same population as *Otis Lennon*. Two or 3 forms. Grades 1–9. Psy Corp.

Stanford Diagnostic Reading Test (1984). Levels: Red (Grades 1.5–4.5); Green (3.5–6.5); Brown (5.5–8.5); Blue (7.5–13.0). Skill areas and grades at which measured: Auditory discrimination—Grades 1.5–6.5; phonetic analysis (sound-symbol associations)—Grades 1.5–8.5; auditory vocabulary (meanings of spoken words)—Grades 1.5–8.5; word reading (word recognition)—Grades 1.5–4.5; reading comprehension (literal and inferential)—all grades; structural analysis (analysis of word parts)—Grades 3.5–13.0; reading rate (ability to read easy material quickly with comprehension)—Grades 5.5–13.0; word parts (knowledge of affixes and root words), vocabulary (understanding meanings of printed words), and skimming and scanning—Grades 7.5–13. Two forms. Grades 1–13. Psy Corp.

Stanford Test of Academic Skills (TASK): Reading (1987). Measures vocabulary (word meaning) and comprehension. Task I (Grades 8.0–12.9); Task II (Grades 9.0–13.9). Two forms. Grades 8–13. Psy Corp.

STS Analysis of Skills—Reading (1974). Criterion-referenced. Three parts: word analysis (discrimination; phonetic analysis—consonants, vowels; structural analysis; word recognition); comprehension (vocabulary in context; literal, inferential, critical comprehension); and study skills (library and reference, organization, pictorial and graphic material). Grades 1–8. STS.

Study Habits Checklist. Yields scores on 37 study skills and habits. Grades 9–14. SRA.

Sucher-Allred Group Reading Placement Test (1986). Two forms, each with 13 word-opposites tests and graded passages (primer–Grade 10). Each 75- to 200-word passage followed by 5 multiple-choice questions (facts, main ideas, inferences, and critical thinking). Scores from both word-meaning and comprehension subtests used to determine instructional level. Grades 2–10. Economy.

Test of Academic Progress (1989). Individual. Reading subtest: word recognition (words read orally) and passage comprehension (read silently, followed by oral questions and answers. Measures literal and inferential comprehension. K–12. Psy Corp.

Test of Reading Comprehension (TORC) (1986). Four subtests: general vocabulary (ability to identify words related to a common concept), syntactic similarities (understanding semantically similar, but syntactically different sentences), paragraph reading (understanding storylike paragraphs) and sentence sequencing. Yields reading comprehension quotient (RCQ), with 85–115 being average. Scaled scores for 4 supplementary tests: math, science, and social studies vocabulary; understanding written directions. Ages 7–17. Pro-Ed.

Tests of Achievement and Proficiency Reading (1986). Reading comprehension test measures ability to define words from context and comprehend prose, poetry, newspaper articles, advertisements, and subject-matter content. Sources-of-information test calls for reading maps, graphs, tables, charts, and reference materials. Normed on same population as *Cognitive Abilities Test.* Levels 15–18 (Grades 9–12). Optional Listening Test. Riverside.

Tests of Individual Needs in Reading (1982). Individual and group. Criterion-referenced. Provides reading level and analysis of reading skills strengths and weaknesses. *Bidwell* form for use with students in western U.S. and Canada; *Red Cloud* form for Native Americans; *Kangaroo* form for use in Australia. *Red Fox* is supplementary group test to evaluate potential for developing word recognition and reading comprehension. Grades 1–7. Council for Indian Education.

The 3-R's Test: Reading (1982). Reading comprehension measured at all levels. Levels 8–18 (Grades 2–12) measure main ideas, explicit and implicit details, and logical relationships/inferences. Levels 9–18 also include words in context, literary analysis, and author's purpose. Vocabulary (word meaning in sentences) measured at Levels 8–18; synonyms also at Levels 8–18. Visual discrimination and sound-symbol association at Levels 6 and 7 (Grades K–1). Study skills at Levels 8–18 (Grades 2–12). Abilities tests (Levels 9–18) measure verbal and quantitative reasoning. Grade-development score (GDS) provides estimate of student's level of reading ability. Grades K–12. Riverside.

Traxler High School Reading Test (1967). Part I measures rate (number words read in 5 minutes) and comprehension (20 questions) of easy material. Part II samples ability to locate main ideas in paragraphs. Two forms. Grades 9–12. Bobbs.

Traxler Silent Reading Test (1969). Yields scores in rate (number of words read in 200 seconds), story comprehension (10 multiple-choice questions based on story used to measure rate), vocabulary (synonyms), and paragraph comprehension. Four forms. Grades 7–10. Bobbs.

Wide Range Achievement Test–Revised (WRAT-R) (1984). Individual. Three subtests: reading, spelling, and arithmetic. Reading subtest primarily measures ability to recognize words in isolation. Level I (Ages 5–11) samples visual discrimination, letter naming, and recognition of up to 75 words. Level II (Ages 12 and up) has a preword section and 74 words. Ages 5 and up. Jastak; Slosson.

Wisconsin Design Tests of Reading Skill Development (1972). Criterion-referenced. Tests measure wide range of word-attack skills at 5 levels: A (Grades K–2), Transition (Grade 1), B (1–3), C (2–4), and D (3–6). Comprehension and study skills measured at 7 levels (K–6). Number of items per subtest greater than found in most CR tests; mastery criterion = 80%. One or 2 forms. Grades K–6. Learning Multi-Systems.

Woodcock Reading Mastery Test–Revised (1987). Individual. Form G has 6 subtests: visual-auditory learning; letter identification; word identification; word attack (decoding nonsense words); word comprehension (synonyms, antonyms, and analogies); and passage comprehension (modified cloze test of sentence comprehension). Form H contains only last 4 of the aforementioned subtests. Two forms. Ages 5–75. AGS.

ADULT BASIC EDUCATION, LITERACY, MINIMAL COMPETENCY

Adult APL Survey (1976). Measures functional literacy at fifth–sixth grade levels. Reading strand has 9 items (of test total of 40) that measure reading in 5 areas of everyday living. Grade 9–adult. American College.

Adult Basic Learning Examination (1986). Measures educational achievement of adults who have had limited formal education. Levels 1 (Grades 1–4), 2 (5–8), and 3 (Grades 9–12) have 4 subtests: listening vocabulary, reading comprehension, spelling, and arithmetic. Levels 1 and 2 also sample grammar, capitalization, and punctuation. Two forms. Ages 17 and up. Psy Corp.

Basic Skills Assessment: Reading (1979). Minimal competency test that uses items such as medicine labels, income tax forms, and job applications. Also measures writing and math skills. Entry norms for Grades 8–9; exit norms for Grade 12. Three forms. Grades 7–12. CTB.

Everyday Skills Tests: Reading (1975). Criterion-referenced test of functional literacy. Measures ability to read labels, want ads, tax forms, and so forth. Fifteen objectives, each with 3 items. Use of reference and graphical materials subtests are norm-referenced. Grades 6–12. CTB.

IOX Basic Skill System (1978). Criterion-referenced measures of minimal competency in reading, writing, and math. Elementary level (Grades 5–6), Secondary level (Grades 7–12). Two forms. Grades 5–12. Psy Corp.

Life Skills: Reading (1980). Criterion-referenced minimal competency test. Measures ability to follow directions (signs, labels, etc.), locate and understand references (phone books, catalogs, etc.), interpret and use information (want ads, lease agreements, etc.), and understand forms (taxes, installment purchases). Two forms. Grades 9–12. Riverside.

Literacy Assessment Battery Contains reading and listening comprehension tests to determine any discrepancy between the two, a vocabulary test to determine the difference between understanding of spoken and written words, and a decoding test. HumRRO.

Performance Assessment in Reading (PAIR) (1981). Criterion-referenced minimal competency test. Seventy-two items sample ability to read warning signs, maps, ads, telephone directory, schedules, and forms. Two forms. Grades 7–9. CTB.

Reading/Everyday Activities in Life (R/EAL) (1972). Criterion-referenced measure of functional literacy (criterion = 80% items correct). Consists of 9 stimulus displays of printed materials used in everyday life (45 fill-in items; 5 per display). Two forms. Ages 15–adult. Westwood.

Senior High Assessment of Reading Performance (SHARP) (1980). Criterion-referenced minimal competency test. Measures ability to apply basic reading skills to life-role situations. Consists of 30 displays representing written materials commonly encountered in daily living. Two forms. Grades 10–12. CTB.

Slosson Oral Reading Test, Form A (1986). Individual. For adults and visually handicapped (words are on separate cards in large print). Same as standard Slosson, but with revised scoring instructions. Adults. Slosson.

SRA Survival Skills in Reading and Mathematics (1976). Criterion-referenced functional literacy tests (norm-referenced scoring can be arranged). Reading tests measure such skills as reading a phone book, street signs, and bills. Grade 6 and up. SRA.

Tests of Adult Basic Education (1987). Reading test comprised of vocabulary and comprehension subtests. Also includes math, spelling, and language tests. Levels E (Grades 2–4); M (Grades 4–6); D (Grades 6–8); and A (Grades 8–12). CTB.

INTELLIGENCE, LEARNING, AND SCHOLASTIC APTITUDE

Arthur Point Scale, Revised Form II (1947). Individual. Nonlanguage scale of mental ability that includes adaptions of 6 tests: *Knox Cube, Seguin Formboard, Arthur Stencil Design, Healey Picture Completion,* and *Porteus Maze.* Requires trained examiner. Ages 5–15. Psy Corp; Stoelting.

British Ability Scales (1983). Designed to help diagnose learning difficulties. Consists of 23 scales measuring a wide range of cognitive abilities that cover 6 areas: speed of information processing, reasoning, spatial imagery, perceptual matching, short-term memory, and retrieval and application of knowledge. Ages $2\frac{1}{2}$–17. NFER-Nelson.

British Picture Vocabulary Scales (1982). Individual. British adaptation of PPVT. Ages 3–18. NFER-Nelson.

Canadian Cognitive Abilities Test (1981). Levels 1 and 2 (Grades K–3) measure verbal, quantitative and nonverbal reasoning, and problem solving. Levels A–H (Grades 3–12) measure scholastic aptitude and abstract reasoning ability. Normed on same population as *Canadian Test of Basic Skills.* Grades K–12. Nelson Canada.

Cognitive Abilities Test (1986). Levels 1 and 2 (Grades K–3) and Levels A–H (Grades 3–12) yield separate scores for verbal, quantitative, and nonverbal reasoning abilities. Normed concurrently with *Iowa Tests of Basic Skills* and *Test of Academic Progress.* K–12. Riverside.

Columbia Mental Maturity Scale (1972). Individual. Brief test that does not require verbal responses and only minimal motor responses. Consists of 92 items arranged in 8 overlapping levels. From a series of drawings, child selects one that does not belong. Ages 3½–10. Psy Corp.

Culture Fair Intelligence Test (Cattell 1933–1977). Measure of general intelligence. Does not require reading and is generally free from cultural and educational influences. Scale 1 (Ages 4–8 and mentally retarded adults) not fully group administrable; Scale 2 (Ages 8–14 and average adult); Scale 3 (Ages 14–superior adult). Scales 2 and 3 have 2 forms and Spanish editions. Ages 4–adult. WPS.

Detroit Tests of Learning Aptitude (1975). Individual. Battery of 19 subtests measure reasoning and comprehension, practical judgment, verbal ability, time and space relationships, number ability, auditory attention, visual attention, and motor ability. Yields MA for each subtest and for total score. Ages 3–adult. Bobbs.

Detroit Tests of Learning Aptitude (DTLA-2) (1985). Individual. Battery of 11 subtests in 4 domains: linguistic, cognitive, attention, and motor. Yields standard scores and percentiles for 8 composite aptitudes: verbal, nonverbal, conceptual, structural, attention-enhanced (STM), attention-reduced (LTM), motor-enhanced (manual dexterity), and motor-reduced (motor-free). General intelligence quotient based on total of 11 subtest scores. Ages 6–17. Pro Ed.

Detroit Tests of Learning Aptitude—Primary (1986). Individual. Eight subtests containing total of 130 items. Types of items include articulation; conceptual matching; design reproduction; digit, letter, object, and word sequencing; draw-a-person; oral directions; picture fragments; sentence imitation; symbolic relations; visual discrimination; and word opposites. Ages 3–9. Pro Ed.

Differential Aptitude Tests (1981). Battery of scholastic aptitude tests. Measures 8 abilities: verbal reasoning, numerical ability, abstract reasoning, clerical speed and accuracy, mechanical reasoning, space relations, spelling, and language usage. Index of scholastic ability based only on verbal reasoning and numerical ability scores. Only verbal reasoning test requires reading ability. Two forms. Grades 8–12, adult. Psy Corp.

Expressive One-Word Picture Vocabulary Test (1980). Individual. Measure of verbal intelligence. Testee continues to name picture shown (110 available) until makes 6 consecutive errors. Yields MA, IQ, percentile, and stanine scores. Ages 2–12. Slosson; WPS.

Expressive One-Word Picture Vocabulary Test—Upper Extension (1983). Individual. Seventy-item measure of verbal intelligence. Ages 12–16. ATP; WPS.

Full-Range Picture Vocabulary Test (Ammons & Ammons 1948). Individual. Measure of verbal intelligence. From 4 pictures, testee chooses one that best illustrates meaning of word spoken by examiner or read by herself. Two forms. Ages 2–adult. Psychological Test.

Goodenough-Harris Drawing Test (1963). Nonverbal test of mental ability. Child's drawings of human figures compared against 12 ranked drawings or scored for the presence of up to 73 characteristics. Separate norms for boys and girls. Ages 3–15. Psy Corp.

Healey Pictorial Completion Tests (1921). Individual. Based on testee's apperceptive ability. In Test I, testee presented a picture with 10 apertures representing 10 incomplete places in the scene. Testee selects and puts in 10 correct inserts from 50 provided. Test II involves selecting 10 squares from 60 choices to complete each of 10 pictures representing, in sequence, daily situations in the life of a school boy. Ages 5 and up. Stoelting.

Henmon-Nelson Test of Mental Ability (1973). Primary battery (Grades K–2) consists of 3 subtests (listening, picture vocabulary, size and number) that measure 9 abilities; does not require reading ability. Tests for Grades 3–6, 6–9, and 9–12 include measures of vocabulary, sentence completion, opposites, general information, verbal analogies, verbal classification, verbal inference, number series, arithmetic reasoning, and figure analogies; reading ability required. Yields IQ (a standard score by age), age and grade percentile ranks, and stanines. Grades K–12. Riverside.

Hiskey-Nebraska Test of Learning Aptitude (1966). Individual. Can be administered entirely via pantomimed instructions; requires no verbal response from testee. Consists of series of performance tasks organized in ascending order of difficulty with 12 subscales. Learning-age score determined by median age level of pupil's performance on subscales. Separate norms for deaf and hearing. Ages 3–17. Hiskey.

Kaufman Assessment Battery for Children (K-ABC) (1983). Individual. Measures intelligence and achievement. Yields 4 global scores: sequential processing, stimultaneous processing, mental processing composite, and achievement; derived scores for subtests (reading scores only in grade equivalents). Only 13 of 16 subtests given to any child. Intelligence assessed through problem solving using simultaneous and sequential memory processes. Sequential Processing Scale comprised of 3 subtests that require child to solve problems by arranging stimuli in sequential or serial order: hand movement (e.g., child performs series of hand movements in same order as examiner), number recall (digit span), and word order (child touches series of silhouettes of common objects in same sequence as names of objects presented orally by examiner). Simultaneous Scale comprised of 7 subtests that require child to solve problems (usually spatial or analogic) in contexts when the input has to be integrated and synthesized in order to produce the appropriate solution (language ability minimized): magic window (identifying pictures that are only partially visible at any one time), face recognition (visual memory of faces), Gestalt closure (visual closure), triangles (assembling triangles into abstract patterns that match models), matrix analogies (selecting pictures or abstract designs that best complete visual analogies), spatial memory (recalling the places of pictures on a page that was exposed briefly), and photo series (putting photographs of an event in chronological order). Achievement Scale measures expressive vocabulary (naming pictured objects); faces and places (naming depicted well-known persons, fictional characters, or places); arithmetic (number and math concepts, counting, computation); riddles (inferring names of concrete or abstract objects when given its characteristics); reading/decoding (naming letters, reading words in isolation); and reading/understanding (acting-out written commands, some of which are single words). Intelligence and achievement tests normed on same population. Ages $2\frac{1}{2}$–$12\frac{1}{2}$. AGS.

Knox's Cube Test. Nonverbal test of mental ability. Measures attention span and short-term memory. KCT Junior (Ages 2–8); KCT Senior (Ages 8–adult). Ages 2–adult. Stoelting.

Kohs Block-Design Test (1919). Individual nonverbal intelligence test consisting of 16 colored cubes used to reproduce 17 colored designs depicted on cards. Similar to block design subtest of *Wechsler* tests. Ages 5–20. Stoelting.

Kuhlman-Anderson Tests (1982). Measure of academic potential. Consists of 8 subtests: 4 verbal, 4 nonverbal. Levels K (Kindergarten); A (Grade 1), B (2), CD (3–4), D (4–5), EF (5–7), G (7–9), H (9–12). Grades K–12. STS.

Leiter International Performance Scale (1969). Nonverbal test of intellectual functioning. Examinee uses blocks to construct designs shown on stimulus cards. Yields MA and IQ scores. Ages 2–18. Slosson; Stoelting.

Lorge-Thorndike Intelligence Tests. Multi-Level Edition (1966) (Levels A–H for Grades 3–13) provides 3 scores: verbal, nonverbal, and composite. Separate Levels Edition

(1962) yields nonverbal score for Levels 1 (K–1) and 2 (Grades 2–3); verbal and nonverbal scores for Levels 3–5 (Grades 4–6, 7–9, 10–12). Two forms. Riverside.

McCarthy Scales of Children's Abilities (1972). Individual measure of general intelligence. Provides 6 scores: verbal, perceptual-performance, quantitative, composite (general cognitive), memory, and motor. Ages $2\frac{1}{2}$–$8\frac{1}{2}$. Psy Corp.

Mill Hill Vocabulary Scales (Raven et al. 1988). Measure of word-meaning knowledge (verbal ability). Uses multiple-choice and open-ended items. Used to supplement information regarding nonverbal reasoning ability as determined by *Raven Progressive Matrices*. Ages $6\frac{1}{2}$–$16\frac{1}{2}$. Psy Corp.

Nonverbal Test of Cognitive Skills (1981). Fourteen subtests measure aspects of reasoning, rote memory, recognition and memory of patterns, visual memory, discrimination, spatial relations, thinking and memory, and visual-motor perception. Instructions can be pantomimed; oral language not required of testee. Ages 6–13. Psy Corp.

Otis-Lennon School Ability Test (1987). Measure of abstract thinking and reasoning ability (scholastic aptitude). Levels: Primary I (Grade 1), Primary II (2–3), Elementary (4–5), Intermediate (6–8), and Advanced (9–12). Reading not required on Primary I and II. Two forms. Grades 1–12. Psy Corp.

Peabody Picture Vocabulary Test—Revised (PPVT-R) (1981). Individual. Measure of verbal intelligence. From 4 choices, child points to picture that best illustrates word spoken by examiner. Two forms. Ages $2\frac{1}{2}$–4. AGS.

PMA Readiness Level (1974). Revision of 1962 edition of Primary Mental Abilities. Five subtests: auditory discrimination, verbal meaning, perceptual speed, number facility, and spatial relations. Grades K–1. SRA.

Porteus Maze (1914–1965). Nonlanguage test of mental ability. Series of 12 mazes of increasing difficulty. Yields qualitative and quantitative scores. Ages 3–14. Psy Corp; Stoelting.

Primary Mental Abilities Test (1962). All 5 levels (K–1, 2–4, 4–6, 6–9, 9–12) sample verbal meaning, number facility, and spatial relations. Perceptual speed tested in K–6 and reasoning ability in 4–12. Grades K–12. SRA.

Quick Test (Ammons & Ammons 1962). Individual test of verbal intelligence. Similar to but shorter (50 items) than *Full-Range Picture Vocabulary Test*. Child selects drawing (4 choices) that best illustrates meaning of word spoken by examiner or read by child. Three forms. Ages preschool–adult. Psychological Services.

Raven Progressive Matrices (1938–1987). Individually administered nonverbal test of mental ability. Requires examinee to solve problems presented in abstract figures and designs. Yields percentile scores. Ages 8–65. Psy Corp.

Receptive One-Word Picture Vocabulary Test (1985). Individual. No verbal response required. Yields stanine, percentile, and language age scores. Normed in San Francisco area. Spanish version available. Ages 2–11. ATP.

Revised Beta Examination (BETA II) (1978). Measure of mental ability that does not require reading ability. Six subtests: mazes, coding, paper form boards, picture completion, clerical checking, and picture absurdities. Yields IQ scores and percentile ranks. Ages 16–64. Psy Corp.

Short Form Test of Academic Aptitude (1970). Four subtests: vocabulary, analogies, sequences, and memory. Yields language and nonlanguage scores. Level 1 (Grades 1.5–3.4), 2 (3.5–4), 3 (5–6), 4 (7–9), 5 (9–12). Grades 1–12. CTB.

School and College Ability Tests (SCAT), Series III (1980). Verbal subtest uses verbal analogies to measure word meaning. Quantitative subtest measures fundamental number operations. Elementary level (Grades 3–6); Intermediate (6–9); Advanced (9–12). Two forms. Grades 3–12. CTB.

Slosson Intelligence Test (1981). Individual. Brief measure of verbal intelligence. Many items *very* similar to those on the Stanford-Binet. Ages 2–18. Slosson; Stoelting.

SRA Pictorial Reasoning Test (1973). Designed "to measure learning potential of individuals from diverse backgrounds with reading difficulties." Entails reasoning with nonverbal, pictorial materials. Consists of 80 sets of 5 pictures or designs. Task is to select the one that differs from the rest. Ages 14 and over. SRA.

Stanford-Binet Intelligence Scale (1972). Individual test of general intelligence (primarily verbal). Test items arranged by age level, with 6 subtests administered at each. Abilities measured include memory, vocabulary, abstract reasoning, and social competence. Yields MA and IQ scores. Ages 2–adult. Riverside.

Stanford-Binet Intelligence Scale, Revised (1986). Fifteen subtests in 4 areas: verbal reasoning (vocabulary, comprehension, verbal relations, absurdities); abstract/visual reasoning (pattern analysis, matrices, paper folding and cutting, copying), quantitative comprehension (quantitative, number series, equation building); and STM (memory for sentences, digits, objects, and beads). Yields scores for each subtest, each of the 4 general areas, and a complete score. Requires trained examiner. Scores correspond to IQs now called "Standard Age Scores." Ages 2–adult. Riverside.

System of Multicultural Pluralistic Assessment (SOMPA) (1978). Individual and group-administered. Assesses cognitive and sensorimotor abilities and adaptive behaviors. Provides estimate of learning potential (ELP) that takes into account differences in family background, SES, etc. Two major components: Parent Interview (adaptive behavior inventory, sociocultural scales, health history inventories) and Student Assessment (physical dexterity, weight by height, visual and auditory acuity, Bender, and WISC-R or WP-PSI). Ages 5–11. Psy Corp.

Test of Cognitive Skills (1981). Measure of scholastic aptitude, reflecting such abilities as reasoning, problem solving, evaluating, discovering relationships, and remembering. Four subtests: sequence (ability to comprehend a rule or principle implicit in a pattern or sequence of figures, letters, or numbers); analogies (ability to understand concrete or abstract relationships and to classify objects or concepts according to common attributes); memory (ability to recall previously presented material); and verbal reasoning (ability to discern relationships and to reason logically). Yields subtest and Cognitive Skills Index (total score). Successor to Short Form Test of Academic Aptitude. Level 1 (Grades 2–3); Level 2 (3–5); Level 3 (5–7); Level 4 (7–9); Level 5 (9–12). Grades 2–12. CTB; PTS.

Test of Nonverbal Intelligence (TONI) (1982). Individual or small-group. Fifty-item, language-free measure; examiner pantomimes instructions and testee responds by pointing. Involves abstract problem solving of increasingly more complex tasks. Two forms. Ages 5–85. Pro-Ed; Slosson.

Wechsler Adult Intelligence Scale–Revised (WAIS-R) (1981). Individual. Yields verbal, performance, and full-scale IQ scores. Verbal scale subtests: information, digit span, vocabulary, arithmetic, comprehension, and similarities. Performance Scale subtests: picture completion, picture arrangement, block design, object assembly, and digit symbol. Requires trained examiner. Ages 16–74. Psy Corp.

Wechsler Intelligence Scale for Children–Revised (WISC-R) (1974). Individual. Yields verbal, performance, and full-scale IQs. Verbal Scale subtests: information, similarities, arithmetic, vocabulary, comprehension, and digit span (supplementary subtest). Performance Scale subtests: picture completion, picture arrangement, block design, object assembly, coding, and mazes (supplementary subtest). Requires trained examiner. Ages 6–16. Psy Corp.

Wechsler Preschool and Primary Scale of Intelligence (WPPSI) (1967). Individual. Yields verbal, performance, and full-scale IQs. Verbal Scale subtests: information, vocabulary, arithmetic, similarities, comprehension, and sentences (supplementary subtest). Performance Scale subtests: animal house, picture completion, mazes, geometric design, and block design. Requires trained examiner. Ages 4–6½. Psy Corp.

Wide Range Intelligence-Personality Test (1978). Measure of global intelligence and personality variables. Ten subtests measure verbal, pictorial, spatial competency, and so on. Also provides cluster scores for language, reality set, motivation, and psychomotor skills. Ages 9½–adult. Jastak.

PERCEPTUAL, PERCEPTUAL-MOTOR, MEMORY, LATERALITY

Auditory Discrimination Test (Wepman 1987). Individual. Forty-item test of ability to distinguish whether two spoken words are exactly the same or differ (in one minimally contrasting phoneme). Two forms. Ages 4–8. Language; WPS.

Auditory Memory Span Test (Wepman & Morency 1975). Individual. Requires ability to retain and recall sets of single-syllable words spoken by the examiner. Sets range from 2 to 6 words. Two forms. Ages 5–8. Language; Stoelting; WPS.

Auditory Sequential Memory Test (Wepman & Morency 1975). Individual. Brief test in which child tries to repeat increasingly longer series of single digits in exactly the same sequence as spoken by examiner. Two forms. Ages 5–8. Stoelting; WPS.

Bender Visual Motor Gestalt Test (1946). Usually individual. Measures perceptual-motor integration. Testee copies, one at a time, 9 abstract designs, which remain in view. Child's reproductions are scored on basis of departures from stimuli. *Bender* often scored using Koppitz system for 5- to 10-year-olds. Pascal and Suttell scoring system often used for older childen and adults. AGS; Psy Corp.

Benton Revised Visual Retention Test (1974). Usually individual. Designed to assess visual perception, visual memory, and visual-motor integration. Ten designs, one at a time, shown briefly, and examinee attempts to draw each. Also yields IQ equivalents. Ages 8–adult. Psy Corp.

Bieger Test of Visual Discrimination (1982). Identifies levels of mastery in identifying larger contrasts, lesser contrasts, and almost identical words and letters. Grades 1–6. Stoelting.

Bruininks-Oseretsky Test of Motor Development (1978). Individual. Used to assess motor development, neurological development and dysfunction. Measures 8 areas of gross and fine motor proficiency. Yields scores for gross motor, fine motor, and battery composite. Short form consists of 14 of the 46 items that constitute complete battery; yields only a general motor proficiency score. Ages 4½–14½. AGS.

Developmental Test of Visual-Motor Integration (1989). Usually individual. Measures ability to integrate visual perception and motor behavior. Pupil copies up to 24 geometric forms of increasing difficulty. Short and long forms. Ages 3–18. MCP.

Frostig Developmental Test of Visual Perception (DTVP) (1966). Five subtests: eye-motor coordination (drawing continuous lines between increasingly narrower boundaries, or drawing lines to connect 2 targets); figure-ground (picking out and outlining geometric forms embedded among other forms); constancy of shape (discriminating among geometric forms of differing sizes, shadings, textures, and positions); position in space (distinguishing between figures in the same or reversed or rotated positions); and spatial relations (joining dots to reproduce forms and patterns shown). Ages 7–8. CPS; Stoelting.

Goldman-Fristoe-Woodcock Test of Auditory Discrimination (1970). Individual. Measures ability to discriminate speech sounds in quiet and in noise. Testee responds to word (on tape) by pointing to 1 of 4 pictures whose names differ in only one sound. Ages 4–adult. AGS.

Goldman-Fristoe-Woodcock Auditory Skills Test Battery (1976). Individual. Battery of 12 tests in four categories: auditory selective attention, auditory discrimination, auditory memory, and sound-symbol tests (which includes measures of auditory analysis, sound blending, and ability to make symbol-sound associations). Age 3–adult. AGS.

Harris Tests of Lateral Dominance (1958). Individual. Set of brief tests of knowledge of left and right; hand preferences; simultaneous writing with both hands; speed and coordination in writing, tapping, and dealing cards; monocular and binocular tests of eye dominance; and foot dominance. Ages 7 and up. Psy Corp.

Jordan Left-Right Reversals Test (1980). Consists of series of numbers, letters, and words printed in correct or left-right reversed spatial orientation. Level 1 (Ages 5–8) contains only single numbers and letters. Level 2 (Ages 9–12) consists of words (many contain reversed letters) and short sentences containing reversed words. Ages 5–12. ATP; Slosson.

Kindergarten Auditory Screening Test (1971). Individual. Recorded test with 3 subtests: listening for speech against a noise background, sound blending, and auditory discrimination. Grades K–1. Follett.

Lincoln-Oseretsky Motor Development Scale (1956). Individual. Consists of 36 items involving a wide variety of motor skills, such as coordination, speed of movement and finger dexterity, eye-hand coordination, and gross activity of the hands, arms, legs, and trunk. Both unilateral and bilateral motor tasks measured. Ages 6–14. Stoelting.

Lindamood Auditory Conceptualization Test (1971). Individual. Consists of 4 parts: precheck (understanding of concepts needed to take the test; e.g., same/different); identifying the number of sounds heard and determining if they are the same or different; indicating the sequence of sounds, and determining the number of sounds in a syllable, and changes in the sound pattern when sounds are added, deleted, changed or repeated. Understanding of task indicated by manipulating colored blocks. Two forms. Ages preschool–adult. DLM.

Memory-for-Designs Test (Graham & Kendall 1960). Usually individual. Design is shown for 5 seconds, then testee attempts to draw it from memory. Each of 15 designs scored 0 to 3 by comparing it to a model. Ages $8\frac{1}{2}$–60. Psychological Test.

Minnesota Percepto-Diagnostic Test (1969). Usually individual. Measure of visual-motor performance. Six designs copied in different settings. Used to diagnose neurological dysfunctions, emotional problems, and personality disorders. Also used to classify LDs as visual, auditory, or mixed. Ages 5–70. Clinical.

Motor-Free Visual Perception Test (1972). Individual. Brief 36-item test that does not require motor skills other than pointing. Child selects (4 choices) the item that is the same as (or different from) the line drawing shown. Section 3 requires visual memory; Section 4, visual closure. Yields perceptual quotient and perceptual age scores. Ages 4–8. ATP; Slosson; Jastek.

Psychoeducational Inventory of Basic Learning Abilities (1968). Individual. Measures 53 basic learning abilities in 6 areas: gross motor development, sensory-motor integration, perceptual-motor skills, language development, conceptual skills, and social skills. Ages 5–12. Fearon.

Purdue Perceptual-Motor Survey (1966). Individual. Series of 11 tasks measuring balance and posture, body image, perceptual-motor skills, ocular control, and form perception. Ages 6–10. PTS; Psy Corp.

Screening Test for Auditory Perception (STAP) (1981). Assesses weaknesses in 5 areas of auditory discrimination: long vs. short vowel sounds, initial single consonants vs. blends, rhyming vs. nonrhyming words, same vs. different rhythmic patterns, and same vs. different words. Grades 1–6. Slosson.

Southern California Motor Accuracy Test (Ayres 1980). Individual. Measures degree of, and changes in, sensorimotor integration of upper extremities. Ages 4–8. WPS.

Southern California Sensory Integration Tests (Ayres 1980). Individual. Battery of 17 short tests: space visualization, figure-ground perception, design copying, motor accuracy, kinesthesia, manual form perception, finger identification, graphesthesia, localization of tactile stimuli, double tactile stimuli perception, imitation of postures, crossing midline of body, bilateral motor coordination, right-left discrimination, and standing balance, eyes open and eyes closed. Ages 4–8. WPS.

Spatial Orientation Memory Test (Wepman & Turaids 1975). Individual. Assesses ability to retain and recall orientation (direction) of visually presented forms. Child responds by pointing to one of a choice of visual stimuli. Two forms. Ages 5–9. WPS; Stoelting.

Test of Lateral Awareness and Directionality (1980). Usually individual. Criterion-referenced. Used to identify children with left-right labeling problems. Pupils classified as high, medium, or low risk. Grades 1–2. ATP.

Test of Non-Verbal Auditory Discrimination (1975). Individual. Nonverbal test of auditory discrimination. Subtests: pitch, loudness, rhythm, direction, and timbre. Ages 6–8. Follett.

Tree/Bee Test of Auditory Discrimination (1978). Usually individual. Assesses phonetic discrimination in individual words, phrases, word pairs, and same/different comparisons. Scored for initial and final consonants, vowel sounds, auditory memory, and ability to follow oral directions. Two forms. Grades K–8. PTS.

Visual Aural Digit Span Test (1978). Individual. Measures short-term memory. Two to 7 digits presented orally or visually for verbal or written repetition. Eleven subtests yield scores for auditory and visual processing, and intrasensory integration. Ages $5\frac{1}{2}$–12. Slosson; ATP.

Visual Discrimination Test (Wepman et al. 1975). Twenty-item test of ability to determine which 2 of 5 nonalphabetic forms are identical. Two forms. Ages 5–8. WPS; Stoelting.

Visual Memory Test (Wepman et al. 1975). Individual. Sixteen-item test of ability to recall unfamiliar forms that cannot be readily named. Two forms. Ages 5–8. WPS; Stoelting.

SENSORY, EYE MOVEMENTS (INDIVIDUALLY ADMINISTERED)

A O Sight Screener (1956). Targets available for both readers and nonreaders of English words and numbers. American Optical.

Eye-Trac. Eye-movement camera. Can determine number and duration of fixations and regressions, span of recognition, and reading rate. Set of 64 reading selections (Grade 1–college) for use with Eye-Trac. G & W Applied Science.

Keystone Tests of Binocular Skill (1938–1949). Adaptation of *Gray Standardized Oral Reading Check Tests* for use with telebinocular. Comparable selections are read orally with each eye separately and with binocular vision. Identifies children who can read better with one eye than with both eyes together. Grades 1–8. Keystone.

Keystone Visual Screening Test (1933–1971). Telebinocular and 15 stereographs provide measure of binocular near- and far-point acuity, muscle balance, depth perception, fusion, and color vision. Short screening test available. Separate School Vision Tests for Massachusetts, Michigan, and New York. Grades 1 and up. Keystone.

Keystone Visual Survey Tests (1933–1961). Uses revision of *Betts Ready to Read Test* with telebinocular. Grade 1 (Grade 2 or 4 for some tests). Keystone.

Ortho-Rater (1958). Stereoscopic instrument (various models) and accompanying stereographic slides used for visual screening. Measures binocular near- and far-point acuity, depth perception, visual discrimination, and color vision. Short test for rapid screening. Grades 1 and up. Bausch and Lomb.

Picture Spondee Threshold Test (1983). Audiometric test used with individuals who cannot function within standard hearing test format that requires them to repeat words. All ages. DLM.

Reading Eye II. Portable eye-movement camera. Measures fixations, duration of fixations, regressions, span of recognition, reading rate with comprehension. Provides 3 ratings: grade level of reading, relative efficiency, directional attack. Includes 64 reading selections. Grade 1–adult. EDL.

School Vision Tester (1974). Consists of 6 tests; tumbling E acuity (each eye), farsightedness (each eye), muscle balance (far, near). Same instrument as Ortho-Rater. Grades K and up. Bausch & Lomb.

Spache Binocular Reading Test (1955). Individual. Measures relative participation of each eye in reading by using stereoscopic slides with different words omitted on each side of the slide. Three levels of difficulty. For use in telebinocular or stereoscope. Test 1 (nonreaders and Grade 1); Test 2 (Grades 1.5–2); Test 3 (Grade 3 and over). Keystone

Titmus Vision Tester (1969). Both School Unit (Grades 1–5) and General Testing Unit (Grades 1–12) duplicate *Massachusetts Vision Test*. Titmus.

OTHER TESTS AND MEASURES

Arithmetic

Diagnostic Test of Arithmetic Strategies (1984). Measures ability to perform addition, subtraction, multiplication, and division calculations. Analysis of performance allows for identification of faulty computational strategies and potential strengths. Grades K–6. Pro-Ed.

Keymath-Revised (1988). Individual. Criterion-referenced. Fourteen subtests. Assesses 3 basic areas of math: content (math concepts), operations (computations), and applications (use of math skills in daily life). Grades K–9. AGS.

Test of Mathematical Abilities (1984). Measures computational and word-problem abilities. Also provides information about attitude toward math, math vocabulary, and understanding of math applications. Grades 3–12. Pro-Ed.

Attitudes

Estes Attitude Scales (1981). Elementary form (Grades 2–6) includes 3 scales for measuring attitudes toward reading, science, and math. Secondary form (7–12) include 5 scales: reading, science, math, English, and social studies. Grades 2–12. Slosson.

Reading Appraisal Guide (1979). Individual. Interview measure of attitudes toward reading and a form for recording errors during oral reading. Grades 5–12. Australian Council; NWRL.

School Attitude Measure. Samples students' stated views of their academic environment and of themselves as learners. Five scales: Motivation for Schooling, Academic Self-Concept—Performance Based, Academic Self-Concept—Reference Based (how others view my school performance), Sense of Control over Performance, and Instructional Mastery (what I need to succeed and learn in school). Levels 4–12 (Grades 4–12). American Testronics.

Language, Spelling

Illinois Test of Psycholinguistic Abilities, Revised (ITPA-R) (1969). Individual. Evaluates abilities in 3 dimensions: channels of communication, psycholinguistic processes, and levels of organization. Twelve subtests: auditory reception, visual reception, auditory association, visual association, verbal expression, manual expression, grammatic closure, visual closure, auditory closure, and sound blending. Ages 2–10. Slosson; WPS.

Northwestern Syntax Screening Test (1971). Individual. Provides quick estimate of syntactic development in receptive and expressive language. Ages 3–8. Northwestern; Stoelting.

Spellmaster Assessment and Teaching System (1987). Subtests include: entry level test; regular-word, irregular-word tests; and homophone test. Yields independent, instructional, and frustration levels for each of 3 word types. Grades K–10. Pro-Ed.

Test of Adolescent Language–2 (1987). Individual. Eight subtests provide information about wide range of language abilities including word meaning and syntax used in listening, speaking, reading, and writing. Yields 10 scores plus adolescent language quotient (ALQ). Grades 6–12. Pro-Ed.

Test for Auditory Comprehension of Language–Revised (1985). Individual. Listening comprehension covering word classes and relations, morphemes, and elaborated sentence constructions. Ages 3–7. DLM.

Test of Awareness of Language Segments (Sawyer 1987). Individual. Three subtests: Sentences-to-Words—9 pairs of sentences read to child who is to repeat each word orally and push forward a block to represent that word; Words-to-Syllables (10 words); and Words-to-Sounds (18 words). Scores: high, average, low; ready for reading instruction, approaching readiness, not ready. Ages 4–6. Aspen.

Test of Language Development–2 (1988). Individual. Primary Edition (Ages 4–8) has 7 subtests that measure various components of receptive and expressive language (word meaning and use, grammar, articulation, auditory discrimination). Intermediate Edition (Ages 8–12) has 6 subtests that measure word meaning and use as well as 3 aspects of syntactic and semantic knowledge. Ages 4–12. Pro-Ed.

Test of Written Spelling–2 (1986). Measures ability to spell phonetically regular and phonetically irregular words. Dictated-word format. Yields spelling quotient and percentile scores. Grades 1–12. Pro-Ed.

Learning and Modality Preferences and Styles

Barsch Learning Style Inventory (1980). Informal 24-item self-report that purports to indicate relative strengths and weaknesses in learning through different sensory channels. Grades 9–16. ATP.

Kerby Learning Modality Test (1980). Individual. Brief screening test to measure visual, auditory, and motor activity strengths and weaknesses. Eight subtests: visual and auditory discrimination, visual and auditory closure, visual and auditory memory, visual and auditory motor coordination. Ages 5–11. WPS.

Learning Style Identification Scale (1981). Identifies 5 learning styles based on testee's internal sources of information (e.g., feelings, beliefs, attitudes) and external sources of information (e.g., other people, events, social institutions). Grades 1–8. PTS.

Medical, Neurological, Neuropsychological

The Anser System (1981). Series of questionnaires regarding pupil's health, education, development, and behavior. Used to assess school adjustment or learning problems. Parent and school forms for each of 3 levels: Form 1 (Ages 3–5), Form 2 (Ages 6–11), and Form 3 (Ages 12–18). Form 4 is self-administered profile for students aged 9 and up. Ages 3–18. EPS.

Halstead-Reitan Neuropsychological Test Battery (1979). Individual. Three batteries: *Reitan-Indiana Neuropsychological Test Battery for Children* (Ages 5–8), 13 tests assessing a broad range of neurological functions; *Halstead Neuropsychological Test Battery for Children* (Ages 9–14), 11 tests; *Halstead Neuropsychological Test Battery for Adults* (Age 15 and up), 13 tests. Ages 5–adult. Neuropsychological Laboratory.

Institutes Developmental Profile (1980). Individual. Used with Doman-Delacato approach to determine child's neurological age. Covers visual, auditory, manual, and tactile competence; language; and mobility. Institutes.

Luria-Nebraska Neuropsychological Battery (1980). Individual. Assesses broad range of neuropsychological functions. Consists of 269 discrete, scored items in 14 scales: motor, rhythm, tactile, visual, receptive and expressive language, writing, reading, arithmetic, memory, intellectual, pathognomonic, left and right hemisphere. Requires trained examiner. Two forms. Age 15 and up. WPS.

Luria-Nebraska Neuropsychological Battery: Children's Revision (1987). Individual. Assesses broad range of neuropsychological functions similar to those listed in test for older individuals. Includes screening and diagnosing general and specific cognitive deficits. Not useful with children who have low verbal ability. Requires trained examiner. Ages 5–12. WPS.

Neurological Dysfunctions of Children (1979). Individual. Screening device for deciding whether to refer child for a neurological examination. Series of 18 yes-no (normal-impaired) items. First 16 items require child to perform simple tasks (e.g., walking along a straight line, touching a finger to nose, and following moving object with eyes). Ages 3–10. AGS.

Quick Neurological Screening Test (1978). Individual. Brief screening test assesses 15 areas of neurological integration. Samples motor development, control of large and small muscles, motor planning and sequencing, sense of rate and rhythm, spatial organization, visual and auditory perception, balance and cerebellar-vestibular function, and attention. Ages 5–adult. Slosson; Psy Corp.

Psychiatric and Personality Disorders

Children's Apperception Test (1980). Individual. Projective technique (basic assumption of projective techniques is that testee will reveal motives, fears, interests, etc.). Ten pictures of various situations shown to child, who tells a story about, or describes, each. Requires trained examiner. Ages 3–10. Stoelting; Psy Corp.

Holtzman Inkblot Technique (1972). Individual. Projective test. Testee is shown 45 blots and asked to describe what he sees. Requires trained examiner. Two forms. Ages 5 and over. Psy Corp.

House-Tree-Person Projective Technique (1966). Individual. Testee makes freehand drawings of a house, a person, and a tree and then discusses each. Requires trained examiner. Ages 3–adult. WPS.

Michigan Picture Test-Revised (1980). Individual. Projective technique. Child responds to 4 pictures. Measure of emotional maladjustment and various personality factors. Requires trained examiner. Grades 3–9. Psy Corp.

Rorschach Psychodiagnostic Test (1951). Individual. Projective technique. Testee is shown 10 "inkblots" and asked to describe what she sees. Requires trained examiner. Ages 3 and over. Stoelting; Psy Corp.

Stroop Color and Word Test (1978). Individual. Very brief test used to investigate personality, cognition, stress response, psychiatric disorders, and other psychological phenomena. Consists of 3 pages: A Word Page on which the names of colors are printed in black; a Color Page with semantically meaningless symbols (Xs) printed in various colors; a Word-Color page on which the words on the first page are printed in the colors presented on the second page, but the name of the color and the color in which it is printed do not match. Grades 2 and up. Stoelting.

Thematic Apperception Test (1973). Individual. Projective technique. Subject shown series of 20 pictures and asked to tell a story about each. Requires trained examiner. Ages 6–adult. Stoelting; Psy Corp.

APPENDIX

B

Series Books for Remedial Reading

Many series have been written specifically to link interest appeal with simplified vocabulary and style. These series have enriched the available resources for corrective and remedial reading.

   One of the most difficult yet most important things to do when working with a poor or reluctant reader is to get him interested in reading. Thus it is important to choose reading material with care. You should select titles that seem likely to appeal to his interests. These materials should be at or below his independent reading level, at least initially. A teacher who has only a rough idea of a child's independent reading level should start with material that is at least two years below the level of material currently being used for reading instruction. If the first book tried seems too easy or too difficult, an adjustment should be made in making the next choice. The reading and interest grade levels shown below are those indicated by the publishers.

Title	Publisher	Reading Grade Level	Interest Grade Level
ANIMAL ADVENTURE SERIES	Benefic	PP–1	1–4
Action adventures of animals based on sound scientific knowledge; 12 realistic stories.			
BUTTERNUT BILL SERIES	Benefic	PP–1	1–4
Adventures of a young boy in the Ozark Mountains in the 1850s; 8 titles.			
TOM LOGAN SERIES	Benefic	PP–1	1–6
Ten books that relate the adventures of a boy growing to manhood in the Old West.			
COWBOY SAM SERIES	Benefic	PP–3	1–6
Western content of these 15 books appeals to many boys.			
MOONBEAM SERIES	Benefic	PP–3	1–6
Ten space-age adventures of a monkey, with adult multiethnic characters as co-stars.			
DAN FRONTIER SERIES	Benefic	PP–3	1–6
Ten adventure books depicting early pioneer life in the Midwest.			
COWBOYS OF MANY RACES	Benefic	PP–5	1–7
Depicts adventures of black American, Spanish-American, and Indian cowboys on the early western frontier; 7 titles.			

Title	Publisher	Reading Grade Level	Interest Grade Level
MANIA BOOKS	Childrens	1	1–5

Sixteen books on such subjects as clowns, animals, and volcanoes; numerous full-page illustrations.

FIRST READING BOOKS	DLM	1	2–3

Written with the easier half of the Dolch Basic Sight Words and the 95 common nouns. Content deals with pets, birds, and wild animals.

DILEMMAS AND DECISIONS	Opportunities for Learning	1–2	9–12

Ten 64-page novels in which teenagers face a variety of difficult decisions.

HELICOPTER ADVENTURE SERIES	Benefic	1–3	1–4

Six adventure stories, some with women in active roles.

FIND OUT ABOUT	Benefic	1–3	1–6

Twelve science books that investigate basic science facts and concepts.

READY, GET SET, GO BOOKS	Childrens	1–3	1–6

Twenty-four books on such topics as dinosaurs, motorcycles, trucks, and dolls.

JIM FOREST READERS	Addison	1–3	2–7

Adventure stories about Jim Forest, a young teenager, and his forest ranger uncle.

JIM HUNTER BOOKS	Fearon	1–3	6–adult

Adventures of a James Bond–type secret agent; 16 titles.

PACESETTERS	Childrens	1–4	4–12

Twenty-four mysteries, suspense stories, science fiction, and adventure stories.

BREAKTHROUGH	Allyn	1–8	7–12

Series of short paperbacks containing modern stories, articles, biographies, and poetry.

A BOOK ABOUT	Raintree	2	2–4

Sixteen books dealing primarily with science topics.

BASIC VOCABULARY BOOKS	DLM	2	3–4

Content about folktales, animals, and Indian folklore.

FIRST HOLIDAY BOOKS	Garrard	2	3–5

Folklore and legends from America and other countries woven into holiday stories.

PRIME TIME ADVENTURES	Childrens	2	4–12

Ten mystery and adventure tales with mature formats.

NEW TRUE BOOKS	Childrens	2–3	1–4

Science subjects appealing to most interests; books contain well-organized, constructive information; 100 titles.

BOXCAR CHILDREN MYSTERIES	Whitman	2–3	3–8

Series of 19 separate mysteries involving the Alden family, who begin their adventures by making their home in a boxcar in order to stay together.

DISCOVERY	Garrard	2–3	4–6

Over 60 biographies of outstanding women, scientists, explorers, reformers, humanitarians, and statesmen.

READ ABOUT SCIENCE	Raintree	2–3	4–6

Fifteen titles covering such topics as space, light and color, and time and clocks.

INTRIGUE SERIES	Benefic	2–3	4–12

Four tales of mystery and intrigue. Map and chart skills developed in the process of unraveling the plots.

CLASSICS LIBRARY	ETA	2–3	5–12

Shortened adaptations including *The Jungle Book, The Last of the Mohicans,* and *Moonstone.*

TOP FLIGHT READERS	Addison	2–3	5–12

Adventures involving various aviation vehicles. Characters of many ethnic backgrounds.

PACEMAKER TRUE ADVENTURES	Fearon	2–3	5–adult

Eleven true stories in paperback; includes historical figures, escape, spies, and pirates.

Title	Publisher	Reading Grade Level	Interest Grade Level
PACEMAKER CLASSICS	Fearon	2–3	5–adult

Sixteen abridged and adapted paperback versions including *The Jungle Book, Two Years Before the Mast,* and *A Tale of Two Cities.*

| ADAPTED CLASSICS | Nat. Assn. Deaf | 2–3 | 6–12 |

Two titles not found elsewhere, *Beowulf* and *The Song of Roland.*

| LAURA BREWSTER BOOKS | Fearon | 2–3 | 6–adult |

Six fast-paced whodunit mysteries and adventures of Laura Brewster, insurance investigator.

| SPORTSTELLERS | Fearon | 2–3 | 6–adult |

Each of eight books focuses on a major sport; subplots explore conflicts and challenges facing today's athletes.

| GALAXY 5 | Fearon | 2–3 | 6–adult |

Six science-fiction stories.

| SPACE POLICE | Fearon | 2–3 | 6–adult |

Six space-age "cops and robbers" books.

| HI-LO PAPERBACKS | Bantam | 2–3 | 7–12 |

Series of 14 contemporary adventure, horror, and mystery stories.

| SPECTER | Fearon | 2–3 | 7–adult |

Series of eight psychic phenomena stories.

| INNER CITY SERIES | Benefic | 2–4 | 2–7 |

Young people solve their problems with imagination, humor, determination; 5 titles.

| EMERGENCY SERIES | Benefic | 2–4 | 2–9 |

Six adventures of a paramedic team, one of whom is a woman.

| WILDLIFE ADVENTURE SERIES | Addison | 2–4 | 3–7 |

Books portray true-to-life experiences of different wild animals.

| MORGAN BAY MYSTERIES | Addison | 2–4 | 3–8 |

Nine well-illustrated mystery books; teenage characters.

| GEMINI BOOKS | Childrens | 2–4 | 3–12 |

Sixteen short books dealing with basic information about such topics as cars, karate, climbing, running, women's sports.

| HORSES AND HEROINES | Benefic | 2–4 | 4–7 |

Six stories involving the adventures of a young girl and her horse.

| SPORTS MYSTERIES SERIES | Benefic | 2–4 | 4–12 |

Teenage boys and girls meet and overcome problems in sports and school activities; 12 titles.

| RACING WHEELS SERIES | Benefic | 2–4 | 4–12 |

Adventures of an inner-city boy and his friends, who learn about the training, equipment, and driving techniques of auto racing; 12 titles.

| CHECKERED FLAG SERIES | Addison | 2–4 | 5–12 |

Fast-moving stories combine a racing setting with the intrigue of mystery. Different types of cars, races, or motorcycles are featured in each book.

| BESTSELLERS I, II, III, IV | Fearon | 2–4 | 6–adult |

Each set contains 10 novelettes with suspense, romance, mystery, or science fiction as themes.

| CRISIS SERIES | Fearon | 2–4 | 6–adult |

Teenagers are confronted by some unhappy realities of life (e.g., alcoholism, adoption, death) in each of 6 books.

| HIWAY BOOKS | Westminister | 2–4 | 7–12 |

Seventeen titles that have adventure, mystery, racing, and interpersonal relationships as their themes.

| ACTION LIBRARIES | Scholastic | 2–4 | 7–12 |

Sixty original paperback novelettes with high-interest plots; characters from various racial and cultural backgrounds.

Title	Publisher	Reading Grade Level	Interest Grade Level
TALESPINNERS, I, II	Fearon	2–4	7–adult

Each set has eight diverse novels that combine believable characters with cliff-hanging predicaments; history, adventure, mystery, and science fiction.

DEEP SEA ADVENTURE SERIES	Addison	2–5	3–8

Twelve adventure and mystery stories about the sea. Mature characters.

WORLD OF ADVENTURE SERIES	Benefic	2–6	4–9

Eight suspense stories built around expeditions.

MYSTERY ADVENTURE SERIES	Benefic	2–6	4–12

Young-adult boy and girl solve mysteries through deductive reasoning, courage, and determination; 6 titles.

SPACE SCIENCE FICTION SERIES	Benefic	2–6	4–12

Adventures of space travelers who visit alien planets and their inhabitants; 6 titles.

TURNING POINT	McCormick	2–6	5–10

Thirty paperbacks ranging in topics from contemporary teenage experiences to the supernatural.

NEW KALEIDOSCOPE READERS	Addison	2–9	7–12

Eight paperbacks covering such topics as careers, sports, and cars. Aimed at reluctant readers.

FOLKLORE OF THE WORLD	Garrard	3	4–5

Fourteen books covering folktales from around the world.

FAMOUS ANIMAL STORIES	Garrard	3	4–6

Each of the 17 titles highlights an animal that displays heroism, devotion, or intelligence.

INDIANS	Garrard	3	4–6

Thirteen biographies of Indian heroines and heroes; history from the American Indian's point of view.

HOLIDAYS	Garrard	3	4–6

History, customs, and traditions in the United States and other lands.

GOOD EARTH BOOKS	Garrard	3	4–7

Science topics dealing with ecology and environmental education.

JUNIOR SCIENCE BOOKS	Garrard	3	4–7

Authentic and well-illustrated books that deal with facts scientifically.

AMERICAN FOLKTALES	Garrard	3–4	4–5

Lively stories about famous folk heroes, regional lore, and exaggerated adventures.

SCOUT SKILL BOOKS	BSA	3–4	5–8

Twelve inexpensive paperbacks on wide variety of topics.

SUPER SPECTOR	Fearon	3–4	6–adult

Six tales of the macabre and bizzare.

SUNDOWN FICTION	New Readers	3–4	7–12

Eighteen titles dealing with courage, dedication, personal triumph and loss, independence, romance, and history.

DOOMSDAY JOURNALS	Fearon	3–4	7–adult

Six suspenseful stories dealing with possible calamities or disasters; science facts.

THAT'S LIFE	Fearon	3–4	9–12

Eight worktexts in which one of 4 ethnic families deals with personal or financial problems, such as medical care and buying a used car.

PLAY THE GAME SERIES	Bowmar	3–5	4–12

Eight stories of famous athletes from various sports.

SEARCH BOOKS	Bowmar	3–5	4–12

Twelve 16-page booklets covering a variety of science topics such as weather, telling time, dolphins, and bird migrations.

DOUBLE ACTION	Scholastic	3–5	7–12

Thirty titles with themes of personal growth, adventure, and mystery.

Title	Publisher	Reading Grade Level	Interest Grade Level
SPOTLIGHT IN LITERATURE	McGraw-Hill	3–6	7–12

Eight books feature the works of over 60 authors including Twain, Shakespeare, and Hemingway.

| WRITERS VOICES | Literacy Volunteers of New York City | 3–6 | 7–adult |

Six books containing excerpts from the works of contemporary writers. Topics include problems encountered by minorites in growing up, divorce, and personal relationships.

| SUM-WAY BOOKS | Fearon | 4 | 4–8 |

Five interactive books. Reader makes decisions as to direction plot will take by solving math word-problems.

| EXPLORING AND UNDERSTANDING SERIES | Benefic | 4 | 4–9 |

Each of the 13 books explores a subject in depth, with special emphasis on science processes.

| CLASSIC PLEASURE READERS | DLM | 4 | 5–7 |

Adaptations of famous stories and legends including Robin Hood, Robinson Crusoe, Aesop, fairytales, and folktales (6 books).

| AMERICANS ALL | Garrard | 4 | 5–7 |

Biographies emphasize character and personal determination of individuals of many races, creeds, and national origins.

| EVERYREADER SERIES | Webster | 4 | 6–8 |

Twenty simplified classics and short-story collections.

| INCREDIBLE SERIES | Barnell-Loft | 4–5 | 7–12 |

Twelve short books that relate unusual historic events.

| FASTBACKS | Fearon | 4–5 | 7–adult |

Six sets whose themes are crime, mystery, science fiction, horror, spies, and romance. Each of 74 novelettes is 32 pages long.

| DOUBLE FASTBACKS | Fearon | 4–5 | 7–adult |

Four titles dealing with the adventures of the Strange Occurrence Squad who investigate unusual phenomena. Each is 64 pages in length.

| YOUNG ADVENTURERS SERIES | Bowmar | 4–6 | 4–12 |

Teenagers in various adventures such as surfing and gliding.

| LANDMARK BOOKS | Random | 4–6 | 5–9 |

Over 65 titles concerned with historical events and important people. Many books written by outstanding authors.

| ALLABOUT BOOKS | Random | 4–6 | 5–11 |

Well-written, factual books on many topics of interest to children.

| SUPERSTARS SERIES | Steck-Vaugh | 4–6 | 7–12 |

Each of 6 books contains short stories about music, movies, television, and sports stars.

| ADAPTED CLASSICS | Globe | 4–8 | 5–12 |

Seventeen simplified and shortened versions including *Moby Dick*, *Tom Sawyer*, *The Scarlet Letter*, and *The Diary of Anne Frank*.

| SPORTS | Garrard | 5 | 5–7 |

Histories of individual sports and biographies of great names in sports.

| JAMESTOWN HANDBOOKS | Jamestown | 5 | 6–12 |

Fourteen books provide information on performing in baseball, basketball, and women's gymnastics.

| JAMESTOWN CLASSICS | Jamestown | 5 | 6–12 |

Twenty-four short adapted versions of stories authored by Jack London, Bret Harte, and Arthur Conan Doyle.

| GREAT UNSOLVED MYSTERIES | Raintree | 5 | 6–adult |

Twenty titles, such as *The Bermuda Triangle*, *Stonehenge*, *UFOs*, and *Killer Bees*.

Title	Publisher	Reading Grade Level	Interest Grade Level
MYTHS, MAGIC, AND SUPERSTITIONS	Raintree	5	6–adult
Twenty books on ghosts, ghouls, haunted houses, great magicians, and so on.			
TOP PICKS	Random	5–7	5–12
Abridged versions of the works of famous authors; 2 or 3 paperbacks on each of 9 topics including comedy, science fiction, sports, and people.			

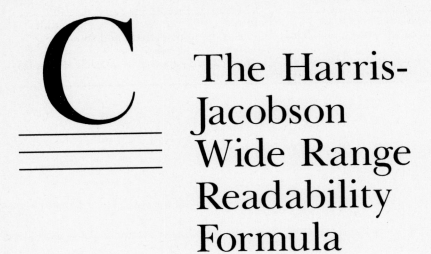

The Harris-Jacobson Wide Range Readability Formula

The readability formula presented here may be used with materials ranging from pre-primer through eighth-reader levels and, by extrapolation, at secondary school and adult levels. It uses two variables: the percentage of hard words (V1) and sentence length (V2).

PREPARING FOR AND USING THE FORMULA

A worksheet comparable to the one on page 737 is useful for tabulating information and using the formula.

Selecting and Counting Samples

Readability is estimated on the basis of representative samples. For a short selection, a minimum of three samples should be used and the readability scores averaged. For a book, a minimum of five samples should be used.

    The samples should be taken at equal intervals through the selection or book. For three samples, divide the work into rough thirds and open at random to one page in each third. For five samples, choose one page at random from each fifth of the work. Do not use the first two paragraphs of selection, in which there is often a concentration of new vocabulary. Do not count numbers or other nonverbal symbols, or the verbal material in figures and tables as words.

Taken from Albert J. Harris and Milton D. Jacobson, *Basic Reading Vocabularies*. New York: Macmillan, 1982, pp. 19–37. Reproduced by permission of the authors and the Macmillan Publishing Co.

Start each sample at the beginning of a paragraph, marking the place with a check in the margin. Count 200 consecutive words and continue counting to the end of the sentence that contains the two-hundredth word. (One-hundred-word samples have been shown to be comparatively unreliable.) Record the page number of the sample and the total number of words on Line A of the worksheet. Count and record the number of sentences in the sample. Count each heading and subheading as a sentence. Record the number of sentences on Line C of the worksheet.

Finding Variable 1

V1 is the percent of hard words in a sample. Hard words are words not on the Readability List. The list is composed of the preprimer through Grade-2 words from the basic Alphabetical List, including the inflectional endings shown. Words in a sample that are not in the list are counted as hard except for proper nouns, which are counted as easy even if they are not on the list. (Numbers, symbols, etc., are not counted at all, as mentioned above.) A hard word is counted as hard only the first time that it occurs in a sample. If a hard word occurs in two samples, it is counted as hard both times. Make a tally mark for each hard word and count the tallies. Record the number of hard words on Line B of the worksheet. The Readability List is found on pages 737–744.

Divide the number of hard words by the number of words in the sample. Multiply the result by 100 to express the result as a percentage. Carry the result to three decimal places. This is the V1 score.

Finding Variable 2

V2 is average sentence length, or mean number of words per sentence. Divide the number of words in the sample by the number of sentences. Carry the result to three decimal places. This is the V2 score.

How to Use the Formula

The following equation is used to find the Predicted Raw Score for a sample.

$$\text{Predicted Raw Score} = .245 \text{ V1} + .160 \text{ V2} + .642$$

The following example may be helpful in clarifying the steps that are followed in finding the Predicted Raw Score and the Readability Score.

Steps in Using the Formula[1]

Sample: Page 21
　　　　　　Number of words (A)　　　207
　　　　　　Number of hard words (B)　　8
　　　　　　Number of sentences (C)　　24
　　　　　　Step 1.　Obtain the V1 score.
　　　　　　　　　　　$8 \div 207 = .0386 \times 100 = 3.865$
　　　　　　Step 2.　Obtain the V2 score.
　　　　　　　　　　　$207 \div 24 = 8.625.$
　　　　　　Step 3.　Multiply the V1 score by .245
　　　　　　　　　　　$3.865 \times .245 = 0.947$

Step 4. Multiply the V2 score by .160
  $8.625 \times .160 = 1.380$
Step 5. Add together the result of Step 3, the result of Step 4, and .642
  (a constant).
  $0.947 + 1.380 + .642 = 2.969$ (the Predicted Raw Score)
Step 6. Round off the Predicted Raw Score to one decimal place.
  $2.969 = 3.0$
Step 7. Find the Predicted Raw Score in Table E.1 and record the
  Readability Score that corresponds to it.
  For 3.0, the Readability Score is 2.9

[1]When using a hand calculator, one may wish to do Step 3 before Step 2. This makes it quicker to calculate the formula because V1 and V2 scores need not be erased from and later reentered into the calculator. The data can be recorded on the worksheet as they are obtained.

The Readability Score is an adjustment of the Predicted Raw Score. Table C.1 gives the Readability Scores that correspond to the Predicted Raw Scores. To find the Readability Score for a selection or a book, add the Readability Scores for each sample and divide by the number of samples. This mean constitutes the Readability Score for the selection or book.

Table C.1 Readability Scores Corresponding to Predicted Raw Scores[a]

Raw Score	Readability Score	Raw Score	Readability Score	Raw Score	Readability Score
1.1	1.0	3.4	3.4	5.7	6.7
1.2	1.0	3.5	3.5	5.8	6.9
1.3	1.0	3.6	3.6	5.9	7.1
1.4	1.1	3.7	3.7	6.0	7.3
1.5	1.2	3.8	3.8	6.1	7.5
1.6	1.3	3.9	3.9	6.2	7.7
1.7	1.4	4.0	4.0	6.3	7.9
1.8	1.5	4.1	4.1	6.4	8.1
1.9	1.7	4.2	4.3	6.5	8.3
2.0	1.8	4.3	4.5	6.6	8.5[a]
2.1	1.9	4.4	4.6	6.7	8.7
2.2	2.0	4.5	4.7	6.8	8.9
2.3	2.1	4.6	4.8	6.9	9.1
2.4	2.2	4.7	5.0	7.0	9.2
2.5	2.3	4.8	5.2	7.1	9.4
2.6	2.4	4.9	5.4	7.2	9.6
2.7	2.6	5.0	5.5	7.3	9.8
2.8	2.7	5.1	5.7	7.4	10.1
2.9	2.8	5.2	5.9	7.5	10.3
3.0	2.9	5.3	6.0	7.6	10.5
3.1	3.1	5.4	6.2	7.7	10.7
3.2	3.2	5.5	6.4	7.8	10.9
3.3	3.3	5.6	6.5	7.9	11.1
				8.0	11.3

[a]Readability Scores above 8.5 have been derived by extrapolation.

Worksheet

Book title_____ Author _____

Publisher _____ Copyright date _____ Scored by _____

Sample Number	1	2	3	4	5
Pages of sample	20,21	46,47	. . . .	. . . .	. . . .
A. No. of words	207	205	. . . .	. . . .	. . . .
B. No. of hard words	8	10	. . . .	. . . .	. . . .
C. No. of sentences	24	22	. . . .	. . . .	. . . .

Step

1. $V1 = B \div A \times 100$	3.865	. . . .			
2. $V2 = A \div C$	8.625	. . . .			
3. $V1 \times .245$	0.947	. . . .			
4. $V2 \times .160$	1.380	. . . .	. . . .		
5. Step 3 + Step 4 + .642 = Predicted Raw Score	2.969	. . . .	. . . .	. . . .
6. Step 5 rounded	3.0	. . . .	. . . .	. . . .
7. Readability Score	2.9	3.3	. . . .	. . . .	. . . .

READABILITY LIST

a	and	awake d	beaver s 's
able r st	angry ier iest	away s	became
about	animal s 's	baby ies 's	because
above	another 's	back s ed ing	become s ing
across	answer s 's ed ing	backyard s	bed s ded ding
act s ed ing	ant s 's	bad dest ly	bedroom s
add s ed ing	any	bag s ged ging	bedtime
afraid	anybody 's	bake s d ing	bee s
after	anymore	ball s 's ed	been
afternoon s 's	anyone 's	balloon s 's ing	before
again	anything	band s ed ing	began
against	anyway s	bang s ed ing	begin s ning
age s d ing	anywhere	bank s 's ed ing	behind
ago	apart	bar s 's red ring	being s
agree s d ing	apartment s	bare s d ing r st ly	believe s d ing
ahead	apple s 's	bark s ed ing	bell s 's ed
air s 's ed y ily	are	barn s 's	belong s ed ing
airplane s 's	aren't	base s 's d ing	below
alike	arm s 's ed ing	baseball s 's	belt s ed
all	around	basement s	bench es ed
alley s	arrow s ed	basket s	bend s ing
almost	art s	bat s 's ted ting	beside s
alone	artist s 's	bath s	best
along	as	be	bet s ting
already	ask s ed ing	beach es ed ing	better s ed ing
also	asleep	bean s	between
always	at	bear s 's ing	beyond
am	ate	beat s ing	big ger gest
an	aunt s 's	beautiful ly	bike s d ing

bill s ed ing
bird s 's
birthday s 's
bit s
bite s ing
black s ed ing er est ly
blackberry ies
blanket s ed ing
blew
block s ed ing y
bloom s ed ing
blow s ing
blue s 's r st
board s 's ed ing
boat s 's ed ing
bob s bed bing
body ies 's
bone s d ing
book s 's ed
boot s ed ing y
born
boss es 's ed y
both
bottle s 's d
bottom s
bought
bow s ed ing
bowl s ed ing
box es ed ing y
boy s 's
brace s d ing
branch es ed ing
brave s 's d r st ly
bread s ed
break s ing
breakfast s 's ed
breath s y
breeze s d
bridge s 's d ing
bright er est ly
bring s ing
broke r
broken ly
brook s
brother s 's ly
brought
brown s ed
brush es ed ing y
bug s ged ging
build s ing
buildings
built

bump s ed ing y
bunch es ed ing
bunny ies
burn s ed ing
bus es
bush es ed y ily
busy ied ier iest
but
butter s 's ed ing y
butterfly ies 's
button s ed ing
buy s ing
by
cage s d y
cake s 's d ing
call s ed ing
came
camp s 's ed ing y
can s ned ning
can't
candle s
candy ies ied
cannot
cap s ped ping
captain s 's
car s 's
card s ing
care s d ing
careful ly
carrot s y
carry ies ied ing
case s 's d ing
castle s 's
cat s 's
catch es ing y
cattle 's
caught
cave s 's d ing
center s 's ed ing
certain ly
chair s 's ed
chance s d
change s d ing
charge s d ing
chase s d ing
cheer s ed ing ily y
cheese s
cherry ies
chest s y
chew s ed ing y
chicken s 's
chief s 's ly

child 's
children 's
chin s
chirp s ed ing
choose s ing
circle s 's d ing
circus es 's
city ies 's
clap s ped ping
class es ed ing y
classroom s
clay s 's
clean s ed ing est ly
clear s ed ing er est ly
clever er est ly
click s ed ing
climb s ed ing
clock s 's ed
close s d ing r st ly
cloth s
clothe s d ing
cloud s ed ing y
clown s 's ed ing
clue s 's d
coat s ed ing
cock s ed ing y
coin s 's ed
cold s er est ly
collect s ed ing
color s ed ing
come s
coming
cook s 's ed ing
cookie s
cool s ed ing er est ly
copy ies 's ied ing
corn y
corner s ed
cost s ing ly
could
couldn't
count s 's ed ing
country ies 's
course s d ing
cover s ed ing
cow s 's ed
cowboy s 's
coyote s 's
crab s bed bing
crack s ed ing
crash es ed ing
crawl s ed ing y

crayon s ed
cricket s
cross es ed ing er ly
crow s 's ed ing
cry ies ied ing
cup s ped ping
curl s ed ing y
cut s ting
dad s 's
daddy 's
dam s med ming
dance s d ing
dandelion s
dark s er est ly
dash es ed ing
daughter s 's
day s 's
daylight s
daytime s
dear s 's er est ly y
decide s d ing
deep s er est ly
deer 's
desk s
detective s 's
did
didn't
die s d
different ly
dig s ging
dine s d ing
dinner s 's
dirt y
dish es ed ing
dive s d ing
do 's ing
doctor s 's ed ing
does
doesn't
dog s 's ged ging
doghouse s
doll s 's y
dollar s 's
don s ned ning
don't
done
donkey s 's
door s 's
doorbell s
doorway s
dot s ted ting
down s ed ing y

downstairs
Dr.
dragon s 's
draw s ing
dream s ed ing ily y
dress es ed ing
drew
drink s ing
drive s ing
driver s 's
drop s ped ping
drove s
drum s med ming
dry ies ied ing ier iest ly
duck s 's ed ing y
dug
during
dust s ed ing y
each
ear s
early ier iest
earth 's ly y
east
easy ier iest
eat s ing
eaten
edge s d ing
editor s 's
egg s ing
eight s 's
either
elephant s 's
elevator s 's
else 's
elves
empty ies ied ing
end s ed ing
enemy ies 's
enough
enter s ed ing
even s ed ly
evening s 's
ever
every
everybody 's
everyday
everyone 's
everything 's
everywhere
exact s ing ly
except ing
exchange s d ing

exercise s d ing
explain s ed ing
explore s d ing
extra s
eye s d ing
face s d ing
fact s ly
factory ies
fair s 's er est ly
fall s 's ing
fallen
family ies 's
far
farm s 's ed ing
farmer s 's
farther
fast ed ing est
faster
fat s ter test
father s 's ed ly
favorite s
fear s ed ing
feather s ed ing y
fed s
feed s ing
feel s ing
feelings
feet
fell s ed ing
felt s
fence s d ing
few er est
field s 's ed ing
fight s ing
fill s ed ing
final s ly
find s ing
fine s d r st ly
finger s 's ed ing
finish es ed ing
fire s 's d ing
first s ly
fish es 's ed ing ily y
fishermen 's
fit s ted ting ter
five s
fix es ed ing
flap s ped ping
flash es ed ing y
flat s test ly
flew
flip s ped ping

float s ed ing
flood s ed ing
floor s ed ing
flour s y
flower s ed ing y
fly ies 's ied ing
fold s ed ing
follow s ed ing
food s
fool s 's ed ing
foot ing
for
forest s ed
forever
forget s ting
forgot
forgotten
forth
found ed ing
fountain s
four s 's
fox es 's ing y
free s d ing r ly
fresh er est ly
Friday s 's
friend s 's ly
frighten s ed ing
frog s 's
from
front s ed
fruit s ed
full er est y
fun
funny ies ier iest
funny-looking
fur s
fuzz y
gallop s ed ing
game s 's ing ly
garage s
garbage
garden s 's ing
gate s 's
gather s ed ing
gave
geese
geography
get s ting
ghost s 's ing ly
giant s 's
girl s 's
give s ing

given
glad dest ly
glass es ed y
go es ing
goat s 's
gold s
golden
gone
good s 's ly
good-by s
goodness
got
gotten
grab s bed bing
grade s d ing
grandfather s 's ly
grandma s 's
grandmother s 's ly
grass es y
gray s ed ing er
great s er est ly
green s ing er est
grew
ground s 's ed ing
grow s ing
growl s ed ing
grown
guess es ed ing
ha
had
hadn't
hair s 's ed y
half
hall s
hammer s ed ing
hand s 's ed ing y ily
hang s ed ing
happen s ed ing
happily
happy ier iest
hard er est ly
has
hat s 's
hate s d ing
have ing
haven't
he
he'd
he'll
he's
head s 's ed ing y
hear s ing

heard
heavy ier iest
held
hello s
help s ed ing
helper s 's
hen s 's
her s
here
here's
herself
hey
hi
hid
hidden
hide s ing
high er est ly
hill s y
him
himself
his
hiss es ed ing
hit s ting
hold s ing
hole s 's d y
home s 's ing ly y
homework 's
honey ed
hop s ped ping
hope s d ing
horn s 's ed y
horse s 's ing y
hose s d
hospital s 's
hot ter test ly
hour s 's ly
house s 's d ing
how
howl s ed ing
hug s ged ging
huge st ly
hum s med ming
hundred s 's
hung
hungry ier
hunt s ed ing
hunter s 's
hurry ies ied ing
hurt s ing
I
I'd
I'll
I'm

I've
ice s d ing
idea s
if
important ly
in
indeed
indoor s
inside s
instead
interest s ed ing
into
invite s d ing
is
island s 's
isn't
it s
it's
itself
jam s 's med ming
jar s 's red ring
jay s 's
jet s ted
job s 's
join s ed ing
joke s d ing
joy s
jump s ed ing y
junk
just ly
keep s ing
kept
key s ed
kick s ed ing
kid s 's ded ding
kill s ed ing
kind s er est ly
king s 's ly
kiss es ed ing
kitchen s 's
kite s 's
kitten s 's
knee s 's d ing
knew
knock s ed ing
knot s 's ted ting
know s ing
known
ladder s 's
lady ies 's
lake s 's
land s 's ed ing
language s

lap s ped ping
large r st ly
last s ed ing ly
late r st ly
laugh s ed ing
lay s ing
lead s ed ing
leaf ed ing y
lean s ed ing er est
leap s ed ing
learn s ed ing
leather y
leave s ing
led
left y
leg s 's ged ging
lemon s ed
lesson s
let s ting
let's
letter s ed ing
library ies 's
lick s ed ing
lie s d
life 's
lift s ed ing
light s 's ed ing er ly
like s ing ly
liked
line s d ing
lion s 's
listen s ed ing
little r st
live s ing
lived
lock s 's ed ing
log s ged ging
lonely ier iest
long s ed ing er est
look s ed ing
loose d ing r ly
lose s ing
lost
lot s 's
loud er est ly
love s 's d ing ly
low ing er est ly
luck ily y
lunch es
lunchroom
lunchtime
lying
ma 's

machine s 's d
mad der ly
made
magic 's
mail s ed ing
main ly
make s
making s
mama 's
man s 's ned ly
many
map s 's ped ping
march es ed ing
mark s ed ing
market s ing
marry ies led ing
mask s ed ing
matter s ed
may
maybe
mayor s 's
me
meadow s 's
mean s ing er est
meant
measure s d ing
meat s y
meet s ing
melt s ed ing
men 's
meow s ed ing
message s
met
mice
middle s
might y ily
mile s 's
milk ed ing y
miller 's
mind s 's ed ing
mine s 's d ing
minute s 's ly
mirror s 's ed ing
miss es ed ing
mix es ed ing
moan s ed ing
mom s 's
Monday s 's
money s 's
monkey s 's
monster s 's
month s 's ly
moo s ed ing

moon s 's ing y
moonlight
more
morning s 's
most ly
mother s 's ed ing ly
mountain s 's
mouse 's d ing y
mouth s 's ed ing
move s ing
moved
movie s
Mr.
Mrs.
Ms.
much
mud
music
must y
my
myself
nail s ed ing
name s 's ing ly
named
nap s ped ping
near s ed ing er est ly
nearby
neck s
need s ed ing y
neighbor s 's ed ing ly
neither
nest s ed ing
net s ted ting
never
new s er est ly
newspaper s 's
next
nice r st ly
night s 's ly
nine s 's
no
nobody 's
nod s ded ding
noise s
none
noon
north 's
nose s d ing y
not
note s d ing
nothing 's
notice s d ing
now

nowhere
number s ed ing
nut s ting
o'clock
ocean s 's
of
off ing
office s 's
officer s 's
often
oh
oil s 's ed ing y
OK
old s er est
on
once
one s 's
only
onto
open s ed ing ly
or
orange s
order s ed ing ly
other s 's
our s
out s ing
outdoor s
outside s
oven s 's
over ly
overhead
owl s 's
own s ed ing
pack s 's ed ing
page s d
pail s
paint s ed ing
painter s 's
paintings
pair s ed ing
pan s ning
pant s ed ing
papa 's
paper s 's ed ing y
parade s 's d ing
park s 's ed ing
parrot s 's
part s 's ed ing ly
party ies 's
pass es ed ing
past
paste d ing
pat s ted ting

patch es ed ing y
path s
paw s ed ing
pay s ed ing
pea s
peanut s
peek s ed ing
pen s ned ning
pencil s ed
penny ies
people s 's d
pepper s ed y
perfect ed ly
person s 's
pet s 's ted ting
phone s 's d
piano s
pick s ed ing y
picnic s
picture s 's d ing
pie s
piece s d ing
pig s 's
pile s d ing
pillow s ed
pin s ned ning
pink s er
pipe s d ing
place s 's d ing
plain s er ly
plan s ned ning
plane s 's d
plant s 's ed ing y
plate s d
play s 's ed ing
player s 's
playground s
please s d ing
pocket s ed ing
poem s 's
point s ed ing y
pole s d ing y
police d
pond s 's
pony ies 's
pool s 's ed
poor er est ly
pop s 's ped ping
popcorn
porch es
possum s
pot s 's ted ting
potato es 's

pound s ed ing
pour s ed ing
practice s d ing
present s ed ing ly
press es ed ing
pretend s ed ing
pretty ied ier iest
prince s 's ly
print s ed ing
prize s d
probably
problem s
promise s d ing
proud er est ly
prove s d ing
puff s ed ing y
pull s ed ing
puppy ies 's
purple s d ing st
purr s ed ing
push es ed ing y
put s ting
puzzle s d ing
quack s ed ing
queen s 's
question s ed ing
quick er est ly y
quiet ed ing er est ly
quilt s ed ing
quite
rabbit s 's
raccoon s
race s 's d ing
radio s 's ed
rail s ing
rain s 's ed ing y
rainbow s 's
raise s d ing
ran
ranch es 's ing
rang
rat s 's
reach es ed ing
read s ing
ready ied ing
real ly
red s 's der dest ly
remember s ed ing
repair s ed ing
rest s ed ing
return s ed ing
rice ing
rich es er est ly

rid s	second s 's ed ly	silver y	spell s 's ed ing
ride s ing	secret s ly	since	spend s ing
right s ed ing ly y	see s ing	sing s ing	spent
ring s ed ing	seed s ed ing	sink s ing	spill s ed ing
river s 's	seek s ing	sir	spin s ning
road s 's	seem s ed ing ly	sister s 's	splash es ed in
roar s ed ing	seen	sit s ting	spoke s
robber s	sell s ing	six es	spoken
rock s ed ing y	send s ing	size s d ing	spoon s 's ed in
rode	sense s d ing	skate s d ing	spot s ted ting
roll s ed ing	sent	sky ies 's	spread s ing
roller s	sentence s d ing	sleep s ing ily y	spring s 's ing
roof s 's ed	set s 's ting	slept	squirrel s 's
room s 's ed ing y	seven s 's	slid	stack s ed ing
rooster s 's	shade s d ing	slide s ing	stage s d ing
root s ed ing	shadow s 's ed ing y	slip s ped ping	stair s
rope s 's d ing	shake s ing	slow s ed ing er est ly	stand s ing
rose s	shall	small er est	star s 's red rin
rough s ed ing er est ly	shape s d ing ly	smart s ed ing er est ly	stare s d ing
round s 's ed ing er est	share s d ing	smell s ed ing y	start s ed ing
row s ed ing	sharp er est ly	smile s ing	state s 's d ing
rub s bed bing	she	smiled	stay s ed ing
ruler s 's	she'd	smoke s 's d ing y	step s ped ping
run s ning	she'll	smooth s ed ing er est ly	stick s ing y
runner s 's	she's	snake s 's d ing	still s ed er
rush es ed ing	sheep 's y	snap s ped ping	stomach s 's
rustle s d ing	sheet s ed	sneaker s ed	stone s 's d
sack s ing	shell s ed ing	sniff s ed ing y	stood
sad der dest ly	shine s d ing	snow s 's ed ing y	stop s ped ping
safe s r st ly	shiny ier iest	so	store s 's d ing
said	ship s 's ped ping	soap s ed y	storm s 's ed in
sail s 's ed ing	shirt s	sock s ed	story ies 's ied
sale s	shoe s	soft er est ly	stove s 's
salt s ed ing y	shook	soil s 's ed	straight er ly
same	shoot s ing	sold	strange st ly
sand s 's ed ing	shop s ped ping	some	stranger s 's
sandwich es ed	shore s d ing	someday	straw s
sandy	short s ing er est ly y	somehow	stream s 's ed i
sang	shot s	someone 's	street s 's
sank	should	something 's	stretch es ed in
sat	shoulder s ed ing	sometime s	strike s ing
Saturday s	shout s ed ing	somewhere	string s ed ing
save s d ing	show s 's ed ing y	son s 's	stripe s d
saw s 's ed ing	shut s ting	song s	strong er est ly
say s ing	shy ied ing est ly	soon er	stuck
scare s d ing	sick er ly	sorry ier iest	stuff s 's ed ing
scary ier iest	side s 's d ing	sound s 's ed ing er ly	such
school s 's ed ing	sidewalk s	soup s	sudden ly
scientist s 's	sigh s ed ing	south 's	sue d ing
scold s ed ing	sight s ed ing ly	space s d ing	suit s 's ed ing
scream s ed ing	sign s 's ed ing	spaceship s 's	summer s 's y
sea s 's	signal s ed ied ing ling	speak s ing	sun s 's ned ni
seat s ed ing	silly ies ier iest	special s ly	Sunday s

sunlight 's
sunny iest
super
supper s 's
suppose d ing
sure r st ly
surprise s d ing
swam
sweet s er est ly
swim s ming
swing s ing
swung
table s
tag s ged ging
tail s ed ing
take s ing
taken
talk s ed ing
tall er est
tap s ped ping
tape s d ing
taste s d ing
tea s
teach es ing
teacher s 's
team s 's ed
tear s ing y
teeth
telephone s d ing
tell s ing
ten s 's
tent s 's
terrible
test s ed ing
than
thank s ed ing
that
that's
the
their s
them
themselves
then
there
there's
these
they
they'll
they're
thin s ned ning ner nest
   ly
thing s 's
think s ing

third s ly
this
those
though
thought s
three s 's
threw
through
throughout
throw s ing
thumb s ed ing
thump s ed ing
thunder s ed ing
Thursday s 's
tickle s d ing
tie s d
tiger s 's
tight s er est ly
till ed ing
time s 's d ing ly
tinkle s d ing
tiny ier iest
tiptoe s d ing
tire s d ing
to
toad s 's
toast s ed ing y
today s 's
toe s d ing
together
told
tomorrow s 's
tonight 's
too
took
tool s ed
top s 's ped ping
toss es ed ing
touch es ed ing y
toward s
towel s
town s 's
toy s ed ing
track s ed ing
trail s ed ing
train s 's ed ing
trap s ped ping
travel s ed led ing
tree s 's
trick s 's ed ing y
tried
trip s ped ping
trot s ted ting

trouble s 's d ing
truck s 's ed ing
true r st
trunk s
truth s
try ies ing
tub s
Tuesday
tug s ged ging
tuna
turn s 's ed ing
turtle s 's
TV 's
twig s
two s 's
ugly ier iest
umbrella s
uncle s 's
under
understand s ing
understood
unhappy ier iest
unite d ing
untie s d
until
up s ped
upon
upset s ting
upside
upstairs
us
use s d ing
valley s 's
van s 's
vegetable s
very
village s 's
vine s
visit s ed ing
voice s d ing
wag s ged ging
wagon s 's
wait s ed ing
wake s d ing
walk s ed ing
wall s ed
wander s ed ing
want s ed ing
warm s ed ing er est ly
was
wash es ed ing
wasn't
watch es ed ing

water s 's ed ing y
wave s d ing
way s 's
we
we'd
we'll
we're
we've
wear s ing
weather s 's ed ing
Wednesday s
weed s ed ing y
week s 's ly
welcome s d ing
well s ed ing
went
were
weren't
west
wet s ting ter ly
what
what's
whatever 's
wheel s 's ed ing
when
whenever
where
where's
wherever
which
while s d
whisper s ed ing
whistle s d ing
white s 's d r st ly
who
who's
whole
why
wide r st ly
wife 's
wild s er est ly
will s ed ing
win s ning
wind s 's ed ing y
window s 's ed
wing s 's ed ing
wink s ed ing
winner s 's
winter s 's ed ing
wire s d ing
wise r st ly
wish es ed ing
with

without	wool ly y	write s ing	you
woke	word s 's ed ing y	writer s 's	you'd
wolf 's ed	work s ed ing	written	you'll
woman 's ly	worker s 's	wrong s ed ly	you're
women 's	world s 's ly	wrote	you've
won	worm s ed ing y	yard s 's	young er est
won't	worn	year s 's ly	your s
wonder s ed ing	worry ies ied ing	yell s ed ing	yourself
wonderful ly	worth y ily	yellow s ed ing er est y	youth s 's
wood s ed y	would	yes	zoo s
wooden ly	wouldn't	yet	

DEVELOPMENT OF THE WIDE RANGE READABILITY FORMULA

The new basic word list in three arrangements provided an opportunity to develop an improved readability formula. The concept of readability was defined, for this purpose, as those characteristics of reading material which make for ease or difficulty in comprehension.

Establishing the Criterion

It was assumed that the average characteristics of eight new series of basal readers would provide a satisfactory criterion scale for developing the readability formula. Each of the series contained preprimers, a primer, a first reader, two second readers, and two third readers. From fourth grade up, if a series had two readers for a grade, they were combined. There were seven primary levels and five levels from fourth grade up, twelve levels in all.

For books above first grade, a computer program was used to select the samples. It divided the book into five equal sections of lines of text and selected a 200-word sample at random in each section, skipping the first two paragraphs of a story and always beginning a sample at the start of a paragraph. For the first-grade books, the samples were selected manually. This provided 40 samples at each level and a total of 480 samples with about 100,000 running words.

Each sample was given a reading difficulty score as follows: preprimer, 1.3; primer, 1.5; first reader, 1.8; low second, 2.2; high second, 2.7; low third, 3.2; high third, 3.7; fourth, 4.5; fifth, 5.5; sixth, 6.5; seventh, 7.5; and eighth, 8.5. It was expected that some samples would be easier and some harder than those assigned criterion scores, and that the effect of this would be to lower somewhat the correlation between readability scores and the criterion.

The Variables

On the basis of previous formulas, two variables were chosen for initial tryout. These were percent of hard words and mean number of words per sentence.

Percent of Hard Words. In developing previous Harris-Jacobson readability formulas, we had found that vocabulary difficulty was the most important variable and that the percent of hard words (words not on a specific list of easy words) was a better measure of vocabulary difficulty than such other measures as mean number of letters per word, mean number of syllables, or percent of words with more than five letters.

In previous formulas we had used either a Short List (first- and second-grade words of the 1972 Core and Additional Lists) or a Long List (first-, second-, and third-grade words). The Short List had a slight advantage at primary levels and the Long List was slightly better at secondary levels. Knowing that the new word list contained substantially more words at first- and second-grade levels than the 1972 list and was intermediate in length between the old Long and Short Lists, we decided to use a Readability List consisting of the roots and inflected forms of first- and second-grade levels in the new word lists. It contains 1462 root words in comparison to 910 roots in the old Short List and 1825 roots in the old Long List.

The V1 score (percent of hard words) is the number of words not in the Readability List divided by the number of words in the sample, in percent. The means and standard deviations for V1 at the twelve levels are shown in table C.2. There is a consistent increase, level by level, with no inversions. The standard deviations also show a gradual increase, with two small inversions.

Mean Words per Sentence.   The V2 means and standard deviations are also shown in Table C.2. The means show a steady increase from level to level with one exception (at high third, the mean V2 score was slightly higher than for fourth grade). The standard deviations for V2 increase gradually from 1.2 to 4.6, with two minor inversions (at high second- and high-third-grade levels). There is some overlapping from level to level.

Deriving the Readability Formula

The first step in developing the formula was to find the correlations of V1 and V2 with the criterion, and the correlation of V1 with V2. These Pearson *r*s are shown in Table C.3. The V1 scores correlate 0.831 with the criterion, a very high result. The V2 correlation is 0.704, a little lower but still good. The correlation between V1 and V2, 0.679, is fairly high, but low enough to warrant the expectation that the combination of two variables will be an improvement over V1 alone.

Multiple Correlation.   The correlations shown in Table C.3 were entered into an iterative multiple-correlation computer program in order to find the maximum multiple correlation and the corresponding regression equation. As shown in Table C.4, R (the multiple coeffi-

Table C.2   Means and Standard Deviations for V1 and V2

Criterion	V1		V2	
	Mean	S.D.	Mean	S.D.
1.3	.30	.441	5.50	1.153
1.5	.37	.377	6.88	1.276
1.8	.87	.972	7.47	1.292
2.2	1.76	1.438	8.40	1.414
2.7	2.91	1.981	8.97	2.052
3.2	4.69	2.822	9.05	1.737
3.7	6.39	2.461	11.10	3.131
4.5	7.94	3.793	10.59	2.810
5.5	9.51	3.517	12.45	3.233
6.5	12.09	4.773	12.57	3.471
7.5	13.54	5.690	14.44	3.783
8.5	14.64	5.168	14.86	4.587

Table C.3   Correlations Among the Criterion, V1, and V2

Variable	1	2	3
1. Criterion scores	1.000		
2. V1 scores	.831	1.000	
3. V2 scores	.704	.679	1.000

cient of correlation) is 0.930, a very high result. This is an improvement of 6% over the Harris-Jacobson Formulas 1 and 2. The regression equation is as follows:

$$\text{Predicted Raw Score} = 0.245 \text{ V1} + 0.160 \text{ V2} + 0.642$$

The use of this equation in finding the Predicted Raw Score has been explained on pages 735–736.

Obtaining the Readability Score.   After the regression equation had been obtained, Predicted Raw Scores were obtained for all 480 samples. The mean Predicted Raw Score was then found for each reader level. These means are shown in Table C.5. One can note that the Predicted means are higher than the criterion scores below fourth-grade level, and lower than the criterion scores from fourth grade up. This is an example of the regression effect, the tendency for predicted scores to be closer to the mean than the scores are that are used to make the prediction.

The Predicted Raw Score means were plotted graphically against the criterion scores and a line of best fit was drawn. For each possible Predicted Raw Score from 1.1 to 8.0, the corresponding adjusted score was read from the graph. These adjusted scores are called Readability Scores and are shown in Table C.1. When several samples have been taken from a work, the mean of their Readability Scores is the Readability Score of the work.

INTERPRETING THE READABILITY SCORE

If we should obtain a Readability Score for every possible sample of a work, the mean of those scores would be the Readability Score of the work. When we estimate a work's readability on the basis of a small number of samples, we can expect that there may be some disparity between the predicted Readability Score and the true readability of the work. The size of the uncertainty is indicated by the standard error of estimate (S.E.est). The higher a correlation, the smaller the S.E.est derived from it; the lower the correlation, the larger the S.E.est.

For the Wide Range Readability Formula, the S.E.est is 0.501, or half a grade. The S.E.est is really the standard deviation of the differences to be found between the Readability Scores of single samples and the true readability of the work. For a sample with a Readability Score of 3.0, the chances are even that the work is below 3.0 or above 3.0. The chances are 68 in 100 that the true readability of the work is ±.5 from 3.0, in other words, between 2.5 and 3.5. The chances are 95 in 100 that the true readability is ±1.0 from 3.0. One should also note that there are 16 chances in 100 that the true value is

Table C.4   Multiple Coefficient of Correlation (R), R^2, and Standard Error of Estimate

R	R^2	S.E.est
.930	.864	.501

Table C.5   Criterion Scores and Predicted Raw Scores

Reader Level	Criterion Score	Mean Predicted Raw Score
Preprimer	1.3	1.594
Primer	1.5	1.831
First reader	1.8	2.049
Low second reader	2.2	2.414
High second reader	2.7	2.789
Low third reader	3.2	3.239
High third reader	3.7	3.982
Fourth reader	4.5	4.280
Fifth reader	5.5	4.963
Sixth reader	6.5	5.614
Seventh reader	7.5	6.270
Eighth reader	8.5	6.605

below 2.5, and 16 chances in 100 that it is above 3.5. There are only 5 chances in 100 that the true value is below 2.0 or above 4.0.

When the mean is obtained for several samples from a work, the chance fluctuations of single samples tend to cancel out, and the margin of uncertainty is reduced. However, it is better to be too cautious than too confident. We recommend that the user of this formula think of an obtained Readability Score as probably within half a grade of the true readability of the work. If the Readability Scores of the samples fluctuate widely, one should realize that an average Readability Score for the work is relatively meaningless.

VALIDITY AND RELIABILITY

Validity

The process of investigating the validity of a measuring instrument involves determining what the instrument measures and how well it functions in a variety of situations in which it can be used (Cronbach & Quirk 1971).

Predictive Validity.   The predictive validity of an instrument is found by obtaining the correlation between scores on the instrument and scores on an independent measure of the characteristic in question, which is called a criterion. For the present formula, the criterion is the scale of grade scores assigned to the twelve basal reader levels. As shown in Table C.4, the multiple correlation between formula scores and the criterion is 0.930, a very high result.

The degree to which predictions from an instrument are better than pure chance is shown by the square of the multiple correlation (R^2). R^2 for this formula is 0.864, indicating that scores predicted from this formula are 86% more accurate than chance guesses would be.

Goodness of Fit.   Goodness of fit refers to the degree to which the Readability Scores obtained from a formula place books or selections at the same level of difficulty as the criterion does. It is possible for a formula to place a number of books in the same sequence as the criterion does, and at the same time to overestimate the difficulty of all the books, or underestimate it. For the present Wide Range formula, the Readability Scores have been adjusted so that the average Readability Score for the 40 samples at each criterion level is exactly equal to the criterion score, from preprimer through eighth-reader level. Readability Scores above 8.5 will place samples in the correct sequence of difficulty, but the accuracy of fit of such Readability Scores has not been verified, since they are derived by extrapolation.

As an example of the importance of goodness of fit, we compared three readability formulas to a criterion consisting of two of the eight series (Houghton Mifflin and Economy) used in the present study (Harris & Jacobson 1980). A three-variable Harris-Jacobson formula agreed with the publishers' designations at all primary levels except high first (1.8), where the Harris-Jacobson score was 2.1. The Spache Formula (1974) agreed with the publishers' designations from preprimer through low second, but underestimated the publishers' designations at the high-second, low-third, and high-third levels; the difference was 0.6 grades at 3^1 and 0.7 grades at 3^2. The Fry Graph (Fry 1968) rated the 2^1 readers as 2.9, the 2^2 readers as 4.0, the 3^1 readers as 4.8, and the 3^2 readers as 6.0. All three formulas placed the books in the correct sequence of difficulty, but there were obvious differences in goodness of fit.

Cross Validation.   As an additional check on validity of the present formula, comprehension scores on exercises taken from the *McCall-Crabbs Standard Test Lessons in Reading* (1961 Edition) were used as a second criterion. These test lessons had been administered to 22,650 Virginia students, from whom a subsample of 18,000 students was selected to match national norms on aptitude and reading comprehension tests. Using a Latin Square design, 51 exercises were administered to fourth graders; 54 exercises to sixth graders; 53 exercises to ninth graders; and 32 exercises to twelfth graders. About 300 pupils took each exercise, without time limit, each pupil taking five test lessons (Grades 6, 9, and 12) or four test lessons (Grade 4).

The mean number of correct answers to the multiple-choice questions included in each test lesson was computed for each of the fourth-grade lessons, and these means provided a comprehension criterion scale at fourth-grade level. Using the Wide Range Formula, Predicted Raw Scores were computed for all fourth-grade test lessons. The correlation of these Predicted Raw Scores with the criterion is 0.66, as shown in Table C.6.

The same procedure was followed at the other three grades, with correlations of 0.53 at sixth grade, 0.55 at ninth grade, and 0.65 at twelfth grade (see Table C.6).

Comparisons with Other Readability Formulas.   At each of the four grades, readability scores were computed for each exercise, using the Dale-Chall Readability Formula. The correlations of Dale-Chall scores with the criterion of mean comprehension scores are shown in Table C.6. The Dale-Chall correlations were approximately the same as the Wide Range correlations at Grades 4, 6, and 9. At twelfth grade, the Wide Range was significantly the higher; using R^2, the Wide Range Formula has an 18% advantage at twelfth grade.

It may be noted that the Dale-Chall correlation we have found is a little lower than the 0.70 reported by Dale and Chall (1948). This may be due to differences between our population and that on which the original McCall-Crabbs grade scores were developed, our use of a more recent edition, or our use of mean comprehension score, whereas Dale and Chall used the grade scores supplied with the test lessons.

A similar procedure was followed for the Fry Readability Formula, with results shown in Table C.6. The Fry Formula had a useful correlation with the criterion only at fourth grade, where it was 10% poorer than both the Wide Range and the Dale-Chall Formulas. At sixth and ninth grade, its correlations with the criterion were low, and at twelfth grade it was not better than chance guessing. These Dale-Chall and Fry results have been previously published (Harris & Jacobson 1976).

We have also correlated two other readability formulas with the McCall-Crabbs criterion, the Wheeler-Smith Formula (1954), and the SMOG Formula (McLaughlin 1969). The results of these two formulas are also shown in Table C.6. These two were

Table C.6   Correlations of the Wide Range Readability Formula and Other Readability Formulas with McCall-Crabbs Comprehension Means[a]

Grade	Wide Range		Dale–Chall		Fry		Wheeler–Smith		SMOG	
	R	R^2	R	R^2	R	R^2	R	R^2	R	R^2
4	.66	.44	.67	.44	.58	.34	.53	.28	.53	.28
6	.53	.28	.53	.28	.30	.09	.43	.18	.41	.17
9	.55	.30	.58	.33	.45	.20	.52	.27	.46	.21
12	.65	.42	.49	.24	.10	.01	.40	.16	.01	.00

[a]Because comprehension is higher when Readability Scores are lower, these correlations are negative. The minus signs have been omitted.

consistently inferior to both the Wide Range and Dale-Chall Formulas at the four grades, and at twelfth grade, SMOG correlated only 0.01 with the criterion.

Problems with the Criterion.   Stevens (1980) has pointed out that although the McCall-Crabbs test lessons have been used as the criterion in the development of at least twelve readability formulas, these exercises were intended to be used as teaching materials and not as tests or as a criterion for readability formulas. In describing the McCall-Crabbs exercises in 1948, Dale and Chall said: "This material, it should be noted, has serious deficiencies as a criterion, but it is the best we have at the present time."

In our computations we ignored the G (grade) scores provided for the test lessons and used, instead, the average comprehension score for the approximately 300 pupils who took the exercise. Our assumption was that these randomly selected groups of 300 were, at each grade, equal in average reading comprehension so that test lessons with lower average scores could be safely assumed to be more difficult (less readable) than test lessons with higher average comprehension scores. To the extent that this may not be completely true, our criterion is imperfect. However, the effect of such imperfection should be to lower the correlations for all readability formulas equally.

It should be noted, also, that a formula tends to have its highest correlation with the criterion used in developing it and lower correlations with other criterion scales. This is true of the Wide Range Formula, which had a much higher correlation with publishers' designations than with McCall-Crabbs. The Dale-Chall Formula was developed using McCall-Crabbs as the criterion. In equaling Dale-Chall results at three grades and surpassing it at one grade, the Wide Range Formula stands the test of cross-validation very well.

Construct Validity.   The degree to which a measure conforms to a theoretical base is called its construct validity. Linguists have emphasized that the ease or difficulty of language is dependent on word meaning (lexical, semantic) and grammatical (syntactic) factors. Early research by Lorge (1944), Dale and Chall (1948), and Spache (1953) indicates that the most satisfactory measure of vocabulary difficulty is the percent of words that are outside a list of common easy words. In a comprehensive review of research on readability, Klare comes to the following conclusions: "A simple 2-variable formula should be sufficient, especially if one of the variables is a word or semantic variable and the other is a sentence or syntactic variable. . . . The word or semantic variable is consistently more highly predictive than the sentence or syntactic variable when each is considered singly. . . . Using a list of familiar words appears to give a slightly more predictive index than counting word length, probably because length is a (secondary) reflection of familiarity" (1974–1975, pp. 96, 97).

The present formula conforms exactly to Klare's specifications. The Readability Word List employed in it is the most up-to-date word list available and contains the first-

and second-grade words used in a majority of eight current series of basal readers. By itself, the V1 score (percent of words not in the list) correlates 0.831 with the criterion, a higher correlation than most formulas that employ two or more variables achieve.

On the average, long sentences are harder to understand than short ones. This does not apply, of course, to single sentences, which may be harder or easier—depending on their word difficulty and syntactic complexity. But when estimating the difficulty of selections or whole books, average sentence length combined with percent of hard words provides as good an estimate of overall readability as can be obtained from two variables.

There have been several attempts in recent years to devise linguistically sound measures of syntactic complexity. MacGinitie and Tretiak (1971) tried out several of them, and reported that none of the measures of sentence depth, when combined with percent of hard words, gave as high a multiple correlation as did the combination of hard words with average sentence length.

It is evident, therefore, that the two variables used in the present formula have strong theoretical as well as statistical justification.

Reliability

As applied to an educational measuring instrument, reliability means the consistency with which the instrument will give the same or closely similar scores on retesting. One way to estimate the reliability of the instrument is to use information concerning its validity. "To be valid a test must be reliable." (Garrett 1958, p. 360). The validity coefficient sets the lower limit of the instrument's reliability, because its correlation with an outside criterion cannot be higher than its self-consistency.

Ordinarily, reliability coefficients of 0.90 or above are considered to be good. The validity coefficient of the Wide Range Readability Formula is 0.930 (see Table C.4), and therefore the reliability must be at least 0.930.

This was checked by dividing the 480 samples into two sets of 240 samples, on an odd-even basis. R was computed for each set, and came out 0.947 for the first set and 0.928 for the second set. Thus the results are stable and reliable.

APPENDIX

 Publisher Abbreviations

The following indicate the full names of the publishers whose names are abbreviated in this textbook: In the text, names in parentheses but not followed by dates are publishers.

Addison: Addison-Wesley Publishing Co.
AGS: American Guidance Service
AIR: American Institute for Research
ALA: American Library Association
Allyn: Allyn & Bacon
American College: American College Testing Programs
American Optical: American Optical Company
Aspen: Aspen Systems Corp.
Aston: University of Aston (England)
ATP: Academic Therapy Publications
Australian Council: Australian Council for Educational Research
Bantam: Bantam Books
Bausch & Lomb: Bausch & Lomb Optical Co.
Benific: Benific Press
Bobbs: Bobbs-Merrill
Borg-Warner: Borg-Warner Educational Systems
Bowker: R.R. Bowker
Bowmar: Bowmar/Noble Publishers
BSA: Boy Scouts of America
Chicago: University of Chicago Press
Childrens: Childrens Press
Clinical: Clinical Psychology Publishing Co.
Consulting: Consulting Psychologist Press

Council for Indian Education: Montana Council for Indian Education
Cove: Cove Publishers
CTB: California Test Bureau; CTB/McGraw-Hill
DLM: DLM Teaching Resources
EDL: Educational Developmental Laboratories, Inc. (McGraw-Hill)
EPS: Educators Publishing Service
Essay: Essay Press
ETA: Educational Teaching Aids
ETS: Educational Testing Service
Fearon: Fearon Education
Follett: Follett Publishing Co.
Gale: Gale Research Co.
Garrard: Garrard Publishing Co.
Globe: Globe Book Co.
Gorsuch Scarisbrick: Gorsuch Scarisbrick Publishers
G & W Applied Science: G & W Applied Science Laboratories
Heinemann: Heinemann Educational Books, Inc.
Hiskey: Marshall Hiskey, 5640 Baldwin, Lincoln, NE 68507
Houghton: Houghton-Mifflin
HumRRO: Human Resources Research Organization
Institutes: Institutes for the Development of Human Potential

IOX: Instructional Objectives Exchange

IRA: International Reading Association

Jamestown: Jamestown Publishers

Jastak: Jastak Associates

Keystone: Keystone View Co.

Klamath: Klamath Printing Co.

Language: Language Research Associates

McCormick: McCormick-Mathers Publishing Co.

MCP: Modern Curriculum Press

Meeting Street: Meeting Street School

Merrill: Charles E. Merrill

Montana: Montana Council for Indian Education

NAEP: National Assessment of Educational Progress

Nat. Assn. Deaf: National Association of the Deaf

NCTE: National Council of Teachers of English

Neuropsychological Laboratory (University of Arizona)

Nevins: Nevins Printing Co.

New Readers: New Readers Press

New Zealand: New Zealand Council for Educational Research

NFER-Nelson: NFER-Nelson Publishing Co. (England)

NIMH: National Institutes of Mental Health

Northwestern: Northwestern University Press

NWRL: Northwest Regional Educational Laboratory

Paradox: Paradox Press

Personnel: Personnel Press

Psychological Test: Psychological Test Specialists

Psy Corp: Psychological Corporation

PTS: Publishers Test Service

Raintree: Raintree Publishers

Random: Random House

Revrac: Revrac Publications

Slosson: Slosson Educational Publications

SRA: Science Research Associates

STS: Scholastic Testing Service

TASA: TASA DRP Services

Test Collection: Test Collection, Educational Testing Service

Teachers: Teachers College Press

Titmus: Titmus Optical Vision Testers

Walch: J. Weston Walch

Walker: Walker Educational Books Corp.

Webster: Webster/McGraw-Hill

Westminster: Westminster Press

Westwood: Westwood Press

Whitman: Albert Whitman & Co.

WPS: Western Psychological Service

Zweig: Zweig Associates

References

AARON, IRA E. Enriching the basal reading program with literature. In B. E. Cullinan (Ed.), *Children's literature in the reading program.* Newark, DE: International Reading Association, 1987, 126–138.

AARON, P. G., & BAKER, CATHERINE. Empirical and heuristic bases for diagnosis. *Topics in Learning and Learning Disabilities,* January 1983, *2,* 27–42.

AARON, P. G.; GRANTHAM, SONTRA L.; & CAMPBELL, NANCY. Differential treatment of reading disability of diverse etiologies. In R. Malatesha & P. Aaron (Eds.), *Reading disorders: Varieties and treatments.* New York: Academic Press, 1982, 449–452.

AASEN, HELEN B. A summer's growth in reading. *Elementary School Journal,* 1959, *40,* 70–74.

ABRAHAMSON, RICHARD F. An analysis of children's favorite picture storybooks. *The Reading Teacher,* November 1980, *34,* 167–170.

ABRAHAMSON, RICHARD F., & CARTER, BETTY (Eds.). *Books for you: A booklist for senior high students.* Urbana, IL: National Council of Teachers of English, 1988.

ABRAMS, JULES C. A dynamic-developmental-interaction approach to reading and related learning disabilities. In S. M. Glazer, et al. (Eds.), *Reexamining reading diagnoses: New trends and procedures.* Newark, DE: International Reading Association, 1988, 29–47.

ABRAMS, JULES C., & KASLOW, FLORENCE. Family stress and the learning disabled child: Intervention and treatment. *Journal of Learning Disabilities,* February 1977, *10,* 86–90.

ACKERMAN, PEGGY T., & DYKMAN, ROSCOE A. Attention and effortful information-processing deficits in children with learning and attention disorders. *Topics in Learning and Learning Disabilities,* July 1982, *2,* 12–22.

ADAMS, ARLENE. *Strategy preferences for assigning pronoun antecedents: A comparison of normal and disabled readers in listening and reading comprehension.* Unpublished doctoral dissertation, State University of New York at Albany, 1986.

ADAMS, ARLENE. *The incidence of reversal errors in normal and learning disabled readers, grades 2, 5, and 8.* Paper given at the annual conference of the American Educational Research Association, New Orleans, April 1988.

ADAMS, ERNEST. A technique for teaching word identification in the content areas. In G. G. Duffy (Ed.), *Reading in the middle school.* Newark, DE: International Reading Association, 1974, 112–116.

ADAMS, MARILYN J. *Failures to comprehend and levels of processing in reading.* Technical Report No. 37. Champaign, IL: Center for the Study of Reading, University of Illinois, April 1977.

ADAMS, MARILYN J. *Models of word recognition.* Technical Report No. 107. Champaign, IL: Center for the Study of Reading, University of Illinois, October 1978.

ADAMS, MARILYN J. Failures to comprehend and levels of processing in reading. In R. Spiro, et al. (Eds.), *Theoretical issues in reading comprehension.* Hillsdale, NJ: Erlbaum, 1980, 11–32.

ADAMS, MARILYN J., & HUGGINS, A. W. F. The growth of children's sight vocabulary: A quick test with educational and theoretical implications. *Reading Research Quarterly,* Spring 1985, *20,* 262–281.

ADELMAN, HOWARD S., & TAYLOR, LINDA. The problems of definition and differentiation and the need for a classification schema. *Journal of Learning Disabilities*, November 1986, *19*, 514–520.

ADLER, SOL. Megavitamin treatment for behaviorally disturbed and learning disabled children. *Journal of Learning Disabilities*, December 1979, *12*, 678–681.

AFFLECK, JAMES Q. et al. Integrated classroom versus resource model: Academic viability and effectiveness. *Exceptional Children*, January 1988, *54*, 339–348.

AIEX, NOLA K. Reading and the elderly. *Journal of Reading*, December 1987, *31*, 280–283.

AIEX, NOLA K. Storytelling: Its wide-ranging impact in the classroom. *ERIC Digest*, No. 9, 1988.(a)

AIEX, NOLA K. Using the newspapers as effective teaching tools. *ERIC Digest*, November 10, 1988.(b)

ALEXANDER, J. ESTILL, & FILLER, RONALD C. *Attitudes and reading*. Newark, DE: International Reading Association, 1976.

ALGARIN, JOANNE P. *Japanese folk literature: A core collection and reference guide*. New York: R. R. Bowker, 1982.

ALGOZZINE, BOB, & YSSELDYKE, JAMES E. The future of the LD field: Screening and diagnosis. *Journal of Learning Disabilities*, August/September 1986, *14*, 394–398.

ALLEN, ELIZABETH G.; WRIGHT, JONE, P.; & LAMINACK, LESTER I. Using language experience to alert pupils' critical thinking skills. *The Reading Teacher*, May 1988, *41*, 904–910.

ALLEN, JOBETH. Inferential comprehension: The effects of text source, decoding ability and mode. *Reading Research Quarterly*, Fall 1985, *20* 603–615.

ALLEN, M. Relationships between Kuhlmann-Anderson Intelligence Tests and academic achievement in grade IV. *Journal of Educational Psychology*, 1944, *44*, 229–239.

ALLEN, MERRILL J. The role of vision in learning disorders. *Journal of Learning Disabilities*, August/September 1977, *10*, 411–415.

ALLEN, ROACH VAN, & ALLEN, CLARYCE. *Language experience activities* (2nd ed.). Boston: Houghton Mifflin, 1982.

ALLEN, ROBERT L. *The verb system of present-day American English*. The Hague: Mouton, 1966.

ALLEN, VIRGINIA G. Developing contexts to support second language acquisition. *Language Arts*, January 1986, *63*, 61–66.

ALLINGTON, RICHARD L. Policy constraints and effective reading instruction: A review. In J. C. Hoffman (Ed.), *Effective teaching of reading: Research and practice*. Newark, DE: International Reading Association, 1986, 261–289.

ALLINGTON, RICHARD L., & JOHNSTON, PETER. Coordination, collaboration and consistency: The redesign of special education interventions. In R. Slavin et al. (Eds.), *Preventing school failure: Effective programs for students at risk*. Boston: Allyn & Bacon, 320–354.

ALLINGTON, RICHARD, et al. What is remedial reading: A descriptive study. *Reading Research and Instruction*, Fall 1986, *26*, 15–30.

ALTWERGER, BESS; EDELSKY, CAROLE; & FLORES, BARBARA M. Whole language: What's new? *The Reading Teacher*, November 1987, *41*, 144–154.

ALVERMANN, DONNA E. Developing lifetime readers. In D. E. Alvermann et al. (Eds.), *Research within reach: Secondary school reading*. Newark, DE: International Reading Association, 1987, 25–36.(a)

ALVERMANN, DONNA E. Integrating oral and written language. In D. E. Alvermann et al. (Eds.), *Research within reach: Secondary school reading*. Newark, DE: International Reading Association, 1987, 109–129.(b)

ALVERMANN, DONNA E. Metacognition. In D. E. Alvermann et al. (Eds.), *Research within reach: Secondary school reading.* Newark, DE: International Reading Association, 1987, 153–68.(c)

ALVERMANN, DONNA E.; DILLON, DEBORAH R.; & O'BRIEN, DAVID G. *Using discussions to promote reading comprehension.* Newark, DE: International Reading Association, 1987.

ALVERMANN, DONNA E.; SMITH, LYNN C.; & READENCE, JOHN E. Prior knowledge activation and comprehension of compatible and incompatible text. *Reading Research Quarterly,* Summer 1985, *20,* 420–436.

ALVERMANN, DONNA E., & SWAFFORD, JEANNE. Do content area strategies have a research base? *Journal of Reading,* February 1989, *32,* 388–394.

American Heritage Dictionary. Boston: Houghton Mifflin, 1985.

AMERICAN PSYCHOLOGICAL ASSOCIATION. *Standards for educational and psychological testing.* Washington, DC: APA, 1985.

AMES, LOUISE B. Learning disabilities: The developmental point of view. In H. R. Myklebust (Ed.), *Progress in learning disabilities,* Vol. I. New York: Grune & Stratton, 1968, 39–74.

AMES, LOUISE B. Learning disability: Truth or trap? *Journal of Learning Disabilities,* January 1983, *16,* 19–20.

AMES, LOUISE B. Ready or not. How birthdays leave some children behind. *American Educator,* Summer 1986, *10,* 30–33, 48.

AMMONS, DICK, & LARRICK, NANCY. *70 favorite paperbacks 1986: Poetry, information and fiction.* Newark, DE: International Reading Association, 1987.

ANDERS, PATRICIA L., & BOS, CANDACE S. Semantic feature analysis: An interactive strategy for vocabulary and text comprehension. *Journal of Reading,* April 1986, *29,* 610–616.

ANDERSON, BETTY. The missing ingredient: Fluent oral reading. *Elementary School Journal,* January 1981, *81,* 173–177.

ANDERSON, CHARLES W., & SMITH, EDWARD L. Children's preconceptions and content area textbooks. In G. Duffy et al. (Eds.), *Comprehension instruction: Perspectives and suggestions.* New York: Longman, 1984, 187–201.

ANDERSON, GARY; HIGGENS, DIANA; & WURSTER, STANLEY R. Differences in the free-reading books selected by high, average, and low achievers. *The Reading Teacher,* December 1985, *39,* 326–330.

ANDERSON, JONATHAN. Lix and Rix: Variations on a little-known readability index. *Journal of Reading,* March 1983, *26,* 490–496.

ANDERSON, LINDA M. What are students doing when they do all that seatwork? In C. W. Fisher & D. C. Berliner (Eds.), *Perspectives on instructional time.* New York: Longman, 1985, 189–202.

ANDERSON, LORIN W. Values, evidence, and mastery learning. *Review of Educational Research,* Summer 1987, *57,* 215–223.

ANDERSON, RICHARD C. (Chair). *The Ohio Reading Recovery Project: Comprehensive report of program evaluation.* Champaign, IL: Center for the Study of Reading, University of Illinois, February 1988.

ANDERSON, RICHARD C., & DAVISON, ALICE. Conceptual and empirical bases for readability formulas. In A. Davison & G. M. Green (Eds.), *Linguistic complexity and text comprehension: Readability issues reconsidered.* Hillsdale, NJ: Erlbaum, 1988, 23–53.

ANDERSON, RICHARD C., & FREEBODY, PETER. Vocabulary knowledge. In H. Singer & R. B. Ruddell (Eds.), *Theoretical models and processes of reading* (3rd ed.). Newark, DE: International Reading Association, 1985, 343–371.

ANDERSON, RICHARD C., & PEARSON, P. DAVID. *A schema-theoretic view of basic processes in reading comprehension.* Technical Report No. 306. Champaign, IL: Center for the Study of Reading, University of Illinois, January 1984.

ANDERSON, RICHARD C.; WILSON, PAUL T.; & FIELDING, LINDA G. Growth in reading and how children spend their time outside of school. *Reading Research Quarterly*, Summer 1988, *23*, 285–303.

ANDERSON, RICHARD C., et al. *Becoming a nation of readers: The report of the Commission on Reading*. Champaign, IL: Center for the Study of Reading, University of Illinois, 1985.

ANDERSON, THOMAS H., & ARMBRUSTER, BONNIE B. Content area textbooks. In R. C. Anderson et al. (Eds.), *Learning to read in American schools: Basal readers and content texts*. Hillsdale, NJ: Erlbaum, 1984, 193–266.(a)

ANDERSON, THOMAS H., & ARMBRUSTER, BONNIE B. Studying. In P. D. Pearson (Ed.), *Handbook of reading research*. New York: Longman, 1984, 657–679.(b)

ANDERSON, THOMAS H.; ARMBRUSTER, BONNIE B.; & KANTOR, ROBERT N. *How clearly written are children's textbooks? Or, of bladderworst and alfa*. Reading Education Report No. 16. Champaign, IL: Center for the Study of Reading, University of Illinois, August 1980.

ANDERSON–INMAN, LYNNE. Bridging the gap: Student-centered strategies for promoting the transfer of learning. *Exceptional Children*, April 1986, *52*, 562–572.

ANSARA, ALICE. The Orton-Gillingham approach to remediation in developmental dyslexia. In R. Malatesha & P. Aaron (Eds.), *Reading disorders: Varieties and treatments*. New York: Academic Press, 1982, 409–433.

AOKI, ELAINE M. "Are you Chinese? Are you Japanese? Or are you just a mixed-up kid?" Using Asian American children's literature. *The Reading Teacher*, January 1981, *34*, 382–385.

APPLEBEE, ARTHUR N.; LANGER, JUDITH A.; & MULLIS, INA V. S. *Who reads best? Factors related to reading achievement in grades, 3, 7, and 11*. Princeton, NJ: Educational Testing Service, February 1988.

ARCHER, MARGUERITE P. Minorities in easy reading through third grade. *Elementary English*, May 1972, *49*, 746–749.

ARGULEWICZ, ED W., & SANCHEZ, DAVID T. Considerations in the assessment of reading difficulties in bilingual children. *School Psychology Review*, 1982, *11*(3), 281–289.

ARMBRUSTER, BONNIE B., & ANDERSON, THOMAS H. *Idea-mapping: The technique and its use in the classroom or simulating the "ups" and "downs" of reading comprehension*. Reading Education Report No. 36. Champaign, IL: Center for the Study of Reading, University of Illinois, October 1982.

ARMBRUSTER, BONNIE B., & ANDERSON, THOMAS H. *Producing "considerate" expository text: Or easy reading is damned hard writing*. Reading Education Report No. 46. Champaign, IL: Center for the Study of Reading, University of Illinois, January 1984.

ARMBRUSTER, BONNIE B.; ANDERSON, THOMAS H.; & OSTERTAG, JOYCE. Does text structure summarization instruction facilitate learning from expository text? *Reading Research Quarterly*, Summer 1987, *22*, 331–346.

ARMBRUSTER, BONNIE B., & GUDBRANDSEN, BETH H. Reading comprehension instruction in social studies programs. *Reading Research Quarterly*, Winter 1986, *21*, 36–48.

ARMBRUSTER, BONNIE B., et al. *What did you mean by that question? A taxonomy of American History questions*. Technical Report No. 308. Champaign, IL: Center for the Study of Reading, University of Illinois, January 1984.

ARMSTRONG, DIANE P.; PATBERG, JUDYTHE; & DEWITZ, PETER. Reading guides—helping students understand. *Journal of Reading*, March 1988, *31*, 532–541.

ARTER, JUDITH A., & JENKINS, JOSEPH R. Differential diagnosis-prescriptive teaching: A critical appraisal. *Review of Educational Research*, Fall 1979, *49*, 517–555.

ASHER, STEVEN R. *Sex differences in reading achievement.* Reading Education Report No. 2. Champaign, IL: Center for the Study of Reading, University of Illinois, October 1977.

ASHER, STEVEN R. *Influence of topic interest on black children's and white children's reading comprehension.* Technical Report No. 99. Champaign, IL: Center for the Study of Reading, University of Illinois, July 1978.

ASHER, STEVEN R. Topic interest and children's reading comprehension. In R. Spiro et al. (Eds.), *Theoretical issues in reading comprehension.* Hillsdale, NJ: Erlbaum, 1980, 525–534.

ASHTON–WARNER, SYLVIA. *Spinster.* New York: Simon and Schuster, 1959.

ASKOV, WARREN; OTTO, WAYNE; & SMITH, RICHARD. Assessment of the de Hirsch Predictive Index tests of reading failure. In R. Aukerman (Ed.), *Some persistent questions in beginning reading.* Newark, DE: International Reading Association, 1972, 33–42.

ATHEY, IRENE. Reading: The affective domain reconceptualized. *Advances in Reading/Language Research,* 1982, *1,* 203–217.

ATHEY, IRENE. Language models and reading. In H. Singer & R. B. Ruddell (Eds.), *Theoretical models and processes of reading.* (3rd ed.). Newark, DE: International Reading Association, 1985, 35–62.(a)

ATHEY, IRENE. Reading research in the affective domain. In H. Singer & R. B. Ruddell (Eds.), *Theoretical models and processes of reading* (3rd ed.). Newark, DE: International Reading Association, 1985, 527–557.(b)

ATKINSON, RICHARD C., & FLETCHER, JOHN D. Teaching children to read with a computer. *The Reading Teacher,* January 1972, *25,* 319–327.

AU, KATHRYN HU-PEI, & MASON, JANA M. Social organizational factors in learning to read: The balance of rights hypothesis. *Reading Research Quarterly,* 1981, *17* (1), 115–151.

AUKERMAN, ROBERT C. *Approaches to beginning reading.* New York: John Wiley & Sons, 1971, 1984.

AUKERMAN, ROBERT C. *The basal reader approach to reading.* New York: John Wiley & Sons, 1981.

AULLS, MARK. Developmental considerations for reading research: Applications to good and poor reader research. In M. Kamil & M. Boswick (Eds.), *Directions in reading: Research and instruction.* Washington, DC: National Reading Conference, 1981, 83–91.

AUSUBEL, DAVID P. The use of advance organizers in the learning and retention of meaningful verbal material. *Journal of Educational Psychology,* 1960, *51,* 267–272.

AUSUBEL, DAVID P. Schemata, cognitive structure, and advance organizers: A reply to Anderson, Spiro, and Anderson. *American Educational Research Journal,* Fall 1980, *17,* 400–404.

AUTEN, ANNE. Understanding other cultures through literature. *The Reading Teacher,* January 1984, *37,* 416–419.

AXELROD, JEROME. Misconceptions some pupils have about remedial reading and themselves. *The English Record,* Fall 1975, *26,* 70–74.

AXELROD, S. *Behavior modification for the classroom teacher.* New York: McGraw-Hill, 1977.

AYRES, A. JEAN. Learning disabilities and the vestibular system. *Journal of Learning Disabilities,* January 1978, *11,* 30–41.

AZARNOFF, PAT. *Health, illness and disability: A guide to books for children and young adults.* New York: Bowker, 1983.

BACKMAN, JOAN. The role of psycholinguistic skills in reading acquisition: A look at early readers. *Reading Research Quarterly,* Summer 1983, *18,* 466–479.

BADIAN, NATALIE A. Auditory-visual integration, auditory memory, and reading in retarded and adequate readers. *Journal of Learning Disabilities*, February 1977, *10*, 108–114.

BADIAN, NATALIE A. The prediction of good and poor reading before kindergarten entry: A nine-year follow-up. *Journal of Learning Disabilities*, February 1988, *21*, 98–103.

BAGFORD, JACK. Evaluating teachers on reading instruction. *The Reading Teacher*, January 1981, *34*, 400–404.

BAILEY, JANIS, et al. Problem solving our way to alternative evaluation procedures. *Language Arts*, April 1988, *65*, 364–373.

BAK, JOHN J., et al. Special class placements as labels: Effects on children's attitudes toward learning handicapped peers. *Exceptional Children*, October 1987, *54*, 151–155.

BAKER, AUGUSTA, & GREENE, ELLEN. *Storytelling: Art and technique.* (2nd ed.) New York: Bowker, 1987.

BAKER, DEBORAH T. What happened when? Activities for teaching sequence skills. *The Reading Teacher*, November 1982, *36*, 216–218.

BAKER, LINDA, & BROWN, ANN L. Cognitive monitoring in reading. In J. Flood (Ed.), *Understanding reading comprehension*. Newark, DE: International Reading Association, 1984, 21–44.(a)

BAKER, LINDA, & BROWN, ANN L. Metacognitive skills and reading. In P. D. Pearson (Ed.), *Handbook of reading research*. New York: Longman, 1984, 353–394.(b)

BAKER, SIDNEY M. Biochemical approach to the problem of dyslexia. *Journal of Learning Disabilities*, December 1985, *18*, 581–584.

BAKKER, DIRK J. Cognitive deficits and cerebral asymmetry. *Journal of Research and Development in Education*, Spring 1982, *15*, 48–54.

BAKKER, DIRK J., & SCHROOTS, H. J. Temporal order in normal and disturbed reading. In G. Pavlidis & T. Miles (Eds.), *Dyslexia research and its application to education*. New York: John Wiley & Sons, 1981, 87–98.

BAKKER, DIRK J.; TEUNISSEN, JETTY; & BOSCH, JOOP. Development of laterality-reading patterns. In R. Knights & D. Bakker (Eds.), *The neuropsychology of learning disorders*. Baltimore: University Park Press, 1976, 207–220.

BAKKER, DIRK J., & VINKE, JAN. Effects of hemisphere specific stimulation on brain activity and reading in dyslexics. *Journal of Clinical and Experimental Neuropsychology*, 1985, *7*(5), 505–525.

BALAJTHY, ERNEST. What does research on computer-based instruction have to say to the reading teacher? *Reading Research and Instruction*, Fall 1987, *27*, 54–65.

BALAJTHY, ERNEST. Computers and instruction. *Reading Research and Instruction*, Fall 1988, *28*, 49–59.

BALDWIN, R. SCOTT; FORD, JEFF C.; & READENCE, JOHN E. Teaching word connotations: An alternative strategy. *Reading World*, December 1981, *21*, 103–108.

BALDWIN, R. SCOTT, & KAUFMAN, RHONDA K. A concurrent validity study of the Raygor Readability Estimate. *Journal of Reading*, November 1979, *23*, 148–153.

BALDWIN, R. SCOTT; PELEG-BRUCKNER, ZEVA; & MCCLINTOCK, ANN H. Effects of topic interest and prior knowledge on reading comprehension. *Reading Research Quarterly*, Summer 1985, *20*, 497–504.

BALMUTH, MIRIAM. *The roots of phonics: A historical introduction.* New York: McGraw-Hill, 1982.

BALMUTH, MIRIAM. Recruitment and retention in adult basic education: What does research say? *Journal of Reading*, April 1988, *31*, 620–623.

BALOW, BRUCE, & BLOMQUIST, M. Young adults ten to fifteen years after severe reading disability. *Elementary School Journal*, 1965, *66*, 44–48.

BALOW, BRUCE; RUBIN, ROSALYN; & ROSEN, MARTHA J. Perinatal events as precursors of reading disabilities. *Reading Research Quarterly*, 1975–1976, *11*(1), 36–71.

BAMBERGER, RICHARD, & RABIN, ANNETTE. New approaches to readability: Austrian research. *The Reading Teacher*, February 1984, *37*, 512–519.

BANKS, ENID M. The identification of children with potential learning disabilities. *Slow Learning Child*, 1970, *17*, 27–38.

BANNATYNE, ALEXANDER D. The color phonics system. In J. Money (Ed.), *The disabled reader*. Baltimore: Johns Hopkins Press, 1966, 193–214.

BANNATYNE, ALEXANDER D. *Language, reading and learning disabilities: Psychology, neuropsychology, diagnosis and remediation*. Springfield, IL: Charles C Thomas, 1971.

BANNATYNE, ALEXANDER D. Choosing the best reinforcers. *Academic Therapy*, Summer 1972, *7*, 483–486.(a)

BANNATYNE, ALEXANDER D. Mirror images and reversals. *Academic Therapy*, Fall 1972, *8*, 87–92.(b)

BANNATYNE, ALEXANDER D. Diagnosis: A note on recategorization of the WISC scaled scores. *Journal of Learning Disabilities*, May 1974, *7*, 272–273.

BANNER, C. N. Child-rearing attitudes of mothers of under-, average-, and over-achieving children. *British Journal of Educational Psychology*, June 1979, *49*, 150–155.

BARCHAS, SARAH E. *Expressed reading interests of children of differing ethnic groups*. Unpublished doctoral dissertation, University of Arizona, 1971.

BARNITZ, JOHN G. *Interrelationships of orthography and phonological structure in learning to read*. Technical Report No. 57. Champaign, IL: Center for the Study of Reading, University of Illinois, January 1978.

BARNITZ, JOHN G. Developing sentence comprehension in reading. *Language Arts*, November/December 1979, *56*, 902–908, 958. Also in A. J. Harris & E. Sipay (Eds.), *Readings on reading instruction* (3rd ed.), New York: Longman, 1984, 286–293.

BARNITZ, JOHN G. Linguistic and cultural perspectives on spelling irregularity. *Journal of Reading*, January 1980, *23*, 320–326.

BARNITZ, JOHN G. Syntactic effects on the reading comprehension of pronoun-referent structures by children in grades two, four, and six. *Reading Research Quarterly*, 1981, *15*(2), 268–289.

BARNITZ, JOHN G. Orthographies, bilingualism and learning to read English as a second language. *The Reading Teacher*, February 1982, *35*, 560–567.

BARNITZ, JOHN G. Toward understanding the effects of cross–cultural schemata and discourse structure on second language reading comprehension. *Journal of Reading Behavior*, 1986, *18*(2), 95–116.

BARON, JONATHAN. Back to basics. *The Behavioral and Brain Sciences*, December 1985, *8*, 706.

BARON, JONATHAN, & TREIMAN, REBECCA. Use of orthography in reading and learning to read. In J. Kavanagh & R. Venezky (Eds.), *Orthography, reading, and dyslexia*. Baltimore, MD: University Park Press, 1980, 171–189.

BARON, JONATHAN, et al. Spelling and reading by rules. In U. Frith (Ed.), *Cognitive processes in spelling*. New York: Academic Press, 1980, 159–194.

BARR, REBECCA C. The influence of instructional conditions on word recognition errors. *Reading Research Quarterly*, Spring 1972, *7*, 509–529.

BARR, REBECCA. The effect of instruction on pupil reading strategies. *Reading Research Quarterly*, 1974–1975, *10*(4), 555–582.

BARR, REBECCA. Influence of reading materials on response to printed words. *Journal of Reading Behavior*, Summer 1975, *7*, 123–135.

BARR, REBECCA. Classroom reading instruction from a sociological perspective. *Journal of Reading Behavior*, 1982, *14*(4), 375–389.

BARR, REBECCA. Observing first-grade reading instruction: Instruction viewed with a model of school organization. In J. A. Niles & R. V. Lalik (Eds.), *Issues in literacy: A research perspective.* Rochester, NY: National Reading Conference, 1985, 30–37.

BARR, REBECCA. What we know and what we need to learn about reading instruction. In J. V. Hoffman (Ed.), *Effective teaching of reading: Research and practice.* Newark, DE: International Reading Association, 1986, 293–315.

BARR, REBECCA, & DREEBAN, ROBERT. A sociological perspective on school time. In C. W. Fisher & D. C. Berliner (Eds.), *Perspectives on instructional time.* New York: Longman, 1985, 109–117.

BARR, REBECCA, & SADOW, MARILYN W. Influence of basal programs on fourth-grade reading instruction. *Reading Research Quarterly*, Winter 1989, *24*, 44–71.

BARRETT, THOMAS C. The relationship between measures of pre-reading visual discrimination and first-grade achievement: A review of the literature. *Reading Research Quarterly*, Fall 1965, *1*, 51–76.

BARRON, BONNIE G., & COLVIN, JUDY M. How to talk to parents. *Journal of Reading*, February 1983, *26*, 452–453.

BARRON, RODERICK W. Development of visual word recognition: A review. In G. MacKinnon & T. Waller (Eds.), *Reading research: Advances in theory and practice*, Vol. 3. New York: Academic Press, 1981, 119–158.(a)

BARRON, RODERICK W. Reading skill and reading strategies. In A. Lesgold & C. Perfetti (Eds.), *Interactive processes in reading.* Hillsdale, NJ: Erlbaum, 1981, 299–325.(b)

BARRON, RODERICK W. Word recognition in early reading: A review of the direct and indirect access hypotheses. *Cognition*, November 1986, *24*, 93–119.

BARTLETT, F. C. *Remembering: A study in experimental and social psychology.* Cambridge, England: Cambridge University Press, 1932.

BASKIN, BARBARA H., & HARRIS, KAREN H. *More notes from a different drummer: A guide to juvenile fiction portraying the disabled.* New York: Bowker, 1984.

BASKIN, BARBARA H.; HARRIS, KAREN H.; & SALLEY, COLEEN C. Making the poetry connection. *The Reading Teacher*, December 1976, *30*, 259–265.

BATES, GARY W. Developing reading strategies for the gifted: A research-based approach. *Journal of Reading*, April 1984, *27*, 590–593.

BAUER, RICHARD H. Information processing as a way of understanding and diagnosing learning disabilities. *Topics in Learning & Learning Disabilities*, July 1982, 2, 33–45.

BAUMANN, JAMES F. A generic comprehension instructional strategy. *Reading World*, May 1983, *22*, 284–294.

BAUMANN, JAMES F. The direct instruction of main idea comprehension ability. In J. F. Baumann (Ed.), *Teaching main idea comprehension.* Newark, DE: International Reading Association, 1986, 133–178.(a)

BAUMANN, JAMES F. (Ed.). *Teaching main idea comprehension.* Newark, DE: International Reading Association, 1986.(b)

BAUMANN, JAMES F. Teaching third-grade students to comprehend anaphoric relationships. *Reading Research Quarterly*, Winter 1986, *21*, 70–90.(c)

BAUMANN, JAMES F. Anaphora in basal reader selections: How frequently do they occur? *Journal of Reading Behavior*, 1987, *19*(2), 141–158.

BAUMANN, JAMES F. Direct instruction reconsidered. *Journal of Reading*, May 1988, *31*, 712–718.

BAUMANN, JAMES F., & SCHMITT, MARIBETH C. The what, why, how and when of comprehension instruction. *The Reading Teacher*, March 1986, *39*, 640–646.

BAUMANN, JAMES F., & SERRA, JUDITH K. The frequency and placement of main ideas in children's social studies textbooks: A modified replication of Braddock's research on topic sentences. *Journal of Reading Behavior*, 1984, *16*(1), 27–40.

BAUMANN, JAMES F.; WALKER, ROBERT N.; & JOHNSON, DALE D. Effect of distractor word variability in children's performance on a word identification test. *Reading Psychology*, Spring 1981, *2*, 88–96.

BEACH, RICHARD, & APPLEMAN, DEBORAH. Reading strategies for expository and literal text types. In A. Purves & O. Niles (Eds.), *Becoming readers in a complex society.* 83rd Yearbook of the National Society for the Study of Education, Part I. Chicago: University of Chicago Press, 1984, 115–143.

BEACH, RICHARD, & WENDLER, LINDA. Developmental differences in response to a story. *Research in the Teaching of English*, October 1987, *21*, 286–297.

BEAN, RITA M., & EICHELBERGER, R. TONY. Changing the role of reading specialists: From pull-out to in-class programs. *The Reading Teacher*, March 1985, *38*, 648–653.

BEAN, THOMAS W. Organizing and retaining information by thinking like an author. In S. M. Glazer et al. (Eds.), *Reexamining reading diagnosis: New trends and procedures.* Newark, DE: International Reading Association, 1988, 103–127.

BEAN, THOMAS W., & ERICSON, BONNIE O. Text previews and three-level study guides for content area critical reading. *Journal of Reading*, January 1989, *32*, 337–341.

BEAN, THOMAS W., et al. Teaching students how to make predictions about events in history with a graphic organizer plus option guide. *Journal of Reading*, May 1986, *29*, 739–745.

BEAUCHAMP, GEORGE R. Background information: Learning disabilities, dyslexia, and vision. *Journal of Learning Disabilities*, August/September 1987, *20*, 411–413.

BEAUCHAMP, ROBERT F. *Selection of books for the culturally disadvantaged ninth grade student.* Unpublished doctoral dissertation, Wayne State University, 1970.

BEAUMONT, J. GRAHAM. Introduction. In J. Beaumont (Ed.), *Divided visual field studies of cerebral organization.* New York: Academic Press, 1982, 1–9. (a)

BEAUMONT, J. GRAHAM. The split-brain studies. In J. Beaumont (Ed.), *Divided visual field studies of cerebral organization.* New York: Academic Press, 1982, 217–232. (b)

BECK, ISABEL L. Comprehension during the acquisition of decoding skills. In J. T. Guthrie (Ed.), *Cognition, curriculum, and comprehension.* Newark, DE: International Reading Association, 1977, 113–156.

BECK, ISABEL L. Reading problems and instructional practices. In G. MacKinnon & T. Waller (Eds.), *Reading research: Advances in theory and practice*, Vol. 2, New York: Academic Press, 1981, 53–95.

BECK, ISABEL L. Reading and reasoning. *The Reading Teacher*, May 1989, *42*, 676–682.

BECK, ISABEL L.; McCASLIN, ELLEN S.; & McKEOWN, MARGARET G. Basal reader's purpose for story reading: Smoothly paving the road or setting up a detour. *Elementary School Journal*, January 1981, *81*, 156–161.

BECK, ISABEL L., & McKEOWN, MARGARET G. Developing questions that promote comprehension: The story map. *Language Arts*, November/December 1981, *58*, 913–918.

BECK, ISABEL L., & McKEOWN, MARGARET G. Application of theories of reading to instruction. In N. L. Stein (Ed.), *Literacy in American schools: Learning to read and write.* Chicago: University of Chicago Press, 1986, 63–84.

BECK, ISABEL L., & McKEOWN, MARGARET G. Toward meaningful accounts in history texts for young learners. *Educational Researcher*, August/September 1988, *17*, 31–39.

BECK, ISABEL L.; McKEOWN, MARGARET G.; & McCASLIN, ELLEN S. Does reading make sense? Problems of early readers. *The Reading Teacher*, April 1981, *34*, 780–785.

BECK, ISABEL L.; McKEOWN, MARGARET G.; & McCASLIN, ELLEN S. Vocabulary development: All contexts are not created equal. *Elementary School Journal*, January 1983, *83*, 177–181.

BECK, ISABEL L.; MCKEOWN, MARGARET G.; & OMANSON, RICHARD C. The effects and uses of diverse instructional techniques. In M. G. McKeown & M. E. Curtis (Eds.), *The nature of vocabulary acquisition.* Hillsdale, NJ: Erlbaum, 1987, 147–163.

BECK, ISABEL L.; OMANSON, RICHARD C.; & MCKEOWN, MARGARET G. An instructional redesign of reading lessons: Effects on comprehension. *Reading Research Quarterly*, 1982, *17*(4), 462–481.

BECK, ISABEL L., et al. Improving the comprehensibility of stories: The effects of revisions that improve coherence. *Reading Research Quarterly*, Spring 1984, *19*, 263–277.

BECKER, GEORGE. *Television and the classroom reading program.* Newark, DE: International Reading Association, 1973.

BECKER, HENRY J. Computers in schools today: Some basic considerations. In N. L. Stein (Ed.), *Literacy in American schools: Learning to read and write.* Chicago: University of Chicago Press, 1986, 23–40.

BEEBE, MONA J. The effect of different types of substitution miscues on reading. *Reading Research Quarterly*, 1979–1980, *15*(3), 324–336.

BEECH, JOHN R. *Learning to read: A cognitive approach to reading and poor reading.* San Diego: College-Hill Press, 1985.

BEECHER, JEFF. Note-taking: What do we know about the benefits? *Eric Digest*, Number 12, 1988.

BEENTJES, JOHANNES, W. J., & VAN DER VOORT, TOM H. A. Television's impact on children's reading skills: A review of research. *Reading Research Quarterly*, Fall 1988, *23*, 389–413.

BEERS, TERRY. Schema-theoretic models of reading: Humanizing the machine. *Reading Research Quarterly*, Summer 1987, *22*, 369–377.

BEGAB, MICHAEL J. Childhood learning disabilities and family stress. In J. I. Arena (Ed.), *Management of the child with learning disabilities: An interdisciplinary challenge.* San Rafael, CA.: Academic Therapy Publications, 1967, 81–87.

BELL, LOUISE C. Supervising reading teachers. *Reading World.* May 1982, *21*, 333–339.

BELLONI, LORETTA F., & JONGSMA, EUGENE A. The effects of interest on reading comprehension of low-achieving students. *Journal of Reading*, November 1978, *22*, 106–109.

BELMONT, IRA, & BELMONT, LILLIAN. Stability or change in reading achievement over time: Developmental and educational implications. *Journal of Learning Disabilities*, February 1978, *11*, 80–88.

BELMONT, LILLIAN, & BIRCH, HERBERT G. Lateral dominance, lateral awareness, and reading disability. *Child Development*, 1965, *34*, 57–71.

BELMONT, LILLIAN, & BIRCH, HERBERT G. The intellectual profile of retarded readers. *Perceptual & Motor Skills*, 1966, *22*, 787–816.

BENDER, LAURETTA. Specific reading disability as a maturational lag. *Bulletin of the Orton Society*, 1957, 7, 9–18.

BENDER, LAURETTA. Use of the visual-motor gestalt test in the diagnosis of learning disabilities. *Journal of Special Education*, Winter 1970, *4*, 29–39.

BENDER, LAURETTA A. A fifty-year review of experiences with dyslexia. *Bulletin of the Orton Society*, 1975, *25*, 5–23.

BENDER, WILLIAM N. Behavioral indicators of temperament and personality in the inactive learner. *Journal of Learning Disabilities*, May 1987, *20*, 301–305.(a)

BENDER, WILLIAM N. Secondary personality and behavioral problems in adolescents with learning disabilities. *Journal of Learning Disabilities*, May 1987, *20*, 280–285.(b)

BENNETT, JOHN E., & BENNETT, PRISCILLA. What's so funny? Action research and bibliography of humorous children's books—1975–1980. *The Reading Teacher*, May 1982, 924–927.

BENSON, D. FRANK. Alexia and the neuroanatomical basis of reading. In F. Pirozzolo & M. Wittrock (Eds.), *Neuropsychological and cognitive processes in reading.* New York: Academic Press, 1981, 69–92.

BENSON, D. FRANK. The neural basis of spoken and written language. In H. Myklebust (Ed.), *Progress in learning disabilities*, Vol. 5. New York: Grune & Stratton, 1983, 3–25.

BENTON, ARTHUR L. *Right-left discrimination and finger localization.* New York: Hoeber, 1959.

BENTON, ARTHUR L. Some conclusions about dyslexia. In A. L. Benton & D. Pearl (Eds.), *Dyslexia: An appraisal of current knowledge.* New York: Oxford University Press, 1978, 451–476.

BENTON, MICHAEL. The methodology vacuum in teaching literature. *Language Arts*, March 1984, *61*, 265–275.

BERGENSKE, M. DIANNE. The missing link in narrative story mapping. *The Reading Teacher*, December 1987, *41*, 333–335.

BERGER, ALLEN. Effectiveness of four methods of increasing reading rate, comprehension, and flexibility. In J. A. Figurel (Ed.), *Forging ahead in reading.* Newark, DE: International Reading Association, 1968, 588–596.

BERGERING, ANTHONY J. An investigation of laryngeal EMG activity and its relation to reading. *Dissertation Abstracts International*, February 1976, *36* (8-B), 4192.

BERGERUD, DONNA; LOVITT, THOMAS C.; & HORTON, STEVEN. The effectiveness of textbook adaptations in life sciences for high school students with learning disabilities. *Journal of Learning Disabilities*, February 1988, *21*, 70–76.

BERGLUND, ROBERT L., & JOHNS, JERRY L. A primer on uninterrupted sustained silent reading. *The Reading Teacher*, February 1983, *36*, 534–539.

BERIETER, CARL, & BIRD, MARLENE. Use of thinking aloud in identification and teaching of reading comprehension strategies. *Cognition and Instruction*, 1985, *2*(2), 131–156.

BERK, RONALD A. Practical guidelines for determining the length of objective-based, criterion-referenced tests. *Educational Technology*, November 1980, *20*, 36–41.

BERK, RONALD A. The value of WISC-R profile analysis for the differential diagnosis of learning disabled students. *Journal of Clinical Psychology*, January 1983, *39*, 133–136.

BERK, RONALD A. An evaluation of procedures for computing an ability-achievement discrepancy score. *Journal of Learning Disabilities*, May 1984, *17*, 262–266.

BERK, RONALD A. A consumer's guide to setting performance standards on criterion-referenced tests. *Review of Educational Research*, Spring 1986, *56*, 137–172.

BERKOWITZ, SANDRA J. Effects of instruction in text organization on sixth-grade students' memory for expository reading. *Reading Research Quarterly*, Spring 1986, *21*, 161–178.

BERLINER, DAVID C. Academic learning time and reading achievement. In J. Guthrie (Ed.), *Comprehension and teaching: Research reviews.* Newark, DE: International Reading Association, 1981, 203–226.

BERQUIST, LEONARD. Rapid silent reading: Techniques for improving rate in the intermediate grades. *The Reading Teacher*, October 1984, 38, 50–53.

BERRES, FRANCES B. *The effects of varying amounts of motoric involvement on the learning of nonsense syllables by male culturally disadvantaged retarded readers.* Unpublished doctoral dissertation, University of California at Los Angeles, 1967.

BERRES, FRANCES, & EYER, JOYCE T. John. In A. J. Harris (Ed.), *Casebook on reading disability.* New York: David McKay, 1970, 25–47.

BERSTEIN, JOANNE E. (Comp.). *Books to help children cope with separation and loss* (2nd ed.). New York: R. R. Bowker, 1983.

BETTENCOURT, EDWARD M., et al. Effect of teacher enthusiasm on student on-task behavior and achievement. *American Educational Research Journal*, Fall 1983, *20*, 435–450.

BETTS, EMMETT A. *Foundations of reading instruction*. New York: American Book, 1946.

BETTS, EMMETT A. *Handbook for the American Adventure Series*. New York: Harper & Row, 1960.

BETTS, EMMETT A. Capture reading motivation. *Reading Improvement*, 1976, *13*, 41–46.

BEYARD-TYLER, KAREN, & SULLIVAN, HOWARD. Adolescent reading preferences for type of theme and sex of character. *Reading Research Quarterly*, 1980, *16*(1), 104–120.

BICKEL, WILLIAM E., & BICKEL, DONNA D. Effective schools, classrooms, and instruction: Implications for special education. *Exceptional Children*, April 1986, *52*, 489–500.

BICKLEN, DOUGLAS, & ZOLLERS, NANCY. The focus of advocacy in the LD field. *Journal of Learning Disabilities*, December 1986, *19*, 579–586.

BIEMILLER, ANDREW. The development of the use of graphic and contextual information as children learn to read. *Reading Research Quarterly*, Fall 1970, 6, 75–96.

BIEMILLER, ANDREW. Changes in the use of graphic and contextual information as functions of passage difficulty and reading achievement level. *Journal of Reading Behavior*, Winter 1979, *11*, 308–318.

BIERLY, KEN P. L. 94–142: Answers to some questions you're asking. *Instructor*, April 1978, 87, 63–65, 72–73.

BINKLEY, MARILYN R. New ways of assessing text difficulty. In B. L. Zakaluk & S. J. Samuels (Eds.), *Readability: Its past, present, & future*. Newark, DE: International Reading Association, 1988, 98–120.

BIRCH, HERBERT G., & BELMONT, LILLIAN. Auditory visual integration in normal and retarded readers. *American Journal of Orthopsychiatry*, October 1964, *34*, 852–861.

BIRMAN, BEATRICE F. How to improve a successful program: Pointers from the National Assessment of Chapter 1. *American Educator*, Spring 1988, *12*, 22–29.

BISHOP, CAROL. *Transfer of word and letter training in reading*. Unpublished master's thesis, Cornell University, 1962.

BISHOP, DAVID M. Motivating adolescent readers via starter shelves in content area classes. In A. Ciani (Ed.), *Motivating reluctant readers*. Newark, DE: International Reading Association, 1981, 44–70.

BISHOP, RUDINE S. Extending multicultural understandings through children's books. In B. E. Cullinan (Ed.), *Children's literature in the reading program*. Newark, DE: International Reading Association, 1987, 60–67.

BISKIN, DONALD S.; HOSKISSON, KENNETH; & MODIN, MARJORIE. Prediction, reflection, and comprehension. *Elementary School Journal*, November 1976, 77, 131–139.

BLACHMAN, BENITA, & JAMES, SHARON L. Metalinguistic abilities and reading achievement in first-grade children. In J. A. Niles & L. V. Lalik (Eds.), *Issues in literacy: A research perspective*. Rochester, NY: National Reading Conference, 1985, 280–286.

BLACHOWICZ, CAMILLE L. Z. Making connections: Alternatives to the vocabulary notebook. *Journal of Reading*, April 1986, *29*, 643–649.

BLACHOWICZ, CAMILLE L. Z. Vocabulary instruction: What goes on in the classroom? *The Reading Teacher*, November 1987, *41*, 132–137.

BLACK, J. L., et al. Dyslexia: Saccadic eye movements. *Perceptual & Motor Skills*, June 1984, *58*, 903–910.

BLACKBURN, G. MERIDETH, & BLACKBURN, LORRAINE A. *Index to poetry for children and young people: 1982–1987*. New York: H. W. Wilson, 1989.

BLAIR, HEATHER. Canadian native peoples in adolescent literature. *Journal of Reading*, December 1982, *26*, 217–221.

BLAIR, TIMOTHY R., & RUPLEY, WILLIAM H. Practice and application in the teaching of reading. *The Reading Teacher*, February 1988, *41*, 536–539.

BLANCHARD, JAY S. What to tell students about underlining. . .and why. *Journal of Reading*, December 1985, *29*, 199–203.

BLANCHARD, JAY S.; MASON, GEORGE E.; & DANIEL, DAN. *Computer applications in reading* (3rd ed.). Newark, DE: International Reading Association, 1987.

BLANK, MARION. A word is a word—or is it? In D. B. Gray & J. F. Kavanagh (Eds.), *Biobehavioral measures of dyslexia*. Parkton, MD: York Press, 1985, 261–277.

BLANK, MARION, & BRIDGER, WAGNER H. Deficiencies in verbal labelling in retarded readers. *American Journal of Orthopsychiatry*, 1966, *36*, 840–847.

BLANTON, LINDA P.; SITKO, MERRILL C.; & GILLESPIE, PATRICIA H. Reading and the mildly retarded: Review of research and implications. In L. Mann & D. Sabatino (Eds.), *The third review of special education*. New York: Grune & Stratton, 1976, 143–162.

BLANTON, WILLIAM E.; MOORMAN, GARY B.; & WOOD, KAREN D. A model of direct instruction applied to the basal skills lesson. *The Reading Teacher*, December 1986, *40*, 299–304.

BLASS, ROSANNE J.; JURENKA, NANCY A.; & ZIRZOW, ELEANOR G. Showing children the communicative nature of reading. *The Reading Teacher*, May 1981, *34*, 926–931.

BLAU, HAROLD, & BLAU, HARRIET. A theory of learning to read. *The Reading Teacher*, November 1968, *22*, 126–129, 144.

BLAU, HAROLD, & LOVELESS, EUGENE J. Specific hemispheric routing—TAK/V to teach spelling to dyslexics: VAK and VAKT challenged. *Journal of Learning Disabilities*, October 1982, *15*, 461–466.

BLEAKLEY, MARY ELLEN; WESTERBERG, VIRGINIA; & HOPKINS, KENNETH D. The effect of character sex on story interest and comprehension in children. *American Educational Research Journal*, Spring 1988, 25, 145–155.

BLOMMERS, PAUL J., & LINDQUIST, E. F. Rate of comprehension of reading: Its measurement and its relationship to comprehension. *Journal of Educational Psychology*, November 1944, *34*, 449–473.

BLOOM, BENJAMIN S. (Ed.) *Taxonomy of educational objectives, Handbook I: Cognitive domain*. New York: David McKay, 1956.

BLOOM, BENJAMIN S. *All our children learning*. New York: McGraw-Hill, 1981.

BLOOMFIELD, LEONARD, & BARNHART, CLARENCE L. *Let's read: A linguistic approach*. Cambridge, MA: Educators Publishing Service, 1961.

BOCK, J. KATHRYN, & BREWER, WILLIAM F. *Discourse structure and mental models*. Technical Report No. 343. Champaign, IL: Center for the Study of Reading, University of Illinois, November 1985.

BOCKS, WILLIAM M. Non-promotion: A year to grow? *Educational Leadership*, February 1977, *34*, 379–383.

BODART-TALBOT, JONI. *Booktalk 3*. New York: H. W. Wilson, 1988.

BODER, ELENA. Developmental dyslexia: A diagnostic approach based on three atypical reading-spelling patterns. *Developmental Medicine and Child Neurology*, 1973, *15*, 663–687.

BOEHNLEIN, MARY M., & HAGER, BETH M. (Comps). *Children, parents, and reading: An annotated bibliography*. Newark, DE: International Reading Association, 1985.

BOND, GUY L. *Auditory and speech characteristics of poor readers*. Contributions to Education No. 657. New York: Teachers College, Columbia University, 1935.

BOND, GUY L., & DYKSTRA, ROBERT. The cooperative research program in first-grade reading instruction. *Reading Research Quarterly*, Summer 1967, *2*, 5–142.

BOND, GUY L.; TINKER, MILES A.; WASSON, BARBARA B.; & WASSON, JOHN B. *Reading difficulties: Their diagnoses and correction* (6th ed.). Englewood Cliffs, NJ: Prentice Hall, 1989.

BONING, THOMAS, & BONING, RICHARD. I'd rather read than . . . *The Reading Teacher*, 1957, *10*, 196–200.

BOODT, GLORIA M. Critical listeners become critical readers in remedial reading class. *The Reading Teacher*, January 1984, *37*, 390–394.

BOOMER, LYMAN W. Special education paraprofessionals: A guide for teachers. *Teaching Exceptional Children*, Summer 1980, *12*, 146–149.

BORKO, HILDA; SHAVELSON, RICHARD J.; & STERN, PAULA. Teachers' decisions in the planning of reading instruction. *Reading Research Quarterly*, 1981, *16*(3), 449–466.

BORKOWSKI, JOHN G.; WEHING, ROBERT S.; & TURNER, LISA A. Attributional retraining and the teaching of strategies. *Exceptional Children*, October 1986, *53*, 130–137.

BORMUTH, JOHN R. Readability: A new approach. *Reading Research Quarterly*, Spring 1966, *1*, 79–132.

BORMUTH, JOHN R. The cloze readability procedure. In J. R. Bormuth (Ed.), *Readability in 1968*. Urbana, IL: National Council of Teachers of English, 1968, 40–47.

BORMUTH, JOHN R. The cloze procedure: Literacy in the classroom. In W. D. Page (Ed.), *Help for the reading teacher: New directions in research*. Urbana, IL: National Conference on Research in English and ERIC/RCS, March 1975, 60–89.(a)

BORMUTH, JOHN R. *The anaphora: Its surface manifestations*. Paper presented at the Annual Meeting of the American Educational Research Association, 1975.(b)

BORMUTH, JOHN R. Literacy is rising, but so is demand for literacy. In L. Reed & S. Ward (Eds.), *Basic skills: Issues and Choices*, *1*. St. Louis: CEMREL, April 1982, 183–190.

BORMUTH, JOHN R. A response to "Is the Degrees of Reading Power test valid or invalid?" *Journal of Reading*, October 1985, *29*, 42–47.

BOS, CANDACE S. Getting past decoding: Assisted and repeating readings as remedial methods for learning disabled students. *Topics in Learning & Learning Disabilities*, January 1982, *1*, 51–57.

BOTEL, MORTON, & GRANOWSKY, ALVIN. A formula for measuring syntactic complexity. *Elementary English*, April 1972, *49*, 513–516.

BOUGERE, MARGUERITE B. Vocabulary development in the primary grades. In J. Figurel (Ed.), *Forging ahead in reading*. Newark, DE: International Reading Association, 1968, 75–85. Also in A. J. Harris & E. Sipay (Eds.), *Readings on reading instruction* (2nd ed.). New York: Longman, 1972, 244–248.

BOWERS, PATRICIA G.; STEFFY, RICHARD; & TATE, ELLEN. Comparison of the effects of IQ control methods on memory and naming speed predictors of reading disability. *Reading Research Quarterly*, Summer 1988, *23*, 304–319.

BOWEY, JUDITH A. Contextual facilitation in children's oral reading in relation to grade and decoding skill. *Journal of Experimental Child Psychology*, August 1985, *40*, 23–48.

BOWEY, JUDITH A. Syntactic awareness and verbal performance from preschool to fifth grade. *Journal of Psycholinguistic Research*, July 1986, *15*, 285–308.

BOYLE, THERESA. Learning disabilities: Miscellaneous information concerning the complex. *American Journal of EEG Technology*, December 1982, *22*, 187–201.

BOZZOMO, LAWRENCE E. Does class size matter? *The National Elementary Principal*, January 1978, *57*, 78–81.

BRADLEY, JOHN M. Evaluating reading achievement for placement in special education. *Journal of Special Education*, Fall 1976, *10*, 237–245.

BRADLEY, JOHN M., & AMES, WILBUR S. Readability parameters of basal readers. *Journal of Reading Behavior*, Summer 1977, 9, 175–183.

BRADLEY, JOHN M., & AMES, WILBUR S. You can't judge a basal by the number on the cover. *Reading World*, March 1978, *17*, 175–183.

BRADY, SUSAN. Short-term memory, phonological processing, and reading ability. *Annals of Dyslexia*, Vol. 36. Baltimore, MD: Orton Dyslexia Society, 1986, 138–153.

BRANSFORD, JOHN D.; VYE, NANCY J.; & STEIN, BARRY S. A comparison of successful and less successful learners: Can we enhance comprehension and mastery skills? In J. Flood (Ed.), *Promoting reading comprehension*. Newark, DE: International Reading Association, 1984, 216–231.

BRASE, D. A., & LOH, H. H. Possible role of 5-hydroxytryptamine in minimal brain dysfunction. *Life Sciences*, 1975, *16*(7), 1005–1016.

BRAUN, CARL; NEILSON, ALLAN R.; & DYKSTRA, ROBERT. Teacher expectations: Prime mover or inhibitor? In Brother L. Courtney (Ed.), *Reading interaction: The teacher, the pupil, the materials*. Newark, DE: International Reading Association, 1976, 40–48.

BRAUN, HENRY I. A new approach to avoiding problems of scale in interpreting trends in mental measurement data. *Journal of Educational Measurements*, Fall 1988, 25, 171–191.

BRAUSE, RITA S., & MAYHER, JOHN S. Teachers, students, and classroom organization. *Research on the Teaching of English*, May 1982, *16*, 131–148.

BRECHT, RICHARD D. Testing format and instructional level with the informal reading inventory. *The Reading Teacher*, October 1977, *31*, 57–59.

BREEN, L. C. Vocabulary development by teaching prefixes, suffixes and root derivations. *The Reading Teacher*, November 1960, *14*, 93–97.

BRENNAN, ALLISON D.; BRIDGE, CONNIE H.; & WINOGRAD, PETER N. The effects of structural variation in children's recall of basal reader stories. *Reading Research Quarterly*, Winter 1986, *21*, 91–104.

BRESCIA, SHELAGH M., & BRAUN, CARL. Associative verbal encoding and sight vocabulary acquisition and retention. *Journal of Reading Behavior*, Fall 1977, 9, 259–267.

BRICKLIN, PATRICIA M. Counseling parents of children with learning disabilities. *The Reading Teacher*, January 1970, *23*, 331–338.

BRIDGE, CONNIE A. Beyond the basal in beginning reading. In P. N. Winograd et al. (Eds.), *Improving basal reading instruction*. New York: Teachers College Press, 1989, 177–209.

BRIDGE, CONNIE A., & WINOGRAD, PETER N. Readers' awareness of cohesive relationships during cloze comprehension. *Journal of Reading Behavior*, 1982, *14*(3), 299–312.

BRIDGES, ETHEL B. Using children's choices of and reactions to poetry as determinants in enriching literary experience in the middle grades. *Dissertation Abstracts International*, 1967, *27*, 3749A.

BRISTOW, PAGE S. Disabled readers: Coping in the classroom. *Reading Today*, December 1987/January 1988, 5, 26.

BRITTON, BRUCE K., et al. Effect of text structure on use of cognitive capacity during reading. *Journal of Educational Psychology*, February 1982, *74* (1), 51–61.

BROD, NATHAN, & HAMILTON, DAVID. Binocularity and reading. *Journal of Learning Disabilities*, November 1973, 6, 574–576.

BROMLEY, KAREN D., & MCKEVENY, LAURIE. Precise writing: Suggestions for instruction in summarizing. *Journal of Reading*, February 1986, *29*, 392–395.

BRONNER, AUGUST F. *Psychology of special abilities and disabilities*. Boston: Little, Brown, 1917.

BROOKS, CHARLOTTE K. (Ed.). *Tapping potential: English and language arts for the black learner*. Urbana, IL: National Council of Teachers of English, 1985.

BROOKS, R. A. *An investigation of the relationship between reading interest and comprehension*, 1972. (ERIC number ED 067 625.)

BROPHY, JERE E. Teacher behavior and student learning. *Educational Leadership*, October 1979, 37, 33–38.(a)

BROPHY, JERE E. Teacher behavior and its effects. *Journal of Educational Psychology*, December 1979, *71*, 733–750.(b)

BROPHY, JERE. Teacher praise: A functional analysis. *Review of Educational Research,* Spring 1981, *51,* 5–32.

BROPHY, JERE E. Research on the self-fulfilling prophecy and teacher expectations. *Journal of Educational Psychology,* 1983, *75*(5), 631–661.

BROPHY, JERE. Principles for conducting first-grade reading group instruction. In J. V. Hoffman (Ed.), *Effective teaching of reading: Research and practice.* Newark, DE: International Reading Association, 1986, 53–84.

BROPHY, JERE E., & EVERTSON, CAROLYN M. *Student characteristics and teaching.* New York: Longman, 1981.

BROWN, ANN L. *Teaching students to think as they read: Implications for curriculum reform.* Reading Education Report No. 58. Champaign, IL: Center for the Study of Reading, University of Illinois, April 1985.

BROWN, ANN L., & CAMPIONE, JOSEPH C. *Psychological theory and the study of learning disabilities.* Technical Report No. 360. Champaign, IL: Center for the Study of Reading, University of Illinois, December 1985.

BROWN, ANN L.; CAMPIONE, JOSEPH C.; & DAY, JEANNE D. Learning to learn: On training students to learn from texts. *Educational Researcher,* February 1981, *10,* 14–21. Also in A. J. Harris & E. Sipay (Eds.), *Readings on reading instruction* (3rd ed.). New York: Longman, 1984, 317–326.

BROWN, ANN L., & DAY, JEANNE D. *Macrorules for summarizing text: The development of expertise.* Technical Report No. 270. Champaign, IL: Center for the Study of Reading, University of Illinois, January 1983.

BROWN, ANN L., & PALINCSAR, ANNEMARIE S. *Inducing strategic learning from texts by means of informed, self-control training.* Technical Report No. 262. Champaign, IL: Center for the Study of Reading, University of Illinois, September 1982.

BROWN, ANN L., & PALINCSAR, ANNEMARIE S. *Reciprocal teaching of comprehension strategies: A natural history of one program for enhancing learning.* Technical Report No. 334. Champaign, IL: Center for the Study of Reading, University of Illinois, April 1985.

BROWN, ANN L., & PALINCSAR, ANNEMARIE S. *Guided, cooperative learning and individual knowledge acquisition.* Technical Report No. 372. Champaign, IL: Center for the Study of Reading, University of Illinois, March 1986.

BROWN, BRIAN., et al. Static postural stability in normal and in dyslexic children. *Journal of Learning Disabilities,* January 1985, *18,* 31–34.

BROWN, ERIC R. A theory of reading. *Journal of Communication Disorders,* November 1981, *14,* 443–466.

BROWN, HARRY J. *Reaction and movement time as related to oral and silent reading in disabled readers.* Unpublished doctoral dissertation, University of Minnesota, 1970.

BROWN, JAMES I. Techniques for increasing reading rate. In J. Merritt (Ed.), *New horizons in reading.* Newark, DE: International Reading Association, 1976, 158–164. Also in A. J. Harris & E. Sipay (Eds.), *Readings on reading instruction* (3rd ed.). New York: Longman, 1984, 397–401.

BROWN, LINDA, & BRYANT, BRIAN R. Reply. *Remedial and Special Education,* July/August 1986, 7, 60–61.

BROWN, LINDA L., & SHERBENOU, RITA J. A comparison of teacher perceptions of student reading ability, reading performance, and classroom behavior. *The Reading Teacher,* February 1981, *34,* 557–560.

BROWNLEE, PHYLISS P. Suggestopedia in the classroom. *Academic Therapy,* March 1982, *17,* 407–414.

BROZO, WILLIAM G., & TOMLINSON, CARL M. Literature: The key to lively content courses. *The Reading Teacher,* December 1986, *40,* 288–293.

BRUCE, BERTRAM, & RUBIN, ANDEE. Readability formulas: Matching tool and task. In A. Davison & G. M. Green (Eds.), *Linguistic complexity and text comprehension: Readability issues reconsidered.* Hillsdale, NJ: Erlbaum, 1988, 5–22.

BRUCK, MAGGIE. The word recognition and spelling of dyslexic children. *Reading Research Quarterly,* Winter 1988, *23*, 51–69.

BRUINSMA, ROBERT. Should lip movements and subvocalization during silent reading be directly remediated? *The Reading Teacher,* December 1980, *34*, 293–295.

BRUMBACK, ROGER A., & STATON, R. DENNIS. Learning disability and childhood depression. *American Journal of Orthopsychiatry,* April 1983, *53*, 269–281.

BRUMBAUGH, F. Reading expectancy. *Elementary English Review,* 1940, *17*, 153–155.

BRUTON, RONALD W. Individualizing a basal reader. *The Reading Teacher,* October 1972, *26*, 59–63.

BRYANT, N. DALE. Modifying instruction to minimize the effects of learning disabilities. *The Forum,* Fall 1980, *6*, 19–20.

BRYANT, N. DALE. *A summary of directions for the "LD–Efficient" teaching manual.* New York: Research Institute for the Study of Learning Disabilities, Columbia University, 1981.

BUCHANAN, MARY, & WOLF, JOAN S. A comprehensive study of learning disabled adults. *Journal of Learning Disabilities,* January 1986, *19*, 34–38.

BUCKLEY, MARILYN H. When teachers decide to integrate the language arts. *Language Arts,* April 1986, *63*, 369–377.

BUCKLEY, ROBERT E. The biobasis for distraction and dyslexia. *Academic Therapy,* January 1981, *16*, 289–301.

BURGESS, JACQUELINE R. Modifying independent leisure reading habits at home. *The Reading Teacher,* May 1985, *38*, 845–848.

BURKE, SUZZANE M.; PFLAUM, SUSANNA W.; & KNAFLE, JUNE D. The influence of black English on diagnosis of reading in learning disabled and normal readers. *Journal of Learning Disabilities,* January 1982, *15*, 19–22.

BURMEISTER, LOU E. A chart for the new Spache Formula. *The Reading Teacher,* January 1976, *29*, 384–385.

BURNS, EDWARD. Linear regression and simplified reading expectancy formulas. *Reading Research Quarterly,* 1982, *17*(3), 446–453.

BURNS, PAUL C., & ROE, BETTY D. *Reading activities for today's elementary schools.* Chicago: Rand McNally, 1979.

BUROS, OSCAR K. (Ed.). *Reading tests and reviews.* New Brunswick, NJ: Gryphon Press, 1968.

BUROS, OSCAR K. (Ed.). *The seventh mental measurements yearbook,* Vols. I & II. Highland Park, NJ. Gryphon Press, 1972.

BUROS, OSCAR K. (Ed.). *Reading tests and reviews II.* Highland Park, NJ: Gryphon Press, 1975.

BUROS, OSCAR K. (Ed.). *The eighth mental measurements yearbook,* Vols. I & II. Highland Park, NJ: Gryphon Press, 1978.

BURRES, LEE, & JENKINSON, EDWARD B. *The student's right to know.* Urbana, IL: National Council of Teachers of English, 1982.

BURSUCK, WILLIAM D., & EPSTEIN, MICHAEL M. Current research topics in learning disabilities. *Learning Disability Quarterly,* Winter 1987, *10*, 2–7.

BUSWELL, GUY T. *Fundamental reading habits: A study of their development.* Supplementary Educational Monographs No. 21. Chicago: University of Chicago Press, 1922.

BUSWELL, GUY T. *Remedial reading at the college and adult levels.* Supplementary Educational Monographs No. 50. Chicago: University of Chicago Press, 1939.

BUSWELL, GUY T. Relationship between rate of thinking and rate of reading. *School Review,* September 1951, *49*, 339–346.

BUTLER, OWEN B. Early help for kids at risk: Our nation's best investment. *NEA Today*, January 1989, 7, 50–53.

BUTLER, SUSAN, et al. Seven-year longitudinal study of early prediction of reading achievement. *Journal of Educational Psychology*, 1985, 77(3), 349–361.

BUTZOW, CAROL M., & BUTZOW, JOHN W. *Science through children's literature.* Englewood, CO: Libraries Unlimited, 1989.

BYERS, J. L., & EVANS, T. E. *Using a lens-model analysis to identify factors in teacher judgment.* Research Series No. 73. East Lansing, MI: Institute for Research on Teaching, Michigan State University, 1980.

BYRNE, BRIAN. Reading disability, linguistic access and short-term memory: Comments prompted by Jorm's review of developmental dyslexia. *Australian Journal of Psychology*, April 1981, 33, 83–95.

CAGNEY, MARGARET A. Children's ability to understand standard English and black dialect. *The Reading Teacher*, March 1977, 30, 607–610.

CAHN, STEVEN M. Restoring the house of intellect. *American Educator*, Fall 1981, 5, 12–13, 37–38.

CALFEE, ROBERT. Cognitive models of reading: Implications for assessment and treatment of reading disability. In R. Malatesha & P. Aaron (Eds.), *Reading disorders: Varieties and treatments.* New York: Academic Press, 1982, 151–176.

CALFEE, ROBERT, & BROWN, ROGER. Grouping students for instruction. In D. Duke (Ed.), *Classroom management.* 78th Yearbook of the National Society for the Study of Education, Part II. Chicago: University of Chicago Press, 1979, 144–181.

CALFEE, ROBERT C., & CURLEY, ROBERT. Structure of prose in the content areas. In J. Flood (Ed.), *Understanding reading comprehension.* Newark, DE: International Reading Association, 1984, 161–180.

CALFEE, ROBERT C., & DRUM, PRISCILLA A. Learning to read: Theory, research, and practice. *Curriculum Inquiry*, Fall 1978, 8, 183–249.

CALFEE, ROBERT C., & DRUM, PRISCILLA A. Research in teaching reading. In M. C. Wittrock (Ed.), *Handbook on teaching* (3rd ed.). New York: Macmillan, 1985, 804–849.

CALFEE, ROBERT; HENRY, MARCIA; & FUNDERBURG, JEAN. A model for school change. In S. J. Samuels & P. D. Pearson (Eds.), *Changing school reading programs: Principles and case studies.* Newark, DE: International Reading Association, 1988, 121–141.

CALFEE, ROBERT C., & PIONTKOWSKI, DOROTHY C. The reading diary: Acquisition of decoding. *Reading Research Quarterly*, 1981, 16, 346–373.

CALFEE, ROBERT C., & SPECTOR, JANET E. Separable processes in reading. In F. Pirozollo & M. Wittrock (Eds.), *Neuropsychological and cognitive processes in reading.* New York: Academic Press, 1981, 3–29.

CAMPIONE, JOSEPH C. Assisted assessment: A taxonomy of approaches and an outline of strengths and weaknesses. *Journal of Learning Disabilities*, March 1989, 22, 151–165.

CANNEY, GEORGE F. Making games more relevant for reading. *The Reading Teacher*, October 1978, 32, 10–14.

CANNING, PATRICIA M.; ORR, R. ROBERT; & ROURKE, BYRON P. Sex differences in the perceptual, visual-motor, linguistic and concept-formation abilities of retarded readers. *Journal of Learning Disabilities*, December 1980, 13, 563–567.

CARBO, MARIE. Making books talk to children. *The Reading Teacher*, November 1981, 35, 186–189.

CARBO MARIE. The evidence supporting reading styles: A response to Stahl. *Phi Delta Kappan*, December 1988, 70, 323–327.

CARLSEN, JOANNE M. Between the deaf child and reading: The language connection. *The Reading Teacher*, January 1985, 38, 424–426.

CARLTON, GLEN; HUMMER, TERRY; & RAINEY, DAVID. Teaching learning disabled children to help themselves. *The Directive Teacher*, Winter/Spring 1984, 6, 8–9.

CARNEGIE CORPORATION OF NEW YORK. Making television better for children: The challenge of ACT. *Carnegie Quarterly*, Spring 1977, 25, 1–3.

CARNINE, DOUGLAS W. Direct instruction: A bottom up skills approach to elementary instruction. In L. Reed & S. Ward (Eds.), *Basic skills: Issues and choices: Approaches to basic skills and instruction 2*. St. Louis: CEMREL, April 1982, 135–146.

CARNINE, DOUGLAS. How to overcome barriers to student achievement. In S. J. Samuels & P. D. Pearson (Eds.), *Changing school reading programs: Principles and case studies*. Newark, DE: International Reading Association, 1988, 59–91.

CARNINE, DOUGLAS; KAMEENUI, EDWARD J.; & COYLE, GAYLE. Utilization of contextual information in determining the meaning of unfamiliar words. *Reading Research Quarterly*, Winter 1984, 19, 188–204.

CARPENTER, DALE. Spelling error profiles of able and disabled readers. *Journal of Learning Disabilities*, February 1983, 16, 102–104.

CARPENTER, PATRICIA A., & JUST, MARCEL A. Cognitive processes in reading: Models based on readers' eye fixations. In A. Lesgold & C. Perfetti (Eds.), *Interactive processes in reading*. Hillsdale, NJ: Erlbaum, 1981, 177–213.

CARPENTER, PATRICIA A., & JUST, MARCEL A. What your eyes do while your mind is reading. In K. Rayner (Ed.), *Eye movements in reading: Perceptual and language processes*. New York: Academic Press, 1983, 275–307.

CARR, EILEEN M.; DEWITZ, PETER; & PATBERG, JUDYTHE P. The effect of inference training on children's comprehension of expository text. *Journal of Reading Behavior*, 1983, 15(3), 1–18.

CARR, EILEEN; DEWITZ, PETER; & PATBERG, JUDYTHE P. Using cloze for inference training with expository text. *The Reading Teacher*, February, 1989, 42, 380–385.

CARR, EILEEN M., & MAZUR-STEWART, MARIANNE. The effects of the vocabulary overview guide on vocabulary comprehension and retention. *Journal of Reading Behavior*, 1988, 20(1), 43–62.

CARR, EILEEN, & WIXSON, KAREN K. Guidelines for evaluating vocabulary instruction. *Journal of Reading*, April 1986, 29, 588–595.

CARR, KATHRYN. The importance of inference skills in the primary grades. *The Reading Teacher*, February 1983, 36, 518–522.

CARR, THOMAS H. Building theories of reading ability: On the relationship between individual differences in cognitive skills and reading comprehension. *Cognition*, February 1981, 9, 73–114.

CARR, THOMAS H., & POLLATSEK, ALEXANDER. Recognizing printed words: A look at current models. In D. Besner et al. (Eds.), *Reading research: Advances in theory and practice*, Vol. 5. New York: Academic Press, 1985, 2–82.

CARROLL, H. C. M. The remedial teaching of reading: An evaluation. *Remedial Education*, February 1972, 7, 10–15.

CARROLL, JOHN B. Review of the Illinois Test of Psycholinguistic Abilities. In O. K. Buros (Ed.), *Seventh mental measurements yearbook*, Vol. I. Highland Park, NJ: Gryphon Press, 1972, 819–823.

CARROLL, JOHN B. Developmental parameters in reading comprehension. In J. T. Guthrie (Ed.), *Cognition, curriculum and comprehension*. Newark, DE: International Reading Association, 1977, 1–15.

CARROLL, JOHN B. The nature of the reading process. In H. Singer & R. B. Ruddell (Eds.), *Theoretical models and processes of reading* (3rd ed.). Newark, DE: International Reading Association, 1985, 25–34.

CARROLL, JOHN B. The National Assessment in Reading: Are we misreading the findings. *Phi Delta Kappan*, February 1987, 68, 424–430.

CARROLL, JOHN B. The Carroll Model: A 25-year retrospective and prospective view. *Educational Researcher*, January/February 1989, *18*, 26–31.

CARROLL, JOHN B.; DAVIES, PETER; & RICHMAN, BARRY. *American Heritage word frequency book*. Boston: Houghton Mifflin, 1971.

CARROLL, JOHN B., & WALTON, MARSHA. Has the reel reeding prablum bin lade bear? In L. Resnick & P. Weaver (Eds.), *Theory and practice in early reading*, Vol. I. Hillsdale, NJ: Erlbaum, 1979, 317–354.

CARTER, BETTY, & ABRAHAMSON, RICHARD F. The best of the high/ lo books for young adults: A critical evaluation. *Journal of Reading*, December 1986, *30*, 204–211.

CARTER, CANDY (Ed.). *Literature—News that stays news: Fresh approaches to the classics*. Urbana, IL: National Council of Teachers of English, 1985.

CARTER, JOHN L., & RUSSELL, HAROLD L. Use of EMG biofeedback procedures with learning disabled children in a clinical and an educational setting. *Journal of Learning Disabilities*, April 1985, *18*, 213–221.

CARVER, RONALD P. Measuring prose difficulty using the Rauding Scale. *Reading Research Quarterly*, 1975–1976, *11*, 660–684.

CARVER, RONALD P. Optimal rate of reading prose. *Reading Research Quarterly*, 1982, *18*(1), 56–88.

CARVER, RONALD P. Is reading rate constant or flexible? *Reading Research Quarterly*, Winter 1983, *18*, 190–215.

CARVER, RONALD P. Reading theory prediction of amount comprehended under different purposes and speed reading conditions. *Reading Research Quarterly*, Winter 1984, *19*, 205–218.

CARVER, RONALD P. How good are some of the world's best readers? *Reading Research Quarterly*, Summer 1985, *20*, 389–419.(a)

CARVER, RONALD P. Is the Degrees of Reading Power test valid or invalid? *Journal of Reading*, October 1985, *29*, 34–41.(b)

CARVER, RONALD P. Measuring readability using DRP units. *Journal of Reading Behavior*, 1985, *17*(4), 303–316.(c)

CARVER, RONALD P. Why is the Degrees of Reading Power test invalid? In J. Niles & R. Lalik (Eds.), *Issues in literacy: A research perspective*. Rochester, NY: National Reading Conference, 1985, 350–354.(d)

CARVER, RONALD P. Should reading comprehension skills be taught? In J. E. Readance et al. (Eds.), *Research in literacy: Merging perspectives*. Rochester, NY: National Reading Conference, 1987, 115–126.(a)

CARVER, RONALD P. Teaching rapid reading in the intermediate grades: Helpful or harmful? *Reading Research and Instruction*, Winter 1987, *26*, 65–76.(b)

CARVER, RONALD P. *Reading rate: Theory and research*. Unpublished manuscript. February 1988.

CARVER, RONALD P., & HOFFMAN, JAMES V. The effect of practice through repeated reading in gains in reading ability using a computer-based instructional system. *Reading Research Quarterly*, 1981, *16*(3), 374–390.

CASKEY, WILLIAM E., JR. The use of the Peabody Individual Achievement Test and the Woodcock Reading Mastery Tests in the diagnosis of a learning disability in reading: A caveat. *Journal of Learning Disabilities*, June/July 1986, *19*, 336–337.

CASTLE, JOYCE B. Vocabulary development: Reading does it. *Reading-Canada-Lecture*, Spring 1986, *4*, 11–15.

CASWELL, HOLLIS L. Non-promotion in the elementary school. *Elementary School Journal*, 1933, *33*, 644–647.

CATTELL, J. M. Ueber die Zeit der Erkennung und Benennung von Schriftzeichen, Bildern, und Farben. *Philosophische Studien*, 1885, *2*, 635–650.

CAZDEN, COURTNEY B. *Child language and education*. New York: Holt, Rinehart and Winston, 1972.

CAZDEN, COURTNEY B. Contexts for literacy: In the mind and in the classroom. *Journal of Reading Behavior*, 1982, *14*(4), 413–427.

CAZDEN, COURTNEY B. *Classroom discourse: The language of teaching and learning.* Portsmouth, NH: Heinemann, 1988.

CEPRANO, MARIA A. A review of selected research on methods of teaching sight words. *The Reading Teacher*, December 1981, *35*, 314–322.

CEPRANO, MARIA A. The effects of pictures on children's initial effort toward learning to read: Review of research. *Reading Improvement*, Spring 1987, *24*, 53–57.

CHABE, ALEXANDER M. *The Russian reading program: A re-examination.* Paper presented at the New York State Reading Association Conference, Kiamesha Lake, NY, November 1983.

CHALL, JEANNE S. *Reading 1967–1977: A decade of change and promise.* Bloomington, IN: Phi Beta Kappa Educational Foundation, 1977.

CHALL, JEANNE S. *Learning to read: The great debate.* New York: McGraw-Hill, 1967, 1983.(a)

CHALL, JEANNE S. *Stages of reading development.* New York: McGraw-Hill, 1983.(b)

CHALL, JEANNE S. Two vocabularies for reading: Recognition and meaning. In M. G. McKeown & M. E. Curtis (Eds.), *The nature of vocabulary acquisition.* Hillsdale, NJ: Erlbaum, 1987, 7–17.

CHALL, JEANNE S. The beginning years. In B. L. Zakaluk & S. J. Samuels (Eds.), *Readability: Its past, present & future.* Newark, DE: International Reading Association, 1988, 2–13.

CHALL, JEANNE S., & CONRAD, SUE S. Resources and their use for reading instruction. In A. Purves & O. Niles (Eds.), *Becoming readers in a complex society.* 83rd Yearbook of the National Society for the Study of Education, Part I. Chicago: University of Chicago Press, 1984, 209–232.

CHALL, JEANNE S.; ROSWELL, FLORENCE C.; & BLUMENTHAL, SUSAN H. Auditory blending ability: A factor in success in beginning reading. *The Reading Teacher*, 1963, *17*, 113–118.

CHAN, LORNA K. S.; COLE, PETER G.; & BARFETT, SHIRLEY. Comprehension monitoring: Detection and identification of text inconsistencies by LD and normal students. *Learning Disability Quarterly*, Spring 1987, *10*, 114–124.

CHANG, FREDERICK R. Mental processes in reading: A methodological review. *Reading Research Quarterly*, Winter 1983, *18*, 216–230.

CHAPMAN, DIANE L. Let's read another one. In D. R. Tovey & S. E. Kerber (Eds.), *Roles in literacy learning: A new perspective.* Newark, DE: International Reading Association, 1986, 10–25.

CHAPMAN, JAMES W. Learning disabled children's self-concepts. *Review of Educational Research*, Fall 1988, *58*, 347–371.

CHAPMAN, L. JOHN. *Reading development and cohesion.* Portsmouth, NH: Heinemann, 1983.

CHAPMAN, L. JOHN. Comprehending and the teacher of reading. In J. Flood (Ed.), *Promoting reading comprehension.* Newark, DE: International Reading Association, 1984, 261–272.

CHARRY, LAURENCE B. Controlling readability factors of teacher-made materials. In B. S. Schulwitz (Ed.), *Teachers, tangibles, and techniques: Comprehension of content in reading.* Newark, DE: International Reading Association, 1975, 93–99.

CHASE, NANCY D., & HYND, CYNTHIA R. Reader response: An alternative way to teach students to think about text. *Journal of Reading*, March 1987, *30*, 530–540.

CHATMAN, STEVEN P.; REYNOLDS, CECIL R.; & WILLSON, VICTOR L. Multiple indexes of test scatter on the Kaufman Assessment Battery for Children. *Journal of Learning Disabilities*, November 1984, *17*, 523–531.

CHAVEZ-OLLER, MARY ANNE, et al. When are cloze items sensitive to constraints across sentences? *Language Learning*, June 1985, *35*, 181–206.

CHEEK, EARL H., & CHEEK, MARTHA C. Organizational patterns: Untapped resources for better reading. *Reading World*, May 1983, *22*, 278–283.

CHERRY, ROCHELLE S., & KRUGER, BARBARA. Selective auditory attention abilities of learning disabled and normal achieving children. *Journal of Learning Disabilities*, April 1983, *16*, 202–205.

CHEYNEY, ARNOLD B. *Teaching reading skills through the newspaper* (2nd ed.). Newark, DE: International Reading Association, 1984.

CHEYNEY, WENDY, & STRICHART, STEPHEN S. A learning stations model for the resource room. *Academic Therapy*, January 1981, *16*, 271–279.

CHING, DORIS C. *Reading and the bilingual child.* Newark, DE: International Reading Association, 1976.

CHITTENDEN, EDWARD A. *Assessment of beginning reading: A framework for coding error patterns in oral reading performance.* Research Report RR-84-19. Princeton, NJ: Educational Testing Service, 1984.

CHOMSKY, CAROL. When you still can't read in third grade: After decoding, what? In S. J. Samuels (Ed.), *What research has to say about reading instruction.* Newark, DE: International Reading Association, 1978, 13–30.

CHOMSKY, CAROL. Approaching reading through invented spelling. In L. Resnick & P. Weaver (Eds.), *Theory and practice of early reading*, Vol. 2. Hillsdale, NJ: Erlbaum, 1979, 43–65.

CHOMSKY, CAROL. Linguistic consciousness-raising in children. *Language Arts*, May 1981, *58*, 607–612.

CHRISTENBURG, LEILA, & KELLEY, PATRICIA P. *Questions: A path to critical thinking.* Urbana, IL: National Council of Teachers of English & ERIC/RES, 1983.

CHRISTIE, JAMES F. The effects of grade level and reading ability on children's miscue patterns. *Journal of Educational Research*, July/August 1981, *74*, 419–423.

CHRISTIE, JAMES F., & ALONSO, PATRICIA A. Effects of passage difficulty on primary-grade children's oral reading error patterns. *Educational Research Quarterly*, Spring 1980, *5*, 41–49.

CIANCIOLO, PATRICIA. Yesterday comes alive for readers of historical fiction. *Language Arts*, April 1981, *58*, 452–462.

CIANCIOLO, PATRICIA J. Responding to literature as a work of art—An aesthetic experience. *Language Arts*, March 1982, *59*, 259–264, 295.

CIANCIOLO, PATRICIA J. No small challenge: Literature for the transitional readers. *Language Arts*, January 1989, *66*, 72–81.

CIANI, ALFRED J. (Ed.). *Motivating reluctant readers.* Newark, DE: International Reading Association, 1981.

CITRON, CHRISTIANE H. Courts provide insight on content validity requirements. *Educational Measurement: Issues and Practices*, Winter 1983, *2*, 6–7.

CLARK, CHARLES H., & BEAN, THOMAS W. Improving advance organizer research: Persistent problems and future decisions. *Reading World*, October 1982, *22*, 2–10.

CLARK, MARGARET M. *Reading difficulties in schools.* Baltimore: Penguin Books, 1970, Exeter, NH: Heinemann, 1979.

CLARKE, JEAN, & BOSTLE, EILEEN (Eds.). *Reading Therapy.* Chicago: American Library Association, 1988.

CLARKE, LINDA K. Invented versus traditional spelling in first graders' writings: Effects on learning to spell and read. *Research in the Teaching of English*, October 1988, *22*, 281–309.

CLAY, MARIE M. *What did I write?* Portsmouth, NH: Heinemann, 1975.

CLAY, MARIE M. *The early detection of reading difficulties* (3rd ed.). Portsmouth, NH: Heinemann, 1985.

CLAY, MARIE M. Implementing Reading Recovery: Systematic adaptations to an educational innovation. *New Zealand Journal of Educational Studies*, 1987, *22*(1), 35–60.(a)

CLAY, MARIE M. Learning to be learning disabled. *New Zealand Journal of Educational Studies*, 1987, *22*(2), 155–173.(b)

CLAY, MARIE M., & IMLACH, ROBERT H. Juncture, pitch, and stress as reading behavior variables. *Journal of Verbal Learning and Verbal Behavior*, April 1971, *10*, 133–139.

CLELAND, CRAIG J. Learning to read: Piagetian perspectives for instruction. *Reading World*, March 1981, *20*, 223–224.

CLEMENTS, SAM D., & BARNES, STEPHEN M. The three R's and central processing training. *Academic Therapy*, May 1978, *13*, 535–547.

CLEWELL, SUZANNE F., & CLIFFTON, ANNE M. Examining your textbook for comprehensibility. *Journal of Reading*, December 1983, *27*, 219–224.

CLEWELL, SUZANNE F., & HAIDEMENOS, JULIE. Organizational strategies to increase comprehension. *Reading World*, May 1983, *22*, 314–321.

CLOER, CARL T., JR. Subvocalization—asset, liability, or both? In P. D. Pearson (Ed.), *Reading: Theory, research, and practice.* Clemson, SC: National Reading Conference, 1977, 209–213.

COHEN, ALICE, & GLASS, GERALD G. Lateral dominance and reading ability. *The Reading Teacher*, January 1968, *21*, 343–348.

COHEN, GILLIAN. Theoretical interpretations of lateral asymmetries. In J. Beaumont (Ed.), *Divided visual field studies of cerebral organization.* New York: Academic Press, 1982, 87–111.

COHEN, JUDITH H. *Handbook of resource room teaching.* Rockville, MD: Aspen, 1982.

COHEN, PETER A.; KULIK, JAMES A.; & KULIK, CHEN-LIN. Educational outcomes of tutoring: A meta-analysis of findings. *American Educational Research Journal*, Summer 1982, *19*, 237–248.

COHEN, SHARON S., & ZIGMOND, NAOMI. The social integration of learning disabled students from self-contained to mainstreamed school settings. *Journal of Learning Disabilities*, December 1986, *19*, 614–618.

COHN, MARVIN, & STRICKLER, GEORGE. Reversal errors in strong, average, and weak letter namers. *Journal of Learning Disabilities*, October 1979, *12*, 533–537.

COLARUSSO, RONALD P., & GILL, SALLY. Selecting a test of visual perception. *Academic Therapy*, Winter 1975–1976, *11*, 157–166.

COLBERT, PAT, et al. Learning disabilities as a symptom of depression in children. *Journal of Learning Disabilities*, June/July 1982, *15*, 333–336.

COLEMAN, J. MICHAEL. Achievement level, social class, and the self-concepts of mildly handicapped children. *Journal of Learning Disabilities*, January 1985, *18*, 26–30.

COLES, GERALD S. The learning-disabilities test battery: Empirical and social issues. *Harvard Educational Review*, August 1978, *48*, 313–340.

COLES, GERALD S. *The learning mystique: A critical look at "learning disabilities."* New York: Pantheon, 1987.

COLLINS, CATHY. Is the cart before the horse? Effects of preschool reading instruction on 4 year olds. *The Reading Teacher*, December 1986, *40*, 332–339.

COLWELL, CLYDE, & HELFELDT, JOHN. The paragraph as a semantic unit: Theory and practice. *Reading World*, May 1983, *22*, 332–345.

COMPTON, CAROLYN. *A guide to 75 tests for special education.* Belmont, CA: Fearon, 1984.

CONDUS, MARIA M.; MARHSALL, KATHLEEN J.; & MILLER, SIDNEY R. Effects of the keyword mnemonic strategy on vocabulary acquisition and maintenance by learning disabled children. *Journal of Learning Disabilities*, December 1986, *19*, 609–613.

CONE, THOMAS E., & WILSON, LONNY R. Quantifying a severe discrepancy: A critical analysis. *Learning Disability Quarterly*, Fall 1981, *4*, 359–371.

CONGRESSIONAL BUDGET OFFICE. *Educational achievement: Explanations and implications of recent trends.* Washington, DC: Superintendent of Documents, United States Printing Office, August 1987.

CONLEY, MARK W. Grouping. In D. E. Alvermann et al. (Eds.), *Research within reach: Secondary school reading*. Newark, DE: International Reading Association, 1987, 130–140.(a)

CONLEY, MARK W. Teacher decision making. In D. E. Alvermann et al. (Eds.), *Research within reach: Secondary school reading*. Newark, DE: International Reading Association, 1987, 142–152. (b)

CONLEY, MARK W., & MURPHY, ANN G. Effective schools/effective teaching research. In D. E. Alvermann et al. (Eds.), *Research within reach: Secondary school reading*. Newark, DE: International Reading Association, 1987, 14–24.

CONNOLLY, CHRISTOPHER. Social and emotional factors in learning disabilities. In H. R. Myklebust (Ed.), *Progress in learning disabilities*, Vol. II. New York: Grune & Stratton, 1971, 151–178.

CONOLEY, JANE C., et al. (Eds.). *Supplement to the ninth mental measurements yearbook*. Lincoln, NE: University of Nebraska Press, 1988.

CONOLEY, JANE C., & KRAMER, JACK J. *The tenth mental measurements yearbook*. Lincoln, NE: University of Nebraska Press, 1989.

COOK, WANDA D. *Adult literacy education in the United States*. Newark: DE: International Reading Association, 1977.

COOKSEY, RAY W.; FREEBODY, PETER; & DAVIDSON, GRAHAM R. Teachers' predictions of children's early reading achievement: An application of social judgement theory. *American Educational Research Journal*, Spring 1986, *23*, 41–64.

COOLEY, ERIC J., & AYRES, ROBERT R. Self-concept and success-failure attributions of non-handicapped students and students with learning disabilities. *Journal of Learning Disabilities*, March 1988, *21*, 174–178.

COOPER, J. DAVID. *Improving reading comprehension*. Boston: Houghton Mifflin, 1986.

COOPER, J. LOUIS. *The effect of adjustment of basal reading materials on reading achievement*. Unpublished doctoral dissertation, Boston University, 1952.

COPELAND, WILLIS D. Teaching-learning behaviors and the demands of the classroom environment. *Elementary School Journal*, March 1980, *80*, 162–177.

COPPERMAN, PAUL. *The literacy hoax: The decline of reading, writing, and learning in the public schools and what we can do about it*. New York: William Morrow, 1978.

COPPOLA, RICHARD. Recent developments in neuro-imaging techniques. In D. B. Gray & J. F. Kavanagh (Eds.), *Biochemical measures of dyslexia*. Parkton, MD: York Press, 1985, 63–69.

CORBETT, EDWARD P. J. A literal view of literacy. In J. Raymond (Ed.), *Literacy as a human problem*. University, AL: University of Alabama Press, 1982, 137–153.

CORDTS, ANNA D. And it's called phonics. *Elementary English*, 1955, *32*, 376–378.

CORLEY, PATRICIA J. A developmental analysis of sentence comprehension abilities in good and poor readers. *Educational Psychologist*, 1988, *23*(1), 57–75.

CORNELIUS, PAULA L., & SEMMEL, MELVYN I. Effects of summer instruction on reading achievement of learning disabled students. *Journal of Learning Disabilities*, August/September 1982, *15*, 409–413.

CORNING, WILLIAM C.; STEFFY, RICHARD A.; & CHAPRIN, IAN G. EEG slow frequency and WISC-R correlates. *Journal of Abnormal Child Psychology*, December 1982, *10*, 511–530.

COTT, ALLAN. *Help for your learning disabled child. The orthomolecular treatment*, New York: Times Books, 1985.

COTTERELL, GILL. A case of severe learning disability. *Remedial Education*, February 1972, *7*, 5–9.

COTUGNO, ALBERT J. Cognitive control functioning in hyperactive and nonhyperactive learning disabled children. *Journal of Learning Disabilities*, November 1987, *20*, 563–567.

COUNCIL FOR EXCEPTIONAL CHILDREN. *Children on medication: A primer for school personnel*. Reston, VA: Council for Exceptional Children, 1986.

COURTNAGE, LEE. A survey of state policies on use of medication in schools. *Exceptional Children*, September 1982, *49*, 75–77.

COWAN, WILLIAM P. Remedial reading in secondary schools: Three-fourths of a century. In H. A. Robinson (Ed.), *Reading and writing instruction in the United States: Historical trends*. Newark, DE: International Reading Association, September 1977, 76–81.

COX, AYLETT R. *Structure and techniques*. Cambridge, MA: Educators Publishing Service, 1977.

COX, JUANITA, & WALLIS, BETH S. Books for the Cajun child—Lagniappe or a little something extra for multi-cultural teaching. *The Reading Teacher*, December 1982, *36*, 263–266.

COX, JUANITA, & WIEBE, JAMES H. Measuring reading vocabulary and concepts in mathematics in the primary grades. *The Reading Teacher*, January 1984, *37*, 402–410.

CRAIN, STEPHEN, & SHANKWEILER, DONALD. Syntactic complexity and reading acquisition. In A. Davison & G. M. Green (Eds.), *Linguistic complexity and text comprehension: Readability issues reconsidered*. Hillsdale, NJ: Erlbaum, 1988, 167–192.

CRANNEY, A. GARR, & MILLER, JANET S. History of reading: Status and sources of a growing field. *Journal of Reading*, February 1987, *30*, 388–398.

CRANNEY, A. GARR, et al. Rate and Reading Dynamics reconsidered. *Journal of Reading*, March 1982, *25*, 526–533.

CRAWFORD, GAIL, & CONLEY, DICK. Meet you in reading lab! *Journal of Reading*, October 1971, *15*, 16–21.

CRISCUOLO, NICHOLAS P. *Look it up! 101 dictionary activities to develop word skills*. Belmont, CA: Fearon-Pitman, 1980.

CRISCUOLO, NICHOLAS P. Ten creative ways to build vocabulary skills. *Wisconsin State Reading Association Journal*, Fall 1981, *26*, 23–26.

CRISCUOLO, NICHOLAS P. Practical ways to motivate children to read and write: A baker's dozen. *New England Reading Association Journal*, Winter 1982, *17*, 25–26.

CRISCUOLO, NICHOLAS P. A treasure trove for building a rich vocabulary. *The Reading Teacher*, January 1984, *37*, 444–446.

CRITCHLEY, MACDONALD. *The dyslexic child*. Springfield, IL: Charles C. Thomas, 1970.

CRITCHLEY, MACDONALD. Dyslexia: An overview. In G. Pavlidis & T. Miles (Eds.), *Dyslexia research and its application to education*. New York: John Wiley & Sons, 1981, 1–11.

CROMER, WARD. The difference model: A new explanation for some reading difficulties. *Journal of Educational Psychology*, 1970, *61*, 471–483.

CRONBACH, LEE J. Test validation. In R. L. Thorndike (Ed.), *Educational measurement* (2nd ed.). Washington, DC: American Council on Education, 1971, 443–507.

CRONBACH, LEE J., & QUIRK, THOMAS J. Test validity. In *Encyclopedia of education*, Vol. 9. New York: Crowell-Collier, 1971, 165–175.

CRONBACH, LEE J., & SNOW, RICHARD E. *Aptitudes and instructional methods*. New York: Irvington, 1977.

CRONNELL, BRUCE. Cause and effect: An overview. *Reading World*, December 1981, *21*, 155–166.

CROSS, DAVID, & PARIS, SCOTT G. Assessment of reading comprehension: Matching test purposes and test properties. *Educational Psychologist*, Summer/Fall 1987, *22*, 313–332.

CUDDIGAN, MAUREEN, & HANSON, MARY BETH. *Growing pains: Helping children deal with everyday problems through reading*. Chicago: American Library Association, 1988.

CULLINAN, BERNICE E. (Ed.). *Children's literature in the reading program*. Newark, DE: International Reading Association, 1987.

CUNNINGHAM, PATRICIA M. Transferring comprehension from listening to reading. *The Reading Teacher*, November 1975, *29*, 169–172.

CUNNINGHAM, PATRICIA M. Investigating the role of meaning in mediated word identification. In P. D. Pearson & J. Hansen (Eds.), *Reading: Theory, research, and practice.* Clemson, SC: National Reading Conference, 1977, 168–171.

CUNNINGHAM, PATRICIA M. A comparison/contrast theory of mediated word identification. *The Reading Teacher,* April 1979, *32,* 774–778. Also in A. J. Harris & E. Sipay (Eds.), *Readings on reading instruction* (3rd ed.). New York: Longman, 1984, 202–207.

CUNNINGHAM, PATRICIA M. Applying a compare/contrast process to identifying polysyllabic words. *Journal of Reading Behavior,* Fall 1980, *12,* 213–223.

CUNNINGHAM, PATRICIA M. A teacher's guide to materials shopping. *The Reading Teacher,* November 1981, *35,* 180–184.

CUNNINGHAM, PATRICIA M. When all else fails. *The Reading Teacher,* April 1988, *41,* 800–805.

CURTIS, MARY E. Vocabulary testing and vocabulary instruction. In M. G. McKeown & M. E. Curtis (Eds.), *The nature of vocabulary acquisition.* Hillsdale, NJ: Erlbaum, 1987, 37–51.

DAHL, PATRICIA, & SAMUELS, S. JAY. Teaching children to read using hypothesis test strategies. *The Reading Teacher,* March 1977, *30,* 603–606.

DAHLBERG, CHARLES C.; ROSWELL, FLORENCE G.; & CHALL, JEANNE S. Psychotherapeutic principles as applied to remedial reading. *Elementary School Journal,* 1952, *52,* 211–217.

DALE, EDGAR, & CHALL, JEANNE S. A formula for predicting readability. *Educational Research Bulletin,* Ohio State University, 1948, *27,* 11–20; *28,* 37–54.

DALE, EDGAR, & O'ROURKE, JOSEPH. *Techniques for teaching vocabulary.* Menlo Park, CA: Benjamin Cummings, 1971.

DALE, EDGAR, & O'ROURKE, JOSEPH. *The living word vocabulary* (3rd ed.). Chicago: World Book-Childcraft International, 1981.

DALE, EDGAR, & O'ROURKE, JOSEPH. The need for a planned vocabulary program. In A. J. Harris & E. Sipay (Eds.), *Readings on reading instruction* (3rd ed.). New York: Longman, 1984, 226–230.

D'ANGELO, FRANK J. Luria on literacy: The cognitive consequences of reading and writing. In J. Raymond (Ed.), *Literacy as a human problem.* University, AL: University of Alabama Press, 1982, 154–169.

D'ANGELO, KAREN. Correction behavior: Implications for reading instruction. *The Reading Teacher,* January 1982, *35,* 395–398.

D'ANGELO, KAREN, & MAKLIOS, MARC. Insertion and omission miscues of good and poor readers. *The Reading Teacher,* April 1983, *36,* 778–782.

DANK, MARION. What effect do reading programs have on the oral reading behavior of children? *Reading Improvement,* Summer 1977, *14,* 66–69.

DANKS, JOSEPH H., & END, LAUREL J. Processing strategies for reading and listening. In R. Horowitz & S. J. Samuels (Eds.), *Comprehending oral and written language.* New York: Academic Press, 1987, 271–294.

DANKS, JOSEPH H., & HILL, GREGORY O. An interactive analysis of oral reading. In A. Lesgold & C. Perfetti (Eds.), *Interactive processes in reading.* Hillsdale, NJ: Erlbaum, 1981, 131–153.

DARCH, CRAIG, & CARNINE, DOUGLAS. Teaching content area material to learning disabled students. *Exceptional Children,* November 1986, *53,* 240–246.

DAVEY, BETH. Using Textbook Activity Guides to help students learn from textbooks. *Journal of Reading,* March 1986, *29,* 489–494.

DAVEY, BETH. Post passage questions: Task and reader effects on comprehension and metacomprehension processes. *Journal of Reading Behavior,* 1987, *19*(3), 261–283.

DAVEY, BETH. The nature of response errors for good and poor readers when permitted to reinspect text during question-answering. *American Educational Research Journal,* Fall 1988, *25,* 399–414.

DAVEY, BETH. Assessing comprehension: Selected interactions of task and reader. *The Reading Teacher*, May 1989, *42*, 694–697.

DAVIDSON, HELEN P. An experimental study of bright, average and dull children at the four-year mental level. *Genetic Psychology Monographs*, 1931, 9, Nos. 3, 4.

DAVIDSON, ROSCOE L. *The effects of an interaction analysis system in the development of critical reading in elementary school children.* Unpublished doctoral dissertation, University of Denver, 1967.

DAVIES, THOMAS R. Project Screen: A followup study of a pre-school screening battery. *Exceptional Child*, November 1980, 27, 151–157.

DAVIS, EVERETT E., & EKWALL, ELDON E. Mode of perception and frustration in reading. *Journal of Learning Disabilities*, September 1976, 9, 448–454.

DAVIS, FREDERICK B. Research on comprehension in reading. *Reading Research Quarterly*, Summer 1968, *3*, 449–545.

DAVIS, FREDERICK B. Psychometric research on comprehension in reading. *Reading Research Quarterly*, Summer 1972, 7, 628–678.

DAVIS, JAMES E., & DAVIS, HAZEL K. *Your reading: A booklet for junior high and middle school students.* Urbana, IL: National Council of Teachers of English, 1988.

DAVIS, JOANNE W. Teaching reading with paperbacks in an elementary school: Three models for classroom organization. *Elementary English*, December 1970, *47*, 1114–1120.

DAVISON, ALICE. Assigning grade levels without formulas: Some case studies. In B. L. Zakaluk & S. J. Samuels (Eds.), *Readability: Its past, present, & future.* Newark, DE: International Reading Association, 1988, 36–45.

DAVISON, ALICE, & KANTOR, ROBERT N. On the failure of readability formulas to define readable texts: A case study from adaptations. *Reading Research Quarterly*, 1982, *17*(2), 187–209.

DAY, KAAREN C., & DAY, H. D. Tests of metalinguistic awareness. In D. B. Yaden & S. Templeton (Eds.), *Metalinguistic awareness and beginning literacy.* Portsmouth, NH: Heinemann, 1986, 187–197.

DEARBORN, WALTER F. Structural factors which condition special disability in reading. *Proceedings of the American Association for Mental Deficiency*, 1933, 266–283.

DEATON, FRANK. A comparison of the effects of reinforcing accuracy and time on-task responses in a programmed remedial program with fourth-grade reading problem children. *Dissertation Abstracts International*, June 1975, *35* (12-B, Pt. 1), 6067–6068.

DE BETTENCOURT, LAURIE U. Strategy training: A need for clarification. *Exceptional Children*, September 1987, *54*, 24–30.

DECHANT, EMERALD V., & SMITH, HENRY P. *Psychology in teaching reading.* Englewood Cliffs, NJ: Prentice-Hall, 1977.

DECI, EDWARD L., & CHANDLER, CHRISTINE L. The importance of motivation for the future of the LD field. *Journal of Learning Disabilities*, December 1986, *19*, 587–594.

DECKER, SADIE N., & BENDER, BRUCE G. Converging evidence for multiple genetic forms of reading disability. *Brain and Language*, March 1988, *33*, 197–215.

DECKER, SADIE N., & VADENBERG, STEVEN G. Colorado twin study of reading disability. In D. B. Gray & J. F. Kavanagh (Eds.), *Biobehavioral measures of dyslexia.* Parkton, MD: York Press, 1985, 123–135.

DEFRIES, J. C. Colorado reading project. In D. B. Gray & J. F. Kavanagh (Eds.), *Biobehavioral measures of dyslexia.* Parkton, MD: York Press, 1985, 107–122.

DE HIRSCH, KATRINA; JANSKY, JEANETTE J.; & LANGFORD, WILLIAM S. *Predicting reading failure: A preliminary study.* New York: Harper & Row, 1966.

DEIGHTON, LEE C. *Vocabulary development in the classroom.* New York: Teachers College Press, 1959.

DELACATO, CARL H. *Neurological organization and reading.* Springfield, IL: Charles C Thomas, 1966.

DELAIN, MARSHA T.; PEARSON, P. DAVID; & ANDERSON, RICHARD C. Reading comprehension and creativity in black language use: You stand to gain by playing the sounding game. *American Educational Research Journal*, Summer 1985, *22*, 155–173.

DELCLOS, VICTOR R.; BURNS, M. SUSAN; & KULEWICZ, STANLEY J. Effects of dynamic assessment on teachers' expectations of handicapped children. *American Educational Research Journal*, Fall 1987, *24*, 325–336.

DE LUKE, SUSAN V., & KNOBLOCK, PETER. Teacher behavior as preventive discipline. *Teaching Exceptional Children*, Summer 1987, *19*, 18–24.

DENCKLA, MARTHA B. Clinical syndromes in learning disabilities: The case for "splitting" vs. "lumping." *Journal of Learning Disabilities*, August/September 1972, 5, 401–406.

DENCKLA, MARTHA B. Learning for language and language for learning. In U. Kirk (Ed.), *Neuropsychology of language, reading and spelling.* New York: Academic Press, 1983, 33–43.

DENCKLA, MARTHA B. Issues of overlap and heterogeneity in dyslexia. In D. B. Gray & J. F. Kavanagh (Eds.), *Biobehavioral measures of dyslexia.* Parkton, MD: York Press, 1985, 41–46.

DENCKLA, MARTHA B.; RUDEL, RITA G.; & BROMAN, MELINDA. Tests that discriminate between dyslexic and other learning-disabled boys. *Brain & Language*, May 1981, *13*, 118–129.

DENK-GLASS, RITA; LABER, SUSAN S.; & BREWER, KATHRYN. *Prevalence of middle ear disease in preschool children*, 1981. Mimeographed.

DENNIS, LYNN; MCKENNA, MICHAEL C.; & MILLER, JOHN W. Project READ:S. Effective design for content area reading. *Journal of Reading*, March 1989, *32*, 520–524.

DENO, STANLEY L. Curriculum-based measurement: The emerging alternative. *Exceptional Children*, November 1985, 52, 219–232.

DENO, STANLEY L. Curriculum-based measurement. *Teaching Exceptional Children*, Fall 1987, *20*, 41–42.

DENO, STANLEY L., & CHIANG, BERTRAM. An experimental analysis of the nature of reversal errors in children with severe learning disabilities. *Learning Disability Quarterly*, Summer 1979, *2*, 40–45.

DENO, STANLEY L.; MIRKIN, PHYLLIS K.; & CHIANG, BERTRAM. Identifying valid measures of reading. *Exceptional Children*, September 1982, *49*, 36–47.

DENO, STANLEY L.; MIRKIN, PHYLLIS K.; & WESSON, CAREN. How to write effective data-based IEPs. *Teaching Exceptional Children*, Winter 1984, *16*, 99–104.

DEPARTMENT OF EDUCATION AND SCIENCE. *A language for life (The Bullock Report).* London: Her Majesty's Stationery Office, 1975.

DEQUIN, HENRY C., & JOHNS, JERRY L. Literacy resources in the U.S. and Canada for visually impaired students. *Journal of Reading*, November 1985, *29*, 148–154.

DE QUIROS, JULIO B. Diagnosis of vestibular disorders in the learning disabled. *Journal of Learning Disabilities*, January 1976, *9*, 50–58.

DE QUIROS, JULIO, & DELLA CELLA, M. La dislexia como sindrome: Estudio estadistico sobre la dislexia infantil en la Ciudad de Rosario—Santa Fe. *Acta Neuropsiquiatrica Argentina*, 1959, 178–193.

DE QUIROS, JULIO B., & SCHRAGER, ORLANDO L. *Neuropsychological fundamentals in learning disabilities.* San Rafael, CA: Academic Therapy Publications, 1978.

DERBY, TOM. Reading instruction and course related materials for vocational school students. *Journal of Reading*, January 1987, *30*, 308–316.

DERRY, SHARON J., & MURPHY, DEBRA A. Designing systems that train learning ability: From theory to practice. *Review of Educational Research*, Spring 1986, 56, 1–39.

DE SANTI, ROGER J. Concurrent and predictive validity of a semantically and syntactically sensitive cloze scoring system. *Reading Research and Instruction*, Winter 1989, *28*, 29–40.

DE SANTI, ROGER J., & ALEXANDER, DOLORES. Locus of control and reading achievement: Increasing the responsibility and performance of remedial readers. *Journal of Clinical Reading*, 1986–87, *2*(1), 12–14.

DE STEFANO, JOHANNA S. Register: A concept to combat negative teachers' attitudes toward black English. In J. S. DeStefano (Ed.), *Language, society and education: A profile of black English*. Worthington, OH: Charles A. Jones, 1973, 189–195.

DEVINE, THOMAS G. *Teaching study skills* (2nd ed.). Boston: Allyn and Bacon, 1987.

DEWITZ, PETER; CARR, EILEEN M.; & PATBERG, JUDYTHE P. Effects of inference training on comprehension and comprehension monitoring. *Reading Research Quarterly*, Winter 1987, *22*, 99–112.

DICKERSON, DOLORES. A study of the use of games to reinforce sight vocabulary. *The Reading Teacher*, October 1982, *36*, 46–49.

DICKINSON, DAVID K. Oral language, literacy skills, and response to literature. In J. R. Squire (Ed.), *The dynamics of language learning: Research in reading and English*. Urbana, IL: ERIC/RCS, 1987, 147–183.

DICKSTEIN, PAUL W., & TALLAL, PAULA. Attentional capabilities of reading-impaired children during dichotic presentation of phonetic and complex nonphonetic sounds. *Cortex*, June 1987, *23*, 237–249.

DIEHL, DIGBY. Readership survey: Good, bad news. *Albany Times Union*, April 20, 1984, B-7.

DIEKHOFF, GEORGE M. An appraisal of adult literacy programs: Reading between the lines. *Journal of Reading*, April 1988, *31*, 624–630.

DIETERICH, THOMAS; FREEMAN, CECILIA; & GRIFFIN, PEG. *Assessing comprehension in a school setting*. Arlington, VA: Center for Applied Linguistics, June 1978.

DIETRICH, DOROTHY M., & MATHEWS, VIRGINIA H. (Eds.). *Development of lifetime reading habits*. Newark, DE: International Reading Association, 1968.

DI LORENZO, LOUIS T., & SALTER, RUTH. Cooperative research in the nongraded primary. *Elementary School Journal*, 1965, *65*, 269–277.

DIRKS, SARAH A., & MOORE, SHARON A. The relationship between the Concepts about Print tests and the Metropolitan Readiness Test. In J. A. Niles & R. V. Lalik (Eds.), *Issues in literacy: A research perspective*. Rochester, NY: National Reading Conference, 1985, 355–361.

DISTAD, LOIS, & PARADIS, EDWARD. The effects of the temporal conjunctions *before* and *after* on reading comprehension by primary grade children. In J. Niles & L. A. Harris (Eds.), *Searches for meaning in reading/language processing and instruction*. Rochester, NY: National Reading Conference, 1983, 95–100.

DI STEFANO, PHILIP P., & HAGERTY, PATRICIA J. Teaching spelling at the elementary level. A realistic perspective. *The Reading Teacher*, January 1985, *38*, 373–377.

DI STEFANO, PHILLIP; NOE, MICHAEL; & VALENCIA, SHEILA. Measurements of the effects of purpose and passage difficulty on reading flexibility. *Journal of Educational Research*, August 1981, *73*, 602–606.

DIXON, ROBERT. Strategies for vocabulary instruction. *Teaching Exceptional Children*, Winter 1987, *19*, 61–63.

DOAKE, DAVID B. Reading-like behavior: Its role in learning to read. In A. Jaggar & M. T. Smith-Burke (Eds.), *Observing the language learner*. Newark, DE: International Reading Association, 1985, 82–98.

DOBO, PAMELA J. Using literature to change attitudes toward the handicapped. *The Reading Teacher*, December 1982, *36*, 290–292.

DOBSON, L. Learning to read by writing: A practical program for reluctant readers. *Teaching Exceptional Children*, Fall 1985, *18*, 30–36.

DOEHRING, DONALD G. *Patterns of impairment in specific reading disability:* A *neuropsychological investigation.* Bloomington, IN: Indiana University Press, 1968.

DOEHRING, DONALD G. Reading disability subtypes: Interaction of reading and nonreading deficits. In B. P. Rourke (Ed.), *Neuropsychology of learning disabilities.* New York: Guilford Press, 1985, 133–146.

DOEHRING, DONALD G.; BACKMAN, JOAN; & WATERS, GLORIA. Theoretical models of reading disabilities, past, present, and future. *Topics in Learning & Learning Disorders,* April 1983, 3, 84–94.

DOEHRING, DONALD G., & HOSHKO, IRENE M. Classification of reading problems by the Q-technique of factor analysis. *Cortex,* 1977, 13, 281–294.

DOEHRING, DONALD G.; HOSHKO, IRENE M.; & BRYANS, B. N. Statistical classification of children with reading problems. *Journal of Clinical Neuropsychology,* 1979, 1(1), 5–16.

DOEHRING, DONALD G., et al. *Reading disabilities: The interaction of reading, language, and neuropsychological deficits.* New York: Academic Press, 1981.

DOLAN, LAWRENCE. A follow-up evaluation of a transition class program for children with school and learning readiness problems. *Exceptional Child,* July 1982, 29, 101–110.

DOLCH, EDWARD W. *A manual for remedial reading.* Champaign, IL: Garrard, 1939.

DOLCH, E. W. How to diagnose children's reading difficulties by informal classroom techniques. *The Reading Teacher,* January 1953, 6, 10–14.

DOLCH, E. W., & BLOOMSTER, M. Phonic readiness. *Elementary School Journal,* 1937, 38, 201–205.

DOLE, JANICE A., & JOHNSON, VIRGINIA P. Beyond the textbook: Science literature for young people. *Journal of Reading,* April 1981, 24, 579–582.

DOLE, JANICE A.; ROGERS, THERESA; & OSBORN, JEAN. Improving the selection of basal reading programs: A report of the textbook adoption guidelines project. *Elementary School Journal,* January 1987, 87, 283–298.

DORE-BOYCE, KATHLEEN; MISNER, MARILYN; & MCGUIRE, LORRAINE D. Comparing reading expectancy formulas. *The Reading Teacher,* October 1975, 29, 8–14.

DORMAN, CASEY. Defining and diagnosing dyslexia: Are we putting the cart before the horse? *Reading Research Quarterly,* Summer, 1985, 20, 505–508.

DOUGAN, MICHAEL. TV may advance interest in reading. *Albany Times Union,* September 22, 1988, A-17.

DOWDY, CAROL A.; CRUMP, W. DONALD; & WELCH, MICHAEL W. Reading flexibility of learning disabled and normal students at three grade levels. *Learning Disability Quarterly,* Summer 1982, 5, 253–263.

DOWHOWER, SARAH L. Effects of repeated reading on second-grade transitional readers' fluency and comprehension. *Reading Research Quarterly,* Fall 1987, 22, 389–406.

DOWHOWER, SARAH L. Repeated reading: Research into practice. *The Reading Teacher,* March 1989, 42, 502–507.

DOWNING, GERTRUDE, et al. *The preparation of teachers for schools in culturally deprived neighborhoods* (The Bridge Project). Cooperative Research Project No. 935. Flushing, NY: Queens College, 1965. Available through University Film Library Services.

DOWNING, JOHN. How society creates reading disability. *The Elementary School Journal,* March 1977, 77, 274–279.

DOWNING, JOHN. Learning to read with understanding. In C. McCullough (Ed.), *Inchworm, inchworm: Persistent problems in reading education.* Newark, DE: International Reading Association, 1980, 163–178.

DOWNING, JOHN. Cognitive clarity: A unifying and cross-cultural theory for language awareness phenomena in reading. In D. B. Yaden & S. Templeton (Eds.), *Metalinguistic awareness and beginning literacy.* Portsmouth, NH: Heinemann, 1986, 13–29.

DOWNING, JOHN, & LEONG, CHE KAN. *Psychology of reading.* New York: Macmillan, 1982.

DOWNING, JOHN; MAY, RICHARD; & OLLILA, LLOYD. Sex differences and cultural expectations in reading. In E. Sheridan (Ed.), *Sex stereotypes and reading: Research and strategies.* Newark, DE: International Reading Association, 1982, 17–34.

DOWNING, JOHN, & THACKRAY, DEREK V. *Reading readiness.* London, England: University of London Press, 1971.

DOYLE, WILLIAM. Classroom organization and management. In M. C. Wittrock (Ed.), *Handbook of research on teaching* (3rd ed.). New York: Macmillan, 1985, 392–431.

DRADER, DARIA. The role of verbal labeling in equivalence tasks as related to reading ability. *Journal of Learning Disabilities,* March 1975, *8,* 53–57.

DREEBEN, ROBERT. Closing the divide: What teachers and administrators can do to help black students reach their reading potential. *American Educator,* Winter 1987, *11,* 28–35.

DREHER, MARIAM H. Spontaneous instantation of general terms. In H. Singer & R. B. Ruddell (Eds.), *Theoretical models and processes of reading* (3rd ed.). Newark, DE: International Reading Association, 1985, 426–433.

DREHER, MARIAM H.; SINGER, HARRY; & LETTEER, CATHERINE A. Explicitedness in sixth-grade social studies textbooks. In J. E. Readence et al. (Eds.), *Research in literacy: Merging perspectives.* Rochester, NY: National Reading Conference, 1987, 177–185.

DREYER, LOIS G. Readability and responsibility. *Journal of Reading,* January 1984, *28,* 334–338.

DREYER, LOIS G.; FUTTERSAK, KAREN R.; & BOEHM, ANN E. Sight words for the computer age: An essential word list. *The Reading Teacher,* October 1985, *39,* 12–15.

DREYER, SHARON S. *The bookfinder: A guide to children's literature about the needs and problems of youth.* Circle Pines, MN: American Guidance Service, 1977.

DRP SERVICES. *Readability report supplement for the seventh edition.* New York: The College Board, 1986. NOTE: The DRP is now published by TASA.

DRUM, PRISCILLA A., & KONOPAK, BONNIE C. Learning word meanings from written context. In M. G. McKeown & M. E. Curtis (Eds.), *The nature of vocabulary acquisition.* Hillsdale, NJ: Erlbaum, 1987, 73–87.

DUDLEY-MARLING, CURTIS; KAUFMAN, NANCY J.; & TARVER, SARA G. WISC and WISC-R profiles of learning disabled children: A review. *Learning Disability Quarterly,* Summer 1981, *4,* 307–319.

DUFFELMEYER, FREDERICK A. A comparison of two noncomputational readability techniques. *The Reading Teacher,* October 1982, *36,* 4–7.(a)

DUFFELMEYER, FREDERICK A. Introducing words in context. *Wisconsin State Reading Association Journal,* Spring 1982, *26,* 4–6.(b)

DUFFELMEYER, FREDERICK A. Main ideas in paragraphs. *The Reading Teacher,* January 1985, *38,* 484–486.

DUFFELMEYER, FREDERICK A., & ADAMSON, SHELIA. Matching students with instructional level materials using the Degrees of Reading Power system. *Reading Research and Instruction,* Spring 1986, *25,* 192–200.

DUFFELMEYER, FREDERICK; BAUM, DALE D.; & MERKLEY, DONNA J. Maximizing reader-text confrontation with an Extended Anticipation Guide. *Journal of Reading,* November 1987, *31,* 146–150.

DUFFELMEYER, FREDERICK A., & DUFFELMEYER, BARBARA B. Are IRI passages suitable for assessing main idea comprehension? *The Reading Teacher,* February 1989, *42,* 358–363.

DUFFY, GERALD G. Maintaining a balance in objective-based reading instruction. *The Reading Teacher,* February 1978, *31,* 519–523.

DUFFY, GERALD G. Fighting off the alligators: What research in real classrooms has to say about reading instruction. *Journal of Reading Behavior*, 1982, *14*(4), 357–373.

DUFFY, FRANK M., et al. Dyslexia: Automated diagnosis by computerized classification of brain electrical activity. *Annals of Neurology*, May 1980, 7, 421–428. (a).

DUFFY, FRANK M., et al. Regional differences in brain electrical activity by typographic mapping. *Annals of Neurology*, May 1980, 7, 412–419. (b).

DUFFY, GERALD G. Models of reading have direct implications for reading instruction: The negative position. In J. A. Niles & R. V. Lalik (Eds.), *Issues in literacy: A research perspective.* Rochester, NY: National Reading Conference, 1985, 398–401.

DUFFY, GERALD G. The relationship between explicit verbal explanation during reading skill instruction and student awareness and achievement: A study of reading teacher effects. *Reading Research Quarterly*, Summer 1986, *21*, 237–252.

DUFFY, GERALD G., & BALL, DEBORAH L. Instructional decision making and teacher effectiveness. In J. V. Hoffman (Ed.), *Effective teaching of reading: Research and practice.* Newark, DE: International Reading Association, 1986, 163–180.

DUFFY, GERALD G., & ROEHLER, LAURA R. Teaching reading skills as strategies. *The Reading Teacher*, January 1987, *40*, 414–418.(a)

DUFFY, GERALD G., & ROEHLER, LAURA R. Improving reading instruction through the use of responsive elaboration. *The Reading Teacher*, February 1987, *40*, 514–520.(b)

DUFFY, GERALD G.; ROEHLER, LAURA R.; & HERMANN, BETH ANN. Modeling mental processes helps poor readers become strategic readers. *The Reading Teacher*, April 1988, *41*, 762–767.

DUFFY, GERALD G., et al. Developing and evaluating measures associated with strategic reading. *Journal of Reading Behavior*, 1987, *19*(3), 223–246.(a)

DUFFY, GERALD G., et al. Effects of explaining the reasoning associated with using reading strategies. *Reading Research Quarterly*, Summer 1987, *22*, 347–368.(b)

DUKER, SAM. *Individualized reading: An annotated bibliography.* Metuchen, NJ: Scarecrow Press, 1968.

DULCAN, MINA K. Comprehensive treatment of children and adolescents with Attention Deficit Disorders: The state of the art. *Clinical Psychology Review*, 1986, 6(6), 539–569.

DULIN, KEN L. Assessing reading interests of elementary and middle school students. In D. Monson & D. McClenathan (Eds.), *Developing active readers: Ideas for parents, teachers, and librarians.* Newark, DE: International Reading Association, 1979, 2–15. Also in A. J. Harris & E. Sipay (Eds.), *Readings on reading instruction* (3rd ed.). New York: Longman, 1984, 344–357.

DUNDON, WILLIAM D., et al. The Bannatyne Recategorization Assessment Procedure: Is it valid for individual diagnosis of LD children? *Learning Disability Quarterly*, Summer 1986, 9, 208–213.

DUNIVANT, NOEL. *The relationship between learning disabilities and juvenile delinquency.* Williamsburg, VA: National Center for State Courts, 1982.

DUNKELD, COHN G. M. *The validity of the informal reading inventory for the designation of instructional levels: A study of the relationships between children's gains in reading achievement and the difficulty of instructional materials.* Unpublished doctoral dissertation, University of Illinois, 1970.

DUNLAP, WILLIAM P., & MCKNIGHT, MARTHA B. Vocabulary translations for conceptualizing math word problems. *The Reading Teacher*, November 1978, *32*, 183–189.

DUNN, RITA. Teaching students through their perceptual strengths or preferences. *Journal of Reading*, January 1988, *31*, 304–309.

DUPUIS, MARY M., & SNYDER, SANDRA L. Develop concepts through vocabulary: A strategy for reading specialists to use with content teachers. *Journal of Reading*, January 1983, *26*, 297–305.

DURKIN, DOLORES. *Children who read early.* New York: Teacher College Press, 1966.

DURKIN, DOLORES. A six year study of children who learned to read in school at age of four. *Reading Research Quarterly*, 1974–1975, *10*(1), 9–61.

DURKIN, DOLORES. What classroom observations reveal about reading comprehension instruction. *Reading Research Quarterly*, 1978–1979, *14*(4), 481–533.

DURKIN, DOLORES. What is the value of the new interest in reading comprehension? *Language Arts*, January 1981, 58, 23–43. Also in A. J. Harris & E. Sipay (Eds.), *Readings on reading instruction* (3rd ed.). New York: Longman, 1984, 249–266.

DURKIN, DOLORES. *A study of poor black children who are successful readers*. Reading Education Report No. 33. Champaign, IL: Center for the Study of Reading, University of Illinois, April 1982.

DURKIN, DOLORES. Is there a match between what elementary teachers do and what basal reader manuals recommend? *The Reading Teacher*, April 1984, 37, 734–744.(a)

DURKIN, DOLORES. *The decoding ability of elementary school students*. Reading Education Report No. 49. Champaign, IL: Center for the Study of Reading, University of Illinois, May 1984.(b)

DURKIN, DOLORES. Reading methodology textbooks: Are they helping teachers teach comprehension? *The Reading Teacher*, January 1986, 39, 410–417.

DURKIN, DOLORES. A classroom-observation study of reading instruction in kindergarten. *Early Childhood Research Quarterly*, September 1987, 2, 275–300.(a)

DURKIN, DOLORES. Influences of basal reader programs. *The Elementary School Journal*, January 1987, 87, 331–341.(b)

DURKIN, DOLORES. Testing in the kindergarten. *The Reading Teacher*, April 1987, 40, 776–780.(c)

DURRELL, DONALD D. *Improvement of basic reading abilities*. New York: World Book, 1940.

DURRELL, DONALD D. *Improving reading instruction*. New York: Harcourt, Brace and World, 1956.

DURRELL, DONALD D. (Ed.). Adapting instruction to the learning needs of children in the intermediate grades. *Journal of Education*, December 1959, *42*, 1–78.

DURRELL, DONALD D. Letter-name value in reading and spelling. *Reading Research Quarterly*, 1980, *16*(1), 159–163.

DURRELL, DONALD D. Letter names controversy. *The Reading Teacher*, May 1984, 37, 880.

DURRELL, DONALD D., & HAYES, MARY T. *Durrell Listening-Reading Series: Manual for listening and reading tests, primary level, Form OE*. New York: Psychological Corp., 1969.

DURRELL, DONALD D., & MURPHY, HELEN A. The auditory discrimination factor in reading readiness and reading disability. *Education*, 1953, 73, 556–560.

DURRELL, DONALD D., & MURPHY, HELEN A. A prereading phonics inventory. *The Reading Teacher*, January 1978, 31, 385–390.

DUTT, ANITA (Comp.). *Fifty creative ways to use paperbacks in the primary grades*. New York: Scholastic Book Services, 1980.

DUVAL, EILEEN V.; JOHNSON, ROGER E.; & LITCHER, JOHN. Learning stations and the reading class. In R. A. Earle (Ed.), *Classroom practice in reading*. Newark, DE: International Reading Association, 1977, 109–118.

DYKSTRA, ROBERT. Auditory discrimination abilities and beginning reading achievement. *Reading Research Quarterly*, Spring 1966, *1*, 5–34.

DYKSTRA, ROBERT. Summary of the second-grade phase of the cooperative research program in primary reading instruction. *Reading Research Quarterly*, Fall 1968, *4*, 49–70.(a)

DYKSTRA, ROBERT. The effectiveness of code- and meaning-emphasis beginning reading programs. *The Reading Teacher*, October 1968, *22*, 17–23.(b)

DYKSTRA, ROBERT. Phonics and beginning reading instruction. In C.C. Walcutt, et al.

Teaching reading: A phonic/linguistic approach to developmental reading. New York: Macmillan, 1974, 373–397.

EAMES, THOMAS H. The effect of correction of refractive errors on the distant and near vision of school children. *Journal of Educational Research*, 1942, *36*, 272–279.

EAMES, THOMAS H. Some neurological and glandular bases of learning. *Journal of Education*, April 1960, *142*, 1–35.

EARLY, MARGARET. Reading in the secondary school. In J. E. Squire (Ed.), *The teaching of English.* 76th Yearbook of the National Society for the Study of Education, Part I. Chicago: University of Chicago Press, 1977, 189–196.

EARP, N. W. Procedures for teaching reading in mathematics. *Arithmetic Teacher*, 1970, *17*, 575–579.

EBERWEIN, LOWELL. What do book choices indicate? *Journal of Reading*, December 1973, *17*, 186–191.

ED 053 881 *Model Programs: Reading. Bloom Township high school reading program,* Chicago Heights, IL, 1971.

ED 053 882 *Model Programs: Reading. Summer junior high schools,* New York, NY, 1971.

ED 053 883 *Model Programs: Reading. Programmed tutorial reading project,* Indianapolis, IN, 1971.

ED 053 884 *Model Programs: Reading. Summer remedial and enrichment program,* Thomasville, GA, 1971.

ED 053 885 *Model Programs: Reading. Elementary reading centers,* Milwaukee, WI, 1971.

ED 053 886 *Model Programs: Reading. Intensive reading instructional teams,* Hartford, CT, 1971.

ED 053 887 *Model Programs: Reading. Yuba County reading-learning center,* Marysville, CA, 1971.

ED 053 888 *Model Programs: Reading. The Topeka reading clinic, centers and services,* Topeka, KS, 1971.

ED 053 889 *Model Programs: Reading. School-within-a-school,* Keokuk, IA, 1971.

ED 053 890 *Model Programs: Reading. Remedial reading program,* Pojoaque, NM, 1971.

EDELSTEIN, RUTH R. Use of group processes in teaching retarded readers. *The Reading Teacher*, January 1970, *23*, 318–334.

EDFELDT, AKE W. *Silent speech and silent reading.* Chicago: University of Chicago Press, 1960.

EDUCATIONAL PRESS ASSOCATION OF AMERICA. *Children's magazine list 1987.* Glassboro, NJ: Glassboro State College, 1987.

EDWARDS, PETER. The effect of idioms on children's reading and understanding of prose. In B. S. Schulwitz (Ed.), *Teachers, tangibles, techniques: Comprehension of content in reading.* Newark, DE: International Reading Association, 1975, 37–46.

EEDS, MARYANN. What to do when they don't understand what they read—Research-based strategies for teaching reading comprehension. *The Reading Teacher*, February 1981, *34*, 565–571.

EEDS, MARYANN. Bookwords: Using a beginning word list of high frequency words from children's literature K-3. *The Reading Teacher*, January 1985, *38*, 418–423.

EEDS, MARYANN. Holistic assessment of coding ability. In S. M. Glazer et al. (Eds.), *Reexamining reading diagnosis: New trends and procedures.* Newark, DE: International Reading Association, 1988, 48–66.

EHRI, LINNEA C. Linguistic insight: Threshold of reading acquisition. In G. Waller & A. MacKinnon (Eds.), *Reading Research: Advances in theory and practice*, Vol. 1. New York: Academic Press, 1979, 63–114.

EHRI, LINNEA. The role of orthographic images in learning printed words. In J. Kavanagh & R. Venezky (Eds.), *Orthography, reading, and dyslexia.* Baltimore, MD: University Park Press, 1980, 155–170.

EHRI, LINNEA C. A critique of five studies related to letter-name knowledge and learning to read. In L. Gentile, M. Kamil, & J. Blanchard (Eds.), *Reading research revisited.* Columbus, OH: Charles E. Merrill, 1983, 143–153.

EHRI, LINNEA C., How orthography alters spoken language competencies in learning to read and spell. In J. Downing & R. Valtin (Eds.), *Language awareness and learning to read.* New York: Springer-Verlag, 1984, 119–147.

EHRI, LINNEA C. Learning to read and spell words. *Journal of Reading Behavior,* 1987, *19*(1), 5–31.

EHRI, LINNEA C. The development of spelling knowledge and its role in reading acquisition and reading disability. *Journal of Learning Disabilities,* June/July 1989, *22*, 356–365.

EHRI, LINNEA C., & WILCE, LEE S. Do beginners learn to read function words better in sentences or in lists? *Reading Research Quarterly,* 1980, *15*(4), 451–476.

EHRI, LINNEA C., & WILCE, LEE S. Recognition of spellings printed in lower and mixed case: Evidence for orthographic images. *Journal of Reading Behavior,* 1982, *14*(3), 219–230.

EHRI, LINNEA C., & WILCE, LEE S. Movement into reading: Is the first stage of printed word learning visual or phonetic. *Reading Research Quarterly,* Winter 1985, *20*, 163–179.

EHRI, LINNEA C., & WILCE, LEE S. The influence of spellings on speech: Are alveolar flaps /d/ or /t/? In D. B. Yaden & S. Templeton (Eds.), *Metalinguistic awareness and learning to read.* Portsmouth, NH: Heinemann, 1986, 101–114.

EHRI, LINNEA C., & WILCE, LEE C. Does learning to spell help beginners learn to read words. *Reading Research Quarterly,* Winter 1987, *22*, 47–65.

EHRLICH, SUSAN F. Children's word recognition in prose context. *Visible Language,* 1981, *15*(3), 219–244.

EKWALL, ELDON E. *Locating and correcting reading difficulties.* (5th ed.) Columbus, OH: Charles E. Merrill, 1988.

ELKONIN, D. B. USSR. In J. Downing (Ed.), *Comparative reading.* New York: Macmillan, 1973, 551–579.

ELIASON, MICHELE J., & RICHMAN, LYNN C. The Continuous Performance Test in learning disabled and nondisabled children. *Journal of Learning Disabilities,* December 1987, *20*, 614–619.

ELLER, REBECCA G.; PAPPAS, CHRISTINE C.; & BROWN, ELGA. The lexical development of kindergartners: Learning from written context. *Journal of Reading Behavior,* 1988, *20*(1), 5–24.

ELLEY, WARWICK B. Vocabulary acquisition from listening to stories. *Reading Research Quarterly,* Spring, 1989, *24*, 174–187.

ELLIOTT, PEGGY G., & STEINKELLNER, LESLEY L. Reading preferences of urban and suburban secondary school students: Topics and media. *Journal of Reading,* November 1979, *23*, 121–125.

ELLIOTT, STEPHEN N., & PIERSAL, WAYNE C. Direct assessment of reading skills: An approach which links assessment to intervention. *School Psychology Review,* 1982, *11*(3), 267–280.

ELLIS, EDWIN S. The role of motivation and pedagogy on the generalization of cognitive strategy training. *Journal of Learning Disabilities,* February 1986, *19*, 66–70.

ELLIS, EDWIN S.; DESHLER, DONALD D.; & SCHUMAKER, JEAN B. Teaching adolescents with learning disabilities to generate and use task-specific strategies. *Journal of Learning Disabilities,* February 1989, *22*, 108–119, 130.

ELLIS, NICK. Visual and name coding in dyslexic children. *Psychological Research,* 1981, *43*, 201–218.

ELLSON, DOUGLAS G. Tutoring. In N. L. Gage (Ed.), *The psychology of teaching methods.* 75th Yearbook of the National Society for the Study of Education, Part I. Chicago: University of Chicago Press, 1976, 130–165.

ELLSON, DOUGLAS G.; HARRIS, PHILIP; & BARBER, LARRY. A field test of programmed and directed tutoring. *Reading Research Quarterly*, Spring 1968, *3*, 306–368.

ELSTER, CHARLES, & SIMONS, HERBERT D. How important are illustrations in children's readers? *The Reading Teacher*, November 1985, *39*, 148–152.

ELTERMAN, R. D., et al. Eye movements in dyslexic children. *Journal of Learning Disabilities*, January 1980, *13*, 11–16.

EMANS, ROBERT, & PATYK, GLORIA. Why do high school students read? *Journal of Reading*, February 1967, *10*, 300–304.

EMMER, EDMUND T.; EVERTSON, CAROLYN M.; & ANDERSON, LINDA M. Effective classroom management at the beginning of the school year. *Elementary School Journal*, May 1980, *80*, 219–231.

ENTIN, EILEEN B., & KLARE, GEORGE R. Some inter-relationships of readability, cloze and multiple-choice scores on a reading comprehension test. *Journal of Reading Behavior*, Winter 1978, *10*, 417–436.

ENTWISLE, DORIS R., et al. The sampling process in first grade: Two samples a decade apart. *American Educational Research Journal*, Winter 1986, *23*, 587–613.

ENTWISLE, DORIS R., et al. Kindergarten experience: Cognitive effects or socialization? *American Educational Research Journal*, Fall 1987, *24*, 337–364.

ERICKSON, LAWRENCE, & STEPHENSON, JUNE. A three-step method for teaching main idea. *The Reading Teacher*, February 1985, *38*, 592–594.

ERICKSON, MARILYN. The Z-score discrepancy method for identifying reading disabled children. *Journal of Learning Disabilities*, May 1975, 8, 308–312.

ERICSON, BONNIE, et al. Increasing critical reading in junior high classrooms. *Journal of Reading*, February 1987, *30*, 930–939.

ERIKSON, ERIK H. *Childhood and society*. New York: Norton, 1950.

ERNHART, CLARE B.; LANDA, BETH; & WOLF, ABRAHAM W. Subclinical lead level and developmental deficit: Re-analysis of data. *Journal of Learning Disabilities*, October 1985, *18*, 475–479.

ESTES, THOMAS H. *Estes Attitude Scales*. Austin, TX: Pro-Ed, 1981.

ESTES, THOMAS H., & RICHARDS, HERBERT C. Habits of study and test performance. *Journal of Reading Behavior*, 1985, *17*(1), 1–13.

EVANS, MARY ANN, & CARR, THOMAS H. Cognitive abilities, conditions of learning, and the early development of reading skill. *Reading Research Quarterly*, Spring 1985, *20*, 327–350.

EVELAND, LARRY W. *Attitudes of elementary school principals and teachers toward individually prescribed instruction*. Unpublished doctoral dissertation, University of Illinois, 1975.

EVERTSON, CAROLYN M.; STANFORD, JULIE P.; & EMMER, EDMUND T. Effects of class heterogeneity in junior high school. *American Educational Research Journal*, Summer 1981, *18*, 219–232.

FADER, DANIEL N. *The new hooked on books*. New York: Berkley, 1977.

FARNAM-DIGGORY, SYLVIA. Commentary: Time now for a little serious complexity. In S. P. Cecci (Ed.), *Handbook of cognitive, social, and neuropsychological aspects of learning disabilities*, Vol. 1. Hillsdale, NJ: Erlbaum, 1986, 123–160.

FARR, ROGER, & CAREY, ROBERT F. *Reading: What can be measured* (2nd ed.). Newark, DE: International Reading Association, 1986.

FARR, ROGER; TULLY, MICHAEL A.; & POWELL, DEBORAH. The evaluation and selection of basal readers. *Elementary School Journal*, January 1987, 87, 267–281.

FARR, ROGER, & WOLF, ROBERT L. Evaluation and secondary reading programs. In A. Purves & O. Niles (Eds.), *Becoming readers in a complex society*. 83rd Yearbook of the National Society for the Study of Education, Part I. Chicago: University of Chicago Press, 1984, 271–292.

FAY, LEO. The status of reading achievement: Is there a halo around the past? In C. McCullough (Ed.), *Inchworm, inchworm: Persistent problems in reading educa-*

tion. Newark, DE: International Reading Association, 1980, 13–21. Also in A. J. Harris & E. Sipay (Eds.), *Readings on reading instruction* (3rd ed.). New York: Longman, 1984, 20–25.

FAYNE, HARRIET R. A comparison of learning disabled adolescents with normal learners on an anaphoric pronominal reference task. *Journal of Learning Disabilities*, December 1981, *14*, 597–599.

FEAGANS, LYNNE, & SHORT, ELIZABETH J. Developmental differences in the comprehension and production of narratives by reading disabled and normally achieving children. *Child Development*, October 1984, 55, 1727–1736.

FEDERAL REGISTER, December 29, 1977, *42*, No. 250.

FEELEY, JOAN T. Interest patterns and media preferences of middle-grade children. *Reading World*, March 1974, *13*, 224–237.

FEELEY, JOAN T. Content interests and media preferences of middle-graders: Differences in a decade. *Reading World*, October 1982, *22*, 11–16.

FEELEY, JOAN T. Help for the reading teacher: Dealing with the Limited English Proficient (LEP) child in the elementary classroom. *The Reading Teacher*, March 1983, *36*, 650–655.

FEINGOLD, BENJAMIN F. Hyperkinesis and learning disabilities linked to the ingestion of artificial food colors and flavors. *Journal of Learning Disabilities*, November 1976, *9*, 551–559.

FEINGOLD, BENJAMIN F. A critique of "Controversial medical treatments of learning disabilities." *Academic Therapy*, November 1977, *13*, 173–183.

FEITELSON, DINA. Sequences and structure in a system with consistent sound-symbol correspondences. In J. E. Merritt (Ed.), *New horizons in reading.* Newark, DE: International Reading Association, 1976, 269–277.

FERNALD, GRACE M. *Remedial techniques in basic school subjects.* New York: McGraw-Hill, 1943.

FERNALD, GRACE M., & KELLER, HELEN. The effect of kinesthetic factors in development of word recognition in the case of nonreaders. *Journal of Educational Research*, 1921, *4*, 357–377.

FERRARO, THOMAS. Fighting illiteracy, the nation's hidden problem. *Albany Times Union*, September 14, 1986. C.2,3.

FESHBACH, SEYMOUR; ADELMAN, HOWARD; & FULLER, WILLIAM W. Early identification of children with high risk of reading failure. *Journal of Learning Disabilities*, December 1974, *7*, 639–644.

FIELDING, LINDA G.; WILSON, PAUL T.; & ANDERSON, RICHARD C. A new focus on free reading: The role of trade books in reading instruction. In T. E. Raphael (Ed.), *The contents of school based literacy.* New York: Random House, 1986, 149–160.

FILLION, BRYANT, & BRAUSE, RITA S. Research into classroom practices: What have we learned and where are we going. In J. R. Squire (Ed.), *The dynamics of language learning: Research in reading and English.* Bloomington, IN: ERIC/RCS, 1987, 201–225.

FILLMER, H. THOMPSON, & MEADOWS, RITA. The portrayal of older characters in five sets of basal readers. *Elementary School Journal*, May 1986, *86*, 651–662.

FILP, JOHANNA. Relationship among reading subskills: A hierarchical hypothesis. *Journal of Reading Behavior*, Fall 1975, *7*, 229–239.

FINCHER, JACK. New machines may soon replace the doctor's black bag. *Smithsonian*, January 1984, *14*, 64–71.

FINUCCI, JOAN M. Approaches to subtype validation using family data. In D. B. Gray & J. F. Kavanagh (Eds.), *Biobehavioral measures of dyslexia.* Parkton, MD: York Press, 1985, 137–153.

FINUCCI, JOAN M. Follow-up studies of developmental dyslexia and other learning disabilities. In S. D. Smith (Ed.), *Genetics and learning disabilities.* San Diego: College-Hill Press, 1986, 97–121.

FINUCCI, JOAN M.; GOTTFREDSON, LINDA S.; & CHILDS, BARTON. A follow-up study of dyslexic boys. In R. L. Cecci et al. (Eds.), *Annals of dyslexia*. Baltimore, MD: Orton Dyslexia Society, Vol. 25, 1985, 117–136.

FINUCCI, JOAN M., et al. Empirical validation of reading and spelling quotients. *Developmental Medicine & Child Neurology*, December 1982, *24*, 733–744.

FINUCCI, JOAN M., et al. Classification of spelling errors and their relationship to reading ability, sex, grade placement, and intelligence. *Brain and Language*, November 1983, *20*, 340–355.

FIRESTONE, PHILIP, et al. The effects of caffeine on hyperactive children. *Journal of Learning Disabilities*, March 1978, *10*, 133–141.

FISHBEIN, DIANA, & MEDUSKI, JERZY. Nutritional biochemistry and behavioral disabilities. *Journal of Learning Disabilities*, October 1987, *10*, 505–512.

FISHER, CAROL J. 55 ways to respond to a book. *Instructor*, April 1979, 88, 94–96.

FISHER, CAROL J., & NATARELLA, MARGARET A. Young children's preferences in poetry: A national survey of first, second, and third graders. *Research in the Teaching of English*, December 1982, *16*, 339–354.

FISHER, SHARON. *Conceptual tempo and oral reading performance*. Unpublished doctoral dissertation, State University of New York at Albany, 1977.

FISK, JOHN L., & ROURKE, BYRON P. Identification of subtypes of learning-disabled children at three age levels: A neuropsychological multivariate approach. *Journal of Clinical Neuropsychology*, 1979, *1*(4), 289–310.

FITE, JUNE H., & SCHWARTZ, LOUISE A. Screening culturally disadvantaged first-grade children for potential reading difficulties due to constitutional factors (Abstract). *American Journal of Orthopsychiatry*, 1965, 35, 359–360.

FITZGERALD, GISELA G. Reliability of the Fry sampling procedure. *Reading Research Quarterly*, 1980, *15*(4), 489–503.

FITZGERALD, JILL. Research on stories: Implications for teachers. In K. D. Muth (Ed.), *Children's comprehension of text*. Newark, DE: International Reading Association, 1989, 2–36.

FLANAGAN, JOHN C. Changes in school levels of achievement: Project TALENT ten and fifteen year retests. *Educational Researcher*, September 1976, 5, 9–12.

FLEISHER, BARBARA M. Oral reading cue strategies of better and poorer readers. *Reading Research and Instruction*, Spring 1988, *27*, 35–50.

FLESCH, RUDOLPH. *Why Johnny still can't read. A new look at the scandal in our schools*. New York: Harper & Row, 1981.

FLETCHER, JACK M. Linguistic factors in reading acquisition. Evidence for developmental changes. In F. Pirozzolo & M. Wittrock (Eds.), *Neuropsychological and cognitive processes in reading*. New York: Academic Press, 1981, 261–294.

FLETCHER, JACK M. Memory for verbal and nonverbal stimuli in learning disability subgroups. *Journal of Experimental Child Psychology*, October 1985, *40*, 244–249.

FLETCHER, JACK M., & SATZ, PAUL. Developmental changes in the neuropsychological correlates of reading achievement: A six-year longitudinal follow-up. *Journal of Clinical Neuropsychology*, 1980, *2*(1), 23–37.

FLETCHER, JACK M.; SATZ, PAUL; & SCHOLES, ROBERT J. Developmental changes in the linguistic performance correlates of reading achievement. *Brain & Language*, May 1981, *13*, 78–90.

FLETCHER, JACK M., et al. Finger recognition skills and reading achievement: A developmental neuropsychological analysis. *Developmental Psychology*, January 1982, *18*, 124–132.

FLETCHER, JACK M., et al. Comparison of cutoff and regression-based definitions of reading disabilities. *Journal of Learning Disabilities*, June/July 1989, *22*, 334–338, 355.

FLOOD, JAMES. The text, the student, and the teacher: Learning from exposition in middle schools. *The Reading Teacher*, April 1986, 39, 784–791.

FLOOD, JAMES, & LAPP, DIANE. Types of texts: The match between what students read in basals and what they encounter in tests. *Reading Research Quarterly*, Summer 1986, *21*, 284–297.

FLOOD, JAMES, & LAPP, DIANE. Reading and writing relations: Assumptions and directions. In J. R. Squire (Ed.), *The dynamics of language learning: Research in reading and English*. Bloomington, IN: ERIC/RCS, 1987, 9–26.

FLOOD, JAMES, & LAPP, DIANE. Conceptual mapping strategies for understanding information texts. *The Reading Teacher*, April 1988, *41*, 780–783.(a)

FLOOD, JAMES, & LAPP, DIANE. A reader response approach to the teaching of literature. *Reading Research and Instruction*, Summer 1988, *27*, 61–66.(b)

FLOOD, JAMES, & LAPP, DIANE. Reporting reading progress: A comparison portfolio for parents. *The Reading Teacher*, March 1989, *42*, 508–514.

FLOOD, JAMES; LAPP, DIANE; & FARNAN, NANCY. A reading-writing procedure that teaches expository paragraph structure. *The Reading Teacher*, February 1986, *29*, 556–562.

FORD, MICHAEL P., & OHLHAUSEN, MARILYN M. Classroom reading incentive programs: Removing the obstacles and hurdles for disabled readers. *The Reading Teacher*, April 1988, *41*, 796–798.

FORELL, ELIZABETH R., & HOOD, JOYCE. A longitudinal study of two groups of children with early reading problems. *Annals of dyslexia*, Vol. 25. Baltimore, MD: Orton Dyslexia Society, 1985, 97–116.

FORESTER, LEONA M. Idiomagic! *Elementary English*, January 1974, *51*, 125–127.

FORGAN, HARRY W., & MANGRUM, CHARLES T. *Teaching content area reading skills* (2nd ed.). Columbus, OH: Charles E. Merrill, 1981.

FORNESS, STEVEN R., & KAVALE, KENNETH A. Psychopharmacologic treatment: A note on classroom effects. *Journal of Learning Disabilities*, March 1988, *21*, 144–147.

FOSS, DONALD J. Experimental psycholinguistics. In M. R. Rosenzweig & L. W. Porter (Eds.), *Annual Review of Psychology*, Vol. 39. Palo Alto, CA: Annual Reviews Inc., 1988, 301–348.

FOTHERINGHAM, JOHN B., & CREAL, DOROTHY. Family socioeconomic and educational-emotional characteristics as predictors of school achievement. *Journal of Educational Research*, July/August 1980, *73*, 311–314.

FOX, BARBARA, & ROUTH, DONALD K. Reading disability, phonemic analysis, and dysphonetic spelling: A followup study. *Journal of Clinical Child Psychology*, Spring 1983, *12*, 28–32.

FRAGER, ALAN M. How good are content teachers' judgments of the reading abilities of secondary school students? *Journal of Reading*, February 1984, *27*, 402–406.

FRAGER, ALAN M., & THOMPSON, LOREN C. Conflict: The key to critical reading instruction. *Journal of Reading*, May 1985, *28*, 676–683.

FRANK, JAN, & LEVINSON, HAROLD N. Dysmetric dyslexia and dyspraxia—Synopsis of a continuing research project. *Academic Therapy*, Winter 1975–1976, *11*, 133–143.

FRANK, JAN, & LEVINSON, HAROLD N. Compensatory mechanisms in cerebellar-vestibular dysfunction, dysmetric dyslexia, and dyspraxia. *Academic Therapy*, Fall 1976, *12*, 5–28.

FRANK, JAN, & LEVINSON, HAROLD N. Anti-motion sickness medications in dysmetric dyslexia and dyspraxia. *Academic Therapy*, Summer 1977, *12*, 411–424.

FRASE, LAWRENCE T. Technology, reading, and writing. In J. R. Squire (Ed.), *The dynamics of language learning: Research in reading and English*. Bloomington, IN: ERIC/RCS, 1987, 294–308.

FRASHER, RAMONA S. A feminist look at literature for children: Ten years later. In E. Sheridan (Ed.), *Sex stereotypes and reading: Research and strategies*. Newark, DE: International Reading Association, 1982, 64–79.

FREASIER, AILEEN W. Teacher self-help IEP rating scale. *Academic Therapy*, March 1983, *18*, 487–493.

FREDERICKS, ANTHONY D., & TAYLOR, DAVID. *Parent programs in reading: Guidelines for success.* Newark, DE: International Reading Association, 1985.

FREDERICKSEN, JOHN R. *A componential theory of reading skills and their interaction.* Technical Report No. 227. Champaign, IL: Center for the Study of Reading, University of Illinois, January 1982.(a)

FREDERICKSEN, JOHN R. *Sources of process interactions in reading.* Technical Report No. 242. Champaign, IL: Center for the Study of Reading, University of Illinois, May 1982.(b)

FREDERICKSEN, JOHN R.; WARREN, BETH M.; & ROSEBERG, ANN S. A componential approach to training reading skills: Part 1. Perceptual units training. *Cognition and Instruction*, 1985, *2*(2), 91–130.

FREEBODY, PETER, & ANDERSON, RICHARD C. Effects of text comprehension of different proportions and locations of difficult vocabulary. *Journal of Reading Behavior*, 1983, *15*(3), 19–39.

FREEMAN, YVONNE S. Do Spanish methods and materials reflect current understanding of the reading process? *The Reading Teacher*, March 1988, *41*, 654–662.

FRIED, ITZHAK, et al. Developmental dyslexia: Electrophysiological evidence of clinical subgroups. *Brain and Language*, January 1981, *12*, 14–22.

FRIEDMAN, GLENN, & REYNOLDS, ELIZABETH G. Enriching basal reader lessons with semantic webbing. *The Reading Teacher*, March 1980, *33*, 677–684.

FRIEDMAN, DIANNE E., & MEDWAY, FREDERIC J. Effects of varying performance sets and outcome on the expectations, attributions, and persistence of boys with learning disabilities. *Journal of Learning Disabilities*, May 1987, *20*, 312–316.

FRIEND, MARILYN, & McNUTT, GAYE. A comparative study of resource teacher job descriptions and administrator's perceptions of resource teacher responsibilities. *Journal of Learning Disabilities*, April 1987, *20*, 224–228.

FRITH, UTA. Unexpected spelling problems. In U. Frith (Ed.), *Cognitive processes in spelling.* New York: Academic Press, 1980, 495–515.

FRITH, UTA. A developmental framework for developmental dyslexia. *Annals of Dyslexia*, Vol. 36. Baltimore, MD: Orton Dyslexia Society, 1986, 69–81.

FRITH, UTA, & FRITH, CHRISTOPHER. Relationships between reading and spelling. In J. Kavanagh & R. Venezky (Eds.), *Orthography, reading and dyslexia.* Baltimore: University Park Press, 1980, 287–295.

FROESE, VICTOR. Cloze readability versus the Dale-Chall formula. In B. S. Schulwitz (Ed.), *Teachers, tangibles, techniques: Comprehension of content in reading.* Newark, DE: International Reading Association, 1975, 23–31.

FROESE, VICTOR. Judging global readability. *The Alberta Journal of Educational Research*, June 1981, *27*, 133–137.

FROST, BARRY P. The role of intelligence "C" in the selection of children for remedial reading. *The Alberta Journal of Educational Research*, 1963, *9*, 73–78.

FROSTIG, MARIANNE. Corrective reading in the classroom. *The Reading Teacher*, April 1965, *18*, 573–580.

FROSTIG, MARIANNE. Visual perception, integrative functions and academic learning. *Journal of Learning Disabilities*, January 1972, *5*, 1–15.

FRY, EDWARD. A readability formula that saves time. *Journal of Reading*, April 1968, *11*, 513–516.

FRY, EDWARD. Fry's readability graph: Clarifications, validity, and extension to level 17. *Journal of Reading*, December 1977, *21*, 242–252.

FRY, EDWARD. Comments on the preceding Harris and Jacobson comparison of the Fry, Spache, and Harris-Jacobson readability formulas. *The Reading Teacher*, May 1980, *33*, 924–926.(a)

FRY, EDWARD. The new Instant Word List. *The Reading Teacher*, December 1980, *34*, 284–289.(b)

FRY, EDWARD. Graphical literacy. *Journal of Reading*, February 1981, *24*, 383–390. Also in A. J. Harris & E. Sipay (Eds.), *Readings on reading instruction* (3rd ed.). New York: Longman, 1984, 337–343.

FRY, EDWARD B. Picture nouns for reading and vocabulary improvement. *The Reading Teacher*, November 1987, *41*, 185–191.

FRY, EDWARD B. Writeability: The principles of writing for increased comprehension. In B. L. Zakaluk & S. J. Samuels (Eds.), *Readability: Its past, present & future*. Newark, DE: International Reading Association, 1988, 77–95.

FRY, EDWARD B. Reading formulas—maligned but valid. *Journal of Reading*, January 1989, *32*, 292–297.

FRY, EDWARD B.; FOUNTOUKIDIS, DONA; & POLK, JACQUELINE K. *The new reading teacher's book of lists*. Englewood Cliffs, NJ: Prentice-Hall, 1985.

FRY, EDWARD; WEBER, JANE; & DEPIERRO, JOSEPH. A partial validation of the kernel distance theory for readability. In P. D. Pearson & J. Hansen (Eds.), *Reading: Disciplined inquiry in process and practice*. Clemson, SC: National Reading Conference, 1978, 121–124.

FRY, MAURINE A., & LAGOMARSINO, LINDA. Factors that influence reading: A developmental perspective. *School Psychology Review*, Summer 1982, *11*, 239–250.

FUCHS, LUCY. Images of Hispanics in 4 American reading series. *The Reading Teacher*, May 1987, *40*, 848–854.

FUCHS, LYNN S. Program development. *Teaching Exceptional Children*, Fall 1987, *20*, 42–44.

FUCHS, LYNN S., & FUCHS, DOUGLAS. Effects of systematic formative evaluation: A meta-analysis. *Exceptional Children*, November 1986, *53*, 199–208.

FUCHS, LYNN S.; FUCHS, DOUGLAS; & MAXWELL, LINN. The validity of informal reading comprehension measures. *Remedial and Special Education*, March/April 1988, *9*, 20–28.

FULLER, GERALD B., & FULLER, DIANE L. Reality therapy: Helping LD children make better choices. *Academic Therapy*, January 1982, *17*, 269–277.

FULLMER, ROBERTA. *Maximal reading and auding rates*. Unpublished doctoral dissertation, Harvard University, 1980.

FUNKHOUSER, G. R., & MACCOBY, N. *Study on communicating science information to a lay audience, Phase II*. Institute for Communication Research, Stanford University, September 1971.

FUSARO, JOSEPH A. *Eye-voice span and linguistic constraints in elementary school children*. Unpublished doctoral dissertation, State University of New York at Albany, 1974.

FUSARO, JOSEPH A. Applying statistical rigor to a validation study of the Fry Readability Graph. *Reading Research and Instruction*, Fall 1988, *28*, 44–48.

FUSARO, JOSEPH A., & CONOVER, WILLIS M. Readability of two tabloid and two nontabloid papers. *Journalism Quarterly*, Spring 1983, *60*, 142–144.

GADDES, WILLIAM H. *Learning disabilities and brain function: A neuropsychological approach*. New York: Springer-Verlag, 1980, 1985.

GALABURDA, ALBERT M. Developmental dyslexia: A review of biological interactions. *Annals of Dyslexia*, Vol. 25. Baltimore, MD: Orton Dyslexia Society, 1985, 21–33.

GALDA, S. LEE. Assessment: Responses to literature. In A. Berger & H. A. Robinson (Eds.), *Secondary school reading: What research reveals for classroom practice*. Urbana, IL: National Council of Teachers of English & ERIC/RCS, 1982, 111–125.

GALDA, LEE. Teaching higher order reading skills with literature: Intermediate grades. In B. E. Cullinan (Ed.), *Children's literature in the reading program*. Newark, DE: International Reading Association, 1987, 89–95.(a)

GALDA, LEE. Teaching higher order reading skills with literature: Primary grades. In B. E. Cullinan (Ed.), *Children's literature in the reading program.* Newark, DE: International Reading Association, 1987, 54–57.(b)

GALDA, LEE. Teaching higher order reading skills with literature: Upper grades. In B. E. Cullinan (Ed.), *Children's literature in the reading program.* Newark, DE: International Reading Association, 1987, 121–123.(c)

GALLAGHER, JAMES J. Learning disabilities and special education: A critique. *Journal of Learning Disabilities*, December 1986, *19*, 595–601.

GALLAGHER, MARGARET C.; GOUDVIS, ANNE; & PEARSON, P. DAVID. Principles of organizational change. In S. J. Samuels & P. D. Pearson (Eds.), *Changing school reading programs: Principles and case studies.* Newark, DE: International Reading Association, 1988, 11–39.

GAMBRELL, LINDA B., & BALES, RUBY J. Mental imagery and the comprehension monitoring performance of fourth- and fifth-grade poor readers. *Reading Research Quarterly*, Fall 1986, *21*, 454–464.

GAMBRELL, LINDA B., & JARRELL, MARY. Summer reading: Description and evaluation of a program for children and parents. *Reading World*, October 1980, *20*, 1–9.

GAMBRELL, LINDA B.; KAPINUS, BARBARA A.; & WILSON, ROBERT M. Using mental imagery and summarization to achieve independence in comprehension. *Journal of Reading*, April 1987, *30*, 638–642.

GAMBRELL, LINDA B.; WILSON, ROBERT M.; & GANITT, WALTER N. Classroom observations of task-attending behaviors of good and poor readers. *Journal of Educational Research*, July/August 1981, *74*, 400–404.

GANAPOLE, SELINA J. The development of word consciousness prior to first grade. *Journal of Reading Behavior*, 1987, *19*(4), 415–436.

GANS, ROMA. *Guiding children's reading through experiences.* New York: Teachers College Press, 1941; 1979.

GARDNER, KEITH. The initial teaching alphabet (i.t.a.) and remedial reading programme. *Slow Learning Child*, 1966, *13*, 67–71.

GARMAN, DOROTHY. Language development and first-grade reading achievement. *Reading World*, October 1981, *21*, 40–49.

GARNER, RUTH. Text summarization deficiencies among older students: Awareness or production ability? *American Educational Research Journal*, Winter 1985, *22*, 549–560.

GARNER, RUTH. *Metacognition and reading comprehension.* Norwood, NJ: Ablex, 1987.(a)

GARNER, RUTH. Strategies for reading and studying expository text. *Educational Psychologist*, Summer/Fall 1987, *22*, 299–312.(b).

GARNER, RUTH, & GILLINGHAM, MARK G. Students' knowledge of text structure. *Journal of Reading Behavior*, 1987, *19*(3), 247–259.

GARREN, RICHARD B. Hemispheric laterality differences among four levels of reading achievement. *Perceptual & Motor Skills*, 1980, *50*, 119–123.

GARRETT, HENRY E. *Statistics in psychology and education* (5th ed.). New York: Longman, 1958.

GATES, ARTHUR I. *The improvement of reading: A program of diagnostic and remedial methods.* New York: Macmillan, 1927; 1935; 1947.

GATES, ARTHUR I. The necessary mental age for beginning reading. *Elementary School Journal*, 1937, *27*, 497–508.

GATES, ARTHUR I. Character and purposes of the yearbook. In N. B. Henry (Ed.), *Reading in the elementary school.* 48th Yearbook of the National Society for the Study of Education, Part II. Chicago: University of Chicago Press, 1949, Chapter I.

GATTEGNO, CALEB, & HINMAN, DOROTHY. Words in color. In J. Money (Ed.), *The disabled reader.* Baltimore: Johns Hopkins University Press, 1966, 175–192.

GAUS, PAULA J. The indispensable reading teacher. *The Reading Teacher*, December 1983, *37*, 269–272.

GAZZANIGA, M. S.; BOGEN, J. E.; & SPERRY, R. W. Observations in visual perception after disconnection of the cerebral hemisphere in man. *Brain*, June 1965, *88* (Part 2), 221–236.

GEE, THOMAS C., & RASKOW, STEVEN J. Content reading specialists evaluate teaching practices. *Journal of Reading*, December 1987, *31*, 234–237.

GEESLIN, DORINE H., & WILSON, RICHARD C. Effect of reading age on reading interests. *Elementary English*, May 1972, *49*, 750–756.

GEIGER, GAD, & LETTVIN, JEROME Y. Peripheral vision in persons with dyslexia. *The New England Journal of Medicine*, May 14, 1987, *316*, 1238–1243.

GELZHEISER, LYNN M. Reducing the number of students identified as learning disabled: A question of practice, philosophy, or policy? *Exceptional Children*, October 1987, *54*, 145–150.

GENTILE, LANCE, & MCMILLAN, MERNA M. Humor and the reading program. *Journal of Reading*, January 1978, *21*, 343–349. Also in A. J. Harris & E. Sipay (Eds.), *Readings on reading instruction* (3rd ed.). New York: Longman, 1984, 369–373.

GENTILE, LANCE M., & MCMILLAN, MERNA M. *Stress and reading difficulties: Research, assessment, intervention.* Newark, DE: International Reading Association, 1987.

GENTILE, LANCE M., & MCMILLAN, MERNA M. Reexamining the role of emotional maladjustment. In S.M. Glazer et al. (Eds.), *Reexamining reading diagnosis: New trends and procedures.* Newark, DE: International Reading Association, 1988, 12–28.

GENTRY, J. RICHARD. An analysis of developmental spelling in GNYS AT WRK. *The Reading Teacher*, November 1982, *36*, 192–200.

GEOFFRION, LEO D., & GEOFFRION, OLGA P. *Computers and reading instruction.* Reading, MA: Addison-Wesley, 1983.

GERMAN, DIANE; JOHNSON, BARBARA; & SCHNEIDER, MARY. Learning disability vs. reading disability: A survey of practitioners diagnositc populations and test instruments. *Learning Disability Quarterly*, Spring 1985, *8*, 141–157.

GERSTEN, RUSSELL; WOODWARD, JOHN; & DARCH, CRAIG. Direct instruction: A research-based approach to curriculum design and teaching. *Exceptional Children*, September 1986, *53*, 17–31.

GESCHWIND, NORMAN. Disconnection syndromes in animals and man, Part I. *Brain*, 1965, *88*, 237–294.

GESCHWIND, NORMAN. Biological associations of left-handedness. *Annals of Dyslexia*, Vol. 33. Baltimore, MD: Orton Dyslexia Society, 1983, 29–40.

GETMAN, GERALD N. A commentary on vision. *Journal of Learning Disabilities*, November 1985, *18*, 505–512.

GETTINGER, MARIBETH, & WHITE, MARY A. Which is the stronger correlate of school learning? Time to learn or measured intelligence. *Journal of Educational Psychology*, August 1979, *71*, 405–412.

GEVA, ESTHER, & RYAN, ELLEN B. Use of conjunctions in expository texts by skilled and less skilled readers. *Journal of Reading Behavior*, 1985, *17*(4), 331–346.

GEYER, JOHN J. Perceptual systems in reading: The prediction of a temporal eye-voice span. In H. K. Smith (Ed.), *Perception and reading.* Newark, DE: International Reading Association, 1968, 44–52.

GHATALA, ELIZABETH S., et al. Training cognitive strategy-monitoring in children. *American Educational Research Journal*, Summer 1985, *22*, 199–215.

GIBBS, DENISE P., & COOPER, EUGENE B. Prevalence of communication disorders in students with learning disabilities. *Journal of Learning Disabilities*, January 1989, *22*, 60–63.

GIBSON, ELEANOR, & LEVIN, HARRY. *The psychology of reading.* Cambridge, MA: MIT Press, 1975.

GICKLING, EDWARD E., & ARMSTRONG, DAVID L. Levels of instructional difficulty as related to on-task behavior, task completion, and comprehension. *Journal of Learning Disabilities*, November 1978, *11*, 559–566.

GILLESPIE, JOHN T. *The elementary school paperback collection*. Chicago: American Library Association, 1985.(a)

GILLESPIE, JOHN T. *The junior high school paperback collection*. Chicago: American Library Association, 1985.(b)

GILLESPIE, JOHN T. *The senior high school paperback collection*. Chicago: American Library Association, 1986.

GILLESPIE, JOHN T., & GILBERT, CHRISTINE B. (Eds). *Best books for children: Preschool through middle grades*. New York: Bowker, 1985.

GILLESPIE, PATRICIA H.; MILLER, TED L.; & FIELDER, VIRGINIA D. Legislative definition of learning disabilities: Roadblocks to effective service. *Journal of Learning Disabilities*, December 1975, 8, 660–666.

GILLIAM, BETTYE; PEÑA, SYLVIA C.; & MOUNTAIN, LEE. The Fry Graph applied to Spanish readability. *The Reading Teacher*, January 1980, *33*, 426–430.

GILLIAM, JAMES E., & COLEMAN, MARGARET C. Who influences IEP committee decisions. *Exceptional Children*, May 1981, *47*, 642–644.

GILLILAND, HAP. The new view of native Americans in children's books. *The Reading Teacher*, May 1982, *35*, 912–916.

GILLINGHAM, ANNA, & STILLMAN, BESSIE W. *Remedial training for children with specific difficulty in reading, spelling, and penmanship* (7th ed.). Cambridge, MA: Educators Publishing Service, 1966.

GILLIS, M. K., & OLSON, MARY W. Elementary IRIs: Do they reflect what we know about text type structure and comprehension. *Reading Research and Instruction*, Fall 1987, *27*, 36–44.

GITTELMAN, RACHEL, & FEINGOLD, INGRID. Children with reading disorders: Efficacy of reading remediation. *Journal of Child Psychology & Psychiatry & Allied Disciplines*, April 1983, *24*, 167–191.

GLASS, ARNOLD L., & PERNA, JOAN. The role of syntax in reading disability. *Journal of Learning Disabilities*, June/July 1986, *19*, 354–359.

GLASS, GENE V., & ROBBINS, MELVYN P. A critique of experiments on the role of neurological organization in reading performance. *Reading Research Quarterly*, Fall 1967, *3*, 5–52.

GLASS, GENE V., et al. *School class size: Research and policy*. Beverly Hills, CA: Sage Publications, 1982.

GLASS, GERALD G. *Teaching decoding as separate from reading*. Garden City, NY: Adelphi University Press, 1973.

GLAZZARD, PEGGY. Kindergarten predictors of school achievement. *Journal of Learning Disabilities*, December 1979, *12*, 689–694.

GLEITMAN, LILA R., & ROZIN, PAUL. Teaching reading by means of a syllabary. *Reading Research Quarterly*, Summer 1973, *8*, 447–483.

GLUSHKO, ROBERT J. Principles for pronouncing print: The psychology of phonology. In A. Lesgold & C. Perfetti (Eds.), *Interactive processes in reading*. Hillsdale, NJ: Erlbaum, 1981, 61–84.

GOELMAN, H; OBERG, A. O.; & SMITH, F. (Eds.). *Awakening to literacy*. London: Exeter, 1984.

GOERTZ, MARGARET E. *State educational standards in the 50 states: An update*. Princeton, NJ: Educational Testing Service, March 1988.

GOERTZ, MARGARET E., et al. *School districts' allocation of Chapter 1 resources*. Princeton, NJ: Educational Testing Service, March 1988.

GOLD, JOYCE, & FLEISHER, LISA S. Comprehension breakdown with inductively organized text: Differences between average and disabled readers. *Remedial and Special Education*, July/August 1986, 7, 26–32.

GOLD, PATRICIA C. Cognitive mapping. *Academic Therapy*, January 1984, *19*, 277–284.

GOLD, YVONNE. Helping students discover the origins of words. *The Reading Teacher*, December 1981, *35*, 350–351.

GOLDBERG, HERMAN K.; SCHIFFMAN, GILBERT B.; & BENDER, MICHAEL. *Dyslexia: Interdisciplinary approaches to reading disabilities*. New York: Grune & Stratton, 1983.

GOLDEN, JOANNE M., & GUTHRIE, JOHN T. Convergence and divergence in reader response to literature. *Reading Research Quarterly*, Fall 1986, *21*, 408–421.

GOLDFIELD, BEVERLY, & SNOW, CATHERINE. Reading books with children: The mechanics of parental influences on children's reading achievement. In J. Flood (Ed.), *Promoting reading comprehension*. Newark, DE: International Reading Association, 1984, 204–215.

GOLDMAN, SUSAN R., & PELLEGRINO, JAMES W. Information processing and educational microcomputer technology: Where do we go from here? *Journal of Learning Disabilities*, March 1987, *20*, 144–154.

GOLDSMITH, JOSEPHINE S.; NICOLICH, MARK J.; & HAUPT, EDWARD J. A system for the analysis of word and context-based factors in reading. In J. Niles & L. A. Harris (Eds.), *New inquiries in reading research and instruction*. Rochester, NY: National Reading Conference, 1982, 185–190.

GOLUB, JEFF (Chair.). *Activities to promote critical thinking*. Urbana, IL: National Council of Teachers of English, 1986.

GOLUB, JEFF (Chair.). *Focus on collaborative learning*. Urbana, IL: National Council of Teachers of English, 1988.

GONZALES, PHILLIP C. How to begin language instruction for non-English-speaking students. *Language Arts*, February 1981, *58*, 175–180.(a)

GONZALES, PHILLIP C. Beginning English reading for ESL students. *The Reading Teacher*, November 1981, *35*, 154–162. Also in A. J. Harris & E. Sipay (Eds.), *Readings on reading instruction* (3rd ed.). New York: Longman, 1984, 443–451.(b)

GONZALES, PHILLIP C., & ELIJAH, DAVID. Stability of error patterns on the informal reading inventory. *Reading Improvement*, Winter 1978, *15*, 279–288.

GOOD, ROLAND H., & SALVIA, JOHN. Curriculum bias in published, norm-referenced reading tests: Demonstrable effects. *School Psychology Review*, 1988, *17*(1), 51–60.

GOOD, THOMAS L., & STIPEK, DEBORAH J. Individual differences in the classroom: A psychological perspective. In G. Fensternmacher & J. Goodlad (Eds.), *Individual differences and the common curriculum*. 82nd Yearbook of the National Society for the Study of Education, Part I. Chicago: University of Chicago Press, 1983, 9–43.

GOODFRIEND, PHYLISS R., & GOGEL, MARGERY. Schoolwide public relations for the reading teacher: A primer. *The Reading Teacher*, January 1987, *40*, 428–432.

GOODLAD, JOHN L., & ANDERSON, ROBERT H. *The nongraded elementary school*. New York: Harcourt, Brace and World, 1959.

GOODMAN, KENNETH S. Reading: A psycholinguistic guessing game. *Journal of the Reading Specialist*, May 1967, *6*, 126–135. Also in A. J. Harris & E. Sipay (Eds.), *Readings on reading instruction* (3rd ed.). New York: Longman, 1984, 45–52.

GOODMAN, KENNETH S. Analyses of reading miscues: Applied psycholinguistics. *Reading Research Quarterly*, Fall 1969, *5*, 9–30.

GOODMAN, KENNETH S. Orthography in a theory of reading instruction. *Elementary English*, December 1972, *49*, 1254–1261.

GOODMAN, KENNETH S. The 13th easy way to make learning to read difficult: A reaction to Gleitman and Rozin. *Reading Research Quarterly*, Summer, 1973, *8*, 484–493.

GOODMAN, KENNETH S. Letters to the editor. *Reading Research Quarterly*, 1981, *16*(3), 477–478.

GOODMAN, KENNETH S. Revaluing readers and reading. *Topics in Learning and Learning Disorders*, January 1982, *1*, 87–93.

GOODMAN, KENNETH S. Unity in reading. In H. Singer & R. B. Ruddell (Eds.), *Theoretical models and processes of reading* (3rd ed.). Newark, DE: International Reading Association, 1985, 813–840.

GOODMAN, KENNETH S. Basal readers: A call for action. *Language Arts*, April 1986, *63*, 358–363.

GOODMAN, KENNETH S., & BIRD, LOIS B. On the wording of texts: A study of intra-text word frequency. *Research in the Teaching of English*, May 1984, *18*, 119–145.

GOODMAN, KENNETH S., & GOLLASCH, FREDERICK V. Word omissions: Deliberate and non-deliberate. *Reading Research Quarterly*, 1980, *16*(1), 6–31.

GOODMAN, KENNETH S., & GOODMAN, YETTA M. Learning about psycholinguistic processes by analyzing oral reading. *Harvard Educational Review*, August 1977, *47*, 317–333.

GOODMAN, KENNETH S., & GOODMAN, YETTA M. Learning to read is natural. In L. Resnick & P. Weaver (Eds.), *Theory and practice of early reading*, Vol. 1. Hillsdale, NJ: Erlbaum, 1979, 137–154.

GOODMAN, KENNETH S., & GOODMAN, YETTA M. A whole-language comprehension-centered view of reading development. In L. Reed & S. Ward (Eds.), *Basic skills issues and choices: Approaches to basic skills instruction, 2*. St. Louis: CEMREL, April 1982, 125–134.

GOODMAN, KENNETH, & GOODMAN, YETTA. Reading and writing relationships: Pragmatic function. *Language Arts*, May 1983, *60*, 590–599.

GOODMAN, KENNETH S; GOODMAN, YETTA M; & HOOD, WENDY (Eds.). *The whole language evaluation book*. Portsmouth, NH: Heinemann, 1989.

GOODMAN, NATALIE C. Girls with learning disabilities and their sisters: How are they fairing in adulthood? *Journal of Clinical Child Psychology*, 1987, *16*(4), 290–300.

GOODMAN, YETTA M. Using children's reading miscues for new teaching strategies. *The Reading Teacher*, February 1970, *23*, 455–459. Also in A. J. Harris & E. Sipay (Eds.), *Readings on reading instruction* (3rd ed.). New York: Longman, 1984, 219–222.

GOODMAN, YETTA. Reading strategy lessons: Expanding reading effectiveness. In W. Page (Ed.), *Help for the reading teacher: New directions in research*. Urbana, IL: ERIC/RCS, 1975, 34–41.

GOODMAN, YETTA M. Miscues, errors and reading comprehension. In J. E. Merritt (Ed.), *New horizons in reading*. Newark, DE: International Reading Association, 1976, 86–93.

GOODMAN, YETTA M., & BURKE, CAROLYN. *Reading miscue inventory*. New York: Richard C. Owen, 1972.

GOODMAN, YETTA, & BURKE, CAROLYN. *Reading strategies: Focus on comprehension*. New York: Holt, Rinehart and Winston, 1980.

GOODMAN, YETTA M.; WATSON, DOROTHY J.; & BURKE, CAROLYN L. *Reading miscue inventory: Alternative procedures*. New York: Richard C. Owen, 1987.

GORDON, BELITA. Teach them to read the questions. *Journal of Reading*, February 1983, *26*, 126–136.

GORDON, CHRISTINE J. Teaching narrative text structure: A process approach to reading and writing. In K. D. Muth (Ed.), *Children's comprehension of text*. Newark, DE: International Reading Association, 1989, 79–102.

GORDON, CHRISTINE J., & RENNIE, BARBARA J. Restructuring content schemata: An intervention study. *Reading Research and Instruction*, Spring 1986, *26*, 162–188.

GORDON, HAROLD W. The learning disabled are cognitively right. *Topics in Learning and Learning Disabilities*, April 1983, *3*, 29–39.

GORE, WILLIAM V., & VANCE, BOONEY. The micro meets the IEP. *Academic Therapy*, September 1983, *19*, 89–91.

GORRITI, CARLOS J. ROBLES, & MUÑIZ, ANA M. RODRIGUEZ. Learning problems in Argentina. In L. Tarnopol & M. Tarnopol (Eds.), *Reading disabilities: An international perspective*. Baltimore: University Park Press, 1976, 27–37.

GOTTLIEB, BARBARA W., et al. Sociometric status and solitary play of LD boys and girls. *Journal of Learning Disabilities*, December 1986, *19*, 619–622.

GOUGH, PAULINE B. Introducing children to books via television. *The Reading Teacher*, January 1979, *32*, 458–461.

GOUGH, PHILIP B. One second of reading. In H. Singer & R. B. Ruddell (Eds.), *Theoretical models and processes of reading* (3rd ed.). Newark, DE: International Reading Association, 1985, 661–686.(a)

GOUGH, PHILIP B. One second of reading: Postscript. In H. Singer & R. B. Ruddell (Eds.), *Theoretical models and processes of reading* (3rd ed.). Newark, DE: International Reading Association, 1985, 687–688.(b)

GOUGH, PHILIP B.; ALFORD, JACK A.; & HOLLEY-WILCOX, PAMELA. Words and context. In O. Tzeng & H. Singer (Eds.), *Perception of print: Reading research in experimental psychology*. Hillsdale, NJ: Erlbaum, 1981, 85–102.

GOUGH, PHILIP B., & TUNMER, WILLIAM W. Decoding, reading, and reading disability. *Remedial and Special Education*, January/February 1986, *7*, 6–10.

GRADEN, JANET L.; CASEY, ANN; & CHRISTENSON, SANDRA L. Implementing a prereferral intervention system: Part I. The model. *Exceptional Children*, February 1985, *51*, 377–384.

GRAHAM, KENNETH G., & ROBINSON, H. ALAN. *Study skills handbook: A guide for all teachers*. Newark, DE: International Reading Association, 1984.

GRAVES, MICHAEL F. Selecting vocabulary to teach in the intermediate and secondary grades. In J. Flood (Ed.), *Promoting reading comprehension*. Newark, DE: International Reading Association, 1984, 245–260.

GRAVES, MICHAEL F. Vocabulary learning and instruction. In E. Z Rothkopf & L. C. Ehri (Eds.), *Review of research in education*. Vol. 13. Washington, DC: American Educational Research Association, 1986, 49–89.

GRAVES, MICHAEL F. The roles of instruction in fostering vocabulary development. In M. G. McKeown & M. E. Curtis (Eds.), *The nature of vocabulary acquisition*. Hillsdale, NJ: Erlbaum, 1987, 165–184.

GRAVES, MICHAEL F.; BOETTCHER, JUDITH A.; & RYDER, RANDALL A. *Easy reading: Book series and periodicals for less able readers*. Newark, DE: International Reading Association, 1979.

GRAVES, MICHAEL F.; BRUNETTI, GERALD J.; & SLATER, WAYNE H. The reading vocabularies of primary grade children of varying geographic and social backgrounds. In J. Niles & L. A. Harris (Eds.), *New inquiries in reading: Research and instruction*. Rochester, NY: National Reading Conference, 1982, 99–104.

GRAVES, MICHAEL, & HAMMOND, HEIDI. A validated procedure for teaching prefixes and its effect on student's ability to assign meaning to novel words. In M. Kamil & A. Moe (Eds.), *Perspectives on reading research and instruction*. Washington, DC: National Reading Conference, 1980, 184–188.

GRAVES, MICHAEL F., & PRENN, MAUREEN C. Costs and benefits of various methods of teaching vocabulary. *Journal of Reading*, April 1986, *29*, 596–602.

GRAY, CLARENCE T. *Deficiencies in reading ability: Their diagnoses and remedies*. Boston: D. C. Heath, 1922.

GRAY, WILLIAM S. *Remedial cases in reading: Their diagnosis and treatment*. Supplementary Educational Monographs, No. 22. Chicago: University of Chicago Press, 1922.

GRAY, WILLIAM S. A modern program of reading instruction for the grades and high school. In G. M. Whipple (Ed.), *Report of the national committee on reading*. 24th Yearbook of the National Society for the Study of Education, Part I. Bloomington, IL: Public School Publishing Co., 1925, 21–74.

GRAY, WILLIAM S. *On their own in reading*. Glenview, IL: Scott, Foresman, 1948.

GRAY, WILLIAM S. Reading. In C. W. Harris (Ed.), *Encyclopedia of educational research* (2nd ed.). New York: Macmillan, 1960, 1106.

GREANEY, VINCENT. Factors related to amount and type of leisure time reading. *Reading Research Quarterly*, 1980, *15*(3), 337–357.

GREANEY, VINCENT. Parental influences on reading. *The Reading Teacher*, April 1986, *39*, 813–818.

GREEN, JUDITH, & BLOOME, DAVID. Ethnography and reading: Issues, approaches, criteria, and findings. In J. Niles & L. A. Harris (Eds.), *Searches for meaning in reading/language processing and instruction*. Rochester, NY: National Reading Conference, 1983, 6–30.

GREEN, JUDITH L., & HARKER, JUDITH O. Reading to children: A communicative process. In J. Langer & M. T. Burke-Smith (Eds.), *Reader meets author/bridging the gap: A psycholinguistic and sociolinguistic perspective*. Newark, DE: International Reading Association, 1982, 196–221.

GREEN, ORVILLE C., & PERLMAN, SUZANNE M. Endocrinology and disorders of learning. In H. R. Myklebust (Ed.), *Progress in learning disabilities*, Vol. II. New York: Grune & Stratton, 1971, 1–17.

GREEN, RICHARD R. *Evaluation of materials designed to improve the balance in reading between comprehension and rate*. Unpublished doctoral dissertation, Boston University, 1971.

GREENBAUM, PAUL E. Nonverbal differences in communication style between American Indians and Anglo elementary classrooms. *American Educational Research Journal*, Spring 1985, *22*, 101–115.

GREENE, JENNIFER C. Individual and teacher class effects in aptitude-treatment studies. *American Educational Research Journal*, Fall, 1980, *17*, 291–302.

GREENEWALD, M. JANE, & PEDERSON, CAROLYN. Effects of sentence organization instruction in reading comprehension of poor readers. In J. Niles & L. A. Harris (Eds.), *Search for meaning in reading/language processing and instruction*. Rochester, NY: National Reading Conference, 1983, 101–103.

GREENLAW, M. JEAN. Reading interest research and children's choices. In N. Roser & M. Frith (Eds.), *Children's choices: Teaching with books children like*. Newark, DE: International Reading Association, 1983, 90–92.

GREENLAW, M. JEAN, & MCINTOSH, MARGARET E. Science fiction and fantasy with teaching to teens. In B. E. Cullinan (Ed.), *Children's literature in the reading program*. Newark, DE: International Reading Association, 1987, 111–120.

GREENLINGER-HARLESS, CAROL SUE. A new cross-referenced index to U.S. reading series, grades K-8. *The Reading Teacher*, December 1987, *41*, 293–303.

GRIESE, ARNOLD A. Focusing on students of different cultural backgrounds—the Eskimo and Indian pupil—special problems in reading comprehension. *Elementary English*, April 1971, *48*, 229–234.

GRIFFITHS, ANITA N. Self-concept in remedial work with dyslexic children. *Academic Therapy*, Winter 1970–1971, *6*, 125–133.

GRINNELL, PAULA C. Reading comprehension and picture usage: A study with first graders. In J. Niles & L. A. Harris (Eds.), *New inquiries in reading research and instruction*. Rochester, NY: National Reading Conference, 1982, 136–139.

GRINNELL, PAULA C. *How can I prepare my young child for reading?* Newark, DE: International Reading Association, 1984.

GRISHAM, J. DAVID, & SIMONS, HERBERT D. Refractive error and the reading process: A literature review. *Journal of the American Optometric Association*, January 1986, 57, 44–55.

GROFF, PATRICK. Research in brief: Shapes as cues in word recognition. *Visible Language*, Winter 1975, 9, 67–71.

GROFF, PATRICK. Blending: Basic process or beside the point? *Reading World*, March 1976, 15, 161–166.

GROFF, PATRICK J. Resolving the letter name controversy. *The Reading Teacher*, January 1984, 37, 384–388.

GROFF, PATRICK, & SEYMOUR, DOROTHY. *Word recognition: The why and the how*. Springfield, IL: Charles C Thomas, 1987.

GROHENS, JOE. Nutrition and reading achievement. *The Reading Teacher*, May 1988, 41, 942–945.

GRONLUND, NORMAN E. *Stating behavioral objectives for classroom instruction*. New York: Macmillan, 1973.

GRONLUND, NORMAN E. *Preparing criterion-referenced tests for classroom instruction*. New York: Macmillan, 1978.

GROSS, ALICE D. The relationship between sex differences and reading ability in an Israeli kibbutz system. In D. Feitelson (Ed.), *Cross-cultural perspectives on reading and reading research*. Newark, DE: International Reading Association, 1978, 72–88.

GROSS, PHILIP P., & SADOWSKI, KAREN. Fog Index—A readability formula for microcomputers. *Journal of Reading*, April 1985, 28, 614–618.

GRUNDIN, HANS U., et al. Cloze procedure and comprehension: An exploratory study across three languages. In D. Feitelson (Ed.), *Cross-cultural perspectives on reading and reading research*. Newark, DE: International Reading Association, 1978, 48–61.

GUERRA, CATHY L., & PAYNE, DELORES B. Using popular books and magazines to interest children in general science. *Journal of Reading*, April 1981, 24, 583–586.

GUILFORD, J. P. Cognitive styles: What are they? *Educational and Psychological Measurement*, Fall 1980, 40, 715–735.

GUNNING, ROBERT. Fog Index of a passage. *Academic Therapy*, March 1979, 14, 489–491.

GUSTAFSON, DAVID J., & PEDERSON, JOYCE. SQ3R and the strategic reader. *Wisconsin State Reading Association Journal*, Fall 1986, 31, 25–28.

GUSZAK, FRANK J. Teacher questioning and reading. *The Reading Teacher*, December 1967, 21, 227–234.

GUTHRIE, JOHN T. Learnability versus readability of texts. *Journal of Educational Research*, February 1972, 65, 273–280.

GUTHRIE, JOHN T. Models of reading and reading disability. *Journal of Educational Psychology*, August 1973, 65, 9–18.

GUTHRIE, JOHN T. Time in reading programs. *The Reading Teacher*, January 1980, 33, 500–502.

GUTHRIE, JOHN T. Acquisition of newspaper readership. *The Reading Teacher*, February 1981, 34, 616–618.(a)

GUTHRIE, JOHN T. Invalidity of reading tests. *Journal of Reading*, December 1981, 25, 300–302.(b)

GUTHRIE, JOHN T. Reading in New Zealand: Achievement and volume. *Reading Research Quarterly*, 1981, 17(1), 6–27.(c)

GUTHRIE, JOHN T. Corporate education for the electronic culture. *Journal of Reading*, February 1982, 25, 492–495.

GUTHRIE, JOHN T. Learning values from textbooks. *Journal of Reading*, March 1983, 26, 574–576.

GUTHRIE, JOHN T. Lexical learning. *The Reading Teacher*, March 1984, 37, 666–667.

GUTHRIE, JOHN T. *Indicators of reading education.* New Brunswick, NJ: Center for Policy Research in Education, Eagleton Institute of Politics, Rutgers University, October 1987.

GUTHRIE, JOHN T.; MARTUZA, VICTOR; & SEIFERT, MARY. Impacts of instructional time in reading. In L. Resnick & P. Weaver (Eds.), *Theory and practice of early reading,* Vol. 3. Hillsdale, NJ: Erlbaum, 1979, 153–178.

GUTHRIE, JOHN T., & MOSENTHAL, PETER. Literacy is multidimensional: Locating information and reading comprehension. *Educational Psychologist,* Summer/Fall 1987, *22,* 279–297.

GUTHRIE, JOHN T., & SEIFERT, MARY. Profiles of reading activity in a community. *Journal of Reading,* March 1983, *26,* 498–508.

GUTHRIE, JOHN T.; SEIFERT, MARY; & KIRSCH, IRWIN S. Effects of education, occupation, and setting on reading practices. *American Educational Research Journal,* Spring 1986, *23,* 151–160.

GUTHRIE, JOHN T.; SEIFERT, MARY; & KLINE, LLOYD W. Clues from research on programs for poor readers. In S. J. Samuels (Ed.), *What research has to say about reading instruction.* Newark, DE: International Reading Association, 1978, 1–12.

GUTHRIE, JOHN T., et al. The maze technique to assess, monitor reading comprehension. *The Reading Teacher,* November 1974, *28,* 161–168.

GUZZETTI, BARBARA J., & MARZANO, ROBERT J. Correlates of effective reading instruction. *The Reading Teacher,* April 1984, *37,* 754–758.

HABAYEB, ALI H. *The effect of illustrations on text comprehension.* Unpublished doctoral dissertation. State University of New York at Albany, 1988.

HABER, LYN R., & HABER, RALPH N. Perceptual processes in reading: An analysis-by-synthesis model. In F. Pirozzolo & M. Wittrock (Eds.), *Neuropsychological and cognitive processes in reading.* New York: Academic Press, 1981, 167–200.

HABER, LYN R.; HABER, RALPH N.; & FURLIN, KAREN R. Word length and word shape as sources of information in reading. *Reading Research Quarterly,* Winter 1983, *18,* 165–189.

HABER, RALPH N., & HABER, LYN R. The shape of a word can specify its meaning. *Reading Research Quarterly,* 1981, *16*(3), 334–335.(a)

HABER, RALPH N., & HABER, LYN R. Visual components of the reading process. *Visible Language,* 1981, *15*(2), 147–182.(b)

HADDOCK, MARYANN. Effects of an auditory and auditory-visual method of blending instruction on the ability of prereaders to decode synthetic words. *Journal of Educational Psychology,* December 1976, *68,* 825–831.

HADDOCK, MARYANN. Teaching blending in beginning reading instruction is important. *The Reading Teacher,* March 1978, *31,* 654–657.

HAERTEL, EDWARD. Construct validity and criterion-referenced testing. *Review of Educational Research,* Spring 1985, 55, 23–46.

HAGGARD, MARTHA R. The vocabulary self-collection strategy: An active approach to word learning. *Journal of Reading,* December 1982, *26,* 203–207.

HAGGARD, MARTHA R. Developing critical thinking with the Directed Reading-Thinking Activity. *The Reading Teacher,* February 1988, *41,* 526–533.

HAINES, DEBORAH J., & TORGESEN, JOSEPH K. The effects of incentives on rehearsal and short-term memory in children with reading problems. *Learning Disability Quarterly,* Spring 1979, *2,* 48–55.

HAINES, L. P., & LEONG, C. K. Coding processes in skilled and less skilled readers. *Annals of Dyslexia,* Vol. 33. Baltimore, MD: Orton Dyslexia Society, 1983, 67–89.

HALE, GORDON A. *Students' prediction of prose forgetting and the effects of study strategies.* Research Report 88–46. Princeton, NJ: ETS, December 1982.

HALEY, BEVERLY. Once upon a time—they lived happily. *Language Arts,* November/December 1975, 52, 1147–1153.

HALL, VERNON C., & TURNER, RALPH R. The validity of the "different language" explanation for poor scholastic performance by black students. *Review of Educational Research*, Winter 1974, *44*, 69–81.

HALL, WILLIAM S., & GUTHRIE, LARRY F. Situational differences in use of language. In J. Langer & M. Smith-Burke (Eds.), *Reader meets author/bridging the gap*. Newark, DE: International Reading Association, 1982, 132–146.

HALLAHAN, DANIEL P., & CRUICKSHANK, WILLIAM M. *Psychoeducational foundations of learning disabilities*. Englewood Cliffs, NJ: Prentice-Hall, 1973.

HALLAHAN, DANIEL P.; MARSHALL, KATHLEEN J.; & LLOYD, JOHN W. Self-recording during group instruction: Effects on attention to task. *Learning Disability Quarterly*, Fall 1981, *4*, 407–413.

HALLAHAN, DANIEL P., et al. A comparison of the effects of reinforcement and response cost on the selective attention of learning disabled children. *Journal of Learning Disabilities*, August/September 1978, *11*, 430–438.

HALLER, EILEEN P.; CHILD, DAVID A.; & WALBERG, HERBERT J. Can comprehension be taught?: A quantitative synthesis of "metacognitive" studies. *Educational Researcher*, December 1988, *17*, 5–8.

HALLER, EMIL J. Pupil race and elementary school ability groupings: Are teachers biased against black children? *American Educational Research Journal*, Winter 1985, *22*, 465–483.

HALLER, EMIL, & WATERMAN, MARGARET. The criteria of reading group assignments. *The Reading Teacher*, April 1985, *38*, 772–781.

HALLIDAY, M. A. K., & HASAN, RUQAIYA. *Cohesion in English*. New York: Longman, 1976.

HALLINAN, MAUREEN T., & SØRENSEN, AAGE B. Ability grouping and student friendships. *American Educational Research Journal*, Winter 1985, *22*, 485–499.

HALPERN, HONEY. Contemporary realistic young adult fiction: An annotated bibliography. *Journal of Reading*, January 1978, *21*, 351–356.

HAMAKER, CHRISTIAAN. The effects of adjunct questions on prose learning. *Review of Educational Research*, Summer 1986, *56*, 212–242.

HAMBLETON, RONALD K., & EIGNOR, DANIEL R. Guidelines for evaluating criterion-referenced tests and test manuals. *Journal of Educational Measurement*, Winter 1978, *15*, 321–327.

HAMBLETON, RONALD K., & EIGNOR, DANIEL R. Competency test development, validation, and standard setting. In R. Jaeger & C. Tittle (Eds.), *Minimum competency achievement testing: Motives, models, measures, and consequences*. Berkeley, CA: McCutchan, 1980, 367–396.

HAMMILL, DONALD D.; COLARUSSO, R. P.; & WIEDERHOLT, J. LEE. Diagnostic value of the Frostig test: A factor analytic approach. *Journal of Special Education*, 1970, *4*, 279–282.

HAMMILL, DONALD; GOODMAN, LIBBY; & WIEDERHOLT, J. LEE. Visual-motor processes: Can we train them? *The Reading Teacher*, February 1974, *27*, 469–478.

HAMMILL, DONALD D., & LARSEN, STEPHEN C. The effectiveness of psycholinguistic training. *Exceptional Children*, September 1974, *41*, 5–14.(a)

HAMMILL, DONALD, & LARSEN, STEPHEN C. The relationship of selected auditory perceptual skills and reading ability. *Journal of Learning Disabilities*, August/September 1974, 7, 429–435.(b)

HAMMILL, DONALD D., & LARSEN, STEPHEN C. The effectiveness of psycholinguistic training: A reaffirmation of position. *Exceptional Children*, March 1978, *44*, 402–414.

HAMMILL, DONALD D., & McNUTT, GAYE. *The correlates of reading: The consensus of thirty years of correlational research*. Austin, TX: Pro-Ed, 1981.

HANEY, DANIEL Q. Ritalin's long history shows few ill effects. *Albany Times Union*, April 4, 1988, A-6.

HANLEY, JOHN, & SKLAR, BERNARD. Electroencephalographic correlates of developmental reading dyslexias: Computer analysis of recordings from normal and dyslexic children. In G. Leisman (Ed.), *Basic visual processes and learning disability*. Springfield, IL: Charles C Thomas, 1976, 217–243.

HANNA, GERALD S.; DYCK, NORMA J.; & HOLEN, MICHAEL C. Objective analysis of achievement—aptitude discrepancies in LD classification. *Learning Disability Quarterly*, Fall 1979, *2*, 32–38.

HANNA, GERALD S., & SCHERICH, HENRY H. An empirical evaluation of three definitions of context dependence. *Journal of Reading Behavior*, Spring 1981, *13*, 75–80.

HANNA, PAUL R.; & HANNA, JEAN S. *Phoneme-grapheme correspondences as cues to spelling improvement*. OE-32008. Washington, DC: U.S. Government Printing Office, 1966.

HANSEN, DONALD A. Family-school articulation: The effects of interactive rule mismatch. *American Educational Research Journal*, Winter 1986, *23*, 643–659.

HANSEN, JANE. The effects of inference training and practice on young children's reading comprehension. *Reading Research Quarterly*, 1981, *16*(3), 391–417.

HANSEN, JANE. Organizing student learning: Teachers teach what and how. In J. R. Squire (Ed.), *The dynamics of language learning: Research in reading and English*. Bloomington, IN: ERIC/RCS, 1987, 321–334.

HANSEN, JANE, & HUBBARD, RUTH. Poor readers can draw inferences. *The Reading Teacher*, March 1984, *37*, 586–589.

HANSFORD, B. C., & HATTIE, J. A. The relationship between self-concept and achievement/performance measures. *Review of Educational Research*, Spring 1982, *52*, 123–142.

HARBER, JEAN R. Achievement in black English. *The Reading Teacher*, April 1982, *35*, 848–849.

HARBER, JEAN R., & BEATTY, JANE N. (Comps.) *Reading and the black English speaking child: An annotated bibliography*. Newark, DE: International Reading Association, 1978.

HARDT, ULRICH H. Literature in the language arts program. In U. Hardt (Ed.), *Teaching reading with the other language arts*. Newark, DE: International Reading Association, 1983, 104–116.

HARDY, MADELINE; STENNET, R. G.; & SMYTHE, P. C. Word attack: How do they "figure them out"? *Elementary English*, January 1973, *50*, 99–102.

HARE, VICTORIA C. Preassessment of topical knowledge: A validation and an extension. *Journal of Reading Behavior*, 1982, *14*(1), 77–85.

HARE, VICTORIA C. What's in a word? A review of young children's difficulties with the construct "word." *The Reading Teacher*, January 1983, *37*, 360–364.

HARE, VICTORIA C., & BORCHARDT, KATHLEEN M. Direct instruction of summarization skills. *Reading Research Quarterly*, Fall 1984, *20*, 62–78.

HARE, VICTORIA C., & CHELSA, LAUREL G. When main idea identification fails. In J. A. Niles & R. V. Lalik (Eds.), *Solving problems in literacy: Learners, teachers, and researchers*. Rochester, NY: National Reading Conference, 1986, 316–325.

HARE, VICTORIA C., & LOMAX, RICHARD G. Readers' awareness of subheadings in expository text. In J. A. Niles & R. V. Lalik (Eds.), *Issues in literacy: A research perspective*. Rochester, NY: National Reading Conference, 1985, 199–203.

HARE, VICTORIA C., & PULLIAM, CYNTHIA A. Teacher questioning: A verification and an extension. *Journal of Reading Behavior*, Spring 1980, *12*, 69–72.

HARE, VICTORIA C.; RABINOWITZ, MITCHELL; & SCHIEBLE, KAREN M. Text effects on main idea comprehension. *Reading Research Quarterly*, Winter 1989, *24*, 72–88.

HARNESCHFEGER, ANNEGRET, & WILEY, DAVID E. Achievement test scores drop. So what? *Educational Researcher*, March 1976, *5*, 5–12.

HARP, BILL. "What do we know now about ability grouping?" *The Reading Teacher*, *February 1989, 42*, 430–431.(a)

HARP, BILL. "What do we do in the place of ability grouping?" *The Reading Teacher*, March 1989, *42*, 534–535.(b)

HARPER, ROBERT J., & KILARR, GARY. The law and reading instruction. *Language Arts*, November/December 1977, *54*, 913–919.

HARRIS, ALBERT J. Lateral dominance, directional confusion, and reading disability. *Journal of Psychology*, 1957, *44*, 283–294.

HARRIS, ALBERT J. A critical reaction to The Nature of Reading Disability. *Journal of Developmental Reading*, 1960, *3*, 238–249.

HARRIS, ALBERT J. Perceptual difficulties in reading disability. In J. A. Figurel (Ed.), *Changing concepts in reading instruction*. Newark, DE: International Reading Association, 1961, 281–290.

HARRIS, ALBERT J. Progressive education and reading instruction. *The Reading Teacher*, November 1964, *18*, 128–138.

HARRIS, ALBERT J. Five decades of remedial reading. In J. A. Figurel (Ed.), *Forging ahead in reading*. Newark, DE: International Reading Association, 1968, 25–34.

HARRIS, ALBERT J. *Casebook on reading disability*. New York: David McKay, 1970.

HARRIS, ALBERT J. A comparison of formulas for measuring degree of reading disability. In R. E. Liebert (Ed.), *Diagnostic viewpoints in reading*. Newark, DE: International Reading Association, 1971, 113–120.(a)

HARRIS, ALBERT J. Psychological and motivational problems. In D. K. Bracken & E. Malmquist (Eds.), *Improving reading ability around the world*. Newark, DE: International Reading Association, 1971, 97–103.(b)

HARRIS, ALBERT J. Some new developments in readability. In J. E. Merritt (Ed.), *New horizons in reading*. Newark, DE: International Reading Association, 1976, 331–340.

HARRIS, ALBERT J. Discussion: Linguistic awareness and cognitive clarity in learning to read. In M. L. Kamil & A. J. Moe (Eds.), *Reading research: Studies and applications*. Clemson, SC: National Reading Conference, 1979, 295–296.(a)

HARRIS, ALBERT J. The effective teacher of reading, revisited. *The Reading Teacher*, November 1979, *33*, 135–140.(b)

HARRIS, ALBERT J. An overview of reading disabilities and learning disabilities in the U.S. *The Reading Teacher*, January 1980, *33*, 420–425.

HARRIS, ALBERT J. How many kinds of reading disability are there? *Journal of Learning Disabilities*, October 1982, *15*, 456–460.

HARRIS, ALBERT J., & JACOBSON, MILTON D. *Basic elementary reading vocabularies*. New York: Macmillan, 1972.

HARRIS, ALBERT J., & JACOBSON, MILTON D. Some comparisons between the Basic Elementary Reading Vocabularies and other word lists. *Reading Research Quarterly*, 1973–1974, *9*(1), 87–109.

HARRIS, ALBERT J., & JACOBSON, MILTON D. Predicting twelfth graders' comprehension scores. *Journal of Reading*, October 1976, *20*, 43–46.

HARRIS, ALBERT J., & JACOBSON, MILTON D. A framework for readability research: Moving beyond Herbert Spencer. *Journal of Reading*, February 1979, *22*, 390–398.

HARRIS, ALBERT J., & JACOBSON, MILTON D. A comparison of the Fry, Spache, and Harris-Jacobson readability formulas for primary grades. *The Reading Teacher*, May 1980, *33*, 920–923.

HARRIS, ALBERT J., & JACOBSON, MILTON D. *Basic reading vocabularies*. New York: Macmillan, 1982.

HARRIS, ALBERT J., & ROSWELL, FLORENCE G. Clinical diagnosis of reading disability. *Journal of Psychology*, 1953, *63*, 323–340.

HARRIS, ALBERT J., & SERWER, BLANCHE L. *Comparison of reading approaches in first-grade teaching with disadvantaged children (the CRAFT Project).* Final Report, Cooperative Research Project, No. 2677. New York: Division of Teacher Education, The City University of New York, 1966. (ERIC Document number ED 010–037.) (a)

HARRIS, ALBERT J., & SERWER, BLANCHE L. The CRAFT Project: Instructional time in reading research. *Reading Research Quarterly*, Fall 1966, *2*, 27–56.(b)

HARRIS, ALBERT J., & SIPAY, EDWARD R. *The Macmillan Reading Readiness Test, RE: Manual for administering, scoring, and interpreting.* New York: Macmillan, 1970.

HARRIS, ALBERT J., & SIPAY, EDWARD R. *Readings on reading instruction.* New York: David McKay, 1972; New York: Longman, 1984.

HARRIS, ALBERT J., & SIPAY, EDWARD R. *How to teach reading: A competency-based program.* New York: Longman, 1979.

HARRIS, ALBERT J., & SIPAY, EDWARD R. *How to increase reading ability.* New York: McKay, 1975; New York: Longman, 1980, 1985.

HARRIS, ALBERT J., et al. *A continuation of the CRAFT Project: Comparing reading approaches with disadvantaged urban negro children in primary grades. Final Report, USOE Project No. 5-05-70-2-12-1.* New York: Selected Academic Reading, 1968. (ERIC Document number ED 020 297.)

HARRIS, EMILY L. The contribution of twin research to the study of the etiology of reading disability. In S. D. Smith (Ed.), *Genetics and learning disabilities.* San Diego, CA: College-Hill Press, 1986, 3–19.

HARRIS, MARGARET, & COLTHEART, MAX. *Language processing in children and adults: An introduction.* Boston: Routledge & Kegan Paul Pic, 1986.

HARRIS, MARY. Family forces for early school development of language fluency and beginning reading. In H. Sartain (Ed.), *Mobilizing family forces for worldwide reading success.* Newark, DE: International Reading Association, 1981, 55–73.

HARRIS, THEODORE L. Reading flexibility: A neglected aspect of reading instruction. In J. Merritt (Ed.), *New horizons in reading.* Newark, DE: International Reading Association, 1976, 27–35.

HARRIS, THEODORE L., & HODGES, RICHARD E. (Eds.). *A dictionary of reading and related terms.* Newark, DE: International Reading Association, 1981.

HARRISON, COLIN. Assessing the readability of school texts. In E. Lunzer & K. Gardner (Eds.), *The effective use of reading.* London: Heinemann, 1979, 72–107.

HARRISON, LUCILE M. *Reading readiness.* Cambridge, MA: Riverside Press, 1936.

HARSTE, JEROME C., & MIKULECKY, LARRY J. The context of literacy in our society. In A. Purves & O. Niles (Eds.), *Becoming readers in a complex society.* 83rd Yearbook of the National Society for the Study of Education, Part I. Chicago: University of Chicago Press, 1984, 47–78.

HARTER, M. RUSSELL, et al. Separate brain potential characteristics in children with reading disability and attention deficit disorder: Color and letter relevance effects. *Brain and Cognition*, February 1988, *7*, 115–140.

HARTLAGE, LAWRENCE C. Vision deficits and reading impairment. In G. Leisman (Ed.), *Basic visual processes and learning disability.* Springfield, IL: Charles C Thomas, 1976, 151–162.

HARTLAGE, LAWRENCE C., & TELZROW, CATHY F. Neuropsychological disorders in children: Effects of medication on learning and behavior modification. *Journal of Research and Development in Education*, Spring 1982, *15*, 55–65.

HARTLEY, JAMES. Typography and executive control processes in reading. In B. K. Britton & S. M. Glynn (Eds.), *Executive control processes in reading.* Hillsdale, NJ: Erlbaum, 1987, 57–106.

HASSILRIIS, PETER. IEPs and a whole-language model of language arts. *Topics in Learning & Learning Disabilities*, January 1982, *1*, 17–21.

HATCH, EVELYN. Research on reading a second language. *Journal of Reading Behavior*, April 1974, *6*, 53–61.

HAVIGHURST, ROBERT J. *Human development and education*. New York: Longman, 1953.

HAYNES, MARIANA C., & JENKINS, JOSEPH R. Reading instruction in special education resource rooms. *American Educational Research Journal*, Summer 1986, *23*, 161–190.

HEALD-TAYLOR, GAIL. How to use predictable books for K-2 language arts instruction. *The Reading Teacher*, March 1987, *40*, 656–661.(a)

HEALD-TAYLOR, GAIL. Predictable literature selections and activities for language arts instruction. *The Reading Teacher*, October 1987, *41*, 6–12.(b)

HEALY, JANE M. The enigma of hyperlexia. *Reading Research Quarterly*, 1982, *27*(3), 319–338.

HEALY, JANE M., & ARAM, DOROTHY M. Hyperlexia and dyslexia: A family study. *Annals of Dyslexia*, Vol. 36. Baltimore, MD: Orton Dyslexia Society, 1986, 237–252.

HEAP, JAMES L. Understanding classroom events: A critique of Durkin with an alternative. *Journal of Reading Behavior*, 1982, *14*(4), 392–411.

HEATHINGTON, BETTY S. What to do about reading motivation in the middle school. *Journal of Reading*, May 1979, *22*, 709–713.

HEATHINGTON, BETTY S., & ALEXANDER, J. ESTILL. Do classroom teachers emphasize attitudes toward reading? *The Reading Teacher*, February 1984, *37*, 484–488.

HEATHINGTON, BETTY S., & KOSKINEN, PATRICIA S. Interest inventory for adult beginning readers. *Journal of Reading*, December 1982, *26*, 252–256.

HECKELMAN, R. G. A Neurological Impress Method of remedial reading instruction. *Academic Therapy Quarterly*, Summer 1969, *4*, 277–282.

HEILMAN, ARTHUR W.; BLAIR, TIMOTHY; & RUPLEY, WILLIAM H. *Principles and practices of teaching reading* (5th ed.). Columbus, OH: Charles E. Merrill, 1981.

HEIMLICH, JOAN E., & PITTELMAN, SUSAN D. *Semantic mapping: Classroom applications*. Newark, DE: International Reading Association, 1986.

HELGREN-LEMPESIS, VALERIE A., & MANGRUM, CHARLES T. An analysis of alternate form reliability of three commercially-prepared informal reading inventories. *Reading Research Quarterly*, Spring 1986, *21*, 209–215.

HELLER, MARY F. How do you know what you know? Metacognitive modeling in the content areas. *Journal of Reading*, February 1986, *29*, 415–422.

HELLRIEGEL, DIANE. *Fifty creative ways to use paperbacks in the middle grades*. New York: Scholastic Book Services, 1980.

HELVESTON, EUGENE M. Management of dyslexia and related learning disabilities. *Journal of Learning Disabilities*, August/September 1987, *20*, 415–421.

HEMBREE, RAY. Correlates, causes, effects, and treatment of test anxiety. *Review of Educational Research*, Spring 1988, *58*, 47–77.

HENDERSON, EDMUND. Understanding children's knowledge of written language. In D. B. Yaden & S. Templeton (Eds.), *Metalinguistic awareness and beginning reading*. Portsmouth, NH: Heinemann, 1986, 65–77.

HENDERSON, LESLIE. *Orthography and word recognition*. New York: Academic Press, 1982.

HENDERSON, LESLIE, & CHARD, JACKIE. The reader's implicit knowledge of orthographic structure. In U. Frith (Ed.), *Cognitive processes in spelling*. New York: Academic Press, 1980, 85–116.

HENDERSON, RONALD W. Social and emotional needs of culturally diverse children. *Exceptional Children*, May 1980, *46*, 598–605.

HENK, WILLIAM A. Adapting the NIM to improve comprehension. *Academic Therapy*, September 1983, *19*, 97–101.

HENK, WILLIAM A. Effects of top-level comparison-contrast text structures in reading comprehension performance. *Reading Research and Instruction*, Fall 1988, *28*, 1–17.

HENK, WILLIAM A., & HELFELDT, JOHN P. How to develop independence in following written directions. *Journal of Reading*, April 1987, *30*, 602–607.

HENK, WILLIAM A.; HELFELDT, JOHN P.; & PLATT, JENNIFER M. Developing reading fluency in learning disabled students. *Teaching Exceptional Children*, Spring 1986, *18*, 202–208.

HENRY, STEPHAN A., & WITTMAN, ROBERT D. Diagnostic implications of Bannatyne's recategorized WISC-R scores for identifying learning disabled children. *Journal of Learning Disabilities*, November 1981, *14*, 517–520.

HERBER, HAROLD L. *Teaching reading in content areas* (2nd ed.). Englewood Cliffs, NJ: Prentice-Hall, 1978.

HERBER, HAROLD L., & NELSON, JOAN. Questioning is not the answer. *Journal of Reading*, April 1975, *18*, 512–517. Also in A. J. Harris and E. Sipay (Eds.), *Readings on reading instruction* (3rd ed.). New York: Longman, 1984, 308–313.

HERBER, HAROLD L., & NELSON-HERBER, JOAN. Planning the reading program. In A. Purves & O. Niles (Eds.), *Becoming readers in a complex society*. 83rd Yearbook of the National Society for the Study of Education, Part I. Chicago: University of Chicago Press, 1984, 174–208.

HERMAN, PATRICIA A., et al. Incidental acquisition of word meaning from expositions with varied text features. *Reading Research Quarterly*, Summer 1987, *22*, 263–284.

HERMANN, HOWARD T.; SONNABEND, NANCY L.; & ZEEVI, YEHOSHUA Y. Bihemifield visual stimulation reveals reduced lateral bias in dyslexia. *Annals of Dyslexia*, Vol. 36. Baltimore, MD: Orton Dyslexia Society, 1986, 154–175.

HERMANN, KNUD. Specific reading disability. *Danish Medical Bulletin*, 1964, *11*, 34–40.

HERR, SELMA E. *Learning activities for reading* (4th ed.). Dubuque, IA: William C. Brown, 1982.

HERRMANN, BETH ANN. Two approaches for helping poor readers become more strategic. *The Reading Teacher*, October 1988, *42*, 24–28.

HICKMAN, JANET. A new perspective on response to literature: Response in an elementary school setting. *Research in the Teaching of English*, December 1981, *15*, 343–354.

HICKMAN, JANET. Classrooms that help children like books. In N. Roser & M. Frith (Eds.), *Children's choices: Teaching with books children like*. Newark, DE: International Reading Association, 1983, 1–11.

HICKMAN, JANET. Children's responses to literature: What happens in the classroom. *Language Arts*, May 1980, *57*, 524–529. Also in A. J. Harris & E. R. Sipay (Eds.), *Readings on reading instruction* (3rd ed.). New York: Longman, 1984, 377–382.

HICKS, CAROLYN. The ITPA visual sequential memory task: An alternative interpretation and implications for good and poor readers. *British Journal of Educational Psychology*, February 1980, *50*, 16–25.

HICKS, CAROLYN, & SPURGEON, P. Two factor analytic studies of dyslexic subtypes. *British Journal of Educational Psychology*, 1982, *52*, 289–300.

HIDI, SUZANNE, & ANDERSON, VALERIE. Producing written summaries: Task demands, cognitive operations, and implications for instruction. *Review of Educational Research*, Winter 1986, *56*, 473–493.

HIDI, SUZANNE, & BAIRD, WILLIAM. Strategies for increasing text-based interest and students' recall of expository texts. *Reading Research Quarterly*, Fall 1988, *23*, 465–483.

HIEBERT, ELFRIEDA H. Developmental patterns and interrelationships of preschool children's print awareness. *Reading Research Quarterly*, 1981, *16*(2), 236–260.

HIEBERT, ELFRIEDA H. An examination of ability grouping in reading instruction. *Reading Research Quarterly*, Winter 1983, *18*, 231–255.

HIEBERT, ELFRIEDA H. Issues related to home influences in young children's print-related development. In D. B. Yaden & S. Templeton (Eds.), *Metalinguistic awareness and beginning literacy*. Portsmouth, NH: Heinemann, 1986, 145–158.

HIEBERT, ELFRIEDA H. The context of instruction and student learning: An examination of Slavin's assumptions. *Review of Educational Research*, Fall 1987, 57, 337–340.

HIER, DANIEL B. Sex differences in hemispheric specialization: Hypothesis for the excess of dyslexia in boys. *Bulletin of the Orton Society*, 1979, 29, 74, 83.

HIER, DANIEL B.; ATKINS, L.; & PERLO, V. P. Learning disorders and sex chromosome aberrations. *Journal of Mental Deficiency Research*, March 1980, 24, 17–26.

HIER, DANIEL, et al. Developmental dyslexia: Evidence for a subgroup with a reverse cerebral asymmetry. *Archives of Neurology*, February 1978, 35, 90–92.

HILDYARD, ANGELA, & OLSON, DAVID P. On the structure and meaning of prose text. In W. Otto & S. White (Eds.), *Reading expository material*. New York: Academic Press, 1982, 155–184.

HILL, CAROL L., & HILL, KENNETH A. Achievement attributions of learning-disabled boys. *Psychological Reports*, December 1982, 51, 979–982.

HILLERICH, ROBERT L. Word lists—Getting it all together. *The Reading Teacher*, January 1974, 27, 353–360.

HILLERICH, ROBERT L. Critical reading for slower learner to gifted (Part I). *Ohio Reading Teacher*, April 1980, 14, 9–12.(a)

HILLERICH, ROBERT L. Critical reading for slower learner to gifted (Part II). *Ohio Reading Teacher*, July 1980, 14, 4–7.(b)

HILLOCKS, GEORGE, JR. *Research on written composition: New directions for teaching*. Urbana, IL: ERIC Clearinghouse on Reading and Communication Skills, 1986.

HILLOCKS, GEORGE, JR., & LUDLOW, LARRY H. A taxonomy of skills in reading and interpretation of fiction. *American Educational Research Journal*, Spring 1984, 21, 7–24.

HILLS, JOHN R. Interpreting grade-equivalent scores. *Educational Measurement: Issues and Practice*, Spring 1983, 2, 15–21.

HINDS, LILLIAN R. Rethinking directions in reading diagnosis, Part III. *Journal of Clinical Reading: Research and Programs*, 1986–1987, 2(1), 1–8.

HINSHELWOOD, JAMES. *Letter, word, and mind-blindness*. London: H. K. Lewis, 1900.

HINSHELWOOD, JAMES. *Congenital word-blindness*. London: H.K. Lewis, 1917.

HISCOCK, MERRILL, & KINSBOURNE, MARCEL. Laterality and dyslexia: A critical review. *Annals of Dyslexia*, Vol. 32. Baltimore, MD: Orton Dyslexia Society, 1982, 178–228.

HISCOCK, MERRILL, & KINSBOURNE, MARCEL. Specialization of the cerebral hemispheres: Implications for learning. *Journal of Learning Disabilities*, March 1987, 20, 130–143.

HITTLEMAN, DANIEL R. Readability, readability formulas and cloze: Selecting instructional materials. *Journal of Reading*, November 1978, 22, 117–122.

HODGES, CAROL A. Toward a broader definition of comprehension instruction. *Reading Research Quarterly*, 1981, 15(2), 299–306.

HODGES, RICHARD E. Language development: The elementary school years. In A. Marquardt (Ed.), *Linguistics in school programs*. 69th Yearbook of the National Society for the Study of Education, Part II. Chicago: University of Chicago Press, 1970, 215–228. Also in A. J. Harris and E. Sipay (Eds.), *Readings on reading instruction* (3rd ed.). New York: Longman, 1984, 59–65.

HODGES, RICHARD E. Research update: On the development of spelling ability. *Language Arts*, March 1982, 59, 284–290.

HOFFMAN, JAMES V. Developing flexibility through ReFlex Action. *The Reading Teacher*, December 1979, 34, 323–329.

HOFFMAN, JAMES V.; O'NEAL, SHARON; & BAKER, CHRISTOPHER. A comparison of inservice and preservice teachers' verbal feedback to student miscues across two difficulty levels of text. In M. Kamil & M. Boswick (Eds.), *Directions in reading: Research and instruction*. Washington, DC: National Reading Conference, 1981, 150–156.

HOFFMAN, JAMES V., et al. Guided oral reading and miscue focused feedback in second-grade classrooms. *Reading Research Quarterly*, Spring 1984, *19*, 367–384.

HOFFMAN, M. S. Early indications of learning problems. *Academic Therapy*, Fall 1971, 7, 23–25.

HOFLER, DONALD B. Word lines: An approach to vocabulary development. *The Reading Teacher*, November 1981, *35*, 216–218.

HOGABOAM, THOMAS W. Reading patterns in eye movement data. In K. Rayner (Ed.), *Eye movements in reading: Perceptual and language processes*. New York: Academic Press, 1983, 309–332.

HOLBOROW, P. L.; BERRY, P.; & ELKINS, J. Prevalence of hyperkinesis: A comparison of three rating scales. *Journal of Learning Disabilities*, August/September 1984, *17*, 411–417.

HOLBROOK, HILARY T. Sex differences in reading: Nature or nuture? *Journal of Reading*, March 1988, *31*, 574–576.

HOLCOMB, WILLIAM R., et al. WISC–R types of learning disabilities: A profile analysis with cross-validation. *Journal of Learning Disabilities*, June/July 1987, *20*, 369–373.

HOLDAWAY, DON. The visual face of experience and language: A metalinguistic excursion. In D. B. Yaden & S. Templeton (Eds.), *Metalinguistic awareness and beginning literacy*. Portsmouth, NH: Heinemann, 1986, 79–97.

HOLDZKOM, DAVID, et al. How communication skill is developed. In D. Holdzkom et al. (Eds.), *Research within reach: Oral and written communication*. St. Louis: CEMREL, 1984, 21–47.

HOLMES, BETTY C. A confirmation strategy for improving poor readers' ability to answer inferential questions. *The Reading Teacher*, November 1983, *37*, 144–147.(a)

HOLMES, BETTY C. The effect of prior knowledge on the question answering of good and poor readers. *Journal of Reading Behavior*, 1983, *15*(4), 1–18.(b)

HOLMES, BETTY C., & ALLISON, ROY W. The effect of four modes of reading on children's comprehension. *Reading Research and Instruction*, Fall 1985, *25*, 9–20.

HOLMES, BETTY C., & ROSER, NANCY L. Five ways to assess readers' prior knowledge. *The Reading Teacher*, March 1987, *40*, 646–49.

HOLMES, C. THOMAS, & MATTHEWS, KENNETH M. The effects of non-promotion on elementary and junior high school pupils: A meta-analysis. *Review of Educational Research*, Summer 1984, *54*, 225–236.

HOLMES, JACK A. The substrata-factor theory of reading: Some experimental evidence. In H. Singer & R. Ruddell (Eds.), *Theoretical models and processes of reading*. Newark, DE: International Reading Association, 1970, 187–197.

HOMAN, SUSAN P. LEA and basals unite! *The Reading Teacher*, March 1983, *36*, 693–694.

HONEL, MILTON F. *The effectiveness of reading expectancy formulas for identifying underachievers*. Unpublished doctoral dissertation, Northern Illinois University, 1973.

HOOD, JOYCE. Is miscue analysis practical for teachers? *The Reading Teacher*, December 1978, *32*, 260–266.

HOOD, JOYCE, & DUBERT, LEE ANN. Decoding as a component of reading comprehension among secondary students. *Journal of Reading Behavior*, 1983, *15*(4), 51–61.

HOOGEVEEN, FRANS, & SMEETS, PAUL M. Establishing phoneme blending in trainable mentally retarded children. *Remedial and Special Education*, 1988, 9(2), 46–53.

HOOPER, STEPHEN R., & HYND, GEORGE W. Performance of normal and dyslexic readers on the Kaufmann Assessment Battery for Children (K-ABC): A discriminant analysis. *Journal of Learning Disabilities*, April 1986, *19*, 206–210.

HOPKINS, CAROL J. Using every-pupil response techniques in reading instruction. *The Reading Teacher*, November 1979, *33*, 173–175.

HOPKINS, LEE BENNETT. *Pass the poetry, please!* (Rev. ed.). New York: Harper & Row, 1987.

HORMANN, ELIZABETH. Children's crisis literature. *Language Arts*, May 1977, *54*, 559–566.

HORN, ALICE. *The uneven distribution of the effects of specific factors.* Southern California Education Monographs, No. 12. Los Angeles: University of Southern California Press, 1941.

HORN, COLLETTE C., & MANIS, FRANKLIN R. Normal and disabled readers' use of orthographic structure in processing print. *Journal of Reading Behavior*, 1985, *14*(2), 143–161.

HORN, JENNIFER L.; O'DONNELL, JAMES P.; & LEICHT, DAVID J. Phonetically inaccurate spelling among learning-disabled, head-injured, and nondisabled young adults. *Brain and Language*, 1988, *33*(1), 55–64.

HORN, WADE F., & PACKARD, THOMAS. Early identification of learning problems: A meta-analysis. *Journal of Educational Psychology*, 1985, *77*(5), 597–607.

HORNE, MARCIA D. Attitudes and learning disabilities: A literature review for school psychologists. *Psychology in the Schools*, January 1982, *19*, 78–85.

HORNE, MARCIA D. *Attitudes toward handicapped students: Professional, peer, and parent reactions.* Hillsdale, NJ: Erlbaum, 1985.

HORNE, MARCIA; POWERS, JAMES; & MAKABUB, PATRICIA. Reader and nonreader conception of the spoken word. *Contemporary Educational Psychology*, October 1983, *8*, 403–418.

HORNER, CATHERINE. *The single-parent family in children's books: An analysis and annotated bibliography with an appendix on audiovisual material.* Metuchen, NJ: Scarecrow, 1978.

HORNICK, ROBERT. Out-of-school television and schooling: Hypotheses and methods. *Review of Educational Research*, Summer 1981, *51*, 193–214.

HORODEZKY, BETTY. Comparative difficulty of beginning reading vocabulary: Set II. *The Alberta Journal of Educational Research*, December 1979, *25*, 259–263.

HOROWITZ, ROSALIND. Text patterns: Part I. *Journal of Reading*, February 1985, *28*, 448–454.(a)

HOROWITZ, ROSALIND. Text patterns: Part II. *Journal of Reading*, February 1985, *28*, 534–541.(b)

HOROWITZ, ROSALIND, & SAMUELS, S. JAY. Reading and listening to expository text. *Journal of Reading Behavior*, 1985, *17*(3), 185–197.

HORWITZ, ROBERT A. Psychological effects of the "open classroom." *Review of Educational Research*, Winter 1979, *49*, 71–86.

HOSKISSON, KENNETH. A response to "A critique of teaching reading as a whole-task venture." *The Reading Teacher*, March 1979, *32*, 653–659.

HOUGH, RUTH A.; NURSS, JOANNE R.; & ENRIGHT, D. SCOTT. Story reading with limited English speaking children in the regular classroom. *The Reading Teacher*, February 1986, *39*, 510–514.

HOWARD, ELIZABETH F. *America as story: Historical fiction for secondary schools.* Chicago: American Library Association, 1988.

HOWE, MARK L.; BRAINERD, CHARLES J.; & KINGSMA, JOHANNES. Storage retrieval processes in normal and learning disabled children: A stages-of-learning analysis of picture-word effects. *Child Development*, August 1985, *56*, 1120–1133.

HOWELL, HELEN. Language, literature, and vocabulary development for gifted students. *The Reading Teacher*, February 1987, *40*, 500–504.

HUBA, MARY E. The relationship between linguistic awareness in prereaders and two types of experimental instruction. *Reading World*, May 1984, *23*, 347–363.

HUCK, CHARLOTTE S. Strategies for improving interest and appreciation in literature. In H. W. Painter (Ed.), *Reaching children and young people through literature*. Newark, DE: International Reading Association, 1971, 37–45.

HUCK, CHARLOTTE S., & HICKMAN, JANET. *Children's literature in the elementary school* (4th ed.). New York: Holt, Rinehart and Winston, 1987.

HUEY, EDMUND B. *The psychology and pedagogy of reading*. New York: Macmillan, 1908. Reprinted by MIT Press, Cambridge, MA, 1968.

HUGGINS, A. W. F., & ADAMS, MARILYN J. Syntactic aspects of reading comprehension. In R. Spiro et al. (Eds.), *Theoretical issues in reading comprehension*. Hillsdale, NJ: Erlbaum, 1980, 87–112.

HUGHES, JOHN R. Electroencephalography and learning disabilities. In H. R. Myklebust (Ed.), *Progress in learning disabilities*, Vol. II. New York: Grune & Stratton, 1971, 18–55.

HUGHES, JOHN R. The electroencephalogram and reading disorders. In R. Malatesha & P. Aaron (Eds.), *Reading disorders: Varieties and treatments*. New York: Academic Press, 1982, 233–253.

HUGHES, JOHN R. Evaluation of electrophysiological studies on dyslexia. In D. B. Gray & J. F. Kavanagh (Eds.), *Biobehavioral measures of dyslexia*. Parkton, MD: York Press, 1985, 71–86.

HUGHES, SONDRA. Finding good literature to supplement contemporary instruction: Bibliographic sources. *The Reading Teacher*, February 1987, *40*, 568–569.

HULME, CHARLES. The effects of manual tracing on memory in normal and retarded readers: Some implications for multi-sensory teaching. *Psychological Research* (Developmental Dyslexia Issue), 1981, *43*, 179–191.(a)

HULME, CHARLES. *Reading retardation and multi-sensory teaching*. Boston: Routledge & Kegan Paul, 1981.(b)

HUMPHREYS, GLYN W., & EVETT, LINDSAY G. Are there independent lexical and nonlexical routes in word processing? An evaluation of the dual-route theory of reading. *The Behavioral and Brain Sciences*, December 1985, 8, 689–740.

HUNT, LYMAN C. Six steps to the individualized reading program (IRP). *Elementary English*, January 1971, *48*, 27–32. Also in A. J. Harris and E. Sipay (Eds.), *Readings on reading instruction* (3rd ed.). New York: Longman, 1984, 190–195.

HUUS, HELEN. Approaches to the use of literature in the reading program. In B. Schulwitz (Ed.), *Teachers, tangibles, techniques: Comprehension of content in reading*. Newark, DE: International Reading Association, 1975, 140–149. Also in A. J. Harris and E. Sipay (Eds.), *Readings on reading instruction* (3rd ed.). New York: Longman, 1984, 363–368.

HUUS, HELEN. A new look at children's interests. In J. Shapiro (Ed.), *Using literature and poetry effectively*. Newark, DE: International Reading Association, 1979, 37–45.

HYMES, JAMES L., JR. *Before the child reads*. New York: Harper & Row, 1958.

HYND, GEORGE W., & HYND, CYNTHIA R. Dyslexia: Neuroanatomical/ neurolinguistic perspectives. *Reading Research Quarterly*, Summer 1984, *19*, 482–498.

HYSLOP, NANCY B., & TONE, BRUCE. Listening: Are we teaching it, and if so, how? *ERIC Digest*, No. 3, 1988.

IDOL, LORNA. Group story mapping: A comprehension strategy for both skilled and unskilled readers. *Journal of Learning Disabilities*, April 1987, *20*, 196–205.

IDOL, LORNA; WEST, J. FREDERICK; & LLOYD, SANDRA R. Organizing and implementing specialized reading programs: A collaborative approach involving classroom, remedial, and special education teachers. *Remedial and Special Education*, 1988, 9(2), 54–61.

ILG, FRANCIS L., & AMES, LOUISE B. *School readiness: Behavior tests used at the Gesell Institute*. New York: Harper & Row, 1964.

INDRISANO, ROSELMINA. An ecological approach to learning. *Topics in Learning & Learning Disabilities*, January 1982, *1*, 11–15.

INGRAM, T.T. S. The nature of dyslexia. *Bulletin of the Orton Society*, 1969, *19*, 18–50.

INGRAM, T. T. S.; MASON, A. W; & BLACKBURN, I. A retrospective study of 82 children with reading disability. *Developmental Medicine & Child Neurology*, June 1970, *12*, 271–281.

INGRAM, T. T. S., & REID, JESSIE F. Developmental aphasia observed in a department of child psychiatry. *Archives of Diseases in Childhood*, 1956, *31*, 131.

INTERNATIONAL READING ASSOCIATION. A position on minimum competencies in reading. *The Reading Teacher*, October 1979, *33*, 54–55.

INTERNATIONAL READING ASSOCIATION. Checklist for evaluating adult basic education reading material. *Journal of Reading*, May 1981, *24*, 701–706.

INTERNATIONAL READING ASSOCIATION. Courts should not make reading policy. *Journal of Reading*, May 1982, 25, 785.

INTERNATIONAL READING ASSOCIATION. *Guidelines for the specialized preparation of Reading Professionals*. Newark, DE: International Reading Association, April 1986.(a)

INTERNATIONAL READING ASSOCIATION. Joint statement on literacy development and prefirst grade. *The Reading Teacher*, April 1986, 39, 819–821.(b)

INTERNATIONAL READING ASSOCIATION. IRA stands against censorship. *Reading Today*, February/March 1989, *6*, 26.

IRVIN, JUDITH L., & CONNORS, NEILA A. Reading instruction in middle level schools: Results of a U.S. Survey. *Journal of Reading*, January 1989, *32*, 306–311.

IRVIN, JUDITH L., & LYNCH-BROWN, CAROL. A national survey of U.S. university reading clinics: Clientele, functions, and tests. *Journal of Reading*, February 1988, *31*, 336–342.

IRWIN, JUDITH W., & DAVIS, CAROL A. Assessing readability: The checklist approach. *Journal of Reading*, November 1980, *24*, 124–130.

IRWIN, PIA., & MITCHELL, JUDY N. A procedure for assessing the richness of retellings. *Journal of Reading*, February 1983, *26*, 391–396. Also in W. Harker (Ed.), *Classroom strategies for secondary reading*. Newark, DE: International Reading Association, 1985, 10–16.

ITO, H. RICHARD. Long-term effects of resource room programs on learning disabled children's reading. *Journal of Learning Disabilities*, June/July 1980, *13*, 322–326.

JACKSON, GREGG B. The research evidence on the effects of grade retention. *Review of Educational Research*, Fall 1975, *45*, 613–635.

JACOBS, JANIS E., & PARIS, SCOTT G. Children's metacognition about reading: Issues in definition, measurement and instruction. *Educational Psychologist*, Summer and Fall 1987, *22*, 255–278.

JACOBS, LELAND. Poetry books for poetry reading. *The Reading Teacher*, 1959, *13*, 45–48.

JACOBWITZ, TINA, & HAUPT, EDWARD J. Retrieval speed in reading comprehension: Failure to generalize. In J. A. Niles & L. A. Harris (Eds.), *Changing perspectives on research in reading/language processing and instruction*. Rochester, NY: National Reading Conference, 1984, 241–246.

JAGGAR, ANGELA M., & HARWOOD, KATHY T. Suggested reading list: Whole language theory, practice, and assessment. In G. S. Pinnell & M. L. Matlin (Eds.), *Teachers and research: Language learning in the classroom.* Newark, DE: International Reading Association, 1989, 142–177.

JALONGO, MARY R., & RENCK, MELLISA ANN. Children's literature and the child's adjustment to school. *The Reading Teacher*, March 1987, *40*, 616–621.

JANIAK, RICHARD. Listening/reading: An effective learning combination. *Academic Therapy*, November 1983, *19*, 205–211.

JANICKE, EUGENE M. Massive oral decoding. *Academic Therapy*, November 1981, *17*, 157–161.

JANIUK, DELORES M., & SHANAHAN, TIMOTHY. Applying adult literacy practices in primary grade instruction. *The Reading Teacher*, May 1988, *41*, 880–886.

JANSEN, MOGENS, et al. Special education in Denmark. In L. Tarnopol & M. Tarnopol (Eds.), *Reading disabilities: An international perspective.* Baltimore: University Park Press, 1976, 155–174.

JANSKY, JEANETTE, & DE HIRSCH, KATRINA. *Preventing reading failure: Prediction, diagnosis, intervention.* New York: Harper & Row, 1972.

JASON, MARTIN H., & DUBNOW, BEATRICE. The relationship between self-perceptions of reading abilities and reading achievement. In W. H. MacGinitie (Ed.), *Assessment problems in reading.* Newark, DE: International Reading Association, 1973, 96–100.

JENKINS, JOSEPH R., & DIXON, ROBERT. Vocabulary learning. *Contemporary Educational Psychology*, July 1983, 8, 237–260.

JENKINS, JOSEPH R., & HEINEN, AMY. Students' preferences for service delivery: Pull-out, in-class, or integrated models. *Exceptional Children*, April 1989, *55*, 516–523.

JENKINS, JOSEPH R.; MATLOCK, BARBARA; & SLOCUM, TIMOTHY A. Two approaches to vocabulary instruction: The teaching of individual word meanings and practice in deriving word meaning from context. *Reading Research Quarterly*, Spring 1989, *24*, 215–235.

JENKINS, JOSEPH R., & PANY, DARLENE. Instructional variables in reading comprehension. In J. Guthrie (Ed.), *Comprehension and teaching: Research reviews.* Newark, DE: International Reading Association, 1981, 163–202.

JENKINS, JOSEPH R., et al. Improving reading comprehension by using paragraph restatements. *Exceptional Children*, September 1987, *54*, 54–59.

JENKINSON, EDWARD B. *Forty targets of the textbook protesters.* 1980. (ERIC number ED 199 716.)

JETT-SIMPSON, MARY. The classroom teacher as an action researcher: Changing the basal reader period. *Wisconsin State Reading Association Journal*, Spring 1986, *30*, 67–72.

JOBE, FRED W. *Screening vision in schools.* Newark, DE: International Reading Association, 1976.

JOHN, ROY E. Neurometric evaluation of brain dysfunction related to learning disorders. *Acta Neurological Scandinavia* (Supplement 89), 1981, *64*, 87–98.

JOHNS, JERRY L. What do inner city children prefer to read? *The Reading Teacher*, February 1973, *26*, 462–467.

JOHNS, JERRY L. Some comparisons between the Dolch Sight Vocabulary and the Word List for the 1970's. *Reading World*, March 1976, *15*, 144–150.

JOHNS, JERRY L. First graders' concepts about print. *Reading Research Quarterly*, 1980, *15*(4), 529–549.(a)

JOHNS, JERRY L. The growth of children's knowledge about spoken words. *Reading Psychology*, Spring 1980, *1*, 103–110.(b)

JOHNS, JERRY L. The development of the Revised Dolch List. *Illinois School Research and Development*, Spring 1981, *17*, 15–24.

JOHNS, JERRY L. Students' perception of reading: Thirty years of inquiry. In D. B. Yaden & S. Templeton (Eds.), *Metalinguistic awareness and beginning literacy*. Portsmouth, NH: Heinemann, 1986, 31–40.

JOHNS, JERRY L., & LUNN, MARY K. The informal reading inventory: 1910–1980. *Reading World*, October 1983, *23*, 8–19.

JOHNS, JERRY L., & WHEAT, THOMAS E. Newspaper readability: Two crucial factors. *Journal of Reading*, February 1984, *27*, 432–434.

JOHNSON, CAROLE S., & GREENBAUM, GLORIA R. Are boys disabled readers due to sex-role stereotyping? *Educational Leadership*, March 1980, *37*, 492–496.

JOHNSON, CAROLE S., & GREENBAUM, GLORIA R. Girls' and boys' reading interests: A review of the research. In E. Sheridan (Ed.), *Sex stereotypes and reading: Research and strategies*. Newark, DE: International Reading Association, 1982, 35–48.

JOHNSON, DALE D., & JOHNSON, BONNIE V. Highlighting vocabulary in inferential comprehension instruction. *Journal of Reading*, April 1986, *29*, 622–625.

JOHNSON, DALE D.; MOE, ALDEN J.; & BAUMANN, JAMES F. *The Ginn word book for teachers: A basic lexicon*. Columbus, OH: Ginn, 1983.

JOHNSON, DALE D., & PEARSON, P. DAVID. *Teaching reading vocabulary* (2nd ed.). New York: Holt, Rinehart and Winston, 1984.

JOHNSON, DALE D.; PITTLEMAN, SUSAN D.; & HEIMLICH, JOAN E. Semantic mapping. *The Reading Teacher*, April 1986, *39*, 778–783.

JOHNSON, DORIS J. Process deficits in learning disabled children and implications for reading. In L. Resnick & P. Weaver (Eds.), *Theory and practice in early reading*, Vol. 2, Hillsdale, NJ: Erlbaum, 1979, 207–227.

JOHNSON, DORIS J., & MYKLEBUST, HELMER R. *Learning disabilities: Educational principles and practices*. New York: Grune & Stratton, 1967.

JOHNSON, LINDA L. Effects of underlining textbook sentences on passage and sentence retention. *Reading Research and Instruction*, Fall 1988, *28*, 18–32.

JOHNSON, MARJORIE S.; KRESS, ROY A.; & PIKULSKI, JOHN J. *Informal reading inventories* (2nd ed.). Newark, DE: International Reading Association, 1987.

JOHNSON, NEAL F. Integration processes in word recognition. In O. Tzeng & H. Singer (Eds.), *Perception of print: Reading research in experimental psychology*. Hillsdale, NJ: Erlbaum, 1981, 29–63.

JOHNSON, RONALD J.; JOHNSON, KAREN L.; & KERFOOT, JAMES F. A massive decoding technique. *The Reading Teacher*, February 1972, *25*, 421–423.

JOHNSON, TERRY; MAYFIELD, MARGIE; & QUORM, KERRY. Organizing for instruction: Exploring different models of reading instruction. In L. Ollila (Ed.), *Handbook for administrators and teachers: Reading in the kindergarten*. Newark, DE: International Reading Association, 1980, 68–84.

JOHNSTON, JAMES C. Understanding word perception: Clues from studying the word-superiority effect. In O. Tzeng & H. Singer (Eds.), *Perception of print: Reading research in experimental psychology*. Hillsdale, NJ: Erlbaum, 1981, 65–84.

JOHNSTON, PETER. *Implications of basic research for the assessment of reading comprehension*. Technical Report No. 206. Champaign, IL: Center for the Study of Reading, University of Illinois, May 1981.

JOHNSTON, PETER. *Reading comprehension assessment: A cognitive basis*. Newark, DE: International Reading Association, 1983.

JOHNSTON, PETER H. Understanding reading disability: A case study approach. *Harvard Educational Review*, May 1985, *55*, 153–177.

JOHNSTON, PETER, & AFFLERBACH, PETER. Measuring teacher and student change in a remedial reading class. In J. Niles & L. A. Harris (Eds.), *Searches for meaning in reading/ language processing and instruction*. Rochester, NY: National Reading Conference, 1983, 304–312.

JOHNSTON, PETER; ALLINGTON, RICHARD; & AFFLERBACH, PETER. The congruence of classroom and remedial instruction. *Elementary School Journal*, March 1985, 85, 465–477.

JOHNSTON, PETER, & PEARSON, P. DAVID. Assessment: Responses to exposition. In A. Berger & H. A. Robinson (Eds.), *Secondary school reading: What research reveals for classroom practice*. Urbana, IL: ERIC/RCS, 1982, 127–141.

JOHNSTON, PETER H., & WINOGRAD, PETER N. Passive failure in reading. *Journal of Reading Behavior*, 1985, 17(4), 279–301.

JOHNSTON, WILLIAM R. Light on heteronyms. *Journal of Reading Behavior*, March 1988, 31, 570–573.

JOLLY, HAYDEN B., JR. Teaching basic function words. *The Reading Teacher*, November 1981, 35, 136–140. Also in A. J. Harris & E. Sipay (Eds.), *Readings on reading instruction* (3rd ed.). New York: Longman, 1984, 215–219.

JONES, B. F.; AMIRAN, M.; & KATIMS, M. Teaching cognitive strategies and text structures within language arts programs. In J. W. Segal et al. (Eds.), *Thinking and learning skills*, Vol. 1. Hillsdale, NJ: Erlbaum, 1985, 259–297.

JONES, KATHRYN M; TORGESEN, JOSEPH K.; & SEXTON, MOLLY A. Using computer guided practice to increase decoding fluency in learning disabled children: A study using the Hint and Hint I program. *Journal of Learning Disabilities*, February 1987, 20, 122–128.

JONGSMA, EUGENE A. *Cloze instruction research: A second look*. Newark, DE: International Reading Association and ERIC/RCS, 1980.

JONGSMA, EUGENE. Homework: Is it worthwhile? *The Reading Teacher*, March 1985, 38, 702–704.

JORDAN, WILLIAM C. Prime-O-Tec: The new reading method. *Academic Therapy Quarterly*, Summer 1967, 2, 248–250.

JORGENSON, GERALD W. An analysis of teacher judgments of reading levels. *American Educational Research Journal*, Winter 1975, 12, 67–75.

JORM, ANTHONY F. Effect of word imagery on reading performance as a function of reading ability. *Journal of Educational Psychology*, February 1977, 69, 46–54.

JORM, ANTHONY F. The cognitive and neurological basis of developmental dyslexia. A theoretical framework and review. *Cognition*, March 1979, 7, 19–33.

JORM, ANTHONY F., et al. Behavior problems in specific reading retarded and general reading backward children. *Journal of Child Psychology and Psychiatry*, 1986, 27(1), 33–43.

JOSE, PAUL E., & BREWER, WILLIAM F. *The development of story liking: Character identification, suspense and outcome resolution*. Technical Report No. 219. Champaign, IL: Center for the Study of Reading, University of Illinois, October 1983.

JUEL, CONNIE. The development and use of mediated word identification. *Reading Research Quarterly*, Spring 1983, 18, 306–327.

JUEL, CONNIE. Support for the theory of phonemic awareness as a predictor of literacy acquisition. In J. Niles & R. V. Lalik (Eds.), *Solving problems in literacy: Learners, teachers and researchers*. Rochester, NY: National Reading Conference, 1986, 239–243.

JUEL, CONNIE. *Learning to read and write: A longitudinal study of fifty-four children from first through fourth grade*. Paper presented at the annual American Educational Research Association Conference. Austin, TX, 1988.

JUEL, CONNIE; GRIFFITH, PRISCILLA L.; & GOUGH, PHILIP B. Reading and spelling strategies of first-grade children. In J. A. Niles & R. V. Lalik (Eds.), *Issues in literacy: A research perspective*. Rochester, NY: National Reading Conference, 1985, 306–309.

JUEL, CONNIE, & HOLMES, BETTY. Oral and silent reading of sentences. *Reading Research Quarterly*, 1981, 16(4), 545–568.

JUEL, CONNIE, & LEAVELL, JUDY A. Retention and nonretention of at-risk readers in first grade and their subsequent reading achievement. *Journal of Learning Disabilities*, November 1988, *21*, 570–580.

JUEL, CONNIE, & ROPER-SCHNEIDER, DIANE. The influence of basal readers on first grade learning. *Reading Research Quarterly*, Winter 1985, *20*, 134–152.

JUST, MARCEL A., & CARPENTER, PATRICIA A. A theory of reading: From eye fixations to comprehension. In H. Singer & R. B. Ruddell (Eds.), *Theoretical models and processes of reading*, (3rd ed.). Newark, DE: International Reading Association, 1985, 174–208.

JUST, MARCEL A. & CARPENTER, PATRICIA A. *The psychology of reading and language comprehension*. Boston: Allyn & Bacon, 1987.

KACHUK, BEATRICE. Relative clauses may cause confusion for young readers. *The Reading Teacher*, January 1981, *34*, 372–377.

KAGAN, JEROME. Reflection-impulsivity and reading abilities in primary grade children. *Child Development*, 1965, *36*, 609–628.

KAMEENUI, EDWARD J.; DIXON, ROBERT C.; & CARNINE, DOUGLAS W. Issues in the design of vocabulary instruction. In M. E. McKeown & M. E. Curtis (Eds.), *The nature of vocabulary acquisition*. Hillsdale, NJ: Erlbaum, 1987, 129–145.

KAMIL, MICHAEL L. Research revisited: Early word recognition studies. *Reading Psychology*, Spring 1980, *1*, 133–136.

KAMMERLOHR, BARBARA; HENDERSON, ROBERT A.; & ROCK, STEVE. Special education due process in Illinois. *Exceptional Children*, February 1983, *49*, 417–422.

KANN, ROBERT. The method of repeated readings: Expanding the neurological impress method for use with disabled readers. *Journal of Learning Disabilities*, February 1983, *16*, 90–92.

KAPELIS, LIA. Early identification of reading failure: A comparison of two screening tests and teacher forecasts. *Journal of Learning Disabilities*, December 1975, *8*, 638–641.

KAPINUS, BARBARA; GAMBRELL, LINDA B.; & KOSKINEN, PATRICIA. Effects of practice in retelling upon the reading comprehension of proficient and less proficient readers. In J. E. Readence et al. (Eds.), *Research in literacy: Merging perspectives*. Rochester, NY: National Reading Conference, 1987, 135–141.

KARWEIT, NANCY L. *Time-on-task: A research review*. Report No. 332. Baltimore: Center for Social Organization of Schools, Johns Hopkins University, January 1983.

KARWEIT, NANCY, & SLAVIN, ROBERT E. Measurement and modeling choices in studies of time and learning. *American Educational Research Journal*, Summer 1981, *18*, 157–171.

KASDON, LAWRENCE M. Some problems in dealing with gain scores. *Reading World*, March 1977, *16*, 178–187.

KATZ, BILL (Ed.). *Magazines for school libraries*. New York: R. R. Bowker, 1987.

KATZ, LEONARD, & FELDMAN, LAURIE B. Linguistic coding in word recognition: Comparisons between a deep and a shallow orthography. In A. Lesgold & C. Perfetti (Eds.), *Interactive processes in reading*. Hillsdale, NJ: Erlbaum, 1981, 85–105.

KAUFFMAN, JAMES M.; GERBER, MICHAEL M.; & SEMMEL, MELVYN I. Arguable assumptions underlying the regular education initiative. *Journal of Learning Disabilities*, January 1988, *21*, 6–11.

KAUFMAN, ALAN S. A new approach to the interpretation of test scatter on the WISC-R. *Journal of Learning Disabilities*, March 1976, *9*, 160–168.

KAUFMAN, ALAN S. The WISC-R and learning disabilities assessment: State of the art. *Journal of Learning Disabilities*, November 1981, *14*, 520–526.

KAVALE, KENNETH. Auditory-visual integration and its relationship to reading achievement: A meta-analysis. *Perceptual & Motor Skills*, December 1980, *51*, 947–955.

KAVALE, KENNETH. Functions of the Illinois Test of Psycholinguistic Abilities (ITPA): Are they trainable? *Exceptional Children*, April 1981, *47*, 496–510.(a)

KAVALE, KENNETH. The relationship between auditory perceptual skills and reading ability: A meta-analysis. *Journal of Learning Disabilities*, November 1981, *14*, 539–546.(b)

KAVALE, KENNETH. The efficacy of stimulant drug treatment for hyperactivity: A meta-analysis. *Journal of Learning Disabilities*, May 1982, *15*, 280–289.(a)

KAVALE, KENNETH. Meta-analysis of the relationship between visual perceptual skills and reading achievement. *Journal of Learning Disabilities*, January 1982, *15*, 42–51.(b)

KAVALE, KENNETH A. A meta-analytic evaluation of the Frostig training program. *Exceptional Children*, July 1984, *31*, 131–141.

KAVALE, KENNETH A., & FORNESS, STEVEN R. Learning disability and the history of science: Paradigm or paradox? *Remedial and Special Education*, July/August 1985, *6*, 12–23.(a)

KAVALE, KENNETH A., & FORNESS, STEVEN R. *The science of learning disabilities*. San Diego, CA: College-Hill Press, 1985.(b)

KAVALE, KENNETH A., & FORNESS, STEVEN R. School learning time and learning disabilities: The disassociated learner. *Journal of Learning Disabilities*, March 1986, *19*, 130–138.

KAVALE, KENNETH A., & FORNESS, STEVEN R. The far side of heterogeneity: A critical analysis of empirical subtyping research in learning disabilities. *Journal of Learning Disabilities*, June/July 1987, *20*, 374–382.(a)

KAVALE, KENNETH A., & FORNESS, STEVEN R. Substance over style: Assessing the efficacy of modality testing and teaching. *Exceptional Children*, November 1987, *54*, 228–239.(b)

KAVALE, KENNETH, & MATTSON, P. DENNIS. "One jumped off the balance beam": Meta-analysis of perceptual-motor training. *Journal of Learning Disabilities*, March 1983, *16*, 165–173.

KAVALE, KENNETH A., & NYE, CHAD. Parameters of learning disabilities in achievement, linguistic, neuro-psychological and social/behavioral domains. *Journal of Special Education*, 1986, *19*(4), 443–458.

KAWI, A. A., & PASAMANICK, B. Association factors of pregnancy with reading disorders of childhood. *Journal of the American Medical Association*, 1958, *166*, 1420–1423.

KAYE, PEGGY. *Games for reading: Playful ways to help your child to read*. New York: Pantheon Books, 1988.

KAYE, STANLEY. Psychoanalytic perspectives on learning disability. *Journal of Contemporary Psychotherapy*, Spring/Summer 1982, *13*, 83–93.

KAZDIN, ALAN E., & BOOTZIN, RICHARD R. The token economy: An evaluative review. *Journal of Applied Behavioral Analysis*, Fall 1972, 5, 343–372.

KEEFE, BARBARA, & SWINNEY, DAVID. On the relationship of hemispheric specialization and developmental dyslexia. *Cortex*, 1979, *15*, 471–481.

KEILITZ, INGO, & DUNIVANT, NOEL. The relationship betwen learning disability and juvenile delinquency: Current state of knowledge. *Remedial and Special Education*, May/June 1986, 7, 18–26.

KELLAM, SHEPPARD G., & SCHIFF, SHELDON K. Effects of family life on children's adaptation to first grade. *American Journal of Orthopsychiatry*, March 1969, *39*, 276–278.

KEMPER, SUSAN. Inferential complexity and the readability of texts. In A. Davison & G. M. Green (Eds.), *Linguistic complexity and text comprehension: Readability issues reconsidered*. Hillsdale, NJ: Erlbaum, 1988, 141–165.

KENNEDY, KEITH. Determining readability with a microcomputer. *Curriculum Review*, November/December 1985, *25*, 40–42.

KEOGH, BARBARA K. The Bender Gestalt with children: Research implications. *Journal of Special Education*, 1961, *3*, 15–22.

KEOGH, BARBARA K. Hyperactivity and learning problems: Implications for teachers. *Academic Therapy*, Fall 1971, 7, 47–50.

KEOGH, BARBARA K. Future of the LD field: Research and practice. *Journal of Learning Disabilities*, October 1986, 19, 455–460.

KEOGH, BARBARA K., & DONLON, GENEVIEVE, M. Field dependence, impulsivity and learning disabilities. *Journal of Learning Disabilities*, June 1972, 5, 331–336.

KEOGH, BARBARA K., & GLOVER, ANNE T. The generality and durability of cognitive training effects. *Exceptional Children Quarterly*, May 1980, 1, 75–82.

KEOGH, BARBARA K., & PELLAND, MICHELLE. Vision training revisited. *Journal of Learning Disabilities*, April 1985, 18, 228–236.

KEPHART, NEWELL C. *The slow learner in the classroom*. Columbus, OH: Charles E. Merrill, 1960.

KERSHNER, JOHN R. Laterality and learning disabilities: Cerebral dominance as a cognitive process. *Topics in Learning & Learning Disabilities*, April 1983, 3, 66–74.

KIBBY, MICHAEL W. The effects of certain instructional conditions and response modes on initial word learning. *Reading Research Quarterly*, 1979, 15(1), 147–171.(a)

KIBBY, MICHAEL W. Passage readability affects the oral reading strategies of disabled readers. *The Reading Teacher*, January 1979, 32, 390–396.(b)

KIES, COSETTE. *Supernatural fiction for teens: 500 good paperbacks to read for wonderment, fear, and fun*. Englewood, CO: Libraries Unlimited, 1987.

KILTY, TED K. *The readability of commonly encountered materials*. Mimeographed. Western Michigan University, Kalamazoo, Michigan, 1976.

KIMMEL, SUSAN, & MacGINITIE, WALTER H. Identifying children who use a perseverative processing strategy. *Reading Research Quarterly*, Winter 1984, 19, 162–172.

KIMMEL, SUSAN, & MacGINITIE, WALTER H. Helping students revise hypotheses while reading. *The Reading Teacher*, April 1985, 38, 768–771.

KING, R. TOMMY. Learning from a PAL. *The Reading Teacher*, March 1982, 35, 682–685.

KINSBOURNE, MARCEL. Models of learning disability. *Topics in Learning & Learning Disabilities*, April 1983, 3, 1–13.

KINSBOURNE, MARCEL, & CAPLAN, PAULA J. *Children's learning and attention problems*. Boston: Little, Brown, 1979.

KINSBOURNE, MARCEL, & WARRINGTON, ELIZABETH K. Developmental factors in reading and writing backwardness. In J. Money (Ed.), *The disabled reader*. Baltimore: Johns Hopkins University Press, 1966, 59–71.

KIRBY, JOHN R., & ROBINSON, GREGORY L. W. Simultaneous and successive processing in reading disabled children. *Journal of Learning Disabilities*, April 1987, 20, 243–252.

KIRBY, KIMBERLY; HOLBORN, STEPHEN W.; & BUSHBY, HARRY T. Word game bingo: A behavioral treatment package for improving textual responding to sight words. *Journal of Applied Behavior Analysis*, Fall 1981, 14, 317–326.

KIRK, SAMUEL A., & KIRK, WINIFRED. On defining learning disabilities. *Journal of Learning Disabilities*, January 1983, 16, 20–21.

KIRK, URSALA. Introduction: Toward our understanding of the neuropsychology of language, reading, and spelling. In U. Kirk (Ed.), *Neuropsychology of language, reading, and spelling*. New York: Academic Press, 1983, 3–31.

KIRSCH, DOROTHY. From athletes to zebras—young children want to read about them. *Elementary English*, January 1975, 52, 73–78.

KIRSCH, DOROTHY I.; PEHRSSON, ROBERT S. V.; & ROBINSON, H. ALAN. Expressed reading interests of young children: An international study. In J. E. Merritt (Ed.), *New horizons in reading*. Newark, DE: International Reading Association, 1976, 302–317.

KIRSCH, IRWIN S., & JUNGEBLUT, ANN. *Literacy: Profiles of America's young adults*. Report No. 16-PL-02. Princeton, NJ: Educational Testing Service, 1986.

KLANDERMAN, JOHN W.; PERNEY, JAN; & KROESCHELL, ZEPHYRINE B. Comparisons of K-

ABC and WISC-R for LD children. *Journal of Learning Disabilities*, November 1985, *18*, 524–527.

KLARE, GEORGE R. Assessing readability. *Reading Research Quarterly*, 1974–1975, *10*(1), 62–102.

KLARE, GEORGE R. A second look at the validity of readability formulas. *Journal of Reading Behavior*, Summer 1976, *8*, 129–152.

KLARE, GEORGE R. Readability. In P. D. Pearson (Ed.), *Handbook of reading research*. New York: Longman, 1984, 681–744.

KLARE, GEORGE R. The formative years. In B. L. Zakaluk & S. J. Samuels (Eds.), *Readability: Its past, present & future*. Newark, DE: International Reading Association, 1988, 14–34.

KLASEN, EDITH. *The syndrome of specific dyslexia: With special consideration of its physiological, psychological, test psychological and social correlates*. Baltimore: University Park Press, 1972.

KLASEN, EDITH. Learning disabilities: The German perspective. In L. Tarnopol & M. Tarnopol (Eds.), *Reading disability: An international perspective*. Baltimore: University Park Press, 1976, 179–191.

KLAUER, KARL J. Intentional and incidental learning with instructional texts: A meta-analysis for 1970–1980. *American Educational Research Journal*, Summer 1984, *21*, 323–339.

KLAUSMEIER, HERBERT J.; SORENSON, JUANITA S.; & QUILLING, MARY. Instructional programming for the individual pupil in the multi-unit school. *Elementary School Journal*, November 1971, *72*, 88–101.

KLEIMAN, GLENN M. *Comparing good and poor readers: A critique of the research*. Technical Report No. 246. Champaign, IL: Center for the Study of Reading, University of Illinois, June 1982.

KLEIMAN, GLENN M., & HUMPHREY, MARY M. *Phonological representations in visual word recognition: The adjunct access model*. Technical Report No. 247. Champaign, IL: Center for the Study of Reading, University of Illinois, June 1982.

KLEINBERG, NORMAN M. *Tachistoscopic vs. pseudo-tachistoscopic training and the Hawthorne effect in improving reading achievement*. Unpublished doctoral dissertation, Columbia University, 1970.

KLIEGL, REINHOLD; OLSON, RICHARD K.; & DAVIDSON, BRIAN J. On problems of confounding perceptual and language processes. In K. Rayner (Ed.), *Eye movements in reading: Perceptual and language processes*. New York: Academic Press, 1983, 333–343.

KLINE, CARL L., & KLINE, CAROLYN L. Follow-up study of 216 dyslexic children. *Bulletin of the Orton Society*, 1975, *25*, 127–144.

KLOEFKORN, MERRILLYN B. Teachers' choices 1987. *Language Arts*, October 1988, *65*, 606–607.

KNOWLES, B. A. Behavior modification and special education. *Slow Learning Child*, November 1970, *17*, 170–177.

KOBASIGAWA, AKIRA; RANSOM, CHRISTINE; & HOLLAND, CORNELIUS. Children's knowledge about skimming. *Alberta Journal of Educational Research*, September 1980, *26*, 169–182.

KOENKE, KARL. Test wiseness: Programs and problems. *Journal of Reading*, February 1988, *31*, 480–483.

KOEPSEL, ERWIN O. *A comparison of teaching reading to educationally handicapped children using Fernald's VAKT method, Blau's AKT method, and existing methods*. Unpublished doctoral dissertation, University of Colorado, 1974.

KOFFLER, STEPHEN L. A comparison of approaches for setting proficiency. *Journal of Educational Measurement*, Fall 1980, *17*, 167–178.

KONOPAK, BONNIE. Eighth graders' vocabulary learning from inconsiderate and considerate text. *Reading Research and Instruction*, Summer, 1988, *27*, 1–14.(a)

KONOPAK, BONNIE C. Effects of inconsiderate vs. considerate text on secondary students' vocabulary learning. *Journal of Reading Behavior*, 1988, *20*(1), 25–41.(b)

KONOPAK, BONNIE C., & WILLIAMS, NANCY L. Using the keyword method to help young readers learn content material. *The Reading Teacher*, March 1988, *41*, 682–687.

KOPPITZ, ELIZABETH M. *The Bender-Gestalt Test for young children*. New York: Grune & Stratton, 1964.

KOŠČ, LADISLAV. Learning disabilities: Definition or specification? A response to Kavale and Forness. *Remedial and Special Education*, January/February 1987, *8*, 36–41.

KOSKINEN, PATRICIA S., & BLUM, IRENE H. Paired repeated reading: A classroom strategy for developing fluent reading. *The Reading Teacher*, October 1986, *40*, 70–75.

KOSKINEN, PATRICIA, & WILSON, ROBERT M. *Have you read any good TV lately? A guide for using captioned television in the teaching of reading*. Falls Church, VA: National Captioning Institute, 1987.

KOSKINEN, PATRICIA, et al. Using closed captioned television to enhance reading skills of learning disabled students. In J. A. Niles & R. V. Lalik (Eds.), *Solving problems in literacy: Learners, teachers, and researchers*. Rochester, NY: National Reading Conference, 1986, 61–65.

KOSKINEN, PATRICIA, et al. Retelling: A strategy for enhancing students' reading comprehension. *The Reading Teacher*, May 1988, *41*, 892–896.

KOSSACK, SHARON, & HOFFMAN, EDWINA. A picture's worth a thousand words: Comprehension processing via the comics. *Journal of Reading*, November 1987, *31*, 174–176.

KREESE, ELAINE C. Using reading as a thinking process to solve math story problems. *Journal of Reading*, April 1984, *27*, 598–601.

KREMIN, HELGARD. Alexia: Theory and research. In R. N. Malatesha & P. Aaron (Eds.), *Reading disorders: Varieties and treatments*. New York: Academic Press, 1982, 341–367.

KRESS, ROY A., & JOHNSON, MARJORIE S. Martin. In A. J. Harris (Ed.), *Casebook on reading disability*. New York: David McKay, 1970, 1–24.

KRETSCHMER, JOSEPH C. Computerizing and comparing the Rix readability index. *Journal of Reading*, March 1984, *27*, 490–499.

KRIPPNER, STANLEY. Hypnosis as verbal programming in educational therapy. *Academic Therapy*, Fall 1971, *7*, 5–12.

KRONICK, DOREEN. *Three families*. San Rafael, CA: Academic Therapy Publications, 1976.

KRUPSKI, ANTOINETTE. Attention problems in youngsters with learning handicaps. In J. K. Torgesen & B. Y. L. Wong (Eds.), *Psychological and educational perspectives in learning disabilities*. New York: Academic Press, 1986, 161–182.

KUCER, STEPHEN B. The cognitive base of reading and writing. In J. R. Squire (Ed.), *The dynamics of language learning: Research in reading and English*. Bloomington, IN: ERIC/RCS, 1987, 27–51.

KUCERA, HENRY, & FRANCIS, W. NELSON. *Comparative analysis of present-day American English*. Providence, RI: Brown University Press, 1967.

KUO, W. F. A preliminary study of reading disabilities in the Republic of China. Collection of papers by National Taiwan Normal University, Graduate School of Education, 1978, *20*, 57–78. Cited by O. Tzeng & D. Hung. Reading in a nonalphabetic writing system: Some experimental studies. In J. Kavanagh & R. Venezky (Eds.), *Orthography, reading, and dyslexia*. Baltimore: University Park Press, 1980, 211–226.

KUYPERS, D. S.; BECKER, W. C.; & O'LEARY, K. D. How to make a token system fail. *Exceptional Children*, October 1968, *35*, 101–109.

KYÖSTIÖ, O. K. Is learning to read easy in a language in which the grapheme-phoneme correspondences are regular? In J. Kavanagh & R. Venezky (Eds.), *Orthography, reading, and dyslexia*. Baltimore: University Park Press, 1980, 35–49.

LABERGE, DAVID, & SAMUELS, S. JAY. Toward a theory of automatic information processing in reading. In H. Singer & R. B. Ruddell (Eds.), *Theoretical models and processes of reading* (3rd ed.). Newark, DE: International Reading Association, 1985, 689–718.

LABOV, WILLIAM. The logic of nonstandard English. In J. S. De Stefano (Ed.), *Language, society, and education: A profile of black English*. Worthington, OH: Charles A. Jones, 1973, 218–237.

LABUDA, MICHAEL (Ed.). *Creative reading for gifted learners: A design for excellence* (2nd ed.). Newark, DE: International Reading Association, 1985.

LABUDA, MICHELE C., & DE FRIES, J. C. Cognitive abilities in children with reading disabilities and controls: A follow-up study. *Journal of Learning Disabilities*, November 1988, *21*, 562–566.

LAKE, MARY L. First aid for vocabularies. *Elementary English*, November 1967, *44*, 783–784. Also in A. J. Harris & E. Sipay (Eds.), *Readings on reading instruction* (2nd ed.). New York: Longman, 1972, 252–254.

LAMB, POSE. Reading and television in the United States. In J. E. Merritt (Ed.), *New horizons in reading*. Newark, DE: International Reading Association, 1976, 370–382.

LAMME, LINDA L. Are reading habits and abilities related? *The Reading Teacher*, October 1976, *30*, 21–27.(a)

LAMME, LINDA L. Self-contained to departmentalized: How reading habits changed. *Elementary School Journal*, January 1976, *76*, 208–218.(b)

LANGER, JUDITH A. Relation between levels of prior knowledge and the organization of recall. In M. Kamil & A. Moe (Eds.), *Perspectives in reading research and instruction*. Washington, DC: National Reading Conference, 1980, 28–33.

LANGER, JUDITH A. Facilitating text processing: The elaboration of prior knowledge. In J. Langer & M. T. Burke-Smith (Eds.), *Reader meets author/bridging the gap: Psycholinguistic and sociolinguistic perspectives*. Newark, DE: International Reading Association, 1982, 149–162.

LANGER, JUDITH A. Examining background knowledge and text comprehension. *Reading Research Quarterly*, Summer 1984, *19*, 468–481.

LANGER, JUDITH A. Levels of questioning: An alternative view. *Reading Research Quarterly*, Fall 1985, *20*, 586–602.

LANGER, JUDITH A. *Children's reading and writing: Structures and strategies*. Norwood, NJ: Ablex, 1986.

LANGER, JUDITH A., & NICOLICH, MARK. Prior knowledge and its relationship to comprehension. *Journal of Reading Behavior*, Winter 1981, *13*, 373–379.

LANGER, PHILIP; KALK, JOHN M.; & SEARLS, DONALD T. Age of admission and trends in achievement: A comparison of blacks and caucasians. *American Educational Research Journal*, Spring 1984, *21*, 61–78.

LAOSA, LUIS M. *Families as facilitator of children's intellectual development at three years of age: A causal analysis*. Research report 81–45. Princeton, NJ: Educational Testing Service, November 1981.

LAPP, DIANE (Ed.). *Making reading possible through effective classroom management*. Newark, DE: International Reading Association, 1980.

LARRICK, NANCY. *A parent's guide to children's reading* (4th ed.). New York: Doubleday, 1975.

LARRICK, NANCY. Classroom magazines: A critique of 45 top sellers. *Learning*, October 1978, *7*, 260–269.

LARRICK, NANCY. *Random notes on recent research reflecting on children's reading*. Paper presented at the International Reading Association Conference, Anaheim, CA, May 1983.

LARRICK, NANCY. Illiteracy starts too soon. *Phi Delta Kappan*, November 1987, *69*, 184–189.(a)

LARRICK, NANCY. Keep a poem in your pocket. In B. E. Cullinan (Ed.), *Children's litera-ture in the reading program.* Newark, DE: International Reading Association, 1987, 20–27.(b)

LARRIVEE, BARBARA. Modality preference as a model for differentiating beginning read-ing instruction: A review of the issues. *Learning Disability Quarterly,* Spring 1981, 4, 180–188.

LARSEN, STEPHEN C., & EHLY, STEWART. Teacher-student interactions: A factor in handi-capping conditions. *Academic Therapy,* January 1978, 13, 267–273.

LARSEN, STEPHEN C.; PARKER, RANDALL M.; & HAMMILL, DONALD D. Effectiveness of psycholinguistic training: A reply to Kavale. *Exceptional Children,* September 1982, 49, 60–66.

LARSON, KATHERINE A. A research review and alternative hypotheses explaining the link between learning disability and delinquency. *Journal of Learning Disabilities,* June/July 1988, 21, 357–363, 369.

LASS, BONNIE. Trade books for black English speakers. *Language Arts,* April 1980, 57, 413–419.

LASS, BONNIE. Do teachers individualize their responses to reading miscues? A study of feedback during oral reading. *Reading World,* March 1984, 23, 242–254.

LASS, BONNIE, & BROMFIELD, MARCIA. Books about children with special needs: An an-notated bibliography. *The Reading Teacher,* February 1981, 34, 530–533.

LASSEN, NIELS A.; INGVAR, DAVID H.; & SKINKØJ, ERIK. Brain function and blood flow. *Scientific American,* October 1978, 239, 50–59.

LASS-WOODFIN, MARY JO (Ed.). *Books on American Indians and Eskimos: A selected guide for children and young adults.* Chicago: American Library Association, 1978.

LAURITZEN, CAROL. A modification of repeated readings for group instruction. *The Read-ing Teacher,* January 1982, 35, 456–458.

LAURITZEN, CAROL, & CHEVES, DEBORAH. Children's reading interests classified by age level. *The Reading Teacher,* April 1974, 27, 694–700.

LAWRENCE, PAUL S., & SIMMONS, BARBARA M. Criteria for reading management systems. *The Reading Teacher,* December 1978, 32, 332–336.

LAWSON, CORNELIA V. *Children's reasons and motivations for the selection of favorite books.* Unpublished doctoral dissertation, University of Kansas, 1972.

LAYTON, JAMES R. A chart for computing the Dale-Chall Readability Formula above fourth grade level. *Journal of Reading,* December 1980, 24, 239–244.

LEBAUER, RONI S. Nonnative English speaker problems in content and English classes: Are they thinking or reading problems? *Journal of Reading,* November 1985, 29 136–142.

LECKY, P. *Self-consistency: A theory of personality.* New York: Island Press, 1951.

LEFTON, LESTER A., et al. Eye movement dynamics of good and poor readers: Then and now. *Journal of Reading Behavior,* Winter 1979, 11, 319–328.

LEHR, FRAN. Reading and the gifted secondary school student. *Journal of Reading,* Feb-ruary 1983, 26, 456–458.

LEHR, FRAN. Peer teaching. *The Reading Teacher,* March 1984, 37, 636–639.

LEHR, FRAN. Suggestopedia. *Language Arts,* November 1987, 64, 778–781.

LEIBERT, ROBERT E. A study of word errors by second, third, and fourth grade pupils reading the Dolch Word List. In J. Niles & L. A. Harris (Eds.), *New inquiries in reading research and instruction.* Rochester, NY: National Reading Conference, 1982, 166–169.

LEINHARDT, GAEA. Transition rooms: Promoting maturation or reducing education? *Jour-nal of Educational Psychology,* 1980, 72(1), 55–61.

LEINHARDT, GAEA, & PALLAY, ALLAN. Restrictive educational settings: Exile or haven? *Review of Educational Research,* Winter 1982, 52, 557–578.

LEINHARDT, GAEA; SEEWALD, ANDREA M.; & ZIGMOND, NAOMI. Sex and race differences in learning disabilities classrooms. *Journal of Educational Psychology*, December 1982, *74*, 835–843.

LEINHARDT, GAEA; ZIGMOND, NAOMI; & COOLEY, WILLIAM W. Reading instruction and its effects. *American Educational Research Journal*, Fall 1981, *18*, 343–361.

LENKOWSKY, RONALD S. Bibliotherapy: A review and analysis of the literature. *Journal of Special Education*, 1987, *21*(2), 123–132.

LENZ, B. KEITH; ALLEY, GORDON, R.; & SCHUMAKER, JEAN B. Activating the inactive learner: Advance organizers in the secondary content classroom. *Learning Disability Quarterly*, Winter 1987, *10*, 53–67.

LEONG, CHE K. Laterality and reading proficiency in children. *Reading Research Quarterly*, 1980, *15*(2), 185–202.

LEONG, CHE K. What does accessing a morphemic script tell us about reading and reading disorders in an alphabetic script? *Annals of Dyslexia*, Vol. 36. Baltimore, MD: Orton Dyslexia Society, 1986, 82–102.

LESGOLD, ALAN M., & PERFETTI, CHARLES A. Interactive processes in reading: Where do we stand? In A. Lesgold & C. Perfetti (Eds.), *Interactive processes in reading*. Hillsdale, NJ: Erlbaum, 1981, 387–405.

LESLIE, LAUREN. The use of graphic and contextual information by average and below-average readers. *Journal of Reading Behavior*, Summer 1980, *12*, 139–149.

LESLIE, LAUREN. Research into practice: Changes in reading assessment. *Reading Today*, April/May 1989, 6, 22.

LESLIE, LAUREN, & SHANNON, ALBERT J. Recognition of orthographic structure during beginning reading. *Journal of Reading Behavior*, 1981, *13*(4), 313–324.

LEVIN, HARRY, & ADDIS, ANN B. *The eye-voice span*. Cambridge, MA: MIT Press, 1979.

LEVIN, HARRY, & COHN, J. A. Effects of instruction on the eye-voice span. In H. Levin, E. J. Gibson, & J. J. Gibson (Eds.), *The analysis of reading skills: A program of basic and applied research*. Final Report, Project No. 5–1213, Cornell University, 1968. (ERIC number ED 034 663.)

LEVIN, HARRY, & KAPLAN, ELEANOR L. Grammatical structure and reading. In H. Levin & J. P. Williams (Eds.), *Basic studies on reading*. New York: Basic Books, 1970, 110–133.

LEVIN, HARRY, & WATSON, J. The learning of variable grapheme-phoneme correspondence. In H. Levin et al., *A basic research program on reading*. Final Report, Cooperative Research Project No. 639, 1963.

LEVIN, JOEL R. On functions of pictures in prose. In F. Pirozzolo & M. Wittrock (Eds.), *Neuropsychological and cognitive processes in reading*. New York: Academic Press, 1981, 203–228.

LEVIN, JOEL R., et al. Mnemonic facilitation of text-embedded science facts. *American Educational Research Journal*, Fall 1986, *23*, 489–506.

LEVINE, KENNETH. Functional literacy: Fond illusions and false economies. *Harvard Educational Review*, August 1982, *52*, 249–266.

LEVINE, MELVIN D. *Developmental variations and learning disorders*. Cambridge, MA: Educators Publishing Service, 1987.

LEVINE, STEVEN G. USSR—A necessary component in teaching reading. *Journal of Reading*, February 1984, *27*, 394–400.

LEVINSON, HAROLD N. *A solution to the riddle dyslexia*. New York: Springer-Verlag, 1980.

LEVISON, BEATRICE. Raphael. In A. J. Harris (Ed.), *Casebook on reading disability*. New York: David McKay, 1970, 117–134.

LEVY, JERRE. Right brain, left brain: Fact and fiction. *Psychology Today*, May 1985, *19*, 40–44.

LEWANDOWSKI, GLEN. A different look at some basic sight-word lists and their use. *Reading World*, May 1979, *18*, 333–341.

LEWIS, JENEVA. *A comparison of kindergarten teachers' perceptions of children's prefer-ence in books with the children's actual preferences.* Unpublished doctoral disser-tation, East Texas State University, 1970.

LEWIS, RAMON, & TEALE, WILLIAM H. Another look at secondary school students' atti-tudes toward reading. *Journal of Reading Behavior,* Fall 1980, *12,* 187–201.

LIBERMAN, ISABELLE Y. A language-oriented view of reading and its disabilities. In H. Myklebust (Ed.), *Progress in learning disabilities,* Vol. 5. New York: Grune & Strat-ton, 1983, 81–101.

LIBERMAN, ISABELLE Y., & SHANKWEILER, DONALD. Speech, the alphabet and teaching to read. In L. Resnick & P. Weaver (Eds.), *Theory and practice of early reading,* Vol. 2. Hillsdale, NJ: Erlbaum, 1979, 109–132.

LIBERMAN, ISABELLE Y., & SHANKWEILER, DONALD. Phonology and the problems of learn-ing to read and write. *Remedial and Special Education,* November/December 1985, *6,* 8–17.

LIBERMAN, ISABELLE Y., et al. Letter confusion and reversals of sequence in the begin-ning reader: Implications for Orton's theory of developmental dyslexia. *Cortex,* June 1971, 7, 127–142.

LIBERMAN, ISABELLE Y., et al. Phonetic segmentation and recoding in the beginning reader. In A. S. Reber & D. L. Scarborough (Eds.), *Toward a psychology of reading.* Hillsdale, NJ: Erlbaum, 1977, 207–225.

LIBERMAN, ISABELLE, et al. Orthography and the beginning reader. In J. Kavanagh & R. Venezky (Eds.), *Orthography, reading, and dyslexia.* Baltimore: University Park Press, 1980, 137–153.

LIBERMAN, ISABELLE Y., et al. Linguistic abilities and spelling proficiency in kindergart-ners and adult poor spellers. In D.B. Gray & J.F. Kavanagh (Eds.), *Biobehavioral measures of dyslexia.* Parkton, MD: York Press, 1985, 163–176.

LIBRETTO, ELLEN V. (Ed.) *High/low handbook: Books, materials, and services for the problem reader.* New York: Bowker, 1985.

LICHT, BARBARA G., & KISTNER, JANET A. Motivational problems of learning-disabled children. Individual differences and their implications for treatment. In J. K. Torge-sen & B. Y. L. Wong (Eds.), *Psychological and educational perspectives in learning disabilities.* New York: Academic Press, 1986, 225–258.

LICKTEIG, MARY JANE. *A comparison of book selection preferences of innercity and sub-urban fourth and sixth graders.* Unpublished doctoral dissertation, University of Oregon, 1972.

LIEBEN, BEATRICE. Attitudes, platitudes, and conferences in teacher-parent relations in-volving the child with a reading problem. *Elementary School Journal,* 1958, 57, 279–286. Also in A. J. Harris & E. Sipay (Eds.), *Readings on reading instruction* (2nd ed.). New York: David McKay, 1972, 420–427.

LILLIE, DAVID L., & ALBERG, JONI Y. The PIAT: Error analysis for instructional planning. *Teaching Exceptional Children,* Spring 1986, *18,* 197–201.

LIMBURG, PETER. *Stories behind words: The origins and histories of 285 English words.* New York: H. W. Wilson, 1986.

LINCOLN, ROBERT D. The effect of single-grade and multi-grade primary school class-rooms on reading achievement of children. *New England Reading Association Jour-nal,* Spring 1982, *17,* 19–24.

LINDFORS, JUDITH W. Understanding the development of language structure. In A. Jaggar & M. T. Smith-Burke (Eds.), *Observing the language learner.* Newark, DE: Interna-tional Reading Association, 1985, 41–56.

LINDSAY, G. A. The Infant Rating Scale. *British Journal of Educational Psychology,* 1980, *50,* 97–104.

LINDSAY, G. A., & WEDELL, K. The early identification of educationally "at risk" children revisited. *Journal of Learning Disabilities,* April 1982, *15,* 212–217.

LINN, ROBERT L., & DRASGOW, FRITZ. Implication of the Golden Rule settlement for test construction. *Educational Measurement: Issues and Practice*, Summer 1987, *6*, 13–17.

LINN, ROBERT L., et al. *An investigation of item bias in a test of reading comprehension.* Technical Report No. 163. Champaign, IL: Center for the Study of Reading, University of Illinois, March 1980.

LIPSON, ALICE M., & ALDEN, LEE. Mainstreaming: Unwanted side effects. *Academic Therapy*, January 1983, *18*, 267–274.

LIPSON, EDEN R. *The New York Times parent's guide to best books for children.* New York: Times Books, 1988.

LIPSON, MARJORIE Y. The influence of religious affiliations on children's memory for text information. *Reading Research Quarterly*, Summer 1983, *18*, 448–457.

LIPSON, MARJORIE Y. Individualizing within basal instruction. In P. N. Winograd et al. (Eds.), *Improving basal reading instruction.* New York: Teachers College Press, 1989, 140–173.

LIPSON, MARJORIE Y., & WIXSON, KAREN K. Reading disability research: An interactionist perspective. *Review of Educational Research*, Spring 1986, *56*, 111–136.

LIVINGSTON, RICHARD. Depressive illness and learning difficulties: Research needs and practical implications. *Journal of Learning Disabilities*, November 1985, *18*, 518–520.

LLOYD, CAROL V., & MITCHELL, JUDY N. Coping with the many concepts in science texts. *Journal of Reading*, March 1989, *32*, 542–545.

LOEHLIN, JOHN C.; WILLERMAN, LEE; & HORN, JOSEPH M. Human behavior genetics. In M. R. Rozenzweig & L. W. Porter (Eds.), *Annual Review of Psychology*, Vol. 39. Palo Alto, CA: Annual Reviews Inc., 1988, 101–133.

LOHNES, PAUL R., & GRAY, MARIAN M. Intelligence and the cooperative reading studies. *Reading Research Quarterly*, Spring 1972, *7*, 466–476.

LOMAX, RICHARD G., & MCGEE, LEA M. Young children's concepts about print and reading: Toward a model of word reading acquisition. *Reading Research Quarterly*, Spring 1987, *22*, 237–256.

LONG, MARGO A. The interracial family in children's literature. *The Reading Teacher*, May 1978, *31*, 909–915.

LONGO, JUDITH A. The Fry Graph: Validation of the college levels. *Journal of Reading*, December 1982, *26*, 229–234.

LORGE, IRVING. Predicting readability. *Teachers College Record*, May 1944, *45*, 404–419.

LORSBACH, THOMAS C., & GRAY, JEFFREY W. The development of encoding processes in learning disabled children. *Journal of Learning Disabilities*, April 1985, *18*, 222–227.

LOVETT, MAUREEN W. Reading skill and its development: Theoretical and empirical considerations. In G. MacKinnon & T. Waller (Eds.), *Reading research: Advances in theory and practice,* Vol. 3. New York: Academic Press, 1981, 1–37.

LOVETT, MAUREEN W. A developmental perspective on reading dysfunction: Accuracy and rate criteria in the subtyping of dyslexic children. *Brain and Language*, May 1984, *22*, 67–91.

LOVETT, MAUREEN W. A developmental approach to reading disability: Accuracy and speed criteria of normal and deficient reading skill. *Child Development*, February 1987, *58*, 234–260.

LOVITT, THOMAS., et al. Adapting science materials for regular and learning disabled seventh graders. *Remedial and Special Education*, January/February 1986, *7*, 31–39.

LOZANOV, GEORGI. The suggestological theory of communicating and instruction. *Suggestology & Suggestopedia*, 1975, *1*, 1–14.

LUCAS, CEIL, & BORDERS, DENISE. Language diversity in classroom discourse. *American Educational Research Journal*, Spring 1987, *24*, 119–141.

LUCAS, PETER A., & MCCONKIE, GEORGE W. The definition of test items: A descriptive approach. *American Educational Research Journal*, Spring 1980, *17*, 133–140.

LUFTIG, RICHARD L. Abstractive memory, the central-incidental hypothesis, and the use of structural importance in text: Control processes or structural features. *Reading Research Quarterly*, Fall 1983, *19*, 28–37.

LUITEN, JOHN; AMES, WILBUR; & ACHERSON, GARY A. A meta-analysis of the effects of advance organizers on learning and retention. *American Educational Research Journal*, Summer 1980, *17*, 211–218.

LUNDAHL, FLEMMING. Split-half classes. In J. E. Merritt (Ed.), *New horizons in reading*. Newark, DE: International Reading Association, 1976, 428–433.

LUNSTRUM, JOHN P. Building motivation through the use of controversy. *Journal of Reading*, May 1981, *24*, 687–691.

LUNSTRUM, JOHN P., & TAYLOR, BOB L. *Teaching reading in the social studies*. Newark, DE: International Reading Association, 1978.

LURIA, A. R. *The working brain: An introduction to neuropsychology*. New York: Basic Books, 1973.

LUTZ, PAMELA B. Staff development. In D. E. Alvermann et al. (Eds.), *Research within reach: Secondary school reading*. Newark, DE: International Reading Association, 1987, 170–186.

LYON, G. REID. Learning-disabled readers: Identification of subgroups. In H. Myklebust (Ed.), *Progress in Learning Disabilities*, Vol. 5. New York: Grune & Stratton, 1983. 103–133.

LYON, KATHLEEN. *The effect on comprehension of increasing the single-word recoding speed of poor readers*. Unpublished doctoral dissertation, State University of New York at Albany, 1984.

LYONS, KEVIN. Criterion referenced reading comprehension tests: New forms with old ghosts. *Journal of Reading*, January 1984, *27*, 293–298.

LYSAKOWSKI, RICHARD S., & WALBERG, HERBERT J. Instructional effects of cues, participation, and corrective feedback: A quantitative synthesis. *American Educational Research Journal*, Winter 1982, *19*, 559–578.

MACGINITIE, WALTER H. When should we begin to teach reading? *Language Arts*, November/December 1976, *53*, 878–882.

MACGINITIE, WALTER H.; KIMMEL, SUSAN; & MARIA, KATHERINE. The role of cognitive strategies in certain reading comprehension disabilities. *The Forum*, Fall 1980, *6*, 10–13.

MACGINITIE, WALTER, & TRETIAK, RICHARD. Sentence depth measures as predictors of reading difficulty. *Reading Research Quarterly*, Spring 1971, *6*, 364–376.

MACLEAN, MORAG; BRYANT, PETER; & BRADLEY, LYNETTE. Rhymes, nursery rhymes, and reading in early childhood. In K. Stanovich (Ed.), *Children's reading and the development of phonological awareness*. Detroit, MI: Wayne State University Press, 1988, 11–37.

MACMILLAN, DONALD L., et al. Impact of Diana, Larry P. and P. L. 94–142 on minority students. *Exceptional Children*, February 1988, *54*, 426–432.

MADAUS, GEORGE F. The influence of testing in the curriculum. In L. N. Tanner (Ed.), *Critical issues in curriculum, Part I*. 87th Yearbook of the National Society for the Study of Education. Chicago: University of Chicago Press, 1988, 83–121.

MADDEN, NANCY A., & SLAVIN, ROBERT E. Mainstreaming students with mild handicaps: Academic and social outcomes. *Review of Educational Research*, Winter 1983, *53*, 519–569.

MAGINNIS, GEORGE H. Measuring underachievement in reading. *The Reading Teacher*, May 1972, *25*, 750–753.

MAGINNIS, GEORGE H. Easier, faster, more reliable readability ratings. *Journal of Reading*, March 1982, *25*, 598–599.

MAGINNIS, GEORGE H. An evaluation of a non-visual method. *Journal of Learning Disabilities*, April 1986, *19*, 215–217.

MAKITA, KIYOSHI. The rarity of reading disability in Japanese children. *American Journal of Orthopsychiatry*, July 1968, *38*, 599–614.

MAKITA, KIYOSHI. Reading disability and the writing system. In J. E. Merritt (Ed.), *New horizons in reading*. Newark, DE: International Reading Association, 1976, 250–254.

MALMQUIST, EVE. *Factors related to reading disabilities in the first grade of the elementary school*. Stockholm: Almquist & Wiksell, 1958.

MALMQUIST, EVE. *Las-och skrivsarigheter hos barn: Analys och behandlings metodik (Reading and writing disabilities in children: Diagnosis and remedial methods)*. Lund, Sweden: Gleerup, 1967.

MALMQUIST, EVE. *Lässvarigheter på grundskolans lagstadium (Experimental studies on reading disabilities at the primary stage)*. Falkoping, Sweden: Utbildningforlaget Liber. Research reports from the National School for Education Research, No. 13, 1969.

MANGIERI, JOHN N., & CORBOY, MARGARET R. Recreational reading: Do we practice what is preached? *The Reading Teacher*, May 1981, *34*, 923–925.

MANGIERI, JOHN N., & HEIMBERGER, MARY J. Perceptions of the reading consultant's role. *Journal of Reading*, March 1980, *23*, 527–530.

MANIS, FRANKLIN R. Acquisition of word identification skills in normal and disabled readers. *Journal of Educational Psychology*, 1985, *77*(1), 78–90.

MANIS, FRANKLIN R., et al. A comparison of analogy- and rule-based decoding strategies in normal and dyslexic children. *Journal of Reading Behavior*, Summer 1986, *18*, 203–218.

MANN, LESTER. Review of the Frostig Developmental Tests of Visual Perception. In O. K. Buros (Ed.), *Seventh mental measurements yearbook*, Vol. 1. Highland Park, NJ: Gryphon Press, 1972, 1274–1276.

MANN, VIRGINIA A. Why some children encounter reading problems: The contribution of difficulties with language processing and phonological sophistication to early reading disability. In J. K. Torgesen & B. Y. L. Wong (Eds.), *Psychological and educational perspectives on learning disabilities*. New York: Academic Press, 1986, 133–159.

MANN, VIRGINIA A.; COWIN, ELIZABETH; & SCHOENHEIMER, JOYCE. Phonological processing, language comprehension, and reading ability. *Journal of Learning Disabilities*, February 1989, *22*, 76–89.

MANN, VIRGINIA A., & LIBERMAN, ISABELLE Y. Phonological awareness and verbal short-term memory. *Journal of Learning Disabilities*, December 1984, *17*, 592–599.

MANN, VIRGINIA A.; TOBIN, PAULA; & WILSON, REBECCA. Measuring phonological awareness through invented spellings of kindergarten children. In K. Stanovich (Ed.), *Children's reading and the development of phonological awareness*. Detroit, MI: Wayne State University Press, 1988, 121–147.

MANNA, ANTHONY L. Making language come alive through reading plays. *The Reading Teacher*, April 1984, *37*, 712–717.

MANNING, GARY L., & MANNING, MARYANN. What models of recreational reading make a difference? *Reading World*, May 1984, *23*, 375–380.

MANZO, ANTHONY V. Expansion modules for the ReQuest, CAT, GRP, and REAP reading/study procedures. *Journal of Reading*, March 1985, *20*, 498–502.

MARIA, KATHERINE, & MacGINITIE, WALTER H. Reading comprehension disabilities: Knowledge structures and non-accommodating text processing strategies. *Annals of Dyslexia*, Vol. 32. Baltimore, MD: Orton Dyslexia Society, 1982, 31–59.

MARIA, KATHERINE, & MacGINITIE, WALTER. Learning from texts that refute the reader's prior knowledge. *Reading Research and Instruction*, Summer 1987, *26*, 222–238.

MARLIAVE, RICHARD, & FILBY, NIKOLA N. Success rate: A measure of task appropriateness. In C. W. Fisher & D. C. Berliner (Eds.). *Perspectives on instructional time.* New York: Longman, 1985, 217–235.

MARMUREK, HARVEY H. C. Reading ability and attention to words and letters in words. *Journal of Reading Behavior,* 1988, 22(2), 119–129.

MARR, MARY BETH, & GORMLEY, KATHLEEN. Children's recall of familiar and unfamiliar text. *Reading Research Quarterly,* Fall 1982, 18, 80–104.

MARSH, HERBERT W.; PARKER, JOHN; & BARNES, JENNIFER. Multidimensional adolescent self-concepts: Their relationship to age, sex, and academic measures. *American Educational Research Journal,* Fall 1985, 22, 422–444.

MARSHALL, NANCY. Discourse analysis as a guide for informal assessment of comprehension. In J. Flood (Ed.), *Promoting reading comprehension.* Newark, DE: International Reading Association, 1984, 79–96.

MARSTON, EMILY. Children's poetry preferences: A review. *Research in the Teaching of English,* Spring 1975, 9, 107–110.

MARTIN, CHARLES E.; CRAMOND, BONNIE; & SAFTER, TAMMY. Developing creativity through the reading program. *The Reading Teacher,* February 1982, 35, 568–572.

MARTIN, L. S., & PAVAN, B. N. Current research on open space, nongrading, vertical grouping, and team teaching. *Phi Delta Kappan,* January 1976, 57, 310–315.

MARTIN, SUSAN G. Reading placement for code switchers. *The Reading Teacher,* January 1989, 42, 278–282.

MARWIT, SAMUEL J., & NEUMANN, GAIL. Black and white children's comprehension of standard and nonstandard English passages. *Journal of Educational Psychology,* June 1974, 66, 329–332.

MARZANO, ROBERT J., & MARZANO, JANA S. *A cluster approach to elementary vocabulary instruction.* Newark, DE: International Reading Association, 1988.

MARZANO, ROBERT J., et al. The Graded Word List is not a shortcut to an IRI. *The Reading Teacher,* March 1978, 31, 647–651.

MASLAND, RICHARD L. Neurological aspects of dyslexia. In G. Pavlidis & T. Miles (Eds.), *Dyslexia research and its application to education.* New York: John Wiley & Sons, 1981, 35–66.

MASON, GEORGE E. High interest-low vocabulary books: Their past and future. *Journal of Reading,* April 1981, 24, 603–607.

MASON, GEORGE E., & MIZE, JOHN V. Twenty-two sets of methods and materials for stimulating teenage reading. *Journal of Reading,* May 1978, 21, 735–741.

MASON, JANA M. *Prereading: A developmental perspective.* Technical Report No. 198. Champaign, IL: Center for the Study of Reading, University of Illinois, February 1981.

MASON, JANA M. *Acquisition of knowledge about reading: The preschool period.* Technical Report No. 267. Champaign, IL: Center for the Study of Reading, University of Illinois, 1982.(a)

MASON, JANA M. *A description of reading instruction: The tail is wagging the dog.* Reading Education Report No. 35. Champaign, IL: Center for the Study of Reading, University of Illinois, August 1982.(b)

MASON, JANA M. An examination of reading instruction in third and fourth grades. *The Reading Teacher,* May 1983, 36, 906–913.

MASON, JANA M. *Kindergarten reading: A proposal for a problem-solving approach.* Technical Report No. 345. Champaign, IL: Center for the Study of Reading, University of Illinois, December 1985.

MASON, JANA M., & ALLEN, JO BETH. *A review of emergent literacy with implications for research and practice in reading.* Technical Report No. 379. Champaign, IL: Center for the Study of Reading, University of Illinois, April 1986.

MASON, JANA; McCORMICK, CHRISTINE; & BHAVNAGRI, NAVAZ. How are you going to help me learn? Lesson negotiations between a teacher and preschool children. In D. B. Yaden & S. Templeton (Eds.), *Metalinguistic awareness and beginning literacy.* Portsmouth, NH: Heinemann, 1986, 159–172.

MASON, JANA; ROEHLER, LAURA R.; & DUFFY, GERALD G. A practitioner's model of comprehension instruction. In G. Duffy et al. (Eds.), *Comprehension instruction: Perspectives and suggestions.* New York: Longman, 1984, 299–314.

MASON, JANA, et al. A schema-theoretic view of the reading process as a basis for comprehension instruction. In G. Duffy et al. (Eds.), *Comprehension instruction: Perspectives and suggestions.* New York: Longman, 1984, 26–38.

MASSON, MICHAEL E. J. Remembering reading operations with and without awareness. In B. K. Britton & S. M. Glynn (Eds.), *Executive control processes in reading.* Hillsdale, NJ: Erlbaum, 1987, 253–277.

MASTROPIERI, MARGO A. Using the keyboard [SIC] method. *Teaching Exceptional Children,* Winter 1988, *20,* 4–8.

MATĚJCĚK, ZDENEK. Dyslexia in Czechoslovakian children. In L. Tarnopol & M. Tarnopol (Eds.), *Reading disabilities: An international perspective.* Baltimore: University Park Press, 1976, 131–154.

MATĚJCĚK, ZDENEK. Specific learning disabilities. *Bulletin of the Orton Society,* 1977, *27,* 7–25.

MATHEWS, MITFORD M. *Teaching to read: Historically considered.* Chicago: University of Chicago Press, 1966.

MATHEWSON, GROVER C. Teaching forms of negation in reading and reasoning. *The Reading Teacher,* January 1984, *37,* 354–358.

MATSUHASKI, ANN, & QUINN, KAREN. Cognitive questions from discourse analysis: A review and a study. *Written Communication,* July 1984, *1,* 307–339.

MATTHEWS, DOROTHY (Ed.). *Getting students to read: New materials and methods.* Urbana, IL: National Council of Teachers of English, 1987.

MATTHEWS, DOROTHY (Ed.). *High interest-easy reading for junior and senior high school students* (5th ed.). Urbana, IL: National Council of Teachers of English, 1988.

MATTINGLY, IGNATIUS G. The psycholinguistic basis of linguistic awareness. In M. J. Kamil & A. J. Moe (Eds.), *Reading research: Studies and applications.* Clemson, SC: National Reading Conference, 1979, 274–278.

MATTIS, STEVEN. Dyslexia syndromes: A working hypothesis that works. In A. L. Benton & D. Pearl (Eds.), *Dyslexia: An appraisal of current knowledge.* New York: Oxford University Press, 1978, 43–58.

MATTIS, STEVEN. Dyslexia syndrome in children: Toward a development of syndrome-specific treatment programs. In F. Pirozollo & M. Wittrock (Eds.), *Neuropsychological and cognitive processes in reading.* New York: Academic Press, 1981, 93–107.

MATTIS, STEVEN; FRENCH, JOSEPH H.; & RAPIN, ISABELLE. Dyslexia in children and young adults: Three independent neuropsychological syndromes. *Developmental Medicine and Child Neurology,* 1975, *17,* 150–163.

MAUGHAN, BARBARA; GRAY, GRACE; & RUTTER, MICHAEL. Reading retardation and antisocial behavior. A follow-up into employment. *Journal of Child Psychology and Psychiatry,* 1985, *26*(5), 741–758.

MAVROGENES, NANCY A. Teaching implications of the schemata theory of comprehension. *Reading World,* May 1983, *22,* 295–305.

MAVROGENES, NANCY A., & GALEN, NANCY D. Cross-age tutoring: Why and how. *Journal of Reading,* January 1979, *22,* 344–353.

MAY, ANN B. All the angles of idiom instruction. *The Reading Teacher,* March 1979, *32,* 680–682.

MAY, JILL P. To think anew: Native American literature and children's attitudes. *The Reading Teacher,* April 1983, *36,* 790–794.

MAY, RICHARD B., & OLLILA, LLOYD O. Reading sex-role attitudes in preschoolers. *Reading Research Quarterly*, 1981, *16*(4), 583–595.

MAYER, RICHARD E. Can advance organizers influence meaningful learning. *Review of Educational Research*, Summer 1979, *49*, 371–383.

MAYER, RICHARD E. Instructional variables that influence cognitive processes during reading. In B. K. Britton & S. M. Glynn (Eds.), *Executive control processes in reading*. Hillsdale, NJ: Erlbaum, 1987, 201–216.

MAYRON, LEWIS W. Allergy, learning, and behavior problems. *Journal of Learning Disabilities*, January 1979, *12*, 32–42.

MAZURKIEWICZ, ALBERT J. The initial teaching alphabet. In J. Money (Ed.), *The disabled reader*. Baltimore: Johns Hopkins Press, 1966, 161–174.

MCAFEE, JACKSON K. *Towards a theory of promotion: Does retaining students really work?* Paper read at the annual meeting of the American Educational Research Association, Los Angeles, 1981. (ERIC number ED 204 871.)

MCANDREW, DONALD A. Underlining and notetaking: Some suggestions from research. *Journal of Reading*, November 1983, *27*, 103–108.

MCBRIDE, RALPH. Visual phrasing cues as an aid to comprehension of simple and complex sentences by learning disabled and normal pupils. *Journal of Research & Development in Education*, 1976, *9*, 109–110.

MCCLAIN, LESLIE J. Study guides: Potential assets in content classrooms. *Journal of Reading*, January 1981, *24*, 321–325.

MCCLURE, ERICA F., & STEFFENSEN, MARGARET. A study of the use of conjunctions across grades and ethnic groups. *Research in the Teaching of English*, October 1985, *19*, 217–236.

MCCONAUGHY, STEPHANIE H. Developmental changes in story comprehension and levels of questioning. *Language Arts*, September 1982, *59*, 580–589.

MCCONAUGHY, STEPHANIE H. Good and poor readers' comprehension of story structure across different input and output modalities. *Reading Research Quarterly*, Winter, 1985, *20*, 219–232.

MCCONKIE, GEORGE W. *Studying the reader's perceptual processes by computer*. Reading Education Report No. 34. Champaign, IL: Center for the Study of Reading, University of Illinois, May 1982.

MCCONKIE, GEORGE W., & HOGABOAM, THOMAS W. *Eye position and word identification during reading*. Technical Report No. 333. Champaign, IL: Center for the Study of Reading, University of Illinois, April 1985.

MCCONKIE, GEORGE W.; WOLVERTON, GARY S.; & ZOLA, DAVID. *Instrumentation considerations in research involving eye-movement contingent stimulus control*. Technical Report No. 305. Champaign, IL: Center for the Study of Reading, University of Illinois, January 1984.

MCCONKIE, GEORGE W., & ZOLA, DAVID. *Eye movement control during reading: The effect of word units*. Technical Report No. 310. Champaign, IL: Center for the Study of Reading, University of Illinois, March 1984.

MCCONKIE, GEORGE W., & ZOLA, DAVID. *Eye movement techniques in studying differences among developing readers*. Technical Report No. 377. Champaign, IL: Center for the Study of Reading, University of Illinois, April 1986.

MCCONKIE, GEORGE W., et al. *Some temporal characteristics of processing during reading*. Technical Report No. 331. Champaign, IL: Center for the Study of Reading, University of Illinois, March 1985.

MCCORMICK, SANDRA. Should you read aloud to your children? *Language Arts*, February 1977, *54*, 139–143, 163.

MCCORMICK, SANDRA, & COLLINS, BETTY M. A potpourri of game-making ideas for the reading teacher. *The Reading Teacher*, March 1981, *34*, 692–696.

McCOWN, RICK R., & MILLER, RAYMOND B. Referential coherence and structural height in text processing. *American Educational Research Journal*, Spring 1986, *23*, 77–86.

McCOY, KATHLEEN M., & PANY, DARLENE. Summary and analysis of oral reading corrective feedback research. *The Reading Teacher*, February 1986, *39*, 548–554.

McDERMOTT, R. P. Achieving school failure: An anthropological approach to illiteracy and social stratification. In H. Singer & R. B. Ruddell (Eds.), *Theoretical models and processes of reading* (3rd ed.). Newark, DE: International Reading Association, 1985, 558–594.

McDONALD, ARTHUR S. Research for the classroom: Rate and flexibility. *Journal of Reading*, January 1965, *8*, 187–191.

McFEELEY, DONALD C. Another look at the VCV controversy. *The Reading Teacher*, October 1981, *35*, 81.

McGEE, LEA M. The influence of metacognitive knowledge of expository text structure on discourse recall. In J. Niles & L. A. Harris (Eds.), *New inquiries in reading: Research and instruction*. Rochester, NY: National Reading Conference, 1982, 64–70.

McGEE, LEA M., & RICHGELS, DONALD J. Teaching expository text structure to elementary students. *The Reading Teacher*, April 1985, *38*, 739–748.

McGEE, ROB, et al. The relationships between specific reading retardation, general reading backwardness and behavioral problems in a large sample of Dunedin boys: A longitudinal study from five to eleven years. *Journal of Child Psychology and Psychiatry*, 1986, *27*(5), 597–610.

McGILL-FRANZEN, ANNE. Failure to learn to read: Formulating a policy problem. *Reading Research Quarterly*, Fall 1987, *22*, 475–490.

McGUIGNAN, F. J. The function of cover behavior ("silent speech") during silent reading. *International Journal of Psycholinguistics*, 1973, *2*, 39–47.

McKENNA, MICHAEL C. Portmanteau words in reading instruction. *Language Arts*, March 1978, *55*, 315–317.

McKENNA, MICHAEL C. Reading interests of remedial secondary school students. *Journal of Reading*, January 1986, *29*, 346–351.

McKENNA, MICHAEL C., & ROBINSON, RICHARD D. *An introduction to the cloze procedure: An annotated bibliography*. Newark, DE: International Reading Association, 1980.

McKENZIE, GARY R. Personalize your group teaching. *Instructor*, August/September 1975, *85*, 57–59. Also in A. J. Harris & E. Sipay (Eds.), *Readings on reading instruction* (3rd ed.). New York: Longman, 1984, 177–180.

McKENZIE, GREGORY G.; NEILSON, ALLAN R.; & BRAUN, CARL. The effects of linguistic connectives and prior knowledge on comprehension of good and poor readers. In M. Kamil (Ed.), *Directions in reading: Research and instruction*. Washington, DC: National Reading Conference, 1981, 215–218.

McKENZIE, ROBERT G., & HOUK, CAROLYN S. The paraprofessional in special education. *Teaching Exceptional Children*, Summer 1986, *18*, 246–252.

McKEOWN, MARGARET G. The acquisition of word meaning from context by children of high and low ability. *Reading Research Quarterly*, Summer 1985, *20*, 482–496.(a)

McKEOWN, MARGARET G. Some effects of the nature and frequency of vocabulary instruction on the knowledge and use of words. *Reading Research Quarterly*, Fall 1985, *20*, 522–535.(b)

McKINNEY, JAMES D. Performance of handicapped students on the North Carolina Minimum Competency Test. *Educational Researcher*, April 1983, *49*, 547–550.

McKINNEY, JAMES D. Longitudinal research on the behavioral characteristics of children with learning disabilities. *Journal of Learning Disabilities*, March 1989, *22*, 141–150, 165.

McKINNEY, JAMES D., & HOCUTT, ANNE M. The need for policy analysis in evaluating the Regular Education Initiative. *Journal of Learning Disabilities*, January 1988, *21*, 12–18.

McLAUGHLIN, G. HARRY. SMOG grading—A new readability formula. *Journal of Reading*, May 1969, *12*, 639–646.

McLEOD, JOHN. Educational underachievement: Toward a defensible psychometric definition. *Journal of Learning Disabilities*, May 1979, *12*, 322–330.

McLEOD, JOHN. *Psychometric identification of children with learning disabilities*, (2nd ed.). Saskatoon, Canada: Institute of Child Guidance and Development, University of Saskatchewan, 1981.

McNAUGHTON, STUART. The influence of immediate teacher correction on self-corrections and proficient oral reading. *Journal of Reading Behavior*, Winter 1981, *13*, 367–371.

McNEIL, JOHN D. *Auditory discrimination training in the development of word analysis skills*. Los Angeles: University of California at Los Angeles, 1967. (ERIC number ED 018 344.)

McNEIL, JOHN D. False prerequisites in the teaching of reading. *Journal of Reading Behavior*, December 1974, *6*, 421–427.

McNEIL, JOHN D. *Reading comprehension: New direction for classroom practice*. Glenview, IL: Scott, Foresman, 1987.

McPHAIL, IRVING P. Toward an agenda for urban literacy: The study of schools where low-income black children read at grade level. *Reading World*, December 1982, *22*, 132–149.

McWHIRTER, J. JEFFRIES. A parent education group in learning disabilities. *Journal of Learning Disabilities*, January 1976, *9*, 16–20.

McWILLIAMS, LANA J. Riding and reading. *Journal of Reading*, January 1979, *22*, 337–339.

MEARES, OLIVE. Figure/ground, brightness contrast, and reading disabilities. *Visible Language*, 1980, *14*(1), 13–29.

MEDLEY, DONALD M. *Teacher competence and teacher effectiveness: A review of process-product research*. Washington, DC: American Association of Colleges for Teacher Education, 1977.

MEDWAY, FREDERICK J., & LOWE, CHARLES A. Causal attribution for performance by cross-age tutors and tutees. *American Educational Research Journal*, Fall 1980, *17*, 377–387.

MEICHENBAUM, DONALD. *Cognitive-behavior modification: An integrative approach*. New York: Plenum Press, 1977.

MEICHENBAUM, DONALD. Cognitive behavior modification with exceptional children: A promise yet unfulfilled. *Exceptional Children Quarterly*, May 1980, *1*, 83–88.

MEICHENBAUM, DONALD, & ASARNOW, J. Cognitive-behavioral modification and metacognitive development: Implications for the classroom. In P. Kendall & S. Hollen (Eds.), *Cognitive behavioral interventions: Theory, research, and procedures*. New York: Academic Press, 1979.

MEINTS, DONALD W. The task system in an individualized reading class. *Journal of Reading*, January 1977, *20*, 301–304.

MEMORY, DAVID M. Record keeping for effective reading instruction. In D. Lapp (Ed.), *Making reading possible through effective classroom management*. Newark, DE: International Reading Association, 1980, 146–185.

MEMORY, DAVID M. Written questions as reading aids in the middle grades: A review of research. In J. Niles & L. A. Harris (Eds.), *New inquiries in reading: Research and instruction*. Rochester, NY: National Reading Conference, 1982, 71–76.

MEMORY, DAVID M. Constructing main idea questions: A test of a depth-of-processing perspective. In J. Niles & L. A. Harris (Eds.), *Searches for meaning in reading/*

language processing and instruction. Rochester, NY: National Reading Conference, 1983, 66–70.(a)

MEMORY, DAVID M. Main idea prequestions as adjunct aids with good and low average middle grade readers. *Journal of Reading Behavior*, 1983, *15*(2), 37–48.(b)

MEMORY, DAVID M., & MOORE, DAVID W. Selecting sources in library research: An activity in skimming and critical reading. *Journal of Reading Behavior*, March 1981, *24*, 469–474.

MERCER, CECIL D., & MERCER, ANNE. The development and use of self-correcting material with exceptional children. *Teaching Exceptional Children*, Fall 1978, *11*, 6–11.

MERLIN, SHIRLEY B., & ROGERS, SUE F. Direct teaching strategies. *The Reading Teacher*, December 1981, *35*, 292–297.

MESSICK, SAMUEL. *Cognitive styles in educational practice.* Research Report 82–13. Princeton, NJ: Educational Testing Service, June 1982.

MESSICK, SAMUEL. Assessment in context: Appraising student performance in relation to instructional quality. *Educational Researcher*, March 1984, *13*, 3–8.

METZGER, R. L., & WERNER, DAVID B. Use of visual training for reading disabilities: A review. *Pediatrics*, 1984, *73*(6), 824–829.

MEWHORT, D. J. K., & CAMPBELL, A. J. Toward a model of skilled reading: An analysis of performance in tachistoscopic tasks. In G. MacKinnon & T. Waller (Eds.), *Reading research: Advances in theory and practice*, Vol. 3. New York: Academic Press, 1981, 39–118.

MEYER, BONNIE J. F. Organizational aspects of text: Effects on reading comprehension and applications for the classroom. In J. Flood (Ed.), *Promoting reading comprehension.* Newark, DE: International Reading Association, 1984, 113–138.

MEYER, BONNIE J. F., & RICE, G. ELIZABETH. The structure of text. In P. D. Pearson (Ed.), *Handbook of reading research.* New York: Longman, 1984, 319–351.

MEYER, LINDA A. The relative effects of word-analysis and word-supply correction procedures with poor readers during word-attack training. *Reading Research Quarterly*, 1982, *17*(4), 544–555.

MEYER, LINDA A. *Long-term academic effects of Direct Instruction Follow Through.* Technical Report No. 299. Champaign, IL: Center for the Study of Reading, University of Illinois, November 1983.

MEYER, LINDA A. Research in implementation: What seems to work. In S. J. Samuels & P. D. Pearson (Eds.), *Changing school reading programs: Principles and case studies.* Newark, DE: International Reading Association, 1988, 41–57.

MEYER, LINDA A.; GREER, EUNICE A.; & CRUMMEY, LORRAINE. An analysis of decoding, comprehension, and story text comprehensibility in four first-grade reading programs. *Journal of Reading Behavior*, 1987, *19* (1), 69–98.

MEYER, SUSAN. What's the word on children's dictionaries? *Learning*, March 1980, *8*, 44–46.

MEYERS, JAMIE. *You can encourage your high school student to read.* Newark, DE: International Reading Association, 1989.

MEZYNSKI, KAREN. Issues concerning the acquisition of knowledge: Effects of vocabulary training on reading comprehension. *Review of Educational Research*, Summer 1983, *53*, 253–279.

MICCINATI, JEANNETTE. The Fernald technique: Modifications increase the probability of success. *Journal of Learning Disabilities*, March 1979, *12*, 139–142.

MICCINATI, JEANETTE L. Using prosodic cues to teach oral reading fluency. *The Reading Teacher*, November 1985, *39*, 206–212.

MICCINATI, JEANETTE L. Mapping the terrain: Connecting reading with academic writing. *Journal of Reading*, March 1988, *31*, 542–552.

MICKLOS, JOHN, JR. Is 1984 upon us? *Journal of Reading*, March 1983, *26*, 486–488.

MICKLOS, JOHN (Ed.). Children's literature sales rise. *Reading Today*, April/May 1988, *5*, 4.(a)

MICKLOS, JOHN (Ed.). School libraries and reading programs: Establishing closer ties. *Reading Today*, December 1987/January 1988, *5*, 1, 18–19.(b)

MIER, MARGARET. Comprehension monitoring in the elementary classroom. *The Reading Teacher*, April 1984, *37*, 770–774.

MIKULECKY, LARRY. Review of *Illiterate America* by Jonathan Kozol. *Journal of Reading Behavior*, 1986, *18*(2), 171–174.

MIKULECKY, LARRY. The status of literacy in our society. In J. E. Readence *et al.* (Eds.), *Research in literacy: Merging perspectives*. Rochester, NY: National Reading Conference, 1987, 211–235.

MILES, J.; FOREMAN, P. J.; & ANDERSON, J. The long and short predictive efficiency of two tests of reading potential. *Slow Learning Child*, November 1973, *20*, 131–141.

MILES, T. R., & HASLUM, MARY N. Dyslexia: Anomaly or normal variation? *Annals of Dyslexia*, Vol. 36. Baltimore, MD: Orton Dyslexia Society, 1986, 103–117.

MILES, W. R., & SEGEL, D. Clinical observation of eye movement in the rating of reading ability. *Journal of Educational Psychology*, 1929, *20*, 520–529.

MILLER, ARTHUR L. A study of reading tastes of children in grades four, five, and six in selected schools in the Lamar area school study council. *Dissertation Abstracts*, 1967, *27*, 2471A.

MILLER, EDITH F. Stimulate reading ... with a dictionary. *Grade Teacher*, February 1962, *79*, 51–52, 106–107. Also in A. J. Harris & E. Sipay (Eds.), *Readings on reading instruction* (3rd ed.). New York: Longman, 1984, 242–245.

MILLER, ETTA. *Relationships among modality preference, method of instruction, and reading achievement.* Unpublished doctoral dissertation, State University of New York at Albany, 1974.

MILLER, GLORIA. The influence of self-instruction on the comprehension monitoring performance of average and above-average readers. *Journal of Reading Behavior*, 1987, *19* (3), 303–317.

MILLER, GLORIA E.; GIOVENCO, ANDREA; & RENTIERS, KATHRYN A. Fostering comprehension monitoring in below average reader through self-instruction training. *Journal of Reading Behavior*, 1987, *19*(4), 379–393.

MILLER, MARGARET J. The primary child in the library. In L. Monson & D. McClenathan (Eds.), *Developing active readers: Ideas for parents, teachers, and librarians*. Newark, DE: International Reading Association, 1979, 43–51.

MILLER, PHYLLIS A. Considering flexibility of reading rate for assessment and development of efficient reading behavior. In S. Jay Samuels (Ed.), *What research has to say about reading instruction*. Newark, DE: International Reading Association, 1978, 72–83.

MILLMAN, JASON, et al. Relation between perseverance and rate of learning: A test of Carroll's model of school learning. *American Educational Research Journal*, Fall 1983, *20*, 425–434.

MILLS, ROBERT E. An evaluation of techniques for teaching word recognition. *Elementary School Journal*, 1956, *56*, 221–225.

MITCHELL, JAMES V., JR. (Ed.). *Tests in print, III*. Lincoln, NE: Buros Institute of Mental Measurements, University of Nebraska, 1983.

MITCHELL, JAMES V., JR. (Ed.). *The ninth mental measurements yearbook*. Lincoln, NE: Buros Institute of Mental Measurement, University of Nebraska, 1985.

MITTERER, JOHN O. There are at least two kinds of poor readers: Whole-word poor readers and recoding poor readers. *Canadian Journal of Psychology*, September 1982, *36*, 445–461.

MOE, ALDEN J., & HOPKINS, CAROL J. Jingles, jokes, limericks, poems, proverbs, puns, puzzles and riddles: Fast reading for reluctant readers. *Language Arts*, November/December 1978, *55*, 957–965, 1003.

MOE, ALDEN; HOPKINS, CAROL J.; & RUSH, J. TIMOTHY. *The vocabulary of first-grade children*. Springfield, IL: Charles C Thomas, 1982.

MOLL, LUIS C. Some key issues in teaching Latino students. *Language Arts*, September 1988, 65, 465–472.

MONAGHAN, E. JENNIFER. A history of the syndrome of dyslexia with implications for its treatment. In C. McCullough (Ed.), *Inchworm, inchworm: Persistent problems in reading education*. Newark, DE: International Reading Association, 1980, 87–101.

MONROE, MARION. *Children who cannot read*. Chicago: University of Chicago Press, 1932.

MONSON, DIANNE L. (Ed.). *Adventuring with books: A booklist for pre-K—grade 6*. Urbana, IL: National Council of Teachers of English, 1985.

MONTAGUE, MARJORIE, & TANNER, MICHAEL. Reading strategy groups for content area subjects. *Journal of Reading*, May 1987, 30, 716–723.

MONTEITH, MARY K. A whole word list catalog. *The Reading Teacher*, May 1976, 29, 844–847.

MONTEITH, MARY K. The magazine habit. *Language Arts*, November/December 1981, 58, 965–969.(a)

MONTEITH, MARY K. The reading teacher vs. children of divorce. *The Reading Teacher*, October 1981, 35, 100–103.(b)

MOON, CHARLES, et al. Main and interactive effects of metallic pollutants on cognitive functioning. *Journal of Learning Disabilities*, April 1985, 18, 217–221.

MOORE, DAVID W. Vocabulary. In D. E. Alvermann et al. (Eds.), *Research within reach: Secondary school reading*. Newark, DE: International Reading Association, 1987, 64–79.

MOORE, DAVID W.; CUNNINGHAM, JAMES W.; & RUDISELL, N. Readers' conceptions of the main idea. In J. Niles & L. Harris (Eds.), *Searches for meaning in reading, language processing, and instruction*. Rochester, NY: National Reading Conference, 1983, 202–206.

MOORE, DAVID W., & MURPHY, ANN G. Reading programs. In D. E. Alvermann et al. (Eds.), *Research within reach: Secondary school reading*. Newark, DE: International Reading Association, 1987, 2–13.

MOORE, DAVID W., & READENCE, JOHN E. Processing main ideas through parallel lesson transfer. *Journal of Reading*, April 1980, 23, 589–593.

MOORE, DAVID W.; READENCE, JOHN E.; & RICKELMAN, ROBERT J. An historical explanation of content area reading instruction. *Reading Research Quarterly*, Summer 1983, 18, 419–438.

MOORE, DAVID W.; READENCE, JOHN E.; & RICKELMAN, ROBERT J. *Prereading activities for content area reading and learning* (2nd ed.). Newark, DE: International Reading Association, 1989.

MOORE, DAVID W., & WILSON, BARRY J. On the search for a characteristic WISC-R subtest profile of reading/learning disabled children. *Reading Research and Instruction*, Winter 1987, 26, 133–140.

MOORE, MICHAEL J., et al. Cognitive profiles in reading disability. *Genetic Psychology Monographs*, February 1982, 105 (1st half), 41–93.

MORETZ, SARA, & DAVEY, BETH. Process and strategies in teaching decoding skills in middle and secondary schools. In L. E. Hafner (Ed.), *Improving reading in middle and secondary schools: Selected readings* (2nd ed.). New York: Macmillan 1974, 76–101.

MORGAN, W. PRINGLE. A case of congenital word-blindness. *British Medical Journal*, 1896, 2, 1543–1544.

MORICE, RODNEY, & SLAGHUIS, WALTER. Language performance and reading ability at 8 years of age. *Applied Psycholinguistics*, 1985, 6(2), 141–160.

MORRIS, DARRELL. Beginning reader's concept of word. In E. Henderson & J. Beers (Eds.), *Developmental and cognitive aspects of learning to spell: A reflection of word knowledge*. Newark, DE: International Reading Association, 1980, 97–111.

MORRIS, JOYCE M. *Standards and progress in reading.* London: National Foundation for Educational Research in England and Wales, 1966.

MORRISON, DELMONT C., & HINSHAW, STEPHEN P. The relationship between neuropsychological/perceptual performance and sociometric status in children with learning disabilities. *Journal of Learning Disabilities,* February 1988, *21,* 124–128.

MORRISON, DELMONT C.; HINSHAW, STEPHEN P.; & CARTE, ESTOE T. Signs of neurobehavioral dysfunction in a sample of learning disabled children: Stability and concurrent validity. *Perceptual and Motor Skills,* December 1985, *61* (Part 1), 863–872.

MORRISON, FREDERICK J. Word decoding and rule-learning in normal and disabled readers. *Remedial and Special Education,* May/June 1984, 5, 20–27.

MORRISON, FREDERICK, & MANIS, FRANKLIN R. Cognitive processes and reading disability: A critique and proposal. In C. Brainerd & M. Pressley (Eds.), *Verbal processes in children: Progress in cognitive development research.* New York: Springer-Verlag, 1982, 59–93.

MORROW, DANIEL H. Dialect interference in writing: Another critical review. *Research in the Teaching of English,* May 1985, *19,* 154–180.

MORROW, LESLEY M. Developing young voluntary readers: The home—the child—the school. *Reading Research and Instruction,* Fall 1985, 25, 1–8.

MORROW, LESLEY M. Retelling: A strategy for reading instruction and assessment. In J. A. Niles & R. V. Lalik (Eds.), *Solving problems in literacy: Learners, teachers and researchers.* Rochester, NY: National Reading Conference, 1986, 73–80.

MORROW, LESLEY M. Promoting voluntary reading: Activities represented in basal reader manuals. *Reading Research and Instruction,* Spring 1987, *26,* 189–202.

MORROW, LESLEY M. Retelling stories as a diagnostic tool. In S.M. Glazer et al. (Eds.), *Reexamining reading diagnosis: New trends and procedures.* Newark, DE: International Reading Association, 1988, 128–149.(a)

MORROW, LESLEY M. Young children's responses to one-to-one story readings in school settings. *Reading Research Quarterly,* Winter 1988, *23,* 89–107.(b)

MORROW, LESLEY M. Creating a bridge to children's literature. In P. N. Winograd et al. (Eds.), *Improving basal reading instruction.* New York: Teachers College Press, 1989, 210–230.(a)

MORROW, LESLEY M. Using story retelling to develop comprehension. In K. D. Muth (Ed.), *Children's comprehension of text.* Newark, DE: International Reading Association, 1989, 37–58.(b)

MORROW, LESLEY M., & WEINSTEIN, CAROL S. Encouraging voluntary reading: The impact of a literature program on children's use of library centers. *Reading Research Quarterly,* Summer 1986, *21,* 330–346.

MORSINK, CATHERINE V., et al. Research on teaching: Opening the door to special education classrooms. *Exceptional Children Quarterly,* September 1986, *53,* 32–40.

MORTON, J. The effects of context upon speed of reading, eye movement, and eye-voice span. *Quarterly Journal of Experimental Psychology,* 1964, *13,* 340–354.

MOSCOVITCH, MORRIS. Right-hemisphere language. *Topics in Language Disorders,* September 1981, *1,* 41–61.

MOSENTHAL, PETER. Psycholinguistic properties of aural and visual comprehension as determined by children's abilities to comprehend syllogisms. *Reading Research Quarterly,* 1976–1977, *12*(1), 55–92.

MOSS, JOY F. Growth in reading in an integrated day classroom. *Elementary School Journal,* March 1972, 72, 304–320.

MOSS, JOY F. *Focus units in literature: A handbook for elementary school teachers.* Urbana, IL: National Council of Teachers of English, 1984.

MOUSTAFA, MARGARET. Comprehensible Input plus the Language Experience Approach: A longterm perspective. *The Reading Teacher,* December 1987, *41,* 276–286.

MOUSTAFA, MARGARET, & PENROSE, JOYCE. Comprehensible input plus the Language Experience Approach: Reading instruction for limited English speaking students. *The Reading Teacher*, March 1985, 38, 640–647.

MUIA, JOSEPH A., & CONNORS, EUGENE T. Legal entanglement of reading clinic's diagnostic procedures. *Journal of Reading*, January 1978, 21, 321–328.

MUTH, K. DENISE. Structure strategies for comprehending expository text. *Reading Research and Instruction*, Fall 1987, 27, 66–72.(a)

MUTH, K. DENISE. Teachers' connection questions: Prompting students to organize text idea. *Journal of Reading*, December 1987, 31, 254–259.(b)

MUTH, K. DENISE. Comprehension monitoring: A reading–mathematics connection. *Reading Research and Instruction*, Spring 1988, 27, 60–67.

MYERS, COLLIN A. Reviewing the literature on Fernald's technique of remedial reading. *The Reading Teacher*, March 1978, 31, 614–619.

MYKLEBUST, HELMER R. Learning disabilities: Definition and overview. In H. R. Myklebust (Ed.), *Progress in learning disabilities,* Vol. 1. New York: Grune & Stratton, 1968, 1–15.

MYKLEBUST, HELMER R. Toward a science of dyslexiology. In H. R. Myklebust (Ed.), *Progress in learning disabilities*, Vol. 4. New York: Grune & Stratton, 1978, 1–40.

MYKLEBUST, HELMER R. Toward a science of learning disabilities. *Journal of Learning Disabilities*, January 1983, 16, 17–18.

NAGY, WILLIAM E. *Teaching vocabulary to improve reading comprehension*. Urbana, IL: National Council of Teachers of English, 1988.

NAGY, WILLIAM E., & ANDERSON, RICHARD C. How many words are there in printed school English? *Reading Research Quarterly*, Spring 1984, 19, 304–330.

NAGY, WILLIAM E.; ANDERSON, RICHARD C; & HERMAN, PATRICIA A. *The influence of word and text properties on learning from context*. Technical Report No. 369. Champaign, IL: Center for the Study of Reading, University of Illinois, January 1986.

NAGY, WILLIAM; ANDERSON, RICHARD C.; & HERMAN, PATRICIA A. Learning word meanings from context during normal reading. *American Educational Research Journal*, Summer 1987, 24, 237–270.

NAGY, WILLIAM E., & HERMAN, PATRICIA A. *Limitations of vocabulary instruction*. Technical Report No. 326. Champaign, IL: Center for the Study of Reading, University of Illinois, October 1984.

NAGY, WILLIAM E., & HERMAN, PATRICIA A. Breadth and depth of vocabulary knowledge: Implications for acquisition and instruction. In M. G. McKeown & M. E. Curtis (Eds.), *The nature of vocabulary acquisition*. Hillsdale, NJ: Erlbaum, 1987, 19–35.

NAGY, WILLIAM E.; HERMAN, PATRICIA A.; & ANDERSON, RICHARD C. Learning words from context. *Reading Research Quarterly*, Winter 1985, 20, 233–253.(a)

NAGY, WILLIAM E.; HERMAN, PATRICIA A.; & ANDERSON, RICHARD C. *Learning word meanings from context: How broadly generalizable?* Technical Report No. 347. Champaign, IL: Center for the Study of Reading, University of Illinois, December 1985.(b)

NAIDEN, NORMA. Ratio of boys to girls among disabled readers. *The Reading Teacher*, February 1976, 29, 439–446.

NARANG, HARBANS L. Bibliotherapy: A review of the research. *Saskatchewan Journal of Educational Research and Development*, Spring 1977, 7, 5–12.

NATIONAL ADVISORY COMMITTEE ON DYSLEXIA AND RELATED DISORDERS. *Reading disorders in the United States*. Washington, DC: Government Printing Office, 1969.

NATIONAL ASSESSMENT OF EDUCATIONAL PROGRESS. *Reading rate and comprehension, 1970–71 assessment*. Report 82–R–09. Denver, CO: Education Commission of the States, December 1972.

NATIONAL ASSESSMENT OF EDUCATIONAL PROGRESS. *Reading, thinking, and writing. Re-*

sults from the 1979–80 National Assessment of reading and literature. Report No. 11–L–35. Denver, CO: Education Commission of the States, July 1981.

NAEP NEWSLETTER, Spring 1982, *15,* 3.(a)

NATIONAL ASSESSMENT OF EDUCATIONAL PROGRESS. *Reading comprehension of American youth: Do they understand what they read? Results from the 1979–80 National Assessment of reading and literature.* Report No. 11–R–02. Denver, CO: Education Commission of the States, July 1982.(b)

NATIONAL ASSESSMENT OF EDUCATIONAL PROGRESS. Linguistic background, achievement linked. *NAEP Newsletter,* Winter 1983, *16,* 3, 5.(a)

NATIONAL ASSESSMENT OF EDUCATIONAL PROGRESS. Low achievers improve reading skills, but top students lose ground in math, science. *NAEP Newsletter,* Winter 1983, *16,* 1–2.(b)

NATIONAL ASSESSMENT OF EDUCATIONAL PROGRESS. New objectives chart course for good writers to follow. *NAEP Newsletter,* Winter 1983, *16,* 4–5.(c)

NATIONAL ASSESSMENT OF EDUCATIONAL PROGRESS. Adult literacy probe moves forward. *NAEP Newsletter,* Spring 1985, *18*(1), 1, 4.(a)

NATIONAL ASSESSMENT OF EDUCATIONAL PROGRESS. *The reading report card: Progress toward excellence in our schools: Trends in reading over four national assessments, 1971–1984.* Report No. 15–R–01. Princeton, NJ: NAEP/ETS, 1985.(b)

NATIONAL COMMISSION ON EXCELLENCE IN EDUCATION. *A nation at risk: The imperative for educational reform.* Washington, DC: Superintendent of Documents, Government Printing Office, 1983. Stock No. 065–000–00177–2. (ERIC number ED 226 006.)

NATIONAL INSTITUTES OF MENTAL HEALTH. *Television and behavior: Ten years of scientific progress and implications for the eighties.* DHMS Publication No. ADM 82–1195. Washington, DC: Government Printing Office, 1982.

NATIONAL JOINT COMMITTEE ON LEARNING DISABILITIES. Learning disabilities: Issues on definition. Baltimore, MD: Orton Dyslexia Society, January 30, 1981. Unpublished manuscript. Also in Jim Leigh, The NJCLD position papers (I–IV). *Learning Disability Quarterly,* Winter 1983, *6,* 4–54.

NATRIELLO, GARY, & DORNBUSH, STANFORD M. Bring behavior back in: The effect of student characteristics and behavior on the classroom behavior of teachers. *American Educational Research Journal,* Spring 1983, *20,* 29–43.

NEGIN, GARY A. The effects of syntactic segmentation on the reading comprehension of hearing impaired children. *Reading Psychology,* 1987, *8*(1), 23–31.

NEGIN, GARY A., & KRUGLER, DEE. Essential literacy skills for functioning in an urban community. *Journal of Reading,* November 1980, *24,* 109–115.

NEILSEN, ALLAN R. An investigation of the relationship of cohesion to linguistic marking, discourse structure, and content familiarity. In M. Kamil (Ed.), *Directions in reading: Research and instruction.* Washington, DC: National Reading Conference, 1981, 209–214.

NEILSEN, ALLAN R.; RENNIE, BARBARA J.; & CONNELL, ARLENE M. Allocation of instructional time to reading comprehension and study skills in intermediate grade social studies classrooms. In J. Niles & L. A. Harris (Eds.), *New inquiries in reading research and instruction.* Rochester, NY: National Reading Conference, 1982, 81–84.

NELL, VICTOR. The psychology of reading for pleasure: Needs and gratifications. *Reading Research Quarterly,* Winter 1988, *23,* 6–50.

NELMS, BEN F. (Ed.). *Literature in the classroom: Readers, texts, and contexts.* Urbana, IL: National Council of Teachers of English, 1988.

NELSON, HAZEL E. Analyses of spelling errors in normal and dyslexic children. In U. Frith (Ed.), *Cognitive processes in spelling.* New York: Academic Press, 1980, 475–493.

NELSON, JOAN, & HERBER, HAROLD L. Organization and management of programs. In A.

Berger & H. A. Robinson (Eds.), *Secondary school reading: What research reveals for classroom practice*. Urbana, IL: National Council for Research in English/ ERIC, 1982, 143–157.

NELSON-HERBER, JOAN. Expanding and refining vocabulary in content areas. *Journal of Reading*, April 1986, *29*, 626–633.

NEMKO, BARBARA. Context versus isolation: Another look at beginning readers. *Reading Research Quarterly*, Summer 1984, *19*, 461–467.

NESSEL, DENISE D. Storytelling in the reading program. *The Reading Teacher*, January 1985, *38*, 378–381.

NESSEL, DENISE. The new face of comprehension instruction: A closer look at questions. *The Reading Teacher*, March 1987, *40*, 604–606.

NEUMAN, SUSAN B. Television, reading, and the home environment. *Reading Research and Instruction*, Spring 1986, *25*, 173–183.

NEUMAN, SUSAN B. The displacement effect: Assessing the relation between television viewing and reading performance. *Reading Research Quarterly*, Fall 1988, *23*, 414–440.(a)

NEUMAN, SUSAN B. Enhancing children's comprehension through previewing. In J. Readence et al. (Eds.), *Dialogues in literacy research*. Chicago: National Reading Conference, 1988, 219–224.(b)

NEUMAN, SUSAN B., & PROWDA, PETER. Television viewing and reading achievement. *Journal of Reading Behavior*, April 1982, *25*, 666–670.

NEVI, CHARLES N. Cross-age tutoring: Why does it help the tutors? *The Reading Teacher*, May 1983, *36*, 892–898.

NEVILLE, DONALD. The relationship between reading skills and intelligence test scores. *The Reading Teacher*, January 1965, *18*, 257–262.

NEVILLE, DONALD D., & SEARLS, EVELYN F. The effect of sentence combining and kernel-identification training on the syntactic component of reading comprehension. *Research in the Teaching of English*, February 1985, *19*, 37–61.

NEWCOMER, PHYLLIS L., & HAMMILL, DONALD D. ITPA and academic achievement: A survey. *The Reading Teacher*, May 1975, *28*, 731–741.

NEWCOMER, PHYLLIS L., & MAGEE, PATRICIA. The performance of learning (reading) disabled children on a test of spoken language. *The Reading Teacher*, May 1977, *30*, 896–900.

NEWHOUSE, ROBERT C., & LOKER, SUZANNE. Does bibliotherapy reduce fear among second-grade children? *Reading Psychology*, January–March 1984, *4*, 25–27.

NEWTON, MARGARET. A neuropsychological investigation into dyslexia. In A. W. Franklin & S. Naidoo (Eds.), *Assessment and teaching of dyslexic children*. London: Invalid Children's Aid Association, 1970, 14–21.

New York Times. A therapy system for young scored. March 7, 1968.

NICHOLS, JAMES N. Foiling students who'd rather fake it than read it or how to get students to read and report on books. *Journal of Reading*, December 1978, *22*, 245–247.

NICHOLS, JAMES N. Using prediction to increase content area interest and understanding. *Journal of Reading*, December 1983, *27*, 325–328.

NICHOLSON, TOM. Reading is not a guessing game: The great debate revisited. *Reading-Canada-Lecture*, Winter 1986, *4*, 239–247.

NICHOLSON, TOM. Using the CIPP model to evaluate reading instruction. *Journal of Reading*, January 1989, *32*, 312–318.

NICHOLSON, TOM; LILLAS, CHRISTINE; & RZOSKA, M. ANNE. Have we been mislead by miscues? *The Reading Teacher*, October 1988, *42*, 6–10.

NICKERSON, RAYMOND S. *Adult literacy and technology*. Technical Report No. 351. Champaign, IL: Center for the Study of Reading, University of Illinois, December 1985.

NILES, J. A., & HARRIS, L. A. (Eds.). *Searches for meaning in reading, language process-ing, and instruction.* Thirty-second yearbook of the National Reading Conference. Rochester, NY, 1983, 202–206.

NILSEN, ALEEN P.; PETERSON, RALPH; & SEARFOSS, LYNDON W. The adult as critic vs. the child as reader. *Language Arts*, May 1980, 57, 530–539.

NILSEN, DON L. F., & NILSEN, ALEEN P. An exploration and defense of the humor in young adult literature. *Journal of Reading*, October 1982, 26, 58–65.

NIST, SHERRIE L., & KIRBY, KATE. Teaching comprehension and study strategies through modeling and thinking aloud. *Reading Research and Instruction*, Summer 1986, 25, 254–264.

NOLTE, RUTH Y., & SINGER, HARRY. Active comprehension: Teaching a process of reading comprehension and its effects on reading achievement. *The Reading Teacher*, October 1985, 39, 24–31.

NORVELL, GEORGE W. The challenge of periodicals in education. *Elementary English*, 1966, 43, 402–408.

NORVELL, GEORGE W. Revolution in the English curriculum. *Elementary English*, May 1972, 49, 760–767.

NORVELL, GEORGE W. *The reading interests of young people.* Ann Arbor: Michigan State University Press, 1973.

O'BRIEN, DAVID G., & MARTIN, MICHAEL A. Does figurative language present a unique comprehension problem? *Journal of Reading Behavior*, 1988, 20(1), 63–87.

OBRZUT, JOHN E., & BOLIEK, CAROL A. Lateralization characteristics in learning disabled children. *Journal of Learning Disabilities*, May 1986, 19, 308–314.

OBRZUT, JOHN E., & HYND, GEORGE W. Cognitive dysfunction and psychoeducational assessment in individuals with acquired brain injury. *Journal of Learning Disabil-ities*, December 1987, 20, 596–602.

O'CONNOR, SHELLY C., & SPREEN, OTFRIED. The relationship between parents' sociomet-ric status and education level, and adult occupational and educational achievement of children with learning disabilities. *Journal of Learning Disabilities*, March 1988, 21, 148–153.

ODLAND, NORINE. Planning a literature program for the elementary school. *Language Arts*, April 1979, 56, 363–367.

O'DONNELL, HOLLY. The hyperactive child and drug treatment. *The Reading Teacher*, October 1982, 36, 106–109.

O'DONNELL, HOLLY. The use of illustrations in textbooks. *The Reading Teacher*, January 1983, 36, 462–464.

O'DONNELL, LINDA E. Intra-individual discrepancy in diagnosing specific learning disa-bilities. *Learning Disability Quarterly*, Winter 1980, 3, 10–18.

O'FLAHAVEN J. F.; HARTMAN, DOUGLAS K.; & PEARSON, P. DAVID. Teacher questioning and feedback practices: A twenty year perspective. In J. Readence et al. (Eds.), *Dialogues in literacy research.* Chicago, IL: National Reading Conference, 1988, 183–208.

OFMAN, WILLIAM, & SCHAEVITZ, MORTON. The kinesthetic method in remedial reading. *Journal of Experimental Education*, 1963, 31, 319–320.

OGLE, DONNA M. The Know, Want to Know, Learn Strategy. In K. D. Muth (Ed.), *Chil-dren's comprehension of text.* Newark, DE: International Reading Association, 1989, 205–223.

OHLAUSEN, MARILYN M., & ROLLER, CATHY M. The operation of text structure and con-tent schemata in isolation and in interaction. *Reading Research Quarterly*, 1988, 23(1), 70–88.

OJEMANN, GEORGE A. Interrelationships in the brain organization of language-related behavior: Evidence from electrical stimulation mapping. In U. Kirk (Ed.), *Neuro-psychology of language, reading, and spelling.* New York: Academic Press, 1983, 129–192.

OLDRIDGE, O. A. Positive suggestion: It helps LD students learn. *Academic Therapy*, January 1982, *17*, 279–287.

OLLILA, LLOYD; JOHNSON, TERRY; & DOWNING, JOHN. Adapting Russian methods of auditory discrimination training for English. *Elementary English*, November/December 1974, *51*, 1138–1141, 1145.

OLSON, ARTHUR V. The questionable value of perceptual tests in diagnosing reading disabilities. *Journal of Research in Reading*, 1980, *3*(2), 129–139.

OLSON, MARY W. Text type and reader ability: The effects on paraphrase and text-based inference questions. *Journal of Reading Behavior*, 1985, *17*(3), 199–214.

OLSON, MARY W.; GEE, THOMAS C.; & FORESTER, NORA. Magazines in the classroom: Beyond recreational reading. *Journal of Reading*, May 1989, *32*, 708–713.

OLSON, MARY W., & LONGION, BONNIE. Pattern guides: A workable alternative for content teachers. *Journal of Reading*, May 1982, *25*, 736–741.

OLSON, RICHARD K. Disabled reading processes and cognitive profiles. In D. B. Gray & J. F. Kavanagh (Eds.), *Biobehavioral measures of dyslexia*. Parkton, MD: York Press, 1985, 215–243.

OLSON, RICHARD K.; FOLTZ, GREGORY; & WISE, BARBARA. Reading instruction and remediation with the aid of computer speech. *Behavior Research Methods, Instruments and Computers*, 1986, *18*(2), 93–99.

OLSON, RICHARD K.; KLIEGEL, REINHOLD; & DAVIDSON, BRIAN J. Eye movements in reading disability. In K. Rayner (Ed.), *Eye movements in reading: Perceptual and language processes*. New York: Academic Press, 1983, 467–479.

OLSON, RICHARD K., et al. Individual and developmental differences in reading disabilities. In T. G. Waller (Ed.), *Reading research: Advances in theory and practice*, Vol. 4. New York: Academic Press, 1985, 1–64.

O'MARA, DEBORAH A. The process of reading mathematics. *Journal of Reading*, October 1981, *25*, 22–30.

OMIZO, MICHAEL M., & MICHAEL, WILLIAM B. Biofeedback-induced relaxation training and impulsivity, attention to task, and locus of control among hyperactive boys. *Journal of Learning Disabilities*, August/September 1982, *15*, 414–416.

O'ROURKE, JOSEPH P. *Toward a science of vocabulary development*. The Hague: Mouton, 1974.

ORTIZ, ALBA A. Choosing the language of instruction for exceptional bilingual instruction. *Teaching Exceptional Children*, Spring 1984, *16*, 208–212.

ORTON, JUNE L. The Orton-Gillingham approach. In J. Money (Ed.), *The disabled reader*. Baltimore: Johns Hopkins Press, 1966, 119–146.

ORTON, JUNE L. *A guide to teaching phonetics*. Cambridge, MA: Educators Publishing Service, 1976.

ORTON, SAMUEL T. *Reading, writing, and speech problems in children*. New York: Norton, 1937.

ORTONY, ANTHONY. *Understanding metaphors*. Technical Report No. 154. Champaign, IL: Center for the Study of Reading, University of Illinois, January 1980.

ORTONY, ANTHONY. Understanding figurative language. In P. D. Pearson (Ed.), *Handbook of reading research*. New York: Longman, 1984, 453–470.

ORTONY, ANDREW; TURNER, TERENCE J.; & LARSON-SHAPIRO, NANCY. Cultural and instructional influences on figurative language comprehension by inner city children. *Research in the Teaching of English*, February 1985, *19*, 25–36.

OSBORN, JEAN. The purposes, uses, and contents of workbooks and some guidelines for publishers. In R. Anderson, et al. (Eds.), *Learning to read in American schools*. Hillsdale, NJ: Erlbaum, 1984, 45–111.(a)

OSBORN, JEAN. Workbooks that accompany basal reading programs. In G. Duffy et al. (Eds.), *Comprehension instruction: Perspectives and suggestions*. New York: Longman, 1984, 163–186.(b)

OSBORN, JEAN. *Reading strategies and reading generalization.* Reading Education Report No. 69. Champaign, IL: Center for the Study of Reading, University of Illinois, September 1986.

OSBORN, JEAN H. Summary: Improving basal reading programs. In P. N. Winograd et al. (Eds.), *Improving basal reading instruction.* New York: Teachers College Press, 1989, 271–296.

O'SHEA, LAWRENCE J., & SINDELAR, PAUL T. The effects of segmenting written discourse on the reading comprehension of low- and high-performance readers. *Reading Research Quarterly,* Summer 1983, *18,* 458–465.

O'SHEA, LAWRENCE J.; SINDELAR, PAUL T.; & O'SHEA, DOROTHY J. The effects of repeated readings and attentional cues on reading fluency and comprehension. *Journal of Reading Behavior,* 1985, *17*(2), 129–142.

OSTERLIND, STEVEN J. Using CRTs in program curriculum evaluation. *Educational Measurement: Issues and Practices,* Fall 1988, 7, 23–30.

OSTERTAG, BRUCE, & RAMBEAU, JOHN. Reading success through rewriting for secondary LD students. *Academic Therapy,* September 1982, *18,* 27–32.

OTTO, WAYNE. *The relationship of retroactive inhibition and school achievement: Theory, research, and implications.* Occasional Paper No. 4. Madison, WI: Research and Development Center for Learning and Re-education, University of Wisconsin, 1966.

OTTO, WAYNE. Evaluating instruments for assessing needs and growth in reading. In W. H. MacGinitie (Ed.), *Assessment problems in reading.* Newark, DE: International Reading Association, 1973, 14–20.

OTTO, WAYNE. Practice makes perfect: always_____ sometimes_____ never_____ . *Journal of Reading Behavior,* November 1985, 29, 189–191.

OTTO, WAYNE; BARRETT, THOMAS C.; & HARRIS, THEODORE L. Research in reading. *Journal of Experimental Education,* Fall 1968, *37,* 65–77.

OTTO, WAYNE; WHITE, SANDRA; & CAMPERELL, KAY. Text comprehension research to classroom application: Developing an instructional technique. *Reading Psychology,* Summer 1980, *1,* 184–191.

OTTO, WAYNE, et al. *A technique for improving the understanding of expository text: Gloss.* Theoretical Paper No. 96. Madison, WI: Wisconsin Center for Educational Research, University of Wisconsin, November 1981.

OWRID, H. L. Hearing impairment and verbal attainments in primary school children. *Educational Research,* June 1970, *12,* 209–214.

PAGE, WILLIAM D., & CARLSON, KENNETH L. The process of observing oral reading scores. *Reading Horizons,* Spring 1975, *15,* 147–150.

PALINCSAR, ANNEMARIE S. The quest for meaning from expository text: A teacher-guided journey. In G. Duffy et al. (Eds.), *Reading comprehension: Perspectives and suggestions.* New York: Longman, 1984, 251–264.

PALINCSAR, ANNEMARIE S. Meta-cognitive strategy instruction. *Exceptional Children,* October 1986, *53,* 118–124.

PALINCSAR, ANNEMARIE S., & BROWN, ANN L. *Reciprocal teaching of comprehension-monitoring activities.* Technical Report No. 269. Champaign, IL: Center for the Study of Reading, University of Illinois, January 1983.

PALINCSAR, ANNEMARIE S., & BROWN, ANN L. Interactive teaching to promote independent learning from text. *The Reading Teacher,* April 1986, *39,* 771–777.

PALINCSAR, ANNEMARIE S., & BROWN, DEBORAH A. Enhancing instructional time through attention to metacognition. *Journal of Learning Disabilities,* February 1987, *20,* 66–75.

PALINCSAR, ANNEMARIE S.; BROWN, ANN L.; & MARTIN, SUZANNE M. Peer interaction in reading comprehension instruction. *Educational Psychologist,* Summer/Fall 1987, *22,* 231–253.

PALINCSAR, ANNEMARIE S., & RANSOM, KATHRYN. From the mystery spot to the thoughtful spot: The instruction of metacognitive strategies. *The Reading Teacher*, April 1988, *41*, 784–789.

PALMER, BARBARA C., & BRANNOCK, VIRGINIA M. Specialized services. In A. Berger & H. A. Robinson (Eds.), *Secondary school reading: What research reveals for classroom practice.* Urbana, IL: NCRE/ERIC, 1982, 159–171.

PALMER, DOUGLAS J. An attributional perspective on labelling. *Exceptional Children*, February 1983, *49*, 423–429.

PALMER, WILLIAM S. What reading teachers can do before the censors come. *Journal of Reading*, January 1982, *25*, 310–314.

PANY, DARLENE, & MCCOY, KATHLEEN M. Effects of corrective feedback on word accuracy and reading comprehension of readers with learning disabilities. *Journal of Learning Disabilities*, November 1988, *21*, 546–550.

PARADIS, EDWARD E. The appropriateness of visual discrimination exercises in reading readiness materials. *Journal of Educational Research*, 1974, *67*, 276–278.

PARATORE, JEANNE R., & INDRISANO, ROSELMINA. Intervention assessment of reading comprehension. *The Reading Teacher*, April 1987, *40*, 778–783.

PARIS, SCOTT G. Teaching children to guide their reading and learning. In T. E. Raphael (Ed.), *The contexts of school-based literacy.* New York: Random House, 1986, 115–130.

PARIS, SCOTT G.; WASIK, BARBARA A; & VAN DER WESTHUIZEN. Meta-metacognition: A review of research on metacognition and reading. In J. Readence et al. (Eds.), *Dialogues in literacy research.* Chicago: National Reading Conference, 1988, 143–166.

PARIS, SCOTT G.; WIXSON, KAREN K.; & PALINCSAR, ANNEMARIE S. Instructional approaches to reading comprehension. In E. Z. Rothkopf (Ed.), *Review of research on education*, Vol. 13. Washington, DC: American Educational Research Association, 1986, 91–128.

PARISH, PEGGY. *Amelia Bedelia.* New York: Harper & Row, 1963; also a Scholastic paperback.

PARK, GEORGE E., & SCHNEIDER, KENNETH A. Thyroid function in relation to dyslexia (reading failures). *Journal of Reading Behavior*, Summer 1975, *7*, 197–199.

PARK, ROSEMARIE. A critical review of developments in adult literacy. In M. Kamil (Ed.), *Directions in reading: Research and instruction.* Washington, DC: National Reading Conference, 1981, 279–289.

PARRISH, BERTA. Put a little romantic fiction into your reading program. *Journal of Reading*, April 1983, *26*, 610–615.

PATBERG, JUDYTHE P.; DEWITZ, PETER; & SAMUELS, S. JAY. The effect of context on the perceptual unit used in word recognition. *Journal of Reading Behavior*, Spring 1981, *13*, 33–48.

PATTERSON, KARLYN E. Neuropsychological approaches to the study of reading. *British Journal of Psychology*, May 1981, *72*, 151–174.

PAUK, WALTER. Speed reading? *Journal of the Reading Specialist*, December 1964, *4*, 18–19.

PAUK, WALTER. The new SQ4R. *Reading World*, March 1984, *23*, 274–275.

PAVLIDIS, GEORGE T. The "dyslexia syndrome" and its objective diagnosis by erratic eye movements. In K. Rayner (Ed.), *Eye movements in reading: Perceptual and language processing.* New York: Academic Press, 1983, 441–466.

PAVLIDIS, GEORGE T. Eye movements in dyslexia: Their diagnostic significance. *Journal of Learning Disabilities*, January 1985, *18*, 42–50.

PEARL, RUTH; BRYAN, TANIS; & DONAHUE, MAVIS. Learning disabled children's attributions for success and failure. *Learning Disability Quarterly*, Winter 1980, *3*, 3–9.

PEARL, RUTH; DONAHUE, MAVIS; & BRYAN, TANIS. Social relationships of learning-disabled children. In J. K. Torgesen & B. Y. L. Wong (Eds.), *Psychological and educa-*

tional perspectives on learning disabilities. New York: Academic Press, 1986, 193–224.

PEARSON, GERALD H. A survey of learning difficulties in children. *Psychoanalytic Study of the Child,* 1952, 7, 372–386.

PEARSON, P. DAVID. Asking questions about stories. *Ginn Occasional Papers, No. 15.* Columbus, OH: Ginn, 1982. Also in A. J. Harris & E. Sipay (Eds.), *Readings on reading instruction* (3rd ed.). New York: Longman, 1984, 274–283.

PEARSON, P. DAVID. *The comprehension revolution: A twenty-five year history of process and practice related to reading comprehension.* Reading Education Report No. 57. Champaign, IL: Center for the Study of Reading, University of Illinois, February 1985.

PEARSON, P. DAVID, & FIELDING, LINDA. Research update: Listening comprehension. *Language Arts,* September 1982, 59, 617–629. Also in A. J. Harris & E. Sipay (Eds.), *Readings on reading instruction* (3rd ed.). New York: Longman, 1984, 74–85.

PEARSON, P. DAVID, & GALLAGHER, MARGARET C. The instruction of reading comprehension. *Contemporary Educational Psychology,* 1983, 8, 317–345.

PEARSON, P. DAVID, & JOHNSON, DALE D. *Teaching reading comprehension.* New York: Holt, Rinehart and Winston, 1978.

PEARSON, P. DAVID, & KAMIL, MICHAEL L. *Basic processes and instructional practices in teaching reading.* Reading Education Report No. 7. Champaign, IL: Center for the Study of Reading, University of Illinois, December 1978.

PEARSON, P. DAVID, et al. The function of metaphor in children's recall of expository passages. *Journal of Reading Behavior,* 1981, 13 (3), 249–261.

PELLEGRINI, ANTHONY D.; DE STEFANO, JOHANNA S.; & THOMPSON, DEBORAH L. Saying what you mean: Using play to teach "literate language." *Language Arts,* March 1983, 60, 380–384.

PELLEGRINI, ANTHONY D., & GALDA, S. LEE. The effects of thematic-fantasy play training in the development of children's story comprehension. *American Educational Research Journal,* Fall 1982, 19, 443–452.

PELOSI, PETER L. The roots of reading diagnosis. In H. A. Robinson (Ed.), *Reading & writing instruction in the United States: Historical trends.* Newark, DE: International Reading Association, September 1977, 69–75.

PELOSI, PETER L. The disabled reader in years past. *Journal of Research and Development in Education,* Summer 1981, 14, 1–10.

PELOSI, PETER L. A method for classifying remedial reading techniques. *Reading World,* December 1982, 22, 119–128.

PENFIELD, W., & ROBERTS L. *Speech and brain mechanisms.* Princeton, NJ: Princeton University Press, 1959.

PENNINGTON, BRUCE F. Issues in the diagnosis and phenotype analysis of dyslexia: Implications for family studies. In S. D. Smith (Ed.), *Genetics and learning disabilities.* San Diego, CA: College-Hill Press, 1986, 69–96.

PENNINGTON, BRUCE F., & SMITH, SHELLEY D. Genetic influences on learning disabilities and speech and language disorders. *Child Development,* April 1983, 54, 369–387.

PERFETTI, CHARLES A. *Reading ability.* New York: Oxford University Press, 1985.

PERFETTI, CHARLES A. Continuities in reading acquisition, reading skill, and reading disability. *Remedial and Special Education,* January/February 1986, 7, 11–21.(a)

PERFETTI, CHARLES A. Reading acquisition and beyond: Decoding includes cognition. In N. L. Stein (Ed.), *Literacy in American schools: Learning to read and write.* Chicago: University of Chicago Press, 1986, 41–61.(b)

PERFETTI, CHARLES A., & LESGOLD, ALAN M. Coding and comprehension in skilled reading and implications for reading instruction. In L. Resnick & P. Weaver (Eds.), *Theory and practice of early reading,* Vol. 1. Hillsdale, NJ: Erlbaum, 1979, 57–84.

PERFETTI, CHARLES A., et al. Phonemic knowledge and learning to read are reciprocal: A longitudinal study of first grade children. In K. Stanovich (Ed.), *Children's reading and the development of phonological awareness*. Detroit, MI: Wayne State University Press, 1988, 39–75.

PERKINS, MARCY R. Minimum competency testing: What? Why? Why not? *Educational Measurement: Issues & Practices*, Winter 1982, *1*, 5–9, 26.

PERKINS, STANLEY A. Malnutrition and mental development. *Exceptional Children*, January 1977, *43*, 214–219.

PETERS, ELLENE E., & LEVIN, JOEL R. Effects of mnemonic imagery strategy on good and poor readers' prose recall. *Reading Research Quarterly*, Spring 1986, *21*, 179–192.

PETERS, MICHAEL. Dyslexia: Why and when the visual-acoustic-kinesthetic-tactile remedial approach might work. *Perceptual & Motor Skills*, April 1981, *52*, 630.

PETERSON, JOE, & CARROLL, MARTHA. The cloze procedure as an indicator of the instructional level for disabled readers. In P. Nacke (Ed.), *Interaction: Research and practice for college-adult reading*. Clemson, SC: National Reading Conference, 1974, 153–157.

PETERSON, JOE; GREENLAW, M. JEAN; & TIERNEY, ROBERT J. Assessing instructional placement with the IRI: The effectiveness of comprehension questions. *Journal of Educational Research*, May/June 1978, *71*, 247–250.

PETERSON, J.; PARADIS, E.; & PETERS, N. Revalidation of the cloze procedure as a measure of the instructional level for high school students. In P. L. Nacke (Ed.), *Diversity in mature reading: Theory and research*. Boone, NC: National Reading Conference, 1973, 144–149.

PETERSON, PENELOPE L. Direct instruction reconsidered. In L. Reed & S. Ward (Eds.), *Basic skills issues and choices: Issues in basic skills planning and instruction*, Vol. 2. St. Louis: CEMEREL, April 1982, 169–176.

PETERSON, SARAH E.; DEGRACIE, JAMES S.; & AYABE, CAROL R. A longitudinal study of the effects of retention/promotion on academic achievement. *American Educational Research Journal*, Spring 1987, *24*, 107–118.

PETRAUSKAS, RYMANTAS, & ROURKE, BYRON P. Identification of subgroups of retarded readers: A neuropsychological multivariate approach. *Journal of Clinical Neuropsychology*, 1979, *1* (1), 17–37.

PETTY, WALTER T.; HEROLD, CURTIS P.; & STOLL, EARLINE. *The state of knowledge about the teaching of vocabulary*. Cooperative Research Project No. 3128. Urbana, IL: National Council of Teachers of English, 1968.

PFLAUM, SUSANNA W. The predictability of oral reading behaviors on comprehension in learning disabled and normal readers. *Journal of Reading Behavior*, Fall 1980, *12*, 231–236.

PFLAUM, SUSANNA W., & PASCARELLA, ERNEST T. Interactive effects of prior reading achievement and training in context on the reading of learning disabled children. *Reading Research Quarterly*, 1980, *16* (1), 138–158.

PFLAUM, SUSANNA W., & PASCARELLA, ERNEST T. Attribution retraining for learning disabled students: Some thoughts on the practical implications of the evidence. *Learning Disability Quarterly*, Fall 1982, 5, 422–426.

PHILLIPS, S. E., & MEHRENS, WILLIAM A. Curricular differences and unidimensionality of achievement test data: An exploratory analysis. *Journal of Educational Measurements*, Spring 1987, *24*, 1–16.

PHLEGAR, JANET M. *Good beginnings for young children: Early identification of high-risk youth and programs that promote success*. Andover, MA: The Regional Laboratory for Educational Improvement of the Northeast and Islands, 1988.

PIAGET, JEAN. *The child's conception of the world*. Paterson, NJ: Littlefield, Adams, 1963.

PICCOLO, JOANNE. Expository text structure: Teaching and learning strategies. *The Reading Teacher*, May 1987, *40*, 838–847.

PIKULSKI, JOHN J. A critical review: Informal reading inventories. *The Reading Teacher*, November 1974, *28*, 141–151.

PIKULSKI, JOHN J., & ROSS, ELLIOTT. Classroom teachers' perceptions of the role of the reading specialist. *Journal of Reading*, November 1979, *23*, 126–135.

PIKULSKI, JOHN J., & SHANAHAN, TIMOTHY. Informal reading inventories: A critical analysis. In J. Pikulski & T. Shanahan (Eds.), *Approaches to the informal evaluation of reading*. Newark, DE: International Reading Association, 1982, 94–116.

PIKULSKI, JOHN J., & TOBIN, AILEEN W. The cloze procedure as an informal assessment technique. In J. Pikulski & T. Shanahan (Eds.), *Approaches to the informal evaluation of reading*. Newark, DE: International Reading Association, 1982, 42–62.

PILLA, MARIANNE L. *The best: High/low books for reluctant readers*. Englewood, CO: Libraries Unlimited, 1989.

PILLAR, ARLENE M. Literature and the language arts for middle grade students. In U. Hardt (Ed.), *Teaching reading with the other language arts*. Newark, DE: International Reading Association, 1983, 117–134.

PILLAR, ARLENE M. Resources to identify children's books for the reading program. In B. E. Cullinan (Ed.), *Children's literature in the reading program*. Newark, DE: International Reading Association, 1987, 156–171.

PILON, A. BARBARA. Reading to learn about the nature of language. In J. Stewig & S. Sebesta (Eds.), *Using literature in the elementary classroom*. Urbana, IL: National Council of Teachers of English, 1978, 1–12. Also in A. J. Harris & E. Sipay (Eds.), *Readings on reading instruction* (3rd ed.). New York: Longman, 1984, 231–236.

PIROZZOLO, FRANCIS J. Eye movements and reading disability. In K. Rayner (Ed.), *Eye movements in reading: Perceptual and language processes*. New York: Academic Press, 1983, 499–509.

PIROZZOLO, FRANCIS J.; DUNN, KAY; & ZETUSKY, WALTER. Physiological approaches to subtypes of developmental reading disability. *Topics on Learning & Learning disabilities*, April 1983, *3*, 40–47.

PIROZZOLO, FRANCIS J., & HANSCH, EDWARD C. The neurobiology of reading disorders. In R. Malatesha & P. Aaron (Eds.), *Reading disorders: Varieties and treatments*. New York: Academic Press, 1982, 215–231.

PIROZZOLO, FRANCIS J., & RAYNER, KEITH. Cerebral organization and reading disability. *Neuropsychologia*, 1979, *17*(5), 485–491.

PIROZZOLO, FRANCIS J., et al. Effects of cerebral dysfunction on neurolinguistic performance in children. *Journal of Consulting & Clinical Psychology*, December 1981, *49*, 791–806.

PLATTS, MARY E. *Anchor: A handbook of vocabulary discovery techniques for the classroom teacher*. Stevensville, MI: Educational Services, 1970.

PLOGHOFT, MILTON, & SHELDON, WILLIAM D. Television viewing skills. In J. Cowen (Ed.), *Teaching reading through the arts*. Newark, DE: International Reading Association, 1983, 11–33.

PODSTAY, EDWARD J. Show me your underlines: A strategy to teach comprehension. *The Reading Teacher*, May 1984, *37*, 828–830.

POIZNER, HOWARD, & TALLAL, PAULA. Temporal processing in deaf signers. *Brain and Language*, January 1987, *30*, 52–62.

POLATAJKO, HELENE J. A critical look at vestibular dysfunction in learning-disabled children. *Developmental Medicine and Child Neurology*, 1985, *27*(3), 283–292.

POLLOWAY, EDWARD A., & POLLOWAY, CAROLYN H. Survival words for disabled readers. *Academic Therapy*, March 1981, *16*, 443–448.

POMERANTZ, HELEN. Subvocalization and reading. *The Reading Teacher*, April 1971, *24*, 665–667.

POPP, HELEN M. Current practices in the teaching of beginning reading. In J. B. Carroll & J. S. Chall (Eds.), *Toward a literate society*. New York: McGraw-Hill, 1975, 101–146.

POVSIC, FRANCES F. Czechoslovakia: Children's fiction in English. *The Reading Teacher*, March 1980, *33*, 686–691.(a)

POVSIC, FRANCES F. Poland: Children's fiction in English. *The Reading Teacher*, April 1980, *33*, 806–815.(b)

POVSIC, FRANCES F. Yugoslavia: An annotated guide to children's fiction in English. *The Reading Teacher*, February 1980, *33*, 559–566.(c)

POVSIC, FRANCES F. Non-Russian tales from the Soviet Union. *The Reading Teacher*, November 1981, *35*, 196–202.(a)

POVSIC, FRANCES F. Russian folk and animal tales. *The Reading Teacher*, December 1981, *35*, 329–343.(b)

POVSIC, FRANCES F. Hungary—Children's fiction in English. *The Reading Teacher*, April 1982, *35*, 820–828.(a)

POVSIC, FRANCES F. The Ukraine—Children's stories in English. *The Reading Teacher*, March 1982, *35*, 316–322.(b)

POWELL, GLEN, & ZALUD, GARRETH. A SQ3R for secondary handicapped students. *Journal of Reading*, December 1982, *26*, 262–263.

POWELL, WILLIAM R. Acquisition of a reading repertoire. *Library Trends*, October 1973, *22*, 177–196.

POWELL, WILLIAM R. Teaching vocabulary through opposition. *Journal of Reading*, April 1986, *29*, 617–621.

POWERS, HUGH W. S., JR. Caffeine, behavior and the LD child. *Academic Therapy*, Fall 1975, *11*, 5–11.

PRESSLEY, MICHAEL; JOHNSON, CARLA J.; & SYMONS, SONYA. Elaborating to learn and learning to elaborate. *Journal of Learning Disabilities*, February 1987, *20*, 76–91.

PRESSLEY, MICHAEL; LEVIN, JOEL R.; & McDANIEL, MARK A. Remembering versus inferring what a word means: Mnemonic and contextual approaches. In M. C. McKeown & M. E. Curtis (Eds.), *The nature of vocabulary acquisition*. Hillsdale, NJ: Erlbaum, 1987, 107–127.

PRESSLEY, MICHAEL; LEVIN, JOEL; & MILLER, GLORIA E. How does the keyword method affect vocabulary comprehension and usage? *Reading Research Quarterly*, 1981, *16*(2), 213–226.

PRESSMAN, RAYMOND. *The relationship of sensory-integration matching abilities and reading instructional approaches to word recognition ability*. Unpublished doctoral dissertation, State University of New York at Albany, 1973.

PRESTON, RALPH C. Reading achievement of German boys and girls related to sex of teacher. *The Reading Teacher*, February 1979, *32*, 521–526.

PRICE, BARRIE JO, & MARSH, GEORGE E. Practical suggestions for planning and conducting parent conferences. *Teaching Exceptional Children*, Summer 1985, *17*, 274–278.

PRIOR, MARGOT, & SANSON, ANN. Attention deficit disorder with hyperactivity: A critique. *Journal of Child Psychology and Psychiatry*, 1986, *27*(3), 307–319.

PRITCHARD, ALLAN, & TAYLOR, JEAN. Suggestopedia for the disadvantaged reader. *Academic Therapy*, September 1978, *14*, 81–90.

PROCTOR, JOHN. Sharing learning: An alternative to resource rooms. *Language Arts*, January 1986, *63*, 67–73.

PROUT, H. THOMPSON, & INGRAM, RICHARD E. Guidelines for the behavioral assessment of hyperactivity. *Journal of Learning Disabilities*, August/September 1982, *15*, 393–398.

Pugh, Sharon L. Teaching children to appreciate literature. *ERIC Digest*, November 1, 1988.

Pumfrey, Peter D. *Reading: Tests and assessment techniques* (2nd ed.). Sevenoaks, Kent, England: Hodder & Stoughton, 1985.

Pumfrey, P. D., & Elliot, C. D. Play therapy, social adjustment and reading attainment. *Educational Research*, June 1970, *12*, 183–193.

Purcell-Gates, Victoria. What oral/written language differences can tell us about beginning instruction. *The Reading Teacher*, January 1989, *42*, 290–294.

Purves, Alan C. *Literature education in ten countries: An empirical study*. New York: John Wiley & Sons, 1973.

Purves, Alan C. The challenge to education to produce literate citizens. In A. Purves & O. Niles (Eds.), *Becoming readers in a complex society*. 83rd Yearbook of the National Society for the Study of Education, Part II. Chicago: University of Chicago Press, 1984, 1–15.

Purves, Alan C. The potential and real achievement of U.S. students in school reading. In N.L. Stein (Ed.), *Literacy in American schools: Learning to read and write*. Chicago: University of Chicago Press, 1986, 85–109.(a)

Purves, Alan C. Testing in literature. *Language Arts*, March 1986, *63*, 320–323.(b)

Purves, Alan C., & Beach, Richard. *Literature and the reader: Research in response to literature, reading, interests, and the teaching of literature*. Urbana, IL: National Council of Teachers of English, 1972.

Purves, Alan C., et al. *Reading and literature: American achievement in international perspective*. Urbana, IL: National Council of Teachers of English, 1981.

Putnam, Ruth A. Cultivating a taste for non-fiction. *Elementary English Review*, 1941, *18*, 228–229.

Pyrczak, Fred, & Axelrod, Jerome. Determining the passage-dependence of reading comprehension exercises: A call for replication. *Journal of Reading*, January 1976, *19*, 279–283.

Quandt, Ivan, & Selznick, Richard. *Self-concept and reading* (2nd ed.). Newark, DE: International Reading Association, 1984.

Rabin, Annette T. Determining difficulty levels of text written in languages other than English. In B. L. Zakaluk & S. J. Samuels (Eds.), *Readability: Its past, present & future*. Newark, DE: International Reading Association, 1988, 46–76.

Rabinovitch, Ralph D. Dyslexia: Psychiatric considerations. In J. Money (Ed.), *Reading disability: Progress and research needs in dyslexia*. Baltimore: John Hopkins Press, 1962, 73–79.

Rabinovitch, Ralph D. Reading problems in children: Definitions and classifications. In A. H. Keeney & V. T. Keeney (Eds.), *Dyslexia: Diagnosis and treatment of reading disorders*. St. Louis: C. V. Mosby, 1968, 1–10.

Radenbaugh, Muriel R. Using children's literature to teach mathematics. *The Reading Teacher*, May 1981, *34*, 902–906.

Rand, Muriel K. Story schema: Theory, research and practice. *The Reading Teacher*, January 1984, *37*, 377–382.

Rankin, Earl F. How flexibly do we read? *Journal of Reading Behavior*, Summer 1970–1971, *31*, 34–38.

Rankin, Earl F. Grade level interpretation of cloze readability scores. In F. Greene (Ed.), *The right to participate*. Milwaukee, WI: National Reading Conference, 1971, 30–37.

Raphael, Taffy E. Teaching questions-answers relationships, revisited. *The Reading Teacher*, February 1986, *39*, 516–522.

Raphael, Taffy E., & Englert, Carol Sue. Integrating writing and reading instruction. In P. N. Winograd, et al. (Eds.), *Improving basal reading instruction*. New York: Teachers College Press, 1989, 231–255.

RAPHAEL, TAFFY E., & GAVELEK, JAMES R. Question-related activities and their relationship to reading comprehension: Some instructional implications. In G. Duffy, et al. (Eds.), *Comprehension instruction: Perspectives and suggestions.* New York: Longman, 1984, 234–250.

RAPHAEL, TAFFY E., & PEARSON, P. DAVID. Increasing students' awareness of sources of information for answering questions. *American Educational Research Journal*, Summer 1985, *22*, 217–235.

RASHOTTE, CAROL A., & TORGESEN, JOSEPH K. Repeated reading and reading fluency in learning disabled children. *Reading Research Quarterly*, Winter 1985, *20*, 180–188.

RASINSKI, TIMOTHY V., & FREDERICKS, ANTHONY D. Sharing literacy: Guiding principles and practices for parent involvement. *The Reading Teacher*, February 1988, *41*, 508–512.

RASMUSSEN, T., & MILNER, B. Clinical and surgical studies of the cerebral speech areas in man. In K. J. Zulch et al. (Eds.), *Otfred Foerster symposium on cerebral localization.* Heidelberg: Springer-Verlag, 1975, 238–257.

RAUCH, SIDNEY J. The administrator and the reading program—What to look for in a reading lesson. *Reading World*, March 1982, *21*, 264–265.

RAUCH, SIDNEY J., & SANACORE, JOSEPH (Eds.). *Handbook for the volunteer tutor* (2nd ed.). Newark, DE: International Reading Association, 1985.

RAYGOR, ALTON L. The Raygor readability estimate: A quick and easy way to determine difficulty. In P. D. Pearson & J. Hansen (Eds.), *Reading: Theory, research and practice.* Clemson, SC: National Reading Conference, 1977, 259–263.

RAYNER, KEITH. Eye movements, perceptual spans, and reading disability. *Annals of Dyslexia*, Vol. 33. Baltimore, MD: Orton Dyslexia Society, 1983, 163–173.(a)

RAYNER, KEITH. The perceptual span and eye movement control during reading. In K. Rayner (Ed.), *Eye movements in reading: Perceptual and language processes.* New York: Academic Press, 1983, 97–120.(b)

RAYNER, KEITH. The role of eye movements in learning to read and reading disability. *Remedial and Special Education*, November/December 1985, *6*, 53–60.

READ, CHARLES. Pre-school children's knowledge of English phonology. *Harvard Educational Review*, February 1971, *41*, 1–34.

READ, CHARLES. *Children's categorization of speech sounds in English.* Research Report No. 17. Urbana, IL: National Council of Teachers of English, 1975.

READ, MERRILL S. Malnutrition, hunger and behavior. In G. Leisman (Ed.), *Basic visual processes in learning disabilities.* Springfield, IL: Charles C Thomas, 1976, 58–72.

READENCE, JOHN E.; BALDWIN, R. SCOTT; & HEAD, MARTHA H. Teaching young readers to interpret metaphors. *The Reading Teacher*, January 1987, *40*, 439–443.

READENCE, JOHN E.; BALDWIN, R. SCOTT; & RICKELMAN, ROBERT J. Instructional insights into metaphors and similes. *Journal of Reading*, November 1983, 27, 109–112.(a)

READENCE, JOHN E.; BALDWIN, R. SCOTT; & RICKELMAN, ROBERT J. Word knowledge and metaphorical interpretation. *Research in the Teaching of English*, December 1983, *17*, 349–358.(b)

READENCE, JOHN E., & MOORE, DAVID. Strategies for enhancing readiness and recall in content areas: The encoding specificity principle. *Reading Psychology*, Fall 1979, *1*, 47–54.

READENCE, JOHN E., & SEARFOSS, LYNDON W. Teaching strategies for vocabulary development. *English Journal*, October 1980, *69*, 43–46.

READENCE, JOHN E., et al. The effect of vocabulary instruction on interpreting metaphor. In J. Niles & R. V. Lalik (Eds.), *Solving problems in literacy: Learners, teachers, and researchers.* Rochester, NY: National Reading Conference, 1986, 87–91.

READING DEVELOPMENT CENTRE. *Games, games, games: Word recognition and listening activities* (4th ed.). Adelaide, South Australia: Education Department of South Australia, 1976.(a)

READING DEVELOPMENT CENTRE. *Resource book on the development of reading skills* (rev. ed.). Adelaide, South Australia: Education Department of South Australia, 1976.(b)

READING TEACHER STAFF. Who profits from self-learning kits? *The Reading Teacher*, January 1978, *31*, 391–392.

REDER, LYNNE M. The role of elaboration in the comprehension and retention of prose: A critical review. *Review of Educational Research*, Spring 1980, *50*, 5–33.

REED, ARTHEA J. S. *Comics to classics: A parent's guide to books for teens and preteens.* Newark, DE: International Reading Association, 1988.

REED, JAMES C. The deficits of retarded readers—Fact or artifact? *The Reading Teacher*, January 1970, *23*, 347–352, 393.

REED, LINDA, & WARD, SPENCER. Basic skills, issues and choices: An introduction. In L. Reed & S. Ward (Eds.), *Basic skills—Issues and choices: Approaches to basic skills instruction*, Vol. 1. St. Louis: CEMEREL, April 1982, 1–24.

REEVE, ROBERT A., & BROWN, ANN L. Metacognition reconsidered: Implications for intervention research. *Journal of Abnormal Child Psychology*, 1985, *13*(3), 343–356.

REEVE, ROBERT A.; PALINCSAR, ANNEMARIE S.; & BROWN, ANN L. *Everyday and academic thinking: Implications for learning and problem solving.* Technical Report No. 349. Champaign, IL: Center for the Study of Reading, University of Illinois, December 1985.

REICHMAN, HENRY F. *Censorship and selection: A manual for school personnel.* Chicago: American Library Association, 1988.

REID, ETHNA R. Practicing effective instruction: The Exemplary Center for Reading Instruction approach. *Exceptional Children*, April 1986, *52*, 510–519.

REIMER, BECKY L. Recipes for language experience stories. *The Reading Teacher*, January 1983, *36*, 396–401.

REINKING, DAVID. Integrating graphic aids into content area instruction: The Graphic Information Lesson. *Journal of Reading*, November 1986, *30*, 146–151.

REINKING, DAVID (Ed.). *Reading and computers: Issues for theory and practice.* New York: Teachers College Press, 1987.

REINKING, DAVID; HAYES, DAVID A.; & MCENEANEY, JOHN E. Good and poor readers' use of explicitly cued graphic aids. *Journal of Reading Behavior*, 1988, *20*(3), 229–247.

RENTEL, VICTOR M. Concept formation and reading. *Reading World*, December 1971, *11*, 111–119.

RESNICK, LAUREN B. Toward a usable psychology of reading instruction. In L. B. Resnick & P. Weaver (Eds.), *Theory and practice in early reading*, Vol. 3. Hillsdale, NJ: Erlbaum, 1979, 355–372.

REUTZEL, D. RAY. A reading mode for teaching arithmetic story solving. *The Reading Teacher*, October 1983, *37*, 28–34.

REUTZEL, D. RAY. Story maps improve comprehension. *The Reading Teacher*, January 1985, *38*, 400–404.

REUTZEL, D. RAY, & HOLLINGSWORTH, PAUL M. Highlighting key vocabulary: A generative-reciprocal procedure for teaching selected inference types. *Reading Research Quarterly*, 1988, *23*(3), 358–378.

REUTZEL, D. RAY; HOLLINGSWORTH, PAUL M.; & DAINES, DELVA. The effect of a direct instruction paradigm using dictated texts on beginning readers' main idea comprehension. *Reading Research and Instruction*, Summer 1988, *27*, 25–46.

REYNOLDS, CECIL R. An examination for bias in a preschool test battery across race and sex. *Journal of Educational Measurement*, Summer 1980, *17*, 137–146.

REYNOLDS, CECIL R. The fallacy of "two years below grade level for age" as a diagnostic criterion for reading disorders. *Journal of School Psychology*, 1981, *19* (4), 350–358.

REYNOLDS, CECIL R. Neuropsychological assessment in education: A caution. *Journal of Research and Development in Education.* Spring 1982, *15*, 76–79.

REYNOLDS, CECIL R. Measuring the aptitude-achievement discrepancy in learning disability diagnosis. *Remedial and Special Education*, September/October 1985, *6*, 37–48.

REYNOLDS, CECIL R. Toward objective diagnosis of learning disabilities. *Special Services in the Schools*, Winter/Spring 1986, *2*, 161–176.

REYNOLDS, CECIL R. Putting the individual into aptitude-treatment interaction. *Exceptional Children*, January 1988, *54*, 324–331.

REYNOLDS, MAYNARD C. A reaction to the JLD special series in the Regular Education Initiative. *Journal of Learning Disabilities*, June/July 1988, *21*, 352–356.

REYNOLDS, MAYNARD C.; WANG, MARGARET C.; & WALBERG, HERBERT J. The necessary restructuring of special and regular education. *Exceptional Children*, February 1987, *53*, 391–398.

RHODES, LYNNE K., & HILL, MARY W. Supporting reading in the home—naturally: Selected materials for parents. *The Reading Teacher*, March 1985, *38*, 619–623.

RICHARDS, I. A., & GIBSON, CHRISTINE M. *English through pictures.* New York: Washington Square Press, 1960.

RICHARDSON, ELLIS. The reliability, validity, and flexibility of the Decoding Skills Test for reading research. In D. B. Gray & J. F. Kavanagh (Eds.), *Biobehavioral measures of dyslexia.* Parkton, MD: York Press, 1985, 279–296.

RICHARDSON, ELLIS; DI BENEDETTO, BARBARA; & BRADLEY, C. MICHAEL. The relationship of sound blending to reading achievement. *Review of Educational Research*, Winter 1977, *47*, 319–334.

RICHARDSON, ELLIS, et al. Relationship of auditory and visual skills to reading retardation. *Journal of Learning Disabilities*, February 1980, *13*, 77–82.

RICHARDSON, SELMA K. *Magazines for children: A selection guide for librarians, teachers, and parents.* Chicago: American Library Association, 1983.

RICHARDSON, SELMA K. *Magazines for young adults: Selections for school and public libraries.* Chicago: American Library Association, 1985.

RICHGELS, DONALD J. Grade school children's listening and reading comprehension of complex sentences. *Reading Research and Instruction*, Spring 1986, *25*, 201–219.

RICHGELS, DONALD J., & HANSEN, RUTH. Gloss: Helping students apply both skills and strategies in reading content texts. *Journal of Reading*, January 1984, *27*, 312–317.

RICHGELS, DONALD J., & MATEJA, JOHN A. Gloss, II: Integrating content and process for independence. *Journal of Reading*, February 1984, *27*, 424–431.

RICHGELS, DONALD J.; MCGEE, LEA M.; & SLATON, EDITH A. Teaching expository text structure in reading and writing. In K. D. Muth (Ed.), *Children's comprehension of text.* Newark, DE: International Reading Association, 1989, 167–184.

RICHGELS, DONALD J., et al. Awareness of four text structures: Effects on recall of expository text. *Reading Research Quarterly*, Spring 1987, *22*, 177–196.

RICHGELS, DONALD J., et al. Kindergartners' attention to graphic detail in functional print: Letter name knowledge and invented spelling ability. In J. Readence et al. (Eds.), *Dialogues in literacy research.* Chicago: National Reading Conference, 1988, 77–84.

RICKARDS, JOHN P. Notetaking: Theory and research. *Improving Human Performance Quarterly*, Fall 1979, *8*, 152–161. Also in A. J. Harris & E. Sipay (Eds.), *Readings on reading instruction* (3rd ed.). New York: Longman, 1984, 331–337.

RILEY, JOHN A., & LOWE, JAMES D., JR. A study of enhancing vs. reducing speech during reading. *Journal of Reading*, October 1981, *25*, 7–13.

RINEHART, STEVEN D.; STAHL, STEVEN A.; & ERICKSON, LAWRENCE G. Some effects of summarization training on reading and studying. *Reading Research Quarterly*, Fall 1986, *21*, 422–438.

RINGLER, LENORE H., & WEBER, CAROL K. Comprehending narrative discourse: Implications for instruction. In J. Langer & M. T. Burke-Smith (Eds.), *Reader meets author/bridging the gap: Psycholinguistic and sociolinguistic perspectives*. Newark, DE: International Reading Association, 1982, 180–195.

RIPICK, DANIELLE N., & GRIFFITH, PENNY L. Narrative abilities of children with learning disabilities and nondisabled children: Story structure, cohesion, and propositions. *Journal of Learning Disabilities*, March 1988, *21*, 165–173.

RISKO, VICTORIA, & ALVAREZ, MARINO C. An investigation of poor readers' use of a thematic strategy to comprehend text. *Reading Research Quarterly*, Summer 1986, *21*, 298–316.

RISPENS, J. Reading disorders as information-processing disorders. In R. Malatesha & P. Aaron (Eds.), *Reading disorders: Varieties and treatments*. New York: Academic Press, 1982, 177–197.

RIST, RAY C. Student social class and teacher expectations: The self-fulfilling prophecy in ghetto education. *Harvard Educational Review*, August 1970, *40*, 411–451.

RIST, RAY C. Do teachers count in the lives of children? *Educational Researcher*, December 1987, *16*, 41–42.

RIVERS, DIANE, & SMITH, TOM E. C. Traditional eligibility criteria for identifying students as specific learning disabled. *Journal of Learning Disabilities*, December 1988, *21*, 642–644.

ROBBINS, LOUISE S. A way out of the book report dilemma. *Journal of Reading*, November 1981, *25*, 165–166.

ROBBINS, MELVYN P. The Delacato interpretation of neurological organization. *Reading Research Quarterly*, Spring 1966, *1*, 57–78.

ROBECK, CAROL P. An investigation of the relationship between concrete operational thought and reading achievement. *Reading World*, October 1981, *21*, 2–13.

ROBERGE, JAMES J., & FLEXER, BARBARA K. Cognitive style, operativity, and reading achievement. *American Educational Research Journal*, Spring 1984, *21*, 227–236.

ROBERTS, CHRISTINE L. A new checklist for evaluating instructional materials in reading. *New England Reading Association Journal*, 1980, *15* (2), 25–34.

ROBERTS, R. W., & COLEMAN, J. An investigation of the role of visual and kinesthetic factors in reading failures. *Journal of Educational Research*, 1958, 57, 445–451.

ROBERTS, TESSA. Auditory blending in the early stages of reading. *Educational Research*, November 1979, *22*, 49–53.

ROBERTSON, JEAN E. Pupil understanding of connectives in reading. *Reading Research Quarterly*, Spring 1968, *3*, 387–417.

ROBINSON, COLIN G. Cloze procedure: A review. *Educational Research*, February 1981, *23*, 128–133.

ROBINSON, FRANCIS P. *Effective reading* (4th ed.). New York: Harper & Row, 1970.

ROBINSON, HELEN M. *Why pupils fail in reading*. Chicago: University of Chicago Press, 1946.

ROBINSON, HELEN M. Perceptual training—Does it result in reading improvement? In R. C. Aukerman (Ed.), *Some persistent questions on beginning reading*. Newark, DE: International Reading Association, 1972, 135–150.(a)

ROBINSON, HELEN M. Visual and auditory modalities related to methods for beginning reading. *Reading Research Quarterly*, Fall 1972, 8, 7–39.(b)

ROBINSON, HELEN M., & WEINTRAUB, SAMUEL. Research related to children's interest and to developmental values of reading. *Library Trends*, October 1973, *22*, 81–108.

ROBINSON, RICHARD D., & PETTIT, NEILA T. The role of the reading teacher: Where do you fit in? *The Reading Teacher*, May 1978, *31*, 923–929.

ROCHE, ALEX F.; LIPMAN, RONALD S.; & OAERALL, WELLINGTON H. The effects of stimulant medication on the growth of hyperkinetic children. *Psychopharmacology Bulletin*, 1980, *16*(3), 13–18.

ROEDER, HAROLD H., & LEE, NANCY. Twenty-five teacher-tested ways to encourage voluntary reading. *The Reading Teacher*, October 1973, *27*, 48–50.

ROEHLER, LAURA R., & DUFFY, GERALD G. Matching direct instruction to reading outcomes. *Language Arts*, May 1982, *59*, 476–480.

ROGERS, CARL R. *Counseling and psychotherapy*. Boston: Houghton Mifflin, 1942.

ROGERS, DOUGLAS B. Assessing study skills. *Journal of Reading*, January 1984, *27*, 346–354.

ROGERS, H. & SAKLOFSKE, D. H. Self-concepts, locus of control and performance expectations of learning disabled children. *Journal of Learning Disabilities*, May 1985, *18*, 273–278.

ROGERS, JANETTE S. Reading practices in open education. *The Reading Teacher*, March 1976, *29*, 548–554.

ROHRLACK, C. R.; BELL, B. J.; & MCLAUGHLIN, T. F. The value of auditory blending skills for reading readiness programs. *Educational Research Quarterly*, Spring 1982, *7*, 41–47.

ROLISON, MICHAEL A., & MEDWAY, FREDERIC J. Teachers' expectations and attributions for student achievement: Effects of label, performance patterns, and special education intervention. *American Educational Research Journal*, Winter 1985, *22*, 561–573.

ROLLER, CATHY M. The influence of normative relative importance on the perceived importance of information. *Journal of Reading Behavior*, 1985, *17*(4), 347–367.

ROSE, CYNTHIA; ZIMET, SARA G.; & BLOM, GASTON E. Content counts: Children have preferences in reading textbook stories. *Elementary English*, January 1972, *49*, 14–19.

ROSE, TERRY; KOORLAND, MARK A.; & EPSTEIN, MICHAEL H. A review of applied behavioral analysis interventions with learning disabled children. *Education and Treatment of Children*, Winter 1982, *5*, 41–58.

ROSENSHINE, BARAK V. Review of Teaching Styles and Pupil Progress by N. Bennett. *American Educational Research Journal*, 1978, *15*, 163–169.(a)

ROSENSHINE, BARAK V. Academic engaged time, content covered, and direct instruction. *Journal of Education*, August 1978, *60*, 38–66.(b)

ROSENSHINE, BARAK V., & BERLINER, DAVID C. *Academic engaged time: Content covered and direct instruction*. Paper presented at the Annual Meeting of the American Educational Research Association, April 1977.

ROSENTHAL, JOSEPH H.; BODER, ELENA; & CALLAWAY, ENOCH. Typology of developmental dyslexia: Evidence for its construct validity. In R. Malatesha & P. Aaron (Eds.), *Reading disorders: Varieties and treatments*. New York: Academic Press, 1982, 93–120.

ROSENTHAL, ROBERT. Pygmalion effects: Existence, magnitude, and social importance. *Educational Researcher*, December 1987, *16*, 37–41.

ROSENTHAL, ROBERT, & JACOBSON, LENORE. *Pygmalion in the classroom*. New York: Holt, Rinehart and Winston, 1968.

ROSER, NANCY L. *Helping your child become a reader*. Newark, DE: International Reading Association, 1989.

ROSER, NANCY, & FRITH, MARGARET (Eds.). *Children's choices: Teaching with books children like*. Newark, DE: International Reading Association, 1983.

ROSER, NANCY L., & WILSON, GEORGENE. Books for reading about reading: Readalouds for children learning to read. *The Reading Teacher*, December 1986, *40*, 282–287.

ROSNER, JEROME. Perceptual skills and achievement. *American Educational Research Journal*, Winter 1973, *10*, 59–67.

ROSNER, JEROME. *The perceptual skills curriculum. Program II—Auditory-motor skills*. New York: Walker, 1976.

Ross, Alan O. *Psychological aspects of learning disabilities and reading disorders.* New York: McGraw-Hill, 1976.

Ross, Elinor P. Checking the source: An essential component of critical reading. *Journal of Reading,* January 1981, *24,* 311–315.

Rosso, Barbara R., & Emans, Robert. Children's use of phonic generalizations. *The Reading Teacher,* March 1981, *34,* 653–658.

Roth, Froma P. Oral narrative abilities of learning-disabled students. *Topics in Language Disorders,* December 1986, 5, 21–30.

Roth, Steven F., & Beck, Isabel L. Theoretical and instructional implications of the assessment of two microcomputer word recognition programs. *Reading Research Quarterly,* Spring 1987, *22,* 197–218.

Roth, Steven F., & Perfetti, Charles A. A framework for reading, language comprehension and language disability. *Topics in Language Disorders,* December 1980, *1,* 15–27.

Rourke, Byron P., & Fisk, John L. Socio-emotional disturbances of learning disabled children: The role of central processing deficits. *Bulletin of the Orton Society,* 1981, *31,* 77–78.

Rourke, Byron P., & Orr, A. Prediction of the reading and spelling performances of normal and retarded readers: A four-year follow up. *Journal of Abnormal Child Psychology,* 1977, *5,* 9–20.

Rowe, Deborah W. Does research support the use of "purpose questions" on reading comprehension tests? *Journal of Educational Measurements,* Spring 1986, *23,* 43–55.

Rowe, Deborah R., & Rayford, Lawrence. Activating background knowledge in reading comprehension assessment. *Reading Research Quarterly,* Spring 1987, *22,* 160–176.

Rowe, Mary B. Wait time: Slowing down may be a way of speeding up. *American Educator,* Spring 1987, *11,* 38–43, 47.

Rowell, Richard B. The effect of tachistoscopic and visual tracking training on the improvement of reading at the second grade level. *Dissertation Abstracts International,* December 1976, *37*(6-A), 3279.

Rozin, Paul, & Gleitman, Lila R. The structure and acquisition of reading II: The reading process and the acquisition of the alphabetic principle. In A. S. Reber & D. L. Scarborough (Eds.), *Toward a psychology of reading.* Hillsdale, NJ: Erlbaum, 1977, 55–141.

Rubenstein, Herbert; Kender, Joseph P.; & Mace, F. Charles. Do tests penalize readers for poor short term memory? *Journal of Reading,* October 1988, *32,* 4–10.

Rubin, Andee. Making stories, making sense. *Language Arts,* March 1980, 57, 285–293, 298, 334.(a)

Rubin, Andee. A theoretical taxonomy of the differences between oral and written language. In R. Spiro, et al. (Eds.), *Theoretical issues in reading comprehension.* Hillsdale, NJ: Erlbaum, 1980, 411–438.(b)

Rubin, Rosalyn. Reading ability and assigned materials: Accommodations for the slow but not the accelerated. *Elementary School Journal,* March 1975, 75, 374–377.

Ruddell, Robert B. *Reading-language instruction: Innovative practices.* Englewood Cliffs, NJ: Prentice-Hall, 1974.

Ruddell, Robert B. Developing comprehension abilities: Implications from research for an instructional framework. In S. J. Samuels (Ed.), *What research has to say about reading instruction.* Newark, DE: International Reading Association, 1978, 108–120.

Ruddell, Robert B. Early prediction of reading success: Profiles of good and poor readers. In M. L. Kamil & A. J. Moe (Eds.), *Reading research: Studies and applications.* Clemson, SC: National Reading Conference, 1979, 150–158.

RUDDELL, ROBERT B. Improving classroom comprehension. In A. J. Harris & E. Sipay (Eds.), *Readings on reading instruction* (3rd ed.). New York: Longman, 1984, 283–286.

RUDDELL, ROBERT B. The effect of oral and written patterns of language structure on reading comprehension. In H. Singer & R. B. Ruddell (Eds.), *Theoretical models and processes of reading* (3rd ed.). Newark, DE: International Reading Association, 1985, 123–128.

RUDDELL, ROBERT B. Vocabulary learning. A process model and criterion for evaluating instructional strategies. *Journal of Reading*, April 1986, 29, 581–587.

RUDDELL, ROBERT, & HAGGARD, MARTHA R. Oral and written language acquisition and the reading process. In H. Singer & R. B. Ruddell (Eds.), *Theoretical models and reading processes* (3rd ed.). Newark, DE: International Reading Association, 1985, 63–80.

RUDDELL, ROBERT B., & SPEAKER, RICHARD B., JR. The interactive reading process: A model. In H. Singer & R. B. Ruddell (Eds.), *Theoretical models and reading processes* (3rd ed.). Newark, DE: International Reading Association, 1985, 751–793.

RUDE, ROBERT T. Objective-based reading systems: An evaluation. *The Reading Teacher*, November 1974, 28, 169–175.

RUDE, ROBERT T. *Teaching reading using microcomputers.* Englewood Cliffs, NJ: Prentice-Hall, 1986.

RUDEL, RITA G. Learning disability: Diagnosis by exclusion and discrepancy. *Journal of the American Academy of Child Psychiatry*, 1980, 19, 347–369.

RUDEL, RITA G., & DENCKLA, MARTHA B. Relationship of IQ and reading scores to visual-spatial and visual-temporal matching tasks. *Journal of Learning Disabilities*, April 1976, 9, 169–178.

RUDMAN, HERBERT C. The informational needs and reading interests of children in grades IV through VIII. *Elementary School Journal*, 1955, 55, 502–512.

RUGG, MICHAEL D. Electrophysiological studies. In J. Beaumont (Ed.), *Divided visual fields studies of cerebral organization*. New York: Academic Press, 1982, 129–146.

RUMELHART, DAVID E. Schemata: The building blocks of cognition. In R. J. Spiro et al. (Eds.), *Theoretical issues in reading comprehension*. Hillsdale, NJ: Erlbaum, 1980, 33–58.

RUMELHART, DAVID E. Understanding understanding. In J. Flood (Ed.), *Understanding reading comprehension*. Newark, DE: International Reading Association, 1984, 1–20.

RUMELHART, DAVID E. Toward an interactive model of reading. In H. Singer & R. B. Ruddell (Eds.), *Theoretical models and processes of reading* (3rd ed.). Newark, DE: International Reading Association, 1985.

RUMELHART, DAVID E., & MCCLELLAND, JAMES L. Interactive processing through spreading activation. In A. Lesgold & C. Perfetti (Eds.), *Interactive processes in reading*. Hillsdale, NJ: Erlbaum, 1981, 37–60.

RUMELHART, DAVID E., & MCCLELLAND, JAMES L. An interactive activation model of context effects in letter perception: II. The contextual enhancement effect and some tests and extensions of the model. *Psychological Review*, January 1982, 89, 60–94.

RUPLEY, WILLIAM H.; MASON, GEORGE; & LOGAN, JOHN W. Past, present, and future job responsibilities of public school reading specialists. *Reading World*, March 1985, 24, 48–60.

RUSH, ROBERT J., & KLARE, GEORGE R. Re-opening the cloze blank issue. *Journal of Reading Behavior*, Summer 1978, 10, 208–210.

RUSH, R. TIMOTHY; MOE, ALDEN J.; & STORLIE, REBECCA L. *Occupational literacy education.* Newark, DE: International Reading Association, 1986.

RUSSAVAGE, PATRICIA M.; LORTON, LARRY L.; & MILLHAM, RHODESSA L. Making responsible instructional decisions about reading: What teachers think and do about basals. *The Reading Teacher*, December 1985, *39*, 314–317.

RUSSELL, DAVID; KARP, ETTA E.; & MUESER, ANNE MARIE. *Reading aids through the grades* (2nd ed.). New York: Teachers College Press, 1975.

RUTTER, MICHAEL. Syndromes attributed to "minimal brain dysfunction" in childhood. *American Journal of Psychiatry*, January 1982, *139*, 21–33.

RYAN, ELLEN B. Identifying and remediating failures in reading comprehension: Toward an instructional approach for comprehenders. In G. MacKinnon & T. Waller (Eds.), *Reading research: Advances in theory and practice*, Vol. 3. New York: Academic Press, 1981, 223–261.

RYAN, ELLEN B.; WEED, KERI A.; & SHORT, ELIZABETH J. Cognitive behavior modification: Promoting active, self-regulatory learning styles. In J. K. Torgesen & B. Y. L. Wong (Eds.), *Psychological and educational perspectives on learning disabilities*. New York: Academic Press, 1986, 367–397.

RYDER, RANDALL J., & GRAVES, MICHAEL F. Secondary students' internalization of letter-sound correspondences. *Journal of Educational Research*, 1980, *73*, 172–178.

RYDER, RANDALL J.; GRAVES, BONNIE B.; & GRAVES, MICHAEL F. *Easy reading: Book series and periodicals for less able readers* (2nd ed.). Newark, DE: International Reading Association, 1989.

SABATINO, DAVID A., & MILLER, TED L. The dilemma of diagnosis in learning disabilities: Problems and potential directions. *Psychology in the Schools*, 1980, *17* (1), 76–86.

SADOW, MARILYN W. The use of story grammar in the design of questions. *The Reading Teacher*, February 1982, *35*, 518–522.

SADOWSKI, MARK. The natural use of imagery in story comprehension and recall: Replication and extension. *Reading Research Quarterly*, Fall 1985, *20*, 658–667.

SADOWSKI, MARK, & LEE, SHARON. Reading comprehension and miscue combination scores: Further analysis and comparison. *Reading Research and Instruction*, Spring 1986, *25*, 160–167.

SAFER, DANIEL J. Nonpromotion correlates and outcomes at different grade levels. *Journal of Learning Disabilities*, October 1986, *19*, 500–503.

SAKAMOTO, TAKAHIKO. Writing systems in Japan. In J. E. Merritt (Ed.), *New horizons in reading*. Newark, DE: International Reading Association, 1976, 244–249.

SAKAMOTO, TAKAHIKO. Beginning reading in Japan. In L. Ollila (Ed.), *Beginning reading instruction in different countries*. Newark, DE: International Reading Association, 1981, 16–25.

SALASOO, AITA. Cognitive processing in oral and silent reading comprehension. *Reading Research Quarterly*, Winter 1986, *21*, 59–69.

SALEND, SPENCER J. Self-assessment: A model for involving students in the formation of their IEPs. *Journal of School Psychology*, Spring 1983, *21*, 65–70.

SALEND, SPENCER J., & MOE, L. Modifying nonhandicapped students' attitudes toward their handicapped peers through children's literature. *Journal of Special Education*, 1983, *19*, 22–28.

SALEND, SUZANNE R. & SALEND, SPENCER J. Writing and evaluating educational assessment reports. *Academic Therapy Quarterly*, January 1985, *20*, 277–288.

SAMPSON, MICHAEL R. A comparison of the complexity of children's dictation and instructional reading materials. In J. Niles & L. A. Harris (Eds.), *New inquiries in reading research and instruction*. Rochester, NY: National Reading Conference, 1982, 177–179.

SAMUELS, BARBARA G. Young adults' choices: Why do students "really like" particular books. *Journal of Reading*, May 1989, *32*, 714–719.

SAMUELS, S. JAY. Effect of distinctive feature training on paired associate learning. *Journal of Educational Psychology*, April 1973, *64*, 147–158.(a)

SAMUELS, S. JAY. Success and failure in learning to read: A critique of the research. *Reading Research Quarterly*, Winter 1973, 8, 200–239.(b)

SAMUELS, S. JAY. Hierarchial subskills in the reading acquisition process. In J. T. Guthrie (Ed.), *Aspects of reading acquisition*. Baltimore: Johns Hopkins University Press, 1976, 141–161.

SAMUELS S. JAY. The method of repeated readings. *The Reading Teacher*, January 1979, 32, 403–408.

SAMUELS, S. JAY. The age-old controversy between holistic and subskill approaches to beginning reading instruction revisited. In C. McCullough (Ed.), *Inchworm, inchworm: Persistent problems in reading education*. Newark, DE: International Reading Association, 1980, 202–221.

SAMUELS, S. JAY. Some essentials of decoding. *Exceptional Education Quarterly*, May 1981, 2, 11–25.

SAMUELS, S. JAY. Diagnosing reading problems. *Topics in Learning Disabilities*, January 1983, 2, 1–11.

SAMUELS S. JAY. Toward a theory of automatic information processing in reading: Updated. In H. Singer & R. B. Ruddell (Eds.), *Theoretical models and reading processes* (3rd ed.). Newark, DE: International Reading Association, 1985, 719–721.(a)

SAMUELS, S. JAY. Word recognition. In H. Singer & R. B. Ruddell (Eds.), *Theoretical models and reading processes* (3rd ed.). Newark, DE: International Reading Association, 1985, 256–275.(b)

SAMUELS, S. JAY. Why children fail to learn and what to do about it. *Exceptional Children*, September 1986, 53, 7–16.

SAMUELS, S. JAY. Factors that influence listening and reading comprehension. In R. Horowitz & S. J. Samuels (Eds.), *Comprehending oral and written language*. New York: Academic Press, 1987, 295–325.(a)

SAMUELS, S. JAY. Information processing abilities and reading. *Journal of Learning Disabilities*, January 1987, 20, 18–22.(b)

SAMUELS, S. JAY. Characteristics of exemplary reading programs. In S. J. Samuels & P. D. Pearson (Eds.), *Changing school reading programs: Principles and case studies*. Newark, DE: International Reading Association, 1988, 3–9.(a)

SAMUELS, S. JAY. Decoding and automaticity: Helping poor readers become automatic at word recognition. *The Reading Teacher*, April 1988, 41, 756–760.(b)

SAMUELS, S. JAY, & DAHL, PATRICIA R. Establishing appropriate purpose for reading and its effect on flexibility of reading rate. *Journal of Educational Psychology*, 1975, 67, 38–43.

SAMUELS, S. JAY, & EISENBERG, PETER. A framework for understanding the reading process. In F. Pirozzolo & M. Wittrock (Eds.), *Neuropsychological and cognitive processes in reading*. New York: Academic Press, 1981, 31–67.

SAMUELS, S. JAY, & KAMIL, MICHAEL L. Models of the reading process. In P. D. Pearson et al. (Eds.), *Handbook of Reading Research*. New York: Longman, 1984, 185–224.

SAMUELS, S. JAY, & MILLER, NANCY L. Failure to find attention differences between learning disabled and normal children on classroom and laboratory tasks. *Exceptional Children*, February 1985, 51, 358–375.

SANACORE, JOSEPH. Guidelines for observing remedial reading lessons. *The Reading Teacher*, January 1981, 34, 394–399.

SANDOVAL, JONATHAN, & HUGHES, RENEE G. *Success in nonpromoted first grade children: Final report*. Davis, CA: University of California. Bethesda, MD: National Institutes of Mental Health, 1981. (ERIC number ED 212 371.)

SARTAIN, HARRY W. The research base for individualized reading instruction. In J. A. Figurel (Ed.), *Reading and realism*. Newark, DE: International Reading Association, 1969, 523–530.

SARTAIN, HARRY W. Research summary: Family contributions to reading attainment. In

H. Sartain (Ed.), *Mobilizing family forces for worldwide reading success*. Newark, DE: International Reading Association, 1981, 4–18.

SATZ, PAUL, & FLETCHER, J. M. Early screening tests: Some uses and abuses. *Journal of Learning Disabilities*, January 1979, *12*, 56–60.

SATZ, PAUL, & MORRIS, ROBIN. Learning disability subtypes: A review. In F. Pirozzolo & M. Wittrock (Eds.), *Neuropsychological and cognitive processes in reading*. New York: Academic Press, 1981, 109–141.

SATZ, PAUL; MORRIS, ROBIN; & FLETCHER, JACK M. Hypotheses, subtypes and individual differences in dyslexias. Some reflections. In D. B. Gray & J. F. Kavanagh (Eds.), *Biobehavioral measures of dyslexia*. Parkton, MD: York Press, 1985, 25–40.

SATZ, PAUL, et al. Some developmental and predictive precursors of reading disabilities: A six-year follow-up. In A. Benton & D. Pearl (Eds.), *Dyslexia: An appraisal of current knowledge*. New York: Oxford University Press, 1978, 313–348.

SATZ, PAUL, et al. The pathological left-handedness syndrome. *Brain and Cognition*, January 1985, *4*, 27–46.

SCARBOROUGH, HOLLIS S. Continuity between childhood dyslexia and adult reading. *British Journal of Psychology*, August 1984, 75 (Part 3), 329–348.

SCHACHTER, SUMNER W. Developing flexible reading rates. *Journal of Reading*, November 1978, *29*, 149–152. Also in A. J. Harris & E. Sipay (Eds.), *Readings on reading instruction* (3rd ed.). New York: Longman, 1984, 402–404.

SCHALE, FLORENCE C. Vertical methods of increasing rates of comprehension. *Journal of Reading*, April 1965, *8*, 296–300.

SCHALE, FLORENCE C. Exploring the potential of the monocularly blind for faster reading. *Academic Therapy*, Summer 1972, *7*, 401–410.

SCHANK, ROGER C. *Reading and understanding: Teaching from the perspective of artificial intelligence*. Hillsdale, NJ: Erlbaum, 1982.

SCHATZ, ELINORE K., & BALDWIN, R. SCOTT. Context clues are unreliable predictors of word meaning. *Reading Research Quarterly*, Fall 1986, *21*, 439–453.

SCHEIRER, MARY ANN, & KRAUT, ROBERT E. Increasing educational achievement via self-concept change. *Review of Educational Research*, Winter 1979, *49*, 131–150.

SCHELL, LEO M. Teaching decoding to remedial readers. *The Reading Teacher*, May 1978, *31*, 877–882.

SCHELL, LEO M. How accurate are oral reading tests? *Reading World*, December 1982, *22*, 91–97.

SCHELL, LEO M., & HANNA, GERALD S. Can informal reading inventories reveal strengths and weaknesses in comprehension subskills? *The Reading Teacher*, December 1981, *35*, 263–268.

SCHELL, VICKIE J. Learning partners: Reading and mathematics. *The Reading Teacher*, February 1982, *35*, 544–548.

SCHNECK-DANZIGER, LOTTE. Probleme der legasthenie. *Schweizerische Zeitschrift fur psychologie und Ihre Anwendungen*, 1960, *20*, 29–48.

SCHEU, JUDITH; TANNER, DIANNE; AU, KATHRYN HU-PEI. Designing seatwork to improve students' reading comprehension ability. *The Reading Teacher*, October 1986, *40*, 18–25.

SCHEU, JUDITH; TANNER, DIANNE K.; & AU, KATHRYN HU-PEI. Integrating seatwork with the basal lesson. In P. N. Winograd et al. (Eds.), *Improving basal reading instruction*. New York: Teachers College Press, 1989, 86–106.

SCHLICHTER, CAROL L. Literature for students who are gifted. *Teaching Exceptional Children*, Spring 1989, *21*, 34–36.

SCHLIEF, MABEL, & WOOD, ROBERT W. A comparison of procedures to determine readability level of non-text materials. *Reading Improvement*, Fall 1974, *11*, 57–64.

SCHMITT, CLARA. Developmental alexia: Congenital word-blindness or inability to learn to read. *Elementary School Journal*, 1918, *18*, 680–700, 757–769.

SCHMITT, MARIBETH C. The effects of an elaborated directed reading activity in the meta-comprehension skills of third graders. In J. Readence, et al. (Eds.), *Dialogues in literacy research.* Chicago, National Reading Conference, 1988, 167–181.

SCHMITT, MARIBETH C., & BAUMANN, JAMES F. How to incorporate comprehension monitoring strategies into basal reader instruction. *The Reading Teacher*, October, 1986, *40*, 28–31.

SCHMITT, MARIBETH C., & O'BRIEN, DAVID G. Story grammars: Some cautions about the translation of research into practice. *Reading Research and Instruction*, Fall 1986, *26*, 1–8.

SCHNAYER, SIDNEY W. *Some relations between reading interest and reading comprehension.* Unpublished doctoral dissertation, University of California at Berkeley, 1967.

SCHON, ISABEL. Recent notorious and noteworthy books about Mexico, Mexicans and Mexican-Americans. *Journal of Reading*, January 1981, *24*, 293–299.

SCHON, ISABEL. Children's books in Spanish: Informational books. *The Reading Teacher*, February 1987, *40*, 566–567.

SCHONHAUT, STEVEN, & SATZ, PAUL. Prognosis for children with learning disabilities: A review of the followup studies. In M. Rutter (Ed.), *Developmental neuropsychiatry.* New York: Guilford Press, 1983, 542–563.

SCHORK, EDWARD J., & MILLER, STEPHEN C. Courts and public education: Possibilities and limits. In R. J. Harper & G. Killar (Eds.), *Reading and the law.* Newark, DE: International Reading Association, 1978, 1–9.

SCHRANK, FREDERICK A.; ENGELS, DENNIS W.; & SILKE, JAMES R. Using bibliotherapy in the elementary school: What does the research say? *Wisconsin State Reading Association Journal*, Winter 1983, *27*, 23–29.

SCHREIBER, PETER A. On the acquisition of fluency. *Journal of Reading Behavior*, Fall 1980, *12*, 177–186.

SCHUBERT, DELWYN G., & WALTON, HOWARD N. Visual screening—A new breakthrough. *The Reading Teacher*, November 1980, *34*, 175–177.

SCHUDER, TED; CLEWELL, SUZANNE F.; & JACKSON, NAN. Getting the gist of expository text. In K. D. Muth (Ed.), *Children's comprehension of text.* Newark, DE: International Reading Association, 1989, 224–242.

SCHULTE, EMERITA S. Independent reading interests of children in grades 4, 5, and 6. In J. A. Figurel (Ed.), *Reading and realism.* Newark, DE: International Reading Association, 1969, 728–732.

SCHULTZ, A. J. *An investigation of the role of interest as a factor in reading comprehension.* Unpublished master's thesis, Rutgers University, 1975 (ERIC number ED 116 152.)

SCHUMAKER, GARY M. Executive control in studying. In B. K. Britton & S. M. Glynn (Eds.), *Executive control in reading.* Hillsdale, NJ: Erlbaum, 1987, 107–144.

SCHUMAKER, JEAN B.; DESHLER, DONALD D.; & ELLIS, EDWIN S. Intervention issues related to education of LD adolescents. In J. K. Torgesen & B. Y. L. Wong (Eds.), *Psychological and educational perspectives on learning disabilities.* New York Academic Press, 1986, 329–365.

SCHUNK, DALE H., & RICE, JO MAY. Enhancing comprehension skill and self-efficacy with strategy value information. *Journal of Reading Behavior*, 1987, *19*(3), 285–302.

SCHUYLER, MICHAEL R. A readability formula program for use on microcomputers. *Journal of Reading*, March 1982, *25*, 560–591.

SCHWANENFLUGEL, PAULA J., & STOWE, RANDALL W. Context availability and the processing of abstract and concrete words in sentences. *Reading Research Quarterly*, Winter 1989, *24*, 114–126.

SCHWANTES, FREDERICK M. Effect of story on children's ongoing word recognition. *Journal of Reading Behavior*, Winter 1981, *13*, 305–311.

SCHWARTZ, ROBERT M., & RAPHAEL, TAFFY E. Concept of definition: A key to improving students' vocabulary. *The Reading Teacher*, November 1985, *39*, 198–205.

SCHWARTZ, STEVEN. *Measuring reading competence: A theoretical-prescriptive approach.* New York: Plenum Press, 1984.

SCHWORM, RONALD W. Hyperkinesis: Myth, mystery, and matter. *Journal of Special Education*, Summer 1982, *16*, 129–148.

SCHWORM, RONALD W., & BIRNBAUM, RICKI. Symptom expression in hyperactive children: An analysis of observations. *Journal of Learning Disabilities*, January 1989, *22*, 35–40, 45.

SCOTT, DEANNA, & BARKER, JEANNE. Guidelines for selecting and evaluating reading software: Improving the decision making process. *The Reading Teacher*, May 1987, *40*, 884–887.

SCOTT, KATHRYN P. Effects of sex-fair reading materials on pupils' attitudes, comprehension, and interest. *American Educational Research Journal*, Spring, 1986. *23*, 105–116.

SCRIBNER, SYLVIA. Literacy in three metaphors. In N. L. Stein (Ed.), *Literacy in American schools: Learning to read and write.* Chicago: University of Chicago Press, 1986, 7–22.

SCRUGGS, THOMAS E., & RICHTER, LORI. Tutoring learning disabled students: A critical review. *Learning Disability Quarterly*, Fall 1985, 8, 286–297.

SEARLEMAN, A. A review of right-hemispheric linguistic capabilities. *Psychological Bulletin*, 1977, *84*, 503–522.

SEARLS, DONALD T.; MEAD, NANCY A.; & WARD, BARBARA. The relationship of students' reading skills to TV watching, leisure time reading and homework. *Journal of Reading*, November 1985, *29*, 158–162.

SEARLS, EVELYN F. *How to use WISC-R scores in reading/learning disability diagnosis.* Newark, DE: International Reading Association, 1985.

SEARLS, EVELYN F., & KLESIUS, JANELL P. 99 multiple meaning words for primary students and ways to teach them. *Reading Psychology*, 1984, 5(1–2), 55–63.

SEAVER, JOANN T., & BOTEL, MORTON. A first-grade teacher teaches reading, writing, and oral communication across the curriculum. *The Reading Teacher*, March 1983, *36*, 656–664.

SEBESTA, SAM L. Choosing poetry. In N. Roser & M. Frith (Eds.), *Children's choices: Teaching with books children like.* Newark, DE: International Reading Association, 1983, 66–78.

SEIDENBERG, MARK S., et al. Word recognition processes of poor and disabled readers: Do they necessarily differ? *Applied Psycholinguistics*, 1985, 6(2), 161–180.

SEIDENBERG, PEARL L., & BERNSTEIN, DEENA K. Metaphor comprehension and performance on metaphor-related language tasks: A comparison of good and poor readers. *Remedial and Special Education*, 1988, 9(2), 39–45.

SELDEN, RAMSEY. On the validation of the original readability formulas. In A. Davison et al. (Eds.), *Text readability: Proceedings of the March 1980 Conference.* Technical Report No. 213. Champaign, IL: Center for the Study of Reading, University of Illinois, August 1981, 10–26.

SEMINOFF, NANCY W. Children's periodicals throughout the world: An overlooked educational resource. *The Reading Teacher*, May 1986, *39*, 889–895.(a)

SEMINOFF, NANCY W. Understanding poetry: Questions to consider. *Wisconsin State Reading Association Journal*, Summer 1986, *30*, 3–16.(b)

SENF, GERALD M. LD research in sociological and scientific perspective. In J. K. Torgesen & B. Y. L. Wong (Eds.), *Psychological and educational perspectives on learning disabilities.* New York: Academic Press, 1986, 27–53.

SERAFICA, FELICISIMA C., & HARWAY, NORMAN I. Social relations and self-esteem of children with learning disabilities. *Journal of Clinical Child Psychology*, Fall 1979, 8, 227–233.

SEWALL, GILBERT. Literacy lackluster. *American Educator*, Spring 1988, *12*, 32–37.

SHAFFER, GARY L. An investigation of the relationship of selected components of readability and comprehension at the secondary school level. In P. D. Pearson & J. Hansen (Eds.), *Reading: Theory, research and practice*. Clemson, SC: National Reading Conference, 1977, 244–252.

SHAKE, MARY C. Bases for grouping decisions. In J. A. Niles and R. V. Lalik (Eds.), *Solving problems in literacy: Learners, teachers, and researchers*. Rochester, NY: National Reading Conference, 1986, 171–177.(a)

SHAKE, MARY C. Teacher interruptions during oral reading instruction: Self-monitoring as an impetus for change in corrective feedback. *Remedial and Special Education*, September/October 1986, 7, 18–24.(b)

SHAKE, MARY C. Teacher questioning: Is there an answer? *Reading Research and Instruction*, Winter 1988, *27*, 29–39.

SHAKE, MARY C. Grouping and pacing with basal materials. In P. N. Winograd et al. (Eds.), *Improving basal reading instruction*. New York: Teachers College Press, 1989, 62–85.

SHANAHAN, TIMOTHY. Predictions and limiting effects of prequestions. In J. A. Niles & R. V. Lalik (Eds.), *Solving problems in literacy: Learners, teachers, and researchers*. Rochester, NY: National Reading Conference, 1986, 92–98.

SHANAHAN, TIMOTHY. The reading-writing relationship: Seven instructional principles. *The Reading Teacher*, March 1988, *41*, 636–647.

SHANAHAN, TIMOTHY, & HOGAN, VIRGINIA. Parent reading style and children's print awareness. In J. Niles & L. A. Harris (Eds.), *Search for meaning in reading/language processing and instruction*. Rochester, NY: National Reading Conference, 1983, 212–217.

SHANAHAN, TIMOTHY, & KAMIL, MICHAEL L. The sensitivity of cloze to passage organization. In J. Niles & L. A. Harris (Eds.), *New inquiries in reading research and instruction*. Rochester, NY: National Reading Conference, 1982, 204–208.

SHANAHAN, TIMOTHY, & KAMIL, MICHAEL L. A further comparison of sensitivity of cloze and recall to passage organization. In J. Niles & L. A. Harris (Eds.), *Search for meaning in reading/language processing and instruction*. Rochester, NY: National Reading Conference, 1983, 123–128.

SHANAHAN, TIMOTHY, & KAMIL, MICHAEL L. The relationship of concurrent and construct validities of cloze. In J. A. Niles & L. A. Harris (Eds.), *Changing perspectives on research in reading/language processing and instruction*. Rochester, NY: National Reading Conference, 1984, 252–256.

SHANKER, ALBERT. Illiteracy: It's not all discouraging words. *On Campus*, December 1988/January 1989, 8, 7.

SHANKER, JAMES L. *Guidelines for successful staff development*. Newark, DE: International Reading Association, 1982.

SHANKWEILER, DONALD, et al. The speech code and learning to read. *Journal of Experimental Psychology: Human Learning & Memory*, November 1979, 5, 531–545.

SHANNON, PATRICK. A retrospective look at teachers' reliance on commercial reading materials. *Language Arts*, November/ December 1982, 59, 844–853.

SHANNON, PATRICK. Conflict or consensus: Views of reading curricula and instruction within one instructional setting. *Reading Research and Instruction*, Fall 1986, *26*, 31–49.

SHAPIRO, JON E. Developing an awareness of attitudes. In J. Shapiro (Ed.), *Using literature and poetry effectively*. Newark, DE: International Reading Association, 1979, 2–7.

SHAPIRO, SHEILA. An analysis of poetic teaching procedures in sixth-grade basal manuals. *Reading Research Quarterly*, Spring 1985, *20*, 368–381.

SHAYON, ROBERT L. *Television and our children.* New York: Longman, Green, 1951.

SHAYWITZ, BENNETT A., & WAXMAN, STEPHEN G. Dyslexia. *New England Journal of Medicine*, May 14, 1987, *316*, 1268–1270.

SHEBILSKE, WAYNE L., & FISHER, DENNIS F. Eye movements and context effects during reading of extended discourse. In K. Rayner (Ed.), *Eye movements in reading: Perceptual and language processes.* New York: Academic Press, 1983, 153–179.

SHEPARD, LORRIE. An evaluation of the regression discrepancy method for identifying children with learning disabilities. *Journal of Special Education*, Spring 1980, *14*, 79–91.

SHEPARD, LORRIE A.; SMITH, MARY LEE; & VOJIR, CAROL P. Characteristics of pupils identified as learning disabled. *American Educational Research Journal*, Fall 1983, *20*, 309–331.

SHEPHERD, MARGARET J.; GELZHEISER, LYNN M.; & SOLAR, ROBERTA. How good is the evidence for a production deficiency among learning disabled students? *Journal of Educational Psychology*, 1985, *77*(5), 553–561.

SHERER, PETER A. Those mystifying metaphors: Students can read them. *Journal of Reading*, April 1977, *20*, 559–566.

SHERIDAN, E. MARCIA. Early reading in Japan. *Reading World*, May 1982, *21*, 326–332.

SHORES, HARLAN J., & HUSBANDS, KENNETH L. Are fast readers the best readers? *Elementary English*, 1950, *27*, 52–57.

SHOUP, BARBARA. Television: Friend, not foe of the teacher. *Journal of Reading*, April 1984, *27*, 629–631.

SHPRINTZEN, ROBERT J., & GOLDBERG, ROSALIE B. Multiple anomaly syndromes and learning disabilities. In S. D. Smith (Ed.), *Genetics and learning disabilities.* San Diego: College-Hill Press, 1986, 153–174.

SHUCARD, DAVID M., et al. Electro-physiological studies of reading-disabled children: In search of subtypes. In D. B. Gray & J. F. Kavanagh (Eds.), *Biobehavioral measures of dyslexia.* Parkton, MD: York Press, 1985, 87–106.

SHUELL, THOMAS J. Cognitive conceptions of learning. *Review of Educational Research*, Winter 1986, *56*, 411–436.

SHUY, ROGER W. The mismatch of child language and school language: Implications for beginning reading instruction. In L. Resnick & P. Weaver (Eds.), *Theory and practice of early reading*, Vol. 1. Hillsdale, NJ: Erlbaum, 1979, 187–207.

SHUY, ROGER W. Four misconceptions about clarity and simplicity. *Language Arts*, May 1981, *58*, 557–561.(a)

SHUY, ROGER W. A holistic view of language. *Research in the Teaching of English*, May 1981, *15*, 101–111.(b)

SIEBEN, ROBERT L. Controversial medical treatments of learning disabilities. *Academic Therapy*, November 1977, *13*, 133–147.

SIEDOW, MARY D; MEMORY, DAVID M.; & BRISTOW, PAGE S. *Inservice education for content area teachers.* Newark, DE: International Reading Association, 1985.

SIEGEL, LINDA S. Deep dyslexia in childhood. *Brain and Language*, September 1985, *26*, 16–27.

SIEGEL, LINDA S., & RYAN, ELLEN B. Development of grammatical-sensitivity, phonological, and short-term memory skills in normally achieving and learning disabled children. *Developmental Psychology*, 1988, *24*(1), 28–37.

SIEGEL, MARY-ELLEN K. *Her way: A guide to biographies of women for young people.* Chicago: American Library Association, 1984.

SILBERBERG, NORMAN E., & SILBERBERG, MARGARET C. A note on reading tests and their roles in defining reading difficulties. *Journal of Learning Disabilities*, February 1977, *10*, 100–103.

SILVA, PHIL A.; CHALMERS, DAVID; & STEWART, IAN. Some audiological, psychological, educational and behavioral characteristics of children with bilateral otitis media with effusion: A longitudinal study. *Journal of Learning Disabilities*, March 1986, *19*, 165–169.

SILVER, ARCHIE A., & HAGIN, ROSA A. A unifying concept for the neuropsychological organization of children with reading disabilities. *Journal of Developmental and Behavioral Pediatrics*, September 1982, *3*, 127–132.

SILVER, LARRY B. The "magic cure": A review of the current controversial approaches for treating learning disabilities. *Journal of Learning Disabilities*, October 1987, *20*, 498–504.

SIMMS, ROCHELLE B. Hyperactivity and drug therapy: What educators should know. *Journal of Research and Development in Education*, 1985, *18*(3), 1–7.

SIMMS, ROCHELLE B., & FALCON, SUSAN C. Teaching sight words. *Teaching Exceptional Children*, Fall 1987, *20*, 30–33.

SIMONS, HERBERT D., & AMMON, PAUL. Primerese miscues. In J. Readence, et al. (Eds.), *Dialogues in literacy research*. Chicago: National Reading Conference, 1988, 115–121.

SIMONS, HERBERT D., & LEU, DONALD J., JR. The use of contextual and graphic information in word recognition by second- fourth-, and sixth-grade readers. *Journal of Reading Behavior*, 1987, *19*(1), 33–47.

SIMONS, SANDRA M. PSRT—A reading comprehension strategy. *Journal of Reading Behavior*, February 1989, *32*, 419–427.

SINGER, HARRY. The SEER technique: A non-computation procedure for quickly estimating readability level. *Journal of Reading Behavior*, Fall 1975, 7, 255–267.

SINGER, HARRY. Theoretical models of reading. In H. Singer & R. B. Ruddell (Eds.), *Theoretical models and processes of reading* (2nd ed.). Newark, DE: International Reading Association, 1976, 634–654.

SINGER, HARRY. IQ is and is not related to reading. In S. Wanat (Ed.), *Issues in evaluating reading*. Arlington, VA: Center for Applied Linguistics, 1977, 43–55.

SINGER, HARRY (Reviewer). Reading miscue inventory. In O. K. Buros (Ed.), *Eighth mental measurements yearbook*, Vol. II. Highland Park, NJ: Gryphon Press, 1978, 1319–1322.(a)

SINGER, HARRY. Research in reading that should make a difference in a classroom instruction. In S. J. Samuels (Ed.), *What research has to say about reading instruction*. Newark, DE: International Reading Association, 1978, 57–71.(b)

SINGER, HARRY. Active comprehension: From answering to asking questions. In C. McCullough (Ed.), *Inchworm, inchworm: Persistent problems in reading education*. Newark, DE: International Reading Association, 1980, 222–232.(a)

SINGER, HARRY. Sight word learning with and without pictures: A critique of Arlin, Scott and Webster's research. *Reading Research Quarterly*, 1980, *15*(2), 290–298.(b)

SINGER, HARRY. Teaching the acquisition phase of reading development: An historical perspective. In O. Tzeng & H. Singer (Eds.), *Perception of print: Reading research in experimental psychology*. Hillsdale, NJ: Erlbaum, 1981, 9–28.

SINGER, HARRY. Hypothesis on reading comprehension in search of classroom validation. In H. Singer & R. B. Ruddell (Eds.), *Theoretical models and processes of reading* (3rd ed.). Newark, DE: International Reading Association, 1985, 920–942.(a)

SINGER, HARRY. Models of reading have direct implications: The affirmative position. In J. A. Niles & R. V. Lalik (Eds.), *Issues in literacy: A research perspective*. Rochester, NY: National Reading Conference, 1985, 402–413.(b)

SINGER, HARRY. The substrata factor theory of reading. In H. Singer & R. B. Ruddell (Eds.), *Theoretical models and processes of reading* (3rd ed.). Newark, DE: International Reading Association, 1985, 630–660.(c)

SINGER, HARRY; & BEAN, THOMAS W. Three models for helping teachers to help students learn from text. In S. J. Samuels & P. D. Pearson (Eds.), *Changing school reading programs: Principles and case studies*. Newark, DE: International Reading Association, 1988, 161–182.

SINGER, HARRY & DONLAN, DAN. *Reading and learning from text* (2nd ed.). Hillsdale, NJ: Erlbaum, 1988.

SINGER, HARRY, & RUDDELL, ROBERT B. (Eds.). *Theoretical models and processes of reading*. Newark, DE: International Reading Association, 1976; 1985.

SINGER, MARTIN H. Insensitivity to ordered information and the failure to read. In M. Singer (Ed.), *Competent reader, disabled reader: Research and application*. Hillsdale, NJ: Erlbaum, 1982, 69–80.

SIPAY, EDWARD R. A comparison of standardized reading test scores and functional reading levels. *The Reading Teacher*, January, 1964, *17*, 265–268.

SIPAY, EDWARD R. Interpreting the USOE cooperative reading studies. *The Reading Teacher*, October 1968, *22*, 10–16.

SIPAY, EDWARD R. Determining word identification difficulties. In B. Bateman (Ed.), *Learning disorders*, Vol. 4. Seattle: Special Child Publications, 1971, 215–247.

SIPAY, EDWARD R. *Manual for the Sipay Word Analysis Tests*. Cambridge, MA: Educators Publishing Service, 1973.

SIPAY, EDWARD R. *Manual for the Diagnostic Decoding Tests*. Cambridge, MA: Educators Publishing Service, 1990.

SIPERSTEIN, GARY N., et al. Social status of learning disabled children. *Journal of Learning Disabilities*, February 1978, *11*, 98–102.

SITTIG, LINDA H. Involving parents and children in reading for fun. *The Reading Teacher*, November 1982, 36, 166–168.

SLATER, WAYNE H., & GRAVES, MICHAEL F. Research on expository text: Implications for teachers. In K. D. Muth (Ed.), *Children's comprehension of text*. Newark, DE: International Reading Association, 1989, 140–166.

SLAVIN, ROBERT E. Best evidence synthesis: An alternative to meta-analytic and traditional reviews. *Educational Researcher*, 1986, *15*(9), 5–11.

SLAVIN, ROBERT E. Ability grouping and its alternatives: Must we track? *American Educator*, Summer 1987, *11*, 32–36, 47–48.(a)

SLAVIN, ROBERT E. Ability grouping and student achievement in elementary schools: A best-evidence synthesis. *Review of Educational Research*, Fall 1987, 57, 293–336.(b)

SLAVIN, ROBERT E. Ability grouping in elementary schools: Do we really know nothing until we know everything? *Review of Educational Research*, Fall 1987, 57, 347–350.(c)

SLAVIN, ROBERT E. Mastery learning reconsidered. *Review of Educational Research*, Summer 1987, 57, 175–213.(d)

SLINGERLAND, BETH H. *A multi-sensory approach to language arts for specific language disability children: A guide for primary teachers*. Cambridge, MA: Educators Publishing Service, 1976.

SMARDO, FRANCES A. Using children's literature to clarify science concepts in early childhood programs. *The Reading Teacher*, December 1982, 36, 267–273.

SMILEY, SANDRA S.; PASQUALE, FRANK L.; & CHANDLER, CHRISTINE L. The pronunciation of familiar, unfamiliar, and synthetic words by good and poor adolescent readers. *Journal of Reading Behavior*, Fall 1976, 8, 289–297.

SMITH, CORINNE R. The future of the learning disabilities field: Intervention approaches. *Journal of Learning Disabilities*, October 1986, *19*, 460–472.

SMITH, DONALD E. P., & CARRIGAN, PATRICIA M. *The nature of reading disability*. New York: Harcourt Brace, 1959.

SMITH, E. A., & KINCAID, J. P. Derivation and validation of the Automated Readability Index for use with technical materials. *Human Factors*, 1970, *12*, 457–464.

SMITH, FRANK. *Understanding reading: A psycholinguistic analysis of reading and learning to read*. New York: Holt, Rinehart and Winston, 1982.

SMITH, FRANK. Reading like a writer. *Language Arts*, May 1983 *60*, 558–567.

SMITH, FRANK, & GOODMAN, KENNETH S. On the psycholinguistic method of teaching reading. *Elementary School Journal*, January 1971, *71*, 177–181.

SMITH, FREDERICK R., & FEATHERS, KAREN M. The role of reading in content classrooms: Assumptions vs. realities. *Journal of Reading*, December 1983, *27*, 262–267.

SMITH, JUDITH, & ELKINS, JOHN. The use of cohesion by underachieving readers. *Reading Psychology*, 1985, *6* (1–2), 13–25.

SMITH, LAWRENCE L., et al. Using grade level vs. out-of-level reading tests with remedial students. *The Reading Teacher*, February 1983, *36*, 550–553.

SMITH, MARY LEE, & SHEPARD, LORRIE A. Kindergarten readiness and retention: A qualitative study of teachers' beliefs and practices. *American Educational Research Journal*, Fall 1988, *25*, 307–333.

SMITH, MAUREEN A., & SCHLOSS, PATRICK J. A "superform" for enhancing competence in completing employment applications. *Teaching Exceptional Children*, Summer 1986, *18*, 277–280.

SMITH, NANCY J. The word processing approach to language experience. *The Reading Teacher*, February 1985, *38*, 556–559.

SMITH, NILA B. The quest for increased reading competency. In H. A. Klein (Ed.), *The quest for competency in teaching reading*. Newark, DE: International Reading Association, 1972, 45–56.

SMITH, NILA B. *American reading instruction* (rev. ed.). Newark, DE: International Reading Association, 1986.

SMITH, PATRICIA L., & TOMPKINS, GAIL E. Structured notetaking: A new strategy for content area readers. *Journal of Reading*, October 1988, *32*, 46–53.

SMITH, RICHARD J., & BARRETT, THOMAS C. *Teaching reading in the middle grades*. Reading, MA: Addison-Wesley, 1974.

SMITH, RONALD A., et al. Labeling theory as applied to learning disabilities. Survey findings and policy suggestions. *Journal of Learning Disabilities*, April 1986, *19*, 195–202.

SMITH, SHELLEY D. Review and recommendations for the future. In S. D. Smith (Ed.), *Genetics and learning disabilities*. San Diego, CA: College-Hill Press, 1986, 205–211.

SMITH, SHELLEY D., et al. Specific reading disability: Identification of an inherited form through linkage analysis. *Science*, March 18, 1983, *219*, 1345–1347.

SMITH, WILLIAM. Intermittent eye malfunctions and their effect on reading. *The Reading Teacher*, March 1984, *37*, 570–576.

SMITH, WILLIAM E., & BECK, MICHAEL D. Determining instructional reading level with the 1978 Metropolitan Achievement Tests. *The Reading Teacher*, December 1980, *34*, 313–319.

SMITH, WILLIAM L. Cloze procedure [Ebbinghaus completion method] as applied to reading. In O. K. Buros (Ed.), *Eighth mental measurements yearbook*, Vol. II. Highland Park, NJ: Gryphon Press, 1978, 1176–1178.

SMITH, WILLIAM L., & COMBS, WARREN E. The effects of overt and covert cues on written syntax. *Research in the Teaching of English*, February 1980, *14*, 19–38.

SMITH-BURKE, M. TRIKA. Classroom practices and classroom interactions during reading instruction: What's going on? In J. R. Squire (Ed.), *The dynamics of language learning: Research in reading and English*. Bloomington, IN: ERIC/RCS, 1987, 226–265.

SNIDER, VICKI. Use of self-monitoring of attention with LD students: Research and application. *Learning Disability Quarterly*, Spring 1987, *10*, 139–151.

SNOWLING, MAGGIE, et al. Segmentation and speech perception in relation to reading skill: A developmental analysis. *Journal of Experimental Child Psychology*, June 1986, *41*, 489–507.

SNYDER, GERALDINE V. Learner verification of reading games. *The Reading Teacher*, March 1981, *34*, 686–691.

SOLAN, HAROLD A. A rationale for the optometric treatment and management of children with learning disabilities. *Journal of Learning Disabilities*, December 1981, *14*, 568–572.

SOLOMON, BERNARD. The television reading program. *Language Arts*, February 1976, 53, 135–136.

SOMMERVILLE, MARY ANN. Dialect and reading: A review of alternative solutions. *Review of Educational Research*, Spring 1975, *45*, 247–262.

SØRENSEN, AAGE B., & HALLINAN, MAUREEN T. Effects of ability grouping on growth in academic achievement. *American Educational Research Journal*, Winter 1986, *23*, 519–542.

SPACHE, EVELYN B. *Reading activities for child involvement* (3rd ed.). Boston: Allyn & Bacon, 1982.

SPACHE, GEORGE. A new readability formula for primary-grade reading materials. *Elementary School Journal*, March 1953, *53*, 410–413.

SPACHE, GEORGE D. Is this a breakthrough in reading? *The Reading Teacher*, 1962, *15*, 258–263.

SPACHE, GEORGE D. *Good reading for poor readers*. Champaign, IL: Garrard, 1974, 1978.

SPACHE, GEORGE D. *Good reading for the disadvantaged reader: Multi-ethnic resources*. Champaign, IL: Garrard, 1975.

SPEAR, L. C. & STERNBERG, R. J. An information-processing framework for understanding learning disabilities. In S. Ceci (Ed.), *Handbook of cognition, social, and neuropsychological aspects of learning disabilities*, Vol. 2. Hillsdale, NJ: Erlbaum, 1986, 2–36.

SPEARRITT, DONALD. Identification of subskills and reading comprehension by maximum likelihood factor analysis. *Reading Research Quarterly*, Fall 1972, 8, 92–111.

SPEARRITT, DONALD. *Measuring reading comprehension in the upper primary school*. Canberra, Australia: Government Publishing Service, 1977.

SPEARRITT, DONALD. Measuring reading comprehension in the upper primary school. *Australian Journal of Reading*, June 1980, 3, 67–75.

SPEECE, DEBORAH; MCKINNEY, JAMES D.; & APPLEBAUM, MARK I. Longitudinal development of conservation skills in learning disabled children. *Journal of Learning Disabilities*, May 1986, *19*, 302–307.

SPENCER, BETH R., & AFFLERBACH, PETER P. Young children's explanation of spaces between words in written text. In J. Readence et al. (Eds.), *Dialogues in literacy research*. Chicago: National Reading Conference, 1988, 69–76.

SPERRY, R. W.; GAZZANIGA, M. S.; & BOGEN, J. H. Interhemispheric relationships: The neocortical commissures: Syndromes of hemisphere disconnection. In R. Vinken & G. Brown (Eds.), *Handbook of Clinical Neurology*, Vol.4. New York: John Wiley & Sons, 1969, 273–290.

SPIEGEL, DIXIE LEE. *Reading for pleasure: Guidelines*. Newark, DE: International Reading Association & ERIC/RCS, 1981.(a)

SPIEGEL, DIXIE LEE. Six alternatives to the Directed Reading Activity. *The Reading Teacher*, May 1981, *34*, 914–920. (b). Also in A. J. Harris & E. Sipay (Eds.), *Readings on reading instruction* (3rd. ed.). New York: Longman, 1984, 391–396.

SPIEGEL, DIXIE LEE. Developing independence in decoding. *Reading World*, March 1985, *24*, 75–81.

SPIEGEL, DIXIE LEE, & FITZGERALD, JILL. Improving reading comprehension through instruction about story parts. *The Reading Teacher*, March 1986, *39*, 676–682.

SPIRT, DIANA L. *Introducing Book Plots 3: A guide for the middle grades.* New York: Bowker, 1988.

SPIVEY, NANCY N., & KING, JAMES R. Readers as writers composing from sources. *Reading Research Quarterly*, Winter 1989, *24*, 7–26.

SPOFFORD, TIM. Niskayuna parent wins suit over child not learning to read. *Albany Times Union*, December 2, 1986, B–2.

SPREEN, OTFRIED. Adult outcomes of reading disorders. In R. Malatesha & P. Aaron (Eds.), *Reading disorders: Varieties and treatments.* New York: Academic Press, 1982, 473–498.

SPRING, CARL, & SANDOVAL, JONATHAN. Food additives and hyperkinesis: A critical evaluation of the evidence. *Journal of Learning Disabilities*, November 1976, *9*, 560–569.

SPYRIDAKIS, JAN H., & STANDAL, TIMOTHY C. Signals in expository prose: Effects on reading comprehension. *Reading Research Quarterly*, Summer 1987, *22*, 285–298.

SQUIRE, JAMES R. *Instructional focus and the teaching of writing.* Ginn Occasional Papers, No 1. Columbus, OH: Ginn, November 1980.

STAHL, NORMAN A.; HENK, WILLIAM A.; & KING, JAMES R. Are drivers' manuals right for reluctant readers? *Journal of Reading*, November 1984, *28*, 166–168.

STAHL, STEVEN A. Three principles of effective vocabulary instruction. *Journal of Reading*, April 1986, *29*, 662–668.

STAHL, STEVEN A. Is there evidence to support matching reading styles and initial reading methods? *Phi Delta Kappan*, December 1988, *70*, 317–322.

STAHL, STEVEN A., & CLARK, CHARLES H. The effects of participatory expectations in classroom discussions on the learning of science vocabulary. *American Educational Research Journal*, Winter 1987, *25*, 541–555.

STAHL, STEVEN A., & ERICKSON, LAWRENCE G. The performance of third grade learning disabled boys on tasks at different levels of language: A model-based exploration. *Journal of Learning Disabilities*, May 1986, *19*, 285–290.

STAHL, STEVEN A., & FAIRBANKS, MARILYN M. The effects of vocabulary instruction: A model-based meta-analysis. *Review of Educational Research*, Spring 1986, *56*, 72–110.

STAHL, STEVEN A., & JACOBSON, MICHAEL G. Vocabulary difficulty, prior knowledge, and text comprehension. *Journal of Reading Behavior*, Fall 1986, *18*, 309–323.

STAHL, STEVEN A., & MILLER, PATRICA D. Whole language and language experience approaches for beginning reading: A quantitative research synthesis. *Review of Educational Research*, Spring 1989, *59*, 87–116.

STAHL, STEVEN A., et al. Prior knowledge and difficult vocabulary in the comprehension of unfamiliar text. *Reading Research Quarterly*, Winter 1989, *24*, 27–43.

STAINBACK, WILLIAM; STAINBACK, SUSAN; & FROYEN, LEN. Structuring the classroom to prevent disruptive behavior. *Teaching Exceptional Children*, Summer, 1987, *19*, 12–16.

STAKE, JAYNE E., & KATZ, JONATHAN F. Teacher-pupil relationships in the elementary school classrooms: Teacher-gender and pupil-gender differences. *American Educational Research Journal*, Fall 1982, *19*, 465–471.

STANLEY, JULIAN C. (Ed.). *Preschool programs for the disadvantaged.* Baltimore: Johns Hopkins University Press, 1972.

STANOVICH, KEITH E. Toward an interactive-compensatory model of individual differences in development of reading fluency. *Reading Research Quarterly*, 1980, *16* (1), 32–71.

STANOVICH, KEITH E. Individual differences in the cognitive processes of reading: I. Word decoding. *Journal of Learning Disabilities*, October 1982, *15*, 485–493. (a)

STANOVICH, KEITH E. Individual differences in the cognitive processes of reading: II. Text-level processing. *Journal of Learning Disabilities*, November 1982, *15*, 549–554.(b)

STANOVICH, KEITH E. Word recognition skill and reading ability. In M. Singer (Ed.), *Competent reader, disabled reader: Research and application.* Hillsdale, NJ: Erlbaum, 1982, 81–102.(c)

STANOVICH, KEITH E. Explaining the variance in reading ability in terms of psychological processes: What have we learned? *Annals of Dyslexia*, Vol. 25. Baltimore, MD: Orton Dyslexia Society, 1985, 67–96.

STANOVICH, KEITH E. Cognitive processes and the reading problems of learning-disabled children: Evaluating the assumption of specificity. In J. K. Torgesen & B. Y. L. Wong (Eds.), *Psychological and educational perspectives on learning disabilities.* New York: Academic Press, 1986, 87–131.(a)

STANOVICH, KEITH E. Matthew effects in reading: Some consequences of individual differences in the acquisition of literacy. *Reading Research Quarterly*, Fall 1986, *21*, 360–407.(b)

STANOVICH, KEITH E.; CUNNINGHAM, ANNE E.; & FEEMAN, DOROTHY J. Intelligence, cognitive skills, and early reading progress. *Reading Research Quarterly*, Spring 1984, *19*, 278–303.

STANOVICH, KEITH E.; CUNNINGHAM, ANNE E.; & WEST, RICHARD F. A longitudinal study of the development of automatic recognition skills in first graders. *Journal of Reading Behavior*, Spring 1981, *13*, 57–74.

STANOVICH, KEITH E.; NATHAN, RUTH G.; & VALA-ROSSI, MARILYN. Developmental changes in the cognitive correlates of reading ability and the developmental lag hypothesis. *Reading Research Quarterly*, Summer 1986, *21*, 267–283.

STANOVICH, KEITH E.; NATHAN, RUTH G.; & ZOLMAN, JUDITH E. The developmental lag hypothesis in reading: Longitudinal and matched reading-level comparisons. *Child Development*, February 1988, *59*, 71–86.

STAUFFER, RUSSELL G. A study of prefixes in the Thorndike list to establish a list of prefixes that should be taught in the elementary school. *Journal of Educational Research*, 1942, 35, 453–458.

STAUFFER, RUSSELL G. (Ed.). *The first grade reading studies: Findings of individual investigations.* Newark, DE: International Reading Association, 1967.

STAUFFER, RUSSELL G. *Directing reading maturity as a cognitive process.* New York: Harper & Row, 1969.

STAUFFER, RUSSELL G. *The language-experience approach to the teaching of reading* (2nd ed.). New York: Harper & Row, 1980.

STEDMAN, LAWRENCE C., & KAESTLE, CARL F. The test score decline is over: Now what? *Phi Delta Kappan*, November 1985, 67, 204–210.

STEDMAN, LAWRENCE C., & KAESTLE, CARL F. Literacy and reading performance in the United States from 1880 to the present. *Reading Research Quarterly*, Winter 1987, 22, 8–46.

STEIN, MARCI. Arithmetic word problems. *Teaching Exceptional Children*, Spring 1987, *19*, 33–35.

STEIN, NANCY L., & TRABASSO, TOM. *What's in a story: An approach to comprehension and instruction.* Technical Report No. 200. Champaign, IL: Center for the Study of Reading, University of Illinois, April 1981.

STELLERN, JOHN; COLLINS, JAMES; & BAYNE, MINA. A dual-task investigation of language-spatial lateralization. *Journal of Learning Disabilities*, November 1987, 20, 551–556.

STENSLAND, ANNA LEE. *Literature by and about the American Indian: An annotated bibliography* (2nd ed.). Urbana, IL: National Council of Teachers of English, 1979.

STEPHENS, BONNIE. Taking the second step in reading. *The Reading Teacher*, April 1989, *42*, 584–590.

STERN, PAULA, & SHAVELSON, RICHARD J. Reading teachers' judgments, plans, and decision making. *The Reading Teacher*, December 1983, *37*, 280–286.

STERNBERG, LES, & TAYLOR, RONALD L. The insignificance of psycholinguistic training: A reply to Kavale. *Exceptional Children*, November 1982, *49*, 254–256.

STERNBERG, ROBERT J. Most vocabulary is learned from context. In M. G. McKeown & M. E. Curtis (Eds.), *The nature of vocabulary acquisition*. Hillsdale, NJ: Erlbaum, 1987, 89–105.

STERNBERG, ROBERT J., & WAGNER, RICHARD K. Automation failure in learning disabilities. *Topics in Learning & Learning Disabilities*, July 1982, *2*, 1–11.

STETZ, F. P., & BECK, M. D. Attitudes toward standardized tests: Students, teachers, and measurement specialists. *Measurement in Education*, 1981, *12*(1), 1–11.

STEVENS, KATHLEEN C. The effect of topic interest on the reading comprehension of higher ability students. *Journal of Educational Research*, July/August 1979, *73*, 365–368.

STEVENS, KATHLEEN C. Readability formulae and McCall-Crabbs Standard Test Lessons in Reading. *The Reading Teacher*, January 1980, *33*, 413–415.

STEVENS, KATHLEEN C. Chunking material as an aid to reading comprehension. *Journal of Reading*, November 1981, *25*, 126–129.

STEVENS, KATHLEEN C. Can we improve reading by teaching background information? *Journal of Reading*, January 1982, *25*, 326–329.

STEVENS, ROBERT J., et al. Cooperative integrated reading and composition: Two field experiments. *Reading Research Quarterly*, Fall 1987, *22*, 433–454.

STEVENSON, HAROLD W. Orthography and reading disabilities. *Journal of Learning Disabilities*, May 1984, *17*, 296–301.

STEVENSON, JIM, et al. A twin study of genetic influences on reading and spelling ability and disability. *Journal of Child Psychology and Psychiatry and Allied Disciplines*, 1987, *28*(2), 229–247.

STEWART, ORAN, & GREEN, DAN S. Test-taking skills for standardized tests of reading. *The Reading Teacher*, March 1983, *36*, 634–638.

STEWIG, JOHN W., & SEBESTA, SAM L. (Eds.). *Using literature in the elementary classroom*. Urbana, IL: National Council of Teachers of English, 1989.

STICHT, THOMAS G. (Ed.). *Reading for working: A functional literacy anthology*. Alexandria, VA: Human Resources Research Organization, 1975.

STICHT, THOMAS G. Rate of comprehending by listening or reading. In J. Flood (Ed.), *Understanding reading comprehension*. Newark, DE: International Reading Association, 1984, 140–160.

STICHT, THOMAS G., & JAMES, JAMES H. Listening and reading. In P. D. Pearson (Ed.), *Handbook of reading research*. New York: Longman, 1984, 293–317.

STICHT, THOMAS G., et al. *Auding and reading: A developmental model*. Alexandria, VA: Human Resources Research Organization, 1974.

STICHT, THOMAS G., et al. *Teachers, books, computers and peers: Integrated communication technologies for adult literacy development*. Unpublished progress report. Naval Post-graduate School and NPRDC, 1986.

STIPEK, DEBORAH, & WEISZ, JOHN R. Perceived personal control and academic achievement. *Review of Educational Research*, Spring 1981, *51*, 101–137.

STONE, NORMAN M. *Reversal errors in reading: Their diagnostic significance and implications for neuropsychological theories of reading disability*. Unpublished doctoral dissertation, University of Iowa, 1976.

STOODT, BARBARA D. The relationship between understanding grammatical conjunctions and reading comprehension. *Elementary English*, April 1972, *49*, 502–505.

STOREY, D. C. Reading in the content areas: Fictionalized biographies and diaries for social studies. *The Reading Teacher*, April 1982, *35*, 796–798.

STOTSKY, SANDRA. The role of writing in developmental reading. *Journal of Reading*, January 1982, *25*, 330–340.

STOTSKY, SANDRA. Research on reading/writing relationships: A synthesis and suggested direction. *Language Arts*, May 1983, *60*, 627–642.

STOTT, DENIS H. *The hard-to-teach child: A diagnostic-remedial approach.* Baltimore: University Park Press, 1978.

STOTT, JON C. In search of the true hunter: Inuit folktales adapted for children. *Language Arts*, April 1983, *60*, 430–438.

STRAHAN, DAVID B., & HERLIHY, JOHN G. A model for analyzing textbook content. *Journal of Reading*, February 1985, *28*, 438–443.

STRANG, RUTH. *Reading diagnosis and remediation.* Newark, DE: International Reading Association, 1968.

STRANGE, MICHAEL. Instructional implications of a conceptual theory of reading comprehension. *The Reading Teacher*, January 1980, *33*, 391–397. Also in A. J. Harris & E. Sipay (Eds.), *Readings on reading instruction.* New York: Longman, 1984, 267–273.

STRICKLAND, DOROTHY. The black experience in paperback (kindergarten through grade 6). In M. J. Weiss (Ed.), *New perspectives in paperbacks.* York, PA: Strine, 1973, 20–23.

STRICKLAND, DOROTHY S. Some tips for using big books. *The Reading Teacher*, May 1988, *41*, 966–968.

STRICKLAND, DOROTHY S., et al. Research currents: Classroom dialogue during literature response groups. *Language Arts*, February 1989, *66*, 192–200.

STRICKLER, EDWIN. Family interaction patterns in psychogenic learning disturbance. *Journal of Learning Disabilities*, March 1969, *2*, 147–154.

STRONG, WILLIAM. *Creative approaches to sentence combining.* Urbana, IL: National Council of Teachers of English, 1986.

STRUEMPLER, RICHARD E.; LARSON, GERALD E,; & RIMLAND, BERNARD. Hair mineral analysis and disruptive behaviors in clinically normal young men. *Journal of Learning Disabilities*, December 1985, *18*, 609–612.

SUBKOVIAK, MICHAEL J. A practitioner's guide to computation and interpretation of reliability indices for mastery tests. *Journal of Educational Measurements*, Spring 1988, *25*, 47–55.

SUCHECKI, MARK S. R. Workers with basic skills more difficult to find. *Albany Times Union*, February 7, 1988, D.1,5.

SUCHER, FLOYD. Use of basal readers in individualized reading. In J. A. Figurel (Ed.), *Reading and realism.* Newark, DE: International Reading Association, 1969, 136–143.

SUCHOFF, IRWIN B. Research in the relationship between reading and vision—What does it mean? *Journal of Learning Disabilities*, December 1981, *14*, 573–576.

SUDERLIN, SYLVIA. *Bibliography of books for children.* Washington, DC: Association for Childhood Education International, 1983.

SULZBY, ELIZABETH. Word concept development activities. In E. Henderson & J. Beers (Eds.), *Developmental and cognitive aspects of learning to spell: A reflection of word knowledge.* Newark, DE: International Reading Association, 1980, 127–137.

SUMMERS, EDWARD G., & LUKASEVICH, ANN. Reading preferences of intermediate-grade children in relation to sex, community, and maturation (grade level): A Canadian perspective. *Reading Research Quarterly*, Spring 1983, *18*, 347–360.

SUNDBYE, NITA. Text explicitness and inferential questioning: Effects on story understanding and recall. *Reading Research Quarterly*, Winter 1987, *22*, 82–98.

SUTHERLAND, ZENA. *The best in children's books*. Chicago: University of Chicago Press, 1986.

SWABY, BARBARA. Varying the ways you teach reading with basal stories. *The Reading Teacher*, March 1982, *35*, 676–680.

SWAIN, EMMA H. Using comic books to teach reading and language arts. *Journal of Reading*, December 1978, *22*, 253–258.

SWAN, T. DESMOND. *Reading standards in Irish schools*. Walkingstown, Dublin, Ireland: Educational Company of Ireland, Ltd., 1978.

SWANSON, H. LEE. Do semantic memory deficiencies underlie learning disabled readers' encoding processes? *Journal of Experimental Child Psychology*, June 1986, *41*, 461–488.

SWANSON, H. LEE. Information processing theory and learning disabilities: An overview. *Journal of Learning Disabilities*, January 1987, *20*, 3–7.(a)

SWANSON, H. LEE. Verbal-coding deficits in the recall of pictorial information by learning disabled readers: The influence of a lexical system. *American Educational Research Journal*, Spring, 1987, *24*, 143–170.(b)

SWETT, SHIELA C. Math and LD: A new perspective. *Academic Therapy*, September 1978, *14*, 5–13.

SWISHER, LINDA, & ATEN, JAMES. Assessing comprehension of spoken language: A multi-faceted task. *Topics in Language Disorders*, June 1981, *1*, 75–85.

SYVALÄHTI, RAIJA. Reading-writing disabilities in Finland. In L. Tarnopol & M. Tarnopol (Eds.), *Reading disabilities: An international perspective*. Baltimore: University Park Press, 1976, 175–178.

SZESULSKI, PATRICIA A., & MANIS, FRANKLIN R. A comparison of word recognition processes in dyslexic and normal readers at two reading-age levels. *Journal of Experimental Child Psychology*, 1987, *44*(3), 364–376.

TABOR, SYLVIA R. Current definition of literacy. *Journal of Reading*, February 1987, *30*, 458–461.

TAFT, MARY LYNN, & LESLIE, LAUREEN. The effects of prior knowledge and oral reading accuracy on miscues and comprehension. *Journal of Reading Behavior*, 1985, *17*, 763–779.

TALLAL, PAULA. Temporal or phonetic processing deficit in dyslexia? That is the question. *Applied Psycholinguistics*, August 1984, *5*, 167–169.

TALLAL, PAULA; STARK, R. E.; & MELLITS, E. D. Identification of language impaired children on the basis of rapid perception and production skills. *Brain and Language*, July 1985, *25*, 314–322.

TARNOPOL, LESTER, & TARNOPOL, MURIEL. Motor deficits that cause reading problems. *Journal of Learning Disabilities*, October 1979, *12*, 522–524.

TARVER, SARA G. Cognitive behavior modification, direct instruction, and holistic approaches to the education of students with learning disabilities. *Journal of Learning Disabilities*, June/July 1986, *19*, 368–375.

TARVER, SARA G., et al. The development of visual selective attention and verbal rehearsal in learning disabled boys. *Journal of Learning Disabilities*, October 1977, *10*, 491–500.

TAYLOR, BARBARA. Toward an understanding of factors contributing to children's difficulty summarizing textbook material. In J. A. Niles & R. V. Lalik (Eds.), *Issues in literacy: A research perspective*. Rochester, NY: National Reading Conference, 1985, 125–131.

TAYLOR, BARBARA M., & NOSBUSH, LINDA. Oral reading for meaning: A technique for improving word identification skills. *The Reading Teacher*, December 1983, *37*, 234–237.

TAYLOR, BARBARA, et al. A comparison of students' ability to read for main ideas in social studies textbooks and to complete main idea worksheets. *Reading World*, March 1985, *24*, 10–15.

TAYLOR, H. GERRY; FLETCHER, JACK M.; & SATZ, PAUL. Component processes in reading disabilities: Neuropsychological investigations of distinct reading subskill deficits. In R. Malatesha & P. Aaron (Eds.), *Reading disorders: Varieties and treatments.* New York: Academic Press, 1982, 121–147.

TAYLOR, H. GERRY; SATZ, PAUL; & FRIEL, JANETTE. Developmental dyslexia in relation to other childhood reading disorders: Significance and clinical utility. *Reading Research Quarterly*, 1979–1980. *15*(1), 84–101.

TAYLOR, INSUP. The Korean writing system. In P. Kolers et al. (Eds.), *Processing visible language*, Vol. 2. New York: Plenum Press, 1980, 67–82.

TAYLOR, INSUP. Writing systems and reading. In G. MacKinnon & T. Waller (Eds.), *Reading research: Advances in theory and practice*, Vol. 2. New York: Academic Press, 1981, 1–53.

TAYLOR, KARL K. Teaching summarization skills. *Journal of Reading*, February 1984, *27*, 389–393.

TAYLOR, KARL, K. Summary writing by young children. *Reading Research Quarterly*, Spring 1986, *21*, 193–208.

TAYLOR, NANCY E. Developing beginning literacy: Content and context. In D. B. Yaden & S. Templeton (Eds.), *Metalinguistic awareness and beginning literacy.* Portsmouth, NH: Heinemann, 1986, 173–184.

TAYLOR, NANCY E.; BLUM, IRENE H. & LOGSDON, DAVID M. The development of written language awareness: Environmental aspects and program characteristics. *Reading Research Quarterly*, Spring 1986, *21*, 132–149.

TAYLOR, NANCY E.; WADE, MARQUET R; & YEKOVICH, FRANK R. The effects of text manipulation and multiple reading strategies on reading performances of good and poor readers. *Reading Research Quarterly*, Fall 1985, *20*, 566–574.

TAYLOR, STANFORD E., et al. *EDL core vocabularies in reading, mathematics, science, and social studies.* New York: EDL/McGraw-Hill, 1979.

TAYLOR, W. L. Cloze procedures: A new tool for measuring readability. *Journalism Quarterly*, Fall 1953, *30*, 415–433.

TEALE, WILLIAM H. Assessing attitudes toward reading: Why and how. *Australian Journal of Reading*, June 1980, *3*, 86–94.

TEALE, WILLIAM H. Parents reading to their children: What we know and need to know. *Language Arts*, November/December 1981, 55, 902–910.

TEALE, WILLIAM H. The beginning of reading and writing: Written language development during the preschool and kindergarten years. In M. Sampson (Ed.), *The pursuit of literacy: Early reading and writing.* Dubuque, IA: Kendall/Hunt, 1986.

TEALE, WILLIAM H. Emergent literacy: Reading and writing development in early childhood. In J. E. Readence et al. (Eds.), *Research in literacy: Merging perspectives.* Rochester, NY: National Reading Conference, 1987, 45–74.

TEALE, WILLIAM H; HIEBERT, ELFRIEDA H.; & CHITTENDEN, EDWARD A. Assesing young children's literacy development. *The Reading Teacher*, April 1987, *40*, 772–777.

TELFER, RICHARD J., & KANN, ROBERT S. Reading achievement, free reading , watching TV, and listening to music. *Journal of Reading*, March 1984, 27, 536–539.

TEMPLETON, SHANE. Using the spelling/meaning connection to develop word knowledge in older students. *Journal of Reading*, October 1983, 27, 8–14.

TEMPLETON, SHANE. Literacy, readiness, and basals. *The Reading Teacher*, January 1986, *39*, 403–409.

TERMAN, LEWIS M., & LIMA, MARGARET. *Children's reading.* New York: Appleton-Century-Crofts, 1937.

TERRY, ELLEN. *Children's poetry preference: A national survey of upper elementary grades*. Research Report No. 13. Urbana, IL: National Council of Teachers of English, 1974.

TERWILLIGER, PAUL N., & KOLKER, BRENDA S. The effects of learning confusable words on subsequent learning of high or low imagery words. *Reading World*, May 1982, *21*, 286–292.

TEST, DAVID W., & HEWARD, WILLIAM L. Teaching road signs and traffic laws to disabled students. *Learning Disability Quarterly*, Winter 1983, 6, 80–83.

TEYLER, TIMOTHY J. *A primer of psychobiology: Brain and behavior*. San Francisco: W. H. Freeman, 1975.

TEYLER, TIMOTHY J. The brain sciences: An introduction. In J. Chall & S. Mirsky (Eds.), *Education and the brain*. 77th Yearbook of the National Society for the Study of Education, Part II. Chicago: University of Chicago Press, 1978, 1–32.

THAMES, DANA G., & READENCE, JOHN E. Effects of differential vocabulary instruction and lesson framework on the reading comprehension of primary children. *Reading Research and Instruction*, Winter 1988, 27, 1–12.

THATCHER, R. W., & LESTER, M. L. Nutrition, environmental toxins and computerized EEGs: A mini-max approach to learning disabilities. *Journal of Learning Disabilities*, May 1985, *18*, 287–297.

THELEN, JUDY. Preparing students for the content reading assignments. *Journal of Reading*, March 1982, 25, 544–549.

THELEN, JUDITH N. *Improving reading in science* (2nd ed.). Newark, DE: International Reading Association, 1984.

THELEN, JUDITH N. Vocabulary instruction and meaningful learning. *Journal of Reading*, April 1986, 29, 603–609.

THOMAS, ADELE. Learned helplessness and expectancy factors: Implications for research in learning disabilities. *Review of Educational Research*, Spring 1979, 49, 208–221.

THOMAS, KAREN F. Early reading as a social interaction process. *Language Arts*, September 1985, 62, 469–475.

THOMAS, KEITH J. Instructional application of the cloze technique. *Reading World*, October 1978, *18*, 1–12.

THOMAS, K. J. The directed inquiry activity: An instructional procedure for content reading. In E. K. Dishner, et al. (Eds.), *Reading in the content areas: Improving classroom instruction* (2nd ed.). Dubuque, IA: Kendall/Hunt, 1986, 278–281.

THOMPSON, RICHARD A., & MERRITT, KING, JR. Turn on to a reading center. *The Reading Teacher*, January 1975, 28, 384–388.

THOMPSON, ROBERT J. The diagnostic utility of WISC-R measures with children referred to a developmental evaluation center. *Journal of Consulting and Clinical Psychology*, August 1980, 48, 440–447.

THOMPSON, STEPHEN J. Teaching metaphoric language: An instructional strategy. *Journal of Reading*, November 1986, 30, 195–209.

THORNDIKE, EDWARD L. *The teacher's word book*. New York: Teachers College Press, Columbia University, 1921.

THORNDIKE, EDWARD L. The vocabulary of books for children in grades 3 to 8. *Teachers College Record*, 1936–1937, 38 (I), 196–205; (II), 316–323; (III), 416–429.

THORNDIKE, ROBERT L. *Children's reading interests*. New York: Teachers College Press, Columbia University, 1941.

THORNDIKE, ROBERT L. *The concepts of over- and under-achievement*. New York: Teachers College Press, Columbia University, 1963.

THORNDIKE, ROBERT L. *Reading comprehension education in fifteen countries: An empirical study*. New York: John Wiley & Sons, 1973.

THORNDIKE, ROBERT L. Reading as reasoning. *Reading Research Quarterly*, 1973–1974, 9(2), 135–147.

THORPE, HAROLD W., & BORDEN, KIM S. The effect of multisensory instruction upon the on-task behaviors and word reading accuracy of learning disabled children. *Journal of Learning Disabilities*, May 1985, *18*, 279–286.

TIERNEY, ROBERT J. Essential considerations for developing basic reading comprehension skills. *School Psychology Review*, 1982, *11*(3), 299–305.

TIERNEY, ROBERT J., & CUNNINGHAM, JAMES W. Research on teaching reading comprehension. In P. D. Pearson (Ed.), *Handbook of reading research*. New York: Longman, 1984, 609–655.

TIERNEY, ROBERT J.; MOSENTHAL, JAMES; & KANTOR, ROBERT N. Classrooom applications of text analysis: Toward improving text selection and use. In J. Flood (Ed.), *Promoting reading comprehension*. Newark, DE: International Reading Association, 1984, 139–160.

TIERNEY, ROBERT J., & PEARSON, P. DAVID. Toward a composing model of reading. *Language Arts*, May 1983, *60*, 568–580.

TIERNEY, ROBERT J.; READENCE, JOHN E.; & DISHNER, ERNEST K. *Reading strategies and practices: A compendium* (2nd ed.). Boston: Allyn and Bacon, 1985.

TIERNEY, ROBERT J., & SCHALLERT, DIANE L. *Learning from expository text: The interaction of text structures with reader characteristics*. August 1982. Final Report ME–G–79–0167.

TIERNEY, ROBERT J., & SPIRO, RAND J. Some basic notions about reading comprehension: Implications for teachers. In J. Harste & R. Carey (Eds.), *New perspectives on comprehension*. Monographs in Teaching and Learning No. 3. Bloomington, IN: School of Education, Indiana University, October 1979, 132–137.

TIMKO, HENRY G. Configuration as a cue in the word recognition of beginning readers. *Journal of Education*, Winter 1970, *39*, 68–69.

TINDAL, GERALD. Investigating the effectiveness of special education: An analysis of methodology. *Journal of Learning Disabilities*, February 1985, *18*, 101–112.

TINDAL, GERALD. Graphing performance. *Teaching Exceptional Children*, Fall 1987, *20*, 44–46.

TINDAL, GERALD, & MARSTON, DOUG. Approaches to assesement. In J. K. Torgesen & B. Y. L. Wong (Eds.), *Psychological and educational perspectives on learning disabilities*. New York: Academic Press, 1986, 55–84.

TINKER, MILES A. Speed versus comprehension in reading as affected by level of difficulty. *Journal of Educational Psychology*, 1939, *30*, 81–94.

TINKER, MILES A. The study of eye movements in reading. *Psychological Bulletin*, 1946, *43*, 93–120.

TINKER, MILES A. Recent studies of eye movements in reading. *Psychological Bulletin*, 1958, *55*, 4.

TINKER, MILES A. *Basis for effective reading*. Minneapolis: University of Minnesota Press, 1965.

TIZARD, J.; SCHOFIELD, W. W.; & HEWISON, JENNY. Collaboration between teachers and parents in assisting children's reading. *British Journal of Educational Psychology*, February 1982, *52*, 1–15.

TIZARD, J., et al. (Advisory Committee on Handicapped Children). *Children with specific reading difficulties*. London, England: HMSO, Secretary of State for Education and Science, February 8, 1972.

TOBIN, AILEEN W., & PIKULSKI, JOHN J. A longitudinal study of the reading achievement of early and non-early readers through sixth grade. In J. Readence et al. (Eds.), *Dialogues in literary research*. Chicago: National Reading Conference, 1988, 49–58.

TOMPKINS, GAIL E., & YADEN, DAVID B., JR. *Answering questions about words*. Urbana, IL: National Council of Teachers of English, 1986.

TOOHEY, KELLEEN. Minority educational failure: Is dialect a factor? *Curriculum Inquiry*, 1986, *16*(2), 127–145.

TOPPING, KEITH. Peer tutoring and paired reading: Combining two powerful techniques. *The Reading Teacher*, March 1989, *42*, 488–494.

TORGESEN, JOSEPH K. Performance of reading disabled children on serial memory tasks: Selective review of recent research. *Reading Research Quarterly*, 1978–1979, *14* (1), 57–87.

TORGESEN, JOSEPH K. Memory processes in reading disabled children. *Journal of Learning Disabilities*, June/July 1985, *18*, 350–357.

TORGESEN, JOSEPH K. Computers and cognition in reading: A focus on decoding fluency. *Exceptional Children*, October 1986, *53*, 157–162.(a).

TORGESEN, JOSEPH K. Computer-assisted instruction with learning-disabled children. In J. K. Torgesen & B. Y. L. Wong (Eds.), *Psychological and educational perspectives in learning disability*. New York: Academic Press, 1986, 417–435.(b)

TORGESEN, JOSEPH K. Learning disabilities theory: Its current state and future prospects. *Journal of Learning Disabilities*, 1986, *19* (7), 399–407.(c)

TORGESEN, JOSEPH K. Cognitive and behavioral characteristics of children with learning disabilities: Concluding comments. *Journal of Learning Disabilities*, March 1989, *22*, 166–168, 175.

TORGESEN, JOSEPH K., & HOUCK, D. G. Processing deficiencies of learning disabled children who perform poorly on the digit span test. *Journal of Experimental Psychology*, 1980, *72*, 141–160.

TORREY, JANE W. Black children's knowledge of standard English. *American Educational Research Journal*, Winter 1983, *20*, 627–643.

TOWNSEND, MICHAEL A. Pupil achievement and adjustment under team and traditional classroom organizations: A review. *New Zealand Journal of Educational Studies*, November 1976, *11*, 113–123.

TRABASSO, THOMAS. On the making of inferences during reading and their assessment. In J. Guthrie (Ed.), *Comprehension and teaching: Research reviews*. Newark, DE: International Reading Association, 1981, 56–76.

TRAUB, NINA. Reading, spelling, handwriting: Traub Systematic Holistic Method. *Annals of Dyslexia*, Vol. 32. Baltimore, MD: Orton Dyslexia Society, 1982, 135–145.

TREIMAN, REBECCA, & HIRSH-PASEK, KATHY. Are there qualitative differences in reading behavior between dyslexics and normal readers? *Memory and Cognition*, 1985, *13*(4), 357–364.

TRELEASE, JIM. *The read-aloud handbook*. New York: Penguin, 1985.

TREVARTHEN, COLWYN. Development of the cerebral mechanism for language. In U. Kirk (Ed.), *Neuropsychology of language, reading, and spelling*. New York: Academic Press, 1983, 45–80.

TRUMBELL, ANN P.; STRICKLAND, BONNIE; & HAMMER, SUSAN E. The Individualized Education Program—Part 1: Procedural guidelines. *Journal of Learning Disabilities*, January 1978, *11*, 40–46.(a)

TRUMBELL, ANN P.; STRICKLAND, BONNIE; & HAMMER, SUSAN E. The Individualized Education Program—Part 2: Translating law into practice. *Journal of Learning Disabilities*, February 1978, *11*, 67–72.(b)

TRUSTY, KAY, & LINK, MARY. Reading teachers: Is aging in your book? *New England Reading Association Journal*, 1980, *15*(3), 6–12.

TUINMAN, J. JAAP. Determining the passage dependency of comprehension questions in 5 major tests. *Reading Research Quarterly*, 1973–1974, 9(2), 206–223.

TUINMAN, J. JAAP; ROWLS, MICHAEL; & FARR, ROGER. Reading achievement in the United States: Then and now. *Journal of Reading*, March 1976, *19*, 455–463.

TULMAN, CHESTER E. Bibliotherapy for adolescents: An annotated research review. *Journal of Reading*, May 1984, *27*, 713–719.

TURNER, SUSAN D. How to look at the testing components of basal reading series. *The Reading Teacher*, May 1984, *37*, 860–866.

TURNER, THOMAS N. Figurative language: Deceitful mirage or sparkling oasis for reading? *Language Arts*, October 1976, *53*, 758–761, 775. Also in A. J. Harris & E. Sipay (Eds.), *Readings on reading instruction* (3rd. ed.). New York: Longman, 1984, 236–240.

TUTOLO, DANIEL J. The study guide—Types, purpose and value. *Journal of Reading*, March 1977, *20*, 503–507. Also in A. J. Harris & E. Sipay (Eds.), *Readings on reading instruction* (3rd ed.). New York: Longman, 1984, 313–317.

TUTOLO, DANIEL. Critical listening/reading of advertisements. *Language Arts*, September 1981, *58*, 679–683.

TWAY, EILEEN (Ed.). *Reading ladders for human relations* (6th ed.). Urbana, IL: National Council of Teachers of English, 1981.

TWAY, EILEEN (Ed.). *Writing is reading: 26 ways to connect*. Urbana, IL: National Council of Teachers of English, 1985.

TYLER, ANDREA, & NAGY, WILLIAM E. *The role of derivational suffixes in sentence comprehension*. Technical Report No. 357. Champaign, IL: Center for the Study of Reading, University of Illinois, December 1985.

TZENG, OVID J. L., & HUNG, DAISY L. Linguistic determinism: A written language perspective. In O. Tzeng & H. Singer (Eds.), *Perception of print: Reading research in experimental psychology*. Hillsdale, NJ: Erlbaum, 1981, 237–255.

UHL, WILLIS L. The use of the results of reading tests as bases for planning remedial work. *Elementary School Journal*, 1916, *17*, 266–275.

UNDERWOOD, GEOFFREY, & ROOT, DAPHNE. Hemispheric asymmetries in developmental dyslexia: Cerebral structure or attentional strategies. *Journal of Reading Behavior*, Summer 1986, *18*, 219–228.

UNDERWOOD, N. RODERICK. *The span of letter recognition of good and poor readers*. Technical Report No. 251. Champaign, IL: Center for the Study of Reading, University of Illinois, July 1982.

UNDERWOOD, N. RODERICK, & MCCONKIE, GEORGE W. Perceptual span for letter distinctions during reading. *Reading Research Quarterly*, Winter 1985, *20*, 153–162.

UNDERWOOD, N. RODERICK, & ZOLA, DAVID. The span of letter recognition of good and poor readers. *Reading Research Quarterly*, Winter 1986, *21*, 6–19.

UTTERO, DEBBRA A. Activating comprehension through cooperative learning. *The Reading Teacher*, January 1988, *41*, 390–395.

VACCA, JO ANNE L. How to be an effective staff developer of teachers. *Journal of Reading*, January 1983, *26*, 293–296.

VACCA, RICHARD T. *Content area reading*. Boston: Little, Brown, 1981.

VAIL, PRISCILLA. 15 reading games you can adapt to any level. *Instructor*, October 1976, *86*, 60–62.

VALENCIA, SHEILA, & PEARSON, P. DAVID. Reading assessment: Time for a change. *The Reading Teacher*, April 1987, *40*, 726–732.

VALERI-GOLD, MARIA. A critical reading skills ladder. *The Reading Teacher*, March 1988, *41*, 739.

VALTIN, RENATE. Dyslexia: Deficit in reading or deficit in research? *Reading Research Quarterly*, 1978–1979, *14*(2), 201–221.

VALTIN, RENATE. Deficiencies in research on reading deficiencies. In J. Kavanagh & R. Venezky (Eds.), *Orthography, reading, and dyslexia*. Baltimore: University Park Press, 1980, 271–286.

VALTIN, RENATE. German studies of dyslexia: Implication for education. *Journal of Research in Reading*, 1984, *7*(2), 79–102.

VANDAMENT, WILLIAM E., & THALMAN, W. A. An investigation into the reading interests of children. *Journal of Educational Research*, 1956, *49*, 467–470.

VAN DEN HONERT, DOROTHY. A neuropsychological technique for training dyslexics. *Journal of Learning Disabilities*, January 1977, *10*, 21–27.

VAN DER VEUR, BARBARA W. Imagery ratings of 1,000 frequently used words. *Journal of Educational Psychology*, February 1975, 67, 44–56.

VANDEVER, THOMAS, & NEVILLE, DONALD D. The effectiveness of tracing for good and poor readers. *Journal of Reading Behavior*, Spring 1972–1973, 5, 119–125.

VAN DE VOORT, LEWIS; SENF, GERALD M.; & BENTON, ARTHUR L. Development of audio-visual integration in normal and retarded readers. *Child Development*, December 1972, *43*, 1260–1272.

VAN METER, VANDELIA. *American history for children and young adults: An annotated bibliographic index*. Englewood, CO: Libraries Unlimited, 1989.

VAUGHN, JOSEPH L. The effect of interest on reading comprehension among ability groups and across grade levels. In G. H. McNinch & W. D. Miller (Eds.), *Reading: Convention and inquiry*. Clemson, SC: National Reading Conference, 1975, 172–176.

VAUGHN, JOSEPH L. Instructional strategies. In A. Berger & H. A. Robinson (Eds.), *Secondary school reading: What research reveals for classroom practice*. Urbana IL: National Council of Teachers of English & ERIC/RCS, 1982, 67–84.

VAUGHN, SHARON, et al. Parent participation in the initial placement/IEP conference ten years after mandated involvement. *Journal of Learning Disabilities*, February 1988, *21*, 82–89.

VEALE, JAMES R., & FOREMAN, DALE I. Assessing cultural bias using foil response data: Cultural variation. *Journal of Educational Measurement*, Fall 1983, *20*, 249–258.

VEATCH, JEANNETTE, & COOTER, ROBERT B. The effect of teacher selection on reading achievement. *Language Arts*, April 1986, *63*, 364–368.

VEATCH, JEANNETTE, et al. *Key words to reading: The language experience approach begins* (2nd ed.). Columbus, OH: Charles E. Merrill, 1979.

VELLUTINO, FRANK R. Alternative conceptualizations of dyslexia: Evidence in support of a verbal deficit hypothesis. *Harvard Educational Review*, August 1977, *47*, 334–354.

VELLUTINO, FRANK R. *Dyslexia: Theory and research*. Cambridge, MA: MIT Press, 1979.

VELLUTINO, FRANK R. Theoretical issues in the study of word recognition: The unit of perception controversy reexamined. In S. Rosenburg (Ed.), *Handbook of applied psycholinguistics: Major thrusts of research and theory*. Hillsdale, NJ: Erlbaum, 1982, 33–197.

VELLUTINO, FRANK R. Childhood dyslexia: a language disorder. In H. Myklebust (Ed.), *Progress in learning disabilities*, Vol. 5. New York: Grune & Stratton, 1983, 135–173.

VELLUTINO, FRANK R. Dyslexia. *Scientific American*, March 1987, *256*, 34–41.

VELLUTINO, FRANK R., & SCANLON, DONNA M. Verbal processing in poor and normal readers. In C. Brainerd & M. Pressley (Eds.), *Verbal processing in children: Progress in cognitive development research*. New York: Springer-Verlag, 1982, 189–264.

VELLUTINO, FRANK R., & SCANLON, DONNA M. Verbal naming in poor and normal readers: Developmental difference in the use of linguistic codes. In D. B. Gray & J. F. Kavanagh (Eds.), *Biobehavioral measures of dyslexia*. Parketon, MD: York Press, 1985, 177–214.

VELLUTINO, FRANK A., & SCANLON, DONNA M. Experimental evidence for the effects of instructional bias on word identification. *Exceptional Children*, October 1986, *53*, 145–154.(a)

VELLUTINO, FRANK R., & SCANLON, DONNA M. Linguistic coding and metalinguistic awareness: Their relationship to verbal memory and code acquisition in poor and normal readers. In D. B. Yaden & S. Templeton (Eds.), *Metalinguistic awareness and beginning literacy*. Portsmouth, NH: Heinemann, 1986, 115–141.(b)

VELLUTINO, FRANK R. & SCANLON, DONNA M. *Auditory information processing in poor and normal readers*. Paper presented at the International Conference on Learning Disabilities, September 2–4, 1987, Amsterdam, The Netherlands.(a)

VELLUTINO, FRANK R. & SCANLON, DONNA M. Linguistic coding and reading ability. In S. Rosenberg (Ed.), *Advances in applied psycholinguistics*, Vol. 2. *Reading, writing, and language learning*. New York: Cambridge University Press, 1987, 1–69.(b)

VELLUTINO, FRANK R. & SCANLON, DONNA M. Phonological coding: phonological awareness, and reading ability: Evidence from a longitudinal and experimental study. In K. Stanovich (Ed.), *Children's reading and the development of phonological awareness*. Detroit, MI: Wayne State University Press, 1988, 77–119.

VELLUTINO, FRANK R., & SHUB, M. JEAN. Assessment of disorders in formal school language: Disorders in reading. *Topics in Language Disorders*, September 1982, 2, 20–33.

VENEZKY, RICHARD L. *The structure of English orthography*. The Hague: Mouton, 1970.

VENEZKY, RICHARD L. The curious role of letter names in reading instruction. *Visible Language*, Winter 1975, 9, 7–23.

VENEZKY, RICHARD L. Harmony and cacophony from a theory-practice relationship. In L. Resnick & P. Weaver (Eds.), *Theory and practice of early reading*, Vol. 2. Hillsdale, NJ: Erlbaum, 1979, 271–284.(a)

VENEZKY, RICHARD L. Orthographic regularities in English words. In P. Kolers et al. (Eds.), *Processing visible language*. New York: Plenum Press, 1979, 283–293.(b)

VENEZKY, RICHARD L. Letter-sound regularity and orthographic structure. In M. Kamil & M. Boswick (Eds.), *Directions in reading: Research and instruction*. Washington DC: National Reading Conference, 1981, 57–73.

VENEZKY, RICHARD L. Steps toward a modern history of American reading instruction. In E.Z. Rothkopf (Ed.), *Review of research in education*, Vol. 13. Washington, D.C.: American Educational Research Association, 1986, 129–167.

VERNON, MAGDALEN D. *Reading and its difficulties: A psychological study*. Cambridge, England: Cambridge University Press, 1971.

VERNON, MAGDALEN D. Varieties of deficiency in the reading process. *Harvard Educational Review*, August 1977, 47, 396–410.

VIK, GRETE HAGTVEDT. Reading disabilities in Norwegian elementary grades. In L. Tarnopol & M. Tarnopol (Eds.), *Reading disabilities: An international perspective*. Baltimore: University Park Press, 1976, 249–264.

VINCENT, DENIS, et al. *A review of reading tests: A critical review of reading tests and assessment procedures available for use in British schools*. Berks, England: NFGR-Nelson, 1983.

VOSNIADOU, STELLA, & ORTONY, ANDREW. The influence of analogy in children's acquisition of new information from text: An exploratory study. In J. Niles & L. A. Harris (Eds.), *Searches for meaning in reading/language processing & instruction*. Rochester, NY: National Reading Conference, 1983, 71–79.

VUGRENES, DAVID E. North American Indian myths and legends for classroom use. *Journal of Reading*, March 1981, 24, 494–496.

VUKELICH, CAROL. Parent's role in the reading process: A review of practical suggestions and ways to communicate with parents. *The Reading Teacher*, February 1984, 37, 472–477.

WADA, J., & RASMUSSEN, T. Intracarotid injection of sodium amytal for the lateralization of cerebral speech dominance: Experimental and clinical observation. *Journal of Neurosurgery*, 1960, 17, 266–282.

WADE, SUZANNE E. A synthesis of the research for improving reading in the social studies. *Review of Educational Research*, Winter 1983, 53, 461–497.

WAGNER, GUY; HOSIER, MAX; & CESINGER, JOAN. *Word power games*. Riverside, NJ: Teachers Publishing, 1972.

WAGNER, LILYA. The effects of TV on reading. *Journal of Reading*, December 1980, *34*, 201–206. Also in A. J. Harris & E. Sipay (Eds.), *Readings on reading instruction* (3rd ed.). New York: Longman, 1984, 358–362.

WAGNER, RICHARD K. Phonological processing abilities and reading: Implication for disabled readers. *Journal of Learning Disabilities*, December 1986, *19*, 623–630.

WAGNER, RICHARD K., & STERNBERG, ROBERT J. Executive control in reading comprehension. In B. K. Britton & S. M. Glynn (Eds.), *Executive control processes in reading*. Hillsdale, NJ: Erlbaum, 1987, 1–21.

WAGONER, SHIRLEY A. Mexican-Americans in children's literature since 1970. *The Reading Teacher*, December 1982, *36*, 274–279.

WALBERG, HERBERT J. Instructional theories and research evidence. In M. C. Wong & H. J. Walberg (Eds.), *Adapting instruction to individual differences*. Berkeley, CA: McCutchon, 1985, 3–23.

WALKER, CHARLES M. High frequency word list for grades 3 through 9. *The Reading Teacher*, April 1979, *32*, 803–812.

WALKER, ELINOR. *Book bait: Detailed notes on adult books popular with young people* (4th ed.). Chicago: American Library Association, 1988.

WALKER, LAWRENCE. Newfoundland dialect interference in oral reading. *Journal of Reading Behavior*, Spring 1975, *7*, 61–78.

WALKER, L., & COLE, E. M. Familial patterns of expression of specific reading disability in a population sample; Part I: Prevalence, distribution, and persistence. *Bulletin of the Orton Society*, 1965, *15*, 12–24.

WALKER, N. WILLIAM. Impulsivity in learning disabled children: Past research findings and methodological inconsistencies. *Learning Disability Quarterly*, Spring 1985, *8*, 85–94.

WALLBROWN, FRED H.; BLAHA, JOHN; & VANCE, BOONEY. A reply to Miller's concerns about WISC-R profile analysis. *Journal of Learning Disabilities*, June/July 1980, *13*, 340–345.

WALLBROWN, FRED H., & WISNESKI, PHILLIP D. Test-retest reliability estimates for eight dimensions of reading attitude. *Psychology in the Schools*, July 1982, *19*, 305–309.

WALLER, T. GARY. *Think first, read later: Piagetian prerequisites for reading*. Newark, DE: International Reading Association, 1977.

WALSH, DANIEL J.; PRICE, GARY G.; & GILLINGHAM, MARK G. The critical but transitory importance of letter naming. *Reading Research Quarterly*, Winter 1988, *23*, 108–122.

WANG, MARGARET C. The development of student self-management skills: Implication for effective use of instruction and learning time. *Educational Horizons*, Summer 1979, *57*, 169–174.

WARD, BARBARA J. (Ed.). Hispanic grade schoolers reading better. *NAEP Newsletter*, Summer 1982, *15*, 1–2.

WARDHAUGH, RONALD. Is the linguistic approach an improvement in reading instruction? In N. B. Smith (Ed.), *Current issues in reading*. Newark, DE: International Reading Association, 1969, 254–267.

WARWICK, B. ELLEY. Cloze procedures (Ebbinghaus completion method) as applied to reading. In O. K. Buros (Ed.), *Eighth mental measurements yearbook*, Vol. II. Highland Park, NJ: Gryphon Press, 1978, 1174–1176.

WATERS, GLORIA S.; BRUCK, MARGARET; & SEIDENBERG, MARK. Do children use similar processes to read and spell words? *Journal of Experimental Child Psychology*, June 1985, *39*, 511–530.

WATSON, JERRY J. A positive image of the elderly in literature for children. *The Reading Teacher*, April 1981, *34*, 792–798.

WATSON, RITA. Learning words from linguistic expressions: Definition and narrative. *Research in The Teaching of English*, October 1987, *21*, 298–317.

WATSON, RITA, & OLSON, DAVID R. From meaning to definition: A literate bias on the structure of word meaning. In R. Hotowitz & S. J. Samuels (Eds.), *Comprehending oral and written language*. New York: Academic Press, 1987, 329–353.

WEAVER, PHYLLIS A. Improving reading comprehension: Effects of sentence organization instruction. *Reading Research Quarterly*, 1979, *15*(1), 129–146.

WEAVER, PHYLLIS A., & RESNICK, LAUREN B. The theory and practice of early reading: An introduction. In L. Resnick & P. Weaver (Eds.), *Theory and practice in early reading*, Vol. 1. Hillsdale, NJ: Erlbaum, 1979, 1–27.

WEBB, NOREEN M. Student interaction and learning in small groups. *Review of Educational Research*, Fall 1982, *52*, 421–445.

WEBBER, ELIZABETH A. Organizing and scheduling the secondary reading program. *Journal of Reading*, April 1984, *27*, 594–596.

WEBER, LAWRENCE (Ed.). No easy answers to improving achievement. *Wisconsin Center for Education Research News*, Winter 1985, 1–3.

WEBER, ROSE-MARIE. The study of oral reading errors: A review of the literature. *Reading Research Quarterly*, Fall 1968, *4*, 96–119.

WEBER, ROSE-MARIE. Review of Findings of Research on Miscue Analysis: Classroom implications. *Journal of Reading Behavior*, Winter 1977, *9*, 416–419.

WEBER, ROSE-MARIE, & SHAKE, MARY C. Teachers' rejoinders to students' responses in reading lessons. *Journal of Reading Behavior*, 1988, *20*(4), 285–299.

WEBSTER, RAYMOND E., & LAFAYETTE ANN D. Distinguishing among three subgroups of handicapped students using Bannatyne's Recategorization. *Journal of Educational Research*, March/April 1979, *73*, 237–240.

WECHSLER, DAVID. *The measurement of adult intelligence* (3rd ed.). Baltimore: Williams & Wilkens, 1944.

WEIGL, EGON. The written language is more than reading and writing. *The Reading Teacher*, March 1980, *33*, 652–657.

WEINSCHENK, CURT, et al. Über die Haufigkeit der kongenitalen legasthenie im zweiten Grund schuljar: II (On the frequency of dyslexia encountered in the second school year: II). *Psychologische Rundschau*, 1970, *21*, 44–51.

WEINSTEIN, CLAIRE E. Fostering learning autonomy through the use of learning strategies. *Journal of Reading*, April 1987, *30*, 590–595.

WEINSTEIN, RHONA S. Reading group membership in first grade: Teacher behaviors and pupil experience over time. *Journal of Educational Psychology*, February 1976, 68, 103–116.

WEINTRAUB, SAMUEL. Two significant trends in reading research. In H. A. Robinson (Ed.), *Reading & writing instruction in the United States*. Newark, DE: International Reading Association, 1977, 59–68.

WEINTRAUB, SAM, & COWAN, ROBERT J. *Vision/visual perception: An annotated bibliography*. Newark, DE: International Reading Association, 1982.

WEIR, BETH. A research base for prekindergarten literacy programs. *The Reading Teacher*, *42*, March 1989, 456–460.

WELLS, JAMES, et al. Newspapers facilitate content area learning: Social studies. *Journal of Reading*, December 1987, *31*, 270–271.

WENDELIN, KARLA H. Taking stock of children's preferences in humorous literature. *Reading Psychology*, Fall 1980, *2*, 34–42.

WESSON, CAREN L.; VIERTHALER, JANINE M.; & HAUBRICH, PAUL A. An efficient technique for establishing reading groups. The *Reading Teacher*, March 1989, *42*, 466–469.

WEST, RICHARD F., et al. The effect of sentence context on word recognition in second- and sixth-grade children. *Reading Research Quarterly*, Fall 1983, *19*, 6–15.

WESTCOTT, JANE. Native American children's literature. *New England Reading Association Journal*, Autumn 1982, *17*, 44–49.

WHALEN, CAROL K.; HENKER, BARBARA; & HINSHAW, STEPHEN P. Cognitive-behavioral therapies for hyperactive children: Premises, problems, and prospects. *Journal of Abnormal Child Psychology*, 1985, *13*(3), 391–410.

WHALEY, JILL F. Readers' expectations for story structure. *Reading Research Quarterly*, 1981, *17* (1), 90–114.

WHALEY, W. JILL. Closing the blending gap. *Reading World*, December 1975, *15*, 97–100.

WHALEY, W. JILL, & KIBBY, MICHAEL W. Word synthesis and beginning reading achievement. *Journal of Educational Research*, November/December 1979, *73*, 132–138.

WHARRY, RHODA E., & KIRKPATRICK, SUE W. Vision and academic performance of learning disabled children. *Perceptual and Motor Skills*, February 1986, *62*, 323–336.

WHEELER, LESTER R., & SMITH, EDWIN M. A practical readability formula for the classroom teacher in the primary grades. *Elementary English*, November 1954, *31*, 397–399.

WHITE, C. STEPHEN. Learning style and reading instruction. *The Reading Teacher*, April 1983, *36*, 842–845.

WHITE, DAVID E. Language experience: Sources of information. *Language Arts*, November/December 1980, *57*, 888–889.

WHITE, THOMAS G.; SOWELL, JOANNE; & YANAGIHARA, ALICE. Teaching elementary students to use word-part clues. *The Reading Teacher*, January 1989, *42*, 302–308.

WHITIMER, JEAN E. Pickles will kill you: Use humorous literature to teach critical reading. *The Reading Teacher*, February 1986, *39*, 530–534.

WHITNEY, PAUL. Psychological theories of elaborative inferences: Implications for schema-theoretic views of comprehension. *Reading Research Quarterly*, Summer 1987, *22*, 299–310.

WICK, JOHN W. Reducing proportion of chance scores in inner-city standardized testing results: Impact on average scores. *American Educational Research Journal*, Fall 1983, *20*, 461–463.

WIDOMSKI, CHERYL L. Building foundations for reading comprehension. *Reading World*, May 1983, *22*, 306–313.

WIEDERHOLT, J. LEE, & HALE, GINGER. Indirect and direct treatment of reading disabilities. *Topics in Learning & Learning Disabilities*, January 1982, *1*, 79–85.

WIENER, MORTON, & CROMER, WARD. Reading and reading difficulty: A conceptual analysis. *Harvard Educational Review*, Fall 1967, *37*, 620–643.

WIESENDANGER, KATHERINE D., & BADER, LOIS A. Teaching easily confused words: Timing makes the difference. *The Reading Teacher*, December 1987, *41*, 328–332.

WIESENDANGER, KATHERINE D., & BADER, LOIS. Children's view of motivation. *The Reading Teacher*, January 1989, *42*, 345–347.

WIGDOR, ALEXANDRIA K. Ability testing: Uses, consequences, and controversies. *Educational Measurement*, Fall 1982, *1*, 6–8, 26.

WIGFIELD, ALLAN, & ASHER, STEVEN R. Social and motivational influences on reading. In P. D. Pearson (Ed.), *Handbook of reading research*. New York: Longman, 1984, 423–452.

WILKINSON, IAN; ANDERSON, RICHARD C.; & PEARSON, P. DAVID. *Silent reading: A best evidence analysis*. Paper presented at the annual meeting of The American Educational Research Association, New Orleans, April 1988.

WILKINSON, IAN; WARDROP, JAMES L.; & ANDERSON, RICHARD C. Silent reading reconsidered: Reinterpreting reading instruction and its effects. *American Education Research Journal*, Spring 1988, *25*, 127–144.

WILKINSON, LOUISE C., & CALCULATOR, STEVE. Request and responses in peer-directed reading groups. *American Educational Research Journal*, Spring 1982, *19*, 107–120.

WILLIAMS, FERN, & COLEMAN, MARGARET. A follow-up study of psycho-educational recommendations. *Journal of Learning Disabilities*, December 1982, *15*, 596–598.

WILLIAMS, JOANNA P. Extracting important information from text. In J. A. Niles & R. V. Lalik (Eds.), *Solving problems in literacy: Learners, teachers, and researchers.* Rochester, NY: National Reading Conference, 1986, 11–29. (a)

WILLIAMS, JOANNA P. The role of phonemic analysis in reading. In J. K. Torgesen & B. Y. L. Wong (Eds.), *Psychological and educational perspectives on learning disabilities.* New York: Academic Press, 1986, 399–416.(b)

WILLIAMS, JOANNA P. Teaching children to identify the main idea of expository texts. *Exceptional Children*, October 1986, 53, 163–168.(c)

WILLIAMS, JOANNA P.; BLUMBERG, ELLEN L.; & WILLIAMS, DAVID V. Cues used in visual word recognition. *Journal of Educational Psychology*, 1970, 61, 310–315.

WILLIAMS, PATRICIA, et al. The impact of leisure time television on school learning: A research synthesis. *American Educational Research Journal*, Spring 1982, 19, 19–50.

WILLIAMS, PETER. Reading and the law: The next step may be up to teachers. *Journal of Reading*, November 1981, 25, 106–112.

WILLIAMS, ROBERT T. A table for the rapid determination of revised Dale-Chall readability scores. *The Reading Teacher*, November 1972, 26, 158–165.

WILLIG, ANN C., et al. Sociocultural and educational correlates of success-failure attributions and evaluation anxiety in the school setting for Black, Hispanic, and Anglo children. *American Educational Research Journal*, Fall 1983, 20, 385–410.

WILLIS, DONALD C. The effect of self-hypnosis on reading rate and comprehension. *American Journal of Clinical Hypnosis*, April 1972, 14, 249–255.

WILLOWS, DALE M.; BORWICK, DIANE; & HAYVREN, MAUREEN. The content of school readers. In G. MacKinnon & T. Waller (Eds.), *Reading research: Advances in theory and practice*, Vol. 2. New York: Academic Press, 1981, 97–175.

WILLOWS, DALE M., & RYAN, ELLEN B. The development of grammatical sensitivity and its relationship to early reading achievement. *Reading Research Quarterly*, Summer 1986, 21, 253–266.

WILMS, DENISE M. *Science books for children: Selection from Booklist, 1976–1983.* Chicago: American Library Association, 1985.

WILSON, PATRICIA J., & ABRAHAMSON, RICHARD F. What children's literature classics do children really enjoy? *The Reading Teacher*, January 1988, 41, 406–411.

WILSON, PAUL T.; ANDERSON, RICHARD C.; & FIELDING, LINDA G. *Children's book reading habits: A new criterion for literacy.* Reading Education Report No. 63. Champaign, IL: Center for the Study of Reading, University of Illinois, January 1986.

WILSON, RICH. Direct observation of academic learning time. *Teaching Exceptional Children*, Winter 1987, 19, 13–17.

WILSON, STEWART P.; HARRIS, CHESTER W.; & HARRIS, MARGARET L. Effects of an auditory perceptual remediation program on reading performance. *Journal of Learning Disabilities*, December 1976, 9, 670–678.

WINEBURG, SAMUEL S. The self-fulfillment of the self-fulfilling prophecy: A critical appraisal. *Educational Researcher*, December 1987, 16, 28–37.

WINKLEY, CAROL K. Building staff competence in identifying underachievers. In H. A. Robinson (Ed.), *The underachiever in reading.* Supplementary Educational Monograph No. 92. Chicago: University of Chicago Press, 1962, 155–162.

WINOGRAD, PETER, & JOHNSTON, PETER. Some considerations for advancing the teaching of reading comprehension. *Educational Psychologist*, Summer and Fall 1987, 22, 213–230.

WINOGRAD, PETER, & NEWELL, GEORGE. *The effects of topic familiarity on good and poor readers' sensitivity to what is important in text.* Technical Report No. 337. Champaign, IL: Center for the Study of Reading, University of Illinois, June 1985.

WIRT, JOHN. Implementing diagnostic-prescriptive reading innovations. *Teachers College Record*, February 1976, 77, 352–365.

WISE, KATHLEEN. Activities for increasing hearing and speaking vocabularies. In A. J. Harris & E. Sipay (Eds.), *Readings on reading instruction* (2nd ed.). New York: Longman, 1972, 249–252.

WITELSON, SANDRA F. Developmental dyslexia: Two right hemispheres and none left. *Science*, January 1977, *195*, 309–311.

WITKIN, H. A., et al. Field-dependent and field-independent cognitive styles and their educational implications. *Review of Educational Research*, Winter 1977, *47*, 1–64.

WITMAN, CAROLYN C., & RILEY, JAMES D. Colored chalk and messy fingers: A kinesthetic-tactile approach to reading. *The Reading Teacher*, March 1978, *31*, 620–623.

WITTROCK, M. C. Education and the cognitive processes of the brain. In J. Chall & A. Mirsky (Eds.), *Education and the brain*. 77th Yearbook of the National Society for the Study of Education, Part II. Chicago: University of Chicago Press, 1978, 61–102.

WITTROCK, M. C. Writing and the teaching of reading. *Language Arts*, May 1983, *60*, 600–606.

WITTY, PAUL A. Studies of the mass media—1949–1965. *Science Education*, 1966, *50*, 119–126.

WITTY, PAUL A., & KOPEL, DAVID. Factors associated with the etiology of reading disability. *Journal of Educational Research*, February 1936, *29*, 440–450.

WITUCKE, VIRGINIA. The book talk: A technique for bringing together children and books. *Language Arts*, April 1979, *56*, 413–421.

WIXSON, KAREN K. Miscue analysis: A critical review. *Journal of Reading Behavior*, Summer 1979, *11*, 163–175.

WIXSON, KAREN K. Level of importance of post questions and children's learning from text. *American Educational Research Journal*, Summer 1984, *21*, 419–433.

WIXSON, KAREN K., & PETERS, CHARLES W. Comprehension assessment: Implementing an interactive view of reading. *Educational Psychologist*, Summer and Fall, 1987, *22*, 333–356.

WIXSON, KAREN K., & PETERS, CHARLES W. Teaching the basal selection. In P. N. Winograd, et al. (Eds.), *Improving basal reading instruction*. New York: Teachers College Press, 1989, 21–61.

WIXSON, KAREN, et al. An interview for assessing students' perceptions of classroom reading tasks. *The Reading Teacher*, January 1984, *37*, 346–352.

WOLF, MARYANNE. The question of essential differences in developmental dyslexia: A response to Seidenberg, Bruck, Fernarolo, and Bachman. *Applied Psycholinguistics*, 1986, *7*(1), 69–76.

WOLF, MARYANNE, & GOODGLASS, HAROLD. Dyslexia, dysnomia, and lexical retreval: A longitudenal investigation. *Brain and Language*, May 1986, *28*, 154–168.

WOLF, RONALD E. What is reading good for? Perspectives from senior citizens. In L. Johnson (Ed.), *Reading and the adult learner*. Newark, DE: International Reading Association, 1980, 13–15.

WOLF, WILLAVENE; KING MARTHA L.; & HUCK, CHARLOTTE S. Teaching critical reading to elementary school children. *Reading Research Quarterly*, Summer 1968, *3*, 435–498.

WONG, BERNICE Y. L. Self-questioning instructional research: A review. *Review of Educational Research*, Summer 1985, *55*, 227–268.

WONG, BERNICE Y. L. A cognitive approach for teaching spelling. *Exceptional Children*, October 1986, *53*, 169–173.(a)

WONG, BERNICE Y. L. Problems and issues in the definition of learning disabilities. In J. K. Torgesen & B. Y. L. Wong (Eds.), *Psychological and educational perspectives on learning disability*. New York: Academic Press, 1986, 3–26.(b)

WONG, JO ANN, & AU, KATHERYN H. The concept-text-application approach: Helping elementary students comprehend expository text. *The Reading Teacher*, March 1985, *38*, 612–618.

WOOD, KAREN D. Free associational assessment: An alternative to traditional testing. *Journal of Reading*, November 1985, *29*, 106–111.

WOOD, KAREN D. Guiding students through informational text. *The Reading Teacher*, May 1988, *41*, 912–920.

WOOD, KAREN D., & MATEJA, JOHN A. Adapting secondary level strategies for use in elementary classrooms. *The Reading Teacher*, February 1983, *36*, 492–496.

WOOD, MARGO. Invented spelling. *Language Arts*, October 1982, *59*, 707–717.

WORLEY, STINSON E. Developmental task situation in stories. *The Reading Teacher*, November 1967, *21*, 145–148.

WRIGHT, GARY. The comic book—a forgotten medium in the classroom. *The Reading Teacher*, November 1979, *33*, 158–161.

WRIGHT, LANCE, & MCKENZIE, CLANCY. "Talking" group therapy for learning-disabled children. *The Reading Teacher*, January 1970, *23*, 339–346, 385.

WYSOCKI, KATHERINE, & JENKINS, JOSEPH R. Deriving word meanings through morphological generalization. *Reading Research Quarterly*, Winter 1987, *22*, 66–81.

YADEN, DAVID B., JR. Reading research in metalinguistic awareness: A classification of findings according to focus and methodology. In D. B. Yaden & S. Templeton (Eds.), *Metalinguistic awareness and beginning literacy*. Portsmouth, NH: Heinemann 1986, 44–62.

YADEN, DAVID B, JR., & TEMPLETON, SHANE. Introduction: Metalinguistic awareness—an etymology. In D. B. Yaden & S. Templeton (Eds.), *Metalinguistic awareness and beginning literacy*. Portsmouth, NH: Heinemann, 1986, 3–10.

YENI-KOMSHIAN, GRACE H.; ISENBERG, DAVID; & GOLDBERG, HERMAN. Cerebral dominance and reading disability: Left visual field deficit in poor readers. *Neuropsychologia*, January 1975, *13*, 83–94.

YNGVE, V. H. Computer programs for translation. *Scientific American*, 1962, *206*, 68–76.

YOAKAM, GERALD A. *Basal reading instruction*. New York: McGraw-Hill, 1955.

YOPP, HALLIE K. The validity and reliability of phonemic awareness tests. *Reading Research Quarterly*, Spring 1988, *23*, 159–177.

YOUNG, LAURENCE R., & SHEENA, DAVID. Eye-movement measurement techniques. *American Psychologist*, March 1975, *30*, 315–330.

YOUNG, PETER, & TYRE, COLVIN. *Dyslexia or illiteracy? Realizing the right to read.* Milton Keynes, England: Open University Press, 1983.

YSSELDYKE, JAMES E., & ALGOZZINE, BOB. Where to begin diagnosing reading problems. *Topics in Learning & Learning Disabilities*, January 1983, *2*, 60–69.

YSSELDYKE, JAMES E., & CHRISTENSON, SANDRA L. Evaluating students' instructional environments. *Remedial and Special Education*, May/June 1987, *8*, 17–24.

YULE, WILLIAM. Predicting reading ages on Neale's Analysis of Reading Ability. *British Journal of Educational Psychology*, June 1967, *37*, 252–255.

YULE, WILLIAM, & RUTTER, MICHAEL. Epidemiology and social implications of specific reading retardation. In R. M. Knights & D. J. Bakker (Eds.), *The neuropsychology of learning disorders: Theoretical approaches*. Baltimore: University Park Press, 1976, 25–39.

YULE, W., et. al. Over- and under-achievement in reading: Distribution in the general population. *British Journal of Educational Psychology*, 1974, *44*, 1–12.

ZAESKE, ARNOLD. The validity of the Predictive Index Tests in predicting reading failure at the end of grade one. In W. D. Durr (Ed.), *Reading difficulties: Diagnosis, correction, and remediation*. Newark, DE: International Reading Association, 1970, 28–33.

ZAKALUK, BEVERLEY L., & SAMUELS, S. JAY. Toward a new approach to predicting text comprehensibility. In B. L. Zakaluk & S. J. Samuels (Eds.), *Readability: Its past, present & future*. Newark, DE: International Reading Association, 1988, 121–144.

ZAKALUK, BEVERLEY L.; SAMUELS, S. JAY; & TAYLOR, BARBARA M. A simple technique for estimating prior knowledge: Word association. *Journal of Reading*, October 1986, *30*, 56–60.

ZANGWILL, O. L. Dyslexia in relation to cerebral dominance. In J. Money (Ed.), *Reading disability: Progress and research needs in dyslexia*. Baltimore: Johns Hopkins Press, 1962, 103–114.

ZECKER, STEVEN G., & ZINNER, TANYA E. Semantic code deficit for reading disabled children on an auditory lexical decision task. *Journal of Reading Behavior*, 1987, *19* (2), 177–189.

ZELLER, LEROY. Prevent summer backsliding. *The Reading Teacher*, April 1980, *33*, 834–835.

ZIGMOND, NAOMI, & MILLER, SANDRA E. Assessement for instructional planning. *Exceptional Children*, April 1986, *52*, 501–509.

ZIMMERMAN, BARRY J., & PONS, MANUEL M. Development of a structured interview for assessing student use of self-regulated learning strategies. *American Educational Research Journal*, Winter 1986, *23*, 614–628.

ZIVIAN, MARILYN T., & SAMUELS, MARILYN T. Performance on a word-likeness task by normal readers and reading-disabled children. *Reading Research Quarterly*, Spring 1986, *21*, 150–160.

ZOROTOVICH, BETTY. The bridge of hope: Hand centers that cause and cure dyslexia. *Academic Therapy*, March 1979, *14*, 469–477.

ZUCKERMAN, DIANA M.; SINGER, DOROTHY G.; & SINGER, JEROME L. Television viewing, children's reading, and related classroom behavior. *Journal of Communication*, Winter 1980, *30*, 166–174.

ZUCKERMAN, SAM. To own a book. *American Education*, November 1977, *13*, 13–16.

Name Index

Subject Index